EUROPEAN NATIONS

ITALY

A REFERENCE GUIDE
FROM THE RENAISSANCE TO THE PRESENT

Roland Sarti

☑®
Facts On File, Inc.

To my granddaughter,
Jeannette R. Beaudet,
with love

Italy: A Reference Guide from the Renaissance to the Present

Copyright © 2004 by Roland Sarti

Facts On File, Inc.
132 West 31st Street
New York NY 10001

Library of Congress Cataloging-in-Publication Data
Sarti, Roland, 1937-
   Italy : a reference guide from the Renaissance to the present / by
   Roland Sarti.
     p. cm.—(European nations)
   Includes bibliographical references and index.
    ISBN 0-8160-4522-4
   1. Italy—History—Dictionaries. I. Title. II. European nations series.
   DG461.S27 2004
   945—dc22   2003062687

Text design by David Strelecky
Cover design by Semadar Megged
Maps by Dale Williams

Printed in the United States of America

VB FOF 10 9 8 7 6 5 4 3 2 1

This book is printed on acid-free paper.

CONTENTS

FOREWORD

This series was inspired by the need of high school and college students to have a concise and readily available history series focusing on the evolution of the major European powers and other influential European states in the modern age—from the Renaissance to the present. Written in accessible language, the projected volumes include all of the major European countries: France, Germany, Great Britain, Italy, and Russia, as well as other states such as Spain, Portugal, Austria, and Hungary that have made important intellectual, political, cultural, and religious contributions to Europe and the world. The format has been designed to facilitate usage and includes a short introduction by the author of each volume, a specialist in its history, providing an overview of the importance of the particular country in the modern period. This is followed by a narrative history of each nation from the time of the Renaissance to the present. The core of the volume consists of an A–Z dictionary of people, events, and places, providing coverage of intellectual, political, diplomatic, cultural, social, religious, and economic developments. Next, a chronology details key events in each nation's development over the past several centuries. Finally, the end matter includes a selected bibliography of readily available works, maps, and an index to the material within the volume.

—Frank J. Coppa, General Editor
St. John's University

INTRODUCTION

Italy is easily recognized on the map as the boot-shaped peninsula that juts out into the Mediterranean Sea. Archaeology tells us something about its early inhabitants and history. There is evidence that pile dwellers, the so-called Villanovian culture, lived in the Po Valley of northern Italy from about 1000 B.C. We know about the Ligurians, a later population that inhabited central and northern Italy, from their custom of cremating their dead and burying their ashes in urns. If the modest artifacts found in their places of burial are any indication, the Ligurians were not a wealthy people, but they were not primitives either. They seem to have brought with them, perhaps from central Europe, the technology of the Iron Age, which in turn may have been learned by contact with ancient Egypt. If that is the case, then the early history of the Italian peninsula confirms the dictum that in ancient times civilization moved from east to west.

Aside from such basic information, the prehistory of the peninsula is mostly uncharted territory. The historic populations, those about which we have written records, are later arrivals, including possibly the Etruscans, whose language is only partly deciphered. Linguistically, they were a population apart from all others, though not culturally, economically, or politically. They ruled a vast territory that stretched from just south of the Po Valley to as far south as Rome, which was initially an Etruscan colony. The Romans were also early immigrants, part of a large flow of Latin-speaking populations that formed confederations of towns known by such names as "Sabini," "Umbri," and "Lucani." These early populations are known collectively as the "Italic people." The principal ethnic ingredients of the future Italian nation were in place by about 1000 B.C.

Greeks, Phoenicians from what is today Lebanon, and Carthaginians from North Africa came later, attracted to the peninsula by its fertile soil and abundant forests. The attraction that the peninsula exerted on these populations is behind the theory that derives the name "Italy" from the Latin word for "calf," *vitulus*. Ancient visitors impressed by the abundance of livestock called those parts of the land that they knew *Vitelia*, the land of calves, then shortened it to *Italia*. Ancient Roman writers were the first to apply the name to the entire peninsula south of the Po Valley. The notion that Italy is a land of plenty survived the centuries in spite of the ravages of man and nature. Overpopulation, wars, deforestation, soil depletion, malaria, earthquakes, and other natural disasters degraded the environment, but the notion that Italy is a land of plenty endured until the 19th century. At that time patriots believed that political independence and unity were all that was needed to develop the rich resources of the peninsula. They were not the first or last to blame economic problems on the shortcomings of government.

This work does not reach into the distant past. It covers approximately the last 500 years of political, economic, social, and cultural developments. Political developments provide the framework because they are the most obvious route to the question of how power develops and is used. We begin with an event that historians recognize as marking a turning point in Italian history, the French invasion of 1494. From that date, bad government, lack of civic spirit, corruption, and divisiveness could be blamed on the foreign powers that controlled the states of the Italian peninsula directly or indirectly. France, Spain, and the Austrian Empire dominated in succession, helped by the fact that Italians had been politically divided and unaccustomed to working together since the decline of the Roman Empire in the fifth century. The question of national independence and unification is therefore the central issue of Italian history in the last 500 years, which is approximately the span of time covered by this work. The movement to achieve national independence and unity is called the Risorgimento, a term that means resurgence and revival. Its use indicates that those Italians who set out to unify the country were inspired by their vision of past glories. These included the power of ancient Rome, the spiritual primacy of the Roman Catholic Church, the commercial feats of medieval communes, and the artistic splendors of the city-states of the Renaissance.

The memory of those glories was the key element in creating a sense of national identity. What was missing after centuries of foreign rule was the sense of what it meant to be Italian. Patriots believe that a population does not constitute a people in the modern sense of the word unless its members share certain fundamental values that transcend divisions of family, region, wealth, and language. The notion that a people share a common identity by virtue of sharing the same history, territory, language, religion, and customs is a modern one. That notion has faced powerful obstacles in Italy due to the internal diversity of the peninsula. Medieval documents occasionally refer to *italicos,* and universities listed students as belonging to an "Italian nation," but the inhabitants of the peninsula were more commonly referred as Lombards, Venetians, Tuscans, Romans, Neapolitans, or Sicilians.

Regional identities have deep roots in Italian history, but that is not to say that *italianità,* the notion of a shared Italian identity, has no basis in history. It has been there as a concept that spread from the top. It was an abstraction formulated by writers looking for a principle of unity in a land that was profoundly divided. The history of the Italian peninsula has provided its inhabitants with many overlapping and sometimes conflicting identities. In ancient times they could think of themselves as members of a particular clan, inhabitants of a particular town, subjects of a particular ruler, or citizens of the multiethnic Roman Empire. In the Middle Ages they could identify with the Catholic Church, with a ruling dynasty, or that nebulous entity called the Holy Roman Empire. What was missing for most people was the intermediate link of *italianità* that connected the particular to the universal. Recent scholarship also tends to neglect that link, looking instead to the regional, cultural, and economic differences that undermine the notion of national identity and relegate the state to the role of secondary agent. This work reflects the belief that in modern times the national state is the chief dispenser and arbiter of power; it is the vital link between the specificity of the local and the abstraction of the universal. The national question remains the central issue of Italian history.

HISTORY OF ITALY

Geography and Population Movements

The search for shared realities begins with geography, which can be thought of as the stage on which humans construct their history. Location, terrain, and climate are geographical constants. The Italian peninsula is the third and most centrally located of three major Mediterranean peninsulas, the Spanish being the most westward and the Balkans the most eastward. The central location in an inland sea has been both an advantage and a handicap. Italy is well situated to take advantage of opportunities to trade, travel, and mix with other populations of the Mediterranean region, but is also confined to that region if barred from access to the wider oceans. The independent communes and city-states of medieval and Renaissance times thrived as long as the Mediterranean was the principal hub of trade and communications. They lagged behind populations situated on the shores of the Atlantic Ocean when trade routes shifted toward the oceans in the 15th and 16th centuries. It was then that power shifted to Spain, France, England, and the Netherlands, which also enjoyed the advantage of political unity. The gap was in economic and political clout, not in cultural matters. It is important to keep in mind that culturally Italy has always been part of Europe. Nothing that happened in Europe left it untouched.

Let us take a closer look at the geography of the peninsula, beginning with the islands of Sicily and Sardinia that are usually left for last and are sometimes overlooked or treated as mere appendages. In ancient times they were far more central to the life of the Mediterranean than most mainland regions. Sardinia, the more isolated of the two, retains its own distinct identity better than most other regions. Settled by a prehistoric population that has left behind thousands of mysterious tower-like structures called *nuraghe,* it was later settled by Phoenicians, Carthaginians, Romans, Greeks, and Arabs. Its history introduces us to an important aspect of Italian history. It points to the fact that Italy is a land where, in the course of centuries, different populations have settled and mixed. We think of Italy as a country of emigrants, but foremost in its history Italy has been a place of reception and settlement of immigrant populations. One more thing needs to be said about the history of Sardinia. Its name crops up frequently in modern Italian history because the island gave its name to the kingdom that played a key role in the Risorgimento. In the 19th century the state called the kingdom of Sardinia comprised, besides the island that gave it its name, the regions of Savoy, Piedmont, and Liguria, all located on the mainland. It was ruled by the House of Savoy, the dynasty that played a central role in the movement for national unification. How the kingdom of Sardinia acquired its name is part of the history of 18th-century European diplomacy that we shall look at further on.

Sicily, the largest and most central of the Mediterranean islands, was an even more attractive place of settlement than Sardinia. Separated from the Italian mainland by the narrow waters of the Strait of Messina, it has had a much closer relationship with the rest of Italy. The Romans took it from the Greeks and Carthaginians in the third century B.C. Since then, no government in power on the mainland has been indifferent to the affairs of Sicily. And no government could ignore the fact that fewer than 100 miles separate the island from the African continent. Arabs from North Africa conquered Sicily in the ninth century and held it for almost 200 years, until evicted by the Normans at the end of the 11th century. It is a favorite point of entry for African and Mediterranean populations making their way to the continent. It is still a favorite, if risky, point of access today for thousands of illegal immigrants on their way to the continent. Sicily became an unwilling part of the Kingdom of Naples in the 13th century. It took a revenge of sorts in the 19th when the Kingdom of Naples was renamed the Kingdom of the Two Sicilies. The island's strategic location and economic importance reinforce Italy's Mediterranean character. While Italy's northern regions pull the country toward the continent, Sicily pulls it toward Africa and the Near East.

The Italian mainland also attracted populations from the continent. Franks, Lombards, Normans, and other Germanic populations arrived in the Middle Ages as conquerors and/or settlers, the distinction between the two being rather unclear. The number of these arrivals is a subject of debate, but most historians agree that these population movements were not on a large scale. They may have come to conquer, but stayed on to govern, cultivate, intermarry, and blend with even earlier settlers. Franks and Lombards formed feudal aristocracies, ruled from their castles in the countryside, and did not look with favor on towns that questioned their authority and wanted independence. But the towns had their way, became independent communes, and developed into city-states that wiped out the feudal nobility, or compelled them to take up residence in the cities. The aristocrats still caused mischief in the cities, because they were a quarrelsome lot and often lived in towers that were the urban equivalents of their rural castles. But the towers of misbehaving lords could be attacked and razed to the ground. Feudal families eventually abandoned their wild ways and became part of the urban landscape. In a nutshell, that is the history of medieval communes. The aristocracies blended in, but their foreign provenance has left traces in the language, names, cuisine, and customs of the Italian peninsula. Italian culture is a composite of many different cultures, partly homogenized by their centuries-old coexistence but still distinct enough to be recognizable for what they once were.

The sea is one geographic constant for the inhabitants of the peninsula, mountains are another. The mountain range of the Alps sets the Italian peninsula apart from the rest of continental Europe. The Apennines, an offshoot of the Alps, cross the northern part of the peninsula from west to east before turning southward toward the southernmost region of Calabria and reemerging on the island of Sicily in somewhat tamer form. In their eastward progress the Apennines mark off the southern edge of the Po Valley, Italy's largest plain and the only one with enough water to sustain a prosperous agriculture. The Italian peninsula would not exist at all were it not for the fact that millions of years ago, enormous natural upheavals raised the Apennines from the sea. These mountains are the backbone of the peninsula and cover about one-third of its territory. The hills that flank the Apennines cover another third. Variations in latitude, elevation, exposure, and terrain in these hilly and mountainous regions make for the multitude of micro-climates that characterize the Italian landscape. In Italy, diversity is a function of geography.

Mountain strongholds and retreats once provided protection from invaders, and many mountain towns and villages still look like the fortified places that they once were. People fled to them for safety, not for comforts. Mountains do not make for easy living. Their impervious terrain makes enormous demands on those who work and travel. The soil is thin, water is scarce in the southern regions, forests were depleted long ago. Families and communities guard their resources jealously. Familism and *campanilismo,* social phenomena that, respectively, denote strong, some would say excessive, dependence on the family unit and local community, are rooted in these hardships of life. The family provided security and, if things worked out well, the way to power. Marriage strategies were part of the pursuit of security and power at all levels of society, from peasant communities to princely states. Kinship networks played a role in the politics of the Renaissance states, in the movement for national unification, and every major aspect of public life. But let's not tar all people with the same brush. Mountain populations were also the first to have small families and to emigrate. The "problem of the mountains" affects all regions from north to south. It was once a problem of overpopulation; today it is a problem of demographic depletion caused by low birth rates and the flight of millions to cities at home and abroad.

Population movements are not unrelated to the state of political affairs. Theoretically, strong government has the option to open or shut the doors to outside populations, while weak government leaves the decision to others. In reality, the choices are not so clear-cut. The power and resources of imperial Rome were both a deterrent and an attraction. Roman armies deterred invaders until the imperial administration fell apart, but the wealth of the court and of important families, the lure of big-city life, of *panem et circenses,* attracted new arrivals. Imperial Rome was a cosmopolitan city, and cities were bases of imperial power. The Roman city was so well rooted in Italy that it outlasted the empire itself. The exodus to the countryside of the early Middle Ages depopulated but did not destroy the cities. Cities survived as religious centers, as administrative headquarters, and as marketplaces. Living in cities carried a social prestige reflected in words that we still use: the word "urbane," meaning educated and socially polished, derives from *urbe,* the Latin word for "city"; a villain (*villano*) was an inhabitant of the countryside, a peasant. Americans idealize life on the land; Italians associate the good life with the amenities and conveniences of city living.

Rome lost its role as the imperial capital in A.D. 331, when Emperor Constantine moved the capital to the city of Byzantium on the Bosporus, but the move did not diminish the attraction that populations on the move felt for Rome and the Italian peninsula. What did diminish was the ability of Rome to guard its frontiers. Byzantium was strong enough to protect its immediate borders, but Rome was not, and Italy was the most attractive prize. It had good land, rich towns, skilled workers, and an educated upper class from which the newcomers could learn the arts of business and public administration. The so-called barbarians may not have been so barbaric after all if they valued living in a settled territory and learning the arts of commerce and government. Waves of newcomers arrived with alarming regularity for some six centuries. The Visigoths shocked the world by sacking Rome in A.D. 410 before moving on to other targets and eventually settling in Spain. In A.D. 476 Germanic troops deposed Romulus Augustulus, the last ruler to hold the title of Roman emperor in Italy. Ostrogoths, Lombards, Muslims, Avars, and Vikings followed. The Lombards settled, the others mostly raided and left. The age of invasions ended around A.D. 1000 with the arrival of the Magyars from central Europe, the last of the marauding tribes. The start of the Crusades in the 11th century signaled a reversal of the trend. Europeans, including many Italians, began to look upon the Near East as a land of conquest and settlement.

THE PAPACY

A closer look at these events throws light on a development with major consequence. The rise of the papacy was a direct consequence of political developments in the early Middle Ages. When the imperial court moved to Byzantium, the bishops of Rome assumed some of its functions. Pope Leo I (440–61) is credited with saving Rome from the Huns and grappling with the problem of how to deal with barbarian kingdoms sprouting from the ruins of the Roman empire. Leo began to elaborate the theory of papal monarchy that enabled his successors to claim spiritual sovereignty over all Christians, including rulers, and to assume the fatherly title of *papa*. The issue of sovereignty became urgent in the next century with the arrival of the Lombards or Longobards (the Long Beards, from their custom of not shaving), who came into Italy in A.D. 568 and established an independent kingdom with its capital at Pavia. Their name lives on in the modern northern region of Lombardy, where they first settled. They practiced Arianism, a form of Christianity considered heretical and therefore unacceptable to Pope Gregory I (590–604), who organized a campaign to convert them. But their conversion was only partial, and the Lombards, as the dominant power in the peninsula, continued to pose a threat to the papacy. Fearful of Lombard power, Gregory's successors called in the Franks. Their king, Pepin the Short (751–68), defeated the Lombards and ceded their territory to the pope, thus laying the foundation of the Papal States. From the political confusion of the eighth century, a low point in the history of Italy, came the temporal power of the popes, which lasted until 1870.

Their defeat by Pepin notwithstanding, the Lombards remained a thorn in the side of popes, who then called in Pepin's son Charlemagne. Charlemagne defeated the Lombards decisively in 774 and became the real power in Italy. Now dependent on Frankish power for military protection, the popes in turn sought to increase the Franks' dependence on the church as the only institution that could impart legitimacy to their rule. On Christmas Day of the year 800 Pope Leo I placed the imperial crown on Charlemagne's head and anointed him emperor. The Holy Roman Empire born on that day lasted in name until 1806, when it was abolished by Napoleon I as a meaningless relic. For much of its millennial history, however, the Holy Roman Empire was far from meaningless. Emperors claimed sovereignty over parts of Italy by virtue of the title and sent armies to enforce their claim.

Thus the papal government, theoretically the most international but in reality the most Italian of all the governments in the peninsula, faced a serious dilemma. As the governing body of the Catholic Church, the papacy identified with the Holy Roman Empire, which was in theory coterminous with the world of Catholic Christianity. In theory there was no conflict, for emperors wielded secular power, which they were expected to use in defense of the church, and popes wielded spiritual power, which was meant to secure the salvation of souls. But the distinction broke down in practice, as popes and emperors quarreled over issues that were both secular and spiritual. The thorniest issue was the appointment (investiture) of bishops, who were simultaneously religious and secular figures with spiritual and administrative duties. As a government based on Italian soil, jealous of its autonomy, and convinced that the secular power it exercised in Italy was essential to the fulfillment of its spiritual mission everywhere, the papacy resented any authority, including the imperial one, that claimed sovereignty in the peninsula. Yet it could not do without secular help, and often called on outside powers to extricate itself from its difficulties in Italy.

The Renaissance historian Niccolò Machiavelli focused on the secular aspects of papal policy when he argued that the papacy was responsible for the miseries and indignities that Italians suffered at the hands of foreigners. The judgment was unjust because all Italian states looked to outside powers when it was in their interest to do so. The problem that Machiavelli saw was rooted not in papal policy, but in the peculiar course of Italy's historical development. The German emperors Frederick II (1220–50) and Manfred (1258–66) were the last to attempt to impose some degree of political unity on the peninsula. After their defeat, city rivalries, factional strife, and murderous politics divided the peninsula into warring states for centuries to come. The so-called Age of the Communes (1000–1300) was a period of internal warfare and political chaos out of which emerged, painfully and paradoxically, the mercantile classes, economic connections, and political institutions of the Renaissance period (1300–1500). While other European countries moved toward centralized monarchy, Italians settled into an arrangement of competing regional states.

RENAISSANCE STATES AND SOCIETY

The largest and most populous of the regional states was the Kingdom of Naples. It had a population of about 1 million around 1500 and 2.1 million in 1595; it covered most of the southern part of the peninsula and the island of Sicily. It stood at the crossroads of Europe, but was never able to take full advantage of its central location in the Mediterranean world. A convenient passageway between the Near East and northern Europe, it was coveted by every power with imperial ambitions. The French Angevins ruled it until 1282 as a united "Kingdom of Sicily." After more than 200 years of war and complicated dynastic successions, during which the mainland monarchs lost the island, island and mainland were reunited in 1504 under Spanish rule. For the next century and a half the Spanish rulers governed the still theoretically separate kingdoms of Naples and Sicily through their viceroys, who tried with limited success to curb the power of independent barons, kept brigandage in check, built a sizable army and navy, and appointed administrators loyal to the Crown. The level of internal violence declined, native industries prospered, and population grew. By the end of the 16th century the kingdom had a population of 2.1 million, and Naples, with a population of over 200,000, was the second-largest city in Europe, exceeded only by Paris in size and splendor. But Spanish rule was not without drawbacks: It limited the autonomy of the kingdom, introduced the Inquisition, expelled Jews, taxed heavily, and generally hindered the expansion of trade. The cities of southern Italy were already lagging behind those of the north in trade at the start of the 16th century, and the gap widened under Spanish administration. The Southern Question has many components. Its roots predate the unification of Italy in the 19th century, when it became a national issue.

Historians no longer contend, as they once did, that Spanish rule was solely responsible for the economic and civic backwardness of the South. But the Spanish rulers did expect much from the possession that they regarded as the jewel of the crown. It was a strategic outpost that protected Spain from the Muslim Turks advancing in the Mediterranean. Spain therefore demanded discipline and obedience from its Italian subjects and expected Naples to contribute significantly to the costs of war. The feudal nobility resisted efforts to centralize the administration with legal maneuvers that created an impossibly complex body of law. Southern jurisprudence was born of the effort to protect local autonomies. The Masaniello revolt of 1647 saw nobility and populace working together to restrain the powers of royal officials. The result was large government that could not act, and a sluggish economy in which an overgrown capital stifled the growth of other urban centers. While other Italian states forged ahead in banking, manufacturing, and trade, the Kingdom of Naples remained primarily agricultural. In the Italian state system, Naples was the giant with feet of clay.

The Papal States, or the States of the Church as they were formally known before 1815, were an agglomeration of territories under the loose control of the papal bureaucracy in Rome. The nobility of the Papal States, like that of Naples, consisted of families with historical roots in their territories, jealous of their prerogatives and independence, supportive of papal authority only if given a free hand in their ancestral possessions. Unlike the Neapolitan aristocracy, they did not provide soldiers and civil servants for the government, for the papacy relied heavily on mercenary troops brought in from other parts of the Catholic world and on clergymen to fill public offices. The presence of the papal court brought pilgrims and business to Rome, but heavy reliance on that premodern equivalent of the tourist trade may not have been good for the economy as a whole. Taxpayers resented the presence of a large nonproductive clergy. Popes and cardinals were great patrons of the arts, but they were also great consumers of revenue. Renaissance popes turned Rome into an impressive showcase, behind which there was little economic substance. On one extreme was the opulence of the churches and palaces of the city, on the other the shabby, dirty, and unsanitary quarters and miserable dwellings of the populace. There was little in between; the middle classes that drove the economy in other parts of Italy were the weakest part of papal society.

More complicated political and territorial arrangements prevailed north of the Papal States. The South was monarchist, the North and center a complicated mix of dynastic states and republics. To be sure, it was not always easy to tell one from the other. Republics were supposedly governed by elected officials in the public interest. Dynastic states, also called principalities because their rulers were princes without royal titles, were ruled by a family. In principalities power was hereditary and princes ruled with the support of other powerful families and groups. Fifteenth-century Florence was a republic in name but a dynastic state in fact because the Medici family ruled by virtue of their wealth and connections. Genoa, Lucca, and Venice were republics, but the majority of their citizens had little say in the affairs of the state. These "aristocratic republics" were governed by their upper classes, which excluded everyone else from public office. State rivalries were the norm regardless of the term of government. The Florentine state showed little interest in expanding territorially beyond the region of Tuscany that was its natural locale because Florentine power rested on banking, trade, and diplomacy. Milan, a dynastic state ruled successively by the Visconti and Sforza families, was expansionist and a threat to its neighbors. Most threatened was the Republic of Venice, an imperial power with far-flung interests in the eastern Mediterranean that was torn by conflicting commitments at home and abroad. Florence, Milan, and Venice were the major players surrounded by lesser states like Parma, Ferrara, and Urbino. Although territorially insignificant, these small states played a large role culturally and politically, thanks to the ambition and vision of their ruling dynasties. The culture of humanism was born and flourished in the courts of Renaissance princes.

How these states fared in the course of the 16th century is a subject of debate. The shifting of trade routes to the Atlantic seaboard, the rise of wealthy banking families in Germany, the consolidation of national monarchies in Spain, France, and England suggest that Italy was relegated to the periphery of European power. But the decline, if that is what it was, is not easily measurable. Italy's population grew from 10 million to 12 million in the course of the 16th century, while Europe as a whole experienced a comparable growth from about 80 million to 100 million. In 1600 the Italian peninsula was the most densely populated region of Europe. After a relative decline in the course of the 17th century, Italy's population resumed a rate of growth comparable to the overall European rate in the 18th century. Italian banking, trade, and manufacturing had done well for most of the 16th century, as Venetian shipping and Genoese

Lorenzo de' Medici, prominent member of the Medici dynasty
(Library of Congress)

banking held on to their previous shares of business and were joined by new trading ports like Livorno and Ancona. Silk manufacturing prospered, except in Venice, and Italians were uncontested masters in the production of luxury goods, including brocades, crystal, laces, leather goods, and jewelry. There is no clear evidence of steady economic decline until the 1630s.

The case that accounts for Italy's political decline rests on the dramatic evidence of the first major foreign invasion of the peninsula by the French in 1494. The Florentine historian Francesco Guicciardini opened his account of events in Italy from 1490 to 1534 with an idyllic description of the state of Italy before the invasion and warned of the dire consequences of foreign rule. Writing in the late 1530s, Guicciardini saw the future in terms of the most recent events. The invasion of 1494 opened the way to other invasions by French and Spanish armies. During the so-called Wars of Italy that stretched from the invasion of 1494 to the Treaty of Cateau-Cambrésis in 1559, Italy was the "battleground of Europe." The original invasion upset the approximate balance of power among the Italian states achieved in 1454–55 with the Peace of Lodi and other diplomatic agreements. After 1494 the Italian states could no longer regulate their own affairs. That fundamental shift may have been masked by the successes of individuals and families. Negotiated agreements and advantageous marriages served the Medici and Farnese families well. Italian advisers and diplomats held positions of power at the French and Spanish courts. Artists who could no longer find commissions at home found them abroad, as far as England and Russia. The military traditions that Italians had developed in the course of centuries of domestic warfare lived on in the deeds of latter-day condottieri, who served with distinction in the armies of foreign powers. Papal diplomacy was sometimes called upon to settle international disputes. In 1571 the Venetian navy played the leading role in the battle of Lepanto, which halted the Turkish advance in the Mediterranean.

The consolidation of dynastic rule that was a feature of 16th-century political life everywhere in Europe from England to Russia occurred in Italy at the level of regional states. The Medici added Siena to their other Tuscan possessions in the 1550s. The process of dynastic concentration developed most notably in what until then had been the most backward and problematic of the Italian states. The possessions of the House of Savoy, tucked away in the Alps where France, Italy, and Switzerland meet, began to merge into something resembling a modern state under the leadership of the ambitious and opportunistic Duke Emanuel Philibert (1553–80). The duke and his successors encouraged the military traditions and vocation of the Savoyard aristocracy, built up a small but reliable army, and employed it profitably. Blocked in one direction by the greater power of France, the *Sabaudi*, as Italians call the members of this dynasty, turned their attention to the fertile Italian plains below. Emanuel Philibert set the premises for the process of expansion by marriage, war, and diplomacy that led to the unification of Italy three centuries later.

While it is possible to overstate the case for Italy's precipitous political decline in the 16th century, there is no doubt that the decline was ultimately real. The loss of political independence was sanctioned by the consolidation of

Spanish rule in Naples and Milan in the course of the 17th century. Military skills fell into disuse in part because they were discouraged by foreign governments. Like the navigators who sought to make their fortunes in the service of countries positioned to take advantage of the new ocean routes, Italian condottieri of the 16th and 17th centuries found it more remunerative to serve in the armies of the Bourbons and Habsburgs. By the 18th century even a normally peace-loving writer like Giuseppe Parini lamented that Italian men had lost the discipline of military life. The stereotypical image of the upper-class Italian male in the 18th century was that of the effete artist or courtier.

The 17th century saw the flight of capital from investments in trade and manufacturing into land and agriculture, a phenomenon described by some historians as the "refeudalization" of the Italian economy. Wealthy families in Venice, Florence, Milan, and other cities became landowners interested primarily in the state of agriculture and social relations in the countryside. There were agricultural innovations, the most significant being the introduction of new crops like maize and rice, which joined chestnuts as staples of mass consumption. Wealthy Italians enjoyed a more varied diet, but meat consumption was low for everyone by north European standards. Much of the wealth produced in the countryside was consumed in the cities, where the wealthy maintained their palatial residences, employed large numbers of servants, and spent lavishly on entertainments. The populations of Milan, Naples, Palermo, Rome, Venice, and other large cities grew in the 17th and 18th centuries, while the populations of smaller cities and towns declined or remained static. The latter were *città del silenzio* (cities of silence), sleepy provincial capitals stuck in the unchanging routine of centuries. The impressions of travelers confirm that northern Europeans came to regard Italy as an economic backwater, and historians generally regard the 17th and 18th centuries as marked by a growing gap between Italy and western Europe.

The gap was less evident in cultural matters. Throughout the period that historians call "early modern" (1500–1800), Italy experienced the same cultural developments as the rest of Europe. The first in order of time was the process of religious reform known variously as the Counter-Reformation, Catholic Reformation, or Catholic Reform. To a degree, the Catholic Reformation accomplished in Italy what secular governments accomplished in other parts of Europe. Sixteenth-century European societies experienced political centralization and greater government control over the activities of individuals and groups. This process was tied everywhere to the imposition of religious uniformity, for there was a general assumption that there could be no political and social stability without religious uniformity. Italy is a particular case of this general trend.

There was no central government authority in Italy to impose religious uniformity as there was in England, France, and Spain, but the influence and power of the Catholic Church cut across the political boundaries that divided the states of the peninsula. Pope Paul III (1534–49) began the process of reform. The Council of Trent formulated the new rules that tightened clerical discipline, required the clergy to keep vital statistics for their parishes, regulated religious orders and lay confraternities, reformed the practice of confession, increased clerical influence over the laity, and controlled the expression of ideas. The principal tools at its disposal were the Inquisition, the Index, and the Jesuit Order. The archbishop of Milan, Carlo Borromeo, provided the practical model of reform adopted throughout Catholic Europe.

Long and controversial, the process of reform caught on slowly. The reforms were essentially complete by the beginning of the 17th century. Even the republic of Venice, the state most jealous of its autonomy and most disposed to resist the encroachments of papal power, eventually fell into line. The Catholic character of Italian culture was definitely consolidated by the reforms of the 16th century as Protestant sympathizers were driven away from the peninsula and dissent was rooted out. There were some spectacular defections to the Protestant camp, but the "heretics" were relatively few. There were probably no more than 300 executions in all of Italy resulting from actions of the Inquisition, a tiny number compared to the numbers in England, France, Spain, or the Netherlands. Jews were confined to ghettoes rather than executed, expelled, or forced to convert. The forcible repression of the Waldensians by the rulers of Savoy in 1655 was the exception to the rule, and it was followed by grudging toleration of the surviving minority. To keep themselves busy, Inquisitors turned their attention to ferreting out cases of magic and witchcraft, but here too the emphasis was on prevention and correction rather than persecution. Repression was relatively mild, perhaps because the Italian church felt secure. The splendors of Baroque art were the outward expression of the church's assertiveness and self-confidence.

War and disease were far more serious dangers for most Italians than religious persecution. In the case of war, Italians benefited from the *Pax Hispanica* that followed the end of the Wars of Italy. They were spared the worst devastation that the Thirty Years' War (1618–48) inflicted on other parts of Europe, notably Germany, where no great power was present to keep out marauding armies. The threat of war was mostly internal as Spain's many commitments prevented it from policing the peninsula effectively. The Castro Wars (1642–49) between the Papal States and the Duchy of Parma over possession of the grain-producing town of Castro in northern Latium was only the most visible of the many obscure conflicts between neighbors that broke out in the course of the 17th century. These local conflicts compounded the tensions and fears aroused by the plague epidemics in 1575–77, 1629–31, and 1656–57. Complete figures are not available, but a few examples suffice to indicate the lethal impact of these epidemics. The epidemic of 1575–77 killed 50,000 of Venice's 200,000 inhabitants; the plague of 1629–31 carried off half of Milan's population of 120,000; in Genoa, 55,000 of its 73,000 perished in the epidemic of 1575–77, which also carried off about one-third of Naples' 300,000 inhabitants. No wonder that the 16th and 17th centuries are sometimes referred to as the age of saints. There were many reasons to look for saints. While the church looked for heroic saints in the fight against Protestantism, ordinary people looked for saints who showed compassion and possessed healing powers.

SECULAR CULTURE IN THE AGE OF THE ENLIGHTENMENT

Secular thought had its own champions. Galileo Galilei (1564–1642) laid the groundwork for modern science. Though the Catholic Church condemned him for his astronomical findings, the combination of mathematical speculation and experimental verification that he practiced is at the core of modern scientific investigation. He did not have many followers in Italy, but those who took up his work contributed to the solution of practical problems of land reclamation, road construction, and the study of anatomy, biology, botany, and medicine. These were the areas of strength of Italian science in the so-called forgotten centuries. Other figures less known than Galileo contributed to the vitality of Italian culture. Francesco Redi (1626–98) was a pioneer scientist who revolutionized the practice of medicine. Lodovico Muratori (1672–1750) anchored the study of history to the use of documents. Giambattista Vico (1668–1744) stressed the fundamental role of culture in the historical process, identified language as the basis of culture, and formulated a comprehensive theory of historical development that anticipated 19th-century romanticism.

With these figures we stand on the threshold of the Enlightenment, the cultural revolution that changed the European cultural landscape in the course of the 18th century. Confident that reason and science are the means to control nature and reform society, the Enlightenment is always traced to English, Scottish, French, and German thought, but Renaissance humanism also challenged traditional notions of divine power and Christian resignation and expressed confidence in reason and free will. Italy's cultural elites responded with enormous interest to ideas that came from abroad because they were the direct heirs of humanist culture. What they received from abroad via correspondence, publications, travel, and the activities of academies they elaborated in light of their own concerns. Freemasonry was a semisecret society that brought together members of the educated middle and upper classes in a common fight against the forces of obscurantism, superstition, and popular religion. In Italy, that meant taking on the Catholic Church. In northern Italy, Francesco Algarotti (1712–64) was the indefatigable and most successful promoter of the new culture. In Milan, Pietro Verri (1728–97) headed a group of intellectuals who pushed for political and economic reforms. There, Cesare Beccaria

(1738–94) won fame for his championing of penal law reforms, and Giuseppe Parini (1729–99) criticized moral laxness and corruption and praised the virtues of honesty, frugality, and simplicity. The *école de Milan* was recognized in France as a distinct version of the new culture. Outside Milan, Luigi Galvani (1737–98) and Alessandro Volta (1745–1827) carried scientific research into the new fields of electricity and magnetism. In the Kingdom of Naples, Pietro Giannone (1676–1748) attacked clerical privilege, Antonio Genovesi (1713–69) and Ferdinando Galiani (1728–87) revised free-trade theories in light of the kingdom's special interests and needs.

What distinguished the figures of the Italian Enlightenment was a pronounced interest in practical reforms and a relative indifference to theoretical speculation. In the 1750s the Republic of Lucca published the first Italian edition of the French *Encyclopédie*, the principal propagator of administrative, economic, and technological reforms. Intellectuals were not the only ones affected by the desire to study, understand, and repair. Governments also responded, hesitantly and cautiously at first. Rulers and ministers considered proposals to improve the machinery of government, expand trade and production, promote education, reduce crime, eliminate food shortages, and alleviate poverty. The need for reform was broadly understood, but Enlightenment ideas circulated initially among the most educated members of society. Reformers knew that they could not count on popular support for avant-garde ideas of change. They relied instead on the initiative of monarchs attuned to the new culture. The centralization of power in the hands of reforming rulers, the so-called enlightened despots, was a prerequisite for change, and the more absolute the monarch the better. Peace was another prerequisite, and Italy was fortunate enough to enjoy such a period of peace from the end of the War of the Austrian Succession in 1748 to the French invasion of 1796.

The governments least interested in reform were those of the aristocratic republics. There were few reforms in the republics of Venice, Genoa, and Lucca, where there were no monarchs to challenge the power of entrenched oligarchies. The most energetic efforts at reform were made in the Habsburg possession of Lombardy, in Tuscany where the House of Habsburg-Lorraine had succeeded the extinct Medicis in 1737, and in Naples and Parma, ruled by the Bourbons. It was the governments of these states that proceeded most energetically to enact the reforms that are associated with 18th-century enlightened monarchy. The monarchs of these states appointed ministers with the vision and energy necessary to reform a system of power that went back to medieval times. The reformers attacked the "liberties" of entrenched groups that were now denounced as undeserved privileges. Nobility, papacy, clergy, religious orders, and guilds were the targets of their attacks.

Absolute monarchs were the new agents of change, and the more absolute their power the greater the scope of reform. In Lombardy under Empress Maria Theresa (1740–80) and her son Joseph II (1780–90), the nobility was initially won over by promises that reforms would not threaten their traditional prerogatives. The government cautiously carried out a land census (1718–59), encouraged agriculture, and enacted administrative and penal reforms. These attempts to obtain accurate information on the ownership of land alarmed landowners large and small. Peasants, weapons in hand, often chased the census takers away. In Tuscany, the governments of Francis of Lorraine (1737–65) and Peter Leopold (1765–90) enacted trade reforms, lowered tolls, abolished guilds, and toyed with religious reform. In Naples, under Charles of Bourbon (1734–59) and in the first years of the reign of his son Ferdinand IV (1759–1825), the government centralized the administration, abolished local autonomies, and reduced clerical privileges. In the Papal States, where four separate popes reigned from 1740 to 1796, there were only half-hearted efforts at reform and little continuity from one pontificate to the next. Enlightenment popes were cultured gentlemen and generous patrons of the arts. Theater, literature, and the arts flourished in 18th-century Rome, but not political reform. What reforms there were dealt with land reclamation, the collection of taxes, and disbursement of public funds. In the Kingdom of Sardinia the rulers of the House of Savoy persevered in their policy of transforming the nobility into servants of the Crown by offering them rewards and careers in the army and public administration. Intellectuals fled the kingdom, some in fear for their lives for having offended the rulers with their ideas of change.

The French Revolution and Napoleon

1789–1815

Interest in reform abated everywhere when it became clear that tampering with government and society risked ushering in revolution. The fear was present all along, but intensified after 1789 when popular revolution actually broke out in France. There was clearly a downside to the power of absolute monarchs that alarmed even the supporters of reform from the top. In the early 1790s even a staunch proponent of reform like the Milanese, Pietro Verri, concluded that it was best to put limits on the power of monarchs. His reasoning was similar to that of the American colonists who said no taxation without representation. The initial response to the news that revolution had broken out in France in 1789 was therefore sympathetic. Calling monarchs to account was something that informed Italians could understand. But fear of the mob soon replaced the fear of royal power. Poor harvests in the late 1780s, the enclosure of common lands, loss of communal rights, abolition of guilds, rising prices, and the proliferation of bandits and beggars created discontent everywhere. The years of reform had primed expectations by whetting the appetite for change and by the dislocations and hardships that change always entails.

The initial mood of mild sympathy for the French Revolution changed to hostility when the import of what was happening in France struck home. The abolition of feudal privileges scared the Italian nobility, the execution of the French monarchs alienated moderate opinion, and the attacks on the French clergy angered the devout. Reformers wanted controlled change, an educated public, and the exclusion of the masses from public life. After 1792 only the most radical intellectuals in Italy sided with the French revolutionaries. They were to be found in schools, secret societies, and the academies. Unlike the French revolutionaries, they lacked government support and a popular following. These Italian Jacobins believed in liberty, equality, and fraternity, and were ready to welcome the French as liberators if they brought revolution with them.

The French army that invaded Italy in the spring of 1796 came to a land where administrative and economic reforms had shaken the authority of throne and altar, and educated elites were ready for change. The invading troops were led by the young and dynamic Napoleon Bonaparte, at age 28 the youngest general in the French army. Of Italian ancestry and fluent in Italian, he was born and bred in Corsica where his family had settled. His quick rise to prominence was due to the Revolution, which he personified. He was an innovator, compulsively driven to change, but not a revolutionary. His attitude was similar to that of an enlightened absolute monarch who distrusted popular initiatives. Beyond that, there was boundless personal ambition and craving for military distinction and glory. Italy was to be his launching pad to greater things. He knew how to motivate. His soldiers, ill-clad and famished, were more interested in booty than in justice, and Bonaparte pointed them toward the fertile plains and cities of Lombardy that lay within their grasp. The Piedmontese army that stood in his way did not pose much of an obstacle, nor did the stronger Austrian forces that he met and routed. Beyond that there was trouble. The depredations and atrocities committed by his soldiers alienated the clergy, peasants, and other ordinary folk who were their victims. That inauspicious start did not dampen Jacobin enthusiasm for the "liberators." The fracture between pro-French and anti-French Italians introduced a new element of civil discord in the body politic.

Bonaparte had a strong proprietary attitude toward Italy, but the French government to which Napoleon was accountable had its own reasons for wanting northern Italy in French hands, for that land was strategically important and rich enough to finance the war that was also being fought on the Rhine. In the first six months after his arrival, Bonaparte sent home the enormous sum of 58 million francs, making the government in Paris financially dependent on the Italian revenues and on himself as their chief provider. Strategically, northern Italy in Austrian hands was a threat to the security of France. In French hands, it was an ideal outpost for defense and offense.

After buying off further Austrian resistance by giving up to them the Republic of Venice, Bonaparte proceeded to change the map of the peninsula. In January 1797 he set up the Cispadane Republic in the territories of Parma, Modena, and Bologna, and carved the sister Transpadane Republic out of Lombard territory. In July 1797 he merged them to form the Cisalpine Republic, which also included the formerly papal territories of Bologna, Ferrara, Forlì, and Ravenna. Jacobin minorities seized power in Genoa, where they installed the democratic Ligurian Republic, in Rome where they abolished papal rule and set up the Roman Republic, and in Naples where, the royal court having escaped to the safety of Sicily, they established the Parthenopean Republic. In a matter of months, Napoleon had changed a political map that had endured for centuries.

These republics set a precedent for further change. In 1798–99 Russo-Austrian troops regained control of most of northern Italy while Napoleon was away on his Egyptian campaign. After returning to Italy in 1800, and defeating the Austrians decisively at the Battle of Marengo, Napoleon restored the Cisalpine Republic, renaming it the Italian Republic in January 1802. The republic was to remain unconditionally loyal to France, but Napoleon flattered Italians by calling them "the first people of Europe" and urging them to fulfill their destiny as a united people behind his leadership. The promise of careers was an added attraction. Francesco Melzi d'Eril (1753–1816), a moderate Lombard who would have preferred to serve a monarch but was willing to go along with a republic, was in charge of day-to-day affairs. The Italian Republic had its own regular army, the administration staffed mostly by Italians. It brought together 3 million Italians who had previously lived under different laws. Its green, white, and red flag was modeled after the blue, white, and red tricolor of revolutionary France. It sent a mixed message, for it stood simultaneously for Italian independence and subordination to France, but in time it came to be associated with national independence only. With one important modification to acknowledge the role of the royal House of Savoy, it became the flag of unified Italy.

Many historians see Napoleon as deliberately encouraging the growth of an Italian national consciousness, but there is little evidence that he envisaged or wanted a truly independent and united Italy. All his initiatives and policies, from road construction to the structuring of the economy, aimed at establishing French hegemony. At the height of his power all of northwestern Italy as far south as Rome, as well as Istria and the Dalmatian coast, were provinces of France. In February 1806 Napoleon's brother Joseph Bonaparte became king of Naples after the French had driven the Bourbons off the mainland and into Sicily for the second time to seek the protection of the British navy. The flamboyant Joachim Murat, Napoleon's brother-in-law and a dashing figure who appealed to the popular imagination, followed Joseph on the Neapolitan throne in June 1808. Murat did call for Italian independence, but he did so *in extremis* when he had no longer anything to lose. Still, thanks to Murat's late conversion to the cause of Italian independence, in southern Italy *murattismo* came to stand for national independence.

On March 15, 1805, after he had been crowned emperor of the French, Napoleon replaced the Italian Republic in northern Italy with a larger Kingdom of Italy. The Italian throne belonged constitutionally to Napoleon and his direct male descendants, but Napoleon did not concern himself with ordinary administration. He did not visit Italy after 1805 and left the state in the hands of his stepson, Eugène de Beauharnais, as his viceroy. There was a legislative body, and the administration, modeled on the centralized administration of France, was in Italian hands. The Kingdom of Italy was expected to be an active participant in the affairs of the Napoleonic empire. For this to happen it needed a sizable army. At its largest, it consisted of some 80,000–90,000 troops. It is estimated that in the course of its existence from 1805 to 1814 the Kingdom of Italy provided Napoleon with some 200,000 soldiers, by far the largest contribution of any of Napoleon's subject states. Thousands of Italian officers demobilized after the defeat of Napoleon in 1815 joined the movement for national unification. Napoleon, who understood the power of patriotism, did make a contribution to the movement for national unification after all.

Ambition and the quagmire of Italian politics drew Napoleon deeper into the affairs of the peninsula. He made peace with the pope in February 1797 (Treaty of Tolentino) after taking over the northern provinces of the Papal States. But papal hostility, the use of papal territory by his enemies, and the political intrigues of Italian Jacobins persuaded him to resume military operations in

January 1798. A convinced atheist who regarded papal authority as a medieval relic, he had the aged and ailing Pope Pius VI removed to France. That move transformed an otherwise unremarkable pope into a martyr and reinforced the image of the revolutionaries as a godless people. The introduction of compulsory military conscription and the efficient collection of taxes did the rest. Disaffection with the French and their local supporters was behind the popular resistance and irregular warfare that plagued the French in the South. The most serious resistance occurred in 1799 when peasant bands led by Cardinal Fabrizio Ruffo and the outlaw Fra Diavolo rose up against the French and their local supporters. On a lesser scale, the same occurred in 1806–08. These were struggles without quarter, marked by unspeakable atrocities on both sides, that introduced a new type of warfare pitting irregular bands against regular troops. *Guerrilla* is a Spanish word, but the French encountered that type of warfare in southern Italy before being discomfited by it in Spain.

The French prevailed in Italy with superior resources, better organization, and the support of critical sectors of society. Public works, administrative reforms, rewards and careers for those qualified to take advantage of opportunities in government and public administration showed the progressive side of French rule. After 1805 the locus of war shifted to central Europe, and Italy enjoyed a few years of peace during which the Napoleonic governments of the peninsula concentrated on enacting reform. The construction of roads and canals, the channeling of rivers, vast projects of urban renewal and land reclamation were the more visible signs of the dynamism of these Napoleonic regimes. In the Kingdom of Naples, the abolition of feudal privileges and *usi civici* (common rights to the land, which impeded land improvements) opened up new possibilities for those members of the middle classes who possessed capital and education. The adoption of the decimal system, of uniform weights, measures, and currencies, of the French civil code, and of uniform penal and commercial laws facilitated legal and business transactions. Most of these beneficial reforms were not rescinded by most post-Napoleonic governments. But their benefits were outweighed by the immediate burdens and impositions of Napoleonic government. Disaffection was on the rise when Napoleon entered the final round of wars that brought him and his system down in 1814–15. What people wanted most of all by then was an end to war, conscription, and high taxes.

THE RESTORATION

1815–1848

The aristocratic leaders of the anti-Napoleonic coalition who settled the affairs of Europe at the Congress of Vienna in 1814–15 brought to the table an agenda that had the double purpose of safeguarding the interests of their class and satisfying the yearning for peace shared by everyone after 25 bloody years of war and revolution. What the victorious allies proposed was an "alliance of throne and altar," respect for traditional institutions and customs, and the cooperation of all conservative governments (the Concert of Europe) to prevent the recurrence of war and revolution. The logical corollary of that principle was the restoration of the papal monarchy and all other "legitimate" dynasties, meaning those deposed by Napoleon, as opposed to the "illegitimate" created by Napoleon. The principle of legitimacy was not extended to the aristocratic republics that had also been victims of Napoleon's innovative zeal. Those republics became spoils of war. The territory of the Republic of Venice went to Austria and that of the Republic of Genoa to the Kingdom of Sardinia. The Republic of Lucca became the Duchy of Lucca, temporarily assigned to the Bourbons who had formerly ruled in Parma. Parma was assigned for the duration of her life to Napoleon's second wife, Marie Louise, who was also the daughter of the Austrian emperor and needed a post suitable to her rank. Parma would revert to the Bourbons at her death, when Lucca would be joined to the Grand Duchy of Tuscany. The Este family returned to the duchy of Modena, the papacy to Rome, and the Neapolitan Bourbons to southern Italy and Sicily. The union of the two parts became official in 1816, and the state was officially renamed Kingdom of the Two Sicilies.

Italy's territorial arrangements reflected more than the desire to restore legitimate monarchs to their thrones. Austria tightened its hold on Italy by incorporating both Lombardy and Venetia in its empire and gaining the right to garrison Parma and the papal towns of Ferrara and Ravenna. The annexation of the former Republic of Genoa by Piedmont-Sardinia could be seen as compensation to the House of Savoy for its loyalty to the conservative cause. Evicted from the continent by Napoleon, the court had retreated to the island of Sardinia to wait out the Napoleonic storm under the protection of the British navy. No dynasty seemed more conservative and less likely to countenance change than the House of Savoy. The annexation of Genoa strengthened this supposed bulwark of conservatism, made it a more effective buffer state against France, and gave it better access to the sea. These territorial adjustments underline the fear of the conservative powers that France might slip into revolution again, attempt to export the revolution by force of arms, and plunge Europe into another round of wars. France was to be hemmed in in every way possible to prevent it from again threatening the peace and stability of the continent. The restoration of Bourbon rule in France in the person of Louis XVIII, France's participation in the conservative Quadruple Alliance, and the strengthening of states bordering on France, including the Kingdom of Sardinia, were measures toward that end.

The "Italian Question" featured prominently in the deliberations of the Congress because Italy was regarded as a potential trouble spot. Large numbers of Italians had supported the Napoleonic regimes, educated minorities had tasted power and aspired to careers in public administration, there were thousands of unemployed and disgruntled former Napoleonic officers, and the members of dozens of secret societies were eager to conspire. Austrian chancellor Prince Clemens von Metternich (1773–1859), the guiding spirit of the Congress of Vienna, was determined to hold these groups in check, but he also understood that the clock could not be turned back to prerevolutionary times. Keeping Italy calm was now Austria's responsibility. Metternich's strategy was to promote the kind of change that did not threaten Austrian hegemony. Administrative reforms to make government more efficient and equitable were acceptable, demands for independence and unity were not. It was at the Congress of Vienna that Metternich made his first references to Italy as a "geographic expression." Italians, according to Metternich, were divided by cultural and historical differences so profound that it made no sense for them to aspire to independence and unity. The only thing they had in common was the shape of the boot; they were better off divided into separate states.

For all his obduracy on the issues of Italian independence and unity, Metternich was too much the political realist to think that it was safe to ignore demands for change. He had no intention of relying solely on military power and repression to keep Italy under Austrian control. He therefore urged Italian rulers to adopt administrative reforms designed to allay discontent. The reforms that he urged on satellite governments were administrative in nature. Metternich called for equitable laws, an honest and efficient judiciary, fair taxation, sound fiscal policies, local self-government, regular consultation between the central government and local councils, careers open to talent, and measures to promote economic development. He was even willing to countenance expressions of cultural patriotism. It was fine for Italians to be proud of Dante as long as the pride was literary. What he did not want to encourage was an autonomous national movement or any concessions to the principle of constitutional monarchy, which he regarded as intrinsically revolutionary.

Metternich's concepts of reform were implemented most readily in the regions of Lombardy and Venetia, where Austria ruled directly because they were integral parts of the empire. The reforms worked best in Lombardy, where the capital city of Milan emerged after 1815 as an important publishing and cultural center, a place where business, the applied sciences, and engineering flourished. Under Austrian rule Milan took on the role of business capital that it retains to this day. This is not to say that all was well. Austria taxed heavily, its trade policies favored other parts of the empire, and Italians were not favored in top administrative and military positions. Still, in the first half of the 19th century Lombardy was economically better off than any other region in Italy. Venetia did not fare as well, largely because of the mountainous nature of its territory, the impoverished state of its peasantry, the loss of trade, and competition from the port of Trieste. Venetians and Italians from the former Venetian territories of Istria and Dalmatia did well in the Austrian navy, where Italian was the official language.

In the states where Austria ruled by proxy, there was less commitment to reform but considerable tolerance. Parma under the easygoing rule of Marie Louise allowed some freedom of expression; the presence of many charities alleviated the plight of the poor. Tuscany was relatively well off, thanks to its prosperous agriculture and the progressive legislation that dated back to pre-revolutionary times. Tuscans welcomed back the House of Habsburg-Lorraine, few opposed the government, much road construction went on, and a relaxed atmosphere prevailed in Florence, where wags said that the only secret society was the Society of Pleasures, open to men and women. That was not entirely correct. An efficient police apparatus kept close watch on the activities of people whose political views were suspect, but the police acted only in extreme cases. Political satire flourished and served as a safety valve. Florence was home to serious intellectuals and reformers, who rallied around Gian Pietro Vieusseux and the review *Antologia*. The Tuscan government was not liberal, but it was shrewd enough to understand that systematic repression was bad for both the government and the economy.

Opposition to Metternich's ideal of "administrative monarchy" came from other Italian states where Austrian influence was indirect, and the opponents were both liberals and conservatives. In the small but strategically located duchy of Modena, Duke Francis IV, a staunch supporter of royal absolutism, was not averse to intriguing with liberals for the sake of territorial gain. In the Papal States, the secretary of state, Cardinal Ercole Consalvi, tried to follow Metternich's advice, but was frustrated by clerical ultraconservatives opposed to his plans to open the public administration to the laity. The clergy's monopoly of public offices would prove to be a major destabilizing factor for the Papal States. Consalvi, who resented Austrian interference in papal affairs, was also determined to show the world that the pope could rule without outside help. Caught between two fires, he pleased neither liberals nor conservatives. The revolutions of 1821 increased conservative fears of revolution, and the election of Pope Leo XII (1823–29) put an end to all efforts at compromise. From then on, papal policy was more conservative than Austrian policy and regarded all efforts at reform as dangerous concessions to the spirit of revolution.

A figure similar to Consalvi guided government policy in the first five years of the Restoration in the Kingdom of the Two Sicilies. As chief adviser to the king, Luigi de' Medici worked to reconcile supporters of the restored Bourbons and of the deposed Napoleonic monarchs. He allowed Neapolitans who had served the Napoleonic governments of Murat and Joseph Bonaparte to retain their posts in the army and public administration. He extended the Napoleonic legislation to Sicily, and outlawed all secret societies, including ultraconservative ones opposed to his policy of the "amalgam." Medici did give censorship powers to church authorities, restored religious congregations abolished under Napoleon, and gave ecclesiastical courts sole jurisdiction over the clergy, provisions that pleased conservatives. As had happened in Rome to Consalvi, Medici's moderate policies won him few friends; they were thoroughly compromised when, in spite of his efforts, revolution broke out in 1821.

Naples' reliance on Austria increased after the revolution, and so did its conservatism in domestic matters. Neapolitan conservatism was reinforced by fear of liberal England, which dominated the Mediterranean and was suspected of encouraging autonomist sentiments in Sicily. In 1812 the English had prevailed on a reluctant King Ferdinand I to issue a constitution that limited his power and made him accountable to an elected legislature. Such precedents were not forgotten; their memory helped drive Naples closer to Austria and Russia, the latter eager to strengthen its position in the Mediterranean with closer ties to the Kingdom of the Two Sicilies. After 1821 political repression increased, the press was tightly controlled, secular education discouraged, enterprise in business was politically suspect. The repressive atmosphere did not encourage economic growth.

Ironically, the state that in the end proved to be most anti-Austrian was the one that was the most conservative in 1815. In 1789–99 the Kingdom of Sardinia bore the brunt of French expansion, eventually losing its independence and all of its mainland provinces to France. King Victor Emmanuel I had fought against Napoleon and lost, but he was not a vindictive man. He banned from court those aristocratic families who had supported Napoleon, but eventually relented. There was no doubt that he dreaded revolution, an obsessive fear reflected also in the writings of one of his diplomats, the ultraroyalist Joseph de Maistre, who was ambassador to Russia from 1803 to 1817. Restored to his possessions and given Genoa as a reward for his loyalty, the king was determined to do all in his power to prevent the recurrence of revolution. He would purge the public administration, diplomatic corps, army, and schools of all Napoleonic appointees. His ministers consulted the court almanac of 1798 to ascertain who held what positions before the French had annexed Piedmont and Savoy. It is alleged, perhaps incorrectly, that the king even considered demolishing a "Jacobin bridge" built by the French. In reality the purge was selective, public servants who were purged at first were soon reinstated, and aristocratic families who had served Napoleon did not suffer for long. These included the family of Camillo Benso, count of Cavour, the future first prime minister of unified Italy.

If fear of revolution was Victor Emmanuel's first passion, hostility toward Austria was a close second. The king confronted the traditional dilemma of his dynasty: how to pursue an expansionist foreign policy while retaining the traditional structures of the state. The territorial ambitions that could only be satisfied in the Lombard plains at the expense of Austria made the Kingdom of

Sardinia an uncertain member of the Concert of Europe and a distrusted ally of Austria. Officers who had served under Napoleon kept their positions in the army, including the future king Charles Albert, who would play a key role in the movement for national independence. The central issue in the affairs of Piedmont-Sardinia after 1815 was how to reconcile territorial expansionism with political conservatism.

In the years of peace that followed the Congress of Vienna, neither the temperamentally cautious Victor Emmanuel I nor his successor Charles Felix had opportunities to engage in military adventures. Any thoughts they may have had of challenging Austrian hegemony in Italy were quickly dispelled by the outbreak of revolution in 1821, when some members of the aristocracy and army officers joined the revolutionaries. The army was considered a mainstay of absolute monarchy, the others being the Catholic Church and the peasantry. The defection of some officers, including Charles Albert, who was serving as royal regent in the temporary absence of Victor Emmanuel I, was a traumatic event. The king resigned the throne in favor of his brother Charles Felix, who carried out a thorough purge of the army, civil service, the schools, and the press. A stickler for legality, Charles Felix took a personal interest in the campaign to root out dissent. The clergy, on which he relied to prevent the spread of dangerous ideas, gained unprecedented influence at court and in the schools.

In the 10 years of Charles Felix's reign, Piedmont-Sardinia was a docile member of Metternich's order, but ironically the seeds of change were planted by the Congress of Vienna itself when it decided to award Genoa to the Piedmontese. That decision greatly complicated the social and political dynamics of the state. Although far from the glory days of its power as a maritime republic, Genoa was still an urban and mercantile center of regional significance. It revered its republican traditions, had an assertive middle class of professionals and businessmen, valued its autonomy, and was anti-Piedmontese at heart. The militarism of the Piedmontese court, the aristocratic tone of Piedmontese social life, and the agrarian basis of the Piedmontese economy clashed with everything that Genoa stood for. The court understood the difficulties it faced in dealing with this city and went out of its way to win acceptance of Piedmontese rule. It encouraged the expansion of Genoese shipping, which became active in the waters of North and South America in the 1820s. The navy patrolled the waters to protect Genoese ships from pirates, which still infested the waters of the Mediterranean, and attacked their bases in North Africa. These and other measures designed to facilitate business had a positive effect in the long run, but tensions were still high in the 1820s when Genoa became a center of political conspiracy. One of the conspirators was a young lawyer, the son of a prominent physician and a recent graduate of the University of Genoa. Giuseppe Mazzini, a leader in the movement for national unification, joined the secret Carboneria society in 1827, shortly after graduating from the university.

ANTI-RESTORATION IDEAS AND MOVEMENTS

1815–1830

Opposition to the Restoration was part of a European movement that drew inspiration from ideas of varying provenance, some traceable to the Enlightenment, others to romanticism, the intellectual reaction to the Enlightenment. The currents of thought that formed liberalism stemmed from those currents of Enlightenment thought critical of absolute monarchy. Liberals rejected royal absolutism, favored limited monarchy, written constitutions, political representation, and civil liberties. Romanticism was not strictly speaking a political movement. It expressed the disillusionment of a younger generation with the rationalism, materialism, and cult of classical forms associated with the Enlightenment, and found expression in literature and the arts. Romanticists were cultural rebels, they challenged norms, and looked inward in their search for truth and beauty. They were fascinated by history, but their historical interests were selective. The romanticist historical imagination was attracted to those periods of the past that classicists ignored or disparaged. While classicists saw beauty in the symmetry and regular lines of ancient Greek and Roman temples, romanticists were fascinated by the asymmetrical, perplexing, mysterious architecture of medieval Gothic cathedrals. The Middle Ages, popular beliefs and practices, religion, and spiritual values were the favorite subjects of romanticist artists and writers. They were interested in the particular rather than the general, in what distinguished individuals and groups, in what made them unique, rather than in what they had in common. Italian romanticists were less enamored of the medieval past than their northern European counterparts, for Italians could not fully reject the glories of the classical civilizations of ancient Rome and the Renaissance without rejecting their own past. But in the Middle Ages they discovered the principle of republican government in the free communes, and that discovery opened their eyes to what they regarded as a democratic alternative to monarchy.

Romanticists did not follow a single political path and took their stand according to personal circumstances and inclinations. Reverence for tradition made conservatives of some, while the cult of individuality and self-expression turned others into rebels. It is easier to equate romanticism with political revolution in Italy than in any other country with the exception of Poland.

Romanticism had an Italian precursor in the Neapolitan philosopher Giambattista Vico, but the movement was born in northern Europe and arrived in Italy at a fairly late date. Its arrival was delayed by the strong influence of the Napoleonic regime, which was highly suspicious and critical of a movement that rejected authority and craved self-expression. In that period, Vittorio Alfieri displayed the rebelliousness and individualism associated with the romanticist outlook, but remained tied to the forms of literary classicism and displayed the classicist dislike of the popular. Romantic literary criticism made its debut in Italy in 1816 when the poet Giovanni Berchet published an essay urging Italian writers to pay attention to what was happening abroad, reject classicism, and seek inspiration from popular culture. The connection between romanticism and political revolt becomes clearer with Ugo Foscolo, who rebelled against both Napoleon and Austria, shared the romanticist obsession with self-expression, believed in Italian independence, and chose to go into exile rather than submit to Austrian demands. Alessandro Manzoni's novel *I promessi sposi* (1827) also fits into romanticism. It did not call for rebellion, but it did castigate the arrogance of the powerful, and saw in the religious faith and simple virtues of ordinary people the way to justice. It was revolutionary in its pacifism, and its appeal to Catholic social conscience was seen as a wake-up call to the Catholic Church. No Italian writer of this period fully fits the definition of "romanticist," but all suggest possible links between romanticism and political action.

The authorities understood and feared the subversive potential of literature. They sensed the subversive message in a poem published by Giacomo Leopardi in 1820. According to an informer reporting to Austrian authorities, Leopardi's seemingly innocuous poem *Ad Angelo Mai* was conceived to arouse patriotic sentiments without seeming to do so by comparing Italy's current state of decline with its earlier greatness. But governments also understood that it took more than indignation and literary fervor to sustain a political movement. While they mostly limited themselves to monitoring the activities of the literati, they dealt more severely with those who engaged in political action. In a closed, repressive society political action took the form of political conspiracy. Secret societies flourished in Italy. Their origins go back to the 18th-century activities of freemasonry, which were more cultural and social than political. Secret political societies cropped up during the Napoleonic period. They attacked the Napoleonic system from two different directions that anticipated their lines of development after 1815. The ultraconservative secret societies of the Right were against the French and against war; they looked to the pope and called for peace. On the Left were societies that rejected Napoleonic rule as absolutist, favored constitutional monarchy, limited representation, and civil liberties. These demands, as we have seen, were the essence of political liberalism, and the secret society committed to this program was the Carboneria.

Restoration government regarded all secret societies as illegal, even the antirevolutionary societies, condemning all as "sects" that promoted special interests by illicit means. Conservative societies blamed governments for retaining Napoleonic laws, failing to purge Napoleonic appointees, and promoting economic innovations that threatened the status quo. Metternich suspected that conservative secret societies were abetted by Russian agents bent on making trouble for Austria in Italy to distract its attention from the Ottoman Empire, on which the Russians had their own designs. In 1816 the Neapolitan government banned all secret societies. In 1817 the first local insurrections sponsored by the Carbonari broke out in the Papal States. These were partly the result of hardship and famine endured by Europeans in the first three years of the Restoration, but were abetted by secret societies. Far more serious were the revolutions of 1820–21, in which the Carbonari also played a leading role. These movements showed that liberal secret societies were strong enough to topple governments, which abandoned their efforts at reform and became more repressive. The revolutions showed that Italian governments could not survive without the military backing of Austria. Thousands of former revolutionaries were purged from the army and public administration, imprisoned, or driven into exile, where they continued to fight and agitate for liberal causes in Spain, France, Greece, Switzerland, England, the United States, and South America. The Italian political diaspora, a phenomenon little studied but significant for both Italy and the countries where exiles were active, began in the 1790s and intensified in the 19th century.

Secret societies never fully recovered from the setbacks of 1821. Their network of cells was still large, but their effectiveness diminished. Government vigilance, internal dissension, defections, and infiltration by spies and saboteurs took a toll. When Giuseppe Mazzini joined the Carbonari in 1827 he discovered to his dismay that his "good cousins," as the members addressed one another, did little more than go through the motions of conspiring against the system. Italian secret societies could only mount a series of minor actions when revolution broke out in France in July 1830. France toppled the absolutist Charles X and installed the moderate monarchy of Louis-Philippe, Belgium won its independence, and Poland made a desperate effort to break away from Russia. Nothing happened in Italy until February 1831, when insurrections occurred and were quickly put down in the duchy of Modena and in Bologna and other towns of the Papal States. The delay was significant, for Italian conspirators had little faith in their own capacity and banked instead on the support of revolutionary France, as they had done in 1796–97. The cautious Louis-Philippe did not intervene, and the governments of the peninsula tightened the noose around the insurgents. The uprisings of 1831 gave the Risorgimento one of its most revered martyrs in the person of Ciro Menotti, who paid with his life for his misplaced hope that the duke of Modena could be won over to the cause of revolution. It was an object lesson in what not to do if one was serious about revolution.

MOVEMENTS OF NATIONAL INDEPENDENCE AND UNITY

1830–1848

Historians often treat the Risorgimento as if it were a single phenomenon, a monolithic movement with clear motives and set objectives. The record suggests otherwise. The insurrections of 1831 in Italy were important not for what they accomplished in the short run, which was little enough. The events of those months are significant because of the debate that they generated, the questions they raised, and the solutions that were proposed. The decade of the 1830s laid the groundwork for what was to come. The often acrimonious debate of tactics outlined alternatives in pursuit of national independence. Most obvious was the differentiation between moderate liberals and democrats. While liberals looked to the constitutional monarchies of France and England, democrats banked on Italians to take up arms, free themselves of foreign rule, and come together as one people. The distinction between liberals and democrats that emerged in the 1830s would be an enduring aspect of the Risorgimento. Another current also made a hesitant and tentative start, looking to the papacy for national leadership. Presaged by Alessandro Manzoni, it found its most explicit advocate in the priest Vincenzo Gioberti, who in the 1830s began to look for an alternative to political revolution. His Neo-Guelf current came into its own in the 1840s in time to play a role in the revolutions of 1848.

A notable consequence of 1830 was the decision by Giuseppe Mazzini to leave Genoa and go abroad. Young Italy, the society that he founded in Marseilles in 1831, rejected secret tactics and commanded its initiates to reach out to the people. It conspired in secret, but also took the revolutionary step of announcing its goals publicly and calling on all Italians to join forces. The goals were national independence and unity, the agents were to be the people, education and revolution were means to the end. Therefore, no more secret programs shared only by the initiated, no more relying on secret cells, but open proselytizing, and readiness for action. These tactics represented a conceptual breakthrough that transformed the Risorgimento from a movement deliberately limited to the select few to one that sought popular support. There was an additional feature to this democratic alternative: an acknowledgment of the seriousness of the social question. Mazzini insisted that patriots fighting for national independence must simultaneously confront social injustice. The national movement must seek to eliminate the extremes of poverty and wealth, put property within everyone's reach, provide for mutual assistance and cooperation across class lines. Mazzini linked the movement for national independence to proposals for social change that were at the heart of the emerging debate on the nature of socialism. His proposals appealed largely to the educated youth whom he addressed in his writings, but workers also responded. They would rally to his message in greater numbers in the years to come.

In that same decade, the hopes of liberals were revived from an unexpected quarter. The succession of Charles Albert of Savoy to the throne of the Kingdom of Sardinia in 1831 opened up new possibilities. A decade earlier, during the revolution of 1821 when he was serving as temporary regent, he had given in to liberal demands for a constitution. He had subsequently retracted and rehabilitated himself in the eyes of conservatives by fighting against liberals in Spain. When he came to the throne he was still trying to live down his youthful indiscretion by surrounding himself with conservative advisers, declaring loyalty to Austria and the Catholic Church, and taking a strong line against liberals. Democrats like Mazzini, of course, he regarded as beyond the pale. When Mazzini attempted to stir up trouble by inciting mutiny in the Sardinian army and navy and organizing armed raids into Savoy from Switzerland and France, Charles Albert came down hard on Young Italy and disrupted its network.

Charles Albert was neither liberal nor conservative at heart; he was above all ambitious and eager to leave his mark on history. Once reassured that revolution was not a threat, he made limited political concessions, simplified the administration, and undertook a course of reform designed to stimulate trade and encourage business. He spent to improve transportation and agriculture, but about 50 percent of the budget went to building up the military, which was Charles Albert's pride and joy. By the 1840s he was ready to break away from Austria and resume the policy of territorial expansion in northern Italy at Austria's expense. Privately, he even expressed support for the Italian independence movement and urged all Italian patriots to have faith in him. Charles Albert, who was anything but a political liberal, played his cards well and gradually regained the confidence of liberals who had been outraged by his betrayal of their principles in 1821.

Another surprising development that heartened liberals was the election of a liberal pope. Pope Pius IX was elected in 1846. The cautious reforms of the early years of his pontificate contrasted sharply with the conservatism of his predecessor, Pope Gregory XVI. The contrast itself was enough to encourage liberal expectations of change that were far in excess of what the new pope had in mind. The Neo-Guelf movement was born of these hopes. In 1843 Vincenzo Gioberti had published his influential book *Del primato morale e civile degli Italiani* (On the moral and civil primacy of the Italians), which augured Italian independence by peaceful means under papal leadership. What had been an unlikely prospect under the conservative Gregory XVI looked like a distinct possibility with a reformist pope. Neo-Guelfism was not an organized movement, it was a wave of enthusiasm that swept through Italy and carried along even the most hesitant and cautious. Only hard-line democrats and conservatives resisted its euphoric appeal. Nearly every one else, even the peasantry that was usually suspicious of liberal schemes of reform, seemed receptive to major political changes in the peninsula under papal leadership.

THE REVOLUTIONS OF 1848–1849

Without realizing what was in store, Italian public opinion was ready for the revolutions that swept through Europe in 1848. Paris is generally regarded as the birthplace of 19th-century revolutions, but the revolutions of 1848 actually began in Italy. In December 1847 the government of Charles Albert sponsored patriotic celebrations to mark the centenary of the Genoese anti-Austrian uprising of 1747. Bonfires appeared all along the crest of the Apennines through the regions of Liguria, Tuscany, and Emilia. On January 1, 1848, the Lombards inaugurated an antismoking campaign that was a form of tax protest against the Austrian government that monopolized the sale of tobacco products. Scuffles between the police and irritated citizens suffering from withdrawal symptoms broke out in the streets of Milan and other cities. On January 3 there was an uprising in the Tuscan seaport of Livorno. On January 12 Palermo rose up against the government of King Ferdinand II and demanded autonomy for Sicily. On January 27 Ferdinand promised a constitution in the hope that the concession would defuse the unrest and restore calm. Within a month Leopold II of Tuscany, Pius IX, and Charles Albert followed suit. Revolution broke out in France on February 22–24 when Parisians overthrew the monarchy of Louis Philippe. It was then that the world took notice of what was happening and revolution spread through Europe like wildfire. On March 13 rioting in Vienna led to Metternich's resignation. On March 15 Hungarians demanded independence from Austria and self-rule. Riots in Berlin on March 15–21 prompted the Prussian king to promise that a national assembly would decide the future of Germany. On March 18–22 fighting broke out in the streets of Milan (the Five Days of Milan), forcing the Austrian troops to abandon the city and retreat to their fortresses in the Quadrilateral.

On March 23 Charles Albert's government declared war on Austria, promising to bring Italians under Austrian rule "the help that a brother expects from a brother, a friend from a friend." The First War of Italian Independence was fought under Piedmontese auspices, and the Italian peninsula would never be the same again. Troops and volunteers from other parts of Italy joined the fight, but hopes of military victory in a regular war against Austria were short-lived, as the Austrians recovered from their initial setbacks after a few months of fighting. On August 6, 1848, Charles Albert agreed to an armistice. Political pressures forced him to resume fighting, but the final defeat was sealed exactly one year after his declaration of war, after the Austrians defeated the Piedmontese army decisively at the Battle of Novara, Charles Albert surrendered, and abdicated in

Pope Pius IX in a
Currier & Ives
lithograph, 1846
(Library of Congress)

favor of his son Victor Emmanuel II. In the meantime the revolution had spread to every part of Italy, the Republic of Saint Mark had been proclaimed in Venice, and the Roman Republic in Rome, where Pius IX was forced to abandon the city. These were heady victories for democrats and republicans, who fought valiantly against overwhelming odds. Giuseppe Garibaldi led a spirited defense of the Roman Republic that, although ultimately unsuccessful, made him a national figure and prepared him for the decisive role that he would play in the future.

The Italian revolutions were ultimately done in by international developments. Austria recovered and sent its armies to restore order in the peninsula. France gave only verbal encouragement to Italian revolutionaries. After Louis Napoleon was elected president of the French Republic in December 1848 the government actually turned against the revolution and dispatched an army to put down the Roman Republic. But the experience of revolution bore fruit regardless. The Kingdom of Sardinia had shown its true colors by declaring war on Austria; it retained the constitution (Statuto) that limited the powers of the king and gave effective powers to an elected legislature, it became a haven for political refugees from other parts of Italy, and it emerged in the 1850s as a constitutional monarchy governed by the Crown and an elected legislature, with a constitution that provided for orderly governance and protected civil liberties. In the eyes of liberals everywhere the state of Piedmont-Sardinia, which only a few decades before stood for the most unenlightened conservatism, now stood for orderly progress. Its new image consigned conservatives and democrats to the opposition and gave liberals authority and respectability. The liberals set out to unify Italy on their own terms. The other Italian states were discredited. The ruling dynasties of Tuscany and the Kingdom of the Two Sicilies had shown that they could not survive without the external support of Austria and other conservative powers. The papacy was most affected, for Pius IX turned against the revolution and called on a coalition of Catholic powers headed by Austria and France to restore Rome to papal rule. Pius IX would never again be tempted to flirt with change. He became an intransigent defender of Catholic political and religious orthodoxy, the champion of strict Catholicism to his admirers and a religious fanatic to his detractors. He had plenty of both. After 1848 the papal curia opposed Italian unification with all the means at its disposal, including police powers and military force. The events of 1848 drew the divide between clerical supporters of the papacy and anticlerical patriots. That divide was destined to last for decades to come.

THE DECADE
OF PREPARATION

1849–1859

The protagonists of the next phase of the unification movement looked back on 1848 as the turning point in their lives and in the course of the unification movement. One important lesson they learned from the defeat of revolution was that it takes more than enthusiasm and high ideals to prevail politically and militarily. Two figures exemplify how the experiences of 1848 affected the Risorgimento. Giuseppe Garibaldi distanced himself from Mazzini, tempered the republicanism of his youth, and became a loyal supporter of King Victor Emmanuel II. A man of the people by family background and personal tastes, he exemplifies the common sense approach that tries to reconcile the ideal with the practical. He had returned to Italy from South America in 1848 to fight for Pius IX under the impression that the pope supported Italian unification. The pope's defection from the national cause turned him into a rabid anticlerical who blamed the papacy and the Catholic Church for the ills of the country and the corruption of the young. The most popular Risorgimento figure, Garibaldi put his popularity in the service of the monarchy, rallied thousands of volunteers to the cause of national unity behind the slogan "Italy and Victor Emmanuel," and bridged the gulf between monarchists and republicans that might otherwise have led to civil war. For that he earned the affection of the people and the gratitude of the ruling dynasty.

Camillo Benso, count of Cavour, is the other exemplary figure. A Piedmontese aristocrat, Cavour was an independent-minded monarchist who did not hesitate to criticize and oppose the king. He became prime minister of Piedmont-Sardinia in 1852, not because Victor Emmanuel liked him, but because he knew how to get his way in a difficult parliament split among conservatives, liberals, and democrats. He used all the tricks of politics and parliamentary procedure with great success in pursuit of his policies, which involved both more and less than he has been given credit for. It involved more because he truly believed in the merits of parliamentary government, in freedom of expression and association, in free trade, and economic progress. Dealing with Victor Emmanuel was particularly difficult for Cavour, for both were headstrong and jealous of their authority. For the most part they were able to put private feelings aside and cooperate on the most important political issues, helped in this challenging task by plain common sense. On major issues Cavour behaved like a principled liberal and not like the political opportunist that his critics charged him to be. The tactics of opportunity he reserved for his dealings in parliament, where he could be treacherous to those who stood in his way. He was less than he has been given credit for because he was not, to use a familiar image, the patient *tessitore* (weaver) who worked tirelessly on a plan to unify Italy. Such a plan he did not have. What he had was a realistic appraisal of the Italian situation, which he thought would evolve toward some form of national unity in time, provided that Austria's hold on Italy was loosened. Evicting Austria did not require a commitment to Italian unification in the short run. It merely required pursuing the traditional strategy of Piedmontese territorial expansion in northern Italy at Austria's expense.

It is the anti-Austrian character of Piedmontese policy under Cavour that must be kept in mind to make sense of the decade of preparation. The administrative and economic reforms that Cavour pushed through showed that Piedmont-Sardinia was a progressive state that deserved the sympathy of liberal powers like France and Great Britain, which were also rivals of Austria. The safety and financial support that the Piedmontese government provided for political refugees from the other Italian states made Piedmont the standard bearer of the struggle against Austria, which brought pressure to bear on the Piedmontese government to deny refuge and support to these political troublemakers. Cavour obliged minimally and reluctantly, just enough to give Austria no reason to make war until Piedmont was ready for it. Getting ready for the showdown meant courting the support of powers stronger than Piedmont, which could provide the military muscle that Piedmont lacked. Participation in the Crimean War as an ally of Great Britain and France was a first diplomatic step in that direction, which earned Cavour the opportunity to have the Italian question raised at the Congress of Paris that ended the war, over the strenuous objections of Austria. Cavour's objective was to isolate Austria further and put the Italian question on the diplomatic agenda. The secret understanding of Plombières (July 1858) between Cavour and Napoleon III was a more aggressive step against Austria, that led directly to the Second War of Independence.

THE YEARS OF DECISION

1859–1861

Cavour practiced the politics of realpolitik, which relied on diplomacy and military power to deal with international issues. Realpolitik was incompatible with the politics of romanticism favored by Mazzinians and democrats, who envisaged liberation by popular revolution and heroic deaths on the barricades. Cavour was successful because he practiced realpolitik, and because he knew how to mix diplomacy and war in the manner most favorable to Piedmont-Sardinia. Shorn of its subtleties, his diplomacy aimed at getting a major power to fight Piedmont's battles. He found that power in the France of Napoleon III. The Second War of Independence (April–July 1859) initiated the conclusive phase of the unification movement. Cavour had envisaged merely an enlargement of Piedmontese territory, incorporating Austrian-ruled Lombardy and Venetia, with some territorial rearrangements in the rest of the peninsula but certainly no unified Italian state as a result of the war. Events did not unfold as planned. The French did most of the fighting in the war, so much in fact and at such great cost in human lives and political risk that Napoleon III decided to end the conflict before Austria was expelled from both Lombardy and Venetia.

The French decision to pull out of the war prematurely enraged Cavour, who resigned as prime minister. But while the war was in progress liberal elements orchestrated uprisings in Tuscany, Parma, Modena, and Bologna. Sometimes described as revolutions, these were really bloodless coups choreographed to make them look like expressions of the popular will. The liberal activists who seized power in these places demanded union with Piedmont-Sardinia and incited patriots in other parts of Italy to follow their example. Without Austria to police the peninsula, the unrest could not be contained. Cavour returned to power in January 1860 to manage the transition toward a larger state different from the one he and Napoleon III had envisaged. In March 1860 well-organized popular plebiscites sanctioned the annexation of Tuscany, Modena, Parma, and the papal Romagna with overwhelming majorities. Piedmont-Sardinia had to renounce Venice for the time being, but it did gain the regions of Lombardy, Emilia, and Tuscany.

Unrest in southern Italy did the rest. A revolt against Bourbon rule that simmered in Sicily gave Garibaldi and his supporters the pretext they needed to

People cheering as Giuseppe Garibaldi rides into Naples on horseback *(Library of Congress)*

mount the expedition of the Thousand that sailed to Sicily in May 1860 from the town of Quarto near Genoa. Cavour did not want that expedition, but did not dare stop it for fear of alienating Garibaldi, his supporters, and patriotic opinion that was now at a boiling point. Garibaldi's volunteers took over the island, crossed to the mainland, and marched triumphantly into Naples on September 7, 1860. Cavour regained the initiative by authorizing the invasion of papal territory by Piedmontese troops, with the excuse that the royal army was needed to maintain order in southern Italy. Garibaldi's readiness to hand over to the Piedmontese the territory liberated by his troops opened the way to the proclamation of the united kingdom of Italy on March 17, 1861.

The proclamation of national independence and unity was a milestone in the history of Italy. It brought to an end the period of occupation and dependency on foreign powers that had been Italy's lot since 1494. Political power was now in the hands of those Italians who had fought for unification under the banner of the House of Savoy. The government of the new state conformed to what was considered progressive and prudent at the time. It had avoided what most considered to be the great leap in the dark, republicanism. It was a constitutional monarchy with a parliament. The lower house of parliament (Chamber of Deputies) was elected and the upper house (Senate) was appointed by the king. The lower house controlled government spending. A restricted franchise gave the right to vote and run for political office to people of considerable wealth and education. Those restrictions enfranchised about 2.4 percent of the population (529,000 out of 21.8 millions), a low figure by later standards, but one that was not out of line with the franchise in other countries at the time, including England, whose government many Italian liberals regarded as a model. Italians had good reasons to congratulate themselves on their achievement, which had the added advantage of a relatively low cost in human lives. Deaths in all the wars of the Risorgimento up to 1860 amounted to no more than 11,200, a modest figure given the scope of the results.

Yet, the new state also faced severe problems. Large regional disparities in economic development, wealth, and education posed a major challenge for the national government. Those disparities were nothing new, but the fact they now coexisted within the same political boundaries made them more glaring. The country as a whole was still overwhelmingly agricultural, but the northern regions of Lombardy and Piedmont were on the threshold of the Industrial Revolution, while the southern regions were still struggling with the last vestiges of a feudal economy; 78 percent of all Italians were illiterate, but that national average disguised regional disparities, from around 50 percent illiteracy in the northern regions to 80–90 percent in the southern. The Southern Question was born in the 1870s when public opinion became aware of the regional disparities between north and south. It is still Italy's preeminent social question.

Church and state were declared enemies, and the enmity meant that many Catholics felt torn by conflicting religious and secular obligations. Cavour, fully aware of how dangerous the religious issue was for the Italian state, proposed a solution based on the principle, A Free Church in a Free State. Rome was still under papal control in 1861, and Cavour proposed that in return for the city of Rome, which all patriots wanted to be the capital of the Italian state, the Italian government would guarantee the full independence of the pope in the exercise of spiritual powers, exclusive papal jurisdiction over bishops and clergy, ownership of all religious buildings and furnishings, compensation for properties lost to the state, and state payment of clerical salaries. The state guaranteed freedom of religion to all. The Holy See rejected these terms and condemned the new state in no uncertain terms. On March 18, 1861, following by one day the proclamation of the Kingdom of Italy, a papal allocution asserted explicitly that the pope could not accept progress, liberalism, and modern civilization. The Syllabus of Errors reiterated these sentiments three years later, and added rationalism, socialism, free thought, religious freedom, and divorce to the list of what the pope could not accept. From the papal perspective, the Kingdom of Italy was an illegitimate robber state that despoiled the church of rightful assets and prerogatives. The internal war was on between clerical supporters of the pope and anticlerical supporters of the secular state.

The unexpected rapidity of the events that brought about national unification helps explain the severity of the problems faced by the Italian state in the first decade of its history. There was not enough time for cooler heads to prevail and for effective solutions to be worked out. The administrative, legal, and military systems of seven different states had to be merged, uniform laws applied, and security assured. The victors cut through the tangle by extending the constitution and laws of Piedmont-Sardinia to the rest of the nation. Hence, the political unification of the peninsula appeared to be a Piedmontese conquest rather than the outcome of a national movement. The results were most unfortunate for parts of the South where the disintegration of the 100,000-strong Neapolitan army let loose thousands of armed men on a society that could not provide for them. The phenomenon of brigandage took on the semblance of all-out civil war in many provinces, aided and abetted by supporters of the deposed Bourbons and by the clergy. The government responded by imposing martial law on many southern provinces and conducting large-scale military operations against the brigands. These operations involved up to 120,000 troops and resulted in an untold number of civilian and military casualties. Exact figures are still not available, but estimates place the casualties somewhere between 20,000 and 74,000 for the period 1861–70, a number far greater than the casualties in all the revolutions and wars of national independence even if we accept the lowest figures. What the Italian state faced in southern Italy after 1861 was a large-scale peasant insurrection caused by long-standing grievances and precipitated by the unexpected dislocations and improvised solutions of the unification movement.

The manner of unification precipitated a political debate that threatened to be as divisive as the widening gap between north and south. The differences between liberals and democrats that were contained while the struggle for independence was going on erupted with full force after unification. Cavour's premature and unexpected death in June 1861 removed from the scene the one figure with the temperament, authority, and prestige needed to manage the conflict and confront the country's many problems. The absence of organized political parties did not make matters any easier, for while political parties were suspected of fomenting partisan hatreds, their absence meant that parliamentary life would revolve around factions and personal clienteles. What was lost in the confusion was a unitary vision of the country's problems and the ability to implement long-range plans to solve them.

The political system that prevailed after 1861 is called liberal because it was based on a written constitution that limited the power of the monarch, granted voting rights, empowered a representative legislature, and provided for the exercise of civil liberties, including freedom of association, expression, and religion. But 19th-century liberalism and democracy were two very different ideologies. Liberals believed in the rule of law, but not necessarily in giving power to the people; they valued personal liberties, and feared that they might be taken away by the masses. Italian liberals had much to worry about, for they knew that they were a minority, their enemies were legion, and that the patriotism that was their passion had shallow roots in the population. In the often-quoted words of the patriot Massimo d'Azeglio, their task after having made the Italian nation was to make the Italian people.

THE POLITICS OF THE
LIBERAL STATE

1861–1901

Liberals and democrats lined up on opposite sides under different names as they debated and argued over the best means to make a people and save the nation. The liberals, styling themselves the "heirs of Cavour" and known to us as the Historical Right (Destra Storica), were the parliamentary majority that governed the country from 1861 to 1876. They were mostly Lombard and Tuscan politicians, who together formed a loose union of interests known as the *consorteria* (clique). The consorteria was far from homogeneous. A subgroup of mostly Piedmontese deputies known as the *permanente* opposed the move to transfer the national capital from Turin to Florence and insisted that only Rome deserved that distinction. They lost out temporarily when the government moved the capital to Florence in 1865, but saw their dream come true in 1870. Another mostly Piedmontese faction wanted to centralize power in the hands of the national government and favored public regulation of private business, while most Lombard and Tuscan representatives wanted economic laissez-faire. The centralizers were led by the Piedmontese, Quintino Sella, the decentralizers by the Romagnole, Marco Minghetti, whose views often coincided with those of the democratic opposition.

Though by no means homogeneous, the Historical Right set out to complete national unity and make the national state politically and economically viable. Rome was still governed by the pope, while Austria still possessed Venice and the mainland region of Venetia. Rome and Venice were powerful symbols in the minds of all patriots. Without Rome, Italy lacked its natural capital; Venice in Austrian hands was a reminder that the historic enemy of national independence was still a power in the peninsula, and poised to strike at Italy's wealthiest regions. The leaders of the Historical Right did not believe in revolution. Unlike the impatient democratic opposition, which wanted Italians to fight and win their own battles in short order, the Right was willing to wait for favorable opportunities. In 1862 and 1867 Garibaldi tried and failed to take Rome with volunteer armies loyal to him rather than to the government. Mazzinians conspired without success to spark revolution in Venetia. Democratic tactics were not successful given the domestic and international realities of the moment. The Right was prepared to fight in a more conventional manner. It obtained Venice and Venetia in 1866 by allying Italy with Prussia against Austria in the Seven Weeks' War, known to Italians as the Third War of Independence.

Taking Rome from the pope was a more complicated affair because Catholic opinion throughout the world supported the pope, and France guaranteed the independence of the little that was left of the Papal States. The Historical Right was ready to defy Catholic opinion, for they were as certain that God was on their side as was the pope that God was on his. Challenging France was much riskier, for France was a major power and Italians still depended on French diplomatic friendship, particularly against Austria. The opportunity came when the fortunes of war turned against the French in the Franco-Prussian War of 1870. After the French withdrew the military garrison that they kept in Rome, the Italian army moved on the city. Pius IX surrendered it after offering token resistance at the city gate of Porta Pia to show the world that he was yielding to force. He retreated to the part of Rome that was left to him and called himself "the prisoner in the Vatican."

After the acquisition of Venice and Rome, the Historical Right showed no desire for military adventures. Financial issues preoccupied the governing majority. Maintaining a large army, paying off a large national debt, financing the construction of railroads that were urgently needed to bind together the different regions and stimulate economic development, gaining the confidence of investors needed to meet the nation's many needs, all these were costly endeavors that placed enormous strain on the national budget. Good fiscal conservatives that they were, the leaders of the Right believed in balanced budgets. So, while on the one hand they pursued the policy of tight spending known as the *politica della lesina,* on the other they raised taxes. They knew that this was not the best way to win popular support, but they did not fear political unpopularity. They relied heavily on indirect taxes that had the advantage of spreading the burden throughout the population: the rich could afford to pay them and the poor, who were hit hardest proportionally, would learn to identify with the state by sharing the costs of government. The introduction in 1869 of the *macinato* (grist tax) levied on the milling of grains caused violent protests in many parts of the country and required calling out the army once again to restore order.

The statist ideology articulated by the most prominent intellectual of the Right, the philosopher Bertrando Spaventa, emphasized that the state was an entity that stood above and transcended all special interests. As the ultimate guardian of law the state had broad obligations. Implicit in this exalted view of the nature of the state was the notion of social paternalism. Two Tuscan members of the Right, Sidney Sonnino and Leopoldo Franchetti, alerted parliament and public opinion to the needs of impoverished peasants and raised the Southern Question. The fear that industrial speculators would gain excessive influence and promote government corruption haunted some members of the Right. That fear was behind the decision to favor the nationalization of railroads. At a time when industrial manufacturing was struggling, the construction and operation of railroads was the most dynamic and lucrative sector of the national economy. Nationalizing the railroads was a means to curb railroad investors and speculators and, coincidentally, to protect the interests of landowners who were the Right's most influential backers. The political fortunes of the Right began to slip in the national elections of 1874, when the leftist opposition won 232 seats out of 508 in the Chamber of Deputies. The Right, with a slim majority of 275, could not prevail in a vote as controversial and contested as the one on the nationalization of railroads. On March 16, 1876, Prime Minister Marco Minghetti announced triumphantly that the government had achieved a budget surplus; two days later it lost the critical parliamentary vote on the railroads and had to resign.

The transfer of power to the Liberal Left (Sinistra Liberale) seemed revolutionary at the time. The new prime minister was Agostino Depretis, a former republican and a parliamentary opponent of Cavour. The Liberal Left included former Mazzinians and current followers of Giuseppe Garibaldi. There was also a geographic shift, as southern representatives occupied 194 of the Left's 232 seats. Depretis was a northerner, but prominent leaders of the Left like Francesco Crispi and Giovanni Nicotera, the new minister of the interior, were southerners. The ideological and regional shifts seemed to promise radical change. The Left promised reduction of taxes, broadening of the suffrage, a stronger stand against clerical influence, and a more active foreign policy. They delivered on all accounts, but not to the expected degree. The Left abolished the grist tax, but did not change the system's reliance on indirect taxes. It extended the suffrage to only 7 percent of the population. It stepped up anticlerical activities, but respected the Law of Guarantees passed by the Right to protect the independence of the papacy. In foreign policy it took the first hesitant steps in the direction of colonialism and formed the Triple Alliance with Austria-Hungary and Germany. It did not encourage irredentism and avoided giving offense to Austria-Hungary over Trento and Trieste. Dissenters distanced themselves from the moderate policies of Depretis, forming the so-called pentarchy that claimed to represent the radical spirit of the liberal Left. Depretis held the coalition together with hard work and political sleight of hand.

Transformism is the label that historians apply to the system of coalition governance that he perfected. It relied on personal understandings, wheeling and dealing, and political back-scratching, and needed a deft hand at the helm to make it work. Transformism aimed at creating working parliamentary majorities out of an assemblage of deputies coming from different political directions, holding divergent views about the future of Italy, and lacking party discipline. Many historians condemn it as politically opportunistic and unprincipled. It was intended to "transform" an assorted political assemblage into a functioning parliament; it may have been unavoidable under the circumstances. Francesco Crispi denounced the practice after succeeding Depretis, who died in office in 1887, but would soon embrace its methods. Crispi, the first southern prime minister, posed as a true democrat and as the "man of destiny" who would bring glory to Italy. He vowed to move ahead with stalled reforms and delivered on his promises during his first government (1887–91) by abolishing the death penalty, revoking anti-strike laws, limiting police powers, reforming the penal system, reorganizing charities, extending the franchise, and passing public health laws and legislation to protect emigrants leaving the country to work abroad.

Crispi's intent was to seek popular support for the state with a program of orderly development at home and expansion abroad. He ran into problems both at home and abroad. At home he had to confront economic crisis and a deteriorating financial situation. Socialism was making inroads among urban and rural workers, and Crispi viewed socialism as a threat to the nation. Socialists in parliament and organized labor were more interested in bread-and-butter issues that in national glory. Crispi's desire to make Italy a colonial power complicated relations with France, which rejected Italian claims to Tunisia and opposed Italian expansion elsewhere in Africa. The two countries engaged in a tariff war that proved more harmful to Italy than to France. Southern exports of wine, olive oil, and fruit were hit particularly hard. Southern discontent and disaffection with the national government reached the boiling point in Sicily in 1893–94 with the uprising of the Fasci siciliani. Crispi was temporarily out of power when the disturbances broke out, but when he returned to power in December 1893, he imposed martial law on Sicily and provinces of central Italy where disturbances also had broken out.

Antagonism with France pushed Crispi into closer relations with Germany and Austria-Hungary. Unlike his predecessors who had tried to advance Italy's interests by balancing between its alliance partners on the one hand and England and France on the other, Crispi relied on the Triple Alliance to pursue his foreign policy goals. These were increasingly focused on East Africa, where Crispi hoped to create a large colonial empire. The attempt ended at Adowa (now Adwa) when Ethiopian forces routed an advancing Italian force with great loss of life.

The ensuing uproar at home and abroad put an end to Crispi's political career and led to the most serious crisis that the country had experienced since national unification. The crisis was more than political. A slump in agricultural production and exports, rising prices, and socialist propaganda were behind the Fatti di maggio, the tumults that broke out in May 1898 in Milan and spread to the rest of the country. Fearing a complete breakdown of law and order, conservatives called for extreme measures. The army restored order with considerable bloodshed. Freedom of the press, the prerogatives of parliament, the legitimacy of political opposition were all called into question in the five years from 1896 to 1901. The presence of new opposition parties that had no direct connection with the Risorgimento meant that new and more troublesome issues were being raised. The Socialist Party (Partito Socialista Italiano, or PSI), the Radical Party, and the Republican Party (Partito Republicano Italiano, or PRI) were critical of the monarchy in a way that the "transformed" liberal Left could never be. Socialists rejected capitalism as a matter of principle; the other parties called for broad political and administrative reforms. Anarchism's challenge to all forms of authority, but mostly the authority of the state, was also disquieting.

It was all too much for members of the older generation brought up to believe that the country would fall apart without domestic solidarity. Conservatives invoked the principles of the founding fathers and, following the lead of Sidney Sonnino, called for a "return to the Statuto." That was the constitution of 1848, still the law of the land but, according to the conservatives, stretched way beyond the intentions of the founders who believed in monarchy, patriotism, and the rule of law. A return to the letter of the Statuto would have expanded the powers of the crown at the expense of parliament and of the army and police at the expense of civil liberties. Conservative attempts to legislate those principles into law caused a furor in parliament and the country. They were beaten back after tumultuous battles by a coalition of radicals, republicans, socialists, and liberals. That victory paved the way toward a new version of liberal government.

THE LIBERALISM OF GIOVANNI GIOLITTI

1901–1914

Giovanni Giolitti was a new type of politician. Too young to have fought the battles of the Risorgimento, he did his apprenticeship in the administration rather than in politics. He turned to politics with a thorough understanding of how the machinery of state works. He could size up changes on the Italian scene in a dispassionate way that struck observers as cold-blooded, calculating, and indifferent to principles. Detractors on the Left called him *ministro della malavita* (minister of the underworld) because they accused him of winning elections with the help of criminal elements. Detractors on the Right suspected him of being a socialist at heart because he courted socialist votes in parliament and reciprocated with political favors. But Giolitti was a man of principles in his own way. He believed firmly in parliament, regarded politics as the art of the possible, did not question the legitimacy of the opposition, thought that government should do what it could to help business and the economy, and wanted the state to be neutral in conflicts between business and labor. Giolitti's program was modern in that it accepted the rise of capital and labor as normal concomitants of economic progress, and recognized that economic and political freedom went hand in hand. He also recognized that the country's political appetites should not exceed its economic possibilities.

The so-called Giolittian era stretched from 1901 to 1914. Giolitti had served as prime minister in 1892–93 with nearly disastrous results for his political career. Government finances were in dire straits and the economy in crisis. His reputation was tainted by the scandal of the Banca Romana and by the agitation of the Fasci siciliani, both occurring on his watch. He had refused to call out the army, a decision that reflected his conviction that the government should not take sides in labor conflicts, but one that alarmed the law-and-order people. It took Giolitti eight years to overcome the stigma attached to him by his first performance as prime minister. He made his political comeback as minister of the interior in the government headed by the ailing Giuseppe Zanardelli in 1901. Giolitti was the real power broker in the government. His assumption of the prime ministry in June 1903 was an important moment because legislation that had stalled started to move forward, but the direction of government was already clear in 1901. There was to be a dialogue between liberals and socialists, government would remain neutral in labor conflicts, reformist unions and worker cooperatives would be encouraged. It was also clear that Giolitti would use all means available to influence the electorate, that the theoretically neutral prefects would play a major role in lining up votes, and that illicit electoral practices would reach a new level, especially in the south where the press was less likely to expose abuses of power.

The Giolittian era covered a critical period. In those years Italy experienced the effects of industrial expansion, mass emigration, the rise of organized labor, and the emergence of an active Catholic political movement. New radical movements appeared at both extremes of the political spectrum, nationalists on the right and revolutionary syndicalists on the left. Both were contemptuous of parliament, which was Giolitti's favorite forum, and both condemned Giolitti's liberalism as a corrupting influence. There was a sharp increase in the frequency and duration of labor strikes, with major ones occurring in 1904, 1906, and 1908. Labor militancy and government neutrality prompted employers to begin organizing on a national scale. The General Confederation of Labor (Confederazione Generale del Lavoro, or CGL) formed in 1906 and the employers' Confederation of Industry (Confindustria) in 1910. Giolitti persisted in his hands-off policy as long as labor contests did not degenerate into public disorders. Southerners experienced the forceful side of Giolitti's labor strategy more frequently than northerners, partly because repression there carried lower political costs, and partly because labor conflicts in the south often turned violent.

Giolitti courted the parliamentary Left and the labor unions with social legislation that included subsidies for low-income housing, preferential awarding of government contracts to worker cooperatives, and old age and disability pensions. The nationalization of the railroads achieved in 1906 by the government of Alessandro Fortis was also part of Giolitti's program, as was the government monopoly on life insurance achieved in 1912. The use of compulsory arbitration was intended to avert the public disorders that would have compelled Giolitti to call out the army.

In the summer of 1911 Giolitti yielded to pressures to take the country to war. At stake were the North African territories of Cyrenaica and Tripolitania that were under nominal Ottoman control and ready to be seized by a colonial power. France had recently won recognition of its control over Morocco. It had disavowed any intention to seize the other two territories and promised to support Italian claims, but the French promise would lapse unless Italy acted quickly. The decision to invade was made and the naval expedition organized quickly to avoid the complications that would result from a long diplomatic debate, but inadequate planning and preparation exacted a price. After the initial seizures of the coastal towns, the campaign bogged down and opposition grew at home and abroad. So did nationalist sentiment and demands for a quick and decisive victory. Socialists condemned the war but, except for a few diehard extremists including the young firebrand Benito Mussolini, who led antiwar demonstrations and ended up in jail, they did little to stop the fighting. In reality, a patriotic frenzy swept the country. Italian emigrants abroad forgot regional differences and came together in support of the war. The Treaty of Ouchy (October 1912) ended formal military operations (a guerrilla war continued for another 20 years) and concluded a peace on moderate terms. The Italian-Turkish War gave Italy the colony of Libya, islands in the Aegean Sea, and greater standing as a colonial and Mediterranean power. It also stirred up Slavic resistance against Ottoman rule in the Balkans. The two Balkan wars of 1912 and 1913 were a direct result of Italy's war, and Balkan unrest was the direct cause of World War I.

The crowning Giolittian achievement was expansion of the suffrage, which became law in June 1912. Giolitti justified it as a reward to the Italian people for the political maturity they had shown and for their patriotic support of the war. Like the war, the reform had unintended consequences. It achieved something close to universal male suffrage, expanded the electorate from 3.3 million to 8.6 million voters, or from 9.4 percent to 24 percent of the total population. It brought Italy into an era of mass participation for which Giolitti's political organization was hardly prepared. It ended parliamentary dominance by strong figures like Giolitti, Crispi, Depretis, and Cavour. The future belonged to organized political parties. The elections of September 1913 were the first in the country's history to involve the people at large. The results changed the way the political system worked. Liberals were still a majority, but at a disadvantage because of their loose organization, competing clienteles, and poor parliamentary discipline. The socialist opposition grew, hard-liners won control of the party, and ideological debate intensified. Catholics also benefited. Some believe Giolitti's liberal coalition held on to a slim majority, thanks to the understanding with Catholics known as the Gentiloni Pact. The elections weakened Giolitti's power base, hardened ideological differences, and polarized parliament. The system was more democratic, more volatile, and harder to manage. Democracy did not bring domestic peace. Antigovernment protests that became outright insurrections broke out in June 1914. Insurgents took over local administrations, proclaimed independent republics, lowered the national tricolor and hoisted the red flag over public buildings, took over transportation and communication facilities, abolished taxes, and disarmed troops. It took 100,000 troops to restore order. Dubbed Red Week, these disorders suggested that a decade of social reform had not pacified the country. Critics pointed out that liberal reforms had only whetted the appetite for more change.

THE GREAT WAR

1915–1918

Giolitti did not have to deal with Red Week because he resigned as prime minister in March 1914. No one knew at the time that the Giolittian era had come to a close because Giolitti's earlier resignations had always resulted in strong comebacks. This time it was different. The outbreak of the Great War, the European conflict that would later be called World War I, had immediate repercussions on the Italian political scene. When fighting broke out in August 1914 the Italian government chose to stay out of the conflict. Permanent neutrality was an option because Italian diplomats could rightly argue that nothing in the Triple Alliance treaty compelled Italy to join its allies in a war that was not defensive in character. Giolitti argued that Italy could obtain a great deal from its allies in return for a promise of neutrality, but his advice was not heeded even though public opinion and many in parliament supported him. Too much the patriot to rock the boat, Giolitti would not press his case in or outside parliament.

His successor, Antonio Salandra, had a different agenda. Instead of negotiating Italian neutrality, he was willing to negotiate the terms of Italian intervention, a decision that worked in favor of supporting the Entente Powers (France, Great Britain, and Russia). Giolitti may have had a parliamentary majority behind him (it is hard to be certain because parliament was never convened to declare war), but for once he had maneuvered himself into irrelevance. The electoral reform had produced an unmanageable parliament. Nationalist sentiments had reached the boiling point. Nationalist propaganda insisted that Italy must go to war to prove that it was a great power, acquire territory, fulfill its colonial aspirations, consolidate a nation under the Italian flag, and end the disgrace of mass emigration. Liberals liked to keep domestic and foreign affairs in separate compartments. Not so nationalists, who regarded foreign and domestic policies as inextricably intertwined.

From August 1914 to May 1915, while the Entente Powers (France, Great Britain, and Russia) fought against Germany, Austria-Hungary, and the Ottoman Empire, Italian diplomats negotiated the terms of Italy's participation in the war. They negotiated with both sides, but to their Triple Alliance partners they offered only neutrality in exchange for territorial concessions by Austria-Hungary, while to the Entente Powers they offered Italian intervention. The

Pact of London, signed in April 1915, set the terms of Italy's intervention on the side of the Entente. But while the negotiations were going on in secret, a very public debate developed in the country over the merits of intervention versus neutrality. That debate had lasting political repercussions. The Socialist Party (Partito Socialista Italiano, or PSI), organized labor, the Catholic Church, the Catholic contingent in parliament, and most Giolittian liberals favored neutrality. Except on the nationalist Right, where interventionist sentiments prevailed, interventionists were in the minority among the country's organized forces. On the Left, Benito Mussolini was expelled from the Socialist Party because of his interventionist views and carried with him a minority of left-wing interventionists. What seemed at the time little more than a party squabble would have major repercussions after the war. Nationalist fervor was rampant among the educated. Students, middle-class professionals, writers, and other intellectuals were ready for war. War would be a great adventure, they could emulate the heroic deeds of their fathers and grandfathers who had unified the country, they would make good on claims that Italy was a great power. It is hard to gauge popular sentiment beyond these minorities because public opinion polls did not exist and the press reflected the views of organized groups. Peasants, who constituted a majority, were influenced by the neutralist sentiments of the church, and urban workers by the Socialist Party and labor unions, which also favored neutrality. The signing of the secret Pact of London, with its stipulation that Italy must go to war within a month, placed the government in the difficult position of choosing a side secretly, with the country divided between neutralists and interventionists, possibly against the wishes of the majority. The constitution allowed the king to declare war without consulting parliament, but in the absence of a parliamentary mandate it was all the more important to have a show of overwhelming popular support. Thus, the four weeks that elapsed between the signing of the Pact of London and the declaration of war saw well-orchestrated events and street demonstrations. The press gave intensive coverage to the public speeches by Gabriele d'Annunzio to delirious urban crowds.

Italy declared war on Austria-Hungary on May 24, 1915. The fact that it did not declare war on Germany until August 28, 1916, points to Italy's limited objectives. The war was being fought to obtain specific territories from the historic enemy of Italian independence. Salandra articulated this narrow vision of the war by invoking the "sacred egoism" of national interest. It was not an uncommon view at the time among government leaders, but it was one that posed special problems for Italy, as its leaders clung tenaciously to this view long after others decided that the war was being fought for grand ideals, including abolishing war itself, outlawing secret diplomacy, providing self-determination for national minorities, and making the world safe for democracy. The decision to go to war was facilitated initially by the opinion of most military experts that the war was bound to be violent but of brief duration. Instead, the opposing armies had bogged down in a war of attrition with no end in sight. The Entente Powers hoped that Italian intervention would tip the scales against Germany and Austria-Hungary, and for that reason had been rather generous with promises of territorial and colonial gains. Italian military leaders prepared for war as best as they could, but there were major deficiencies in armaments and supplies, due in part to the recent war in North Africa, that Italian industry could not easily make up. Heavy artillery and machine guns were in short supply, there were not enough trained officers, and the Austrian border was poorly defended because, by the terms of the Triple Alliance, Austria should have been an ally rather than the enemy.

Had the Austrians been better prepared they conceivably could have scored the rapid victory sought by the Italians. But neither side prevailed. Both had to contend with the forbidding nature of the mountainous terrain, deficiencies in armaments, and outmoded military thinking. The front was 400 miles long, but most of the fighting occurred along a 60-mile stretch in the northeastern sector along the Isonzo River from the town of Tolmino in the Alps to the Adriatic Sea. The 11 "battles of the Isonzo" fought between May 1915 and August 1917 won the Italians some terrain, but were enormously costly in lives and materiel. The creation of the Arditi shock troops was an effort to break the stalemate and restore movement to what had become a bloody war of attrition. The 12th battle was almost decisive, but not as the Italians had hoped. It resulted in the nearly disastrous Austro-German breakthrough at Caporetto that drove the Italians back to the Piave River and cost them thousands of casualties and prisoners. It took the Italians nearly a year to recover. Much changed in that last year. A government of national unity, led by Vittorio Emanuele Orlando, took steps to restore civilian morale and improve relations with the army. The new army commander, General Armando Diaz, was much better than his competent but insensitive and rigid predecessor, General Luigi Cadorna, at dealing with soldiers and civilian leaders. Troop morale improved, civilians rallied behind the war effort, and the public perceived the war as one of national defense rather than conquest. The final offensive was well timed. In October 1918 the army resumed the offensive against an exhausted enemy ready to collapse, and the Austrians signed an armistice at Villa Giusti on November 4. The Italians were the only ones to end the war victorious on enemy territory. World War I ended seven days later when the Germans signed the armistice of Compiègne. The Italian army, almost defeated a year earlier, had made a remarkable recovery and beaten both enemies and allies in the drive to secure peace.

A war fought so hard and for so long was bound to have major repercussions on the home front. A striking characteristic of the Italian political scene was that the end of fighting saw a resumption of the old polemics between neutralists and interventionists. Alone among European socialist parties, the Italian Socialist Party, in favor of Italian neutrality before the war, had adopted during the war a policy of neither supporting nor sabotaging the war effort (*né aderire né sabotare*). That ambiguous stand left them vulnerable to accusations of defeatism, of having undermined troop morale with their antiwar propaganda, of having brought on the defeat at Caporetto, and of working for communist revolution in Italy, as the Bolsheviks were doing in Russia. War and the Russian Revolution split the Italian left. Republicans, radicals, and social democrats rallied behind the government. Some socialists, impressed by the victory of communism in Russia, did want a communist revolution, while others thought that Italian workers should press for a greater share of the fruits of victory, including better wages and benefits, and shorter working hours. In reality it was not always possible to distinguish between reformists and revolutionaries, for any form of labor militancy could easily be seen as part of a revolutionary plan. The urban unrest and "bread riots" of the summer of 1917 seemed a prelude to revolution similar to what was happening in Russia. The war also intensified the traditional antagonism between city and countryside, for the mostly peasant infantry had carried the burden of fighting, while large numbers of industrial workers had remained at home with military deferments to work on jobs deemed critical to the war effort. Peasant families, on the other hand, suffered from high casualties, lost income, requisitions of produce and livestock, and decreased consumption. The government promised land and jobs to boost troop morale. Veterans expected to cash in on those promises at war's end.

THE POSTWAR CRISIS
AND THE RISE OF FASCISM

1918–1922

Italy was represented at the Paris Peace Conference by Prime Minister Vittorio Emanuele Orlando and Foreign Minister Sidney Sonnino. Their insistence on full implementation of the territorial provisions of the Pact of London, plus additional compensations for the prolonged nature of the war and the changed situation in the Balkans due to the unanticipated demise of the Austro-Hungarian Empire, clashed with the expectations of Italy's wartime allies. The Caporetto debacle, although hardly worse than the reverses suffered by the others, gave the allies a pretext to disparage Italy's contribution to the joint war effort and oppose its demands. Their propaganda in turn enflamed Italian nationalists, who accused the government of being too accomodating at the peace table and called the result a "mutilated victory." Their anger focused on President Woodrow Wilson, whom they held chiefly responsible for opposing Italy's demands. Wilson was a formidable opponent because he personified the idealism of the war effort and was immensely popular in Europe. The enthusiastic receptions he received during a trip to Italy in January 1919 attested to his popularity among Italians. He appealed directly to the Italian people over the heads of their representatives in Paris to mitigate their demands and respect the principle of self-determination for the Slavic populations of the new state of Yugoslavia.

That meant that Italians should gave up their claim to the city of Fiume, whose transfer to Italy had not been included in the Pact of London. As a major seaport it was more important for the Yugoslavs than for the Italians, who acquired the even more important port city of Trieste. The self-determination argument was perhaps less compelling because the city was Italian-speaking, but the majority in the suburbs and countryside was Croatian. The Italian delegation abandoned the peace conference in protest when it could not get its way, then returned to participate in the final sessions, but Orlando's prestige was badly shaken at home and he resigned as prime minister in June 1919. Matters took an unexpected turn in September when Fiume was seized and occupied by a band of Italian paramilitary "legionnaires" led by Gabriele d'Annunzio. In Fiume d'Annunzio assumed the title "comandante" and created many of the patriotic rituals, including military parades, salutes, war cries, the cult of youth, and speeches from the balcony that would become part of fascism. The fate of Fiume became a highly emotional issue that complicated post-war politics. The government refused to accept the city from the legionnaires and evicted them by force, after the city had proclaimed its independence and even declared war against Italy. Italy eventually got the city, minus the suburbs and countryside, with international approval. But that conclusion was far off in the future. The fact that the legionnaires were mostly disgruntled army officers, and that more flocked to join them after the seizure of the city, suggested deteriorating military discipline, that the government had a tenuous hold on the armed forces, that nationalist passions could put to a severe test the loyalty and discipline of the armed forces, and that the country might face the danger of civil war.

Rapidly escalating social conflicts also seemed to portend civil war. The years 1919–20 are remembered as the *biennio rosso* (Red Years). Labor strikes reached unprecedented levels of frequency and intensity. They culminated in the occupation of the factories by workers in September 1920, after which the agitation abated. But the forcible eviction of management from the factories, and the government refusal to intervene, scared employers, who began to think in terms of self-defense and to look for new political allies. A new electoral law of August 1919 introduced the system of proportional representation. The elections held in November 1919 on the basis of that law produced a parliament that reflected accurately the political divisions of the country. An assortment of political formations that could be broadly defined as centrist, including liberals, democrats, radicals, republicans, and social democrats, accounted for 252 seats out of a total of 508 seats in the Chamber of Deputies. Socialists won 156 seats, and the Catholic Popular Party (Partito Popolare Italiano, or PPI) 100 seats. A parliament so configured could not produce stable governments because the liberal center was not homogeneous and the two major parties would cooperate neither with liberals nor with one another. Coalition governments headed by Francesco Saverio Nitti (1919–20), Giovanni Giolitti (1920–21), and the lesser figures of Ivanoe Bonomi (1921–22) and Luigi Facta (1922) governed precariously in the face of mounting economic discontent and popular unrest.

The demobilization of millions of veterans, unemployment, inflation, food and fuel shortages, food rationing, strikes, and outbreaks of politically motivated street demonstrations were salient features of the Italian scene in 1919–20. To make matters worse, in 1918–19 Italy, like other countries, suffered from a lethal influenza (*la spagnola*) that deepened people's fears and sense of insecurity. Instead of bringing the promised peace and prosperity, the end of the war ushered in a period of crisis that played into the hands of political extremists and fringe groups. Political success for these initially small groups depended on inventive leadership, ability to transform the issues of the moment into a set of easy propositions, and build a political base that cut across traditional social divides.

Fascism rose against this grim background of fear, resentments, and desperate grasping for new ideas to confront a crisis that was the direct result of war. Benito Mussolini founded the *fasci di combattimento* in Milan, Italy's leading industrial city, on March 23, 1919. He pitched his message specifically at war veterans, whom he called the *trincerocrazia* (aristocracy of the trenches) and welcomed as a new and decisive political force. A former socialist, interventionist, and war veteran, he had the requisite qualifications to address the enormous mass of veterans that he predicted would shake the very foundations of society. He was also a talented political journalist. His personal newspaper, *Il Popolo d'Italia,* was an effective vehicle for the dissemination of his views and those of his movement. And the "fascism of the first hour," the first and most radical version of fascism, did promise radical change. It rejected monarchy and called for a republic; it demanded abolition of the Senate because it was appointed rather than elected; it promised universal suffrage for men and women, a system of political representation that took into account the economic role and professional qualifications of individuals and groups, and a voice for workers in the process of production. The program condemned socialism, not because it was socialist but because it was anti-national. Instead of class war and the dictatorship of the proletariat, fascism promised class cooperation. It condemned the bourgeoisie, but not capitalism. The bourgeoisie was a state of mind, capitalism was a system of production. The enemy was not capitalism but the state, which shackled the process of production with high taxes and excessive regulation. Not wealth redistribution, but "productivism" would solve the social problems of the nation.

Fascism promised its own revolution, distinct from that of the socialists. The Fascist revolution began in April with the sacking and burning of the Milan premises of *Avanti!,* the Socialist Party newspaper. It was the first of many "punitive expeditions" carried out against political opponents by paramilitary "squads" answering to Mussolini and other leaders of the movement. The *squadristi* were for the most part war veterans, some from the elite Arditi troops, usually former officers who found it difficult to reenter civilian life and could not abandon the habit of command that they had acquired during the war. Fascism was initially an urban movement of the North, but it soon spread into the countryside and to other parts of the country. The growth was rapid after the occupations of the factories by workers in September 1920. The occupations, and the government's failure to evict the occupiers, frightened employers and landowners. They were also emboldened by the failure of the occupations into thinking that they could now launch a successful counteroffensive against the unions and the socialists with their own resources and the help of *squadristi.* Thus began in the course of 1921 the conversion of fascism from a movement that promised radical change to one that insisted on the restoration of law and order as a precondition for change. While industrial employers tried to maintain a certain distance from fascism, landowners relied increasingly on the Fascist action squads to attack and destroy union headquarters, worker cooperatives, and mutual aid societies. Fascists also directed their organized attacks against socialist newspapers and party headquarters. As they became better organized and bolder, they removed local elected officials and took over local administrations. The young Italo Balbo was particularly successful in his native province of Ferrara and throughout the Po Valley, where the network of worker organizations was most developed. Balbo deluded himself into thinking that he was attacking not socialism but "those other Austrians," in other words enemies of the nation, as he called the socialists who organized workers and incited them to act against employers and landowners.

The *squadristi* did not apologize for using violence against legitimate organizations and elected officials. The cult of the minority as the repository of the national interest was an integral part of Fascist ideology. Mussolini had said in his founding speech that majorities are static, and minorities are dynamic, and he explicitly endorsed "the dictatorship of will and intelligence" over the inert masses. There was always that fundamental contradiction at the core of Fascist ideology, that on the one hand it held up the Italian people as a model of civilization, while on the other it rejected "the masses" as the deadweight of history. The contradiction did not matter much in practice, for Fascists arrogated to themselves the right to speak for the people and coerce the masses, but it did force the Fascists into performing a delicate balancing act. They had to convince Italians that they wanted to have and do what the Fascists wanted them to have and do. That was a feat seemingly beyond the power of the Fascist movement in its early days. The lack of discipline and the unpredictability of local Fascist bosses, or *ras*, as these independent-minded potentates were called, worried Mussolini. Hence his attempts to rein in his undisciplined followers, develop a uniform ideology, and transform the movement into a regular political party. In the elections of May 1921 he and 34 other Fascists were elected to parliament in the list of government candidates sponsored by Giolitti. The old political wizard hoped that being represented in parliament would help "transform" the Fascists into law-and-order people. In August 1921 Mussolini engineered the Pact of Pacification between Fascists and Socialists, over the strenuous objections of the most belligerent *ras*. At Mussolini's insistence, the Fascist movement became the Partito Nazionale Fascista (PNF) in November 1921. Controlling the squads proved more difficult. It occurred more than a year later in December 1922, after the Fascists had come to power, when the squads were organized into a centrally run party militia. Moderate opinion looked favorably on these developments. They suggested that fascism might yet be channeled into the ways of legality.

Containing fascism was too much of a challenge for postwar governments. Resting on shaky parliamentary majorities and coalitions, these governments were at the mercy of political parties that were locked in ideological conflicts and incapable of forming a common front. Government policy wavered, sometimes taking a hard line on issues of law and order, sometimes closing an eye to what many liberals regarded as acts of justified violence against the subversives of the left. Nitti instituted the Royal Guard (Guardia Regia), a military police force trained to deal with street disorders. Giolitti hoped to engage the Fascists in the give-and-take of parliamentary politics, but he also ordered the police to shoot them down if they misbehaved seriously in the streets. That was an act of political courage, as was the decision to abolish budget-breaking government subsidies to keep the price of bread artificially low. Giolitti resigned when the elections of May 1921 failed to give him the majority he needed to govern. Mussolini had intimated in the campaign preceding the election that the Fascists intended to seize power with a "march on Rome" that would give them control of the capital and the national government. The scenario proved more complicated, as Mussolini adopted a twofold strategy of encouraging and preparing his followers to make the big move on the capital, while maneuvering politically behind the scenes to eliminate or minimize opposition to the move. It was a time-consuming but ultimately successful tactic. The squads began to gather and move on Rome in the last days of October 1922. Mussolini waited out the events in Milan, keeping open his options, which included beating a hasty retreat into nearby Switzerland if matters turned ugly for the Fascists, until the refusal of King Victor Emmanuel III to sign the martial law decree that would have ordered the army to put down the Fascist squads told him that he had nothing to fear from the king and the army. He then demanded and received the king's invitation to form his own government. On October 31, 1922, Italy had a new prime minister in the person of Benito Mussolini. He would remain in that post, with significant changes of title, until July 25, 1943.

THE SEIZURE OF POWER

1922–1925

When Mussolini was appointed prime minister the Fascists were a parliamentary minority that needed the help of other parties and groups to govern constitutionally. Not that there was any doubt that they would rule one way or another. Mussolini made that quite clear when he said that "Our program is simple: We want to rule Italy," and when he told the Chamber of Deputies in his maiden speech as premier that had he chosen to do so he could have transformed that "gray chamber" into a bivouac for his troops. But he was saved from having to govern dictatorially right away by the willingness of most liberal and Catholic deputies to cooperate with the new government in the hope that the responsibilities of power would dampen the Fascists' enthusiasm for radical change. Mussolini accepted the help of those willing to cooperate with his government and even went so far as to make overtures to moderate socialists, perhaps to further divide them and to introduce into his government a new element that would make it look more representative and pro-labor. His overtures to the socialists did not pan out, but that still left his government with a majority that was willing to give him the benefit of the doubt. Parliament voted his government extraordinary powers for a period of one year in budgetary and fiscal matters. His first finance minister was Alberto De Stefani, an economic liberal and free trader who set about the difficult task of balancing the budget, cutting back on government regulations, reducing the size of the bureaucracy, improving communications and transportation, and helping an economic recovery that was already underway.

The search for allies across the political spectrum and the pursuit of administrative reforms suggest perhaps a desire to de-escalate ideological conflict and create an atmosphere of relative calm in which urgently needed technical reforms could be discussed and implemented. Domestic concerns were certainly uppermost in Mussolini's mind in his first three years of government. In that time the conduct of foreign policy was left mostly in the hands of career diplomats in the ministry of foreign affairs, managed by Salvatore Contarini, who held the post of secretary-general of that ministry from 1920 to 1925—mostly but not entirely in the hands of professional diplomats, for in 1923 Mussolini provoked a show of force with Greece and sent a naval force to occupy the Greek island of Corfu. He backed off under pressure from the British government, but won a significant victory the following year when he pressured Yugoslavia into giving up its claims to Fiume and annexed that long-disputed town. The seizure of Corfu remained an isolated episode for the time being and the annexation of Fiume could hardly be seen as anything but an overdue settlement. The overall record of government in these early years suggested that the liberals might have been right in thinking that the responsibilities of government would tame Mussolini and his Fascist followers. But such hopes would have been misplaced because there were other and less reassuring aspects of Fascist government from the very start. Mussolini was never content with mere administrative reforms. He told the Fascist Grand Council, a new body that he created in December 1922 and that was destined to take on important functions of government, that fascism had not carried out the march on Rome to engage in ordinary administration. He also wanted to make parliament more cohesive and compliant. Parliament appointed a commission headed by the Fascist deputy Giacomo Acerbo to study electoral reform. It came up with a proposal that was approved by a majority in June 1923. Most liberals, including Giovanni Giolitti, supported the reform, as did many Catholic representatives. Only the socialists and communists voted against it.

The new electoral law enabled the Fascists to win control of parliament in the national elections of April 1924, but their victory was marred by charges that they had terrorized the opposition and manipulated the vote. On May 30, 1924, the socialist leader Giacomo Matteotti presented parliament with a well-documented exposé of electoral irregularities and demanded the nullification of the elections. On June 10 he was abducted while on his way to parliament, spirited away in a car, severely beaten, and killed by a group of Fascist enforcers. Matteotti's disappearance and the discovery of his remains in August precipitated a crisis that nearly brought down Mussolini's government. About 150 opposition deputies abandoned parliament in protest to meet as a counter-parliament in the so-called Aventine Secession. King Victor Emmanuel III did not answer their appeal to dismiss Mussolini. The degree of Mussolini's personal responsibility in the crime has never been ascertained. He may have wanted Matteotti punished physically but not killed, he may not have known when or how the action would take place, but orders to proceed against Matteotti probably originated from within his government. When Matteotti's death was ascertained all government figures suspected of collusion in the crime and the attempted coverup were dismissed from their posts, including Minister of the Interior Emilio De Bono. Mussolini wanted to reassure public opinion, but tensions rose throughout the summer and fall of 1924. In December a group of hard-line Fascists confronted Mussolini and demanded decisive action. Mussolini responded on January 3, 1925, with a speech in parliament that ended all doubts about where he stood. He assumed the political but not criminal responsibility for what had happened, dared his opponents to bring charges against him, and promised a quick restoration of order and calm in the country. The Aventine secessionists were not allowed to return to parliament, the opposition was muzzled, dissident groups driven underground, and press censorship became systematic.

The Matteotti crisis ushered in a new phase of Fascist rule that saw an expansion of government that would have been hard to predict in the earlier "liberal" phase. Opponents of the regime coined the term "totalitarian" to condemn fascism's pursuit of absolute power. Mussolini adopted the term triumphantly, boasting that fascism intended to go beyond the customary political functions of government to penetrate and organize all aspects of social life, become a daily presence in the lives of ordinary people, and shape the attitudes and behavior of individuals. The "Fascist regime" was the machinery devised in pursuit of that goal, starting in 1925. Parliament was reduced to a rubber-stamping body and its makeup and functions were radically transformed by corporative reforms, its membership handpicked by the Fascist Party and various other official organs. Only the Fascist Party operated legally, all the other parties having been disbanded or driven underground. Mussolini was now the Duce, his title no longer that of prime minister but of head of government responsible to the king. Mussolini was outwardly deferential toward the king, but inwardly resented the "dyarchy" or formal sharing of power—a formal sharing only, because the king reigned but did not rule. Worker strikes and employer lockouts were banned and only government-approved labor unions and employer associations were authorized to engage in collective bargaining. Government arbitrators stood ready to settle unresolved labor disputes. The Opera Nazionale Balilla (later renamed Gioventù Italiana del Littorio) enrolled boys and girls ages six to 15. The National Organization for the Protection of Mothers and Infants, founded in December 1925, promoted the regime's policy of population growth and racial health. Other public health initiatives included campaigns to contain and eradicate rampant diseases like malaria and tuberculosis. Fascism's *politica della razza* (racial policy) began as a drive to promote not racial purity but the physical and mental health of Italians, who were now urged to live actively, participate in sports, enjoy the outdoors, eat and drink soberly. The Opera Nazionale Dopolavoro discounted meals, provided centers for cultural and recreational activities, sponsored theatrical performances, and organized group excursions. It was the regime's most popular innovation, perhaps because it avoided overt political propaganda.

THE FASCIST REGIME IN ACTION

1925–1935

Putting in place this machinery of government and social control was a lengthy and complicated process that continued into the 1930s. "Deals" among different and rival interest groups were an integral part of the process. Negotiations with the Catholic Church settled the long-standing Roman Question. The Lateran Pacts and Concordat of 1929 established formal relations between the Holy See and the Italian government, guaranteed the church full independence in the exercise of spiritual powers, established Catholicism as the religion of the state, expanded religious instruction in the schools, acknowledged the jurisdiction of the church on questions of marriage, and compensated the church for expropriated properties and financial losses. The potential for friction in some sensitive matters was never eliminated. The organization of youth was a case in point, the adoption of racial policies by the regime in the late 1930s was another. But generally, after 1929 church and state got along reasonably well, to the relief and approval of millions of Italians who, in March 1929, gave the regime a resounding vote of confidence in the first national referendum held after the march on Rome. Just as important was the accommodation with the army, to achieve which the regime refrained from creating an independent militia loyal to the Duce and the party. The militia that evolved after 1925 was never a serious rival to the regular army. It was subject to army rule and discipline and lost much of its military effectiveness through deliberate neglect. Army officers still pledged loyalty to the king. The army, the church, and the Crown backed the regime.

Other important compromises occurred in the areas of economic and social policy. Workers lost freedom of association, had to accept leaders and spokesmen that they did not choose, and suffered wage cuts in times of economic crisis. In return they obtained considerable job security and benefits in the form of family allowances, paid vacations, health and old age insurance. Social welfare came to Italy with fascism. Employers benefited in many ways. They no longer had to contend with rebellious unions and worker demands that threatened managerial prerogatives. The government favored heavy industry and rescued industrial firms on the verge of bankruptcy. In return they had to accept an unprecedented degree of regulation by cartels, ministries, and various other public agencies, including the powerful Institute for Industrial Reconstruction (Istituto per la Recostruzione Industriale, or IRI). The protectionist policies of the late 1920s and 1930s benefited domestic industries that were deemed strategically valuable, particularly those related to the production of armaments. The cartelization of industries in the 1930s protected even the least efficient producers by guaranteeing existing firms a share of the national market and quotas of scarce raw materials.

Landowners benefited from the campaign to expand agricultural production that started in 1925. The centerpiece of that campaign was the "battle for wheat" that the regime touted as an all-out effort to modernize agriculture. By 1938 Italian farmers produced enough wheat to meet the domestic need, at great cost to the taxpayers who subsidized the program and to the detriment of livestock production and meat consumption. The regime spent the huge sum of nearly 16 billion lire on land reclamation from 1922 to 1939. Land reclamation, another showpiece project, was expected to contribute to the *sbracciantizzazione* ("deproletarization") of the agricultural labor force by turning landless workers into small peasant proprietors and break their traditional ties to the political parties of the left in parts of north and central Italy. In the south, the regime's primary motivation was to win support for the regime in a part of the country that, with few exceptions, was indifferent to fascism. The battle for wheat, the use of machinery and artificial fertilizers, training of agrarian experts, land reclamation, and incentives to keep families on the land were part of a concerted effort to win the support of the country's rural population.

In reality, most of the rural population derived little benefit from the regime's economic and social programs. Few peasants belonged to any of the regime's formal organizations, with the possible exception of the Dopolavoro. The Massaie Rurali, an organization for peasant housewives, was established only in 1935 and was poorly funded. For most rural workers, finding employment outside agriculture was difficult because of laws that restricted internal migration to those who already had an offer of work. Anti-migration laws were an important part of the program of "ruralization" that was designed to keep people on the land and regulate the movement of people to the industrial cities. "Ruralization" offered few material advantages to ordinary peasants, but it did offer some moral compensation. The peasant family, life on the soil, and the simple pastimes of country life were praised in art and song as social models and ideals.

Mussolini was the central figure of the regime because of his uncommon ability to win the trust of powerful interests and manipulate the many contending factions and pressure groups that regarded him as the indispensable mediator. His ability to be many things to many people was a powerful asset. Although it is usually obscured by his carefully cultivated public image as a domineering figure, the key to his acceptance and longevity in power was the ability to strike compromises, make decisions that left many doors open, threaten only declared enemies, and keep alive the hopes of collaborators. Such temporizing did not sit well with everyone, and throughout the 1920s there was a steady exodus of discontents from the ranks, including Fascist anticlericals who objected to the cozy relations with the church, labor activists who wanted more for workers, laissez-faire liberals opposed to government regulation, assorted hard-liners impatient with the slow pace of change, and insiders revolted by the evidence of collusion and corruption. The Fascist Party, home to many discontents, was purged of dissidents and entrusted to the care of Achille Starace, a Fascist who could be relied on to follow Mussolini's directives blindly. Mussolini disliked independent-minded collaborators and surrounded himself with obedient automatons like Starace or industrious civil servants like police chief Arturo Bocchini. Mussolini the zealous bureaucrat is a little-known figure worth studying.

The Fascist Party did not have much influence on state policy in the 1930s but was very active in public life, where it performed highly visible ritual functions. The organization of rallies, parades, community projects, and propaganda campaigns was its specialization. The party's primary task was to organize popular "consensus" for the regime, a troublesome and controversial issue if ever there was one. The evidence suggests that by the mid 1930s there was indeed broad popular support for the regime, which could boast of some significant achievements in social policy and the pacification of the country. The generation born during and right after the war was now coming of age and knew of no other system. The regime appealed to the young and made much of them as the hope of the future. Those among their elders who were not happy with the status quo grumbled cautiously. Above and beyond the arrangements and deals discussed earlier that tied specific interest groups to the regime, the overarching themes of nationalist propaganda had broad appeal. Those with the most formal education were influenced the most, for they were the ones most exposed and receptive to the regime's official propaganda. Support for the regime was therefore most noticeable among the educated middle classes, which also benefited from the expansion of career opportunities in government and the public sector of the economy. Students in secondary schools and universities, graduates, teachers, civil servants, and professionals, both men and women, were drawn to the regime. The less educated of both sexes, the peasantry of north and south, were the least affected by the various patriotic myths popularized by the regime, including the cult of ancient Rome (*romanità*), of the Duce as the father of his people, and of Italy as the cradle of civilization. What all of this bought the regime was the active support of many among the educated, and passive support by the rest of the population.

FOREIGN POLICY AND THE ROAD TO WAR

1935–1940

By 1935 most opponents of the regime had been driven out of the country, the few who were in the underground at home posed no threat, the economy had been spared the worst ravages of the Great Depression, and corporative reforms were in place. Foreign governments accepted the regime, seeing it as a bulwark against communism and as a necessary corrective to the individualism and anarchic tendencies of the Italian people. But the order that prevailed at home and the acceptance of the regime abroad were also signs that fascism had reached an impasse. Mussolini was fully aware that what had been achieved fell far short of what had been promised. Still unrealized was the promise of national greatness and empire. The 1920s had not been propitious for dramatic gestures and shows of force. During that decade Italian diplomacy had generally seconded multilateral peaceful initiatives like the Treaties of Locarno (1925) that confirmed the inviolability of existing political boundaries, signed friendship treaties with a number of countries, including Ethiopia and Albania, which would soon bear the brunt of Italian expansionist ambitions, and shown due regard for the authority of the League of Nations and the system of collective security. There were exceptions, like the seizure of Corfu in 1923 and repeated efforts in the 1920s to foment discord in the neighboring state of Yugoslavia, but not enough to suggest that Fascist diplomacy was substantially different from that of other powers.

Matters were somewhat different at home, where military parades, a cult of uniforms, nationalist indoctrination, the paramilitary organization of youth, and the spreading cult of *romanità* nurtured dreams of empire. Mussolini's attention shifted from domestic to foreign affairs after 1929 when he felt that the regime was securely established at home. The rise of Hitler and national socialism in Germany opened new prospects for playing off Germany against France and Great Britain to Italy's advantage. Mussolini followed German developments with the closest attention and ambivalent feelings. On the one hand, he recognized the similarities between fascism and national socialism and was flattered by Hitler's attention and praise. Hitler always acknowledged Mussolini as his ideological predecessor and hailed him as a historical figure of the first rank. Mussolini valued the admiration for the political ascendancy it gave him, but also worried about national socialist claims to Austria and the southern Tyrol, and was aware that the ideologies of fascism and national socialism differed in important ways. On the subject of the Tyrol Hitler was cautious, but his closest collaborators made no mystery of their intention to incorporate the German-speaking populations of the Trentino–Alto Adige into the Third Reich. There were ideological differences on the issue of race. Biological racism was the central tenet of national socialism; it played no role in Fascist ideology. Italian fascism had made peace with the Catholic Church, while national socialism viewed the church as a rival and enemy.

Mussolini's interest in foreign policy grew as Hitler came closer to seizing power. In July 1932 the Duce added the post of foreign minister to his other duties. Libya was finally pacified after a 20-year struggle against native resistance. In December 1932 Mussolini commissioned General Emilio De Bono to prepare plans for war in Ethiopia. The choice of De Bono was significant, for De Bono was the army general most closely associated with fascism, and Mussolini wanted a military triumph with a clear Fascist imprint. Hitler's appointment as German chancellor in January 1933 focused Mussolini's attention on the issue of European borders. The Four Power Pact, also known as the *Patto Mussolini,* called on France, Germany, Great Britain, and Italy to collaborate toward peaceful revisions of the borders set by the Versailles Treaty. A series of amendments rendered it meaningless, but the fact the Mussolini attached great importance to it suggests that he was positioning himself to act as mediator between Nazi Germany and the two western democracies.

That was Italy's customary role in European diplomacy and did not necessarily imply aggressive designs, but Mussolini sought leverage to pursue a dynamic foreign policy. Ethiopia was an objective, but he was also mindful of Italy's continental role and European interests, which now seemed threatened by Germany. He was committed to Austrian independence because the unification of Austria and Germany (*Anschluss*) demanded by the Nazis would have put Germany on Italy's borders and threatened Italy's control of the southern Tyrol. Italy's influence in Hungary and the rest of central Europe was also threatened by Germany's rising power. Hitler and Mussolini met for the first time in Venice in June 1934. The meeting was not the disaster that reports made it out to be, but it did not resolve all differences. Hitler assured Mussolini that Germany had no designs on the Italian Tyrol, but the question of Austrian independence was unresolved. The two countries almost came to blows in July when Austrian Nazis attempted unsuccessfully to overthrow the Austrian government and killed Chancellor Engelbert Dollfuss, Mussolini's protégé, while the Mussolinis were playing host to Dollfuss's family. The dispatch of four Italian army divisions to the border at the Brenner Pass was a dramatic gesture that caught the attention of the world. The show of force reinforced Mussolini's image as a decisive leader who was capable of holding Hitler in check.

In April 1935 the representatives of France, Great Britain, and Italy met at the Stresa Conference to discuss the formation of a common front against Germany. Mussolini pressed hard for a strong condemnation of Germany, but came away with the impression that France and Great Britain were not serious about containing Germany. He also came away from the conference with the impression based on what was not said that the two western powers were willing to give Italy a free hand in Ethiopia. That was more than he needed to move ahead with plans that were already formulated. In December 1934 a border incident in the oasis of Walwal heightened tensions. Mussolini pressed ahead with plans for full-scale war. Italian troops crossed the border from the Italian colonies of Eritrea and Somalia into Ethiopia on October 3, 1935.

The Ethiopian War was a foreign policy turning point. Roundly condemned by most governments and by the League of Nations, it isolated Italy diplomatically. Only Germany refused to condemn the aggression, thereby earning Hitler Mussolini's steadfast gratitude. Relations between the two countries improved steadily after 1935. The economic sanctions against Italy imposed by the League of Nations did not stop the war effort, which dragged on until Italian troops entered the Ethiopian capital on May 5, 1936, and Mussolini declared victory to an enthusiastic nation. Italian public opinion perceived the war as a settling of the old score of the Battle of Adowa and as a rightful effort to earn Italy "a place in the sun" alongside other colonial powers. Beyond that generic expectation there was a more specific intent in Mussolini's mind. Possession of Ethiopia, Eritrea, and Somalia would give Italy a strong base of operations on the Red Sea and Indian Ocean. It was no longer a question of re-creating the ancient Roman Empire around the shores of the Mediterranean Sea. *Mare nostrum* was not enough. Italy needed access to the oceans in order to transcend the limitations of that inland sea and reach out to other parts of the world.

Victory in Ethiopia signaled a qualitative jump in Italian imperial aspirations. Carried away by visions of colonial empire, Mussolini lost interest in the affairs of central Europe, in preserving Austrian independence, and blocking Germany's search for *Lebensraum.* He implicitly accepted the international role that Hitler had seen for Italy in *Mein Kampf:* Italy was to be a Mediterranean and African colonial power, while Germany fulfilled its destiny north of the Alps and in eastern Europe. That was the division of spheres of influence that more than anything else accounts for the formation of the Rome-Berlin Axis (1936). Italian-German friendship and cooperation were reinforced by the exchange of official visits. Mussolini received a splendid reception in Germany in September 1937, and Hitler was likewise feted in Italy in May 1938. By then the two countries were fighting on the same side in the Spanish civil war; Hitler had remilitarized the Rhineland and annexed Austria without incident. Italy's relations with France deteriorated badly, but Mussolini still kept up the pretense of maintaining equidistance between Germany and the western democracies. A gentlemen's agreement between Italy and Great Britain signed in January 1937 promised to respect the status quo in the Mediterranean. To Mussolini it meant defusing anger over Italian intervention in Spain and gaining precious time to pursue other goals. In November 1937 Italy joined the Anti-Comintern Pact between Germany and Japan, which was the first official understanding among the three countries that would fight as allies in World War II. The publication of the *Manifesto of Fascist Racism* in July 1938 made anti-Semitism official policy. It marked a startling change from the rejection of racial doctrines that Mussolini had expressed in 1934. The adoption of biological racism was not due solely to the influence of Nazi Germany. The perceived need to separate Italians and natives in Ethiopia also played a role, but there is no doubt that Mussolini was eager to show Hitler that fascism and national socialism were aligned on the racial question. Laws banning Jews from the professions, business, and the schools followed the publication of the manifesto. In September 1938 Mussolini played the role of honest broker at the Munich Conference in what may have been the high point of his diplomatic career. But the plan that he proposed to settle the Sudeten question was perfectly compatible with what the Germans wanted for the time being.

The road to that alliance was not smooth. Italy's contacts with Japan were marginal, but not with Germany. Japan was potentially useful as an ally against the Soviet Union, Great Britain, and the United States, but the Japanese sphere of influence was far away in Asia where Italy had no ambitions. Not so the German sphere of influence, which was right next door. The distinction between the Italian and German spheres of influence mentioned earlier was a rough one that left many possibilities for friction, if not outright conflict. Italy had given up on Austria but continued to regard Hungary as a client state. German agents were active in nearby Croatia. When Italians protested their activities there, the German diplomats backed down and reassured their Italian colleagues that Germany regarded Croatia and the Balkans as being within Italy's sphere of influence. In March 1939 German troops moved into Czechoslovakia and took over the regions of Bohemia and Moravia. Mussolini was taken aback by that move. Perhaps to redress the balance of power in Italy's favor, but also to position Italian troops for further action against Greece and Yugoslavia, he ordered the invasion and takeover of Albania in April 1939. The next month, on May 22, 1939, Italy and Germany signed the Pact of Steel that formalized and sealed the alliance between the two regimes

The Pact of Steel was an unusual diplomatic document in that it gave both signatories carte blanche to do very much what they liked and committed them to come to one another's aid with all the forces at their disposal. That was not the language of conventional diplomacy, which normally tried to gauge and limit commitments. The pact was particularly risky for Italy because Germany was the country most likely to take the initiative and incur the risks of retaliatory action by other powers. On August 23, 1939, Germany and the Soviet Union shocked the world by concluding the Pact of Non-Aggression. That opened the way to the German invasion of Poland in September and the start of World War II. The Italians were spectators as these events unfolded. Hitler informed Mussolini but did not consult with him. The Pact of Steel had given Hitler the freedom of action that he sought and tied the hands of the Italian dictator, who approved of neither the Non-Aggression Pact nor the decision to attack Poland.

On September 3, 1939, when France and Great Britain declared war on Germany, Italian diplomats faced a most difficult dilemma. On the one hand, the language of the Pact of Steel left them little room to maneuver: They should have gone to war on the side of Nazi Germany with no questions asked. On the other hand, they knew perfectly well that Italy was unprepared for war militarily and financially. The army was large (Mussolini had vowed to put into the field "8 million bayonets") but ill equipped. The most serious deficiencies were in heavy artillery and armor. Training also left much to be desired, especially that of noncommissioned officers. The first large-scale mobilization of troops revealed an appalling lack of basic facilities and equipment. Serious shortages of coal and gasoline hampered transportation and industrial production. Only about 600 of the air force's estimated 2,300 airplanes were combat-ready. The navy was in better shape, but battleships that should have been ready were still under construction and its plans did not envision rapid action against the enemy. The primary role for the navy was to guard supply lines with the colonies. Things were no better on the economic side. Foreign currency reserves were exhausted, and the government was on the verge of bankruptcy. Years of fighting in Ethiopia and Spain had taken a toll on the armed forces and the treasury. Publicly acknowledging these deficiencies was out of the question. Mussolini felt humiliated, but agreed to inform Hitler that Italy could not join the fight without massive help from Germany. In the words of the Italian foreign minister, the list of urgently needed armaments and supplies was big enough to choke a bull.

Hitler, although eager to have Italy join the fray, did not press for intervention, thus making it easier for Mussolini to announce Italian "nonbelligerency." He was careful to avoid any mention of "neutrality," with its memories of Italy's defection from the Triple Alliance in 1914–15 and connotations of equidistance between the warring sides. Nonbelligerency meant that Italy was on Germany's side, but not as a fighting partner for the time being. That face-saving formula did not sit well with the Duce, who felt that a great power could not afford to stay out of a major conflict being fought on its doorstep. Italy's descent into war was as slow as it had been in 1914–15, but different in substance. This time there was never any chance that the government might abstain permanently or change sides. Unless Germany was defeated quickly, a most unlikely prospect in 1939, Italy would intervene at the opportune moment. Everyone was looking for signs of a quick German victory. The signs seemed clear enough in spring 1940 after Germany overran Belgium, the Netherlands, and Denmark, and the French army reeled under Germany's blitzkrieg. In May 1940 police informers reported that ordinary people were asking themselves why the government was not going to war after years of touting war as the ultimate test of a country's will to prevail. Shrewd businessmen who knew that the country lacked the resources and industrial apparatus to engage in a long war of attrition thought that victory was within the grasp of the Axis powers because the Germans were moving so quickly. Even the normally ultracautious Victor Emmanuel III thought that it was time to stop hesitating.

WAR AND THE DOWNFALL OF THE FASCIST REGIME

1940–1945

After telling his generals not to worry about the poor state of the armed forces, and that sacrificing a few thousand dead would allow him to sit at the peace table to claim a share of the spoils of war, he took the fateful step. On June 10, 1940, he announced to a frenzied crowd and somber nation listening on the radio that Italy declared war on France and Great Britain. Italy's intervention had the effect of spreading the war beyond Europe. The short campaign that the army fought against the French in the Alps was a minor event, except that it revealed a serious lack of preparation. Given that hardly any fighting had taken place, Mussolini decided against making territorial demands on France and agreed to a separate armistice that was signed on June 24. Mussolini's decision reveals his way of thinking about the war. Italian intervention was timed to take advantage of an impending German victory, in the expectation that it would not be so rapid as to prevent the Italians from conducting some successful military operations on their own. Without that evidence of Italy's ability to fight independently of Germany, Mussolini's regime would be discredited, Italy could not demand major gains, and the victory would be hollow. Hence Mussolini's insistence that the armed forces mount a decisive campaign against the British by invading Egypt from Libya and capturing the Suez Canal. But the Libyan campaign ran into difficulties from the start. Italo Balbo was governor and commander of military operations in the colony. He died in an airplane crash, accidentally shot down by friendly fire on June 28, 1940. Marshall Rodolfo Graziani, who succeeded him, resisted Mussolini's demands for quick action, alleging all sorts of equipment and supply deficiencies. In September his troops moved 60 miles into Egypt and took up defensive positions. British armored forces counterattacked in December and drove the Italians far back into Libya.

Seeking a rapid victory elsewhere, in October 1940 Italian troops attempted to invade Greece from their bases in Albania. Bad weather prevented effective use of the air force, the infantry bogged down in the mud of the mountains, confusion reigned in the shipping ports of southern Italy where thousands of troops were assembled, the Greeks fought stubbornly, and the British rushed to help them. On November 11, 1940, the British air force launched a surprise attack on Italian warships anchored in the port of Taranto and in one stroke put out of commission three capital ships. A complete debacle was narrowly avoided because the troops fought tenaciously through the winter and halted the Greek advance toward the Adriatic, but the campaign was a major embarrassment. Mussolini fumed and fired Badoglio as chief of staff. Italian forces in East Africa surrendered to the British in spring 1941. The country settled down for what now promised to be a long and hard war. The setbacks in Africa and the Balkans indicated how difficult it would be for the country to fight that kind of conflict. Mussolini had started out hoping that Italy could fight its own "parallel war" alongside Germany and earn some credible victories in short order. That was no longer possible, and he resigned himself to calling for German help. The Germans responded, knocked Yugoslavia and Greece out of the war, and Erwin Rommel led offensive operations in North Africa that brought Italian and German troops within 70 miles of Alexandria by July 1942. The British forced them back in October–November 1942. That same month Allied forces landed in North Africa and began to squeeze the Italians and Germans from east and west. Italian troops fought well in Tunisia before being evicted from that last foothold on African soil in May 1943. By then Italian cities were under steady attack from the air, the home front was beginning to crack, and Mussolini was scrambling to save his government.

The defeats of 1940 left Italy at the mercy of its stronger German ally, which understandably demanded a stronger voice in Italian affairs for shouldering the greater burden. Mussolini's strategy now shifted from one of gaining independent victories to one of making a credible effort as a subordinate partner. After Germany invaded the Soviet Union in June 1941, he insisted on sending a large Italian expeditionary force to fight on that front. He followed Japan's attack on Pearl Harbor with an Italian declaration of war against the United States on December 11, 1941. The United States, he claimed in his war speech, was the last bastion of capitalism and the ultimate guardian of the world order that denied Italy its place in the sun. The crowd was still there to cheer him, but ordinary Italians did not see the logic behind this declaration of war. The war was becoming less national and more Fascist as it spread to parts of the world and involved countries with which Italy had no quarrel. Mussolini could still claim some gains. In 1941–42 Italian troops occupied parts of Greece, Yugoslavia, and southern France, extending Italian dominion to regions that had long been coveted by the Fascist regime. They were not puppets of the Germans. Italian commanders refused to hand over Jews and opposed German designs on the territories under their jurisdiction. None of this altered the fact that Italy was now Germany's junior partner. Nazi leaders showed their contempt by calling Mussolini their most important *Gauleiter* (district leader).

On July 10, 1943, came the blow that everyone expected, without knowing precisely where it would land. Allied troops landed in Sicily and marched inland, meeting little resistance from the Italian troops stationed to defend the island. Only a few days earlier Mussolini had vowed the island's defenders would stop the invaders dead at the tideline. The *discorso del bagnasciuga,* as that rash pronouncement came to be known, and the fact that German troops bore the brunt of defending the island, made the loss of Sicily all the more galling. The loss of Sicily put the regime on the ropes, not from the threat of popular revolt but from disaffection at the top. Two conspiracies converged to bring down Mussolini and the regime. On the one hand, disaffected Fascists pressured Mussolini into summoning a meeting of the Grand Council, which was theoretically the highest consultive body of the regime. On the other, the king decided it was time to reassert his authority as head of state and commander in chief. Military officers still took an oath of loyalty to the king, and it was to them that Victor Emmanuel turned in the hour of crisis. Meeting far into the night of July 24–25, 1943, the Grand Council voted no confidence in Mussolini and called on the king to take command of the armed forces. That was the signal that the king was waiting for. On the afternoon of July 25, Mussolini reported to the king without suspecting what was in store. After a tense meeting, during which the king vented his resentment at Mussolini's usurpation of royal prerogatives, the Duce was taken into custody and spirited away by an armed detachment waiting outside the king's villa.

Perhaps the most astounding aspect of the crisis of July 1943 was the absence of a Fascist response to Mussolini's ouster. The Fascist militia and other special forces supposedly loyal to Mussolini acquiesced in the bloodless coup. When news of Mussolini's ouster reached the people, there were celebrations in the streets and crowds attacked the monuments and symbols of the regime. But the rejoicing was premature. Marshall Pietro Badoglio, the new head of government appointed by the king, had a most difficult task ahead of him. The imperative need to get out of the war could not be acknowledged for fear of German retaliation. Badoglio promised publicly that the war would continue, but he authorized secret negotiations for an armistice with the Allies. His emissary, General Giuseppe Castellano (1893–1977), signed the secret armistice that amounted to an unconditional surrender on September 3, 1943. It was not to be announced publicly until the Italian government had taken steps to protect Rome from German retaliation with the help of Allied troops, but when the Allied commanders realized that Rome was doing little to protect itself, they went ahead and announced the armistice on September 8, 1943. The events of the next few hours had disastrous repercussions. The royal court, government, and high command left Rome in such haste that the move had all the appearances of headlong flight. Even worse, they left the army without clear orders, allowing it to dissolve into thin air within days, as officers and enlisted men jettisoned their uniforms and weapons, donned what civilian clothing they could find, and started making their way home as best they could.

The Germans wasted no time in repairing the situation to their advantage. Hitler was not fooled by Badoglio's commitment to continue fighting, and ordered additional German divisions to pour into Italy and begin taking over strategic posts and facilities. A few Italian formations opposed them bravely after the announcement of the armistice, but they were quickly overwhelmed. The Germans corralled stragglers, put them in concentration camps, and eventually shipped them to Germany as prisoners of war or to work as laborers. On

A U.S. armored column rolls through the streets of Palermo, Sicily, on July 22, 1943. *(National Archives)*

the Greek island of Cephalonia where Italian commanders, acting on their own initiative, took up arms against the Germans, thousands were massacred. Hitler still regarded Mussolini as a viable leader and a valuable asset, but Mussolini was under arrest in an unknown place. Discovering his whereabouts and freeing him became a high priority. German paratroopers carried out the daring rescue in the mountains of the Gran Sasso in the Abruzzo region and took him to Germany, where Hitler prevailed on him to return to Italy and set up a new government. Mussolini's state of mind in those days is difficult to assess, for resuming his political career was apparently not his first choice. He later claimed that he gave in to Hitler's request to spare Italy the threatened consequences of a hostile German occupation, but a desire for personal vindication, rancor against those who had abandoned him, particularly the king, as well as a sense of honor may have played a role in his decision to set up the Italian Social Republic that, until the last days of the war, governed those parts of Italy controlled by the Germans.

Italy was a divided country from September 1943 when the armistice was signed to May 1945 when the war ended. The Allies achieved their essential military goals in Italy in 1943 with the Italian surrender, collapse of the Fascist regime, and elimination of the Italian armed forces. They gained complete control of the Mediterranean and of enough Italian territory south of the Gustav Line to launch air operations against Germany from the south. From then on, the Italian theater was of secondary importance to the Allies. After the liberation of Rome in June 1944 the Allies decided to divert forces from Italy to France and the Normandy front. The war dragged on in Italy as the Allies made slow progress up the peninsula, hampered by mountainous terrain, bad weather, and stiff German resistance.

The king governed nominally in the so-called Regno del Sud (Kingdom of the South), which consisted initially of a few provinces that the Allies left under Italian administration. His situation was similar to that of Mussolini, who governed nominally in the North under even stricter German control. The Kingdom of the South, recognized by the Allies as the only legitimate Italian government, declared war against Germany and fielded an army to fight alongside the Allies. Its existence assured the juridical continuity of the Italian state in the eyes of the victorious powers. As the war continued with no end in sight, Italians found themselves at the mercy of invading armies. Left without public services and often without basic necessities, they showed immense resourcefulness. They turned to family and friends for support, sought refuge from bombardments and other ravages of war in makeshift accommodations in villages and countryside, and found ways to bypass the crumbling structures of the official economy. What public services could no longer provide enterprising individuals offered for a price. The industrious dabbled in the mushrooming black market or sought out odd jobs, like the *sciuscià* (shoeshine boys) of Naples who became figures of folklore. Prostitution flourished, as it always does where armies are present; the Mafia surfaced again in Sicily after having laid low for most of the Fascist period, aided perhaps by its new American connections. The enormous quantities of occupation currency from the Allied Military Administration put a lot money in the hands of Allied troops and, in the process, all but destroyed the value of the lira.

Problems in the German-occupied North were of a different nature. There was more order, inflation was less severe, most public employees and industrial workers kept their jobs and were paid until the very last days of the war; the black market was less exuberant than in the South. Enterprising individuals accumulated sizable fortunes at considerable risk: they bought cheaply on the German side, transported goods illegally across the front line, and sold dearly in Allied-controlled territory where prices were high. Basic necessities could also be procured by buying directly from peasant producers, who accumulated considerable savings by selling part of their meager produce. The most serious issues were political. Mussolini's Italian Social Republic could not shake off the negative connotations of being associated with German occupation. The thousands of Fascist diehards who rallied to its defense were a small minority. Passive resistance was more common, and more common still was the attitude of *attendismo* (wait and see), whereby millions of Italians steered clear of politics while waiting for the Allies to arrive. By 1944 most Italians sensed that an Allied victory was only a matter of time and were not fooled by propaganda reports that German secret weapons would soon reverse the fortunes of war.

Passive resistance and *attendismo* could develop into something more threatening for the Germans and for Mussolini's puppet regime: They could lead to active resistance. When the government of the Social Republic called up the "class of 1924" for service in its armed forces, thousands of young men did not answer the call. They did not relish the prospect of fighting for a discredited government that was clearly on the ropes, and dreaded the very real prospect of being sent to Germany as forced laborers. They joined small groups of what the authorities called "rebels" operating in the mountains. History remembers them as the Partisans, freedom fighters who took up arms against fascism and the German occupiers. The anti-Fascist resistance arose for many reasons. Its first manifestations were in the South, but it developed fully in the North where German occupation lasted the longest. With the country split in two and politically conscious Italians taking sides one way or the other, the resistance was part civil war, part war of liberation, and part social war as communist leaders took charge of many of its formations. The Committee of National Liberation of Northern Italy (Comitato di Liberazione Nazionale per Alta Italia, or CLNAI), later renamed National Liberation Committee (CLN), became a de facto government in many parts of northern Italy. It was recognized as a legitimate authority by the Allies and by the royal government in the South.

The resistance was significant militarily because it engaged thousands of German and Italian Fascist troops that otherwise would have been used against the Allies, and because it destabilized the government of the Social Republic. In the last days of the war resistance troops liberated the cities of northern Italy before Allied troops got there. The resistance was even more significant politically. Its existence showed that Italians were willing to fight for their own liberation from fascism and German occupation; it served as a crucible in which anti-Fascist groups and political parties met and mixed; it became a source of reference and inspiration after the war, when antifascism was the only ideology shared by most political parties. With the sole exception of the neo-Fascist Italian Social Movement (Movimento Sociale Italiano, or MSI) and various other right-wing groups, which together were never more than a small minority in the country, the "myth" of the resistance as a united national effort against fascism held the country together after 1945.

POSTWAR RECONSTRUCTION

1945–1950

The principal contenders for power in postwar Italy were the political parties born of the resistance, the Allies, the monarchy, and the church. The Italian Communist Party (Partito Comunista Italiano, or PCI) had played a major role in the resistance and had strong anti-Fascist credentials. Many of its leaders had lived in exile during the Fascist period, had fought against fascism in Spain, and had the military experience needed to take up the fight in Italy after 1943. The party's close ties to the Soviet Union made it suspect in the eyes of the Allies, but Palmiro Togliatti, the party's postwar leader, insisted that Communists would cooperate with other parties in the task of reconstruction and would abide by the ground rules of political democracy. Only with the onset of the cold war in 1947 did the PCI take a militant stand against the United States, adopting the Soviet line that the Marshall Plan, ostensibly about economic reconstruction, was in reality an American effort to interfere in the internal political affairs of other countries. The Italian Socialist Party (Partito Socialista Italiano, or PSI), the other great party of the Left, felt compelled to align itself with the more popular PCI in order to maintain its credibility among workers. Its leader, Pietro Nenni, did not trust the Communists, but was equally afraid that failure to make a common front with them against the forces of reaction might lead to a resurgence of fascism, perhaps in a more moderate but still dangerous guise. Christian Democracy (Democrazia Cristiana, or DC) was the other mass party. It had played a secondary role in the resistance, but its close ties to the Catholic Church, clergy, and religious associations gave it a secure base throughout the country. These forces stepped into the power vacuum left by the collapse of state administration in the final phase of the war; they negotiated with Partisans and Allies, opposed the Communists, and played to the fears of social revolution from the left. The capable leadership of Alcide De Gasperi assured that the DC would be the party of the future. The other notable party was the Action Party. It occupied the political space between the parties of the Left and the DC, rejected communism and clericalism, and embraced social democracy. It was a prestigious party that appealed to intellectual minorities, but not the masses. Its elitist image doomed it from the start, and it succumbed to the populist spirit and partisan atmosphere of Italian politics after 1945.

Alcide De Gaspari
(European Union)

Another victim was the monarchy, which went down to defeat in the referendum of June 1946. Its association with fascism and the war was too much of a political liability. The Allies were divided, the British supporting the monarchy and the Americans opposing it; they left the decision to the voters. The last-minute abdication of the old king in favor of his son Umberto II did not gain the monarchy enough votes nationwide. The election returns did show a division between the South, which voted for the retention of the monarchy, and the rest of the country that voted overwhelmingly for the republic. Once the monarchy was abolished, monarchists formed the National Monarchist Party (Partito Nazionale Monarchico, or PNM), which along with the neo-Fascist MSI

(Movimento Sociale Italiano) constituted the right wing of Italian politics after the war. The constitution in effect precluded their coming to power singly or in combination, but their presence was useful. It enabled the DC to present itself as a party of the center, opposed to both fascism and communism, and deserving the support of everyone who believed in political democracy.

A constituent assembly set to work on a constitution for the Italian republic. When the new constitution went into effect on January 1, 1948, it put in place the political system that prevailed until the 1990s. Its salient features were the renunciation of war as an instrument of national policy, suffrage for men and women (women had already voted for the first time in the elections and referendum of 1946), protection of civil freedoms, a weak executive, dominant legislature, safeguards against fascism and dictatorship, and commitment to social welfare. The constitutional description of the state as "A democratic republic based on work" pleased the parties of the Left, which accused the dominant DC of playing to conservative interests, without spelling out precisely what it was that the republic should do for workers. That would be a contentious issue in the decades to come. Other ambiguous or contentious provisions in the constitution were also cause for debate. The constitution called for administrative decentralization and regionalism without specifying the functions and powers of local and regional councils. It endorsed the Lateran Pacts and Concordat of the Fascist regime, thereby acknowledging that the church had sole say in matters of marriage and family, including abortion, birth control, divorce, and religious instruction in the schools.

Other aspects of postwar political life were related indirectly to the spirit or provisions of the constitution. The constitution said nothing about political parties, but the system of strict proportional representation that was deemed most appropriate to the democratic spirit of the constitution produced a large number of parties, none of which could rule alone for long. With few and brief exceptions, postwar Italy was governed by party coalitions that required periodic adjustments of political course. The most important element of continuity was the dominance of the DC from 1945 to the early 1990s. The coalition governments of the immediate postwar period were governments of national unity dominated by Christian Democrats with the participation of Communists and Socialists. The tensions of the cold war split the parties of the Left and put an end to their participation in government. Social democrats bolted from the PSI and formed the Italian Social Democratic Party (Partito Socialista Democratico Italiano, or PSDI), which collaborated with the DC. In May 1947 De Gasperi reshuffled his government to exclude Communists and Socialists. The decision was influenced by the imperative need not to jeopardize American economic aid that was being funneled to Italy and other European countries through the Marshall Plan. Until the 1960s the DC governed with the support of the three small parties of the center, the pro-business Italian Liberal Party (Partito Liberale Italiano, or PLI), the Italian Republican Party (Partito Republicano Italiano, or PRI), and the Italian Social Democratic Party (Partito Socialista Democratico Italiano, or PSDI). As De Gasperi intended, their support freed the DC from having to rely entirely on the Catholic vote and the support of the church.

Economic reconstruction took precedence in the immediate postwar years. In 1945 the Italian economy was in a dreadful state, with unemployment and inflation at record levels, savings depleted, transportation facilities destroyed, industrial output at a quarter of the 1938 level, agricultural production at 55 percent, and national income at about half of what it had been in 1938. Yet, recovery was fairly rapid. Production was back to the 1938 level within three years. By 1960 national income doubled and the economy hummed along, buoyed by exports and low labor costs. The guiding principles were monetary stability, fiscal restraint, and tight government spending, policies associated with Luigi Einaudi, an economic liberal and sound money advocate who served as deputy premier and budget minister in 1947–48. The large state-owned holding company (Istituto per la Recostruzione Industriale, or IRI), a legacy of the Fascist period, had not yet been corrupted by political patronage. It actually helped the private sector by relieving it of unprofitable industries that could not compete in the free market. By September 1949 the government had accumulated enough reserves of foreign currency and brought prices, budget, and balance of payments sufficiently under control to stabilize the exchange rate of the lira at 625 to the dollar. It remained at that level with only minor fluctuations until the 1970s, a sign that the economy had stabilized at a new plateau. The 1950s were the years of Italy's economic miracle.

The impoverished South was a source of cheap labor to the industrial cities of the North. Mass migration alleviated the plight of the South, but the economic gap between the two parts of the country continued to grow. Land reform broke up the *latifundia* (large estates), and redistributed some 700,000 hectares of land by 1962, benefiting 113,000 peasant families. It was only a tiny fraction of the rural population and the inexperienced and underfunded new owners did not do well. Eventually the land issue disappeared from public view and another took its place. In 1950 the government set up the Cassa per il Mezzogiorno (Fund for the South) to promote the South's economic development. It funneled billions to the South in public and private investments. Its activities contributed to the diversification of the southern economy, parts of which did quite well while others lagged behind. Government programs did not solve the Southern Question, but they did impact southern regions in different ways. Funds flowed to selected parts of the South with the construction of expensive infrastructures and capital-intensive industrial projects. Selective industrialization had its drawbacks. It did not help the South as a whole, but it did have considerable benefits *in loco*. More effective were improvements in education, transportation, public health, emigrant remittances, and social welfare. By the 1980s the Southern Question had dissolved into as many questions as there were local economies in the South—this according to experts who had the specialized knowledge to understand that the South was evolving in complex and diversified ways. Public opinion, especially in the North, did not alter its view that the question of the South was really the "problem of the South."

CHRISTIAN DEMOCRATIC DOMINANCE AND CENTRIST PARTY POLITICS

1948–1958

In the elections of April 1948 the Christian Democratic Party (Democrazia Cristiana, or DC) came tantalizingly close to winning an absolute majority with 48.5 percent of the popular vote. It did win a majority in the Chamber of Deputies with 305 out of 574 seats. Technically, the DC could have ruled alone, but De Gasperi chose to continue governing with party coalitions that freed the DC from having to rely entirely on the Catholic vote and the support of church and clergy. The center parties of the coalitions that governed until the end of the 1950s ranged from the pro-business Partito Liberale Italiano (PLI) to the Partito Socialista Democratico Italiano (PSDI), which was liberal in the American sense of the word. Like the DC, they were anticommunist, pro-American, and committed to parliamentary democracy. Communists and Socialists formed the opposition. In the 1948 elections, they won 31 percent of the popular vote running on a joint ticket. Anticipating an even stronger showing in the next elections, the DC introduced a bill that would have given the party or coalition of parties that won at least 50 percent of the popular vote two-thirds of the seats in the Chamber of Deputies, where governments were made and unmade. The bill passed over the vehement opposition of the parties on the Left and vocal dissidents from the center parties, who named the new law the *legge truffa* (swindle law). The DC and the center parties won 49.85 percent, barely short of the 50 percent needed to trigger the effect of the law, which was subsequently annulled. Thereafter, shaky coalition governments would be the norm in Italian politics.

The short-lived nature and instability of governments was mitigated to some degree by the fact that the same figures served repeatedly, often playing a game of musical chairs with ministerial posts. In fact, the achievements of the governments of the 1950s were far from negligible. They confronted a domestic scene recovering from the ravages of war, plagued by high unemployment, labor strife, disorder in the streets, rampant lawlessness in many parts of the country, and regional separatism. Communist rhetoric was often at odds with the official party line of loyalty to the democratic process. *Il vento del nord* (the wind from the north), a reference to the revolutionary thrust of the Communist Resistance, was expected to bring the proletariat to power and cleanse the country of corruption. Northern workers occupied factories and southern peasants carried out land seizures, all in the name of social justice. In Sicily, the bandit Salvatore Giuliano, said to be in the pay of the Mafia and large landlords, led a separatist movement. Following an attempt on the life of Communist leader Palmiro Togliatti on July 14, 1948, violent demonstrations broke out throughout the country. The insurgents gained control of communications facilities in central Italy and of the city of Genoa. Communists controlled the local administrations of the "Red Belt," which comprised most of Liguria, Tuscany, and Emilia-Romagna.

Whether Italy was actually on the verge of revolution after the elections of 1948 is a moot issue. The official party line imposed by Togliatti disavowed any revolutionary intentions, but close collaborators like Luigi Longo and Pietro Secchia disagreed and favored a more aggressive approach. The Communist victory in Yugoslavia and the civil war raging in Greece were worrisome developments. The center parties confronted the pressing issue of domestic security decisively. Minister of the Interior Mario Scelba was the law-and-order man of the moment. The *Celere* police squads mounted on American military surplus Jeeps were one response to disorder in the streets, special laws limiting civil freedoms and expanding police powers were another. The police regularly found and seized large quantities of weapons illegally stashed away by former Resistance fighters. But not all responses were repressive. Governments passed and implemented land reform measures, established the Fund for the South, and created new public agencies for economic development. Ente Nazionale Idrocarburi (ENI), set up to develop energy resources but soon branching out into road construction, gasoline distribution, and the construction of highway facilities, was the most dynamic and the one that caught the public imagination with a publicity campaign that catered to the sense of national pride. The labor front calmed down considerably in the early 1950s, partly because the labor movement split along political lines and partly because management orchestrated an effective campaign against the more aggressive unions, replacing older militants with more docile younger workers brought in from the countryside.

Christian Democrats were often accused of lacking a "sense of the state," meaning that they were prone to put the interests of their party, of their voters, and of interest groups against the general interest. More pointedly, they were charged with running a corrupt government. There is no evidence that they deliberately encouraged corrupt practices, but they did strengthen the party financially and looked after the interests of party voters and supporters. Clientelism, the dispensation of favors small and large to individuals and networks of backers, is an apt description of their political tactics. They were not the only party that operated in the manner of old-fashioned American political bosses, but as the party in power with the greatest access to the resources of government, they were the ones most vulnerable to charges of profiteering. They lost ground in the elections of 1953 with 40.1 percent of the popular vote, recovered partially in the elections of 1958 with 42.4 percent, and slipped to 38.3 percent in 1963. Their share of the vote held steady at around 38–39 percent in the 1960s and 1970s, but the other center parties did not do as well. The gains were on the right and left, but most notably on the latter where the Communist Party popular vote rose from 22.6 percent in 1953 to 34.4 percent in 1976, coming that year close to four points behind the Christian Democrats. The Socialist Party actually declined from its high point of 14.2 percent in 1958 to 9.6 percent in 1976. The extremes were gaining at the expense of the "vital center" of the political spectrum.

THE OPENING
TO THE LEFT

1958–1980

Dwindling electoral support for the parties of the center was the mathematical reason for the shift in political alliances that began to take place in the late 1950s. Behind the shift were profound social changes. The "economic miracle" changed the character of Italian society from predominantly agricultural to predominantly industrial. A major population shift from the countryside to the cities and from south to north accompanied the change. Labor unions grew and became more militant as workers demanded an increasing share of the benefits of the economic miracle. Millions of Italians, displaced by the dislocations that economic change always entails and attracted by economic opportunities, emigrated abroad, mostly to the countries of northern Europe, South America, North America, and Australia in that order. Migration to the cities of the North from both the South and the surrounding countryside made demands on urban services that few local governments could meet. The most successful in this respect were the city administrations run by the Communists, that of Bologna being the best example. The white-collar sector of the economy, which included public services, was actually the fastest-growing, with future implications for the Communist strategy of relying on the support of workers and landless peasants. A consumer revolution was under way as Italians began to buy appliances, cars, and television sets; roads were clogged with traffic. Paradoxically, as society was becoming increasingly atomized and the culture hedonistic, the traditional attachment to family and home survived. There was continuity in change. In other words, Italy was beginning to experience all the contradictions of modernization.

Social revolution is too strong a word for the changes occurring in those years, for there were still important elements of continuity with the past. Italians by and large remained culturally conservative, attached to family, traditional gender roles, and the ceremonial aspects of religion, even if they voted for the parties of the Left. Communists and Socialists were ideologically in favor of women's rights, abortion, and divorce, but cautious in practice because they understood the mentality of most of their constituents. Feminism, the gay movement, environmentalism, and prison reform were new issues that found their strongest advocates outside the mainstream political parties. The "opening to the Left" was the cautious political response to a country moving painfully toward a new equilibrium. The left fringes of Christian Democracy had always favored a more open and receptive attitude toward the non-Communist left. They opposed consumerism and the "Americanization" of Italian society as much as they opposed communism. In the elections of 1958, the Christian Democratic vote rose from 40.1 percent to 42.4 percent, and the Socialist vote from 12.7 percent to 14.2 percent. Even before the elections, Amintore Fanfani, a Catholic sensitive to social problems who was the new Christian Democratic political boss, proposed an alliance with the Socialists to invigorate the governing coalition and facilitate social planning. After the elections the idea was taken up by the DC centrist group known as the Dorotei and by Aldo Moro, the new party secretary. The Dorotei and Moro dominated the DC for the next decade. An experiment in government supported by the neo-Fascists failed when street protests forced the resignation of Fernando Tambroni in 1960. U.S. president John F. Kennedy, recently elected, reversed American opposition to center-left coalitions, Pope John XXIII made known his support, and the Soviet Union of Nikita Khrushchev looked less menacing than that of Stalin. The Socialists had their own reason for wanting to cooperate with the Christian Democrats. Alliance with the Communists had not worked to their advantage, they wanted some of the fruits of power, Pietro Nenni feared that the Christian Democrats would turn to the right if the Socialists failed to collaborate, and party intellectuals argued that the Socialists could capture the state from within.

In March 1962 Amintore Fanfani formed the first center-left government with the active support of the Republican and Social Democratic Parties and the passive support of Socialists, who abstained from voting against it. The government took the drastic and controversial step of nationalizing the electrical industry, legislated a tax on dividends, and made secondary schooling compulsory to the age of 14. The nationalization of the electrical industry was a bitterly contested step that Fanfani wanted in order to give the government control over energy prices and a handle on the entire economy. Ente Nazionale per l'Energia Elettrica (ENEL) was the new regulatory state agency that was supposed to rationalize the industry and reduce energy costs. In the event, it did neither. The school reform led to an explosion in university admissions that would soon have major repercussions on the social scene. Fanfani moved fast, too fast for many in and outside his party who either opposed the reforms in principle or were afraid that they might succeed all too well, to the advantage of the DC and its partners.

In the regularly scheduled elections of 1963, the DC dropped from 42.4 percent to 38.3 percent of the popular vote. That setback left the party no choice but to move closer to the Socialist Party, which temporarily patched up its differences with the Social Democratic Party (presumably a sign of its new moderation) and managed to obtain 14.5 percent of the vote. Aldo Moro formed the first genuinely center-left government in December 1963. Nenni was his vice-premier, and the Socialist Antonio Giolitti, grandson of Giovanni Giolitti, was budget minister. The new government promised to enact many overdue reforms, including administrative decentralization, reform of higher education, popular housing, and the legalization of divorce. But first it had to deal with a serious economic recession (the *congiuntura*), and may have made matters worse by taking steps to curb inflation, internal demand, and public spending. Rumors of secret plots to organize a military coup were in the air. It is highly unlikely that the army wanted or could have carried out a coup, but the rumors kept growing into the late 1960s. Three consecutive center-left governments headed by Aldo Moro from 1953 to 1968 had little to show in the way of reform. The legalization of divorce, admittedly a major development in a Catholic country like Italy, took effect in 1970 and was confirmed by popular referendum in 1974. Even more controversial was the legalization of abortion. Both measures reflected changes in social attitudes that the political parties struggled to reflect. There was a strong economic recovery in the private sector, which was derailed by the repercussions of the oil crisis of the early 1970s. The public sector grew, but its contribution to the recovery was questionable. State agencies were turning into breeding grounds for political patronage, clientelism, and ill-conceived projects that diverted capital from more productive investments.

In the elections of 1972 both the Christian Democrats and the Socialists lost some ground, but the Socialists were the biggest losers, as they dropped from 14.5 percent to 9.6 percent of the popular vote. The experiment in center-left government was not working to their advantage. The center-left seemed to actually be benefiting the Communists who gained slightly; they could now present themselves as the only party of the left that was unsullied by corrupt government. Profound changes were underway by 1972. Organized workers demanded major salary and workplace concessions, university students were in open revolt, a mood of rebellion spread among the young, public services were mired in red tape, and public confidence in government was at a low point. The reasons for the crisis of the state and society that unfolded in the late 1960s and early 1970s are complicated. Poor employment prospects, particularly dire for university graduates, the Vietnam War that called into question Italy's ties to the United States, the infectious example of the Cultural Revolution in China and of protest movements in the United States, the keen interest in Marxist social theory on the part of university students, the rejection of consumerist values, demands for gender equality and sexual liberation, encouragement of change by the Catholic Church, all these were ingredients in the explosive mix that was being brewed in the 1960s. In 1967–68 student protests erupted at the University of Trento (public but strongly influenced by Catholic liberation theology), the Catholic University of Milan, the University of Turin, and the University of Rome. The movement spread from these prominent centers of student activism to virtually every other university, and even to some secondary schools.

Student protesters linked up with disgruntled workers. This was the aspect that set the Italian protest movement apart from protest movements in other countries and seemed to pose the greatest threat to the state. For by 1968–69 labor protests seemed to be on the verge of escaping the control of the labor unions and political parties with which the unions were affiliated. The workers who came into the factories in the 1960s were better educated than the workers of an earlier generation, many came from the better-off parts of the South, some had had experience working abroad, and some with no previous experience of factory work were unaccustomed to the rituals of collective bargaining. Small but active minorities were drawn to political organizations and fringe groups that promised more than salary increases and benefits. They insisted instead on giving workers a voice in the process of production, they intimidated managers, took over some factories, and proclaimed the factory as the logical birthplace of the revolution. In the *autunno caldo* (Hot Autumn) of 1969 the country appeared to be on the verge of revolution, as it had been in the "Red Years" of 1919–20. Grassroots worker militancy certainly prodded the labor unions into taking an aggressive stance. Collective bargaining agreements negotiated in this climate yielded great benefits to the workers in the form of higher wages, shorter working hours, longer paid vacations, and generous bonuses and pensions. The rising cost of labor was not matched by increases in productivity because the worker movement also successfully opposed the introduction of labor-saving techniques that would have speeded up assembly lines and threatened jobs.

Matters took an even more ominous turn outside the workplace where the cult of violence was definitely in the air. The New Left of the 1960s was not just about flowers, peace, and making love. There was a violent component to it that was very much in evidence in Italy, where self-proclaimed revolutionary groups bent on violence proliferated in a crowded political underground. The "strategy of tension" that they adopted targeted prominent and not-so-prominent business, political, and cultural figures who were seen as part of the establishment. The intellectual fuzziness and anarchism typical of this way of thinking defied conventional political classifications and distinctions. Left and right met and mingled in the murky world of political conspirators. Their intent was to destabilize the state, bring it down, and create a better society out of the resulting chaos. What that society might look like was left to the individual imagination. Particularly upsetting to the young Marxists who rallied to extra-parliamentary and underground groups of the Left was the prospect that the Communist Party (PCI) might be drawn into the political mire. That seemed a definite possibility after the elections of 1976 brought the popular vote of the PCI to within four percentage points of the DC. It seemed as if it was now poised to benefit from its embrace of political democracy by becoming a credible partner in government. The "historic compromise" (*compromesso storico*) between the DC and the PCI never came to full fruition, but the possibility that it might drove Marxist dissidents over the edge.

Terrorism is not too strong a word for the violence that permeated public life after the explosion of a bomb that killed 16 people in front of a bank in Milan on December 12, 1969. The *anni di piombo* (years of lead) followed that first incident. The campaign of terror culminated in the 1978 kidnapping and assassination of Aldo Moro, whose bad luck it was to be perceived as the architect of the political system. Moro's death did not bring down the system, but it did stop dead in its tracks the historic compromise that he and Communist Party leader Enrico Berlinguer were bent on promoting. Communist deputies cooperated with government in the spirit of national solidarity, but not as legitimate partners. Moro's death, which was supposed to deliver a fatal blow to the state, according to the conspirators, had the opposite effect. Public opinion definitely turned against the violence that many Italians had almost excused until then as an understandable reaction against corrupt and incompetent government. The reaction was firm but not exaggerated. It took into account the fact that the dissidents who practiced terror were never more than a small minority even among the disaffected. The government increased surveillance, created special antiterrorist forces (the so-called *teste di cuoio*—leather heads—from the masks that they wore to protect their anonymity), and gave special powers to the police and the judges, without seriously infringing on civil liberties. The antiterrorist reaction was a responsible performance that partly redeemed the state for the years of inaction and aimless drifting.

PROFILE AND POLITICS OF A CHANGING WORLD

It was not terrorism that altered the face of Italian society after 1980, but the forces of economic change, international developments, and the will of the people. In the elections of 1979 held while the country was still feeling the trauma of the Moro assassination, the Democrazia Cristiana (DC) maintained its strength, but the Partito Comunista Italiano (PCI) popular vote dropped from 34.4 percent to 30.4 percent. The party had unequivocally denounced terrorism, but voters were not disposed to absolve it entirely of responsibility for what the country was going through. The party decided to abandon the policy of informal cooperation with the DC, leaving the dominant but struggling DC little room for political maneuvering. A bright spot on the political scene was the election of Sandro Pertini to the presidency of the republic in 1978. The patent honesty and simplicity of this old-time Socialist and anti-Fascist caught the public imagination and helped restore trust in government. In 1981 Pertini used his presidential power to invite Giovanni Spadolini, of the PRI, to become prime minister. For the first time since 1945 the prime minister was not Christian Democrat. This seemingly superficial novelty had in reality profound political implications. However, the significance was not immediately evident because Spadolini headed two short-lived governments in the course of 16 months. The elections of 1983 dealt a disastrous blow to the DC, which dropped from 38.3 percent to 32.9 percent of the popular vote; the Socialist vote rose from 9.8 percent to 11.4 percent.

The way was open for the Socialist leader, Bettino Craxi, to become prime minister, and to hold that post for a postwar record of four years. Public opinion welcomed the stability that a long tenure brought to politics and rewarded the Socialist Party with 14.3 percent of the popular vote in the elections of 1987. But Craxi's dynamic personality and longevity in office proved to be mixed blessings. He became the target of heated and sometimes vicious attacks by political opponents and in the media. He was accused of corruption and of harboring dictatorial ambitions, likened to Mussolini. Governing coalitions headed by Christian Democrats followed Craxi's resignation, and they were all hampered by the growing rivalry between Socialists, who had sharpened their appetite for power, and Christian Democrats loath to surrender to their Socialist partners and rivals. By the end of the 1980s the political system that had been in place for nearly 45 years was at the end of its rope, the public debt was at dizzying heights, inflation rampant, capital draining out of the country, and confidence in government at an all-time low.

International developments dealt the final blows to a system that had reached a dead end all by itself. A close relationship with the United States, allegiance to NATO, fear of the Soviet Union, and opposition to communism had been constants of Italian foreign policy since the end of World War II. Craxi had struck an independent note by questioning American hegemony and gotten in trouble for it. The American connection was an integral part of the system of power that could not be questioned. The end of the cold war did what Craxi could not do, by removing the threat of Soviet power and thereby diminishing the value of NATO and America as impediments to communism. The end of the cold war removed these important props to the system and potentially opened the way to major changes unthinkable just a few years before. Political and business leaders became the targets in the Mani Pulite and other corruption scandals in the early 1990s. The investigations were led by judges who claimed to be apolitical, but the fact that most of the accused belonged or had ties to the Socialist and Christian Democratic Parties suggested the presence of political motivations. The public initially supported the investigations and the examining magistrates, but lost interest as the process dragged on interminably and as it became clear that it was not easy to blame individuals for practices that seemed to be universal. At the start of the 21st century, 10 years after the investigations began, it seemed to be business as usual in the area of public life where economics met with politics.

Institutional reform of government made slightly more headway. Public opinion polls and political referenda showed strong support for reforming voting procedures, abolishing the system of proportional representation, and strengthening the presidency. Those were precisely the reforms that did not sit well with political parties, but political parties were now in crisis and fighting for survival. Secret voting by deputies was abolished in 1988 to eliminate the tendency of "free-shooters" to vote down bills approved by their parties that they did not dare oppose openly. In 1993 parliament introduced single-member districts for 75 percent of the seats in the legislature, the other 25 percent still being represented proportionally. That did not reduce the number of parties. As the old ones died out, new ones appeared. The Christian Democrats, Socialists, Communists, and neo-Fascists voted themselves out of existence, but were reborn with different names and philosophies. The Movimento Sociale Italiano (MSI) renounced fascism and became the National Alliance (Alleanza Nazionale, or AN) under the leadership of Gianfranco Fini; the PCI renounced communism and was reborn as the Democratic Party of the Left (Partito Democratico della Sinistra, or PDS). DC members migrated to other parties of their choice, but some chose to stay on under the old label of the Popular Party (Partito Popolare Italiano, or PPI). The greater novelty was the rise of completely new parties. The most prominent was Forza Italia (Go, Italy!) founded by Silvio Berlusconi, which by its very name expressed the kind of national pride voiced by sports fans cheering on their favorite team. The Northern League founded by Umberto Bossi was an even greater novelty because it seemed to

call into question the sacrosanct traditions of the Risorgimento and the achievement of national unity.

The general elections of 1994 were the first to be held by the new rule of single-representative constituencies, with the participation of a new panoply of political parties. The Liberty Pole coalition comprising Forza Italia, the National Alliance, and the Northern League won a majority of seats in the lower house of parliament, enough for Berlusconi to form his first government. It rested on an uneasy alliance between the ultrapatriotic National Alliance (which won big in the South and in Rome), the only slightly less patriotic Forza Italia, and the Northern League, whose patriotism was directed toward Padania, an imaginary separate nation of the north. The electoral reform having failed to stabilize the system (there were still 14 parties in parliament), it became necessary to call for early elections. This time it was the Olive Tree Coalition (L'Ulivo) that prevailed and inaugurated five years of left-of-center governments headed by Lamberto Dini, Romano Prodi, Massimo D'Alema, and Giuliano Amato. They had the unenviable task of preparing Italy for admission to the European Monetary Union by 1999, which required strict spending limits on government and

Prime Minister Silvio Berlusconi (left) and President George W. Bush in 2001 *(Hulton/Archive)*

reductions of social expenditures. To nearly everyone's surprise the center-left coalition succeeded, but success rendered it superfluous. The House of Freedoms, Berlusconi's new coalition, won majorities in both houses of parliament in the elections of 2001. The coalition was more stable this second time around because the Northern League and National Alliance were chastened by electoral losses and were subordinate to an invigorated Forza Italia. In the year 2004 Berlusconi seems poised to break the postwar record for longevity in power set by Bettino Craxi.

Major economic, social, and cultural developments were behind these political changes. The media dismissed the 2001 elections as a popularity poll between Berlusconi and the head of the rival coalition, the former mayor of Rome, Francesco Rutelli. Public opinion polls held before the elections showed that most voters did indeed prefer the young and photogenic Rutelli, but that they still intended to vote for Berlusconi's political right. It was not looks that swayed voters, but programs and promises. Berlusconi's coalition promised privatization of public services, less waste in government, lower taxes, and economic prosperity. Close relations with America, a country that Berlusconi regards as the standard bearer of freedom throughout the world, are at the heart of Berlusconi's foreign policy. He is lukewarm toward the European Union, which he regards with suspicion because of its tendency to interfere in the internal affairs of member nations. To the extent that Forza Italia has an ideology, it is one of individualism, free-market economy, and indifference if not contempt for intellectual and nonproductive endeavors. Last but not least, Berlusconi also appealed to national pride, a sentiment previously soft-pedaled outside the far right. The fact that he is under suspicion of having engaged in bribery and other corrupt practices as a businessman does not make him less popular. He personifies the ideology of individual success that appeals to a generation of voters who have reached maturity in the age of triumphant consumerism. This is not to say that his pro-business attitude is rooted in traditional economic liberalism or that his patriotism derives from political currents born of the Risorgimento. He is a new phenomenon without roots in tradition.

The changes underlying the Berlusconi phenomenon are traceable to the 1980s, when the country overcame the economic and political crises of the preceding decade and took the road that made it the fifth or sixth economic power of the world. Italy's economic rise benefited from expansion of all the economies of the western world in that decade. It was marked by management's successful counteroffensive against organized labor. Fiat led the fight in 1980 when it fired thousands of workers for business reasons and defeated a protest strike backed by the PCI leadership. Business consolidations and shake-outs thinned the ranks of industrial workers throughout that decade, sending the labor movement on a slide from which it never recovered. Most new jobs were in the services and white-collar occupations that were most resistant to unionization. Also, the biggest expansions occurred in small businesses, an area of economic strength where unions were weak. The indexation of wage increases to the rise in the cost of living, a feature of many labor contracts, was abolished in 1992. There was also an influx of cheap foreign labor, both legal and illegal, that undercut the ability of unions to negotiate advantageous contracts for their members. The presence of foreign laborers in turn inflamed xenophobic resentments that played into the hands of the Northern League, National Alliance, and Forza Italia, the three parties that donned the mantle of patriotism and were also pro-business.

At the start of the 21st century, Italy stands at a crossroads. Membership in the European Union requires adjustments that not everyone welcomes. Stringent budgetary requirements that apply to all members may hinder the ability to deal with national problems and issues. Pensions are a most difficult issue for Italy because its population is aging, the labor force is shrinking, and funding is a costly business. The government reforms of the 1990s have not gone far enough, and political instability is a permanent problem. Italian foreign policy has to adjust to the changes brought on by the end of the cold war. Italy now stands on the world's most unstable political fault line, the one that separates the prosperous countries of the Northern Hemisphere from the impoverished countries to the south. During the cold war Italy was situated geographically on the second line of defense; now it stands on the frontline. Being shielded from war has been a great blessing, but it has done little to prepare public opinion for new responsibilities. Italian defense spending has seldom exceeded 2 percent of the national budget since the 1950s; that may have to change. Its Mediterranean position, proximity to the trouble spots of the Middle East, and the vulnerability of its exposed territory and transportation facilities make it a prime target for political terrorism.

Foreign policy is not formed in a vacuum. For it to change there must be changes at home, and Italians are not likely to agree on an international role for the country unless they can come together at home. The political system may have to change for that to happen. The issues of the moment are serious but not unmanageable. There is public support for a decisive fight against organized crime; the state of public finances was worse in the recent past, when government rose to the challenge; in 2003 budgets deficits were high, but not as high as those of France and Germany. Regional tensions are less intense than they were a decade ago. Correctives to the denounced ills of rampant individualism and the loss of social cohesiveness exist in the traditional institutions of family and strong attachment to the local community. In Italy, public mindedness and civic spirit flourish at the local level. In the economy also, small is beautiful. Small-scale business firms are still the backbone of the Italian economy, a useful corrective to the impersonal nature and potential for massive corruption of large-scale businesses. In 2004, the financial difficulties experienced by FIAT and other major firms, as well as the Parmalat financial scandal, are reminders of the familiar shortcomings of big business. None of this, however, is exclusively Italian. Italy's future will most likely resemble that of other Western nations, particularly that of its partners in the European Union. If history is any guide, Italians will meet the new challenges with their customary flair for combining the old with the new.

HISTORICAL
DICTIONARY
A–Z

A

abortion

The campaign to legalize abortion in Italy was spurred by the apparent frequency of illegal abortions. The campaign for abortion on demand gained momentum after the legalization of DIVORCE in 1970. The Catholic hierarchy, the dominant Christian Democratic Party, and many doctors and nurses opposed the feminist-led campaign. "A woman's right to choose" proved to be a popular slogan that found broad support even among Catholics. The fight for abortion was led in parliament by the small but vocal RADICAL PARTY and by Socialists. Parliament legalized abortion in July 1975, but the controversial Law 194 regulating it was not passed until May 1978. The law allows unrestricted abortion in the first 90 days of pregnancy, but restricts its use progressively after that point, allowing it in the final stages of pregnancy only to save the life of the mother. About two-thirds of the country's doctors refused to perform abortions after its legalization, but enough cooperated to make possible about 200,000 legal abortions every year in the first years after passage of the law. Annual rates of induced abortions have declined from about 16 per 1,000 women ages 15–49 in the early 1980s to less than 10 per 1,000 in the late 1990s. Currently, about 150,000 legal abortions are being performed every year, and perhaps an additional 50,000–60,000 illegal abortions in advanced stages of pregnancy. Organized opposition from the Catholic Church forced two national referenda on the issue in May 1981. An overwhelming 88.5 percent of voters rejected a Radical Party demand for freely chosen abortion, while 67.9 percent turned down a Catholic proposal to strictly limit abortion to cases of immi-

nent danger to a woman's life or health. Catholic groups continue to wage their fight against legalized abortion, with little chance of repealing a measure that enjoys broad popular support. The figures indicate that abortions contribute significantly to the negative growth rates of the population in recent years (in 1999, for instance, the population registered a natural loss of over 34,000).

Abravanel, Judah (ca. 1465–ca. 1535)
Jewish scholar of Spanish origin influential in Italian humanist circles

Also known as Leone Ebreo, Judah Abravanel (also spelled Abarbanel) was the son of the Jewish theologian Isaac Abravanel (1437–1508). Father and son fled from Portugal to Spain in 1483 to escape persecution. Judah fled from Spain to Naples, which was then under Spanish rule, after the Jews were expelled from Spain in 1492. In Naples he served as personal physician to the Spanish viceroy, then moved on to Genoa, Rome, and perhaps Venice. In Italy, Abravanel discovered NEOPLATONISM and became one of its most influential advocates. His most important work, the *Dialoghi d'amore* (Dialogues on love, 1535), developed the Neoplatonist concept of love as the binding force of the universe. Love, according to Abravanel, enables the intellect to appreciate higher levels of truth and beauty, eventually drawing the individual to spiritual union with God. The *Dialoghi* were widely read in Europe, helping to spread Neoplatonism in Italy and beyond. It is thought that Abravanel's writings influenced GIORDANO BRUNO and Baruch Spinoza.

Abruzzo (or Abruzzi)

The region of Abruzzo (pop. 1.3 million), lies in the central part of the peninsula, bordered on the north by the region of the MARCHES, on the west by LATIUM, the south by MOLISE, and on the east by the ADRIATIC SEA. Its capital city of L'Aquila is located in the heart of the APENNINES. It is a picturesque town still completely surrounded by medieval walls, rich in churches and monuments dating from the Middle Ages, with relatively few tourists in spite of recent road and other transportation improvements. The region's other principal cities and provincial capitals are Chieti, Pescara, and Teramo. The region is divided topographically into two distinct areas. A mountainous western part includes the highest elevations of the Apennines (the peak of the Gran Sasso at 9,558 feet [2,914 meters] above sea level, and the massif of the Maiella at 8,168 feet (2,795 meters). The eastern hilly area slopes down gradually to the coastal towns and beaches of the Adriatic coast. The region's rivers that flow from the mountains to the Adriatic provide hydroelectric power, but are of limited use for purposes of agricultural irrigation. The temperate climate of the coastal region contrasts sharply with the cold temperatures and abundant snowfalls of the mountains. Agricultural production has been hampered by the prevalence of small properties, a characteristic of mountain regions that is especially marked in Abruzzo. In the past, the mountains have provided a steady stream of emigrants to the cities and to foreign countries. Today the region is one of the most sparsely populated in the country. Commercial agriculture has made some progress in the hilly regions at elevations below about 2,000 feet (600 meters). Grapes, olives, flowers, and horticultural products destined for Roman markets are the major commercial crops grown in the region. Forests of ash, chestnut, oak, and beech prevail at elevations of 2,000–2,600 feet (600–800 meters) and higher. Pastoral activities are in decline. Almost gone is the traditional pattern of transhumance (migration of sheep from the mountains to the plains in early fall, returning to the mountains in the spring). Industrial production is limited to a few areas, most notably around the town of Pescara on the Adriatic coast. Fishing is still an economically significant activity. Tourism is growing, due mostly to the natural attractions of the region. Winter sports are popular in the mountains, and both mountains and beaches attract summer vacationers. The Parco Nazionale d'Abruzzo, the largest national park in the country with more than 98,800 acres (40,000 hectares) of protected land, is home to the country's last surviving wild bears, wolves, deer, and wildcats. Although located in central Italy, the region is considered to be part of the South. It was the northernmost province of the KINGDOM OF THE TWO SICILIES before national unification. The region's struggling economy qualified it for inclusion in the CASSA PER IL MEZZOGIORNO, the government agency charged with promoting the economic development of the South.

Abyssinia   See ETHIOPIA.

academies
private local societies that promoted cultural activities and civic involvement

In the 15th and 16th centuries the term *accademia* designated any organized group of professional or dilettante scholars coming together for purposes of study. Founded and named after Plato's Academy in ancient Athens, the academies helped propagate the culture of HUMANISM. Artistic, literary, and philosophical interests prevailed, but the academies also played a role in propagating interest in experimentation and the study of nature. The first academy was the Accademia Fiorentina formed in FLORENCE in the 1460s under the patronage of COSIMO and LORENZO DE' MEDICI to further the study of Plato's philosophy. It folded shortly after the death of Lorenzo in 1492, but by then the example had caught on in other cities and spread further in the 1500s, becoming a veritable movement. Many of the new academies were little more than private clubs operating for the benefit of their members. The most prestigious were the Accademia della Crusca founded in Florence in 1582 and the Accademia dei Lincei founded in Rome in 1603. The Roman group consisted of younger scholars interested in literature, mathematics, and natural history. GALILEO was a member. The Accademia della Crusca turned to the study of language, and in 1612 published its famous *Vocabolario della Crusca,* which helped to make Tuscan the language of educated Italians. Another Roman academy founded in 1690, the Arcadia Romana, gave its name to the Arcadian movement, which set out to reform and purify the language of poetry. When the pastoral style of the Arcadian writers became itself an affectation, as stylized and ornate as the language it had sought to replace, anti-Arcadian writers carried on the linguistic campaign that the Arcadians had initiated. An innovative feature of Arcadian societies was that they were open to women, who through them gained a foothold in literary circles. Many academies took on fanciful names of uncertain meaning and derivation, such as the *Addormentati* (Sleepers) and *Confusi* (Confused) of Genoa, *Intronati* (Stunned) and *Rozzi* (Uncouth) of Siena, and the *Erranti* (Wanderers) of Brindisi. The diffusion of academies promoted interest in literature, science, and scholarship in minor cities and towns. Many still function. Often derided as frivolous and amateurish, academies have played a vital role in Italian culture.

Acerbo, Giacomo (1888–1969)

Fascist figure and legislator active in the early days of fascism

Born near Pescara, Acerbo studied agrarian science, volunteered for military service in WORLD WAR I, organized war veterans, joined the Fascist Party in August 1920, and founded the first Fascist squad in his native Abruzzo region. The following year he was elected to the Chamber of Deputies on the Fascist ticket, served as secretary of the Fascist parliamentary delegation, and chaired an economic commission. He was one of

the architects of the short-lived pacification pact between Fascists and Socialists that was concluded in August 1921. He also helped transform the Fascist movement into a regular political party. Considered a moderate, a few weeks before the march on Rome Acerbo announced the Fascist Party's support for the monarchy, thus removing a major obstacle to the appointment of BENITO MUSSOLINI as prime minister. Acerbo sponsored the electoral reform bill approved by parliament in July 1923, commonly known as the Acerbo Law. The new law abolished the system of proportional representation and assigned two-thirds of the seats in the chamber to the party or coalition of parties with at least 25 percent of the popular vote. That law gave the Fascists and their allies control of parliament in the elections of April 1924. That same year Acerbo received the title of baron of Aterno. Accused of complicity in the murder of GIACOMO MATTEOTTI, Acerbo stepped down from his cabinet post as undersecretary of state. He returned to the government as minister of agriculture (1929–35) and served as minister of finance from February to July 1943. A member of the Fascist Grand Council, on July 25, 1943, he voted for the motion of no confidence that toppled Mussolini's dictatorship. He escaped Fascist retribution by going into hiding. Eventually tried and sentenced for his role in the regime, Acerbo was pardoned after serving two years of a 30-year sentence.

Action Party (Partito d'Azione)

anti-Fascist political party with roots in the resistance movement

The Action Party sought to unify noncommunist groups opposed to fascism during and immediately after WORLD WAR II. Founded in 1942, it was inspired by ideals of social democracy and attracted the support of prominent members of the anti-Fascist movement GIUSTIZIA E LIBERTÀ. The Action Party played a prominent role in the RESISTANCE. Seeking a radical break with the past, and national renewal, the Action Party was uncompromisingly anti-monarchist, anti–big business, and pro-labor. It called for regional and local autonomies, economic reform, special programs to help the South, and European federation. FERRUCCIO PARRI was its austere and idealistic founder and leader. Two other prominent *azionisti*, UGO LA MALFA and EMILIO LUSSU, represented two distinct currents within the party. La Malfa's group favored small and medium-sized business, while Lussu's favored labor, land reform, and the development of the South. Parri headed the first postwar government (June–November 1945) that began the difficult transition to peacetime. It disarmed the resistance, led in the campaign to abolish the monarchy, and began purging Fascists from government. The party's achievements did not improve its popular image, which was one of being overly intellectual and out of touch with the common people. It was also the object of unremitting attacks by the Communist Party (PCI) and the Christian Democratic Party (DC). The elections of 1946 gave the Action Party only 1.5 percent of the popular vote; the party dissolved and its members joined other political groups.

Acton, John Francis Edward (1736–1811)
English supporter of the Neapolitan Bourbon monarchy

Born in France to a family of English baronets, Acton served with distinction in the French and Tuscan navies before being invited to reorganize the Neapolitan navy in 1778. Favored by Queen MARIE CAROLINE, to whom he was linked romantically by court gossip, Acton served as navy minister and as prime minister (1785–1806). He promoted administrative, naval, and military reforms, gaining respect for his political acumen. Acton's influence increased immeasurably after 1799 when the armies of NAPOLEON forced the Neapolitan rulers to abandon their capital and withdraw to Sicily. The court returned to Naples when the pro-French PARTHENOPEAN REPUBLIC fell later that year, remaining in the capital until 1806, when the French once again forced them back to Sicily. But by 1806 Acton had incurred

the displeasure of the royal couple. His preference for Great Britain over Austria displeased the queen, who was the daughter of Empress MARIA THERESA of Austria. Acton seemed more interested in keeping Sicily under British protection than regaining the mainland, as the Neapolitan rulers urged him to do. An ill and dispirited Acton resigned as prime minister in August 1806. In retirement he regained the queen's goodwill but not his political influence. When he died in 1811, the Neapolitan rulers were still in Sicily under the protection of the British navy.

Adelfi See SECRET SOCIETIES.

Adowa, Battle of See BARATIERI, ORESTE; COLONIALISM.

Adrian VI (1459–1523)
pope (1522–1523)

Born Adrian Florensz at Utrecht in the Netherlands, Adrian succeeded LEO X as a compromise choice. As a young clergyman, he had served as tutor to the future emperor CHARLES V. Adrian became cardinal in 1517. Interested in learning, and particularly attracted to the ideas of reform-minded religious humanists, Adrian had little interest in the secular aspects of Renaissance culture, was a tight spender, and insisted on purging the Catholic Church of corrupt practices like simony (the purchase of spiritual benefits and religious offices) and nepotism (the appointment of relatives to lucrative positions). Nor was he a strong believer in the temporal rights of the PAPACY, which he thought embroiled the church in political affairs and distracted it from its spiritual duties. Neither the papal court nor the Roman populace cared much for him. At his death after only 20 months in office, the Roman crowd cheered the physician who had attended to him in his last days. His successor, CLEMENT VII, did not pursue the reforms favored by Adrian and left the way open to the advance of Protestantism. Adrian was the last non-Italian pope before the election of JOHN PAUL II in 1978.

Adriatic Sea See MEDITERRANEAN SEA.

Africa, Italian colonies in See BARATIERI, ORESTE; COLONIALISM; RUBATTINO, RAFFAELE; SAPETO, GIUSEPPE.

AGIP (Azienda Generale Italiana Petroli)
agency for the exploration, production, and distribution of energy resources
AGIP was established in 1926 as a government-controlled operation to prospect for oil, extract, refine, and market its findings, as part of the Fascist regime's developing campaign to reduce reliance on imported fuels. Its explorations yielded little of value in the short run, including in Libya where oil was detected but could not be brought to the surface by the technology of the day. AGIP was more successful in Iraq and Romania, where its findings gave the Italian oil industry its first foothold in these oil-rich lands. AGIP was not producing enough to significantly alleviate national dependence on foreign sources by the time the country went to war in 1940. Gas discoveries in the Po Valley in 1946 and 1949 gave it a new lease on life. When it was absorbed by ENI in 1953, AGIP was producing more than 2 billion cubic meters of methane gas and supplying 9.4 percent of the country's energy needs.

Agnelli family See FIAT.

Agnesi, Maria Gaetana (1718–1799)
scholar and mathematician, author of pioneering texts for teaching mathematics
Born to a family of Milanese silk merchants, she was the oldest of the 21 children that her father, Pietro Agnesi, had with his three wives. Her father took a great interest in her education and hired capable private tutors. At age nine, reportedly already fluent in Greek, Hebrew, Latin, French, German, Italian, and Spanish, Agnesi published a Latin translation of an essay written by one of her tutors advocating higher education for women. An admirer of Sir Isaac Newton, as a young woman she engaged in philosophical debates and pursued her interests in the natural sciences, presenting her views in the book *Propositiones philosophicae* (1738). Her most famous publication was a two-volume textbook, *Istituzioni analitiche ad uso della gioventù italiana* (Analytical precepts for the use of Italian youth, 1748–49), which brought together the elements of algebra and calculus for beginners. The book brought her international recognition, a papal letter of commendation, and an offer of appointment from the University of Bologna. It is not clear whether she accepted the appointment or ever taught. She insisted on living a simple life out of the public eye, in near seclusion, concentrating on the solitary study of religion and mathematics. After the death of her father in 1752 she expended most of her considerable inheritance on charitable works. She is remembered most often today for her cubic curve known as the "Witch of Agnesi." The term "witch" in this case has no connection with witchcraft. It is a corruption of the Latin term *versoria* (a turning around) into the Italian *versiera,* or wife of the devil, a most unfair and cruel development for someone so pious.

agriculture
Agriculture was the backbone of the Italian economy until the middle of the 20th century. The prevalence of hilly and mountainous territory in the peninsula, the diversity of terrain, microclimates, and labor techniques have made Italian agriculture extremely diversified. The products are diversified, and so are the forms of habitat, employment, family organization, and land tenure associated with agriculture. Geography

and history have both played a role. Where water is abundant and irrigation technically feasible, as in the Lombard plains of the Po Valley, a highly developed, capital-intensive, market-oriented agriculture developed in early modern times to serve the needs of growing urban populations. In the South, where water was scarce, labor plentiful, and urban growth limited, production took place on large estates (*latifundia*). Unlike the commercial agriculture of the North, which provided city markets with a broad range of goods, southern agriculture specialized in the production of cereals for export. In central Italy a form of sharecropping known as MEZZADRIA supported family-based agriculture that aimed to satisfy the needs of both the producers and the market. In the lowlands and hills of Tuscany, the Marches, and Umbria where *mezzadria* prevailed, the major crops were olives, grapes, cereals, and a variety of fruit and vegetables. At the higher elevations in the ALPS and APENNINES, peasant families aimed at attaining maximum self-sufficiency, minimizing recourse to market, and seeking supplementary sources of income outside agriculture, often by resorting to emigration (see MOUNTAINS, PROBLEM OF THE). Families concentrated on producing a few staple crops like chestnuts, maize, or rye, and tending sheep and goats for their milk and milk products. Mountain agriculture aimed at survival rather than profit.

The course of agricultural production has also been influenced by political developments at home and abroad. Governments have taken different approaches to LAND REFORM. Public and private programs of land reclamation have brought new lands under cultivation. Reclaimed lands in the lower Po Valley have become important producers of commercial crops like sugar beets, maize, and wheat. The production of cereals was stimulated enormously by the policy of AUTARKY adopted by the Fascist regime. The agricultural policies pursued today by the EUROPEAN UNION favor enterprises that are internationally competitive, encourage specialization, and adopt labor-saving techniques. Italian agriculture is responding with mechanization, increased use of artificial fertilizers, cheap immigrant labor, and better marketing. In spite of these advances, the role of Italian agriculture in the national economy has declined steadily. In the 1860s, agriculture accounted for about two-thirds of the gross national product. Its share fell to about half at the start of the 20th century, and to about a quarter in the 1950s. In 1998, agriculture contributed only 2.6 percent to the gross national product, and accounted for 6 percent of total employment. The shifting of population out of agriculture into the manufacturing and service industries has been accompanied by a general increase in income levels. The decline of Italian agriculture is part of a larger trend evident in all the advanced economies of the western world and of the greater integration that is the most important aspect of the global economy.

AIDS

The first case of AIDS (acquired immunodeficiency syndrome) was diagnosed in Italy in 1983. There were sharp yearly increases in the number of diagnosed cases from the late 1980s to the mid 1990s, the highest number of 5,659 occurring in 1995. There was a significant drop thereafter, down to 1,926 in 1998, the last year for which official figures are available. From 1982 to 1999, there were a total of 44,183 cases diagnosed, the highest number of 13,277 registered in the region of Lombardy, the lowest number of 31 in the region of Molise. The highest concentrations were in the urban centers of northern Italy and in Rome. Nearly half the diagnosed cases (21,281) were reportedly attributable to intravenous drug use, 6,619 to homosexual contact, and 5,320 to heterosexual contact. Making drug use a crime in 1990 led to a sharp increase in the number of prison inmates afflicted with AIDS. On the related issue of HIV infections, women and infants account for about 20 percent of cases and prison inmates for about one-third. Annual HIV infection increases were estimated at 5,000–10,000 in the late 1990s. Less than one third of all subjects infected by HIV are thought to be receiving treatment. A national campaign to control the spread of HIV infection was organized in 1987–90 after parliament adopted legislation to protect the confidentiality of medical tests. Advocates of coordinated public health measures to stop the spread of AIDS, including public education on the use of and free distribution of condoms, had to overcome the political opposition of the CATHOLIC CHURCH and the Christian Democratic Party (DC). An internationally organized and highly controversial gathering of homosexuals held in Rome in July 2000 ignited debate on gay sex and AIDS. Sex education in schools, thought to be an effective way of controlling AIDS and other sexually transmitted diseases, is a hotly debated issue. While Italians are very much aware of the presence of AIDS, political groups have approached the issue with caution and reluctance (see GAY MOVEMENT).

Aix-la Chapelle, Peace of See AUSTRIAN SUCCESSION, WAR OF THE.

Albania

Located on the Balkan shore at the entrance to the ADRIATIC SEA and separated from Italy by only 50 miles of water, Albania has long attracted the attention of whatever power happens to dominate the Italian peninsula. In the 11th century the Republic of VENICE established colonies in the territory of modern Albania to secure safe passage into the MEDITERRANEAN SEA. In the 13th century Albania was ruled by the Angevin dynasty of NAPLES. In the 15th century Venice and Naples supported the unsuccessful Albanian struggle against the Ottoman Turks. It remained under Turkish rule until 1913, when the European powers recognized the political independence of Albania largely because Austria and Italy could not agree on how to dispose of its territory. Austrians, Greeks, Italians, and Serbians contended for control of Albania during WORLD WAR I. The PARIS PEACE CONFERENCE ratified Albanian independence in 1919 on the basis of national self-determination. Italian influence increased steadily after 1925 as Albania became increasingly dependent on Italian economic and financial help. Its ruler, Ahmed Zogu, who was crowned King Zog in 1928, tried to resist Italian encroachment. In April 1939 Italy invaded Albania militarily, King VICTOR EMMANUEL III adding the title of king of Albania to his other royal titles. Italy used Albania as a staging ground for its attack on Greece in WORLD WAR II. After the war a newly independent Albania was ruled for 40 years by a communist regime led by Enver Hoxha, a leader of the anti-Fascist resistance during World War II. In those years of mounting international isolation for Albania, Italian influence was felt largely through television, Italian programs that easily reached the country giving Albanians visions of Western affluence and lifestyles unimaginable in their impoverished land. The collapse of the communist regime was followed in the early 1990s by a mass exodus of tens of thousands of Albanian refugees to Italy, prompting Italian countermeasures to stem the flow. In 1992 the Italian army sent troops back into Albania, this time on humanitarian missions to oversee the distribution of food aid and provide security in an increasingly tense and lawless situation. Operation Pelican, as the relief mission was called, was subsequently formally taken over by the EUROPEAN UNION, but Italy remains an important player as Albania goes through the transition toward a free-market economy and political democracy.

Alberoni, Giulio (1664–1752)
cardinal and political figure
Born in Piacenza of humble parentage, Alberoni was educated by the Jesuits and ordained a priest in 1689. Early on he demonstrated a talent for ingratiating himself with influential people who could further his career. In 1696 he followed his patron, Bishop Giorgio Barni of Piacenza, to Rome, where he continued his education. Alberoni began his diplomatic career in 1702 as a part of a mission sent by the duke of

Parma to negotiate with French forces during the WAR OF THE SPANISH SUCCESSION. Alberoni took over the mission a year later and remained in French service until 1708. In 1710 he accompanied the duke of Vendôme, the French commander, on a diplomatic mission to Spain, where they successfully championed the candidacy of the grandson of King Louis XIV of France, who reigned as Philip V (1700–46). In 1713 Louis XIV promoted Alberoni's appointment as envoy of the duchy of PARMA at the Spanish court. He was instrumental in arranging the marriage of Elisabetta Farnese to the recently widowed Philip V in 1714. The marriage made Alberoni the most influential courtier and adviser at the court of Spain. In that capacity, Alberoni promoted administrative and military reforms to revive the declining power of the Spanish monarchy. He improved the collection of revenues, reformed the currency, expanded manufacturing, modernized the merchant marine, established model farms, and curtailed smuggling. In 1717 he was made cardinal. His fortunes began to decline as the Spanish monarchy embarked on a series of military adventures, starting with a successful invasion of SARDINIA (1717) and a failed invasion of SICILY (1718). Alberoni was blamed for the war with England and France that broke out as a result of these initiatives. His life in danger, Alberoni left Spain in 1719, only to be arrested and tried in ROME on charges of having abused his power. He was exonerated after a three-year trial that ended in 1723. He served several popes during the remaining years of his life, most notably as legate for the Romagna provinces of the PAPAL STATES (1735–43). In 1732 he founded an ecclesiastical college in his native Piacenza, to which he bequeathed all his possessions.

Albertario, Davide (1846–1902)
radical Catholic activist and journalist
Born in the province of Pavia to a family of well-to-do landowners, Albertario first studied in seminaries where his conservative parents hoped he would be shielded from liberal influences, then went on to obtain a degree in theology from the Gregorian University of Rome in 1868. He was ordained into the priesthood a year later in Milan. This "journalist priest" immediately took up the conservative Catholic crusade against the Italian state inspired by Pope PIUS IX, joining the staff of the Milanese paper *L'Osservatore Cattolico*. He became its director in 1870, and immediately accentuated its conservative bent with the slogan *Col Papa e per il Papa* (With the Pope and for the Pope), challenging not only the liberal state but also Catholics who hoped for the reconciliation of CHURCH AND STATE. Albertario urged Catholics to boycott the state by staying away from the polls and to demand a national Catholic university to train future leaders of the movement. He looked to the rural masses to counteract liberal influences. Polemical and outspoken, he aroused strong feelings for and against his person and his views. His clerical superiors censured him after he criticized the policies of Pope LEO XIII as too liberal. The censure did not make him less popular among young activists who flocked to him. His slogan *Preparazione nell'astensione* (Preparation in abstention) expressed the intention of taking political power by organizing the religious masses against liberals. "Democracy," he insisted, "must be Christian, or it must not be." He was arrested after the FATTI DI MAGGIO of 1898, sentenced to three years in jail, and released in 1899. More radical than conservative, Albertario expressed and inspired the views of the most doctrinaire and intransigent Catholics who saw no redeeming virtues in liberal ideology. His strategy of organizing Catholics to take over the state paid off in the long run with the rise of Christian Democracy (see DC), but Albertario did not live to see its success and Christian Democrats have seldom acknowledged him as a precursor.

Alberti, Leon Battista (1404–1472)
Renaissance scholar, scientist, and architect
Alberti is often cited as the best example of the many-talented Renaissance man, or *uomo universale*, broadly knowledgeable, conversant with

many disciplines and arts. Alberti's interests covered literature, the visual arts, engineering, music, and mathematics. He was born in GENOA, the illegitimate son of a wealthy Florentine merchant in political exile from his city. In Venice, where he followed his father and spent his youth, Alberti studied classical Greek, Latin, mathematics, the liberal arts, church law, and practiced a variety of sports. At age 24 he obtained a degree in law. Like FILIPPO BRUNELLESCHI, he studied ancient ruins in Rome, and his writings on the subject spread the cult of classical design. In 1430 he was allowed to take holy orders in spite of his illegitimate birth, which normally would have excluded him from the religious life. In Florence, where he settled in 1534, he emerged as a theorist of a new approach to the visual arts, education, and family life. Most influential were his treatises *De pittura* (On painting, 1436), *De statua* (Of sculpture, ca. 1464), and the all-important *De re aedeficatoria* (On building), which he wrote over a period of many years and was published after his death. The treatise on building was based on his close study of Roman ruins, carried on in Rome after Pope Nicholas V (1447–55) had called on him to study and plan the reconstruction of the city. Particularly noteworthy is Alberti's concept of church architecture, examples of which are the façade of Santa Maria Novella in Florence, of Sant'Andrea in Mantua, and the Tempio Malatestiano in the church of San Francesco in Rimini. Alberti argued that advances in technology and engineering enabled his contemporaries to replicate the achievements of the ancients in building and the visual arts. He urged painters and sculptors to study anatomy so that they could render nature and the human form more realistically. It was also proper for art, he argued, to expand its themes beyond the religious, to include mythology, nature, and history. His contributions extended to philosophy and religious studies. As a member of the Florentine Academy (see ACADEMIES), he was instrumental in the effort to reconcile Plato's philosophy with the Christian faith.

Albertini, Luigi (1871–1941)
journalist, political commentator, and public figure

A leading figure of Italian JOURNALISM, Albertini was born in Ancona to a wealthy business family that experienced hard times in the early 1890s after the bankruptcy and death of the father. He graduated from the University of Turin and taught political economy, sharing the economic liberalism of his friend LUIGI EINAUDI. A stint as an apprentice journalist in London in 1894–95 convinced him that Italian journalism should rise above political partisanship and adopt the model of factual reporting exemplified by the London *Times*. After working as an economic journalist in Rome, in 1898 Albertini was hired by Milan's *Corriere della Sera*. As manager, Albertini modernized the printing facilities, launched the popular illustrated Sunday supplement *La Domenica del Corriere*, and introduced a special book review section. In 1900 he became the *Corriere's* chief editor, making it the most authoritative and respected paper in the country. Interpreting political independence as freedom from government control, Albertini was a severe critic of Prime Minister GIOVANNI GIOLITTI, whose policies he regarded as corrupt and corrupting. Constitutional government, patriotism, legality, administrative honesty, and economic liberalism were values that Albertini regarded as nonpolitical. The paper attracted the most prestigious names of Italian journalism, including GIOVANNI AMENDOLA, LUIGI BARZINI SR., and GIUSEPPE ANTONIO BORGESE. GABRIELE D'ANNUNZIO and LUIGI PIRANDELLO contributed to the paper's *terza pagina* (third page), which covered art and literature. Albertini's political sympathies were with conservative liberals like ANTONIO SALANDRA and SIDNEY SONNINO. He supported the ITALIAN-TURKISH WAR, opposed broadening the suffrage, resented clerical meddling in politics, and favored Italian intervention in WORLD WAR I. He was made a senator in 1914. After the war, he represented Italy at the Washington Naval Conference (1921). Initially tolerant of FASCISM as a remedy against communism, he opposed it after it came to power, and condemned its political use of violence against opponents. In 1922 he turned down Mussolini's offer to serve as ambassador to Washington. Political pressure evicted him and his brother Alberto from the leadership of the *Corriere* in November 1925. Albertini then turned to agriculture, with a land reclamation project in the Roman countryside that he financed and supervised. He moved to Rome in 1926 and devoted the last years of his life to research and writing.

Aldrovandi, Ulisse (1522–1605)
scientist, collector, and classifier of natural objects

Aldrovandi, a celebrated naturalist from Bologna, devoted his professional life to collecting, describing, and classifying natural objects. His collection of familiar and exotic animals, fossils, stones, gems, and metals formed a private museum that he called a "theater of nature." Visitors from all over Europe came to study, exchange ideas, and satisfy their intellectual curiosity. Aldrovandi's goal was to promote the understanding of nature, demystify its processes, discover recurring patterns in natural phenomena, and ultimately write a definitive history of the natural world. He saw himself as carrying on the work of Aristotle by testing and verifying the factual observations of the ancient master using logic and independent empirical investigation. The concept of assembling and ordering natural objects in a single space in the museum had a lasting impact on the methodology of learning. Aldrovandi's museum was a social space devoted to communal investigation and cooperative scholarly discourse, radically different from the private libraries prevalent at the time as places of study for isolated individuals. Aldrovandi was not only a scientist, but also an effective publicist of the new methodology based on the importance of empirical observation and the accumulation of facts. His fame and influence endured in part because the city of Bologna maintained his collection for several decades after his death. His many admirers and students saw to the posthumous publication of his voluminous writings, tables, and illustrations.

Aleardi, Aleardo (1812–1878)
poet and patriot dear to the romantic imagination

A most popular poet in his own time, Aleardi's literary reputation has suffered greatly since his death. Born to a noble family of Verona, baptized Gaetano Maria Aleardi, he studied law at the University of Padua, where he showed far greater enthusiasm for the rowdier aspects of student life than for scholarship. His most notable interests were poetry, country, and women, not necessarily in that order. Although love of women was a recurring theme of his poetry, he never married, but in *Il matrimonio* (1842), one of his early poems, he did acknowledge the importance of marriage. Sympathy for the sufferings of the poor and disinherited was a sign of his generosity. Politically, he was decisively democratic. He sided with the Venetian revolutionaries in 1848. In 1852 and 1859 he was arrested and jailed for his political views. Noble but not wealthy, he pursued the writer's life in the face of deprivation. His first popular poem was *Lettere a Maria* (1846), which expressed platonic love for an unidentified woman. Aleardi's verse, unlike his actions, exalted pure, platonic love, and mystical connections with women, nature, and the life of the spirit. He appealed to the romantic imagination of his time. After national unification Aleardi was honored as a poet and patriot. His *Canto politico* (1862) called for liberating ROME from papal rule. His appointment as senator in 1873 recognized him as one of the country's leading public figures. He lived the last years of his life in Florence, where he also taught at the Fine Arts Institute. Critics had begun to question his literary merits well before his death, chastising his verse as sentimental and mannered. The criticism was too harsh. An unprejudiced reader often senses genuine sentiments behind the overly refined language. Rejecting the Arcadian poetry of the 18th century as frivolous, Aleardi wanted art to confront real issues and express real sentiments. In that sense, he was an authentic figure of the romantic age.

Aleramo, Sibilla   See FACCIO, RINA.

Alexander VI (1431–1503)
pope (1492–1503)

Born near Valencia (Spain) to a noble Catalan family and baptized Rodrigo de Borja y Borja, he was known in Italy as Rodrigo Borgia. In 1456 Rodrigo received a degree in canon law from the University of Bologna. That same year an uncle became Pope Callistus III (1455–58), made the nephew a cardinal, and appointed him to several lucrative ecclesiastical posts. A skillful politician and able administrator, Rodrigo became an influential member of the Roman curia, engineering the election of several popes before arranging his own election in 1492. His success was made possible by the support of influential families, most notably the ruling SFORZA FAMILY of Milan. A handsome man of vigorous physique, the new pope was known to be a womanizer (he had at least four illegitimate children) and to appoint family members to lucrative public posts (nepotism). But he also used family members to advance his own policies, as he did by arranging marriages of his daughter Lucrezia Borgia. None too popular in Rome where he was resented as a foreigner, he had to contend with an organized opposition that lost no opportunity to portray him in the most unfavorable light. Indeed, it is easy to see him as the personification of the lust, simony, and nepotism that critics have attributed to RENAISSANCE popes. While his personal failings are undeniable, recent studies have also drawn attention to his considerable achievements. Elected pope, he sought reconciliation with his opponents and worked to create a united front of Italian rulers to prevent a French invasion of the peninsula. His efforts failed, the French took Rome in December 1494,

and Alexander had little choice but to get along with the dominant new power. He seconded the efforts of his son, Cesare Borgia, to enlarge the PAPAL STATES at the expense of neighboring MILAN and VENICE. Alexander's most formidable critic and opponent within the church was GIROLAMO SAVONAROLA, whom he excommunicated in 1497 and pressured the Florentine state to proceed against. Alexander then made some feeble efforts at church reform that can be seen as anticipating the more successful efforts of his successors. Looking beyond Europe, Alexander encouraged Spanish expansion in the non-Christian world. A papal bull of 1493 fixed the line of demarcation between the overseas possession of Portugal and Spain in such a way that the entire American continent was within the Spanish sphere. But the Treaty of Tordesillas (1494) altered the line so as to put the territory later known as Brazil under Portuguese rule. Alexander died while apparently trying to engineer his own succession to the papal throne. His behavior as pope reflected and magnified the faults of his age, but he must also be numbered among those Renaissance popes who sought to restore power and dignity to the papacy by giving it a viable territorial basis and role in world affairs, and by patronizing the arts.

Alfa Romeo   See FIAT.

Alfieri, Vittorio (1749–1803)
writer and patriotic figure

Recognized as a forerunner in the search for a modern Italian identity, Alfieri was born to a noble Piedmontese family from Asti. His pursuit of literary fame took him far from his family and region culturally and emotionally. While he admired the aristocracy's ethic of honor, he came to despise that class and Piedmontese society generally for being provincial and anti-intellectual. In his writings, Alfieri protested against all forms of servility and conformism dictated by society. Nevertheless, he remained too much the aristocrat to be truly democratic, and his contempt extended to the conformism of the crowd, whose tyranny he feared as much as he feared and resented the tyranny of monarchs. He came to these views after a restless life that began predictably enough for a member of his class with years of study at the Royal Academy of Turin (later the Military Academy), from which he graduated in 1762. He served as an officer in the Piedmontese army until 1774, traveling to other parts of Italy and Europe, and everywhere enjoying access to the most select circles thanks to his family background. Travel opened his mind to the ideas of the ENLIGHTENMENT. Back in Italy, Alfieri resolved to devote himself to a life of writing, making Italian the language of choice. In his writings, which included plays based on the stories about Cleopatra, Antigone, Agamemnon, Brutus, and Orestes, Alfieri looked back to ancient Greece and Rome. Civic virtue and heroic individualism were the two themes that he celebrated in his writings. In *Della tirannide* (Of tyranny, 1777), he praised ancient Romans for their spirit of republican pride and independence, and castigated his contemporaries for their servility. In *Del principe e delle lettere* (Of the prince and letters, 1778–86), he urged writers to keep their distance from the powerful, maintain their independence, and speak out uncompromisingly for liberty. His love and open relationship with the countess of Albany, wife of the Stuart pretender to the English throne, was both a deeply felt passion and an assertion of independence from social conventions. Initially an admirer of the American and French revolutions, Alfieri turned against the FRENCH REVOLUTION for its mob violence and cult of equality. His antagonism toward everything French deepened after the French invasion of Italy in 1796. The virulence of his feelings finds full expression in the verses of the anti-French diatribe *Il misogallo* (1793–99). In the account of his life that he gave in *Vita* (1790–1803), Alfieri saw himself as struggling to perfect his art, find his own voice, and be an example to his contemporaries. The notion that writers have an obligation to confront real issues

through their art and inspire virtue in others is a legacy that Alfieri passed on to his successors.

Alfonso I of Naples (1396–1458)
king of Naples (1443–1458)

The son of Ferdinand I of Aragon and Sicily, he inherited the crowns of Aragon and Sicily from his father in 1416, ruling over these lands as Alfonso V. He acquired the crown of Naples in 1443, after more than 20 years of costly and bloody wars against rival claimants to the throne. The one constant of his tortuous diplomacy was to consolidate Aragonese control of the western Mediterranean. In 1420 he invaded the island of Sardinia, which provided him with a convenient base of operations against the Italian mainland. In 1421 Queen Giovanna II of Naples (1414–35) asked for his help against French claimants to her throne. Giovanna's adoption of Alfonso provided the basis for his claim to her throne upon her death, a claim that he successfully defended against the French.

Alfonso devoted himself entirely to Italian affairs after taking up residence in Naples in 1443 and left his Spanish possessions under the care of his wife and brother. His expansionist inclinations embroiled him in unsuccessful wars for control of Milan (1447–53). After hesitating, he signed the Peace of Lodi (1454) that brought a measure of political stability to Italy. He increased the power of the crown at the expense of the already weakened feudal nobility of the kingdom. Styling himself *Rex Sicilie citra et ultra farum* (King of Sicily on both sides of the lighthouse), a reference to a lighthouse that guided ships through the Strait of Messina, he concentrated power in the royal household, with limited autonomy granted to local councils and parliaments of the nobility. The concentration of power in royal appointees was not without benefits: banditry was virtually eliminated, the arbitrary powers of local officials curbed, corruption of public officials reduced, and laws made more uniform. Government revenue increased substantially with the introduction of direct taxes, which weighed disproportionately on the poorer classes. Much was spent on the army, consisting of Italians, Spaniards, and mercenaries, and on the navy, which Alfonso used to extend Neapolitan power to the eastern Mediterranean.

Under Alfonso's leadership, Naples reached the height of its power and influence in Italy and the Mediterranean region. That power was based on the close relationship that he maintained with Spain, but the relationship tilted heavily in Spain's favor after Alfonso's death. Alfonso, called the Magnanimous because of his generous patronage of the arts, turned his court into a major center of humanistic culture. He himself was well educated, versed in philosophical studies, an eloquent speaker, affable and patient when it suited him. He was also exceedingly jealous of his royal prerogatives and was a determined state-builder, according to the most progressive notions of royal power at the time. Admired and praised by the artists and writers whom he patronized, he was resented by many of his Neapolitan subjects, especially by the nobility whose privileges he attacked, for his autocratic ways and for the preferential treatment of Spaniards at his court.

Algarotti, Francesco (1712–1764)
writer, literary critic, and publicist for the new science

Algarotti was born in Venice to a wealthy merchant family, studied in Venice, Rome, and Bologna, was drawn to the study of science, and wrote the treatise *Newtonanismo per le dame* (Newtonism for the ladies, 1737), which in spite of its frivolous title was really a serious interpretation of Newtonian science as a continuation of the work of GALILEO. The book brought Algarotti instant celebrity. His travels took him to many European countries, including France, England, Prussia, and Russia, everywhere received as an honored guest. In 1746 he was appointed court chamberlain to Frederick II of Prussia, whom he served until 1753. He was Voltaire's friend and correspondent. His writings, covering a broad range of topics, treat all the major issues of his time with elegance and wit. As a linguist and literary critic, Algarotti urged writers to write in their own native language to express authentic cultural values. After returning to Italy in 1753, Algarotti founded a school in Bologna, promoted the publication of his own writings, and carried on a busy correspondence with his many acquaintances in Italy and the rest of Europe. Algarotti was an effective publicist for the culture of the Enlightenment in Italy, for Italy's contributions to that culture, and for the use of Italian as the language of the educated.

Alitalia Airline See IRI.

Alleanza Nazionale See MSI (ITALIAN SOCIAL MOVEMENT).

Allies See WORLD WAR II.

Almirante, Giorgio See MSI (ITALIAN SOCIAL MOVEMENT).

Alps

The great mountain range of the Alps that arches over northern Italy in an east-west direction separates Italy from France, Switzerland, Austria, and Slovenia. The territory known as the Italian Alps covers the western, southern, and eastern slopes. In the west, where the Alps separate Italy from France and sweep northward from the Riviera across the region of Piedmont, the range is no more than 60 miles deep, but contains the highest peaks. The tallest of all, Mont Blanc, is in French territory close to where the borders of Italy, France, and Switzerland meet. It is part of a massif that reaches an elevation of 15,571 feet (4,807 meters). Long ridges and deep valleys descend from the flanks of the Alps toward the Po Valley, carrying rivers and streams that irrigate the fertile plains of the region of LOMBARDY.

In the central part of the Alps, the Brenner Pass facilitates communications between Italy and Austria. The Brenner border, following the high peaks of the Alps in this central portion, was attained by Italy at the end of WORLD WAR I, a conflict that Italy fought almost entirely in the difficult territory of the central and eastern Alps. The eastern Alps bordering on Slovenia are not as clearly demarcated as the other portions of the chain. They are characterized by lower summits of no more than 8,500 feet and mountain passes that invite population movements. Italian and Slavic-speaking populations have mixed freely in the course of centuries, generally without producing the kind of ethnic conflicts frequent in other parts of the region. Although the Alps present a formidable obstacle on paper, they have never prevented military incursions into Italy. From the time when Hannibal carried out his legendary crossing with elephants in the third century B.C. to the French invasions of the 15th century, or the German takeover in WORLD WAR II, the Alps have been a porous border.

The economy of the Alps has been traditionally agricultural, characterized by small family plots that do not encourage the use of modern methods of production. Sizable family farms survive in the region of TRENTINO–ALTO ADIGE where German-speaking populations hold on to their traditional custom of passing farms intact from one generation to the next. But in the Italian-speaking areas, where the practice of divisible inheritance prevails, land ownership is extremely fragmented. In recent years, cooperative ventures, especially in pasturage and wine production, have ameliorated the situation. Historically, the population had recourse to emigration. In the past the incidence of emigration from Alpine territories, particularly in the region of VENETIA, has at times been higher than from Italy's impoverished South. Significant manufacturing activities have developed in some towns at the foot of the Alps, such as Como, Lecco, and Varese. Today, tourism is the major resource of the Alpine economy. Spectacular scenery, lakes, summer retreats, and superb skiing facilities attract visitors from all over the world.

Alto Adige   See TRENTINO–ALTO ADIGE.

Alvaro, Corrado (1895–1956)
writer inspired by the traditions and folklore of the Italian South

This noted journalist and fiction writer was born in Reggio Calabria to a lower-middle-class family (his father was an elementary school teacher), studied in Naples and Rome, served as an infantry officer in WORLD WAR I, and earned a degree in letters from the University of Milan in 1920. Although his experiences carried him away from his native CALABRIA, most of his writings are inspired by the folklore, customs, and mentality of his native region. Politically liberal and a dissenter from FASCISM, he avoided overt criticism of the regime and stayed in Italy. But his novels and short stories can be read as warnings against the dangers that totalitarian governments, both Fascist and communist, pose to culture. His message was that intellectuals should maintain their independence from all political creeds. His fame was secured by the publication in 1930 of a collection of short stories entitled *Gente in Aspromonte* and of the novel *Vent'anni* (Twenty years). *Gente in Aspromonte*, his most widely read work, tells the story of a family of hardworking shepherds who wreak revenge against an oppressive landlord and are driven to break the law by their elemental thirst for justice. Because a strong southern perspective animates all of Alvaro's writings, he is credited with drawing public attention to the seriousness of the SOUTHERN QUESTION in the postwar years.

Amadeus Ferdinand Maria of Savoy (1845–1890)
(Amedeo Ferdinando Maria di Savoia)
duke of Aosta, member of the Italian ruling dynasty, and king of Spain

Amadeus, second son of VICTOR EMMANUEL II, accepted the crown of Spain in 1870 after it had been left vacant by the forced resignation of Queen Isabella in 1868. His candidacy was put forth with the approval of other European powers partly to forestall a German claim to the throne, to thwart the establishment of a republic in Spain, and satisfy the dynastic ambitions of his father. Powerful conservative interests opposed his candidacy, including the Carlists, who found him too liberal and objected to the anticlerical policies of the HOUSE OF SAVOY. Amadeus accepted the Spanish crown reluctantly. After escaping several attempts on his life and threatened by rebellion, Amadeus resigned as king of Spain in 1873 and returned to Italy. His candidacy has been seen as part of a policy of Italian expansion, but it seems that Foreign Minister EMILIO VISCONTI-VENOSTA yielded out of concern that a refusal would lead to the establishment of a Spanish republic.

Amari, Michele (1806–1889)
Sicilian scholar, patriot, and foremost orientalist of his generation

Amari was born in Palermo to a middle-class family of lawyers and civil servants. His admiration for English and French Enlightenment authors, developed when he was a student at the University of Palermo, made him politically suspect in the repressive atmosphere of the KINGDOM OF THE TWO SICILIES. Amari had decidedly democratic tendencies, resented aristocratic privileges, and opposed Neapolitan rule over his island. When his father was arrested in 1822 for conspiring against the government, Amari assumed financial responsibility for his family as a civil servant. His efforts to contain the cholera epidemic of 1837 took on a coloring of political opposition. He resented his transfer to Naples in 1838, returned to Sicily in 1840, and in 1842 completed his first major work, *La Guerra del Vespro siciliano* (History of the War of the Sicilian Vespers), which was the first attempt at a historical reconstruction of the popular revolt of 1282 against the French. Amari's account stressed the popular character of the uprising and downplayed the role of the aristocracy. Amari then went to Paris, where he studied Ara-

bic and began research on the period of Muslim rule in Sicily, and made contact with GIUSEPPE MAZZINI, the champion of Italian independence. He welcomed the revolution of 1848, was elected to the Sicilian parliament, and served as finance minister in the revolutionary government. He returned to Paris as a political exile in 1849, eventually distancing himself from the more radical patriots and becoming a lukewarm supporter of CAVOUR's moderate policies. He completed his study of Muslim rule in Sicily with the publication of his *Storia dei musulmani in Sicilia* (History of the Muslims in Sicily, 1854–72), which was hailed as a major contribution to the study of the Muslim expansion. He was appointed senator in 1861 and served as minister of education (1862–64). He retired from teaching in 1866 and devoted the rest of his life to his scholarly pursuits.

Amato, Giuliano (born 1939)
former socialist, prime minister

Born in Turin, Amato joined the Italian Socialist Party (PSI) at age 20. He was elected to parliament in 1983, served as deputy prime minister in the government headed by Bettino Craxi (1983–87), was treasury minister in 1987, and prime minister from June 1992 to April 1993. As prime minister, Amato pursued a policy of tight spending with considerable success, and led a crackdown against organized crime and government corruption. His deft handling of policy matters earned him the sobriquet, Doctor Subtle. He is also known as *Topolino* (Mickey Mouse) because of his small stature and decisive manner. Amato maintained personal credibility in the upheavals of the early 1990s because he was not personally implicated in the political scandals that ruined the Socialist Party and ended the political career of his former mentor Craxi. He served as minister for constitutional reform and again as treasury minister under MASSIMO D'ALEMA. Amato returned to the prime ministry as an independent in April 2000 following the resignation of D'Alema. His second coalition government took the country into the EUROPEAN UNION. Unabashedly intellectual, Amato was thought to lack the charisma to compete successfully in the general elections of May 2001. Rome's photogenic former mayor Francesco Rutelli headed the Olive Tree coalition in his place, losing to SILVIO BERLUSCONI, who succeeded Amato as prime minister in June 2001.

Ambrosio, Vittorio (1879–1958)
army general and chief of staff

General Ambrosio was born in Turin and began his military career as a cavalry officer. He fought in the ITALIAN-TURKISH WAR, in WORLD WAR I, and continued to serve in the 1920s as an army commander in Sicily. In WORLD WAR II he commanded an army in Yugoslavia in 1941 and was appointed army chief of staff in January 1942. Ambrosio developed a reputation for political tact in difficult situations and for being able to defuse professional rivalries. By 1943 he was convinced that Italy could not win the war and sought to convince BENITO MUSSOLINI that Italy should break away from Germany and conclude a separate peace. In February 1943 he replaced UGO CAVALLERO as general chief of staff in charge of all military services and began to plan the withdrawal of Italian troops from abroad. In early July, after concluding that Mussolini would not break away from Germany, Ambrosio began secret preparations to transfer military power from Mussolini to the king. He was instrumental in carrying out the coup of July 25, 1943, that removed Mussolini from power. Keeping his post after the coup, Ambrosio played a role in the secret armistice negotiations with the Allies. He is held partly responsible for the state of confusion that led to the complete collapse of the army when the armistice was announced on September 8, 1943. He stepped down as general chief of staff in July 1944, retired from the army, and lived quietly after the war, never commenting on his role in the controversial events of 1943.

Amendola, Giorgio (1907–1980)
anti-Fascist activist and Communist Party leader

Giorgio Amendola, the son of GIOVANNI AMENDOLA, carried on his father's battle against fascism from a position further to the left. Born in Rome, he joined the Italian Communist Party (PCI) in 1929. Arrested in 1932 for seditious activities against the regime, he spent the next five years in jail. As an expatriate in France in the late 1930s, he took charge of party activities in that country. He escaped to Tunisia during the German occupation of France, returned to Italy in 1943, participated in the RESISTANCE, and was a member of the Rome Committee of National Liberation. In April 1945 he organized the takeover of the city of Turin by the resistance prior to the arrival of the Allies. He served in parliament as a member of the Communist Party in all the postwar legislatures and was a member of the party's central committee from 1955. He carved out a position for himself as an expert on economic issues and on the SOUTHERN QUESTION, and led the fight for internal democracy within the party. He took a strong stand against TERRORISM, favored closer ties to Western Europe, and was elected to the European parliament in 1979. In 1975 he initiated the national debate with historian RENZO DE FELICE on the historical role of the resistance and the relationship between fascism and the Italian republic. Amendola pursued the course set for the Communist Party by PALMIRO TOGLIATTI, pursuing power by electoral means, organizing workers and intellectuals, and reaching out to the middle classes. The policy of gradual penetration of government and society was reformist, but Amendola and other members of what was called the right wing of the Communist Party saw it as the only practical way to restructure Italian society in an egalitarian direction. Amendola's hope of creating a unified, democratic party of the left committed to fundamental change came to fruition 10 years after his death with the founding of the Democratic Party of the Left.

Amendola, Giovanni (1882–1926)
political journalist, member of parliament, and anti-Fascist activist

This Neapolitan journalist, remembered for the brave opposition to fascism that cost him his life, actually started out on the fringes of the political right as a nationalist collaborator of GIOVANNI PAPINI and other young radicals opposed to the liberalism of GIOVANNI GIOLITTI. He served in WORLD WAR I, and in 1916 joined the staff of the Milanese daily *Corriere della Sera.* He parted company with the nationalists after the war by advocating a policy of friendship and collaboration with the new state of Yugoslavia. He ran for parliament successfully in 1919, 1921, and 1924 as a radical democrat close to FRANCESCO SAVERIO NITTI. By this time he could be described as a liberal who believed in political diversity and parliamentary government, but feared the consequences of universal suffrage and proportional representation. Full democracy might give too much power to voters unprepared to use it responsibly and play into the hands of demagogues on the political left and right. In 1922 he served as minister of colonies in the government headed by LUIGI FACTA. He was not an immediate opponent of fascism, hoping that drawing Fascists into the government and giving them a share of power would educate them politically. He did oppose the march on Rome and turned resolutely against fascism in 1923 when it became clear the Fascists were out to seize full control of government. He coined the term "totalitarian" to describe the nature of fascism and waged a courageous war against the emerging regime from the pages of his newspaper *Il Mondo* (1922–26). He led the constitutional opposition in parliament and the AVENTINE SECESSION after the murder of GIACOMO MATTEOTTI in June 1924. As leader of the opposition he urged the king to remove BENITO MUSSOLINI from power, and sought to mobilize public opinion against the emerging regime. He left the country for France after suffering a savage beating at the hands of Fascist thugs in 1925 and died a year later from the aftereffects of the beating.

Amicizia Cristiana See SECRET SOCIETIES.

anarchism
social theory and movement that sees the power of the state as the main impediment to a just society

The anarchist movement developed in Italy largely at the initiative of the Russian agitator MICHAEL BAKUNIN, who was present in Italy from 1864 to 1874. Initially an emissary of Karl Marx, Bakunin set off the anarchist movement when he decided to strike out on his own. Convinced that Italy was ripe for social revolution, he looked to the impoverished peasantry of the South to start the revolution. To make headway, anarchism had to battle the rival influences of Karl Marx and GIUSEPPE MAZZINI. The rivalry intensified in 1871 in the wake of the repression of the Paris Commune. Anarchism had some appeal for intellectuals and workers. Italian anarchists maintained loose ties with Marx's International Workingmen's Association until expelled in 1896. CARLO CAFIERO and ERRICO MALATESTA inspired and steered the movement. The anarchist creed, fundamentally antiauthoritarian, was also atheistic and favored government decentralization, local autonomy, and small-scale economic organization. It called for individual, revolutionary, violent action ("propaganda of the deed") to set off larger conflagrations. Self-proclaimed anarchists practiced political assassination and other forms of terrorism. Sante Caserio (1873–94), a baker, assassinated the president of France in 1894. Luigi Luccheni (1873–1910) assassinated Empress Elizabeth of Austria in 1898. Gaetano Bresci (1869–1901), a textile worker, assassinated King UMBERTO I in 1900. The fact that Caserio and Luccheni were Italians working abroad points to the appeal of anarchism among politically conscious Italian emigrants. Sizable colonies of Italian anarchists existed in Marseilles; New York City; Paterson, New Jersey; and Barre, Vermont. Anarchism lost much of its appeal in Italy after the dismal failure of anarchist-led uprisings. ANDREA COSTA openly disavowed the tactics of violence and insurrection in favor of the reformist, electoral politics of socialism after the last unsuccessful anarchist uprising in southern Italy in 1877 (Moti del matese, uprising of the matese—a rugged mountain region northeast of Naples). Anarchism remained a presence in Italy until the Fascist regime suppressed it entirely. Traces of anarchist mentality linger on in the antiauthoritarianism of libertarians and radicals who distrust the power of government.

Andrea del Sarto (1486–1531)
Renaissance painter

Overshadowed and influenced by his older contemporaries LEONARDO and RAPHAEL, the Florentine painter Andrea del Sarto is often consigned to the second rank of RENAISSANCE artists. He stands out for his adherence to the principles of classical representation at a time when artists were beginning to strive for the dramatic visual effects that culminated in MANNERISM. Andrea del Sarto's paintings are characterized by balanced composition, clarity of line, delicate colors, and the use of chiaroscuro. The overall effect is one of gentle expressiveness and quiet melancholy. A good example of his style of painting is the altarpiece of the *Madonna of the Harpies* (1517), a representation of the Virgin and Child, on display in the Uffizi Gallery in Florence. A later painting, *The Lamentation* (1524), done after Andrea had left Florence with his family to escape an outbreak of the plague, shows figures grieving over the body of the dead Christ (Andrea's wife, Lucrezia del Fede, posed for the figure of the Virgin). It stresses the redeeming message of Christ's sacrifice rather than his sufferings, reflecting perhaps the piety beginning to permeate Florentine popular culture at the onset of the CATHOLIC REFORMATION. While not a mannerist, Andrea del Sarto's meticulous craftsmanship influenced mannerist artists of a later generation, including GIORGIO VASARI, who deemed his works faultless. The combination of craftsmanship and expressiveness evident in Andrea del Sarto's paintings caught the imagination of later generations. Robert Browning imagined him as an artist driven by a relentless creative urge, unappreciated by those close to him, particularly by his wife, who was portrayed as the bane of his artistic life. That can all be ascribed to poetic license. Andrea del Sarto's work suggests an artist highly disciplined, given to understatement, isolated, and prone to go his own way.

Andreotti, Giulio (1919–   )
prime minister and Christian Democratic leader

Born into a Roman family of modest means, he studied law at the University of Rome. A devout Roman Catholic, from his student days he gravitated toward Catholic organizations and formed close ties with religious and lay figures destined to play an important role in his rapid rise to power and prominence. These included the future pope, PAUL VI, and the Christian Democratic leaders ALCIDE DE GASPERI, and ALDO MORO. Elected to parliament in 1947, Andreotti has occupied important posts as minister of finance, treasury, defense, industry and commerce, and budget. He was prime minister three times, in 1972–73, 1976–79, and 1989–92. An adroit and devious politician, he has played a major role in Italian politics whether in or out of power. He has been the architect of political alliances and coalition governments that aimed at keeping the Communists out of power and Italy firmly anchored in the Western camp during the years of the cold war. In the United States he was regarded as a key ally. He was nevertheless instrumental in shaping the so-called Historic Compromise of 1976 that should have led to formal communist participation in government. He was prime minister during the years of extreme unrest and political terrorism that saw the kidnapping and murder of Aldo Moro by the RED BRIGADES in 1979. He was again prime minister when the end of the cold war doomed the political system that sustained his power. His lengthy political presence, pursuit of controversial policies, wily methods, and involvement in murky political deals aroused suspicion and hostility. His political career was terminated in 1993 when prosecutors charged him with conspiring with and protecting the MAFIA. In 1999 a jury acquitted him of the serious charge that he had conspired in the 1979 murder of muckraking journalist Carmine Pecorelli. Andreotti was acquitted of all charges in October 2003 by the country's highest court (*corte di cassazione*) after a 10-year ordeal. He remains a highly controversial figure who speaks out on public issues and calls himself the victim of political vendettas and betrayal by enemies and former friends. He is also a prolific, witty, and often entertaining writer of light and serious works.

Annali Universali di Statistica See

SCIENCE.

Ansaldo Company

This manufacturer of steel, ships, locomotives, rolling stock, and armaments was founded in 1852 by Giovanni Ansaldo (1819–63), a Genoese entrepreneur who started out as an architect (one of his projects was the design for Genoa's monumental cemetery at Staglieno) and as a teacher of mathematics. He went into business in the 1850s at the urging of Count CAVOUR, the Piedmontese prime minister who wanted to encourage industrialization. Ansaldo started out manufacturing locomotives, railroad and naval equipment, diversifying after national unification into the production of steel and armaments. In 1903 the company was reorganized into a joint-stock operation with the help of British capital, undergoing a major expansion in the next 10 years. When WORLD WAR I broke out, Ansaldo supported Italian intervention on the side of the Entente powers. The firm experienced unprecedented growth during the war as the country's major manufacturer of arma-

ments, producing enough heavy artillery without government authorization to meet the military emergency after the BATTLE OF CAPORETTO. At war's end, Ansaldo was the country's largest industrial complex. In 1920, under the aggressive management of the brothers Mario and Pio Perrone, it attempted to gain control of the Banca Commerciale Italiana (see BANKING) to secure urgently needed capital. When the takeover failed, Ansaldo was rescued from bankruptcy by the government in 1922, setting a precedent for later public rescues of private firms. The company was kept alive in the 1920s by the government's program of naval expansion. It was eventually absorbed by IRI in 1932, ceasing its operations as a private firm and becoming part of the public sector of the economy.

Anselmi, Tina See PROPAGANDA 2.

anticlericalism

Resentment and opposition to the secular influence and political power of the CATHOLIC CHURCH has been a feature of Italian life for centuries. It was present in the writings of NICCOLÒ MACHIAVELLI, the culture of the ENLIGHTENMENT, FREEMASONRY, and in the politics during and after the RISORGIMENTO. The church's opposition to national unification and to the Italian state fueled and exacerbated feelings of anticlericalism, particularly among educated Italians. Efforts by the Italian state to guarantee papal sovereignty and compensate the church for its economic losses did not lessen the conflict between CHURCH AND STATE. Anticlerical feelings were shared by most 19th-century patriots. They were particularly strong among members of the LIBERAL LEFT that won control of parliament in 1876. In the 1880s and 1890s Prime Minister Francesco Crispi was determined to wage a fight to the finish against supporters of the pope, who were referred to disparagingly as *papalini* (little papists). The government openly encouraged antipapal activities, and clashes between clericals and anticlericals often turned violent. National associations like the Società del Libero Pensiero (Society for Free Thought), founded in 1872, and the even more militant Giordano Bruno Society, dominated by Freemasons, organized anticlerical demonstrations and disseminated anticlerical literature. The government dissolved many Catholic organizations after the FATTI DI MAGGIO of 1898. Government-sponsored anticlerical measures abated in the first decade of the century as Prime Minister GIOVANNI GIOLITTI sought the political support of Catholics. Many Fascists shared anticlerical sentiments, but anticlericalism found little government support under FASCISM, once the regime had come to terms with the church. After WORLD WAR II, anticlericalism was a significant source of popular support for the parties of the political left, especially the Communist Party (PCI). Communist anticlericalism diminished in the 1970s when the party sought an accommodation with the church in its bid to share power with the dominant Christian Democratic Party (DC). The election in 1978 of Pope JOHN PAUL II, the first non-Italian pope in almost 500 years, had the probably unintended consequence of reducing papal interference in Italian politics, thereby defusing the political resentments that fueled anticlericalism. Political anticlericalism seems to be on its way to extinction. It is perhaps being replaced by indifference to religion, as suggested in declining rates of church attendance and to the church's teachings on controversial issues like ABORTION and DIVORCE.

Anti-Comintern Pact

The Anti-Comintern Pact was initially an anticommunist understanding between Germany and Japan concluded in November 1936. Italy joined the pact in November 1937. Italian interest in reaching an understanding with Germany and Japan predated its adherence to the pact. The Italian aim was to reach an anti-British alliance with Japan in the wake of the ETHIOPIAN WAR, hoping that it would distract British attention from the Mediterranean. Since the Japanese

were unwilling to antagonize the British at that moment, the Italian government settled for a three-way understanding directed against the Soviet Union that aimed at containing communism. Thus, the Italian government responded favorably to German solicitations to join the pact. Even without specific provisions for its implementation, the pact signaled the ideological and diplomatic alignment of the three powers, leading the way to the TRIPARTITE PACT and the alliance of the three powers in WORLD WAR II.

antifascism

Anti-Fascist movements and ideas originated from different political directions and for different reasons. Slow to develop because most observers did not believe at first that BENITO MUSSOLINI intended to enact far-reaching constitutional changes, anti-Fascist initiatives gained momentum after 1924 when it became clear that the government was out to crush all opposition. Most political parties and observers misread Fascist intentions during the first two years of Fascist rule. Liberals and Catholics thought that fascism was an unpleasant but necessary antidote to the rising influence of socialists and communists who had scored impressive gains in the elections of 1919 and 1921. Even socialists and communists, who were the frequent targets of Fascist attacks, did not seem unduly alarmed. To them, fascism was merely a more naked version of capitalist reaction, different in form but not in substance from the reaction of liberal governments.

Anti-Fascist movements developed when it became clear that the Fascists were set on changing the political ground rules. The Catholic leader, LUIGI STURZO, was one of the first to sound the alarm, joined quickly by the moderate socialist leader FILIPPO TURATI and the liberal maverick, GIOVANNI AMENDOLA. Others who were critical of fascism were reluctant to speak out as long as Fascists confined their assaults to members of the far left. It was the assassination of GIACOMO MATTEOTTI that galvanized and united the opponents of fascism. In the AVENTINE SECESSION, parliamentary opponents tried to oust Mussolini by boycotting parliament. Their failure, and the repressive laws enacted by the Fascist government in 1925–26, signaled the beginning of a new phase in the fight against fascism. Without freedom of expression, opponents of the regime could no longer come together openly. The special laws legalized political persecution, drove the opposition underground, or forced it to leave the country. Official police figures show that by 1929 5,046 suspected subversives, most of them communists, were referred to the special tribunal set up to weed out political opponents. Of these, 901 were condemned to serve prison terms, and an undetermined number were subjected to forced confinement or police surveillance.

By the early 1930s domestic opposition to fascism had ceased to exist for all practical purposes. With the exception of a few isolated communist cells that managed to survive underground until 1932, and Catholic dissenters who found cover in religious organizations or the Vatican, resistance continued from abroad. France, Switzerland, Belgium, England, the United States, and the Soviet Union were the major countries where anti-Fascist expatriates found refuge. In 1927 liberals, republicans, and socialists founded the Anti-Fascist Concentration in Paris to help political refugees and work for the restoration of political freedoms in Italy. The leader of the concentration was the socialist elder statesman Filippo Turati. Other prominent socialists held important positions. The movement Giustizia e Libertà, launched in 1929 by CARLO ROSSELLI, appealed to non-communists, distanced itself from existing parties, and promised a democratic republic after the fall of fascism. That the Fascist regime would fall seemed most unlikely in the early 1930s. Not only was the regime secure at home, but Hitler's rise to power in January 1933 promised to facilitate the spread of fascism abroad. That prospect, and the threat that it posed to communism and the Soviet Union, convinced communists to make common cause with other anti-Fascists in so-called Popular Front movements and governments. One such leftist governing coalition in

Spain triggered the military reaction led by General Francisco Franco. In the ensuing Spanish civil war (1936–39), Germany and Italy supported Franco militarily, while anti-Fascist volunteers, about 5,000 of them Italians organized in the Garibaldi Brigade commanded by RANDOLFO PACCIARDI, rallied in defense of the Popular Front government. For these and other anti-Fascist fighters, the Spanish civil war was a dress rehearsal for what they hoped would be a decisive military showdown in Italy.

They had to wait for Italy's defeat in WORLD WAR II for that showdown to happen. A complete military defeat was required to topple the regime. Political divisions and personal rivalries prevented anti-Fascists from forming a united front until Mussolini was ousted from power by a palace coup in July 1943. Although anti-Fascists had no role in Mussolini's ouster, they did play an important role in the RESISTANCE movement that followed. At that point, the history of antifascism becomes part of the struggle to liberate Italy from fascism and from German control. The unity of political forces of the resistance in their common fight against fascism made antifascism the sustaining ideology of the Italian republic founded in 1946.

anti-Semitism See JEWS IN ITALY.

Antologia (L') See JOURNALISM.

Antonelli, Giacomo (1806–1876)
cardinal and Vatican diplomat
Giacomo Antonelli, chief adviser to Pope PIUS IX, was born near the town of Terracina, in the Papal States, to a prosperous merchant family. He attended the seminary and university in Rome, earned a doctorate in canon and civil law, and entered the papal civil service in 1830. His intelligence and competence opened the way to steady advancement; in 1844 he was appointed papal treasurer and was made a cardinal in 1847.

Antonelli supported political reforms during the first years of Pius IX's pontificate, but changed course when reform gave way to revolution in 1848. Thereafter, second in command in the Vatican as secretary of state and chief adviser to the pope, he was a hard-line defender of traditional papal prerogatives and power. He opposed the movement for Italian unification because it threatened the pope's temporal power. When Italy was unified in spite of papal opposition, Antonelli effectively seconded the pope's campaign against the Italian state, making the conflict of CHURCH AND STATE the central issue of papal policy. Antonelli's many critics saw him as the real power behind the papal throne, and he was disparaged and vilified like no other figure in the clerical camp, not only by political opponents, but also by papal supporters bent on saving the pope's reputation as a man of reason and compromise. The debate still goes on, but the evidence suggests that Antonelli was the scapegoat for the pope's unpopular or controversial decisions.

Antonioni, Michelangelo (1912–   )
film director, cultural interpreter, and commentator

Antonioni was born to a middle-class family. He studied economics and business at the University of Bologna, filmmaking in Rome, was a newspaper film critic in the 1930s, and wrote for the screen in the early 1940s. His first film was *Gente del Po* (1943), conceived in the realist style of social commentary. His career developed after the war with films that were controversial for their extreme realism. *I vinti* (Losers, 1952) was banned in Italy and France for its graphic descriptions of criminal life. Antonioni gradually developed a distinctive style marked by an obsessive preoccupation with the inner life of his characters, who were often uprooted, restless individuals suffering from the depersonalization and anomie of contemporary life. *L'avventura* (The adventure, 1960), *L'eclisse* (The eclipse, 1962), and *Deserto rosso* (Red desert, 1964) show Anto-

nioni's filmmaking in its most introverted mode. His choice of subjects and cinematic technique, which seems episodic and disjointed, has puzzled critics, but his films have generally done well at the box office. He has been most admired in Anglo-Saxon countries, particularly the United States, where his descriptions of contemporary life have struck a chord. His first English-language film, *Blow-Up* (1966), confirmed his standing as a major cultural figure. He has also done a number of documentaries. Failing health in the 1980s forced him to cut back and abandon several projects. His most important contribution has been as a witness to the travails of a generation caught in the flux of rapid cultural change.

Aosta   See VALLE D'AOSTA.

Apennines

The Apennine mountain range stretches over 300 miles from the Ligurian ALPS to the Strait of Messina, forming the backbone of the Italian peninsula. The chain reemerges across the strait on the island of SICILY, completing an arc that marks the eastern edge of the TYRRHENIAN SEA. The highest peak of the Gran Sasso in the region of ABRUZZO rises to 9,558 feet (2,914 meters) above sea level. While the range is not notable for high altitudes, the terrain is frequently steep and unstable. The narrow mountain backbone running the length of the peninsula impedes the formation of large rivers below the Po Valley. Of the rivers originating in the Apennines, only the Arno and Tiber have a steady if markedly uneven water flow all year. Most of the other rivers behave like raging torrents in the rainy season, only to all but dry up in the summer months. Difficulties of transportation attributable to the Apennine landscape have been largely overcome by extensive road building, tunneling, and bridge construction, at which Italians have excelled out of necessity.

The Apennine range shows different characteristics in different parts of the peninsula. The northern and central parts from LIGURIA through the Abruzzi are generally more forested than the southern portions, with oak, beeches, chestnuts, and conifers covering the slopes up to about 4,500 feet above sea level. Above that zone lie plateaus called *alpi,* which serve as grazing grounds. The practice of transhumance, whereby in the fall shepherds migrate with their flocks from these high plateaus to the lowlands and return to the higher elevations in the spring, was common until the 1950s. It is now practiced on a much smaller scale. Apennine agriculture has undergone a similar decline due to intensive depopulation. The cultivation of cereals and chestnuts needed for local sustenance has been replaced in part by the introduction of commercial crops. Olives, grapevines, and flowers are cultivated at elevations below 2,000 feet.

The southern Apennines suffer from extensive deforestation, lower levels of precipitation, clayish soils, erosion, sparse vegetation, and an exceedingly complex topography marked by a maze of valleys. The Sila Mountains of CALABRIA are an exception to this generally bleak picture. There, extensive forests and wet grazing lands provide a favorable environment for pasturage, lumbering, charcoal production, and other related activities. Catering to tourists and vacationers is becoming the principal resource for many areas of the Apennines, particularly where natural attractions like thermal waters, skiing slopes, and fishing are available. Government programs of reforestation, the designation of national park areas, and enforcement of measures to protect the environment now make many parts of the Apennines attractive for hunting, fishing, skiing, hiking, camping, and other recreational activities.

Apofasimeni See SECRET SOCIETIES.

Apulia See PUGLIA.

Aquinas, Thomas See SCHOLASTICISM.

Arcadian Movement See ACADEMIES.

architecture

Every architectural period from the prehistoric to the contemporary, and the building styles of all populations that have had contacts with the peninsula, including Greeks, Arabs, Byzantines, Normans, and Germans, are represented in the architectural legacy of the Italian peninsula. Given such variety and diversity, all generalizations are questionable. But it is possible to simplify the picture by concentrating on the styles associated with periods of exceptional creativity. The classical style of ancient Rome, the Romanesque style of the medieval period, the neoclassical revival of the RENAISSANCE, the BAROQUE of the 17th and 18th centuries, the experimental architecture of the early 20th century, and the contemporary style mark such moments. None, however, were purely national; models and techniques of varying provenance influenced all.

The Roman style of construction was inspired by classical Greek forms, which the Romans could see firsthand in those parts of southern Italy previously settled by Greek-speaking populations, and which can still be admired in the temples of Agrigento and Paestum. Roman architecture differed from Greek in making use of the arch and vaulting (possibly of Etruscan origin), and in the monumental scale of many of its projects. The Roman Colosseum, by far the best-known example of the Roman style, illustrates the scale of Roman construction and its use of columns and arches for both decorative and structural purposes. The golden age of Roman architecture coincides approximately with the first two centuries of the Christian era. The expansion of the Roman Empire during that period required the planning of new towns, the construction of roads and bridges, aqueducts, public baths, triumphal arches for victorious generals, popular housing for the growing urban multitudes, palaces and villas for the wealthy. Marble replaced brick as the material of choice for public buildings and the more opulent pri-

Interior of the Colosseum, Rome, ca. 1909 *(Library of Congress)*

vate residences. Architecture was the craft that glorified and preserved the empire.

In the medieval period, the decline of the empire and rise of the PAPACY saw a shift toward ecclesiastical architecture. Early Christian churches replicated the form of Roman basilicas with their straight naves. This style soon incorporated Byzantine features, most notably domes, decorative frescoes, and mosaics. The period from about 1000 to 1250 saw the emergence of the Romanesque style in the building of churches, cathedrals, and monasteries. Its characteristics are massive walls needed to bear the heavy weight of vaulted roofs, emphasizing horizontal lines rather than height, with a separate bell tower (*campanile*) and baptistery, small windows, and the heavy use of exterior decorative sculptural details. A good example of Romanesque architecture is the cathedral complex at the *Piazza dei Miracoli* in Pisa, which includes the famous Leaning Tower. While there are many examples in Italy of the Gothic style (most notably in the Cathedral of Milan, begun in the 14th and completed in the 19th century), Gothic remained the style of northern Europe, influencing Italian architecture indirectly and sporadically.

The Renaissance style of architecture for which Italy is known is best seen in the works of FILIPPO BRUNELLESCHI, dating from the early part of the 15th century. The inspiration came from the study of ancient Greek and Roman structures. Large vaults and domes cover vast spaces, symmetry and balance inform the layout, and a feeling of light pervades the interior, in stark contrast with the impression of darkness and mystery typical of both the Romanesque and Gothic styles. Florentine churches, particularly the cathedral designed by Brunelleschi, afford some of the best examples of Renaissance ecclesiastical architecture. Palaces and villas built for the wealthy reflect similar concerns with symmetry and light, with concessions made to the needs of security at a time when city life could be extremely turbulent. Thus, Renaissance residences, like the Palazzo Venezia in Rome and the Pitti Palace in Florence, show few and small openings on the lower floors to facilitate defense, while the exteriors have a plain or rustic look. Ground-floor quarters were often spacious warehouses and shops to store or display the goods of the buildings' merchant owners. Country villas, on the other hand, reflected the desire of the wealthy to enjoy the pleasures of life in grand settings reminiscent of ancient Greece and Rome. ANDREA PALLADIO's villas in the Venetian countryside exemplify the craving for both comforts and dignified repose in a carefully controlled bucolic setting. Civic architecture also flourished in the Renaissance, as city governments often competed with ecclesiastical authorities to erect buildings that proclaimed the secular power of the state. The Palazzo Pubblico and the Piazza del Campo in Siena, built at the end of the 13th century, attest to the passion for public life that surged through the late-medieval and Renaissance city.

Architecture in the baroque period reflected the resurgence of religious and spiritual values of the late Renaissance and the CATHOLIC REFORMATION. The baroque style was classical in concept, but characterized by the dynamic use of curves, columns, and ornamentation to create dramatic contrasts and vistas. With the decline of the baroque at the end of the 18th century, Italian architecture entered an imitative phase. But impressive examples of private and public architecture, town planning, and use of new materials and techniques of production abound in 19th-century Italy. A good example of 19th-century public architecture is the covered Vittorio Emanuele Gallery in Milan, designed by Giuseppe Mengoni (1829–77) but inspired by London's Crystal Palace. In Italy the Art Nouveau style popular in northern Europe at the end of the 19th century was dubbed *stile floreale* and *stile Liberty*. An example of stile Liberty is the grandiose monument to VICTOR EMMANUEL II built in Rome and inaugurated in 1911 to mark the 50th year of national unification. Dubbed the Wedding Cake by its many disparagers, and the Altare della Patria by those who revere it as a symbol, this enormous white-marble structure features a profusion of columns, staircases, and ascending levels.

In reaction to the rhetorical strivings or affectations of the *stile Liberty*, FUTURISM proclaimed the functional mission of the arts, including architecture, in a world dominated by the machine and the factory. Futurist architecture envisioned industrial cities transformed and embellished by rationally designed housing, places of work, and public spaces, as in the daring designs of Antonio Sant'Elia (1880–1916), featuring skyscrapers connected by bridges, intricate public transportation systems, and apartment buildings rising to dizzying heights. Functionality and rhetoric coexisted and competed for official approval and endorsement under FASCISM. The Santa Maria Novella train station in Florence (built 1933–36) is a good example of the functional style. The coeval central railway station in Milan is more traditional in its striving for monumentality. The more or less official architect of the Fascist regime was Marcello Piacentini (1881–1960), who stood out for his ability to reconcile traditional and modern schools of thought, and who ultimately came out on the side of individual inspiration.

A more creative phase of Italian architecture developed after 1950. Although many of its practitioners were formed in the years before WORLD WAR II, they made their mark during the period of postwar reconstruction when architectural vision and skill were needed to help repair the damages of war. The principle of functionality still prevailed, but it was joined to concern for good craftsmanship, attractive design, and original use of quality materials. Reinforced concrete was used liberally and creatively to achieve daringly projecting surfaces, span valleys with sleek viaducts for modern highways, build new housing, sports complexes, and other public spaces catering to multitudes of people. The most notable figure of this most recent phase is Pier Luigi Nervi (1891–1979), who prided himself on being the kind of architect who understood the practical aspects of construction. His works, like the Palazzetto dello Sport in Rome and the George Washington Bridge Bus Terminal in New York, combine efficiency, economy of line, and an impression of airiness and lightness in a harmonious whole.

ARCI (Associazione Ricreativa Culturale Italiana) See GAY MOVEMENT; OPERA NAZIONALE DOPOLAVORO; SPORTS.

Ardigò, Roberto (1828–1920)
philosopher and teacher, leading thinker of Italian positivism

Born near Cremona, this influential philosopher was the acknowledged leader of philosophical POSITIVISM in Italy. Ordained a priest in 1851, he left the priesthood in 1871 after a protracted polemic with his clerical superiors who wanted him to renounce certain publicly stated views on matters of faith that were deemed incompatible with Catholic belief. Ardigò taught philosophy at the secondary level before his writings won him a regular appointment as professor of philosophy at the University of Padua in 1881. His writings on the importance of science and the scientific method appealed at a time when the country was trying to catch up with scientific advances elsewhere in Europe. Perhaps his most influential work was *La morale dei positivisti* (The positivist morality, 1879), in which he argued that reason must be cultivated to conquer instinct and foster the common good. Ardigò followed Herbert Spencer in placing natural evolution at the center of his philosophical system, but insisted on the autonomous development of his thought from the naturalistic premises of RENAISSANCE philosophy. According to Ardigò, nature evolves gradually from a state of inchoate confusion toward specific forms. From a shapeless beginning, the world assumes an infinite variety of forms, both material and spiritual, all of which stem from the original matter. The mind, being a product of this process, is capable of understanding reality in all its aspects through the senses. There is no problem that reason cannot solve given time and resources. Although a strong believer in science and evolution, Ardigò rejected purely materialistic notions that reduced consciousness and mental activity to mere chemical and biological processes. Rejecting absolute material determinism, he argued that mind and matter have evolved as distinct and equally important entities. His philosophy appealed to movements of the democratic left, particularly turn-of-the-century RADICALISM, that looked for a progressive philosophy of social action, believed in individual choice, and rejected the strict materialism and historical determinism of the Marxist left.

Arditi

These highly trained and motivated shock troops were founded and saw action in WORLD WAR I. They were meant to attack enemy lines, engage in hand-to-hand combat, and open the way for massive attacks by regular infantry troops. Recruited from ultranationalists, adventurous youths, and jailed criminals, battalions of Arditi were deployed after the disastrous BATTLE OF CAPORETTO and played an important role in halting the Austro-German advance in northern Italy. They also participated in the final battles of the war that saw the collapse of the Austrian army. About 10,000 Arditi joined the political association Arditi d'Italia, founded in November 1918, which called on war veterans to take a political stand. The politicization of the corps and the Arditi's frequent breaches of military discipline alarmed the government, which disbanded their military formations in January 1919. Arditi veterans played a prominent role in the seizure of the city of FIUME by GABRIELE D'ANNUNZIO in September 1919. Many former Arditi joined the Fascist squads, contributing to fascism's tactics of violence, its cult of youth, warlike imagery, and rituals. The Fascist Militia was initially modeled on the Arditi, but was later diverted toward policing rather than purely military roles.

Aretino, Pietro (1492–1556)
Renaissance writer, courtier, and public figure

Scandalous behavior, irreverent, biting, and scurrilous writings did not prevent Aretino from enjoying the patronage and friendship of some of the keenest minds and most influential personages of his time, including Cardinal Giulio de' Medici (the future pope CLEMENT VII). Many were willing to overlook Aretino's glaring personal faults because of his wit and literary talents. He was born in Arezzo to a family of modest means (his father was a cobbler), and adopted the name of his native city as his own, perhaps to disguise his humble origins. He received his first education from an uncle who was a cleric and from a local nobleman who was the lover of Aretino's attractive mother. He left Arezzo at age 18 to live the life of an itinerant intellectual. Between 1510 and 1527, he lived in PERUGIA, SIENA, ROME, and MANTUA, everywhere enjoying the support of wealthy and influential patrons, who glossed over his misbehavior and protected him from his many enemies. In Perugia he wrote his first poems, but it was in Rome that he gained a reputation as a writer of unmatched wit, evident in the public lampoons of prominent figures, known as *pasquinate,* into which Aretino poured all his venomous talent. His older contemporary LUDOVICO ARIOSTO rightly called him the Scourge of Princes. Aretino had to leave Rome in 1525, after barely surviving an attempt on his life. He found refuge in Venice where he lived from 1527 to the end of his life, showing his gratitude by calling that city the fatherland of all lovers of liberty. In Venice he fell in love with a woman whom he credited with converting him to the love of women, had several illegitimate children with various mistresses, but also continued to carry on the homosexual affairs that had made him notorious. His reputation as a writer and satirist rests on his lampoons, letters, sonnets, dialogues, and plays, but that reputation was for a long time clouded by his obsessive interest in and depiction of sexual matters. A famous portrait by TITIAN shows a portly Aretino proudly displaying the necklace that was a prized gift from the king of France.

Ludovico Ariosto *(Library of Congress)*

Ariosto, Ludovico (1474–1533)
(or Lodovico)
inspiring literary figure and indifferent public servant

Born in Reggio Emilia to a family of the nobility, Ariosto was raised and educated in FERRARA, where he entered into the service of the ruling ESTE FAMILY. Although his desire to devote himself to literature was thwarted by family respon-

sibilities and by his obligations of diplomatic service to the Estes, Ariosto managed nevertheless to write profusely. Latin poetry and plays written in the vernacular poured from his pen, the latter being performed in the court theater at Ferrara, where he also served as theatrical director. His masterpiece is the epic poem *Orlando furioso* (1532), which he intended as a sequel to the unfinished poem by Matteo Boiardo (1441–94), the *Orlando innamorato.* Ariosto's poem flattered his patrons by introducing the ancestors of the Este family in the heroic tales that he recounted. The opening verse of "I sing of ladies, knights, weapons, and loves" introduces the tale of the medieval knight Orlando (Italian for *Roland,* the knight of Carolingian epic), who is hopelessly in love with Princess Angelica (hence the adjective *furioso,* as madly in love), and is driven by his passion to spectacular feats of heroism. Duels, sieges, and shipwrecks see Orlando and fellow fighters pitted in deadly struggle against infidel Muslims, who are eventually defeated by the Christian warriors. Ariosto's account of this traditional material shows nostalgia for the waning world of medieval chivalry. But, along with affection for the past, there is also an ironic detachment from the ethos of knightly culture that was being challenged by new forms of statecraft and warfare. When Ariosto wrote his poem, Europe was girding itself to confront the twin threats of Muslim expansion and religious wars unleashed by the Protestant Reformation. It was an open question whether the wealthy bourgeois class that was replacing the old titled nobility would be up to the task. The poem thus touched a raw nerve with its idealization of the past and tacit acknowledgment of a crisis of values in the Christian world. Ariosto's poem reflects concerns similar to those evident in Miguel de Cervantes's *Don Quixote*. The immediate popularity of *Orlando furioso* was due as much to the nature of the message as to the lyrical beauty of Ariosto's verses. The poem is an enduring classic of Italian literature.

aristocracy

This least studied of social classes has played a prominent role in every economic, social, and political development of the last 500 years. The term covers a variety of groups and figures at the top of the social ladder, some distinguished by titles of nobility (counts, barons, dukes, princes), others recognized as an elite by virtue of their lineage, wealth, and historical role. Titles of nobility are of royal origin, bestowed by monarchs as rewards for service, often but not exclusively for service of a military nature. Popes also bestowed titles of nobility in their capacity as temporal rulers, giving rise to what later would be called the "black aristocracy" of Rome. Titles were more than marks of distinction, as they often entailed special privileges of dress and precedence and economically valuable conces-

sions, such as immunities from taxation and the right to collect fees for the administration of justice. The old republics of VENICE, GENOA, and LUCCA did not bestow titles of nobility, but were nevertheless governed by aristocracies (patriciates) that enjoyed special rights in government and public life. LOMBARDY and TUSCANY also had aristocracies that lacked formal titles of nobility, but that were recognized nevertheless as privileged orders. The MEDICI are perhaps the best example of an aristocratic family that rose to be de facto rulers of a state without special titles of nobility, until receiving them in the 16th century by imperial concession.

Historians tend to look upon the aristocracy as a class in decline since the 18th century, but recent studies point to its ability to adjust and profit from historical changes. There are indeed many examples of aristocratic families and individuals who have been economic innovators, provided bureaucrats and officers for modern states and armies, espoused progressive political ideals, and even supported revolutions. The Piedmontese aristocracy is often cited as an example in this regard, Count CAMILLO BENSO OF CAVOUR being its best example of a modernizing, politically progressive aristocrat. The aristocracies of other Italian states were also important players in movements for reform, as attested by such names as BELGIOIOSO, CARACCIOLO, CONFALONIERI, PALLAVICINO, and RICASOLI, to name a few prominent aristocrats active in progressive causes. The novel by the Sicilian nobleman Giuseppe di Lampedusa, *The Leopard* (1960), is a classic account of the aristocracy's talent for accommodation and survival.

Arlacchi, Pino (1951–)
sociologist and international authority on organized crime

A sociology professor at the University of Florence, Arlacchi has studied and written extensively on the MAFIA and international crime. In 1997 he resigned from the Italian senate to devote himself full time to his duties as director of the United Nations' Office for Drug Control and Crime Prevention. In the United Nations, he is responsible for directing the international campaign against drug traffic and the illegal transportation of people for purposes of exploitative employment and prostitution. According to his estimates, in the 1990s the traffic in human beings has involved more than 30 million people from Southeast Asia alone. His studies emphasize the businesslike nature of organized crime and its need for government collusion and protection to carry on its activities. His writings include *The Mafia Ethic and the Spirit of Capitalism* (1986).

armed forces

Four services make up Italy's armed forces: army, navy, air force, and the self-contained corps of the carabinieri, which serves as a national police force in peacetime and as military police in wartime. The armed forces of the unified state were formed by amalgamating three distinct entities: the Piedmontese army that played a major role in the movement for national unification, the paramilitary forces composed of volunteers at the command of GIUSEPPE GARIBALDI, also an important component of the unification movement, and the armies of pre-unification states that had opposed national unification. The most important by far among the last was the army of the KINGDOM OF THE TWO SICILIES. The amalgamation of these forces created friction, as the Piedmontese insisted on imposing their military organization and practices on this heterogeneously composed national army. Soldiers were required to swear loyalty to King VICTOR EMMANUEL II, who was the nominal commander in chief. The army was based on long terms of service of four to five years on active duty and six in the reserve, with conscripts chosen by lot. To compensate for deficiencies of training and equipment, the army relied on elite troops like the Bersaglieri, mobile troops trained for rapid action present in the old Piedmontese army since 1836.

The first challenge faced by the army was the repression of BRIGANDAGE in the South, for which some 100,000 troops were mobilized and deployed in a brutal civil war. Internal policing would always be an important duty of the army, making it the object of popular resentment. On the other hand, the army was expected to endear itself to the people, to make them proud of being Italian, instilling in them a sense of discipline and collective mission, taking on educational responsibilities, like teaching conscripts how to read and write. Financial support for the army varied from a high of around 40 percent of state expenditures in the 1860s to around 20 percent in later years. Naval expenditures increased greatly in the 1880s when the government committed itself to a program of naval expansion that was designed to turn Italy into a world-class naval and colonial power. The army's performance against Austria in the Third WAR OF NATIONAL INDEPENDENCE (1866) exposed serious deficiencies of preparation and command, prompting a general reorganization by General Cesare Ricotti Magnani (1822–1917) from 1870 to 1876. The term of regular service was reduced to three years, the peacetime strength of the army was set at 224,000, expandable to 800,000 by calling up the reserves, and specialized mountain troops, the *Alpini,* were deployed to defend the northern border. This military organization remained essentially unchanged until WORLD WAR I.

Although military expenditures were high in relation to total government spending, they were inadequate to maintain an efficient army and navy of the size contemplated. The ITALIAN-TURKISH WAR (1911–12), in which airplanes were first used in combat, drained military resources, leaving the country ill prepared to face WORLD WAR I. By 1914, when European powers were using costly armaments and engaged in naval races, Italy's finances were strained to the utmost to maintain an army of 750,000 and a navy that ranked fifth in the world in tonnage, behind Great Britain, Germany, the United States, and France, but ahead of Austria-Hungary and Russia. That the country's armed forces were too large for its economic resources is also evident from the fact that Italy was the power that spent the least on the individual soldier, a mere $67 a year (in 1914 dollars), compared with $1,000 for the United States, $352 for Great Britain, $148 for France, and $136 for Germany.

World War I posed the most severe challenge ever faced by the Italian armed forces. Five million men were mobilized, the dead numbered close to 600,000, the disabled 1.7 million. Demobilization proceeded rapidly once the war was over, but little effort was made to reorganize the military. Proposals made by General Antonino Di Giorgio (1867–1932), who served as war minister in 1924–25, to reduce the size of the peacetime army and spend more on training and equipment ran into opposition from fellow officers. In 1925 General PIETRO BADOGLIO became the chief of staff, a position that he retained until 1940. With fascism in power, and BENITO MUSSOLINI eager to play a personal role in military matters, the army closed ranks around Badoglio, whose loyalty to the Fascist regime was more a matter of convenience than conviction. It relegated the Fascist Militia, which aspired to become a full-fledged military force, to a secondary paramilitary role as an internal police force. Army and navy officers remained loyal to the king, refused to join the party, and resisted efforts at "fascistization." The one exception was the air force, which became an independent branch of the military in 1925 on a footing of parity with the army and navy, and was considered to be the most Fascist branch of the armed forces. In the 1930s infantry divisions were reduced from three to two regiments to give them greater mobility in what military experts expected to be the "wars of rapid decision" of the future.

While Italian military doctrine envisaged highly mobile forces of great firepower, military training and equipment reflected the mentality of trench warfare typical of World War I. The outbreak of WORLD WAR II in September 1939 found Italy seriously unprepared for the conflict. Mussolini's decision to go to war in June 1940 was based on the erroneous estimate that a German victory was imminent. The military command acquiesced in what they saw as a political deci-

sion that they should not question. When the German war machine stalled and the prospects of rapid victory evaporated, the Italian military faced a long war for which neither the armed forces nor the country as a whole were prepared. Serious deficiencies in armored weaponry, heavy artillery, antiaircraft defense, air power, and poor coordination among the three services hampered performance, with often disastrous results.

Defeat brought dramatic changes to the Italian armed forces. With the monarchy gone, the army lost much of its political clout, and the loss of colonies deprived the military of a claim to a large share of the nation's resources. Postwar governments renounced the great-power ambitions of Fascist and pre-Fascist foreign policy and settled for a cautious course in international relations that left little scope for military action. The PEACE TREATY imposed severe limits on the size of the army, navy, and air force. The new CONSTITUTION renounced war as an instrument of international relations and gave command of the armed forces to the figurehead president. The ministry of war was renamed the ministry of defense. Military spending has been a low priority since World War II, generally running well below 2 percent of the gross domestic product. The armed forces have adjusted to their reduced role, not without pain or resentment, and not without arousing suspicion of harboring designs to undermine or bring down democratic government. But as a rule the armed forces have acknowledged the authority and legitimacy of civilian control. Military conscription remains in force, with short 10-month periods of service and with provisions for performing alternative social service.

In recent years the armed forces have come under severe public scrutiny for their antiquated facilities, harsh treatment of recruits, and inadequate support services. A reform is underway that aims to make the armed forces more professional, with long-term recruitment, improvement of training methods, and modernization of equipment. The Italian armed forces are fully integrated within NATO and have participated in various international actions, including interventions in Lebanon (1982), Somalia (1992), Croatia (1996), Kosovo (1999), and ALBANIA. The end of the cold war and the shifting of tensions toward the Middle East and the Mediterranean area have changed the international landscape and Italy's strategic position. The change is bound to affect the future role of its armed forces domestically and internationally even as public opinion remains deeply suspicious and averse to military commitments—witness the strong public resistance to government support of the recent (2003) war in Iraq. The government of SILVIO BERLUSCONI has committed 3,000 troops to police duty in postwar Iraq in spite of domestic opposition to the deployment.

Armed Revolutionary Nuclei See
ORDINE NUOVO.

Artusi, Pellegrino (1820–1911)
author credited with inventing the idea of a national Italian cuisine

The fact that Artusi was born in Forlimpopoli, a town in the ROMAGNA region renowned for its cuisine, may indeed be the key to his fame. Born to a merchant family, Artusi developed a good sense for business, which served him well as a silk merchant, investor, and banker. By age 50 he had achieved sufficient financial security to retire from business and pursue his true interests, which consisted of conversing, socializing, and eating well. As he explained in the book that made him famous, *La scienza in cucina e l'arte di mangiar bene* (The science of cooking and the art of eating well, 1891), the principal needs of the human race are nutrition and reproduction. While he had little to say about the latter, at least in print, he was a veritable fount of wisdom when it came to eating. The book gave advice on good hygienic habits in the kitchen, the nutritive value of foods, how to make the best use of ingredients, proper deportment at table and, most of all, it presented a profusion of recipes that is cred-

ited with creating the very concept of an Italian national cuisine. Italy was still a country of regions when the book was published 30 years after national unification. By the very fact of presenting in one book recipes from different parts of the peninsula, describing cooking methods easily followed in ordinary kitchens, discussing the variety of ingredients and ways of blending them into tasty and unpretentious dishes, stressing the importance of freshness, sound cooking techniques, and simple but attractive presentations, and deploring the tendency of chefs to slavishly follow French cuisine, he established the style of cooking that would be known as Italian. His book was an immediate success, went through many editions both plain and lavish, and sold millions of copies. Artusi did for Italians at table what CAVOUR, GARIBALDI, and MAZZINI did for Italians in politics: He gave them a common frame of reference that became part of their national identity. *The Art of Eating Well* (1996), a recent translation, makes Artusi's classic accessible in English.

Aspromonte, Battle of See GARIBALDI, GIUSEPPE.

Astrolabio (L') See ROSSI, ERNESTO.

Austerlitz, Battle of See NAPOLEON I.

Austrian Empire
Territories inhabited by Italian-speaking populations were an integral part of the Austrian Empire throughout its entire history. The proximity of the Tyrol, TRENTINO–ALTO ADIGE in Italian, a hereditary possession of the ruling HABSBURG DYNASTY since the 14th century, oriented the territorial and political ambitions of the Habsburgs toward Italy. Habsburg influence in Italy became dominant in the wake of the WAR OF THE SPANISH SUCCESSION with the incorporation of LOMBARDY into a vast multinational empire extending from

eastern Europe to the Low Countries. The Austrian position in Italy was further strengthened by the accession of the HABSBURG-LORRAINE DYNASTY to the Tuscan throne in 1737. In 1797 the Habsburgs annexed Venetia by the terms of the Treaty of Campoformio concluded with NAPOLEON. French domination replaced Austria's during the Napoleonic period, but the Austrians returned in force after Napoleon's decisive defeat in 1814–15. Lombardy and Venetia became once again lands of the Austrian Empire as an autonomous "Lombardo-Venetian Kingdom" headed by an Austrian viceroy. Austrian princes ruled in TUSCANY, PARMA, and MODENA, while the governments of the PAPAL STATES and the KINGDOM OF THE TWO SICILIES relied on the support of Austrian arms. After 1815 Austria was the ultimate guarantor of a peace settlement that was based on keeping the peninsula politically divided. As such, the Austrian Empire was the most formidable enemy of Italian political unification. Austrian rule survived the REVOLUTIONS of 1848–49, but suffered a fatal setback after being defeated by France and the Kingdom of SARDINIA in the Second WAR OF NATIONAL INDEPENDENCE (1859). That defeat led to the unification of Italy in 1860–61. Austria held on to VENETIA until 1866, when it was forced to cede that region as part of the peace settlement following the Third War of National Independence. Austria retained control of other Italian-speaking territories in the Trentino and around the port city of TRIESTE until the end of WORLD WAR I. The nature of Austrian rule in Italy is still the subject of historical controversy. Patriotic Italian scholarship has traditionally emphasized the oppressive character of Austrian rule, pointing out that Austria levied more in taxes in its Italian possessions than it spent there, that Italians were discriminated against in public service, and that Austrian rule rested ultimately on the use of violence and military repression. Dissenting voices have pointed out that Austrian administration was more efficient and honest than the administration provided by native governments, its taxation fairer, and its economic policies more progressive. The debate appears to have been stoked by recent developments. Northern SEPARATISM and membership in the EUROPEAN UNION once again raise questions about the strength of ties among Italian regions and the country's relationship to the rest of Europe, questions that were once discussed in the context of Italy's role in the Austrian Empire.

Austrian Succession, War of the

The war broke out in 1740 after the accession of MARIA THERESA of Austria after the death of her father, the Holy Roman Emperor Charles VI (1711–40). Austria was attacked by a combination of powers eager to seize Habsburg territories. The anti-Austrian coalition included Prussia, France, Spain, Bavaria, Poland, and Saxony, while Austria was supported by England and Russia. The war was fought in Central Europe, France, the Low Countries, and Italy. In Italy, the king of Sardinia, Charles Emmanuel III (1730–73), first joined the anti-Austrian coalition, but switched sides in 1742 after being promised part of Lombardy. His army rendered a signal service to Maria Theresa by protecting Austria's southern flank against the French and Spaniards, but in the end Charles Emmanuel had to be content with merely rounding out his Piedmontese territories to the historical boundary of the Ticino River, leaving the greater prize of Lombardy in Austrian hands. In the south, King CHARLES OF BOURBON sided with Spain, and consolidated his rule by defeating an Austrian army at the Battle of Velletri (1744). The Peace of Aix-la-Chapelle (1748), which ended the war, acknowledged Piedmontese gains and the independence of Naples, and awarded the duchy of PARMA to the Bourbon ruler, Philip, son of ELISABETTA FARNESE. The settlement left the Italian peninsula under the control of foreign powers. Austria was the dominant power, but Spain maintained a foothold with Bourbon rulers installed in Naples and Parma. Italian patriots would later complain that the peace settlement turned Italy into a vast tourist playground at the mercy of foreign masters. Nevertheless, Austrian hegemony gave the peninsula nearly 50 years of political stability, until the Napoleonic invasion of 1796. During those 50 years Italy contributed to the culture of the ENLIGHTENMENT, enjoyed close ties with the rest of Europe, and experienced economic and political reforms that set the stage for further progress in the 19th century.

autarky
pursuit of national economic self-sufficiency
BENITO MUSSOLINI proclaimed autarky as official policy in March 1936, but the pursuit of national economic self-sufficiency had been underway since the mid-1920s when the Fascist regime had launched campaigns to expand production of wheat and enacted protectionist measures to shield domestic manufacturers from foreign competition. The official adoption of autarky was a result of the ETHIOPIAN WAR and the economic sanctions against Italy adopted by the League of Nations. National economic self-sufficiency was presented as a necessary precondition for the conduct of an independent foreign policy and preparation for future military conflicts. But full economic self-sufficiency was unattainable by Italy given its almost total dependence on imported fuels and key raw materials. The country did achieve self-sufficiency in grain production by 1938, and domestic substitutes were developed to compensate in part for the lack of certain raw materials. The production of artificial fibers, hydroelectric power, chemicals, shipping, armaments, and machinery was boosted by the pursuit of autarky. The regime touted these results as major achievements, while critics pointed to the high costs of substitutes and the diversion of scarce resources from potentially more profitable or useful investments. Autarky did entail costly public subsidies for production and the creation of a vast public sector of the economy (see IRI).

Autunno caldo See LOTTA CONTINUA.

Avanguardia Socialista See LABRIOLA, ARTURO.

Avanti! See JOURNALISM.

Aventine Secession
parliamentary protest against the Fascist regime
In June 1924, within days of the assassination of socialist leader GIACOMO MATTEOTTI by Fascist toughs, a group of about 150 anti-Fascist deputies left parliament in protest. The move, named after the plebeians of ancient Rome who had withdrawn to the Aventine Hill in protest against the power of the patricians, initiated an organized effort to bring down the government of BENITO MUSSOLINI. It was led by GIOVANNI AMENDOLA, who hoped that the protest would give King VICTOR EMMANUEL III justification to dismiss Mussolini, as it was his constitutional prerogative to do. The king's refusal doomed the Aventine secession to failure. The gesture had major resonance in the country and left Mussolini momentarily isolated. But it also had the unintended consequence of leaving Mussolini vulnerable to the pressure of die-hard Fascists who demanded that he move ruthlessly against all political opponents. Mussolini responded by doing precisely what they, and perhaps he, wanted to do all along, calling on the Fascist squads to crack down on opponents of the regime. The Catholic, communist, republican, and socialist deputies who had bolted from parliament reclaimed their seats in the course of 1925, but emergency decrees issued by the government a year later declared them forfeited and expelled the former secessionists from the lower house of parliament. The political wisdom of the secession has been questioned because it removed the regime's opponents from parliament and made it easier for Mussolini to enact legislation that clamped down on civil liberties and laid the foundations of his personal dictatorship. Nevertheless, the Aventine Secession was a morally significant gesture that exposed the Fascist regime's ultimate reliance on violence.

Avogadro, Amedeo (1776–1856)
mathematician and scientist

Born in TURIN to a family of the Piedmontese nobility (he held the title of count of Quaregna), Avogadro received degrees in civil and canon law from the University of Turin in 1795 and 1796, and served in the courts during the French occupation and the RESTORATION. His passion was for the study of physics and mathematics, which he pursued first as an amateur. He was appointed to teach physics and mathematics at the University of Turin in 1814–22 and 1834–50. A theoretical physicist with little interest in experimentation, he pioneered the developing field of physical chemistry. In 1811 he formulated the hypothesis, since known as Avogadro's Law. It states that under the same conditions of pressure and temperature, equal volumes of gases contain the same number of molecules. Using Avogadro's Law, other physicists were able to determine that the number of molecules present in the gram molecular volume is the same for all gases, and called that number (6.02 times 10 to the 23rd power) Avogadro's number. Modest and self-effacing, Avogadro was a prolific writer with many publications to his credit. His scientific papers and essays, published in French and Italian, have gained him a posthumous reputation as a major contributor to the atomic theory of matter.

Axis, Rome-Berlin
political alliance of Fascist Italy and Nazi Germany

The Axis, as the political and military alliance between Fascist Italy and Nazi Germany is commonly known, developed in the late 1930s. As late as 1934 major differences divided the two countries over such issues as the fate of Austria (which Fascist Italy wanted to keep separate from Nazi Germany as a buffer state between the two countries), racial policies (which BENITO MUSSOLINI condemned as nonsensical until 1934), and the international Fascist movement (which both sides wanted to control). Until 1935 Hitler showed much more interest in an alliance with Italy than Mussolini showed in an alliance with Germany. This changed in the aftermath of the ETHIOPIAN WAR, which left Italy isolated and consequently more interested in establishing closer ties with Germany. In his speech of November 1, 1936, Mussolini referred to the developing connection with Germany as "an axis around which can revolve all those European states with a will to collaboration and peace." In Mussolini's mind, if not in Hitler's, considerations of political expediency weighed more heavily than the ideological affinities between the two regimes. Later, Italy joined the ANTI-COMINTERN PACT signed by Germany and Japan and concluded the PACT OF STEEL with Germany, thus transforming the informal understanding known as the Rome-Berlin Axis into a formal military alliance.

Azeglio, Luigi Taparelli d' See CIVILTÀ CATTOLICA.

Azeglio, Massimo d' (1798–1866)
writer, painter, patriot, and political figure

This Piedmontese nobleman is remembered chiefly as a patriot who espoused the cause of Italian unification under the leadership of the HOUSE OF SAVOY. He was also a painter and writer of considerable renown in his time, particularly admired for patriotic novels like his *Ettore Fieramosca* (1833), which stirred national pride by pointing to the military valor of Italians in earlier times. His political pamphlet *Gli ultimi casi di Romagna* (On recent events in Romagna, 1846) condemned both the abuses and the corruption of papal government and the extreme views of conspirators like GIUSEPPE MAZZINI. D'Azeglio thus carved out a political space in the national movement for the moderate leadership of the House of Savoy, which he served faithfully. He was wounded fighting against Austria in 1848. As prime minister to King VICTOR EMMANUEL II (1849–52) he supported constitutional government, secured parliamentary approval of the anticlerical Siccardi Laws (1850), which abolished ecclesiastical courts, limited property donations to religious bodies, and decriminalized the nonobservance of religious obligations. He resigned as prime minister in November 1852, outmaneuvered by CAVOUR. Less flexible than Cavour, d'Azeglio feared an alliance with radical patriots surrounding GIUSEPPE GARIBALDI, seeing in them the vanguard of republicanism and social chaos. He played no significant role in the events of 1859–60 that culminated in the unification of Italy. He regarded national unification with some apprehension, for fear that the South would be a drag on the North. In the autobiographical *I miei ricordi,* published posthumously in 1867, d'Azeglio warned Italians of the difficulties ahead. Although the phrase, "Now that we have made Italy we must make the Italian people," attributed to him does not appear in precisely that form in his memoirs, it does reflect his view that political unification was just the beginning of a long and difficult process of national fusion.

Azione Cattolica Italiana See CATHOLIC ACTION.

B

Baccarini, Alfredo See LIBERAL LEFT.

Baciocchi, Elisa Bonaparte (1779–1820)
*sister of Napoleon I, ruler of Lucca (1805–1809)
and Tuscany (1809–1814)*

This younger sister of NAPOLEON I, married in 1797 to Felice Baciocchi (1762–1841), a Corsican officer whom Napoleon elevated to the rank of prince, ruled along with her husband the principalities of LUCCA and Piombino from 1805 to 1809. Elisa wielded effective power, displaying immense energy and clarity of purpose in enacting reforms in her domains. Penal and civil laws were brought into compliance with French legislation, and schools, hospitals, aqueducts, and roads were built or improved. Urban renewal changed the appearance of many parts of the city. She bowed to her brother's will under pressure, confiscating ecclesiastical assets even though she recognized that attacking the church would render her unpopular. One privilege that was much appreciated by her subjects was the exemption from military service. Elisa was ambitious to rule beyond the two small principalities assigned to her in 1805. In 1809 she obtained from her brother the title of grand duchess of Tuscany and moved to Florence, while continuing to exercise her sovereignty over Lucca and Piombino. In Tuscany, which was then annexed to France, her powers were limited. Her popularity declined in the final years of the Napoleonic period, partly as a result of economic hardship resulting from the trade restrictions of Napoleon's Continental System. She was forced into exile and deposed following Napoleon's military defeats in 1814–15.

Badoglio, Pietro (1871–1956)
chief of staff and prime minister

Badoglio is a notable and controversial military figure of the period 1914–45. Piedmontese by birth, he pursued a military career with single-minded concentration, rising quickly from colonel to general during WORLD WAR I. The exploit that is associated with his name and opened his way to advancement was the capture of the important Austrian position of Monte Sabotino (August 1916), which led to the capture of the city of Gorizia. He suffered a setback a year later when the army he commanded crumbled at the BATTLE OF CAPORETTO, but his career did not suffer. In the aftermath of that disaster, he helped reorganize the army in preparation for the battle of the Piave River, which halted the last Austrian offensive in June 1918.

After the war Badoglio served as army chief of staff (1919–21). For his known anti-Fascist sentiments he was consigned to the minor post of Italian ambassador to Brazil (1923–24), but BENITO MUSSOLINI called him back and appointed him to the newly created post of chief of general staff (*capo di stato maggiore*), which he held from May 1925 to December 1940. He was responsible for advising Mussolini on all military matters, coordinating the activities of the army, navy, and air force, and overseeing all military planning. Mussolini was ultimately responsible for military policy, but Badoglio bears much responsibility for the failure to modernize Italy's ARMED FORCES. He failed to coordinate planning for the army, navy, and air force, did not appreciate the importance of air power, paid scant attention to motorization, mechanization, and use of heavy armor. He remained very much a traditionalist who relied on numbers and infantry.

Badoglio was at his best in organizing and conducting colonial wars. Without relinquishing his post as chief of general staff, he assumed command of the military operations that brought Libya under full Italian control (1928–33). In 1935, as tensions mounted in the Mediterranean, he warned Mussolini about the dangers of a naval conflict with Great Britain should Italy launch an invasion of Ethiopia. But once the ETHIOPIAN WAR was underway, he made clear his interest in assuming command. Mussolini obliged him by appointing him to succeed General EMILIO DE BONO in November 1935. Badoglio thus prepared and led the final offensive that broke the back of the organized resistance in May 1936. Badoglio's lavish rewards for that feat included promotion to the rank of marshal and the title of duke of Addis Ababa. But while reaping these rewards Badoglio made his dissent from some of the regime's policies known. He favored an alliance with France against Germany, expressed opposition to Italian intervention in the Spanish civil war and to Italian intervention in WORLD WAR II. But he was always cautious, never took an unqualified stand, and always yielded when Mussolini showed resolve. He was silent when Mussolini took Italy into war in June 1940.

Badoglio was forced out as chief of staff in December 1940 after the armed forces had suffered a series of humiliating reverses. Although he was blamed for the poor military performance, the regime took no steps against him and he dropped out of the public eye. From this semiretirement, he positioned himself to succeed Mussolini as Italy's defeat drew nearer. King VICTOR EMMANUEL III appointed him to head the new government after removing Mussolini on July 25, 1943. Badoglio then attempted the risky maneuver of negotiating a secret armistice with the Allies and changing sides in the war, while simultaneously assuring Hitler that Italy would continue to fight as Germany's ally. The gambit failed, Badoglio abandoned Rome to the Germans, fled to the South with the royal court to seek protection from the Allies, and left the armed forces without orders. Those decisions destroyed the armed forces and assured the collapse of the monarchy after the war. But Badoglio was not done yet. As head of two successive governments operating under strict Allied control, he made Italy a "cobelligerent" in the war against Germany (October 1943) and oversaw the army's limited role in the fighting. He resigned under pressure after the liberation of Rome on June 18, 1944, and retired to private life. His book *Italy in the Second World War* (1948) is self-serving, but contains some interesting documentation.

Baffi, Paolo   See BANCA D'ITALIA.

Bakunin, Michael   (1814–1876)
Russian anarchist active in Italy
This Russian anarchist chose post-unification Italy as the place to practice his philosophy of revolution, banking on peasant discontent in the South, a discontented intelligentsia, and the fragility of the recently unified state. Born to a family of the Russian aristocracy, Bakunin attended military school, resigned his commission, traveled to Europe, and gravitated toward socialism. Arrested by the Prussian police for his part in the REVOLUTIONS of 1848, he was extradited to Russia, where he spent 10 years in a Siberian prison camp (1851–61). He escaped, found his way back to Europe via North America, approached GIUSEPPE MAZZINI and Karl Marx in London, and made his way to Italy in January 1864 claiming to speak for both. He founded the Alliance for Social Democracy as a section of Marx's First International. Winning the confidence and support of young radicals, Bakunin decided to go his own way. From his bases in Florence and Naples he orchestrated unsuccessful insurrections in 1867, 1870, and 1874. More of an inspirational figure than an organizer,

Bakunin undermined Mazzini's appeal and laid the foundations for Italian ANARCHISM. Antiauthoritarian by temperament and creed, he opposed the centralized state, nationalism, and religion. The failure of his insurgencies and severe government repression dimmed his appeal. By the late 1870s many of his followers were turning to socialism, which they saw as the wave of the future.

Balabanoff, Angelica (1869–1965)
Russian-born radical active in Italian socialism
Balabanoff forsook her privileged family background to pursue radical causes outside her homeland. She studied in Brussels and Rome, was influenced by the Marxist theoretician ANTONIO LABRIOLA, and joined the Italian Socialist Party (PSI). As a socialist, she championed feminist issues. In Switzerland (1903–07), she propagandized among Italian workers and met the young expatriate BENITO MUSSOLINI, whom she took under her wing. She was instrumental in furthering Mussolini's journalistic career in the Socialist Party, until 1914 when they broke over the issue of Italian intervention in WORLD WAR I. Thereafter she became an unswerving critic of Mussolini and his policies. Balabanoff went back to Switzerland when Italy went to war in 1915. As an internationalist, Balabanoff disapproved of the war and sought to end it. In 1916 she adopted Lenin's position that pacifists should take advantage of the war to promote socialist revolution. She returned to Russia in May 1917 and supported the Bolshevik regime until 1921 when she left for Stockholm, Vienna, and eventually Paris (1926), where she linked up once again with Italian socialists in exile from Fascist Italy. She went to the United States in 1936 and returned to Italy in 1948, by then a critic of both FASCISM and Leninism. Her memoirs, *My Life as a Rebel* (1938), provide some fascinating insights into the world of radical politics.

Balbo, Cesare (1789–1853)
writer, political strategist, and patriot
Count Balbo was born in Turin to a family of the provincial aristocracy transplanted into the capital city. Of liberal sentiments, he was drawn to politics at an early age, held office during the Napoleonic occupation, and accompanied his father into political exile in Spain (1817–19). His political ideas matured in Spain. As a moderate liberal he favored a limited constitutional monarchy. Returning to Piedmont, he joined a group of moderate advisers around Prince CHARLES ALBERT, urging him in 1821 to accept a constitution but to avoid political conspiracies. His moderate views did not save him from internal exile for 10 years when the REVOLUTION of 1821 was suppressed. More a scholar than man of action, Balbo studied and wrote during his years of enforced political inactivity. He is remembered principally as the author of *Le speranze d'Italia* (On the Hopes of Italy, 1844). The book was dedicated to VINCENZO GIOBERTI, whose views on the future of Italy Balbo shared in part. Unlike Gioberti, however, Balbo was very much aware of Italy's economic backwardness, did not believe in Gioberti's notion of Italian "primacy" in the modern world, argued that free trade and economic development were necessary preconditions for political unity, and did not believe that the pope could serve as president of a national confederation. According to Balbo, unity should take the form of a confederation of autonomous states led by Piedmont-Sardinia. Thus, while the book was dedicated to Gioberti, it was really addressed to Charles Albert who had come to the throne in 1831. Balbo's book also held out the prospect that Austria could be persuaded to accept Italian unification and the attendant loss of territory by territorial compensations in eastern Europe at the expense of the Ottoman Empire. Thus, according to Balbo, Italian unification could be achieved without having to fight the Austrians. Such arguments appealed to moderate patriots who wanted to avoid both war and revolution. In 1847 Balbo and CAVOUR founded

the periodical *Il Risorgimento,* which reflected the views of moderate patriots. Balbo served as prime minister of Piedmont's first constitutional government in March–July 1848, was active in parliament after stepping down as prime minister. His writings, which included *Sommario della Storia d'Italia* (Summary of the history of Italy, 1846), continued to shape public opinion, making a case for a peaceful resolution of the national question, loyalty to the HOUSE OF SAVOY and the CATHOLIC CHURCH, and warning of the dangers of revolution.

Balbo, Italo (1896–1940)
Fascist leader and military figure
Italo Balbo was born and raised in Ferrara in a middle-class family connected to the local nobility of the city and of Piedmont. Outgoing, impetuous, somewhat undisciplined in his youth, and also motivated by the patriotic traditions of the family, Balbo abandoned his studies to volunteer for military service in WORLD WAR I. Returning to civilian life as a decorated veteran, he graduated from the prestigious Cesare Alfieri Institute of Florence in 1920. In 1921 he joined the rising Fascist movement, organized action squads in the province of Ferrara, and soon emerged as a powerful *ras* (local chieftain) of the movement. An able organizer, he led punitive actions against political opponents in nearby provinces, until the Fascists controlled the entire Po Valley. In October 1922 he took charge of the military organization of the march on Rome. As head of the Fascist Militia, Balbo was responsible for many acts of violence and intimidation against political opponents. He was among the party leaders who pressured Mussolini to crack down on anti-Fascists during the GIACOMO MATTEOTTI crisis. As minister of aeronautics (1929–33) Balbo laid the basis of the modern Italian air force. He won international attention by personally leading team flights (*crociere*) across the Atlantic, the most famous involving 24 seaplanes that flew from Italy to Chicago and back

Italo Balbo *(Library of Congress)*

(1933). An international celebrity, his fame is said to have aroused Mussolini's jealousy and fear that Balbo could develop into a political rival. On his return from Chicago, Mussolini appointed him governor of the Italian colony of Libya, an honorific post that had the advantage of keeping Balbo away from Italy. But the appointment did not keep Balbo out of the public eye. The well-publicized projects that Balbo undertook in the colony included construction of the *Via Balbia,* a modern motor road 1,118 miles (1,800 kilometers) long along the Mediterranean coast from Tunisia to Egypt, and the settlement of 30,000 Italian agricultural colonists in Libya (1938–39). By 1940 there were approximately 100,000 Italian settlers in Libya among a native population of 800,000. Balbo did not hide his opposition to the Fascist regime's racial policies and the alliance with Nazi Germany. His command of Italian forces in Libya in WORLD WAR II was cut short when his plane was accidentally shot down by friendly fire on June 28, 1940, less than three weeks into the war. His death gave rise to the unfounded rumor that Mussolini had planned his death to rid himself of a dangerous rival. Balbo's death, coming as it did before the humiliating military reverses that followed, reinforced the image of Balbo as a dissident who could stand up to Mussolini. While that view may exaggerate Balbo's political courage, there is little doubt that both in life and death he personified the Fascist ideal of the man of action.

Baldini, Nullo See COOPERATIVISM.

Balilla, Opera Nazionale See GIOVENTÙ ITALIANA DEL LITTORIO.

Balkans

The Balkans, or the Balkan Peninsula, comprises ALBANIA, Greece, Bulgaria, Romania, the former state of Yugoslavia, and the European part of Turkey (the territory northwest of the Dardanelles). This is an area of historical interest for Italy because of the geographic proximity of Albania and Yugoslavia and the strategic importance of the Balkan Peninsula in the Mediterranean. Opportunities for trade and economic expansion have beckoned since the early Middle Ages when Venetian traders established bases and settlement colonies in the Balkans and resisted the Turkish advance toward the Adriatic Sea. Situated at a historic crossroad where Mediterranean and continental populations meet and mix, the Balkans have been contested ground throughout the centuries. In modern times, the Ottoman, Austrian, and Russian Empires have annexed or controlled parts of the region, aspiring to become dominant throughout. In the 19th century Great Britain emerged

as an important player in the politics of the region because of its interest in securing the Mediterranean lifeline of its empire. Italy has been a secondary player in the area since the decline of Venetian power in the 17th century. Before national unification, the Kingdom of Sardinia and the Kingdom of the Two Sicilies had commercial contacts with the Balkans and some Italian political exiles found refuge there.

Italian interest in the Balkans grew after national unification with the growth of trade and shipping. The marriage of the future king VICTOR EMMANUEL III to Princess Elena of Montenegro in 1896 was both a symptom and a cause of escalating Italian designs on the Balkans. In the first decade of the 20th century the Venetian businessman GIUSEPPE VOLPI established a strong Italian commercial presence in Montenegro and Albania. The recognition of Albanian independence in 1913 was an attempt by the great powers to head off competing Austrian and Italian claims to that country. Italian forces occupied Albania, Montenegro, and parts of Serbia during WORLD WAR I. After the war, and particularly during the period of FASCISM, Italian foreign policy aimed to establish complete control over Albania, destabilize and isolate Yugoslavia, gain possession of the coast of DALMATIA, and use those bases as the starting point for conquest or control of the rest of the Balkan Peninsula. The marriage of Princess Giovanna, daughter of Victor Emmanuel III, to King Boris III of Bulgaria in 1930 was part of Italy's Balkan strategy. French and British opposition to Italian designs on the Balkans was one factor behind the Italian-German alliance that developed after 1935. But German and Italian policies also conflicted in the Balkans and, especially after Germany's annexation of Austria in 1938, the two countries behaved more like rivals than partners in that part of Europe.

The Italian military occupation of Albania in April 1939 was a response to the German occupation of Bohemia in March of that year. Italian military bases in Albania were directed against both Yugoslavia and Greece. It was from Albania that Italian forces launched their unsuccessful attack on Greece in October 1940. The botched aggression opened up new opportunities for Germany in Bulgaria and Romania. Both countries were pressured by Germany into entering WORLD WAR II on the side of the Axis powers. Germany intervened militarily in Yugoslavia in April 1941 to help the Italians still fighting on the Greek front and to consolidate Germany's dominance of the Balkans. The armistice of September 1943 eliminated the Italian troops as an independent presence, some becoming German prisoners of war, others joining the fight against Germany, and some choosing to fight on to protect Italian lives and interests in Istria and Dalmatia.

The Italian presence in the Balkans since World War II has been mainly economic and cultural. Italian television introduced Western products and cultural models to parts of the Balkans under communist rule. In this new guise, Italy carried on its traditional role of communicator and mediator between Western and Eastern Europe. An Italian presence, both civilian and military, has existed in Albania and parts of the former independent state of Yugoslavia since the early 1990s, as part of United Nations programs and NATO operations. A close economic, cultural, and political relationship prevails with the independent state of Slovenia, which is territorially adjacent to northern Italy.

Banca Commerciale Italiana See
BANKING; CUCCIA, ENRICO.

Banca d'Italia (Bank of Italy)
The Bank of Italy, the country's central bank, was established in 1893 following the scandal of the BANCA ROMANA that rocked the Italian financial world. Until 1926, when it became the sole bank of issue, it shared the authority to issue paper currency with the Bank of Naples and Bank of Sicily. The Bank of Italy has played a central role in the economic development of the country. Under the capable leadership of Bonaldo Stringher (1854–1930), who was its director from 1900 to 1930, it regulated the supply of money, maintained a stable exchange rate, and

provided credit to fuel economic growth. As the lender of last resort, it extended emergency loans and prevented business bankruptcies. As a state institution open to public scrutiny, it inspired trust in public policy, the stability of the currency, and the reliability of financial markets. The economic growth of the period 1900–13 was due in great measure to the steady course set by Stringher. The bank tightened its grip on the economy in the 1920s and 1930s, when it became a full-fledged bankers' bank, with exclusive rights of issue and regulatory powers over other banks. Stringher was the first in a series of remarkable public servants who have headed the bank. Under the directorship of LUIGI EINAUDI (1945–47) and Donato Menichella (1947–60), it brought inflation under control and stabilized the exchange rate at 620–630 lire to the American dollar. The stable exchange rate contributed to the postwar reconstruction of the economy. Under Guido Carli (1960–75) and Paolo Baffi (1975–80), it steered the economy through recession and political instability. Under CARLO AZEGLIO CIAMPI (1980–92), it reduced the public debt, curbed inflation, and strengthened the currency to prepare the country for admission to the European Monetary System. In 1992 the Banca d'Italia took over from the treasury responsibility for setting the official exchange rate and was no longer obliged to lend to the government. These and other measures, including privatization of some of its assets, were designed to free the bank from political party pressures that might otherwise compromise its regulatory role. In 2004 the bank was challenged by the Berlusconi government, which tried unsuccessfully to curb its regulatory powers. It will be redefined as the country is fully integrated into the EUROPEAN UNION.

Banca Romana, scandal of
The Roman Bank was founded in 1835 by French and Belgian investors. It became the official bank of the PAPAL STATES in 1851. In 1874 the Italian government made it one of six national banks authorized to issue currency under pub-

lic regulation. An audit of the bank carried out in 1889 revealed serious irregularities in the activities of the bank, including issuing of currency beyond set limits and printing of false banknotes. The government suppressed the report, fearing that a major scandal would rock the economy and undermine public confidence in government. The scandal broke nonetheless in December 1892, when members of the political opposition read excerpts of the report into the parliamentary record and leaked it to the press. GIOVANNI GIOLITTI, then in his first term as prime minister, sponsored a banking reform (1893) that liquidated the Roman Bank and restricted currency issuance to the newly founded BANCA D'ITALIA and to the banks of Naples and Sicily. Giolitti's reform was well conceived, but his reputation suffered because as treasury minister in 1889 he had agreed to the suppression of the original report, borrowed money from the Bank of Rome for government purposes, and nominated the bank's governor, Bernardo Tanlongo (1820–96), to the senate. The political aftershocks of the scandal continued to reverberate for years, tarnishing the reputations of both Giolitti and FRANCESCO CRISPI, who preceded and succeeded Giolitti as prime minister.

Banco Ambrosiano, scandal of

Financial improprieties in the affairs of this Milanese bank that came to light in 1980 showed a deficit of some $790 million and $1.4 billion in unsecured loans to foreign subsidiaries. The prospect of bankruptcy and collapse of public confidence in the banking system prompted the government to take extraordinary measures, including the temporary closing of the stock market and the start of an investigation that pointed to a network of connections linking the Banco Ambrosiano to the Vatican, the activities of convicted financier Michele Sindona (1921–86), who was then serving a prison sentence in the United States for financial fraud, the MAFIA, the shadowy world of Licio Gelli's Masonic lodge PROPAGANDA 2, and various public figures. The

Ambrosiano's president, Roberto Calvi (1921–82), ousted and convicted of currency fraud, escaped during his appeal and was found hanging from Blackfriars Bridge in London. His secretary committed suicide by jumping out a window, an investigating magistrate was assassinated, and Sindona died mysteriously in jail of cyanide poisoning. There was enough to justify subjecting the financial operations of the Vatican to close scrutiny. The Ambrosiano went bankrupt two months after Calvi's death, leaving more than $1 billion in debts. The scandal, the many unresolved issues associated with it, and the press campaign that suggested widespread corruption in the business and political worlds contributed to the crisis of public confidence that gripped the country in the 1980s and led to the political reforms in the 1990s.

Banco di Napoli   See BANKING.

Banco di Roma

Founded in 1880 by a group of investors with close ties to the Vatican, the Bank of Rome expanded beyond its regional base to become the first Italian bank with a strong presence abroad. The opening of a branch in Paris in 1902 was the start of a major expansion of its branches throughout the Mediterranean area. In the following decade the bank opened branches in Egypt, Malta, Spain, and in Constantinople. When the ITALIAN-TURKISH WAR broke out in 1911, the Bank of Rome had 18 branches in Libya. Its presence in lands that were part of the Ottoman Empire, and presumably the Vatican's religious interest in these Muslim lands, made the Bank of Rome a supporter of Italian political expansion in North Africa and the Near East. The fact that one of the bank's directors, Romolo Tittoni, was the brother of the Italian foreign minister TOMMASO TITTONI also suggests that there may have been a connection between the bank's interests and the government's colonial policy. After WORLD WAR I the bank opened additional branches in Lebanon, Palestine, and Syria. But its expansion was inadequately financed and poorly administered. In the postwar years the bank experienced a severe financial crisis, from which it was rescued in 1923 by the newly installed government of BENITO MUSSOLINI, which had a stake in preserving the bank's positions abroad and in healing the conflict of CHURCH AND STATE. The overextended network of foreign branches brought considerable financial losses to the bank, requiring additional subsidies from the government in the 1930s. The bank's industrial holdings were nationalized as part of these rescue operations and absorbed by the Institute for Industrial Reconstruction (IRI). In the 1930s the international operations of the bank were an integral part of the Fascist regime's expansionist policies. WORLD WAR II put an end to both the regime's and the bank's designs, forcing the bank to relinquish many of its positions abroad. The Vatican distanced itself from the bank in 1942, when Pope PIUS XII established the Institute for Religious Works as an independent bank for the administration of religious funds.

Banco di San Giorgio See BANKING.

Banco di Sicilia See BANKING.

Bandiera brothers

*patriots and martyrs for the cause of Italian
independence*

Attilio, born in 1810, and his brother Emilio, born in 1819, were sons of a Venetian family serving the AUSTRIAN EMPIRE. Their father, Francesco Bandiera (1785–1847), held the rank of admiral in the Austrian navy, and his two sons were also commissioned naval officers. Many sailors and officers in the Austrian navy came from Austria's Italian provinces and Italian was the navy's official language. The Bandiera brothers founded a secret society called Esperia that was committed to fighting for Italian indepen-

dence. Given the Austrian government's opposition to Italian independence and the brothers' oath of loyalty to the empire, that commitment was tantamount to treason. In June 1844, acting on false and misleading information possibly planted by spies, Attilio and Emilio went to the aid of what they believed to be an ongoing insurrection against the Neapolitan government. Landing on the coast of CALABRIA with 19 companions, they were all quickly captured by government troops. Those who survived the initial encounter, including the Bandiera brothers, were executed by firing squad on July 25, 1844. Regarded as martyrs to the cause of national independence, the story of the Bandiera brothers became part of the heroic saga of the RISORGIMENTO. The affair had an important aftermath in England, where the political exile GIUSEPPE MAZZINI charged that the British government had violated the privacy of his correspondence by intercepting his mail with the Bandiera brothers and passing on compromising information to the Austrian government. The ensuing scandal embarrassed the British government and generated public support for the Italian movement in England. With its public and private dramas and murky background, the affair of the Bandiera brothers was a cause célèbre that focused public attention on the Italian question.

Bandini, Sallustio Antonio
(1677–1760)

public figure and economic reformer

Born to a prominent family of Siena, Bandini received a degree in philosophy and civil law (1699) and held the chair of canon law at the city's university (1700–05). Choosing to pursue an ecclesiastical career in 1705, he became an influential adviser to the archbishop of Siena, promoted reforms in the Sienese administration, and encouraged scientific education and research. Like many public administrators of his time, Bandini was concerned with promoting agricultural and commercial reforms that would ensure a steady supply of cereals, a concern dictated by a growing population and by the fear of popular unrest. His experiences as a landowner and administrator made him aware that state regulations often interfered with production. He proposed a vast program of land reclamation in the depopulated Tuscan *maremma,* a desolate land in the southern part of the region, government protection of agriculture, and limited free trade in cereals. Although not an advocate of unrestricted free trade, Bandini nevertheless began to question the mercantilist doctrines that regulated both trade and the money supply. His ideas moved cautiously away from the pursuit of agricultural self-sufficiency toward the ideal of free trade. Bandini's pragmatic reformism influenced the economically liberal legislation of the Tuscan state after his death.

banditry See BRIGANDAGE.

Banfield, Edward C. See FAMILISM.

banking
Italian banking families dominated the field of domestic and international finance from the 14th to the 16th centuries. Devising ways of circumventing the Catholic Church's prohibition against charging interest on loans (usury), Italian bankers became rich and powerful by lending, changing, and transferring money across Europe, and trading in goods as a collateral activity. The Bardi family of Florence did well initially by lending to the English royal dynasty, but went bankrupt in 1345–46 when Edward III defaulted on his debts. More fortunate were the MEDICI, who founded their own bank in 1397, and became the wealthiest family of Europe, before also going into decline during the 16th century. Their financial demise was part of the larger crisis of 16th-century Italy, which some banking institutions managed to survive. The Banco di San Giorgio of Genoa remained profitable by tak-

ing advantage of lending and investment opportunities in Spain and its far-flung colonial empire. Founded in 1407, it shut its doors in 1816. Another survivor was the Monte dei Paschi of SIENA. Founded in 1369 to guarantee repayment of the Sienese public debt from the leasing of grazing lands (*paschi*), by the 17th century it had developed into a full-fledged banking operation, probably the first of its kind in Europe. It is today one of the oldest and most successful banking institutions in the world. At a more modest level, charitable institutions called *monti di pietà* were founded in the 15th century to free ordinary borrowers from dependence on pawnshops and reduce popular hostility and violence toward the Jews who owned these shops. The *monti* were the precursors of modern savings banks that deal with ordinary depositors.

The modern Italian banking system developed after national unification from such precedents. Six different banks inherited from pre-unification states were authorized to issue banknotes and engage in lending operations. With minimal coordination and lax government supervision, speculative ventures and questionable lending practices came to a head in the early 1890s. A crisis in the building industry, the resulting collapse of the overexposed BANCA ROMANA, and a string of bank failures between 1889 and 1893 revealed the inadequacies of the national banking system. The ensuing reform established the BANCA D'ITALIA (1893) as the national bank, sharing currency issuance with the Banco di Napoli and the Banco di Sicilia. In the private sector, the Banca Commerciale Italiana, founded in 1894, adopted the German model of "mixed" banking, which used depositors' money to extend medium- and long-term loans to industry. Used aggressively by its long-time director Giuseppe Toeplitz (1866–1938), the system funneled savings toward industry, fueled rapid industrial expansion, and established the close relationship between industry and banking that has been the enduring feature of the Italian financial system.

In the 1920s the bankers first beat back efforts by industrialists to gain control of the banks, then consolidated their control of major industrial sectors. What the industrialists could not do in the 1920s, the government did in the 1930s when industrial production slumped and industry could not repay its huge debts to the banks. The government bailed out the banks, took their industrial share holdings as collateral, and gained control of much of private industry. Thus was born the public sector of the Italian economy that was managed by the Institute for Industrial Reconstruction (IRI). In the process of restructuring the banking system, the Banca Commerciale, Banco di Roma, and Credito Italiano became publicly owned institutions subject to government control. The Banking Act of 1936 prohibited banks from extending long-term credit to industry, leaving industrialists largely dependent on the stock market, which could not meet the needs of industry. Government lending came with strings attached.

This centralized banking system survived the fall of FASCISM. In the period of postwar reconstruction (1945–50), it stabilized the CURRENCY and brought inflation under control. The system performed a similar function after the economic setbacks of the 1970s. By the 1990s Italian banking, which until then had been shielded from foreign competition, was feeling pressure from the outside. In the years of protection, banks had made major investments in noncompetitive industries like steel, machinery, chemicals, and in costly ventures for the economic development of the South. They could no longer do so in the new climate of "globalization" and economic integration. The slow and painful process of restructuring and adjustment that began in the early 1990s continues to this day. The privatization of the Bank of Italy in 1992 was followed by the privatization of the other public banks, including the Banca Commerciale, in the late 1990s. Major mergers are still going on to make Italian banking competitive in the context of European economic integration.

Baratieri, Oreste (1841–1901)
colonial governor and army general

Born near Trent under Austrian rule, Baratieri fought as a volunteer under GIUSEPPE GARIBALDI in 1860, then transferred to the regular army. He distinguished himself for bravery in the unfortunate Battle of Custoza (1866) and fought again under Garibaldi in the Franco-Prussian War with the rank of captain. He won recognition for his military writings and administrative ability. Appointed governor of the colony of Eritrea in 1892, he improved the administration, reordered the judiciary, and made the colony financially self-supporting. In 1894–95 he led successful sorties against rebellious populations. Favored by Prime Minister FRANCESCO CRISPI, who approved of his political past and admired his élan, Baratieri was put in command of a punitive expedition against the Ethiopian emperor Menelik II, who had gone to the aid of Eritrean insurgents. Urged to act by Crispi, who wanted a quick colonial victory, Baratieri yielded to political pressure. Against his better judgment, he launched an offensive that ended in disaster near Adowa in Ethiopian territory. Inaccurate maps, poor reconnaissance, and incompetent leadership led 16,500 troops into an ambush that in one single day cost the Italians 6,000 dead and 1,900 prisoners. News of the defeat rocked the country and brought down Crispi's government. Baratieri was recalled and tried by a military tribunal. Although he was exonerated, the defeat put an end to his military career. His other achievements forgotten, he is remembered as the general responsible for humiliation that rankled nationalist feelings until the defeat of Adowa was "avenged" by the invasion of Ethiopia in 1935–36.

Barberini family

The Barberini family rose to power thanks to its close ties to the CATHOLIC CHURCH and Spain in the 16th and 17th centuries. Originally from Siena, they moved first to Florence and then

Rome, where they rose to prominence. Maffeo Barberini became Pope URBAN VIII in 1623. He consolidated the power of the family by appointing relatives to major civil and ecclesiastical positions. With Spain on their side, the Barberini seemed poised to become the dominant power in Italy, until other ruling families formed a coalition against them, backed by France. The two sides clashed in the so-called War of Castro (1642–44), in which the combined forces of Modena, Parma, Tuscany, and Venice were able to check papal power and curb the Barberini. The family was banished from Rome after the death of Urban VIII in 1644 and its riches confiscated. Cardinal Jules Mazarin (1602–61), chief adviser to the French monarchy, took up their cause and used military force to restore the Barberini to their position and wealth in Rome. Thenceforth, the family avoided dangerous political causes and entanglements, solidifying its power with advantageous marriages and profitable investments. The imposing Barberini Palace in Rome, begun in 1625, was the family residence. Its once-rich art collection was sold and dispersed long ago. The Barberini's enthusiasm for building construction was proverbial. Their quarrying of materials from ancient Roman buildings for their own projects prompted the saying, *Quod non facerunt Barbari facerunt Barberini* (What the Barbarians didn't do, the Barberini did).

Bardi family See BANKING.

Baretti, Giuseppe (1719–1789)
literary critic and polemicist
Like other Piemontese intellectuals of his generation, Baretti, born in Turin, fled his native region for places abroad that were more receptive to the life of the mind. Baretti went to London in 1751, struck up a friendship with Samuel Johnson, and became part of his literary circle. He returned to Italy in 1760 to launch a journal of literary criticism modeled on the English *Spectator*. The *Frusta Letteraria* (The Literary Lash)

made quite a splash in its brief but stormy life (1763–64). While reviewing the major literary works of the time, the journal lashed out at just about every contemporary Italian writer, accusing some of aping foreign fashions and others of being obtusely traditional. He was particularly hard on the rival journal *Il Caffè*, which he accused of imitating the French, and on the Accademia della Crusca, the self-appointed guardian of linguistic purity that stood in the way of change. The efforts at language reform by the Arcadian movement he dismissed as superficial and childish. What did Baretti stand for? Some have seen him simply as a cantankerous figure driven by personal passions and resentments. While his personality may have had much to do with the tone of his polemics, the issues that he raised were timely and legitimate. His insistence that there was such a thing as a common and unique Italian culture anticipated the later concerns of ROMANTICISM. Above all, Baretti advised aspiring Italian writers to have faith in themselves as individuals, follow their personal inclinations, and be critical both of tradition and current fashions. The Italian language, whose use he advocated for writers throughout the peninsula, should be allowed to develop freely, respectful of the past but in touch with the present. It was his tone more than his message that irritated many of his compatriots. When his journal shut down, Baretti returned to England where he promoted the study of Italian language and culture.

Bari, city of
The capital of the region of PUGLIA, Bari (pop. 332,000) is southern Italy's major port on the Adriatic Sea and the country's most important contact point for trade with the countries of the eastern Mediterranean and the Near East. An annual trade fair, the *Fiera del Levante*, showcases Italian products for trade purposes. Probably founded by Balkan populations, the city prospered under the Greeks and Romans. In the Middle Ages it was contested and controlled at

various times by Goths, Byzantines, Lombards, Saracens, Germans, and Normans. In the 11th century it became part of what later would be called the KINGDOM OF THE TWO SICILIES, which was absorbed by the Italian state in 1860. The old part of the city (*Bari vecchia*) is a maze of alleys close to the port and around the ancient Basilica of Saint Nicholas, the city's patron saint. The modern city (*Bari nuova*) was begun after 1800, expanded after 1860 with the arrival of the railroad, and was further amplified by the Fascist regime to stimulate trade and extend Italian influence in the Near East. The new city is laid out in a well-planned geometrical pattern. It comprises both an industrial zone and popular residential quarters. Its industrial firms are mostly small and medium-scale, specializing in construction materials, textiles, engineering, and petrochemicals. The University of Bari is an important cultural center for the entire region.

Baronio, Cesare (1538–1607)
(Baronius)
church scholar and religious reformer

Born near Frosinone, Baronio studied law, was ordained a priest in 1564, appointed cardinal in 1596, chief church librarian in 1597, and served as personal adviser and confessor to Pope Clement VIII. He is credited with prevailing on the pope to accept the conversion to Catholicism of King Henry IV of France. Baronio's papal candidacy was blocked by Spain in 1605. A disciple of religious reformer Saint Filippo Neri (1515–95), Baronio took it upon himself to show by historical research that the reforms proposed by the COUNCIL OF TRENT were rooted in the traditions of the church and were not simply a response to Protestantism. His intensive labors over more than 20 years produced the 12 large volumes of the *Annales ecclesiatici* (Church annals, 1588–1607). The *Annales* provided answers to practical questions of religious reform by tracing the historical development of doctrinal issues and religious practices over the course of centuries. The unfinished work was continued by his suc-

cessors, but he had done enough to secure his position as the foremost church historian of his time and founder of modern church history.

baroque

The term *baroque,* probably derived from *barroco* (an irregular pearl), designates an artistic style that prevailed from the early part of the 17th to the middle of the 18th century. The term, coined in the 18th century, reflected the distaste that the artists of the ENLIGHTENMENT felt for a style rooted in the preceding century. To them, baroque meant misshapen, odd, irregular, confused, and confusing. The large scale and profusion of forms and colors typical of baroque art aimed for theatrical effect. The baroque style in architecture and the visual arts aimed to overwhelm the onlooker with a display of dynamic forms and expressions of emotional intensity. Critics objected to its rejection of the classical norms of balance, symmetry, and restraint. Like MANNERISM, which preceded it in time, the Baroque spread from Italy to other parts of Europe, particularly to the possessions of the Spanish and Austrian Habsburgs, including the Spanish possessions in America. It had little influence in France, where the monarchy favored the classical style. Although the baroque style permeated secular art, as evident in the many palaces of the aristocracy and works of art commissioned by lay patrons, the spread of the new style was closely associated with the COUNCIL OF TRENT and the Catholic revival that aimed at reclaiming the territories lost to Protestantism. The monumentality of baroque religious art and the richness of its ornamentation were meant to draw the faithful into a world of visual splendor. The use of columns made possible the construction of enormous buildings with impressive façades, large interiors, and enormous enclosed plazas like St. Peter's Square in Rome, with its colonnaded arms that reach out as if to embrace the faithful. Baroque paintings teeming with figures covered enormous canvases painted in striking colors. Small-scale works in the spirit of baroque were the exception. Statues depicted the human form in contorted poses meant to express intensity of feeling. In Italy, GIAN LORENZO BERNINI best represents the baroque style in architecture and sculpture.

Bartali, Gino See SPORTS.

Barzini, Luigi, Sr. (1874–1947), and Barzini, Luigi, Jr. (1908–1984)
father and son, journalists and political commentators

Barzini Sr. was a popular and influential journalist and war correspondent who covered world events for major newspapers, including the liberal *Il Corriere della Sera* and the Fascist *Il Popolo d'Italia*. After visiting the United States in 1921 to cover the Washington Naval Conference, he decided to launch a newspaper for Italian-Americans. *Il Corriere d'America* started to publish in 1923. Barzini sold it in 1931 when he returned to Italy. His pro-Fascist sentiments gave him entry into the highest political circles of the Fascist regime. BENITO MUSSOLINI made him a senator in 1934. As a correspondent for *Il Popolo d'Italia*, Barzini covered the Spanish civil war and the Russian campaign in WORLD WAR II. He continued to collaborate with Mussolini in the period of the ITALIAN SOCIAL REPUBLIC. For an example of his early reporting, see his *Peking to Paris: A Journey across Two Continents in 1907* (1972).

The son, Luigi Barzini Jr., also a journalist and a writer of note, was particularly popular in the English-speaking world. Born in Milan, he attended Columbia University in New York City and began his journalistic career working for the *New York World*. He returned to Italy in 1931, worked for *Il Corriere della Sera,* and frequented the group of young dissidents that gravitated around GALEAZZO CIANO. He was arrested in April 1940 on charges of leaking confidential information to the enemy and making disparaging remarks about Mussolini. After WORLD WAR II he

wrote for major newspapers and magazines as an independent journalist. Staunch anticommunist, he represented the Liberal Party (PLI) in the chamber of deputies from 1958 to 1976. His book *The Italians* (1965), written for the general reader, was a major publishing success that introduced many Anglo-Saxon readers to Italian life and culture.

Basilicata

The southern region of Basilicata (pop. 606,000), formerly called Lucania from the name of its ancient inhabitants, occupies the instep of the peninsula, bordering on the Gulf of Taranto in the Ionian Sea, the region of CALABRIA to the south, the Tyrrhenian Sea to the southwest, the region of CAMPANIA to the north, and the region of PUGLIA to the northeast. It is the most mountainous and least densely populated of the southern regions. The rugged interior, difficult communications, arid soil, and malaria in the lowlands have discouraged settlement. Heavy deforestation from the latter part of the 19th century has caused major problems of erosion and soil instability. The forests that covered most of the region in ancient times now occupy less than 10 percent of the territory. Emigration abroad and to the industrial cities of northern Italy has siphoned off a large part of the population. The two principal cities are Potenza, which is the regional capital, and Matera. Matera is known for its picturesque section of *I Sassi* dating back to the eighth century. It is a cluster of cave-like dwellings, churches, narrow alleys, and small piazzas carved out of the mountainside, inhabited until the middle of the 20th century. The economy of the region has been traditionally agricultural, with a small but developing industrial sector dominated by small and medium-sized firms. Cereals, olives, grapes, and other fruits are the principal agricultural products. The range of industrial products includes textiles, processed food, wine, building materials, and wood products. Public administration is the principal source of white-collar employment.

It has been historically difficult to enforce government authority in this region. The bloody repression of BRIGANDAGE by the army in the 1860s did not endear the national government to the local population and contributed to the massive exodus of people from the region. As perhaps the most economically depressed region, Basilicata exemplifies the seriousness and complexity of the SOUTHERN QUESTION.

Bassani, Giorgio See JEWS IN ITALY.

Basso, Lelio (1903–1978)
political figure, writer, and public
commentator
Born near the Ligurian city of Savona, Basso was an intellectual prominent in public debate and a political activist of the Left. He received a law degree in 1925. A critic of bourgeois society and an anti-Fascist, he collaborated with PIERO GOB-ETTI. He was arrested in 1928 and interned in a concentration camp in 1939–40. Anticipating the collapse of the Fascist regime, Basso began to work for the revival of socialism in Italy. In 1943 he launched the Movement for Proletarian Unity (Movimento di Unità Proletaria, or MUP), which later gave life to a new socialist party, the Italian Socialist Party for Proletarian Unity (PSIUP), which was meant to bridge the gap between socialists and communists. When socialists and communists emerged from the war as separate entities, Basso and his followers stayed with the Italian Socialist Party (PSI) during its period of collaboration with the communists. Basso served as PSI secretary-general in 1947–49 and represented it in parliament. When the PSI changed tactics in 1963, distanced itself from the Communist Party (PCI), and sought an accommodation with the Christian Democratic Party (DC), Basso and his followers revived the PSIUP in January 1964 to promote unity of action on the Left. Basso served as PSIUP president until his resignation in 1970. An unbending critic of NATO, of the Vietnam War, of American foreign policy, and

of capitalism in every form, Basso spoke for an intransigent socialist minority that opposed political accommodation with the parties in power, called for political action by the masses, and for major structural reforms of the economy. Marginalized politically in his later years, Basso was a respected and effective figure in public debate until his death.

Battisti, Cesare (1875–1916)
socialist journalist and irredentist
A leading figure of Italian IRREDENTISM, Battisti was born to a well-off family of businessmen in Austrian-ruled TRENT. In 1893 he entered the University of Florence where he studied literature and joined socialist circles. As a journalist in his native city, he published reviews that propagandized for both socialism and irredentism, calling simultaneously for protection of workers and of Italian national identity within the multinational AUSTRIAN EMPIRE. BENITO MUSSOLINI was one of his collaborators in this struggle. Elected to the Austrian parliament in 1911, Battisti demanded administrative autonomy for the Italian-speaking TRENTINO. When WORLD WAR I broke out in August 1914, Battisti urged the Italian government and public opinion to declare war against Austria-Hungary. He volunteered for military service when Italy did go to war in May 1915, and distinguished himself for valor in several actions. Captured by the Austrians, he was tried for treason and executed by hanging in July 1916. Battisti was reviled in Austria as a traitor and revered in Italy as a national martyr. The Fascist regime eulogized his memory and every schoolchild learned of his love and sacrifice for Italy.

Bauer, Riccardo (1896–1982)
journalist, anti-Fascist activist, social
philosopher, and political commentator
Bauer was born in Milan, studied economics, served as a volunteer in WORLD WAR I, and began a career in journalism in the 1920s as an anti-

Fascist. He was editor of the anti-Fascist weekly *Il Caffè*, collaborated with PIERO GOBETTI and FERRUCCIO PARRI, and helped political prisoners escape from jail. He was arrested in 1927 and released a year later. Arrested again in 1930, he was sentenced to a 20-year prison term. In jail Bauer met CARLO ROSSELLI, with whom he collaborated in launching the movement Giustizia e Libertà. He was a founding member of the ACTION PARTY and an organizer of the armed RESISTANCE. Bauer's antifascism was rooted in his commitment to the ideals of individual freedom and social justice. He rejected communism, class warfare, and interpreted the resistance as a movement to affirm the principle of creative freedom. His struggle was against authority, hierarchy, and social subordination. A revolutionary in principle, Bauer rejected terrorist violence and relied on education to foster the spirit of freedom. He continued to speak out for democratic ideals as a journalist after the war, showing no interest in holding political office.

Bazzi, Giovanni Antonio See SODOMA.

Beauharnais, Eugène de (1781–1824)
Napoleonic viceroy and reformer
The son of Josephine Bonaparte from her first marriage, Eugène served his stepfather NAPOLEON I loyally from 1798 when he went with him on the Egyptian campaign until his fall in 1815. Napoleon adopted Eugène, appointed him viceroy of the Kingdom of Italy in 1805, and in 1806 designated him to be his successor should he die without a male heir. As viceroy, Beauharnais turned the capital city of MILAN into a vibrant and magnificent court center, introduced administrative reforms, and created an Italian army loyal to Napoleon. The favoritism that he showed toward the French in his appointments, the high taxes that he levied to help finance Napoleon's war machine, and the fact that he was a foreigner created resentment among his Italian subjects. He was nevertheless respected,

and under his leadership the Kingdom of Italy was perhaps the best administered of Napoleon's satellite states. He commanded an Italian force of 27,000 during the Russian campaign and assumed command of the entire French army in Russia during the disastrous retreat. Even in defeat, he refused to distance himself and the Kingdom of Italy from Napoleon. Deposed like all other Napoleonic rulers by the CONGRESS OF VIENNA, Beauharnais received compensation in the form of titles of nobility and a life pension.

Beccaria, Cesare (1738–1794)
Enlightenment writer and reformer
Born to a noble family of Milan, Beccaria was educated by Jesuits and took a degree in law at the University of Pavia. Influenced by the ideas of the ENLIGHTENMENT, he joined a group of young Milanese reformers around the journal *Il Caffè*. Under their influence, he wrote the study that would make him famous. The book *Dei delitti e delle pene* (Of crimes and punishments, 1764), gained immediate attention and brought him fame as a progressive, innovative thinker. Condemning the indiscriminate use of torture to obtain confessions from suspects and the frequent application of the death sentence for even minor crimes, Beccaria made a case for abolishing torture, making punishment proportionate to the crime, rehabilitating criminals, and reserving the death penalty only for the most heinous crimes. The book, a classic text of modern criminology, has influenced penal reform throughout the western world. Beccaria also wrote on art, economics, government, taught, and served in the public administration, but his name is indelibly tied to the book that made him famous.

Belgioioso, Cristina (1808–1871)
Milanese noblewoman, radical patriot, and
pioneering feminist
Born in Milan to the patrician family of the Trivulzio, she was raised by a liberal stepfather who saw to it that she received a good educa-

tion. Unhappy at home where parental discord prevailed, at the age of 16 she married Prince Emilio Barbiano di Belgioioso (1800–58) against the wishes of her family. She thus acquired the title of princess, which she retained after the couple's separation. She joined the secret sect of the CARBONERIA as a *giardiniera* (auxiliary) and became an exuberant if somewhat indiscreet political conspirator. Her commitments to the causes of Italian independence, social justice, and women's liberation never wavered, but her enemies seized upon her unconventional and often disorderly personal life, punctuated by many love affairs, to undermine her credibility. She was an early backer of GIUSEPPE MAZZINI, whose republicanism she shared at this stage of her life. From 1831 to 1848 she wrote for newspapers and traveled in France, Italy, and England, meeting some of the most notable artistic and political personalities of her time, including the future NAPOLEON III, who may have been one of her lovers. She participated in the REVOLUTIONS of 1848 in Milan, Naples, and Rome. In 1849 she organized a military nursing corps in Rome that predated Florence Nightingale's similar initiative by four years. From 1849 to 1853, perhaps to avoid arrest in western Europe, where she was on a wanted list, she traveled extensively in eastern Europe and Asia Minor, going as far as Jerusalem and penning highly colorful descriptions of her travels. She returned to Paris in 1853 in poor health and probably suffering from an addiction to opium formed during her travels. By then her politics had turned moderate, she had abandoned republicanism, and welcomed the unification of Italy under the HOUSE OF SAVOY, of which she published a laudatory history in 1860. She lived the last years of her life in retirement.

Bellarmine, Robert (1542–1621)
Roman Catholic prelate and scholar
This prominent Jesuit scholar, cardinal, and canonized saint, was born in the Tuscan town of Montepulciano to a family prominent in church affairs. He was ordained in 1570 and took up the chair of religious studies at the Jesuit Roman College in 1576. From that position, and later as rector of the school and adviser to the pope, he contributed to the most important religious and theological debates of his time. He generally took a moderate position on most issues, thus incurring the displeasure of both innovators and traditionalists. He was made a cardinal in 1599. On the issue of relations between popes and secular rulers, Bellarmine argued that the pope could depose rulers who abused their trust. He even went on to argue the daring proposition that while God established the secular power, the people should have a voice in how it was exercised. In the famous controversy with GALILEO over the nature of the solar system, Bellarmine took the position that Galileo had a right to propound his views as long as he presented them as theoretical constructs capable of explaining observed phenomena, and not as an unassailable representation of reality. Learned and subtle, Bellarmine's work attempted to reconcile traditional dogma with the new understanding of politics and nature.

Belli, Giuseppe Gioacchino (1791–1863)
popular poet and satirist
Although born to a well-off Roman family, Belli was orphaned at an early age and spent much of his life in straitened circumstances. Driven by intellectual curiosity, he made up what he lacked in formal education by reading widely on his own. He is chiefly remembered for his writings in the Roman dialect, recognition for which came to him fairly late in life. His decision to write in dialect reflected his conviction that only by using the everyday language of ordinary people could literature capture the vitality of a living language and the culture of the people. Using the sonnet as his form, he portrayed Roman life realistically, depicting its seamier aspects in the coarse language of the streets. His realism reflected an aspect of the culture of ROMANTICISM, which drew attention to the daily

struggles, beliefs, and aspirations of the people. But unlike most romantic writers, Belli did not idealize the people. Christian acceptance of flawed human nature made him tolerant of their shortcomings. He valued the sincerity, spontaneity, and common sense that he found among ordinary people, and condemned the hypocrisy of the educated. Belli's populist sympathies had no adverse political consequences. Valuing domesticity and the quiet life, he avoided giving offense to the PAPACY or political interests.

Bellini, Vincenzo (1801–1835)
opera composer

Born to musicians in the Sicilian city of Catania (his father was an organist), Bellini's musical talent was nurtured at an early age by the family, before the young man was sent to study at the Naples conservatory in 1819. In his relatively brief career, cut short by early death, Bellini won public acclaim for his unique melodic gift and ability to express sentiment in long musical phrases ideally suited to the human voice. His distinctly personal style reflects the influence of his older contemporary GIOACCHINO ROSSINI and of Sicilian and Neapolitan folk music. His first successful productions in Naples earned him an invitation to write for the most prestigious opera house in Italy, Milan's La Scala, where he staged the opera *Il pirata* (1827) with enormous success. He was again successful in Venice with the staging of *I Capuleti ed i Montecchi* (1830), based on the story of Romeo and Juliet. His two best-known operas, *La sonnabula* and *Norma,* were both produced in 1831. Bellini lived in Milan from 1827 to 1833, when he left that city for extended visits to Paris and London. Wherever he went, he basked in the adulation of enthusiastic fans. In Paris he struck up a close friendship with Chopin, who considered Bellini the most gifted melodist of their generation. In London he met and fell madly in love with the soprano Maria Malibran (1808–36), but that was just one of several passionate affairs he had with leading

Vincenzo Bellini *(Library of Congress)*

ladies of the operatic stage. *I puritani,* his last opera, was performed to major acclaim in Paris in January 1835, with the Milanese soprano Giulia Grisi (1811–69) in the principal female role. Bellini died in a Paris suburb in September of that same year, probably of amebic dysentery, although legend soon had it that a jealous husband had poisoned him. Rossini, GIUSEPPE VERDI, and Richard Wagner all admired Bellini's music. Although Bellini had no discernible political views, his music did not fail to inspire Italian patriots fighting for national unification. GIUSEPPE GARIBALDI is thought to have been inspired by the duet *Suoni la tromba* (Let the trumpet sound) from *I puritani,* in which two rivals in love come together to fight in the cause of liberty. Bellini's music appealed irresistibly to the romantic sensibility that expected music and theater to express strong feelings and high ideals.

Bembo, Pietro (1470–1547)
writer, linguist, and literary critic

Bembo was born to a family of the Venetian nobility, spent his youth abroad in the company of his father who was in the diplomatic service, and received the humanistic education fashionable in his day. He served in the papal diplomatic corps and became a cardinal in 1539. An accomplished Latinist, Bembo chose to write in the Florentine vernacular accessible to a wide lay readership. On the use of Latin, he argued that contemporary writers should go back to the Latin of Cicero and Virgil. In the *Prose della volgar lingua* (Prose writings in the vulgar language, 1525) he argued that the standard for the use of Italian was set by the major writers of the 14th century, particularly by GIOVANNI BOCCACCIO in prose and PETRARCH in verse. Bembo called their noble and inspiring language the *volgare*. That designation, not meant to be denigrating, has been in use ever since. The linguistic criteria adopted by Bembo, covering such matters as grammar, spelling, and syntax, later became the basis of the first vocabulary of the Italian language published by the Accademia della Crusca in 1612. Bembo's contributions to the development of the Italian language illustrate the decisive role played by the literati is shaping the official language, which has always differed substantially from the everyday language of ordinary Italians. Bembo's theories were hotly debated in his day, but prevailed nevertheless due in no small measure to his personal charm and the gracefulness and elegance of his writings.

Benedict XIV (1675–1758)
pope (1740–1758)

Cardinal Prospero Lambertini came to the papacy the long way. He was 65 when elected and it took the College of Cardinals five months to pick him. Admired in his own time for his intellect, scholarly accomplishments, openness to new ideas, and genial disposition, Benedict stands out as one of the great popes of the ENLIGHTENMENT. In religious matters he simplified ritual, reduced feast days, acknowledged the legitimacy of Eastern Christian rites in communion with Rome, and urged caution in placing books on the INDEX. Perhaps his greatest challenge came in dealing with Catholic governments determined to challenge and curb the power of the church. He responded with skillful diplomacy, steering a middle course between critics and supporters, to ward off the more serious threats to papal power. He turned Rome into an artistic and intellectual center, founded new schools, established chairs for the study of science, mathematics, and medicine, and expanded the Vatican Library and archives. Renowned artists and scholars came to Rome from all parts of Europe to study and work. Benedict XIV exemplifies the papacy's identification with the culture of the Enlightenment before the onset of revolution and the conclusion of later popes that Enlightenment culture and Christianity were not compatible.

Benedict XV (1854–1922)
pope (1914–1922)

Born Giacomo Della Chiesa in Genoa to a family of the aristocracy, his surname (Of the Church) proved prophetic. He was ordained in 1878 and entered on a career in the Vatican's diplomatic corps, holding various posts in Rome and abroad. In 1907 he was named archbishop of Bologna and made a cardinal in 1914. He was elected pope in September of that same year. Given the timing of his election, WORLD WAR I was the most urgent issue of his papacy. He opposed Italy's intervention in the war and condemned the diplomatic negotiations preceding it, which excluded the Vatican from participation in any future peace settlement. The war itself he denounced as a crime against God and humanity. Benedict pursued a neutral stance, committed to seeking a peaceful solution that would enable him to mediate the conflict. However, his overtures were rebuffed as each side suspected him of secretly siding with the other. A detailed proposal of August 1917 called for a negotiated peace, freedom of the seas, no territorial gains, gradual disarmament, and an international tribunal for the peaceful settlement of international disputes. It was similar in many respects to President Woodrow Wilson's celebrated Fourteen Points, but received scant attention from governments. Benedict condemned the Treaty of Versailles as punitive and a cause of future wars. In Italian politics he took steps to stem the threat of communism and encouraged the formation of the Italian Popular Party (PPI) to mobilize the Catholic vote. By the time of Benedict's death in January 1922 the Popular Party had become the second-largest party in the country.

Beneduce, Alberto (1877–1944)
financial expert and public administrator
Beneduce, a statistician, demographer, agricultural and insurance expert, as well as a teacher, business manager, and public servant, was a pivotal figure in business and government in the first four decades of the 20th century. It complicates matters that he was also a socialist dedicated enough to name his daughter Idea Socialista (she later married the banker ENRICO CUCCIA), was well connected in the world of high finance, and collaborated with the Fascist regime. In 1914 he called for Italian intervention in the war and volunteered for military service. After the war he served as minister of labor in the government headed by the social democrat IVANOE BONOMI (1921–22). Initially opposed to fascism, he came on board after 1925 when the regime abandoned laissez-faire policies in favor of economic interventionism. GIUSEPPE VOLPI, the new minister of finances, made way for him in business and government because he valued Beneduce's expertise. BENITO MUSSOLINI, also impressed by Beneduce's

competence and loyalty, relied on him for advice in the campaign to revalue the CURRENCY. In 1933 Mussolini appointed Beneduce head of the Institute for Industrial Reconstruction (IRI), and Beneduce used his power to put private banks and industrial firms under government control. In this roundabout fashion, he realized the socialist goal of expanding government control of the economy. Made senator in 1939, the next year he resigned all his public offices because of poor health, but retained his important positions on the boards of private businesses. Often overlooked because of his deliberately low-key public personality, Beneduce was the real *duce* of the 20th-century Italian economy.

Benetton
Headquartered in the northern city of Treviso, Benetton exemplifies the typically Italian transition from small family enterprise to global conglomerate. Luciano Benetton, the company's founder, started out as a shop assistant, sold his bicycle to buy a sewing machine, went into business (1955), and sold sweaters knitted by his sisters. Eventually he hit upon a winning idea, manufacturing pastel-colored sweaters, marketing them in carefully selected locations in shops bearing the Benetton name, and cultivating a youthful, sporting image for the merchandise. Benetton shops are actually owned by independent retailers who have contracted to buy directly from Benetton and who are solely responsible for selling the merchandise. Benetton does little manufacturing of its own, mostly contracting out to local suppliers. A network of agents oversees the apparel chain, checking for quality and monitoring the operations of outlets. The system has the advantage of maximizing profits on a relatively small investment of capital. The Benetton image is something of a cross between trendy boutique and large-scale producer. The apparel line has lost some of its appeal in recent years, prompting the family to diversify into unrelated areas of business, including telecommunications and the operation of toll roads. Benetton's success

in the apparel line has reinforced Italy's image as a fashion and design leader.

Bentinck, William (1774–1839)
(Lord William H. Cavendish Bentinck)
British diplomat and adviser to the Bourbon monarchy in Sicily, governor-general of India

Lord William Bentinck arrived in Sicily as British envoy in July 1811. The court of FERDINAND IV had settled in Palermo after being driven from the mainland by the French armies of NAPOLEON I. Bentinck, who had previously served as military commander and governor in India, was a blunt, soldierly type who did not hesitate to pressure the king and his entourage into adopting policies deemed desirable by the British. Bentinck, a Whig, was very much in favor of limited, constitutional monarchy. It was at Bentinck's insistence that Ferdinand issued the so-called Sicilian constitution of 1812, which provided for an elected legislature with the power to tax, gave voting rights to the wealthy, and abolished feudal privileges dear to the nobility. The constitution appealed to the liberal nobility of the island, but was resented by the court and the conservative nobility. Its acceptance changed the nature of the anti-Napoleonic struggle from conservative reaction to liberal reform. Bentinck also seems to have entertained the possibility that Sicily could become a British possession. Nevertheless, his reforms encouraged Italian patriots to expect some form of Italian independence from the British. They were soon disillusioned. The conservative British government removed Bentinck from Sicily in July 1814, disavowed his liberal policies, and acquiesced to Austrian dominance in Italy. In 1816 Ferdinand IV abolished the Sicilian constitution and made Sicily a province of the KINGDOM OF THE TWO SICILIES. The Sicilian constitution of 1812 was a model for moderate liberals in the RISORGIMENTO.

Bentivoglio family See BOLOGNA.

Berchet, Giovanni (1783–1851)
poet, patriot, and political exile

Berchet was born in Milan to a family of French-Swiss origin. Love of literature did not mix easily with his duties as a government clerk and he soon gave up the security of steady employment. Familiar with European writers, he translated into Italian modern British and German authors of the romantic school. His pamphlet entitled *Semiserious Letter by Chrysosthom to his Son* (1816) urged readers to pay attention to what was happening abroad in order to renew Italian culture, in the good-humored tone of a father giving advice to a son. Berchet saw Italy as part of the European cultural mainstream, but he also argued for the distinctive character of Italian culture within the framework of European letters. He did not limit himself to writing, but also took part in political conspiracies, and fled abroad after the REVOLUTION of 1821 to avoid arrest. He lived seven years in London working as a bank clerk and writing the romantic verses that gave him fame as a writer and patriot. During the revolutions of 1848 Berchet was a member of the provisional government of Lombardy and supported union with the KINGDOM OF SARDINIA. He found refuge in Piedmont after the revolution and served briefly in the Piedmontese parliament. Hardly read today and all but forgotten by literary critics, Berchet was an important figure in his time.

Berio, Luciano (1925–2003)
prolific and innovative avant-garde composer

Born in the Ligurian coastal town of Oneglia to a family of professional musicians, Berio studied music at the Milan Conservatory (1945–50). His fellow students included the American soprano Cathy Berberian, whom he married in 1950, and who influenced him to adopt modernist idioms. Berio quickly made a name for himself as an innovative composer open to new ideas. In the 1950s he pioneered in the use of electronic instruments and experimented with 12-tone music. His first composition for the stage was

Passaggio (1963), which premiered at the Piccola Scala of Milan. Its expression of the social pressures at work on its sole female character was indicative of the political tone of Berio's early works. His later works lost much of their political immediacy and were more introspective and lyrical. His musical idiom is a synthesis of the contemporary and the traditional, showing the influence of composers as different as CLAUDIO MONTEVERDI, GIUSEPPE VERDI, and Igor Stravinsky. In addition to instrumental music, Berio also wrote for the voice on texts by contemporary authors such as UMBERTO ECO. He traveled and worked extensively abroad, including the United States, where he lived for many years. He taught at Tanglewood and the Julliard School, where he founded the Julliard Ensemble and took up conducting. He returned to Italy in 1972 and established his own school of music in Florence in 1980. On television and in concerts, he has tried to interest popular audiences in contemporary music. Perhaps the best example of his style is the five-movement work for orchestra and voices entitled *Sinfonia* (1967–68). With an international following among devotees of avant-garde music, Berio is regarded as Italy's major postwar composer.

Berlinguer, Enrico (1922–1984)
Communist Party leader and reformer
Berlinguer, descended from a family of the Sardinian nobility, rose through the ranks of the Italian Communist Party (PCI) after joining its youth section in 1943. In 1945 he became a member of the party's central committee and was elected to parliament in 1968. He succeeded LUIGI LONGO as general secretary of the party in 1972 and held that top post until his death. He steered the party through a particularly difficult period marked by political terrorism, labor unrest, and a changing international situation. Domestically, he pursued the HISTORIC COMPROMISE with the dominant Christian Democratic Party (DC), distanced his party from extra-parliamentary and terrorist groups, reaffirmed the

party's commitment to parliamentary democracy, and sought to contain labor unrest. Internationally, he broke with the Soviet Union by embracing EUROCOMMUNISM, favoring European economic integration, and accepting NATO. In the late 1970s, following the assassination of ALDO MORO, faced by public rejection of TERRORISM and electoral losses for his party, he adopted a more confrontational attitude toward the Christian Democrats, which effectively ended the historic compromise. Berlinguer was widely respected for his personal and political integrity, but his policies were controversial within and outside his party, none more so than the strategy of sharing power with the Christian Democrats.

Berlusconi, Silvio (1936–)
media tycoon and political leader
Born in Milan, the son of a bank employee, Berlusconi attended Catholic schools and earned a law degree from the University of Milan. His enterprising spirit manifested itself when he helped pay his way through college by performing as a crooner on cruise ships. Business talent and good timing earned him a fortune in real estate deals in the 1960s. He took advantage of state deregulation of the television industry in the 1970s to develop a network of private stations that today controls about 80 percent of the commercial market. His vast fortune, estimated at about $12 billion in 2001, also rests on ownership or control of a vast media empire that includes newspapers, magazines, advertising agencies, and the AC Milan soccer team. He turned to politics in the 1980s as a political protégé of Socialist Party leader BETTINO CRAXI, but, in addition to his media empire, his rise was also aided by the political scandals of the early 1990s that ended Craxi's career and brought down the old political establishment. In 1993 Berlusconi launched his own political party, named FORZA ITALIA. In 1994 he headed a short-lived coalition government that collapsed after only seven months in power. Berlusconi then headed the parliamentary opposition to the center-left gov-

ernments. In the elections of May 2001 he campaigned largely on his image as a "can-do" businessman, promised to eliminate waste and corruption in government, modernize public services, fight crime, curb illegal immigration, and give the country greater international visibility and a stronger role in NATO and the EUROPEAN UNION. He capitalized on his image as a political outsider. His inventive campaign ploys included signing a formal contract with the voters to deliver on his promises and mailing a glossy biography of himself to millions of households. His image apparently appealed particularly to a younger generation of middle-class voters attracted by the promises of economic progress and prosperity, and motivated by a patriotic fervor similar to the enthusiasm of sport fans for their favorite team. The second coalition government that he formed in June 2001 has been much more durable than the first. Berlusconi shows amazing resilience in the face of attacks that would doom less resourceful politicians. He faces opposition for his pro-business policies, strong identification with American foreign policies, attempts to cut government spending, particularly in the sensitive area of pension benefits, and in the courts for alleged bribery of public officials by him or his subordinates in business. His second government was still in power in April 2004.

Berni, Francesco (1497–1545)
writer

Born in Tuscany, Berni is remembered as the writer of witty, satirical verse written in Roman dialect. His association with Rome came from his years in the service of prelates in that city. Berni's verse appealed to the contemporary taste for the paradoxical use of highly polished language that praised the unexpected or cast ridicule on prominent people and events. Berni's language was down to earth, often to the point of vulgarity and indecency. The realism of his writings contrasts with the lyricism traceable to the influence of PETRARCH. Because of that contrast, Berni is seen as representing the anti-lyrical and antisentimental strain of the Italian literary tradition. His reworking of Matteo Maria Boiardo's unfinished epic poem *Orlando innammorato* was even more popular than the original. Berni dubbed his own style of writing *poesia bernesca*, and the label has been applied to a vast body of 16th- and 17th-century burlesque literature that satirizes ideals and idealists. He did not live without risk, and may have died poisoned by a victim of his wit.

Bernini, Gian Lorenzo (1598–1680)
sculptor, architect, and painter

The leading artist of the Italian BAROQUE was born in Naples, the son of a Florentine father who was also a sculptor and a Neapolitan mother. Contemporaries remarked that his art combined the meticulous craftsmanship of Tuscany with the love of gesture and emotionality of Naples. His artistic talent manifested itself early in life. His earliest surviving sculptures, from around 1615, showing the influence of ancient Greek and Roman models, reveal his ability to render the human body with anatomical precision while also imparting to his figures a sense of motion and emotional dynamism. Gesture, passion, and emotional intensity were the dominant traits of his mature art, which strives to make a strong impression, and to capture and hold the attention of the viewer. Bernini worked in Rome for most of his life. There, his talent can be admired in the design of churches, fountains, statues, and public monuments. His patrons included the BORGHESE FAMILY and several popes. Among his more notable works are the Cathedra Petri, which enshrines Saint Peter's seat inside Saint Peter's Basilica, and the colonnade embracing Saint Peter's Square. Perhaps his best-known and most discussed statue is the Ecstasy of Saint Teresa in the Church of Santa Maria della Vittoria. The Triton Fountain in Piazza Barberini and the Fountain of the Four Rivers in Piazza Navona are his most celebrated outdoor compositions. Bernini is noted for his successful integration of sculpture and architecture. As the papacy's official artist, his influence was felt throughout the Catholic world, making him the most ubiquitous and influential figure of the baroque style. Celebrated as an unparalleled genius in his lifetime, his reputation suffered at the hands of later critics, including classicists and contemporary functionalists who object to the rhetorical, extroverted character of his works.

Bertani, Agostino (1812–1886)
leader of the radical opposition before and after national unification

This energetic and tireless RISORGIMENTO figure was born to a prominent Milanese family, practiced medicine and surgery, and was irresistibly drawn to politics. After traveling abroad to perfect his medical skills, Bertani fought on the barricades during the Five Days of Milan in the REVOLUTIONS of 1848. When the revolution was suppressed in Milan Bertani moved on to organize medical services for the revolutionaries in Rome. A convinced republican, Bertani formed a strong attachment to GIUSEPPE MAZZINI. Throughout the 1850s, while Mazzini was in London, Bertani organized support for him in Genoa and founded sharpshooting clubs to train patriots for war. In 1859 he organized medical assistance for the volunteers fighting for GIUSEPPE GARIBALDI. He also joined Garibaldi's expedition to Sicily in 1860, when he favored prolonging the military campaign to take Rome from the pope. In the national parliament (1860–80, 1880–82) he was a vocal critic of both the HISTORICAL RIGHT and the LIBERAL LEFT. During the campaign against BRIGANDAGE in the South, Bertani criticized the government and the army for the use of arbitrary and excessive force. At his insistence the government began an investigation of the living conditions of workers and peasants tied to the investigation headed by STEFANO JACINI into the conditions of agriculture. Bertani carried on his opposition in the halls of parliament, condemned recourse to political violence, and rejected social-

ism, which he saw as a threat to the state and national unity.

Bertolucci, Bernardo (1940–   )
film director and screenwriter

Bertolucci was born in Parma to a family that encouraged the boy's artistic interests. His father was a poet, film critic, and art history professor. The son started out as a writer with the publication of *In cerca di mistero* (In search of mystery, 1960), a book of poetry. His career in film began while he attended the University of Rome (1958–61) as assistant director to PIER PAOLO PASOLINI. Bertolucci left the university without graduating to pursue filmmaking independently. His first successful feature film, *Prima della rivoluzione* (Before the revolution, 1964), inspired by Stendhal's novel *The Charterhouse of Parma,* displayed the distinguishing characteristics of his style: sensitivity to personal drama and psychological tension, portrayed against a broad social canvas that adds poignancy and historical significance to the personal situations of his characters. His work suggests an intellectual debt to Italy's operatic tradition and to the more recent and fashionable influences of Sigmund Freud and Karl Marx. After a pause of six years attributable to fund-raising difficulties, Bertolucci produced *La strategia del ragno* (The spider's strategy, 1970). This film, inspired by a short story by Jorge Luis Borges, traces a son's investigation of his father's murder by Fascists, expecting to find out about his father's anti-Fascist past, only to discover that his father had been a Fascist informer executed by his own friends to preserve his good name as an anti-Fascist. *Il conformista* (The conformist, 1971), based on the novel by ALBERTO MORAVIA, is regarded as Bertolucci's masterpiece. Set against the backdrop of Fascist Italy, it tells the story of a young man from a wealthy family who goes along with fascism to hide his own sense of insecurity and resolve his own personal conflicts. *Ultimo tango a Parigi* (Last tango in Paris, 1972), Bertolucci's most controversial film, is often denounced as obscene because of its depiction of sexual politics. Its tremendous success worldwide established Bertolucci as a major cinematic presence and gave him freedom to pursue projects of his own liking at a leisurely pace. *Novecento* (1900, 1976) was an almost six-hour-long epic that resorts to Freudian and Marxist insights to illuminate the transition from liberalism to fascism and ends in 1945 with the triumph of socialism in Bertolucci's Po Valley. Bertolucci again captured worldwide attention wth the filming of *The Last Emperor* (1987), his last major success. The winner of many Academy Awards, this film tells the story of the last Chinese emperor Pu Yi, who began as a child ruler and ended his life working as a gardener in communist China. Bertolucci's career connects the Italian postwar cinematic tradition, with its focus on the personal, intimate, and small-scale, with the American and international preference for the epic, grandiose spectacle, and striking visual effects.

Betti, Ugo (1892–1953)
playwright
Betti's reputation as a writer rests on his works for the stage. As a dramatist, he can be ranked next to LUIGI PIRANDELLO. Betti was born in the university town of Camerino, studied law, and began writing in his spare time in the 1920s while pursuing a career as a judge. He wrote steadily and his plays were performed in the 1930s; he received prizes for his work, and showed no discernible political inclinations. He was one of many artists who found it possible to express himself and pursue his intellectual interests within the fairly broad parameters of artistic license allowed by the Fascist regime. A strong moralistic tone pervades his plays, in which characters wrestle with questions of conscience. It has been suggested that his experiences on the bench made him aware of the complexities of human relationships and account for his concern with issues of individual responsibility, guilt, and atonement. Such concerns also reflect his ongoing consideration of religion and the attendant issues of free will, forgiveness, and

redemption. Betti's reputation as a dramatist rose appreciably after WORLD WAR II. In the climate of Christian Democracy that prevailed after 1945, Betti openly embraced Catholicism and the church. Italian critics have tended to ignore or minimize Betti's work. He is better known and appreciated in the Anglo-Saxon world, where his moralizing tendencies strike a chord with audiences. Several of his 27 plays have been translated into English.

Bianchi, Michele See FASCISM.

Bianco di Saint-Jorioz, Count Carlo (1795–1843)
military writer and political conspirator
Born to a noble family of Piedmont, orphaned at an early age, Bianco studied law at the University of Turin, then pursued a military career, rising to the rank of captain in the elite regiment of the king's dragoons. His republican sentiments drew him toward the SECRET SOCIETIES that rose in Piedmont after 1815. Compromised by his role in the REVOLUTION of 1821, he escaped to Spain, where he fought for the liberal cause in the 1820s, then found refuge in Gibraltar, Greece, and MALTA. In Malta he wrote and published his treatise *Della guerra nazionale d'insurrezione per bande* (On the national war of insurrection by bands, 1828), which became a classic text for conspirators in the European underground. Regarded as a fundamental text of guerrilla warfare, Bianco's book explained how the tactics of irregular warfare could defeat regular armies. Political assassination, physical intimidation, acts of terrorism and sabotage like the poisoning of water supplies, and hit-and-run raids against designated targets were among the tactics that Bianco considered legitimate in wars of national liberation. In 1831 Bianco linked up with GIUSEPPE MAZZINI and FILIPPO MICHELE BUONARROTI. Both expected that Bianco, as head of the secret military society of the Apofasimeni (Those Who Have Vowed to Die), would recruit

and train conspirators for their respective projects of insurrection. But Bianco was better as a theoretician than as an organizer or field commander. Bianco committed suicide and very little came of his efforts in the short run. But his ideas lived on in the Italian revolutionary tradition. His conceptualization of "war by bands" had an impact on Mazzini, CARLO PISACANE, ANARCHISM, and 20th-century terrorist groups like the RED BRIGADES.

Biblioteca Italiana (La)   See JOURNALISM.

Binda, Alfredo   See SPORT.

birth control

Italian birthrates, once among the highest in Europe, have declined steadily since the mid-19th century. That decline suggests that Italians have practiced birth control regardless of religious injunctions and public controversy. The decline has affected all parts of the country, but national averages do obscure significant regional variations. Birthrates remain higher in the South than in the North and rural families tend to be larger than urban families. Still, the gap in birthrates between North and South, between urban and rural, and between the middle and working classes is closing. Families of small landowners have long had the lowest birthrates. Surveys indicate that lacking easy access to contraceptives, Italian couples have limited the number of children by other means. The campaign to legalize the sale and distribution of contraceptives and introduce sex education in the schools encountered the opposition of the CATHOLIC CHURCH. It should also be pointed out that the pro-natal policies of the Fascist regime left behind legislation that banned the sale and distribution of contraceptives. After 1945, governments dominated by the Christian Democratic Party (DC) generally adhered to church policy on birth control and sex education. Opposition to

restrictions on birth control came from the parties of the Left and their subsidiary organizations. The Unione Donne Italiane (UDI) and other feminist organizations campaigned vigorously for lifting restrictions. The sale of contraceptives and dissemination of birth control information were legalized in 1971. Legislation providing for family-planning clinics passed in 1975. The battle to legalize and facilitate birth control intersects historically and ideologically with the concurrent struggle to legalize ABORTION. Individual choices, social trends, and legislative policies have given Italy one of the lowest birth rates in the world. In 1995–2000 the population grew by less than 1 percent; in 2002 women had a fertility rate of only 1.2, and the crude birthrate stood at 8.5 per 1,000 (lower than the death rate of 10.3 per 1,000). At the start of the 21st century Italy faces the prospects of a rapidly aging population and population decline.

Bissolati, Leonida   (1857–1920)
moderate socialist, journalist, and government minister

A founding member of the Italian Socialist Party (PSI), Bissolati made his political debut as a republican after completing law studies at the University of Bologna. His interest in social problems drew him to socialism as an organizer of agricultural workers and journalists. From 1896 to 1903, and again from 1908 to 1910, he was editor in chief of the party newspaper *Avanti!*. From his first election to parliament in 1897, Bissolati worked to win more electoral support for the party and greater leverage in parliament. The revolutionary wing of the party, and even many moderates, opposed his policy of collaboration with Prime Minister GIOVANNI GIOLITTI. His support of the government's foreign policy and his vote in favor of military spending for the ITALIAN-TURKISH WAR further isolated him. Expelled from the Socialist Party in 1912, Bissolati founded the Socialist Reformist Party, which won little voter support. Bissolati at first favored Italian neutrality in WORLD WAR I, then opted for Italian intervention on the side of England and France. At age 57 he volunteered for military duty, served on the frontline, and was wounded. In 1917 he became minister for military affairs in the government of national unity headed by PAOLO BOSELLI. Bissolati favored a policy of friendly relations with the Slavic nationalities of the former Austrian Empire and opposed the annexation of ethnic minorities. Differences with the government on these and other issues led to his resignation as minister for military affairs in December 1918. In the politically surcharged atmosphere of the postwar years, Bissolati became a highly controversial figure reviled by extremists of the Left and Right. BENITO MUSSOLINI cast him in the role of national villain, although he made partial amends after Bissolati's death. Bissolati was a voice of reason and moderation that was drowned out by raging political passions.

Bixio, Gerolamo (1821–1873)
(Nino)
*conspirator in the fight for national
unification, political and military figure*
This Genoese patriot, an adventurous daredevil to an extreme, loved the sea and military combat in about equal measure. Born to a family of liberal sentiments, he sailed at an early age, enrolled in the Sardinian navy, and left it to roam the Indian Ocean, eventually finding his way back to Genoa by sailing around the world. An active conspirator, he organized republican elements in Genoa in the 1840s. In the REVOLUTION of 1848 he fought with GIUSEPPE GARIBALDI and was seriously wounded in Rome in 1849. He went back to the sea in the 1850s, fought again with Garibaldi in 1859, and played a major role at his side in the Sicilian campaign of 1860 as second in command, and was again wounded in combat. Admitted to the regular army, he rose to the rank of general. He commanded troops in 1866 against Austria and in the taking of Rome in 1870. Bixio, an irascible and intemperate

commander, often acted impetuously, offended many, and stood in awe only of Garibaldi. He showed a more moderate side of his personality as a member of the first Italian parliament after 1860 when he tried to mediate the conflict between Garibaldi and CAVOUR and reconcile moderates and democrats. He was appointed senator in 1870, but impatient with political maneuverings and unsuccessful in business, he returned to life on the sea. In 1872 he sailed with his own ship to the Indian Ocean in search of opportunities for Italian commercial expansion. It was his last adventure. He died in Malaysia, the victim of a cholera epidemic.

Black Shirts See FASCISM.

Blasetti, Alessandro (1900–1987)
film critic and director
The most innovative and successful film director of the Fascist period was born in Rome, received a law degree, but turned his attention to the new field of film criticism. From the columns of *Cinematografo*, the review that he founded in 1926, Blasetti called for revitalizing the Italian film industry, which had declined from its prewar position of eminence. Starting with the film *Sole* (Sun, 1929), now almost entirely lost, he began to treat topical themes approved by the regime in a true-to-life style that critics say anticipated postwar cinematic NEOREALISM. *Sole* presented one of the regime's proudest achievements, the draining of the Pontine marshes, as a victory of willpower over the forces of inertia. In *Terra madre* (Mother Earth, 1930), Blasetti made peasants the heroes of his story, glorified life on the land, and presented urban life as corrupting and enervating. In *1860* (1932), Blasetti tackled the story of Italian unification from the perspective of a Sicilian peasant couple (played by real peasants) who expect social justice from the movement for national unification. *Vecchia guardia* (The old guard, 1934) idealized Fascists "of the first hour" who had taken to the streets to save

the country from communism. With the exception of *Vecchia guardia,* Blasetti did not trumpet the messages of Fascist propaganda. His seems to have been more a case of spontaneous identification with the regime. His films were all the more effective, and undeniably popular, for their understated manner and the documentary filming techniques. Blasetti's style began to change in the late 1930s when his films turned to look at the historical past, employed costumed actors in baroque settings, and strove for spectacular effects. He survived the fall of the Fascist regime and continued to make films that had some commercial success. *Europa di notte* (Europe by night, 1958) and *Io amo, tu ami* (I love, you love, 1961), catered to the erotic interests of audiences, using fiction to look at sexual mores.

Boccaccio, Giovanni (1313–1375)
writer and scholar, precursor of humanist culture

The writer who is acknowledged as the father of Italian prose was born either in Florence or Certaldo. He was the illegitimate son of a merchant who acknowledged his paternity, accepted him into the family, and trained him for a career in trade and banking. In 1327 the young Boccaccio accompanied his father to Naples and worked there with him for the next 13 years. The son's literary vocation and scholarly interests manifested themselves fully during the years of his adolescence in Naples, as did his youthful exuberance, pursuit of worldly pleasures, and social ambitions. Boccaccio was accepted in court circles and hobnobbed with the city's young aristocrats. Fiammetta, the young woman with whom he fell in love and who appears idealized in several of his writings, may have been the illegitimate daughter of Naples's King Robert (1309–43). His familiarity with merchants and aristocrats may explain Boccaccio's admiration for the feudal concept of honor and merchant-like concern for the concrete and palpable. The tension between commercial endeavor and gentlemanly detachment manifests itself in many of his writings. His most important work of the Neapolitan period is the long prose narrative entitled the *Filocolo* (1336–38). It tells the story of the young prince Florio and his impoverished sweetheart Biancifiore. In love since childhood, they are separated and eventually reunited. The story narrates Florio's long and trying quest for his lost love, their reunion, conversion to Christianity, and marriage. The conventional plot, clearly derived from medieval sources, is enlivened by episodes and description that ring true to life. The story shows Boccaccio's talent for storytelling and for depicting places, passions, and incidents with an eye for their diversity and uniqueness.

Boccaccio's return to Florence in 1341 opened a less happy period of his life. Civil strife, war, and economic crisis threatened the city. Florence nevertheless provided him with many opportunities to mingle with learned scholars and creative artists. The most important and lasting connection of his Florentine years was with the poet PETRARCH, whom Boccaccio admired above all his contemporaries. Inspiration also came to him from two other figures of the recent past, Giotto and DANTE. Giotto he admired for the realism of his figures and Dante for his pursuit of eternal ideals. The outbreak of the plague in 1348 compounded Florence's problems (in two years the epidemic carried off about two-thirds of the population). It also provided Boccaccio with the occasion to write the masterpiece of his life. The *Decameron,* written around 1350, imagines a group of 10 young men and women who take refuge in the countryside to escape the epidemic. To pass away the time, they take turns telling tales. The book's 100 tales range far and wide in tone and topic. The influence of traditional chivalric literature is evident, but the tone is strikingly new. Human vices and the pleasures of the flesh are abundantly depicted, but so are bravery and generosity. The stories illustrate the acquisitive ethic of the merchant class, the innocence of youth, the egoism of old age, the corruption of the clergy, and the chivalric code of the aristocracy.

His contemporaries did not immediately appreciate Boccaccio's versatility and genius. They tended rather to condemn the bawdiness of the tales, the irreverence, and the apparent refusal to pass judgment on immoral behavior. A closer reading might have revealed embedded in the very structure of the book the same striving for eternal truth that Boccaccio admired in Dante. It was for later generations of readers to appreciate the *Decameron*'s originality, its rich gallery of characters, and its thoroughly secular spirit. In that sense, Boccaccio can be seen as a major precursor and inspirer of the culture of HUMANISM. His influence reached far and wide, as evident in Chaucer's *Canterbury Tales.* In his final years, grossly overweight and infirm, Boccaccio sought peace and solitude in Certaldo. He left his ancestral town reluctantly, when the Florentine government entrusted him with some mission. By putting his experience and learning at the service of the state, Boccaccio exemplified another characteristic of humanism: the ideal of the informed citizen active in the public arena.

Bocchini, Arturo (1880–1940)
Fascist chief of police

While keeping a low public profile as chief of police (1926–40), Bocchini was largely responsible for creating and operating the repressive apparatus of the Fascist regime. Born in the southern province of Benevento, he graduated from the University of Naples in 1902 with a law degree, and took on an entry-level position in the interior ministry the following year. He moved gradually and methodically up the ladder, gaining complete mastery of the administration, until BENITO MUSSOLINI appointed him chief of police in September 1926. The choice reflected Mussolini's preference for dealing with functionaries rather than party zealots. Bocchini's appointment coincided with the reorganization of the state that came in the wake of the MATTEOTTI crisis. Bocchini provided better training and pay for police officers, introduced uniform criteria for appointment and advancement,

and coordinated the activities of the various security services. He took full advantage of the laws that expanded the powers of the police, assuring Mussolini the complete loyalty of the forces, organizing a nationwide system of informers, nipping political opposition in the bud with preventive arrests, and reporting directly to Mussolini on a daily basis. Such access to the ultimate source of authority inevitably aroused opposition from party figures who obstructed and criticized him, to little effect. Mussolini relied on information received from Bocchini to gauge the state of public opinion. Bocchini kept the Duce's confidence by observing his general directives and telling him what he thought he wanted to hear. When he disagreed with policy decisions, as he apparently did in the case of anti-Semitic legislation, he did not question them in principle, but did what he could to delay or dilute their application. He died unexpectedly in office in November 1940 after having put the police on a war footing. Bocchini made discreet use of police powers, but ubiquitous informers, preventive measures, and frequent arrests created a climate of intimidation that frightened people into political acquiescence. The popular consensus behind the regime owed much to Bocchini's discreet and efficient use of police powers.

Boccioni, Umberto (1882–1916)
futurist painter and sculptor

The son of a civil servant, Boccioni was born in Reggio Emilia but moved frequently as a child as his father was posted to different places. In 1897 he graduated from a technical school in Catania, moved to Rome in 1901, and began his artistic career painting commercial posters. In 1906 he visited Paris and traveled to Russia. In 1907 he settled in Milan, where he met FILIPPO TOMMASO MARINETTI, the founder of the futurist movement. Like all futurists, Boccioni wanted to break decisively with tradition, but stood out for his exceptionally innovative techniques and for his ability to articulate the intentions of the cultural revolution of FUTURISM. The new art was to be dynamic, reflecting the restlessness of the machine age and the excitement of industrial society. His essays on painting and sculpture became basic texts of the new art, while his works conveyed the excitement of experimentation. Objects were barely recognizable, shapes became all important, tumultuous movement and blurring of lines and colors dominated the canvases. Boccioni welcomed the advent of war in 1914, campaigned for Italy's participation in the conflict, and volunteered for military service in May 1915 when Italy went to war. He died in the army, the victim of a horse-riding accident.

Bodio, Luigi See STATISTICS.

Boiardo, Matteo See ARIOSTO, LUDOVICO; PANIZZI, ANTONIO.

Boito, Arrigo See SCAPIGLIATURA.

Bologna, city of

Bologna (pop. 381,000), the capital city of the EMILIA-ROMAGNA region, lies in the Po Valley at the foot of the APENNINES. The Etruscans founded it in the sixth century B.C. and called it Felsina. Gauls took it over two centuries later, and then came the Romans who called it Bonomia. Byzantines, Lombards, and Franks ruled it successively after the collapse of Roman administration in the fifth century. The founding of its famous university, the oldest in Europe, around 1088 made the city an international center of learning, a distinction that it still retains. Bologna was one of the first cities to be organized as an independent commune in 1144. In the following centuries the town was torn by the factional conflicts between Guelfs and Ghibellines that afflicted most Italian cities. Ruled intermittently by the Bentivoglio family from 1401 to 1512, it became part of the PAPAL STATES in the 16th century. The city remained under papal rule until

1860 when it became part of the kingdom of Italy. Its diversified and prosperous economy combines agriculture, industry, commerce, and tourism. Small and medium-sized firms dominate the industrial sector, producing shoes, textiles, chemicals, and food products. Bologna is renowned for its rich cuisine, which has earned it the name, *Bologna la Grassa* (Bologna the Fat). Considered a model city for the efficiency and comprehensiveness of its public services, it was the boast of the Italian Communist Party (PCI) that administered it for many decades after 1945.

Bonaparte, Joseph (1768–1844)
king of Naples (1806–1808) and Spain (1808–1813)

Accepting the crowns of Naples and Spain to please his younger brother NAPOLEON I, Joseph (Giuseppe) had little of his brother's enthusiasm for military glory. Handsome, charming, intellectually alive, and receptive to new ideas, Joseph was easygoing and of moderate temperament. Napoleon relied on him because he was genuinely fond of his brother and knew that he could trust him. He made Joseph king of Naples, expecting no military help from the Neapolitans but wanting to use the southern Italian kingdom as a source of revenue and as a base for his Mediterranean policy. Joseph had studied at the University of Pisa, knew Italy well, and governed more independently than his brother expected. He organized the government with ministries along French lines, abolished feudalism, shut down religious organizations that performed no useful social function, reorganized government finances, improved the collection of taxes, reduced the public debt, and introduced military conscription. Implementation of these reforms was slow and gradual because Joseph did not want to alarm the powerful nobility and clergy. The nobility were to be fully compensated for the loss of feudal rights and would retain ownership of most of the land. Many religious communities were spared, Neapolitans were appointed to important positions in the government, and military conscription was light. Joseph also resisted his brother's exorbitant demands for money. He resented the restrictions that the Continental System placed on free trade, did what he could to enforce the system, but was unable to stop contraband and illicit trade. Joseph ruled by decree without a parliament, but shortly before becoming king of Spain in 1808 he issued a constitution that provided for limited representation. JOACHIM MURAT, Joseph's successor in Naples, showed more interested in military matters than government administration. Joseph's policies were popular with some reform-minded members of the aristocracy and middle classes. Later in the 19th century, the policies of Joseph and Murat became reference points for moderate liberals who wanted change without revolution.

Bonaparte, Napoleon See NAPOLEON I.

Bonaparte family (Buonaparte family)

The precise place of origin of the Bonaparte (or Buonaparte) family is unclear, but in all likelihood they migrated from Tuscany or Liguria to Corsica in the 16th century, settling in the capital city of Ajaccio. A family of some influence, they received patents of nobility from the grand duke of Tuscany in 1757 and 1759. For a time, family members sported their noble status by signing themselves de Buonaparte. Carlo Bonaparte (1746–85) studied law in Pisa, and married Letizia Ramolino in 1764. They had 13 children, eight of whom survived: JOSEPH (born 1768), NAPOLEON (born 1769), Lucien (born 1775), Elisa (born 1777), Louis (born 1778), Pauline (born 1780), who married into the BORGHESE FAMILY, Caroline (born 1782), who married JOACHIM MURAT, and Jerome (born 1784). The family supported PASQUALE PAOLI's struggle for Corsican independence from the republic of GENOA, and from France after the Genoese ceded the island to the French in 1768. However, the family quickly seized the opportunities brought by

French rule. The young Napoleon was able to attend the French military academy at Saint-Cyr thanks to a scholarship that the French government made available to impoverished members of the nobility. Joseph became king of Naples, ELISA (who married FELICE BACIOCCHI) was princess of Lucca and Tuscany. The Bonapartes were active in Italian affairs in the 19th century after the defeat of Napoleon, including Carlo Luciano, prince of Canino (1803–57), a son of Lucien, who sided with the revolutionaries in Venice and Rome in 1848–49, Napoleon Joseph, nicknamed Plon-Plon (1822–91), son of Jerome, who married the daughter of King VICTOR EMMANUEL II, and Louis Napoleon, the future NAPOLEON III, who was a political conspirator in Italy in the 1830s.

Bonghi, Ruggero (1826–1895)
(or Ruggiero)
journalist and political figure

Born in Naples, Bonghi studied law, philosophy, and classical languages, identified with no particular school of thought, and displayed intellectual independence throughout his career as a journalist, political commentator, and member of parliament. Politically liberal in his youth, he was a revolutionist in 1848, and a political exile in Turin in the 1850s. CAVOUR encouraged him to return to Naples in 1860 to influence public opinion in favor of the national government. Bonghi was elected to parliament in 1861, founded the Turin newspaper *La Stampa* in 1862, held various academic appointments at the universities of Naples, Pavia, and Turin teaching law, history, and philosophy. In parliament he sat with the HISTORICAL RIGHT and served as minister of public education (1874–76). He showed a particular interest in the ROMAN QUESTION, which he would have liked to see settled on terms favorable to the state. He believed that civil life had to rest on a strong religious foundation, but he was anticlerical enough to want government controls on the power of the clergy. His goal was an alliance of CHURCH AND STATE against the forces of materialism and socialism, which he saw as a mounting threat in the last years of his life. Bonghi was a severe critic of the LIBERAL LEFT after it came to power in 1876. He criticized the TRIPLE ALLIANCE, the governments of FRANCESCO CRISPI and GIOVANNI GIOLITTI, and campaigned for a strong Italian cultural presence abroad. He was a founder of the DANTE ALIGHIERI SOCIETY for the promotion of Italian language and culture. Bonghi looked upon politics as the active pursuit of values and ideals, and a form of cultural war.

Boniface VIII See COLONNA FAMILY; DANTE ALIGHIERI.

Bonino, Emma See RADICAL PARTY.

Bonomelli, Geremia See SCALABRINI, GIOVANNI BATTISTA.

Bonomi, Ivanoe (1873–1951)
moderate socialist prime minister
The political career of this social democratic leader spanned 60 years from the early 1890s to his death. Born in Mantua, Bonomi studied and practiced law. He became a socialist activist in his 20s as an organizer of farm workers. Closely identified with the reformist politics of FILIPPO TURATI, Bonomi sought to address social issues by parliamentary action. His book *Le vie nuove del socialismo* (The news ways of socialism, 1907) made a case for the revisionist policy of legality and collaboration with progressive groups outside the socialist camp. In 1912 he was expelled from the Italian Socialist Party (PSI) for his refusal to follow the party line of opposition to the ITALIAN-TURKISH WAR. With LEONIDA BISSOLATI he founded the moderate Socialist Reformist Party, which gathered little support. Becoming progressively more nationalist, Bonomi served as minister of public works (1916–17, 1919) and minister of war (1920–21). As prime minister

(July 1921–February 1922), he negotiated the TREATY OF RAPALLO. During the Fascist period (1922–43) Bonomi retired to private life, practiced law, and wrote scholarly works on Italian foreign policy and the national unification movement. The regime did not disturb him. In 1942–43 he formed and led a coalition of anti-Fascist parliamentarians but avoided involvement in the RESISTANCE. As prime minister from June 1944 to June 1945 he persuaded the Allies to give Italy the status of cobelligerent against Germany and restore Italian administration in occupied provinces. At the time of his death he was serving as president of the senate (1948–51). Bonomi lacked political charisma but was respected for his personal tact, diplomatic skills, and deep understanding of the country's problems.

Bonomi, Paolo See COLDIRETTI.

Bontempelli, Massimo See NOVECENTO MOVEMENT.

Bordiga, Amadeo (1889–1970)
Communist Party founder and leader
This prominent Marxist theoretician and political figure, born in Naples, was among the socialist dissidents who left the Italian Socialist Party (PSI) in 1921 to found the Communist Party of Italy, precursor of the Italian Communist Party (PCI), and served as its first secretary. The success of Lenin's Bolshevik faction in Russia in 1917 confirmed Bordiga's belief that only a highly disciplined and ideologically uncompromising political party could lead the working class to a successful revolution. He rejected parliamentary politics, grassroots organizations, the factory councils advocated by ANTONIO GRAMSCI, and the notion of revolutionary spontaneity among workers. Arrested and confined by the Fascist regime, he was allowed to practice his profession as an engineer after being released in 1930. Bordiga dropped out of politics and was expelled

from the party, but his intellectual influence was still felt after 1945 by Marxists who rejected the Communist Party's line of accommodation with liberal democracy.

Borgese, Giuseppe Antonio
(1882–1952)
writer and literary critic

Born in Palermo, Borgese was initially drawn to the school of philosophical idealism headed by BENEDETTO CROCE, but soon joined the ranks of young intellectuals who rejected all rigid philosophies as culturally limiting and stifling. Borgese was attracted to German culture and taught German literature at the universities of Rome and Milan from 1910 to 1931. His interest in German culture had more to do with the appeal of ROMANTICISM than admiration for German militarism. He favored Italy's intervention in WORLD WAR I and headed the government's press and propaganda bureau from 1917 to 1919. He was a witness and participant in the political and ideological dilemmas of the postwar years. In his novel *Rubè*, published in 1938 but written in 1921, he portrayed the state of political confusion in the mind of its protagonist, who seems unable to choose between the extremes of socialism and fascism. Borgese rejected both. He lived in Italy until 1931, when he refused to take the oath of loyalty that the regime required of all university professors and left the country. In self-imposed exile in the United States, he taught at the New School for Social Research, Smith College, and the University of Chicago. In *Goliath: The March of Fascism* (1937), Borgese portrayed fascism as a cultural malady afflicting the petty bourgeoisie, which he saw as a sick class infected by nationalism and the Nietzschean cult of the superman. During WORLD WAR II Borgese was active in anti-Fascist politics. After the war he helped draft a constitution for a new world order based on economic justice, shared resources, and equal representation of the world's regions in an international organization having real power.

Borgese returned to Italy in 1948 and resumed his old chair of literature at the University of Milan.

Borghese, Prince Junio Valerio
(1906–1974)
naval officer and political figure

This member of the BORGHESE FAMILY carried on the family military tradition. His personal charisma, independence of mind, military professionalism, and ability to inspire loyalty suggest similarities with the Renaissance CONDOTTIERI of his ancestry. His well-planned attacks on ships supplying the anti-Franco forces during the Spanish civil war could not be publicized at the time because Italy was not officially at war, but they caught the attention of BENITO MUSSOLINI and gave Borghese access to Italy's highest military and political circles. He developed new techniques of naval attack using small submarines, torpedo boats (MAS), and human-guided torpedoes. During WORLD WAR II he led successful attacks with human-guided torpedoes against British ships in Gibraltar and Alexandria. After Italy's surrender to the Allies in September 1943, Borghese was among the few naval officers who sided with Mussolini and continued to fight against the Allies. As commander of the battalion *Decima Mas* he fought against Italian and Yugoslav partisans. His insistence on independent action led to his temporary arrest for insubordination, but he was too popular with the troops to be detained. The slogan of his corps was *Tutti per Junio, Junio per tutti* (All for Junio, Junio for all). His troops attempted to keep Tito's Yugoslav forces out of Italian territory. A tribunal sentenced him to 12 years in jail after the war, but he was released almost immediately. In postwar politics he was active in the neo-Fascist Italian Social Movement (MSI). In March 1971 he staged a coup against the government with a ragtag band of followers that was quickly dispersed. He fled to Spain to avoid arrest. His funeral in Rome brought out large numbers of personal admirers and political sympathizers. His book of memoirs covering the years 1935–43 was published in English under the title *Sea Devils* (1952).

Borghese family
family of the Roman aristocracy

This family of the Roman aristocracy traces its origins back to 13th-century Siena. They moved to Rome in the 16th century, gaining influence in the Catholic Church and the court of Spain. Camillo Borghese became Pope PAUL V; other family members were cardinals, senators, and soldiers. Marcantonio Borghese (1598–1658), nephew of Pope Paul V and the largest Roman landowner, received from the Spanish king the titles of prince and grandee of Spain. Breaking with the family tradition of loyalty to papacy and monarchy, Prince Camillo Borghese (1775–1832) sided with the JACOBINS in 1798 and supported the Napoleonic regime. He married Pauline Bonaparte (1780–1825), a sister of NAPOLEON I, at the emperor's request, became a general in the French army, and governor of Napoleon's Italian possessions. The Borghese did not support the movement for Italian unification and remained loyal to the PAPACY. They belonged to the so-called Black Aristocracy of Rome that made peace with the Italian state slowly and grudgingly. The family's monumental Palazzo Borghese, a splendid example of aristocratic architecture, was an exclusive meetingplace for national and international celebrities. The Borghese Museum and Gallery, open to the public, house the extensive art collections of the family.

Borgia family
family of Spanish origin connected to Italy through the papacy

The Borjas of Spain, having acquired notoriety beyond all proportion to their role in Italian history, continue to intrigue historians. The first member of the family to gain prominence was Cardinal Alonso de Borja, who became Pope Calixtus III (1455–58). Feeling isolated as a foreign pope and none too sure of the loyalty of his Roman subjects, Calixtus called many of his Catalan relatives to Rome, including his nephew Rodrigo Borjas who became Pope ALEXANDER VI in 1492.

Controversy surrounds Alexander VI and his two children, Cesare and Lucrezia Borgia, who are euphemistically described as the pope's "nephews." Cesare (1475–1507) was made bishop in 1492 and cardinal in 1493, but renounced the clerical life to pursue worldly goals and glory after his older brother was murdered in 1498. He led the military campaigns designed to consolidate papal rule in the Romagna region and against families of the Roman nobility unwilling to acknowledge papal authority. His considerable political and military skills brought him success in these campaigns. His reward was power and the title of duke of Romagna, bestowed on him by his father in 1501. Formally a papal vassal, Cesare set out to create a model state within the papal domain. He earned the gratitude of his subjects by suppressing BRIGANDAGE, establishing a popular militia, providing tax relief, and applying laws equitably. But his efforts to centralize power in his own hands and curb local autonomies and the privileges of powerful families encountered opposition, which Cesare could not overcome despite his well-deserved reputation for ruthlessness. Faced by internal revolts, by the opposition of King Louis XII of France who did not want to see a strong papal state, poor health, and undermined finally by the pope's premature death in 1503, Cesare's power began to unravel. Forced out of the PAPAL STATES, he fled to Naples, Spain, and Navarre. He was killed in battle fighting for the king of Navarre, who was his brother-in-law. NICCOLÒ MACHIAVELLI regarded Cesare as a model ruler defeated by bad luck, but posterity has viewed him rather as an excessively ambitious, unscrupulous, and cruel despot.

Cesare's sister Lucrezia (1480–1519) has acquired an unfounded reputation for deviousness, immorality, and sexual license. Her alleged proclivity for poisoning lovers and rivals has fueled endless stories. The record suggests a less lurid life. Brought up at the papal court and utterly loyal to her family, she was a pawn in the

An artist's depiction of Cesare Borgia (left) seated with Machiavelli *(Library of Congress)*

hands of her father and brother. Her three marriages were designed to further their political designs. With her third and final marriage (1501) into the ESTE FAMILY, she became duchess of Ferrara. She ruled capably and compassionately, attracted artists and writers of note to her court, and brought cultural distinction to the city. Her subjects mourned her death from complications following the birth of her seventh child. The unsavory reputation of Alexander VI, Cesare, and Lucrezia can be ascribed to rumors spread by Romans who resented the dominance of a foreign family.

Borromeo, Carlo (1538–1584), and Borromeo, Federico (1564–1631)
church figure and religious reformer

Cardinal Carlo Borromeo, archbishop of Milan and major figure of the CATHOLIC REFORMATION, was born to a family of the Lombard nobility. In

1560 his uncle Pope Pius IV (1559–65) called him to Rome to serve as his personal secretary. In that capacity, Borromeo helped plan the work of the last sessions of the COUNCIL OF TRENT. He was ordained into the priesthood in 1563 and appointed archbishop of Milan in 1564. He took up residence in Milan after the death of his uncle, turning his diocese into a laboratory of religious reform. His intent was to renew the church, regain the religious initiative in Europe, contain the spread of Protestantism, and recover lost territory. He insisted on strict clerical discipline, made priests accountable to the bishop, resisted secular interference in clerical affairs, promoted spiritual practices and rituals, and strengthened bonds between clergy and laity. Central to his reform were the practices of confession and penance as means to reclaim souls and assert the spiritual primacy of the clergy. Borromeo understood religious reform as an essentially spiritual undertaking to be carried out in an almost military manner by model priests who could influence the beliefs and behavior of the laity. His canonization in 1610 showed that he made a deep impression on his contemporaries. Federico Borromeo, appointed archbishop of Milan in 1595, completed the reforms left unfinished by his older cousin.

Borsellino, Paolo See MAFIA.

Bosco, Giovanni (1815–1888)

religious reformer, educator, and social worker
This Catholic priest, popularly known as Don Bosco, was born to a peasant family near the town of Asti in the region of PIEDMONT. He worked as a fieldhand, was able eventually to attend school on a regular basis, and was ordained into the priesthood in 1841. His religious vocation went hand in hand with an equally strong motivation to teach. In the 1840s he preached and taught orphans, peasant and working-class boys, encouraged and helped by the archbishop of Turin, Luigi Fransoni (1789–1862), who was later expelled from Piedmont for his opposition to government control of clerical affairs. Don Bosco shared Franzoni's hostility to secular power, to the REVOLUTION of 1848, and the anticlerical laws promulgated by the government in the 1850s. But he did take advantage of constitutional provisions protecting freedom of the press and of association to publish a Catholic journal and establish mutual aid societies among young workers. He complied reluctantly with, and partly circumvented, laws expanding the role of public education. The Salesian movement, which he started in the 1850s, developed into an international organization that combines spiritual guidance with secular schooling. In 1860–61 he was accused of conspiring against the state, but the government produced no evidence to substantiate these charges. Don Bosco was respectful toward the monarchy, but feared the influence of anticlerical elements in the national government. His

efforts to resolve the conflict of CHURCH AND STATE failed. In trying to reach a compromise, he alienated both liberals and conservatives. PIUS IX supported Don Bosco's grassroots initiatives to broaden the church's popular base. Don Bosco did much to enhance the popular appeal of the church, particularly among rural populations, which saw him as a model of spirituality and social activism on their behalf. He was canonized in 1934. The English translation of his autobiography is entitled *Memoirs of the Oratory* (1984).

Bosco, Rosario Garibaldi See FASCI SICILIANI.

Boselli, Paolo (1838–1932)

political figure and prime minister
Boselli represented his native district of Savona in parliament from 1870 to 1919 as a moderate conservative. A lawyer, professor of finance at the University of Rome, and an expert on maritime law, he enjoyed a reputation for professional competence and fairness. The highlight of his political career was his appointment as prime minister in June 1916 as head of a government of national unity during WORLD WAR I. As prime minister, he had to contend with deep political divisions that were barely disguised by the need for wartime unity. A fluent and learned speaker, Boselli excelled at patriotic oratory. Already in poor health when he became prime minister, he was forced to resign in October 1917 in the aftermath of the defeat at CAPORETTO. Appointed senator in 1921, a supporter of the Fascist regime, and the last surviving member of the parliament of 1870 that had taken Rome from the pope, Boselli in March 1929 was given the honor of presenting to the senate for ratification the law that settled the ROMAN QUESTION and ended the conflict of CHURCH AND STATE. A nervous tic that caused him to shake his head prompted the quip that Boselli was the perfect politician because he could say yes with his mouth and no with his head.

Bossi, Umberto (1941–   )
*political figure, leader of northern Italy's
separatist movement*

Born near Varese in 1941, Bossi studied medicine and law at the universities of Pavia and Padua. A student in the 1960s, he was attracted to the political movements of the Left and to environmental causes. He gained attention in the late 1970s by calling for regional autonomy and loosening the grip of the central government over the regions. In 1982 he founded the newspaper *Lombardia Autonomista* and in 1984 he was a cofounder and secretary of the Lega Lombarda (Lombard League), named after the alliance of medieval cities that had fought for regional independence. Heading the league's ticket, he was elected to the senate in 1987. The movement caught on, with Bossi calling for separation of the northern regions from the rest of the country or for a redistribution of power in favor of regional governments. In 1991 he founded the Lega Nord (Northern League) that aimed at creating a united front among northern separatists. In the elections of 1992 the Northern League won 8.7 percent of the popular vote and sent Bossi to parliament as its leading representative. On the national stage, Bossi won attention for his outspoken, blunt, politically incorrect, and often downright crude language and demeanor. While his appeal was limited to the northern regions, he nevertheless became a national figure by playing on resentment of big government, regional animosities, and anti-immigration sentiments. In 1994 he formed a short-lived tactical alliance with SILVIO BERLUSCONI, but pulled out quickly when the connection appeared to undermine his appeal among voters. Although the Northern League has lost much of its appeal at the polls, Bossi remains popular among certain voters. He rejoined Berlusconi in his second government, formed in June 2001, serving as a minister without portfolio. Bossi's message, if not his style, has mellowed considerably since the early days of the movement. Today he calls for greater regional autonomy rather than separation, smaller government, and economic growth. He lists himself as a journalist and writes regularly for *Padania,* the newspaper of the Northern League.

Botta, Carlo (1766–1837)
*liberal historian, literary critic, and public
figure*

Botta, a historian active in public life, influenced the development of liberal ideology in 19th-century Italy. A supporter of the FRENCH REVOLUTION and NAPOLEON, Botta served in Napoleon's army as a medic in 1796–97 and continued to serve the French government in various capacities until Napoleon's downfall in 1814, when Botta retired from public service. Afterward, he held various academic posts in France and devoted himself principally to writing. His initial admiration for the French Revolution and Napoleon are not evident in his mature writings. It is largely through these that he exerted influence on his contemporaries. His principal works are a history of the American Revolution, *Guerra d'indipendenza degli Stati Uniti d'America* (The American war of independence, 1809), and two volumes on the history of Italy, *Storia d'Italia dal 1789 al 1814* (History of Italy from 1789 to 1814, 1824) and *Storia d'Italia continuata da quella del Guicciardini* (History of Italy, continued from Guicciardini's, 1832). In these works, he developed interpretations of Italian history that are considered fundamental. Drawing from the disillusionment with Napoleonic rule that was shared by many of his contemporaries, in his work on the American Revolution Botta compared George Washington to Napoleon, the American general personifying the virtuous citizen and Napoleon the despot. Botta found little to admire and much to deplore in the attitude of Italian JACOBINS who welcomed French rule. While he gave them credit for being motivated by generous sentiments, he questioned their overly optimistic view of human nature, deplored their utopian expectations, and their fanatical zeal. Botta, a literary classicist, was also critical of the culture of ROMANTICISM, which he saw as foreign and alien to the classical spirit of Italian culture.

Botta's works, widely read by his contemporaries, influenced the thinking of liberals seeking a middle path between the status quo and revolution.

Bottai, Giuseppe (1895–1959)
Fascist leader, journalist, and social theoretician

Born in Rome to a lower-middle-class family, Bottai was that rare figure who finds equal satisfaction in politics, war, art, and the life of the mind. Attracted to FUTURISM as early as 1914, in 1915 he interrupted his studies to volunteer for military service in WORLD WAR I. During the war he joined the elite ARDITI shock troops. Back in civilian life, he was a founder of the Roman section of the Fascist movement and its leader after breaking his ties with futurism. No one more than Bottai felt the irresistible spell of BENITO MUSSOLINI, whom he would always regard as an exceptional personality. His Fascist faith never wavered, even as he suffered repeated setbacks within the Fascist Party. He argued for making the party democratic, for keeping it in touch with public opinion, creating and giving real power to the Fascist corporations, and broadening access to the schools. The corporate reforms of 1926–34 owed much to Bottai, who was deeply involved in theoretical debates and legislating. But things did not go his way. The Fascist Party became progressively more bureaucratic and isolated from the rest of the country, the corporations never acquired the functions and autonomy favored by Bottai, and the regime became entirely dependent on Mussolini. He did make some headway as minister of national education (1936–43). The school reform of 1939 that he sponsored and which took his name provided for manual labor training at the primary level, a single secondary school track at the middle school level, and improved technical training at the secondary level. The compulsory study of Latin at the secondary level was designed to make the universities accessible to all students who completed secondary schooling at age 14. The imminence of military defeat in WORLD WAR II made Bottai rethink his allegiance to fascism and Mussolini.

As a member of the Fascist Grand Council, he played a primary role in the plot that removed Mussolini from power in July 1943. Wanted by the authorities of the ITALIAN SOCIAL REPUBLIC, he escaped and served in the French foreign legion for the remainder of the war. Bottai was notable for keeping his internal dissidence within limits acceptable to the regime. His critical intelligence was fully displayed in the reviews that he directed, *Critica Fascista* (1923–43), *Archivio di Studi Corporativi* (1930–43), *Primato* (1940–43), and *ABC* (1953–59).

Botticelli, Sandro (1445–1510)
artist whose paintings reflect the religious and secular concerns of Renaissance humanism

A towering figure among the giants of RENAISSANCE painting, Botticelli learned the craft as an apprentice to Filippo Lippi (1432–69) and perhaps Andrea del Verrocchio (1435–88). His complete command of color, perspective, and composition enabled him to achieve extraordinary harmony of line and intensity of feeling in his paintings. His best-known works, including the *Primavera* and *Birth of Venus* dating from the 1470s and '80s, show the influence of NEOPLATONISM. The central figure in the *Primavera* sums up Botticelli's ability to combine a pagan appreciation of physical beauty with a sense of spirituality that bridges the gap between paganism and Christianity. During this period of his career Botticelli moved in the select circle of artists and scholars who surrounded LORENZO DE' MEDICI. His later works reflect the extreme religious intensity inspired by the preaching of GIROLAMO SAVONAROLA, whom Botticelli followed and admired. Because Botticelli's art mirrored the ideas of his time, his works have both artistic and historical value.

Bourbons
dynasty of French origin that ruled in France, Spain, and Italy

The royal Bourbon dynasty takes its name from the castle of Bourbon, the family seat in central

France. In 1589 Henry IV became the first Bourbon king of France. A branch of the family ruled in Spain from 1700 to 1931, a second branch in the Kingdom of NAPLES and the KINGDOM OF THE TWO SICILIES from 1735 to 1860, and a third in PARMA from 1748 to 1859, in all cases with interruptions along the way due to the fortunes of war and revolution. The Bourbons of Naples are particularly important in the history of Italy. The history of the Kingdom of the Two Sicilies unfolds in the successive reigns of CHARLES OF BOURBON, FERDINAND I, FRANCIS I, FERDINAND II, and FRANCIS II. The Spanish Bourbons were established in Italy by hereditary right to the duchy of Parma. Charles of Bourbon was the son of the first Bourbon king of Spain, Philip V, and ELISABETTA FARNESE of Parma. Charles ruled first as duke of Parma and Piacenza (1731–35) and then as king of Naples (1735–1759). He left Naples to become king of Spain, where he ruled as Charles III (1759–88). His son Ferdinand I succeeded him as king of Naples. With Ferdinand the dynasty became fully acclimated to Naples, took on the language, manners, and color of the place, and cut its ties to Spain.

Although the Bourbons and HABSBURGS were rivals in many parts of Europe, in Italy the two dynasties worked together. Both Bourbons and Habsburgs backed away from government reforms after the outbreak of the French Revolution in 1789, fearful that concessions to their dissatisfied subjects would only fuel demands for more change, lead to revolution, and the loss of their thrones, as had happened to the Bourbons in France. Liberal insurrections in 1821 and 1848 reinforced the Bourbons' determination to hold the line against concessions. In both instances the Bourbons had to rely on Austrian troops to put down the revolts and reestablish their authority. Bourbon monarchs did not lack support at home, for they were popular with peasants, the urban lower classes, and the conservative aristocracy. In the city of Naples where many people were employed at court or benefited from royal largesse, the Bourbons could usually rely on the lower orders, often derogatively called the *lazzaroni* (riffraff), who in times of trouble could be expected to make common cause with the monarchy against middle-class liberals and intellectuals who wanted a voice in government. The undisguised hostility of educated liberals toward a monarchy that resisted demands for change made the Bourbons suspicious of intellectuals in general. Hence their dislike of all *pennaruli* (pen pushers) and their fear of the educated and of education in general.

The imprisonment of prominent Neapolitans for expressing their disapproval of government caused scandal throughout western Europe. As time went by the Bourbons became increasingly dependent on the support of conservative powers like Austria and Russia. Austria's defeat in the Second WAR OF NATIONAL INDEPENDENCE (1859) brought the Bourbon dynasts to the verge of collapse. GIUSEPPE GARIBALDI evicted them from Naples in 1860 when the Kingdom of the Two Sicilies became part of the unified kingdom of Italy. Seen as the epitome of blind reaction at the time of national unification, the memory and image of Bourbon rule improved by the 1890s, as many Neapolitans came to question the advantages of national unification. The saying "We were better off when we were worse off" reflected some nostalgia for the days of Bourbon rule. Something similar occurred a century later as southerners reassessed the past and their place in the national state in the light of separatist movements and new tensions between North and South.

Bramante, Donato (1444–1514)
Renaissance artist who set the pace and style of architectural design

Born in Urbino, Bramante was trained as a painter but is remembered primarily as an architect. He first appears as an architect working in Milan in 1485 at the court of Duke LODOVICO SFORZA. His Milanese projects, which include the rebuilding of the Church of Santa Maria delle Grazie (1492), reveal Bramante's preference for the use of circular forms and superimposed orders. The rounded forms give a compact look to the exteriors of Bramante's buildings while imparting a sense of spaciousness and light to the interiors. In 1499 Bramante left Milan for Rome, where he became chief papal architect. Placed in charge of large-scale projects of urban renewal that involved tearing up of old quarters, Bramante became affectionately known as *Il Ruinante* (The Wrecker). Perhaps Bramante's most influential building is the small Tempietto (little temple) alongside the Church of San Pietro in Montorio built in 1502 on the spot where Saint Peter is thought to have been martyred. The Tempietto marks the culmination of Bramante's fascination with circular shapes, use of columns, and superimposed orders. It is a compact structure that provides a textbook demonstration of the classical style typical of RENAISSANCE architecture. Bramante also designed and oversaw the start of the rebuilding of the Basilica of Saint Peter in 1506, launching the fateful project that would soon help ignite the Protestant Reformation by arousing the anger of northern Europeans at such lavish papal expenditures. MICHELANGELO later altered the design of Saint Peter's drastically, but Bramante's influence is still noticeable in the cruciform shape of the structure (which Bramante designed with four equal arms) and the enormous dome surmounting it. To satisfy JULIUS II's impatience for rapid results, Bramante devised quick techniques of construction and ornamentation, such as the use of stucco and cast vaults. His pervasive influence makes him the founder of Renaissance architecture.

Brenner Pass   See ALPS; TRENTINO–ALTO ADIGE.

Bresci, Gaetano   See ANARCHISM; FATTI DI MAGGIO; TERRORISM; UMBERTO I.

brigandage

The term *brigandage* refers to the armed resistance that the recently unified kingdom of Italy faced from 1861 to 1865 in the provinces of the former KINGDOM OF THE TWO SICILIES. *Brigandage*

reflects the national government's desire to present acts of rebellion as instances of criminal behavior rather than as a form of popular resistance against the state. Instances of organized popular resistance against government were by no means unknown in the South, but the phenomenon of the 1860s was much more pervasive than its predecessors. It was the direct result of the events of 1860, when soldiers from the disbanded Neapolitan army roamed the countryside, the deposed BOURBONS intrigued to regain their lost throne, and expectations of rapid improvement were frustrated. The extension of Piedmontese law to the new territories, military conscription, high taxes, rising food prices, lack of land reform, and a cultural acceptance of the outlaw as a popular hero figure contributed to the spread of brigandage. The country experienced a form of undeclared civil war that resembles in some ways the Civil War that was then being fought in the United States. In both cases, a unionist North prevailed over a secessionist South, martial law prevailed, and the period of reconstruction was marked by the imposition of northern law on a recalcitrant population.

However, unlike the American, the Italian southern resistance had no government of its own, encountered strong opposition within the South itself, and pitted urban groups generally supportive of national unification and the state against a disaffected rural population. Resistance was strongest in the regions of BASILICATA, CALABRIA, and PUGLIA, where martial law was widely applied. The insurgents were organized in bands that were occasionally strong enough to take over entire towns, but never strong enough to maintain stable control over a large territory. They waged guerrilla warfare against the regular army, their combined strength at the height of the resistance in 1862 being estimated at approximately 80,000. Against them the government deployed an army of about 120,000. Official sources give the figures of 5,212 for the number of rebels killed in combat or otherwise executed, and of 5,044 for those who were detained. The number of army casualties is not known.

The severe repression restored law and order in the South but left behind a legacy of regional animosity and bitterness with long-term consequences in national politics. Brigandage put the SOUTHERN QUESTION on the national agenda, made northerners aware of the problems of the South, and initiated the still ongoing debate on the coexistence of North and South within the same state. Brigandage tends to recur when the authority of the state weakens, as it did in Sicily in the aftermath of World War II under SALVATORE GIULIANO, when rebelliousness also expressed a desire for regional autonomy. It is also connected to the illegal activities of the MAFIA, which have at times taken the form of armed resistance against the state.

Brunelleschi, Filippo (1377–1446)

Florentine architect, sculptor, goldsmith, and clockmaker

This versatile artist is remembered primarily as the designer and engineer of the enormous dome that surmounts Florence's cathedral, the Church of Santa Maria del Fiore. Brunelleschi gained public recognition in 1401 for his design of the doors to the cathedral's baptistery, the commission for which eventually went to his lifelong rival LORENZO GHIBERTI. Whatever Brunelleschi's talents as a sculptor may have been, he is remembered as a supreme architect and builder. Brunelleschi won the commission to build the dome on the cathedral in 1418 after a grueling competition. The secretive, cantankerous architect produced a successful model whose engineering features, like the supposed use of iron chains embedded in the structure, continue to puzzle the experts. The dome of Santa Maria del Fiore was designed to surpass in size that of the Pantheon, the largest building of ancient Rome. To preserve the towering effect envisaged by Brunelleschi, the city of Florence forbids the construction of any higher structure. Other works by Brunelleschi, all in Florence, include the Foundling Hospital (begun in 1419), the Churches of San Lorenzo (1420), Santo Spirito (1436), and

Santa Maria degli Angeli (1437), the Pazzi Chapel (1433), and possibly the façade of the Pitti Palace. Some of these works were completed after his death. Brunelleschi's study of classical buildings in Rome inspired him to make extensive use of arches supported by columns. His style is characterized by spare use of ornamental devices and the dominance of pure lines, which he regarded as the hallmark of ancient Greek and Roman architecture. His search for symmetry and proportion led him to study and apply mathematics to architecture and engineering. He is considered to be the most influential architect of his generation, bridging the gap between medieval and Renaissance styles of construction. Buried under the spectacular dome that he built, his tomb was rediscovered in 1972.

Bruni, Leonardo (1370–1444)

Renaissance scholar and leading humanist figure

Bruni was the dominant figure of Florentine HUMANISM in the first half of the 15th century. Of modest social origin, Bruni gave up the study of law to devote himself to the study of classical Greek with the Greek scholar Manuel Chrysoloras. Admired for his scholarly accomplishments, Bruni led the revival of learning with translations of Aristotle, Plato, Plutarch, and Xenophon into Latin that set a new standard in classical studies. His familiarity with ancient texts enabled him to speak with authority on the issues of the day. In *Laudatio Florentinae urbis* (In praise of the city of Florence), published in 1401, Bruni held up Florentine republican government as a model for others to emulate. This text is considered to be the manifesto of civic humanism. In his *Historiarum florentini populi* (History of the Florentine people), begun around 1415 and left unfinished at his death, Bruni covered the history of Florence chronologically from its origins to 1404, using sources critically and interpreting events. His message was that the success of the Florentine state was due to its republican origins. Bruni may have written his history to make a case for Florence against its rival city of Milan, governed despotically by the VISCONTI FAMILY, but his argument that republican institutions nurture a strong civic spirit, prevent the rise of political despots, and promote economic prosperity made a deep impression on his contemporaries and influenced political thinking. Bruni worked for the Florentine government and the PAPACY. In Florence he held the high office of chancellor of the republic and was a successful diplomat. Greatly admired for his vast learning and unmatched eloquence, Bruni was buried with state honors in the Church of Santa Croce.

Bruno, Giordano (1548–1600)
scholar, theologian, and religious dissenter

Bruno was born in the town of Nola, near Naples, to an impoverished family of the local nobility. *Il Nolano* (The Nolan), as Bruno was often called, was admitted to the Dominican order in 1565, ordained into the priesthood in 1572, and awarded a doctorate in theology in 1575. In 1571 he was invited to Rome to instruct the pope in mnemotechny (the art of memorizing), which Bruno had mastered, but the pontiff's favor did not save him from arrest and eviction from Naples in 1576 on charges of practicing magic. Thus began Bruno's life of wanderings, which took him to northern Italy, Switzerland, France, England, and Germany. Wherever he went he was embroiled in disputes with Aristotelian academics, whose views Bruno assailed mercilessly. In 1591 he accepted an invitation to tutor a young Venetian nobleman in the *ars memoriae*. His young student denounced him to the Holy Office on a variety of charges, including womanizing (Bruno made light of his admitted fondness for women), blasphemy, practicing magic, holding that there were many worlds and that the universe is eternal.

The last two charges were particularly serious because of their heretical implications. If there were many inhabited worlds, for whom had Christ died? If the universe was eternal, what

became of God's omnipotence? Bruno's pantheism (the belief that God resides in all natural things) brought into question the sacramental role of the clergy, for if God is in all things then recourse to the clergy may not be necessary. The Venetian authorities who examined Bruno decided to turn him over to the Holy Office in Rome, where he was subjected to a second trial. He was questioned, tortured, and his writings were examined. When he refused to acknowledge his errors after a seven-year ordeal, the INQUISITION turned him over to the secular authority for execution. On February 17, 1600 (a Jubilee Year when Rome was crowded with pilgrims from all over the Catholic world), Bruno was burned at the stake in Rome's Campo dei Fiori.

Bruno's philosophy remains enigmatic, for it is not easy to find a logical thread through his many writings that have survived. He was unquestionably attracted to magic, to the mysteries of the ancient Egyptians and Hebrews, and believed in the pursuit of knowledge by intuition rather than reason. His disputatious, downright quarrelsome temper, won him many enemies. Although he rejected Protestantism, Protestants regarded him as a martyr because he had challenged papal authority. Nineteenth-century anticlericals made him a hero for the same reason (see ANTICLERICALISM). The statue raised to him in Campo dei Fiori in 1887 has been the site of anticlerical demonstrations ever since; the anticlerical Giordano Bruno Society is named after him.

Buonarroti, Filippo Michele (1761–1837)
political conspirator, founder and leader of secret societies

A lifelong commitment to conspiracy and revolution made Buonarroti a cult figure among radicals of his and later generations. Born in Pisa to a patrician family of magistrates and lawyers whose ancestors included MICHELANGELO, he studied law, music, and philosophy at the University of Pisa. Influenced by his reading of Jean Jacques Rousseau, he espoused the dogmas of equality and popular sovereignty, to which he added a commitment to overthrow governments by violent means. He joined his first secret lodge in 1786, enthused over the French Revolution, and worked for the revolutionary government in CORSICA promoting religious and land reforms. Robespierre appointed him revolutionary commissioner for the town of Oneglia (1794–95). In 1796 he participated in the Conspiracy of Equals that tried and failed to take over the French government. He spent most of the Napoleonic period under house arrest, treated leniently by NAPOLEON I, who seems to have felt affection for Buonarroti. That did not prevent Buonarroti from conspiring against Napoleon. In 1809–10 he launched the secret society of the Sublime and Perfect Masters, whose members were expected to infiltrate governments and other subversive secret societies. When that society was discovered and dismantled in 1824, he turned his attention to the CARBONARI, reorganized the association, and controlled its activities. Buonarroti clashed with GIUSEPPE MAZZINI, a younger conspirator whom Buonarroti regarded as a rival. For several years each sought to control the other's network, until the police repressed both. There were significant differences between Buonarroti and Mazzini. Buonarroti relied on secret conspiracies, Mazzini called for popular revolt; Buonarroti expected France to lead the revolution, Mazzini wanted the initiative to come from Italy. Buonarroti's secret society I Veri Italiani (True Italians) competed with Mazzini's Giovine Italia (YOUNG ITALY). Buonarroti became a legendary figure of the Left and his book *Babeuf's Conspiracy for Equality* (1828) was obligatory reading for all radicals. Karl Marx read it and may have been inspired by Buonarroti's theory of revolution to conceptualize communists as the revolutionary vanguard.

Buonarroti, Michelangelo See
MICHELANGELO BUONARROTI.

Buontalenti, Bernardo See MANNERISM.

Buozzi, Bruno (1881–1944)
socialist labor organizer and anti-Fascist
Buozzi belonged to the moderate reformist wing of the Italian Socialist Party (PSI). Born in the province of Ferrara where there was intense labor strife, a mechanic by trade, he devoted himself to organizing workers, always putting their concrete interests ahead of ideological considerations or questions of party loyalty. In 1911 he became secretary of the national union of metal workers. He opposed Italian intervention in WORLD WAR I, but helped mobilize workers when the country went to war. After the war he called for the eight-hour day and negotiated wage improvements. He led strikes for concrete economic gains, but condemned strikes that were politically motivated. He was elected to parliament in 1919, 1921, and 1924, and served as secretary of the General Confederation of Labor in 1925–26. Buozzi's efforts to find space for a labor movement free of political ties led to discussions with the government of BENITO MUSSOLINI, but the discussions came to nothing. In 1926 Buozzi joined the anti-Fascist exiles in France, hoping to keep an independent labor movement alive abroad. The Gestapo arrested him in France in 1941. Freed in July 1943, he resumed his activities as a labor organizer, settled strikes in Turin, and negotiated agreements between Catholic and communist labor organizations. He was again arrested by the Germans in Rome in January 1944 and executed by them during their retreat from Rome.

Burlamacchi, Francesco (1498–1548)
political dissenter and conspirator
Belonging to one of the influential mercantile families of LUCCA, unlike most members of his class who preferred to tend to their business interests, Burlamacchi showed interest in political life and public office. In 1533 he became *gonfaloniere* (head of government) of the Republic of

Lucca. Raised again to the same office in 1546, he led a secret conspiracy against Florentine dominance in Tuscany. His supporters were political malcontents from nearby PISA and Pistoia, and rivals of the ruling MEDICI family. Burlamacchi apparently planned to use the rural militia of his city to consolidate his control of the government in Lucca, move against Florence, and topple Medici rule. The conspirators hoped to replace the Medici government with a confederation of self-governing cities and to promote religious reform, but they lacked the resources to carry out their ambitious plan. Burlamacchi was probably influenced by Protestant sympathies common among the merchant aristocracy of Lucca. When the conspiracy was discovered, the Medici pressured Lucca into bringing Burlamacchi to justice. Arrested and tortured, he went to his death without revealing the names of his accomplices. Burlamacchi was rehabilitated as a patriot and anticlerical reformer during the RISORGIMENTO and a statue to him was erected in the central square of his city.

Busoni, Ferruccio See GOZZI, CARLO.

Buttiglione, Rocco See COMUNIONE E LIBERAZIONE.

C

Cabot, John (ca. 1450–1498), and Sebastian (ca. 1474–1557)
navigator and explorer

The explorer known to the English as John Cabot was born Giovanni Caboto in Genoa, became a Venetian citizen in 1476, sailed the eastern Mediterranean Sea in the service of Venetian trade, and journeyed at great risk to Mecca before going to England, probably in the 1480s. Like CHRISTOPHER COLUMBUS, Cabot believed that the rich lands of the East could be reached directly by sailing west over the Atlantic Ocean, but Cabot intended to use England as a springboard. From England he sailed to Iceland and Greenland in search of fish before receiving a patent from King Henry VII in 1496 to explore the Atlantic Ocean farther west. He reached the coast of North America in a first voyage (1497) and returned a year later to carry on further exploration. It is likely that in his 1498 voyage he sailed as far south as Chesapeake Bay. It is also likely that he died on this second voyage. The fate of this second expedition is unknown, but the English crown invoked it to justify its territorial claims to North America. Thus, John Cabot has been called the real discoverer of North America. John's son, Sebastian Cabot, continued his father's exploration in his unsuccessful search for the Northwest Passage to the Far East. The two Cabots were part of the diaspora of pilots from the Italian peninsula who used their maritime skills in pursuit of fame and fortune on Europe's new Atlantic frontier in the service of foreign powers.

Cadorna, Luigi (1850–1928)
army general and chief of staff in World War I

General Luigi Cadorna was the son of General Raffaele Cadorna (1815–97) who had led Italian troops in the taking of Rome in September 1870. This Piedmontese family had a military tradition of long standing. Luigi Cadorna was commissioned in 1868. In July 1914 he was appointed army chief of staff and commanded the Italian army in WORLD WAR I until forced to resign in November 1917 in the wake of the CAPORETTO disaster. Self-assured to a fault, impervious to criticism, and a strict disciplinarian, Cadorna brooked no interference with his command from anyone, including government ministers whose support he needed to carry on with his duties. He was a competent and careful organizer, but his approach to war, like that of most generals at the time, was traditional and unimaginative. Under his command the army maintained a steady pressure on the Austrians and insisted on launching frontal attacks against entrenched positions. The territorial gains produced by those tactics came at an enormous cost in lives. Cadorna held the army together with strict discipline, sacked subordinate commanders for even minor infractions, and acted with little regard for the morale of troops. When the enemy caught the army by surprise at Caporetto and forced a retreat with huge losses in lives and prisoners, Cadorna committed the capital error of publicly blaming the disaster on the troops. The government sacked him unceremoniously, replacing him with the more tactful ARMANDO DIAZ. A military inquest (1919) faulted Cadorna on several accounts, including disregarding intelligence of enemy plans, poor deployment of troops, and lack of cooperation with civilian authorities. But Cadorna's defenders argued that the charges against him were politically motivated to disparage the army. They praised Cadorna for his patriotism, pointed to his successes before Caporetto, and the effectiveness of the resistance that he organized in the days after the rout. The case divided public opinion for many years, with nationalists strongly supporting Cadorna against his critics from the Left and the liberal center. The Fascist government promoted Cadorna to the rank of army marshal in 1924 in an effort to placate the army and the political Right.

Cadorna, Raffaele (1889–1973)
army general and formal commander of the resistance in World War II

Raffaele, the son of LUIGI CADORNA, kept his distance from the Fascist regime and, like most army officers, remained loyal to the monarchy and King VICTOR EMMANUEL III. Cadorna followed the royal court to southern Italy when the king abandoned Rome in September 1943, worked closely with the Allies, and led Italian regular troops who took the field against the Germans in 1944. That same year he was parachuted into northern Italy to take command of the armed RESISTANCE. He took steps to organize the fighters along military lines, curb the independent authority of field commanders, and neutralize the political influence of communists. Thanks to his organizational efforts, military units of the resistance were able to take control of northern cities from the retreating Germans in the final days of WORLD WAR II prior to the arrival of the Allies. After the war he served as chief of staff of the armed forces (1945–47) and as senator (1948–63). His writings are an important source of information on military and political aspects of the resistance movement.

Caffè (Il) See VERRI, PIETRO.

Cafiero, Carlo See ANARCHISM; MALATESTA, ERRICO.

Cagliostro, Alessandro (1743–1795)
adventurer, impostor, and confidence man popular in high society

Alessandro, count of Cagliostro, was the assumed name of the Sicilian-born Giuseppe Balsamo, an adventurer who made a name for himself throughout Europe as a magician and physician allegedly possessing miraculous curative powers. His wife, Lorenza Feliciani, was his capable accomplice. The renown that he acquired gave him access to the highest social circles, which accepted him in spite his lowborn status. Cagliostro promised to raise the spirits of the dead, transform base metals into gold, claimed to have spoken with Egyptian pharaohs and to have witnessed the crucifixion of Christ, Nero's burning of Rome, and crusaders setting off for the Holy Land. His displays of hypnotic power were popular events that drew crowds. He introduced a new Egyptian rite in FREEMASONRY, and membership in that brotherhood facilitated his movements in Europe and opened doors to exclusive circles in London, Paris, Rome, and St. Petersburg. In Paris he was implicated in the Affair of the Queen's Necklace, which contributed to discrediting the French monarchy on the eve of the FRENCH REVOLUTION. He left Paris just ahead of the police. Arrested in Rome in 1789, he was tried, found guilty of founding a Masonic lodge in the city, and sentenced to die. The government commuted the death sentence to life imprisonment, which he served to the end of his days in the remote fortress of St. Leo. He refused the offer of holy sacraments on his deathbed. His adventurous life offers an intriguing look at the side of ENLIGHTENMENT culture that was fascinated by the supernatural, magic, mysticism, and the irrational.

Cairoli, Benedetto (1825–1889)

Risorgimento patriot and prime minister

Benedetto Cairoli was born in Pavia to Carlo Cairoli (1777–1849) and Adelaide Bono (1806–71), the first of five sons, all patriots active in the movement for national unification. All but Benedetto died fighting for the cause. The mother became a symbol of patriotic motherhood. Benedetto fought against the Austrians in 1848, conspired with GIUSEPPE MAZZINI in the 1850s as a republican, but made his peace with the Piedmontese monarchy after the failure of republican conspiracies. After a period of exile in Switzerland, he returned to Italy in 1854. He fought as a volunteer under the command of GIUSEPPE GARIBALDI in 1859 and 1860. A member of the national parliament for the LIBERAL LEFT from 1861 until his death, he criticized his own party and Prime Minister AGOSTINO DEPRETIS for the slow pace of political reform. He confronted difficult issues in his three appointments as prime minister between 1878 and 1881. A moment of popularity came his way when he was credited with saving the life of King UMBERTO I in November 1878 by standing between him and an assailant, suffering a knife wound in the process. Nationalists censured his cautious foreign policy, blaming him for Italy's failure to demand territorial gains at the Congress of Berlin (1878) and for the French seizure of Tunisia (1881). On the other hand, Austria held him responsible for nationalist agitation over TRENT and TRIESTE. Cairoli resigned under fire from all sides, and his political reputation never recovered from these setbacks. Admired for his courage and selfless patriotism, he has been regarded as an ineffectual politician.

Calabria

Calabria (pop. 2,050,000) occupies the tip or "toe" at the southernmost extreme of the peninsula. It borders on the region of Basilicata on the north; the Tyrrhenian Sea lies to its west, the Ionian Sea to its east, and it is separated from the island of SICILY on the south by the Strait of Messina. Its complex topography is dominated by mountains, which cover most of its surface. In this part of the peninsula, the APENNINES are known as the Sila Mountains, with peaks that reach almost one and a quarter miles (2,000 meters) in elevation. The southernmost part of the mountain range is known as the Aspromonte (Harsh Mount), a name that reflects the jagged, impervious nature of the land. Although precipitation is plentiful in the mountains, rapid runoff into rivers and torrents that empty quickly into the sea makes for chronic water shortages. Historically, its system of land tenure consisted of many very small properties alongside very large estates (*latifundia*) owned by absentee landlords, run by middlemen, and worked by ill-paid day laborers. Land reform has broken up the large estates, but agriculture has not flourished. The production of wheat, the traditional commercial staple of Calabrian agriculture, has declined. Its most valuable products are now olives, citrus fruit, wine grapes, sugar beets, and potatoes. Industry (construction materials, food processing, textiles, paper, and wood products) is underdeveloped, and small firms are the norm. The region has enormous tourist potential in its beaches and mountains. There are also historical and artistic treasures left behind by the region's many rulers over the centuries (Greeks, Romans, Byzantines, Normans, Germans, and Spaniards) that wait to be discovered by visitors. As in the other regions of the underdeveloped South, government is the largest provider of jobs. The principal cities of the region are Catanzaro, Cosenza, and the regional capital of Reggio Calabria, which was completely destroyed by an earthquake in 1908 and rebuilt along modern lines. Emigration abroad and to the industrial cities of northern Italy siphoned off approximately 1 million people from this region between the 1870s and 1970s. Since then, the population outflow has diminished.

Calixtus III   See BORGIA FAMILY.

Calvi, Roberto See BANCO AMBROSIANO,
SCANDAL OF.

Calvino, Italo (1923–)
author

Born in Havana, Cuba, to Italian parents working on the island as agronomists, Calvino
returned to Italy with his family in 1925, and he
was raised in the town of San Remo on the Italian Riviera. He studied agronomy at the University of Turin, where his father was professor of
tropical agriculture. Calvino served in the paramilitary Fascist youth organization and in the
Italian occupation of France in World War II. He
joined the anti-Fascist RESISTANCE in 1943 and
the Italian Communist Party (PCI) in 1944. He
left the PCI in 1957 to protest the Soviet invasion of Hungary. Since then, he has been leery
of espousing political causes, but continues to
view events from a generally left-wing perspective. His widely read novels show a whimsical
imagination, avoid realistic representations, and
conform to no political school. Calvino's first
novel, *Il sentiero dei nidi del ragno* (The path to the
spider's nest, 1947), shows that his intellectual
nonconformism is of long standing. It presents
the resistance movement, a sacred icon of the
political Left, through the eyes of a child who
cannot comprehend the issues of the adult
world. The novel conveys the message that the
movement attracted participants who themselves had no clear perception of what they were
fighting for. The failure of the resistance to revolutionize Italian society, deplored by the Italian
Left, becomes more understandable from this
perspective. Calvino often sets his novels in the
past, using lightly sketched historical background for exotic effect. *Il visconte dimezzato* (The
cloven viscount, 1952) portrays a 17th-century
aristocrat who returns from the Turkish wars
split in two by a cannon ball. The good half fights
against the bad half until the two are sewn
together again after fighting a duel over a
woman. The viscount is thus restored to his normal condition, but without deriving any notice-

Italo Calvino *(Library of Congress)*

able intellectual or emotional improvement
from his ordeal. In *Il Barone rampante* (The baron
in the trees, 1957), Calvino looks at the Enlightenment, French Revolution, and Napoleonic
period through the eyes of a nobleman who
chooses to sit out these historical events in a tree.
These last two novels, and a third one entitled
Il cavaliere inesistente (The nonexistent knight,
1959), have been published in English translation as part of a trilogy entitled *Our Ancestors*
(1980). The tone of detachment and ironic pessimism that permeates these and other writings
is part of Calvino's style. He has derived inspiration in part from popular folklore, finding it a
rich source of fantastic characters and plots. The
result was his retelling of folktales in the splendid collection entitled *Italian Folktales* (1980),
which became an American best-seller.

Camerini, Mario See DE SICA, VITTORIO.

Camorra See MAFIA.

Campanella, Tommaso (1568–1639)
philosopher and religious dissident

This Dominican friar, philosopher, visionary, and political agitator, who confronted the most controversial issues of his time and acted on his beliefs, was regarded as intolerably radical and dangerous by religious and secular authorities in his time. He continued to speak out in spite of torture and imprisonment, eventually gaining recognition for the originality and brilliance of his ideas and leaving a legacy of daring philosophical speculation and social thinking. Campanella was born to poor parents (his father was a cobbler) in the region of Calabria. He was baptized Giovan Domenico (Tommaso was the name he took on as a Dominican) and studied philosophy as part of his religious training. From his earliest writings, he stood out as a critic of the Aristotelian tradition that dominated medieval learning. Arrested in Naples in 1592 on charges of consorting with the devil and showing contempt for the church, Campanella chose to run away rather than retract his philosophical views. Pursuing him in Rome and Venice, the INQUISITION forced his return to Calabria in 1598. Campanella saved his own life by feigning insanity, but spent the next 27 years in prison. In his imprisonment he wrote profusely, including the piece for which he is best remembered, the description of an imaginary society in *Città del sole* (The city of the sun, 1602). This classic of utopian literature describes an ideal city free from human vices, based on common ownership of property, ruled by a philosopher-king, and peopled by an educated, virtuous citizenry. Campanella was freed in 1626, went to Rome where he was befriended by Pope URBAN VIII, and left Italy for Paris in 1634. In Paris he found a warm welcome at court and in intellectual circles. Death in the refuge of the French capital interrupted the publication of his works. With his far-reaching interests, vision of the world of learning as a unified whole, and faith in the value of direct experience, Campanella sums up and concludes the course of the RENAISSANCE.

Campania

The region of Campania (pop. 5,781,000) is a key region of the South. It borders the regions of LATIUM to the northwest, MOLISE to the north, PUGLIA to the northeast, and BASILICATA to the south. Its complicated topography divides essentially into a large coastal plain and a mountainous interior. The APENNINE range is less rugged in this region than in the north, but is still impervious enough to isolate the populations of the interior from those of the coastal plain. Campania links the southern regions with central and northern Italy by road and railroad. It is a hub of maritime communications, has a well-developed agriculture, and a major industrial center around the capital city of NAPLES. The mild climate of the coastal areas, fertile volcanic soil, and diversity of products explain its ancient designation as *Campania Felix*. Its principal cities and provincial capitals are Naples, Avellino, Benevento, Caserta, and Salerno. Campania has the highest population density in the country due to intensive urban concentration in the capital city and its environs. Rural districts have seen a major exodus of people to Naples, cities of the North, and abroad. Native Samnite populations, who contested Roman rule in southern Italy, Greeks, Romans, Lombards, Byzantines, Normans, and Spaniards have inhabited the region in the course of history. Each has left a distinctive legacy in the architecture, dialects, and customs of the region. Evidence of the opulence of some ancient settlements can be seen in the Greek temples of Paestum and the excavated parts of Roman Pompeii and Herculaneum, buried by an eruption of the still active volcano of Mount Vesuvius in A.D. 79. The height of the volcano changes with each eruption; at last count it stood at 4,196 feet. The seaside town of Amalfi was the first independent commune to achieve commercial importance. In the 11th century it rivaled GENOA and PISA, controlled the western Mediterranean routes, and traded with the Near East, North Africa, and Spain. Norman rule put an end to Amalfi's independence and introduced feudalism to the region, with lasting consequences for its economic and political development. The Norman monarchs and their successors up to the unification of Italy in 1860 maintained a system of government in which the court at Naples shared power with families of the nobility that controlled the countryside. Naples was the first southern city to benefit from laws to encourage industrialization (1907). Some of the bloodiest fighting of WORLD WAR II occurred in this region on the beaches of Salerno and around the town and abbey of Monte Cassino in 1943–44.

campanilismo

The term *campanilismo* describes the intense feeling of identification and loyalty that Italians feel toward the local community. The term derives from *campanile* (bell tower), traditionally the highest and most visible physical feature of the Italian town, and therefore the symbol of the town itself. In the Italian lexicon, the term *paesano,* describing a fellow townsman, stands next in line to *parente* (relative) in terms of attachment and identification. The *paese* is a shared ground for social events, business activities, and religious and political rituals. Italian emigrants in far-off places maintain ties among themselves based on the town of origin. The reality of *campanilismo* as a distinctive component of Italian culture is seldom questioned, but its significance is a subject of debate. The common view that *campanilismo* was an obstacle to national unity seems mistaken. Often it was precisely the identification and attachment to the local community, be it village, town, or city, that facilitated identification with the Italian nation as a way of surmounting subnational divisions and rivalries. A citizen of Siena or Pisa might prefer the authority of a national government to that of a

more powerful neighbor like Florence. Similarly, strong identification with the local community would give concrete meaning to the idea of a nation once the incorporation of the community in the national state was an accepted fact. For many Italians, the local community was and remains the only setting in which they can be active participants in public affairs. In other words, *campanilismo* is not the same as parochialism. While parochialism implies closure to the outside world, *campanilismo* can be a way of connecting with the outside world. Questions remain about the future of *campanilismo:* As power shifts from local to national and international centers, the outside world imposes foreign fashions and models, and means of global communication reach to the grass roots of society.

Campoformio, Treaty of See DALMATIA; NAPOLEON I; VENICE.

Canaletto (1697–1768)
(Antonio Canal)
Venetian painter notable for the documentary character of his works

The Venetian painter Antonio Canal, known as Canaletto, is notable chiefly for his depictions of Venetian scenes (*vedute*). Much admired for the realism of his paintings, which reproduce faithfully the striking architecture of the city, Canaletto found a ready market for his scenes among well-to-do visitors from abroad, who bought his paintings as souvenirs of the city. Because of their realism, his paintings document not only the appearance of the city but also the fashions, rituals, and social customs of his time. His skill as a designer, mastery of perspective, feeling for color, and delicate touch made him internationally popular. He was both an artistic and a commercial success. He was especially admired in England where he lived and worked from 1746 to 1756, and where some of his best works can be seen today. He is not to be confused with his apprentice and nephew Bernardo Bellotto

(1720–80), who was also called Canaletto. Bellotto was an even more prolific painter than his uncle, whose style he copied. Bellotto worked from London to Warsaw, and his works show up in collections across the continent.

Cannizzaro, Stanislao   See SCIENCE.

Canova, Antonio (1757–1822)

*Venetian sculptor who catered to the
neoclassical taste of the Enlightenment*

Inspired by the art of ancient Greece and Rome, which he studied from samples found in the house where he was born, Canova strove for purity and simplicity of line in reaction to the convoluted style of the ROCOCO. Working mostly in Rome and Naples, Canova sculpted mythological figures, the tombs of popes and other prominent personages, busts and statues of NAPOLEON I and his family. Napoleon admired his art and commissioned many works from him. Canova's nude statue of Napoleon's sister Pauline (see BORGHESE FAMILY) reveals Canova's art at its sensuous best. A shrewd marketer of his talent, Canova was successful artistically and commercially.

Cantù, Cesare (1804–1895)

patriotic writer and educator

This Lombard writer set out to reach and educate a large public with historical works and novels that preached the ethic of personal responsibility and self-help. He joined Mazzini's YOUNG ITALY but did not play an active part in it. Of liberal sentiments, Cantù shied away from political conspiracy and radical ideologies. His Catholic faith prevented him from actively opposing or criticizing papal politics. He believed that national independence would come about gradually with the evolution of existing institutions. For his involvement in the Mazzinian movement, Cantù was arrested and spent some time in jail in 1833–34. His novel *Margherita*

Antonio Canova *(Library of Congress)*

Pusterla (1833), set in 14th-century Milan, idealized medieval culture based on local attachments and Christian values, the loss of which he blamed on the rise of the tyrannical government. His most ambitious work was a multivolume history of the world, *Storia universale* (1836–42), which brought him fame and commercial success. After his brush with the law, Cantù avoided political entanglements. He deplored the rift between PIUS IX and the national movement, and the conflict of CHURCH AND STATE. In his later writings he addressed the social question as a moderate who sought harmony in the workplace. His novel *Portafoglio d'un operaio* (Dossier of a worker, 1871) told the story of a worker who made his way in life by being industrious, sober, and devoted to his family. Like the contemporary novels of Samuel Smiles, it emphasized the importance of honesty and personal responsibility, and the dangers that political activism and radical ideologies posed for workers. Cantù urged employers to take a personal interest in the welfare of workers, and dedicated his novel to ALESSANDRO ROSSI, the most paternalistic employer of his generation. Cantù served briefly in parliament (1860–61), but his real commitment was to educating with his writings. He belongs to the ranks of intellectuals who sought to bridge the gap between ordinary people and the intelligentsia. A prolific writer, Cantù put his faith in gradual progress, Christian resignation, and the work ethic.

Capello, Bianca (1548–1587)

grand duchess of Tuscany

Born to a family of the Venetian aristocracy, Capello shocked her contemporaries by eloping at age 15 with a penniless Florentine bank clerk, presumably in rebellion against the rigid seclusion that was the lot of upper-class Venetian women. Her outraged father had her declared an outlaw but she found protection in FLORENCE, where she lived unhappily, attending to domestic chores in the household of her in-laws. Her beauty caught the eye of Francesco de' Medici (see MEDICI FAMILY), heir to the Tuscan throne, who publicly made her his mistress. Her husband was mysteriously assassinated (1569). Francesco, who became grand duke of Tuscany in 1574, married her in 1578 after his own wife had died in childbirth. In her new role as grand duchess, Bianca worked successfully to ease the political rivalry between Florence and Venice. It was one of her great disappointments that she was never able to produce an heir to the throne, and that her attempt to pass off another's baby as the desired heir was quickly discovered. As mistress and wife, Bianca held a brilliant court that attracted the best and brightest of Florentine society. Many prominent Florentine families resented her as an outsider and protested her marriage to the grand duke. The couple died under suspicious circumstances within two days of one another. She was refused honorable burial, and her body was cast in a common grave. Rumors of a deliberate poisoning were never substantiated. Writers of later generations have embroidered profusely on her experiences. Bianca Capello's adventurous life, assertiveness, and courage to follow her own inclinations have made her a romantic heroine and a symbol of feminine emancipation.

Caporetto, Battle of

This WORLD WAR I battle takes its name from the extreme northern town of Caporetto, where Austrian and German troops broke through the Italian front line on October 24, 1917. Within a few days of the breakthrough, the Italian troops were in disorderly retreat. They regrouped along the Piave River some four weeks later, but by then their casualties numbered about 10,000 dead and 30,000 wounded. Some 300,000 were prisoners in the hands of the enemy and 350,000 had become separated from their units in the chaos of the retreat. About one-third of Italy's 1.8 million troops were knocked out of action by the Austro-German offensive. In addition, the Italians lost more than half of their artillery and machine guns, and an enormous quantity of supplies. That the most serious defeat suffered by the Italian army in any war did not result in complete collapse was due to the tough fight put up by units that were still operational, and to the inability of the Austrians to exploit their initial success. British and French troops, who arrived after the Italians had stopped the advance, had a positive effect on morale. The rout had major military and political repercussions. ARMANDO DIAZ replaced LUIGI CADORNA as commander in chief, and VITTORIO EMANUELE ORLANDO replaced PAOLO BOSELLI as prime minister. The new leaders took steps to improve the morale of soldiers and civilians, and to mobilize the economy for all-out resistance. Public opinion swung behind the war effort with renewed determination. New draftees (the "class of 1899") replenished the ranks and were called upon to carry on to victory. In the long term, however, Caporetto left a legacy of recriminations that embittered the political scene, until they were silenced by the Fascist dictatorship.

Capponi, Gino (1792–1876)
liberal patriot, reformer, and educator

This member of one of the most prominent families of the Florentine aristocracy was educated in Vienna and Florence, frequented the Tuscan court during Napoleonic times and in the RESTORATION, traveled widely in Italy and Europe to acquaint himself with the latest educational methods, and was a founder of the *Antologia,* the Florentine journal that promoted economic and educational reforms. A political moderate, Capponi believed in a *filosofia del buon senso* (philosophy of common sense) that avoided generalizations and served as a guide to concrete reforms. Intimately religious, he claimed that Christianity stood for charity, equality, and human dignity, but denied that it could have any political content or affiliation. As a historian of medieval and Renaissance Italy and of Christianity he insisted on the importance of objectivity and rejected the idea that the study of history could serve the interests of the moment. Of scholarly temperament and blind at the age of 40, Capponi played a limited role in public affairs in 1848. As an independent intellectual, he attracted and inspired the most progressive and reform-minded elements of his time, casting a cultural influence far greater than his limited public role would suggest.

Capuana, Luigi See VERISMO.

Capuchins See CATHOLIC REFORMATION.

carabinieri

The military corps of the carabinieri was founded in 1814 as part of the army of the Kingdom of SARDINIA. It was conceived as a lightly armed, highly mobile police force equipped with the latest precision weapon, the carbine, from which the corps derives its name. It is a fully militarized police force of about 80,000 in peacetime, capable of carrying out full-scale military operations, commanded by a regular army general, and subject to military discipline. The carabinieri are under the jurisdiction of the ministry of the interiors in peacetime and under the ministry of defense in wartime. Its policing duties include patrolling the countryside, securing military installations, fighting organized crime, conducting internal surveillance, carrying out rescue missions by land, air, and sea, recovering stolen art works, and apprehending art thieves. In wartime the carabinieri serve as military police. Its description as the *Arma Benemerita* (Deserving Corps) reflects the general respect that the corps has earned for its discipline, concern for the safety and rights of citizens, and its apolitical character. The corrazzieri (cuirrassiers) are a special unit of the corps that guards the head of state and the QUIRINAL PALACE.

Caracciolo, Domenico, marquis of Villamarina (1715–1789)
Neapolitan nobleman and political reformer

Caracciolo was born in Spain, studied law, and served as Neapolitan ambassador to Turin (1754–64), London (1764–71), and Paris (1771–81). Influenced by ENLIGHTENMENT ideas, Caracciolo undertook administrative and political reforms in SICILY, where he served as the king's viceroy (1781–86). He suppressed the INQUISITION, closed monasteries and guilds, taxed clerical properties, and curtailed religious festivals. He ran into severe resistance when he attacked the fiscal and jurisdictional privileges of the Sicilian nobility, which successfully resisted his efforts. Called by the king to Naples to serve as prime minister (1786–89), he encountered the hostility of Queen MARIE CAROLINE and her favorite, JOHN ACTON. Caracciolo died before the monarchy's fearful reaction to the FRENCH REVOLUTION ended attempts at administrative and political reform.

Caravaggio *(Library of Congress)*

Caravaggio (1573–1610)

unconventional painter known for his naturalistic effects

Michelangelo Merisi took his art name from the Lombard town of Caravaggio, where he was born. The son of a poor family, trained in Milan, he worked in Rome, Naples, Malta, and Sicily. His violent, quarrelsome temper landed him in trouble with the authorities wherever he went. He died on his way to Rome from a wound received in a brawl, leaving behind an artistic legacy of some 40 paintings. Reacting against the excesses of MANNERISM, Caravaggio strove to paint in a more natural fashion, depicting mythical and religious figures as ordinary folk engaged in worldly tasks, as when he depicted the executioners of Saint Peter as street toughs. Critics have seen Caravaggio as expressing a new

sense of piety rooted in everyday life, but it may also be that he was driven to create scandal with his paintings, as he did with his actions. Whatever his motives, there is no doubt that his work forces itself on the attention of the viewer. Massive bodies thrust into the foreground, expressive gestures, the contrast of light and shadow are element of his style. Caravaggio dominated Italian painting and cast his influence throughout Europe, due in part to a host of imitators and copyists. Dutch painters, including Rubens and Rembrandt, were particularly affected by his striving for naturalism.

Carboneria

most important of the secret societies agitating for Italian independence

The secret society of Carboneria emerged as the most important element in the secret political opposition to constituted government after 1815. The romantic imagination pictured the carbonari as mysterious conspirators practicing secret rites. The origins of the name, usually translated as "charcoal burners," are obscure. Conceivably, the term may refer to Masonic rituals practiced by the members, or to the actual occupation of the first carbonari, or to the secret nightly meetings held in forests in the light of charcoal fires. The secret society was formed in Naples in 1807–10 during the reign of JOACHIM MURAT, probably by Neapolitan military officers opposed to NAPOLEON I who wanted some form of representative government. During the Napoleonic period, the society may have enjoyed the covert support of Austria and England in their struggle to topple Napoleonic rule. When Austria replaced France as the dominant power in the peninsula after the CONGRESS OF VIENNA, the carbonari turned against Austria.

Their moderate agenda differed from that of the more radical JACOBINS who preceded them and were still active in the political underground. The carbonari sought change by winning the confidence of or putting pressure on monarchs and other influential people, in the spirit and manner of 18th-century FREEMASONRY. Constitutional monarchy, limited voting rights, parliamentary government, and access to public office by qualified people were their objectives. They conspired, staged coups, and resorted to street action, but seldom drew on people from outside their own ranks. It is possible that the innermost councils of Carboneria harbored republican convictions, but most members favored constitutional monarchy, and limitation of voting rights to people of property and education; they feared popular initiatives. In their view, national independence could be achieved without unifying the peninsula politically. They preferred to work with established monarchs and avoided attacking the privileged orders of society, with the exception of the clergy.

The group's political program was moderate, but internally the Carboneria was more open and democratic than most other secret societies. Most members were middle-class professionals, marginally employed intellectuals, and military officers, but the membership encompassed a cross-section of society from aristocrats to workers, and included some women. The members regarded one another as *buoni cugini* (good cousins), regardless of social extraction. The secret network spread from Naples to the rest of Italy and into France, connected with other secret societies, and orchestrated various uprisings starting in 1817. In the 1820s the conspirator FILIPPO MICHELE BUONARROTI centralized control of the Carboneria in his own hands and reorganized the network on an international basis. The political effectiveness of the Carboneria is a matter of dispute, but it seems that its membership reached the considerable figure of about 60,000. Governments were alarmed by its activities, repressed it where they could, and waged an intensive propaganda campaign against it. The carbonari played prominent roles in the REVOLUTIONS OF 1820–21 and 1830. The failure of these revolutions, the passing of the older generation, emergence of new leaders, and spread of more radical ideologies diminished the appeal of Carboneria after 1830. Giuseppe Mazz-

ini's YOUNG ITALY challenged it for control of the national movement. There was little left of Carboneria by 1848, when popular revolutions broke out in most parts of Italy. A few cells survived into the 1850s and 1860s, when the movement for national independence was out in the open and looked toward the new figures of CAVOUR and GIUSEPPE GARIBALDI.

Cardano, Girolamo (1501–1576)
late Renaissance scholar and natural philosopher

Born in Pavia and raised in Milan, Cardano was a mathematician, physician, astrologer, and student of magic. The combination of scientific rigor and belief in the supernatural makes him one of the most intriguing figures of the RENAISSANCE. At the universities of Pavia , Padua, and Bologna he made a name for himself as a pioneer in the development of algebra, and for his mechanical inventions, and knowledge of medicine. Cardano lived at a time when the boundaries between what we think of as science and magic were blurred. He saw both as legitimate quests to attain a better understanding of nature. In his view, science was a way of studying measurable phenomena, while magic sought to make sense of and control phenomena that escaped measurement. Sensation and human fate were among the latter. His special interest was astrology, which he practiced by applying mathematics to the behavior of celestial bodies. He developed precise tables to ascertain the conjuncture of celestial and terrestrial phenomena, in order to predict the fate of individuals and the course of human events. He defended astrology against its many critics, insisting that its failures were due to the inadequate training and shoddy practices of many of its practitioners, not to the nature of the subject. His suggestion that Christ's divine powers were in some measure attributable to astrological influences exposed him to charges of impiety. As his self-confidence grew with his fame, Cardano came to think of himself as uniquely qualified to understand and control natural processes. For his own self-assessment, see his autobiography, *De propria vita* (The book of my life, 1643, English translation 1930 and 2002).

Carducci, Giosuè (1835–1907)
major poet of the postunification period

The most celebrated Italian poet of the postunification period was born in Tuscany, graduated from the Scuola Normale of Pisa (1856), taught in secondary schools, and published *Rime*, his first book of poetry, in 1857. From 1860 to 1904 he taught at the University of Bologna. He later organized his poetical writings into chronological and stylistic groups entitled *Juvenilia* (1850–60), *Levia Gravia* (1861–71), *Giambi ed epodi* (1867–79), *Rime nuove* (1861–87), *Odi barbare* (1877–89), and *Rime e ritmi* (1887–99). Reacting to what he regarded as the degeneration of romantic poetry into mere sentimentality, Carducci returned to the classical style that represented to him the only authentic Italian literary tradition. But for Carducci classicism was not merely a matter of style. For him, classicism meant vigorous engagement with the issues of the day, which is what he did with his poetry to instill in his fellow countrymen the sense of civic responsibility that he deemed appropriate to the age of national independence. Never a cloistered figure, he engaged vigorously with all the issues of the day, using his academic post to broadcast his views and form a retinue of disciples who continued his secular apostolate. Carducci tried to clear the ground of cultural deadwood, railing against the influence of religion, which he equated with the most retrograde superstition. In the provocative *Inno a Satana* (Hymn to Satan, 1863), he hailed Satan as the symbol of human revolt and the liberation of reason from the tyranny of authority. His anticlerical and strongly republican sentiments mellowed with the passage of time, until an open profession of monarchist sentiments brought his conversion to a logical conclusion and led to his acceptance as the authoritative voice of unified Italy. In his later poetry he often shows sensitivity for matters of the spirit and avoids the rhetorical emphasis that mars some of his poetry. The ultimate international accolade came a few months before his death when he received the Nobel Prize in literature.

Carli, Gian Rinaldo (1720–1795)
economist and Enlightenment reformer

Born in Capodistria (now Kopen in Slovenia) when it was under Venetian rule, Carli emerged as one of the leading figures of the Italian ENLIGHTENMENT. After teaching at the University of Padua, he moved to Milan in the service of the Austrian government. He was one of the first intellectuals to take up the public campaign against belief in magic and witchcraft, arguing that observation and reason were the only reliable foundations of knowledge. He is remembered mostly for his economic writings, in which he questioned the physiocratic faith in free trade for agricultural products and argued for state control and regulation of manufacturing and trade to protect developing enterprises. As economic minister of Milan under Austrian rule, Carli carried out a land census (*catasto*) to give government officials and landowners objective data on land values for more equitable taxation. Feared at first by landowners, the land census revealed its usefulness when it resulted in increased valuations without higher taxes and promoted more efficient use of land resources. Carli also oversaw the minting of new coins to eliminate debased currency. To encourage public acceptance of vaccination against smallpox and show that the procedure was not dangerous, Carli staged the public vaccination of his son. A faithful servant of the HABSBURG dynasty, Carli saw no incompatibility between being part of the Habsburg multinational empire and asserting the uniqueness and unity of Italian culture, which he defended in the essay *Della patria degli italiani* (On the Italian fatherland), published in the Milanese review *Il Caffè* in 1765. The essay was not well received by the cosmopolitan intellectuals of Milan. PIETRO VERRI challenged Carli on this and other issues. Carli was deeply suspicious of theorists and abstractions. His pragmatic bent and his interest in concrete remedies for specific problems clashed with the search for broad principles of reform that engaged most of his contemporaries.

Carli, Guido   See BANCA D'ITALIA.

Carlo III di Borbone   See PARMA, CITY OF.

Carlo Lodovico di Borbone (1799–1883) (or Ludovico)

king of Etruria (1803–1807), duke of Lucca (1824–1847), duke of Parma (1847–1849)

This member of the Spanish BOURBON family reigned as a minor as king of Etruria (Tuscany) from 1803 to 1807 under the regency of his mother, Marie Louise of Bourbon. NAPOLEON I deposed them for failing to honor the trade blockade against Great Britain. The CONGRESS OF VIENNA assigned the Duchy of PARMA to his mother, but allowed Napoleon's second wife, Marie Louise of Habsburg, to govern that duchy until her death. In the meantime, the Bourbons were assigned the Duchy of LUCCA, which Carlo Lodovico's mother ruled until her death in 1824. Lodovico succeeded his mother as duke of Lucca and governed that city until 1847, when he took over the Duchy of Parma at the death of the Habsburg, Marie Louise. Lodovico's rule in Lucca was distinguished by his easygoing style of government, love of leisurely pastimes, and general bonhomie. He permitted Protestants to worship and allowed them to build their own chapel at Bagni di Lucca, partly to encourage foreign tourism. His weakness for the company of gamblers and adventurers did not go unnoticed. Conservatives regarded him as liberal, but the liberals of Lucca were not won over by his moderate politics. Organized demonstrations against him on the eve of the REVOLUTIONS of 1848 prompted him to leave the city in great haste and turn it over to the Grand Duchy of Tuscany, thus putting an end to Lucca's existence as an independent state. In Parma he ruled as Carlo II, signed a military pact with Austria, and resigned in March 1849 in favor of his son Carlo III, who was assassinated in 1854 under mysterious circumstances. Carlo Lodovico lived out the rest of his life in quiet and easy retirement. Easygoing and likable, he did not deem himself born to political life.

Carnera, Primo (1906–1967)

world heavyweight boxing champion and national symbol

The only Italian boxer to hold the world heavyweight title, Carnera was born into a family of modest means in the Friuli region, learned carpentry, and practiced his trade in France as a teenager. Having impressive size and strength (he was 6' 9" tall and weighed 250–270 pounds), Carnera began his career as a circus strongman. His boxing debut occurred in 1928 and he quickly became a popular attraction in France and England. In 1930–33 he repeatedly toured the United States to establish his credentials as a legitimate contender for the heavyweight title. While the reactions of the press were mixed, Carnera was an immediate success with Italian-Americans. He took the world heavyweight title from Jack Sharkey in June 1933. Carnera's success also caught the attention of Fascist leaders in Italy, including BENITO MUSSOLINI, who congratulated him on his victory. The Fascist press hailed him as an example of Italian physical prowess and daring. Flattered by the attention and motivated by genuine patriotism, Carnera praised the Fascist regime and donned the black shirt. The official adulation stopped after Max Baer took the title from him in June 1934. Although he remained personally popular in Italy, his boxing career went into irreversible decline after he lost to Joe Louis in June 1935. His high earnings from boxing were mostly diverted into the pockets of managers and middlemen. He returned to Italy to pursue a brief and unremarkable career in Italian cinema. He married in 1939, spent the war years in Italy, returned to the United States in July 1946, and became an American citizen in 1953. His success as a professional wrestler in the 1950s brought him the financial security that had eluded him as a boxer. Carnera's boxing career was dogged by rumors of fixed fights and control by shady crime figures. Some of his encounters were indeed fixed, as was customary in the boxing world when a promising contender was being groomed for the title. But his key career matches were apparently legitimate. A man whose fierce appearance disguised a caring and gentle disposition, Carnera prevailed as a fighter by diligence and hard work rather than by natural talent. His life was fictionalized in the film *The Harder They Fall* (1956).

Carracci, Annibale See RENI, GUIDO.

Carta del Lavoro See CORPORATISM.

Caruso, Enrico (1873–1921)
opera star, singing idol, and national symbol
The most admired Italian operatic singer of all time was born in Naples to a family of modest means, the only one of his mother's first 18 children to survive (she would give birth to three more, two of whom survived childhood). He began singing in a local church and gradually won local renown for the beauty and passionate quality of his tenor voice. His success was rapid after he made his debut in 1895 in PIETRO MASCAGNI's opera *Cavalleria rusticana.* He sang in all major opera houses, but his career was centered on New York's Metropolitan Opera House. He was New York's favorite tenor from the time of his first Metropolitan appearance in 1903 to the year of his untimely death from pleurisy. Italian-Americans idolized him, and he in turn drew them into the opera house by the thousands. Caruso popularized the Italian opera

repertory in the United States, to the dismay of the devotees of French and German opera, which dominated the American stage until his arrival. Those who did not hear him in person could appreciate him through his recordings. Caruso's career happened to coincide with the beginning of the recording industry, and he took to the new medium seriously and enthusiastically, recording some 240 selections in the course of his career. He was the first singer to reach a vast public beyond the opera house and to bridge the gap between classical and popular music.

Casanova, Giacomo (1725–1798)
adventurer, confidence man, and talented self-promoter renowned for his amorous escapades
Giovanni Giacomo (or Jacopo) Casanova was born in Venice. The son of actors, he was abandoned by his mother at an early age, studied for the clergy but was expelled before being ordained, and tried his luck as a soldier and a violinist without success, before taking up the life of wandering that made his name a byword for adventure and scandal. A man of great charm, he ingratiated himself with powerful people, made his living as a confidence man, gambler, spy, and magician, usually managing to keep one step ahead of the law. Jailed in Venice for recruiting for FREEMASONRY (1755), he wrote a book about his daring escape from the infamous Piombi prison. Highly popular in Paris, he introduced the lottery to France and made a great deal of money as its director. He wrote his memoirs in French, the language of most of his writings, commenting shrewdly on figures and events of his time and making no effort to disguise his own libertine nature. Particularly proud of his amorous escapades, which he often described graphically, he probably exaggerated his success with women. He has come nevertheless to be thought of as the epitome of the seducer. Driven out of the great capitals of Europe by his unsavory reputation, he spent the last 13 years of his life

employed as a librarian in the castle of his friend Count Waldstein in Bohemia, where he shared the servants' quarters and grumbled about their lack of respect for him. Like his contemporary CAGLIOSTRO, Casanova personified the 18th-century stereotype of the charming, quick-witted, unscrupulous Italian who lived by stratagems, but he can also be seen more favorably as the embodiment of a secular mentality intolerant of unexamined, religiously based injunctions and restraints. His multivolume *Memoirs* and various abridgements of the same can be read in English editions.

Casati Law

Named after Minister of Public Instruction Gabrio Casati (1798–1873) who sponsored it, this law was adopted by the Piedmontese parliament in November 1859 shortly after the annexation of Lombardy. The law, which was extended to the entire national territory after unification, established a centralized system of national education based on the Napoleonic model, in which a central ministry of education set national curricula, and teacher certification requirements, and supervised and enforced teaching and learning standards for the entire nation. Popularly elected local school boards under the control of PREFECTS were held responsible for establishing and funding public elementary schools. Only kindergartens, vocational schools, and naval and military academies were exempt from regulation. The law was criticized for requiring fundamental scholastic choices that determined careers at too young an age, the elitist nature of the secondary school curriculum, the Latin requirement that worked against students from poor backgrounds, and the sharp distinction between humanistic and technical curricula that made it all but impossible to switch from one to the other. The Casati Law remained in force with only minor revisions until 1923.

Casati, Teresa See CONFALONIERI, FEDERICO.

Caserio, Sante See ANARCHISM.

Cassa per il Mezzogiorno
national fund established to promote the economic development of the southern regions

The Cassa per il Mezzogiorno (Fund for the South) was established by law in August 1950 to finance, plan, and implement programs for the economic development of the South. The Cassa's initial objectives were land reclamation, water control, irrigation, road construction, and other projects specifically related to agricultural development. It was to be funded for 10 years at annual levels of 100 billion lire. In 1952 and 1957 the duration, level of funding, and scope of its activities were expanded to include industrial development, schooling, tourism, urban renewal, public health, and the construction of economic infrastructures. To speed up its operations, the Cassa was exempt from the bureaucratic red tape of other government agencies. From the mid-1950s to the mid-1970s it achieved some spectacular breakthroughs. It funded the construction of modern steel mills at Bagnoli and Taranto and of chemical plants and oil refineries in the regions of Puglia and Sicily. In 1970–74 the South absorbed 32 percent of the country's industrial investment largely as a result of public funds funneled there through the Cassa. Its projects had significant impact on local economies, but did not solve the larger problems of unemployment, emigration, inadequate schooling, and organized crime that continued to plague vast areas of the South. Its industrial investments never recovered from the setbacks caused by the oil crisis of the early 1970s. Nothing done for agriculture stopped the exodus of people from the countryside. In the meantime, the Cassa fell prey to the practices of feather-bedding, clientelism, and political manipulation that plagued the public sector. The vast sums spent in the South by the Cassa and by government ministries and bureaus to address the SOUTHERN QUESTION created a political backlash in other parts of the country. The Cassa was abolished in 1984 and its functions assigned to a multiplicity of national, regional, and local agencies. The operating principle of the new policy is that public funds must be directed toward all depressed regions regardless of their geographic location. The South should continue to receive substantial funding commensurate with the lower levels of public spending typical of the first years of the 21st century.

Cassino, Battle of See WORLD WAR II.

Castelfidardo, Battle of See CIALDINI, ENRICO.

Castelli, Benedetto See TORRICELLI, EVANGELISTA.

Casti, Giambattista (1724–1803)
satirical writer and social critic
This versifier and playwright delighted in satirizing the personages, manners, and pretensions of his time. Showing little inclination for the life of the celibate priest that he was ordained to be, Casti wandered throughout Europe observing and commenting on what he saw in Vienna and St. Petersburg, where he was court poet, in Milan where he lived, and in Paris where he died. His facility as a writer was exceeded only by his cynicism, which was not always misplaced. In his *Poema tartaro* (1778) he ridiculed the pretensions of the Russian court of Catherine II and the civilized veneer that was superimposed on Russia's rustic culture. The men and ideas of the FRENCH REVOLUTION fared no better in his *Gli animali parlanti* (The talking animals), written in the 1790s but published in 1802. His talking animals imagine that they can govern themselves wisely with written constitutions, but their wicked nature triumphs over their good intentions, and they govern worse than their predecessors. NAPOLEON I paid the work the compliment of banning it. The sexual innuendo of his *Novelle galanti* showed him at his titillating best and gave him a

reputation as a licentious writer. His serious and downright censorious contemporary GIUSEPPE PARINI took Casti to task for his frivolous tone and tolerant attitude.

Castiglione, Baldassarre (1478–1529)
courtier, diplomat, soldier, and scholar
Castiglione personified the qualities of the cultured and versatile gentleman that he described in his famous book *Il cortegiano* (The courtier). Born near Mantua to a family of small landowners, Castiglione was educated at the courts of LODOVICO SFORZA and the GONZAGA FAMILY, where learning and chivalry were held in high regard. He later served in diplomatic capacities at court in Urbino, Mantua, and Rome. He wrote *Il cortegiano* between 1508 and 1516 after serving in Urbino, where the art of gentlemanly (and ladylike) behavior was cultivated with the greatest care. The book, written in polished Italian for easier access, is cast in the form of a dialogue among the men and women of the court. The ideal gentleman (courtier) must be of noble blood, loyal to the prince, skilled in the arts of war, physically fit, adept at sports, familiar with foreign languages, well read, educated in many different fields, and not overly specialized. He must display his qualities and accomplishments nonchalantly, with natural ease, as if they cost him no effort, that whole demeanor being described as *sprezzatura*. It will not do for a gentleman to seem overly preoccupied with anything, except possibly the preservation of his honor, which he must guard with the greatest care. Courtly ladies must be good domestic managers, well educated, and always gracious. It must be emphasized that Castiglione was describing a code of behavior considered appropriate to the noble orders of society (the courtiers), not to commoners who had to contend with the needs of daily life. Although Castiglione was clearly describing an ideal that was nowhere fully attainable, his book was translated in many languages after its publication in 1528 and served as a guide to etiquette until the 19th century. Castiglione was less fortunate than his book. He is said to have died of

a broken heart after failing on a diplomatic mission entrusted to him by Pope CLEMENT VII.

Castracani, Castruccio See LUCCA, CITY OF.

castrati

A new type of singer made its debut at the papal court in late-16th-century Rome, where the religious zeal of the CATHOLIC REFORMATION kept women off the stage. The voices of the castrati ranged from contralto and mezzo to full soprano, the unnatural tone having been secured by castration (the surgical removal of the sex glands) at age seven or eight, before the onset of puberty. Church authorities never officially endorsed the practice but allowed it to continue. What had been a religiously motivated practice soon took on a momentum of its own as castrati singers met with overwhelming popular favor, and impoverished parents sacrificed their boys to secure a better future for them. By the 18th century the castrati were the great stars of Italian OPERA. Castration did not guarantee artistic success, and indeed the overwhelming majority of the thousands of boys subjected to the operation found employment in occupations less respectable than singing. But the successful ones, like Farinelli (Carlo Broschi, 1705–82), who was considered the greatest artist of them all, were idolized throughout Europe and lavishly compensated. They were international stars of the first magnitude with popular followings similar to those of contemporary pop idols. The castrati rendered a tremendous service to music by bringing the art of singing to an unprecedented and possibly never equaled level of technical perfection. Connoisseurs found their singing particularly affecting with its combination of pathos and power. Their voice control enabled them to perform the most amazing vocal feats. Interest in the castrati waned quickly in the 19th century as women took to the stage, but castrati continued to sing in the choir of the Sistine Chapel into the early years of the 20th century. The last singing castrato was Alessandro Moreschi

(1858–1922), who made several recordings in Rome in 1902–03.

Castro, War of See BARBERINI FAMILY.

Cateau-Cambrésis, Treaty of (or Peace of)

Signed in the French town of Cambrai on April 3, 1559, this treaty addressed some long-standing rivalries among European powers. England gave up its claims to Calais in France, and France recognized Spanish control over Milan, Naples, Sicily, and Sardinia. The French thus acknowledged the Spanish domination of the Italian peninsula. The French also withdrew from Piedmont and Savoy, restoring those territories to the rule of the HOUSE OF SAVOY, agreed that Siena should be part of the Medici state (see MEDICI FAMILY), and ceded the island of CORSICA to the Republic of GENOA. With this treaty, France gave up on the dream of controlling Italy. The House of Savoy began the slow process of Italian expansion that resulted in national unification in the 19th century. VENICE maintained its policy of neutrality and continued its losing battle against the Turks in defense of its overseas empire. Milan, Tuscany, Naples, and the Papal States were formally independent but under the direct or indirect control of Spain. The Italian states, unable to defend themselves against the greater powers, gained the protection of Spain (later replaced by Austria), and some domestic peace, but lost their independence. There would be many more wars and territorial changes in Italy before national independence, but the Treaty of Cateau-Cambrésis determined Italy's place in the international order for the next three centuries.

Catholic Action

Catholic Action is an association of lay Catholics working closely with the clergy to promote Catholic interests and values. It is an international organization whose origins can be found in the papal pronouncements of the 1860s encouraging the faithful to resist secular ideologies and the demands of modern states. Its precursor in Italy was the Opera dei Congressi, which PIUS X dissolved in 1903 because he deemed it too independent of clerical control. Pope BENEDICT XV established Catholic Action in Italy in 1915 to lead and coordinate the activities of various Catholic economic, political, and social organizations. Pope PIUS XI, who reorganized it, saw Catholic Action as the main secular arm of the church reaching out to school-age children with a strong cultural and spiritual message. Its expansion created a potential for conflict with the Fascist regime, which saw it as a dangerous rival in its efforts to win the hearts and minds of Italians. The regime acknowledged the legitimacy of Catholic Action in 1929, but attacked it in 1931 to gain exclusive control of all youth organizations. Catholic Action survived the confrontation by promising to concern itself with purely religious matters. Nevertheless, many figures in the Christian Democratic Party (DC) of the post-Fascist era were formed by their experiences in Catholic Action and relied on its support in their postwar campaigns. The lay character and scope of Catholic Action were restored after 1946, spawning a multiplicity of lay organizations in schooling, scouting, sports, entertainment, social welfare, and political action. It became an umbrella organization with subsidiaries in every corner of Italian society. The organizations of the political Left stood up to Catholic Action only in the heart of Italy's "red belt." Its organizations reached a total membership of 2.7 million at the heyday of its power in the mid-1950s. Until the 1970s Catholic Action was an important part of the political machinery of the DC, helping it to spread its message and bring out the vote, and generally playing the role of a reserve clergy. But not all its members followed the course set by the church. Some actually joined movements of the opposition, including the most radical extra-parliamentary groups of the Left. Its political importance has declined in recent years, particularly since the

demise of the DC in 1994 and the church's retreat from direct involvement in Italian politics.

Catholic Church

The Holy Catholic and Apostolic Church, as the Catholic Church is properly called, stands for different things. To the devout, the church is the divinely ordained institution that stands between man and God and is the sole means of salvation. In a secular frame of reference, however, the church stands for people, organizations, structures, and rituals that advance clerical interests. This is particularly true in Italy where the Catholic Church is palpably present in countless ways. Its imprint is evident on land and towns, in politics, the economy, and the way of life. To Italians, the church (*la chiesa*) is a daily presence with a large historical legacy. The PAPAL STATES were for centuries a politically sovereign entity in the heart of the peninsula. The PAPACY is firmly planted on Italian soil and shares ROME, the national capital, with Italy's political leadership. Thus, in Italy, CHURCH AND STATE often compete for the same space claim allegiance from the same people.

Neither the Catholic Church nor the Italian state can afford to ignore one another. Their relations require constant monitoring and adjustment. About 98 percent of Italians are nominally Catholic, and although less than one-third attend mass regularly, the overwhelming majority marry in church, have their children baptized, and are buried with religious rites. In Italy the sanctity and closeness of the family is both a religious principle and a dominant social attitude. The church exerts a cultural influence in Italy that is far greater than the level of religious observance might suggest. Such influence, however, has never gone unchallenged. Opposition to the secular role of the church has found expression in the many forms of ANTICLERICALISM. Italians have rebuffed the church in politics by voting communist by the millions and on family matters by practicing contraception and legalizing divorce and abortion.

The church has responded to these and other challenges by mobilizing the clergy, organizing at the grass roots to combat secular tendencies, supporting certain political parties for reasons of opportunity or principle, and using the media to influence public opinion. The most widely distributed publication in Italy today is *La Famiglia Cristiana,* a religiously inspired journal that carries the word of the church to millions of households. The church constantly adjusts its tactics to confront change and promote its agenda. The changes that have diminished the influence of the church in the last 100 years are primarily economic and social. They include the decline of agriculture, the virtual disappearance of the peasantry as a social class, large-scale migrations from countryside to city and from South to North, the undermining of hierarchical relationships in the home, workplace, and civil society, and the spread of consumerism and secular entertainment. The church has responded with the reforms of Vatican II, updating its practices and rituals, reaching out to the laity, and shaping its messages to reflect more accurately the values of middle-class churchgoers.

This process of *aggiornamento* (renewal) has not been without problems. It has alienated Catholics who remain attached to the old traditions, and generated fears that the church is moving too fast, or not fast enough. Italian Catholics are divided on such issues as the celibacy of priests and the ordination of women. In sum, the church faces the same challenges in Italy that it does in the rest of the world, with added immediacy and urgency due to physical proximity and interdependence of church and state.

Catholic Reformation

religious and administrative reform of the Roman Catholic Church in the 16th and 17th centuries

The term Catholic Reformation is preferred to the once common Counter-Reformation because the latter implies that the religious reforms were a reaction to the challenge of Protestantism rather than a spontaneous development within the Catholic Church. It is true that the call for reform of the church was sounded before the rise of Protestantism. It came from humanist scholars like LORENZO VALLA and from bishops and monarchs, from lay movements and new religious orders like the Oratory of Divine Love. Popular support for GIROLAMO SAVONAROLA showed that the masses were also eager for reform. Luther's challenge to the papacy heightened the sense of urgency, but it could not have induced the movement for reform all by itself. Pope PAUL III took the initiative soon after his election in 1534 by naming cardinals sympathetic to reform and appointing a commission to begin the process. It took 30 years for the COUNCIL OF TRENT to agree, and another 30 years before the council's recommendations were implemented. The more visible innovations were the INDEX, the ROMAN INQUISITION, and the JESUIT ORDER.

Most important was the implementation of clerical discipline from pope to bishops and bishops to lower clergy. Parish priests were held to more rigorous standards of conduct, required to involve the laity in church activities, and keep accurate records. The earliest birth, baptismal, marriage, and death records in most Italian parishes date from the beginning of the 17th century, for it took that long to implement the new rules. Important changes occurred also among the monastic orders. The Capuchins, founded in 1536 and named after the shape of their hood (*cappuccio*), were an offshoot of the Franciscan order that drew ordinary people into the life of the church. Religious reforms could not change the political realities of the Italian peninsula. Under the control of powerful rulers, the PAPACY was no longer politically independent. Its political fate was controlled by the Spanish monarchy, which was the dominant power in Italy and the Continent.

The Catholic Reformation affected Spain and the Italian states most directly. Protestant minorities in these countries were silenced and their leaders forced into exile, the clergy tightened its hold on education, and the expression of ideas was monitored carefully for signs of heresy. The arts were mobilized to glorify the church. Places of worship were redesigned and embellished to encourage attendance and participation in religious rituals. While Protestants shunned artistic displays, Catholics reveled in the glories of BAROQUE art. With the reorganization of the church, affirmation of traditional Catholic doctrines, founding of new schools, and adoption of new rituals and art forms, the Catholic Reformation had an enormous and controversial impact on Italian culture. Critics deplore the stifling effects of enforced religious conformity in Catholic countries like Italy and Spain, forgetting perhaps that Protestant countries were equally repressive. GIORDANO BRUNO, TOMMASO CAMPANELLA, and GALILEO were the most prominent victims of this repressive climate. Critics also charge that the Catholic Reformation isolated Italy from the most progressive parts of Europe where the economic and political institutions of the modern world were being developed. Many Italians who shared these perceptions opposed the church and rallied to the cause of ANTICLERICALISM.

Cattaneo, Carlo (1801–1869)
economist, historian, government critic, and reformer

Cattaneo was born in Milan to a family of modest means, studied jurisprudence, and graduated from the University of Pavia in 1824. Drawn to the study of social problems and statistical investigations, he contributed to DOMENICO ROMAGNOSI's *Annali universali di statistica* (1833–38), and in 1839 founded his own review, *Il Politecnico*, which called for economic and political reforms. Averse to political conspiracy, Cattaneo initially hoped to promote reforms within the framework of the AUSTRIAN EMPIRE, to which his native region of Lombardy belonged and which he hoped could be transformed into a federation of equal nationalities. Italian independence would be a gradual consequence of such a federal system. Disillusioned by the lack of interest in reform shown by the Austrian authorities, Cat-

taneo supported the REVOLUTION of 1848 and served as head of the revolutionary war council that took charge of Milan during the revolution. His republican sentiments became manifest when he opposed the plan to unite Lombardy to the kingdom of Piedmont-Sardinia, commenting that he preferred rule by an enlightened Austria to rule by a backward Piedmont. Although a republican, Cattaneo also opposed GIUSEPPE MAZZINI's view of Italy as a centralized republic, arguing that a loose federation was preferable, given Italy's regional diversity. Forced into exile by the failure of the revolution, Cattaneo settled in Switzerland, where he remained until 1859. He was disappointed that the liberation of the South in 1860, which he supported, resulted in a centralized monarchy. He refused to take a seat in the Italian parliament, to which he was elected in 1860 and 1867, so as not to take the oath of loyalty to the king that was required of all elected members. He lived out his last years in Lugano, Switzerland. Cattaneo's intellectual influence was felt across political divides. He introduced POSITIVISM to Italy, promoted the study of statistics and social problems, and inspired scholars and political activists critical of the monarchy. His essay on the key role of cities in Italian history (1858) established the field of urban studies.

Cavallero, Ugo (1880–1943)
military and industrial expert, general and army chief of staff

Highly regarded for his professional competence, this commander played a major role in the preparation and conduct of military operations in WORLD WAR II. Born into a prominent Piedmontese family, Cavallero received his first commission as a lieutenant in 1910. In 1911 he ranked first in his class at the war college and volunteered for duty in the ITALIAN-TURKISH WAR. Promoted to the rank of captain and awarded a bronze medal for military valor, in May 1915 he was appointed to the general staff of General LUIGI CADORNA. Cavallero's skills as a military planner were instrumental in halting the Austro-German offensive after the BATTLE OF CAPORETTO and in reorganizing the army for the final battles of the war. In 1918 he was promoted to brigadier general and later served as Italian military representative at the PARIS PEACE CONFERENCE. In 1920 he resigned from the army to work for private industry. BENITO MUSSOLINI sought his advice and appointed him undersecretary of war in 1925. Cavallero was apparently instrumental in having General PIETRO BADOGLIO appointed chief of staff, but disagreements with his chief led Cavallero to resign as undersecretary in 1928. Back in civilian life, Cavallero took on the presidency of the ANSALDO STEEL WORKS and reorganized the firm during his tenure (1928–33). Called back into service, in 1937 he succeeded RODOLFO GRAZIANI as commander of Italian forces in East Africa. After the conclusion of the Pact of Steel between Italy and Germany, he assumed responsibility for coordinating military preparations of the two countries and became identified with the Fascist regime's pro-German policies. In December 1940 Cavallero replaced Badoglio as chief of staff after the armed forces had suffered serious military reverses in Africa and Albania. His willingness to let the German high command assume principal responsibility for the conduct of the war on all fronts put him on a collision course with fellow officers critical of Germany, and also with Mussolini's initial resolve to fight a "parallel war" without German help. As chief of staff, Cavallero did not press to reduce the size of the armed forces and improve their armament, yielding instead to Mussolini's desire to maintain a numerically large army. Mussolini dismissed him in February 1943 as part of a general reshuffling of top positions. Badoglio had him arrested after Mussolini's ouster from power on July 25, 1943. While in prison, Cavallero wrote an exculpatory memorandum, which magnified his differences with Mussolini and his role in the events leading up to the dictator's ouster. Badoglio may have deliberately allowed a copy of Cavallero's memorandum to fall into German hands to compromise him. Cavallero apparently committed suicide on September 13, 1943, under circumstances that have never been fully clarified, perhaps to avoid being forced to cooperate with the Germans after the Italian army surrendered to the Allies on September 3, 1943.

Cavalli, Francesco See OPERA.

Cavallotti, Felice (1842–1898)
charismatic political agitator, journalist, and Radical Party leader

Cavallotti caught the public imagination as an opponent of the monarchy and of parliamentary corruption. Born in Milan, he interrupted his studies to fight as a volunteer for GIUSEPPE GARIBALDI in 1860 and 1866. That same year he graduated from the University of Padua with a law degree, but chose to pursue a career as a journalist, political commentator, poet, and playwright. Elected to parliament in 1873, he joined the LIBERAL LEFT, where he distinguished himself for his stand against the practices of political TRANSFORMISM. When the Liberals came to power in 1876, he moved further to the left, calling for universal suffrage and for a "social republic" that would close the gap between rich and poor, government and the people. Cavallotti rejected the idea of insurrection and looked to parliament to carry on the struggle on behalf of the people. The so-called Pact of Rome that he drew up for the movements of the Left called for the protection of civil rights, administrative decentralization, free elementary education, reduced military spending, and restraints on the power of the king. As leader of the first Radical Party, Cavallotti led the opposition to the government of FRANCESCO CRISPI, whom he called corrupt and a threat to democracy. His vehement denunciations of political practices and opponents aroused both admiration and hatred. He died from a fatal wound suffered while fighting his 33rd political duel. The Radical Party embarked on a more moderate course after his death, which came just as the political system that he condemned experienced a crisis from which the parties of the Left emerged stronger.

Cavazzoni, Sefano See PPI.

Caviglia, Enrico (1862–1945)
*army general who played a major role in
World War I*
Caviglia served as a lieutenant in Ethiopia in
1896 and in Japan as a military observer during the Russo-Japanese War. He distinguished
himself as a field commander in WORLD WAR I.
He was a key figure in the aftermath of the BAT-
TLE OF CAPORETTO, when he directed the rede-
ployment of the divisions that halted the
Austrian advance. He was also largely responsible for planning the final offensives of the war.
These achievements earned him the rank of
army general. He served briefly as war minister
in 1919 and was appointed senator the same
year. He commanded the troops that evicted
Gabriele D'Annunzio's legionnaires from FIUME
in December 1920. Initially a Fascist sympathizer, Caviglia turned against fascism during the
MATTEOTTI crisis. He was promoted to the rank of
marshal in 1926, but generally kept out of the
public eye during the Fascist period, pursuing his
professional military interests as a writer and
international observer, and working quietly
behind the scenes to undermine his rival, Marshal PIETRO BADOGLIO. Caviglia retained the
king's confidence throughout these years. He
played an advisory role in the king's ouster of
BENITO MUSSOLINI in July 1943, was mentioned
as a possible successor to Mussolini as head of
government (the king chose Badoglio instead),
commanded the short-lived defense of Rome
against the Germans, and surrendered the city
on September 10, 1943.

Cavour, Camillo Benso, Count of
(1810–1861)
*chief architect of Italian unification and first
Italian prime minister*
The first prime minister of the kingdom of Italy
was born to a family of the Piedmontese nobility. He attended military school (1820–26), pursued a military career, but left the army in 1831
to pursue farming and management of family-
owned lands. Successful as a landlord and financially independent, he turned his attention to
public affairs. He was an advocate of childhood
education, agricultural association, free trade,
and civil liberties. He entered politics in 1847
when new laws on freedom of the press gave
him the incentive to launch *Il Risorgimento*, a
newspaper that gave its name to the movement
for national unification. He was among those
liberals who in January 1848 called on King
CHARLES ALBERT to grant a constitution. In June
1848 he was elected to Sardinia's first parliament, where he supported the war against Austria and the annexation of LOMBARDY and
VENETIA. Reelected in 1849, he led the political
center against supporters of absolute monarchy
and the clericals on the Right, and democrats
and republicans on the Left.

Cavour's political and economic principles
were firmly fixed. He opposed the clerical right
and democratic left, was for constitutional monarchy, limited voting rights, parliamentary government, freedom of the press, and free trade.

In 1850–52 Cavour held cabinet posts as minister of agriculture and commerce and minister
of finance. He became prime minister in November 1852, and held that post with only one brief
interruption until his death. As prime minister
he took firm control of parliament and directed
both domestic and foreign policy. He presided
over an ambitious and successful program of
railroad construction, naval expansion, and
industrialization that gave Piedmont the economic lead among the Italian states. His dislike
of Austria, support of political dissidents and
exiles from other Italian states, and reliance on
parliament made him popular among liberals in
Italy and abroad. Austrian opposition prompted
Cavour to look for allies among those liberals. In
Italy he relied on the support of liberals who
wanted national independence, abroad he
looked for governments that shared his liberal
principles and were prepared to challenge Austrian hegemony in Italy. Cavour admired the

British system of government, but could not get British support because the government would not abandon its policy of neutrality. NAPOLEON III, on the other hand, was prepared to align France with Piedmont-Sardinia against Austria.

Cavour's decision to go to war alongside England and France against Russia in the CRIMEAN WAR opened up new diplomatic prospects. One result was the secret AGREEMENT OF PLOMBIÈRES, concluded in July 1858 by Cavour and the French emperor. By its terms, France agreed to come to Piedmont's aid in a war against Austria in return for territorial and other compensations from Piedmont. The agreement went into effect when Cavour provoked Austria into declaring war on Piedmont-Sardinia in April 1859. But the Second WAR OF NATIONAL INDEPENDENCE did not go quite as Cavour had hoped. France pulled out before Austria was decisively defeated, and a chagrined Cavour stepped down as prime minister in July 1859. He returned to office in January 1860 to preside over the unexpected annexation of central Italy, the spectacular success of GIUSEPPE GARIBALDI's expedition to Sicily and Naples, and the incorporation of the South into the newly formed Kingdom of Italy.

None of this was part of a predetermined plan. Individual initiatives, fortuitous circumstances, and chance played a large role in these events. Nevertheless, Cavour showed his political skill in being able to turn unexpected developments to Piedmont's advantage. It is not that he was a mere opportunist, as some of his critics have charged, for he was a convinced liberal and an Italian patriot in his own way. He simply did not envisage such a rapid conclusion to the process of national unification, which he would have preferred to see happen in a more gradual manner. He did not approve of Garibaldi's expedition to Sicily, tried to stop it, and when he realized that he could not do so, went along with it to prevent the more impetuous and politically suspect republican patriots from controlling it, gaining the upper hand, and turning the South into a center of republican agitation. It was to advance his vision of moderate, constitutional

government that he and King VICTOR EMMANUEL II decided to send the Piedmontese army to the South, with the consent of France. To get there, they invaded, occupied and never relinquished a large slice of papal territory, which also became part of the Kingdom of Italy. Cavour would have preferred a more orderly process, but was ready nevertheless to seize the opportunities that came his way. He decided to extend Piedmontese law to the annexed territories and ratify the process by means of well-orchestrated popular plebiscites that returned large majorities in favor of national unification under the monarchy of Victor Emmanuel II.

His constitutional but high-handed procedures left bitter political legacies. Southern resentment found expression in BRIGANDAGE; democrats and republicans, including Garibaldi, protested vehemently against the cession to France of the province of NICE and the REGION OF SAVOY, which was part of Cavour's bargain with Napoleon; the PAPACY denounced the loss of its territory and refused to recognize the new state. Thus was born the conflict of CHURCH AND STATE that bedeviled Italian politics until it was settled in 1929. Many issues were unresolved when Cavour died unexpectedly on June 6, 1861, but the unification of Italy under the HOUSE OF SAVOY was unquestionably his great achievement and his most important legacy.

Cellini, Benvenuto (1500–1572)
Renaissance artist and autobiographer

The candid self-portrait that this Florentine goldsmith and sculptor gave of himself in his *Autobiography* makes him seem remarkably modern. It is the story of an ambitious, assertive, and resourceful individual, who prevails by his talent and quick wit, and is not shy about broadcasting his merits. His family background was ordinary, but not without surprises. The father, a mason, wanted his son to take up the same trade, but allowed him to take up the arts when he saw the young man's passion and talent for drawing. Cellini latched onto powerful patrons.

Benvenuto Cellini *(Library of Congress)*

From 1519 to 1540 he worked mostly at the papal court in Rome, and from 1519 to 1540 at the French court in Paris. After 1540 he worked mostly for the MEDICI FAMILY in Florence. Most of his Roman works were lost when he melted them to provide precious metal for the pope just before the SACK OF ROME. The saltcellar that he cast for Francis I displays his goldsmith's talent for meticulously conceived and executed miniature detail. The most important work of his Florentine period is the statue of Perseus beheading Medusa. This and his few other surviving works suggest an artist more preoccupied with realistic representation than with conveying emotion. Cellini's intense pride in his artistic skill is a recurring theme of his *Autobiography*. It reflects not only his sense of personal achievement but also the sentiment shared by artists of his gen-

eration that they had brought the visual arts to perfection. The *Autobiography* is a carefully constructed self-portrait that mixes personal pride with candid assessments of strengths and weaknesses. It parades its subject as brave, quarrelsome, boastful, generous, candid, deceitful, devoted to art, and totally self-absorbed. As the portrait of a genuine human being it reflects the interest in the individual that was the notable novelty of the culture of Renaissance HUMANISM.

Cena, Giovanni   See FACCIO, RINA.

Cesi, Federico (1585–1630)
natural scientist and cultural innovator,
Prince of Sant'Angelo and San Polo
Born to a family of the Roman nobility, Prince Federico received the best education available in his day. His mastery of classical Latin placed him at the forefront of humanist scholarship, but his most impressive intellectual attribute was a lively curiosity and an encyclopedic mind that reached out to all branches of knowledge. At age 18 he helped found the Roman Accademia dei Lincei in 1603 (see ACADEMIES), an interdisciplinary group that cultivated the study of the natural sciences and mathematics. Cesi visited Naples to familiarize himself with the scientific studies of Giambattista Della Porta and his school of southern philosophy. After 1613, Cesi became a convert to the school of GALILEO, adopting the mathematical and experimental methods associated with the Florentine scientist. Cesi's adoption of Galilean methodology is thought to have oriented Italian science away from the study of magic and the supernatural and in the direction of exact measurement and experimental verification. Cesi exercised great influence on his contemporaries because of his personal prestige, social connections, and indefatigable work as a publicist. He was responsible for the publication of important scientific works, illustrations of flora and fauna specimens, collection of natural objects, use of precision instruments, and the

staging of scientific demonstrations for the public. While not himself a practicing scientist, Cesi was instrumental in propagating scientific knowledge and interest in experimentation among educated Italians, thus helping to keep scientific culture alive at a time when it was suspect in the eyes of religious and political authorities in the peninsula.

CGIL (Confederazione Generale Italiana del Lavoro)

As the major union of workers in Italy, the CGIL directs and coordinates the activities of its member federations in the various sectors of the economy. Worker representatives from the major political parties, the Christian Democrats (DC), Communists (PCI), and Socialists (PSI) founded it in wartime Rome in June 1944. The union called for a national plan of reconstruction, new labor contracts, full employment, land reform, and comprehensive social assistance for all workers. Irreconcilable political and organizational differences with communists caused ACLI (Associazione Cristiana dei Lavoratori Italiani), the labor organization of the Christian Democrats, to leave the CGIL in September 1948 and to found the rival, DC-dominated CISL (Confederazione Italiana dei Sindacati dei Lavoratori) in 1950. The CGIL remained dominant in large industry and among agricultural laborers and sharecroppers in the areas of northern and central Italy that voted for the PCI. From 1949 to 1952 it campaigned unsuccessfully for a national labor plan based on the nationalization of the electrical industry, land reclamation, construction of public housing, schools, and hospitals. Although formally independent, it flexed its organizational muscle for political purposes related to the objectives of the PCI. In July 1948 it called a national strike in the wake of the failed attempt on the life of communist leader PALMIRO TOGLIATTI. It did the same in July 1960 to bring down the center-right government headed by FERNANDO TAMBRONI. Opposing parties and employer groups concluded that the CGIL's objectives were more political than economic, and stiffened in their resolve to defeat its proposals. The 1950s saw organized labor fighting a defensive battle against employers who were emboldened by the spectacular recovery of the ECONOMIC MIRACLE.

In 1955 the CGIL abandoned the tactic of negotiating contracts centrally on a national basis, and allowed its trade federations and local sections to bargain autonomously. It adopted a more militant stance in the 1960s when it encouraged frequent recourse to strikes and organized political protests. By the late 1960s the CGIL was noticeably more militant than the PCI, intransigent in labor negotiations, and sympathetic to the street actions of left-wing activists. In the protests of the "hot autumn" of 1969 unions belonging to the CGIL and CISL made common cause with each other and with the workers and students who took to the streets. Over the next few years, unions stepped up their recruiting and obtained major concessions from employers on wages, benefits, and direct worker involvement in labor negotiations through local factory councils. Wage increases automatically pegged to the rate of inflation (*scala mobile*) became a standard feature of labor contracts. Governments were pressured into increasing pension, housing, and education benefits. In July 1972 the three major unions, CGIL, CISL, and the socialist UIL (Unione Italiana del Lavoro) signed a pact of cooperation that was supposed to blossom into a full merger. Euphoric labor leaders envisaged the possibility of making the labor movement a vehicle for political and social reform, but the anticipated unity of the labor movement foundered on political differences among the unions and their respective political patrons.

The CGIL was by far the most militant of the three major confederations through most of the 1970s. Economic crisis and the PCI strategy of pursuing the HISTORIC COMPROMISE with the dominant DC put an end to CGIL militancy in the late 1970s. The decline of labor militancy that began in the 1980s continues to this day, due to many causes. The CGIL found itself at the losing end of many confrontations throughout the 1980s and 1990s. In 1985 a public referendum abolished the *scala mobile*. Reductions in government spending, a global economy that enables employers to move resources to places friendly to business, the influx of nonunionized workers from developing countries, and declining membership continue to sap the power of labor unions and cut into social benefits. The prosperity of the 1990s benefited large strata of the population, workers entered the ranks of the middle classes, and middle-class individualism supplanted working-class collectivism as the dominant ethic. The CGIL is still an important presence on the labor scene, but can no longer aspire to the role of national reformer that it envisaged for itself in the heyday of its power in the 1970s.

Charles V (1500–1558)

king of Spain (1516–1556) and Holy Roman Emperor (1519–1558)

Charles V enters Italian history, as he does the history of many other places in the world, by royal inheritance. From his grandfather Ferdinand II of Aragon, he inherited Naples, Sicily, and Sardinia. Possession of these territories involved Charles in a dynastic conflict with Francis I of France for control of the Italian peninsula. But as the self-proclaimed defender of Catholicism against the spread of Protestantism, he also had an interest in the viability of the PAPACY and its possessions. Consequently, Italy played a large role in his designs, although his main efforts would always be directed against Protestant inroads in Germany and the Netherlands, and against the Ottoman Turks who threatened Christian Europe from the east. Charles's Italian policy was inspired and implemented by his principal adviser, the Italian-born Mercurino Arborio, marquis of Gattinara (1465–1530). It was Gattinara who prevailed upon Charles to fight the French for control of Milan, thus involving the emperor in the quagmire of

Italian politics. When France, Milan, Venice, Florence, and Rome formed the alliance known as the League of Cognac (1526), Charles responded by sending an army into Italy. It consisted largely of Lutherans from the empire's German provinces, and they gleefully carried out the SACK OF ROME (1527), which shocked the Catholic world. Pope CLEMENT VII accepted a costly peace settlement and agreed to crown Charles as Holy Roman Emperor (1530). Charles's control of Italy was still far from secure as Francis allied himself with the Ottoman Turks to recover his position in the peninsula. French influence would be eliminated with the TREATY OF CATEAU-CAMBRÉSIS, while the Turkish threat to Italy persisted long after the death of the emperor in 1558. Although Charles treated Italy as a base of operations against the Turks and taxed his Italian subjects to finance his wars, the costs of his Italian campaigns probably exceeded the revenues he raised in the peninsula. He spent his last years in solitary retirement in Castile after abdicating as king of Spain in 1556, and died knowing that he had failed to restore the religious unity of Christian Europe and to fend off the Turkish threat. He came closest to succeeding in Italy, which became part of the Habsburg Empire of his descendants, thanks to his persistent challenge of French dominance.

Charles VI   See AUSTRIAN SUCCESSION, WAR OF THE; MARIA THERESA.

Charles Albert (1798–1849)

king of Sardinia (1831–1849)

Charles Albert had an unconventional upbringing for a ruler of his time. His father Charles Emmanuel, who belonged to a lateral branch of the HOUSE OF SAVOY, sympathized with the FRENCH REVOLUTION and served in the army of NAPOLEON I. Charles Albert was educated in France and Switzerland, received the title of count from Napoleon and also served in the French army. Returning to Piedmont after

Napoleon's downfall, he was suspected of harboring liberal tendencies. Since neither his uncle King VICTOR EMMANUEL I nor the king's brother CHARLES FELIX (1765–1831) had any male heirs, Charles Albert was in line to inherit the throne. On friendly terms with liberal members of the Piedmontese nobility, he was drawn into the conspiracy that resulted in the failed REVOLUTION of 1821 during which, acting as regent in the temporary absence of the king, he acceded to liberal demands for a constitution. Victor Emmanuel I resigned and Charles Felix, who succeeded him, quickly disavowed the constitution. Charles Albert, now in disgrace with the new king, went into temporary exile in Florence. He was rehabilitated in 1823 when he led troops fighting against the liberals in Spain.

Charles Albert inherited the Sardinian throne at the death of Charles Felix. He ruled as an absolute monarch, persecuted and put down political conspiracies and subversive organizations, including Mazzini's YOUNG ITALY, and sought the support of conservative governments. But when fear of revolution receded in the late 1830s, Charles Albert enacted administrative and economic reforms. He adopted a uniform code of laws for the entire kingdom, comprising PIEDMONT, SAVOY, and SARDINIA, created a council of state to advise him on government, abolished feudal obligations in the island of Sardinia and internal tolls throughout the state, negotiated commercial treaties with Great Britain and France, encouraged maritime trade, and the expansion of the port of Genoa. Unwilling to sacrifice any of his royal prerogatives, he nevertheless made cautious overtures to liberal elements, hinting privately that he favored the cause of Italian independence.

The chance to fight for Italian independence presented itself in 1848 when revolution broke out in Austrian-ruled Lombardy. Charles Albert granted the Statuto, which later became the first Italian CONSTITUTION, declared war on Austria, and fought the first of the WARS OF NATIONAL INDEPENDENCE. After his defeat at the battle of Novara in March 1849, he abdicated in favor of his son VICTOR EMMANUEL II and went into exile in Portugal, where he died in July 1849. An enigmatic and controversial figure, Charles Albert was dubbed *Re tentenna* (King Waffle) for his changes of political direction and apparent vacillating between repression and reform. His pursuit of self-serving dynastic interests went hand in hand with selfless patriotism and a willingness to take risks for the cause of Italian independence. The debate goes on. Perhaps he can be seen as an absolute monarch who wanted to preserve the full powers of the crown while pursuing policies that encouraged liberals, whose political objectives he did not share. The liberal cause of Italian independence was not incompatible with the expansionist policies that the House of Savoy had pursued for nearly three centuries. His youthful brush with the French Revolution and Napoleon had left in him a craving for controlled change and for personal glory that he tried unsuccessfully to combine with the principle of absolute monarchy.

Charles Emmanuel II of Savoy   See
WALDENSIANS.

Charles Emmanuel IV   See SAVOY, HOUSE OF.

Charles Felix   (1765–1831)
king of Sardinia (1821–1831)
Charles Felix (Carlo Felice), became king of Piedmont-Sardinia in 1821 following the abdication of his older brother VICTOR EMMANUEL I. His immediate concern was to repress the insurgents who had pressured his nephew CHARLES ALBERT, who had taken over as regent in his uncle's absence, into granting a constitution. Charles Felix called on the Austrian army to put down the insurgents and exiled his nephew to Florence. Charles Felix was determined to prevent the recurrence of revolution, oppose political liberalism in all its forms, and assert his authority as an absolute monarch. His purge of

officers suspected of harboring liberal sentiments undermined the efficiency of the army, which he valued as the ultimate guardian of order and stability. Fearful that secular schooling was ultimately responsible for the loss of faith in traditional values and institutions, Charles Felix favored clerical control of education at all levels and encouraged the JESUITS to assume control of universities. His policies drove political dissenters into exile in Spain, France, and England, from where they carried on their struggle against absolute monarchy and the provisions of the CONGRESS OF VIENNA. Charles Felix showed a more progressive side of his character in matters of public administration and economic policy. While he expanded police powers to crack down on political dissenters, he also insisted on following correct judicial procedures against political suspects. GIUSEPPE MAZZINI may have been a beneficiary of Charles Felix's insistence on correct judicial proceedings. Charles Felix encouraged the growth of Genoese shipping, ordered expeditions against Muslim strongholds that imperiled travel and commerce in the Mediterranean, and succeeded in reconciling most Genoese to the loss of political independence and acceptance of Piedmontese rule. He died childless, the last direct descendant of the main branch of the House of Savoy, and was succeeded by Charles Albert, the first monarch of the Savoia-Carignano branch that ruled Italy until 1946.

Charles of Bourbon (1716–1788)
king of Naples and Sicily (1735–1759)
Son of Philip V, king of Spain, grandson of Louis XIV of France, and designated heir to the Grand Duchy of Tuscany upon the expected extinction of the Medici dynasty, Charles chose instead to claim the crowns of Naples and Sicily, which had been occupied by Austria in 1707 during the WAR OF THE SPANISH SUCCESSION. In 1734 Charles (also known as Don Carlos) led a Spanish army into southern Italy, defeated the Austrians who were embroiled in the War of the Polish Succession, and assumed the crowns of Naples and

Sicily. He was crowned in 1735 and ruled until 1759, when he succeeded to the Spanish throne as Charles III. As King Charles of Naples and Sicily, without any numeration to his name, he regained political independence for the kingdom after more than 230 years of foreign domination, won international recognition for the state, and founded the Neapolitan BOURBON dynasty that ruled in Naples and Sicily until 1860. Charles devoted his energies to building up the power of the monarchy, curtailing feudal and clerical privileges, creating an army, reforming the complex legal system, founding schools, initiating a land census, encouraging agriculture and commerce, and building the impressive royal palace and gardens of Caserta. He appointed able counselors, most notably BERNARDO TANUCCI, who served as chief adviser in domestic and foreign affairs. Charles was succeeded by his third-born son as FERDINAND IV, a minor who governed under the tutelage of advisers. Ferdinand's ministers carried out the reforms envisaged by his father, until fear of revolution and the influence of conservative advisers put an end to the reforms in the 1780s. Charles is remembered as Naples' most progressive monarch who made the Bourbon dynasty popular and brought his kingdom into the mainstream of the ENLIGHTENMENT.

Cherubini, Maria Luigi (1760–1842)
opera composer, active mostly abroad and most influential in France
Cherubini was born in Florence, where he studied music under his father and other local musicians. Evidence of his talent for musical composition persuaded his father to send him to BOLOGNA and the Tuscan grand duke to finance his education there under the renowned composer Giuseppe Sarti (1729–1802). After producing several comic and serious operas in Italy and London, Cherubini took up residence in Paris in 1788. During the turbulent years of the French Revolution he composed choral numbers and hymns for public festivals staged by the government to stimulate patriotic support for the

Revolution. *Médée* (1797), based on the Greek myth of Medea, is considered to be his masterpiece, but in his time Cherubini's artistic reputation rested on a great many other compositions for the stage, sacred music, and various orchestral pieces. The stage drama *Les deux journées* (The two days, 1800) was considered his finest piece at the time. It catered to the taste generated by the French Revolution for strong action and dramatic situations and was performed to acclaim in France and Germany. Beethoven heard it in Vienna and expressed great esteem for its composer. Cherubini's stay in France was not without problems, some personal and some professional. An unhappy marriage and, most of all, Napoleon's dislike for Cherubini's operas, which he found heavy, slow-moving, and uninspiring, complicated his life and brought about a temporary withdrawal from musical composition. Cherubini's influence was felt mainly in French opera, where he bridges the gap between CLASSICISM and ROMANTICISM. He was less influential in Italy, where *Medée* was not performed until 1909 in translation as *Medea,* and was revived in the 1950s, again in its Italian version, by the soprano Maria Callas. He belongs to the group of 18th- and early 19th-century composers, which included his younger contemporary GASPARO SPONTINI, who sought primary recognition outside Italy and addressed European audiences.

Christian Democracy See DC.

church and state

In the 19th century, the process of Italian national unification brought to a head tensions between church and state that were already evident in the 18th century. The appointment of bishops, the legal status of the clergy, tax exemptions for religious orders and communities, accumulation of property in the hands of religious groups, and the role of the JESUIT ORDER were issues of contention between church and state that predated the movement for national unifi-

cation. The claims of modern governments to full authority over their people and territory clashed with the traditional powers that the church regarded as necessary conditions for the fulfillment of its spiritual mission. Political liberals and religious reformers attempted in vain to reconcile or mediate the conflict. The NEO-GUELFS thought that the PAPACY could lead the movement for national independence. They were encouraged by the election of Pope PIUS IX in 1846, until the papal response to the REVOLUTION of 1848 made it clear that the papacy would not put in jeopardy its relations with Catholic powers by supporting a nationalist movement.

The papacy's conviction that it could not carry out its spiritual duties without territorial sovereignty put the church on a collision course with the Italian national movement. While papal policy insisted on retention of political sovereignty over papal territory, Italian patriots looked upon papal territory as an integral part of the nation and on ROME as the natural capital of the unified state. The seizure of papal territory by the Piedmontese army in 1860 and 1870 gave rise to the ROMAN QUESTION. The formula of a "free church in a free state" proposed by Cavour shortly before his death proved unacceptable to Pius IX, who called himself a "prisoner in the Vatican" and refused to recognize the Italian state. The state expropriated church properties, shut down churches, religious communities, and charities, and engaged in anticlerical polemics. The papacy responded by calling on Catholics to boycott the state. The papal policy of *non expedit* adopted in the 1870s warned Catholics that it was "not expedient" for them to participate in the political life of the nation, and advised them not to vote or run for office in national elections. New religious associations, missionary drives, and mass rituals sought to rally the faithful behind their religious leaders. The state also reached out to the masses, encouraging secular education and fostering ANTICLERICALISM.

Only in the first decade of the 20th century did the clashes and diatribes between clericals and anticlericals abate. Alarmed by the rise of socialist movements, the governing liberals let up on their anticlericalism and the papacy relaxed the *non-expedit* to allow Catholics to vote in support of designated candidates. The conflict between church and state ended officially with the signing of the Concordat and the Lateran Pacts in 1929. There was still the potential for conflict between the Fascist regime that sponsored the accords and the church in the sensitive areas of family legislation, education, youth organization, and racial legislation. The fall of fascism and the rise of Christian Democracy after 1945 opened up a new chapter in the history of church-state relations in Italy. Christian Democrats relied on the church to rally voters and help them win their political battles, and the church relied on the governing Christian Democratic Party (DC) to ward off the threat of communism and help it propagate Christian values.

But while relations between church and state were cordial in the years of DC hegemony, the same cannot be said for relations between the religious hierarchy and society in general. The church and the DC suffered serious defeat on the issues of legalized ABORTION, contraception, and DIVORCE. The question of church and state became more and more the question of church and society. In February 1984 church and state negotiated a new concordat that revised the provisions of 1929 on several key issues. Catholicism was no longer defined as the official religion of the state, compulsory religious instruction in public schools was abolished, church property was made fully taxable, Vatican financial deals had to conform to Italian law, state salaries for priests were replaced by voluntary contributions through the income tax system. The dire consequences for the church predicted by opponents of the revisions did not materialize. Public opinion polls show that 75–80 percent of Italians consider themselves religious, marry in church, and raise their children to be observant. The election of a non-Italian pope, JOHN PAUL II, in 1978 may have contributed to the easing of tensions between church and state. Under this pope the papacy has distanced itself from Italian politics. The pope's official visit to the Italian parliament in the year 2003 was a clear sign of easing tensions.

Cialdini, Enrico (1811–1892)
military and political figure

Cialdini rose to commander in chief of the Italian army after a long apprenticeship that began with his participation in the REVOLUTION of 1831 in his native city of Modena. A political exile in the 1830s and 1840s, he fought on the liberal side in Portugal and Spain, returning to Italy in 1848 to fight against Austria in the papal army. In 1849 he joined the Piedmontese army, fought in the CRIMEAN WAR, and commanded a division in the Second WAR OF NATIONAL INDEPENDENCE (1859). In 1860 he led the Piedmontese troops that defeated the papal army at the battle of Castelfidardo, giving the Piedmontese control of the regions of Marches and Umbria. In November of 1860 he took charge and won the surrender of the last Neapolitan troops holding out in Gaeta and Messina. Those successes gained him the title of duke of Gaeta. As commander of troops in the recently occupied South he took the first measures against BRIGANDAGE (1861) but was quickly replaced by his archrival, General ALFONSO LA MARMORA. In the Third War of National Independence he shared command of field operations with La Marmora. That unwise arrangement contributed to the Italian defeat at the Battle of Custoza because the two commanders did not agree on tactics. He took over as sole army commander following La Marmora's dismissal after the battle. The two generals and their respective backers engaged in bitter polemics after the war. Cialdini served in the chamber of deputies (1861–64), was appointed to the senate (1864), and as ambassador to Madrid (1870) and Paris (1876). He retired from public life in 1882.

Ciampi, Carlo Azeglio (1920–   )
economist, banker, prime minister and
president of the republic

Ciampi was born in Livorno to a family of opticians, served in the army during WORLD WAR II in

Kosovo, supported the short-lived ACTION PARTY after the war, then distanced himself from other political parties. Untainted by political scandal, he maintained a reputation for professional competence and impartiality. An observant Catholic, he does not make public display of his religion. His long tenure as governor of the BANK OF ITALY (1979–93) confirmed his reputation for honesty and administrative effectiveness. He defended the CURRENCY successfully at a time of monetary crisis, launched long overdue reforms of the banking system, and freed the Bank of Italy from political interference and the supervision of the Ministry of the Treasury. In April 1993 President OSCAR LUIGI SCALFARO appointed him prime minister, the first nonparliamentarian to hold that top government post. He picked his ministers for their competence and reliability, without reference to their politics, forming a broadly based government to deal with the most urgent problems of the moment. Ciampi achieved spending cuts, economic privatization, monetary stability, and political reforms during his eight months in office. He resigned in January 1994, after parliament had approved his austerity budget, to force new general elections that he felt were necessary to help the country deal with the spreading political scandal of TANGENTOPOLI. Appointed treasury minister in 1996, he prepared the country for admission to the European monetary system. His broad popularity with the public and the political establishment brought about his election to the highest office in the land, the presidency of the republic, in May 1999. His term of office will expire in 2005.

Ciano, Costanzo (1876–1939)
military and political figure
Born in Livorno, Ciano graduated from the city's naval academy in 1896, saw action in the ITALIAN-TURKISH WAR (1911–12), and distinguished himself in WORLD WAR I commanding torpedo boats in small-scale surprise actions known as *beffe* (jests), which won public acclaim. Repeatedly decorated, he was later promoted to the rank of admiral and received the title of count of

Cortellazzo, named after one of his exploits. He was an early Fascist who participated in the March on Rome and held important ministerial posts, including the ministry of communications (1924–34). As minister of communications he carried out the reforms that enabled BENITO MUSSOLINI to boast that trains finally ran on time. He was also president of the chamber of fasces and corporations (1934–39). In 1926 Mussolini secretly designated him as his successor in case of his own death. Political boss of Livorno, Ciano's influence was felt throughout Tuscany. His extensive properties included a grandiose villa in the town of Borgo a Mozzano, near Lucca. His holdings included the Livorno newspaper *Il Telegrafo*. Rumors of illicit wealth accumulations dogged him and his son GALEAZZO CIANO, contributing to the unpopularity of the Fascist regime in its final phase. A nationalist, an admirer of Mussolini, politically conservative but given to radical solutions, Costanzo Ciano was one of the most typical figures of the Fascist regime.

Ciano, Galeazzo (1903–1944)
Fascist diplomat and foreign minister
The only son of COSTANZO CIANO, his rapid rise was paved by his father's wealth and connections. The young Ciano's image as a privileged and spoiled child of the regime contributed to his reputation as a political lightweight playing out of his league. He was actually a quick learner and a successful student who received a law degree from the University of Rome in 1925, looked forward to a literary career, and liked to rub shoulders with artists and intellectuals. A taste for life in fashionable circles and an irresistible attraction to women competed with, and often won out over, his more serious interests. He chose to pursue a career in the diplomatic corps after graduation. By 1930 he had successive postings in Rio de Janeiro, Buenos Aires, Beijing and the Holy See. In that same year he married Edda Mussolini (1910–95), the Duce's daughter. The newlyweds sailed for China, where Ciano served as consul-general in Shanghai before returning to

Beijing as plenipotentiary minister (1930–33). Back in Italy, he served as undersecretary for press and propaganda (1934–35) and as minister of the same when that bureau became a ministry (1935). That same year he volunteered for military duty in the ETHIOPIAN WAR, serving as a bomber pilot. His previous diplomatic experience, military record, and marriage opened Ciano's way to the foreign ministry, which he took over in June 1936. His pro-German sentiments were known at the time, and the appointment was interpreted correctly as signaling BENITO MUSSOLINI's desire for closer relations with Nazi Germany. Ciano favored alliance with Germany in his early years as foreign minister, but wavered in the face of British hostility to the ROME-BERLIN AXIS and his own personal dislike for Hitler and German foreign minister Joachim von Ribbentrop. By 1939 he was fearful that Germany would drag Italy into a major war for which the country was unprepared. But Ciano's personal preferences did not count for much. Mussolini definitely had the last word in foreign policy and kept Ciano on as foreign minister because of his son-in-law's political submissiveness and boundless admiration for him. Ciano orchestrated the Italian invasion of ALBANIA in April 1939. He later tried to keep Italy out of WORLD WAR II, but gave in as usual when the Duce decided to fight alongside Germany. He bungled the political planning for the attack on Greece in October 1940, which capped the military's humiliating performance. Becoming increasingly suspicious toward Germany during the war and fearful of military defeat, he turned against Mussolini, but continued to work at his side, hoping that a compromise peace would allow Italy to leave the war honorably. Mussolini dismissed him as foreign minister in February 1943 and appointed him as ambassador to the Holy See. A member of the Fascist Grand Council, on the night of July 24–25 Ciano voted for the motion that called on Mussolini to resign. He was later captured by the Germans, handed over to Mussolini's puppet regime in northern Italy, tried, and found guilty of treason for signing the grand council's motion. On January 11, 1944, Ciano was executed with four other Fascists who had also voted against Mussolini. His secret diary is a revealing document of Fascist diplomacy and backstairs politics.

cicisbeism

Cicisbeism was a custom prevalent among the upper classes in 18th-century Italy whereby married women kept at their side young men known as cicisbei, or *cavalier serventi,* as devoted and solicitous companions. These young men attended to the needs of their ladies from morning till night, having access to their homes, looking after their toilettes, assisting them at mealtime, and escorting them to social gatherings. It was generally assumed for the sake of propriety that the relationship was not sexual, but suspicions to the contrary were common, especially among foreign visitors who were shocked by the ubiquitous custom. It was considered bad form for husbands to be jealous, and indeed many may have welcomed the presence of cicisbei, who relieved them of tiresome social duties. At a time when husbands were not known for being solicitous toward their wives, the custom of cicisbeism may have made marriage more bearable for many women. In Venice, marital contracts sometimes required and named a **cicisbeo,** who could be a relative or friend of the family. The custom was certainly more prevalent in the northern than in the southern states, where family customs were stricter and ladies had servants, but not cicisbei. It must be stressed that the status of cicisbeo was an honorable one, although not everyone was in favor of the idea. GIUSEPPE PARINI, who could be a dour moralist when it came to the failings of others, condemned the custom as frivolous or worse. Nevertheless, its prevalence suggests a tolerant disposition among the upper classes, a desire for attentive companionship, and the need for a socially acceptable pastime for young males.

Cimarosa, Domenico See OPERA.

Cisalpine Republic   See NAPOLEON I.

CISL   See CGIL; SYNDICALISM.

Civiltà Cattolica (La)

This biweekly journal published by the JESUITS is an authoritative Vatican mouthpiece. Its policies are formulated and its articles written by a board of writers of proven loyalty to the PAPACY. Founded in Naples in 1850, the journal reflected a conservative viewpoint hostile to revolutionary movements, including LIBERALISM and the RISORGIMENTO. Its outlook reflected papal clashes with revolutionary movements in 1848–49, which had the effect of solidifying papal ties to the absolute monarchies of Austria and Naples. But the journal also held that absolute monarchy was incompatible with papal independence and moved its headquarters from Naples to Rome. When Italian troops seized Rome in 1870, *Civiltà Cattolica* moved from Rome to Florence. The journal kept up its battle against the Italian state until the Roman Question was settled in 1929. Its general philosophy was articulated forcefully by one of its early writers, Luigi Taparelli d'Azeglio (1793–1862), who rejected rational philosophy as inherently subversive, insisted on the inadequacy of reason and the flawed nature of human beings, and asserted that authority is the necessary foundation of human society. The journal's outlook was very much in line with the conservatism of PIUS IX but was also favored by the more liberal LEO XIII.

CLN and CLNAI   See RESISTANCE.

Clement VII (1478–1534)

pope (1523–1534)

Born Giulio de' Medici, the natural son of Giuliano de' Medici (1453–78), and therefore nephew of LORENZO DE' MEDICI, Giulio was made archbishop of Florence in 1513 and cardinal in

Pope Clement VII *(Library of Congress)*

1517 by his cousin Pope LEO X. He succeeded ADRIAN VI to the papacy in 1523 as head of the group of cardinals who supported the imperial faction. A very political pope, Clement was primarily concerned with maintaining papal independence by playing off Emperor CHARLES V against King Francis I of France, the two archrivals for power in Italy. His support of Francis angered the emperor, who unleashed his troops against Clement and brought on the SACK OF ROME in 1527. Clement was forced to acknowledge the power of Charles V by crowning him in 1530. Charles obliged him by restoring Medici rule in Florence. Dependence on the emperor did not prevent Clement from continuing to cultivate close ties with the French ruling house and arranging the marriage of Catherine de' Medici (see MEDICI FAMILY) with Francis's son Henry, with fateful consequences for the future of the French monarchy. Clement was so preoccupied with politics that he failed to appreciate the significance of Martin Luther's challenge to papal authority and England's separation from the Church of Rome during his pontificate. Turning a deaf ear to the emperor's request that he summon an ecumenical council to take up the issue of religious reform, Clement lost precious time and was unable to contain the spread of Protestantism. Clement has been judged harshly by contemporaries and historians for his political and religious shortcomings.

Clement VIII See BARONIO, CESARE; TASSO, TORQUATO.

Clement XI (1649–1721)
pope (1700–1721)

Gian Francesco Albani, born in Urbino, who became pope as Clement XI, was caught in the ongoing dynastic struggle between Habsburgs and BOURBONS over the succession to the Spanish throne. In the ensuing WAR OF THE SPANISH SUCCESSION, Clement took the side of the Bourbons, reasoning that dominance of the peninsula by a Bourbon dynasty lodged in Spain was preferable to dominance by the more assertive Austrian Habsburgs. Victory in the war gave the Austrians control of the important states of Milan and Naples. The PAPAL STATES were not threatened, but the Habsburgs began to challenge papal claims to feudal lordship in other parts of Italy, thus beginning to chip away at the concept of papal political sovereignty. VICTOR AMADEUS II of Savoy also successfully challenged papal feudal claims to the island of Sicily recently acquired by the House of Savoy. Far more attuned to religious than to political issues, Clement agonized over JANSENISM, a Catholic reform movement suspected of heresy. When he finally issued a condemnation of the movement in the bull *Unigenitus* (1713), French Catholics split over the issue, threatening for a while the unity of the church. The split was healed, but the

controversy left a legacy of ANTICLERICALISM that affected figures of the ENLIGHTENMENT. Clement was more successful in his cultural and social endeavors, overseeing important projects of urban renewal, establishing public workshops, reducing unemployment, encouraging textile manufacturing, reorganizing the Roman university of the Collegio Romano, welcoming and providing financial support for artists and scholars. A man of his times, Clement believed that Catholics should be familiar with developing secular trends in order to defend the faith from its enemies.

Clement XIV (1705–1774)
pope (1769–1774)

Giovanni Vincenzo Ganganelli, born in the Romagna region, took on the name of Clement XIV when he was elected pope in 1769. Prior to his election he had been a popular preacher. In Rome since 1740, he was familiar with the ways of papal bureaucracy and government. The defining issue of his pontificate was the future of JESUITS, which he was under great pressure to abolish. The attacks came from intellectuals of the ENLIGHTENMENT who saw in the Jesuits the personification of obscurantist cultural traditions and stifling authority, and from monarchs who resented the independent power of the PAPACY, of which the Jesuits were a mainstay. Clement reluctantly abolished the order in 1773, thanking it for its previous services and expressing regret that it had outlived its time. The controversial decision defused tensions between the papacy and ruling monarchs, particularly the Bourbon monarchy of France, which had insisted on the suppression of the order. The dispersed Jesuits carried on a slanderous campaign against Clement, which led to rumors that they had caused his death by poisoning. His premature death put an end to educational reforms championed by JANSENISM that would have given a greater role to the secular clergy. To protect the artistic treasures of Rome, which were being despoiled and dispersed to other parts of Italy and Europe, Clement established the Vatican Museum to gather and secure in one place paintings, sculptures, and other artistic artifacts. In the spirit of the Enlightenment, special attention was paid to gathering and preserving the pagan art of ancient Greece and Rome. Clement began the policy of state-sponsored artistic preservation that was designed to make Rome the center of Italian art and a favorite destination of tourists.

Cola di Rienzo (ca. 1313–1354)

Roman reformer who sought to restore the glory of classical Rome

The son of an innkeeper, Cola di Rienzo was a public notary. He rose to a position of dominant power in Rome during the absence of the papacy, with the title of tribune. He held power in May–December 1347 and August–October 1354. Presenting himself as a champion of the people against the greedy nobility, Cola found inspiration in the writings and ruins of ancient Rome, called for popular election of an emperor, extension of Roman citizenship to all Italians, and a federation of Italian cities. His ideal of a rejuvenated Italy inspired a few contemporaries, including PETRARCH, who briefly championed Cola's cause. Cola's message was lost on most of his contemporaries, while his bizarre behavior and demands provoked popular outrage. He was hacked to death by an angry mob while trying to escape from the city. Later generations were more appreciative. Cola's vision of a virtuous citizenry based on the republican ideals of ancient Rome struck a chord in the ENLIGHTENMENT period. Cola the visionary attracted 19th-century romanticists and patriots. A life of Cola was found in Napoleon's baggage after Waterloo, a novel based on Cola's life inspired Richard Wagner to compose *Rienzi,* his first successful opera, and GABRIELE D'ANNUNZIO wrote a life of Cola. Cola's extravagant expectations, drive for personal glory, and tragic death at the hands of an angry mob have also been seen as anticipations of the life and death of BENITO MUSSOLINI.

Coldiretti

The Confederazione Italiana Coltivatori Diretti (Italian Confederation of Small Farmers), usually referred to as Coldiretti or Coltivatori Diretti, was founded in October 1944 by Paolo Bonomi (1910–85), who was its president until 1980. Although its charter described it as secular and apolitical, it was in fact an avowedly Catholic organization that supported the Christian Democratic Party (DC), using its political clout to help small peasant landowners and sharecroppers. Family farms are the grassroots members of Coldiretti. Above them, an intricate pattern of local councils and provincial federations culminates in a national council. The national council reserves seats for the representatives of farming women. The organization grew rapidly, reaching a membership of close to 3.6 million family farmers in 1962. It was particularly strong in the regions of the South and in mountainous areas throughout the country where small landownership prevailed. With a large delegation in parliament and control of the Ministry of Agriculture, Coldiretti was able to deliver technological services in the form of machinery and fertilizers, credit assistance, pensions and subsidies, and cooperatives to grow and sell produce. Popular support for Coldiretti was also due in no small measure to its ideology. It held up the farming family as the basic unit of society, praised the family values that went with it, and upheld private ownership as a social ideal. It packed a strong anticommunist message that appealed particularly to small landowners. The enthusiasm of small farmers for their organization was summed up in the comment of one member that he believed only in God and in Bonomi. Coldiretti's membership has declined since the 1960s due to the crisis of small-scale farming and the rural exodus to the cities. Presently (2004), Coldiretti represents some 568,000 agricultural entrepreneurs. In its heyday, Coldiretti was a mainstay of Christian Democratic government.

Colleoni, Bartolomeo See CONDOTTIERI.

Colletta, Pietro (1775–1831)
military officer and revolutionary figure
This Neapolitan military officer joined the army in 1796, fought against the French in 1798, but sided with the French-sponsored PARTHENOPEAN REPUBLIC and with the monarchy of JOSEPH BONAPARTE. Drawn to these regimes by his liberal sentiments, Colletta rose to the military rank of marshal, received the title of baron, and held important administrative posts. He emerged during the Napoleonic period as the most typical representative of the liberal minority of the upper middle class and aristocracy that supported French rule. After Napoleon's defeat in 1814–15, Colletta helped negotiate a peace settlement that included retention in rank of military officers like him who had served the previous regime. In the REVOLUTION of 1821 he sided with the insurgents, probably intending to keep in check the more radical democratic elements present in the movement. The government sent him to Sicily to suppress a separatist uprising on the island; he also served as army and navy minister (1821). Colletta was imprisoned after the absolute monarchy was restored. Liberated in 1823, he went into exile in Tuscany, where he collaborated with the liberals around GIAN PIETRO VIEUSSEUX. While living in Florence he wrote a history of Naples, the *Storia del Reame di Napoli dal 1734 al 1825* (History of the kingdom of Naples, 1734–1825, 1834, English translation 1858), which reflected his dislike of both absolute monarchy and popular democracy. Colletta equated the latter with mob rule. His praise of the reforms of the Napoleonic ruler JOACHIM MURAT influenced later generations of patriots and laid the groundwork for a Muratist movement that called for national independence and representative government.

Colletti, Lucio (1924–2001)
political writer and theorist
This social philosopher was born in Rome and studied philosophy at the University of Messina with the Marxist philosopher Galvano Della Volpe (1895–1968). Colletti taught philosophy at the University of Rome. He joined the Italian Communist Party (PCI) in 1949 and emerged as an important cultural party figure. His reflections on Marxism centered on the distinction between appearance and reality, a notion that Colletti derived from his understanding of Immanuel Kant. For Colletti, Marxism is an empirical method of inquiry that stays in touch with the real rather than a philosophical system with a predetermined outcome. Colletti argued that the value of labor, a concept central to Marx's economic analysis, is determined by the social context in which labor occurs, a position that leads to questioning Marx's axiom that labor is what creates value. Never an orthodox Marxist, Colletti broke with the PCI in 1964. His highly abstract writings were influential in the 1970s as Marxists sought ways of reconciling Marxist philosophy with the complexity of capitalism. Colletti began to drift steadily toward the right, pausing in the 1980s to identify with socialist leader BETTINO CRAXI. In the 1990s he served in parliament as a representative of the right-of-center FORZA ITALIA. The itinerary from left to right that Colletti followed, while not unusual among western intellectuals in the latter part of the 20th century, was highly controversial in Italy. See his *From Rousseau to Lenin* (1972, 1974) and *Marxism and Hegel* (1973, 1979).

Collodi, Carlo (1826–1890)
writer famous for his children's stories, author of Pinocchio
This was the literary pseudonym, derived from the Tuscan town of Collodi where he spent his youth, adopted by Carlo Lorenzini. After fighting in the REVOLUTION of 1848, Lorenzini turned to journalism, showing in his writings a vivacious style and a sense of humor that appealed to readers. Also a talented caricaturist, he penned amusing, good-natured portrayals of the main personages and events of Florence in his day, which were later published in volume form. He was eventually attracted to writing for children. Starting with translations of fairy tales, he published two successful books of his own, *Giannet-*

tino (1876), which was intended for school children, and *Minuzzolo* (1877). His fame rests almost entirely on the phenomenal success of *The Adventures of Pinocchio*, which first appeared in newspaper installments (1881) and then in book form (1883). This is a deceptively simple work that can be read on many different levels. The tale of the wooden puppet that gets into trouble for not resisting the temptation to play, skip classes, run away from home, and associate with undesirable companions, who is eventually redeemed by his own generous impulses, and becomes a person of flesh and blood, has stimulated endless discussion. While children enjoy the whimsical aspects of the story, adults have pondered its political, social, and psychological messages. It has been seen as patriotic, capitalist, and Freudian. It is doubtful that Lorenzini saw it as anything more than an entertaining tale that would bring him the money that he desperately needed to pay his many gambling debts and get by in life with some decorum. However one might interpret it, the richness of Lorenzini's imagination, his felicitous style, and basic optimism have made *Pinocchio* one of the most widely read books. In Italy it has the status of a classic, familiar to every Italian in the original, which is much more realistic and earthy than the expurgated versions served up to American children.

colonialism

Italy's pursuit of colonial empire was controversial and divisive from the start. Advocates touted the importance of colonies for trade and settlement, critics argued that the country's limited resources would be better spent domestically on education, promoting economic development, and reducing regional disparities. The historical memories of imperial Rome, of the maritime empires of medieval city-states, and the desire to be recognized as a modern power were powerful stimuli. However, as a latecomer to the race for colonies Italy had to confront the ambitions and rivalry of established states, which enjoyed a head start and had already staked claims to the more economically or strategically attractive territories.

Italian colonial ambitions were directed to certain African territories by the need to follow the lead of other powers and by Italy's Mediterranean position. The country joined in the "scramble for Africa" in 1869, the year that the Suez Canal was opened, with a lease to the Bay of Assab on the Red Sea coast by the shipping company founded by RAFFAELE RUBATTINO. It was a formally private venture, launched to establish a coaling station that would facilitate Italian shipping toward the Indian Ocean. The government backed the deal and purchased the concession outright in 1882. Thus began Italy's historic concern with the region known as the Horn of Africa. By then, France had frustrated Italian ambitions for Tunisia by declaring a protectorate over that territory (1881), reinforcing Italy's interest in the Horn of Africa.

Italian penetration of that east African region was aided indirectly by Catholic missionary efforts, particularly by the work of Cardinal Guglielmo Massaia (1809–89), whose writings describing his work among the Galla populations of Ethiopia were published in 1885–95. The explorations and writings of GIUSEPPE SAPETO also stimulated public interest in Africa. In 1889 Italy and Ethiopia concluded the TREATY OF UCCIALLI, by which the Ethiopian emperor Menelik II (1844–1913), in return for Italian military aid, acknowledged the Italian occupation of the Bay of Assab, over which Menelik claimed sovereignty. The Italian government also interpreted the treaty as giving Italy a protectorate over Ethiopia, but Menelik rejected that interpretation and actively opposed further Italian inroads into his territories. The same year that the Treaty of Uccialli was signed, the Italian government declared a protectorate over the entire Benadir coast on the Indian Ocean, which eventually became Italian Somaliland. In 1890 the Bay of Assab territory became the Italian colony of Eritrea, the forerunner of modern independent Eritrea.

With operational bases on the Red Sea and the Indian Ocean coasts, Italy was now poised to enforce its interpretation of the Treaty of Uccialli. Italian military penetration of Ethiopia came to a sudden and disastrous end on March 1, 1896, when an Italian expeditionary force was surrounded and defeated by a large Ethiopian army at the Battle of Adowa. The defeat put an end to Italian colonial activity in East Africa for the time being, but the nationalist press kept the memory of that national humiliation alive. The Fascist regime would tout its conquest of Ethiopia in 1935–36 in the course of the ETHIOPIAN WAR as revenge for the humiliation suffered at Adowa 40 years before. In the interim, Italy seized the opportunity to acquire the territories of Cyrenaica and Tripolitania from the Ottoman Empire by force of arms in 1911–12 in the course of the ITALIAN-TURKISH WAR. Italian control over these territories, which were merged to form the colony of Libya, was consolidated in the 1920s.

The Ethiopian War resulted in the consolidation of the territories of Ethiopia, Eritrea, and Italian Somaliland into a single entity called Italian East Africa and in the formal proclamation by Benito Mussolini of an Italian Empire. In WORLD WAR II the colonies served as bases for Italian military operations against British forces in Egypt and in East Africa. The loss of all of Italy's colonies at the end of World War II was widely lamented in the press, but proved to be a great blessing in disguise. Italy's colonies yielded none of the economic advantages anticipated by colonialists, and were a constant drain on the Italian economy. Italian Somaliland was a United Nations trust territory under Italian administration from 1950 to 1960, when it joined British Somaliland to form independent Somalia. Thus ended the last direct vestige of the Italian colonial empire, born of great power aspirations and lost providentially as a result of military defeat.

Colonna, Vittoria (1492–1547)
writer, and friend and inspirer of Renaissance artists

This prominent member of the COLONNA FAMILY gained attention as a writer, a friend of artists and scholars, and as the hostess of gatherings in Rome and Viterbo that attracted some of the most important cultural figures of her generation. PIETRO BEMBO, BALDASSARRE CASTIGLIONE, MICHELANGELO, and the English cardinal Reginald Pole were among her friends and correspondents. Her literary output consists of some 300 sonnets, the first 100 of which she wrote to relieve her pain and distress at the death of her husband Francesco d'Avalos, a Spanish nobleman whom she married in 1509 and who died in 1525. She lived most of the rest of her life as a secular nun in seclusion in a Roman convent. The combination of sensitivity and highly polished style evident in the sonnets made her the leading woman poet in the eyes of her contemporaries. Literary critics of later generations were less kind to her, faulting her for a tightly controlled style that hindered spontaneity of expression. Having a deeply religious temperament, she was influenced by Calvinism but did not renounce her Roman Catholic faith. A representative of the new piety that stressed purity of faith, charity, and generosity, she avoided the public eye, contributing to the reform of the church with her writings, correspondence, and personal influence. Her late-life friendship and correspondence with Michelangelo, whom she met when she was 49 years old, has been the subject of intensive study pointing to the influence of her religious views on Michelangelo's art.

Colonna family

It was not uncommon for Italian noble families to claim direct descent from the nobility of ancient Rome. That claim may not be far-fetched in the case of the Colonna family, given its centuries-old association with the city of Rome. But that claim is not substantiated. The first documented references to the Colonnas date from the middle of the 11th century. From then on the family name figures prominently in the affairs of Rome and the PAPACY right up to our times. While many other Italian noble families sought to become ruling dynasties at the head of independent states, the Colonnas gained by serving the papacy. That does not mean that relations with individual popes were always friendly. A member of the Colonna family, Stefano the Elder (1265–1349), was instrumental in consigning Pope Boniface VIII (1294–1303) to King Philip the Fair of France, who then removed the papacy to Avignon during the so-called Babylonian Captivity of the Church (1309–78). Conflicts with individual popes did not lessen loyalty to the papacy as an institution. It was a member of the Colonna family, Pope Martin V (1417–31), who restored the papacy to Rome, ended feuding within the city, revived the lucrative pilgrim trade, and began the process of renovation that made Rome a center of Renaissance culture. During the Babylonian Captivity, the Colonnas ruled the city with the cooperation of other noble families, including their traditional rivals the ORSINI FAMILY. The Colonna family produced a series of notable CONDOTTIERI who served both the popes and the Spanish viceroys in southern Italy. Marcantonio II (1535–84) played an important role in the Christian victory over the Turks at the naval BATTLE OF LEPANTO (1571). The family maintains close ties to the Vatican to this day. It is a prime example of the so-called "black aristocracy" that prides itself on its loyalty to the CATHOLIC CHURCH. Princess Isabella Colonna (1889–1984) was regarded as the doyenne of high Roman society until her death. In recent years, the family has been torn by internal feuds and has attracted more than its share of media attention. It has set something of a record by maintaining its prominent social position over the course of nearly a thousand years.

Coltivatori Diretti See COLDIRETTI.

Columbus, Christopher (1451–1506)
navigator whose voyages opened the American continent to European settlement
Known as Cristoforo Colombo by Italians and as Cristóbal Colón by Spaniards, Columbus's ethnic identity has been the subject of considerable controversy. Most scholars are satisfied with the accuracy of Columbus's own assertion that he was born in Genoa, but his precise connection with the city of his birth and with Italy in general is far from clear. Still, visitors to Genoa are shown a Casa di Colombo that is reputed to be his place of birth. The mapping and seafaring traditions of the city may have had much to do with Columbus's interest in navigation, but opportunities to sail and explore were far greater in the countries facing the Atlantic seaboard than in his native city. He turned to sailing after spending some years in his father's trade as a weaver. He was shipwrecked near the Portuguese coast in 1476, joined his brother Bartholomew who was working as a mapmaker in Lisbon, worked for a Genoese merchant who was trafficking in sugar off the coast of Africa, and in the process developed the skills that would make him an accomplished mariner. Contrary to popular opinion, Columbus was not unique in believing that the earth was round and that the Indies could be reached by sailing westward. Those beliefs were actually shared in his time by most educated people. What distinguished Columbus was the single-minded determination with which he pursued his goal of reaching the Asian continent by traveling westward. Familiarity with the maps of the cartographer PAOLO TOSCANELLI may have confirmed his resolve.

Repeatedly rebuffed by the rulers of Portugal and Spain, he finally prevailed upon King Ferdinand and Queen Isabella of Spain to sign a contract authorizing the famous expedition of three ships that sailed from the port of Palos on August 3, 1492. After an adventurous voyage, he landed probably on a small island in the Bahamas on October 12, 1492. The "discovery of America" opened up a new era in the history of the western world, for although Viking sailors had indeed already reached the new continent, it was Columbus's voyage that initiated the era of regular contacts and exchanges between Europe and the Americas. For his achievement, the Spanish sovereigns named him admiral of the ocean sea, and governor of the lands he had discovered. He sailed again three times, in 1494, 1498, and 1502, carrying on further explorations of the Caribbean, reaching Trinidad, and probably the South American mainland around the mouth of the Orinoco River in present-day Venezuela.

Columbus's reputation suffered from failure to bring back the expected riches and from reports of poor administration of the lands under his jurisdiction. In 1500 a royal official had him transported back to Spain in chains and briefly imprisoned. By then, Columbus may have suspected that he had stumbled across a new continent, but persisted in thinking that further exploration might vindicate him. The fourth and final voyage failed to provide the evidence he was looking for that he had indeed reached Asia. He never regained the admiration and stature accorded him after his first voyage. Italians largely forgot him for centuries. Much later, in the course of the RISORGIMENTO, his name became a symbol of patriotic pride. Genoa erected a monument in his honor in 1846. Still later in the century, Italian-Americans adopted Columbus as a symbol of their ethnic identity, transforming Columbus Day into a celebration of the Italian identity and their collective contribution to American life.

commedia dell'arte

This form of theatrical representation originated in Italy around the middle of the 16th century and spread rapidly to other parts of Europe. It was particularly popular in France, where it influenced the comical theater of Molière. Its name derives from the fact that its actors were highly skilled professionals who were expected to improvise or embroider on the plot sketched out by the playwright. That does not mean that the improvisation was extemporaneous, for actors prepared and rehearsed their roles and the pranks (*lazzi*) that they expected would make the audience laugh. In time actors specialized in the stock characters (*maschere*) that were typical of commedia dell'arte: the boastful soldiers (Cap-

tain Fracassa, Spaccamonte, Spaventa); the clever, thieving, or foolish servants (Arlecchino, Truffaldino, Pulcinella); the elderly, good-natured master (Balanzone); the flirtatious maid (Colombina, Diamantina); lovers young and old; and so on. Actors danced, performed acrobatics, and could address the audience directly. Puppetry also adopted characters and situations from commedia dell'arte. Highly popular, the great artistic drawback of commedia dell'arte was that its fixed characters did not allow for psychological insight and elaboration: the fool was always the fool, the villain the villain, and the outcome invariably predictable. Sophisticated audiences, and especially playwrights, began to tire of these stock situations and looked for more realistic portrayals of people and situations. Eighteenth-century critics and authors like CARLO GOLDONI delivered some mighty blows against commedia dell'arte. The genre survived as a form of popular entertainment well into the 20th century, and contemporary social satirists like DARIO FO have adopted it successfully for their purposes.

Common Man's Movement See UOMO QUALUNQUE (L').

communism See PCI.

Communist Refounding See PCI.

Comunione e Liberazione

This lay Catholic organization was founded in Lombardy in 1969. By 1979 it had about 60,000 members, all volunteers with a deeply rooted commitment to Catholic orthodoxy and particularly close to Pope JOHN PAUL II, whose theological views they uphold and defend. Its fundamentalist approach has appealed particularly to students in secondary schools and universities. The organization is active among urban workers and the poor. It runs its own social services and industrial and commercial enterprises that provide employment. It is a small but very visible and influential part of a network of lay Catholic associations in Italy that had about 4 million members in 1990. It exerted great influence on the old Christian Democratic Party (DC). Following the DC's demise in 1994 it joined the more politically conservative United Democratic Christians of Rocco Buttiglione, which has supported the governments of SILVIO BERLUSCONI. However, the theological conservatism of Comunione e Liberazione does not necessarily translate into political conservatism. The organization also maintains ties with Catholic political figures that look to the Left.

Conciliatore (Il) See JOURNALISM; ROMANTICISM.

Concordat See ROMAN QUESTION.

condottieri

Condottieri ("they who lead") were familiar figures in the military landscape of medieval and Renaissance Italy. Soldiers of fortune who looked upon war as a business enterprise, they organized and led mercenary military formations (*compagnie di ventura*) on the basis of agreements that stipulated the size and armament of the force, the duration of service, and compensation. They were the product of the endemic state of warfare that prevailed among the many states of the peninsula in the 13th and 14th centuries. Famous condottieri included FRANCESCO SFORZA, Gattamelata (1370–1443), Niccolò Piccinino (1386–1444), and Bartolomeo Colleoni (1400–75). Successful condottieri often developed political ambitions of their own and sought to establish themselves as independent rulers, as did the Sforzas in Milan. Their approach to warfare was highly professional and their tactics relied more on thorough preparation and expert maneuver than bloody combat. The relative

degree of political stability procured by the PEACE OF LODI reduced opportunities for profit and advancement through war in Italy. The French and Spanish invasions of the peninsula provided opportunities for Italian condottieri to fight in the service of foreign powers, as did many members of the COLONNA, MALATESTA, and ORSINI families. Highly regarded for their military skills, these latter-day condottieri lacked the military autonomy and political prospects of their predecessors, and operated within a hierarchical chain of command that called for greater discipline. The condottieri therefore represent an intermediate stage of military development between the mercenary armies of medieval times and modern armies based on training and hierarchical command. The presence of condottieri in the armies of Spain, France, and the HOLY ROMAN EMPIRE gave Italians a military reputation that lasted well into the 17th century.

Confalonieri, Federico (1785–1846)
educational and economic reformer, advocate of Italian independence

Count Federico Confalonieri was a Lombard nobleman of liberal views. Born in Milan, married in 1806 to Teresa Casati (1787–1830), who also belonged to a prominent Milanese family, he refused to become part of the Milanese Napoleonic court where his wife was a lady-in-waiting. His known anti-Napoleonic sentiments earned him a place in the Lombard delegation that in 1814 tried unsuccessfully to win autonomy for Lombardy under French rule. Confalonieri also opposed Austrian rule after 1815. He traveled to France, England, and Belgium to familiarize himself with industrial and technological advances in the more economically developed countries of western Europe. In Lombardy he sponsored the progressive journal *Il Conciliatore* and proposed a broad range of economic and social reforms that included the improvement of popular education through the use of the Lancastrian method of teaching, steamship navigation on the Po River, gas illumination, and mechanization of the textile industry. Convinced that Austrian rule was the chief impediment to reform, Confalonieri worked with the CARBONERIA to win independence for Lombardy. In the REVOLUTION of 1821 he cooperated with Piedmontese conspirators, assuming responsibility for forming a provisional government in Milan and orchestrating an anti-Austrian uprising. The Austrian authorities arrested and tried him, and condemned him to death, but the sentence was commuted to life imprisonment. He was released in 1835 thanks to the intercession of his wife and her influential family, was deported to the United States (1837), returned to Europe and eventually to Milan, where he lived under police surveillance. In the last years of his life he traveled in western Europe and the Near East.

Confindustria

The General Confederation of Italian Industry, better known as Confindustria, is the chief lobby organization of Italian industrialists. Founded in Turin in 1910 to deal with organized labor and lobby the government, it was reorganized in 1919 on a national basis. From the beginning it reflected the views of the larger firms in the auto, metals, and mechanical industries. Small firms, textile and other manufacturers oriented toward export markets contested its claim to speak for all of industry. Confindustria prevailed thanks to several developments. One was the determination of Gino Olivetti (1880–1942), no relation to the manufacturers of office machines, who served as Confindustria secretary from 1919 to 1934. The other was the rise of FASCISM, which in 1926 granted to Confindustria the monopoly of industrial representation that it sought. As the sole legally recognized representative of all industrial employers, Confindustria had an official role in the system of Fascist CORPORATISM, and was entitled to representation in the organs of government. Its directives had the force of law in its areas of competence. After the fall of the Fascist regime, Confindustria lost its

official status, no longer spoke for small producers and state enterprises, and reverted to its former role as a private lobby group. It was influential in the period of national reconstruction, when its laissez-faire philosophy informed government economic policy. It was on the defensive in the turbulent 1960s and early 1970s, but recovered much of its clout in the subsequent decades. It undermined the power of labor unions, organized the successful antilabor initiatives of the 1980s and 1990s, and is working to restructure Italian industry in the face of globalization and mounting competition from abroad. It maintains considerable influence as a pressure group, thanks to its organizational efficiency, political contacts, influence in the relevant government ministries, and the quality of its national leadership, which includes the top names of Italian industry.

Congress of Vienna (1814–1815)

The aim of the Congress of Vienna was to establish a system of international relations that would prevent the recurrence of war and revolution. Although attended by the representatives of many governments, the congress was dominated by the major powers that had defeated NAPOLEON I, namely, Austria, Great Britain, Prussia, and Russia. France was also represented because the government of King Louis XVIII, which had replaced Napoleon's government, was deemed an acceptable partner in the reconstruction of Europe.

The congress paid considerable attention to the affairs of Italy. Territorial changes were designed to restore Austrian dominance of the Italian peninsula, which Napoleon had put completely under French dominance. Legitimacy, meaning that only pre-Napoleonic dynasties had a right to rule, was the principle that guided the congress. The principle of legitimacy was not extended to the Republics of GENOA, LUCCA, and VENICE, which existed before the Napoleonic Wars but were not restored by the Congress of Vienna. The regions of Lombardy and Venetia were incorporated into the AUSTRIAN EMPIRE as a royal possession called the Kingdom of Lombardy-Venetia. Members of the imperial HABSBURG family were put on the thrones of other Italian states: FERDINAND III became grand duke of Tuscany, MARIE LOUISE, daughter of the Austrian emperor, became duchess of Parma, and FRANCIS IV, who was also related to the Habsburgs, became duke of Modena. The other three major states of the peninsula, the KINGDOM OF SARDINIA, KINGDOM OF THE TWO SICILIES, and the PAPAL STATES, relied on Austria for protection.

Italy was thus divided into small states, none strong enough to challenge Austrian dominance. The Kingdom of Sardinia was the one state that gained considerable territory. Its king, VICTOR EMMANUEL I, had a well-deserved reputation as one of Europe's most conservative monarchs. The congress authorized the Kingdom of Sardinia to annex the former territory of the Republic of Genoa, thereby broadening its access to the sea, enabling it to improve its economy, and strengthening its role as a buffer state against France. This was a case in which the principle of legitimacy was applied in tandem with the principle of balance of power. After 1815 Austria played the role of policeman, was the enemy of revolution, and served as the ultimate obstacle to Italian political independence and unity.

Connubio See CAVOUR, CAMILLO BENSO, COUNT OF; RATTAZZI, URBANO.

Consalvi, Ercole (1757–1824)
papal adviser and diplomat
Serving as papal secretary of state from 1800 to 1823, Cardinal Consalvi steered papal policy during a particularly difficult period. He played a key role in securing the election of PIUS VII, who rewarded him by making him cardinal (without Consalvi's having taken holy orders) and secretary of state. A political realist, Consalvi acted according to his belief that the world had changed profoundly as a result of the FRENCH REVOLUTION. He ended the conflict with France by negotiating the Concordat with NAPOLEON I (1801), which recognized Catholicism as the religion of the majority in France and provided for government payment of clergy. His resistance to further Napoleonic claims on the CATHOLIC CHURCH landed him in exile and prison. His persecution gave him renewed prestige and authority after Napoleon's fall in 1814. As papal representative at the CONGRESS OF VIENNA, Consalvi won full territorial restoration of the PAPAL STATES. His principal concerns after 1815 were reform of the state administration, particularly the admission of laymen to public office, and a conciliatory policy toward supporters of the former Napoleonic regime. Unfortunately, he ran into the opposition of the political extremists known as the *zelanti*, who blocked his proposals. He welcomed the support of Austria, but resisted Prince Metternich's claims to tighter control of papal policy. Consalvi's influence ended with the election of the *zelanti*'s candidate, Pope Leo XII (1823–29). Consalvi died in January 1824, four months after the election of the new pope.

consociativismo See HISTORIC COMPROMISE.

Constituent Assembly See CONSTITUTIONS.

constitutions
Written constitutions contain a set of rules regulating the conduct of government. Such documents are today an accepted feature of political life in western democracies. However, their acceptance came after long and often violent struggles to limit the power of absolute monarchs. In the 18th century only a few progressive monarchs, most notably PETER LEOPOLD of Tuscany, considered granting constitutions, but were quickly dissuaded from implementing such projects by fear of revolution. Constitutions were adopted in Spain and Sicily in 1812 and in France in 1814. These became models for Italian liber-

als in the 19th century. The Spanish constitution was favored by the more democratic elements because it was founded on the principle of popular sovereignty, provided a fairly broad suffrage, and an elected parliament. The French charter appealed to more moderate elements because it was in the form of a royal concession and was based on a narrow suffrage and a bicameral legislature, one branch of which was elected and the other appointed by the king. The Sicilian constitution also provided for an elected legislature based on narrow suffrage, partial compensation for abolished feudal rights, and administrative autonomy for the island. It was revoked by the Bourbon government in 1816, but it, too, remained a point of reference for 19th-century liberals.

SECRET SOCIETIES and liberal groups called for constitutions in the REVOLUTIONS of 1820–21, 1830, and 1848. The rulers of Naples, Piedmont-Sardinia, and Tuscany granted constitutions in 1848, but only the Piedmontese constitution (Statuto) survived the defeat of revolution. Granted by King CHARLES ALBERT in February 1848, it gave real powers over budgets and legislation to a lower house of parliament (chamber of deputies) elected on the basis of a narrow suffrage, provided for an upper house (senate) appointed by the king, and gave the king command of the armed forces, war, peace, and foreign policy. The Statuto was the fundamental law of the Kingdom of SARDINIA from 1848 to 1861 and of the kingdom of Italy from 1861 until the monarchy was abolished in 1946. It did not provide for the principle of ministerial responsibility to parliament, which nevertheless became generally accepted political practice by the end of the 19th century, when prime ministers and their cabinets were expected to resign if they lost the support of the majority on important issues in the elected chamber.

Along with the broadening of the franchise in 1882, 1912, and 1919, the Statuto served as the basis of an increasingly democratic system of government until FASCISM changed the system of voting and political representation after 1922.

The king's appointment of BENITO MUSSOLINI as prime minister in October 1922 was strictly speaking a constitutional act since the Statuto gave the king the power of appointment, but it was against the normal practice of appointing a leader of a party well represented in parliament. The Statuto remained the fundamental law of the land throughout the Fascist period. Although Fascist legislation and Mussolini's ambition diminished the power of the king, the retention of the Statuto gave the king a constitutional basis for dismissing Mussolini in July 1943, thus bringing to an end the period of Fascist rule. The Statuto lapsed when a majority voted against the monarchy and for a republican form of government in the national plebiscite and elections of June 1946.

The constituent assembly elected by the voters framed the constitution of the Italian republic. The republican constitution went into effect on January 1, 1948, and is still the fundamental law of the land. The main objective of the framers was to establish a system of government that would provide the strongest safeguards against a recurrence of fascism and dictatorship. It defines Italy as "a democratic Republic based on work," guarantees civil liberties, free enterprise, the separation of CHURCH AND STATE, recognizes the family as a natural association founded on marriage, renounces war, provides for a bicameral parliament elected by universal suffrage and for local and regional autonomies, gives a largely ceremonial role to the office of president of the republic, vests executive power in the office of prime minister and the council of ministers (cabinet), establishes a supreme court to judge the constitutionality of laws and popular referenda to affirm or repeal contested laws, and provides for a parliamentary procedure to amend the constitution. National unity and the republican form of government are not subject to amendment.

Not all provisions of the republican constitution were implemented immediately. Provisions for regional governance were not fully implemented until the 1970s. The concept of separation of church and state required more specific definition. In February 1984 the Italian government and the Holy See negotiated a new Concordat to replace that of 1929 that had been endorsed by the constitution of 1948. The new agreement omitted the reference to Catholicism as the sole religion of the Italian state, made religious instruction in state schools optional, and abolished state subsidies for the clergy. Critics blame the constitution for a weak executive, a poor sense of the state, neglect of the public interest, bureaucratic corruption, and insufficient separation of church and state. Still, there are many things that can be said in its favor. It has effectively dispelled the threat of fascism and personal dictatorship, made government broadly representative, and protected individual freedoms. It gave the state the power it needed to deal with political TERRORISM. Since the early 1990s there has been much debate over the future of the present constitution and the nature of a "second republic" with a different constitutional foundation: a strong presidency, a two-party system, administrative decentralization, and less bureaucracy. While public opinion seems to appreciate the gains realized with the current constitutional system, there is also strong public support for changing the system of governance.

cooperativism

Cooperatives of consumers and producers have a long history in Italy. Able to function only under a political system that protects freedom of association, cooperatives emerged first in Piedmont-Sardinia under the CONSTITUTION of 1848. Under its provisions, workers were free to organize mutual aid societies, labor unions, and cooperatives. The first cooperatives, in the retail trades, provided merchandise at cut prices. Next were producer cooperatives among glassmakers, tailors, printers, stonemasons, and carpenters. They produced at competitive prices and provided employment, social services, and pensions. Government authorities kept a close watch on worker cooperatives, suspecting them of sub-

version, but allowed them to function as long as they did not engage in political activities. Cooperatives spread to other regions after the unification of Italy. A notable development of the postunification period was the movement to form popular savings banks and rural credit unions in the regions of Venetia, where liberal and Catholic organizers competed for the allegiance of workers and peasants. Socialists also came forward to promote cooperatives among landless day workers and sharecroppers of the Po Valley and Romagna areas.

Various legislative acts passed in the 1880s recognized mutual aid societies and cooperatives as juridical entities that could enter into contracts and assume collective responsibilities. In 1893 the National League of Cooperatives was set up, representing 117 out of an estimated 2,500 cooperatives active in the country. By the end of WORLD WAR I the league represented 2,321 cooperatives. The National Confederation of Cooperatives founded in 1919 set out to organize Catholic cooperatives throughout the country. The cooperative movement as a whole grew enormously in the years 1919–22. Its strong political coloration aroused fears that the movement could become the cutting edge of economic and political revolution. The growth of the cooperative movement was checked by FASCISM, which directed its attacks against both socialist and Catholic cooperatives. But once established, the Fascist regime chose to control and regulate rather than eliminate cooperatives. In 1926 the Fascist National Agency for Cooperation took over 7,131 cooperatives, which grew to 14,576 by 1942.

Cooperatives emerged from the devastation of WORLD WAR II with enough political clout to win a secure place in the postwar economy. The three-way organizational split among cooperatives associated with left-wing parties (PCI and PSI), Catholic cooperatives associated with the DC, and cooperatives associated with the PRI and PSDI later diminished their influence. Nevertheless, cooperatives have flourished economically, adopting modern methods of management and responding well to changing market demands. What they have lost is the ability cherished by the pioneers of the movement to change the nature of the economy from one based on laissez-faire principles to one based on the principle of association. For the approximately 500,000 workers of about 160,000 cooperatives currently operating, cooperatives represent an unqualified economic success.

Coppi, Fausto See SPORT.

Corfù Crisis See FASCISM.

corporatism

Corporatism, or corporativism, is an ideology of cooperation that cuts across class lines, uniting workers, entrepreneurs, and government officials in economic activities, carried out in the public interest or the interests of the state. Corporatism aims at eliminating conflicts of interest among labor, business, and government. FASCISM adopted and institutionalized corporatism, but the origins of the ideology predate the rise of fascism. Catholic social doctrine embodied corporatist principles derived from Christian notions of spirituality, charity, and human solidarity. An idealization of medieval guilds as fundamentally harmonious associations of employers and workers was also part of Catholic corporatist thinking. The encyclicals of Pope LEO XIII and the writings of GIUSEPPE TONIOLO are important sources of Catholic corporatist doctrine. Nationalists also adopted corporatism as a means of securing domestic harmony, developing the economy, and strengthening the state. Both Catholic and nationalist corporatism aimed at combating the influence of socialism and eliminating class conflict.

The Fascist corporatist state was the brainchild of social theoreticians like ALFREDO ROCCO and GIUSEPPE BOTTAI. Both were determined to give fascism a social doctrine that transcended the perceived limitations of economic liberalism and socialism, emphasized social cooperation, appealed to ideal values, and enhanced the power of the state. Before corporatist reforms could be enacted, the Fascist regime had to eliminate domestic opposition, gain control of organized labor, and reassure and pressure employers into accepting a system of economic controls. The enactment of corporatist reforms was therefore gradual. It began in 1926 with the passage of laws eliminating independent labor unions, and creating the Ministry of Corporations. A national council of corporations was set up in 1930 as an advisory body on economic questions. Twenty-two national corporations were set up in 1934, each with jurisdiction over a specific sector of the economy, regulated by councils representing labor, management, and government, and coordinated at the top by the national council and Ministry of Corporations.

The regulatory powers of the 22 corporations were limited, but they did play a role in labor relations, helped in the formation of business cartels, and conducted studies for the benefit of government experts. The corporations were caught in the contradictions of Fascist economic policy. On the one hand, the proliferation of government agencies interfered with the work of the corporations by dispersing decision-making powers in different directions. On the other, the policy of AUTARKY adopted by the regime required even more centralized economic planning than could be provided by 22 separate corporations. A final reform in 1938 transformed parliament's chamber of deputies into the chamber of fasces and corporations, its members now representing the corporations, the Fascist Party, and other officially recognized associations. By that time, however, parliament had lost all meaningful legislative functions. The entire corporative structure was abolished after the fall of the Fascist regime in 1943, but an expanded bureaucracy and increased red tape were lasting legacies of Fascist corporatism.

Social theoreticians have also seen its traces in the practice of formal and informal cooperation of private business, organized labor, and government officials that is a feature of all modern economies. That form of "societal corporatism" is significantly different in structure and scope from the official institutionalized "state corporatism" and is best seen as a distinct and separate form of corporative interaction with its own historical and economic derivations. In any case, in whatever form it takes, corporatism has always appealed almost exclusively to intellectuals and social engineers who are intrigued by its theoretical possibilities. Unlike other modern "isms," corporatism is an ideology without a mass following.

Corradini, Enrico (1865–1931)
journalist, founder and inspirer of the nationalist movement

This Florentine political writer and journalist played a major role in orienting Italian NATIONALISM toward colonial and territorial expansion. A graduate of the University of Florence, he began as a high school teacher of literature, joined the cultural battle against philosophical POSITIVISM, fell under the spell of GABRIELE D'ANNUNZIO, and like D'Annunzio was not content with a purely aesthetic approach to life. The Italian military defeat at the BATTLE OF ADOWA (1896) drew him into public debate. Corradini made avenging that defeat the message of his writings. He sought to do so by promoting a sense of nationalist pride and cohesiveness by applying the socialist notion of class struggle to international relations. According to his creed, the world was divided between rich and poor nations, just like nations were divided between the rich and poor classes. Rich and poor nations competed for the world's resources. Rich bourgeois nations like Great Britain and France that had grown rich with empire prevented "proletarian nations" like Italy from claiming their rightful share of territory and resources. Italy was the chief proletarian nation. It was hampered internally by class divisions and externally by the will of wealthy nations. It must overcome the former by seeking colonies for the settlement of its poor and the latter by protecting its nascent industries necessary for warfare from foreign competition. It must prepare for the inevitable showdown that would simultaneously affirm its status as a great power and solve the social question. Corradini singled out Italian emigration as a national calamity and humiliation, arguing that colonies would provide places of settlement where Italians could work under the protection of their own flag. His most important publication was the review *Il Regno* (1903–06), which touted the message that Italy could overcome scarcity of natural resources by an act of collective will power. He was a founder of the ITALIAN NATIONALIST ASSOCIATION (1910), supported the ITALIAN-TURKISH WAR (1911–12), Italian intervention in WORLD WAR I, and FASCISM. He collaborated with the Fascist regime, served as senator, and helped restructure the Fascist state according to the theory of CORPORATISM. Private papers that came to light after his death showed that he disapproved of the personality cult surrounding BENITO MUSSOLINI. The Fascist regime eulogized him as a national hero and precursor of fascism.

Corridoni, Filippo (1888–1915)
political activist of the extreme Left and revolutionary syndicalist

A political activist of the extreme Left, Corridoni was drawn to radical ideologies that promised social regeneration by violent means. His political itinerary took him from Mazzinian republicanism to socialism and REVOLUTIONARY SYNDICALISM. Inspired by Georges Sorel's faith in the revolutionary fervor of the working class and the myth of the general strike as the weapon of revolution, Corridoni rejected the Italian Socialist Party (PSI) and the leadership of organized labor as reformist, and founded his own Syndicalist Union (1913), with which he hoped to wrest control of organized labor from the reformist General Confederation of Labor. He failed in that objective, but his personal charisma, public eloquence, and courage made him a highly visible and popular figure at a relatively young age. When his hopes of revolution were dashed by the failure of the RED WEEK uprisings of June 1914, he put his faith in a general war that would shake the system to its foundation and launch the social revolution. When BENITO MUSSOLINI came around to that view in October 1914, it looked like the making of an alliance between two charismatic leaders. But Corridoni did not live long enough to see the results of that alliance. Acting on his conviction that war was the necessary prelude to revolution, he volunteered for military service and died in combat in October 1915. The Fascist regime hailed him as a martyr and precursor.

Corriere della Sera See ALBERTINI, LUIGI; JOURNALISM.

Corsica

Part of France since 1769, the island of Corsica was previously under the nominal rule of the republic of GENOA. Genoese policy excluded natives from administrative and political office, attacked the seigneurial rights of the nobility, and favored commercial elements in the hope of creating a new social class loyal to the republic. But Genoese efforts could not control the fierce family feuds that plagued the island. Its state of chronic revolt persuaded the Genoese government to cede the island to France in 1769. Pasquale Paoli (1735–1807) emerged as the hero in the Corsican struggle for independence, a struggle that he waged against both Genoa and France until he was forced into exile in England. Corsica's most famous figure is NAPOLEON I, who quickly gave up on his family's association with the cause of Corsican independence and identified entirely with France. During the RISORGIMENTO, Corsica served as a staging ground for operations by SECRET SOCIETIES fighting for Italian independence. The island's cultural and linguistic affinities with Italy have attracted the attention of Italian nationalists. The Corsicans have shown little interest in being part of Italy, and relations between Italy and France have been friendly for the most part. FASCISM was the exception. In the late 1930s Fascist propaganda claimed Corsica for Italy, and Italian troops invaded the island in 1942.

corso forzoso See CURRENCY.

cosa nostra See MAFIA.

Cossiga, Francesco (1928–   )
Christian Democratic leader and president of the republic

Born in Sardinia, Cossiga was active in the Catholic movement as a university student, rose through the ranks of the Christian Democratic Party (DC) to hold the highest office in the land, and served as president of the republic from 1985 to 1992. He joined the DC in 1945, was elected to the chamber of deputies in 1958, and held his first ministerial post in 1966. He was interior minister in charge of national security in 1976–78. The intensification of TERRORISM during his watch, culminating in the kidnapping and assassination of ALDO MORO, who had been Cossiga's political mentor, led to his resignation from that post the day after the kidnapping. That gesture saved his reputation as a man willing to acknowledge his responsibility for failing to protect Moro and the country from terrorists. He went on to serve unremarkably as prime minister in 1979–80 and to hold the post of senate president. He was elected president of the republic in 1985 with strong support across the political spectrum. The presidency brought out aspects of Cossiga's personality that had not been evident earlier. Public reticence gave way to talkativeness. He clearly meant to use the moral power of the nation's highest office to push for political reforms. His method was to address the country directly through a series of pronouncements (*esternazioni*) that drew attention to the inadequacies of the political system, parliamentary misbehavior, financial corruption, and the influence of organized crime. His persistent efforts played a role in getting the process of reform underway in the early 1990s. In the process, Cossiga acquired a reputation as a political maverick and loose cannon. The image of volatility was reinforced by his unexpected decision in April 1992 to resign from the presidency just 10 weeks before the normal expiration of his mandate. That same year he was made senator for life. The breakup of the DC in 1994 left Cossiga at political loose ends, but in 1998 he tried to revive the party with a new name, the Democratic Union for the Republic (UDR). With 5 percent of the seats in the chamber of deputies, UDR gave the former communist MASSIMO D'ALEMA the majority that he needed to form his center-left government in October of that year.

Costa, Andrea (1851–1910)
social activist and founder of Italian socialism
Costa has a strong claim to being considered the founder of Italian socialism. Born to a family of modest means in the Po Valley town of Imola, his passion for politics developed during his first year at the University of Bologna, which he left when he was denied a scholarship. His journalistic ventures and organizational activities among workers brought him regional prominence. Costa's stand in support of the Paris Commune led to a break with GIUSEPPE MAZZINI and the republican movement. Costa turned to ANARCHISM as a seemingly more promising movement for the Left, and was jailed for his subversive activities (1874–76). After his release, Costa left for Paris, where he discovered Marxism and began his long relationship with the Russian radical ANNA KULISCIOFF. The failure of repeated attempts at insurrection convinced Costa that the use of violence discredited the cause of revolution and strengthened the opposition. Costa decided that the best way to safeguard the interests of workers and advance the cause of socialism was to adopt the legal tactics of large-scale organization

and parliamentary action. In 1881 he founded the newspaper *Avanti!* to spread the socialist gospel. In 1882 he became the first socialist to win a seat in parliament. In 1892 he helped form the first national party of workers, from which sprang the Italian Socialist Party (PSI). He encouraged workers to organize and fought in parliament for the right to strike. Costa obtained the ultimate seal of political respectability when he was elected vice president of the chamber of deputies. Socialism by then was an integral part of the political system of GIOVANNI GIOLITTI. The debate over the nature, tactics, and goals of socialism was still going on when Costa died. His successors struggled to reconcile the tactic of legal action that he espoused with that of violent revolution that he rejected.

Council of Trent See TRENT, COUNCIL OF.

Counter-reformation See CATHOLIC REFORMATION.

Craxi, Bettino (1934–2000)
Socialist Party leader, prime minister, and political outcast
Born in Milan, the son of a lawyer, christened Benedetto but always known as Bettino, Craxi was drawn to socialist politics from an early age by family tradition. He joined the Socialist Party (PSI) at age 18, and briefly attended Milan University law school. He became leader of the Socialist Party in 1976, put his followers in key positions, reorganized the party, and distanced it from communism. The 11.4 percent of the vote that his party received in the elections of 1983 positioned him to head a coalition government with the numerically dominant but divided Christian Democratic Party (DC). He was the first socialist to serve as prime minister. His four-year government lasted until March 1987, setting a postwar record for longevity. Those four years were marked by economic growth, rising con-

sumption of goods, and increase in leisure time. An unusually active foreign policy saw the commitment of Italian troops to Lebanon as part of an international peacekeeping force, a controversial decision to accept NATO nuclear missiles on Italian soil, and a rare clash with the United States over the arrest of Arab terrorists by American authorities on Italian soil. On the sensitive issue of Middle East policy, Craxi tilted toward support for the Palestinians. In the elections of 1987 held shortly after Craxi's resignation as prime minister, the Socialist Party reached its highest vote of 14.3 percent. His tenure was nevertheless highly controversial. Suggestions of political corruption dogged Craxi because of the system of patronage and political contributions that he controlled. Socialists did gain much influence in government and state-run institutions during the Craxi years. The attacks against him intensified as his power and popularity grew, stirred by the fears of rival parties and figures. The 1992 investigation of the MANI PULITE (Clean Hands) bribery scandal in Milan in 1992 eventually implicated Craxi and he resigned as PSI secretary in February 1993. He fled to Tunisia in May 1994 to avoid prosecution in what he charged was a politically motivated trial. He was subsequently convicted of graft and corruption and an international warrant was issued for his arrest, but he was never extradited. He died of a heart attack in Tunisia.

Crimean War

Fought in 1853–56, the Crimean War pitted Russia against a coalition consisting of the Ottoman Empire, Great Britain, France, and the Kingdom of SARDINIA. The Kingdom of Sardinia intervened in the war in January 1855, dispatched a corps of 15,000 troops, and sent Prime Minister CAVOUR to the Congress of Paris that ended the war. Italian intervention was solicited by Great Britain and France partly to reassure Austria that it would have nothing to fear on its Italian border if it joined the anti-Russian coalition and partly for the additional troops that Sardinia could provide. The Sardinian contingent of 15,000 troops fought one significant engagement and

performed well militarily. Like all other combatants, the Sardinians suffered more casualties from disease than from combat. The once-accepted interpretation that Cavour deliberately sought involvement in the war to advance the cause of Italian unification is not borne out by recent research. It seems rather that the French and British pressured the Kingdom of Sardinia into going to war. There were no immediate gains for Sardinia, but the fact that it was represented at the Congress of Paris, that the great powers acknowledged the existence of an "Italian Question," and that Austria was left diplomatically isolated did indirectly advance the cause of Italian independence. Closer relations with France yielded political dividends in 1859 when France and Sardinia went to war against Austria, while Great Britain looked on the unification of Italy with benevolence.

Crispi, Francesco (1808–1901)
Risorgimento patriot, leader of the democratic opposition, and prime minister

Crispi's career took him from the role of political conspirator to the office of prime minister in the course of a life filled with controversy and marked by unfulfilled promise. He was born into a Sicilian family of grain merchants of Albanian origin. At the University of Palermo he studied law and literature, received a law degree (1837), and pursued a career in journalism. He moved to Naples in 1845 to take a judgeship, but returned to Sicily after revolution broke out there in January 1848. As a journalist and member of the Sicilian parliament, he supported the separatist movement that sought to break ties with Naples. As a political exile in Turin, Paris, London, and other European cities from 1849, he immersed himself in the politics of the national movement, abandoning Sicilian separatism, and identifying with the republicanism of GIUSEPPE MAZZINI, with whom Crispi collaborated closely until 1859. That year marked the beginning of his turn toward the HOUSE OF SAVOY and the monarchy as the institution most likely to succeed in unifying Italy. In 1860 he played a key role in persuading GIUSEPPE GARIBALDI to lead the famed expedition of the Thousand that freed Sicily from Bourbon rule.

He was elected to the first Italian parliament in 1861 and in all successive legislatures for the rest of his life. In 1864 he took the public stand that "the monarchy unites us, a republic would divide us," which signaled the final break with Mazzini. As a member of the parliamentary opposition, he criticized both the governments of the HISTORICAL RIGHT and LIBERAL LEFT. Although he was himself part of the Liberal Left, and served as president of the chamber of deputies when the Liberal Left was in power, he joined the so-called PENTARCHY that opposed the Liberal Left governments led by AGOSTINO DEPRETIS. When Depretis died in office in July 1887, Crispi succeeded him as prime minister and foreign minister. He dominated the political scene until 1896, serving as prime minister and in various other capacities for all but almost three years (1891–93). With his carefully cultivated image as a man of destiny, Crispi sought to govern energetically. In his first years in office his government enacted many desirable reforms. He took steps to improve the functioning of the courts, broadened the franchise in local elections, introduced programs of public sanitation, reformed the welfare and penal systems, and sponsored laws for the protection of emigrants. More controversially, he also took steps to increase the powers of the executive at the expense of parliament and strengthened the authority of PREFECTS.

His foreign policy was assertive, actively pursuing recognition for Italy as a major power, engaging in a tariff war with France, and seeking a close understanding with Germany. After some hesitation, he also backed the policy of colonial expansion. The negative consequences of the trade war with France and a deteriorating domestic economy forced his resignation as prime minister in February 1891, but he returned in December 1893 with an enhanced reputation as man of action and savior of the country. However, this time he had to face unprecedented domestic and foreign difficulties. He declared martial law to repress rebellions in Sicily and central Italy, antagonized powerful industrialists and landowners by proposing new forms of taxation to balance the budget, and had to confront the political storm that followed the defeat of Italian troops in Adowa in March 1896. Forced out of office and subjected to official investigations to ascertain responsibility for that military debacle, he lived in retirement until his death in 1901. Crispi remains something of an enigma, a democrat with irresistible authoritarian impulses, a patriot turned aggressive nationalist, a villain to the Left and a hero to the Right.

Critica (La) See CROCE, BENEDETTO.

Critica Sociale See PSI; TURATI, FILIPPO.

Croce, Benedetto (1866–1952)
leading philosopher and public figure
Considered the most prominent Italian intellectual of his generation, Croce's cultural influence was felt in many fields in Italy and abroad. Primarily a philosopher, he also influenced historical scholarship, literary criticism, art, and politics. Born in the small town of Pescasseroli in the Abruzzo region to a well-off family of landowners, in 1883 he lost his parents in an earthquake, went to live with his uncle SILVIO SPAVENTA in Rome (1883–86), where he attended the university and was influenced by the Marxist theoretician ANTONIO LABRIOLA. He then settled in Naples, where he lived and worked for the rest of his life as an independent scholar. He never sought or held an academic appointment, traveled widely, and developed a keen interest in contemporary politics and political ideologies. His essay *On the Materialistic Interpretation of History* (1896) rejected materialism as a guide to the interpretation of history and signaled a break with Labriola. Croce questioned not only the validity of Marxist historical analysis but, more generally, of POSITIVISM as a way of understanding reality, turning instead to an idealist philosophy of Hegelian origin.

Benedetto Croce *(Library of Congress)*

In his journal *La Critica* (1903–44) Croce carried out a campaign to breathe new life into Italian culture, combat the influence of positivism, and assert the primacy of spirit over matter. In this and other ventures he had the backing of his then friend and disciple GIOVANNI GENTILE and the publisher Giovanni Laterza (1873–1943). Their intent was to form a political leadership for the 20th century. Croce was appointed senator in 1910 and served as minister of public education (1920–21), but political activism was not his ideal. He saw himself rather as a cultural presence influencing politics from the outside. He broke with the Socialist Party (PSI) openly in

1911, charging that socialist agitation intensified class antagonisms and undermined the spiritual unity of the country. He later opposed FASCISM as a historical aberration. Croce saw history as the progressive realization of liberal ideals and as "the religion of liberty." He looked to the state as the impartial enforcer of the law, believed in private property, individual freedom, open debate, and political pluralism. His liberalism did not go as far as to embrace political democracy and majority rule. That limit explains his initial sympathy for fascism as a necessary corrective to democracy, but then his later opposition once it became clear that fascism meant the arbitrary and repressive use of power. Croce's liberalism also made him anticlerical. He criticized papal policy for its hostility toward the Italian liberal state and its sympathy for fascism.

Croce's long-standing opposition to Marxism reasserted itself after 1945 when he saw resurgent communism as a threat to liberal values. But after 1945 Croce's cultural influence was challenged by the rising influence of Marxism, particularly in the version elaborated by ANTONIO GRAMSCI. It can be said with much justification that for about two decades after 1945 Italian intellectuals were either Crocean or Gramscian. Croce's critical appraisal of his own ideas appears in *Contributo alla critica di me stesso* (1915), translated and published in English by his friend and admirer, the philosopher R. G. Collingwood as *An Autobiography* (1927, repr. 1970). For his interpretation of history see his *History of Europe in the Nineteenth Century* (1933) and *Storia d'Italia dal 1871 al 1915* (History of Italy from 1871 to 1915, 1928).

Crusca, Accademia della See ACADEMIES;
BEMBO, PIETRO.

Cuccia, Enrico (1908–2000)
financier and business facilitator
Cuccia is regarded as the most influential Italian banker of the second half of the 20th century, a role partially disguised by his public reticence.

Born in Rome of Sicilian parents, he started out working for the BANCA D'ITALIA. In 1934 he joined the recently established Institute for Industrial Reconstruction (IRI), a state-owned holding company that dominated the public sector of the economy. In 1938 Cuccia joined the staff of the Banca Commerciale Italiana, the most prestigious of Italy's banking institutions. In 1939 he married the daughter of IRI's founder and chairman, ALBERTO BENEDUCE. In 1946 Beneduce appointed his son-in-law to start up Mediobanca, a credit institution that extended medium-term credit to big industry. Using its leverage as lender, Mediobanca arranged major financial operations, including the 1966 merger of the Montecatini and Edison firms to form the chemical giant MONTEDISON. Cuccia proved extremely adept at arranging complicated financial deals among the giants of Italian industry. In the 1980s he helped revitalize FIAT, arranging for the buyback of shares sold by Fiat's owners, the Agnelli family, to Libyan leader Muammar el-Qaddafi in 1976. Cuccia's power began to wane in the 1990s with the gradual privatization of the state-controlled enterprises, which eroded Cuccia's role as effective broker between the private and public sectors. He remained honorary chairman of Mediobanca until his death in Rome in June 2000. In a bizarre aftermath, grave robbers snatched Cuccia's body and held it for ransom. Upon being apprehended, they explained that they had settled for Cuccia dead because he had been too well guarded while alive.

Cultura Sociale (La) See MURRI, ROMOLO.

Cuoco, Vincenzo (1770–1823)
historian and political writer
Cuoco was a participant and first historian of the period 1799–1815, which witnessed revolution, and the rise and fall of NAPOLEON I. He was born in a small town in the region of Molise, the son of a lawyer who wanted him to follow in his own professional footsteps. Cuoco went to the University of Naples in 1787, where he took up the study of economics and political philosophy. He avoided politics until he became a sympathizer of the PARTHENOPEAN REPUBLIC proclaimed in 1799. Although he took no active part in the government, his sympathies for the republic brought him a sentence of exile when the Bourbon monarchy was temporarily restored in 1800. After visiting Marseilles and Paris, in 1804 he settled in Milan, where he founded the periodical *Giornale Italiano*. His publication raised and publicized the issue of national identity and independence, earning Cuoco a place among the forerunners of the RISORGIMENTO. His *Saggio sulla Rivoluzione napoletana* (Essay on the Neapolitan revolution, 1801), assessed the events of 1799 from a moderate perspective that favored gradual change and rejected revolution. According to Cuoco, the JACOBINS who led the revolution of 1799 pursued utopian goals, were out of touch with the common people, and were responsible for its failure. He described the revolution as "passive" because it disregarded the needs of the people, who turned against it at the first opportunity. His chief complaint was that the Jacobins had ignored history, putting too much distance between themselves and the masses that were attached to the traditions of the kingdom. In spite of this assessment, Cuoco was no populist reformer, for he also believed that the most needed reforms were those that would stimulate the economy, and not reforms that would give land to the landless or provide support for the poor. Cuoco's ideal of good government was the monarchy of JOSEPH BONAPARTE and his successor, JOACHIM MURAT, whom Cuoco served faithfully in various administrative capacities. The RESTORATION did not deprive him of all his offices but Cuoco, emotionally frail, became increasingly despondent in his remaining years. His influence helped steer the movement for national unification in the moderate direction that it took under the guidance of CAVOUR. Leftist writers and theoreticians used Cuoco's concept of "passive revolution" against revolutionaries deemed too timid to mobilize the masses.

Curcio, Renato See RED BRIGADES.

currency

The Italian currency is the lira, a name derived from the Roman word for pound (*libra*), The *libra,* weighing approximately 325 grams, was used as the reference point for the weight of coins in circulation. When Charlemagne introduced uniform coinage in the eighth century, the lira became the unit of currency throughout his empire, which included Italy as far south as Rome. For centuries, however, the lira remained only a nominal currency. No coins actually bore that name, but the lira (pound), or fraction thereof, referred to the amount of metal actually present in a coin. In the Middle Ages the lira was usually defined as 340 grams of silver. In 1745 the Republic of GENOA minted the first coin that was actually called a lira. During Napoleonic times and later in the 19th century, the terms lira and franc were often used interchangeably, the amount of precious metal in the lira varying, however, from state to state, and the lira remaining a unit of measure rather than an actual coin. The lira of Piedmont-Sardinia became the Italian lira after national unification. The Italian lira was a silver coin weighing 4.5 grams, equivalent to 0.29 grams of gold, with a gold/silver ratio of 1:15.5. The lira remained on this bimetallic standard until 1866, when the government was forced to abandon the convertibility of the lira into gold (*corso forzoso*) to meet its obligations and avoid bankruptcy. By the 1890s the lira had regained its value and the government repealed the *corso forzoso,* or policy of nonconvertibility.

In 1900–14 the exchange rate of the lira was pegged at five to the U.S. dollar, and this is considered to be the lira's period of greatest stability and prestige. The cost of WORLD WAR I and the postwar economic crisis triggered an unprecedented inflation and depreciation of the lira. The Fascist regime took up the defense of the lira (Bat-

tle of the Lira) in 1926–27, partly for financial reasons and partly for reasons of national prestige. It stabilized the lira at the exchange rate called QUOTA 90. Monetary stability kept inflation at bay and gave the regime the domestic stability that it needed to conduct an aggressive FOREIGN POLICY. The defeat of the Fascist regime in WORLD WAR II brought on an unprecedented monetary crisis. The value of the lira plunged as the Allies issued vast amounts of occupation currency, inflation ran rampant, and efforts at price controls actually stimulated a black market with unregulated prices.

Recovery was slow and difficult in the new international economy dominated by the American dollar. Strengthening the currency was a primary objective of postwar economic policy, and by the early 1950s the lira achieved a stable exchange rate of approximately 620 to the dollar, a rate that remained stable until the early 1970s. Since then, the lira has floated broadly in response to changing domestic and international economic developments. In the late 1990s the government was able to meet the monetary requirements for admission to the EUROPEAN UNION by curtailing spending, limiting public borrowing, and raising taxes. Like the currencies of other European Union members, the Italian lira was gradually replaced by the euro, the new European Union currency. The lira went out of circulation officially in March 2002.

Curtatone, Battle of See MONTANELLI, GIUSEPPE.

Custoza, Battle of See CIALDINI, ENRICO; LA MARMORA, ALFONSO; WARS OF NATIONAL INDEPENDENCE.

Cyrenaica See COLONIALISM.

D

D'Alema, Massimo (1949–)
leader of the political Left and prime minister
Born into a family long associated with the Italian Communist Party (PCI), D'Alema visited the Soviet Union as a young man, headed the Young Communist League, and served as chief editor of the party newspaper *L'Unità* (1988–90). Following the breakup of the Communist Party in 1991, D'Alema was founding member of its successor, the DEMOCRATIC PARTY OF THE LEFT. Formally renouncing communism, D'Alema headed the new party and became its chief spokesman for a new brand of democracy and popular government based on economic growth, political freedom, and social justice. He became prime minister in October 1998, the first former communist to occupy that post. He faced the difficult task of meeting stringent budget requirements to qualify Italy for entry in the European Monetary Union on January 1, 1999. His government met that goal, but not without severe disagreements with its coalition partner, the unreconstructed communists of *Rifondazione Comunista,* whose dissent weakened the governing coalition. D'Alema's government pursued an unusually active foreign policy, committing Italian troops to peacekeeping missions in Albania and Bosnia, and combat planes to the 1999 NATO campaign against Slobodan Milošević in Kosovo, as well as assuming responsibility for policing parts of Kosovo province. The government also had to deal with a short-lived crisis in relations with the United States after an American air force jet brought down a cable car carrying 20 tourists in February 1999. D'Alema's budget-cutting measures alienated many of his supporters on the Left, including the labor unions and many members of his own party. He resigned as prime minister in April 2000, after the parties of the governing center-left coalition lost votes in regional elections to the opposition groups led by SILVIO BERLUSCONI. As head of the Democratic Party of the Left and a leader of the opposition, D'Alema continues to work for his brand of social democracy.

Dalla Chiesa, Carlo Alberto (1920–1982)
military officer in charge of the fight against political terrorism and the Mafia
This general of the CARABINIERI military corps proved himself a man of courage and an efficient organizer in the fight against political TERRORISM (1978–82), following the kidnapping and assassination of ALDO MORO. His next assignment showed the limits of police power in the absence of adequate political cover. In April 1982 Dalla Chiesa accepted the invitation from Prime Minister GIOVANNI SPADOLINI to become prefect of Palermo and take charge of the government's campaign against the MAFIA. The government, however, did not grant his request for broad police powers throughout Sicily. Dalla Chiesa understood the Mafia as a gigantic business operation with strong political connections. Fighting it required a skillful combination of old-fashioned police methods with the latest tools of electronic surveillance. On September 3, 1982, Dalla Chiesa was gunned down in his car along with his wife and chauffeur. A crime that shocked the nation almost as much as the Moro assassination, the death of Dalla Chiesa energized parliament into passing a series of measures that made "association with the Mafia" a

crime, broadened police powers, and led to the arrest of thousands of suspected Mafia members and accomplices. Suspicions that highly placed political figures conspired or colluded in his assassination were rife in the press at the time and continue to this day.

Dalmatia

Dalmatia, currently a province of the independent state of Croatia, and formerly part of Yugoslavia, occupies the coast of the Adriatic Sea and its immediate hinterland from the city of Fiume (Rijeka) to the gulf of Kotor. Zara (Zadar) is the capital; other important cities are Fiume, Sebenico (Sibenik), and Dubrovnik. The population is mostly Roman Catholic. Historic ties to Italy date back to the first century B.C. when Dalmatia became a Roman province. It later fell under the rule of the Ostrogoths, the Byzantine Empire, the Ottoman Turks, and Venice. Venetians settled in its coastal cities and islands, fighting off attempts by the Turks to occupy the region. NAPOLEON I forced Venice to surrender Dalmatia to Austria in 1797 by the Treaty of Campoformio, which ended Venetian independence. From 1805 to 1809 it was part of the Napoleonic Kingdom of Italy; it was part of the French Empire from 1809 to 1815, when the Congress of Vienna restored it to Austrian rule. It remained under Austrian rule until the end of WORLD WAR I. The Treaty of Paris awarded most of Dalmatia to the new state of Yugoslavia in spite of the fact that the province had been assigned to Italy by the secret PACT OF LONDON to entice Italy into declaring war on Austria. GABRIELE D'ANNUNZIO took over Fiume illegally in 1919, and the city was assigned to Italy in 1924. The Treaty of Rapallo (1920) gave Italy the city of Zara and the islands of Cres, Losinj, Palagruza, and Lastovo in the upper Adriatic. Italian military forces occupied most of Dalmatia in WORLD WAR II but lost control of it to Germany in 1943 when Italy pulled out of the war. The communist partisans of Marshall Tito took over Dalmatia in 1945 and began to systematically expel its

Italian-speaking population. The population is now overwhelmingly Serbo-Croatian.

D'Annunzio, Gabriele (1863–1938)
writer and public figure

Born in Pescara to a family of the upper-middle class (his father was a successful merchant prominent in local affairs), D'Annunzio attended the exclusive live-in Cicognini College in Prato, where he spent seven years. His first volume of poems, *Primo vere* (1889), published while he was a student, announced him as a new and disturbing literary presence. Sensuous and self-indulgent, D'Annunzio's writings appealed to a generation eager for new sensations. As a journalist, D'Annunzio introduced a large readership to the gossip and scandals of Roman social life, in which he fully participated. The novel *Il piacere* (Pleasure, 1889) is based on his intimate knowledge of Roman high society. It confirmed D'Annunzio's reputation as a scandalmonger and womanizer. Andrea Sperelli, the novel's sensuous and self-indulgent protagonist, can be seen as modeled on the author, who, like his hero, also liked to pose as a Nietzschean superman exempt from the rules of conventional morality. He liked the dramatic gesture. In 1897 D'Annunzio was elected to parliament as a member of the conservative Right, but, bored by parliamentary routine, three years later he defected clamorously to the socialist Left. He was not reelected. A well-publicized affair with the actress ELEONORA DUSE brought him more public attention. In 1911 he left Italy for France to escape his many creditors, who recouped their losses by auctioning off his furniture and collections of artistic and rare objects. In France he wrote poems glorifying the ITALIAN-TURKISH WAR. He returned to Italy in May 1915 to campaign for Italian intervention in WORLD WAR I and immediately volunteered for military service. During the war he participated in several well-publicized exploits, most notably an air raid over Vienna, during which the Italian planes dropped propaganda leaflets over the enemy's capital. A genuine war hero, he loudly criticized the government's failure to obtain maximum territorial compensations at the PARIS PEACE CONFERENCE. His reference to Italy's "mutilated victory" fed the anger of frustrated nationalists. In September 1919 he led a band of armed volunteers who forcibly took over the contested city of FIUME. At the head of the self-proclaimed state, called the Reggenza del Carnaro, he held out in the city against the wishes of the great powers and the Italian government until January 1921. During those 15 months Fiume became a stage for D'Annunzio's brand of theatrical politics. He assumed the title of *Comandante,* staged parades and mass rallies, addressed the crowd from his balcony in the presidential palace, invented patriotic slogans and war cries, designed and donned military uniforms for himself and his followers, and threatened to "march on Rome." When the Italian troops finally evicted him, he retired to private life in a villa overlooking Lake Garda, which he refurbished and named *Il Vittoriale.* It is not surprising that D'Annunzio was later dubbed the John the Baptist of fascism, but the truth is that his relations with fascism and BENITO MUSSOLINI were often strained. The regime subsidized him generously, partly out of genuine admiration and partly to keep him happy and quiet. The association with the Fascist regime cast a long shadow on D'Annunzio as a literary figure. Dismissed after the war as a bombastic writer with a genius for staying in the public eye, D'Annunzio's literary reputation is now being reassessed without political partisanship. The picture that emerges is that of a writer of immense talent who in his life and writings reflected the travails, passions, and foibles of Italians before and after WORLD WAR I.

Dante Alighieri (1265–1321)

major literary figure and national symbol
Dante's influence is so pervasive that his name must be included in any coverage of Italian culture. Born to a family of the Florentine lower nobility, he was active in the public life of his city

Dante Alighieri in a portrait from the *Divine Comedy* (*Library of Congress*)

at a time of intense and perilous factional strife. Caught in the struggle between popes and emperors, he sided with the faction known as the White Guelfs that opposed Pope Boniface VIII. When the Black Guelfs won out, he was banished from the city and his possessions confiscated. He lived the rest of his life in exile, wandering from court to court in central and northern Italy.

Literary references to him as the *Ghibellin fuggiasco* (Wandering Ghibelline), Ghibellines being supporters of the emperors, overlook the fact that he did not support the imperial cause in Florentine politics. But the Ghibelline label does point to his belief that universal empire was the proper mode of political organization for the Christian world. In his view, secular rulers were the rightful holders of political power, and the church was the depository of spiritual power. In the RISORGIMENTO, anticlerical patriots overlooked Dante's preference for a universal mode of political organization (more akin to a united Europe than to one divided into national states), seizing instead on his opposition to the PAPACY, which they regarded as an obstacle to national unification. Dante was thus transformed into a patriotic icon and a forerunner of modern ANTICLERICALISM.

Dante also assumed significance as a symbol of Italian nationality because of his literary role in shaping and propagating the use of the Tuscan dialect as the national language. The poetic masterpiece that he composed during his exile, called *Commedia* by him and *The Divine Comedy* by later generations, became the holy book of Italian culture, playing a role for educated Italians similar to that of Homer's *Iliad* and *Odyssey* for educated Greeks. Its verses are studied for their poetic power and for what they reveal about Dante's attitude toward the affairs of Italy, its place and mission in the world, and the moral values of Italian culture. In the 19th century, UGO FOSCOLO and GIUSEPPE MAZZINI were instrumental in developing Dante's image as a forerunner of Italian national identity.

Dante Alighieri Society

The poet's name was claimed by the Dante Alighieri Society, founded in 1889 by RUGGERO BONGHI and others to help Italian emigrants abroad maintain a sense of their Italian identity. Its mission developed into that of promoting the expansion of Italian culture abroad by encouraging the study of the Italian language, funding lectures and libraries, and sponsoring and disseminating publications. It was a private association with close ties to government. Those ties became even closer during the Fascist period when the government used it for outright propaganda purposes. It suffered from the Fascist connection in the postwar years, but gradually regained some of its former vitality as a cultural institution by coordinating its efforts with those of other groups in an area where government

policy has been weak to nonexistent. In 1989, the centenary of its foundation, the Italian state recognized it officially as part of its national commission for the promotion of Italian culture abroad.

Da Ponte, Lorenzo (1749–1838)
writer and educator

Born Emanuele Conegliano to a Jewish family of Venice, he took the name of Lorenzo Da Ponte when he converted to Christianity in 1763. After a brief stint in a seminary, he launched on an adventurous life marked by scandal. Expelled from Venice in 1782, he found refuge in Vienna, where he served as librettist at the imperial theater from 1783 to 1790. In that capacity he wrote lyrics for several composers, including Antonio Salieri (1750–1825) and Mozart. The libretto for Mozart's opera *Don Giovanni* is considered his masterpiece. He resumed a life of wandering after the death of his patron, Emperor JOSEPH II. Settling in London in 1791, he worked again as a librettist, contracted an unhappy marriage, taught Italian, ventured into the bookselling business, went broke, and left for the United States in 1805. After a brief stint as a medicine salesman in Pennsylvania, he settled in New York City, where he earned a living by teaching Italian. Columbia University appointed him professor of Italian language and literature in 1830. He encouraged the performance of Italian opera in the city, creating a taste that has endured. Da Ponte is in many ways typical of 18th-century Italian intellectuals and artists who felt limited in Italy, wandered abroad, and in the process helped to establish an Italian cultural presence in foreign lands.

D'Aragona, Ludovico See SYNDICALISM.

DC (Democrazia Cristiana)

The initials DC stand for the political party of Christian Democracy that dominated Italian politics from 1945 to the early 1990s. The movement from which the party sprang had its roots in Catholic social thought of the late 19th century. It was an attempt to update Catholic social doctrine in light of the social transformations brought on by the Industrial Revolution, including opposition to the spread of socialism and materialist doctrines. Christian democracy asserted the principle of social solidarity, condemned class warfare, and called on workers and employers to come together in a spirit of mutual understanding and cooperation. Its fundamental principles were set out after 1890 in the encyclicals of Pope LEO XIII, the writings of GIUSEPPE TONIOLO, and the political initiatives of ROMOLO MURRI. Strong opposition from elements of the clergy and laity, the conflict of CHURCH AND STATE, and the election of Pope PIUS X hindered the rise of a Christian Democratic movement before WORLD WAR I. Christian Democracy was the ideology of the popular party (PPI) founded in 1919 by the priest LUIGI STURZO. Hostile to FASCISM, the party was dissolved at the demand of Benito Mussolini to improve relations between the CATHOLIC CHURCH and the Italian state. Facing political persecution and deprived of papal support, the PPI dissolved in 1925.

ALCIDE DE GASPERI, the PPI's last secretary, gave the name of Christian Democracy to the party that he organized following the collapse of the Fascist regime in 1943. Its anti-Fascist credentials were strengthened by De Gasperi's own past and by the party's participation in the RESISTANCE. Its program called for land reform, an end to state monopolies, modernization of the public administration, and cooperation across class lines. It embraced family values, private property, and social services for the indigent. Unlike other political parties that targeted particular classes or groups, the DC appealed to a broad cross-section of society. It was a Catholic party, but De Gasperi was careful to assert the DC's lay character and to distance it from the Catholic hierarchy. Nevertheless, the church gave strong support to the party, especially at election time. The DC emerged as the single largest political party in the coun-

try in the elections of June 1946 and gained an absolute majority in the elections of 1948. After that triumph, it was the leading vote-getter but never again a party of the absolute majority. It governed in coalition with other parties out of choice and necessity. The parties that supported the DC were those of the center (PLI, PRI, and PSDI) in the 1950s and the PSI (socialists) in the 1960s after the so-called OPENING TO THE LEFT.

Anticommunism was the strongest political card that the DC played for the duration of the cold war, but in the 1970s and 1980s declining voter support and internal party pressures led to the informal understanding with the communists known as the HISTORIC COMPROMISE. It involved sharing power without actually admitting communists into the national government. The result was a critical blurring of ideological distinctions, political disorientation among voters, and the rise of political TERRORISM on the extreme Left and Right. Signs of the DC's political decline were the appointment of the first non–Christian Democratic prime minister in the person of GIOVANNI SPADOLINI in 1981 and the long government headed by the socialist BETTINO CRAXI in 1983–87. The DC reached a low point in the elections of 1992 when it won only 29 percent of the popular vote. It was still the single largest party, but in the eyes of most voters it was tainted by years of political corruption, government inefficiency, and scandal. The end of the cold war and the MANI PULITE scandal of the early 1990s administered the final blows to the DC. In January 1994 it renamed itself the Italian Popular Party (PPI) in an effort to return to its origins as a party of reform, but attempts to restructure it produced more discordant factions. Some former Christian Democrats joined the Democratic Party of the Left (PDS), others the rightist National Alliance. For all its undeniable inadequacies, the DC presided over a critical period of history when political democracy struck deep roots, the economy prospered, regional imbalances were reduced, schooling became universally accessible, and the depths of deprivation (la miseria) became a thing of the past.

De Ambris, Alceste (1874–1934)

*labor organizer and revolutionary
syndicalist*

Born to a middle-class family in the province of
Massa Carrara (Tuscany), where there were
strong anarchist and socialist influences, De
Ambris became politically active at an early age,
joined the Socialist Party (PSI) in 1892, organized
workers, and wrote for socialist publications.
Jailed twice, in 1898 he left Italy for Brazil, where
he organized Italian emigrants. Expelled by the
Brazilian government in 1903, he returned to
Italy, resumed his journalistic and organizational
activities first in the town of Savona, then in
Parma (1907), where he became secretary of the
local chamber of labor. With Parma as his base of
operations, he encouraged Italian workers to use
the strike as a political weapon and aim at the
seizure of power by constant agitation. His tactics were inspired by the ideas of Georges Sorel
and REVOLUTIONARY SYNDICALISM. That orientation caused him to break with the PSI and the
General Confederation of Labor. In 1908 he led
a bitterly contested and ultimately unsuccessful
agricultural strike, after which he once again fled
to Brazil. Elected to parliament by the workers
of Parma, he returned to Italy in 1913 protected
by parliamentary immunity. His experiences
abroad convinced him that worker solidarity
broke down in the face of national differences.
He concluded that Italian workers should rely
only on themselves. His turning away from internationalism prepared his conversion to a form of
nationalist socialism. When WORLD WAR I broke
out, he joined BENITO MUSSOLINI in urging Italian
intervention. During the war he developed an
ideology of national revolution and CORPORATISM
that alienated him further from the socialist Left.
The Union of Italian Labor (UIL) that he helped
found in 1914 later gravitated toward FASCISM.
De Ambris supported GABRIELE D'ANNUNZIO'S
seizure of FIUME in 1919 and wrote the *Carta del
Carnaro* (Charter of the Carnaro), which outlined a corporatist form of political organization
for Fiume that anticipated the corporatism of the
Fascist state. But De Ambris disapproved of Mussolini's political tactics and suspected him of
seeking an accommodation with conservative
interests. He did not therefore support the Fascist seizure of power, left the country for France
in 1923, and spoke out against the regime.
Regarded with suspicion by anti-Fascist groups,
he lived politically isolated. In 1926 the Fascist
government stripped De Ambris of his Italian
citizenship.

De Amicis, Edmondo (1846–1908)

popular writer and patriotic publicist

De Amicis entered on a military career at age 19
and served as an infantry officer in the war of
1866. As editor of the review *L'Italia Militare,* he
published sketches of military life, later gathered
in the volume *La vita militare* (1868), that presented service in the army as a school of patriotism. Encouraged by this first success, De Amicis
left the army to pursue a career as writer and
journalist. He was present at the seizure of Rome
in 1870, traveled widely in Europe and the Near
East, always putting his impressions in writing
with only moderate commercial and literary success. His strength was fictional narrative that
conveyed strong moral messages. The book that
displays De Amicis at his best is *Cuore* (1886)
where, as the title indicates, he speaks from and
to the heart. It is a collection of stories focusing
on the lives of ordinary people struggling with
hardship and poverty, surviving by courage and
hard work, often with the help of better-off compatriots. De Amicis deplored the plight of emigrants, wanted broad access to education, and
called on members of the privileged classes to
help the less fortunate. His paternalistic message
resonated strongly among middle-class Italians,
who found in De Amicis a champion of the poor
who spoke the reassuring language of social solidarity and did not threaten revolution. Literary
critics dismissed him as sentimental and social
critics as paternalistic. De Amicis is often referred
to as a "rosewater socialist" and the term *socialismo deamiciasiano* is synonymous in Italy with
well-meaning but ineffective social concern.

Cuore was once one of the most widely read books in Italy and is not entirely forgotten even today. Many of De Amicis's writings have been published in English, including several editions of *Cuore: The Heart of a Boy* between 1887 and 1986.

De Benedetti, Carlo   See OLIVETTI S.P.A.

De Bono, Emilio   (1866–1944)
military figure, commander of Fascist action squads and militias, chief of police, army commander in the Ethiopian War
General De Bono was one of the few high-ranking military officers who openly sided with FASCISM before the party came to power in October 1922. His career before the advent of fascism had been fairly undistinguished. He was made captain in 1897, in the ITALIAN-TURKISH WAR he had his first experience of colonial administration, and was promoted to general in 1916. He turned to fascism after being decommissioned in 1920. BENITO MUSSOLINI welcomed him and assigned to him a prominent role as one of four "Quadrumvirs" (commanders) of the march on Rome that brought the Fascists to power. De Bono identified completely with the Fascist regime, serving as chief of police and commander of the Fascist Militia (1922–24), governor of the colony of Tripolitania (1925–28), and minister of colonies (1929–35). Implicated in the coverup of the murder of GIACOMO MATTEOTTI, he had to step down as chief of police in 1924. As minister of colonies he was instrumental in planning for the ETHIOPIAN WAR. Mussolini appointed him military commander in Ethiopia at the start of operations in October 1935, in order to have a Fascist general in charge, but replaced him with General PIETRO BADOGLIO less than two months later to speed up operations. De Bono was promoted to army marshal, but to De Bono's chagrin Badoglio enjoyed the honors and material rewards of victory. For the remainder of his career an embittered De Bono also had to confront charges of profiteering and bad administration under his colonial rule. Soured by Mussolini's refusal to defend him against his critics, De Bono was further alienated by his aversion to the alliance with Nazi Germany. He played no role in WORLD WAR II, but as a member of the Fascist Grand Council he voted on July 24, 1943, for the motion that called on Mussolini to resign. For that he was considered a traitor to the regime, imprisoned, tried, and executed by diehard Fascists in January 1944.

De Felice, Renzo   (1929–1996)
historian, biographer of Mussolini, and political critic
Perhaps Italy's most controversial contemporary historian, De Felice left his mark on scholarship and public life mostly with a monumental biography of BENITO MUSSOLINI that took up most of his productive life. He began his teaching career at the University of Salerno in 1968 and later became a tenured professor of contemporary history at the University of Rome. A student of Delio Cantimori with whom he studied at the University of Florence, De Felice followed his mentor's lead in at least two ways. Intellectually, he pursued Cantimori's interest in utopian thinkers and social reformers with his early studies of Italian JACOBINS. He followed Cantimori politically by joining the Italian Communist Party (PCI). An activist who believed in taking his beliefs to the people, De Felice was arrested in 1952 for distributing anti-American and anti-NATO propaganda. But neither Cantimori nor De Felice could stay with any one movement for very long, and both distanced themselves from the PCI after 1956. For De Felice that also meant distancing himself from Marxist historiography. By the early 1960s his interests had shifted to the 20th century, and particularly to the study of FASCISM, which he pursued for the rest of his life. After his *Storia degli ebrei italiani sotto il fascismo* (History of Italian Jews under fascism, 1961) came many other works on fascism, including the eight-volume biography of Mussolini (1965–97).

His revisionist view of Mussolini and fascism was controversial from the start. He argued that fascism derived from the ideologies and movements of the Left, that its composite character allowed it to move in different directions, that Mussolini was its central figure because he had political savvy and shrewdness, that his foreign policy operated within a traditional balance-of-power framework, and that popular consensus, not coercion, sustained the regime. By making Mussolini the key figure and downplaying the role of social and cultural forces, De Felice thus suggested that fascism was a one-time phenomenon not likely to recur. That notion challenged the view favored by the Left that fascism was an ever-present threat and that antifascism was therefore an indispensable ingredient of a democratic society. De Felice went on to question the importance of the RESISTANCE, thus challenging another premise of the Left. De Felice did not set out to rehabilitate fascism, but he did argue that its role had to be assessed without political partisanship. He thus goaded a reluctant public into debating the nature and role of fascism in Italian life. The debate that he sparked continues to reverberate in Italian political life.

De Felice-Giuffrida, Giuseppe   See FASCI SICILIANI.

De Gasperi, Alcide (1881–1954)
anti-Fascist figure, Christian Democratic leader, and prime minister

De Gasperi was Italy's dominant political figure of the reconstruction period after WORLD WAR II. Born to a lower-middle-class family (his father was a police officer) in a village of the Trentino region that was part of the AUSTRIAN EMPIRE, De Gasperi nurtured a strong sense of Italian cultural identity in that region of mixed German and Italian populations. Equally strong was his identification with the Roman Catholic Church and the progressive political aspirations of Christian Democracy (DC), in which he made his political debut in the late 1890s. From 1900 to 1905 he was simultaneously a student of philology at the University of Vienna and a political activist. His political activities included journalism, organizing Italian workers, and defending Italian cultural identity in the multinational Austrian Empire. De Gasperi, who looked upon his political activities as a religious apostolate, clashed with Italian anticlerical socialists in the Trentino, most notably with CESARE BATTISTI, and BENITO MUSSOLINI when he visited the region. From 1911 to 1918 De Gasperi served in the Austrian parliament, pressing the government for concessions to his Italian-speaking constituents, opening an Italian university in TRIESTE, and banking on the TRIPLE ALLIANCE to protect the interests of the Italian minorities in the Austrian Empire. During the war he followed the lead of Pope BENEDICT XV in urging a peaceful solution to the conflict.

De Gasperi entered Italian politics when the Trentino became part of Italy at the end of WORLD WAR I. In 1919 he joined the newly founded Popular Party (PPI) and was elected to the Italian parliament on its ticket in 1921. He was clear about the differences between his party and the Fascists, but favored taking the Fascists into the government in order to avert civil war. He continued to favor collaboration with Mussolini's government until the elections of 1924, when he campaigned publicly against the Fascists and their allies. He became political secretary of the Popular Party in May 1924. Now a major target of Fascist attacks, De Gasperi resigned his post as party secretary and was evicted from parliament. Jailed for 16 months for attempting to leave the country illegally, he found employment in the Vatican Library for the rest of the Fascist period.

De Gasperi resumed political activity in 1942–43 as an organizer of the Christian Democratic Party (DC) that governed Italy for almost half a century after the war. He served as head of his party and as prime minister without interruption from December 1945 until July 1953, guiding the country through the peacemaking process, the adoption of a new constitution, participation in NATO, and taking the first steps toward European economic cooperation and political integration. His first governments included Communists and Socialists, but in May 1947 he adopted the four-party politics of cooperation among Christian Democrats, Social Democrats, republicans, and liberals. These centrist coalitions and the subsequent OPENING TO THE LEFT kept Fascists and Communists out of power until the 1990s.

In spite of his own definition of Christian Democracy as a party of the center moving gradually toward the Left, De Gasperi favored centrist coalitions and policies. He insisted that the party uphold Christian values, while remaining politically independent of the CATHOLIC CHURCH, hence his commitment to governing with the help of lay parties even when the Christian Democrats had the votes to go it alone. Intimately suspicious of secular values, De Gasperi pursued the ideal of a society based on principles of social solidarity, committed to personal freedoms and private property, and opposed to materialism and class conflict. Shifting political loyalties and party rivalries deprived him of the parliamentary majority that he needed to govern, and he resigned as prime minister in July 1953. Already in poor health when he left office, De Gasperi died in his native Trentino in August 1954.

Del Carretto, Saverio See FRANCIS I.

Deledda, Grazia (1871–1936)
novelist inspired by the folklore and customs of her native Sardinia

Winner of the 1926 Nobel Prize for literature, in her novels and short stories Deledda delved into the popular beliefs, primordial myths, and superstitions of her native Sardinia. Human passions are at the core of her narratives. After her first novel, *Fior di Sardegna* (Flower of Sardinia, 1892) came 40 more, turned out at regular intervals, including *Elias Portòlu* (1903), *Cenere* (Ashes, 1903), *L'Edera* (Ivy, 1908), *Colombe e sparvieri* (Doves and hawks, 1912), *Marianne Sirca* (1915), *Il segreto dell'uomo solitario* (The secret of a solitary

man, 1921), and *Annalena Bilsini* (1927). She turned some of her novels into plays that were successful on the stage. *Cenere* was made into the only film that starred ELEONORA DUSE. Love, betrayal, guilt are the driving forces of Deledda's characters, with social background serving as backdrop. What emerges from the filter of her imagination is not a realistic picture of life in Sardinia, but rather a parade of psychologically ambiguous characters. Her characters could not exist without the regional setting, but it is the emphasis on the psychology of human passions that gives her work the broad appeal that earned her the Nobel Prize. Several of her novels have been translated into English.

Della Casa, Giovanni (1503–1556)
papal diplomat, administrator, and writer

Della Casa served as bishop of the southern Italian town of Benevento and as papal nuncio (ambassador) to Venice. An able administrator, he is remembered primarily as a secular writer. He wrote elegant verse, but his name is associated primarily with the famous book of manners, *Il Galateo* (1558) that was published after his death. It became hugely popular throughout Europe after being translated into English, French, German, Latin, and Spanish. It helped to popularize what was considered appropriate and amiable behavior for gentlemen in the manner of BALDASSARRE CASTIGLIONE's *The Courtier*, which it imitated. Della Casa takes his place among RENAISSANCE writers who tried to inculcate gentlemanly habits and manners in the upper reaches of society.

Della Volpe, Galvano See COLLETTI, LUCIO.

De Lorenzo, Giovanni (1907–1973)
army chief of staff suspected of planning a military coup

General De Lorenzo was born in Sicily, studied naval engineering at the University of Genoa, served on the Russian front in WORLD WAR II, and was a member of the RESISTANCE. Continuing his military career after the war, he was appointed chief of Italian military intelligence (SIFAR) in 1955 and commander in chief of the CARABINIERI in 1962. As head of SIFAR and as commander of the Carabinieri, he modernized the services; he cooperated with the American CIA to train and equip special forces to deal with political subversion. In 1966 confidential documents leaked to the press revealed that he had compiled personal dossiers on prominent political figures. De Lorenzo, who had been promoted to army chief of staff in 1965, was then accused of having harbored secret designs to take over the government at a moment of political crisis in the summer of 1964, possibly in collusion with President ANTONIO SEGNI. It was never clarified whether this so-called Solo Operation was designed to actually carry out a coup d état or was a precautionary counterinsurgency measure against outside forces. The very existence of the plan alarmed the parties of the Left that saw themselves as its targets. De Lorenzo was promptly relieved of his army command in 1966. Once decommissioned, De Lorenzo was elected to parliament for the Monarchist Party (PNM) and later switched his allegiance to the neo-Fascist Italian Social Movement (MSI). A parliamentary inquest censured his methods but recommended no further action.

De Mauro, Tullio   See ITALIAN LANGUAGE.

Democratic Party of the Left   See PCI; PDS.

De Nicola, Enrico (1877–1959)
*member of parliament and first head of state
of the Italian republic*

De Nicola was a renowned lawyer in his native Naples before turning to politics as a progressive liberal. Elected to parliament in 1909 as a follower of GIOVANNI GIOLITTI, he served as under-secretary of colonies (1912–14) and treasury (1919), and as president of the chamber of deputies (1920–23). He was reelected to parliament in 1924 on the national ticket that included liberals and Fascists, was made senator in 1929, but abstained from political activity. De Nicola did not actively oppose FASCISM and was later criticized for his passive acceptance of the regime. He returned to politics in 1943–44 as a liberal identified with BENEDETTO CROCE. He played a key role in working out the political compromise that enabled UMBERTO II to replace his father on the throne until the elections of June 1946. After the elections, De Nicola served as the provisional head of state of the Italian republic, and became the first president of the republic when the new CONSTITUTION went into effect on January 1, 1948. LUIGI EINAUDI succeeded him as the first regularly chosen president in May 1948. De Nicola presided over the senate from 1948 to 1953 and over the constitutional (supreme) court from 1956 to 1958. De Nicola was respected as a legal expert and for his personal integrity.

Denina, Carlo (1731–1813)
Enlightenment figure, writer, and reformer

An important figure in the cultural life of his native Piedmont, this clergyman was inspired by the ideas of the ENLIGHTENMENT. Born to a poor farming family, he was able to complete his university studies thanks to a state scholarship. While teaching in secondary school he published works on church history and the history of literature. His most celebrated work was *Delle rivoluzioni d'Italia* (On the revolutions of Italy, 1769–72), in which the term *revolution* refers to cultural changes over the centuries. The focus on Italy encouraged other scholars to look for connections and similarities across the political divides of the peninsula, thus playing a role in the rise of cultural nationalism. The book was also notable for the larger perspective that situated Italian culture in the European context. Appointed to teach Italian and Greek languages at the University of Turin, Denina undertook studies on the history of the ruling HOUSE OF SAVOY. In *Dell'impiego delle persone* (On the employment of people) he urged ecclesiastical reforms. His efforts to have the book published without official approval angered the clergy and caused him to be dismissed from his university post (the book was published in 1803). In 1782 he found a warm welcome at the court of Frederick II of Prussia. A history of Piedmont that he wrote during this period was published as *Istoria dell'Italia occidentale* (A history of western Italy, 1809). In Prussia he also wrote on German history and literature and corresponded with Italian intellectuals. Denina's stay at Frederick's court was a moment of intense interaction with the cultural trends of the Enlightenment, which reached Italians in part through Denina's writings and correspondence. In his last years Denina was employed as librarian at the court of NAPOLEON I.

De Pinedo, Francesco (1890–1933)
aviator and national hero
This celebrated aviator was born to a patrician family in Naples and served in the ITALIAN-TURKISH WAR as a naval officer. He began to fly during WORLD WAR I. He won international acclaim in 1925 with a flight from Italy to Australia, Japan, and back that covered more than 34,000 miles (55,000 kilometers). A similar exploit took him from Italy to North and South America and back in 1927. These and other flights helped publicize the new Italian air force and the Savoia-Marchetti airplanes that won many international flight records. In 1929 De Pinedo was promoted to general and served as deputy air force chief of staff. A personal rivalry with aviation minister ITALO BALBO, whose handling of air force matters De Pinedo criticized in reports to BENITO MUSSOLINI, put an early end to De Pinedo's career in the air force in 1933. He sought to revive his fortunes by staging a record long-distance flight from New York to Tokyo, but died in New York when his heavily loaded airplane crashed on takeoff.

Depretis, Agostino (1812–1887)
prime minister and dominant political figure
Depretis belonged to the generation that fought for Italian independence. Born to a well-to-do family of Piedmontese landowners, Depretis studied law at the University of Pavia. In the 1840s he joined the ranks of republican conspirators who gravitated toward GIUSEPPE MAZZINI. He made his debut in politics when he was elected to the first Piedmontese parliament in June 1848. He retained his seat in the preunification parliament of Piedmont-Sardinia and later the Italian parliament, always known as the "representative from Stradella," the Piedmontese town with which Depretis's name was always associated. In the preunification parliament he sat with the democratic faction who regarded Cavour as insufficiently patriotic. After the death of URBANO RATTAZZI in 1873, Depretis became the leader of the LIBERAL LEFT. In that capacity, he served three times as prime minister between 1876 and 1887, a period that is often described as the era of Depretis because of his political dominance. An accomplished politician, Depretis defeated the HISTORICAL RIGHT in parliament and brought in a new generation of representatives, including many from the South. Depretis renounced the republican sentiments of his youth, and worked to limit the prerogatives of the crown and broaden the suffrage. He also promised to repeal the unpopular MACINATO (grist tax), give more power to local administrations, and make elementary schooling compulsory. These and other reforms were slowed and compromised by the difficulties of governing with a divided majority, by inadequate funding, and by the fear that broadening the suffrage would give more leverage to the Catholic Church and its refusal to recognize the Italian state. During his last and longest ministry (1881–87), Depretis orchestrated the repeal of the grist tax, extended the suffrage, and enacted administrative reforms, including the reorganization of the national railroad system. His major achievement in foreign policy was the conclusion of the TRIPLE ALLIANCE with Austria-Hungary and Germany, which

Depretis regarded as compatible with good relations with Great Britain and France. He perfected the practice of TRANSFORMISM, sidestepping dissenters from the Liberal Left and seeking the support of the Historical Right on specific bills. His readiness to take support wherever he found it, manipulation of parliamentary majorities, the use of patronage to sway voters, and other questionable electoral practices, gave Depretis an unsavory reputation. Critics accused him of stifling debate, avoiding questions of principle, and governing by personal rule. A more sympathetic view sees him as adept in the arts of compromise, committed to gradual reform, and able to maintain parliamentary consensus in a difficult political environment.

De' Ricci, Scipione See RICCI, SCIPIONE DE'.

De Ruggiero, Guido (1888–1948)
political writer and public figure
This distinguished Neapolitan scholar studied law and taught the history of philosophy at the universities of Messina and Rome (1923–25). A political liberal, De Ruggiero viewed LIBERALISM as a gradual process that enfranchised broad segments of the population, promoted involvement in civic affairs, and led toward democracy. In perceiving liberalism as an open road toward democracy, De Ruggiero distanced himself from BENEDETTO CROCE, with whom he was nevertheless close politically and philosophically. De Ruggiero came to liberalism from nationalistic positions that made him favor Italian intervention in WORLD WAR I. The war changed his perspective, drawing him toward the radical liberalism of PIERO GOBETTI. A silent opponent of FASCISM, De Ruggiero continued to live and teach in Italy under the regime. His *Storia del liberalismo europeo* (The history of European liberalism, 1925) was very influential in guiding a younger generation of intellectuals toward a positive reappraisal of the country's liberal past. Its reprinting (1941) caused his dismissal from

his university post a year later. A founder of the ACTION PARTY, in 1943 he was appointed rector of the University of Rome by the government of PIETRO BADOGLIO. He also served as minister of education (1944) in the government of IVANOE BONOMI (1944). Other works include a multivolume *Storia della filosofia* (History of philosophy, 1918–48) and *Il ritorno della ragione* (The return of reason, 1946).

De Sanctis, Francesco (1817–1883)
historian, literary critic, government minister, and public figure
A member of the generation that fought for Italian independence, De Sanctis was also a major intellectual figure. His influence was felt through his teaching and his writings as a historian and literary critic. He was born in Avellino, studied privately in Naples, and began to teach in 1839. Radicalized by the influence of philosophical IDEALISM, De Sanctis fought on the barricades in the REVOLUTION of 1848 alongside his students. For that indiscretion he lost his teaching position and was incarcerated. Sentenced for deportation to America (1853), he jumped ship and made his way to Turin and Zurich, where he taught Italian literature (1856–59). He returned to Naples in 1860, was elected to the first Italian parliament, and was active in journalism. As minister of education (1878–79) he upheld the separation of CHURCH AND STATE, insisted on maintaining the lay character of public education, and on combating illiteracy. His political stance was that of a typical 19th-century liberal, but the nature of his intellectual legacy is more complex. He distanced himself from the school of literary criticism that looked for moral lessons in literature. In his two-volume masterpiece, *Storia della letteratura italiana* (History of Italian literature, 1870–71), also published in English (1931, 1960, 1968), he studied literature historically and approached it as an integral part of the culture of the people. His survey of Italian literature from medieval times to the 19th century derives vitality and validity from the conceptualization of lit-

erature as an expression of national culture. Its combination of rigorous scholarship and imaginative understanding shows De Sanctis poised uneasily between ROMANTICISM and POSITIVISM. His cultural influence and legacy is still the subject of debate.

De Sica, Vittorio (1901–1974)

actor, singer, and film director

De Sica's 50-year career as an entertainer began in the 1920s as an actor in musical comedies and vaudeville. De Sica was raised in Naples, worked briefly as an office clerk, turned to the theater, and scored his first big success with the lead part in *Gli uomini, che mascalzoni* (What rascals men are, 1932), a film directed by Mario Camerini (1895–1981). Success in various sentimental comedies established him as Italy's most popular actor in films like *Il signor Max* (Mr. Max, 1939) and *Grandi magazzini* (Department stores, 1939). These films catered to popular taste by poking gentle fun at the very wealthy and showing ordinary people happily coming to terms with their modest lot in life. De Sica turned to more serious stage roles and film directing in 1940, interpreting stage plays by Noel Coward, Bernard Shaw, and R. B. Sheridan that were often revelations for Italian audiences, and directing films with a more serious social content. In *I bambini ci guardano* (The children are watching us, 1943), he told the story of a mother who abandons husband and children to live with her lover. The film depicts the complexity of marital relationships, suggests sympathy for the woman's search for fulfillment outside an unhappy marriage, but also shows the tragic effects of a broken marriage on family life. Critics have seen in the films that De Sica directed between 1940 and 1944 hints of the forthcoming style of NEOREALISM. The neorealist style is evident in films that De Sica codirected with Cesare Zavattini (1902–89). In *Sciuscià* (Shoeshine, 1946) and *Ladri di biciclette* (Bicycle thieves, 1948), De Sica gave sympathetic portrayals of human beings traumatized by war, poverty, unemployment, and moral con-

fusion. In these films De Sica was especially sensitive to the plight of children in war-ravaged Italy. *Miracolo a Milano* (Miracle in Milan, 1950) is a fairy tale excursion into the lives of marginal people who end their search for happiness by flying away from this world on broomsticks. *Umberto D* (1952), perhaps the most sophisticated and complex of De Sica's films, explores the not-always-attractive personality of a retired civil servant who reacts against the indignities and hardships of retirement by closing in on himself and contemplating suicide. De Sica continued to act and direct in both light and serious veins until 1970, displaying great acting versatility and ability as a storyteller.

De' Stefani, Alberto (1879–1969)

economist and Fascist political figure

Born in Verona, De' Stefani was a laissez-faire economist who acquired a solid academic reputation teaching and writing on quantitative economics and statistics before turning his attention to politics after WORLD WAR I. He favored Italian intervention in the war and volunteered for military service. He joined the Fascist Party and was elected to parliament in 1921. A leader of Fascist action squads, he engaged in several large-scale actions, including the occupation of the city of Bolzano by the Fascists at the beginning of October 1922. As the first Fascist minister of finances (1922–25), De' Stefani oversaw a partial dismantling of government regulatory agencies, reduced tariffs and taxes on business, cut government expenses, balanced the budget, pursued a deflationary policy, and strengthened the CURRENCY. Domestic producers who could not compete resisted his free-trade policies, and investors were angered by his attempts to curb stock market speculations. In July 1925 BENITO MUSSOLINI replaced De' Stefani with GIUSEPPE VOLPI as minister of finances. Mussolini later put De' Stefani in charge of the regime's program of extensive LAND RECLAMATION projects and used him in various advisory capacities. As a member of the Fascist Grand Council he voted to oust

Mussolini on July 25, 1943. A political crimes tribunal dismissed charges against him after the war. Economic liberalism and illiberal politics coexisted uneasily in De' Stefani.

Destra Storica See HISTORICAL RIGHT.

De Vecchi, Cesare Maria (1884–1959)
prominent figure of the Fascist regime
An officer in WORLD WAR I, De Vecchi received the title of Count of Val Cismon in recognition of a wartime action. After the war, he organized and controlled the Fascist movement in his native Piedmont. A conservative royalist, he had little sympathy for the radical aspirations of FAS-CISM. His appointment as one of the four leaders (*quadrumviri*) of the march on Rome was intended to reassure the king that fascism was well disposed toward the monarchy. De Vecchi would have preferred a government headed by the conservative liberal ANTONIO SALANDRA rather than one headed by BENITO MUSSOLINI. As commander of the Fascist militia, the outspoken and blunt De Vecchi was often a political embarrassment for Mussolini, who appointed him governor of the distant colony of Somalia to get him out of the way. De Vecchi "pacified" the colony during his tenure (1923–28) by disarming tribes, subduing recalcitrant warlords, and pursuing rebels into Ethiopia. He also laid claims to Ethiopian territory. Back in Italy, he served as ambassador to the Holy See (1929–35), minister of education (1935–36), and governor of the Dodecannese Islands (1936–40). He antagonized the pope, irritated administrators, teachers, and colonial subjects. After doing his best to provoke war with Greece by sinking a Greek submarine, when war broke out he resigned as governor, claiming inadequate military support from the government. After calling on Mussolini to step down in July 1943, De Vecchi went into hiding and eventually made his way to South America. After the war he got off with a light sentence at a war crimes tribunal, returned to Italy, and

joined the neo-Fascist ITALIAN SOCIAL MOVEMENT. His clean-shaven head and handlebar mustache gave him a distinctive look in harmony with his truculent character.

De Viti De Marco, Antonio (1858–1943)
economist, journalist, and publicist
Born in the southern town of Lecce in the region of Puglia, De Viti De Marco was among the *MERIDIONALISTI* who brought national attention to the SOUTHERN QUESTION. After teaching at several universities, he was appointed professor of economics and finance at the University of Rome (1887). He also sat in parliament as a member of the Radical Party (1900–21). Economic liberalism coexisted in his thinking with a concept of the state as an active economic agent. He argued for free trade to develop southern agriculture, deplored economic protectionism, and charged that the government's spending and fiscal policies diverted capital from productive private investments. But in the treatises for which he is best known, *Il carattere teorico dell'economia finanziaria* (Theoretical aspects of financial economy, 1888) and *Principii di economia finanziaria* (Principles of financial economy, 1928), he theorized that government should use resources in pursuit of defined national economic goals. Politics, according to De Viti De Marco, should mediate and resolve conflicts between the economic principles of laissez-faire and the need for public intervention and government spending. His writings reached an influential public through such journals as the *Giornale degli Economisti*. He lost his university post in 1931 when he refused to take the obligatory oath of allegiance to FASCISM.

Diaz, Armando (1861–1928)
military officer, army commander, and war minister
General Diaz was born in Naples to a noble family of Spanish origin. His first active command was as an infantry officer in the ITALIAN-TURKISH WAR, in which he was wounded in action.

Assigned to the general staff in 1914, during WORLD WAR I he was promoted to general, given first a divisional command (1916) and then an army command (1917). That same year he replaced LUIGI CADORNA as army commander in chief after the BATTLE OF CAPORETTO. The surprise appointment was ascribed chiefly to Diaz's reputation for political tact and understanding of soldiers' needs and psychology at a time of national crisis. Diaz's military judgment and capabilities were vindicated by his successful reorganization of the army, bolstering of troop morale, and by the success of the final offensive of the war. For his role in the war he received the title of *duca della Vittoria*. Sympathetic toward fascism, which he regarded as a patriotic movement, Diaz is said to have advised King VICTOR EMMANUEL III not to call out the army against the Fascist squads marching on Rome in October 1922. He served as minister of war in the Fascist government (1922–24). He was appointed senator and was the first officer promoted to the newly created top rank of military marshal (1924).

Di Giorgio, Antonino   See ARMED FORCES.

Dini, Lamberto (1931–   )
prime minister
Born in Florence, Dini graduated with a degree in economics from the University of Florence and studied in the United States as a Fulbright scholar. A member of the International Monetary Fund since 1959, he became its director in 1976. From 1979 to 1994 he was the director of the BANK OF ITALY. He entered politics because of his economic expertise, without any party affiliation, and was treasury minister from May 1994 to January 1995 in the first government of SILVIO BERLUSCONI. He succeeded Berlusconi as prime minister from January 1995 to May 1996. As prime minister, Dini moved the country toward new national elections and won approval for a controversial austerity budget that kept Italy on track for admission to the European Monetary Union.

In the national elections of May 1996 he was elected to parliament as leader of Rinnovamento Italiano (Italian Renewal), a small party of the political center that he founded, which is still his personal vehicle. Dini has also served as foreign minister in the governments of MASSIMO D'ALEMA (1998–2000) and GIULIO AMATO (2000–01). As foreign minister, Dini confronted some major issues, including the arrival of thousands of illegal immigrants, the policing of Albania and other territories in former Yugoslavia, and the crisis in Kosovo. His steady hand in the conduct of foreign policy reinforced his reputation as a moderating and reassuring political presence.

Di Pietro, Antonio (1950–   )
magistrate who led the fight against political corruption
Born to a peasant family in the southern region of Molise, Di Pietro caught the national imagination as the most visible magistrate in the MANI PULITE (Clean Hands) investigation that pursued corruption in high places. As a young man he emigrated to Germany to work as a manual laborer, returned to Italy to fulfill his military obligation, joined the police force, attended university and law school, eventually qualifying for a position in the courts (1981). After an undistinguished and troubled start, he was assigned to Milan where the Clean Hands investigation began in February 1992. Di Pietro became the most visible member of the panel of judges that took charge of the investigation. His modest background contributed to his image as a man of the people fighting for honesty and justice in public life. Hard work and effective use of computer technology led to the arrest of thousands of suspects among businessmen and public officials. Public opinion polls at the height of the investigation ranked Di Pietro as the most popular man in the country. His resignation from the investigation in December 1994 was sudden and unexpected. The resignation followed charges, later dropped, that he abused his judicial powers, but may also have been motivated

by disagreement with the political motivations of the investigation. After resigning, Di Pietro turned to teaching and politics, served briefly as minister of public works in the government of ROMANO PRODI (1996), resigned after clashing with fellow ministers, and won a senate seat in the center-left coalition (1997). In the elections of May 2001 he ran on his own ticket, which he called Italia dei Valori (Italy of Values), but failed to win the minimum 4 percent of the vote required to obtain a seat in parliament. He is no longer the popular figure that he was in the 1990s and his political future is uncertain.

Di Vittorio, Giuseppe (1892–1957)
political figure and labor leader

Di Vittorio was the son of poor day laborers from the southern region of PUGLIA where he joined the radical labor movement in 1911. He was elected to parliament for the Socialist Party (PSI) in 1921 but switched to the Communist Party (PCI) in 1924. Condemned in absentia to 12 years in jail for political sedition by a Fascist tribunal, Di Vittorio escaped to France where he was active in the international labor movement. He served in the Spanish civil war as a communist political commissar. After the war he served in parliament from 1946 but his most important contribution was as the chief organizer of the General Confederation of Labor, which he headed from 1945 to 1957. Di Vittorio failed to keep organized labor united, as the movement split along political lines. In October 1949 he proposed a *piano del lavoro* (labor plan), backed by the PCI, for the reconstruction of the postwar economy. It envisaged the nationalization of the electrical industry, extensive LAND RECLAMATION and irrigation projects especially for the South, and large-scale construction of popular housing. The plan was to be financed by progressive taxes and would provide 700,000 jobs. Di Vittorio called for massive strikes and demonstrations in support of the plan and raised the prospect of social revolution if the government turned it down. Agitation for the plan continued through the early 1950s, against

Giuseppe Di Vittorio *(Library of Congress)*

mounting opposition from organized business and the ruling Christian Democratic Party (DC), which saw the plan as a stalking horse for economic collectivism. The defeat of the labor plan foreclosed the prospects of economic reconstruction along socialist lines and marked a turning point in the history of postwar Italy.

divorce law

The legalization of divorce was an issue in Italy from the time of national unification. Opposed by the CATHOLIC CHURCH on the ground that matrimony was an indissoluble sacrament, legalization had the support of anticlericals but found few champions in the national parliament. The civil code of 1865 allowed civil marriage, promptly condemned by the church as invalid, but made no provisions for divorce. The issue was taken up by socialists, who called for legalized divorce as part of their campaigns on behalf of illegitimate children, unmarried mothers, and the rights of women. Parliament took up the question perhaps a dozen times between 1870 and 1920 without ever finding enough votes to make it into law. The CONCORDAT of 1929 put the question to rest for the time being by recognizing the legal validity of religious marriages and the sole jurisdiction of ecclesiastical courts on marriage annulments. The incorporation of the Concordat in the CONSTITUTION of the Italian republic was an important victory for the church, but one that also put the issue back on the national agenda. A socialist proposal to legalize divorce reached parliament in 1965, but was promptly blocked by the Christian Democratic Party (DC). Organized campaigning by various political and feminist groups in the late 1960s helped turn public opinion in favor of legalization. After long debate, parliament passed a law that made divorce legal as of December 1, 1970. But the battle was not over, as various militant Catholic groups forced a national referendum on the issue. The results of the referendum of May 1974 were unequivocal: 59 percent favored legalized divorce, 41 percent opposed it. Approximately 90,000 divorces were granted in 1970–74, as many couples took advantage of the new law to regularize de facto separations. The initial high numbers fanned fears that the law would undermine the institution of marriage. But the Italian divorce rate soon stabilized to one of the lowest levels in Europe, validating the arguments of pro-divorce advocates who predicted that the law would be used to rectify only the most untenable marriage situations. The church continues to uphold the sacramental nature of marriage and to claim sole jurisdiction over the dissolution of marriages.

Dodecanese Islands See COLONIALISM.

Dolci, Danilo (1924–1997)
writer and educator
A social activist with a pacifist approach to the solution of social problems, Dolci was born in the Yugoslav town of Sesana. He was brought up in comfortable circumstances in northern Italy and trained as an engineer. Visiting Sicily in 1952 to study its ancient Greek temples at Segesta, he remained on the island to work with the chronically unemployed and destitute. He settled down in the rural settlement of Trappeto near Palermo, married a local widow with five children, and organized the first *sciopero a rovescio* (reverse strike) in which local people went to work to repair a road without authorization or compensation. It was the beginning of many such peaceful actions, for which Dolci served time in jail on charges of trespassing on public property. He then turned his attention to education by persuading parents to send their children to school. Land reform, irrigation, urban poverty, infant mortality, malnutrition, and bureaucratic inertia were additional issues that prompted responses from Dolci in the form of organized protests and hunger strikes. He was also a crusader for world peace. His peaceful methods won him recognition as the Gandhi of Sicily, brought him international sympathy and support. Being in the public eye protected him from retaliation by the MAFIA, which did not look kindly on his initiatives. Dolci relied on community action, organized self-help, and avoided ties to political parties. His nonpolitical approach was appreciated more readily abroad than in Italy. He was particularly popular in the Anglo-Saxon world, where volunteers raised funds for his activities. Dolci's *Report from Palermo* (1956) won international acclaim as a sociological investigation of life among the poor of that city. Many of his other works have been translated into English.

Domenica Letteraria (La) See MARTINI, FERDINANDO.

Donatello (1386–1466)
Renaissance sculptor admired for the expressiveness of his works
The foremost Florentine sculptor of the early Renaissance was born Donato di Niccolò di Betto

Bardi. His first known employment was as an assistant to LORENZO GHIBERTI on the famed doors of the Florence Baptistry in 1404–07. Donatello sculptures in Florence include the marble statue of Saint George (1416) in the National Museum, the prophet Habakkuk (1427), the Annunciation (1433) in the Church of Santa Croce, the bronze David (1440), made for the MEDICI FAMILY and now in the Bargello, and Mary Magdalene (1453–55) in the Baptistry, carved in wood. In 1432–33 Donatello journeyed to Rome to study the city's ancient works. The statue of Marcus Aurelius inspired him to strive for a similar massive effect, evident in the striking monument to the condottiere Gattamelata (1444–47), the first equestrian statue made since ancient times, which stands in front of the basilica of Saint Anthony in Padua, where Donatello worked from 1443 to 1452. After 1452 he divided his time between Florence and Siena, creating in his final years some of his most dramatic and poignant works. The statue of Saint John the Baptist in the Cathedral of Siena is a good example of the emotionally charged, highly expressive, surrealistically imagined figures of his final years. The emotional intensity of his works was not to everyone's liking. He was faulted for straying from the balanced, serene style of his contemporaries, particularly that of the much admired Ghiberti. Donatello's influence was nevertheless immense, inspiring later artists to strive for the same level of technical skill and expressiveness.

Donati, Giovanni Battista See SCIENCE.

Donizetti, Gaetano (1797–1848)
opera composer of the romantic period
The renowned composer who wrote more than 60 operas was born in Bergamo to a poor family without roots in the musical world. A free music school opened by a local charity and the patronage of the composer Johannes Simon Mayr enabled him to acquire musical training (1806–14). His first successful opera, *Zoraida di*

Granata, was performed in Rome (1822), but his first international triumph came with *Anna Bolena* (1830), performed in Paris and London. Other successes came with *L'elisir d'amore* (1832), *Lucrezia Borgia* (1833), *Lucia di Lammermoor* (1835), *La fille du régiment* and *La favorite,* both staged for the Parisian theater in 1840, *Linda di Chamounix* (1842), and *Don Pasquale* (1843). His health began to deteriorate seriously in 1843. His erratic behavior, uncontrollable fits of temper, and recurring memory lapses were attributed to syphilis. A prolific master of both comic and serious opera, he felt constrained by traditions ingrained in the Italian stage and looked to the rest of Europe for modes of musical expressions. Free from the repressive political atmosphere of Italy, he expressed sympathy for GIUSEPPE MAZZINI and his patriotic movement, but politics was not a dominant concern for Donizetti. Depiction of strong passions, human conflicts, and dramatic situations make him the outstanding Italian representative of ROMANTICISM in music. Immensely popular in his time, then seriously neglected except for a few of his tuneful comic operas, he regained the favor of audiences and critics in the second half of the 20th century, when talented singers like Maria Callas, Leyla Gencer, and Beverly Sills breathed new life into Donizetti's romantic heroines.

Dopolavoro See OPERA NAZIONALE DOPOLAVORO.

Doria, Andrea (1466–1560)
Genoese military figure and political reformer
This member of the powerful Genoese family of the Doria spent his youth as a soldier of fortune in the service of the pope, the king of Naples, and other Italian lords. He helped put down rebellions by rival families against the Republic of GENOA, fought with the French against the Spaniards, and managed to restore Genoese independence after imperial Spanish forces had seized the city. But he then switched sides and

received from the Spaniards rich compensation for his military services and a commitment that they would respect the independence of Genoa (1528). He proceeded to enact a series of political reforms that gave control of the republic to the leading aristocratic families of his city, foremost among them his own family, and excluded commoners from government. Andrea Doria held no official title and was careful to preserve the trappings of representative institutions, but was in fact the real power. Stability at home enabled him to turn his attention to military ventures abroad. As an admiral in the imperial navy he led several expeditions against the Turks and helped clear the Mediterranean of piracy. In 1547–48 he put down with brutal efficiency revolts against his rule led by the rival Fieschi and Cybo families. In 1559 he recovered the island of CORSICA from the Spaniards with the help of the French. Andrea Doria exemplifies the style of the CONDOTTIERI who pursued personal gain through warfare and public office. His political reforms make him the real founder of the aristocratic republic of Genoa that survived until 1797. Members of the Doria family held top political office in Genoa until the middle of the 17th century and positions of power in other Italian states until the beginning of the 19th.

Dorotei   See MORO, ALDO.

Dossetti, Giuseppe (1913–1996)
Christian Democratic radical and social reformer

This politically active priest stood for a socially radical version of Christian democracy in Italy after 1945. Dossetti took part in the RESISTANCE movement and served as deputy secretary of the newly formed Christian Democratic Party (DC). As head of the DC's left wing, Dossetti was critical of capitalism and envisaged an evangelical political movement that spoke directly to Catholic workers, the needy, and the disinherited. Solidarity across class lines was the principle behind

Dossetti's evangelical and political work. In foreign policy, he pleaded for Italian neutrality in the cold war and for keeping Italy out of NATO. His presence lent credibility to the image of the DC as a socially progressive force and contributed to the party's overwhelming victory in the elections of 1948. But the climate of the cold war was not conducive to the kind of politics envisaged by Dossetti. Having lost the support of the party leadership and confined to speaking for an isolated and ineffective minority, in 1951 Dossetti withdrew from public life and retired to live a life of seclusion in a monastery. Even in retirement his charismatic presence drew followers who organized themselves in communities. In 1994 he took a public stand against the government of SILVIO BERLUSCONI, urged reforming the DC along progressive lines, and supported the center-left government of MASSIMO D'ALEMA.

Douhet, Giulio (1869–1930)
military theorist and advocate of the supremacy of air power

Remembered primarily as a military figure and theoretician of the use of air power in modern wars, Douhet was a man of many talents who wrote on a wide variety of subjects, authored plays, and exercised his sharp wit at the expense of military bureaucrats. He commanded the first contingent of Italian pilots (1912–15), served on the general staff (1915–16), was promoted to colonel (1917), and promptly ran afoul of military justice by criticizing the unimaginative and costly frontal-assault tactics of the commander in chief, General LUIGI CADORNA. Imprisoned after the BATTLE OF CAPORETTO, he retired from military service in 1919. He saw in overwhelming air power the way to avoid the appalling carnage of wars of attrition as seen in WORLD WAR I. Dominance of the air was to be achieved by building enormous fleets of strategic bombers and employing them ruthlessly against military and civilian targets alike to destroy enemy morale and war-making capabilities. Ground forces would play a purely defensive role and would be used to occupy enemy territory after wars were won from the air. Douhet's theories may have had some influence on Fascist air force chief ITALO BALBO, but Fascist Italy did not try to build the kind of dominant air force envisaged by Douhet. His ideas were taken more seriously in Germany and the United States. General William Mitchell is thought to have been influenced by Douhet's writings. To the extent that Douhet's theories were taken seriously in Italy, they may have had a negative effect by downplaying the importance of fighter aircraft, antiaircraft defenses, and coordination of air force, army, and navy operations, in favor of squadrons of large bombers. The effectiveness of air dominance and heavy bombing in WORLD WAR II offered a partial vindication of Douhet's theories, but the prophetic nature of his vision would become fully evident in the conflicts that broke out in the Balkans, Afghanistan, and Iraq at the end of the 20th and beginning of the 21st century. His book *Il dominio dell'aria* (1921) was published in English as *The Command of the Air* (1942, 1983).

Du Tillot, Guillaume-Léon (1711–1774)
Enlightenment figure and reformer
As chief adviser to Philip of Bourbon, duke of Parma (1748–65), the Frenchman Du Tillot, son of one of Louis XIV's officials, attempted to reform the government and public administration of the duchy of PARMA. Du Tillot challenged the economic and legal privileges of the CATHOLIC CHURCH, limited the powers of the INQUISITION, expelled the JESUITS, and proposed an integrated system of public education from elementary schooling to university studies. He tackled the problem of state finances with little success, due to the heavy expenditures of the court and the fiscal privileges of clergy and nobility. His encouragement to agriculture and commerce paid off in improved productivity and a higher standard of living. During Du Tillot's tenure as chief minister, Parma was regarded as the "Athens of Europe" because of its generous patronage of artists and

scholars. Du Tillot's influence declined after the death of Philip. A typical reformer of the Enlightenment, Du Tillot's reforms were partly undone after his dismissal in 1771.

Duse, Eleonora (1859–1924)
actress and public personality
Born to a family of the theater, Duse made her stage debut at the age of 14 in the role of Juliet, then went on to win international acclaim as *La Duse* for her roles in Italian, French, and German plays. Her uncanny ability to identify with characters gave enormous emotional impact to her interpretations. Her acting method was notable for its simplicity. She avoided makeup and grand theatrical gestures. Interested in contemporary

Eleonora Duse *(Library of Congress)*

drama, she introduced Ibsen to the Italian stage and championed the plays of GABRIELE D'ANNUN-ZIO, with whom she carried on a highly publicized and stormy love affair from 1897 to 1904. She presented his plays to an initially hostile public. Her persistence paid off as audiences began to respond to the allure of her acting and to D'Annunzio's resonant rhetoric and eroticism. Duse helped spread the cult of D'Annunzio that affected several generations of educated Italians.

Perhaps more important, she renewed the prestige of the Italian theater at home and abroad. D'Annunzio repaid her by revealing intimate details of their relationship in his novel *Il fuoco* (The Fire, 1900). In 1916 she appeared in the film *Cenere* (Ashes). She competed for international acclaim with her contemporary Sarah Bernhardt. Duse was well past her prime when she gave her farewell performance in New York in 1923.

E

Ebreo, Leone See ABRAVANEL, JUDAH.

Eco, Umberto (1932–)
writer, literary critic, and social theorist

A cultural presence in Italy and abroad, Eco is known for his contributions to linguistics, communication studies, philosophy, literary criticism, journalism, and fiction. He was born in 1932 in the town of Alessandria (Piedmont), studied philosophy at the University of Turin, and graduated in 1954 with a dissertation on the esthetics of St. Thomas Aquinas. He has taught at the universities of Bologna, Florence, Milan (where he resides), and Turin, and has been a visiting professor at Yale University. In the 1970s he emerged as a major figure in the new discipline of semiotics, which pursued the ambitious goal of developing a uniform research methodology that cut across fields and unified different social disciplines. The starting point of semiotics is that all knowledge is a form of communication. While some semiologists have pushed this claim to the extreme postmodernist conclusion that knowledge is therefore an artificial form of representation that has meaning only in the context of individual experience, Eco has generally stopped short of such a radical conclusion. His position seems to be that modes of expression (signs) only impose an artificial order on the real world. Eco set out his views on the nature of the new discipline in *A Theory of Semiotics* (1976). His major works have been translated into English, including his best-selling novel *The Name of the Rose* (1983), which explores philosophical issues in detective fashion by telling the story of a crime committed in a medieval monastery. *Foucault's Pendulum* (1989) is another novel by Eco that uses fiction to address serious intellectual issues. In Italy, Eco is also known as a political commentator and polemicist in the tradition of intellectuals speaking out on public issues, a position which Eco defends in his writings as a social obligation. Eco speaks from a generally liberal position in the American sense of the term, without identifying with particular political parties.

economic miracle

The expansion of the ECONOMY in the 1950s is often described as Italy's economic miracle. Before the expansion could occur, the country had to recover from the devastation of the war. The recovery was achieved by the early 1950s with the help of American aid through the Marshall Plan, the reconstruction of the transportation system, and the stabilization of the currency. Recovery was also facilitated by the relatively minor damage suffered by the large industrial complexes of the North during the war, the availability of cheap migrant labor from the South, the ethic of hard work, inventiveness of management, and the cooperative attitude of labor unions in the early years of the recovery. Government investments in the South helped to create a national market. Government ownership of steel-making, communications, transportation, and energy production and distribution shifted the cost of these capital-intensive industries from the private to the public sector. Manufacturing and exports drove the economic expansion of the 1950s. Autos, domestic appliances, office equipment, shoes, and textiles led the exports market. Domestic consumption rose slowly until the mid-

1960s as wages remained fairly stable, while savings and investments grew.

All this suggests that the economic miracle was less a miracle than it was the result of preparation, ingenuity, hard work, and delayed consumer gratification. The boom lasted from 1951 to 1963, was interrupted in 1964–65 by a temporary recession (*congiuntura*), resumed in 1966–67, and continued until it was ended by the oil crisis of the early 1970s. The 1970s saw a major shift as the labor unions became more demanding and militant, workers won major concessions from management, and the country entered a period of political instability and turbulence. Flight from the countryside and massive emigration from the South, rapid growth of urban populations and city slums, loosening of family and community ties, and inadequate investment in public services were the price paid for rapid growth. The economic miracle brought on decisive transformations: industry overtook agriculture, millions moved from the countryside and small towns into large cities, consumption levels rose, social mobility increased, and rapid social change became the norm.

economy

Italy has always been a country with many economies. Regional distinctions, differences between North and South, the coexistence of a large government-owned or -managed public sector with private entrepreneurship are characteristics of economic life in the Italian peninsula that complicate discussions of the Italian economy. Different regions and forms of economic activity have interacted if for no other reason than their geographical proximity, and their interaction is what has formed the Italian economy over the centuries. Regional economic differences were already pronounced in the Middle Ages, when the states of northern and central Italy underwent economic transformations that produced large accumulations of private wealth. Trade, manufacturing, and banking transformed Florence, Venice, Genoa, Milan,

and many other city-states into economic powerhouses. Their wealth sustained RENAISSANCE culture in all its glory well into the 16th century. What sapped the economic vitality of the Renaissance city-states is still the subject of debate. War, foreign competition, Turkish control of the eastern Mediterranean, the displacement of trade routes from the MEDITERRANEAN SEA to the Atlantic Ocean, growing aversion to risk, all these played a role.

The Kingdom of Naples, the largest state in the peninsula, was also a center of Renaissance culture but its economy was agricultural and rural, reliant on cultivation and trade in grains and closely tied to Spain economically and politically. It was also more exposed to hostile Turkish incursions. In Naples, the state claimed a greater share of resources through taxation, and siphoned capital away from productive investments. The North had many thriving urban centers, the South had only one, Naples, where the court and nobility resided and provided employment for a large urban proletariat.

Economic downturns may have diminished regional differences in the 17th century, but only temporarily. The 18th saw efforts at economic reform in both North and South, but the North soon forged ahead. The greatest progress occurred in the region of LOMBARDY. Under Austrian rule, 18th-century Lombardy began to assert the primacy that would make it and its capital city of Milan the economic heartland and business capital of modern Italy. But what was most glaring by the beginning of the 19th century was not the phenomenon of regional imbalances, but rather the growing economic distance between the peninsula as a whole and the developing industrial economies of northwestern Europe.

In the industrial age, all the Italian regions and states were variously disadvantaged by distance from the principal areas of business activity, lack of key resources like coal and iron, scarcity of capital, and inadequate infrastructures in transportation, BANKING, and EDUCATION. The RISORGIMENTO movement for national unification reflected in part the desire to join the economic mainstream. Political divisions and tariff barriers hindered trade in the peninsula, and Austrian dominance stood in the way of creating a national market. The lead taken by the Kingdom of SARDINIA in the movement for national unification is largely attributable to the success of the economic policies promoted by Prime Minister CAVOUR.

National unification did not produce the expected economic miracle, but it did pressure the government to stimulate the economy. In partial retreat from the free-trade policies of the early years of national unification, the government adopted protective tariffs in 1878 and 1887 to help domestic manufacturers. Government economic interventionism in the form of protective tariffs, contracts, subsidies, regulation, management, and outright ownership of the means of production has been a constant feature of Italian economic life since national unification. Railroads, shipbuilding, machinery, steel, electricity, and chemicals are some of the sectors that would not have developed in Italy without government protection or stimulation.

War and economic crisis also induced the state to play an active economic role. WORLD WAR I tightened ties between government and private business. The founding of IRI (Institute for Industrial Reconstruction) further blurred the line between private and public enterprise. This state holding company founded in 1933 to bail out banks that were on the verge of bankruptcy became a lasting feature of the Italian economy. Through it, the state controlled and managed vast sectors of the economy that were deemed essential for national defense and security. This "mixed economy" in which private and public enterprise coexist was a legacy of FASCISM. It survived the fall of fascism to play a role in the postwar ECONOMIC MIRACLE by relieving the private sector of responsibility for the largely uncompetitive enterprises that were concentrated in the public sector. By the 1970s mismanagement and political interference aggravated the problems of the public sector, making it increasingly burdensome for taxpayers. The process of priva-

tization that has been underway since the late 1980s aims at reducing the scope of public initiative, pursuing greater efficiency, and developing those sectors of the economy that can compete successfully in global markets. Food processing, fashions, and design excel in this climate, while heavy industries have not fared well.

In the 1970s the Italian economy crossed the line from the industrial to the postindustrial stage as the service industries overtook manufacturing industries as principal producers and job providers. Small and medium-sized firms prevail in all sectors of the economy. They are more flexible and respond readily to changes in demand and market conditions. Many thrive in the *economia nera* (underground economy) where they avoid taxes and cut labor costs. Seen in its totality over the course of 140 years since national unification, the record of the Italian economy is a positive one. The standard of living has improved for most Italians at a pace comparable to that of other western countries, the gap between North and South has been reduced, and the Italian economy ranks today among the top seven in the world. Italy may not have pioneered in economic innovation or created a distinctive model of development in modern times, but it has prospered by riding global economic trends with impressive success.

Edison See MONTEDISON.

education
Obligatory schooling and standardized curricula came to Italy after national unification. Until then, educational requirements and standards varied from state to state. Universities were the pride of all preunification states. First was the University of Bologna, founded in the 11th century, then came Padua (1222), Naples (1224), Rome (1303), Perugia (1308), Florence (1321), Modena, (1329), Pisa (1348), Siena (1357), Turin (1365), Ferrara (1361). With another nine universities founded between 1500 and 1800, at the

start of the modern era Italy led other European countries in the number of its institutions of advanced learning. Law and medicine were the subjects most commonly taught, but the humanities (*studia humanitatis*), including grammar, rhetoric, ethics, poetry, and history, were also popular. But all was not well. In the 17th century Italian universities began to lag behind universities elsewhere in Europe in research and teaching in the natural sciences. They have struggled to keep pace with scientific teaching and research ever since. At the primary and secondary levels instruction was a matter of family choice. Literacy rates in premodern times are a matter of conjecture, but we do know that knowledge of reading and writing was not limited to the highly educated. The clergy controlled teaching at all levels until some 18th-century states, particularly Austrian Lombardy and Tuscany, passed laws to secularize education and teacher training.

The educational system of the Italian state after unification was regulated by the CASATI LAW (1859). Although it was mostly concerned with higher education, the Casati Law was the basis of the first sustained efforts to make elementary education obligatory, standardize curricula, and establish and enforce national standards. Attendance was made compulsory for the first two grades in 1877, raised to the first three grades in 1888, and to fifth and sixth in 1904–11. There were large local and regional differences, most glaring between North and South, because until 1911 the law made local administrations responsible for funding elementary education. But education for the masses was now a reality. National literacy levels rose from 31.2 percent of the population over age six in 1871 to 62.1 percent in 1911. The battle against illiteracy had patriotic overtones. Without the ability to read, large segments of the population would not receive the messages that they were one people with rights and duties as citizens. Universal military conscription also played an important role in the battle against illiteracy as illiterate recruits were taught to read and write as part of their basic training.

Compulsory schooling also affected traditional gender roles. More girls than boys seem to have attended school regularly at the elementary levels. Women of the middle and upper classes had access to secondary education on an equal footing with men. The teaching profession became an important avenue of social mobility for women. Secondary schools designed specifically for women provided academically rigorous training and physical education, putting Italy at the forefront in this particular area of instruction before 1914.

The campaign to improve schooling intensified under FASCISM. The philosopher GIOVANNI GENTILE, the regime's first education minister, enacted the first reform in 1923, and GIUSEPPE BOTTAI enacted the second in 1939. Gentile set out to improve standards and imposed a uniform national curriculum that included the compulsory study of Latin at the secondary level. The elitist intent of Gentile's reform was summed up in the slogan "few but good," which meant that schools should be selective and concentrate on producing quality graduates. But in reality school attendance and graduation increased at all levels during the Fascist period. Bottai's reform, coming some 16 years after Gentile's, took cognizance of the changing role of education. It raised the age at which important career decisions were made from age 11 to 14, and sought to broaden access to secondary and advanced education. WORLD WAR II prevented the implementation of Bottai's reforms, but on the eve of war the regime could rightfully claim that it had drastically reduced illiteracy and broadened access to postelementary education.

The most thorough transformations have occurred since 1945 under the democratic laws of the Italian republic. In 1951 87.1 percent of people over age six were literate. By 1971 literacy stood at 94.8 percent, thanks also to the use of national television broadcasting to reach all strata of the population. Today illiteracy is virtually nonexistent in Italy, but that achievement does not speak to proficiency, as many literate adults in reality possess only the basics of reading and writing. Other issues that continue to draw attention are the nature of the curriculum (still heavily weighted toward the classics at the secondary level), the age at which students have to make career-affecting decisions, the ability of the system to prepare people for the current economy (still weak in technical schooling), and the relationship between public and private (mostly Catholic) education. Requirements have been liberalized, students can choose today from a variety of secondary schools and specializations, and since 1969 any student with a senior secondary-school diploma may attend a university. The overwhelming majority of students attend public schools, but private schooling is protected by the CONSTITUTION. Religious instruction in public schools, made compulsory in 1929, is today voluntary. Administrative decentralization has made it possible for some districts to develop educational models of international renown (as in Reggio Emilia), but local success stories are part of a national picture that is less encouraging. Funding for education and teacher salaries remains low nationwide, and broad regional disparities still prevail. Scientific and technical education still lags behind education in other fields. University enrollments are still heavily weighed toward law, medicine, civil service employment, and humanistic and social science fields. Graduates in the humanities and social sciences find that there are few job openings in their fields. Educational reform remains at the top of the national agenda. The Organization for Economic Cooperation and Development publishes periodic updates on Italian education, the most recent in 1998.

EIAR (Ente Italiano Audizioni Radiofoniche) See JOURNALISM.

Einaudi, Luigi (1874–1961)
economist, journalist, and political figure
Born near Cuneo in the region of Piedmont, Einaudi graduated from the University of Turin, taught economics in Turin and Milan, and published extensively in the fields of economic theory and finance. An economic liberal and free trader, his views were not in favor during the Fascist period, but he nevertheless remained in Italy until forced to escape to Switzerland in 1943. After the war he served as governor of the BANK OF ITALY (1945–46), treasury minister (1947), and as president of the Italian republic (1948–55). He reached a broad public with his writings and teaching. As a journalist he wrote for influential papers like *Corriere della Sera* and *La Stampa*. He ranks as the most influential Italian economist of the first half of the 20th century and as one who remained consistent and true to his convictions while holding public office. His most notable achievement in the public arena was his successful campaign as governor of the Bank of Italy and treasury minister to stabilize the currency. That victory against runaway inflation was the necessary precondition for the postwar economic recovery and for the ECONOMIC MIRACLE of the 1950s. He returned to academic life and journalism after serving as president of the republic.

Elba, island of
Elba (86 square miles), located six miles off the coast of southern Tuscany, is the largest of seven islands forming the Tuscan Archipelago (the others are Gorgona, Capraia, Pianosa, Montecristo, Giglio, and Giannutri). Etruscans, who settled Elba in pre-Roman times, used iron ore from its mines to support a thriving metallurgical industry. Extraction of iron ore has continued into modern times. However, its production has never been sufficient to satisfy the domestic need. Elba's smelting facilities were not rebuilt after sustaining heavy damage in WORLD WAR II, but iron ore continues to be mined on the island in small quantities. AGRICULTURE and tourism are the island's most important resources. Etruscans, Greeks, and Romans controlled the island in ancient times. In the Middle Ages it was ruled by PISA. It passed to Spain in the 15th century, then

to the Kingdom of NAPLES and the Grand Duchy of TUSCANY before becoming part of Italy in 1860. From May 1814 to February 1815 it was an independent principality ruled by NAPOLEON I, who was confined there by a decision of the CONGRESS OF VIENNA and escaped to try his military luck again, before being decisively beaten at Waterloo. During his brief stay Napoleon carried out many improvements that can still be seen. The residence where he held court is today a tourist attraction.

elections and electoral systems

Election to public office is a key aspect of modern democracy. The practice, common in the ancient world among Greeks and Romans, was also known in the medieval city-states of Italy before they were transformed into dynastic monarchies. Electoral practices survived until the end of the 18th century in the aristocratic republics of GENOA, LUCCA, and VENICE, with voting rights limited to families of their respective aristocracies. Popular sovereignty and election to public office were principles of government that were brought to Italy by the ideas of the ENLIGHTENMENT and the armies of the FRENCH REVOLUTION. Italian JACOBINS adopted these principles far more readily than the masses. The lesson of popular resistance to change was not lost on the SECRET SOCIETIES that carried on the fight for government reform in the first part of the 19th century. Reform movements during this period generally stopped short of demanding voting rights for all citizens. The right to vote was to be limited to the minorities of property holders and the educated. It was only democratic movements like Giuseppe Mazzini's YOUNG ITALY that called for universal suffrage and popular government in the first part of the 19th century.

The REVOLUTION of 1848 called for constitutions and representative government. Only the CONSTITUTION granted by the Kingdom of SARDINIA survived the defeat of revolution. It became the constitution of the unified Kingdom of Italy from 1861 to 1946, when the monarchy was abolished and a new constitution was enacted. Known as the Statuto, the old constitution provided for an elective lower house of parliament (Chamber of Deputies) and an upper house (Senate) appointed by the king. A voting law accompanying the Statuto prescribed that only males could vote who were 25 or older and paid at least 40 lire per year in taxes. By these rules, only 2 percent of the population could vote. The electoral reform of 1882 enfranchised approximately 7 percent of the population by reducing the tax requirement to 20 lire per year and introducing a schooling or literacy alternative to the payment of taxes.

Although gradual, these reforms alarmed conservatives and others who feared the consequences of a broader suffrage. Discontent with the electoral system contributed to the political crisis of 1896–1901, when constitutional guarantees and civil freedoms were threatened by a conservative backlash. But the crisis was followed by the period of liberalization and electoral reform associated with GIOVANNI GIOLITTI (1901–14). The electoral reform of 1912 extended the right to vote to males who had fulfilled their military obligation, increased the electorate from 3.3 million to 8.7 million, enfranchised about 25 percent of the population, and brought mass politics to Italy for the first time. In the elections of 1919 and 1921 about 30 percent of the population was eligible to vote. The number of eligible voters who actually voted varied greatly. It was less than one-half in the period 1861–82, but increased steadily to very high levels in 1919–21.

Free elections were eliminated under FASCISM. The elections of the Fascist regime resembled plebiscites in which voters could vote yes or no, and only for candidates handpicked by the party and other official agencies of the regime. Fascist electoral laws were also based on the principle that individuals should be represented not as free citizens but as members of recognized corporate bodies. The regime claimed that its electoral reforms were inspired by a notion of democracy that put the interests of the nation ahead of those of the individual. Fascism redefined democracy by giving priority to the interests of the group as defined by the government and party officials.

Liberal democracy came to Italy after the fall of the Fascist regime. The elections of 1946 were the first held on the basis of unrestricted universal suffrage for both men and women. Voters abolished the monarchy and chose representatives to a constitutional assembly charged with preparing a constitution for the Italian republic. The new constitution went into effect on January 1, 1948. Voters who were 21 or older could vote for representatives to the lower house of parliament (Chamber of Deputies); 25-year-olds could also vote for representatives to the upper house (Senate). In 1978 the voting age was lowered to 18.

Important changes in electoral procedures accompanied the expansion of the franchise. In 1919 proportional representation replaced the uninominal district system. With the uninominal system one winner took all, while proportional representation gave political parties the same proportion of seats in the legislative branch that they receive in the popular vote. Proportional representation is more democratic, uninominal voting makes for more stable politics. Proportional representation was adopted after the war because it was more democratic and safeguarded against the recurrence of one-party dictatorship, such as Italians had experienced under fascism. It made the parliaments of the republic broadly representative of all political parties, prevented single-party dominance, and made government by multiparty coalitions necessary.

Proportional representation was at the core of the political system that governed Italy from 1946 to the early 1990s. It produced coalition governments controlled by the Christian Democratic (DC) and other center parties in 1948–63, by the DC and the Socialist Party (PSI) in 1963–83, and by various combinations of Christian Democrats, Socialists, and other parties of the center and left in 1983–92. The familiar party system broke down after the election of 1992 as voters reacted to the end of the cold war and to the evidence of political corruption revealed by the Clean Hands (MANI PULITE) investigation. The dominant Christian Democratic, Socialist, and Communist Parties dissolved, new political groups formed, and public opinion supported proposals to reform the electoral system. In 1993 parliament introduced uninominal districts for 75 percent of seats in parliament, but retained proportional representation for the remaining 25 percent. The change did not reduce the number of parties, and short-lived coalition governments remain the norm to this day. Proposals to do away with proportional representation entirely, strengthen the executive branch of government, and introduce direct election of the president of the republic have lost the momentum gathered in the 1990s. Public opinion still favors reform, but the political will to carry it out seems to have flagged.

Emanuel Philibert (1528–1580)
(Emanuele Filiberto)

military commander, member of the House of Savoy, founding figure of the state of Piedmont-Sardinia

Upon becoming duke of Savoy in 1553, Emanuel Philibert, nicknamed *Testa di ferro* (Ironhead), regained the family possessions in the ancestral region of Savoy that had been lost in war by his father Charles III. The son was known for his brilliant generalship, demonstrated in the course of a military career that began at age 17 fighting for Emperor Charles V. By age 25 Emanuel Philibert was commander in chief of the emperor's armies. His principal aim as duke of Savoy was to secure for his dynasty additional territories in Piedmont, Savoy, and Switzerland. He succeeded, except that he failed to regain control of the Protestant town of Geneva, which passed permanently to the Swiss. Emanuel Philibert centralized the administration, simplified the justice system, raised taxes, reorganized and expanded the standing army to a force of 20,000 (expandable to 36,000 in times of war), imposed compulsory military service on a reluctant nobility, adopted Italian and French as the official languages of the state, built roads, and encouraged economic development. The loss of Swiss territories, the strength of the French monarchy to the north, and the transfer in 1562 of the capital city from Chambéry in Savoy to Turin in Piedmont oriented the foreign policy of the dynasty toward Italy, where it was destined to play a key role in the process of national unification. Emanuel Philibert's courageous, cunning, and at times ruthless leadership thus laid the basis for the only Italian state capable of conducting an autonomous and opportunistic foreign policy in the subsequent three centuries, giving this mountain state a political leverage out of all proportion to the 1.5 million subjects and the modest resources at its command.

emigration See MIGRATION.

Emilia-Romagna

Emilia-Romagna (pop. 3,981,000), the sixth largest Italian region, occupies a strategic position between the regions of Lombardy, and Venetia to the north, Piedmont to the west, Liguria, Tuscany, and the Marches to the south. The region stretches funnel-like from the west toward the Adriatic Sea, where it covers a broad expanse of shoreline. The PO RIVER marks its northern boundary, the crest of the APENNINE MOUNTAINS the southern. The Emilia portion of this hyphenated region covers the provinces of Piacenza, Parma, Reggio Emilia, Modena, and Bologna (the regional capital); the Romagna covers the Lower Po Valley provinces of Ferrara, Forlì, and Ravenna. The name Emilia derives from the Via Aemilia, the ancient Roman road that still traverses the region. Byzantines, Lombards, and Germans controlled the region in medieval times. German emperors recognized papal authority over Bologna and the Romagna provinces in the 13th century. Those territories remained part of the PAPAL STATES until 1859,

when they joined the Kingdom of Italy with the rest of the region.

The relatively simple topography consists of mountains that seldom exceed 1.25 miles (2,000 meters) in elevation, a hilly region traversed by many streams that empty into the Po River, and a large fertile plain along the southern bank of the river, where commercial agriculture thrives. The plains of the Romagna have been home to masses of landless day laborers. These *braccianti*, hired from day to day by large landowners, poorly paid, and often unemployed, turned to socialism in the 19th century and have been the backbone of social protest movements and political parties of the Left. Political activism has given the *romagnoli* a reputation for political extremism and volatility. BENITO MUSSOLINI hailed from the province of Forlì. The hills and mountains of the region are less suitable for commercial agriculture than the plains, more thinly populated, home to many small landowners, and more moderate politically.

Agriculture remains the principal economic resource of the region, with fruit, wheat, sugar beets, vegetables, and grapes its most profitable products. Industry is present but not in great concentrations. Small and medium-sized firms are common in food processing, farm machinery, racing cars, clothing, and ceramics. Parmigiano-Reggiano cheese, Parma *prosciutto* (cured ham), *zampone* (pig trotter stuffed with meats and spices), balsamic vinegar, and Lambrusco wine are some of the renowned food products of the region. Production of chemicals and natural gas extraction has brought large-scale industry to the provinces of Ferrara and Ravenna. Tourism is important in Bologna and along the Adriatic shore, where sandy beaches, efficient organization, and reasonable prices attract large numbers of tourists from Germany and northern Europe. The Byzantine churches of Ravenna are also a major attraction. Emilia-Romagna is in many ways an ideal region: it is prosperous, generally peaceful now that it has shed its tradition of turbulent politics; its medium-sized towns and cities have a tradition of efficient administration and good public services and are mostly free of congestion and industrial pollution.

ENAL (Ente Nazionale Assistenza Lavoratori) See OPERA NAZIONALE DOPOLAVORO.

ENEL (Ente Nazionale Energia Elettrica)
former national electricity supplier and distributor, now partly privatized

ENEL, the National Electrical Energy Agency, was founded in 1962 to run the recently nationalized electrical industry. It created an integrated grid for the distribution of electrical energy throughout the national territory, oversaw a shift from hydroelectric to thermal production, reduced regional disparities, and unified rates. In the process, ENEL gained almost complete control of the national market for production and distribution of electrical power. As a state monopoly it was exempt from normal criteria of business profitability, ran growing deficits, and was over-administered. It showed little interest in the development of nuclear energy, partly because of strong public opposition to the construction of nuclear plants. Italy's four nuclear plants provided 4 percent of national production by the mid 1980s. Further construction of nuclear plants was banned in 1987 by popular referendum in the wake of the Chernobyl disaster in the U.S.S.R. Since then, ENEL has encouraged research into the use of renewable energy resources and has become one of the world's largest suppliers in this market. Under mounting public criticism, in 1992 ENEL became a public corporation under the jurisdiction of the Italian treasury and subject to privatization. In 1999 the government decided to deregulate the production and trade of electricity while maintaining a state monopoly for its distribution. Under this arrangement, ENEL retained control of the distribution grid, had to divest itself of all other operations, and offer shares of stock to private investors. It could also set up separate companies to produce, trade, and distribute elec-

tricity. This partial and gradual privatization has avoided major shocks to the market but has disappointed free-market advocates who blame ENEL for defending its monopoly and seeking to survive by diversifying its investments into fields unrelated to energy. As of 2004, the Italian government still owns about two-thirds of ENEL's stock. ENEL is now using cash generated by divesting itself of many of its nonenergy holdings to establish itself as a major energy supplier and distributor in the United States.

ENI (Ente Nazionale Idrocarburi)

ENI, the National Fuels Agency, was founded in 1953 as a state holding company charged with finding and developing oil deposits in the Po Valley, where earlier discoveries of large natural gas deposits suggested their presence. When no oil discoveries were made, ENI turned to oil exploration and development abroad under the energetic leadership of its first president ENRICO MATTEI. It obtained concessions from Egypt, Iran, Libya, and Morocco on the basis of a 75-25 profit-sharing formula that gave the larger share to the oil-producing country, thus breaking the 50-50 split offered by the major oil companies at the time. In 1960 it contracted to buy and sell oil from the Soviet Union. These forays into international waters stirred resentment and controversy in the oil world, where ENI and Mattei were seen as upstarts and troublemakers. At home, ENI carried out a systematic prospecting of the national territory looking for new sources of energy, found oil deposits off the coast of Sicily, built extensive oil refining facilities, and developed a national network for the distribution of oil and gasoline. Its emblem, a six-legged dog, became a familiar feature of Italy's industrial and commercial landscape. Mattei made shrewd use of his political ties to the Christian Democratic Party (DC) to expand his empire into areas unrelated to oil, including textiles, machinery, and the press, to influence public opinion, but otherwise ran a tight ship and fended off political interference with his operations. After his death in a mysterious plane crash in 1962, ENI succumbed to political pressures and became part of the spoils system of the DC. A state-controlled agency, it was criticized for corrupt practices and poor management. Calls for reform mounted until its holdings began to be privatized in 1995. By the year 2000 the state owned only about one-third of its holdings, enough to control appointments and operations. In its heyday, ENI was credited with supplying the country with the energy resources it needed to fuel the ECONOMIC MIRACLE. Regarded as an example of how public and private enterprise could complement one another, it was thought to have pioneered a new concept of power based on the interaction of economics and politics.

Enlightenment

Enlightenment is a term that describes a movement guided by those ideas of reform that spread throughout Europe and the New World during the 18th century. Its beginnings can be traced to the Scientific Revolution of the 17th century, and the writings of pioneering figures like John Locke, Adam Smith, and Montesquieu. Their ideas spread by means of publications, correspondence, travel, and religious and secular reform movements like JANSENISM and FREEMANSONRY. Enlightenment ideas emanated from the educated minorities, made converts in the upper reaches of society, including the so-called Enlightened Monarchs who had the power to implement reforms. The leaders of the Enlightenment were prepared to apply the tests of rationality and efficiency to religious, political, economic, and social practices of the time. They congratulated themselves on living in the "century of lights" and condemned the preceding centuries as times of darkness, prejudice, and ignorance.

Beyond these general traits of Enlightenment culture, every region and country had a specific set of issues on its agenda. In Italy, the fundamental issue of the Enlightenment was the search for a new relationship between the Catholic Church and secular governments. Defining the proper limits of ecclesiastical authority (jurisdictionalism) was the principal concern of early figures of the Italian Enlightenment like PIETRO GIANNONE and LODOVICO MURATORI. The most acclaimed and universally admired figure of the Italian Enlightenment was CESARE BECCARIA, whose book *On Crimes and Punishments* (1764) subjected the existing system of justice to a devastating critique, denounced its brutality, argued that punishments must be proportional to the seriousness of the crime, and that incarceration should aim at rehabilitating criminals. ANTONIO GENOVESI and FERDINANDO GALIANI addressed the issues of free trade and the supply of food. GIUSEPPE PARINI castigated the frivolous habits of the upper classes and the low levels of public morality and civic spirit.

Those who turned their attention to the forms of government generally looked to absolute monarchy as the institution most likely to succeed in carrying out desired reforms. The rulers of Italian states that embraced the idea of reform with the greatest enthusiasm were King CHARLES OF BOURBON in Naples, Emperor JOSEPH II in Austrian Lombardy, and Grand Duke PETER LEOPOLD in Tuscany. All expanded the power of government, improved the public administration, curbed the privileges of the church, encouraged economic growth, and promoted public education. Government reform was felt to a lesser extent in papal Rome, where Enlightenment popes did, however, encourage literature and the visual arts. The strongest opposition to reforms came from the extremes of society. At the upper end, some members of the ARISTOCRACY feared the loss of fiscal and social privileges. The grassroots opposition to reform came from peasants and lower clergy, who resented the attacks of the intelligentsia on traditional religion and feared the loss of traditional collective rights to the land. Historians still debate the nature of the Italian Enlightenment. Some see it as rooted in the culture of the Italian Renaissance, others as a European phenomenon, or as presaging the spirit of 19th-century nationalism. What is certain is that

Italy participated in the culture of the Enlightenment, experienced Enlightened reform, and nurtured a legacy that survived later attempts to undo those reforms. The search for concrete solutions to economic, political, and social problems; an aversion to abstract speculation; and a spirit of practicality were the distinguishing traits of the Italian Enlightenment.

Eritrea See COLONIALISM.

Este Family

The Este family ruled the city and territory of FERRARA for some 300 years, from the end of the 13th to the end of the 16th century. The family began its ascent as part of the rural nobility of PADUA in Carolingian times. The ancient origin was a matter of great pride, since it provided a rationale for claiming precedence over rival families, particularly over the rival MEDICI FAMILY of Florence, with whom the Este often clashed. The Este were lords of Ferrara by the end of the 13th century, but they did not achieve the status of a regional power until the rule of Niccolò III (1383–1441), who began construction of the massive castle that still dominates the center of the city. The high point of Este rule was reached in the 16th century. Ercole I (1421–1505) ruled with the title of duke after 1471. His offspring married well. Isabella (1474–1539) married into the GONZAGA FAMILY of Mantua, made a name for herself as a friend and patron of the arts, and earned the title of First Lady of the Renaissance, bestowed on her posthumously by admiring scholars. Beatrice (1775–97) married LODOVICO SFORZA of Milan. Ercole's son Alfonso's second wife was Lucrezia Borgia (see BORGIA FAMILY), who was much admired as duchess of Ferrara. Marriage alliances, patronage, and dynastic ambitions gave the Este remarkable political and cultural clout. But, surrounded by hostile powers, the Este had to tread carefully. They had to deal with the hostile Medici, the suspicious republic of VENICE, and the grasping PAPAL STATES. Alfonso

(1476–1534) faced divisive family feuds, the enmity of Pope JULIUS II, and the French military power in the ITALIAN WARS. The Este were plucky but unlucky. Ferrara became a papal fief, and the last member of the family to rule over the city was the childless Alfonso II (1533–97). The city passed under direct papal rule in 1598 and the Este moved to the duchy of MODENA, where they ruled until 1859. Ferrara prospered and became an important center of humanist culture under the rule of the Este. The poets LODOVICO ARIOSTO and TORQUATO TASSO served the family; music, the visual arts, and printing flourished; the city grew and acquired imposing churches and palaces.

Este, Isabella d' See ESTE FAMILY.

Ethiopia See COLONIALISM; ETHIOPIAN WAR.

Ethiopian War

This conflict between Italy and Ethiopia broke out in October 1935. Its antecedents go back to 1896 when the Ethiopians destroyed an Italian expeditionary force at the BATTLE OF ADOWA. The nationalist press kept the memory of Adowa alive and urged revenge for the humiliation. The Fascist regime took up the call, but it was only in the early 1930s that international developments opened up possibilities for a move against Ethiopia. In 1932 BENITO MUSSOLINI took charge of the foreign ministry and made Ethiopia a priority. While he began diplomatic negotiations to give Italy a free hand in Ethiopia, his military advisers drew up contingency plans for military action. In December 1934 border incidents between Ethiopia and the Italian colony of Somalia provided the pretext he was looking for. Lengthy logistical operations required to transport and equip a large army of nearly half a million soldiers followed. Military operations began in early October 1935. Italy had a decisive superiority in numbers and armaments, which included mech-

Four soldiers taking aim during the Italian campaign in Ethiopia *(Library of Congress)*

anized means of transportation, tanks, airplanes, and poison gas. Nevertheless, progress was slowed by the need to build roads and by the cautious attitude of General EMILIO DE BONO. In November 1935 the more competent and energetic General PIETRO BADOGLIO replaced De Bono. Badoglio sped up operations that resulted in the capture of the capital city of Addis Ababa in May 1936. Italian superiority in armaments, air power, and the use of poison gas proved decisive. Mussolini immediately proclaimed military victory in Ethiopia and announced that Italy had gained an empire. Guerrilla resistance against Italian rule continued into WORLD WAR II, when British forces and Ethiopian guerrillas forced the Italians to surrender.

Fascist propaganda touted the conquest of Ethiopia as the supreme achievement of the regime. Much was made of the fact that the victory put an end to the institution of slavery in Ethiopia. The war was undeniably popular at home, where it was perceived as a national victory against international opposition orchestrated by Great Britain, France, and the League of Nations, which imposed economic sanctions against Italy in an unsuccessful attempt to halt the aggression. The government claimed that the victory gave Italy a place among the great colonial powers, provided land for Italian settlers, and unlocked the natural riches of Ethiopia. These promises were not realized. The venture was a drain on the national treasury, diverted scarce capital into unproductive investments, and overextended the country militarily. The political repercussions of the war were equally negative. Seeing the war as a challenge to the system of collective security and the authority of the League of Nations, and pressured by public opinion, the British and French governments opposed Italy's aggression. Nazi Germany did not. Relations with Britain and France never recovered. Italy became dependent on German economic and political support, abandoned its policy of containing Germany and preventing its union with Austria. The origins of the ROME-BERLIN AXIS and PACT OF STEEL can be traced back to the Ethiopian War.

Eugene of Savoy (1663–1736)
(Eugen, Eugène de Savoie-Carignan)
military commander in Austrian service

This prince of the HOUSE OF SAVOY was born and raised in Paris. After being refused a commission in the French army, he entered into the service of the Holy Roman Emperor Leopold I in his war against the Turks. He played a role in the relief of Vienna besieged by the Turks and pursued the Turkish armies into the Balkans, where he helped capture the stronghold of Belgrade. Appointed imperial commander in Hungary, he inflicted further defeats on the Turks. As his military fortunes rose, opposition against him intensified at the imperial court. The emperor made him commander in chief in the WAR OF THE SPANISH SUCCESSION. In that conflict, Eugene defeated the French in northern Italy and, together with the English, at the battle of Blenheim in Bavaria (1704), once again removing a serious threat to Vienna and putting an end to French territorial designs. Further military victories in Flanders and the Rhineland in the same war and against the Turks in other campaigns (1716–18) confirmed his reputation as a formidable military leader. Revered and feted, Eugene amassed the large fortune that enabled him to live out the last years of his life in splendor. The Belvedere Palace that he built in the outskirts of Vienna as his summer home in 1714–23, with the art collection that attests to his good taste, is a major tourist attraction.

Eugenius IV See MARTIN V.

Eurocommunism

A phenomenon of the late 1960s and 1970s, Eurocommunism signaled a shift in tactics by several European Communist parties, including the Italian Communist Party (PCI). Distancing itself from Moscow after the 1968 Soviet invasion of Czechoslovakia, the PCI turned its attention to Western Europe, reaffirmed its support for the principles of political democracy, freedom of speech and association, and cooperation with other political parties. In foreign policy the PCI endorsed Italian membership in NATO and European economic integration. These were the principles of Eurocommunism that Party Secretary ENRICO BERLINGUER upheld and defended against critics within the party. In 1975 Berlinguer went so far as to state publicly that the party was better off in the West than in the Soviet sphere because Western democracy allowed it to pursue its own road to socialism. When the French and Spanish Communist Parties took up a similar line, the phenomenon of Eurocommunism was in full sway. It was not a movement capable of developing independently. It was rather a policy favored by political circumstances. It played to the need to distance the Communist parties of Western Europe from the Soviet Union, from political TERRORISM, and to reassure voters that Communists would wield power responsibly. In Italy, Eurocommunism coincided with the campaign to bring about the HISTORIC COMPROMISE with the Christian Democratic Party (DC). Eurocommunism faded from the scene when cold war tensions revived in the early 1980s, terrorism waned, and power-sharing prospects dimmed. Its legacy was a lasting commitment to Western Europe taken up by the PCI's successor, the Democratic Party of the Left.

European Union (EU)

The EU is the latest and probably definitive designation for the project of European economic and political integration that began after WORLD WAR II. Appalled by the destruction caused by the war, a number of European leaders took the initiative to create a network of mutually beneficial economic and political contacts among the countries of Western Europe that would link them and make war unthinkable in the future. The founding figures and promoters of the European project included the economist Jean Monnet, French foreign minister Robert Schuman, German chancellor Konrad Adenauer, and Italian prime minister ALCIDE DE GASPERI. The first step toward the creation of a common market area in which goods and people could cross national boundaries freely was the creation in 1951 of the European Coal and Steel Community (ECSC) consisting of Belgium, France, Germany, Italy, Luxembourg, and the Netherlands. In 1957 the same six countries signed the Treaty of Rome, which set up the European Economic Community (ECC) and a separate treaty that established the European Atomic Energy Commission (EAEC). The ESCS, ECC, and EAEC merged in 1967 to form a single body, which was later named the European Community (EC). Great Britain, Denmark, and Ireland joined the EC in 1973, Greece in 1981, Spain and Portugal in 1986, Austria, Finland, and Sweden in 1995. In 1992 EC members agreed to adopt uniform tariff regulations, business and social welfare measures, and rules governing border crossings and transportation. By that time the movement toward greater economic and political integration had gained irresistible momentum. The Maastricht Treaty (1994) gave the name of European Union (EU) to the EC to emphasize its commitment to complete economic and political unification. The EU is governed by a commission made up of government-appointed civil servants who wield considerable power, a council of ministers, and a parliament elected directly by the voters of member countries. The powers of the EU's governing bodies are still evolving. The most important and controversial EU decision so far has been the adoption of a common European Currency Unit (ECU), more generally known as the euro, which replaced the national currencies of member nations in the first three months of 2002. In order to belong to the common currency area, member countries must meet stringent financial and monetary requirements designed to insure the stability of the common currency. After heated domestic debates, Italian governments met these requirements in the late 1990s by reducing public spending, the public debt, and social benefits, and raising taxes. Italians have been enthusiastic supporters of the European project from its inception. Public support has held steady in spite of the considerable sacrifices made to meet the criteria for full membership.

Evola, Julius (1898–1974)

Fascist philosopher and neo-Fascist guru figure
Baron Giulio Cesare Andrea Evola was born to a family of the Roman nobility. A man of many talents, Evola was initially influenced by FILIPPO TOMMASO MARINETTI to paint and write poetry in the Futurist manner. A reading of Oswald Spengler's *The Decline of the West* launched Evola on a lifelong quest for a principle that would rejuvenate western culture. That quest led him to the discovery of eastern religions and esoteric strains of spiritualism embedded in western culture. That same path also led him to FASCISM, in which he saw an antidote to the materialism, individualism, and cosmopolitanism that he thought sapped western creativity and the will to prevail. But Evola was never entirely at home in fascism and never joined the Fascist Party. In fascism he valued tradition, leadership, and inspiration, but rejected its populism and modernizing aspirations. He was attracted to fascism as a vehicle for combating the political consequences of the FRENCH REVOLUTION and the social consequences of the Industrial Revolution. In *Imperialismo pagano* (Pagan imperialism, 1928) Evola urged the Fascist regime to reject Christianity and

embrace the pagan worldview of ancient Rome. This did not sit well with the Fascist leadership at a time when the regime was pursuing an accommodation with the CATHOLIC CHURCH. In other writings he rejected capitalism (America) and communism (Soviet Union) as equally objectionable forms of materialism. His rejection of modernity and the idea of progress found full expression in *Rivolta contro il mondo moderno* (Revolt against the modern world, 1934). His writings on race include *Il mito del sangue* (The blood myth, 1935) and *Sintesi di dottrina della razza* (Synthesis of racial doctrine, 1941), in which he developed a theory of racial differences that rejected biological determinism and insisted on the spiritual foundations and attributes of racial identity. The spiritual basis of his racism did not prevent him from espousing pronounced anti-Semitic views. Benito Mussolini regarded Evola as a maverick but accepted his concept of race because it differentiated Italian racial thought from the German version. Evola stuck by Mussolini to the end and did not renounce his views after the fall of the regime. Neo-Fascists and extra-parliamentary groups of the political Right hailed him as their principal philosopher in postwar Italy. In that role he became something of a cult figure (the "Marcuse of the right, only better," said one of his admirers) and cast a long shadow over the culture of the radical Right.

F

Faccio, Rina (1876–1960)
journalist, novelist, and early feminist

Known by her pen name of Sibilla Aleramo, Faccio is remembered principally as the author of the groundbreaking feminist novel *Una donna* (A woman, 1906, English-language edition 1980, with a biographical and critical introduction). Partially autobiographic, the novel told the story of a woman who, trapped in an unhappy marriage, abandoned husband and child to seek personal fulfillment as a writer. A secondary theme of the novel was the clash between the more progressive culture of the North where the protagonist was born and educated and the archaic social mores of the South where she was transplanted. The novel also reflected her real-life anguish at the abandonment of her child and their forced separation. Immediately controversial, the novel won international acclaim, went through several editions, and was translated in all the major European languages. Giovanni Cena (1870–1914), an influential poet, novelist, and critic, was her mentor and lover during this period. Faccio took up feminist causes as a journalist. A series of well-publicized love affairs with prominent intellectual figures gave her an image as a sexually liberated woman. Her politics were complex. She rejected "social feminism" in favor of "individual feminism." In the course of her life she was a socialist, a Fascist, and a communist. Besides *A Woman,* she also wrote *Il passaggio* (The passage, 1919), which was a reflection on another love affair, the collection of essays *Andando e stando* (Going and staying, 1921), *Dal mio diario 1940–1944* (From my diary, 1940–1944, 1945) and a book of poems *Luci della mia sera* (Lights of my evening, 1956).

Facta, Luigi (1861–1930)
last liberal prime minister before the advent of fascism

Were it not for the fact that Facta was prime minister at the time when the Fascists took over the government, he would have remained an obscure politician. A member of parliament from 1892 to 1924, he held several posts in governments headed by GIOVANNI GIOLITTI, whose lead Facta generally followed. Facta was invited to form a government in February 1922 when parliament could not agree to bring back Giolitti. Once in office Facta thought that he could go it alone, but foundered on his inability to contain Fascist street violence. Losing the support of the majority, he resigned in July 1922, but was asked to form a second government when no one else would agree to face the impending crisis. Fascist squads took over towns and staged the "march on Rome" in the last days of October. Facta reacted constitutionally by asking King VICTOR EMMANUEL III to proclaim a state of siege in the country, which would have authorized the army to disperse the Fascists by force. The king at first promised, then changed his mind, leaving Facta little choice but to resign as prime minister (October 29, 1922). The king asked BENITO MUSSOLINI to form a government, thus bringing the government crisis to a close and opening the way to 20 years of Fascist rule. Appointed to the senate in 1924, Facta faded into the political obscurity that he richly deserved.

factory councils See GRAMSCI, ANTONIO.

Falcone, Giovanni See MAFIA.

Fallaci, Oriana (1930–)
journalist and public commentator
Born in Florence, Fallaci belongs to the generation that was formed by the experiences of
WORLD WAR II and the RESISTANCE. Brought up in
the socialist tradition, she has avoided identification with political parties and maintains an
independent position. Her outspokenness is legendary, as is the individuality of her views on
issues of current interest. As a feminist, she supported the campaigns to legalize divorce and
abortion, but always with great sensitivity to the
moral aspects of these controversial issues. She
has exposed the use of police brutality, criticized
American involvement in Vietnam, nuclear
armaments, and repressive regimes around the
world. In a recent interview she has criticized
Italian intellectuals for their failure to condemn
world terrorism. In the 1990s she made her
home in New York, where she still resides. Her
writings in English include *The Useless Sex* (1964),
about women in contemporary society; *If the Sun
Dies* (1966), about the American space program;
Nothing, and So Be It (1972), about the Vietnam
War; *Letter to a Child Never Born* (1976), about
motherhood and society; *Interview with History*
(1976), a series of interviews with world leaders;
A Man (1980), about the Greek freedom fighter
Alexandros Panagoulis; and *Insciallah* (1992), a
novel about life in war-torn Beirut.

familism
Familism is a social science concept that attributes decisive cultural and social importance to
the institution of the family. It derives from
anthropological and sociological studies of Italian
society and is often employed in a pejorative
sense to denote low levels of public spirit, weak
associational habits, and lack of social cooperation beyond the limits of the family among Italians. The American anthropologist Edward C.
Banfield coined the term "amoral familism" in his
Moral Basis of a Backward Society (1958). According to this influential and controversial study of
a southern Italian community, amoral familists
strive to maximize the immediate material
advantage of the nuclear family and assume that
everyone else behaves accordingly. In such a culture there is no place for the concept of a shared
public interest; low levels of civic spirit, association, and cooperative behavior are the norm.
Banfield cautioned that because his research was
limited to one community, his findings should
not be extrapolated indiscriminately. Other
scholars were less cautious, and the controversy
triggered by Banfield's study still reverberates in
the social sciences. Some see amoral familism as
a general trait of Italian society, others find it particularly applicable to southern Italy, and some
reject the concept altogether. Critics point out
that the ethos of a particular community should
not be generalized to a larger society, that empirical research requires historical explanation, and
that Banfield's American perspective distorted his
observations. A criticism less frequently heard is
that attachment to the family is not necessarily
confining, that the family links its members to
the rest of society, is a channel for the diffusion of
social values, and is an essential part of the social
fabric. In other works Banfield himself has seen
in the weakness of family ties the principal reason for the crisis of urban America. With all these
reservations, the concept of familism continues
to influence interpretations of Italian society in
areas as diverse as politics, demography, business,
emigration, and crime. The main difficulty lies in
striking the right balance between the contrasting notions of the family as a limiting institution
and the family as a link in the social chain.

Fanfani, Amintore (1908–1999)
economist and Christian Democratic leader
Born in Arezzo, this prominent political figure of
the postwar era attended the Catholic University
of Milan, held teaching appointments in economics at the Catholic University (1936–55) and
the University of Rome (1955–83). He authored

several important studies, including *Storia del capitalismo* (History of capitalism, 1933), *Catholicism, Protestantism, and Capitalism* (1935, 1984), *Dal mercantilismo al liberalismo* (From mercantilism to economic liberalism, 1936), and *Storia delle dottrine economiche dall'antichità al XIX secolo* (A history of economic thought from ancient times to the nineteenth century, 1955). Like other faculty members at the Catholic University, in the 1930s Fanfani favored economic CORPORATISM and supported the Fascist regime's racial and geopolitical policies. During WORLD WAR II he took refuge in Switzerland and joined the anti-Fascist RESISTANCE as a Christian Democrat. In 1946 he was appointed to the national directorate of the Christian Democratic Party (DC) and represented the party in the constituent assembly that prepared the CONSTITUTION of the Italian republic. He was a parliamentary deputy (1948–63) and senator (1968–72). In 1972 he was appointed senator for life in recognition of his outstanding public service. As party secretary (1954–59) he centralized power in the hands of the national directorate, reduced the influence of local bosses, loosened party ties to the CATHOLIC CHURCH, and worked to bring about the OPENING TO THE LEFT. He served repeatedly as prime minister (1954, 1958–59, 1960–63, 1982–83, 1987) and was also minister of the interior and foreign minister in various governments. As foreign minister, Fanfani attempted to give Italy a more active and independent role in foreign affairs. A fixture of the political scene until the 1980s, Fanfani was also one of the more colorful and charismatic figures of a political system that was impervious to charisma.

Fanfulla della Domenica (Il) See

MARTINI, FERDINANDO.

Farinacci, Roberto (1892–1945)
Fascist local boss, party strongman, and critic of Benito Mussolini

Farinacci was born in the southern town of Isernia to a family of modest means. The family moved to Cremona when Roberto was 16. Temperamentally unsuited to study, he dropped out of school and began working as a telegraph operator for the state railways at the age of 17. His political debut was as a labor organizer and follower of the moderate socialist LEONIDA BISSOLATI. Farinacci favored Italian intervention in WORLD WAR I, served in the army, severed his ties with the Socialist Party at the end of the war, and joined Mussolini's Fascist movement in 1919. Taking advantage of special laws for war veterans, he completed his secondary studies, and obtained a law degree with a plagiarized dissertation (1923). By then FASCISM was in power and Farinacci was a powerful political figure. As an intransigent Fascist he demanded more power for the Fascist Party and criticized Mussolini for being too accommodating toward the opposition. During the MATTEOTTI crisis he called for repressive actions to silence the opposition and eliminate dissent within the country. BENITO MUSSOLINI appointed him to the post of party secretary in February 1925. In that role, he set the foundations of the regime by muzzling the press, eliminating the opposition in and outside parliament, and expanding the role of the party. Mussolini dismissed him in March 1926 to curb his growing power. Farinacci then retreated to his fief in Cremona, where he spoke out as a Fascist dissident with his newspaper *Cremona Nuova*. In 1934 Farinacci and Mussolini were reconciled, and Farinacci was admitted to the Fascist Grand Council that was theoretically in charge of party affairs. He served in the air force during the ETHIOPIAN WAR, when he accidentally lost his right hand fishing with explosives. In the late 1930s Farinacci became an ardent admirer of Hitler and the Nazi regime and an outspoken anti-Semite. In 1939 he urged Mussolini to go to war on Germany's side. He served again in the military during WORLD WAR II. When Mussolini was ousted in July 1943, Farinacci took refuge in Germany, where he broadcast messages praising the German army and urging Italians to keep fighting on Germany's side. He collaborated with the Germans during the period of the ITALIAN

SOCIAL REPUBLIC, was arrested by resistance fighters while trying to escape to Switzerland and shot on April 28, 1945. His steady criticism of Mussolini's policies earned him the nickname of "mother-in-law of the regime."

Farinelli See CASTRATI.

Farini, Luigi Carlo (1812–1866)
political conspirator and patriot
Born in Ravenna, Farini was drawn into political conspiracy against the papal government at an early age. He took a degree in medicine at the University of Bologna after participating in the REVOLUTION of 1831. His ties to SECRET SOCIETIES interfered with his medical practice and research, forcing him to abandon the PAPAL STATES and find refuge in more liberal Tuscany. The accession of PIUS IX to the papal throne in 1846 and the pope's early reforms drew Farini back to the Papal States. He served as secretary general in the Ministry of the Interior (1847–48), as liaison to King CHARLES ALBERT of Piedmont-Sardinia, as a deputy in the first elected Roman parliament, and adviser to Prime Minister PELLEGRINO ROSSI. Moderately liberal, Farini favored constitutional monarchy and opposed the ROMAN REPUBLIC OF 1849. After 1848 Farini became a Piedmontese citizen, collaborated with CAVOUR, was elected to the Piedmontese parliament (1849–60) and the Italian parliament (1860–65). In 1859 as "dictator" of Emilia-Romagna, he forced the union of that region with Piedmont, which hastened the process of national unification. He also rendered important services to the cause of national unification in 1860 as viceroy in southern Italy. Such activity took its toll. By the time he was appointed Italian prime minister (1862–63) he was on the verge of mental collapse. Erratic behavior and moments of outright insanity (he reportedly threatened the king with a knife for refusing to declare war on Russia) cut short his term of office and ended his political career.

Farnese, Alessandro (1545–1592)
military commander serving the Spanish monarchy
This member of the FARNESE FAMILY held the title of duke of Parma and Piacenza (1586–92) and was a distinguished military commander. He began his military training in his early teens, developed into an excellent horseman and marksman, and established his reputation with individual acts of valor that caught the attention of powerful personages. He stood out for bravery at the BATTLE OF LEPANTO (1571), caught the eye of Philip II of Spain, and was appointed governor of the Spanish Netherlands in 1577. He succeeded in recovering for the Spaniards the southern provinces lost to the forces of the Protestant ruler William of Orange. Farnese's success permanently separated the northern provinces from the southern, marking the modern boundary between Belgium and the Netherlands. His next assignment was to assemble troops and ships for a projected invasion of England. The failure of the Spanish Armada (1588) tarnished Farnese's reputation. He assumed the title of duke of Parma and Piacenza at the death of his father in 1586 but never took personal charge of his domain. He died from battle wounds suffered in a military campaign against the Protestant forces of Henry IV of France and was buried in Parma.

Farnese, Elisabetta See ALBERONI, GIULIO; FARNESE FAMILY.

Farnese family
The Farnese family ruled the duchy of PARMA and Piacenza from 1545 until 1731. The family fortunes were always closely tied to those of the PAPACY from the time of its return to Rome from France in the early 15th century. The men, soldiers first of all, managed by force of arms to carve a small state out of disparate family holdings. Emperor CHARLES V bestowed on them the ducal title at the urging of Pope PAUL III, a family member who raised their fortunes to new heights. The

first duke, Pier Luigi Farnese (1503–47), was an ambitious ruler who centralized power in his own hands, built fortresses, rebuilt Piacenza, and was murdered by a jealous political rival. Subsequent dukes held on to their domains by military ruthlessness, adroit diplomacy, and advantageous marriages. The marriage in 1538 of Ottavio Farnese (1524–86) to Margaret of Austria, the natural daughter of Charles V, broadened the scope of Farnese politics from Italy to the rest of Europe. ALESSANDRO FARNESE, son of Ottavio and Margaret, took full advantage of the new opportunities to play an important role in the wars of the Spanish Empire. The Farnese dynasty became extinct upon the death of Antonio Farnese (1679–1731), the last male member of the family, who died childless, and the duchy became a possession of the Spanish BOURBONS. The last female member of the family was Elisabetta Farnese (1692–1766). A niece of Antonio Farnese, Elisabetta became queen of Spain in 1714 by marrying King Philip V at the urging of Cardinal GIULIO ALBERONI. Gaining much influence at court, she worked to recover territories lost during the WAR OF THE SPANISH SUCCESSION and secure thrones for her children. Her son CHARLES OF BOURBON ruled in Parma and Piacenza, Naples and Sicily, establishing the Bourbon dynasty securely on Italian soil.

Fasci Siciliani
Sicilian protest movement

The movement known as the Fasci Siciliani owes its name to the *fasci* (clubs or leagues) of workers that were formed on the island of Sicily in the early 1890s. Giuseppe De Felice Giuffrida (1859–1920) and Rosario Garibaldi Bosco (1865–1936) founded the first fasci in Catania (1891) and Palermo (1892) respectively. These urban centers provided direction for popular unrest that spread throughout the island in 1893–94 in the wake of a severe crisis of agricultural exports brought on by a tariff war with France. At the same time, competition from American producers hurt the sulfur industry in the western part of the island. Bosco and De Felice Giuffrida put a socialist

imprint on the unrest, but the demonstrators who roamed the island defied simple political characterization. Religion motivated some, others were monarchists who called for justice from the king, still others were republicans. Demands included the abolition of taxes, land reform, reform of local administrations, and new labor contracts. Leaders claimed a membership of 300,000 and political candidates sponsored by the fasci won seats in local councils. By the end of 1893 there were illegal occupations of land, unauthorized gatherings, and confrontations with the police. FRANCESCO CRISPI became prime minister in December 1893, imposed martial law, and dispatched 40,000 troops to the island. Crispi regarded the fasci as part of a larger subversive plan to destabilize the government and separate Sicily from the rest of Italy. His fears played into the hands of local notables who feared losing control of municipal administrations. The repression restored law and order, but also intensified regional distrust of national government, encouraged organized crime, and accelerated emigration from the island.

fascism
political ideology behind the regime and personal dictatorship of Benito Mussolini

The term *fascism* derives from *fascio*, a "bundle of sticks" carried by ancient Roman officials, the lictors, as a symbol of their authority and of the power of unity. Fascists often referred to their movement as the *fascio littorio* to link their movement and regime to ancient Rome. The cult of ancient Rome, or *romanità*, was an important component of Fascist ideology. Fascism saw the empire of ancient Rome as an inspiring example and believed that ancient Romans succeeded because they stood united, willingly sacrificing their personal interests for the greater good of Rome. Fascism insisted that individuals find fulfillment in the state as the modern embodiment of the collective good.

A more recent derivation of the term points to another important aspect of fascism. In 19th-century Italian politics, individuals and groups of different political provenance sometimes formed a *fascio* to press a specific issue or agenda. (The FASCI SICILIANI were an example of one such formation.) In this latter sense, therefore, a *fascio* (*fasci* in the plural) is the Italian equivalent of the French *ligue* or the German *Bund*, which also indicated the union of disparate political elements in pursuit of a common goal.

In the spirit of unity of action, FILIPPO CORRIDONI and BENITO MUSSOLINI formed the Fasci di Azione Rivoluzionaria (Fasces for Revolutionary Action) to push for Italian intervention in WORLD WAR I. Fasci di Combattimento (Fighting Fasces) was the name of the movement that Mussolini founded in Milan on March 23, 1919. It, too, brought together people of differing political persuasions united to demand adequate compensation for war veterans' and Italy's contributions to the war effort. Fascism, born from the euphoria of military victory, differed from all other political ideologies of the 20th century in idealizing war and combat as positive goods. Men were born to be warriors. In Mussolini's striking phrase, "War is to man what motherhood is to woman."

But there was more to fascism than the pursuit of military triumphs and national glory. As GIOVANNI GENTILE, the leading philosopher of Italian fascism, pointed out, fascism did not subscribe to any rigid ideology, for to subscribe to any fixed set of beliefs was to renounce the right to stay in touch with changing reality, and staying in touch with reality was necessary for political survival and success. Fascism could not follow set rules, conventional wisdom, or majority opinion. It needed a leader with a well-developed political sense who could negotiate the shifting currents of history, adjust his political course accordingly, and compel others to follow his lead. In the eyes of many Fascists, Mussolini was precisely such a leader. Fascism was therefore in danger of becoming a personality cult, and indeed many made no distinction between *fascismo* and *mussolinismo*. In time, the cult of the Duce (Leader) took precedence over all other considerations. Attempts to define fascism consequently run into the difficulty

that fascism did not want to be defined. Perhaps the best way to understand fascism in its many manifestations is to stop looking for general definitions and to reflect instead on how specific "fascisms" responded to historical developments.

In Italy, fascism was a product of war. In 1919 Mussolini understood very clearly that the way to gain immediate political leverage was to play to the sentiments of millions of demobilized war veterans hungry for compensation and recognition. He appealed to them as the "aristocracy of the trenches" who had won the right to govern the country by fighting and winning the war. In war they had acquired the skills of combat that could be put to political use; indeed, the Fascist squads injected military discipline and organized violence into Italian politics from the start. The movement was designed to appeal to men formed by the experience of war. Many were former officers who had found fulfillment in combat, were accustomed to command, and unwilling or unable to reenter civilian life. Such men were useful but also difficult to control for political purpose. To gain a better hold on his followers, Mussolini insisted on transforming the movement into a regular party.

The National Fascist Party (PNF) was thus born in November 1921 with an ideology that set it apart from the other main ideologies of the moment. Fascism rejected communism, socialism, and liberal democracy as unpatriotic: communism and socialism because they called for class struggle and put class interests ahead of the national interest, and liberal democracy because it was individualistic and prey to party politics. Fascism's emphatic call for national unity seemed all the more urgent at a time when the Bolsheviks had come to power and communism seemed poised to spill outside the Soviet Union. That apparent threat scared many who might not otherwise have turned to fascism. The church, landowners, industrialists, and middle-class professionals of all descriptions accepted fascism as an alternative to communism, even when they did not share its warlike ethic and desire for radical change. They were willing to accept Fascist violence, hoping that it was a passing phenomenon justified by the dangers of the moment.

Fascism could not have come to power without the active and passive support of these *fiancheggiatori* (fellow travelers). In 1921–22 Fascist Black Shirts, so called because of the uniform they wore, stepped up their violence against political opponents. They targeted Socialists, Catholics, and liberals individually and collectively. In August 1922 they defeated a general strike called by the Socialists, then systematically began to seize control of towns and local administrations.

The transformation of the movement into a party controlled from the top met resistance from local bosses, or *ras*, jealous of their autonomy and suspicious of Mussolini. ITALO BALBO and ROBERTO FARINACCI were typical *ras* who managed to retain a measure of independence. *Rassismo* was a centrifugal force that was never completely eradicated. Fascism remained to the end a tense union of political bosses, each a small-scale replica of the Duce, jealous of their power and prerogatives, reluctant to acknowledge a superior authority, but demanding blind obedience from their subordinates. Mussolini's dominance rested on his persuasive abilities, which he exercised effectively in speech and writing, his political intelligence, ability to exploit rivalries among his subordinates, and make himself the ultimate arbiter of disputes. The Fascists seized power at the national level in the last days of October 1922, with the so-called March on Rome. Some 30,000 Black Shirts converged on the capital city, King VICTOR EMMANUEL III refused to sign a decree ordering the army to disperse them by force, and invited Mussolini to form a government. The king's invitation ran counter to the established practice of having a majority leader form the government, but there were precedents for it, so it was not strictly speaking unconstitutional. Mussolini headed a small Fascist delegation in parliament but could count on the support of deputies from other political parties, including many liberals who were willing to give the Fascists a chance to govern.

Mussolini's appointment as prime minister proved to be only the first step toward the consolidation of power in Fascist hands. The so-called Acerbo Law (see GIACOMO ACERBO) of 1923 gave the Fascists and their closest allies the opportunity to become the governing majority. The national elections of April 1924 gave them a decisive majority in parliament. Socialist leader GIACOMO MATTEOTTI denounced Fascist electoral irregularities, was promptly murdered by Fascist henchmen, and Mussolini's government tottered in the ensuing political scandal and crisis. After temporizing indecisively for several months, Mussolini called on the Fascist squads to silence the opposition.

The speech of January 3, 1925, in which he took historical (but not legal) responsibility for the assassination of Matteotti and the use of violence, marks the beginning of Mussolini's personal dictatorship and of the Fascist regime. The special laws of 1925–26 curtailed civil liberties, established special political tribunals, and eliminated the last vestiges of political opposition. A secret police organization, known cryptically as OVRA, was set up to identify and root out political opponents. Legal reforms broadened Mussolini's power. He no longer had to rely on parliament to maintain his position, was no longer simply head of government, but head of the state responsible only to the king. Multiparty elections were abolished, and only officially approved candidates could run for public office. Workers and employers had to join officially recognized associations, the only ones authorized to bargain collectively for all employers and workers. CORPORATISM was the social ideology of the regime. A ministry of corporations and a national council of corporations were designed to guide labor relations and economic policy. They never had full power, but their existence bolstered the regime's claim that it was engaging in a daring and novel social experiment. Roberto Farinacci, appointed party secretary in 1925, purged dissidents and tightened party discipline. Local administrations were no longer run by elected municipal councils, but by Fascist officials called *podestà*. The powers of PREFECTS were expanded, giving the central government more control over local affairs. Prefects and *podestà* were the regime's two poles of power, the first representing the authority of the state, the second that of the party. State authority generally prevailed.

The regime did not rely solely on force and repression. It won popular support and consolidated power with new agencies to assist people in need, protect the health and well-being of mothers and children, eradicate disease and illiteracy, organize sports, promote physical fitness, and reclaim unproductive land. The party organized patriotic rituals and mass demonstrations. The OPERA NAZIONALE DOPOLAVORO (After-Work, or Leisure Time, Organization), founded in 1925, was by far the most popular innovation of the regime. All the more effective for avoiding outright political propaganda, it brought mass entertainments and recreational activities to millions of people in cities and the countryside. It organized excursions and group vacations, prepared meals, presented plays and movies at reduced prices, or brought people together to socialize and listen to the radio. The settlement in 1929 of the ROMAN QUESTION that ended the conflict of CHURCH AND STATE was also popular. The result was an overwhelming endorsement of the regime in the national plebiscite of 1929. The vote was not free, but an overwhelming majority did feel that fascism had brought order to the country, improved the economy, reduced social differences, and promoted national pride. Internal resistance to the regime all but ceased in the early 1930s.

FOREIGN POLICY took precedence over domestic affairs in the 1930s. Fascism never disguised the fact that its intention was to make Italy into a great military power, but it began cautiously. The state of the armed forces was a topic of constant discussion. The regime courted military officers and went out of its way to eliminate potential causes of friction between the regular armed forces and the voluntary armed militia that served the party. But there were few opportunities for military adventures in the 1920s. In that decade Italian diplomacy behaved sensibly

and generally favored peace initiatives. The occupation of the Greek island of Corfu in 1923 was the exception, but it was a short-lived and isolated incident. The 1930s were different. The Great Depression, the rise of Nazi Germany, rampant nationalism, rising tensions in Asia, and the inability of the League of Nations to deal with major international crises upset the balance of power.

Mussolini took over the office of foreign minister in 1932, thereby assuming personal control of foreign policy and sidelining career diplomats whom he found too cautious and peace loving. He instructed his military experts to prepare plans for war against Ethiopia, a land that Italy had long coveted as a colony. Achieving a spectacular victory in Africa became the principal goal of his personal diplomacy. It meant making sure that Italy would not face a military threat in Europe or the Mediterranean while conducting a military campaign far from home, hence, the FOUR-POWER PACT, the STRESA CONFERENCE, and the moves to contain the power of Nazi Germany. Mussolini was determined to prevent the union of Germany and Austria, which would have rendered Italy's northern border less secure and altered the balance of power in Europe. Military success in the ETHIOPIAN WAR came at high political cost. Mussolini seriously underestimated the negative international reaction. The war overextended Italy militarily and financially, inflicted lasting damage on Italy's relations with Great Britain and France, and left Mussolini with little choice but to avoid diplomatic isolation by drawing closer to Nazi Germany. The alliance was cemented by Italian-German cooperation in the Spanish civil war, the ROME-BERLIN AXIS, and the PACT OF STEEL that tied Italy to Germany. With Germany increasingly assertive and dominant on the European continent, Italian ambitions focused on Africa and the Mediterranean region. *Romanità,* the cult of ancient Rome, took on concrete meaning. By calling the Mediterranean *Mare nostrum* (Our sea), fascism claimed for Italy a role of dominance like that of ancient Rome. The slogans "Book and Rifle" and "War Is to Man What Motherhood Is to Woman" reflected the unabashed warlike ethic of fascism. Fascism has the dubious distinction of being the only modern ideology that openly endorses war and conquest as positive benefits.

Mussolini took no pleasure in the role of mediator that he played at the Munich Peace Conference of September 1938. There he was credited with having saved the peace of Europe by averting a military showdown over the fate of Czechoslovakia, but he preferred to be hailed as the warrior who gathered the spoils of war. Awed by Hitler, but also jealous of his successes, in April 1939 he ordered the occupation of ALBANIA to counteract his fellow dictator's invasion of Czechoslovakia. By then he was only able to react to the initiatives of others. Torn between the desire for conquest and fear of the consequences of a major war, he hesitated when Great Britain and France declared war on Germany in September 1939. Bellicose tendencies, the warlike ethic of fascism, and the prospect of a rapid German victory made it difficult and embarrassing to keep Italy out of war. When Mussolini did commit Italy to WORLD WAR II in June 1940, he hoped to have just enough time to perform credibly in war and occupy some territory before claiming even bigger spoils at the peace table, in view of the certain victory. The expectation of a decisive success proved to be the fatal gamble that resulted in defeat and ruin. It was a tragic but logical conclusion for a regime that considered war the ultimate test of success. In the end fascism got what it wished for.

Fatti di maggio

Disturbances throughout Italy in May 1898 have gone down in history as the Fatti di maggio, or Events of May. There was widespread resentment of high taxes, military conscription, arbitrary police methods, repression of labor unions, government corruption, and limited voting rights. Socialist propaganda fanned the discontent, but the immediate cause of the demonstrations was the disruption in the supply of wheat caused by a bad harvest in 1897 and impediments to trade attributable to the Spanish-

American War. Cries of "bread and work" were raised in demonstrations that spread from south to north in places like Bari, Naples, Rome, Florence, and throughout the Po Valley. Violence broke out in Milan May 7–10 when demonstrators clashed with the police. Workers went out on strike, the government called out the army and put the city under martial law. Eighty demonstrators and two soldiers were killed, and 450 others were wounded in street fights. Thousands were arrested, including the most prominent leaders of the socialist and clerical opposition. The military overreaction brought down the government, created a constitutional crisis, and strengthened the opposition. When King UMBERTO I conferred a military decoration on the general in charge of the repression, popular hatred of the monarchy reached new heights. Gaetano Bresci (1869–1901), an immigrant and anarchist working in Paterson, New Jersey, resolved to avenge the victims of repression. He went back to Italy and, on July 29, 1900, shot the king to death. The Fatti di maggio marked the height of popular discontent with government, but also set in motion a series of events that led to liberal reforms.

Fattori, Giovanni See MACCHIAIOLI.

federalism

In Italy and other European countries federalism stands for decentralization of government power and devolution of the powers of the national government to regional or local administrations. Since national unification, Italy has had strong national government modeled on the French or Napoleonic system of centralized administration. But critics of that model have argued that centralized administration is poorly suited to Italy's historical and cultural traditions. They have pointed to the diversity of Renaissance city-states and preunification regional states, the vitality of regional cultures, and the complex GEOGRAPHY as reasons for decentralized government. CARLO CATTANEO and VINCENZO GIOBERTI,

among others, raised the issue in the RISORGI-
MENTO, arguing that Italy should be unified as a
loose federation of states. GIUSEPPE MAZZINI
believed in a national government with broad
political powers, but also believed in strong local
administrations. The issue was decided in favor
of strong national government by extending the
administration of the Kingdom of SARDINIA to
the entire national territory.

Federalists kept up the fight after national
unification, charging that the national government was responsible for a variety of problems,
including BRIGANDAGE and the SOUTHERN QUES-
TION. Opponents of federalism responded that a
strong national government was needed to
maintain the fragile unity of the state, reduce
regional disparities, and give Italy international
clout. FASCISM used that last argument to further
centralize power in the hands of public officials.
Federalists had a new opportunity to press their
case after the fall of the Fascist regime. The issue
figured prominently in the proceedings of the
constitutional assembly that produced the CON-
STITUTION of the Italian republic, which has been
in effect since 1948. The republican constitution
endorses REGIONALISM based on a division of
powers between the national government and
regional administrations. But according to the
constitution the powers of regional administration are derivative. They are granted by the
national government, and all powers not specifically granted to the regions belong to the national
government. In a truly federal system the opposite would be the case.

Federalism is once again on the national
agenda. "League movements" dating to the 1980s
demand administrative decentralization, curbs
on the powers of the national government in
Rome, and reduced national taxation and public
spending. UMBERTO BOSSI and his LEGA NORD initially insisted on outright separation of North and
South, but have scaled down their demands in
favor of limiting the power of the national government to redistribute resources among the
regions. Reductions in public spending and Italian membership in the EUROPEAN UNION and the
European Monetary System have taken the wind

out of their sails. At the beginning of the 21st
century the issue is no longer separation of the
regions but a redistribution of powers between
the national and regional governments.

Federati See SECRET SOCIETIES.

Federterra (Federazione Nazionale dei Lavoratori della Terra)

Founded in 1901 in Bologna, Federterra (the
National Federation of Agricultural Workers) set
out to organize landless workers and sharecroppers. Federterra was affiliated with the General
Confederation of Labor (CGL) and was supported
politically by the Socialist Party (PSI), but set its
own policies and goals. It was the largest organization of land workers and an important
source of mass support for the Socialist Party, the
only one that could claim a large following
among land workers. In 1914 it represented
almost 283,000 workers and 2,089 local leagues;
87 percent of its members were landless workers from the Po Valley, where large-scale agriculture was most developed, but it also
represented workers from the southern regions
of Puglia and Sicily. Its slogan was *la terra ai con-
tadini* (land to the peasants), but it did not seek
to transform landless workers into peasant proprietors, nor did it seriously pursue land expropriation and collectivization. It concentrated
instead on becoming the sole representative of
landless workers, establishing employment
offices, and negotiating labor contracts. It also
adopted an aggressive policy of using strikes to
pressure landlords and state officials into making concessions. It declared its intent to look
after the interests of poorer workers and equal-
ize earnings. It became less militant after engaging in costly strikes and losing members in
1904–06. It distanced itself from the Socialist
Party, avoided using strikes for political purposes, concentrated on providing services for its
members, and sought government support for
worker cooperatives. Like the Socialist Party,
Federterra never resolved the contradiction

between its long-term goals of radical social change and the day-to-day pursuit of piecemeal reforms. After a period of intense activity in 1919–20, it suffered losses at the hands of Fascist armed squads, aided by landlords. Fascist repression forced it out of existence in 1926.

Federzoni, Luigi (1878–1967)
journalist, polemicist, nationalist, and Fascist figure

Born and educated in Bologna, Federzoni started out as a novelist, essayist, and literary critic for several newspapers. In 1910 he was among the founders of the ITALIAN NATIONALIST ASSOCIATION and served on the editorial board of the association's review *L'Idea Nazionale,* which backed Italy's conquest of Libya in the ITALIAN-TURKISH WAR, attacked FREEMASONRY and the Italian Socialist Party (PSI). Federzoni was one of six nationalists elected to parliament in 1913. He held his parliamentary seat as a nationalist until 1923. As a member of parliament, secretary of the Italian National Association, and journalist, Federzoni worked to promote Italian intervention in WORLD WAR I. Volunteering for military service, he served in the artillery and air force, and was decorated three times for bravery. He did not support BENITO MUSSOLINI's bid for power and was not enthusiastic about the fusion of NATIONALISM and FASCISM that took place in 1923. Still, Federzoni served the Fascist regime well in various capacities. As minister of colonies (1922–24, 1926–28) he reorganized the colonial administration. As interior minister (1924–26) during the MATTEOTTI crisis he saw to it that Mussolini was protected from his opponents. Although he did this to safeguard the authority of the state rather than to protect the Fascists, he nevertheless rendered fascism a signal service at a moment of grave crisis. Federzoni's policies in effect set the course for the Fascist regime by relying more on the authority of the state and the power of the police, and discouraging the radical aspirations of Fascist ideologues. He was not well liked by many Fascists, who saw him as a conservative impediment to their notions of

radical reorganization. Mussolini respected but never fully trusted him. Federzoni was aloof, professorial, and more loyal to the king than the Duce. Mussolini therefore relegated Federzoni to prestigious but politically innocuous posts, including the presidency of the senate (1929–39) and of the ITALIAN ACADEMY (1938–43). In July 1943 Federzoni was among those members of the Fascist Grand Council who voted to oust Mussolini and give powers of command to the king. He thus helped bring down the curtain on the Fascist regime. In 1945 he was sentenced to life imprisonment as a Fascist collaborator, but was amnestied in 1947. He taught Italian literature in Portugal for a time, and returned to Italy unmolested in 1951.

Fellini, Federico (1920–1993)
innovative film director

Familiar to millions of moviegoers as the director of such renowned films as *La strada* (1954), *Le notti di Cabiria* (1956), *La dolce vita* (1959), and *8 1/2* (1963), Fellini began his career in the movies in wartime Italy as a scriptwriter. Born in the Romagna region, in 1939 he moved to Rome where he worked for a while as a newspaper cartoonist. In 1943 he married the actress Giulietta Masina (1921–94), met ROBERTO ROSSELLINI in 1945, and was caught up in the rise of cinematic NEOREALISM. With *I vitelloni* (1953), a tale of five pathetic youths trapped in the boredom of provincial life, he scored his first commercial success. It was also the first film to show Fellini's distinctive talent for rendering states of mind. In that sense, *I Vitelloni* marked a break with Neorealist attempts to portray the details of daily life. Fellini's characters struggle with questions of identity, confront existential problems, and look for meaning in life, issues that seemed particularly relevant to audiences at a time when accelerated social change threatened familiar ways and values. Fellini's films blur the distinction between the real and the perceived; the dilemmas that they confront are those of postmodern man groping his way in a world of uncertainty. The film that blurs the line between the real and

Federico Fellini *(Library of Congress)*

the imagined most successfully is *8 1/2*. Perhaps autobiographical in that it depicts a film director's search for truth and meaning, *8 1/2* seems to be the most felt and revealing of Fellini's films. Existential agonizing points to nostalgia for a past imagined as simpler than the present. Fellini also expressed that sense of nostalgia in *Amarcord* (I Remember, 1973), a dream-like depiction of life in the Romagna of Fellini's childhood. Never one to deliver political messages or diatribes, in *Amarcord* Fellini recollects the Fascist period as a kind of carnival diversion from the realities of everyday life and as a period of almost childlike innocence. More than any other film director, Fellini faithfully interpreted the mood and outlook of the postwar generation. Besides being great entertainment, his films stand out as cultural documents.

Feltrinelli, Giangiacomo (1926–1972)
publisher and political radical
This successful publisher showed a perplexing combination of shrewd business savvy and political extremism. Largely self-educated (he completed one term at an exclusive secondary school),

he joined the Communist Party (PCI) in 1945, took over the business interests of his wealthy Milanese family, and used his financial resources in support of various left-wing causes. In 1951 he founded the Feltrinelli Institute in Milan, with an impressive library and archive for the study of socialism and organized labor. In 1955 he launched the Feltrinelli Publishing House, which distinguished itself for the originality and high quality of its publications. Its two most successful ventures were the publication of Boris Pasternak's novel *Dr. Zhivago* (1957), which was smuggled out of the Soviet Union and given to Feltrinelli by a member of the Italian Communist Party, and of Giuseppe di Lampedusa's novel *Il gattopardo* (*The Leopard*, 1958). Both proved to be huge commercial and literary successes that confirmed Feltrinelli's reputation as a shrewd and discerning publisher. He left the Communist Party in 1958, moving ideologically toward the more radical positions of the New Left in the 1960s. Nuclear disarmament, environmentalism, radical psychiatry, and anticolonialism became the consuming causes of his final years. He linked up with anarchist groups, expressed contempt for formal learning, filled his bookshops with radical literature, and called for a general strike to bring down the capitalist system. He traveled to developing countries to stoke the fires of revolution against the former colonial powers. Feltrinelli disappeared from circulation in 1969, adopted the underground name of Osvaldo, and joined the ranks of terrorists who hoped to bring down the state with acts of violence. He died when a bomb he was attaching to an electric pylon blew up accidentally. As a successful businessman turned terrorist, Feltrinelli holds a unique place in the annals of Italian business and radicalism.

feminism
movement for women's rights in the home, workplace, and public life
Feminism has encountered strong opposition in Italy. Powerful groups, including the CATHOLIC CHURCH and its political allies and the weight of

public opinion have hindered the spread of feminist ideas, which have nevertheless made extensive gains. The role of women in society has been a constant issue and feminist voices have been heard since national unification. GIUSEPPE MAZZINI called on women to join the fight for national independence and social justice and promised them the vote. One of his followers was ANNA MARIA MOZZONI, who is considered the founder of the Italian feminist movement. In 1881 she founded the League for the Advancement of Women's Rights, calling on women to fight their own battles and not rely on movements and institutions that they themselves did not control.

In Mozzoni's time it was not feminism that took women out of the home, but modernization changes in the economy that put women in factories, offices, and classrooms. As workers, women joined labor unions, strikes, and demonstrations. As teachers and students they acquired and imparted educational skills that made for greater social mobility and independence. SIBILLA ALERAMO's widely read feminist novel *A Woman* (1906) dramatized the plight and struggle for personal liberation of an educated woman trapped in an archaic system of social relations. ANNA KULISCIOFF insisted that socialists pay attention to women's issues. Her call made the Italian Socialist Party (PSI) an important vehicle for women's rights. It demanded better treatment for women in the workplace and under the law, but was also a limited vehicle because it championed the rights of women as members of the working class rather than as women and citizens.

The advent of FASCISM was a setback for the feminist movement. Fascist ideology valued women as mothers and wives, encouraged large families, criminalized birth control and abortion, and favored men in the workplace. Nevertheless, women did make advances in education during the Fascist period, joined organizations that took them out of the home in large numbers, benefited from health measures and domestic programs designed specifically for them, and generally supported the regime much as men did. Women showed more resistance than men to Fascist idealization of war and militarism. During WORLD WAR II women joined or collaborated with the anti-Fascist RESISTANCE movement. In September 1944 women from the resistance and from the southern provinces recently liberated by the Allies founded the *Unione Donne Italiane* (UDI), which carried on the struggle for women's rights into the postwar period. Women's most important political gain after the war was the right to vote, exercised for the first time in the elections of 1946. UDI's weekly *Noi Donne* (We Women) had a wide distribution. Although closely tied to the Communist Party (PCI), it downplayed politics and focused on women's practical needs at home and in the workplace.

A more combative and ideological generation of feminists came of age in the 1970s. The student revolts of 1968–69, the emergence of the New Left, changing notions of personal liberation and fulfillment influenced Italian feminism in that crucial decade. ABORTION, BIRTH CONTROL, DIVORCE, family rights, sexual violence, women's ownership and control of their bodies were the new issues. The new feminist periodical *effe* (for the Italian pronunciation of the letter "f," as in feminism) struck a militant tone that appealed to radical feminists, but disconcerted traditional feminists and their political allies. In the 1970s Italian feminism won some impressive victories, but also splintered into small groups pursuing different agendas, distanced itself from the PCI, which many women found too moderate or hesitant, and relied instead on the much smaller but more vocal Radical Party. Perhaps more important in the long run than specific victories on the issues of abortion, birth control, divorce, and family legislation is the feminist campaign to change cultural attitudes toward sexual differences, encourage new forms of socializing between men and women, and strike the proper balance between gender equality and recognition of the special needs of women as women.

Ferdinand I (1751–1825)
king of Naples and Sicily (1759–1825)
This member of the BOURBON dynasty ruling in Naples appears with different numerations.

From 1759 to 1815 he ruled in Sicily as Ferdinand III and in Naples as Ferdinand IV, the two territories being considered distinct possessions of the monarch. He became Ferdinand I when the two territories were united in 1816 as the KINGDOM OF THE TWO SICILIES. The drop in numeration prompted the malicious quip that with one more political change he would become Ferdinand 0. Ferdinand responded to fundamental shifts in culture and international relations that occurred during his long reign in a manner typical of most sovereigns of his generation. Assuming the throne as a minor, he had to rely heavily on advisers and on the authority of his father CHARLES OF BOURBON, who in 1759 exchanged the throne of Naples for that of Spain, but continued to run the affairs of Naples from afar. When Ferdinand came of age in 1767 he relied heavily on the advice of BERNARDO TANUCCI, who continued the process of reform begun under Charles. In 1776 Ferdinand married MARIE CAROLINE, a daughter of Empress MARIA THERESA of Austria.

Caroline played an important role in Ferdinand's life and in the affairs of the court. His devotion to her was such that detractors blamed her for many things that went wrong in Ferdinand's reign. Marie Caroline's influence probably was decisive in orienting Ferdinand's foreign policy away from Spain and toward Austria. The shift had profound implications when Naples sided with Austria during the Napoleonic Wars. The royal couple was also blamed for forsaking reform, but backing away from reform was a general European trend in the 1790s and after the FRENCH REVOLUTION. The pro-French Jacobin uprising of 1799 forced the royal family to seek refuge in Sicily. When Ferdinand returned to Naples, he carried out a thorough repression of the Jacobins that gave him a reputation for cruelty and ruthlessness. Forced out of Naples again in 1806 by the French, the royal family retreated once again to Sicily, protected by the British navy.

Pressured by Lord WILLIAM BENTINCK, Ferdinand issued a CONSTITUTION in 1812, a move that he quickly regretted and promptly rescinded when the CONGRESS OF VIENNA restored him to power as Ferdinand I, king of the KINGDOM OF THE TWO SICILIES. He adopted a generally conciliatory policy after 1815 inspired and executed by his chief adviser LUIGI DE' MEDICI. The REVOLUTION of 1821 forced him to grant a constitution even more liberal than that of 1812, which he again renounced after having promised to uphold it. His experience made him completely distrustful of LIBERALISM and reform. Indifferently educated, devoted to hunting, fishing, and life in the outdoors, Ferdinand took an interest in government and cut a fine figure in public. He spoke Neapolitan dialect fluently and liked to mix with ordinary people. His human qualities endeared him to many of his subjects, but have not done much for his image in history.

Ferdinand II (1810–1859)
king of the Two Sicilies (1830–1859)

Assuming the crown of the KINGDOM OF THE TWO SICILIES at the death of his father FRANCIS I, Ferdinand II began his reign auspiciously. The 20-year-old ruler was self-confident, energetic, and eager to learn. The plebeian manners that he adopted and that offended cultivated people actually endeared him to the populace. After his accession Ferdinand visited all corners of the kingdom, encouraged the study of social conditions, received subjects from all walks of life, spent generously on charity, granted a political amnesty, built roads, ports, and other public works. Intellectual curiosity was not his strength, but in 1845 he took the daring step of hosting the first congress of Italian scientists. He pursued a more independent foreign policy, distanced himself from Great Britain, and sought closer ties with Austria and Russia. Those were the actions of a young ruler who thought that he could improve the administration and the economy by decree, without surrendering any of his royal prerogatives, with the collaboration of experts loyal to the throne. But the method favored by 18th-century rulers was no longer adequate in Ferdinand's time. Uprisings in Sicily and the mainland provinces indicated discontent with his policies. The REVOLUTION of 1848 forced him to summon a parliament and grant a constitution; he dismissed both at the first opportunity. He was a reluctant participant in the war against Austria. The troops that political pressure forced him to send had orders not to press across the Po River. When Sicily took advantage of the revolution to break away from Naples, Ferdinand subdued the island by force. The shelling of Messina earned him the nickname of *Re Bomba* (King Bomb). The experience of revolution soured him on reform, made him suspicious of intellectuals, and fearful of public debate. The arrest and jailing of thousands of political dissidents turned European public opinion against him. William Gladstone described his government as the denial of God turned into a system. But Ferdinand no longer courted public opinion and dismissed those who sought to influence it with their writings as *pennaruli* (pen pushers). After 1848 Ferdinand understood that the ultimate protection of his throne was the conservative power of the AUSTRIAN EMPIRE. To liberals he personified tyranny, patriots saw him as an obstacle to national independence. In 1856 an attempt on his life by a soldier during a military review left him in a state of terror and increased his isolation. His death came after a long and painful illness.

Ferdinand III (1769–1824)
grand duke of Tuscany (1790–1824)

Ferdinand III, second-born son of PETER LEOPOLD, succeeded to the Tuscan throne in 1790 when his father stepped down to become Austrian emperor. Afraid that revolution might break out in his realm after it broke out in France in 1789, Ferdinand took a strong stand against reform. Afraid that concessions might encourage demands for further change, he revoked some of his father's most progressive measures, relied on the conservative nobility, and revived clerical privileges. The policy of neutrality that he adopted in the conflicts between France and Austria did not prevent the French from invading Tuscany in 1799 and evicting Ferdinand. The temporary

victory of the anti-French coalition in 1799 restored him to his throne, but the peace settlement of 1801 forced him to relinquish it once again in exchange for the German Grand Duchy of Würzburg. The CONGRESS OF VIENNA restored Tuscany to him in 1814. Ferdinand's policies during the RESTORATION were generally moderate and conciliatory. He kept many reforms introduced by the French, encouraged commerce, carried out a land census to make taxation more equitable, undertook ambitious programs of land reclamation, road construction, and urban renewal. Mild censorship allowed some criticism of the government and the expression of progressive views in print. The course of public policy reflected the moderately liberal views of the Tuscan aristocrats that Ferdinand called to his side, particularly those of Count Vittorio Fossombroni (1754–1844), who served as his prime minister from 1815 to 1844.

Fermi, Enrico (1901–1954)
expatriate nuclear physicist and Nobel Prize winner

This Roman-born nuclear physicist showed an exceptional aptitude for science at an early age. His precocious talent earned him admission to the prestigious *Scuola Normale Superiore* of Pisa, from where he graduated in 1922. After doing postgraduate work in Germany with the physicist Max Born, Fermi taught physics and mathematics at the universities of Florence and Rome. In 1926 the University of Rome appointed him to a newly created chair of theoretical physics. In Rome, Fermi also headed a team of scientists conducting pioneering research in nuclear physics. In 1929 he became the youngest member of the recently founded Royal Academy of Italy. His experiments with neutrons at the university produced promising results, showing how elements could be made radioactive and how the level of radioactivity could be controlled. Experimenting with uranium, Fermi's team produced a variety of radioactive substances, one of which was thought to be a new chemical element. Although the discovery could not be confirmed at the time,

Enrico Fermi *(Library of Congress)*

the results inspired other scientists in Europe and America to delve further into the process of splitting the atom and creating radioactive man-made elements. Later experiments by German scientists showed that the new element was barium. Fermi's research won him the Nobel Prize in physics in 1938 for his identification of new radioactive elements produced by neutron bombardment and his discovery of nuclear reactions by means of slow neutrons. The Fascist press trumpeted Fermi's work as a major Italian contribution to world science. However, by 1938 Fermi's team had broken up and he had all but abandoned laboratory experimentation.

That same year that Fermi won the Nobel Prize, the anti-Semitic laws just enacted by the Fascist regime threatened Fermi's Jewish wife Laura, whom he had married in 1928. They never returned to Italy from Stockholm, where they had gone to receive the Nobel Prize. In the United States, which Fermi had already visited several times in the 1930s, Fermi did team

research at Columbia University to construct an "atomic pile" that would produce a controllable nuclear reaction. The government funded Fermi's work in view of its military potential, and appointed a special committee to track the progress of the research. In July 1942 the Fermis moved to the University of Chicago. There, in December of that year Fermi and his team achieved the first controlled, self-sustained nuclear chain reaction. That was the critical breakthrough needed to develop a new source of energy and build the atomic bomb. The government-sponsored "Manhattan Project" developed the first atomic bombs that were dropped on Japan in 1945. Fermi became an American citizen in 1944 and remained involved in the project as an assistant to Robert Oppenheimer. In 1946 Fermi received the Congressional Medal of Merit for his work. He continued with his experimental work, served on the Atomic Energy Commission, and lectured widely in Europe and the United States. In his last major research project carried out before his death, Fermi applied rudimentary computers to simulate the behavior of subatomic particles. Diagnosed with cancer in 1952, he died two years later.

Ferrara, city of

Ferrara (population 132,000) is a provincial capital in the Emilia-Romagna region and an important agricultural and industrial center. First mentioned in eighth-century documents when the Lombards seized it from the Byzantines, it saw fierce fighting among rival Guelf and Ghibelline families. The ESTE FAMILY ruled the city from 1240, expanded its territory, and made it an important SIGNORIA. Rivalries within the family encouraged the ambitions of neighboring PAPAL STATES and the Republic of VENICE. In 1332 the pope asserted his authority over the city by investing its rule in the Este family, which thereby became a papal vassal. Ferrara became a major RENAISSANCE cultural center, home to illustrious artistic and literary figures, including TORQUATO TASSO. Religious reformers with Protestant sympathies disseminated their ideas from Ferrara until driven out in the 16th century. The government invested heavily to reclaim swampy land, thereby laying the foundations for the province's prosperous agriculture. In 1598 Ferrara became part of the Papal States. The economic decline that had set in by then continued in the 17th century as private investments dried up and the government abandoned the land reclamation projects begun by the Este family. Improvements resumed near the end of the 18th century and were stepped up under the Napoleonic administration (1801–14). The CONGRESS OF VIENNA restored the city to the Papal States on condition that Austria be allowed to maintain a military garrison there. In March 1860 Ferrara became part of the Kingdom of Italy. The expansion of large-scale commercial agriculture and concentration of landless day laborers made the *Polesine,* the countryside around Ferrara, a hotbed of social radicalism and a Socialist Party (PSI) stronghold. In 1919–21 Ferrara was the scene of violent confrontations between workers and landowners. Socialists and Fascists fought it out, the latter led by ITALO BALBO, who became the city's powerful boss. From 1945 to the early 1990s Ferrara was a communist stronghold.

Ferrara, Francesco (1810–1900)
liberal economist and political reformer
Regarded as the first of the modern Italian economists, Ferrara is known for his unwavering advocacy of free-market and free-trade principles derived from his study of Adam Smith, Thomas Malthus, David Ricardo, and James Mill. Born in Palermo and trained in religious schools, Ferrara was a liberal Catholic who combined religious faith with faith in representative government. His liberalism brought about his arrest in Sicily in January 1848. Liberated by insurgents, he served in the Sicilian parliament and voted for separation from Naples. He favored forming a federation of Italian states under Piedmontese leadership and was part of the delegation that in 1848 offered the crown of Sicily to the future VICTOR EMMANUEL II. A political exile in Piedmont in the 1850s, he collaborated with Prime Minister CAVOUR, whom he nevertheless criticized for not being rigorously laissez-faire. In 1858 he was suspended from his chair of political economy at the University of Turin on charges of inciting student unrest. After national unification Ferrara supported the government's policy of tight spending and budget balancing. He served in parliament (1867–80), was briefly minister of finance (1867), and was appointed senator (1881). Ferrara, temperamental and doctrinaire, was a respected scholar and a controversial public figure. The many volumes of his *Biblioteca dell'Economista* (1850–70) brought the classical texts of British and French liberal economists to the attention of Italian readers.

Ferrari, Giuseppe (1811–1876)
political theorist and social reformer
Ferrari navigated his way through the currents of 19th-century radical thought to give social direction and content to the movement for national independence. Born in Milan to a family of small businessmen and landowners, Ferrari received a secular education and obtained a law degree from the University of Pavia (1832). Interested in social issues, he joined the circle of scholars around GIAN DOMENICO ROMAGNOSI, became friends with CARLO CATTANEO, and immersed himself in study. From Romagnosi he derived a strong sense of the importance of economic factors in modern society. The European dimension, particularly important in Ferrari's thought, was reinforced by his move to Paris in 1838. French socialist thought exerted a lasting influence on Ferrari. He earned a doctorate in Paris and taught in Strasbourg, but as a socialist, an anticlerical, and a foreigner he encountered powerful political opposition. Ferrari reflected on Italian events as an admirer of the FRENCH REVOLUTION. Italian patriots were angered by his criticism that they were unrealistically optimistic about Italy's readiness for the modern world, that their movement lacked a social program and offered little to the masses. Social revolution, or revolutionary war, was the

means to independence proposed by Ferrari. His ideal was a decentralized federal republic that respected the diversity of regional cultures. He distanced himself from the major currents of the RISORGIMENTO before and after the REVOLUTIONS of 1848. An isolated figure with no following, he played a small role in the movement for national unification, but his criticism that the Risorgimento failed as a social revolution influenced radical thinkers of later generations. A member of the Italian parliament from 1860 to 1876, he accepted the monarchy reluctantly. He used his position to accuse the government of social irresponsibility, demanded educational reforms, and raised the SOUTHERN QUESTION.

Ferrero, Guglielmo (1871–1942)
writer and public figure

Ferrero was an influential intellectual who wrote for a broad public and took strong stands on contemporary issues. Born in Naples, he studied in Bologna and Turin. He was influenced by the criminologist CESARE LOMBROSO, with whom he coauthored a study of female criminality and prostitution, *La donna delinquente* (1893). This study reflected Ferrero's Darwinian sociology and his belief that genetic heredity was the key to character formation. Ferrero later enlarged his focus to take into account sociological influences. His major work is a five-volume history of ancient Rome, *Grandezza e decadenza di Roma* (1902–07). Translated as *The Greatness and Decline of Rome* (1909), this was a sociological account of the Roman transition from republic to empire. It provoked strong negative reactions from BENEDETTO CROCE and other idealist philosophers who rejected Ferrero's philosophical POSITIVISM. Also controversial was the attack on modern capitalism of Ferrero's *Fra i due mondi* (1913), translated as *Ancient Rome and Modern America: A Comparative Study of Morals and Manners* (1914), which argued that modern capitalism and mass production are fundamentally incompatible with notions of quality and moral worth. In politics, Ferrero came out strongly in favor of Italian intervention in WORLD WAR I on the side of France, again crossing swords with Croce. A social democrat fearful of mass culture, Ferrero rejected both communism and fascism. Kept under police surveillance as an opponent of the Fascist regime, Ferrero left for Switzerland in 1930. His courses on the history of the FRENCH REVOLUTION taught in Geneva produced some important publications. Ferrero saw the French Revolution and NAPOLEON I as precursors of 20th-century-mass-based totalitarian regimes. He found in the principle of legitimacy adopted by the CONGRESS OF VIENNA a valid safeguard against the threat of mob rule and dictatorship stemming from the revolutionary tradition.

Ferri, Enrico (1856–1929)
criminologist and political figure

A student of ROBERTO ARDIGÒ and a philosophical positivist, Ferri stressed the importance of environmental factors on character formation and behavior. In his *Sociologia criminale* (1896), translated as *Criminal Sociology* (1900), Ferri argued for the removal of the environmental and social causes of crime as the first step toward crime reduction. He taught penal law in several universities, including the University of Rome, from 1884 to 1925. Elected to the Italian parliament in 1886 as a member of the Radical Party, Ferri turned to socialism in 1893. His *Socialismo e scienza positiva* (1894), translated as *Socialism and Modern Science* (1904), presented socialism as a logical synthesis of the ideas of Darwin, Spencer, and Marx. Within the Socialist Party (PSI), Ferri headed the revolutionary elements opposed to the moderate line of party leader FILIPPO TURATI, but for the sake of party unity refrained from pushing his opposition to the breaking point. From 1903 to 1908 he was editor in chief of the party newspaper *Avanti!*. To the general surprise and dismay of fellow socialists, in 1909 Ferri began to favor collaboration of socialists and nonsocialists. His influence within the party declined rapidly. In 1912 he was the only socialist to vote for the annexation of Libya but, again unpredictably, he supported the party line of nonintervention in WORLD WAR I. After the war he chaired a government commission charged with proposing revisions to the penal code. Its liberal recommendations were adopted in 1921 but repealed by the Fascist regime in the 1920s. Ferri expressed support for FASCISM and denounced socialism as empty rhetoric. He claimed to see in BENITO MUSSOLINI's facial features, especially his protruding jaws, scientific evidence of strength of character. A grateful Mussolini had him appointed senator in 1929, but Ferri died before taking his seat. A respected legal expert and powerful orator, Ferri is still a political enigma.

Ferrucci, Francesco (1489–1530)
Renaissance military commander and patriotic icon

The historical figure of Ferrucci is encrusted in patriotic legend. This Florentine merchant turned military commander was brought up in republican Florence after the ouster of the MEDICI FAMILY. He held public office in various parts of the state and gained military experience fighting in defense of the Florentine republic. In recognition of his demonstrated talent for military affairs, the government appointed him commander against the troops of Emperor CHARLES V. Ferrucci mounted a spirited campaign against overwhelming odds, managing to hold off the superior forces of the imperial and papal armies arrayed against him. In a final desperate ploy to catch the enemy from the rear, Ferrucci led his soldiers through the APENNINES, but an imperial force caught up with him near the village of Gavinana (Pistoia) and defeated his small band of exhausted followers. Ferrucci was among the last to die, finished off by an Italian imperial officer named Maramaldo. To 19th-century patriots Ferrucci was the epitome of the brave Italian fighting against foreign domination, and Maramaldo a symbol of national betrayal. Democrats fostered a veritable cult of Ferrucci for his republicanism. Schoolchildren were taught that the

dying Ferrucci reproached his killer with the words *Vile, tu uccidi un uomo morto* (Coward, you are killing a dead man). A memorial in the main square at Gavinana attracts patriotic visitors.

FIAT

FIAT (Fabbrica Italiana Automobili Torino) is Italy's largest privately owned firm and a major manufacturer of motor vehicles. It was founded in 1899 by Giovanni Agnelli (1866–1945). The economic fortunes of FIAT, the Agnelli family, and the city of Turin have been intertwined ever since. Agnelli, a former military officer, began modestly as a motor-tricycle shop worker and carriage shop owner. In the FIAT venture, he initially had several partners, including members of the Turinese aristocracy, who gradually lost interest or were bought out, leaving Agnelli in sole control. He revealed exceptional managerial talents, guided the company's growth, won government contracts, diversified production, and cultivated the export market. Roller bearings, auto components, buses, and trucks were added to the manufacture of automobiles under Agnelli's leadership. In organizing assembly-line production, Agnelli followed the example of Henry Ford, whom he met during visits to the United States and greatly admired. Agnelli led employer resistance to organized labor after WORLD WAR I, supported the liberal GIOVANNI GIOLITTI, switching his support to FASCISM in 1921. The Fascist government made him a senator in 1923, and he took advantage of the government's pro-business policies to integrate production along vertical lines, establish factories in Spain and the Soviet Union, and gain firm control of the domestic market. In 1927 he founded IFI (Istituto Finanziario Industriale) to generate funds for capital investment. IFI became a holding company, which controls a variety of enterprises in disparate sectors of the economy.

The death of Giovanni's son Edoardo (1892–1935) in a car accident opened the way to the grandson, also named Giovanni but always referred to as Gianni Agnelli (1921–2003), and

Woman in a FIAT at the international automobile show in Turin, 1955 *(Library of Congress)*

known popularly, as *L'avvocato* (The Lawyer). General manager Vittorio Valletta (1883–1967) ran FIAT from 1946 to 1966, when Gianni took personal control. He headed FIAT until his formal retirement in 1996 when Cesare Romiti (born 1923) replaced him as head manager, but Gianni stayed on until his death as honorary chairman in overall control of the family's vast holdings. His brother Umberto Agnelli (born 1934) succeeded him. In 1986 FIAT acquired control of the prestigious automaker Alfa Romeo (founded in 1915) as part of its strategy to expand its control of the Italian market and strengthen its presence abroad, especially in the American market through an understanding with General Motors. The gambit to penetrate the American market failed, but the 1980s and early 1990s were nevertheless a period of great growth. By 1996 FIAT had a workforce of 237,000, annual revenues of $46 billion, and accounted for almost 5 percent of the country's domestic product. Today the family is busy diversifying its holdings, seeking advantageous connections or mergers with major foreign manufacturers, including General Motors, and establishing a foothold in the potentially lucrative field of energy production and distribution. Ironically, car manufacturing is the most financially troubled division of the Agnelli empire, raising questions about its economic viability and survival.

Ficino, Marsilio (1433–1499)
Renaissance philosopher and scholar

Ficino's exceptional promise was recognized by COSIMO DE' MEDICI, who took the six-year-old son of a Florentine physician under his wing and directed him toward the study of ancient classics. Admitted to the Medici household at age 18, Ficino took up the study of philosophy and classical Greek. Constantinople, the last stronghold of the Byzantine Empire and depository of ancient Greek classical learning, was about to be

Marsilio Ficino *(Library of Congress)*

to the most spiritual essence. Central to Platonism was the concept of love, which Ficino viewed as a passion that attached itself to objects, people, and principles, enlarging human understanding from the material and carnal to the spiritual, with love of God as the ultimate attainment. Critics seized on the subversive implications of the Neoplatonic worldview, arguing that it blurred necessary distinctions between truth and falsehood, between good and evil. Ficino, who saw no contradiction between Plato and Christian theology, became a priest in 1473. LORENZO DE' MEDICI continued the patronage of Ficino and the academy begun by his grandfather Cosimo. The synthesis of Christian and pagan philosophy proposed by Ficino gave philosophical coherence and respectability to the art and culture of the RENAISSANCE.

Figli della Lupa See GIOVENTÙ ITALIANA DEL LITTORIO.

Filadelfi See SECRET SOCIETIES.

Filangieri, Gaetano (1752–1788)
Enlightenment philosopher and political reformer

Filangieri, prince of Arianello, born to a family of the Neapolitan nobility, was destined for a military career. He left his military post in 1769 to study law, completed his law degree at the University of Naples in 1774, and immediately published a commentary commending a royal decree against abuses in the courts. A sign of things to come, this study eventually led to his seven-volume work *Scienza della legislazione* (Science of legislation, 1780–85). It is the ultimate and most comprehensive expression of the Neapolitan ENLIGHTENMENT. Its global sweep covers events in every part of the world, from the American Revolution, which Filangieri supported, to the nature of government in China, which he also admired for its role in maintaining

overrun by the Turks. To preserve the Greek heritage, western scholars would have to develop the necessary linguistic and critical skills. Ficino was most prominent among the scholars and philosophers who took on the challenge. The villa that Cosimo presented to him became the center of a group of scholars who set out to revolutionize philosophical thought. The Florentine Academy, as the group became known, was wholly devoted to studying, translating, and propagating the thought of Plato in the updated version known as NEOPLATONISM. Ficino, who led the academy, presented his understanding of Plato in his *Platonic Theology* (1482). He devoted himself entirely to the mission of recovering manuscripts, translating, defending Plato and his interpreters from their Aristotelian detractors, who looked upon Neoplatonists as dangerous philosophical radicals. Neoplatonists developed a hierarchical view of the universe in which every object and passion found a place, in an ascending scale that went from grossest matter peace and prosperity in the land, to the African slave trade, which he deplored. But while ranging far and wide, Filangieri never loses sight of his principal goal, which is to make a case for progressive monarchy. Filangieri hoped to go beyond describing the right form of government, as Montesquieu had done in *The Spirit of Laws* (1748), to mapping out a course of action whereby an enlightened monarch could improve public administration, eliminate destructive social privileges, and secure economic prosperity. It was essential to abolish the special privileges of the nobility and clergy in matters of justice, ownership of land, inheritance, and education. Filangieri assigned to his own social class, the nobility, an important role as a check on the power of the monarch and as an intermediary between the monarch and the rest of society. A strong monarch was needed to carry on the process of reform, and an aristocracy open to people of talent was also needed to help the monarch. Filangieri made no distinction between the interests of the monarch and the interests of the state. In his thinking, monarchy and state stood above special interests and partisan politics. This idealized concept of the state is a strong feature of Neapolitan Enlightenment thought and a lasting contribution to Italian political theory. Filangieri's premature death deprived political science of a mind that was both synthesizing and original at a time when the revolutionary changes that he had anticipated would surely have prompted further reflections on the role of state and government. Filangieri's work was widely known in Europe and in the American colonies.

Fini, Gianfranco See ITALIAN SOCIAL MOVEMENT.

FIOM (Federazione Impiegati e Operai Metallurgici)

The Federation of Metal Workers is the largest trade union in the Italian labor movement. Since 1906 it has been affiliated with the General Confederation of Labor (CGL), the country's largest

grouping of labor unions with ties to the parties of the Left. In Italy, the designation "metal workers" covers anyone who works with metals at any stage of production, from extraction to finishing operations in all industries except shipbuilding. The union therefore represents a variety of occupations, including steel, auto, and machinery. FIOM was founded in Livorno in 1901 but quickly moved to Turin in Italy's developing industrial heartland. In 1906 under BRUNO BUOZZI's leadership, it wrung some important concession from employers, including salary increases and the right to establish grievance committees within the factories. These grievance committees gave FIOM a strong presence on the shop floor. FIOM kept in close touch with its members, distanced itself from CGL's leadership, and often set the tone for the rest of the labor movement. It helped organize the war effort during WORLD WAR I. At the end of the war it demanded formal recognition of *commissioni interne* (factory councils) to give workers a say in management. The demand for factory councils acquired strong political and ideological significance in the labor conflicts of the postwar years, but FIOM did not generally support linking worker demands and political issues. It concentrated instead on concrete issues of wages and working hours that mattered most to its members. In 1919 it signed a nationwide agreement that introduced the eight-hour day in industry. It played a major role and scored other important successes in the intense labor conflicts of 1919–20, but could not stand up to the Fascist offensive against organized labor that developed in 1921–22. The Fascist regime forced FIOM to dissolve in 1926. It was reconstituted in 1944–45 as part of CGL's reincarnation, the CGIL. It was in the forefront of labor conflicts in the "hot years" of 1968–73, and remains an active and important presence on the Italian labor scene to this day.

Fiume, city of

Fiume (Rijeka) was part of Italy from 1924 to 1945, when the forces of Josip Broz Tito occupied it at the end of WORLD WAR II and incorporated it into Yugoslavia. Located in the ISTRIA region at the head of the Adriatic Sea, the city was founded in Roman times, was held by Franks and Croatians in the Middle Ages, became part of Habsburg Austria in 1466, was part of France during the Napoleonic period, and returned to Austrian rule in 1814. It became a free port in 1723 and a major port in the 19th century, when it was the point of embarkation for many emigrants departing from Eastern and Central Europe. WORLD WAR I disrupted its traffic. In the immediate postwar years the city was claimed by both Italians and Yugoslavs, the Italians claiming it on the ground that most of its inhabitants were of Italian nationality because they spoke Italian. The Yugoslavs claimed it on geographical, political, and strategic grounds. President Woodrow Wilson supported Yugoslav claims at the PARIS PEACE CONFERENCE. The impasse was cut short when Italian legionnaires (free corps troops) led by GABRIELE D'ANNUNZIO occupied the city in September 1919. When the Italian government refused to accept the city in this irregular fashion, D'Annunzio settled in, called his diminutive state the *Reggenza del Carnaro,* and turned it into a symbol of vehement Italian nationalism. To keep up the enthusiasm of his followers and show the world that Italians were determined to hold on to the city, he developed colorful rituals, complete with popular rallies, speeches from a balcony, Roman salutes, black uniforms, and marching troops, claiming for himself the title of comandante. For these colorful innovations, D'Annunzio is sometimes referred to as the John the Baptist of FASCISM. Italian troops forced D'Annunzio and his legionnaires out of Fiume in December 1920 to eliminate a source of internal subversion and restore credibility to the government. The TREATY OF RAPALLO (1920) made Fiume a free state, but Italian troops again occupied the city in 1922. The Treaty of Rome (1924) divided the territory, giving the city to Italy and the surrounding countryside to Yugoslavia with the suburb of Porto Baros (Susak). The 1947 PEACE TREATY gave Fiume and most of the Istrian peninsula to Yugoslavia. Fiume is now part of the Republic of Croatia.

Florence, city of

Florence (pop. 376,700) is the regional capital of Tuscany. It is located in a plain below the foothills of the APENNINES, on the banks of the Arno River. Florence began as the Roman settlement of Florentia. Its later development is poorly documented. In the Middle Ages it was the seat of a bishopric, a center for the education and training of clergy, and a military stronghold. Florence became an independent commune in the 12th century, extending its territory, and assuming in 1197 the leadership of an anti-imperial league that protected its independence and facilitated its expansion. It expanded at the expense of the neighboring cities of Arezzo, LUCCA, PISA, and SIENA to rule the area occupied by the modern region of Tuscany. Bloody factional struggles marked its domestic history, pitting Guelfs versus Ghibellines and nobility versus merchants. Guelfs were often merchants, Ghibellines aristocrats. The Guelfs won out in the 14th century, supported by the church. Merchants, bankers, and manufacturers governed the town through guilds and city councils, excluding the less privileged. Neither war nor domestic turmoil halted the growth of the city, which reached 90,000 inhabitants in 1338. The Black Death did what neither war nor civil strife could do, carrying off half of the city's population when it struck in 1348. More internal turmoil followed as high taxes and famine drove poor people to desperate extremes. The 1378 revolt of the Ciompi (marginal workers in the wool industry) was an early example of class warfare. Representative government seemed less workable under these conditions. Politics became largely a matter of family interests and rivalries. Order was restored when the MEDICI FAMILY established its rule. While the struggle was going on, there was lively public debate over the best form of government. That debate was at the heart of the culture of HUMANISM with its ideals of citizenship and public service. Humanist scholars played into the hands of the Medici by arguing that Florence was the best example of republican government, even as the family's power increased and everyone else lost interest or access to government.

Whatever its political drawbacks, the 60 years of Medici rule (1434–94) were an astonishingly creative period in the history of Florence. The French invasion of 1494 interrupted Medici rule, gave GIROLAMO SAVONAROLA his moment in history, and brought forth the political interlude of the Florentine republic, which found its champion in NICCOLÒ MACHIAVELLI. The Medici returned in 1512, were forced out again in 1527, and restored to power in 1530 by the armies of CHARLES V, which laid siege to the city and ended the dream of republican government. There was little room for Florentine autonomy in the new era dominated by the superpowers of Spain and France. In compensation for their lost autonomy, the Medici received the titles of grand dukes and Florence consolidated its hold over the rest of Tuscany.

In the "forgotten centuries" that followed, Florence retained some of its cultural vitality, but lost much of its economic and all of its political power. This was nevertheless the age of GALILEO, when science sank its roots in Florentine soil. The dynasty of HABSBURG-LORRAINE replaced Medici rule in 1737 and governed as a dependency of the Austrian Empire until 1859. Florence was the capital of the unified kingdom of Italy from 1865 to 1871. By then it was well on its way to reclaiming its historical role as the country's cultural capital. The review *Antologia* (1821–33) had attracted major literary figures to Florence. By the 1850s it was home to the MACCHIAIOLI school of painting. In the 20th century writers like GIOVANNI PAPINI, GIUSEPPE PREZZOLINI, CURZIO MALAPARTE, and Vasco Pratolini were either born in Florence or made Florence their cultural home. Today Florence displays its past in the museums, palaces, and monuments that cluster in the city center. Its present state defies easy definition. As a provincial and regional capital, Florence is an important administrative center. It is a transportation hub for air, road, and railroad traffic. A major tourist attraction, it draws millions of visitors every year. Industrial activity takes place in outlying areas. Not far from Florence, the town of Prato is the historic center of textile production. Immigrants from distant countries have taken over manufacturing activities that native Florentines no longer practice in great numbers. But the Florentines are as argumentative, witty, and irreverent as they were reputed to be in medieval times.

Florio family   See RUBATTINO, RAFFAELE.

Fo, Dario (1926–   )
playwright and actor

Dario Fo is known as a biting and often wacky political satirist. His career in show business began in 1952 on Italian television with a series of comic monologues poking fun at conventional interpretations of the past, debunking heroes, and casting historical villains in a favorable light. In 1954 he married the talented writer and performer Franca Rame (1926–   ). The two have worked together ever since. Their theater harks back to premodern models. The writing is deceptively simple and direct, the acting often improvisational, the audience is encouraged to participate, and the political messages are delivered in unambiguous terms. Fo often appears as a jester aiming his barbs at government, the police, big business, and the Catholic Church. Always against the establishment, Fo and Rame have embraced left-wing causes without following any strict party line. Once Communist Party (PCI) members, in the 1970s Fo and Rame sided with extra-parliamentary groups and criticized the PCI from a perspective further to the left. The play *Accidental Death of an Anarchist* (1970) is typical of the most radical phase of Fo's career. Based on a real-life incident that made headlines, it presents the story of a young anarchist who according to police reports fell to his death from a window while in custody. In this play, a seemingly incoherent Harlequin appears as the voice of reason, while the police and judges sound truly crazed. Fo's popularity in Italy peaked in the late 1970s, while his reputation abroad has grown enormously since. In 1997 Fo won the Nobel Prize in literature. His satire is much more acceptable today than it was 30 years ago.

Fogazzaro, Antonio (1842–1911)
liberal Catholic writer

Much of the high-minded agonizing that one finds in Fogazzaro's writings reflected his own experience of life. Born in Vicenza to a middle-class family of modest means, his father opposed his desire to devote himself to literature, insisted that he follow a career in the law for which the son had little aptitude, and kept him on a tight financial leash for much of his life. An Italian patriot at heart, illness and lack of initiative prevented Fogazzaro from participating actively in the struggle for national unification. Hence the self-doubting, generational struggles, tension between personal inclinations and the demands of duty, and conflicts of principle that dominate his novels. A religious conversion experienced sometime in his late 20s added the dominant concern with the role of faith in personal growth and social behavior. He found solace in Catholicism, but a Catholicism that in his mind confronted the challenges of modern thought. His reflections revolve around the dualism between faith and reason, spirit and matter, mysticism and sensuality, authority and freedom. His commitment to updating Catholicism in light of contemporary thought makes him a founder of Catholic MODERNISM. Literary critics have noted that his characters are incarnations of high-minded principles rather than recognizable human beings. It was a source of great suffering and humiliation to him that modernists found him too timid, while traditionalists found him too controversial. Fogazzaro's last two novels, *Il Santo* (The Saint, 1905) and *Leila* (1911), were placed on the INDEX after PIUS X condemned modernism. *Piccolo mondo antico* (1895), translated as *The Patriot* (1906), is considered to be his masterpiece.

Fonseca, Eleonora Pimentel de (1752–1799)
early political radical and journalist

Eleonora Pimentel, marchioness of Fonseca, a Neapolitan noblewoman of Portuguese parentage, was a prominent member of the radical minority that installed and supported the PARTHENOPEAN REPUBLIC of 1799. Her compositions in verse and dramas won her admission to the Arcadian Academy but social concerns soon overshadowed her literary ambitions. She turned her attention to questions of reform, contributing to public debates on economic policy, law, and education, in the spirit of enlightened reform. When hopes that King FERDINAND I would lead the reform movement were dashed, she defended the FRENCH REVOLUTION and was among the first JACOBINS who welcomed French troops as liberators. During Naples' short-lived experiment in republican government, she almost single-handedly edited and published the radical paper *Il Monitore Napoletano.* In the columns she championed republican ideals and principles of democracy, fully aware that her views would not be understood by the majority. When the BOURBONS were restored to Naples, Fonseca was sentenced to death and executed. Later generations revered her as a political martyr whose ideas were far ahead of her time.

foreign policy

Italian foreign policy begins with national unification because the foreign policies of preunification states clashed more often than not. Geographical, economic, and political realities have shaped the foreign policy of the Italian state. Above all, Italian foreign policy must take into account what happens in the Mediterranean Sea, where the choice can be put in stark terms. For the sake of security, trade, and communications with the outside world, Italy must either control or be on friendly terms with whoever controls the Mediterranean. Italian control of the Mediterranean has not been a feasible option since ancient times, when the Romans built their empire around that sea. The city-states of medieval and Renaissance times gained enough control to safeguard their trade routes, but never enough to impose their political will on surrounding populations. The most powerful of these city-states, the Republic of VENICE, dominated the eastern part of the Mediterranean for about three centuries before yielding to the Turks in the 16th and 17th centuries. In modern times, only the Fascist regime aspired and attempted to dominate the Mediterranean. Its challenge to British supremacy ended in its defeat in WORLD WAR II.

With the possible exceptions of Venice and Fascist Italy, the governments and states of the peninsula have had to come to terms with the power or powers that control the Mediterranean. After the end of the Napoleonic Wars, that meant conducting a foreign policy that recognized the reality of British naval supremacy. Since the end of World War II when American naval power replaced the British, Italian foreign policy has had to take into account the reality of American supremacy. "Taking into account" has usually meant staying on friendly terms with the dominant power. That overriding need has not deprived Italian foreign policy of maneuvering room. For one thing, no power is ever fully dominant, and adroit diplomacy can exploit areas of weakness and international rivalries. Italian diplomats have done so with considerable success. Medieval and Renaissance states exploited the rivalry between the CATHOLIC CHURCH and the HOLY ROMAN EMPIRE.

In the centuries of foreign domination of the peninsula that began with the French invasions of the 1490s, Italian states exploited the rivalry of France and Spain. They did so from a position of weakness and could only respond to what others decided. But at least one state showed that international rivalries could be used to advantage even from a position of weakness. In the 16th century the Duchy of SAVOY, sitting astride the French and Italian ALPS, made opportunistic alliance with rival powers to gain territory. By the 18th century the Duchy of Savoy had become the Kingdom of Sardinia, and in 1860 the Kingdom of Sardinia became the Kingdom of Italy. The Duchy of Savoy became the kingdom of Italy by exploiting the ongoing rivalries of BOURBONS and HABSBURGS, France and Austria, concluding alliances and changing sides, fighting wars and making peace at opportune moments.

Italian foreign policy kept up that tradition in the decades after national unification. Under the new label of balance-of-power diplomacy the governments of the postunification period also sought to gain by exploiting the ambitions and rivalries of greater powers. Germany was the dominant power on the continent after 1870. Italian diplomats took that reality into account, loosened Italy's diplomatic ties to France, and for the sake of German friendship even accepted alliance with Austria, the archenemy of Italian unification. In 1882 Italy joined with Germany and Austria-Hungary to form the TRIPLE ALLIANCE. But, mindful that Britain ruled the Mediterranean, Italian diplomats stipulated that the alliance implied no hostility toward the British.

A major cause of the Triple Alliance was the Italian-French rivalry over Tunisia, which the French claimed for themselves in 1881. Defensive in nature, the Triple Alliance was of limited use as a tool for territorial expansion. In one major respect it was a real hindrance, because the ethnically Italian territories of TRENTINO and ISTRIA, claimed by Italian patriots, belonged to Austria-Hungary, Italy's partner in the Triple Alliance. Italy and Austria also competed for influence in the BALKANS. In 1896 Italian COLONIALISM suffered a setback when the Ethiopians defeated an Italian expeditionary force at the BATTLE OF ADOWA. The Triple Alliance was of little help if Italy was interested in colonial or territorial gains. It was not in Italy's interest to be wholly bound to it.

In 1902 Italy and France put aside their rivalries and concluded the secret Prinetti-Barrère Agreements. Italy acknowledged French interests in Tunisia, France did the same for Italian interests in Libya, and Italy agreed to remain neutral should Germany attack France. The agreements began the process of Italian detachment from the Triple Alliance and led to the ITALIAN-TURKISH WAR that gained Italy the colony of Libya, its biggest colonial prize before 1914. Again, Italian diplomacy advanced Italian claims by playing off the rivalries of greater powers within the framework of balance-of-power diplomacy. This was the policy of preponderant- or decisive-weight diplomacy that enabled Italy to exploit international rivalries to its own advantage. It was this diplomacy that sustained Italy's role as "the least of the great powers" after national unification.

When WORLD WAR I broke out Italian diplomats negotiated with both sides, signed the PACT OF LONDON, and went to war on the side of Great Britain, France, and Russia, against its former Triple Alliance partners. The war introduced the most active period of Italian diplomacy. The victory raised Italy's international status, encouraged NATIONALISM and FASCISM, and raised expectations of greater gains in the future. The change was not merely quantitative. Italian diplomacy in the Fascist period changed fundamentally, pursuing not carefully calculated and calibrated gains in the balance-of-power framework, but goals of Mediterranean dominance, empire, and glory. But the change was gradual. In the 1920s domestic concerns took precedence, professional diplomats controlled the foreign ministry, and the international situation was not conducive to adventurous initiatives. The one false step was the temporary occupation of the Greek island of Corfu in 1923, a move that seemed prophetic only in retrospect.

Much changed in the 1930s. By then BENITO MUSSOLINI had full personal control of foreign policy, the Great Depression intensified nationalist rivalries, and international tensions rose. Eager to score a big success that would solidify support for the regime, Mussolini requested plans for a military campaign in Ethiopia, and began diplomatic preparations to smooth the way. Like his predecessors, he counted on international tensions, which intensified after Adolf Hitler came to power in January 1933, to divide opponents, create conflicts, and give him room to maneuver. The FOUR-POWER PACT (1933) showed his desire to maintain a balance of power in Europe that would give him a free hand elsewhere. The STRESA CONFERENCE (1935) gave him the illusion of support for war in Africa. Mussolini launched the ETHIOPIAN WAR in

the mistaken impression that France and Great Britain would accept Italy's conquest of Ethiopia for the sake of Italian support against Nazi Germany. The war had the unintended effect of damaging beyond repair Italy's relations with the western democracies and tying Italy to Germany. The ROME-BERLIN AXIS was a natural consequence of the Ethiopian War. The PACT OF STEEL (1939) tied Italy to Germany. It was an ideological alliance that made no distinction between the interests of fascism and those of the Italian state. It left little wiggle room for diplomacy. Fascist Italy could not work the balance of power without ceasing to be Fascist.

That was the road that led to WORLD WAR II, to Italy's loss of part of its national territory and of all its colonies, and its demotion from the role of "least of the great powers" to that of a regional power. The CONSTITUTION of the Italian republic repudiates war as an instrument of international diplomacy. Italian governments since 1945 have tended to regard foreign affairs as a distraction from more pressing domestic issues, spending little on defense, relying for security on American military power and NATO. The United States now controlled the Mediterranean, and friendship with the United States has been a constant of Italian foreign policy since 1945. The one foreign policy issue that was truly felt in Italy after the war had to do with the fate of TRIESTE, and that was settled with the return of the city to Italy in 1954.

Although the notion that Italy ought to strive for neutrality or equidistance in the postwar struggle between East and West surfaced periodically in public debate, Italy's pro-Western commitment never wavered during the cold war. A trace of the old balance-of-power and preponderant weight approach is perhaps noticeable in the view occasionally voiced by Italian political figures that Italy can serve as a model of social democracy more humane than that of American capitalism or Soviet-style socialism. Both diplomacy and public opinion have generally been more pro-Arab in Italy than in the United States. Dependence on Middle East oil is one reason for the pro-Arab orientation of Italian foreign policy. Other reasons are public opinion, the power of political parties that rely on voter support, and the need to maintain good relations with neighboring Arab and Muslim populations. Italy's deliberately low international profile is sometimes criticized, but public opinion polls indicate that most Italians support it. Most Italians also expect international endorsement for commitments abroad. Italian diplomacy prefers to work within the framework of NATO, the European Union, or the United Nations. Peacekeeping missions conducted by the Italian military in the Balkans, Afghanistan, and the Middle East in recent years had broad political and popular support. Recent government decisions supporting war in Iraq and challenges to the authority of the European parliament suggest that official policy does not always reflect the popular desire to have international backing. An intensification of rivalries and conflicts in the Mediterranean region and Middle East may well increase the level of public attention and raise foreign policy near the top of the national agenda.

Forlani, Arnaldo See HISTORIC COMPROMISE; PROPAGANDA 2.

Fornovo, Battle of See ITALIC LEAGUE.

Fortis, Alessandro (1841–1909)
patriot and political figure
Fortis belonged to the generation that participated in the final struggles of the Risorgimento and claimed positions of prominence in the unified state. Born in Forlì, a republican follower of GIUSEPPE MAZZINI in his youth, Fortis fought as a volunteer under GIUSEPPE GARIBALDI in 1866 and 1867. The failure of republican conspiracies in the 1870s convinced him of the futility of illegal actions against the monarchy. A member of parliament after 1880, he gravitated toward moderate positions, serving as undersecretary of the interior under FRANCESCO CRISPI (1887–90) and

minister of agriculture under LUIGI PELLOUX (1898–99). He resigned in 1899 and joined the liberal opposition to uphold constitutional liberties threatened by Pelloux's legislation. From then on he identified with the moderate liberal policies of GIOVANNI GIOLITTI, whom he served loyally. Fortis stepped up to the post of prime minister (1905–06) when Giolitti stepped down temporarily. As prime minister, Fortis confronted a railroad strike that threatened to paralyze transportation. Attacked by socialists as subservient to business interests, Fortis nationalized the railroads, making railroad workers public employees and depriving them of the right to strike. He was a lightening rod to Giolitti, taking the heat for controversial actions that Giolitti hesitated to carry out. An able lawyer, brilliant speaker, and an adroit politician, Fortis was a typical representative of the political generation that governed the liberal state.

Fortunato, Giustino (1848–1932)
writer, political figure, social critic, and advocate for the South
Born in the southern region of Basilicata, Fortunato made it his mission in life to educate public opinion about the realities of life in the South. He was conservative politically, like LEOPOLDO FRANCHETTI and SIDNEY SONNINO with whom he collaborated as a journalist. In parliament, where he served as a deputy from 1880 to 1909 and as a senator from 1909 until his death, he belonged to the group that followed Sonnino. His major work, *Il Mezzogiorno e lo Stato italiano* (The South and the Italian state, 1912), challenged the myth that the South was a land of natural riches made poor by bad administration and political corruption. Fortunato showed that the root causes of southern poverty were deforestation, inadequate rainfall and irrigation, soil erosion, excessive reliance on production of cereals, absentee landlordism, lack of capital, and antiquated agricultural practices. The remedies that he proposed reflected his changing understanding of the economy. His initial prescriptions focused on tax relief, but by the end of the 19th century he came

around to the idea that the best solution was the adoption of free-market policies to encourage the specialization of agriculture. His political stand in favor of a two-party system that gave voters a clear choice between free trade and state intervention reflected his dislike of TRANSFORMISM and desire for political clarity. A stickler for constitutional correctness, Fortunato urged liberals to resist FASCISM. The Fascist regime kept him under surveillance but did not persecute or try to silence him.

Foscolo, Ugo (1778–1827)
poet, literary critic, and inspirational patriotic figure

Born and raised on the Greek island of Zazinthos (Zante) in the Ionian Sea, Foscolo joined his mother in Venice in 1792, continued his studies and frequented the intellectual salons of the city. In 1797 he made his debut as a playwright with the successful performance of the tragedy *Tieste* that harked back to the classical Greek theme of conflict between private sentiments and public duty. Politically suspect in Venice, Foscolo welcomed NAPOLEON I as a liberator and joined the Napoleonic army of the Cispadane Republic. Welcomed back in Venice by the newly established democratic republic, he left the city for Milan when the TREATY OF CAMPOFORMIO assigned Venice to Austria. In Milan he was responsible for the publication of the republican newspaper *Il Monitore Italiano* (1797–98). From 1798 to 1806 he held civilian and military positions in Bologna, Florence, Milan, and France. In 1799 he took part in the defense of Genoa besieged by the Austrians. In 1802 he published the *Ultime lettere di Jacopo Ortis* (Last letters of Jacopo Ortis), a romantic novel that was an immediate success. The novel, inspired by Goethe's *The Sorrows of Young Werther,* was also autobiographical. It described Foscolo's hopeless love for another man's wife (in his case Teresa Pickler, the wife of his friend and fellow poet VINCENZO MONTI) and his love for Italy, the two frustrated passions driving the hero of the novel to suicide. Foscolo wrote some of his best poetry in the form of odes

and sonnets, and translated Homer's *Iliad.* In the *Orazione a Bonaparte* (1802) he had the courage to warn Napoleon that he risked becoming a tyrant. Returning to Italy after spending almost two years in France, he wrote his poetic masterpiece, the ode entitled *Dei sepolcri* (Of sepulchers, 1807). In it Foscolo praised the memory and cult of the dead as an organic link between past and present and a source of pride for Italians, who could revere their most glorious dead entombed in the sepulchers of the Church of Santa Croce in Florence. It was an explicit protest against the Napoleonic legislation that banished funerary monuments and prescribed equality of burial for all citizens. Foscolo left Italy in 1815 to avoid life under Austrian rule, went to England in 1816, and spent the rest of his life in London. His last years were beset by poverty and scandal, for Foscolo seldom curbed his passionate nature, sexual appetites, and extravagant spending habits. Buried near London, his remains were transported and buried in the Church of Santa Croce in 1871. His adventurous life, political courage, and love of Italy made him a hero in the eyes of Italian patriots who venerated his memory and propagated his cult as a great Italian.

Fosse Ardeatine, Massacre of the

A sandstone quarry located on the ancient Ardeatine road on the southern outskirts of Rome, the Fosse Ardeatine was the site of a mass execution of Italian prisoners by German troops on March 24, 1944. In retaliation for a terrorist attack by RESISTANCE fighters against a German column, in which 33 Germans had been killed, German and Fascist authorities ordered the execution of 10 hostages for every German casualty. The victims were chosen from among political prisoners who were already incarcerated, men arrested near Via Rasella where the attack had taken place, Jews, and randomly selected civilians, for a total of 335. The mass execution by gunfire took place in the quarry, which was then mined and collapsed on top of the bodies. The exhumation and identification of the victims took place after the liberation of Rome by Allied troops in June 1944. The somber memorial built on the site reminds visitors of the atrocities of war.

Fossombroni, Vittorio See FERDINAND III.

Four-Power Pact

Anticipating a resurgent Germany under Nazi leadership, in a speech of October 1932 BENITO MUSSOLINI floated the idea of a four-power pact by Italy, France, Great Britain, and Germany (deliberately excluding the Soviet Union) to resolve future international conflicts by peaceful means outside the framework of the League of Nations. Mussolini formally proposed such a pact to a receptive British delegation in March 1933, less than two months after Hitler had come to power in Germany. Mussolini was perhaps trying to forestall the German annexation of Austria that was the Nazis' immediate goal and that he saw as a threat to Italy's security, but he was also eager to drive a diplomatic wedge between France and its east European allies, including the Soviet Union, on which France relied for security against Germany. Mussolini hoped to enmesh France in a pact that he could dominate because of his friendly relations with both Germany and Great Britain. The pact would increase Italy's international leverage and enable it to further its colonial ambitions. The text of the pact that was initialed on June 6, 1933, by representatives of the four powers contained revisions that watered it down considerably. Never officially approved by all four governments, the Four-Power Pact was soon a dead letter. It is nevertheless revealing as an attempt by Mussolini to seize the diplomatic initiative and make Italy the lynchpin of European diplomacy.

Fra' Diavolo (1771–1806)
outlaw, guerrilla fighter, and popular figure
Under the nom de guerre of Fra' Diavolo (Brother Devil), Michele Pezza led bands of armed peasants against French troops in the area of Gaeta, near the Roman-Neapolitan border.

Born in the town of Itri to a family of modest means, Pezza had some formal education and could read and write. His turbulent temperament won him his colorful nickname long before he came to public attention. In trouble with the law, he may have taken up arms against the French in defense of the king in the hope of rehabilitating himself. In 1798–99 he led his bands against the French-sponsored PARTHENOPEAN REPUBLIC. He cooperated with Cardinal Fabrizio Ruffo and other irregular fighters around Rome, thus keeping communications open with Austrian troops operating against the French in central and northern Italy. For his daring actions and apparent loyalty to the monarchy he won support from the English, who subsidized him. King FERDINAND IV made him a colonel in the Neapolitan army. Fra' Diavolo took up arms again in 1806 but was less effective against the well-organized and ruthless army of Joseph Bonaparte. Fra' Diavolo's bands committed many atrocities in a drawn-out fight in which neither side gave quarter. Dubbed a bandit and captured, he was executed in 1806. Within a few years of his death he was enshrined in popular memory as a champion of the oppressed, contributing to the southern myth of the good bandit who defends the weak against the strong. Historically, Fra' Diavolo represents the populist element on the side of conservative monarchy, aristocracy, and clergy. Against the traditional view of Fra' Diavolo as a ruthless bandit, recent interpretations present him as a precursor and practitioner of modern guerrilla warfare.

Franchetti, Leopoldo (1847–1917)
*publicist for land reform, problems of the
South, and colonial settlement*
A Florentine landowner, Franchetti turned his attention to issues of LAND REFORM and their political implications. In collaboration with SIDNEY SONNINO, Franchetti brought the SOUTHERN QUESTION to public attention in the 1870s. From the columns of the Florentine review *La Rassegna Settimanale* (1878–82), he and other champions of land reform argued for an enlightened con-

servatism that addressed the needs of the masses and promoted moderate reform. Franchetti's ideal was a rural democracy and a state supported by and responsive to the needs of a landowning peasantry. He saw COLONIALISM as a possible solution to the scarcity of land in Italy, promoted a land settlement venture in the colony of Eritrea in the 1890s, and later proposed similar settlements in Libya and Asia Minor. He was a member of the chamber of deputies from 1882 to 1909 and of the senate from 1909 until his death. He committed suicide in November 1917, after hearing of the defeat at CAPORETTO.

Francis I (1777–1830)
king of the Two Sicilies (1825–1830)

Succeeding his father FERDINAND I, Francis ruled as king of the KINGDOM OF THE TWO SICILIES from 1825 to his death in 1830. Previously, he had ruled in his father's stead in Sicily during the constitutional government imposed by the British envoy Lord WILLIAM BENTINCK (1812–14), and again briefly during the constitutional interlude during the REVOLUTION of 1821. Hopes that he might make liberal concessions during his reign, based on his previous acceptance of constitutional government, were quickly dashed. A devoted husband and father, Francis was more drawn to the pleasures of domestic life and to his favorite pastime of hunting than to the responsibilities and demands of government. Nevertheless, he was not an inactive ruler. He sought to repress brigandage, reform the army, and contain the enormous budget deficits, with disappointing results in all areas. He countenanced reforms that did not threaten his royal prerogatives, including a new forestry law, improvements in the system for collecting import duties, abolition of common rights to land in Sicily, the founding of the state archive, and encouragement of cultural associations. In 1827 he negotiated the withdrawal of Austrian troops stationed in his kingdom since 1821. He did not encourage industry for fear of its social consequences, exercised strict vigilance over the activities of SECRET SOCIETIES, and repressed a liberal uprising in the Cilento region

in 1828. His chief of police, Francesco Saverio Del Carretto (1777–1861), was most effective in rooting out political dissidents. The last issue to occupy the king's attention was the marriage in 1829 of his daughter Maria Christina (1806–78) to the much older King Ferdinand VII of Spain. The marriage set the stage for the outbreak of the long and bloody Carlist Wars in Spain that pitted conservatives against liberals. His son FERDINAND II succeeded Francis to the throne.

Francis II (1836–1894)
king of the Two Sicilies (1859–1860)

Francis II, the last ruling member of the Neapolitan BOURBON DYNASTY, came to the throne at the death of his father, FERDINAND II, in May 1859. Francis continued his father's policy of neutrality in the Second WAR OF INDEPENDENCE. Following his own inclinations and the advice of Austria, Francis turned down CAVOUR's overtures for a friendly understanding with Piedmont-Sardinia, resisted British pressure to grant political reforms, and refused to make liberal concessions at home. A result of his resistance to reform was that liberals abandoned the monarchy and made common cause with the Piedmontese. Francis thus found himself isolated at home and abroad after Austria was defeated in the war. The final crisis began with an uprising in Sicily in April 1860, which the government was unable to repress. News of the uprising persuaded GIUSEPPE GARIBALDI to launch the expedition of the Thousand, which led to the unification of Italy and the dethronement of the Bourbons. Francis stayed with troops loyal to the monarchy while they were besieged in the town of Gaeta, until forced to surrender in February 1861. Subsequent attempts to regain the throne were fruitless. Shortly before being crowned he had married Maria Sofia of Bavaria (1841–1925) who was at his side in the final years of the kingdom and accompanied him in exile to Rome and Paris. Her role in the demise of the Kingdom of the Two Sicilies has been the subject of controversy. A heroine to supporters of the old regime, she was an arch-villain in the eyes of liberals.

Charges that she was responsible for the king's resistance to reform and for instigating BRIGANDAGE in the South after 1860 have not been substantiated.

Francis IV (1779–1846)
duke of Modena and Reggio (1815–1846)

A descendant of the ESTE FAMILY through his mother, Maria Beatrice d'Este, he succeeded Ercole III (1727–1803) as duke of Modena and Reggio by right of inheritance through his mother. His father was Emperor Ferdinand of Austria (1835–48). Forced out by the French, Francis regained his throne in 1815. Francis nurtured ambitious political designs. In rivalry with his cousin CHARLES ALBERT of Piedmont-Sardinia and imagining himself capable of operating independently of Austria, he intrigued to put himself at the head of a movement of national independence. Although he was a convinced absolutist, he may have encouraged the liberal conspirators who plotted the revolution of 1831 by promising to grant a constitution. But it is also possible that he played a double game to entrap the conspirators. What is certain is that the conspirators were arrested at the last minute. His role in the events of 1831 is still unclear, but his decision to cut ties with the conspirators resulted in the arrest and execution of their leader, CIRO MENOTTI, and the imprisonment of many others. Francis abandoned Modena when revolution spread to the PAPAL STATES, but was soon reinstated by Austrian troops. An enigmatic figure, Francis stands out for his failed attempt to use the movement for national independence for conservative purposes.

Francis Joseph (1830–1916)
(Franz Joseph)
emperor of Austria (1848–1916)

More familiarly known to Italians, both affectionately and derisively, as *Cecco Peppe*, Austrian emperor Francis Joseph ruled over LOMBARDY, VENETIA, TRIESTE, ISTRIA, and the TRENTINO as part of his HABSBURG inheritance. He became emperor while the REVOLUTIONS of 1848 threatened to tear apart the Austrian Empire. Temporarily forced to evacuate most of Lombardy and Venetia, his troops soon regained control of these regions, defeated the Piedmontese, and restored Austrian authority in the Italian peninsula. But he now had to contend with a stronger national movement and with a rival on the European scene in the person of NAPOLEON III, who also had designs on Italy. Defeated in the Second WAR OF INDEPENDENCE by the combined forces of France and Piedmont-Sardinia (1859), Francis Joseph ceded Lombardy to Piedmont-Sardinia. In 1866 the Austrian army lost again in the Seven Weeks' War. Italians know that conflict as the Third WAR OF INDEPENDENCE, because the recently formed Kingdom of Italy fought against Austria as Prussia's ally. Although the Austrians won militarily against the Italians, Prussia's victory forced Francis Joseph to relinquish Venetia to Italy. Although not a friend of the Italian state, he did his best to diminish tensions, visiting Venice in 1875, welcoming King UMBERTO I to Vienna in 1881, and accepting Italy as an ally in the TRIPLE ALLIANCE. These steps did not defuse Italian IRREDENTISM, which continued to clamor for Austrian territories inhabited by Italian-speaking populations. The problem of nationalities within the Austrian Empire plagued Francis Joseph for the rest of his reign. The memory of his Italian losses influenced his decision to declare war on Serbia in 1914 to prevent that state from leading a successful secessionist movement, as Piedmont had done in the 19th century. He did not live long enough to see the loss of Trieste, the Trentino, and Istria to Italy and the dissolution of the Austrian Empire at the end of WORLD WAR I. As the ruler of a multinational empire, Francis Joseph struggled to come to terms with nationalism, the sentiment that stood between him and his Italian subjects.

Francis of Assisi (Saint) See ITALIAN LANGUAGE.

Francis Stephen of Habsburg-Lorraine (1708–1765)

grand duke of Tuscany (1737–1765)

Francis ruled as duke of the French-speaking region of Lorraine by inheritance (1729–37). As part of the settlement that ended the War of the Polish Succession (1733–35), Francis agreed to exchange Lorraine for the grand duchy of TUS-CANY at the expected extinction of the MEDICI FAMILY dynasty, which occurred in 1737. From his marriage to Empress MARIA THERESA of Austria (1736) came the dynasty of HABSBURG-LOR-RAINE that ruled Tuscany until 1859. Francis Stephen, after an initial visit of one year, ruled Tuscany through an appointed council while residing in Vienna at his wife's side as nominal coruler of the empire after she became empress in 1740. In 1745 he was elected Holy Roman Emperor, a largely honorific title that carried little power but enhanced his prestige. Although Francis ruled over Tuscany in absentia, he initiated and oversaw major administrative reforms. He limited the censorship powers and fiscal immunities of the CATHOLIC CHURCH, improved the collection of taxes, simplified the administration of justice, and verified titles of nobility. Resistance by clergy and nobility, and the need to raise revenue for Austria's wars, slowed down the process of reform and imposed a heavy burden on the Tuscan treasury. The reform process had come to a virtual standstill by the time Francis died, but his son and successor, the Grand Duke PETER LEOPOLD, resumed it with enthusiasm. Francis deserves credit for initiating the process of reform that made 18th-century Tuscany one of the most progressive states in Europe.

Fransoni, Luigi See BOSCO, GIOVANNI.

Frederick II of Hohenstaufen See ITALIAN LANGUAGE; TWO SICILIES, KINGDOM OF THE.

freemasonry

Freemasonry spread from Britain to the European continent and to North America in the 18th century as a secret organization committed to propagating the ideas of the ENLIGHTENMENT. Masonic lodges appeared in France and Italy in the 1720s, propagating the secular message that reason and education were the necessary antidotes to the poisons of traditional religion and popular superstition. Freemasonry became a secular religion that preached faith in progress and reform. Its period of greatest growth in Italy was the decade of the 1730s. The PAPACY condemned it in 1738 but the network continued to spread into the 1780s, attracting the support of aristocrats, government officials, and rulers, who looked upon the Freemasons as allies in their efforts to curb the power of the church and carry out economic and political reforms. Membership was open to the educated regardless of social extraction, and members were enjoined to deal with one another on a basis of equality. Masonry lost the support of rulers as the revolutionary implications of its ideology and practices became clearer in the course of the 18th century.

After the outbreak of the FRENCH REVOLUTION, governments looked upon freemasonry as a subversive organization, persecuted its members, and drove them underground. Masonic lodges attracted JACOBINS, who supported the French armies that invaded Italy in 1796–99. NAPOLEON I supported the Masons and allowed the formation of the first Grand Orient of Italy in 1805. Freemasonry survived the hostility of conservative governments during the RESTORATION. It played a role in the movement for national unification as a breeding ground for SECRET SOCIETIES. There were probably links between Freemasons and CARBONARI conspirators. Among the major figures of the unification movement, GIUSEPPE GARIBALDI was a Freemason. In the conclusive phase of the unification movement, Italian freemasonry split into three branches, based in Turin (1859), Palermo (1860), and Naples (1861). They came together in 1887 under the first national grand master, Adriano Lemmi (1822–1906), a patriot and businessman, who headed the national society from 1885 to 1895. Ernesto Nathan (1845–1921), a mayor of Rome (1907–13), headed the Freemasons in 1896–1904 and again in 1917–19. Under Lemmi and Nathan, freemasonry became an important carrier of radical ideology opposed to the extremes of left and right. Clericalism and socialism were its declared enemies.

In 1908 the national organization split into two branches, known respectively as the lodges of Palazzo Giustiniani and Piazza del Gesù. Opponents attacked both, charging that the society was in effect a state within the state, wielded immense power, and was the source of political corruption. The advent of FASCISM presented freemasonry with its most serious crisis. Even though many prominent Fascists were Freemasons, as of 1923 no Fascist Party member could be a Freemason. The regime banned freemasonry outright in 1925. The organization survived abroad and reconstituted itself in Italy in 1943–44. The CONSTITUTION of the Italian republic banned all secret organizations, but freemasonry circumvented that provision by making its membership lists available to public officials upon request. More than 500 Masonic lodges are thought to be active in Italy today. Although the organization has never regained the political clout that it enjoyed in the heyday of its power at the beginning of the 20th century, the parties of the Left have frequently accused it of plotting to overthrow democratic government. The involvement of high government officials in the secret Masonic cell known as PROPAGANDA DUE (P2) corroborated the impression that freemasonry plays an occult role in Italian public life.

French Revolution, Italy and the

Histories of modern Italy often start with the French Revolution. The main reason for doing so is that Italians were among the first to feel the repercussions of the revolution that developed in France between 1789 and 1799. News of events

in France spread in Italy through the press and by word of mouth as travelers brought back dramatic accounts of popular violence and government upheavals. Reactions varied. Italians dissatisfied with conditions in their states hoped that changes in France would induce changes at home. Support for the revolution was especially marked among educated Italians who had lost faith in the capacity of governments to bring about needed political and economic reforms. But the reported excesses of French revolutionaries also caused alarm. The persecutions of clergy and nobility, the abolition of the monarchy and executions of Louis XVI and Marie Antoinette alarmed traditionalists in all walks of life.

The polarization of views between sympathizers and critics of the French Revolution laid the groundwork for later divisions among conservatives, liberals, and radicals. Everywhere in Europe, including Italy, the political ideologies and currents of the 19th century reflected different responses and interpretations of events in revolutionary France. Italian conservatives supported the traditional order based on papacy and monarchy, liberals looked for constitutional government and limited monarchy similar to that of France in 1789–92, and radicals hoped for democratic government, economic justice, and national unity, such as the French had experienced in 1792–94 under so-called Jacobin rule.

The force of these ideas grew in Italy as a result of NAPOLEON's invasion of 1796. The French military presence silenced the conservatives and gave the upper hand to Italians who were eager for change. Those who welcomed the French and sympathized with the revolution were called JACOBINS regardless of their precise political position. Jacobins took advantage of French support and freedom of expression to air their views in the press, radical societies, and salons. Governments like those of the PARTHENOPEAN REPUBLIC and ROMAN REPUBLIC gave Jacobins access to power. These governments fell when the French temporarily withdrew in 1798–99, and Jacobinism was no longer in favor when the French returned in 1800. Napoleon was no longer the leader of revolutionaries, but an ambitious general on his way to becoming an emperor. He looked for subservient governments and subjects. Italy would soon become part of the French Empire.

Napoleonic rule banned radical discourse, but it did bring revolutionary change to Italy in the form of centralized administration, uniform laws, a new commercial code, the decimal system, and the green, white, and red flag patterned after the French tricolor that became a powerful symbol of Italian identity. The free and open debates of the 1790s also left a legacy. They were remembered as signs of intellectual ferment and political effervescence. The memory of these debates and of experiments in republican government appealed to radical patriots. The recollections created the myth that revolution was a popular and unstoppable phenomenon and informed a generation of Italians ready to break with the past. Many joined secret societies like the CARBONARI, which opposed Napoleonic and later Austrian rule in the name of French-inspired ideals of liberty, equality, and national independence. After 1815 most Italians who wanted change looked back on the French Revolution as a model, and most conservatives regarded it is the fount of all evils. Either way, Italians reacted strongly to the French Revolution. Their reactions were at the core of the public debate that developed in the 19th century.

Friuli-Venezia Giulia

Part of the AUSTRIAN EMPIRE until 1918, Friuli-Venezia Giulia (pop. 1.2 million) is situated in Italy's northeastern corner. It borders on the region of Venetia to the west and the republics of Austria, Slovenia, and Croatia to the north, east, and southeast. Friuli-Venezia Giulia is what is left of the pre–World War II region of Venezia Giulia after the territorial changes sanctioned by the PEACE TREATY of 1947. In addition to its current provinces of TRIESTE, Gorizia, Pordenone, and Udine, Venezia Giulia included the provinces of FIUME (Rijeka) and Pola (Pula), and large areas of

the current provinces of Gorizia and Trieste. The name Friuli derives from Forum Iulii, a settlement of ancient Rome, while Venezia Giulia derives from the Julian Alps that cover the region's northern portion. A border region of mountains and plains, with Germanic and Slavic linguistic minorities, and a distinct dialect, Friuli-Venezia Giulia has enjoyed regional autonomy since 1963. The provinces of Gorizia, Udine, and Pordenone saw extensive fighting in WORLD WAR I and were the scene of the disastrous battle and retreat at CAPORETTO. Its principal river, the Tagliamento, flows southward from the Alps to the head of the Adriatic Sea. The major industry is shipbuilding, centered on the shipyards of Monfalcone. Agriculture also plays a role, but is limited by the mountainous terrain, prevalence of small peasant holdings, and the use of land for military purposes over the centuries. Fruit, sugar beets, cereals and, most of all, quality grapes for wine production, are the most important agricultural products of the region. The monumental military ossuary at Redipuglia holds the remains of thousands of soldiers who died in World War I. The Carso (Karst) area around Trieste, riddled with chasms and caves, is a major natural attraction. Roman ruins, winter sports, and the beaches of the Adriatic Sea are important tourist attractions.

Frusta Letteraria See BARETTI, GIUSEPPE.

Fucini, Renato See VERISMO.

Fuller, Margaret (1810–1850)
American writer

An influential writer, leading figure among the New England Transcendentalists, and a pioneering feminist, Fuller met GIUSEPPE MAZZINI in London in 1846 and became a devoted follower of this republican radical. Immediately captivated by his democratic ideology and fervor, she visited Florence, Venice, Milan, Rome, and Naples, making political contacts in radical circles in his behalf on the eve of the REVOLUTION of 1848. Her letters to the *New York Tribune* described the situation in Italy before and during the revolution, creating much sympathy and support for the revolution among Americans. In Rome she married the Marquis Giovanni D'Ossoli against the wishes of her family. Along with her friend Princess CRISTINA DI BELGIOIOSO, Fuller served as a nurse during the defense of the ROMAN REPUBLIC. Her manuscript on the revolution was lost in the shipwreck off Fire Island that took her life and the lives of her husband and their two-year-old son in July 1850.

Fund for the South See CASSA PER IL MEZZOGIORNO.

futurism

artistic, literary, and political movement of the early part of the 20th century

A cultural movement related to cubism, futurism enthusiastically welcomed the promise and prospects of industrial society, expressed disillusionment and rejection of middle-class values, and denounced *passatismo,* the cult of tradition and the past. Its tenets were formulated by a group of young artists and intellectuals led by FILIPPO TOMMASO MARINETTI, who wrote the movement's original manifesto. Published in the Parisian newspaper *Le Figaro* in February 1909, the *Futurist Manifesto* welcomed industrial production and mechanical inventions as liberating innovations. It hailed machinery, giant ships, airplanes, and automobiles as exciting inventions that brought new freedoms. What futurists admired about the modern was the excitement of change, speed, and creativity. The craving for the material comforts of mass production they despised as a product of decadent bourgeois mentality. Futurist art celebrated the fast-paced rhythms of modern life. In his *Cucina futuristica* (1932), Marinetti urged Italians to forsake the starchy diet that made them lethargic and adopt an eating regimen that would thin and invigorate them. Although the *Futurist Manifesto* was issued in Paris, industrial Milan was the futurists' spiritual home, and bureaucratic Rome was their nemesis. In exuberant language, they called for daring and rebellion, and sang "the love of danger, the habit of energy and boldness." In the works of UMBERTO BOCCIONI, Giacomo Balla (1874–1958), Carlo Carrà (1881–1966), Luigi Russolo (1885–1947), Gino Severini (1883–1966), and other futurist painters and sculptors one sees the intent to provoke and shock that characterized all futurist art. Twisted shapes convey motion, striking geometrical layouts and vivid colors catch the eye. Futurist architecture envisaged sleek structures of steel and glass, cities of skyscrapers, and fast-moving means of transportation. Futurism's aesthetic of violence and blood conveyed political messages. Glorification of war as the only hygiene of the world, rejection of democracy and humanitarianism, and assertion of iconoclastic values were part and parcel of its political message. Futurists welcomed WORLD WAR I. Many volunteered for military service, some died in action. The movement was a victim of the war and never regained its former cultural vitality. Its glorification of violence and war and its rejection of democracy, but not its spirit of rebellion and anarchic individualism, lived on in FASCISM.

G

Galiani, Ferdinando (1728–1787)
*Neapolitan economist and Enlightenment
philosopher*

Galiani was born in the town of Chieti (Abruzzi),
the son of a minor government official. His uncle,
who was an archbishop and rector of the University of Naples, saw to it that he received an
excellent education, suitable appointments
within the church, and an adequate income.
Galiani took the vow of celibacy and the clerical
tonsure required to qualify for his sinecures, but
the young abbé promptly disregarded the vow
and wore a wig to cover the tonsure. The talented youngster also caught the eye of BERNARDO
TANUCCI, minister of justice and chief royal
adviser. The publication of Galiani's major work,
Della moneta (On money, 1751) brought him public renown. Intervening in the debate on money
current at the time, Galiani developed the theory
that economic value is a function of the rarity
and usefulness of goods. Posted to Paris as
embassy secretary in 1759, Galiani became a regular and admired frequenter of Parisian salons.
He was a close friend of Denis Diderot, Louise
d'Epinay, and Melchior Grimm. An admirer of
French culture, he nevertheless criticized the
Physiocrats for their faith in free trade. In his *Dialogues sur le commerce des blés* [Dialogues on the
Grain Trade] (1770), he argued that trade policies should reflect the specific conditions of time
and place rather than adhere blindly to free-trade
doctrines. Galiani argued that it was the duty of
government to ensure an adequate supply of
wheat for the people to avoid the calamities of
famine and public disorder, even if that meant
curbing the free exportation of grains. Galiani
was devastated when a diplomatic indiscretion
on his part caused his recall to Naples in 1769.
His subsequent correspondence with Madame
d'Epinay and others provides marvelous insights
into the culture of the ENLIGHTENMENT.

Galileo Galilei (1564–1642)
*astronomer, mathematician, and physicist,
pioneer of modern science*

Like other pioneers of modern science, Galileo is
best understood as a "natural philosopher" subscribing to the Renaissance notion of the fundamental unity of knowledge. Hence his interest
and exploration of diverse fields, including mathematics, physics, astronomy, and engineering in
science and technology, and rhetoric, literature,
theology, and metaphysics in the humanities.
Endowed with a penetrating mind, he was also
an accomplished stylist and formidable debater.
Born to a family of the Florentine aristocracy,
Galileo attended the University of Pisa where he
switched to the study of mathematics after a
brief encounter with medicine. His most fundamental contribution to modern science was the
application of geometry and mathematics to the
study of the behavior of objects in motion. That
breakthrough enabled him to formulate in 1604
the law governing the theoretical behavior of
falling objects, which states that the distance
covered by a free-falling body is in squared proportion to the time of the fall. Although this law
is expressed as $s = gt^2$, in which g stands for
gravity, the discovery of the role of gravity would
be left to Isaac Newton in the next generation of
scientists.

Although physics was Galileo's primary
field of interest, he is best remembered for his

Galileo Galilei *(Library of Congress)*

contributions to astronomy. The breakthrough was his application of the telescope. He built a telescope in 1610 on the basis of earlier discoveries by others and used it to carry out systematic observations of stars, planets, and other bodies in space. With his *cannocchiale* (eye cane), as he called the new instrument, he explored the surface of the Moon, activity on the Sun, and the composition of the Milky Way. He observed that the surface of the Moon was uneven and mountainous, that the Milky Way consisted of a large number of separate stars, that the planet Jupiter had four large satellites, and that the Sun showed changing spots. These discoveries revolutionized our understanding of the universe by challenging the accepted notion that change and decay were processes found only in the imperfect sublunary world of Earth, and that the rest of the universe was immutable. Modern space travel is possible because Galileo's conceptual breakthrough showed that Earth and the rest of the universe show similar phenomena.

Galileo left his teaching post at the University of Padua in 1610 to become chief philosopher and mathematician to the grand duke of Tuscany, a position that freed him from the obligation to teach and enabled him to devote himself entirely to research and writing. By then, Galileo was a convinced Copernican, believing on the basis of Copernicus's writings and of his own observations that the Earth revolved around the Sun rather than vice versa. Warned in 1616 by religious authorities in Rome not to openly proclaim the Copernican view, which was considered contrary to the traditional teachings of the church and therefore heretical, Galileo kept public silence on the issue until 1632, when he published his *Dialogue on the Two Chief Systems of the World.* The publication unleashed a public controversy that overwhelmed Galileo. In 1633 he was brought to Rome, put on trial by the ROMAN INQUISITION, and forced to renounce the Copernican theory upheld in the *Dialogue.* After making the abjuration, Galileo is said to have reiterated his belief: *Eppur si muove* (And yet it moves).

After temporary confinement in Siena, Galileo spent the last years of his life at his villa in Arcetri, near Florence. His stature as a pioneer of modern science and precursor of Isaac Newton is unquestioned. His clash with the church has also cast him in the role of a champion of freedom of thought, wrongly muzzled by religious ignorance and arrogance. The church's effort to suppress his ideas may have had negative consequences on the course of scientific inquiry in Italy. While scientific activity in Italy continued to flourish long after Galileo's condemnation, Italian scientists after Galileo avoided theoretical investigations that might arouse suspicion. While the history of Italian science cannot be explained in terms of the church's treatment of Galileo, it would appear that the fear of official sanction by religious and secular authorities did have some influence on the course of scientific work in Italy. Italian scientists turned to the study of practical problems of engineering, like flood control and building construction, and toward collecting, cataloguing, and classifying natural specimens, rather than risking official censure by engaging in potentially controversial pursuits. Technology did not suffer but the tradition of theoretical speculation that is at the heart of modern science was set back by the church's censure and condemnation of Galileo's work. In the year 2001, Pope JOHN PAUL II formally rescinded the church's condemnation of Galileo.

Galvani, Luigi (1737–1798)
anatomist and pioneer in the study of electricity

Trained as a physician and noted as a surgeon, Galvani was appointed to teach anatomy at the University of Bologna in 1775. While dissecting and preparing frog specimens for laboratory work, Galvani noticed that the leg muscles contracted when touched by an electrically charged metal. In 1791, after experimenting with an electrical arc (discharge) that induced muscle contractions in the frogs, Galvani went public with his results, arguing that the electricity originated in animal tissue. ALESSANDRO VOLTA challenged Galvani's conclusion, arguing correctly that the electrical charge came from the metals in Galvani's experiment. The debate stimulated public interest in electricity and its possible therapeutic uses. Galvani's name lives on in such scientific terms as galvanometer (an instrument used to measure electrical currents) and galvanizing (process of covering a metal object with a protective or decorative coating of zinc).

GAP (Gruppi d'Azione Patriottica)
See RESISTANCE.

Gardini, Raul See MONTEDISON.

Garibaldi, Giuseppe (1807–1882)
patriot, commander of volunteer fighters, and leading Risorgimento figure

Unswerving commitment to the cause of national independence and a reputation for per-

Giuseppe Garibaldi *(Library of Congress)*

sonal honesty, selflessness, and courage give Garibaldi unique status among the political figures of modern Italian history. Born to a family of modest means (his father was a short-haul sea trader) in the town of NICE (part of France when he was born), Garibaldi was largely self-educated. By reading on his own he developed a good knowledge of mathematics, the classics, history, political theory, and modern literature. Raised in a bilingual environment, he was equally at home in French and Italian. His preference for Italian was an early indication of his sense of national identity.

The picture of Garibaldi as a man of action short on intellect is a crude caricature of the historical figure. While Garibaldi showed no great inclination for theoretical speculation, he was widely read, keenly interested in ideas, and steadfast in his commitment to a few simple political principles. His egalitarian temperament made him suspicious of all forms of privilege. He was a republican because he saw monarchy as the ultimate expression and guarantor of aristocratic privilege. Furthermore, he did not see himself as fighting for the independence of any one country in isolation, but rather as engaged in an international struggle for the liberation of all countries from foreign rule.

Having followed in his father's footsteps and gone to sea at the age of 16 as a merchant seaman, he voyaged to the countries of the eastern Mediterranean and was eventually called up for service in the navy of the Kingdom of SARDINIA. At sea he became acquainted with followers of the French radical thinker Henri de Saint-Simon who introduced him to the ideas of their teacher. His republican sentiments account for his first foray into politics as a follower of GIUSEPPE MAZZINI. Compromised in a failed conspiracy in 1834, Garibaldi escaped a death sentence by fleeing abroad. From 1835 to 1848 he was in South America, where he fought for various causes, most notably and successfully for the independence of Uruguay from Argentina. He returned to Italy in 1848 to fight in the revolutions of that year. His unsuccessful but heroic defense of the ROMAN REPUBLIC in 1849 made him a charismatic figure in his own land. In the course of those dramatic events he suffered the death of his pregnant South American wife, Anita Ribeiro da Silva Garibaldi (1821–49).

Forced into exile again, he lived with compatriots on Staten Island, New York, visited Central America, and sailed the Pacific Ocean as a trader. In 1855 he returned to Italy, bought land on the island of Caprera off Sardinia, and set himself to building a house and farming the land. Politics and war took him away from these domestic occupations. In 1859, during the Second WAR OF INDEPENDENCE, he commanded a corps of volunteers with considerable success. His historical moment came in 1860 when he led the group of volunteers who have gone down in history as the Thousand to topple BOURBON rule in Sicily and southern Italy. In the final phases of the campaign Garibaldi commanded a force of more than 40,000. The liberation of the South, pulled off successfully against overwhelming odds, is the central event of the RISORGIMENTO. It made the unification of Italy possible and gave a strong political voice to the democratic elements attracted to Garibaldi. His success, republican sentiments, and radical following aroused the suspicions of moderate politicians, including CAVOUR, who did not attack him publicly but worked behind the scenes to undermine his influence.

Garibaldi's plans to complete the process of national unification by taking Rome from the pope were thwarted twice. The Italian army stopped him and his volunteers in 1862, to prevent international complications that would have followed the attack. Garibaldi was wounded in the clash with regular Italian troops that occurred in the mountains of Aspromonte in the region of Calabria. French troops stopped him in 1867 at the Battle of Mentana. These two setbacks did not harm his reputation for bravery or skillful command. His last military campaign took place in 1871 when he led an international force of volunteers against the Prussians in defense of the recently proclaimed French republic.

The focus of intense national and international interest and admiration, Garibaldi was both an expert guerrilla fighter and an effective leader in conventional warfare. In the last decade of his life he was all but immobilized by the effects of his many wounds and by arthritis. Too independent to be a successful politician, he nevertheless remained active politically, served in the Italian parliament, campaigned for a citizens' army to defend the country and for political reforms, including universal suffrage. The "myth" of Garibaldi as a man of the people and fighter for political independence and social justice lived on after him, as attested by the innumerable monuments, inscriptions, piazzas, and streets named after him throughout the country. He is generally regarded as the country's most popular public figure.

Gasparri, Pietro (1852–1934)
Catholic diplomat and legal expert

Cardinal Gasparri, born in Macerata, was ordained into the priesthood in 1877. An expert in canon law, he was chiefly responsible for the codification of canon law in the monumental *Codex iuris canonici* (Code of canon law, 1904–17). He served as secretary of state from 1914 to 1930 under Popes BENEDICT XV and PIUS XI. During this long tenure in the second most important political post in the Vatican, Gasparri steered papal diplomacy through the difficulties of WORLD WAR I and postwar politics. The preeminent issues of his tenure in office were the role of the Vatican in wartime, the rise of communism in the Soviet Union, and of FASCISM in Italy. A staunch opponent of communism, Gasparri did not favor fascism but was willing to negotiate with BENITO MUSSOLINI. He is remembered principally for the role he played in settling the ROMAN QUESTION and normalizing relations of CHURCH AND STATE in Italy. He directed the long negotiations between the Vatican and the Fascist government, which resulted in the signing of the LATERAN PACTS in February 1929. An able negotiator, Gasparri protected the financial interests and doctrinal positions of the church on such key issues as marriage and education. Less admiring of Mussolini and more critical of fascism than Pius XI, he was replaced as secretary of state in 1930 by Eugenio Pacelli (the future PIUS XII). Mussolini took the unusual step of having Gasparri, a prelate, appointed to membership in the ITALIAN ACADEMY (1933) in recognition of his expertise as a jurist and for his diplomatic services.

Gattamelata   See CONDOTTIERI; DONATELLO.

Gattinara, Mercurino Arborio Marquis of   See CHARLES V.

gay movement

The Italian gay movement began in Milan in May 1971 at the initiative of gay militants who found little or no support from the political parties of the Left, which they considered to be their natural allies. Gay militants mostly from Milan, Turin, and Rome formed FUORI, meaning "out" (Fronte Unitario Omosessuale Rivoluzionario Italiano), which led the movement. In 1974 FUORI decided to join the RADICAL PARTY to avoid financial bankruptcy and political isolation. Some gay groups objected to the merger and decided to go their own way, initiating the process of internal splintering that has characterized the Italian gay movement ever since. More controversy and internal fighting followed FUORI's adoption of the tactics of legal action. Against its pursuit of reform by legislation, dissident militants turned to street action, organized national gatherings and gay camps, and called for uncontrolled personal freedom. These activities, and student revolts in 1977 in which gay issues surfaced, caught the attention of the public but generated little support in the country at large. In the 1980s the Italian Communist Party (PCI) came around to supporting gay demands. The communist administration of Bologna made headlines and stirred controversy by leasing public space to local gays. ARCI, the cultural and recreational association controlled by the PCI, accommodated gays within its organizational structure. In 1984 Arcigay became the major national gay organization as FUORI went into decline. The spread of the AIDS epidemic in the 1980s absorbed its attention and united the various currents among gay militants to lobby for preventative and health care measures. By the 1990s openly gay candidates were being elected to political office at the local, regional, and national levels. There is now acceptance of gays in public life, but the issue of "Gay Pride" remains controversial in the country at large. The CATHOLIC CHURCH, political parties of the Right, and conservative groups openly condemn homosexuality. A gay pride parade held in Rome in July 2000 was condemned by the church, which called the parade an act of provocation deliberately timed to coincide with the Jubilee Year. The Italian gay movement remains internally divided, with a weak national organization, many splinter groups, and divisions between gays and lesbians, lesbians generally preferring to associate with feminist organizations rather than male gay groups. National leaders also find little support among rank-and-file gays, who are suspicious of what they see as attempts to regulate individual behavior. Compared to gay movements in other western countries, the Italian movement is small, politically isolated, and relatively ineffective.

Gazzettino Rosa (Il) See JOURNALISM.

Gedda, Luigi (1902–2000)
geneticist, political figure, and voter organizer
for the Christian Democratic Party
Born in Venice, Gedda received a medical degree, taught medicine, and did pioneering research on the conception of twins. He was president of the youth section (1934–36) and of the men's section (1946–50) of CATHOLIC ACTION. In 1948 he spearheaded the drive to found local civic committees that gave Catholic Action a strong grassroots presence. As president of Catholic Action (1951–61), Gedda used the civic committees to compensate for the party's organizational weakness, mobilize the popular vote, and give the Christian Democratic Party (DC) a dominant role in government. Gedda represented the intransigent Catholic element that opposed compromise with the parties of the Left and resisted the OPENING TO THE LEFT and all efforts to bring socialists into the government. Pope JOHN XXIII removed him as head of Catholic Action to reduce the political role of the Catholic Church and facilitate the admission of socialists into the government.

Gelli, Licio See PROPAGANDA 2.

Gemelli, Agostino (1878–1959)
conservative Catholic educator and
philosopher
Gemelli, a Franciscan friar, founder and rector of the Catholic University of the Sacred Heart of Milan, emerged in the interwar years as a leading Catholic intellectual and link between the Catholic Church and the Fascist regime. Trained in science, he received a medical degree from the University of Pavia in 1902 and won international recognition for his work in experimental psychology. Gemelli took religious orders in 1903 after experiencing a spiritual crisis that was resolved by his reflections on the message of Saint Francis of Assisi. Eager to engage the enemies of the faith on intellectual grounds, he founded the *Rivista di Filosofia Neoscolastica* (1908), which professed a neo-Thomist philosophy critical of the two dominant philosophical currents of the moment: POSITIVISM and the Hegelian idealism of GIOVANNI GENTILE. After the war, Gemelli was both supporter and critic of the Italian Popular Party (PPI), seeing it as politically useful but insufficiently Catholic in its program and orientation. The University of the Sacred Heart, which opened in December 1921, was the centerpiece of his crusade to revitalize Catholic culture. With the support of Pope PIUS XI, who was a friend of Gemelli, the government approved it in 1924 as a "free university" endowed with considerable autonomy in spite of its professed confessional status. Its press and best-known review, *Vita e Pensiero*, aimed at nonspecialist readers, helped propagate a religious ideology that stressed the affinity of interests between Catholicism and the Italian state. At the same time, the university attracted the best-qualified Catholic students, training an elite that would play a major political role after the fall of the Fascist regime. Gemelli, an avowed supporter of the Fascist regime, welcomed the settlement of the ROMAN QUESTION, Fascist CORPORATIVISM, anticommunism, and anti-Semitism. Most of all, Gemelli was attracted to Benito MUSSOLINI for his deference toward the church and the restraints he placed on anticlericals.

Genoa, city of (Genova)
Genoa (pop. 636,000), capital of the region of Liguria, emerged as a major sea power after achieving political independence as a free commune in the 11th century. The Republic of Genoa

waged war successfully against the rival maritime city-state of PISA, winning control of SARDINIA, CORSICA, and SICILY in the course of the 13th century when its trade and commercial settlements reached Spain, North Africa, the Black Sea, and the Near East. Its expansion in the eastern Mediterranean region was opposed by VENICE, but Genoese shipping held its own until internal disputes weakened the government of the republic in the course of the 14th century. Constant warfare with Venice and Spain absorbed Genoese resources to the point that the city could no longer defend itself. It was ruled by the French (1396–1409, 1499–1506) and by MILAN (1421–99). Forced out of the eastern Mediterranean by the Venetians and the Turks, Genoese trade still controlled the western Mediterranean, while the city's credit institution, the BANCO DI SAN GIORGIO, played an important role in the finances of Milan and the Iberian peninsula. Genoa suffered during the wars of the early 16th century and was sacked by imperial troops (1522). In 1528 the commander ANDREA DORIA won imperial recognition of the city's autonomy and inaugurated the system of aristocratic government that lasted until NAPOLEON I annexed Genoa to France (1805). The CONGRESS OF VIENNA refused to restore the independent republic and assigned Genoa to the KINGDOM OF SARDINIA. By then, the city was but a shadow of its former self. A gradual revival of its economic fortunes began in the 1820s with government encouragement of the shipping industry and policing of Mediterranean waters against Barbary pirates. Genoese shipping companies reached out to the Atlantic trade and Genoese settlements established an Italian presence in the port cities of the United States, Brazil, and Argentina. Birthplace of GIUSEPPE MAZZINI, Genoa played an important role in the movement for national unification. It was Italy's principal seaport and an important shipbuilding center until the 1960s when both its shipping and shipbuilding began to decline. Today Genoa is a busy commercial emporium and transportation center at the southern end of Italy's "industrial triangle" that has Milan and TURIN as its other terminals.

Genoa, Conference(s) of

From April 10 through May 19, 1922, the Italian government hosted a 34-nation conference in Genoa to discuss postwar economic reconstruction and open relations between the Soviet Union and the noncommunist nations. Prime Minister LUIGI FACTA and Foreign Minister Carlo Schanzer (1865–1953) represented Italy. They were particularly interested in gaining access to Central European markets, reaching an agreement with the Soviets over repayment of czarist and war debts, and opening up the Soviet Union to foreign investment. Soviet and German representatives signed a separate treaty at the nearby town of Rapallo that settled the question of debts between the two countries and gave Germany access to the Soviet market. The bilateral agreement undermined the Genoa Conference, which broke up on May 19 without settling any of the issues that had prompted its calling.

Another international conference opened in Genoa on July 20, 2001, when representatives of the world's leading industrialized nations (the so-called G8 group composed of Canada, France, Germany, Great Britain, Japan, Italy, Russia, and the United States) met to discuss ways of promoting free trade and the integration of production and exchange across national borders. Opponents of globalization, as the movement toward world economic integration is known, also gathered in Genoa to protest against what they regarded as a capitalist plot to dominate the world economy in disregard of environmental and social concerns. The strong police reaction to street protests resulted in one death and many injuries and arrests of demonstrators. The conference closed on July 22 after meeting behind closed doors with extraordinary security measures. Antigovernment protests and a parliamentary investigation into police behavior followed its closing, to the embarrassment of the government of Prime Minister SILVIO BERLUSCONI, which staunchly defended the police. In spite of the protests, a parliamentary majority and public opinion generally backed the government's actions.

Genovesi, Antonio (1713–1769)
Neapolitan economist, philosopher, and Enlightenment reformer

Genovesi was born near Salerno to a family of landowners, entered the priesthood in 1737 at his family's insistence, and undertook the study of contemporary French and English philosophy that was his real interest. His familiarity with Descartes, Newton, Locke, and the economists of his time made him a leading and influential representative of ENLIGHTENMENT culture. After teaching metaphysics and ethics, in 1754 he was appointed to the newly created chair of commerce at the University of Naples. Genovesi lectured and wrote in Italian rather than Latin in order to reach a larger audience and influence public policy. His course lectures were published in two volumes as *Lezioni di commercio* (Lessons of Commerce, 1765–67). Genovesi's awareness of the social and public policy implications of economic decision making justify regarding him as a founder of the discipline of political economy. In practice, his ideas were a blend of traditional mercantilist notions that assigned an important economic role to government, and innovative laissez-faire, free-trade doctrines. Generally, Genovesi favored abolition of feudal privileges, unimpeded domestic economic exchanges, government protection of fledgling industries to encourage domestic manufacturing, and protection of agriculture to assure a sufficient supply of grains. Most of all, he argued for the importance of general education to dispel ignorance and prejudice, and impart practical, productive skills. He supported the reforms promoted by BERNARDO TANUCCI, looked to the enlightened nobility to carry on the reform movement, and favored restricting the power of the clergy. His last political campaign was against the JESUITS. When the Jesuits were expelled from the Kingdom on Naples in 1767 Genovesi was asked to draw up a plan for the improvement of education. However, the economic reform movement had run its course by that time, and the plan was never implemented. Often consulted by the government, Genovesi's proposals were usually stymied by strong opposition from traditionalists. His cultural influence was nevertheless great in southern Italy where he trained and influenced a generation of scholars who carried on his work.

Gentile, Giovanni (1875–1944)
philosopher and educator, strongly nationalist and closely identified with the Fascist regime

Born in Castelvetrano (Sicily), Gentile discovered his vocation for the study of philosophy at the prestigious *Scuola Normale* of Pisa, which he entered in 1893. His dissertation on ANTONIO ROSMINI-SERBATI and VINCENZO GIOBERTI signaled the beginning of a lifelong concern for the state and development of Italian philosophical thought. After teaching at the secondary level for several years, Gentile was called on to teach philosophy at the University of Palermo (1907–14) and at the *Scuola Normale,* where he remained for the rest of his life as teacher and president. Interest in Marxism brought him into contact with the older BENEDETTO CROCE. The two philosophers exerted strong intellectual influence on one another until philosophical and political differences drove them apart starting around 1914. Gentile's LIBERALISM was more authoritarian than Croce's. Gentile's philosophical IDEALISM insisted on the religious nature of all effective systems of belief, while Croce's was secular. Both were anticlerical, but Gentile set out to imbue lay education and culture with the same sense of passion and commitment toward the nation that traditional religion directed toward other-worldly concerns.

In 1914 Gentile favored Italian intervention in WORLD WAR I, while Croce favored neutrality. Gentile blamed the military defeat at CAPORETTO on the inadequacies of the school system, which in his judgment had failed to instill a strong spirit of patriotism in the Italian people. Gentile looked to the social body rather than to the individual, hence his belief that the individual finds fulfillment in the life of the state. Deeming it his duty as a philosopher and educator to foster a sense of national unity, he accepted BENITO MUSSOLINI's invitation to become minister of education (1922–24), joined the Fascist Party, and promoted school reform (May 1923). Gentile's principle was *pochi ma buoni* (few but good). The educational process was to be highly selective at the secondary level, allowing only the few that met its stringent requirements to go on to universities.

During the MATTEOTTI crisis Gentile wrote and promoted the *Manifesto of Fascist Intellectuals* (1925) that expressed the solidarity of a number of prominent cultural figures with the Fascist government. After 1925 he was not part of the government, but played an important role as mediator between the Fascist regime and the country's intellectuals. Gentile was the regime's most prestigious intellectual and a powerful cultural organizer. From 1926 to his death in 1944 he was chief editor of the monumental *Enciclopedia Italiana*. Perhaps the most ambitious and successful cultural enterprise of the regime, this multivolume reference tool was a model of serious scholarship, enriched by the contributions of the country's leading authorities. The encyclopedia entry on *Fascism*, signed by Mussolini, was partially written by Gentile. Published separately and translated in many languages, it went around the world as the most authoritative and comprehensive statement of Fascist doctrine.

Gentile continued to support the Fascist regime in spite of mental reservations concerning its racial policies and alliance with Nazi Germany. His loyalty did not waver even after Mussolini was deposed and arrested in July 1943. To show his continuing commitment at a time when most intellectuals were defecting to the opposition, he accepted the compromising post of president of the ITALIAN ACADEMY. Anti-Fascist guerrilla fighters shot him dead in front of his home on April 15, 1944. Only his one-

time friend and rival Benedetto Croce exceeded Gentile in intellectual influence in Italy. The publication of Gentile's *Opere complete* (1969–96) attests to the ongoing interest and importance of his work. There are translations of his writings in English and other languages, but Gentile's philosophical idealism has had little influence outside Italy. For an example of his work, see his *Genesis and Structure of Society* (1966).

Gentileschi, Orazio (1562–1647), and Gentileschi, Artemisia (1593–ca. 1652)
father and daughter painters of the late Renaissance period

Born to a family of painters, father and daughter responded to the influence of CARAVAGGIO in very personal and distinctive ways. Orazio was born in PISA, worked in the region of the Marches, Genoa, Paris, and in London at the court of Charles I. In his paintings, which include *Flight into Egypt* and *Lot and His Daughters*, the delicate shaping of the figures and soft contours attenuate the sense of drama typical of the school of Caravaggio. Artemisia began her training under her father, worked mostly in Florence, Naples, and in Madrid at the court of Philip IV. Her presence in Naples after 1630 helped reinvigorate painting in the South. Her works, which include a particularly striking and gory rendition of *Judith Beheading Holofernes* and a *Mary Magdalen*, show a vigorous style and the skillful use of light and dark (chiaroscuro). The choice of female subjects and violent situations may have been influenced by her own experience as a victim of rape by an art instructor hired by her father, but her strong manner and choice of heroic poses suggest anything but an attitude of victimization. Her personal reputation suffered as a result of allegations made by her attacker in the course of a bitterly contested trial that ended in a light sentence for the accused rapist. Both father and daughter were much in demand, particularly as portraitists, and their works appear in different parts of Europe. The father's artistic reputation eclipsed the daughter's, until she was

Artemisia Gentileschi *(Library of Congress)*

rediscovered and reappraised by feminist art historians in the latter part of the 20th century. Her life is fictionalized in a French film, *Artemisia* (1998) starring Valentina Cervi.

Gentiloni, Vincenzo Ottorino
(1865–1916)
Catholic activist and political organizer

Count Gentiloni, born near Ancona (Marches), entered politics in the early 1890s as an organizer of Catholic voters interested in resolving the conflict between CHURCH AND STATE. Appointed in 1909 as president of the Catholic Electoral Union, he is credited with having played a key role in swinging Catholic support behind Prime Minister GIOVANNI GIOLITTI. The lifting of the papal prohibition against Catholic

participation in national elections gives credence to the belief that in 1913 Gentiloni and Giolitti agreed to direct Catholic votes toward candidates who endorsed the church's position on a number of issues, including education, divorce, and freedom of association. This so-called Gentiloni Pact supposedly enabled Giolitti's Liberal Party to maintain its dominant political position in the national ELECTIONS of 1913. Radicals and socialists roundly condemned the alleged deal, seeing it as an attempt to undermine the parties of the Left. Their attacks helped bring on Giolitti's resignation as prime minister in March 1914, before the onset of the international crisis that led to WORLD WAR I. Giolitti's absence from government during that crisis is thought to have made it easier for interventionists to bring Italy into the war. Gentiloni resigned as president of the Catholic Electoral Union shortly before his death in 1916.

geography

The most obvious feature of the geography of the Italian peninsula is its complexity. Varieties of climate, topography, landscape, and human habitat make all generalizing inherently risky. The easily recognizable "boot" that extends from the European continent into the MEDITERRANEAN SEA toward Africa contains mountains, forests, farmlands, beaches, isolated dwellings, villages, and large cities, all symbiotically related in an environment in which human labor has left an indelible imprint on the natural landscape. The most esthetically appealing parts of the peninsula are those in which nature and human effort blend harmoniously, as they do in the central regions of the MARCHES, TUSCANY, and UMBRIA, but that may be a matter of personal preference. The peninsula's 116,318 square miles (slightly larger than the state of Arizona) cover a territory that is approximately one-third mountains, one-third hills, and one-third plains or lowlands. The ALPS and APENNINES are its principal mountain ranges. The national territory includes the large islands of SARDINIA and SICILY. The many smaller islands include Capri, Elba, Ischia, Lampedusa, and Pantelleria, and the Egadi and Lipari island groups off the coast of Sicily.

The continental part comprises the Alps and the country's largest plain, the well-irrigated and fertile Po River Valley (Val Padana). Alpine streams flow into the scenic lakes of northern Italy, including Lake Garda and Lake Como, and into the tributaries that come together to form the country's longest watercourse, the PO RIVER. Water is less abundant in the rest of the peninsula, which is dominated by the mountainous backbone of the Apennines. South of the Po Valley, only the Arno River, which flows through the region of Tuscany, and the Tiber River, which flows through the region of LATIUM, are large enough to maintain a fairly steady supply of water throughout the year. Below Rome, the rivers are mostly seasonal streams that dry up in summer. Southern agriculture has traditionally had to contend with scarcity of water. Nevertheless, agricultural production has done well in many areas of the South, particularly in the volcanic soil around the city of NAPLES and in the Conca d'Oro (Golden Bowl) plain around PALERMO. The large plain (Tavoliere) that covers much of the PUGLIA region was once an important winter grazing ground for sheep.

North, Center, and South are sufficiently different geographically to justify this customary three-way distinction and merit individual attention. Geographers suggest, however, that there are other useful ways of conceptualizing the geography of the peninsula. One alternative model identifies "three Italies" that do not coincide with North, Center, and South or with the administrative boundaries of existing regions. According to this now generally accepted partition, there is a Northwest characterized by established large-scale industries, a North-East-Center with newer, expanding small and medium-scale industries, and a South marked by slower economic development. However one may define it, the Italian land mass is surrounded by water on three sides, making the sea another dominant reality. A mountainous interior hindering internal communications and transportation combined with the accessibility of the sea have invited Italians to look beyond their shores. Many of Italy's towns and cities historically have found economic opportunity on the sea. Medieval GENOA, PISA, and VENICE grew wealthy from seagoing commerce. The proximity of the sea has facilitated MIGRATION in and out of the peninsula and the long, exposed coastline has influenced Italian politics and FOREIGN POLICY. See also AGRICULTURE, URBANIZATION, and the entries on Italy's regions.

Georgofili, Accademia Economico-Agraria dei

The Academy of the Georgofili (lovers of the fields) was founded in 1753 by a group of Florentine aristocrats to encourage the revival of AGRICULTURE according to French and English notions of agricultural improvement. It was the first of many such agricultural societies interested in the diffusion and adoption of practical remedies to improve agricultural production that soon spread throughout Italy. One of its first endeavors was to organize a tree-planting contest that led to increased Tuscan production of olive oil and wine by the 1780s. The Georgofili were also responsible for the introduction of new grains resistant to disease, crop diversification, and improved soil techniques, all of which helped make Tuscan agriculture a model of its kind. In the 19th century the academy was a rallying point for progressive landowners interested in the development of a national market and therefore receptive to both economic and political changes in the peninsula. There were limits to the academy's championing of progressive agriculture. Improvements in productivity were limited by the prevalence of *mezzadria*, a sharecropping system approved by the Georgofili that had the advantage of stability but did not encourage agricultural progress. Although technologically progressive, the Georgofili represented the views of landowners who were ultimately more interested in economic security and social peace in the countryside than in maximizing production and profits in agriculture. It has nevertheless played an important educational role, helped educate peasant landowners and workers, and has sponsored prestigious publications. The *Atti* of the academy have been published regularly since 1792.

Ghiberti, Lorenzo (ca. 1378–1455)
Florentine sculptor and goldsmith
Ghiberti is best remembered as the creator of the famous Baptistery doors in Florence. He won that commission in 1401 in a competition to design and construct a door to match an earlier one by Andrea Pisano. The panels that he designed depicted scenes from the life of Christ, the Evangelists, and Church Fathers, in bas-relief, and in a style reminiscent of Pisano's Gothic. In Florence, where he lived and worked most of his life, he created several other works, including statues of Saint John the Baptist, Saint Matthew, and Saint Stephen, for the Church of Orsanmichele. After returning from a short trip to Venice in 1424, he took up work on the third door to the Baptistery, on which he continued to work for some 28 years. The Gates of Paradise, as his admiring fellow Florentines dubbed these portals, consist of 10 panels depicting scenes from the Old Testament framed by bands with niches from which the figures of ancient prophets protrude in a striking display of small-scale sculpting bravura pointing to his training as a goldsmith, the effect being emphasized by the gilded surface, recently cleaned to reveal its original brightness. Five panels that were heavily damaged by the flood of 1966 have also been fully restored. The minutely detailed compositions of figures, landscaped backgrounds, and architectural features come together as a harmonious whole. The impression that these doors made on Ghiberti's contemporaries was enormous. He was hailed as the master of a new style that utilized varying grades of relief in a gamut of subtle gradations that ran from the representation of virtually flat figures (a technique called *schiacciato*) to fully rounded ones protruding from the surface. He was seen as a daring inno-

vator, although the view of himself that emerges from his *Commentarii,* an autobiography and commentary on art written around 1450, is that of a follower of trends set by GIOTTO, Duccio di Boninsegna, Andrea Pisano, and other late medieval and early Renaissance artists.

Ghirlandaio, Domenico   See
MICHELANGELO BUONARROTI.

Giambologna   See MANNERISM.

Gianni, Francesco Maria (1728–1801)
Tuscan economist and political reformer
Descended from an old family of the Florentine aristocracy and extremely wealthy, Gianni bore his family name and influence with an excessive pride that made him unpopular even among his social peers. Nevertheless, he was an influential public figure highly respected by Grand Duke PETER LEOPOLD, who relied on him for advice in carrying out economic and political reforms. Gianni learned the ways of bureaucracy by working his way through the financial administration of the Grand Duchy of TUSCANY, including the post of director of customs in Pisa to which he was appointed in 1754. He became senator in 1761 and state councilor in 1789. Although he shared the reforming zeal of his contemporary POMPEO NERI, the two often disagreed and gave conflicting advice to the grand duke. Practical above all else, Gianni was always ready to question doctrinaire views and never willing to admit his own errors. A landowner and free trader at heart, he nevertheless questioned the Physiocrats' blind faith in agriculture and free trade, arguing for protection to encourage urban manufactures. He did favor free trade in grains in principle, but acknowledged that controls were desirable to ward off domestic shortages and social unrest. He was nevertheless identified with free traders and fell into disfavor after the grain shortages of the late 1780s and the bread riots of 1790. His political influence declined, but some

degree of popular resentment was still evident in 1799, when his estate was sacked by a mob and Gianni fled abroad in fear for his life.

Giannini, Guglielmo See UOMO QUALUNQUE.

Giannone, Pietro (1676–1748)
Neapolitan historian, legal expert, and political reformer

Born to a family of modest means, Giannone was able to study law at the University of Naples, thanks to the help of a relative in the priesthood. He practiced law with some success after graduation (1698), but he also found time to pursue his passion, which was the study of history. A 20-year study of Neapolitan legal history resulted in the publication of his *Istoria civile del Regno di Napoli* (Civil history of the Kingdom of Naples, 1723). The theme of his work is the relationship between CHURCH AND STATE. Giannone's documentation exposed the false basis of clerical claims to privileged status within the state, including the papal claim of feudal lordship over the Neapolitan monarchy symbolized by the yearly homage gift of a white mare (*chinea*) from the king to the pope. His defense of civil authority and attack on clerical privilege earned him the hostility of the pope. Giannone was excommunicated, his work placed on the INDEX, his career ruined, and he was forced into exile. He continued his researches in Vienna (1723–34), where he completed the three-volume study *Triregno,* which expanded on his earlier work and fleshed out the historical evidence for a reform of the state. His life made difficult in Vienna, then attracted to VENICE, where he found little support, Giannone was well received in Protestant Geneva (1735–36). Although attracted theologically to Protestantism, he refused to convert in order to carry on his campaign against clerical privilege as a Catholic. That decision infuriated Catholic authorities. Tricked into visiting Catholic SAVOY, he was arrested and detained in various prisons by the local authorities for the rest of his life, but they did not consign him to papal justice. Among the works that he wrote in prison was the *Vita scritta da lui medesimo* (A life written by himself), which took his story up to 1741 and is an important social document on life in Naples and Vienna. Various unreliable versions of the *Vita* and *Triregno* were published in the 19th century. A reliable edition of the *Vita* was published in 1904 and of *Triregno* in 1940. JACOBINS and 19th-century anticlerical patriots regarded Giannone as a precursor and martyr.

Gigli, Beniamin See OPERA.

Ginzburg, Natalia See JEWS IN ITALY.

Gioberti, Vincenzo (1801–1852)
Catholic philosopher, Risorgimento patriot, and political figure

Born in Turin to a family of the lower middle class, educated by priests, he received a degree in theology in 1823, was ordained a priest in 1825, and continued his theological studies at the University of Turin. In 1831 he was appointed professor of theology at the same university, as well as court chaplain. Suspected of political subversion, arrested, and expatriated in 1833, Gioberti lived and wrote in Paris and Brussels until 1848 when he returned to Italy in the wake of revolution. His fame as writer and scholar, won during his years of exile, propelled him to the position of prime minister of the kingdom of SARDINIA in 1848–49. Exiled once again after the revolution, Gioberti spent the few remaining years of his life in France. The salient biographical facts of Gioberti's short but influential life can be thus summed up, but the nature of his ideas is more elusive. Influenced as a young man by the republican ideals of the FRENCH REVOLUTION and by the fiery patriotism of VITTORIO ALFIERI and UGO FOSCOLO, the young Gioberti internalized the patriotic passion of the generation of ROMANTICISM. But his political convictions were moderated by a scholarly, contemplative temperament that was incompatible with all forms of extremism. He seems to have found his religious faith after his ordination and struggled thereafter to reconcile it with his commitment to an independent Italy. Attracted briefly to Giuseppe Mazzini's YOUNG ITALY, he soon rejected its principle of revolutionary action and sought attainment of national independence and unity by a gradual process. Accord with the PAPACY, reliance on international diplomacy, and popular education were the means that Gioberti proposed to other patriots.

Intent also on promoting church reform, he challenged the authority of the JESUITS which he held responsible for the papacy's rejection of LIBERALISM. His political vision emerged fully developed in his most influential work, *Del primato morale e civile degli italiani* (On the moral and civil primacy of the Italians, 1843). Its argument that Catholicism was the essential ingredient of the Italian national identity and that the papacy was therefore the natural leader of the movement for national independence was immediately controversial. Gioberti argued that papal leadership of the national movement would avert the danger of revolution, reassure the world, and give Italy independence without recourse to revolution or war. The pope would be compensated for the loss of temporal power by becoming president of a federation of Italian states.

Gioberti's program pleased those who wanted to reconcile religion with patriotism and enraged others who could not countenance papal leadership or imagine a peaceful solution to the national question. Gioberti's book inspired the NEO-GUELF movement, which gained strength with the unexpected election of Pope PIUS IX in 1846. With a seemingly liberal pope at the helm, Gioberti was the man of the moment. It was this popularity, and his willingness to work with the monarchy of CHARLES ALBERT, that gave Gioberti political prominence in 1848. But that prominence was of short duration. The pope's rejection of the national cause and of liberal reform cut the ground from under Gioberti and the Neo-Guelfs. His prime ministry was controversial and short (December 1848–February 1849).

After his moment in the limelight, Gioberti went back into political exile, living out the last years of his life in Paris in straitened financial circumstances. Deprived of papal support, his writings placed on the INDEX, Gioberti reformulated his vision of Italy's future in his *Rinnovamento civile d'Italia* (Civil renewal of Italy, 1851), which assigned to Piedmont the role of national leader, with recourse to war if necessary, as long as it remained a constitutional monarchy. He still considered Catholicism the essential ingredient of the Italian national identity, but saw the need for reform within the church and called for a progressive, reforming papacy. The influence of French socialist thought in the last years of his life also opened Gioberti's mind to the importance of the social question in the movement for national unification. By tying national independence to religious reform, Gioberti sought to provide spiritual guidance for the Italian people and political advice for the church. His effort to resolve the issue of CHURCH AND STATE found partial fruition in the principles and politics of Christian Democracy (DC).

Gioia, Melchiorre (1767–1829)
economist, political writer, and reformer

Born in Piacenza, Gioia is a prominent figure of the Italian ENLIGHTENMENT. Influenced by JANSENISM and an admirer of Jacobin government in France, Gioia took holy orders in 1793 but renounced them to pursue political journalism. Jailed for his public support of revolution, he was liberated by NAPOLEON I. In 1797 he wrote a prize-winning essay on the theme "Which Form of Free Government Can Best Secure the Happiness of Italy?" Gioia's answer was that Italy should be governed as an independent, unified republic. That under the circumstances such a republic would have to be pro-French and anti-Austrian was not lost on the pro-French judges who awarded the prize. But Gioia was also a critic of the French administration for giving Venice to Austria and limiting the powers of the Italian governments. He did well as an economist and statistician in the employ of the Napoleonic administrations. In 1801 he was made the official historian of the Cisalpine Republic and put in charge of collecting statistics (1806–08). Politically suspect after the fall of Napoleon, he wrote in favor of economic protectionism to encourage industrialization in LOMBARDY and collaborated with GIAN DOMENICO ROMAGNOSI in founding the influential review *Annali Universali di Statistica*. He is seen in retrospect as a precursor of the RISORGIMENTO.

Giolitti, Giovanni (1842–1928)
liberal leader, statesman, and dominant political figure

In the period that is commonly known as the Giolittian era (1901–14), Giolitti served as minister of the interior (1901–03), was three times prime minister (1903–05, 1906–09, 1911–14), and wielded decisive political influence when out of office as leader of the liberal forces in parliament. He earned a law degree from the University of Turin (1860) and chose to pursue a career in public administration. That decision cost him the chance to participate in the conclusive battles of the Risorgimento, for which Giolitti was not suited by temperament. He served in various administrative capacities, learning the nuts and bolts of government and gaining insight into the nature of the political process. He entered parliament in 1882 as a member of the LIBERAL LEFT. At the core of Giolitti's liberalism was his respect for parliament. He made parliament the center of power at a time when its role was being challenged, worked with parliament to enact his political program, and protected it from attack by extraparliamentary forces, including the monarchy.

Giolitti's political career had its stormy moments. As minister of the treasury (1889–90), he clashed with the impetuous FRANCESCO CRISPI, whom he succeeded briefly as prime minister (1892–93). That first stint as head of government nearly ruined him politically, as he was caught up in the scandal of the BANCA ROMANA and faced charges of corruption. His refusal to invoke martial law during the uprising of the FASCI SICILIANI

left him open to charges that he was soft on law and order and socialism. His comeback occurred after the country's prolonged political crisis of 1896–1901, when the ailing GIUSEPPE ZANARDELLI asked him to serve as his minister of the interior. With Zanardelli ill, Giolitti became the real political power even before assuming the prime ministry in November 1903. His many critics accused him of manipulating ELECTIONS, and Giolitti was indeed adept at piling up majorities with the restricted suffrage of those years. His use of PREFECTS for electoral purposes was nothing new, but he did perfect the practice in the elections of 1904 and 1909 that gave the liberals comfortable majorities. Such manipulations became much more problematic after Giolitti steered through parliament the electoral reform bill of 1912 that expanded the electorate from 3 million to 8.5 million voters. This, his most daring political move, may have hastened the end of the Giolittian era, for Giolitti's followers controlled relatively fewer seats in parliament after the elections of 1913.

It was Giolitti's practice to seek parliamentary support from wherever he could find it. He reached out to all parliamentary groups willing to cooperate with him, including socialists and Catholics who had been previously ostracized from government. To engage the socialists, he instituted a policy of government neutrality in labor disputes, whereby the government limited itself to maintaining law and order and intervened only if violence broke out. Giolitti also courted socialist backing by awarding public contracts to worker cooperatives. Although an anticlerical at heart, he welcomed the support of Catholic deputies, repaying them for their support by holding back on a divorce bill and appointing them to positions of influence. Giolitti's decision to fight the ITALIAN-TURKISH WAR pleased Catholics and right-wing nationalists, who were also gaining a foothold in politics. Catholic support may have given Giolitti enough votes to retain a precarious majority in the elections of 1913.

Monetary stability, moderate protectionism, and government encouragement of production sustained the economic expansion of the Giolittian era. But economic progress came at the price of serious social dislocations. EMIGRATION reached unprecedented levels between 1900 and 1914. The rapid industrialization of the North widened the gap between North and South. Giolitti was aware of the economic plight of the South and steered through parliament the first laws to promote its development. GAETANO SALVEMINI and other *MERIDIONALISTI* accused Giolitti of favoring the businessmen and workers of the industrial North at the expense of the mostly peasant South. Salvemini's charge that Giolitti was the *ministro della malavita* (rackets minister) stuck and clouded Giolitti's political reputation.

Controversy continued to swirl around Giolitti during and after WORLD WAR I because he was known to have opposed Italian intervention. In the electoral campaign of 1919 he charged that an aggressive minority had dragged the country into war against the will of the majority and vowed that it must never be allowed to happen again. That position put him at odds with FASCISM, which Giolitti did not perceive right away as a serious threat to the liberal state. He returned to power as prime minister with his fifth and final government (June 1920–June 1921) at a time of grave crisis. Faced by the workers' occupation of the factories in September 1920, he refused to intervene as employers urged him to do. He isolated D'Annunzio in FIUME to prevent nationalism from sweeping through the country, took steps to contain Fascist violence, and curbed government expenditures to reduce the huge spending deficit. That program alienated the political extremes and won him few supporters in the middle.

Gambling that the mood of the country was swinging in his favor, he called for new elections in May 1921. The disappointing results brought about his resignation. Out of power but still head of the liberals, Giolitti did not resist the country's drift toward fascism, banking perhaps that the responsibility of power would tame the Fascists, weaken the Left, and make for a return of stability. He voted for the Fascist-sponsored ACERBO law that changed the electoral system and favored the Fascist electoral triumph of 1924. After the elections, Giolitti joined the opposition. He broke openly with the Fascist government only months before his death in July 1928. A pragmatic reformer above all else, Giolitti avoided enunciating grandiose programs and visions, set limited goals, and was an effective administrator with a realistic and perhaps too narrow view of the possibilities of change. He made his case in his *Memoirs of My Life* (1923).

Giordano, Umberto See OPERA.

Giornale de' Letterati Italiani See MAFFEI, SCIPIONE.

Giovanna II of Naples See ALFONSO I OF NAPLES.

Gioventù Italiana del Littorio (GIL)
umbrella organization of Fascist youth groups, with mandatory membership

The Fascist youth organization derived its name from the lictor's rods that were the symbol of authority in ancient Rome. It was formed in 1937, replacing the Opera Nazionale Balilla founded in 1926. It covered all youth organizations. The Figli e figlie della lupa (Sons and Daughters of the She-Wolf), again a reference to the symbolism of ancient Rome, enrolled children ages six to eight; the Balilla was for eight- to 15-year-old boys, the Avanguardisti for boys 15 to 18. Girls had their own auxiliary organizations, the Giovani italiane and Giovani fasciste. The purpose of GIL was to infuse Fascist ideals in the young, prepare them for their responsibilities in Fascist society, and inculcate in them the cult of the Duce. Boys underwent various stages of military training, starting with marching exercises and mock rifle drills and culminating in realistic simulations of combat at the Avanguardist level. Male graduates of the youth movement were encouraged to continue their military training and careers in the Fascist Militia. For women, the emphasis was on preparation for motherhood and other domestic duties. Non-Fascist youth groups were banned in 1928 and membership in Fascist youth organizations was made compulsory in 1938. The Catholic Church opposed the Fascist monopoly. The Fascist organization reached 8.8 million members in 1942. It gave the regime a pervasive presence at the grass roots of society and a foothold in every family. The regime attached great importance to the youth movement, banking on it to prepare future generations for war and to perpetuate Fascist values.

Giovine Italia See YOUNG ITALY.

Giovio, Paolo (1483–1552)
Renaissance historian, art critic, and humanist writer

Giovio's fame rests primarily on his historical and biographical writings. Born in Como, orphaned at an early age, and raised by his older brother Benedetto, who was a writer of note, he studied medicine and philosophy in Milan (1506–15) before concluding his studies in Padua and Pavia. He practiced medicine in Rome, but his good reputation as a physician was soon overshadowed by his fame as a historian who wrote in elegant Latin for educated readers. Pope CLEMENT VII admired Giovio and conferred Roman citizenship on him (1524). Giovio was at the pope's side in 1527 during the infamous SACK OF ROME when the papal court found refuge behind the walls of Castel Sant'Angelo. Clement made him a bishop and Francis I of France granted him a pension. Giovio's villa in Como contained a remarkable collection of portraits of distinguished contemporaries (the only coeval portrait of CHRISTOPHER COLUMBUS is thought to have been part of his collection). The collection in turn inspired him to write "great lives" of his contemporaries and to urge GIORGIO VASARI to do the same. Giovio is best

remembered for his *Commentari delle cose de Turchi* (Commentaries on Turkish affairs, 1531), an account of the Turkish threat to the Christian world, and his *Historia sui temporis* (History of his own times, 1550–52). His lively style, the rapid translation of his works from Latin to Italian and vice versa, his personal familiarity with major figures and events of his time, and the anecdotal nature of his writings make Giovio the first historian capable of reaching a broad educated public. Modern scholars question the reliability of some of his accounts, and he admitted that he wrote to please those who paid him. Nevertheless, Giovio provides unique insights into the events and figures of his time and is indispensable reading for those who wish to understand 16th-century Italy.

Girardengo, Costante See SPORTS.

Giuliano, Salvatore (1922–1950)
Sicilian outlaw, leader of an autonomist movement

The most notorious Italian bandit of the 20th century, Giuliano was born to a poor Sicilian family of Castelvetrano. His career as an outlaw began in 1943 when he killed a policeman who had caught him smuggling flour, a practice quite common in wartime. In the civil chaos of the war and postwar years, Giuliano became the head of a band of outlaws who operated in and around the town of Montelepre in western Sicily. With the connivance of the MAFIA and of the Sicilian separatist movement that wanted independence for the island, Giuliano was able for years to defy thousands of police and army troops that were sent to capture him. On May 1, 1947, he led an ambush at a locality called Portella delle Ginestre against a peaceful communist-led demonstration calling for land reform, killing 11 demonstrators. The Italian Communist Party (PCI) called for a parliamentary investigation, charged that Giuliano acted for the Mafia, and was tied to the ruling Christian

Democratic Party (DC) and the Sicilian separatist movement. The minister of the interior, MARIO SCELBA, also a Sicilian, took charge of the campaign against Giuliano, which resulted in Giuliano's killing in July 1950 by a member of his own band, Gaspare Pisciotta, who was later poisoned while awaiting trial in prison. The handsome, swaggering Giuliano was dubbed the king of Montelepre, received much attention from the press and caught the imagination of the public. The weakness of the Italian state after the war, the fear of communism, idealization of the bandit as a champion of the people, and separatist aspirations worked in Giuliano's favor for a while. His death marked the end of the period of state reconstruction and the return of political stability based on regional autonomy and the dominance of Christian Democracy.

Giulio Romano (1492–1546)
Renaissance artist known for the dramatic impact of his compositions

Baptized Giulio Pippi, this painter and architect served as RAPHAEL's assistant until his master's death in 1520. Influenced by both Raphael and MICHELANGELO, Romano developed a distinct style that blended Raphael's gracefulness with Michelangelo's gravity. His internal decorations cover entire walls, are full of classical allusions, and convey the sense of motion and high drama that is typical of the BAROQUE. His work as architect and painter is shown at its best in the fantastic design and decorations of the Palazzo del Tè in Mantua, which he built for the GONZAGA FAMILY in 1527–34. Its rustic exterior conforms to the palace's original rural setting. Columns and windows are set out in a seemingly irregular yet perfectly balanced fashion that teases the eye and calls for close scrutiny of the design. The interior consists of a series of rooms, with walls and ceilings fully covered by pictorial decorations. The most striking is the Sala dei Giganti (Hall of Giants), where Romano painted enormous frescoes that depict the destruction of the rebellious giants by Zeus. It was painted to welcome the Emperor CHARLES V in 1532, a salute to the ruler who was expected to bring order to Italy after the anarchy of war, represented in the murals by the rebellious giants. Here Romano stands out as a painter in the spirit of MANNERISM.

Giusti, Giuseppe (1809–1850)
Tuscan writer, patriot, and political commentator

Giusti was born in the Tuscan village of Monsummano near Pistoia to a prominent local family. As a law student at the University of Pisa (1826–29) he showed far more enthusiasm for carousing than for studying, prompting his father to recall him home. He returned to Pisa to complete his studies in 1834, graduated, but never showed much enthusiasm for the practice of law. His literary writings won him fame as a political satirist. His satire expressed patriotic sentiments shared by moderate liberals who opposed Austrian dominance and wanted national independence without conspiracies, popular violence, or revolution. Education, gradual reforms, and moderate government were the core values of his liberalism. Giusti aimed his sharp barbs at absolute monarchs, papal power, clerical influence, and political hypocrisy. His carefully crafted verses were intended for popular consumption rather than critical acclaim. He can be enjoyed at his best in the poem *In Sant'Ambrogio,* where he describes his own feelings as he watches Austrian soldiers devoutly attending mass. In that poem Giusti's humanity comes out, and political satire combines with genuine pathos. His premature death from tuberculosis deprived the literary scene of someone who could bring literature to the people. His popularity contributed to making Tuscan the national language.

Giustizia e Libertà   See ANTIFASCISM; ROSSELLI, CARLO.

Gladio   See TAVIANI, PAOLO EMILIO.

Gobetti, Piero (1901–1926)

liberal literary critic, journalist, and anti-Fascist political commentator

Social and literary criticism come together in Gobetti's work to produce a devastating critique of the course of Italian history from the RISORGIMENTO to the rise of FASCISM. While still a student at the University of Turin he published the review *Energie nuove* (1918–20), which called for a broader participation in political life, new leadership, and reform of the state administration. Gobetti sympathized with the efforts of his friend ANTONIO GRAMSCI to organize and mobilize workers for political action, but did not share Gramsci's Marxist faith. Gobetti believed that civil liberties, universal suffrage, education, open debate, and political competition were indispensable attributes of sound social organization. Like Gramsci, he assigned an important role to intellectuals, who were to carry on a "liberal revolution" by working with and interpreting the needs of the masses. *Rivoluzione liberale* was the title of the review published by Gobetti (1922–25). His political philosophy put him on a collision course with fascism. Repeatedly arrested, he was severely beaten by Fascist toughs in September 1925. He died the following year in Paris as a result of his injuries. Gobetti is remembered as an eloquent and impassioned anti-Fascist who posthumously influenced the opposition movement GIUSTIZIA E LIBERTÀ.

Goldoni, Carlo (1707–1793)

Venetian playwright who changed the direction of Italian theater

Goldoni revolutionized Italian theater with his more than 150 plays written in Italian and Venetian dialect. Born to a professional family, he studied and practiced law before running away to Milan (1733), where he took up writing for the theater. While the traditional COMMEDIA DELL'-ARTE featured stock characters and improvised dialogue, Goldoni insisted on the importance of actor fidelity to written text, restrained acting, and realistic delineation of character. His theater is often described as a comedy of manners. People caught in comic domestic situations familiar to the audience were his stock-in-trade. In the dialect comedy *I rusteghi* (The clods, 1760) he recounts the conflicts between tight-spending husbands and their wives and daughters, who scheme endlessly to force their men to loosen the purse strings. Goldoni avoided the use of vulgar language, which had become common in comic plays, and aimed instead at humorous decorum. His characters represented a cross-section of society, from nobility and wealthy merchants to ordinary people at home and in the streets. He drew his characters sympathetically, showing their weaknesses and foibles without moralizing, with a tolerance that seems to have been an integral part of his personality. Popular with the public, he was the target of attacks from rivals who accused him of disregarding the noble traditions of the Italian theater and condoning immoral behavior. Good theater, his plays are also valuable as social documents reflecting the customs and values of his time. Embroiled in literary and political controversy provoked by his rival CARLO GOZZI, Goldoni left Venice for Paris in 1762. He was welcomed and honored in the French capital and at the royal court of Versailles. Voltaire praised his plays for their realism, Louis XV invited him to teach Italian to members of the royal family. A royal pension enabled Goldoni to leave service at court and return to Paris in 1780. Out of favor with the revolutionaries who retracted his pension in 1790, he lived his last years in poverty and poor health, looked after by his wife and nephew.

Gonella, Guido (1905–1982)

leader of conservative wing of Christian Democracy, member of parliament, and education minister

Gonella was born in Verona, studied and taught philosophy and law, was active in Catholic youth organizations, and wrote for Catholic publications before making his political debut as a founding member of the Christian Democratic

Party (DC). Gonella belonged to the staunchly anticommunist and conservative wing of the DC. He appealed to middle-class voters, upheld the importance of the family, and proposed educational reforms to provide for school choice, reduce the role of the state, expand the role of private education, and give parents a strong voice in school matters. Strongly opposed by the parties of the Left and by rival currents within his own party, Gonella's proposals made little headway at the time, even though he served as minister of education (1946–51). A member of the constituent assembly (1946–48) and of parliament after 1948, he held various posts in governments controlled by the DC.

Gonzaga family

Members of the Gonzaga dynasty ruled in MANTUA, Guastalla, Sabbioneta, and other principalities from 1328. They rose to prominence by conquest and marriage, acquired titles of nobility, and developed a reputation as formidable CONDOTTIERI. Mantua's exposed position in the Po Valley made the city vulnerable to attack from more powerful neighbors, forcing the Gonzagas to fortify their possessions and turning them toward military pursuits. Francesco I (1366–1407) built the Castle of San Giorgio in Mantua and defended the city against the VISCONTI of Milan. Lodovico III (1412–78) was a distinguished captain who held out against VENICE and undertook an ambitious program of urban reform. The Gonzagas generally kept on good terms with the PAPACY, except for Federico II (1500–40) who fought for Emperor CHARLES V against Pope CLEMENT VII. It was a timely switch. Federico was well rewarded, acquired the duchy of Monferrato, and hired GIULIO ROMANO to build and decorate the Palazzo del Tè. The Gonzagas were generous patrons of artists and scholars. Under their rule, Mantua became an important center of RENAISSANCE culture. The direct Gonzaga line died out with Vincenzo II in 1627.

Gothic line See WORLD WAR II.

government

What is described here is the government of the Italian republic. Its organization and operation are regulated by the CONSTITUTION of 1948 and by evolving political practices. To avoid confusion, one should distinguish between two distinct meanings of the term "government." The term is often used as a synonym for cabinet, or council of ministers. The cabinet or council of ministers is the "government" in charge at any one time. It consists of the prime minister (head of government) and other ministers in charge of specific ministries or appointed for some other purpose (ministers without portfolio). The council of ministers stays in power as long as it has the support of a majority in parliament. There have been more than 50 such "governments" in Italy since the end of WORLD WAR II.

As used here, the term refers to the way the state functions, regardless of what political party or group of parties may control the levers of power at any one time. The organization of government in that sense is based on the constitution, which defines Italy as a parliamentary republic governed by a bicameral legislature (chamber of deputies and senate), a president, an independent judiciary, a supreme court, and by regional and local administrations. The constitution makes the legislature (parliament) the most powerful branch of government. Members of either branch of parliament (or cabinet members) may initiate bills, which must be approved by a majority of both branches of parliament before becoming law. A distinctive feature of the Italian legislative process is that either parliament or the cabinet may enact decree-laws (*decreti legge*). These are measures that go into effect immediately, subject to later approval by parliament within a specified period of time, usually 60 days. Until the ELECTIONS of 1994 the system of proportional representation and voting by party list guaranteed seats in parliament to virtually all political parties no matter how small. The change toward single-member, winner-take-all constituencies, meant to reduce political fragmentation, has changed the composition of parliament but has not stopped the proliferation of small parties or organized groups within it. Since no single party dominates parliament, Italy is usually governed by multiparty coalitions.

The constitution describes the president of the republic as the head of the state and assigns to him the function of representing "the unity of the nation." The power of the Italian presidency is limited. The president is not elected directly by the people, but by both houses of parliament sitting jointly for a seven-year term of office. The president's most important function is to designate new prime ministers, who must then be approved by parliament to carry out their duties, and to call for new elections if no parliamentary majority can be formed. Otherwise the office of president is mostly ceremonial. Still, individual presidents have made effective use of the "bully pulpit" to raise issues of national concern and sway public opinion. An issue that is currently the subject of national debate is whether to provide for direct popular election of the president and increase the power of the office. It is important to keep in mind that the largely ceremonial nature of the presidency is not an accident. The weakness of the executive branch is a deliberate feature of the Italian system of government, which was put in place to prevent the kind of personal dictatorship or one-party control that Italians experienced under FASCISM.

An independent judiciary (*magistratura*), whose members are civil servants appointed for life, and a supreme court (*corte costituzionale*) that rules on the constitutionality of laws, are designed to guarantee the impartial and nonpolitical application and interpretation of the law. The independence of the judiciary is also a matter of political contention. As civil servants, judges are supposed to stand above politics. Parliament sets the laws that govern the magistrates.

Besides the provisions of the constitution, Italian government also reflects customs, historical precedents, and political realities. Representative government has had relatively little impact on the bureaucracy, which sees itself as an entity apart and guards its prerogatives jealously. Its sense of entitlement has grown due to the lack of political direction attributable to the frequent changes of ministries, weakness of the executive, and lack of political continuity. The president of the republic may be a largely ceremonial figure, but the powers of the local policeman or postal clerk can be quite intimidating. PREFECTS are still powerful officials within the public administration. Judges who are supposed to be impartial and apolitical have played a controversial political role in the MANI PULITE investigations. Prime Minister SILVIO BERLUSCONI, currently under investigation by judges for alleged business malpractices, is a vocal critic of the judiciary for its alleged leftist political biases. The complexities of Italian government have long been a source of puzzlement to outsiders, particularly to Anglo-Saxon observers who have difficulty grasping its subtleties and apparent contradictions. For all the justified criticisms of government, it should be remembered that it has avoided anarchy and dictatorship, protected civil liberties, encouraged free expression, and provided support for an expanding economy and major improvements in the standard of living.

Gozzi, Carlo (1720–1806)
Venetian dramatist, literary critic, and social commentator

Gozzi, born to an impoverished family of the Venetian nobility, came to writing by family tradition. His older brother Gasparo Gozzi (1713–86) was a noted writer, journalist, and educational reformer, better known in his time than his younger playwright brother. Financial need directed Carlo toward a career in the military and he served with the Venetian army in DALMATIA (1741–44). Retired from the army, he took up writing as a critic and rival of CARLO GOLDONI. He granted that Goldoni had literary talent, but attacked his plays for their social realism. According to Gozzi, Goldoni's depiction of human weaknesses and foibles lacked inspirational power, encouraged immorality, undermined the aristocratic ethos of the republic, and was therefore politically subversive. It was largely Gozzi's attacks that forced Goldoni to leave Venice. Gozzi preferred the traditional style of COMMEDIA DELL'ARTE with its puppetry, stock characters and situations. His plays, written from 1761 to 1765 in the form of fables, conformed to that traditional style. Popular with audiences, many were later set to music. *L'amore delle tre melarance* (*The Love of Three Oranges*), which contained an attack on Goldoni, was set to music by Sergei Prokofiev. *Turandot,* the dramatic tale of the Chinese princess who yields to the ardent suitor Calaf, was the basis for operas with the same title by Ferruccio Busoni (1866–1924), GIACOMO PUCCINI, and other composers. *La donna serpente* (*The Serpent Woman*) inspired Richard Wagner to compose his first opera, *Die Feen.* The long poem *La Marfisa bizzarra* (1772) was an ironic diatribe against the social customs of his time. Gozzi relished attacking his literary rivals and was often at the center of literary controversies. His autobiography, curiously entitled *Memorie inutili per servire alla vita di Carlo Gozzi* (Useless memoirs on the life of Carlo Gozzi, 1797–98), is an important source of information on Venetian theater, popular tastes, and political attitudes of the time.

Gramsci, Antonio (1891–1937)
Marxist theoretician, Communist Party founder and leader

Gramsci was born near Cagliari (Sardinia) to a lower-middle-class family of Greek-Albanian origin. The family experienced financial and social trauma when the father, a civil servant, was jailed for embezzlement of public funds. The son, a hunchback and in frail health since early childhood, was a brilliant student who studied at the University of Turin on a scholarship. He entered the university in 1911, joined the Socialist Party (PSI) in 1912, and left the university in 1913 to take up journalism. Like other young radicals of his generation he was initially captivated by the activism of BENITO MUSSOLINI and may have favored Italian intervention in WORLD WAR I under the impression that war would hasten the outbreak of revolution. Physically unfit for military service, Gramsci worked as a jour-

nalist and pondered how as an intellectual he could reach out to workers and peasants. The issue that preoccupied him then and in the years to come was how to forge a revolutionary union of workers and peasants, of North and South.

The success of the Russian Revolution convinced Gramsci that a socialist revolution was imminent in Italy, and that workers and intellectuals like himself and his comrades were destined to lead it. Gramsci asserted that culture must inform political action, and vice versa, a view that implied a close (organic) link between workers and intellectuals. His closest collaborators were ANGELO TASCA, UMBERTO TERRACINI, and PALMIRO TOGLIATTI. The weekly *L'Ordine Nuovo* (New Order) founded by Gramsci and his companions in 1919 became the vehicle for the dissemination of ideas and tactics associated with the group and with the movement that was named after the newspaper. Gramsci's awareness that a new social order required a working class capable of running a complex industrial society convinced him that workers must acquire the technological and organizational skills possessed by the bourgeoisie. These were not only the skills of the shop floor and assembly line, but also those of industrial management and political organization.

Factory councils (*consigli di fabbrica*) run by workers were Gramsci's solution to the problem of worker education. These shop-floor organizations, similar to the soviets of the Russian Revolution, were to be essential adjuncts to the political party and labor unions. After the war Gramsci lost faith in the revolutionary potential of the Socialist Party and labor unions, questioned the tactics of reform of the Socialist Party, and put his faith in the revolutionary potential of factory councils. The occupation of the factories by workers in September 1920 seemed to justify his confidence in the revolutionary potential of factory councils. The *Ordine Nuovo* group and others seceded from the Socialist Party and founded the Communist Party of Italy in January 1921. The timing was off. The revolutionary tide was about to subside and Gramsci, aware of the change, turned his attention to studying the communist experiment underway in the Soviet Union and the new phenomenon of FASCISM. In the course of a long stay in Moscow and Vienna (1922–24), he met Lenin, was active in the Third Communist International (Comintern), and met Giulia Schucht, his future wife.

Gramsci returned to Italy in 1924 to take his seat in parliament as a member of the Communist Party. His major concern was how to oppose the Fascist regime that was taking shape under his eyes. He agreed with the Marxist analysis that fascism was a reactionary movement in defense of bourgeois interests, but he also acknowledged that it appealed to the lower-middle classes (petty bourgeoisie) and the masses. How to win mass support for a communist revolution under these conditions? Close collaboration between the industrial workers of the North and the peasant masses of the South was the key feature of Gramsci's revolutionary strategy. He advocated a broad anti-Fascist political alliance that cut across class lines and urged the party to stay in close touch and responsive to the rank and file. Disagreement flared up within the party. AMADEO BORDIGA and other party leaders rejected collaboration with noncommunists, insisted on centralized leadership and an elitist party of true believers.

Gramsci's ideas, condensed in the so-called Lyons Theses, prevailed at the party meeting that was held in January 1926 in Lyons, France, to escape the Fascist police. With Moscow's support, Gramsci became party leader, but was arrested in November and sentenced to 20 years in jail. From jail he carried on an intensive correspondence and wrote reflections on history, culture, and politics that were later published as his *Prison Notebooks*. In these writings Gramsci penned some of his most penetrating analyses of capitalist society, culture and politics, education and political consensus, intellectuals and the masses. The concept of cultural hegemony developed by Gramsci in these writings insists on the critical importance of ideas and values in forming a revolutionary consciousness. No revolution can succeed unless it captures and maintains control of the cultural high ground, and uses its cultural dominance to bring about fundamental changes of ideas and values.

In prison, Gramsci, always in fragile health, succumbed to depression and a fatal combination of physical ailments. He died in April 1937 in a Roman clinic to which he had been sent when it became clear that he was dying. His fame and influence were largely posthumous. After 1945 Togliatti and the PCI found guidance and inspiration in Gramsci's writings. As these writings became better known in Italy and abroad, Gramsci became a cultural icon and an obligatory point of reference for social theorists pondering the nature of capitalism, communism, and the tactics of revolution. The preeminent role that Gramsci assigned to intellectuals earned him privileged treatment in the writings of other intellectuals. Also intriguing was Gramsci's notion that revolution could be carried out by cultural means. That prospect had special appeal in Italy and elsewhere in the western world once it became clear that revolution Soviet-style would not likely occur. Gramsci's influence peaked in the 1960s when the New Left, feminists, and radicals of various persuasions, looked for a democratic version of Marxism. His complete writings are available in Italian. English-language selections appear in *Letters from Prison* (1973); *The Modern Prince and Other Writings* (1957); *Selections from Cultural Writings* (1985); *Selections from Political Writings, 1910–1926* (1977–78), 2 vols.; and *Selections from the Prison Notebooks* (1971).

Grandi, Dino (1895–1988)

early Fascist activist, diplomat, and internal critic of Mussolini

Born to a landowning family of the Romagna, in his youth Grandi was attracted to radical ideologies of the Left, which conflicted with his religious faith and patriotism. The outbreak of WORLD WAR I resolved that conflict in favor of patriotism. Military service interrupted Grandi's law studies at the University of Bologna and his

Dino Grandi *(Library of Congress)*

work as a budding journalist. He served with distinction in the war, reentered civilian life to complete his law studies (1919), and joined the Fascist movement in November 1920. A squad leader, he led armed expeditions against political opponents. In May 1921 he was elected to parliament as a Fascist. Grandi emerged within FASCISM as a critic of Mussolini's political tactics and personal dominance. But he always dissented with enough discretion to maintain his political standing. He served as undersecretary of the interior (1924–25), foreign ministry undersecretary (1925–29), foreign minister (1929–32), ambassador to London (1932–39), and minister of justice (1939–43). Strongly pro-British in foreign policy, he did not favor the alliance with Nazi Germany, and opposed war against France and Great Britain. As minister of justice and a

member of the Fascist Grand Council, he wrote and proposed the motion of no confidence that led to Mussolini's arrest on July 25, 1943. He escaped the death sentence issued against him in January 1944 by a Fascist tribunal by going into hiding. In 1947 he was absolved of charges that he had committed crimes against the state. After living in Portugal and South America, Grandi returned to Italy in the 1950s to establish a model farm and write his memoirs. Talent for survival was his most notable quality, ambiguity the hallmark of his political career.

Gravina, Gian Vincenzo See METASTASIO, PIETRO.

Graziani, Rodolfo (1882–1955)
military commander and political figure of the Fascist period
Graziani began his military career in African colonial conflicts before 1914. In WORLD WAR I he was promoted from captain to major. After the war he was given command of colonial operations in Libya, where Italian colonial authority was under attack by organized native resistance. His hard-hitting actions against the rebels (1924–32) earned him a reputation for ruthless efficiency. In 1932 he was promoted to general and given a command in Italy. Appointed governor of the colony of Somalia in 1935, during the ETHIOPIAN WAR Graziani established a southern front and led a vigorous campaign that won him national attention, the title of marshal, and appointment as viceroy in Ethiopia after the end of large-scale military operations. As Ethiopian viceroy (1936–38), Graziani eliminated the last vestiges of organized military resistance. His harsh measures provoked an attempt on his life and a general revolt that lingered until Italian forces were expelled from Ethiopia in WORLD WAR II. Graziani was always a controversial figure, highly sensitive to criticism, and prone to make enemies. His rivals included the formidable PIETRO BADOGLIO, a less colorful figure but a better politician. Graziani remained out of the pub-

lic eye until October 1939 when he was named army chief of staff and supervised military preparations for war. In July 1940 he was given command of Italian forces in North Africa. In that post he incurred the wrath of BENITO MUSSOLINI for delaying an offensive against British forces in Egypt. When after much prodding he did move, the offensive stalled and was soon repulsed. His lackluster performance caused his recall in February 1941, after which Graziani retired to private life. He was among the minority of generals who rallied to Mussolini after his ouster from power in July 1943. For his loyalty and name, Mussolini appointed him defense minister and chief of staff of the ITALIAN SOCIAL REPUBLIC (1943–45). Graziani remained faithful to Mussolini until the end, waging war against the Allies and the RESISTANCE movement, asserting that he was only doing his duty as a good Italian. Graziani did not see himself as a Fascist, but as a patriot fighting for Italy. A postwar tribunal sentenced him to 19 years in jail as a war criminal, but he was released in May 1950.

Gregory XIII (1502–1585)
pope (1572–1585)

Ugo Boncompagni, born in Bologna, took on the name of Gregory XIII when he became pope at age 70. A man of scholarly temperament, he studied and taught law in Bologna, took part in the COUNCIL OF TRENT, became bishop in 1558, and in 1565 was sent as papal legate to Spain where he made an excellent impression. His pontificate was marked by intense religious strife in Europe. Gregory set out to contain the spread of Protestantism. He supported the JESUITS, took steps to improve the education of the clergy, improve papal finances and diplomacy, and set an example of personal rectitude and devotion. The Jesuit school in Rome was renamed the Gregorian University in his honor. With the help of a more competent and committed clergy and active diplomacy, Gregory halted the spread of Protestantism in Germany and reclaimed the Rhineland, Bavaria, the Tyrol, Austria, and Poland for Catholicism. He was not successful in England and the Netherlands, where he relied on the military and naval power of Spain to accomplish his goals. He condoned the attempt to suppress the Huguenots in France, which resulted in the St. Bartholomew's Day massacre (1572). Gregory is also remembered for the calendar reform that took on his name. The Gregorian calendar promulgated in 1582 lopped 10 days from that year to align the dating with the vernal equinox. Accepted in the Catholic world, it was rejected by Protestant and Eastern Orthodox authorities. Great Britain and its American colonies adopted it in 1752, while the Greek Orthodox Church resisted the change until the 20th century. Gregory is also remembered for promoting a revised edition of the body of canon law, the *Corpus Juris Canonici* (1582), for initiating a grandiose and costly urban renewal project, and sponsoring archaeological exploration and scholarly study of the relics of Christian Rome, including the catacombs. Gregory's costly initiatives required heavy taxation and a diversion of funds from economic investment to political expenditure. Opposition from the nobility, economic hardship, and brigandage were legacies that Gregory passed on to his successor Sixtus V.

Gregory XVI (1765–1846)
pope (1831–1846)

Born in Belluno (Venetia), Bartolomeo Alberto Cappellari took on the name of Gregory XVI upon his election to the papacy in February 1831. Neither his temperament nor his education prepared him to deal with the social and political turbulence of his pontificate. He was a monk of the Camaldolese Order, ordained a priest in 1787. Utterly devout, he was more attuned to the austerity of life in the monastery and the solitary studies and contemplation in his cell than the responsibilities of public life. His most pronounced trait was to regard most forms of change with undisguised suspicion and hostility. He opposed liberal movements, secularism, laissez-faire economics, socialism, and Italian independence. He deplored industrialization, railroads, secular education, and freedom of expression. His first public action as pontiff was to condemn the REVOLUTION of 1831 that broke out a few days after his election. He called on the Austrian army to put it down. That decision, and the harsh treatment of political prisoners, earned Gregory the lasting enmity of liberals and patriots. Gregory was also troubled by calls for the separation of CHURCH AND STATE and for reform within the church. In the encyclical *Mirari vos* (1832) he condemned the writings of the French liberal priest Felicité de Lamennais and their call for freedom of conscience and reforms within the church. His resistance to innovation alarmed even his supporters. Austrian chancellor Klemens von Metternich pressured Gregory to promote administrative reforms, to little avail. For Gregory, the bottom line was that subjects owed allegiance to their God-appointed rulers, of which the pope was one as a temporal ruler in Italy, and that papal power was incompatible with democratic government. He was succeeded by PIUS IX, who seemed to promise change and innovation.

Grimaldi family See MONACO.

Grisi, Giulia See BELLINI, VINCENZO.

Grist Tax See *MACINATO*.

Gritti, Andrea (1455–1538)
Venetian merchant, military expert, and political figure
Gritti turned his attention to public affairs after engaging in trade; he served as *doge* (head of state) from 1523 to 1538. As a merchant in Constantinople he successfully mediated conflicts between Muslims and Christians. Although he preferred diplomacy to war, he also had the military expertise to lead Venetian forces in the war against the League of Cambrai (1509–10). The French took him prisoner in a renewal of hostilities in 1512 but released him a year later. In

1517 Gritti prepared a report on the state of military defenses that became the basis of the Venetian system of fortifications on the mainland. He was also instrumental in preparing the maritime defenses that enabled Venice to withstand a direct Turkish threat in 1537. His grasp of public administration and military matters made him a formidable presence in Venetian politics. The Venetian aristocracy looked upon him as an outsider and resented his authoritarian and high-handed manner, but his reputation was such that he was spared the attacks that might have ruined the career of a lesser figure. A generous patron of the arts, he helped create Venice's image as a cultural center. A strong guide in a time of trouble, Gritti was the last *doge* to exert personal dominance of Venetian affairs. After him came the period of collective aristocratic rule that marked the decline of Venice's power. Titian's portrait of Gritti in Washington's National Gallery conveys something of the inner strength and stamina of the person.

Gronchi, Giovanni (1887–1978)
prominent Christian Democratic leader and president of the republic
Gronchi was born in Pontedera (Pisa), studied to be a teacher, and joined the Catholic labor movement as an organizer. He volunteered for military service in WORLD WAR I, was a founder of the Italian Popular Party (PPI), and was elected to parliament in 1919. His first government post was as undersecretary of industry and commerce in the coalition government that BENITO MUSSOLINI formed in October 1922. Gronchi resigned and joined the opposition in April 1923 to protest Fascist violence against Catholic organizations. Deprived of his seat in parliament by the Fascist government in 1926, Gronchi withdrew from public life and gave up his teaching position. For the remaining years of the Fascist regime he worked as an industrial manager. He joined the Christian Democratic Party (DC) in 1943, served as party contact person with the RESISTANCE movement, and was a member of the

constituent assembly (1946–47) that wrote the CONSTITUTION of the Italian republic. He was president of the chamber of deputies after the 1948 elections and served as president of the republic (1955–62). As president he was exceptionally active and visible, making effective use of that largely ceremonial office to influence the course of politics. He was among the first Christian Democrats to advocate the OPENING TO THE LEFT and the sharing of power with the Socialist Party (PSI). In foreign policy he favored a neutralist course, partial disengagement from NATO and the United States, and a policy of peaceful coexistence with the communist bloc. He traveled widely, visiting the Soviet Union, the United States, and the Latin American countries that had a strong Italian presence. Opposition from within his own party frustrated Gronchi's efforts to change the course of domestic and foreign policy and strengthen the office of president.

Guareschi, Giovanni (1908–1968)
(Giovannino)

writer, political satirist, and social commentator

Guareschi was born in a small town of the Po Valley, the setting of his best writings. His father was a colorful local character attracted to vaguely leftist political causes and to disastrous financial schemes, his mother a highly respected schoolteacher whose modest salary kept the family going. The son inherited the father's bizarre imagination and the mother's zest for hard work. A fun-loving, brilliant student, Guareschi studied law to satisfy his parents but his real interests were writing and drawing. His first successful venture was as a cartoonist and writer for the satirical review *Bertoldo* (1936–43). His barbs during World War II against the Fascist regime got him into trouble with Fascist officials, and he joined the army to escape retribution. When the government tried to withdraw from the war in September 1943, Guareschi was taken prisoner by the Germans and barely survived the war in concentration camps. He returned to Italy, resumed his career as a journalist, and founded the weekly review *Candido,* which enjoyed great popularity. Guareschi became the most visible journalist in Italy, resuming his role as a political satirist, and took aim at both the Christian Democratic (DC) and Communist (PCI) Parties. He was found guilty of libel and sentenced to one year in jail after he charged that ALCIDE DE GASPERI, the Christian Democratic leader, had urged the Allies to bomb Rome in 1944 to hasten their advance on the city. Guareschi regarded the monarchy as a symbol of national unity and was sorely disappointed when Italians voted for a republic in June 1946. In a series of memorable short stories that first appeared in *Candido* and were later published in book form, he invented the characters of Don Camillo, a formidable parish priest, and his stalwart communist antagonist Peppone. Their amusing scrapes, carried out in a truculent but ultimately harmless manner, conveyed the message that Italians shared a common culture transcending their political differences. That message was not well received in the surcharged political atmosphere of the postwar years. Ordinary Italians enjoyed the stories, while literary critics and politicians ignored him or attacked him as a disguised Fascist. After his death his appeal to national unity was seen as an anticipation of the HISTORIC COMPROMISE. The stories of Don Camillo were the basis of five highly successful films in which the roles of Don Camillo and Peppone were interpreted respectively by Fernandel and Gino Cervi. For translations of his writings see *The Don Camillo Omnibus* (London: Gollancz, 1974).

Guerra, Learco See SPORTS.

Guerrazzi, Francesco Domenico (1804–1873)

Risorgimento patriot, writer, and political figure

Born in LIVORNO, Guerrazzi personified the loud and stormy politics of his native port city. After graduating from the University of Pisa (1824), he turned to journalism. Through *L'Indicatore Livornese*, a radical newspaper that he founded in 1829, he made contact with GIUSEPPE MAZZINI. Both were convinced republicans, but their clashing personalities precluded any close political understanding. In 1830 and 1833 Guerrazzi served several months in jail for political subversion. He made his literary mark with the publication of *La battaglia di Benevento* (The battle of Benevento, 1825) and *L'assedio di Firenze* (The siege of Florence, 1836), two historical novels that looked at military clashes in medieval and Renaissance Italy and praised Italian valor. Guerrazzi's fiction catered to the prevailing romantic taste for dramatic encounters and horrific situations recounted in overblown, turgid language. His denunciation of abuses by the powerful and idealization of the people appealed to democrats. Guerrazzi was a vehement anticlerical who often cast the PAPACY as the villain. He was more influential as a writer than as a politican. He was head of government in Tuscany during the REVOLUTION of 1848–49, was jailed in the aftermath and found refuge in Corsica. When he returned to Italy in 1857 he chose to live in Genoa. Temperamental to a fault, he refused to go back to Tuscany where he felt unappreciated. Elected to the Italian parliament in 1860, from the benches of the democratic opposition he lashed out at the monarchy and at the governing HISTORICAL RIGHT. Guerrazzi was a flamboyant figure, given to flowery language and theatrical gestures that appealed to the generation of ROMANTICISM. His style can be sampled in translation in *Beatrice Cenci: A Historical Novel of the Sixteenth Century* (1858) and *Manfred, or the Battle of Benevento* (1875).

Guicciardini, Francesco (1483–1540)
Florentine historian, political commentator, and diplomat

Guicciardini was born to a patrician family of Florence, received a law degree from the University of Pisa in 1505, and pursued a career in public service. In 1511 the government of the Florentine republic appointed him to the important diplomatic post of ambassador to Spain. His ability to adjust to changing political circumstances secured his advancement regardless of changes of government. In 1516 he left the service of Florence for that of the papacy under LEO X. He remained in the service of the papacy for almost 20 years in various administrative positions. In the struggle between the French and Spaniards for control of Italy, Guicciardini made the mistake of siding with the losers. When the Spaniards defeated the French and established their hegemony in the peninsula, Guicciardini found himself out of favor. He continued to serve both Rome and Florence, but his career was at a dead end. In the last three years of his life, retired in his villa in the hills above Florence, he wrote the book that made him famous, the *Storia d'Italia* (History of Italy), published posthumously in 1561–64. It narrated the history of Italy from about 1490 to 1534, placing Italian events in the larger context of the struggle by France and Spain for European dominance. He sounded the alarm for what he called the "misfortunes of Italy" under foreign rule. Using his own extensive experience in politics and diplomacy, Guicciardini went beyond appearances to consider the decisive forces of history, namely, the use of power and conflicts of interest. His detailed accounts of Italian politics point to the intentions of the powerful as the decisive element. But Guicciardini was also aware that historical events are often driven by accident and unpredictability. In writing his major work Guicciardini made extensive use of notes that he had penned over many years in public life, which were partially published as his *Ricordi* in 1576–85. An earlier work, the *History of Florence*, written in 1508–09 but published only in 1859, shows his pride in the achievements of his native city and points to his sense that the richness of Italian culture is due to the diversity and competitiveness of its city-states. Unlike his contemporary and friend NICCOLÒ MACHIAVELLI, Guicciardini valued the independence of Italy from foreign rule, but did not advocate its political unification. His *History of Italy* is available in a good English translation by Sidney Alexander (1969).

Guinigi, Paolo   See LUCCA, CITY OF.

Gullo, Fausto (1887–1974)
Communist legislator and advocate of land reform

Born in Catanzaro (Calabria), a lawyer by profession, Gullo joined the Italian Communist Party (PCI) and was elected to parliament in 1924, but served only briefly before being arrested by the Fascist police. He was politically prominent during and after WORLD WAR II when he served as minister of agriculture (1944–45), and minister of justice (1945–46). He was also a member of the constituent assembly that wrote the CONSTITUTION of the Italian republic (1946–47) and was elected to represent the Communist Party in parliament in 1948. Gullo is best remembered for the so-called Gullo decrees that he promulgated as minister of agriculture. Responding in part to spontaneous occupations of land by southern peasants, Gullo's decrees redrew agrarian contracts in favor of sharecroppers, legalized peasant seizures of land, encouraged the formation of peasant cooperatives, and sought to eliminate middlemen who worked for the interests of large landowners. These highly controversial measures mobilized southern peasants behind a program of land reform that challenged the dominance of large landowners and aimed at changing the structure of southern agriculture. Rural agitations inspired by these measures lasted into the early 1950s, linking protests of peasants in the South with the strikes and agitations of industrial workers in the North. Peasant support for communism increased, but the determined resistance of large landowners, MAFIA violence, and the Communist Party policy of accommodation at the national level eventually foiled the attempt to reform southern agriculture.

Gustav line   See WORLD WAR II.

H

Habsburg-Lorraine dynasty
ruling house of the Grand Duchy of Tuscany
from 1737 to 1859

The union of the Habsburg and Lorraine dynasties occurred through the marriage of MARIA THERESA, heir to the Austrian throne, and FRANCIS STEPHEN OF LORRAINE in 1736. In 1735, as a result of the peace settlements that ended the WARS OF THE AUSTRIAN and SPANISH SUCCESSIONS, Francis Stephen renounced his claim to the duchy of Lorraine in exchange for a commitment that he would become grand duke of Tuscany at the death of Gian Gastone de' Medici, last of the Medici line. Gian Gastone died in 1737, and Francis Stephen succeeded him but governed Tuscany mostly in absentia through a council of regents. His second son, PETER LEOPOLD, who succeeded him in 1765, took up residence in Florence, transformed Tuscany into a model state, and planted the Habsburg-Lorraine dynasty firmly on Tuscan soil. In 1790 Peter Leopold succeeded his older brother JOSEPH II as ruler of the AUSTRIAN EMPIRE. The Tuscan throne passed on to Peter Leopold's second son, who ruled as FERDINAND III. His son succeeded him as LEOPOLD II but was forced out of Tuscany in 1859 by a bloodless uprising that preceded the union of Tuscany and Piedmont-Sardinia. Leopold II was the last member of the Habsburg-Lorraine dynasty to rule in Tuscany. The possession of the Tuscan throne by a member of the dynasty was an important element of the hegemony that Austria exercised over Italy until national unification. The dynasty of Habsburg-Lorraine stood out among the ruling dynasties of the period for its moderate tone, progressive policies, mild repression of political dissidents, and genuine attachment to Tuscany and its people.

Haile Selassie, Emperor See ETHIOPIAN WAR.

Hamilton, Emma See MARIE CAROLINE.

heresies

It was customary in Italy to designate as heresies all religious movements that dissented from Roman Catholicism. In pre-Reformation times, these included the Cathari, WALDENSIANS, Humiliati, and the followers of the 12th-century monk Joachim of Fiore. These movements rejected the authority of the pope, the hierarchical structure of the CATHOLIC CHURCH, and the sacramental role of the clergy. Heretical movements often began as attempts to reform the church from within and moved gradually toward a rejection of the institutional church, eventually claiming that they embodied the true Christian faith. All had been condemned and persecuted by the church since the Middle Ages. The Humiliati and Waldensians survived into the 16th century, when they succumbed to the church's offensive against Protestantism, with which the dissenters had doctrinal similarities.

Identifying and ferreting out heresies and heretics became a major concern of the JESUITS and the INQUISITION. Protestant doctrines appealed to many Italians, and those who held on to them in the face of papal condemnation had to find refuge outside Italy. Religious exiles included prominent figures like BERNARDINO OCHINO, FAUSTO AND LELIO SOZZINI, and PETER MARTYR VERMIGLI. The condemnation of suspected dissenters like GIORDANO BRUNO, TOMMASO CAMPANELLA, and GALILEO occurred against this background of mounting concern and intolerance. Individuals and groups were condemned for holding ideas that, although not primarily religious, as in the case of Galileo, had doctrinal implications unacceptable to the church. Papal condemnation extended even to JANSENISM, which was not strictly speaking a heretical movement because it did not question the role of the church as the necessary vehicle of salvation. Jansenism straddled the dividing line between religious and political reform. The connection between Jansenism and republicanism cast a suspicion of heresy on political movements that challenged traditional political institutions, promising radical change and a utopian future. The Catholic Church's rejection of ideas associated with the ENLIGHTENMENT and the FRENCH REVOLUTION, the alliance of throne and altar during the RESTORATION period, and the condemnation of modern ideologies of change derive historically from the perception of heresy as a form of dissent that has both religious and secular implications.

Hermetism

literary and philosophical trend concerned with the hidden meaning of words and symbols

The term Hermetism is used in two different contexts. In the context of RENAISSANCE culture, it refers to a body of ideas based on writings attributed to the ancient Egyptian god of wisdom Thoth, whom the ancient Greeks renamed Hermes Trimegistus, whence the term Hermetism. The Hermetic books dealt with various forms of magic. Renaissance scholars studied them to understand the fundamental unity of nature in all its aspects. Imaginative understanding rather than reason would reveal the divinely ordained secrets of the natural world. MARSILIO FICINO translated these esoteric writings into Latin (1471) and made them part of the canon of NEOPLATONISM. In to the 17th century they were recognized as forgeries. The Hermetic writings appealed to intellectuals seeking alternative paths to knowledge and power.

In the second sense, the term Hermetism refers to a literary movement dominant in the 1930s characterized by the use of allusive, cryptic, often impenetrable language that suggested rather than described meaning. The movement is sometimes seen as a reaction against the bombastic, rhetorical use of language associated with FASCISM. It should be pointed out, however, that influential figures of the regime like GIUSEPPE BOTTAI and GALEAZZO CIANO patronized writers identified with the movement. The poet Giuseppe Ungaretti (1888–1970) is considered the founder and representative figure of literary Hermetism. Hermetism went out of fashion quickly after the war, perhaps because writers were no longer compelled to wrap their thoughts in obscure language. Content became more important than form, as evident in the cinematic and literary NEOREALISM of the 1950s. The allusive use of language to express politically suspect ideas typical of Hermetism can be seen in Elio Vittorini's novel *Conversazione in Sicilia* (1938–39), translated *Conversation in Sicily* (1988).

Historic Compromise

The Historic Compromise (*compromesso storico*) was an attempt to formalize the de facto political cooperation of the Christian Democratic Party (DC), the Italian Communist Party (PCI), and the Italian Socialist Party (PSI), which was already in partnership with the Christian Democrats. Communist Party leader ENRICO BERLINGUER broached the idea in a series of articles that appeared in the review *Rinascita* in the fall of 1973. Berlinguer wished to avoid extreme political polarization and the possibility of a right-wing, CIA-inspired coup similar to what had happened previously in Chile. At the social level, the Historic Compromise signified the alliance of workers and middle classes, and the convergence of communism and Catholicism against reactionary forces. The DC could be won over with reassurances that a government of national unity such as he envisaged would protect the interests of its middle-class constituents as well as the interests of workers. The proposal, inspirational but vague, was opposed by conservative Christian Democrats, socialists, intransigent communists, and extra-parliamentary groups of the Left and Right. The flare-up of TERRORISM in the late 1970s, capped by the kidnapping and assassination of ALDO MORO, helped put an end to the project. The failed effort was followed in the 1980s by an unofficial partnership of communists and Christian Democrats known as *consociativismo* (associationism). That watered-down version of the Historic Compromise was opposed successfully by Socialist Party leader BETTINO CRAXI and by Christian Democratic leaders Arnaldo Forlani and GIULIO ANDREOTTI.

Historical Right

The Historical Right, or Destra Storica, was a political bloc that controlled government through parliament after national unification. Members of the Piedmontese, Lombard, and Tuscan aristocracies and upper-middle classes were prominent among its leaders. They did not constitute a formal party, but were held together by a shared philosophy of government and by common interests as members of the privileged classes. Sometimes referred to as the *Consorteria,* they were a self-conscious elite who expressed a paternalistic concern for the welfare of the masses but rejected universal suffrage and local autonomy. They believed in constitutional government, civil liberties, separation of CHURCH AND STATE, and laissez-faire economics. Their commitment to constitutional procedures and civil liberties clashed at times with their exalted concept of the state as the ultimate guarantor of legality. Their faith in the state expressed itself as

a preference for centralized administration, strict law enforcement, and rigorous taxation.

The Historical Right confronted serious issues that threatened the recently achieved national unity. It took the first steps to regulate relations between church and state, fought a war against Austria (1866), acquired Rome and Venice, repressed BRIGANDAGE, began construction of a national system of railroads, improved public education, balanced the budget, and gave financial credibility to the government. The Historical Right was never popular, and most of its leaders would have found it unbecoming to court popularity. They lost control of parliament to the LIBERAL LEFT in 1876 and became the party of the constitutional opposition. The leaders of the Historical Right before 1876 were GIOVANNI LANZA, MARCO MINGHETTI, BETTINO RICASOLI, and QUINTINO SELLA. After 1876, its most notable figures were ANTONIO STARABBA DI RUDINI ANTONIO SALANDRA, and SIDNEY SONNINO. The Historical Right is not to be confused with the new or nationalist right of the early 20th century, which rejected constitutional, parliamentary government and espoused extreme NATIONALISM.

Holy League   See LÉPANTO, BATTLE OF.

Holy Roman Empire

Holy because blessed by papal authority and Roman because it sought to emulate ancient Roman rule, the Holy Roman Empire was a medieval political construct with imprecise and shifting geographic boundaries. What it lacked in geographical precision it made up in longevity, for the title lasted from the coronation of the German king Otto I as Holy Roman Emperor in 862 until 1806 when Napoleon I forced the last Holy Roman Emperor, Francis II of Austria, to renounce the title. The title was supposed to reflect the superiority of the emperor over other kings and princes of the Christian world. In reality, the universal authority of Holy Roman Emperors was constantly challenged and often

Panoramic view of St. Peter's Basilica and Square in Vatican City, ca. 1909 *(Library of Congress)*

ignored. The title was meaningful for those rulers who had the resources and power to enforce it. It has relevance in Italian history because Holy Roman Emperors had dual authority and sometimes conflicting interests as rulers of German and Italian lands. Germany and most of northern and central Italy as far south as the kingdom of NAPLES were nominally part of the Holy Roman Empire in the Middle Ages. The claims of medieval emperors over Italian territories produced a backlash in the form of tax revolts and struggles for municipal independence, thus playing a role in the emergence of independent communes and city-states. By the 15th century the imperial title was monopolized by the Habsburg and, later, the HABSBURG-LORRAINE dynasties. With the Habsburgs, imperial interests shifted from Germany to Austria, but interference in Italian affairs continued. During the Reformation, emperors sided with the PAPACY against German princes, but CHARLES V often used his imperial authority to control the pope and to adjudicate territorial disputes and succession claims in Italy. In the course of the 17th and 18th centuries, imperial administration deteriorated, and opposition increased from rival dynasties and emerging nation-states. The Napoleonic Wars dealt the final blows to the Holy Roman Empire.

Holy See

The term Holy See (*Santa Sede*) has two distinct meanings. In its broadest sense, it refers to the governing body of the Catholic Church, consisting of the pope and the various clerical offices that advise him and administer church affairs. In this broad sense, the Holy See is often also designated as the Roman Curia and is responsible for the material and spiritual guidance of the church as an organization and of Catholics as a body of the faithful. In a narrower sense, the term Holy See designates the government of the independent state of Vatican City, occupying an area of about 109 acres enclosed by the Leonine Wall on the west bank of the Tiber River within the city of ROME. Within its boundaries lie Saint Peter's Basilica and its adjacent square, the Castel Sant' Angelo, and the vast Vatican Museum and Library, which contain some of the world's most precious collections of art objects, books, and ancient manuscripts. It also has jurisdiction over the pope's summer residence at Castel Gandolfo outside Rome and over important churches and other buildings outside the Vatican walls in the city of Rome. All papal buildings enjoy rights of extraterritoriality and are governed by the Holy See. The Italian government recognized the independence of Vatican City when the ROMAN QUES-

TION was settled in 1929 with the conclusion of the Lateran Pacts and Concordat. The Italian government recognized the free state of the Vatican and guaranteed its unrestricted access to the outside world. The Vatican has its own citizenship, currency, postal service, and diplomatic corps. Church law (canon law) governs it, and the pope appoints all its officials. The pope, an absolute sovereign, is surrounded by an elaborate ceremonial, and has the last word in matters of faith (doctrine of papal infallibility). Swiss guards serve as the pope's personal bodyguards, but the security of the Vatican State is also the responsibility of the Italian government. Relations between the Holy See and the Italian government are generally cordial, but important political differences between the two have emerged from time to time since 1929, particularly on issues of education, sexuality, family life, and the status of Rome as national capital and holy city.

homosexuality See GAY MOVEMENT.

humanism

Humanism is synonymous with the culture of the Italian Renaissance. In the 15th century, the term *humanista* designated a professional teacher of the *studia humanitatis,* a set of disciplines consisting of Latin, Greek, grammar, rhetoric, history, poetry, and ethics, with particular emphasis on the writings of ancient Greece and Rome. The term entered scholarly discourse in the 19th century. Nineteenth-century German scholarship set the pace, drawing attention to the new interests and questions of Renaissance intellectuals who studied the ancient classics, admiring these ancient texts for their elegance and practical usefulness in tackling problems of government, public policy, and morality. The study of history in particular was thought to hold lessons valuable for policymakers and citizens alike.

Humanism thus took on a broad meaning that transcended the original definition as a program of studies. Today the term is used to describe what is seen as a fundamental shift from religious to secular concerns traceable to the culture of the Renaissance. The theological concerns that dominated medieval culture gave way among the educated to questions that concerned the here and now. This is not to suggest that humanists turned against religion. On the contrary, most were sincerely religious. LORENZO VALLA, the most prominent humanist of his generation, sought ways to eliminate clerical abuses and restore the spiritual authority of the Catholic Church. Northern European humanists showed a particular disposition to put their learning in the service of religion and religious reform. The study of the classics provided humanists with new models of education, new definitions of the good life, and new ways of understanding the natural world. Scholars sought out and studied ancient texts to understand how Greeks and Romans defined the good life, good government, and the role of nature. While many of the texts prized by humanists had been known and studied in the Middle Ages, humanist scholars approached them with new questions and a fresh sensitivity to their hidden meanings.

FLORENCE is commonly seen as the cradle of humanist culture, but recent research points to the prevalence of humanist currents in many other cities of northern and central Italy. The revival of interest in classical texts seems to have started in PADUA around the middle of the 13th century. Florentine scholars did play a major role in turning the interest in ancient texts into a new form of learning, expressed in the Florentine vernacular (Tuscan) spoken by educated lay people. Humanists everywhere became involved in public affairs and in the service of the state. Italian artists and scholars pioneered and helped spread the new culture in Italy and beyond. GIOVANNI BOCCACCIO and PETRARCH are early humanists. In their 13th-century writings one finds appreciation of worldly pleasures, human affections, and natural beauty. Their 15th- and 16th-century successors showed great interest in political and civic issues, often serving as public officials and political counselors to ruling princes. FRANCESCO GUIC-

CIARDINI and NICCOLÒ MACHIAVELLI put their learning in the service of government and political philosophy. Nineteenth-century scholars, taking their cue from the Swiss historian Jacob Burckhardt, detected in the Italian Renaissance the historical turning point that ushered in the modern era. Humanism is the term that they used to describe the cultural shift toward secular concerns inspired by the study of the ancient classics.

Humbert I See UMBERTO I.

Humbert II See UMBERTO II.

Humiliati See HERESIES.

I

idealism

Applicable to ways of thinking about art, ethics, and philosophy, idealism denotes the tendency to assign highest status to perceptions, ideas, and spiritual values to understand the world of the senses. Philosophically, idealism is the opposite of materialism and its direct derivatives, philosophical POSITIVISM and modern science, which seek to understand the real world by measuring and quantifying material entities and phenomena. Idealism is traceable in western culture to the philosophy of Plato, who looked upon the changing material world as a reflection and approximation of immutable concepts (ideas), which he thought of as eternal forms that give meaning to material objects.

Modern idealism stresses the fundamental role of mind, reason, and perception in shaping reality, as opposed to the role of objects (materialism) or will (existentialism). Particularly influential in Italian culture has been the idealism of the 19th-century German philosopher Georg Wilhelm Hegel. His view of history as a dialectical process leading to the realization of the concept of liberty, and of the state as the embodiment and guardian of that concept, influenced BERTRANDO and SILVIO SPAVENTA, and through them BENEDETTO CROCE, the most authoritative intellectual of his generation. The idealization of the state as a neutral entity enforcing the law above political passions found particular favor with the HISTORICAL RIGHT, which Croce took to be a model of good government. In Croce's hands, idealism became a powerful weapon against Marxist socialism, which he condemned because of its materialistic foundation.

In a different variant, idealism was the dominant philosophy behind FASCISM. GIOVANNI GENTILE took the idealization of the state to a different level when he saw it not only as the guardian of law and legality but as an entity that needed and should seek the support of the people, for he recognized that the modern state cannot function without a popular basis. Gentile's idealism was ultimately incompatible with the principles of natural rights, personal freedom, and civil rights at the core of liberal ideology. The concept of TOTALITARIANISM was rooted in Gentile's notion of the powerful and popular state. Philosophical idealism lost much of its intellectual appeal and following after World War II, partly because of its association with fascism and its rejection by the political Left, which turned its attention and fell under the spell of the subtle Marxism of ANTONIO GRAMSCI. But from the 1860s to the 1940s, idealism was the dominant philosophy among Italian intellectuals, who drew different conclusions from a common basis, some seeing it as the foundation of legality, others as the necessary premise for the active state that transcends the distinction between public and private.

Illustrazione Italiana (L') See JOURNALISM.

Imbriani, Matteo See IRREDENTISM.

immigration See MIGRATION.

Index (Index Librorum Prohibitorum)

The Index of prohibited books contains titles that are deemed morally dangerous or incompatible with Catholic doctrine. Lists of unacceptable books were drawn up in the early days of the publishing industry, the first being issued in 1515. But these were uncoordinated lists subject to the discretion of local bishops. Pope PAUL IV issued the first papal list of prohibited books in 1557 as part of the Catholic campaign to combat the spread of Protestantism. The COUNCIL OF TRENT issued directives on book censorship in 1563, and in 1571 Pope PIUS V established the Congregation of the Index to evaluate books suspected of containing heretical opinions and make recommendations to the INQUISITION, or Holy Office. For all its influence, the Index was never meant to identify and condemn all books deemed dangerous for Catholics. It reviewed only titles that were submitted to it, and exclusion from the Index was in no way an endorsement of a book's contents. However, excommunication could be the penalty for reading and propagating the views contained in condemned books. Some books that were once included were later removed, most notably those dealing with the Copernican view of the universe. The list of condemned books includes titles by some of the most prominent figures in western culture. The Holy Office updated its lists regularly, but the last edition of 1948 was never published. In 1966 the Congregation for the Propagation of the Faith, which the year before had replaced the Holy Office, removed all penalties and downgraded the Index to a mere recommendation for the moral guidance of the faithful.

industrialization

Italy experienced the Industrial Revolution later than most western European countries. Its transformation from a predominantly agricultural to a predominantly manufacturing ECONOMY was delayed by natural and political causes. The natural deposits of iron, copper, tin, and other metals that had sustained Italian trade and manufacturing in ancient and medieval times could not be worked profitably in the industrial age of mass production. Italy also lacked coal and oil, the two most important sources of energy in the industrial age. Late political unification hindered the formation of a national market and the low incomes of the agricultural economy held back consumption and demand. Investment capital for industrial ventures was also scarce, as Italians preferred to put their money in land, housing, government bonds, and private savings.

At the time of Italy's unification in 1860–61, industrial production was limited. It was heavily concentrated in textiles, particularly the manufacture of cotton and silk fabrics, in the northern regions of LOMBARDY and PIEDMONT. Regional imbalance has been a constant feature of Italian industrial production, which remains highly concentrated in the Italian northwest, particularly in the so-called Industrial Triangle (the area between the cities of TURIN, MILAN, and GENOA). The construction of a national system of transportation based on railroads was both a precondition and an important aspect of the process of industrialization. That task was essentially completed by the end of the 19th century. By then the country had also moved beyond a series of economic crises marked by scandals in building construction and BANKING, a ruinous tariff war with France, and economic depression.

Domestic manufacturers benefited from protective tariffs enacted in 1878 and 1887 and by government contracts. The government's commitment to a costly program of naval rearmament was a boon to struggling steel and mechanical industries. The Terni Steelworks, founded in 1884, were intended largely to provide rolled steel and plating for the naval program. Iron deposits in the island of ELBA and soft coal deposits in SARDINIA were exploited. The development of hydroelectric power from the early years of the 20th century went some way toward compensating for the scarcity of industrial fuels. The Italian industrial takeoff, achieved in the period 1898–1908, enabled the country to meet the demands of WORLD WAR I. The war itself provided further stimulus for the expansion of heavy industry and the concentration of ownership and management.

These trends continued under FASCISM. After a period of free-trade policy (1922–25) that benefited exporting industries like textiles and food processing, the Fascist regime pursued a policy of national economic self-sufficiency, or AUTARKY, that encouraged the diversification of industrial production. The chemical, metals, machinery, and shipbuilding industries benefited particularly from the policy of autarky. Automobiles, road construction, and the entertainment industries (cinema and radio) were also the beneficiaries of Fascist economic policy. The other major development of the Fascist period was the rise of a public sector, with the founding of the Industrial Reconstruction Institute (IRI) in 1933. In the 1930s the value of industrial production exceeded that of agricultural production for the first time in the country's history.

The goal of the regime's industrial policy was to prepare the country for war, but the industrial apparatus could not meet the country's needs in WORLD WAR II. Postwar recovery was facilitated by the limited physical damage to industrial plants. While the transportation system and shipping suffered heavy damage, factories suffered much less. The recovery was well underway by the early1950s, stimulated by injections of funds from the Marshall Plan, by the government's monetary policies, and a supply of cheap labor from the southern regions. Exports of domestic appliances, textiles, and shoes established an Italian industrial presence in foreign markets in the 1950s and 1960s. Auto production enjoyed a virtual monopoly of the national market, but also won important positions in sales and manufacturing in Latin America, Spain, and the Soviet Union. Other sectors to make headway were natural gas production and oil refining, due largely to the operations of the national fuels agency ENI and its dynamic director, ENRICO MATTEI.

But the great strength of Italian industrial production from the postwar years to this day has been the sector of small- and medium-sized production. Firms with fewer than 1,000 workers have shown great resiliency and adaptability in the face of changing economic and market needs. Costs of production have been kept low by the widespread practice of *lavoro nero* (unreported workers and undocumented labor activities), which has relied heavily on the work of illegal immigrants. Industrial design, which relies on well-established traditions of good craftsmanship, has given Italian industry global visibility and renown. Services, the most important being those that cater to the health and tourist industries, account today for the greater share of the national product, signaling that the Italian economy has passed from the industrial to the postindustrial phase. The manufacturing industries are still a mainstay of the Italian economy, which ranks in fifth or sixth place among the developed nations.

Innocent VIII See WITCHCRAFT.

Innocent XI (1611–1689)
Pope (1676–1689)
Benedetto Odescalchi, born in Como, became pope at a time when the international prestige of the papacy was at a low point after repeated clashes with King Louis XIV, who was determined to assert royal control over the church. Innocent successfully asserted papal control of church affairs, assumed leadership of efforts to resist the Turkish advance in central Europe and the relief of the city of Vienna besieged by the Turks in 1683, and promoted the Christian counteroffensive that pushed the Turks out of Hungary and part of the Balkans. The enmity between Louis and Innocent was not alleviated even by Louis's revocation of the Edict of Nantes in 1685, which ended the policy of toleration of Protestants in France. Innocent praised the measure but condemned its harsh application. The

conflict with France was not resolved at the time of Innocent's death, with Louis XIV rejecting papal jurisdiction over the appointment of bishops in France, questioning papal claims to ultimate authority in matters of faith, and threatening military action against the PAPAL STATES. A man of saintly character, Innocent showed no tolerance for deviant behavior within the church. He demanded the highest moral standards among the clergy, strengthened the authority of bishops, condemned displays of wealth, silenced religious dissenters, and put the church on a solid financial footing. French resentment of Innocent blocked his canonization for a long time. It occurred in 1956 under PIUS XII.

Innocent XII See MALPIGHI, MARCELLO.

Inquisition, Roman

The institution took its name from the title of its chief official, the *inquisitor,* who was a papal appointee charged with identifying and condemning Christians guilty of heresy. What is commonly known as the medieval Inquisition was established in 1223 to root out dissenting Christians in southern France, northern Italy, and Germany. Then and later, the primary task of the Inquisition was not to condemn heretics but, rather, to make them see the errors of their ways, confess, and reenter the ranks of the orthodox faithful. But if brought to trial the accused were often tortured, found guilty of heresy, and turned over to the secular arm of government for the punishment of death. Burning at the stake was the usual form of execution for convicted heretics. In 1478 King Ferdinand and Queen Isabella established the Spanish Inquisition, which was independent of the medieval. Authorities used it to impose religious uniformity and loyalty to the monarchs by identifying Jews and Muslims who were suspected of having falsely converted to Christianity. In 1542 Pope PAUL III injected new life into the medieval Inquisition by assigning it to the Congregation of the Inquisition, or Holy Office, with jurisdiction over the entire Christian world. This reformed institution is often referred to as the Roman Inquisition. It had jurisdiction over the entire Christian world and superseded all other tribunals. It was moderate in its judgments compared to its forebears, and highly successful in ferreting out and uprooting Protestants from Italy and Spain. It is also remembered for the role it played in condemning such prominent figures as TOMMASO CAMPANELLA, GIORDANO BRUNO, and GALILEO. In 1965 the Congregation for the Propagation of the Faith took over the Inquisition's functions and to this day remains the church's principal watchdog in matters of faith.

Invernizio, Carolina (1851–1916)
popular and prolific novelist who catered to the taste for the sinister and the macabre

Invernizio was born in Voghera (Piedmont) to a middle-class family, studied in Florence, married a military officer, and led a life of utter respectability totally at variance with the dark, violent, and scandalous deeds that she narrated in her novels. The commercial success of her more than 100 books indicates that she satisfied the needs of a large public. She was to a popular readership what Sigmund Freud was to the intelligentsia: a guide to the subconscious and the inexpressible substratum of the human personality. Between the covers of her books readers found stories of incest, rape, and violent death that were frightening, horrifying, and thrilling. The heroines that are the main characters of her novels are also often the victims of violence and treachery. They respond with a mixture of innocence, resilience, and strength that must have appealed to the women that constituted most of her public. Among her most successful novels are *Rina o L'angelo delle Alpi* (Rina, or the angel of the Alps, 1877), *Il bacio di una morta* (The kiss of a dead woman, 1886), *La vendetta di una pazza* (The revenge of a mad woman, 1894), and *La sepolta viva* (The woman who was buried alive, 1896). Usually dismissed by literary critics as a mere raconteur who provided cheap thrills for a barely literate public, Invernizio is actually one of the most intriguing literary figures of her generation, both for the dissonance between her respectable private life and her scandalous writings and for the cultural and social messages conveyed by her novels.

Ionian Sea   See MEDITERRANEAN SEA.

IRI (Industrial Reconstruction Institute)

The Istituto per la Ricostruzione Industriale was established in 1933 by the Fascist regime to bail the country's major banks out of financial crisis during the Great Depression. IRI assumed the debts and obligations owed by the banks and took over the banks' practically worthless industrial shareholdings. IRI was originally intended to be a temporary stopgap solution, but when its rescue job was completed in 1937 it was reorganized on a permanent basis. IRI was left with a controlling interest in steel, machinery, shipping, electricity, and communications. All these were areas of strategic importance for the war economy that the regime wanted to create in conjunction with the policy of AUTARKY. IRI's first director was ALBERTO BENEDUCE, who as a former socialist was alleged to entertain a secret plan for nationalizing the economy. In reality, the industries were not nationalized, for IRI operated them on the basis of market criteria, the firms that it controlled issued their own stock, and IRI officials generally refrained at least initially from interfering with management. BENITO MUSSOLINI was careful to keep IRI in the hands of technocrats like Beneduce and away from advocates of state CORPORATISM, who might have wanted to use the institute for their social experiments. By 1939 IRI's holdings represented almost a fifth of the country's total capital assets.

The relationship between IRI and the government changed after WORLD WAR II. Under Christian Democratic (DC) leadership, IRI expanded, became increasingly politicized, and was often used for purposes of patronage by the governing party. It built roads, developed communications, and invested in the economic development of the South. It moved into sectors having nothing to do with its original mandate, like food production and distribution, controlled the national airline Alitalia, and the national communications network RAI. ROMANO PRODI served as its director in 1982–89 and 1993–94. By the 1990s IRI had become an enormous financial drain on the treasury. With yearly losses running into the trillions of lire, it contributed to the devaluation of the CURRENCY and threatened the entire economy. Under pressure from the EUROPEAN UNION and the national treasury, IRI began to divest itself of assets in the mid 1990s. Its residual holdings and funds realized from the sale of assets were transferred to the treasury at the end of the year 2000. Thus ended the Italian experiment in state ownership of the means of production begun by FASCISM and prolonged by Christian Democracy. In the current economic climate favoring privatization, judgments of IRI's operations are mostly negative. However, it arguably contributed to Italy's postwar ECONOMIC MIRACLE by relieving the private sector of unprofitable holdings, overseeing the construction of essential infrastructures, and facilitating cooperation between private and public capital.

irredentism

The independent kingdom of Italy, formed in 1861, did not include all the territories that patriots wished to see united in one nation. They claimed these "unredeemed" lands on historical and linguistic grounds, arguing that Italy had a rightful claim to them because they had belonged to Italian states in the past, or that their populations spoke Italian or dialects closely related to Italian, or that Italy needed those lands for strategic and security reasons. Historical, cultural, and geographic arguments were inextricably mixed in irredentist claims, usually in such a way as to maximize territorial demands. In 1861 the city of ROME and its adjacent territory, the regions of VENETIA, TRENTINO–ALTO ADIGE, ISTRIA, NICE, SAVOY, the islands of CORSICA and MALTA, and Italian-speaking towns in DALMATIA were not part of united Italy. At one time or another Italian irredentists claimed all these lands. After Italy gained Venetia in 1866 and Rome in 1870, irredentist sentiment focused on those Italian-speaking populations and lands still under Austro-Hungarian rule, particularly the Trentino, Istria, and Dalmatia. The cities of TRENT, capital of the Trentino, and TRIESTE, chief city of the Istrian peninsula, became irredentist symbols.

Italy's partnership with Austria-Hungary in the TRIPLE ALLIANCE required that the government officially disavow irredentist claims to Austro-Hungarian territories. Irredentism remained popular among students, the intelligentsia, and democrats and republicans opposed to the monarchy. Italians living under Austrian rule were often passionately irredentist. The most extreme contemplated and carried out acts of violence to express their hatred of Austria and assert their Italian identity. Guglielmo Oberdan (1858–82), a student of republican convictions born to an Italian-speaking family of Trieste, was condemned to death and executed by the Austrians for planning, without actually attempting, to assassinate Austrian emperor FRANCIS JOSEPH. The chief spokesman for the movement was the republican journalist Matteo Imbriani (1843–1901), who fought in the WARS OF NATIONAL INDEPENDENCE, founded the Italia Irredenta Association, and coined the term *terre irredente* (unredeemed lands) that gave the movement its name. From his seat in parliament and with his writings, Imbriani made irredentism and the pursuit of Italy's natural frontiers a national issue. The socialist journalist CESARE BATTISTI agitated for autonomy and eventually for union with Italy for his native Trentino.

As the irredentist campaign gained momentum, Italian governments found it increasingly hard to justify the alliance with Austria-Hungary and the official disavowal of irredentist aims. Austrian and German support for Italian COLONIALISM was motivated in part by the desire to distract Italy's attention from irredentist goals. Irredentist arguments were used to justify Italy's defection from the Triple Alliance and its declaration of war against Austria-Hungary in WORLD WAR I. The war itself was billed at home as Italy's "Fourth War of National Independence." Austria's defeat and the acquisition of Italian-speaking lands ended irredentist claims against Austria. FASCISM eventually resurrected the old Italian claims to Corsica, Nice, and Savoy against France and to Malta against Great Britain, but this latter-day irredentism lacked the popular appeal of the earlier anti-Austrian movement. The loss of Italian-speaking territories to Yugoslavia at the end of WORLD WAR II sustains some irredentist sentiments to this day, almost entirely confined, however, to the right-wing fringes of NEO-FASCISM. Irredentist claims are politically insignificant in the current climate of international cooperation.

ISTAT (Istituto Centrale di Statistica) See STATISTICS.

Istria

Istria (Istra in Serbo-Croatian) is a mountainous peninsula on the eastern side of the upper Adriatic Sea. Its principal cities and seaports are TRIESTE, FIUME (Rijeka), and Pola (Pula). Romans, Byzantines, and Venetians ruled it successively. VENICE governed much of Istria until the end of the 18th century, but the HABSBURGS began to establish their presence in the 15th century. Habsburg rule generally left Venetian settlers in place. Venetians settled in the port cities and provided seamen and officers to the Austrian navy. In Napoleonic times Istria changed hands from Venice to Austria (1797), from Austria to France (1805), and back to Austria (1815). These outside powers imposed their laws and people on the ancient Illyrian tribes and the Slavic-speaking populations who settled the countryside. A frontier region where Italian and Slavic-speaking populations met and mingled, Istria's ethnic composition has always been mixed. Italians were the majority in the cities, while Serbo-Croatians predominated in the countryside. The presence of Italian-speaking urban majorities fueled Italian IRREDENTISM. The peace settlement of 1919 assigned the entire territory to Italy, over the objections of Yugoslavia. Italian rule ended in 1945 when Yugoslav partisan forces loyal to Marshal Tito occupied the area and expelled most of the Italian-speaking population. The PEACE TREATY of 1947 assigned most of the area to Yugoslavia, with the exception of the area around Trieste, which was restored to Italy in 1954. Istria is today part of the independent republic of Croatia, a state born from the breakup of Yugoslavia in the 1990s.

Italia dei Valori   See DI PIETRO, ANTONIO.

Italia Irredenta Association   See
IRREDENTISM.

Italian Academy (Accademia d'Italia)

The Accademia d'Italia was created by the Fascist regime in 1926 and officially inaugurated by BENITO MUSSOLINI in 1929. It was launched with great fanfare to attract prestigious intellectuals to the regime and for the greater glory of the nation. Its declared purpose was to promote national culture, keep it free of foreign influences, and promote its expansion in the world. It promoted folk studies and was behind the campaign to purge the ITALIAN LANGUAGE of foreign terms. Like the much older, prestigious French Academy, after which it was modeled, the Italian Academy bestowed official accolades and funding on the country's scholars, artists, writers, and scientists. The most eminent and cooperative rose to high positions. Its presidents were TOMMASO TITTONI, GUGLIEMO MARCONI, GABRIELE D'ANNUNZIO, LUIGI FEDERZONI, and GIOVANNI GENTILE. Prominent academicians included ENRICO FERMI and LUIGI PIRANDELLO. The academy was part of the Fascist regime's campaign to create a national culture from above by enticing the country's most creative individuals into patron-client relationships with the state. The academy was officially abolished in 1944, and all its assets assigned to the Roman Accademia dei Lincei.

Italian language

Derived from Latin, Italian belongs to the Romance group of Indo-European languages that includes French, Spanish, Portuguese, and Romanian. Its evolution from Latin occurred gradually between the 10th and 13th centuries. By the end of the 13th century the Tuscan dialect spoken in FLORENCE gained dominance over other regional dialects because of Florence's rising power in the peninsula and the eminence of its writers. German emperor Frederick II of Hohenstaufen (1194–1250) first promoted the use of Tuscan as a literary language at his court in PALERMO, a gathering place for poets and scholars from all over Italy. Saint Francis of Assisi (1182–1226) used this vernacular in his famous *Cantico di Frate Sole* (Song of brother sun) to stimulate religious fervor among ordinary Italians who did not understand Latin. DANTE was the most eminent of the early writers who gave luster to the language, followed by GIOVANNI BOCCACCIO and PETRARCH.

Outside of Tuscany, and neighboring parts of central Italy where local dialects were closely related to Tuscan, only educated people understood or spoke the national language. People without formal education spoke local and regional dialects that were only distantly related to Tuscan and were all but incomprehensible to outsiders. The diffusion of Tuscan from the educated to the general population was a slow and contested process. Even among the intelligentsia, the dominance of Tuscan was a contentious issue until the end of the 18th century. Its acceptance by eminent non-Tuscan patriotic writers such as VITTORIO ALFIERI, UGO FOSCOLO, GIACOMO LEOPARDI, and ALESSANDRO MANZONI made it the national language in the 19th century. It is estimated that when the country was unified in 1861 only about 630,000 Italians (2.5 percent of the total population) spoke the national language.

The adoption of a single language for the entire peninsula has been both cause and effect of the process of national unification. Its diffusion from the top down required concerted efforts by writers, educators, and public officials. Compulsory military service, the spread of literacy, and the advent of mass media have made Italian the language spoken today by almost every native of Italy. It is the official language of 57 million Italians living in Italy, of the REPUBLIC OF SAN MARINO, and of the VATICAN. An estimated additional 20 million people speak Italian in other parts of the world, particularly in South and North America where Italians and their descendants have settled in large numbers, and in those parts of Africa affected by Italian COLONIALISM. There is little government support today to promote the teaching and use of Italian abroad. Nevertheless, the study of Italian outside Italy has increased greatly in the last 20 or 30 years, and thousands of students go to Italy every year to study the language.

Italian has evolved significantly in the course of time, but the Italian used by Dante is readily recognized and understood by today's educated Italians. It consists of about 261,000 words, 2,000 of which are used conversationally and 7,000 are generally understood. After FASCISM fought and lost its battle to keep Italian free of foreign influences, the language incorporated a large number of foreign words, particularly from English, and has expanded in response to developments in science, business, and communications. The most recent reference work is the *Grande Dizionario dell'Uso* (Turin: UTET, 2000), edited by the authoritative linguist and former education minister Tullio De Mauro.

Italian National Society See CAVOUR;

GARIBALDI, GIUSEPPE; LA FARINA, GIUSEPPE; MANIN, DANIELE; RISORGIMENTO; SOCIETÀ NAZIONALE ITALIANA.

Italian Nationalist Association See

NATIONALISM.

Italian Social Movement See MSI.

Italian Social Republic (RSI)

Italian Social Republic (Republica Sociale Italiana) is the official name of the government formed by BENITO MUSSOLINI in German-occupied northern Italy after his rescue from prison by German paratroopers in September 1943. Its unofficial name was Republic of Salò, after the small town on Lake Garda that served as the government's headquarters. Mussolini apparently agreed to head the new Fascist government under threats of German reprisals against the population if he refused. Once reinstated, he resolved to refurbish the image of fascism by going back to the movement's radical beginnings. Hence the rejection of the monarchy and the adoption of a republican form of government, promises to restructure the economy in a socialist direction, give workers a voice in management, adopt profit-sharing and land reform, nationalize big industry, and fight international capital.

With the exception of republicanism, none of these promises were realized or even seriously pursued. Germany had no interest in promoting social experiments in Italy and opposed any policies that might interfere with the prosecution of war. Mussolini soon reverted to his old tactic of seeking political support across the board and cracking down hard on stubborn opponents. His government, composed of die-hard Fascists, concentrated on rebuilding the army to fight alongside the Germans, suppressing internal opposition, and fighting the anti-Fascist RESISTANCE movement. The government's efforts to conscript Italians for military service led many potential draftees to join the resistance. Mussolini was well aware of his limited margin of autonomy, but justified his decision to carry on at Germany's side by claiming that he could thus protect Italians from the kind of deadly retaliation that the Germans visited on other subject populations. He was only partly successful, for in the final year of the war Germany annexed Italian territories, refused to release Italian troops interned in Germany, raided the country's industrial apparatus, rounded up Italian civilians, used them as the equivalent of slave labor to build war fortifications, and generally imposed a harsh military rule. There was much talk about organizing a last-ditch military defense of the Social Republic in the mountains, but nothing came of it in the end. The Social Republic ended with the execution of Mussolini on April 28, 1945. It left behind a legacy of discord and hatred that haunts the Italian public to this day.

Italian-Turkish War (1911–1912)

Also known as the Libyan War, this conflict broke out in September 1911 with an Italian declaration of war against the Ottoman Empire. Prime Minister GIOVANNI GIOLITTI was induced to favor the war by the acquiescence of the major European powers, the weakness of the Ottoman Empire, and the desire to appease nationalists with a show of force on the 50th anniversary of national unification. The war met with strong opposition at home from socialists. It did stir national sentiment at home and abroad among Italians who saw the war as an affirmation of Italian power. Catholics eager to make inroads in Muslim lands, and critics of Italian emigration looking to settle Italians in a colonial territory under the national flag also supported the war.

Military operations proved to be more difficult than anticipated. Italian troops occupied the major coastal towns quickly, but then ran into determined resistance from Turkish troops and natives who declared jihad against the Christians and resorted to guerrilla warfare tactics. The conflict dragged on, required the deployment of 100,000 troops, and expenditure of enormous quantities of war materiel. To force the Ottomans to the peace table, the navy carried the war to the Dardanelles, the Aegean Sea, and the eastern Mediterranean. In April–July 1912 a naval expedition headed by Admiral Enrico Millo (1865–1930) penetrated the Dardanelles and occupied the Dodecannese Islands. The bombing of Beirut and other towns produced an outcry of indigna-

tion in the Arab world. The Ottoman government agreed to negotiate when attacked by Bulgaria, Greece, Montenegro, and Serbia in the conflict known as the First Balkan War. European governments, alarmed by the spread of the conflict, also urged a quick settlement. The Treaty of Ouchy (October 1912), also known as the Treaty of Lausanne, acknowledged Italian occupation of Libya and the Dodecannese Islands, without formally recognizing Italian sovereignty. In Libya, resistance to Italian rule continued on and off until the early 1930s. A serious unintended consequence of the Italian-Turkish War was the destabilization of the Balkans, a major cause of WORLD WAR I.

Italian Wars   See RENAISSANCE.

Italic League

An alliance formed in August 1454 soon after the signing of the PEACE OF LODI by the states of MILAN, VENICE, and FLORENCE to maintain acquired positions and balance of power among the states of the peninsula. Proposed by FRANCESCO SFORZA, the league eventually included the PAPAL STATES and NAPLES, thus encompassing all the major Italian states. It provided for a defensive military alliance for a period of 25 years, and military cooperation in case of war, and banned separate alliances or peace treaties. The league did not prevent conflicts and did not deter the French invasion of 1494, but did make it possible for the Italian states to form the army that convinced the French to beat a hasty retreat back to France after having reached Naples. The army fielded by the league engaged the French at the battle of Fornovo (July 1495). The encounter was inconclusive. The Italian side remained in control of the field of battle, but did not prevent the French from continuing their orderly march back to France.

J

Jacini, Stefano (1827–1891)
Lombard economist, agrarian expert, and conservative political figure

Born to a family of large landowners in the province of Cremona, the young Jacini studied agriculture, avoided politics, traveled widely in Europe, and published *Proprietà fondiaria e le popolazioni in Lombardia* (1854), a landmark study of landownership in the region of Lombardy. It revealed his vocation as an agricultural modernizer and his understanding of the links between agriculture and public policy. An observant Catholic, Jacini held aloof from the movement for national unification, opposed the struggle against the PAPACY, but agreed to serve as minister of public works under CAVOUR (1860) and again under ALFONSO LA MARMORA (1864–66). His election to parliament as a member of the HISTORICAL RIGHT in 1867 was annulled because of alleged irregularities, but he was appointed to the senate in 1870. In 1877 Jacini took charge of a parliamentary investigation into the state of agriculture and the condition of land workers. The Inchiesta agraria, also known as the Inchiesta Jacini, published 15 volumes (1881–85) documenting the state of agriculture in various parts of Italy. The concluding volume, written by Jacini, stated that the purpose of the investigation was to ascertain the needs and problems of production rather than prescribe solutions. He stressed that the problems of agriculture were not due to landlords' ignorance, greed, or lack of capital resources. The fundamental problems of Italian agriculture were fragmentation of landownership, excessive labor, and low productivity. Jacini's remedy was to let free-market forces take their course, respect freedom of contract between landlords and workers, and encourage the productive use of private capital with appropriate fiscal measures. Jacini failed in his intention to rally support for his plan by launching a conservative party, but the findings of the inquest became a reference point for a national debate on the needs of agriculture. The radical deputy AGOSTINO BERTANI led a separate investigation that stressed the needs of agricultural workers and rural populations.

Jacobins

The term Jacobin derives from the radical political club established in the St. Jacques monastery in Paris in 1789. Their ideology, Jacobinism, attracted considerable attention among educated Italians in the early 1790s. In Italy, the designation of Jacobin applied to those who sympathized with the FRENCH REVOLUTION, demanded republican government, universal suffrage, the separation of church and state, and economic equality. Italian Jacobins welcomed the French invasion of 1796 as a liberating event and held positions of power during the *triennio* (1796–99), the first three years of French rule. Although inspired and energized by the French Revolution, Italian Jacobinism also had had autonomous roots in 18th-century FREEMASONRY and JANSENISM. Italian Jacobins were not blind followers of their French counterparts. Basically anticlerical, many nevertheless looked to the egalitarian spirit of Christianity rather than the secular ideologies of the ENLIGHTENMENT. More isolated than their French counterparts, they ran into strong popular hostility and found little support for their programs. Italian Jacobins also had to contend with moderates who were intrinsically fearful of the masses and whose zeal for reform was tempered by the desire to benefit from revolutionary change. Land reform in the PARTHENOPEAN REPUBLIC was mostly for the benefit of those who had capital to buy land.

Major changes were nevertheless legislated by the governments of Jacobin republics during the *triennio*. The most radical change was the replacement of monarchies with representative governments. The Parthenopean Republic abolished feudalism, the CISALPINE REPUBLIC ended primogeniture (sole right of inheritance by firstborn males), allowed women to own property, and instituted civil marriage. The changes were radical enough to alarm the church, the traditional ruling dynasties, and their many supporters. Republican governments were toppled during the crisis of Napoleonic power in 1798–99. In many places in central and southern Italy, peasants and urban workers turned against the republicans, whom they regarded as traitors to church and monarchy. Bands led by Cardinal FABRIZIO RUFFO and the outlaw FRA DIAVOLO showed particular ferocity against Jacobins and their supporters. When French dominance was restored in 1800, the new republican governments were more moderate, cautious, and subservient to NAPOLEON BONAPARTE. Napoleon reined in the more radical elements to make his rule acceptable to the majority of Italians. Jacobin revolutions, according to the Neapolitan commentator VINCENZO CUOCO, were "passive" in that they failed to address the social issues that mattered most to the common people.

Jansenism

Jansenism was based on the teachings and writings of the Dutch Roman Catholic theologian Cornelis Jansen (1585–1638). Jansen's theology stressed that salvation came solely from the power of God (predestination). However, glorification of the power of God was combined in Jansenist thought with an equally strong emphasis on fulfillment of Christian duties, hence the insistence on the regular partaking of communion as a sign of individual resolve. Politically minded Jansenists emphasized the duties of Christians in the public realm, concluding that republics were most conducive to the active involvement of Christians in civic matters. Jansenism insisted that salvation and civic virtue were attainable only within the CATHOLIC CHURCH, but clashed with the church over the doctrine of predestination, papal authority, and the role of the JESUITS, which Jansenists saw as the most powerful obstacle to reform within the church and in society. Pope CLEMENT XI condemned Jansenism in the bull *Unigenitus* (1713). In 18th-century Italy the Jansenist polemic against the papacy and the Jesuits merged with the efforts of monarchs to assert power over the PAPACY. The Habsburg rulers JOSEPH II and PETER LEOPOLD were in the forefront of the antipapal campaign. Jansenist professors at the University of Pavia in Austrian Lombardy supported their campaigns by subjecting the papal claims to critical scrutiny. In Peter Leopold's Tuscany, Bishop SCIPIONE DE RICCI introduced daring ritual changes inspired by Jansenism. The republics of GENOA and VENICE welcomed Jansenists ostracized by other states. Jansenism lost official support when the outbreak of the French Revolution created fear of change among monarchs, clergy, and nobility. Jansenist influences continued to permeate Catholic culture informally. There is evidence of Jansenist influences in the family backgrounds of CAVOUR, GIUSEPPE MAZZINI, and ALESSANDRO MANZONI.

Jesuit Order

The Jesuit religious order, formally known as the Society of Jesus, was founded by the Spaniard Ignatius Loyola and officially approved by Pope PAUL III in 1540. Known for their rigorous training, strict discipline, and loyalty to the PAPACY, the Jesuits have always attracted attention for their real or suspected influence within and outside the CATHOLIC CHURCH. Jesuits have been hailed as defenders of the faith, rigorous educators, and the intellectual elite of the church, and

Interior of the Jesuits' Church, Venice, ca. 1890 *(Library of Congress)*

vilified as devious counselors to the powerful, corruptors of morals, enemies of the secular state and of progress. The Jesuits' close ties to the papacy, opposition to the national unification movement, and involvement in cultural and political affairs have made them particularly controversial in Italy. In the 17th century the Jesuits combated JANSENISM and opposed secular trends in politics, philosophy, and science. They did not oppose philosophic or scientific speculation as such, but sought to reconcile modern philosophy and science with the traditional teachings of the church and the authority of the papacy.

Reaching the height of power around the middle of the 18th century, the Society of Jesus soon came into conflict with rulers bent on consolidating their own power and the authority of

the secular state. Jesuits were expelled from Portugal (1759), France (1764), Spain (1767), the kingdom of NAPLES (1768), and the duchy of PARMA (1769). Pope CLEMENT XIV dissolved the order in 1773 under pressure from the Bourbon dynasty. Reconstituted in 1814 by Pope PIUS VII, it adopted an intransigent, antiliberal stance, and was a mainstay of the alliance of throne and altar during the RESTORATION. The order condemned SECRET SOCIETIES and opposed constitutional monarchy, civil liberties, and national movements. VINCENZO GIOBERTI, a liberal Catholic, denounced the Jesuits as enemies of progress. The revolutions of 1848 reinforced the political conservatism of the order. The Jesuit review *CIVILTÀ CATTOLICA* carried on a polemic against patriots and liberals and backed the intransigent conservatism of Pope PIUS IX. Patriotic animosity against the Jesuits continued after national unification and has fueled ANTICLERICALISM ever since.

Jews in Italy

Jews have lived in Italy since at least the second century B.C., when Roman sources mention their presence. During the reign of Emperor Tiberius (A.D. 14–37) 200 years later, some 50,000–60,000 Jews lived in the city of Rome. More came after the capture of Jerusalem by Titus in A.D. 70. Tradition has it that today's Roman Jews are the descendants of those early settlers. Jewish communities were present throughout the Middle Ages and the RENAISSANCE. The majority of Jews held menial positions, but many stood out in the arts and professions. Jewish doctors were prominent in Europe's first medical school founded in Salerno in the ninth century.

Italian Jews experienced bouts of repression for religious and economic reasons, but until the 16th century, on the whole they suffered less discrimination and were better integrated than Jews in other parts of Europe. The Aragonese rulers of southern Italy followed the Spanish lead, forcing Jews out of their lands after 1492. The segregation of Jews from the rest of society was a consequence of the CATHOLIC REFORMATION and of state politics. The term *ghetto*, derived from *getto* (casting), refers to the section of VENICE where metal foundries were located and Jews were confined in 1516. Segregation became systematic under Pope Paul IV (1555–59), when all Jews were confined to walled ghettoes, forbidden to own land, evicted from the professions, and required to wear distinctive signs of their religious identity. The expulsion of Jews from the PAPAL STATES in 1569 (except for those living in Rome and the port city of Ancona) was an example followed by other states.

Jewish communities continued to exist in Venice, FLORENCE, and in the region of PIEDMONT. The Tuscan government welcomed Jews to the free port city of LIVORNO after 1590. Papal policy also wavered, some popes pursuing a hard line, others showing tolerance. Pope Sixtus V (1585–90) was among the latter and relied on Jews to help him straighten out Vatican finances. Most Jews experienced life in the ghettoes as degrading and downright dangerous, due to overcrowding, poor housing, and bad sanitation. Forced out of the professions, Jews often resorted to menial occupations as ragpickers, street peddlers, used-goods dealers, and pawnbrokers.

The 18th century brought improvements for Jews in those states of the peninsula that were most affected by the culture of the ENLIGHTENMENT. The Habsburg possessions of LOMBARDY and TRIESTE, the Grand Duchy of TUSCANY, and the Duchy of PARMA enacted emancipating laws. The FRENCH REVOLUTION put Jewish emancipation on the political agenda of all the Italian states and emancipating laws were brought to Italy by NAPOLEON. Jewish support of the French occupation produced a popular backlash that resulted in anti-Jewish pogroms. The RESTORATION regimes of 1815–48 enacted restrictive laws, but Jewish communities were now better organized to look after their members and take advantage of business and educational opportunities. Under the CONSTITUTION of 1848, the Jews of Piedmont-Sardinia enjoyed the rights of all

citizens. Many Jews participated in the movement for national unification. Most politically active Jews supported the moderate policies of CAVOUR, but some rallied to the democratic movement of GIUSEPPE MAZZINI.

National unification benefited Italian Jews who were ready to take advantage of new opportunities in schooling, business, and public service. In 1861 only 5.8 percent of Italian Jews above the age of 10 were illiterate, compared to 54.5 percent for the general population. In the next half-century Jews made headway in the academic world, business, government, and the military. Giuseppe Ottolenghi (1838–1904), the most famous member of this distinguished Piedmontese family, fought for Italian independence, was decorated for bravery, taught military science, was promoted to general (1888), served as war minister (1902–03), and was appointed to the senate (1903). LUIGI LUZZATTI, an economist, was prime minister (1910–11). Ernesto Nathan (1845–1921), a Freemason, born to a family that was close to GIUSEPPE MAZZINI, served as mayor of Rome (1909–13). The liberal period from national unification to the outbreak of World War I was a promising moment for Italian Jews. However, not all was well even in this "Silver Age" that promised a golden future. Anti-Semitism was rife in some quarters, and individual success stories disguise the reality that most Jews lived ordinary lives and many were downright poor. In 1912 one-third of Italy's Jews were dependent on community charity, the poorest being the Jews of Rome.

Assimilation continued until the late 1930s, when the Fascist regime enacted anti-Semitic laws. Until then some 7,300 Jews out of a population of about 45,000 belonged to the Fascist Party, a considerably higher proportion than for the population as a whole. BENITO MUSSOLINI was not anti-Semitic, had a Jewish mistress and cultural mentor in the person of MARGHERITA SARFATTI, and before the late 1930s publicly condemned anti-Semitism and racism in general. The ETHIOPIAN WAR and the ROME-BERLIN AXIS changed his attitude and gave unexpected leverage to anti-Semites like GIUSEPPE PREZIOSI and ROBERTO FARINACCI. The Racial Laws of November 1938 banned Jews from government, business, and the professions, and banned inter-marriage between Jews and Aryans. Lax application of the laws, bureaucratic inefficiency, corruption, and widespread popular sympathy mitigated the effects of the anti-Semitic legislation, but the overall effects were devastating. Italian Jews were forced to leave the country or become second-class citizens.

Passive and active resistance to the regime and anti-German sentiments alleviated the plight of Italian Jews in WORLD WAR II. The army refused to deport Jews out of the areas of the Balkans and France that were under its jurisdiction, and Jews from other parts of Europe still found some protection in Italy. Massive deportations occurred after Italy tried to pull out of the war in September 1943. The single largest roundup of Jews in German-occupied Italy occurred in Rome on October 16, 1943, when 1,259 Jews were seized and deported. In 1943–45, 7,749 Italian Jews died in Nazi camps and the Italian Jewish population declined to about 28,000. It was back to 35,000 by 1975 and has remained stable around that number since then. A disproportionately large number of Jews were active in the anti-Fascist RESISTANCE during the war. The memory of persecution and questions of identity have animated the writings of Italian Jewish authors of the war and postwar generations. They include PRIMO LEVI's *Se questo è un uomo* (If this is a man, 1947), Giorgio Bassani's *Il giardino dei Finzi-Contini* (The garden of the Finzi-Contini, 1962), and Natalia Ginzburg's *Lessico familiare* (The things we used to say, 1963). The largest Jewish communities in Italy today are those of Rome, Milan, and Trieste. Italian law fully protects the rights of Jews and other minorities, and Jews are well integrated into Italian society. Anti-Semitism nevertheless lingers on in the far quarters of the political Right and can be stoked by events in the Middle East and by widespread sympathy for the plight of Palestinians.

John XXIII (1881–1963)
pope (1958–1963)

Angelo Giuseppe Roncalli, born near Bergamo (Lombardy) to a family of sharecroppers, attended seminary (1892–1900). In 1904 he was ordained into the priesthood and received a doctorate in theology. At the start of his ecclesiastical career as secretary to the bishop of Bergamo (1905–14) he demonstrated his concern for social problems and established his reputation as a church historian. The publication of a five-volume life of CARLO BORROMEO (1936–52) was the result of research begun in these early years. After serving as a military chaplain in the Italian army in WORLD WAR I, he held several posts in Rome and traveled widely in Europe. Made archbishop in 1925, he was appointed papal representative to Bulgaria (1925), Turkey, and Greece (1935), papal nuncio to liberated Paris (1944), and observer to UNESCO (1951). He became cardinal and patriarch of Venice in 1953. In his diplomatic posts Roncalli displayed the human warmth, tact, and sense of humor that were his hallmark, but it was in Venice that he demonstrated the pastoral style that made him beloved.

His election as pope in October 1958 was a surprise. The new pope, warm, approachable, and chatty, was in every respect the opposite of his predecessor, the aloof and austere PIUS XII. He was also an innovator who launched the *aggiornamento* (updating) of the CATHOLIC CHURCH. Eager to show his benevolence toward the Italian state, he was the first pope to pay an official call on President ANTONIO SEGNI in the Quirinal Palace, the former papal residence. John initiated the ecumenical dialogue with other churches that sought cooperation and ultimate union among Christians of all denominations. He also reached out to non-Christians and lifted the ancient condemnation of Jews as killers of Christ. His reforms aimed to put the church in touch with the realities of the industrial world, showing concern for workers, the underprivileged, and the socially marginal, including convicts and the homeless. In the encyclical *Mater*

Pope John XXIII *(Library of Congress)*

et Magistra (Mother and teacher, 1961), he called on the church to support social reform, avoid the extremes of communism and capitalism, assure a just wage for workers, and assist developing countries. The pope encouraged international dialogue. The fact that John's pontificate coincided with the presidency of John F. Kennedy in the United States and the government of Nikita Khrushchev in the Soviet Union contributed to the prospect of peaceful coexistence.

John's principal concern was to promote ecclesiastical reform. To that end he appointed an unprecedented number of new cardinals to reflect diversity within the church and summoned a general council. The Second Vatican Council (Vatican II) opened in Rome in October 1962. It addressed issues of vital importance, such as the role of laity and hierarchy within the church, interfaith dialogue, clerical duties, and church rituals. The council's opening marked the high point of John's pontificate. The expectations aroused by its summoning had not yet been fulfilled when John died of cancer in June 1963. The council concluded its deliberations under John's successor, Pope PAUL VI.

John Paul I   See JOHN PAUL II.

John Paul II (1920–   )
pope since 1978

Born in a small village near Krakow (Poland) and baptized Karol Wojtyla, the son of a retired army officer and a mother who died young, he studied at the University of Krakow. When the German invasion of Poland shut down the university in September 1939, Karol studied secretly for the priesthood during the war while hiding in the palace of the archbishop of Krakow. He was ordained in 1946, and spent two years in Rome, where he obtained a doctorate in theology before returning to Poland. Bishop of Krakow in 1958, archbishop in 1964, and Poland's youngest-ever cardinal in 1967, he was a highly popular figure who led the fight against Poland's communist regime.

His election to the papacy followed the brief 33-day pontificate of his predecessor John Paul I (1912–78), whose name he chose to continue. At age 58 John Paul II was one of the youngest popes on record and the first non-Italian pope since 1522. In his long and eventful pontificate John Paul has shown an inclination to use the power of his office for political purposes. His continuing fight against communism is believed to have contributed to the downfall of communist regimes in Poland, Eastern Europe and the Soviet Union. An assassination attempt on his life in May 1981 may have been motivated by political resentments and fears. Seriously wounded, John Paul resumed his papal duties after a convalescence of several months.

A pope with a truly global perspective, John Paul travels widely and frequently. His broad outlook and non-Italian background may have contributed to the shift in papal policy toward the Italian state and lessened clerical interference in Italian affairs. In 1984 a revision of the CONCORDAT of 1929 brought about the complete separation of CHURCH AND STATE in Italy. He still speaks out forcefully in matters of education and family life that he considers questions of faith, firmly rejecting abortion, birth control, domestic partnerships, and attempts to redefine marriage. Internationally, John Paul has continued the policy of LEO XIII and JOHN XXIII of condemning both communism and capitalism, seeking to reconcile the demands of social justice with personal rights and private property. He has called upon the clergy to combat social injustice mindful of their spiritual obligations and duties as members of the clergy. A socially progressive but theologically conservative pope, John Paul II has condemned clerical abuses and misbehavior, but makes no concessions to reformers who would abolish clerical celibacy, open the priesthood to women, or give the laity a stronger voice in church matters. Universally popular in the early years, John Paul's papacy has become controversial and divisive among Catholics in what appears to be its concluding phase, following in this regard a course similar to that of the pontificate of PIUS IX, whom John Paul wants to see canonized.

Jommelli, Niccolò See OPERA.

Joseph II (1741–1790)
Austrian emperor (1780–1790)
The son of Empress MARIA THERESA of Habsburg and Holy Roman Emperor FRANCIS OF LORRAINE, Joseph ruled jointly with his mother after his father died in 1765, assuming sole control of the empire after the death of his mother in 1780. Impatient with the slow speed of reform under his mother, he moved speedily to abolish serf-

dom and feudal privileges, impose imperial control on religious orders, adopt freedom of worship, abolish the use of torture and the death penalty, and initiate a land survey to ascertain the extent of private wealth. Convinced that absolute power was necessary to carry out reform, Joseph curtailed the autonomy of nobility and clergy within his lands, limited the role of local administrations, reorganized the imperial administration, and expanded the power of imperial bureaucrats in Vienna. Joseph is often seen as a typical exponent of enlightened monarchy, but his impatience, haste, and lack of political tact suggest a ruler lacking the political realism possessed by most monarchs of the ENLIGHTENMENT. In Italy he alienated the ARISTOCRACY and PAPACY, turned them against the imperial administration, and drove them into the arms of the reaction that followed the outbreak of the French Revolution in the last year of his reign. In Lombardy, the reaction to Joseph's policy of administrative centralization and taxation of landed wealth was voiced by a group of disgruntled aristocrats led by PIETRO VERRI, who near the end of Joseph's reign sought remedy in limited, constitutional monarchy. Joseph's untimely death brought to the throne his younger brother PETER LEOPOLD, grand duke of Tuscany. Although imposed in haste, most of Joseph's reforms survived the years of reaction after his death to the benefit of the AUSTRIAN EMPIRE.

Jotti, Nilde (1920–1999)
Communist personality, member of parliament, champion of women's rights
Nilde (Leonilde) Jotti was born in Reggio Emilia, attended the Catholic University of Milan, and became a teacher. She joined the underground as a member of the Communist Party (PCI) during the Fascist period. A member of the RESISTANCE, she founded and led the Women's Defense Groups that played an important role in the fight against FASCISM. She credited the resistance with giving Italian women a prominent political role

for the first time in the nation's history. As a member of the committee of the constituent assembly (1946–47), Jotti was instrumental in preparing the final version of the republican CONSTITUTION that went into effect in 1948. She followed the party line reluctantly when she agreed to the constitutional endorsement of the CONCORDAT, which preserved the privileged position of the Catholic Church and the indissoluble nature of marriage, and banned divorce. She was elected to parliament in 1948 and served continuously until 1999, when she retired for health reasons. From 1979 to 1992 she served as elected speaker (leader) of the chamber of deputies, the highest political position held by a woman in Italy. The most prominent and influential woman in the PCI, she became a member of the party's central committee in 1956. She supported the abolition of the PCI in 1991 and joined the Democratic Party of the Left (PDS) as its rightful successor. Her career spanned the entire history of the PCI from its founding to its dissolution.

journalism

Printed sheets began to disseminate information, news, and views in 16th-century FLORENCE, GENOA, and VENICE. Venice soon took the lead, thanks to the relative leniency of its government in matters of censorship. The word "gazette" common in journalism derives from the *gazeta*, a Venetian coin that was the price of a newspaper in 1563. After suffering a loss of momentum in the 17th century, Italian journalism revived in the 18th with the publication of the *Gazzetta Veneta* (1760–62), GIUSEPPE BARETTI's *Frusta Letteraria* (1763–65), and PIETRO VERRI's *Il Caffè* (1764–66). All were modeled on the British *Spectator* and oriented toward practical issues of agricultural and economic development. MILAN challenged and surpassed Venice as the publishing and journalistic center of the peninsula in the 18th century, and was in turn challenged but not surpassed by Florence.

Italian journalism became explicitly political after the outbreak of the FRENCH REVOLUTION.

NAPOLEON's arrival in 1796 and the rise of the JACOBINS opened the floodgates to revolutionary publications that inundated the peninsula during the first three years of Napoleonic rule (1796–99). The most notable of the republican publications was *Il Monitore Italiano* of Milan (1798). It published for only a few months but inspired similar publications in other major cities. The authoritarian change of direction that occurred after 1799 brought about stricter government control of newspapers, but saw also the expansion of journalism in new directions. The Milanese *Il Corriere delle Dame* (1804–72) reached out to women, publications began to feature paid advertisements, expanded their coverage to cultural events, adopted industrial techniques of production, and even provided home delivery. The first years of the RESTORATION period witnessed some new journalistic initiatives, the most notable being the Milanese literary review *La Biblioteca Italiana* (1816–41), supported by the government in the hope that it would persuade the intelligentsia to rally around Austrian rule. The government was less tolerant toward another Milanese review, *Il Conciliatore* (1818–19), which catered to a more radical readership. The Florentine progressive monthly *Antologia* (1821–33), which called for educational and economic reforms, survived in the tolerant Tuscan climate until suppressed in the aftermath of the REVOLUTION of 1830–31. The most radical political journal of the period was the *Giovine Italia* (1832–34), published clandestinely in Marseilles by GIUSEPPE MAZZINI and smuggled into Italy.

Political journalism was the norm during the REVOLUTIONS of 1848 everywhere in the peninsula. It survived the revolution in Piedmont-Sardinia, where the CONSTITUTION guaranteed enough freedom of expression to sustain a free press: 117 periodicals were published in the Kingdom of Sardinia in 1858, compared to 68 in Lombardy-Venetia, 27 in Tuscany, 16 in Rome, and 50 in the entire South. National unification stimulated political debate. Most newspapers favored national government, but the press reflected a broad range of views. Opposed to national unification was the Vatican newspaper *L'Osservatore Romano,* which began publishing in 1851. By 1874 18 more or less regular publications expressed Catholic views. Opposed to the government from the Left was Milan's *Il Gazzettino Rosa* (1867–74) and a host of other publications that appeared more or less regularly whenever they could escape confiscation by the police. The weekly *L'Illustrazione Italiana* began publication in 1875 for a middlebrow readership interested in everything from fashions to exotic places.

The first modern daily that sought to reach a truly popular clientele was Milan's *Il Secolo,* which started in 1866, sold at five cents a copy, and had broad distribution. The *Corriere della Sera,* founded in 1876, replaced it as the most widely read and prestigious daily in the country. Modeled on London's *Times* and politically moderate, under the direction of LUIGI ALBERTINI, the *Corriere* established itself as a reliable source of information with a moderate slant on politics. Unapologetically political was the Socialist Party (PSI) newspaper *Avanti!,* which began publishing in 1896, directed by LEONIDA BISSOLATI. It played an important role in all the political struggles of the coming decades, starting with the campaign to protect freedom of the press during the political crisis that gripped the country from 1898 to 1901.

The decade before the outbreak of World War I was the golden age of journalism. In those years the printed word was virtually the sole means for disseminating information. Literacy levels rose, political passions spread, and a rising standard of living meant that more people could afford to buy newspapers. Among the rising stars of Italian journalism in those years was BENITO MUSSOLINI, who rose to be chief editor of *Avanti!* (1912–14) and was in his youth an eagerly read political commentator. An important innovation unique to Italian journalism was the introduction of the *terza pagina,* the third page, dedicated entirely to commentary and reviews of art, literature, and theater by prestigious figures of the cultural world.

FASCISM transformed journalism and the journalistic profession. As a former journalist who understood the importance of the printed word, Mussolini cajoled and pressured the press into slavishly supporting the regime. Freedom of the press was all but eliminated in Italy by 1926. While journalistic content declined, the appearance of newspapers and the technical aspects of production improved. Journalism became a modern industry with improved facilities for collecting news, printing, and distribution. Radio and motion pictures supplemented and eventually surpassed newspapers as conduits of information and communication. Starting in 1930, daily news bulletins presented by the Ente Italiano Audizioni Radiofoniche (EIAR) gave listeners the official and sole version of national and world events. The Fascist regime relied heavily on its ability to control public opinion in peace and war by manipulating all means of information.

Today, freedom of the press is protected by constitutional safeguards. The constitution of the Italian Republic provides for freedom of the press, with certain restrictions to safeguard public morality and safety. Newspapers may be sued for libelous reporting. Political parties have taken full advantage of freedom of the press to launch their own newspapers (*stampa politica*) and carve out spheres of influence in radio and television. The Christian Democratic Party (DC) had broad press support during its period of political dominance, but the communist (PCI) *L'Unità* and the socialist (PSI) *Avanti!* also had large readerships. Unaffiliated newspapers like *Corriere della Sera* and *La Stampa,* both moderately conservative, and the moderately liberal *La Repubblica* (founded in 1976), constitute the so-called informational press (*stampa informazione*) and have the largest circulation. A truly independent journalist like INDRO MONTANELLI, who followed no party line, had to struggle to be heard. Political parties dominated radio and television broadcasting until 1974–75, when court decisions and a new law ended the monopoly of the state-run broadcasting corporation RAI (Radio Audizioni Italiane), deregulated the media, and opened them up to private competition. SILVIO BERLUSCONI was one of the first, and the most successful entrepreneur, to take advantage of the new opportunities for commercial television. Changes of ownership, consolidations, and competitive programming are the norm in Italian journalism at the beginning of the 21st century. With the unprecedented degree of freedom that Italian journalism enjoys today comes also an unprecedented sense of uncertainty and questioning of the public role and responsibilities of the media.

Julius II (1443–1513)
pope (1503–1513)

Born in Savona to a family of the nobility, the ecclesiastical career of Giuliano della Rovere benefited at first from the nepotism of his uncle, Pope Sixtus IV (1471–84), who appointed him to important posts and made him a cardinal. But papal favoritism, and the considerable influence that the nephew exercised at his uncle's court backfired when jealous cardinals elected Giuliano's archrival, ALEXANDER VI, as pope. Giuliano had to wait for the death of Pope Pius III, Alexander's short-lived successor, to get his turn on the papal throne. Julius II was a secular-minded pope who plunged into politics with energy and passion. A warrior pope, he often took the field at the head of his troops, and awed his contemporaries who called him *Il papa terribile* (the dreaded pope). Julius put aside his personal enmity toward the BORGIA FAMILY to complete the task of consolidating papal control over central Italy. He fought against antipapal VENICE and resisted the efforts of the French monarchy to dominate Italy. Seen later as a champion of Italian independence, Julius did not want to unify the peninsula under papal leadership. His aim was to maintain a balance of power that would give the papacy freedom of action. A patron of the arts, Julius employed the best artists of his time, including MICHELANGELO, who painted the Sistine Chapel for him and sculpted the Moses that sits on the pope's tomb in the Church of San Pietro in Vincoli. He also began the construction of St. Peter's basilica. In spite of his lavish expenditures on war, there

Pope Julius II *(Library of Congress)*

was a sizable surplus in the papal treasury at the time of Julius's death. His pontificate is still the subject of controversy. Detractors argue that he undermined the church's spiritual authority by enmeshing the papacy in politics, waging war, and squandering resources on artistic embellishments. Favorable historians point to the gain in territorial security, without which the church could not function independently. His patronage enriched the artistic patrimony of Rome. Nineteenth-century Italian patriots admired Julius for his crusading ardor against foreigners.

Julius III See PALESTRINA, GIOVANNI PIERLUIGI DA.

Juvara Filippo (1678–1736)
(or Juvarra)

*baroque architect known for his lavish
elaborations of classical motifs*

Born in Messina (Sicily), Juvara studied in Rome and did most of his work in northern Italy, particularly in Turin, where he settled in 1715 in the employ of King VICTOR AMADEUS II. Juvara was the dominant artistic presence in the city for more than 20 years as the king's first architect. He also designed churches, altars, private palaces, squares, and streets, leaving his imprint on the geometrical layout of the expanding city. He was known for his monumental, large-scale designs, evident in his masterpiece, the basilica of Superga, situated high above the city and built in thanksgiving for the liberation of the city in 1706 and as a mausoleum for members of the HOUSE OF SAVOY. The Palazzo Madama (1718), which served as the meeting place of the first Italian parliaments in 1860–65, set the style for palatial constructions throughout Europe. Juvara knew how to adjust his designs to the specific purposes of his constructions, showing flair for both austere lines and lavish ornamentation, depending on the need. His influence helped transform Turin into an architectural showplace. His reputation as a master architect won Juvara a royal summons to Madrid, where he was put to work on the new palace that replaced the one destroyed by fire in 1734. He died in the Spanish capital.

K

Kuliscioff, Anna (1857–1925)

Russian-born political radical who played an important role in Italian socialism

Born Rosenstein to a well-off family in a small Crimean town, Kuliscioff studied medicine in Zurich. There she joined a group of Russian revolutionaries and launched her career as a lifelong radical activist. In France she met ANDREA COSTA, with whom she lived and had a daughter. Drawn to ANARCHISM, Costa and Kuliscioff went to Italy, where they were arrested in 1879 and accused of plotting to overthrow the government. Acquitted, Anna turned to socialism and influenced Costa to do likewise. Costa went on to become the most prominent socialist of his generation. In 1885 Kuliscioff met and became the lifelong companion and political partner of FILIPPO TURATI, who replaced Costa as the leader of Italian socialism. She had great influence on Turati, who treated her as an intellectual equal and was guided by her toward the idea of social democracy. Their close relationship and mutual influence makes it difficult to separate one from the other. Kuliscioff had a distinct personality and well-defined ideas. She was a close student of Marx, whom she interpreted in a democratic vein, and communicated her appreciation of Marx to Turati, whose socialism lacked rigorous philosophical grounding. She urged Turati to formulate for the Socialist Party (PSI) a political strategy mindful of the needs of the peasantry and of the South. Her advice did not change the socialist northern strategy that relied primarily on the support of industrial workers. The Kuliscioff-Turati correspondence documents an ongoing dialogue that was mutually beneficial. Her salon in Milan was an important gathering place for intellectuals and a center for the diffusion of socialist ideas.

L

labor unions See SYNDICALISM.

Labriola, Antonio (1843–1904)
*revisionist Marxist philosopher and socialist
propagandist*

Born in Cassino (Naples), Labriola absorbed
Hegelian philosophy from his teacher BERTRANDO
SPAVENTA, but interest in social psychology oriented him toward POSITIVISM and SOCIALISM. In
1874 he was appointed to teach philosophy at
the University of Rome, a post that he kept to
the end of his life. The study of Marxism and historical materialism was his central concern from
about 1889. He approached Marxism critically,
fascinated by its apparent ability to explain all of
history but also aware of the problems inherent
in its interpretation of history as a process driven
by material forces in the production process.
Labriola's revision of Marx's teachings made
room for the role of consciousness in history,
pointing to the role of such factors as education
(he was a tireless crusader for popular education), individual awareness, and public opinion.
Labriola did insist on the scientific nature and
universal validity of socialism. As Italy's most
prominent Marxist theoretician, he had considerable influence on the development of Italian
socialism in the 1890s. His model was German
social democracy, which Labriola saw as a movement sensitive to changing social realities, and
therefore pragmatic, but also anchored in Marxist understanding. Italian socialism struck Labriola as lacking philosophical rigor, mired in
politics, torn by internal contradictions, and
utterly opportunistic. While FILIPPO TURATI worked
to give the Italian Socialist Party (PSI) a mass fol-

lowing, Labriola favored a small, disciplined
party willing to sacrifice short-term political success for long-term struggle. Labriola's awareness
of the importance of cultural factors for the success of socialist revolution seems to anticipate
ANTONIO GRAMSCI's concept of cultural hegemony. The Italian Marxist tradition owes much
to Labriola's conceptualization of revolution as a
cultural and political phenomenon. Labriola was
an intellectual who lacked the common touch.
He made his influence felt with his writings, his
correspondence with a wide range of personalities, including BENEDETTO CROCE, Georges Sorel,
Friedrich Engels, and Karl Kautsky, and his well-
attended courses at the University of Rome. His
writings include *Essays on the Materialist Conception of History* (1903) and *Socialism and Philosophy*
(1907).

Labriola, Arturo (1873–1959)
*economic writer, journalist, revolutionary
socialist, and labor organizer*

Born in Naples, Labriola studied economics, and
tutored in political economy at the University of
Messina. His economic training and roots in the
underdeveloped South convinced him that the
road to progress was through industrialization
and worker revolution. His faith in a worker revolution may have been based on his observations of southern workers' strong negative
reactions to industrialization, and resentment of
socialist tactics seen as benefiting primarily
northern workers. A founder of REVOLUTIONARY
SYNDICALISM, in 1902 Labriola moved from
Naples to Milan, Italy's business capital, to challenge the Socialist Party (PSI) on its home

grounds. The paper *Avanguardia Socialista* that he published in Milan from 1902 to 1906 took a hard line against the party leadership. Labriola, an enthusiastic disciple of Georges Sorel, preached worker violence and the "general strike" to bring down capitalism and government. The failure of the general strike of September 1904 was a serious setback for Labriola. Repeated strike failures in the coming years convinced him that the inspiration for revolution was more likely to come from proletarian nationalism. Believing that nationalist exaltation and the violence of war would lead to revolution, Labriola supported the ITALIAN-TURKISH WAR (1911–12) and Italian intervention in WORLD WAR I. As his nationalism intensified, his demands for domestic change moderated. He was elected to parliament in 1913 as an independent socialist. In parliament he pursued the same reformist tactics that he had previously criticized. After the war he served as minister of labor in GIOVANNI GIOLITTI's last government (1920–21). He opposed FASCISM and went into voluntary exile in 1927. He returned to Italy in 1935 to express his support for the Fascist regime during the ETHIOPIAN WAR, still believing that war would lead to social revolution. Still clinging to his personal version of socialism, he was elected to the republican constituent assembly (1946–47) and to the senate in 1948.

La Farina, Giuseppe (1815–1863)

Risorgimento figure and moderate political leader, who helped forge the alliance between moderates and democrats that unified the national movement

This Sicilian patriot played an important but often overlooked role in the process of national unification as a journalist and organizer. Born in Messina, he received a law degree in 1835, lived in Florence in the 1840s, and returned to Sicily to play a leading role in the unsuccessful REVOLUTION of 1848 as one of its more radical elements. The political repression that ensued drove him into political exile, first in France (1849–53), then in PIEDMONT, where he joined the thousands of political exiles from other parts of Italy who were active in Piedmontese politics. In Turin he published a review, the *Rivista Enciclopedica Italiana* (1855–56). It conveyed the message that political independence, liberty, and economic prosperity are inseparable. La Farina hoped that the message would reach and convert moderate opinion to the cause of national unification. This stance showed La Farina distancing himself from the more radical currents of the RISORGIMENTO toward the moderate positions of CAVOUR. He was recognized as a spokesman for Cavour's moderate policies, but he also worked to reconcile moderates and radicals. In 1857 he became secretary and principal organizer of the SOCIETÀ NAZIONALE ITALIANA, which attracted thousands of members to the national cause and became the basis of his political power. La Farina wanted to see his native Sicily part of unified Italy, but feared that radical elements would control Giuseppe Garibaldi's expedition to liberate the island. In June 1860 Cavour dispatched La Farina to Sicily to bring about its immediate annexation to Piedmont, thereby depriving Garibaldi of an independent base. Garibaldi unceremoniously evicted La Farina from Sicily and sent him back to Piedmont. For his role as Cavour's agent, La Farina earned the enmity of many patriots, including his fellow Sicilian FRANCESCO CRISPI who questioned La Farina's motives and integrity. Elected to parliament, La Farina headed a weakened but still active National Society and worked closely with the governing majority. La Farina proved himself a capable political boss, adept at securing patronage for his followers, and at making and unmaking governments. Widely distrusted, he never achieved the important role in national politics that he felt was due to him.

La Malfa, Giorgio See MANI PULITE.

La Malfa, Ugo See PRI.

La Marmora, Alfonso Ferrero de (1804–1878)

Piedmontese general, administrator, and political figure

Born in Turin, La Marmora studied at the city's military academy, served as instructor to the royal princes, and gained a reputation for military skill and valor fighting against the Austrians in 1848. He demonstrated his loyalty to the monarchy by repressing the insurrection that broke out in Genoa in 1849. As minister of war and chief of staff, he was responsible for the reorganization of the Piedmontese army in the 1850s. In 1855 La Marmora commanded the Piedmontese expeditionary corps in the CRIMEAN WAR. In 1859 he served on the king's staff in the war against Austria and was prime minister from July 1859 to January 1860. As governor of Milan (1860) and Naples (1861), he was in charge of those cities during the transition to Italian rule. Prime minister once again in 1865–66, La Marmora negotiated the military alliance with Prussia. When the Third WAR OF INDEPENDENCE broke out, he stepped down as prime minister to become army chief of staff, but his performance in that post was far from brilliant. He agreed to split command of military operations with his rival, General ENRICO CIALDINI, who insisted on operating independently. Confusion in the field and in the lines of command led to the military debacle of CUSTOZA, where the Austrians checked the numerically superior Italians. La Marmora shouldered much of the blame and retired to private life.

Lambruschini, Raffaello (1788–1873)

liberal Catholic, political reformer, and educator

Lambruschini was born to a well-off family of Genoa and followed uncles who were prominent in the church into an ecclesiastical career. Exiled for his opposition to Napoleonic rule, he returned to Rome in 1814 to resume his ecclesiastical duties. At odds with the conservative policies of the papal government, he renounced his ambitions and retired to a family estate in Tuscany. There he joined the group of liberal reformers that gravitated to GIAN PIETRO VIEUSSEUX's review *L'Antologia*. He called for free trade, agricultural reforms, savings banks, kindergartens and vocational schools, and teacher training. Politically, he supported national independence, civil liberties, and the separation of CHURCH AND STATE. He opposed papal temporal power, which he regarded as an obstacle to religious reform. After national unification he was appointed to the senate (1860) and held prominent posts in public administration, scholarly and educational associations.

Lampedusa, Giuseppe di See
ARISTOCRACY; FELTRINELLI, GIANGIACOMO.

land reform

Land reform was a major issue in Italy until the second half of the 20th century. The need for agricultural improvements in many regions, the pressure of POPULATION on the land, scarcity of fertile soil, presence of a large, landless rural population, and the social importance attached to land ownership called for changes in existing land arrangements. Land hunger was prevalent everywhere in Italy until the 1950s and 1960s, when nonagricultural occupations became more attractive and remunerative. But the land question presented itself differently, depending on the region, nature of the terrain, and type of land tenure. In the Po Valley, one of the few areas in Italy where large-scale, capital-intensive agriculture was feasible and where marginally employed day laborers prevailed, land reform meant land reclamation to put more land under cultivation, and worker cooperatives operating alongside and competing with privately owned farms. In central Italy, where property was more fragmented and *MEZZADRIA* prevailed, land reform envisaged expropriation, formation of worker cooperatives, or, alternatively, creation of peasant-owned and -operated family-sized farms. In the South, where large estates (*latifundia*) coexisted alongside tiny peasant holdings and a landless rural population, land reform meant breaking up the large estates and creating an independent peasantry of small and middle-sized landowners. Mountain peasants who could barely eke out a living on the small parcels of land faced a series of special problems that gave rise to the problem of the MOUNTAINS.

Attempts at land reform were feeble in the 18th century. Stimulating trade and improving agriculture seemed the best solutions to the problem of how to feed a growing number of mouths. In the South, land reform was tied to questions of feudal rights and use of common lands. The Napoleonic regimes took the drastic steps of abolishing feudal rights and putting common lands on the market. These measures benefited mostly investors who had the capital to acquire land, but may have actually worsened the lot of impoverished peasants and rural workers. Few voices were raised calling for land reform in the RISORGIMENTO. Few leaders were willing to raise an issue that was more likely to divide than to unite Italians behind the movement for national unification. When GIUSEPPE GARIBALDI did call for land reform in Sicily in 1860, the forcible land seizures and peasant violence that ensued seemed to justify those fears.

Calls for land reform became a staple of socialist agitation after national unification. Rural workers and sharecroppers organized and agitated for land redistribution, but generally settled for better contracts from landowners. Demands for land reform intensified after WORLD WAR I, as organized war veterans pressured the government to expropriate land and staged illegal land occupations. Turmoil in the countryside was a decisive factor in the rise of FASCISM, which opposed expropriations but acknowledged the need for land reform. Fascism repressed worker agitations against landowners, but also promised reclamation and land for the landless, and saw small peasant landowners as the social backbone of the regime. Fascist land reform relied on land reclamation at home and the acquisition of colonies abroad to create an independent peasantry. Land reform was again a hot issue in the

early years of the Italian republic, when both the Communist Party (PCI) and the Christian Democratic Party (DC) endorsed it. But they did not agree on what land reform meant. To Christian Democrats it meant encouraging property ownership and supporting the small landowners who voted for them. Communist land reform meant improving the lot of landless workers and sharecroppers, discouraging landownership, and looking upon landowners as class enemies. The agrarian reform of 1950 aimed at abolishing large-scale absentee landlordism in designated parts of the peninsula, including the lower Po Valley, parts of central Italy, the continental South, Sicily, and Sardinia. For the first time, the government expropriated and redistributed vast areas of land. While the economic consequences of the reform are still the subject of debate, it seems clear that the liquidation of many large estates in the South and on the islands, and the formation of small and middle-sized farms did not change the basic structure of Italian agriculture, which remained polarized between the extremes of large, market-oriented, and generally profitable commercial operations and small, fragmented, and inefficient family holdings.

Structural change occurred when employment opportunities outside agriculture improved, peasants and rural workers abandoned the land, and international competition forced landowners to modernize. Employment opportunities and emigration eliminated the cheap labor on which agricultural employers relied; competition forced farmers to consolidate their holdings and adopt more efficient methods of production. Land reform lost its urgency as agriculture took a backseat to manufacturing, trade, and services.

The role of land reform in the formative years of the national economy has long been a contentious issue. ANTONIO GRAMSCI argued that the absence of land reform estranged the masses from the movement for national unification and the national state. The historian ROSARIO ROMEO defended the agrarian policies of the founders, arguing that land redistribution through land reform would have reduced productivity and prevented the capital accumulations needed to sustain economic progress.

Lanza, Giovanni (1810–1882)
Piedmontese political figure, parliamentary leader, last of the "heirs of Cavour"

Lanza, a brilliant university student with degrees in medicine (1832) and surgery (1833), was a rare figure who combined patriotic sentiments with a strong interest in science and economic reform. A member of scientific societies, he volunteered to fight against the Austrians in 1848. He was elected to parliament that same year, and in every election thereafter until his death. Initially a member of the LIBERAL LEFT, he moved gradually toward the HISTORICAL RIGHT that controlled parliament from 1861 to 1876. Lanza took CAVOUR as his model, backed the parliamentary monarchy, and resisted the pressures of royalists who wanted to strengthen the powers of the king at the expense of parliament. In parliament he was president of the chamber of deputies (1860–61, 1867–69), minister of education (1855–58), finance (1858–59), interior (1864–65), and prime minister (1869–73). He kept Italy out of the Franco-Prussian War of 1870 and took advantage of the situation to seize ROME from the pope and make it the capital of Italy. Faced by mounting government deficits, he reluctantly supported the policy of high taxes and tight spending that made possible the balancing of the budget after he left office. The unpopularity of his policies forced him to resign as prime minister. Lanza combined administrative competence with a reticent, low-key personality that earned him the respect of those who knew him well, but that did not serve him well politically. Unpopular in his time, he should be recognized as a key figure in the formation of the Italian state.

Lanzillo, Agostino (1886–1952)
legal expert, journalist, and Fascist theoretician

Born in Reggio Calabria, Lanzillo studied and practiced law, served in parliament and on gov-

ernment commissions that mapped the development of the Fascist state. A follower and protégé of Georges Sorel, Lanzillo did not share Sorel's hope that a general workers' strike could bring about revolution. He did believe that the working class could bring off a successful socialist revolution if properly educated to take on the responsibilities of power. As a socialist, Lanzillo opposed party leader FILIPPO TURATI and his reformist tactics. Lanzillo gravitated instead toward the revolutionary extremism of BENITO MUSSOLINI. His break with socialism occurred in 1914 when he joined Mussolini to campaign for Italian intervention in WORLD WAR I. He volunteered for military service and was wounded in action. He joined the Fascist movement in 1919, carrying on an effective polemic against the Socialist Party (PSI). Fascist conservatives effectively opposed his call that the party take up worker demands to break the socialist hold on working-class representation. Always something of a maverick, Lanzillo's political usefulness to the regime declined in the 1920s. From his post as professor of political economy at the University of Rome, he spoke out in measured tones against the increasingly conservative orientation of the regime. A convinced free trader, Lanzillo also incurred political displeasure by speaking out against the regime's policy of AUTARKY. In 1935 he was appointed rector of the Advanced Institute of Economy and Commerce in Venice. That he was never in complete disgrace with the regime was due to his fundamental agreement with Fascist doctrine and his profound antidemocratic beliefs.

La Pira, Giorgio (1904–1977)
Christian Democratic mayor of Florence, Christian Democratic party leader

La Pira was born in Ragusa (Sicily), received a law degree from the University of Messina, and taught jurisprudence at the University of Florence. He joined the Christian Democratic Party (DC) in 1944, was a member of the constituent assembly that drew up the new CONSTITUTION, and was elected to parliament in 1948. In the elections of that year he and GIUSEPPE DOSSETTI called for the party to reach out to the *povera gente* (poor folks) who were attracted to communism. In 1950 Prime Minister ALCIDE DE GASPERI included La Pira in his government as undersecretary for labor and social welfare. In 1951–57 and again in 1961–65 he served as mayor of FLORENCE. A devout Roman Catholic, La Pira found justification for his social principles in scripture and church doctrine, insisting that social activism was a logical corollary of his Catholic faith. In 1960 he led a worker takeover of the Officine Galileo, an industrial complex that threatened to dismiss workers. La Pira was also a peace activist who agitated for peaceful coexistence between the United States and the Soviet Union, human rights, international disarmament, assistance to developing countries, and an end to the war in Vietnam, with a definite anti-American slant. A special concern of his was to promote better relations between Italy and the Middle East. His stance on domestic and international issues generated strong opposition and he was not reelected mayor of Florence in 1965.

Lateran Pacts   See ROMAN QUESTION.

Laterza, Giovanni   See CROCE, BENEDETTO.

latifundia   See AGRICULTURE.

Latin

Latin is the foundation of all modern Romance languages, including Italian. Originally one of several Italic languages spoken in the region where the city of ROME is located, its use spread as Roman power expanded beyond the region. The adoption of Latin as the language of the educated was part of the process of "Romanization" in Italy from about 350 B.C. to 50 B.C. As the official language of Roman imperial administration, Latin provided a degree of cultural unity, and continued to play such a role even as Roman imperial power declined. A division developed between the learned, who were familiar with the literary language (classical Latin), and the uneducated, who spoke a popular version (vulgar Latin). Medieval Latin and modern Romance languages are derived mostly from the popular Latin spoken by ordinary people. Use of Latin was an important legacy of the Roman Empire to the Roman Catholic Church, which adopted it as the language of religious ritual, clerical administration, and education. Thus, Latin remained the foundation of cultural unity among the educated throughout Europe in the Middle Ages. A shared knowledge of Latin facilitated communication among clerics, scholars, government officials, and professionals until at least the 17th century, when modern Romance languages began to replace it. In Italy, the study of Latin was a prerequisite for university admission until the 1960s. Critics challenged the requirement as elitist, defenders upheld it as the sign of a rigorous and well-rounded education. The controversy still simmers, but educated Italians generally regard knowledge of Latin as an important cultural attribute.

Latium

Latium (Lazio), population 5.3 million, is a region in central Italy facing the Tyrrhenian Sea on the west, bordered on the north by the regions of TUSCANY, UMBRIA, and the MARCHES, and by CAMPANIA and MOLISE to the south. Geographically diverse, Latium comprises several distinct land areas. East of the coastline lies a large plain with vast tracts of reclaimed land, several distinct groups of hills (including the picturesque Alban Hills), and a tract of the APENNINE range. The Tiber (Tevere, in Italian), the region's major river, originates in the Apennines, flows southward through ROME, and empties into the sea near Fiumicino, the site of one of the country's principal airports. The national park of Mount

Circeo, in the southern stretch of the region facing the sea, covers approximately 8,400 hectares.

The region's history reflects the fortunes of Rome and the PAPACY. After the decline of Roman imperial power in the fourth century A.D., Latium fell under Byzantine control. In the following century it began to form the basis of the papacy's temporal power, a role that it retained until the 19th century. The region's powerful families gained control of the papacy in the 10th century and established a feudal system that was the source of much civil conflict. Latium became the site of violent clashes between papal and imperial forces when the German emperors moved south in the 11th century and a series of strong popes backed by the emperors challenged the privileges of local families. The consolidation of papal power largely prevented the phenomenon of communal independence that affected other parts of Italy in the 12th and 13th centuries. The economy of the region suffered from the absence of the papacy in the 14th century, when it was forcibly removed to Avignon, in France, but recovered after the papal court returned to Rome in 1377. The Renaissance papacy further tightened its control over the region and kept it under papal control until the kingdom of Italy annexed it in 1860–70 in the course of the RISORGIMENTO.

The present boundaries and administrative structure of the region were set in 1927–34 as part of the administrative restructuring and land-reclamation projects undertaken under FASCISM. Latium today includes the provinces of Rome, Frosinone, Latina (founded in 1932 with the name of Littoria), Rieti, and Viterbo. Rome, the national capital and a major transportation hub, has 55 percent of the region's population. The regional economy historically has relied heavily on public employment by the papal government before national unification and by the national government after national unification. Approximately 73 percent of the labor force is employed in the service sector, which includes government and tourism. Industrial employment is a fairly recent development, but is substantial and diversified enough to give the regional economy a broader base than in the past.

Lazzaretti, Davide (1834–1878)
popular preacher, religious leader, and social reformer

Lazzaretti is that rare figure in modern Italian history: a layman who found inspiration for social reform in religion. Born to a family of modest means in Arcidosso, a small town in the province of Grosseto in southern Tuscany, Lazzaretti worked as a carter in his native region. Although he considered himself loyal to the pope, he fought in the Italian army in 1860 when it invaded the PAPAL STATES. He showed little interest in religion until he experienced a religious conversion in 1868. Economic crisis and peasant unrest in his native region may have precipitated the spiritual crisis that prompted him to seek a life of spiritual meditation. His spreading fame as a holy man won him followers in the region of Mount Amiata in southern Tuscany. Literate, he prophesied by word and in writing the coming of a new messiah who would liberate poor people from the tyranny of the greedy and would reconcile CHURCH AND STATE. He envisaged himself as precisely such a messiah. Lazzaretti imagined that the hour of resolution was approaching after both Pope PIUS IX and King VICTOR EMMANUEL II died in 1878. Excommunicated by the Vatican, Lazzaretti found enthusiastic followers among the peasantry of the Mount Amiata area. On August 18, 1878, as he and his followers descended from the mountain to proclaim the day of liberation, they were met by army troops with orders to turn them back. The troops fired when Lazzaretti refused to obey their order. Lazzaretti and several of his followers were killed. A cult of Lazzaretti developed among the local populations that survived underground until the early 1940s, when the last of his followers died. While there is little doubt that the "Savior of Mount Amiata" saw himself primarily as a religious leader, the enthusiasm he aroused among small landowners, sharecroppers, and artisans had definite social overtones that make the *Lazzarettiani* an example, common in Protestant societies but rare in Italy, of popular social radicalism inspired by religious sentiment.

Lazzari, Costantino (1857–1927)
pioneering labor organizer and socialist leader
Born in Cremona (Lombardy), Lazzari joined the workers' movement at an early age. A metal worker with a technical school degree, Lazzari believed in *operaismo,* direct action by workers "with blistered hands." Lazzari distrusted intellectuals and plans of social reform based on abstract ideologies. Never a Marxist in the doctrinal sense, he was nevertheless a socialist pioneer. In 1882 he founded the Italian Workers Party (Partito Operaio Italiano) for the stated purpose of supporting and directing strikes by workers and peasants. In the 1880s Lazzari was repeatedly arrested and jailed for organizing workers and for political agitation. Committed to organized labor and direct action by workers, the Workers Party was an important constituent of the Italian Socialist Party (PSI). Within the PSI Lazzari opposed the reformists who relied on parliamentary politics to advance the interests of the movement. He also opposed COLONIALISM, military expenditures, and all forms of cooperation with government. His record and uncompromising opposition to all forms of militarism earned him the position of party secretary from 1912 to 1919. In that capacity he opposed intervention in WORLD WAR I. He was behind the motion to expel BENITO MUSSOLINI from the party on the issue of nonintervention. His slogan to "neither support nor sabotage" the war effort after Italy intervened in the conflict defined the Socialist Party position for the duration of the war. After the war he tried unsuccessfully to heal the breach that led to the socialist secession and the founding of the Communist Party of Italy in 1921. He was elected to parliament in 1919, 1921, and 1924, and forcibly expelled by the Fascists in 1926. He died destitute shortly after being released from a Fascist prison.

Leghorn   See LIVORNO, CITY OF.

Legnano, Battle of   See MILAN, CITY OF.

Lemmi, Adriano   See FREEMASONRY.

Leo X (1475–1521)
pope (1513–1521)
Giovanni de' Medici, son of LORENZO DE' MEDICI, took the name of Leo X after being elected pope in 1513. A cardinal at the age of 13, he was head of the Medici family after the death of his father and during the period of political exile. Easygoing and very much a man of the world, he welcomed the election as an opportunity to "enjoy the papacy that God has seen fit to give us." And enjoy it he did. He is remembered as a generous

Pope Leo X (center) with two cardinals, by Raphael
(Library of Congress)

patron of arts and letters. His ambitious building plan for the city of Rome, which included completion of Saint Peter's basilica, proved costly, forcing him to borrow heavily and to undertake questionable fund-raising activities, including the large-scale sale of ecclesiastical offices and indulgences. It was the organized sale of indulgences throughout Christian Europe that prompted Martin Luther to issue the challenge to the papacy that started the Protestant Reformation (1517). Leo did not take the challenge seriously enough to halt his questionable practices. He excommunicated Luther and others who insisted on reform, concluded an alliance with Emperor CHARLES V to repress heresy, and left to his successors the arduous task of dealing with the consequences of his actions.

Leo XII See CONSALVI, ETTORE.

Leo XIII (1810–1903)
pope (1878–1903)

Gioacchino Pecci, born near Frosinone to a family of the lesser nobility, was ordained into the priesthood (1837), served as archbishop of Perugia (1846–77), and was made cardinal in 1853. Elected pope in 1878 after the death of PIUS IX, he reversed the course chosen by his predecessor against the forces of modernization. Leo XIII opened doors for Catholics eager to play a role as citizens of modern states. He saw the expansion of Catholic scholarship and education as a central aspect of this process of *aggiornamento*. He opened the secret Vatican archives to scholars, encouraged biblical studies, sought to reconcile science and faith, and sponsored new programs and schools, including the Catholic University of Washington, D.C. At the time of his accession the papacy was in conflict with the governments of Italy over the ROMAN QUESTION, Germany, in the battle of ideologies known as the *Kulturkampf*, and France over their anticlericalism. Leo's conciliatory attitude led to improved relations with France and Germany. There was no improve-

ment in Vatican relations with Italy, which actually reached a low point during his pontificate. The aggressiveness of anticlerical groups in Rome stiffened his resolve to oppose the secular state and he called on Catholic governments to back him in his confrontation with the Italian government. His progressive social views were summed up in the encyclical *Rerum novarum* (Of new things, 1891), which steered Catholic social doctrine toward a middle position between capitalism and socialism, pleading that workers were entitled to fair pay and treatment and that it was the duty of employers to care for workers. The encyclical condemned both capitalism and socialism as materialistic, rejecting both individualism and collectivism as equally objectionable. In other writings he condemned class conflict and called for cooperation across class lines. His philosophy laid the foundation for the movements of Christian Democracy (DC) and Christian CORPORATIVISM and informed the thinking of Catholic reformers, including GIUSEPPE TONIOLO, ROMOLO MURRI, and LUIGI STURZO. Leo's embrace of modernity was a major change in papal policy, but in doctrinal matters and on the Roman Question he was as intransigent as his predecessors, hence his hostility toward Italian anticlericals and the government.

Leonardo da Vinci (1452–1519)
Renaissance artist and forerunner of modern experimental science

Leonardo was born in the Tuscan town of Vinci, from which comes his last name. He was the illegitimate son of a local notary and a peasant woman. His father acknowledged him as his natural son and looked after his education. In 1456 he moved to Florence, apprenticed in the workshop of VERROCCHIO to learn painting and sculpture, and met major artists, including SANDRO BOTTICELLI and Domenico Ghirlandaio. Little is known about Leonardo's life and work before age 30, but it was during this early period that he painted the famous unfinished *Adoration of the Magi*, now in the Uffizi Gallery.

Leonardo da Vinci *(Library of Congress)*

da Vinci's *Mona Lisa (La Gioconda) (Library of Congress)*

A man of many talents, Leonardo's interests encompassed painting, sculpture, architecture, engineering, mathematics, botany, physiology, and anatomy. He favored a hands-on approach and experimented widely, to satisfy his curiosity and test ideas and theories by direct observation. Around 1482 he moved to Milan to serve Duke LUDOVICO SFORZA as a consultant on town planning, architecture, land reclamation, and military engineering. In the 16 years he spent in Milan, he painted two versions of the *Madonna of the Rocks* (one is now in the Louvre and the other in the London National Gallery) and the even more famous fresco of the *Last Supper* in the Church of Santa Maria delle Grazie, recently restored but still badly deteriorated.

After the fall of Ludovico Sforza in 1499, Leonardo went to Mantua, Venice, Florence, and Rome, where he served CAESAR BORGIA as a military engineer. In 1503 he was back in Florence, commissioned to paint a fresco of the battle of Anghiari in competition with his younger rival MICHELANGELO. The work was never completed, and the completed portions deteriorated rapidly, but it is thought to have had a major influence on the artists who flocked to study it. What is perhaps the most celebrated painting of the Renaissance, the *Mona Lisa,* also belongs to this period of Leonardo's life.

In 1506 he returned to Milan, now under French rule, and remained there for the next 10 years, working for King Louis XII. His interest in the natural sciences apparently increased during this period, with new investigations and projects in anatomy, hydraulics, and military engineering. He spent the last three years of his life in

France, in the service of King Francis I, who left him free to pursue his own interests. The more than 5,000 pages of his secret *Notebooks,* which he probably began during his first stay in Milan and kept up until near the end of his life, document his versatility and inventiveness. Anatomical sketches, drawings of animals and plants, designs for flying machines, submarines, artillery, and tanks are all in evidence. To some of his contemporaries, and to critical scholars of later generations, the very breadth of Leonardo's interests and the many projects he left unfinished suggest an unfocused mind and the talents of a dilettante. The more common view is that Leonardo is the very model of the accomplished "Renaissance Man," an artist of great sensitivity and grace, and a scientific investigator who anticipated the mentality of the modern scientist by insisting on direct observation and a critical attitude toward received knowledge.

Leoncavallo, Ruggiero (1858–1919)

composer, librettist, and musical critic

Leoncavallo is remembered as the composer of the successful one-act OPERA *I Pagliacci* (1892), for which he wrote both the libretto and the music. This tale of the tragic consequences of love and jealousy among a troupe of traveling performers was an immediate success. Its portrayal of steamy passions and violence makes it perhaps the best example of the VERISMO style in music. For this work, Leoncavallo wrote music that expresses raw passions vividly and melodramatically. The action develops quickly and the characters are driven by elemental urges that speak for themselves. Although the well-known prologue philosophizes about the meaning of art and life, the work as a whole plays to the emotions rather than the intellect. Leoncavallo composed other operas, including *La Bohème* (1897), less well known than GIACOMO PUCCINI's opera by the same title, and *Zazà* (1900), both musically appealing. But none of his other operas equaled the success of *I Pagliacci.* His song *Mattinata* was made famous by the tenor ENRICO CARUSO who recorded it in 1904 and made it one of the first best-sellers in the new medium. Leoncavallo also made history in 1907 with a recording of *I Pagliacci* that he supervised, the first complete recording of an opera.

Leone, Giovanni (1908–2001)

Christian Democratic leader and president of the republic

The sixth president of the Italian republic was born near Naples, earned a law degree at that city's university in 1929, and went on to teach at several universities, including his alma mater and the University of Rome. He served in the army in WORLD WAR II, and was a founding member of the Christian Democratic Party (DC), which he represented in parliament. His reputation as a legal scholar enhanced his image as a serious political figure. First elected to the chamber of deputies in 1948, he served as its president (1955–63), was twice briefly interim prime minister (1963 and 1968), and a senator. He was instrumental in working out the political compromise that assured passage of the controversial DIVORCE LAW. He was elected president of the republic in 1971 but resigned in June 1978, six months before the end of his term of office. The resignation was motivated by press charges that he had received payoffs from the Lockheed Aircraft Corporation for government contracts. The charges were never proven, and Leone claimed that he resigned only to spare the country more political turmoil in the aftermath of the kidnapping and assassination of ALDO MORO. His presidency was also marred by charges that he was in thrall to his wife, Donna Vittoria, who was said to be the real power behind the throne. Leone continued to serve in the senate after resigning as president, but gradually distanced himself from politics. Generally aligned with the party's conservative wing, he disapproved of the party's attempted opening toward the communists and resented what he considered to be its failure to support him adequately when he was attacked by the press.

Leopardi, Giacomo (1798–1837)
poet, social philosopher, and commentator on the human condition

Born in Recanati (Marches) to a family of the local nobility, the young Leopardi was educated by private tutors and by his father, Count Monaldo Leopardi (1776–1847), a strict law-and-order man loyal to the papal regime and opposed to political innovation. Aside from what he learned under his father's rigorous tutelage, the young Leopardi was largely self-taught. In seven years of intensive study he mastered classical Latin, studied Greek and Hebrew, and wrote on philological topics. The grueling pace and isolation compounded the effects of congenital physical ailments. Leopardi was in frail health throughout his short life.

From his study of the classics Leopardi derived a sense of form and a spare style. But he was not a classicist in the larger sense, for the introspection and sensitivity of his writings suggest self-absorption, pathos, and an affinity with the prevailing school of ROMANTICISM. The philosophical reflections of his *Operette morali* (1827) express the strict materialism and pessimism that are distinctive characteristics of *leopardismo*. He renounced religion, faith in progress, and sentimentality. Deprived of the comforts of friendship and romantic love, Leopardi found fulfillment in his work. In his best poetical compositions, a lyrical understanding of human emotions and the world of nature balance his pessimism. Two cantos published in 1818, *All'Italia* (To Italy) and *Sopra il monumento a Dante* (On the monument to Dante), express a longing, then fashionable, for the past glories of Italy, but civic sentiments were always peripheral in Leopardi.

His imagination and sensitivity are best appreciated in lyrical odes like *L'Infinito, Alla luna* (To the Moon), *La sera del dì di festa* (The Evening of the Feast Day), and *Il Sabato del villaggio* (The Village Saturday). His masterpiece may well be his last ode *La ginestra* (The Broom Plant), which projects his personal pessimism onto the human condition in a tone of calm reflection and resignation. Regarded as Italy's major 19th-century poet, Leopardi's influence was felt after the political preoccupations of the Risorgimento ebbed and readers could appreciate his command of language and poetic imagination.

Leopold I See PETER LEOPOLD.

Leopold II (1797–1870)
member of the House of Habsburg-Lorraine, grand duke of Tuscany, 1824–1859

Son of FERDINAND III, Leopold succeeded his father at a time when the strict political controls of the first years of the RESTORATION could be relaxed. His leniency created a political climate in Tuscany that allowed for the expression of moderately dissenting views. His efficient police, however, kept close surveillance on political suspects. Leopold carried out administrative and educational reforms, and ambitious programs of road construction and land reclamation. Encouraged by the example of Pope PIUS IX, in 1847 Leopold granted freedom of the press, joined other states in a customs union, and issued a constitution (February 1848). The rise of a radical democratic movement alarmed Leopold, and when the democrats came to power in the course of revolution, he left Tuscany. Restored to his throne by the intervention of the Austrian army, he revoked the constitution, introduced the death penalty for political crimes, and cracked down on dissenters. When the kingdom of SARDINIA and Austria went to war in 1859 in the Second WAR OF INDEPENDENCE, liberal elements orchestrated an uprising and Leopold chose to leave Tuscany peacefully, never to return. His posthumous memoirs entitled *Il governo di famiglia in Toscana* (Family government in Tuscany, 1987) is a fascinating document of the royal mentality and attitude toward government.

Lépanto, Battle of
Catholic and Turkish fleets fought the naval battle of Lépanto, the largest in European history since ancient times, on October 7, 1571, off the Greek town of Navpaktos (Lépanto in Italian). It

was a concerted effort by Catholic states to halt the Turkish advance in the Mediterranean. The Turks had laid siege to MALTA in 1565, evicted the Venetians from Cyprus in 1570, advanced along the Mediterranean coast of Africa, threatened Venetian positions in DALMATIA, and raided Italian towns. Before the loss of Cyprus VENICE had stayed aloof from papal efforts to form a Holy League against the Muslim Turks. Now the Venetians backed the efforts of Pope Pius V (1566–72) to put Catholicism on the offensive against both Turks and Protestants. Venice, GENOA, the PAPAL STATES, Spain and its Italian possessions, all contributed forces to the large Catholic fleet that assembled off the Greek coast. The Venetians made the single largest contribution. About half the soldiers and most of the crews were of Italian origin. Casualties were heavy on both sides, Christian losses reaching about 9,000 dead and Muslim losses about 30,000. The Turkish fleet was destroyed, and Turkish progress in the Mediterranean was disrupted. Venice ignored papal advice to continue the fight and made peace with the Turks in 1574, trusting that it could preserve its commercial positions with diplomacy. The Turks, stymied in the Mediterranean, continued their advance toward central Europe by land until halted at the gates of Vienna in 1683. The battle of Lépanto thus had the effect of diverting the Turkish threat from Italy toward the Habsburg possessions to the north. The battle marked the last concerted effort by Italian city-states against a foreign power.

Levi, Carlo (1902–1975)

anti-Fascist writer and member of the resistance movement

Born in Turin, Levi received a medical degree but showed more interest in painting and writing than medicine. Part of a group of avant-garde painters known as the "Group of Seven," Levi was arrested for his anti-Fascist activities and confined to a remote village in the BASILICATA region of southern Italy (1935–36). He joined the anti-Fascist RESISTANCE in 1943–45

Carlo Levi *(Library of Congress)*

and the ACTION PARTY. After the war he represented the Communist Party (PCI) as an independent senator. His most notable literary work is the novel *Cristo si è fermato a Eboli* (Christ stopped at Eboli, 1946). Based on his experience of confinement, it was written in Florence in 1943–44 while fighting raged in the city. The novel places Levi's experience of persecution in the context of the ongoing fight for liberation. It exposes the unbridgeable gap between the Fascist regime's grandiose claims of glory and the seamy realities of daily life in Italy's Deep South. It also contrasts the profound humanity of the peasants with the rhetorical pretensions of fascism and the pettiness of its local petty bourgeois supporters. The novel, published shortly after the end of WORLD WAR II, struck a chord with the public, helping many to come to terms with the recent Fascist experience. While not a great work of literature, it is a deeply felt and moving work. Its success was even greater in the English-speaking world after it appeared in translation in

1947. Levi's other writings include the novel *L'orologio* (The clock, 1950), and commentaries based on his travel experiences in Sicily, *Le parole sono pietre* (Words are stones, 1953) and *Il futuro ha un cuore antico* (The future has an ancient heart, 1956), which he revised and published as *Tutto il miele è finito* (All the honey is finished, 1964), about life in the Soviet Union. None of Levi's other writings matched the success of *Christ Stopped at Eboli*.

Levi, Primo (1919–1987)
writer known for his eyewitness accounts and commentaries on life in concentration camps

Born in Turin to a middle-class Jewish family that was fully assimilated to Italian culture, Levi was trained and worked for almost 30 years as an industrial chemist. Awareness of his Jewish identity was forced upon him by the Fascist regime's anti-Semitic laws of 1938 and by his subsequent experience of deportation and life in a concentration camp. That experience inspired his first book of memoirs *Se questo è un uomo* (If this is a man, 1947), which passed almost unnoticed at the time. His testimony continued with *La tregua* (The truce, 1963) and *I sommersi e i salvati* (The drowned and the saved, 1986). Well before that last book was published, Levi had become an international celebrity, a role with which he never felt comfortable. A notable trait of Levi's writings is the ability to transcend the Jewish experience of suffering, and present the Holocaust as a human tragedy. Never a religious person, Levi looked for messages of human meaning in all aspects of his life, including his commitment to science. His literary masterpiece may well be *Il sistema periodico* (The periodic table, 1975), a series of mostly autobiographical stories named after chemical elements whose properties inspire reflections on history, science, and personal identity. His one novel, *Se non ora, quando?* (If not now, when?, 1982), tells the story of a group of European Jews who fight behind the lines against the Nazis and leave at the end of the war to settle in Palestine. It has

never been clarified whether his death from a fall down a stairwell was an accident or suicide. Most of his writings are available in English translation. Indeed, Levi's writings may be more popular in the Anglo-Saxon world than in Italy.

Levi-Montalcino, Rita (1909–)
Italian expatriate and internationally renowned scientist

Levi-Montalcino was born in Turin to a Jewish family. She obtained a degree in medicine from the University of Turin (1936) and worked there as an assistant in neurobiology and psychiatry (1938–40). The racial laws of the Fascist regime forced her to leave her post, but she was able to continue her research privately. She lived in hiding in Florence in 1943–44. After the Allies liberated the city in July 1944 she provided medical care for refugees. She returned to the University of Turin as an assistant professor of anatomy in 1945, but left for the United States in 1947, attracted by opportunities in the field of neurological research. She was on the teaching faculty at Washington University in St. Louis (1947–58) and later rose to the position of director of the Neurology Research Center at that school. Her many publications established her as an authority in the field of neurological research. In 1986 she was a corecipient of the Nobel Prize in medicine for her work on growth factors. She resumed her professional connection with Italy as a member of the national research council and served on its board until 1995. She was also elected to the Academy of Arts and Sciences (1966), National Academy of Sciences (1968), Accademia Nazionale dei Lincei (1976), the French Académie des Sciences (1989), and the Royal Society of London (1995). In 2001 she was appointed senator for life.

Liberal Left

In the RISORGIMENTO the term "left" designated those groups that drew inspiration from the ideas of GIUSEPPE MAZZINI, looked to GIUSEPPE GARIBALDI for leadership in action, favored a republican form of government, and opposed the moderate liberalism of CAVOUR. Also known as democrats, they were antiaristocratic, mostly of middle-class extraction, and often of southern origin. They called for a broad suffrage, lower taxes, popular education, and administrative decentralization. During the first 15 years of national unification (1861–76) when the HISTORICAL RIGHT controlled parliament, the Liberal Left acted as the opposition. But neither it nor the governing majority was organized as a political party. Each was a loose political coalition torn by factions and personal rivalries, held together by memories of the past, symbolic figures, and political convenience.

The Liberal Left came to power on March 18, 1876, when the governing majority lost a critical vote and fell apart. AGOSTINO DEPRETIS, leader of the Liberal Left, became prime minister and placed trusted followers in key posts in the national administration. The elections of November 1876 completed the defeat of the Historical Right and consolidated the Left's hold on power. The change seemed much more revolutionary at the time (observers described it as a "parliamentary revolution") than in retrospect. The new government supported the monarchy, promised to protect civil liberties, extend the suffrage, lower taxes, secularize the schools, and pursue a cautious FOREIGN POLICY. Republicans looked on the parliamentary victory as the first step toward the abolition of the monarchy.

But the left coalition split into factions once in power. A faction known as the Pure Left was loyal to the monarchy but critical of Depretis. The Pure Left included a group known as the Pentarchy for its five leaders: Alfredo Baccarini (1826–90), BENEDETTO CAIROLI, FRANCESCO CRISPI, GIOVANNI NICOTERA, and GIUSEPPE ZANARDELLI. They accused Depretis of weakness and corruption, were aggressively patriotic, and assertive in foreign affairs. More radical still was the faction of the Extreme Left led by AGOSTINO BERTANI and FELICE CAVALLOTTI. They wanted universal suffrage, radical school reforms, public health programs, and redistribution of taxes and land for the benefit of the poor. The Liberal Left is not to be confused with the socialist Left that appeared on the political scene in the 1880s. By then, the Liberal Left was the governing majority. It had made its peace with the monarchy and supported the status quo, while socialists were diehard republicans, who demanded wealth redistribution and voting rights for the disfranchised.

The Liberal Left had a mixed record in power. Under Depretis, it abolished the grist tax, broadened the suffrage, and made education compulsory to age nine. But its electoral and parliamentary practices smacked of political corruption. It made TRANSFORMISM the rule in government, abused police powers, ran high budget deficits, exacerbated relations with the CATHOLIC CHURCH, and its foreign policy antagonized France and imposed a heavy burden of military expenditures. When Crispi took over from Depretis in 1887, the Liberal Left enacted some administrative reforms, but became mired in financial corruption and was ultimately undone by its policy of COLONIALISM. By the 1890s the old distinctions between Liberal Left and Historical Right were becoming irrelevant. They eventually merged into the liberalism of GIOVANNI GIOLITTI, which was a composite of the two. Giolittian liberalism incorporated both the more progressive aspirations of the Liberal Left and its questionable parliamentary practices.

Liberal Party See PLI.

liberalism

Historically, the political ideology of liberalism developed in opposition to the institution of absolute monarchy. Liberalism called for constitutions to limit the theoretically absolute power of monarchs, voting rights for the qualified, parliamentary government, civil liberties, and economic progress. Liberalism was the principal ideology of the RISORGIMENTO, which was simultaneously a movement to unify Italy and give it representative government. The policies of CAVOUR best expressed the expectations of Italian liberals in the movement for national unification. Cavour's program appealed particularly to the middle classes who possessed the economic means and educational qualifications to take advantage of political rights.

Liberalism was firmly committed to economic progress, but the Italian language differentiates between political and economic liberalism. *Liberalismo* stands for political liberalism, with its emphasis on representative government and constitutionally guaranteed civil rights. Economic liberalism, meaning capitalism, laissez-faire economics, and free trade, is referred to in Italian as *liberismo*. *Liberalismo* and *liberismo* were firmly joined in Cavour's mind, but not in the thinking of his successors who governed Italy after national unification.

Italian liberalism stood for economic and political progress by gradual reform. It favored a restricted franchise, which it was willing to broaden gradually, as more people acquired property and education, so as not to give power to its many enemies on the left and the right. Universal suffrage might be the ultimate goal of liberals, but for many it represented a leap in the dark that they were not eager to make. Liberals often regarded popular democracy and uneducated masses as a danger to personal liberty. Liberalism affirmed the rights of the individual and protected those rights from the power of government, while democracy spoke the language of universal rights and expected government to play a strong role in securing those collective rights. In the 19th century, liberalism and democracy were distinct ideologies. GIOVANNI GIOLITTI's decision to give the liberal state a popular basis by broadening the suffrage was a courageous experiment that had the unintended consequence of bringing on the crisis of the liberal state.

Liberalism opposed all potentially totalitarian ideologies and regarded both fascism and socialism as threats to personal liberty. But fear of popular democracy and socialism often prevailed, and predisposed liberals to tolerate attacks on mass movements and organizations. Thus, many sincere liberals initially acquiesced in the Fascist use of violence against enemies of the liberal state, including socialists and Catholics, only to condemn FASCISM at a later date, when its illiberal sentiments became manifest. BENEDETTO CROCE was the philosophical voice of Italian liberalism. His writings reflect the virtues and shortcomings of Italian liberal thought.

Liberty Pole See POLO DELLA LIBERTÀ.

Libya See COLONIALISM.

Libyan War See ITALIAN-TURKISH WAR.

Ligorio, Pirro See MANNERISM.

Liguria

The region of Liguria (population 1.6 million) covers the stretch of coastline known as the Italian Riviera. It gives its name to the Ligurian Sea, the most northwestern part of the Mediterranean Sea. Liguria borders on France to the west, the regions of PIEDMONT and EMILIA-ROMAGNA to the north, and TUSCANY to the east. Its long, arching coastline divides into a western stretch known as the *Riviera di Ponente*, facing southeast, and the eastern part called *Riviera di Levante*, facing southwest. The entire coastline, from Ventimiglia near the French border to Lerici near the Tuscan, is dotted with tourist resorts popular with international visitors since the middle of the 19th century. The principal coastal towns are Ventimiglia, Imperia, San Remo, Savona, GENOA (regional capital), Portofino, Santa Margherita, Rapallo, Chiavari, Sestri Levante, and La Spezia. Of exceptional, unspoiled beauty are the isolated coastal villages of the Cinque Terre in the eastern part of the region near La Spezia. The APENNINE MOUNTAINS cover most of the region and plunge precipitously into the sea, giving the coastline its characteristic jagged aspect. The mountainous interior is thinly populated, 90 percent of the regional inhabitants living in the coastal towns, with 39 percent living in the regional capital of Genoa, which dominates the region. The region consists of four provinces: Genoa, Imperia, La Spezia, and Savona. Agriculture is of minor importance, although production of flowers, fruit, vegetables, and prized olive oil is significant for certain towns. Industry has been the principal source of employment since the latter part of the 19th century, when Liguria began to emerge as the southern anchor of Italy's so-called Industrial Triangle, consisting of Liguria, LOMBARDY, and Piedmont. Tourism and commercial services provide employment for about two-thirds of the labor force. The most important manufacturing industries are steel, engineering, oil refining, and shipbuilding, concentrated along the coastline between Genoa and Savona. Shipbuilding, the dominant industry until the 1960s, now specializes in the construction of small craft and leisure boats. Ligurian seafarers have pioneered in exploration and trade through the ages.

Lincei, Accademia dei See ACADEMIES; ITALIAN ACADEMY.

Lippi, Filippo See BOTTICELLI, SANDRO.

Lissa, Battle of See WARS OF NATIONAL INDEPEDENCE, THIRD.

Livorno, city of

The city of Livorno (population 161,700), often rendered in English as Leghorn, is a provincial capital and port city in TUSCANY. Ruled by PISA in the 14th century when it was little more than a small village, it became a walled military stronghold and passed under the rule of GENOA in 1405. FLORENCE acquired it in 1421. The Medici (see MEDICI FAMILY) ruling house, which ruled all of Tuscany in the 16th century, developed it when the nearby port of Pisa silted up. The rational layout of its streets attests to its origins as a planned town. Declared a free port in 1590, it rose quickly to maritime and commercial prominence. The flourishing seaport attracted large numbers of foreign merchants and bankers, including JEWS who formed a permanent colony in the city. One of the more economically dynamic cities of the peninsula, Livorno displayed the social tensions and conflicts typical of thriving seaports. Its economic dynamism was anomalous in 19th-century Italy, where few cities experienced rapid commercialization. Workers from Livorno played a role in the REVOLUTIONS of 1848 and generally supported the more radical democratic factions in the RISORGIMENTO. The city expanded rapidly after national unification, competing with GENOA as a commercial and shipbuilding center. Its naval academy is the major training school for Italian naval officers. Left-of-center politics are a tradition among the *livornesi.* During the Fascist period, the city was controlled politically by the Ciano family, which also owned the city's newspaper *Il Tirreno.* Allied bombing heavily damaged the city during WORLD WAR II. It served as the major port of entry for Allied troops moving north to fight the Germans along the GOTHIC LINE. The city has been a communist stronghold since the war. Today Livorno is a thriving seaport and an industrial city with shipyards, oil refineries, and chemical plants. Important industrial plants are also located in the town of Piombino. The island of ELBA is also part of the province of Livorno, from where it can be reached by regular ferry service.

Lodi, Peace of See ALFONSO I OF NAPLES; RENAISSANCE.

Lombard League See BOSSI, UMBERTO; MILAN, CITY OF.

Lombardy

The region of Lombardy (Lombardia), population 8.9 million, borders on Switzerland to the north, the regions of EMILIA-ROMAGNA to the south, TRENTINO–ALTO ADIGE and VENETIA to the east, and PIEDMONT to the west. It is Italy's most populous region. MILAN, the regional capital, is the country's second-largest city and its business capital. The zones of mountains, hills, and plains make for a diverse natural environment that sustains a rich and varied agriculture. It is rich in water. The Ticino River marks the region's historic border with Piedmont. The Adda, Mincio, and Oglio rivers flow from the ALPS into the PO RIVER. Lake Maggiore, Lake Lugano (mostly in Switzerland), Lake Como, Lake Iseo, and Lake Garda (the largest in Italy) are the region's principal lakes. Milan has dominated Lombardy's history and economy, its urban area spreading irresistibly over the countryside and incorporating other towns into one sprawling megalopolis. Its other provinces are Bergamo, Brescia, Como, Cremona, MANTUA, PAVIA, Sondrio, and Varese. Its mountain areas in the provinces of Bergamo, Sondrio, and Varese are economically depressed, but the region as a whole enjoys the highest standard of living in the country, comparable to that of the most advanced countries in Europe. Regional prosperity has not been without drawbacks. A large influx of immigrants has caused urban sprawl and put pressure on public services. High rates of crime and drug use, environmental pollution, and traffic congestion are realities of everyday life. Political resentments tend to focus against the national government and central bureaucracy, which many Lombards regard as drains on private business and the regional economy. UMBERTO BOSSI's antigovernment movement was born in Lombardy.

Lombroso, Cesare (1835–1909)

anthropologist and criminologist known for his theories of criminal behavior

Lombroso was born in Verona, studied medicine, worked as an army physician, and taught medical law and psychiatry. He outlined his theory of

Cesare Lombroso *(Library of Congress)*

criminal behavior in a pamphlet published in 1876, later expanded into the book *L'uomo delinquente* (Criminal man, 1878). His theory, based on anthropological measurements of the skulls of convicted criminals, proposed that criminals were identifiable by certain physical features that revealed a congenital predisposition to break the law. Particularly revealing, according to Lombroso, is the shape of the skull, which he regarded as providing scientific proof of predisposition to criminal behavior. Phrenology is the name given to this field of inquiry. According to Lombroso, the somatic characteristics (physiognomy) of criminals were throwbacks to those of our early human ancestors, a phenomenon known as atavism. Lombroso also argued that criminality tended to manifest itself in women as prostitution.

Lombroso probably based his theory on Darwinian evolution and reflected confidence that human behavior had materialistic, physiological determinants, as earlier phrenologists had also argued. Lombroso's contribution was to provide empirical evidence and point to cranial shape and facial characteristics as basic determinants. Such features as high cheekbones and protruding jaws were seen as telltale signs of criminal predisposition. Lombroso acknowledged the role of social environment, but chose not to pursue that line of inquiry. He did acknowledge that financial greed and monetary considerations can lead to a life of crime, even in the absence of physiological traits. Lombroso's emphasis on somatic traits puts him in the social science school that sought to explain human behavior in terms of inherited physiological characteristics.

To the extent that these characteristics were then seen as being racial, Lombroso's thought can also be seen as part of the development of racial ideology. There were racial implications in Lombroso's thinking, evident in the tendency to associate criminal behavior with somatic traits common among southerners. Lombroso even included Jews among the groups of undesirables, on the basis of their adherence to ancient practices, including circumcision, even though he was himself a Jew. But seen in their proper context, Lombroso's theories also had progressive and liberal connotations. If criminal behavior was not a matter of personal choice, as the prevailing school of jurisprudence maintained, but was rather the result of an individual's congenital makeup, then penalties should not aim at punishing, for punishment implied deliberate transgression. Penalties should aim instead at restraining and correcting criminal behavior in a humane manner. Such a view was compatible with Lombroso's progressive politics, which put him close to the movements of the Left. His translated works include *Criminal Man* (1911), which is an abridged version of *L'uomo delinquente,* and *Crime: Its Causes and Remedies* (1912). His daughter, Gina Lombroso-Ferrero (1872–1944), an important figure in her own right, was his collaborator.

London, Pact of

Secret military alliance concluded on April 26, 1915, after protracted negotiations by Italy and the Entente Powers (the United Kingdom, France, and Russia), just prior to Italy's intervention in WORLD WAR I. Italy had declared its neutrality in the conflict in August 1914, on the grounds that Austria-Hungary and Germany, its TRIPLE ALLIANCE partners, were the aggressors and had failed to consult before launching military operations. Italian diplomats negotiated with their Austrian and German counterparts, seeking territorial concessions from Austria in return for Italian neutrality. They also negotiated simultaneously with the Entente Powers for territorial gains and other compensations as the price of Italian intervention. The Entente Powers enjoyed a great advantage in these negotiations, in that they could satisfy Italian demands by giving up territories that belonged not to them, but to Austria-Hungary. The Entente Powers agreed that at war's end, Italy would receive TRENT and the surrounding region, TRIESTE, ISTRIA, DALMATIA, a sphere of influence in the BALKANS, and colonial compensations. The Italian government committed itself to entering the war within a month of signing the treaty. It then orchestrated an intensive pro-war campaign at home and declared war against Austria-Hungary on May 24, 1915, without consulting parliament. The declaration of war against Germany, not contemplated by the Pact of London, came more than a year later, on August 28, 1916. The secret pact and the declaration of war without parliamentary approval were permitted by the constitution, which left those decisions to the king. But they were highly controversial actions that left a legacy of domestic discord and hampered the prosecution of the war. The feelings for and against intervention exploded full force after the war, poisoned the political climate, and contributed directly to the rise of FASCISM.

Longo, Luigi (1900–1980)
*Communist Party leader, resistance
commander, and member of parliament*
Longo was born near Alessandria (in Piedmont) to a peasant family, studied engineering, was

Luigi Longo *(Library of Congress)*

drafted for military service in 1920, joined the Socialist Party (PSI), and was a founder of the Communist Party of Italy. Arrested in 1927, he fled to Switzerland and France, where he remained active in the anti-Fascist movement. In the Spanish civil war he served as political commissar and inspector general of the Communist International Brigades. Arrested by the French police in 1939 and turned over to Italian authorities, he spent the next four years in political confinement on the island of Ventotene. He joined the RESISTANCE in 1943 and served as second-in-command of its communist military formations. He was elected to the constituent assembly in 1946 and to parliament in 1948. He succeeded PALMIRO TOGLIATTI as secretary general of the Italian Communist Party (PCI) in 1964 and served in that capacity until 1972, when ENRICO BERLINGUER took over that post. Longo remained faithful to Togliatti's political strategy of accommodation with the CATHOLIC CHURCH and the

Christian Democratic Party (DC). Acceptance of parliamentary democracy and rejection of armed revolution were logical corollaries of that stance. Longo nevertheless indulged in occasional gestures of support for hard-line communists. In the 1960s he tried to promote dialogue between the PCI and the militant student groups of the New Left, without much success. Longo was an organizer and administrator rather than a political strategist.

Lorenzetti, Ambrogio See SIENA.

Lorenzini, Carlo See COLLODI, CARLO.

Loria, Achille (1857–1943)
political economist, author of influential tracts on private property, monetary theory, and historical materialism

Born in Mantua, Loria was appointed to teach political economy at the University of Siena (1881), University of Padua (1891), and University of Turin (1902). He was the most influential Italian social theoretician at the turn of the century. His influence reached well beyond Italy, and shows up in the writings of Frederick Jackson Turner, Charles Beard, and other social scientists. The global scope of his economic analysis is evident from the principles of economic development that he formulated in *La rendita fondiaria e la sua elisione naturale* (Land income and its natural extinction, 1880). According to that analysis, the use of land of European countries and their colonies is a function of population density, and the economic development of colonies replicates that of the European economies from primitive times to the present.

Attracted by, yet critical of, Marxist economics, Loria was an economic materialist who questioned Marx's conclusions. In Loria's scheme of things, land, not labor, is the source of all value, and it is the exploitation of agricultural rather than industrial workers that results in the accumulation of capital. Friedrich Engels, ANTO-

NIO LABRIOLA, ANTONIO GRAMSCI, and other Marxists disparaged Loria's economics and argued that modern economies cannot be understood simply in terms of land use. For a period of time Loria's economics did influence Italian socialist thinking, due, perhaps, to the important role that land and land workers played in the Italian socialist movement. Loria defended his theories until the end of his days, when he was still fighting yesterday's battles. See his *Economic Foundations of Society* (1899).

Lotta Continua

New Left extra-parliamentary radical group of the late 1960s and early 1970s

Lotta Continua (Continuing Struggle) was the best known of many New Left radical groups that sprang up in the late 1960s. *Liberare tutti* (free everybody), the title of a song about prison inmates, conveyed its message. Tactically, it professed a Leninist-Maoist version of communism that emphasized the role of a tightly knit avant-garde elite, leading the masses on the model of the Cultural Revolution then going on in China. It addressed itself principally to factory workers in the industrial cities of the North and helped radicalize the labor strikes and agitations of the Autunno caldo (Hot Autumn) of 1969. Always a small minority within the labor movement, Lotta Continua received intense public attention because of its activism and intransigent hostility to capitalism and the state. Lotta Continua's commitment to social revolution was at odds with the Communist Party (PCI) strategy of collaboration with Christian Democracy (DC). In 1976 Lotta Continua experienced a crippling internal crisis when worker's and women's factions decided to go their own way. The political space occupied by Lotta Continua and similar groups was taken over by organizations advocating and practicing political TERRORISM.

lottizzazione

The term *lottizzazione* refers to the practice of parceling out spheres of influence among the various political parties. The presence of numerous political parties and the coalition nature of Italian politics encourage the practice of sharing spoils. To benefit from *lottizzazione* a party has to be able to contribute significantly to the governing coalition. The major beneficiaries of this practice are the parties that can swing the largest number of votes, and their benefits are roughly proportional to their political strength, regardless of ideology and questions of principle. The major beneficiaries of *lottizzazione* have been the Christian Democratic Party (DC), Communist Party (PCI), and Socialist Party (PSI). Christian Democrats and Socialists were most deeply involved because of their history of collaboration going back to the early 1960s. The Communist Party benefited, even though it was not officially part of any governing coalition at the national level, by cooperating unofficially with the DC and other parties at both national and local levels. *Lottizzazione* has been an important part of the political system known as *partitocrazia* (rule by political parties). It is a widespread impression in Italy that real power resides ultimately in political parties rather than in the government itself. The term *lottizzazione* denotes political corruption and lack of principle, and is particularly associated with the nature of Italian politics since 1945. But the practice is not uniquely Italian. Spoil-sharing is the lubricant of coalition politics everywhere. So-called pork-barrel legislation is a rough American equivalent of *lottizzazione*.

Louis Napoleon See NAPOLEON III.

Lucca, city of

Lucca (population 85,500), a provincial capital situated in northwestern TUSCANY, lies in the middle of a fertile plain irrigated by the Serchio River and its tributaries. Founded by a pre-Roman people known as the Ligurians, it was taken over by the Etruscans and became a Roman colony in the year 89 B.C. It developed under Roman rule into an important center on the Aurelian and Cassian roads that converged near the city. From around A.D. 750 it served as the capital of the Lombard territory of Tuscia, the predecessor of modern Tuscany. It continued as capital under the rule of the Franks in the ninth and 10th centuries. Imperial edicts in the 11th and 12th centuries made it a self-governing commune. It remained independent for more than 700 years, in seemingly perennial conflict with neighboring PISA. By the 13th century Lucca thrived on silk manufacturing, trade, and banking. Under the military lordship of Castruccio Castracani (1320–28), Lucca extended its dominion over most of western Tuscany and challenged FLORENCE for dominance of the region. Its political and economic fortunes declined after Castracani's premature death, but the businessmen of the city maintained their positions in France, England, and the Low Countries. Under the rule (*signoria*) of Paolo Guinigi (1400–30), Lucca took on the trappings of a typical Renaissance city-state. But on the whole Lucca retains the aspect of a medieval town, with its encircling walls and an intricate urban layout. The 16th century was marked by economic and political crisis.

An independent republic, antipapal, and in close commercial contact with northern Europe, Lucca was a natural center of evangelical activity in the 16th century. The activities of its chief magistrate, FRANCESCO BURLAMACCHI, confirmed fears that it might become a center of religious and political subversion, and brought upon it the hostility of Florence and the papacy. The republic managed to maintain its independence, thanks to the protection of CHARLES V, a state-of-the-art system of walls, and prudent diplomacy. It was governed by its aristocracy, which excluded commoners from positions of power. NAPOLEON I overthrew the aristocratic republic in 1799 and replaced it with a democratic republic on the French model. But in 1805 Lucca became a principality governed by Napoleon's sister ELISA BACIOCCHI.

The CONGRESS OF VIENNA made it the Duchy of Lucca and assigned it to Marie Louise of the Spanish Bourbons (1817–24) and her son CARLO LODOVICO (1824–47). The extremely devout

Marie Louise favored the clergy, built churches, and encouraged religious charities. Her policies made Lucca a most Catholic city, a characteristic that it retains to this day. Marie Louise's easy-going son was more interested in worldly pleasures than in the responsibilities of government, but under the rule of mother and son, Lucca saw much road construction, urban renewal, and economic growth. In 1847 the Duchy of Lucca was incorporated into the Grand Duchy of Tuscany. A notable feature of its history was its sizable emigration from the poorer mountain districts to the countries of northern Europe, North and South America, and Australia. Lucca is a provincial capital with a diversified economy and a comfortable standard of living. The city maintains its medieval character, but small-scale industries and commercial establishments thrive in its suburbs and countryside.

Luccheni, Luigi See ANARCHISM.

Ludovico Sforza (Il Moro) See SFORZA FAMILY.

Luria, Salvatore See SCIENCE.

Lussu, Emilio (1890–1975)
anti-Fascist political activist and social reformer
Lussu was born near Cagliari (Sardinia) to a family of prosperous landowners, received a law degree, and served with distinction in WORLD WAR I. The Sardinian Action Party that he founded in 1920 demanded autonomy for the island, a republican form of government for the nation, social legislation, and policies to promote the economic development of the South. Lussu organized political resistance to FASCISM in Sardinia and was elected to parliament in 1921 and 1924. He was arrested in 1926, suffered imprisonment and political confinement, but managed

to escape and leave Italy in 1929. In France, he founded the movement *Giustizia e Libertà* with CARLO and NELLO ROSSELLI, but left it in 1935 because it would not move in a socialist direction. In 1943 he joined the ACTION PARTY and the RESISTANCE. He joined the Socialist Party (PSI) in 1947, held cabinet posts in the governments of FERRUCCIO PARRI and ALCIDE DE GASPERI, and served in the senate from 1948 to 1964. He was also a leader of the ultra-leftist Italian Socialist Party of Proletarian Unity (PSIUP) founded by LELIO BASSO. His writings include *Road to Exile: The Story of a Sardinian Patriot* (1936).

Luzzatti, Luigi (1841–1927)
economic expert, political figure, and moderate liberal reformer

Luzzatti was born to a Jewish family in Venice, studied and taught law and economics at the Universities of Padua and Rome. His long public career covered a period of 50 years from the period of the HISTORICAL RIGHT to the rise of FAS-CISM. He contributed to balancing the budget in the 1870s, helped develop commercial policies in the 1880s and 1890s, was treasury minister in 1891, 1896, and 1903–06, minister of agriculture (1909–10), and prime minister (1910–11). He was at the forefront of the movement to form popular banks and encourage private savings. A fiscal conservative who believed in budgetary responsibility and monetary stability, Luzzatti also campaigned for educational and land reforms, extension of the suffrage, religious freedom, and the separation of CHURCH AND STATE. He fought to contain the scourges of pellagra, alcoholism, and pornography. His foreign policy favored France, and he supported Italian intervention in WORLD WAR I. His last government post was as treasury minister under FRANCESCO NITTI (1920). GIOVANNI GIOLITTI named him senator in 1921. Respected across the political spectrum, Luzzatti was a great facilitator who could work with individuals and groups of different political persuasions and who promoted moderate reforms.

M

Macchiaioli
group of avant-garde painters

The term Macchiaioli, derived from the Italian word *macchia* (spot or blot), refers to a group of artists who combined commitment to art with political activism. The group formed in Florence in the 1850s and became prominent in the 1860s. The ostensible purpose of the group was to challenge the dominance of the conservative Florentine Academy, which insisted on a rigid, dogmatic approach to the study of art. The challenge was politically subversive because the academy was the guardian of the official culture, which was in turn associated with the rule of the HABSBURG-LORRAINE DYNASTY and Austrian political dominance. The Macchiaioli adopted a naturalistic approach to art that contrasted sharply with the formalism of their predecessors. They strove to depict nature as the eye perceives it, conveying vivid first-sight impressions using the *macchia,* or patch of color. Their naturalist bent may have been a response to the challenge posed by the new art of photography, which many feared would make painting obsolete. Macchiaioli painters often depicted scenes from the struggle for national unification and generally identified with the more democratic currents of the RISORGIMENTO. Ordinary people engaged in the daily routines of work and home were a favorite subject, and GIUSEPPE GARIBALDI was their hero. The Macchiaioli are regarded as anticipators of the French Impressionists, though unlike the Impressionists, they were soon forgotten outside Italy. Giovanni Fattori (1825–1908) is the most notable figure among the artists of this group. The rediscovery of the Macchiaioli has produced several important studies of their art in recent years.

Macciocchi, Maria Antonietta (1922–   )
political activist and leader of the postwar Italian feminist movement

A leading voice of Italian FEMINISM, Maciocchi is known as a dissident who speaks out in idiosyncratic and disconcerting ways. Born near the southern city of Frosinone, Macciocchi joined the Communist Party (PCI) in 1942, went on to direct the party papers *Noi Donne* (We Women, 1949–55) and *Vie Nuove* (New Ways, 1956–61), and was a correspondent for the daily, *L'Unità* (1961–68). She received a doctorate in political science from La Sorbonne (Paris) and taught at the University of Vincennes. She was elected to the European parliament in 1968 as a PCI representative. In 1972 she moved to France. In her book *La donna "nera"* (The "black" woman, 1976), she charged that Italian women had been won over to fascism by a subconscious attraction to forms of authoritarian control and male dominance. She raised similar questions about women's presence in the PCI and about the party's stand on women's issues, seeing in Marxist parties' championing of women's causes condescension and desire for control. Women's issues, she argued, should not be subsumed under the rubric of class struggle, as Marxist parties insisted on doing. Differences with the party line on these and other issues led to a parting of the ways in 1977. In 1979 she was reelected to the European parliament as a representative of the RADICAL PARTY, where she found more latitude for the expression of her personal views. On the question of abortion, she has deplored recourse to clinics where abortions are performed with inhuman impersonality on an industrial scale. A self-styled political heretic, Macciocchi has spoken for women from a humanistic perspective independent of party affiliation.

Machiavelli, Niccolò (1469–1527)
historian, playwright, diplomat, and political theorist

Seen variously as the founder of modern political thought, the advocate of political immorality ("the end justifies the means"), or the defender of popular government and republican liberty, Machiavelli's legacy is still the subject of debate. The facts of his life are less controversial. Of his education we know little, except that he drew inspiration from the writers of ancient Greece and Rome. Born to a family of the old Florentine nobility that had seen better days, he found employment in the government of the Florentine republic in 1498, after the death of GIROLAMO SAVONAROLA, whose religious zeal he did not share. In the government of the republic, Machiavelli held an important position similar to that of a modern secretary of state. In that post, which he held until the end of the republic in 1512, he discharged important diplomatic missions abroad, came to know and observe the political personalities of his time, and familiarized himself with the intricacies of Italian politics.

His writings reflect his familiarity with the political ways of his time, but do not necessarily show the political realism that is attributed to him. In writing about military matters, he argued for the superiority of popular militias over the mercenary armies employed by governments. His faith in popular militias was well intentioned but misplaced. The Florentine militia that he organized did not perform well. It was defeated in 1512 by mercenary troops fighting for Spain. Medici (see MEDICI FAMILY) rule was restored, Machiavelli lost his position in government, was imprisoned and tortured, and retired to live on a small family estate in the countryside. In 1513–17 he wrote or completed the two most important works for which he is still remembered, the *Discourses on the First Ten Books of Livy* and *The Prince*, both published posthu-

Niccolò Machiavelli *(Library of Congress)*

mously in 1531–32. Allowed to return to Florence around 1518–19, he wrote poetry and plays, including *La mandragola,* a comedy that shows an irreverent Machiavelli making fun of corrupt clergymen and credulous husbands.

The interpretation of the political Machiavelli depends to a large degree on whether one attaches more importance to one or the other of these two works. The *Discourses* show the Machiavelli who admired the republican spirit of ancient Rome and saw in the Roman republic a model for the modern state. In *The Prince*, dedicated to the restored Medici ruler in the partly realized hope of regaining political favor, Machiavelli dispenses advice on how to get on with the business of government. His experience of politics taught him that politics was not about the pursuit of abstract ideals of justice, but about the effective use of power. Cesare Borgia (see BORGIA FAMILY) made a strong and mostly positive impression on Machiavelli, but the prince of the title is not any particular ruler. He is rather an ideal figure, a ruler effective in war and a good administrator, one who can secure the survival of the state in a treacherous world.

His advice to rulers is that they should strive to make themselves loved and feared. But if they find that they cannot make themselves loved, then they must make themselves feared. Machiavelli proffered such advice at a time when Italian states were under constant threat of attack and invasion by foreign forces. The Italian Wars that began in 1494 ended only in 1559 with the TREATY OF CATEAU-CAMBRÉSIS. Machiavelli's advice to rely on force may not have been particularly useful to Italian rulers at a time when force was slipping from their hands. But Machiavelli also advised rulers to be both lion and fox, to combine force and cunning, and great cunning could compensate for inadequate force. There was not much evidence of national feeling in Italy in Machiavelli's time, but in the last chapter of *The Prince*, Machiavelli asserted that all of Italy was waiting for an effective ruler to drive the French and Spaniards from the peninsula. Under the seemingly practical and hard-nosed advice to rely on force, there was the utopian notion that, with effective leadership, Italians could defeat more powerful nations.

The call on Italians to expel foreign invaders made Machiavelli a hero in the eyes of 19th-century patriots. Others saw Machiavelli in a more ambivalent or downright negative light, seeing in the advice that he dispensed in *The Prince* an encouragement to govern amorally, with concern only for political survival, and indifference toward ideals and values. In 1559 Machiavelli's works were placed on the INDEX. In Anglo-Saxon and Protestant countries, Machiavelli stood for Catholic corruption, and "machiavellian" meant immoral and unscrupulous. The term still retains those connotations in common usage. Machi-

avelli certainly did not intend to encourage immoral behavior. But the public spirit that he admired in ancient Romans, and would have liked to see more in evidence among his contemporaries, was at odds with the advice to be cunning and ruthless that he dispensed in *The Prince*. We can see in the totality of Machiavelli's works and correspondence the unacknowledged idealist at odds with the self-proclaimed political realist. Interpreters still struggle to reconcile Machiavelli the idealist with Machiavelli the realist.

macinato

The term *tassa del macinato* (grist tax), or simply *macinato*, refers to a tax levied on the milling of grains. Always unpopular because the tax disproportionately affected low-income taxpayers, the grist taxes levied by pre-unification governments were abolished by the national government when the country was unified in 1860–61. They fell disproportionately on people of modest means, particularly peasants and rural workers who had to pay millers directly when they took their grains to be milled. Debate over grist taxes flared up in the 1860s, when the leaders of the governing HISTORICAL RIGHT proposed adoption of a grist tax to help balance the budget. Parliament approved the new tax after much debate in July 1868. When the tax went into effect on January 1, 1869, riots broke out in the regions of Emilia-Romagna and Tuscany. Troops quelled the rioting, lives were lost, and fear of social revolution spread. Grist tax increases in the 1870s kept the controversy alive. The LIBERAL LEFT promised to abolish the tax and did so gradually, after coming to power in 1876. It was abolished completely in 1880. It is estimated that the *macinato* raised about 5 percent of government revenues during its duration. It helped balance the budget, but left behind a bitter legacy of popular resentment and played into the hands of social agitators.

Maestri, Pietro See STATISTICS.

Maffei, Scipione (1675–1755)
economist, historian, social critic, playwright,
pioneer of Enlightenment culture

Born in Verona to a family of the nobility, Maffei studied in Jesuit schools in Parma and Modena, fought in the WAR OF THE SPANISH SUCCESSION, and traveled extensively in France, England, and the Low Countries. Everywhere an attentive observer of customs and trends in government, politics, and economy, Maffei looked with a critical eye on the state of Italian culture. In his *Scienza chiamata cavalleresca* (On the science called chivalry, 1710), which was ostensibly an attack on the custom of dueling, he developed a definition of *virtù* (bravery) that placed public service and social usefulness above noble birth and military accomplishments. Through the Venetian review *Giornale de' Letterati d'Italia* (1710–40), of which he was a founder, he stimulated discussion of developments in other parts of Europe, always with an eye to closing the gap between the culture of Italy and that of more progressive countries. In his book *Impiego del denaro* (The use of money, 1744) he deplored the Catholic prohibition against lending at interest (usury), arguing that the unrestricted use of money accounted for the economic dynamism and strength of Protestant countries. Deploring the political weakness of the Venetian state, in the pamphlet *Consiglio politico* (Political advice, 1737), Maffei proposed a form of government based on a division of powers between executive and legislative branches and giving real power to the provincial nobility that was excluded from government. Maffei's advice was not heeded. Later generations found in his writings prophetic admonitions of cultural lag and decadence.

Mafia

The beginnings, development, and current scope of the criminal organization known as the Mafia, even the origins and meaning of the name, are unclear. In current discourse, "Mafia" generally refers to organized, profitable illegal activities (gambling, smuggling, prostitution, drug traffick-ing, influence peddling), supported by certain strata of the population in an identifiable territory, exerting informal but effective control over economic activity in that territory, carrying on with the connivance of public officials, and having a loosely structured hierarchical chain of command that cuts across regional and even national lines. Along with this definition of "Mafia" as organized illegal activity (Mafia with a capital "M"), there has always been a looser definition of mafia (with a small "m") that sees it as a set of cultural values that may lead to organized illegal activities under specific circumstances.

Mafia as a cultural phenomenon rests on distrust of the state and its system of justice, which is seen as indifferent to the interests of and incapable of providing security for individuals and businesses. The local chieftain, or *capo mafioso*, is a "man of respect" who provides what the state cannot. Respect is an attribute of all members of the group, who are thought of as "men of honor." They are bound by their ties of "honor" to support one another, deliver on their promises, and keep silent before the law. Silence before the law (*omertà*) is what makes prosecution of mafia activities problematic under the best circumstances. The concept of personal honor permeates all levels of the mafia, creating a profound sense of differentiation between it and the outside world. The frequent designation of the mafia as Cosa Nostra (Our Thing) reflects this sense of corporate identity among members of the in-group.

Originally, the Mafia was a phenomenon confined to western Sicily, where state authorities noted its presence immediately after national unification. Local *mafiosi* forged ties with the political leadership by delivering votes in national elections, a phenomenon prevalent until FASCISM put an end to electoral campaigns. The Fascist regime cracked down hard on the Mafia, disabling the organization (or, depending on the interpretation, merely forcing it underground) for the duration of the regime. It reemerged rapidly in 1943, in the wake of the Allied invasion of Sicily in WORLD WAR II, allegedly with the complicity or tacit acceptance of the Allies, who may have utilized the Mafia to "soften" Sicily for the invasion and help them administer it. Mafia groups were behind the movement for Sicilian independence that found a colorful champion in the outlaw SALVATORE GIULIANO. The state's vigorous reaction, Giuliano's death in 1950, and American refusal to countenance Sicilian separatism put a quick end to the island's movement for independence.

By the 1960s the Mafia was no longer confined to western Sicily. Mafia-like entities known as the Camorra and 'Ndrangheta developed in NAPLES and the region of CALABRIA, respectively. In the 1980s the Mafia took hold in the region of PUGLIA, where it specializes in the smuggling of drugs, weapons for the BALKANS, and illegal immigrants. By the 1990s Mafia cells had spread beyond the South to some central and northern regions. The spread of the Mafia far beyond its traditional areas, the expanding volume and nature of its activities, bloody feuds that broke out regularly between rival mafia groups, evidence of growing collusion between organized crime and the political system, and assassinations of public officials, created enormous alarm and clamor. Anti-mafia popular rallies in Sicily and elsewhere made headlines. In 1982 the government sent General CARLO ALBERTO DALLA CHIESA to Sicily to crush the Mafia. His assassination produced an enormous outcry throughout the country. The judge Giovanni Falcone (1939–92) was appointed special investigator with broad prosecutorial powers. Hundreds of suspects were arrested, some breaking the code of silence for the first time. Many were found guilty and sent to jail. Falcone and his colleague Paolo Borsellino (1940–92), also a determined Mafia antagonist, were both assassinated in 1992.

By 1992 the parliamentary system that protected the Mafia was also under attack. It would soon collapse, dispatched by members of the same judiciary that bore the brunt of the anti-Mafia crusade. A controversial episode of the crusade was the prosecution of Christian Democratic leader GIULIO ANDREOTTI on charges of col-

lusion with the Mafia. In the late 1990s the fight against the Mafia took on an international character as police cooperation across national lines improved. The United Nations is also playing an important role in the international effort to root out Mafia organizations, which display a remarkable ability to emerge wherever there are opportunities to profit by illegal trafficking. New Mafias are springing up, not only in Italy and the United States, where they have traditionally operated, but also in Asia, eastern Europe, and Latin America. The traditional identification of the Mafia with Italians or Italian-Americans of Sicilian extraction is called into question as the phenomenon reproduces itself wherever the right conditions materialize.

Magenta, Battle of　See NAPOLEON III; WARS OF NATIONAL INDEPENDENCE.

Magliani, Agostino (1824–1891)
economist and political figure known for his manipulation of state finances

Magliani was born near Salerno in southern Italy, studied and lived in Naples, served in the state administration, and moved to Turin in 1860 to work in the national government's accounting bureau. His financial expertise, reputation for personal honesty, and rhetorical flair won him appointment as senator (1871) and minister of finance (1877–88). As minister of finance in the governments of AGOSTINO DEPRETIS he was responsible for a major shift in financial policy. Taking advantage of the balanced budgets achieved by the HISTORICAL RIGHT, Magliani increased spending on armaments, railway construction, and other public works. His critics dubbed his spending policies *finanza allegra* (merry finance). High levels of government spending and borrowing produced deficits, and encouraged creative accounting practices designed to disguise them. In spite of deficits, Magliani halted the erosion in the value of the CURRENCY, kept it on a level of parity with the French franc, and abolished the hated MACINATO tax, thus fulfilling promises made by the LIBERAL LEFT before coming to power. His tenure in office coincided with a period of prosperity that masked the problems inherent in his financial policies, which included heavy reliance on consumer taxes. His failure to anticipate bad times and build up sufficient reserves left the government unprepared for the financial crises of the 1890s, to the lasting detriment of his reputation as minister and financial expert.

Maistre, Joseph de See ROMANTICISM.

Malaparte, Curzio (1898–1957)
writer and internal critic of the Fascist regime

Malaparte (real name Kurt Erich Suckert) was born in Prato (in Tuscany) to a German father and an Italian mother. His father was a factory foreman, and the young Erich grew up in close contact with workers, for whose language and ways he developed a close affinity reflected in his own salty prose. He studied at the exclusive Collegio Cicognini of Prato (1911–14), joined the Republican Party (1913), volunteered for military service, and was a decorated veteran of WORLD WAR I. Sharing the concern of many intellectuals of his generation that European culture was in decline, he looked for a political movement capable of reversing the trend and found it in FASCISM. Attracted to the Fascist labor movement headed by EDMONDO ROSSONI, he joined the Florentine section of the Fascist Party in September 1922. His activity as a Fascist labor organizer had little or no significance in his work or subsequent career. In the early 1920s Malaparte emerged as an important figure on the Italian literary and journalistic scene. After the Fascist seizure of power in October 1922 Malaparte challenged BENITO MUSSOLINI's policy of accommodation with the political opposition.

His highly personal and idiosyncratic view of fascism as an antimodernist movement based on local traditions, peasant culture, and Catholicism (understood by Malaparte essentially as respect for the principle of authority) was opposed by leading Fascist figures. Malaparte published the weekly review *La Conquista dello Stato* (1924–28), but gave up on trying to change the course of the regime in 1925–26. He did take occasional potshots at individual figures, including ITALO BALBO and Mussolini. In 1926 he launched the current known as Strapaese (Small Town) that praised the country's agrarian traditions, and the creative energy of the early Fascist squads, and condemned the modernizers of what Malaparte called Stracittà (Big City). After shutting down his review, Malaparte served as editor of the Turinese daily *La Stampa* (1929–31), then left for Paris where he published *Technique du coup d'État* (1931). In that controversial book, communism and Lenin came out as truly revolutionary. Fascism and Mussolini, on the other hand, were seen as having carried out a coup d'état, without changing the character of Italian society.

Definitely out of political favor, in 1933 Malaparte was expelled from the party and sentenced to five years' confinement. In confinement and after his liberation, Malaparte avoided political controversy and turned his attention to literary matters. As correspondent for the daily *Corriere della Sera* he covered the Russian front in WORLD WAR II. His experiences there inspired the documentary novel *Kaputt* (1943), which revisited the theme of European decadence in the modern world. In 1944–45 he served as a liaison officer between the Allies and the Italian army. Writing was Malaparte's almost exclusive concern after the war. His novels *La pelle* (The skin, 1949) and *Mamma marcia* (Rotten mother, 1959), the latter published posthumously, elaborated further on the theme of cultural decadence. The vitality of local culture was the dominant theme in the collection of essays entitled *Maledetti toscani* (Those cursed Tuscans, 1956). An accomplished writer, attentive observer, and perceptive commentator, Malaparte's reputation is tainted by charges of unprincipled opportunism and obsessive self-promotion.

Malatesta, Errico (1854–1932)

socialist dissident, anarchist, and conspirator

Malatesta was born in Santa Maria Capua Vetere (Naples) to a noble and wealthy family. He studied medicine at the University of Naples but abandoned his studies to become a political militant. A republican admirer of GIUSEPPE GARIBALDI in his youth, he was later a socialist and an anarchist. Inspired and radicalized by the insurrection of the Paris Commune, he formed a close bond with the Russian anarchist MICHAEL BAKUNIN and with Carlo Cafiero (1846–92). In 1872 he helped launch the Italian section of Karl Marx's First Workingmen's International. Malatesta believed in "propaganda of the deed," the notion that practicing revolutionary violence regardless of its prospects of immediate success was the best way to prepare workers and peasants for revolution. In Europe and in South and North America, always on the move to avoid arrest, he called on workers to rise against the state. In 1880 he opened an electrical repairs shop in London, where he felt relatively safe. He returned to Italy clandestinely in 1894 to participate in the insurrections of the FASCI SICILIANI. In 1896 he represented Spanish workers at the London meeting of the Second International that expelled anarchists from its ranks. Arrested again in Italy for his role in the FATTI DI MAGGIO of 1898, he escaped abroad and was welcomed by the Italian anarchists of Paterson, New Jersey. Condemned in Italy in 1911 for his denunciation of the ITALIAN-TURKISH WAR, he was saved from deportation from Great Britain by street protests. Back in Italy in 1913, he instigated the uprisings of RED WEEK, after which he escaped abroad once again. Returning to Italy in November 1918, he immediately began to agitate for revolution. He had little faith in the revolutionary ability of the socialist leadership. Briefly, he hoped that GABRIELE D'ANNUNZIO might lead a revolution from FIUME. He spent the last years of his life under house arrest in Rome. The Fascist regime did not fear him and even accorded him a measure of respect. Underlying Malatesta's anarchist beliefs was an optimistic faith in the ability of individuals to govern themselves responsibly and a visceral distrust of

government and all forms of authority. His principal work *L'Anarchia* (Anarchy) is available in English translation (1900).

Malatesta family

The Malatesta family ruled the city-state of Rimini and other towns of the ROMAGNA region from 1295 to 1528. Early on, members of this family acquired a reputation for political deviousness and ruthlessness, a reputation remarkable for a time when violence was common and often extreme. The surname Malatesta (Hard Head) was given to an early member of the family who showed his ability to stand up (*tener testa*) to his enemies. Their policy of generally siding with the Guelf factions of their region kept them on friendly terms with the PAPACY and won them much territory. However, the Malatestas did not hesitate to support the imperial side as opportunity dictated. Generally distrusted, they feuded constantly with their neighbors, particularly the MONTEFELTRO FAMILY of Urbino, and their hold on power and territory was precarious. The most notable member of the family was Sigismondo Malatesta (1417–68), who was known for his military prowess, cruelty, lust, and homicidal tendencies. The fact that he was also an accomplished poet and patron of the arts did not spare him from excommunication and papal condemnation as the "prince of all wickedness." Dante immortalized the family in the *Divine Comedy* by recounting the story of the unlucky lovers Paolo and Francesca, murdered by the repulsive Gianciotto Malatesta, Francesca's jealous husband and Paolo's brother.

Malibran, Maria See BELLINI, VINCENZO.

Malpighi, Marcello (1628–1694)

anatomist and pioneer of modern science

Malpighi was born into a well-off family of Crevalcuore (Bologna), studied and taught medicine at the University of Bologna (1653–56, 1659–62, 1666–91), the University of Pisa (1656–59), and the University of Messina (1662–66). In the last three years of his life (1691–94) he served as personal physician to Pope Innocent XII (1691–1700). Like many naturalists of his time, Malpighi's interests ranged far and wide. Highly regarded as a physician, Malpighi is remembered largely for his pioneering use of the microscope in anatomical studies. While GALILEO explored the skies with the telescope, Malpighi studied small organisms and anatomic features with the instrument that he called a "flea glass." He ascertained that the capillaries complete the circulation of the blood from arteries to veins by studying frogs' lungs ("I have sacrificed almost the whole race of frogs . . .," he wrote to a friend). That discovery provided the missing link to William Harvey's theory of blood circulation. A side result of his research was the correct explanation of the function of lungs. Malpighi argued the then controversial theses that animal and human anatomy were related, and that sound medicine required anatomical knowledge. Other important discoveries include the role of taste buds, the structure of glands, skin, kidneys, and spleen. His study of eggs and of chick embryos led him to state that *omne vivum ex ovo* (all life comes from the egg). Malpighi relied on direct observation and blamed grand theorizing for leading scientists astray. But he did enunciate the general anatomical principle that more complex organisms have more specialized organs. In 1689 a religious tribunal condemned aspects of Malpighi's work as incompatible with Catholic doctrine. The condemnation did not prevent Innocent XII from calling him to Rome and showering him with honors in the last years of his life.

Malta

Malta, today an independent nation of approximately 400,000 inhabitants, is a former British colony with traditionally close ties to Sicily and the Italian mainland. Consisting of three islands located south of Sicily, its strategic location near the geographical center of the MEDITERRANEAN SEA has attracted the attention of many powers.

Romans, Byzantines, Arabs, Normans, Spaniards, French, and English have ruled it at various times. The military order of the Knights Hospitalers, also known as the Knights of Malta, received the island from Emperor CHARLES V in 1530. They built the fortified capital city of Valletta, and in 1565 defended the islands against the Ottoman Turks, thereby preserving the islands' ties with Europe and the Christian world. Overwhelmingly Roman Catholic and devout, the Maltese people have cultivated close ties with the Vatican. The knights held and governed the islands until 1798, when they were ousted by NAPOLEON I, who in turn was ousted by the British two years later. The British turned Malta into an important naval base and governed it as a colony. With British connivance, in the 19th century Malta served as a base of operations for Italian patriots organizing to fight for Italian independence. The Fascist government claimed Malta for Italy as part of its policy of Mediterranean dominance. The failure to capture the islands during WORLD WAR II was a major military setback for the Fascist regime. Heavy bombardments by the Italian and German air forces generated strong anti-Italian sentiments. There are still linguistic and cultural affinities between Malta and Italy, as attested to by the frequency of Italian surnames and place names on the islands. There are two official languages in Malta, Maltese and English, but Italian is a second or third language for many Maltese. Relations with Italy have been generally cordial since Malta became independent in 1964. There are close economic ties between the two countries, and Italy has extended economic aid to ease Malta's transition from colonial status to full independence.

Mameli, Goffredo (1827–1849)
poet and Risorgimento martyr figure

Mameli was born in Genoa to a distinguished family. His father, Giorgio Mameli (1798–1871), was an admiral in the Piedmontese navy and his mother, Adelaide Zoagli (1805–84), belonged to one of Genoa's oldest aristocratic families. The young Mameli took a degree in law from the

University of Genoa but was soon carried away by enthusiasm for the republican ideals of the exiled GIUSEPPE MAZZINI, who as a young man had courted his mother. Active in the patriotic underground, in March 1848 Mameli fought against the Austrians in Lombardy. In December 1848 he went to Rome, where he helped establish the ROMAN REPUBLIC. He then called on Mazzini to go to Rome to lead the republican government. Mameli died from a wound suffered fighting for the Roman Republic. He holds a preeminent place among the heroic figures of the RISORGIMENTO. A promising writer, he wrote the lyrics that were set to music by Michele Novaro (1822–85) and became the Italian national anthem, also know as the *Inno di Mameli.*

Mamiani della Rovere, Terenzio (1799–1885)

liberal philosopher and political figure

Mamiani was born in Pesaro (Marches), studied in Rome, and joined liberal Catholics who urged the PAPACY to adopt progressive policies. For his support of the REVOLUTION of 1831 he was imprisoned and exiled. In Paris he emerged as a leader of liberal exiles who favored constitutional monarchy. He wrote and published extensively, and was recognized as a thinker who looked for the *juste milieu* (middle course) in politics. Mamiani returned to the PAPAL STATES in 1847, served as minister of the interior and foreign minister, and proposed national resistance to Austria. A political moderate, he opposed the radical elements who established the ROMAN REPUBLIC. Forced out of office by their victory, he went to Turin. In 1856 he was elected to the parliament of Piedmont-Sardinia. He supported CAVOUR's domestic and foreign policies, organized support for the war against Austria, and served as minister of education (1860–61). He was appointed to teach philosophy at the universities of Turin (1857) and Rome (1871), served as ambassador to Greece (1861) and Switzerland (1865), and was made a senator in 1864. He steered through the senate the Law of Guarantees (1871) that regulated relations between CHURCH AND STATE. Mamiani's reputation as a philosopher has not held up well. GIACOMO LEOPARDI declared him a shallow optimist, BENEDETTO CROCE found his philosophy lacking in rigor and originality. Mamiani was an effective publicist for moderate government, education, and gradual reform.

Mancini, Pasquale Stanislao (1817–1888)

legal expert, journalist, and Risorgimento political figure

Born near the southern city of Avellino, Mancini earned a law degree from the University of Naples. His first publication revealed liberal sentiments that made him suspect in the eyes of the Neapolitan government. The REVOLUTION of 1848 allowed him to express his liberalism openly as a journalist and member of the elected Neapolitan parliament. The reaction that followed the failure of the revolution forced him to seek refuge in PIEDMONT, from where he continued his attacks on the Neapolitan monarchy. He taught jurisprudence at the University of Turin and was elected to parliament in 1855 and 1859. Elected to the national parliament in 1860, he joined the opposition. His first task was to supervise the integration of the southern provinces into the national state. His ANTICLERICALISM led him to curb clerical privileges and expropriate religious properties. His political prospects improved with advent of the LIBERAL LEFT to power in 1876. As minister of justice (1876–78), he extended freedom of the press and abolished imprisonment for debt. His most important post was as foreign minister (1881–85). In that capacity he concluded the TRIPLE ALLIANCE, negotiated commercial treaties with France, Germany, Spain, and Switzerland, and pursued a policy of COLONIALISM in Africa. Mancini counted on British support for Italian colonial ventures, but turned down a British invitation to have Italy as a partner in the administration of Egyptian affairs. He resigned as foreign minister and

Pasquale Stanislao Mancini *(Library of Congress)*

retired to private life in June 1885 after losing parliamentary support for his colonial policies.

Mani Pulite

The police investigation known as Mani Pulite (Operation Clean Hands) began on February 17, 1992, when the police raided the offices of a Milanese charitable institution and discovered evidence of illicit deals between local businessmen and public officials. The charity being investigated was shown to have received kickbacks from funeral parlors for every cadaver delivered for burial from the charity's old folks' home. The continuing investigation, led by the magistrate ANTONIO DI PIETRO, brought to light a network of connections involving bribes, kickbacks, and sweetheart deals that touched many branches of the city administration. The city of Milan, reputed until then to be a model of business efficiency and administrative propriety, became known in the press as Tangentopoli (Bribesville). "Tangentopoli" turned into a national scandal that implicated prominent public figures, including the Socialist mayor of Milan, his brother-in-law and former prime minister BETTINO CRAXI, Republican Party secretary Giorgio La Malfa, and SILVIO BERLUSCONI. The scandal terminated Craxi's political career and tarnished the reputation of the Italian Socialist Party (PSI). The police arrested several thousand suspects, detained them for long periods of time, and extracted confessions that implicated ever more suspects. Concerned that the investigation was running out of control, ruining the lives of innocent people, and trampling on civil rights, higher magistrates and political leaders, including the president of the republic, curtailed the powers of the investigators. Critics charged that the investigators were really "revolutionaries in judges' robes" who used the system of justice for political ends for the benefit of the Democratic Party of the Left (PDS). Coinciding with other investigations involving the MAFIA, Operation Clean Hands gave the impression of pervasive corruption in business and politics. It undermined public trust in government and fueled demands for political change. The public revolt was largely responsible for the political reforms of the 1990s to curb the power of political parties. By the end of the decade the public had lost interest and political reforms stalled.

Manin, Daniele (1804–1857)
Venetian patriot and Risorgimento figure
Manin was born in Venice to a family of Jewish ancestry that had converted to Christianity in the 18th century and changed its name from Fonsecca to Manin, after the last doge of the Venetian republic. Manin followed in his father's footsteps as a lawyer, graduating from the University of Padua in 1821, and practicing law in

Venice. Manin came to politics by way of economics. In 1847, alarmed by Venice's economic decline under Austrian rule, Manin took the position that the city needed closer economic ties with the rest of Italy. His firm commitment to the use of legal means (*lotta legale*) wavered when revolution broke out in 1848. Manin was chosen president of the independent Venetian republic when the Austrians evacuated the city. A convinced republican, Manin sacrificed his personal conviction and agreed to union with Piedmont-Sardinia for the sake of national unity. As a political exile in Paris in the 1850s, Manin earned a living by giving Italian lessons. He condemned the tactics of political conspiracy and insurrection used by GIUSEPPE MAZZINI as the "theory of the dagger" and urged patriots to rally behind CAVOUR and constitutional monarchy. Manin and GIORGIO PALLAVICINO cofounded the SOCIETÀ NAZIONALE ITALIANA in 1856 to promote national unity and constitutional monarchy. Physically frail and in poor health, Manin died four years before his program for Italy's unification came to fruition.

mannerism

Mannerism is a style of artistic representation in painting, sculpture, and architecture that emerged in the 16th century (High Renaissance). It can be thought of as an intermediary phase of artistic development between Renaissance classicism and the BAROQUE. The term itself came into use in the 17th and 18th centuries. It derives from the Italian word *maniera* (manner), probably in the sense of having good manners, being stylish and refined. Indeed, mannerist artists were preoccupied with expressing sentiments in a way that was pleasant to the eye and showed the artist's mastery of technique and craftsmanship. Mannerism developed after artists had mastered the conventional techniques of drawing, perspective, and coloring and were striving for new effects. The desire to show off technical mastery often led artists to depict densely peopled and complex scenes suggestive of movement and

drama. They often represented the human form in elongated, twisting poses, and made whimsical use of structural elements in building construction. The intent to transcend conventional techniques can be detected in the later works of Michelangelo, who is sometimes considered a precursor and inspirer of mannerism. Representatives of the mannerist style in Italy include the painters Parmigianino (1503–40), GIULO ROMANO, and Sodoma (1477–1549), the sculptors BENVENUTO CELLINI, BARTOLOMEO AMMANNATI, and Giambologna (Giovanni Bologna; 1529–1608) and architects Pirro Ligorio (1510–83) and Bernardo Buontalenti (1531–1608).

Mantegazza, Paolo (1831–1910)
anthropologist, physiologist, and science publicist

The experiments of this pioneer biologist, conducted in the 1860s, anticipated the findings of modern endocrinology by positing a relationship between substances secreted by sex glands and certain sexual characteristics. Descended from an old family of the Milanese aristocracy, Mantegazza led an adventurous life, traveling widely in exotic places, studying and comparing the habits of unfamiliar populations in Latin America, Africa, and Asia. From these studies he derived a sense of the relativity of social customs, but continued to believe in values that differentiate civilized from uncivilized populations. He preached that scientists must be free to pursue their researches in all directions, but must also be sensitive to social norms. He served in the parliament, as a deputy from 1865 to 1876 and as a senator from 1876 until his death. The holder of a chair of pathology at the University of Pavia (1861) and of anthropology at the University of Florence (1869), he popularized SCIENCE, POSITIVISM, and Darwinian evolution. His hugely popular books the *Physiology of Pleasure* (1854) and *Physiology of Love* (1873) introduced Italians to sex education. In his work and writings he used psychological insights to explain human behavior. According to Mantegazza, scientific understanding was socially valuable because it enabled individuals to control their emotions. In the novel *Testa* (The Head, 1887), he advised young readers to control the impulses of the heart with a "head screwed on right." Self-control and self-reliance were the moral values preached by Mantegazza, who wielded enormous influence over several generations of Italian readers. His major works were translated in many languages, including English.

Mantegna, Andrea (ca. 1431–1506)
Renaissance painter, engraver, and archaeologist

Born in a small village near PADUA, Mantegna was adopted and trained by a local painter and businessman who farmed out his services to local patrons. His first paintings for the Ovetari chapel in the Church of the Eremitani in Padua (1457) were almost totally destroyed by Allied bombings in WORLD WAR II, but photographs and the few remains show Mantegna's lifelong preoccupation with technical problems of perspective. That concern reflected the influence of Tuscan artists, to which Mantegna brought a characteristically northern Italian concern with naturalistic representation of daily objects and anatomic details. His use of light for special effects is a particularly noteworthy feature of his works. Mantegna honed his artistic skills by studying and drawing ancient artifacts, some of which he may have unearthed in the company of a group of humanists who met on the shores of Lake Garda near VERONA. More intensive study of classical antiquities probably occurred when Mantegna visited ROME in 1488. Other important paintings by Mantegna appear in the Church of San Zeno in Verona. Starting in 1460, Mantegna worked for the GONZAGA FAMILY in Mantua. In the famous murals (1474) that line the Camera degli Sposi in Mantua's Ducal Palace, we see Mantegna's genius for portraiture and visual illusion at its zenith. These murals anticipate the development of the BAROQUE. Mantegna's canvases are found in many museums, including the Uffizi Gallery in Florence, Brera Gallery in Milan, Louvre in Paris, and National Gallery in London.

Mantua, city of

Mantua (Mantova), population 48,300, is a provincial capital situated on the right bank of the Mincio River in the region of LOMBARDY. Originally an Etruscan settlement, it was later colonized by the Romans in the third century B.C. Byzantines, Lombards, and Franks occupied it, attracted by its strategic location protected on three sides by water and by the rich soil of the Lombard plain. The rule of bishops brought it some stability, but factional fights between supporters of emperors and popes disturbed its history in the Middle Ages. In the 12th century it became an independent commune, joined with other Lombard towns to resist imperial power, and was part of the anti-imperial alliance that secured papal dominance of northern Italy in the 13th century. The rule of the GONZAGA FAMILY over the city, which began in 1328 and lasted until 1627, ushered in a period of economic gain and artistic distinction. Under Gonzaga rule Mantua became an important center of RENAISSANCE culture and grew in political importance. The end of Gonzaga rule was followed by a period of renewed warfare that ended with the start of HABSBURG rule in 1707. NAPOLEON conquered it in 1797, lost it to the Austrians in 1799, and regained it in 1801. Under Napoleonic rule (1801–14) it was first part of the pro-French Cisalpine Republic and kingdom of Italy. Under renewed Austrian rule (1814–66) it became an important military base and a linchpin, along with VERONA, Legnago, and Peschiera, of the defensive system known as the Quadrilateral. While the Austrians surrendered Lombardy in 1859, they held on to the Quadrilateral, including the city of Mantua, until 1866 when they surrendered it at the end of the Third WAR OF NATIONAL INDEPENDENCE. In the subsequent decades the landless workers of the province flocked to the Socialist Party (PSI). The Mantuan countryside was the site of violent clashes between Socialists and Fascists after WORLD WAR I. The agriculture of the province benefited from the protectionist policies of the Fascist regime. Mantua is still an important agricultural center. The artistic legacy of Gonzaga rule also makes it a tourist attraction.

Manuzio, Aldo (1449–1515)

humanist printer and scholar who set the highest standards for book production

Aldo Manuzio (Aldus Manutius), also known as Manuzio the Elder to distinguish him from his grandson Aldo the Younger (1547–97), who also carried on the family printing business, was born near Rome and studied in Rome and Ferrara. At about age 45 he set up his printing business in VENICE, where he enjoyed considerable freedom to publish. A student of classical Latin and Greek, Manuzio oversaw both the scholarly and production aspects of his editions. His Greek printings, including a five-volume edition of the works of Aristotle (1494), were particularly important both for their scholarly accuracy and visual presentation. Manuzio also published dictionaries, grammars, and textbooks for both Greek and Latin in formats that ranged from large folio to small octave formats for affordability and portability. Also noteworthy were his editions of such "moderns" as DANTE, PETRARCH, and BEMBO. Manuzio was the first to use Old Times Roman instead of Gothic as the standard typeface, to adopt italics as a form of cursive, and to base his illustrations on the paintings and drawings of major artists. The demand for a typical volume seems to have increased from about 200 to 1,000 copies thanks to Manuzio's reputation for good craftsmanship and accuracy. His Aldine Press made Venice the most important publishing center in Europe. After his death the family printing business was carried on by his father-in-law, his son Paolo (1512–74), and grandson Aldo the Younger, whose standards of production are considered to be much inferior to his grandfather's.

Manzoni, Alessandro (1785–1873)

novelist, poet, playwright, and national icon

Born in Milan to a family of the Lombard aristocracy, he was educated privately by religious teachers. His literary talent showed early in poems that enthused for the revolutionary ideals of liberty, equality, and fraternity. Joining his mother, Giulia Beccaria (daughter of CESARE BECCARIA), in Paris in 1805, he read and followed French rationalist thinkers. The influence of Enrichetta Luigia Blondel, a Calvinist from Geneva whom he married in 1808, turned him away from secularism and back to religion. The conversion to Catholicism was completed in 1810 when Alessandro and Enrichetta remarried in the Roman Catholic rite. They returned to Milan that same year. The *Inni sacri,* composed from 1812 to 1822, were the first literary manifestation of his renewed religious faith. In these odes, Manzoni reflects on religion as an experience of suffering and redemption. The consolation and redeeming power of religion are also the themes of his plays *Il conte di Carmagnola* (The count of Carmagnola, 1819) and *Adelchi* (1822).

His masterpiece, the novel *I promessi sposi* (The betrothed, 1827), ranks among the great literary masterpieces. Conceived on a grand scale, it tells the story of Renzo and Lucia, who prevail against the arrogant powerful and their minions to achieve their dream of marriage. Set in 17th-century Lombardy, the novel was inspired by Manzoni's belief in the power of God to punish the corrupt and protect the humble and weak. It also sketches a cultural portrait of 17th-century Lombardy that displays Manzoni's critical intelligence and sense of history. The final reworking of the novel, completed in 1840–42, contains an appendix entitled *La colonna infame* (The infamous stele), an account of the plague epidemic of 1630 that condemns the trials and executions of individuals accused of spreading the disease.

I promessi sposi marks a milestone in the development of modern Italian. Manzoni, after composing a preliminary version that left him dissatisfied, lived in Florence and rewrote the novel in a literary Tuscan that set the standard for linguistic correctness. Manzoni's political influence was not as great. Although an Italian patriot at heart, he was too timid to play a role in public life. His faith in the redeeming power of religion may also have been an obstacle. Few of Manzoni's contemporaries shared his religious intensity, and activists deplored that his writings conveyed messages of passivity and resignation. But time muted the critics, and in his old age Manzoni was universally admired and revered for his literary accomplishments, compassion, and sense of social justice. GIUSEPPE VERDI composed his solemn *Requiem Mass* to commemorate him.

Maraini, Dacia See MORAVIA, ALBERTO.

Marcellus II See PALESTRINA, GIOVANNI PIERLUIGI.

March on Rome See FASCISM.

Marches

The region of the Marches (Marche) in central Italy, population 1,461,000, borders on the Adriatic Sea to the east, the regions of EMILIA-ROMAGNA to the north, TUSCANY, UMBRIA, and LATIUM to the west, and ABRUZZO to the South. The republic of SAN MARINO lies within its borders. Its provinces and chief cities are Ancona, Ascoli Piceno, Macerata, PESARO, and URBINO. The geography is mostly mountainous, but the elevations of the Apennine Mountains are not particularly high in this regional stretch. The shoreline is flat and sandy for long stretches, but broken occasionally by rocky outcrops. The isolated massif of Mount Conero, which rises to an elevation of 572 meters (1,876 feet), is a picturesque coastal enclave. The name Marches derives from the military administration of this boundary land (mark) in early medieval times. From Frankish military rule it passed to ecclesiastical administration in the eighth century, but

local feudal families soon exercised effective power in the region. These included the MONTE-FELTRO and MALATESTA FAMILIES. The church maintained its authority largely by playing off the rivalries of powerful local lords, consolidating its hold on the region in the 16th and 17th centuries. Thereafter the region followed the history of the PAPAL STATES until it became part of the Kingdom of Italy in 1860. It was often the scene of bitter social struggles. Anarchists, republicans, and socialists were active in street protests and insurgencies, most notably during the agitations of RED WEEK in June 1914. Today, the standard of living is slightly below the national average. Agriculture still provides much of the region's production and employment. Farming, formerly based on sharecropping (see *MEZZADRIA*), is now practiced mostly by small and medium-sized family-owned farms, which does not make for efficiency but does provide opportunities for employment. Small-scale manufacturing businesses are also an important source of employment and are often combined with family farming. Paper, textiles, footwear, furniture, and musical instruments are typical products of these establishments. Oil refineries, chemicals, food processing plants, and shipyards are located on the coast. The regional capital of Ancona is the busy center of such activities. Seaside resorts attract large numbers of tourists, while many picturesque and historically significant towns in the hilly interior await discovery by the outside world.

Marconi, Guglielmo (1874–1937)
physicist and entrepreneur, inventor of wireless telegraphy

Marconi was born in Bologna to an Irish Protestant mother who had come to Italy to study singing and married a Bolognese landowner. To his parents' dismay, he showed little interest in schooling of any type, but did display an avid curiosity for the developing field of electricity. His mother saw to it that he was provided with the latest literature and that he received private

Guglielmo Marconi *(Library of Congress)*

from the use of long-wave to short-wave signals, which proved much more suitable for long-distance communication. His communication devices were used with some success by the Italian army in WORLD WAR I. In 1924 Marconi succeeded in sending spoken radio messages from England to Australia, thus inaugurating the era of modern long-distance radio broadcasting. That same year the first Italian radio station began to broadcast from Rome. Marconi won exceptional recognition and honors for his discoveries. He was made senator in 1914 at the minimum required age of 40, received the tile of marquis, served as president of the Italian Academy, and was an honorary member of the Fascist Grand Council. Strongly patriotic, he served as an officer in the Italian army and navy during World War I, later discharged diplomatic missions, and in 1935 volunteered for service in the ITALIAN-ETHIOPIAN WAR. That same year he was appointed to the chair of electromagnetic studies that was established for him at the University of Rome. It was rumored that in the last years of his life he was engaged in highly secret research to develop a *raggio della morte* (death ray), which presumably was some kind of laser weapon.

instruction in that subject. At the University of Bologna Marconi audited a course taught by the physicist Augusto Righi (1850–1921), who was doing research on electromagnetic waves and was surrounded by a group of enthusiastic assistants. Marconi's earliest experiments, carried out at home in 1894–95 with makeshift equipment, convinced the young scientist that electromagnetic waves could carry signals over long distances using antennas instead of connecting wires. In 1896 he went to London to patent his system of transmission and establish a business for the commercial exploitation of his discovery. In 1899 he transmitted signals across the English Channel and in 1901 across the Atlantic from Cornwall to Newfoundland. The first practical applications of wireless transmission were in shipping, but Marconi was extremely diligent in pursuing all other practical uses. An important decision that he made was to shift his research

Marengo, Battle of   See NAPOLEON I.

Maria Cristina of Naples and Spain
See FRANCIS I.

Maria Sofia of Bavaria and Naples   See FRANCIS II.

Maria Theresa (1717–1780)
Austrian archduchess and empress, queen of Bohemia and Hungary (1740–1780)
As heiress to the Habsburg possessions, Maria Theresa ruled over LOMBARDY, which was known then as the state of Milan. Geographically separated from the main body of her imperial possessions in central Europe, Lombardy was important

to Maria Theresa because of its strategic position and economic wealth. It was her only secure possession in Italy, the Austrians having lost ground in the peninsula during the WAR OF THE AUSTRIAN SUCCESSION. The Austrian government recovered much of its influence after the war, thanks to Maria Theresa's policies of cautious reform and marriage alliances. Her husband, FRANCIS STEPHEN OF HABSBURG-LORRAINE, governed Tuscany after the demise of the Medici family, and her daughter MARIE CAROLINE married the king of Naples. In Lombardy, Maria Theresa ruled directly through appointed civil servants who carried out important reforms. They were able to complete a land census (*catasto*) that became the basis for an efficient and equitable system of taxation based on the assessed value of land, abolished the system of farming out the collection of taxes to private individuals and groups, curbed the privileges of the nobility and the church, and laid the foundation for a state bureaucracy based on merit and qualifications. Knowing that the Lombard aristocracy opposed many of these reforms, Maria Theresa urged her administrators to proceed gradually and cautiously. Her moderation persuaded the more enlightened members of the aristocracy to work with her. It was most notably PIETRO VERRI who collaborated with the reformers as long as Maria Theresa lived. After 1765 Maria Theresa ruled jointly with her son JOSEPH II. She restrained his reforming zeal, which, finding no impediment after her death, alienated many of his Lombard subjects.

Marie Caroline (1752–1814)
*queen of Naples and the Two Sicilies
(1768–1814)*

Marie Caroline, daughter of Empress MARIA THERESA of Austria, married King Ferdinand IV of Naples (later King FERDINAND I of the Two Sicilies) in 1768. The marriage was not a happy one, and rumors of infidelity and political intrigue dogged Marie Caroline's reputation from the early years of her reign. Her authority increased when she was admitted to the council of state in 1775.

Strong-willed and definitely pro-Austrian, Marie Caroline sought to eliminate Spanish influence at the court of Naples. In this endeavor she was seconded by her English favorites Sir JOHN FRANCIS ACTON and Lady Emma Hamilton (ca. 1765–1815), who saw the change in foreign policy as advantageous for British interests. Marie Caroline and Ferdinand continued the reforms initiated by Ferdinand's father, King CHARLES OF BOURBON, until the 1790s. The fears provoked by the outbreak of the FRENCH REVOLUTION, and pressure from Austria and Great Britain, caused a reversal of policy that put the Kingdom of Naples on a collision course with France. The royal family abandoned Naples when the pro-French PARTHENOPEAN REPUBLIC came to power in 1799. When they returned later that year, Marie Caroline was blamed for the harsh repression that discredited the ruling dynasty in the eyes of liberal Europe. During the Napoleonic Wars Marie Caroline incurred the displeasure of the British commander Lord WILLIAM BENTINCK by opposing his proposals for political reform. After the royal family returned to Naples in the wake of Napoleon's defeat in 1814, the British forced Marie Caroline to abandon her court. She returned to Vienna and there she died.

Marie Louise of Bourbon   See LUCCA, CITY OF.

Marie Louise of Habsburg   See PARMA, CITY OF.

Marinetti, Filippo Tommaso (1876–1944)
literary and political maverick, founder and promoter of Italian Futurism

Born in Alexandria, Egypt, to a wealthy Italian family, after completing his first studies in that city he continued his education in Paris, Pavia, and Genoa, where he received a law degree. Milan became Marinetti's physical and spiritual home after the family moved there from Alexandria. Influenced more by French than Italian culture, his first major writings were in French. The strongest Italian influence came from GABRIELE D'ANNUNZIO, with whom he shared a fascination for war and a talent for self-promotion. However, Marinetti's writings were anything but D'Annunzian in style, as Marinetti scorned tradition and strove desperately for novelty in all forms of expression. His prose flouted the rules of grammar, syntax, and punctuation, and often resorted to visual gimmicks like the use of geometrical shapes and symbols to make a point rapidly and efficiently. His *Futurist Manifesto* (1909), published in Paris but reflecting the dynamism of industrial Milan, expressed boundless admiration for modern industrial technology and the fast pace of urban living. Marinetti was an effective showman who promoted FUTURISM with countless gimmicks. His activism and glorification of violence and war showed an intellectual affinity for FASCISM, which he supported from beginning to end. Marinetti was initially attracted to fascism by its animal vigor, proclaimed love of danger and adventure, and glorification of the individual. The Fascist regime honored Marinetti and made him a member of the prestigious ITALIAN ACADEMY. A part of the regime's cultural establishment, Marinetti appeared to embrace or condone the official culture that he had previously scorned. The close association with fascism has cast enough of a dark shadow on Marinetti's reputation to stand in the way of a proper appreciation of his originality. Developments in popular culture and the arts attest to his prophetic vision. The flouting of conventional rules of expression, the anti-intellectualism of his intellect, staging of "happenings" for artistic and political purposes, substitution of visual images for words, as in comic books, are all developments that Marinetti anticipated.

Marino, Giambattista (1569–1625)
poet admired for the virtuosity of his language and flamboyant imagery

From an early age Marino showed his willful personality by defying his father, who wanted him to study law, seeking instead the protection of Neapolitan noblemen who were willing to indulge his passion for writing and literature. Born in Naples, Marino lived an adventurous life in Rome, Turin, and Paris, always with the patronage of highly placed personages, including King Louis XIII of France, who idolized him. A self-promoter, Marino relished public attention, mocked other writers, and incurred their hatred. The Genoese poet Gaspare Murtola (died 1624) attempted to assassinate him. Marino returned from Paris in 1623 hailed as Italy's major poet, envied and imitated like no other. His major work, *Adone* (1623), tells the story of the love of Venus for Adonis, depicting the progress of their love from the sensual to the intellectual, and its tragic conclusion with the death of Adonis, who had incurred the jealousy of Mars. In this and many other compositions in verse, Marino displayed a vivid imagination and, most of all, a technical mastery of meter and rhyme that astonished his contemporaries. Marino believed that poetry should strive to amaze and entertain. To do so he often resorted to florid language, extreme elaboration, and bizarre imagery. Known derogatively as *marinismo*, his style is the literary equivalent of the BAROQUE in the visual arts. Carried to excess by Marino's many imitators, *marinismo* has been severely condemned by literary critics as a cerebral and artificial exercise in linguistic virtuosity. It has also been judged negatively because of its association with a low point in Italian political history.

Mario, Alberto (1825–1883)
journalist, volunteer fighter, and publicist for Italian independence

Born in Lendinara (Rovigo) under Austrian rule, educated in a seminary, Mario frequented Italian patriotic clubs in Austrian-ruled Rovigo, and Ferrara where he studied. His friendship with the poet and patriot ALEARDO ALEARDI is said to have filled him with enthusiasm for the cause of Italian independence. During the REVOLUTION of 1848 Mario met GIUSEPPE MAZZINI in Milan and joined the republican movement. In Genoa in the 1850s, he was a newspaper editor and Mazzinian conspirator. Arrested in 1857 with Jessie Meriton White for their role in the CARLO PISACANE affair, the two married in 1858 in England. That same year they toured the United States to raise money for the Italian national cause. They returned to Italy in 1859 to take part in the war against Austria. Although still a republican, Mario distanced himself from Mazzini after the war, drawn to the federalism of CARLO CATTANEO and the charismatic figure of GIUSEPPE GARIBALDI. He followed Garibaldi to Sicily in 1860. Elected to the first national parliament, Mario refused to take the required oath of allegiance to the monarchy and was not allowed to take his seat. He continued to conspire to liberate VENICE and ROME. He was with Garibaldi again in 1867 in the unsuccessful attempt to seize Rome. After 1867 he devoted himself primarily to journalism and writing.

Mario, Jessie Meriton White (1832–1906)

English follower of Mazzini, journalist, and historian

Born in Portsmouth to a family of shipbuilders, she became an enthusiastic supporter of the cause of Italian independence after meeting GIUSEPPE GARIBALDI in 1854. A later meeting with GIUSEPPE MAZZINI turned her into a lifelong admirer and devotee of the Genoese patriot. She abandoned the study of medicine to devote herself to the cause of Italian independence. With her medical knowledge, she was valuable as a nurse in Garibaldi's corps in 1860 and 1870. She was arrested in Genoa in 1857 and jailed for four months on suspicion of conspiring with Mazzini. Upon her return to England in 1858 she married ALBERTO MARIO. Passionate, combative, impetuous, and generous, she developed a lifelong political devotion to Mazzini that caused some friction with her husband, but they continued to collaborate until his death. A tireless and prolific writer, her popular biographies of Garibaldi (1884), Mazzini (1886), and other Risorgimento figures exuded democratic sentiments and helped propagate patriotism among the younger generations. Her journalistic exposé of urban squalor in Naples (1877) brought national attention to the SOUTHERN QUESTION. She deplored the fact that the movement for national independence had brought the monarchy to power and failed to improve the material conditions of the Italian people. Her book *The Birth of Modern Italy* (1909) is an enthusiastic account of the unification movement from a radical-democratic perspective.

Maroncelli, Piero   See PELLICO, SILVIO.

Martin V (1368–1431)
pope (1417–1431)

Oddone Colonna, a member of the powerful COLONNA FAMILY, was elected pope by the Council of Constance (1414–18) that sought to end the Great Schism and reunify the church. The council hoped that the pope would govern by consultation with the cardinals, but Martin V had other ideas. Distrustful of representative assemblies and convinced that the proper administration of church affairs required a strong hand at the helm, Martin enforced papal authority. Taking up residence in Rome in 1420, he faced the awesome task of reconstructing the city that had fallen to ruin during the years of papal residence in Avignon. He was the first of the RENAISSANCE popes to begin the reconsolidation of Christian unity under papal leadership, restore the spiritual authority of the PAPACY, and give it a secure territorial basis. Martin waged successful fights against sovereigns and anti-popes who were reluctant to acknowledge his authority, subdued feudal lords accustomed to governing independently, and brought distinguished artists to Rome to renovate and beautify the city. The work that Martin V initiated was completed by his immediate successors, Eugenius IV (1431–47) and Nicholas V (1447–55). The restoration of the papal monarchy was accomplished by 1450, when Pope Nicholas V proclaimed a jubilee year to draw pilgrims and business to Rome.

Martini, Ferdinando (1841–1928)

writer, political figure, cultural organizer, and publicist

Born in Florence, Martini taught literature and made his literary debut as a journalist and playwright. He was elected to parliament in 1875 and served uninterruptedly in the chamber of deputies until voted out in 1919. In his 44 years in parliament he held important posts in the ministries of education and colonies. In 1884 he became undersecretary in the ministry of public instruction and served as its minister in 1892–93. He was governor of the colony of Eritrea (1897–1907) and minister of colonies (1914–16). In 1914–15 he was a persuasive advocate of Italian intervention in WORLD WAR I, a stand that may have cost him reelection after the war. He was made senator in 1923 and named minister of state in 1927. Readers knew him as a vivacious journalist and elegant writer. He was founding editor of the reviews *Il Fanfulla della Domenica* (1879) and *Domenica Letteraria* (1882) and author of important books of memoirs. His *Diario eritreo* (Eritrean Diary, 1946) is a rare firsthand account of Italian colonial administration.

Masaccio (ca. 1401–1428)

early Renaissance painter and artistic innovator

This Florentine painter, whose real name was Tommaso (Maso) di Ser Giovanni di Mone, is considered the founder of RENAISSANCE painting. Taking up where Giotto (1267–1337) had left off, Masaccio's paintings created the illusion of reality. Few of his paintings have survived. The most important are his frescoes depicting the expulsion of Adam and Eve from the Garden of Eden, and the paying of tribute money, in the Brancacci Chapel in the Church of Santa Maria del Carmine in Florence (1425). His frescoes revolutionized the art of painting by creating the illusion of three-dimensionality in imitation of sculpture, by careful attention to proportion, and by the use of perspective and light to catch and direct the attention of the viewer. His unprece-dented mastery of technique contributed to making his paintings not only lifelike but, more important, capable of conveying powerful messages. Aside from these technical accomplishments, Masaccio excelled at capturing the emotions of the figures and moments that he depicted. His uncanny ability to convey the human element is still evident today, although the contemporary viewer must struggle to recapture the astonishment experienced by Masaccio's contemporaries, who thought that they were seeing life itself in his compositions. The most important artists who came after him studied his paintings and were strongly influenced by them, including RAPHAEL and MICHELANGELO.

Masaniello (1620–1647)

popular leader of an insurrection in Naples

Born Tommaso Aniello in Naples, orphaned at an early age, illiterate, this young fisherman is remembered for his role as the leader of a popular uprising in his native city. The revolt that broke out on July 7, 1647, against the Spanish authorities that governed the city was triggered by a tax on the sale of fruit and the lowering of the official weight of a loaf of bread. Even as they proclaimed their loyalty to the Spanish king, the insurgents burned legal documents, sacked the residences of the nobility, and released prisoners. The popular thinking behind the revolt was that an alliance between the people and the monarch, bypassing the greedy nobility, was the foundation of sound government. Acknowledged as leader of the revolt, Masaniello abolished duties on food, appointed men of the people to administrative posts, and organized a popular militia to defend the city. Masaniello's triumph, however, was short-lived, for he was assassinated one week after winning these concessions from the Spanish viceroy. The revolt continued without him for several months, until it was finally suppressed in the summer of 1648. The Spanish government was alarmed enough by what had happened to initiate a series of reforms. Lowering taxes, curbing the power of the nobility, and appointing commoners to public office pleased the common people, but alienated the nobility from the Spanish crown.

Mascagni, Pietro (1863–1945)
opera composer and conductor

Mascagni was born in Livorno. His father, a baker, wanted his son to become a lawyer. Showing his headstrong nature, the young Mascagni studied music instead. After gaining recognition in his city with some early compositions, in 1882 he began to study music at Milan's prestigious conservatory with help from a wealthy patron. He profited from nearly three years of study under expert teachers, including the composer AMILCARE PONCHIELLI. But he left the conservatory before completing the course of study, impatient to start on his own, eager for recognition, and averse to discipline. Years of deprivation followed. Mascagni joined a traveling operetta troupe, gave piano lessons, quarreled with his family, married, and chafed at the prospect of a dreary life in a small southern town where he had landed his first steady position. In 1888 he entered a contest sponsored by the publishing house of Sonzogno for a one-act opera. The result was the immediate and unexpected success of *Cavalleria rusticana*. Performed in Rome in 1890, it made Mascagni a national celebrity. Mascagni set to music the story of a real-life "crime of honor" as told by GIOVANNI VERGA in a celebrated short story and play. It is a taut drama that depicts dispassionately the passions and actions of ordinary people without any romantic gloss. It was the musical equivalent of literary VERISMO.

Unlike the music of Richard Wagner that appealed to Italy's cultural elites, Mascagni's melodious music and effective theatricality drew popular audiences. Enthusiasm for the opera and its composer ran so high that critics spoke of an epidemic of "Mascagnitis." Mascagni wrote 14 operas after *Cavalleria*, including *L'amico Fritz* (1891), *Guglielmo Ratcliff* (1895), *Iris* (1898), *Le maschere* (1901), *Isabeau* (1911), *Lodoletta* (1917), *Il piccolo Marat* (1921), and *Nerone* (1935). These

Pietro Mascagni *(Library of Congress)*

melodically rich and musically sophisticated compositions reveal Mascagni as an accomplished dramatist and musician, but none was as successful as *Cavalleria rusticana*. Mascagni could never come to terms with the lack of popular success of his later operas. His *Cavalleria* is usually performed today in tandem with RUGGERO LEONCAVALLO's one-act opera *I Pagliacci*. Peevish to a fault, Mascagni feuded with rivals, complained about lack of recognition, and importuned public officials for favors. His efforts to ingratiate himself with BENITO MUSSOLINI are notorious. They were at least partly motivated by the need to dispel the erroneous impression that he was an anti-Fascist. Mascagni was something of a populist, but held no deep political beliefs; he lived for his music, career, and reputation. He died in straitened circumstances in war-torn Rome, complaining to the end that his musical talent was not adequately recognized or rewarded.

Masina, Giulietta See FELLINI, FEDERICO.

Massaia, Guglielmo See COLONIALISM.

Mattei, Enrico (1906–1962)
public entrepreneur, developer of energy resources, and political figure

Born to a working-class family in the small town of Acqualagna (Marches), Mattei began as a factory worker, was active in the Catholic movement, and served as a commander of Christian Democratic formations in the RESISTANCE movement. After the war he was a member of the national council of the Christian Democratic Party (DC) and served in the chamber of deputies (1948–53). Charged immediately after the war with closing down AGIP, the national petroleum agency founded by the Fascist regime, Mattei used his position to undertake exploration of oil and natural gas in the Po Valley (1946–47). The discovery of sizable gas deposits and his strong political connections enabled Mattei to replace AGIP with ENI, the new national oil agency, in 1953. As president of ENI, Mattei promoted energy development, distribution, and consumption, often resorting to political pressure and bribery to obtain favors and concessions. Determined to break the hold of American companies on Italy's oil supplies, in 1957 he signed an agreement with Iran, later extended to Morocco, whereby ENI assumed the costs of extracting oil in return for only 25 percent of the profits rather than the 50 percent demanded by other oil companies. In 1960 Mattei also concluded a deal with the Soviet Union to import Russian oil. American oil producers and government officials suspected that he might be moving toward a neutralist foreign policy and aiming to withdraw Italy from NATO. His death in a plane crash fueled conspiracy theories alleging involvement by business competitors, the CIA, and the MAFIA. Public and private investigations have confirmed nothing. Mattei's controversial energy policies are credited with contributing to the Italian ECONOMIC MIRACLE by increasing the supply of energy fivefold in the 1950s.

Matteotti, Giacomo (1885–1924)
Socialist Party leader and opponent of the Fascist regime

Matteotti was born to a prosperous family of landowners in the Po Valley town of Fratta Polesine, received a law degree from the University of Bologna, and was an active organizer for the Socialist Party (PSI) in his native region. A moderate Socialist in the manner of FILIPPO TURATI, whom he followed, Matteotti was elected to parliament in 1919. He was respected for his sober style and solid preparation. In 1924 he became party secretary. Following the national elections of May 1924, in which the Fascists and their supporters had won a large majority, Matteotti delivered in parliament a well-documented denunciation of Fascist abuses and intimidations in the electoral campaign. He asked parliament to annul the elections in which the Fascists and their allies had won a decisive majority. The speech angered BENITO MUSSOLINI and inflamed political passions. On June 10, 1924, Fascist toughs abducted Matteotti on his way to parliament. He was killed, apparently in the ensuing struggle inside the abductors' automobile. His body was discovered buried in the Roman countryside on August 15. The political crisis that followed threatened the survival of the Fascist regime. Fascists close to Mussolini were implicated in the assassination, including EMILIO DE BONO, who as minister of the interior was the official ultimately in charge of law and order. De Bono resigned. The actual perpetrators, all minor figures, were brought to trial, found guilty, and given light prison sentences. Mussolini himself came under suspicion, but charges that he had personally ordered the action were never proven. Mussolini rode out the storm. The protests eventually subsided. King VICTOR EMMANUEL III did not use his constitutional powers to remove him from office. Addressing parliament on January 3, 1925, Mussolini dared the opposition to bring charges against him. Fascist squads took to the streets and imposed a reign of terror against opponents of the regime. The subsequent purging of political opponents from parliament, the use of the secret police, and the enactment of special laws eliminating freedom of speech and political liberties inaugurated one-party rule and Mussolini's personal dictatorship.

Matteucci, Carlo See SCIENCE.

Mazzei, Filippo (1730–1816)
writer, traveler, diplomat, friend and adviser to Thomas Jefferson
Mazzei was typical of educated Italians who, in the Age of ENLIGHTENMENT, traveled widely and took advantage of opportunities outside Italy. He was born in Poggio a Caiano, near Florence, studied and practiced medicine, traveled widely in Europe, Asia Minor, and the American colonies. Wherever he went he won the confidence of important personages who made use of his services. In London, where he taught Italian and dabbled in commerce, he met Benjamin Franklin, who advised him to go to Virginia. Arriving there in 1773, he was befriended by the leaders of that colony, including Thomas Jefferson. As a gentleman farmer, with the help of Jefferson he introduced into the colonies European crops and plant species, including varieties of grapevines for wine production. He returned to Europe in 1779 to seek support for the American Revolution, but was captured by the English. He was back in Virginia in 1783. In 1785 he joined Jefferson in Paris. From 1789 to 1792 he was the Paris representative of the king of Poland. His dispatches throw light on the course of the French Revolution. In 1792 he moved to Warsaw. The partition of Poland that year put an end to Mazzei's diplomatic career. In his retirement in Pisa he wrote profusely, including a book of memoirs translated into English as *Philip Mazzei: My Life and Wanderings* (1980). He also wrote a four-volume history of the United States of America published in French (1788). In 1797 Mazzei caused a political furor in the United States when he published a letter from Jefferson imputing monarchist sentiments to his Federalist opponents.

Mazzini, Giuseppe (1805–1872)
inspirer of the Italian unification movement, tireless conspirator, and democrat
Born in Genoa to a family of the upper middle class (his father was a respected medical doctor and university professor, his mother a well-educated woman), Mazzini received a law degree from the University of Genoa (1827). As a student he was attracted more to literature and political conspiracy than to law, which he practiced briefly. He joined the secret CARBONERIA society, was arrested and jailed. In 1830 he chose to go into voluntary exile in France rather than submit to political confinement. In Marseilles he founded YOUNG ITALY, a patriotic society committed to republicanism and democracy. Its members swore to proselytize and fight for democracy, national independence, and unity, and to wage relentless war on tyrants. Thousands of exiles and recruits from different parts of Italy joined the organization. In 1833 Mazzini moved to Geneva, from where he planned insurrections in Italy. When his attempts failed, he turned his attention to Europe. Young Europe, which he founded in 1834, sought to stir revolution among oppressed nationalities from Ireland to Russia.

Mazzini was the first to envisage a coordinated European revolutionary movement based on popular support. FILIPPO MICHELE BUONARROTI, a rival, relied instead on the secret methods of the Carbonari and on professional conspirators.

Political persecution forced Mazzini to leave Switzerland for England in 1837. He made London his headquarters and spent most of the rest of his life there, trying to stir up revolution in Italy and other countries in Europe. He opened a school for the children of Italian workers, reorganized Young Italy, supported conspiracies, engaged in political debates, and won international recognition as the voice of oppressed nationalities. Although he devoted his life to the fight for national independence, he refused to call himself a nationalist. He regarded family and nation as institutions that brought individuals together and connected them to humanity as a whole. Loyalty to the nation could not become the ultimate form of allegiance without breaking that essential continuity between the individual and humanity.

He returned to Italy when revolution broke out in 1848, took charge of the ROMAN REPUBLIC, and defended it against French, Austrian, Neapolitan, and Spanish troops sent to suppress it. The failure of revolution in 1848–49 did not discourage Mazzini. He continued to agitate for national unity, for the abolition of papal rule, and for Rome as the national capital. In Mazzini's eyes, Rome stood for Italy's greatness and universal mission in the modern world. Rome governed by the Italian people was to be a beacon of civilization in the modern world. Throughout the 1850s he continued to work for Italian unification, as control of the movement slipped out of his hands and was taken over by moderate liberals who did not share Mazzini's vision or his republican sentiments. CAVOUR and GIUSEPPE GARIBALDI took the lead in the political events of 1859–60 that saw the country unified as a monarchy.

Mazzini's republicanism differentiated him from both monarchists and socialists. Well before 1848 he had made clear his differences with socialists. He championed worker interests and appealed for worker support on the basis of an associational philosophy that called for cooperation across class lines. Unity of workers and employers, educated and uneducated, was an essential precondition for the triumph of demo-cratic movements. Anything else would lead to forms of tyranny, whether by individuals or groups. In 1860 he published *Doveri dell'uomo* (The duties of man). It was addressed to workers, to remind them that they had both rights and obligations, to urge them to be aware of both their material and spiritual needs and forge alliances among themselves and across class lines.

The reference to spiritual needs underlies the importance that Mazzini attached to religion. He was deeply religious, but in a way that did not conform to any established creed or theology. He believed in God and in the immortality of the soul, but rejected the doctrinal and ritual aspects of Christianity. He condemned papal authority, but admired the universal spirit and institutional basis of the CATHOLIC CHURCH. He would have liked to see the Catholic Church adopt a form of democratic governance, but felt that the Protestant denominations had gone too far in that direction. In the final years of his life, he had good reason to be disappointed. Italian unification was an accomplished fact, but not as he wanted it. Italy was governed by a monarchy, the young were indifferent to his ideas, workers turned to socialism, and papal authority grew stronger. Mazzini returned to Italy in 1871 when he had only a few months left to live. He returned under an assumed name because the government still banned him as a dangerous radical. A controversial figure in his lifetime, Mazzini was eventually revered as the "soul" of the RISORGIMENTO.

Meda, Filippo (1869–1939)
member of parliament, journalist, pioneering figure of Christian Democracy

Meda was born in Milan to an observant Catholic family. A lawyer and teacher, he turned to journalism in 1889, becoming editor and publisher of the Milanese paper *L'Osservatore Cattolico* (1898–1902). The paper urged Catholics to play an active role in society, abandon their intransigent opposition to the state, and reclaim their lost political influence. Catholics had to form a political movement of their own and engage in electoral politics at both the local and national levels. Meda became the chief spokesman for this brand of political Catholicism, and took advantage of the relaxation of the papal prohibition against voting in national elections to run for parliament. Elected in 1909, he led a group of about 20 Catholics in parliament, and was one of the architects of the so-called GENTILONI PACT that advised Catholics to vote for liberal candidates who opposed anticlericals and socialists. Meda did not advocate automatic cooperation with the liberal majority. He supported the government on the crucial question of intervention in WORLD WAR I and urged Catholics to support the war effort. He served as finance minister (1916–19) and treasury minister (1920–21). A founder of the Popular Party (PPI), Meda turned down invitations to form his own government in 1922, deferring to party leader LUIGI STURZO, who did not want to cooperate with liberals. Failed cooperation of liberals, socialists, and Catholics is thought to be a major reason for the victory of FASCISM. Meda's own role in this regard is mixed. He urged Catholic deputies not to participate in Mussolini's government, but supported the ACERBO LAW that enabled Fascists to consolidate their hold on parliament. He withdrew from politics in 1925, refusing a government offer of a senate seat. In private life he served as president of the Banca Popolare of Milan and was a founder of the Catholic University of the Sacred Heart.

Medici, Cosimo de' (1389–1464)
banker, founder of Medici rule in Florence, patron of artists and scholars

Cosimo the Elder was the effective founder of Medici rule in Renaissance FLORENCE. He inherited wealth from his father, Giovanni di Bicci, but to wealth Cosimo added political clout. Acceptance did not come easily. Families of the old aristocracy like the Albizzi and Strozzi regarded Cosimo as an upstart, feared him, and had him banished from Florence in 1433. He returned a year later to a tumultuous welcome, praised as the fair and generous champion of the people. Cosimo was careful to preserve the trappings of republican government, did not assume princely airs or titles, professed himself a good citizen of Florence and a devout Christian. He preferred the velvet glove to the iron fist and diplomacy to war. A practical man, he understood that artists and intellectuals could burnish his image, and encouraged them accordingly. His many construction projects included the Medici palace, which was the largest structure built up to that time. He bought manuscripts and founded libraries. Under his stewardship Florence became the center of HUMANISM. His far-flung business interests and broad vision made him look beyond the Florentine state. Perhaps his most important foreign policy decision was to end the traditional rivalry between Florence and Milan by signing the Peace of Lodi with FRANCESCO SFORZA (1454). At his death, the Florentines bestowed on him the title of *Pater Patriae* (Father of the Country).

Medici, Giulio de' See CLEMENT VII.

Medici, Lorenzo de' (1449–1492)
prominent member of the Medici dynasty, diplomat, patron of the arts

Dubbed *Il Magnifico* (The Magnificent) in recognition of his special status as the unofficial head of the Florentine state and of his generosity as a patron of the arts, Lorenzo personifies the Renaissance ruler. Without ever holding a princely title and while maintaining the trappings of representative republican government, Lorenzo dominated Florentine politics after the death of his father, Piero de' Medici, in 1469. Piero, who had inherited his position from his father, COSIMO the Elder, had not been an effective ruler. His five-year rule had been marred by civil unrest. The 23 years of Lorenzo's rule were a period of relative peace and security for Florence. Lorenzo was not a good administrator, squandering much of the family patrimony, but the Florentine economy did well.

Intelligent and well educated, he was a discerning patron of artists and writers, whose careers he advanced both directly and indirectly by commissioning works for himself and by recommending them to other wealthy patrons. He was himself a writer of considerable talent. He could be ruthless against political opponents, of which there were many among the families of the Florentine nobility. Members of the Pazzi family plotted to assassinate him and his younger brother Giuliano. They struck in church on April 26, 1478. Lorenzo escaped with his life, and struck back with an orgy of executions, sentences of exile, and confiscations that terrified all his opponents. But that was an exceptional case. Lorenzo was not overbearing as a rule, for he did not want to antagonize unnecessarily.

His diplomacy aimed at containing and managing conflicts of interest among the Italian states and avoiding war. He made Florence the linchpin of a system of alliances designed to prevent dominance by any single state. Florence gained territory without upsetting the balance of power on which his diplomacy rested. Lorenzo's achievements did not make him universally popular. Prominent families felt threatened by his power and prominence, but there was little they could do as long as he lived. In the last years of Lorenzo's life, his enemies began to rally around the popular friar GIROLAMO SAVONAROLA, a critic of the Medici whom Lorenzo himself had invited to preach in Florence in 1490. The revolt came against Lorenzo's son and successor, Piero, who ruled from 1492 to 1494. The insurgents expelled the Medici from Florence and enacted constitutional reforms to prevent a recurrence of personal rule. The MEDICI FAMILY returned to rule Florence in 1512, after years of war and domestic conflict.

Medici, Luigi de' (1759–1830)
Neapolitan political figure, reformer, and diplomat

A descendant of the Neapolitan branch of the MEDICI FAMILY, Luigi Medici received a law degree and practiced law. In 1783 he joined the state administration and was appointed to a politically

influential judicial post. JOHN ACTON, perhaps jealous of his mounting influence, had him arrested in 1795 on the false charge that he sympathized with revolutionary JACOBINS. Medici eventually regained political favor and held important posts in Sicily under Bourbon rule (1806–14). He represented the Kingdom of Naples at the CONGRESS OF VIENNA (1814–15), presided over the fusion of Naples and Sicily and the birth of the KINGDOM OF THE TWO SICILIES (1816), and negotiated a concordat between Naples and the PAPACY (1818). He was in effect the king's chief minister and the dominant influence in Naples in the early years of the RESTORATION. His opposition to constitutional monarchy angered liberals, but Medici was evenhanded in other respects. He banned both liberal and conservative secret societies; he did not restore confiscated properties to religious orders but gave religious authorities the power to ban undesirable publications; he kept political reprisals to a minimum and retained civil servants who had worked for the Napoleonic administration. Medici was essentially a pragmatic functionary who sought to keep politics out of the public administration. An expert in financial matters, he worked to keep the government solvent, encouraged economic development, and steered a middle course between reaction and revolution. Temporarily ousted by the REVOLUTION of 1821, Medici returned to power after the revolution and shaped government policy until his death. An important achievement of his last years was the negotiated withdrawal of Austrian troops from Naples in 1827.

Medici del Vascello, Giacomo (1819–1882)
patriot, military figure, and public official

Born to a politically liberal Lombard family, Giacomo followed his father into political exile in Spain, where the father fought against the conservative Carlists. A follower of GIUSEPPE MAZZINI (who sent Giacomo to summon GIUSEPPE GARIBALDI back from South America), Giacomo was one of the first to abandon Mazzini for Garibaldi in the REVOLUTIONS of 1848. Medici played an important role in the defense of Rome in 1849, holding out against overwhelming odds in a fortified position called the Vascello, hence the title of marchese del Vascello that he received in 1876. He was at Garibaldi's side again in 1859 and 1860, after which he transferred to the regular army with the rank of general. In 1866, again at Garibaldi's side, he was awarded a gold medal for military valor. His efficient repression of the antigovernment uprising of September 1866 and vigorous law enforcement won him the enmity of democrats, who accused him of selling out to the monarchy and betraying the people. Perhaps better than any other RISORGIMENTO figure, Giacomo Medici illustrates the conversion from republicanism to monarchism and from moderately liberal to moderately conservative positions, common among those who fought for national independence.

Medici family
Florentine banking family that ruled in Florence and Tuscany

The richest family in Europe ruled the Florentine republic first, then the grand duchy of Tuscany, intermarried with the most powerful families, gave two queens to France, and three popes to the CATHOLIC CHURCH. The Medici emerged from rural obscurity in the 13th century. They may have started out as pharmacists or physicians, as suggested by the three round shapes, which may represent pills, in the family coat of arms. The shapes were interpreted variously at the time. Supporters and detractors alike often called out *palle, palle* (balls, balls) to express their feelings. The first prominent member of the family was Giovanni di Bicci (1360–1429), who consolidated the family business in banking and money-changing. He fathered two sons, COSIMO (called the Elder) and Lorenzo, and from them sprang the two main branches of the family. Cosimo's descendants included LORENZO the Magnificent, Giulio (Pope CLEMENT VII), Gio-

vanni (Pope LEO X), and Catherine (1519–89), who married King Henry II of France. Lorenzo's descendants included the famed and feared captain of fortune Giovanni delle Bande Nere (1498–1526), Marie (1573–1642), second wife of King Henry IV of France, and a long list of grand dukes of Tuscany, who inherited the throne after the death of the last direct descendant of Cosimo, Duke Alessandro (1510–37). Alessandro, an unworthy scamp, is the ruler to whom NICCOLÒ MACHIAVELLI dedicated *The Prince*. The third Medici pope, Leo XI (1605), lived a mere three months after his election.

The Medici were evicted from Florence in 1494, but returned in 1512. Caught in the rivalry between France and Spain, they sided with the Spanish imperial cause, receiving the hereditary title of dukes of Florence from Emperor CHARLES V in 1532. Cosimo I (1519–74) ruled as duke of Florence (1537–69) and as grand duke of Tuscany (1569–74). A ruler of vision, he curbed the power of nobles, eliminated the last vestiges of republicanism, and created a centralized state administration. His successors were Francesco (1574–87), Ferdinand I (1587–1609)), Cosimo II (1609–21), Ferdinand II (1621–70), Cosimo III (1670–1723), and Gian Gastone (1723–37). Like Cosimo the Elder and Lorenzo the Magnificent, these latter-day Medici were liberal patrons of artists, scholars, and scientists. GALILEO was one of their protégés. But unlike their better-known predecessors, they were not economic powerhouses and ruled with the support of foreign powers. The dynasty ended with the death of the childless Gian Gastone in 1737. Its demise came at a bad time for native Italian rulers, who were being replaced by foreign families. The great powers awarded the Grand Duchy of Tuscany to FRANCIS OF LORRAINE, husband of Empress MARIA THERESA of Austria. Italian states were becoming possessions of foreign rulers, mostly for the benefit of the Austrian Habsburgs.

Mediobanca See CUCCIA, ENRICO.

Mediterranean Agreements

Two international agreements were signed in 1887 to protect the status quo in the Mediterranean area and provide compensations if changes in the status quo occurred. The diplomatic representatives of Great Britain, Italy, Austria-Hungary, Germany, and Spain signed the first Mediterranean Agreement in February 1887. The signatories agreed to respect the status quo and to compensate Italy with territorial concessions in North Africa and/or the Balkans should changes occur. The second Mediterranean Agreement, signed in December 1887 by the representatives of Great Britain, Austria-Hungary, and Italy, referred specifically to maintaining the status quo in the eastern Mediterranean and Black Sea regions. The first agreement was directed against France, the second against Russia. The agreements marked a victory for Italian diplomacy, and most signally for the policies of Foreign Minister Count Carlo Felice Nicolis di Robilant (1826–88). Robilant's diplomacy increased Italy's security in the Mediterranean, created obstacles to French designs on Morocco and Tripolitania, improved relations with Great Britain, and gave Italy a say in Balkan affairs. The Mediterranean Agreements were a step on the road to COLONIALISM and the acquisition of Libya.

Mediterranean Sea

In the world's largest inland sea (Mediterranean means "in the middle of land" in Latin), the Italian peninsula occupies a central position. This geographical reality has important consequences for Italy. Three of the Mediterranean's four subdivisions surround the peninsula: the Tyrrhenian Sea to the west, Ionian Sea to the South, and Adriatic Sea to the east. The Aegean Sea, the Mediterranean's fourth subdivision, is not far, and Italian states have always followed developments in that body of water that touches the shores of Greece and Turkey. From the time of ancient Rome's struggle against Carthage, Italian states have faced the dilemma of dominating the

Mediterranean or establishing a modus vivendi with another dominant sea power. The empire of ancient Rome was essentially a Mediterranean empire. The Pax Romana (Peace of Rome) brought security and stability to the Mediterranean world, and the empire declined when Rome could no longer control the sea. Italian maritime city-states eventually wrested control of the Mediterranean from Byzantines and Muslims. From the 13th century to the 16th, the fleets of GENOA and VENICE, with some competition early on from PISA, plied the waters of the Mediterranean from Spain to the Near East. Control of Mediterranean trade routes was the geopolitical and economic basis of the Italian RENAISSANCE. Venice, the most successful and enduring of these maritime powers, was the key intermediary between the Near East and Europe.

The period of Spanish dominance of the Mediterranean saw the Kingdom of NAPLES rise in importance as a Spanish vice royalty. But Naples was never able to capitalize on its privileged central position. Politically dependent on outside powers and confined to the southern half of the peninsula, separated from the rest of Europe by rival states, it could not play the role of intermediary. An unlikely candidate, the Kingdom of SARDINIA, took up that role in the 19th century. Almost landlocked until it acquired Genoa in 1815, it built up a respectable navy, repressed piracy, and developed new trade routes in the Mediterranean and Atlantic. CAVOUR, the kingdom's prime minister in the 1850s, built railroads to move goods, improved communications with northern Europe, expanded the navy, and negotiated advantageous trade treaties.

The opening of the Suez Canal in 1869 augured well for Mediterranean commerce and Italy's economic future, but also intensified international rivalries. Great Britain was now the dominant naval power and the Mediterranean was part of the imperial lifeline to India. Italy could not afford to antagonize such a power. Maintaining friendly relations with Great Britain became an axiom of Italian FOREIGN POLICY. Its international commitments, including those to Great Britain's rivals or enemies, were not allowed to jeopardize the British connection. The large navy that Italy built in the 1880s was never meant to challenge British control of the Mediterranean, but rather to serve as an adjunct to the British in case of conflict with France, for France was the country that Italy saw as its main Mediterranean and colonial rival.

Only the Fascist regime reversed the established policy of friendship with Great Britain, pursuing instead the alternative of Italian dominance of *mare nostrum* (Our Sea). Indeed, Fascist foreign policy looked beyond Italy's position in the Mediterranean. The capture of the British strongholds of Gibraltar and Suez would give Italy unrestricted access to the oceans. Adequate resources never backed this grand vision. Italy's decisive defeat in WORLD WAR II ended the Fascist regime's dreams of dominance. It also had a lasting impact on Italian policy, which reverted to the alternative of staying on good terms with the dominant power. The fact that the new power was that of the United States meant that Italian foreign policy would be pro-American. The U.S. Sixth Fleet, stationed in the Mediterranean since the end of World War II, visits Italian ports regularly and has access to Italian bases. The Italian navy plays a significant but subsidiary role in military and humanitarian interventions in the Balkans and eastern Mediterranean.

The realignment of world politics since the end of the cold war puts Italy on the north-south fault line of political instability that runs through the Mediterranean Sea. Italy remains sensitive and vulnerable to developments in the troubled regions of the Mediterranean world. Its long, exposed coastline attracts large numbers of legal and illegal immigrants from North Africa, the Balkans, and places farther east. Italy appears to be reverting to its ancient role as a place of arrival for millions of people. How Italians respond to developments in the Mediterranean remains to be seen. What is clear is that they will be intimately affected by what happens in and around the body of water that belongs to a multitude of people.

Melzi d'Eril, Francesco (1753–1816)
Lombard aristocrat, collaborator of Napoleon, and political reformer

Count Francesco Melzi belonged to a distinguished Milanese family prominent in the cultural and political life of Lombardy. Well traveled, of refined tastes, a lover of the arts, fluent in Italian, French, Spanish, and German, Melzi sat on Milan's administrative council and held various diplomatic posts in the service of Austria under JOSEPH II and PETER LEOPOLD. These two monarchs personified for Melzi the ideal of the good ruler and he joined other Lombard reformers in supporting their governments. Melzi believed in reform but was personally hostile to revolution, republicanism, and democracy. Initially well disposed toward revolutionary France, he disavowed the revolution when it turned radical. NAPOLEON trusted Melzi and in 1802 appointed him vice president of the Italian republic, over which he himself presided. With Napoleon busy elsewhere, Melzi had much discretion in northern Italy and used his power to promote reform in the spirit of the ENLIGHTENMENT. His legislation regulated the church, made education the criterion for appointment to civil service posts, curbed local autonomies, expanded the power of central government, created a ministry of public education, and enacted laissez-faire reforms to stimulate the economy. Even as he followed Napoleon's lead, Melzi claimed maximum autonomy for his administration. For that reason he is seen as a precursor of the Italian independence movement, but his ideal was a robust kingdom of northern Italy allied to France, rather than a truly independent national state. He left public service in 1805 when Napoleon transformed the Italian republic into the Kingdom of Italy. Napoleon was intent on establishing his own family dynasty and appointed his brother-in-law EUGENE DE

BEAUHARNAIS as viceroy. In 1807 Napoleon rewarded Melzi by conferring on him the title of duke of Lodi.

Menabrea, Luigi Federico (1809–1896)
*general, political figure, loyal to the ruling
House of Savoy*

Menabrea was born in Chambéry (Savoy), studied engineering in Turin, joined the engineering corps of the Piedmontese army as a lieutenant, and taught geometry and mechanical engineering at Turin's military academy (1839–49). His politics during this period of his life leaned toward the democrats, but the REVOLUTIONS of 1848, and fear of republicanism and socialism turned him in the opposite direction. Fearful that constitutional government might degenerate into something more radical, he called for curbs on freedom of expression and defended the Catholic Church against its critics. He served in the Piedmontese parliament from 1848 to 1860, not openly opposed but critical of CAVOUR's policies. He returned to military service in 1859, conducted operations against the Austrians and against the papal army, and was made senator in the Italian parliament in 1860. He served as minister of the navy (1861–62), public works (1862–64) and in several other political and diplomatic posts before becoming prime minister (1867–69). Suspected of being the king's tool and of harboring antiparliamentary designs, Menabrea became the target of violent attacks by the LIBERAL LEFT. He was the prime minister who ordered the arrest of GARIBALDI after he tried to take Rome by force in 1867. That lost him the confidence of parliament, but the king retained him in office nevertheless, confident that he was the man to deal with the political and financial crisis facing the government. Menabrea took the politically dangerous step of adopting the hated *MACINATO* tax, repressed popular disturbances, and governed with the help of experts rather than politicians. Implicated in a financial scandal involving the operations of the state tobacco monopoly and accused of being a reactionary, he was forced to resign against the wishes of King VICTOR EMMANUEL II. In 1870 he took the politically unpopular position of opposing the transfer of the national capital to Rome out of a sense of legitimacy and respect for the pope. The posts of ambassador to London (1876–82) and Paris (1882–92) were the last that he held before retiring from public life.

Mengoni, Giuseppe See ARCHITECTURE.

Menichella, Donato See BANCA D'ITALIA.

Menotti, Ciro (1798–1831)
*patriotic figure, political conspirator, and
victim*

Menotti was born near the town of Carpi in the Duchy of MODENA, was a textiles merchant by profession, and a political liberal by avocation. In the 1820s he was active in the CARBONERIA and in contact with its secret master Filippo Buonarroti. In the course of murky secret understandings that have never been fully clarified, with the Modenese conspirator Enrico Misley (1801–63) acting as mediator, Menotti attempted to involve Duke FRANCIS IV, ruler of Modena, in a plot that would give the duke the title of king over an enlarged state, including eventually the territories belonging to Charles Albert of Piedmont, in return for the duke's promise to govern as a constitutional monarch. The duke seems to have encouraged Menotti to proceed with the plot. It is not clear whether he did so in the hope of actually enlarging his domain (he was known to want to govern a larger state than the tiny duchy) or to keep track of the plot in order to quash it at the right moment. The fact remains that in February 1831 the duke had Menotti arrested and took the prisoner with him when he was forced to leave Modena after an uprising of his subjects. Menotti was tried, found guilty of political subversion, and executed in May 1831. Menotti's martyrdom became part of

RISORGIMENTO history and patriotic mythmaking. He is a good example of the type of patriot still tied to the conspiratorial tactics of the SECRET SOCIETIES, who relied on the collaboration of rulers to carry out their programs of reform.

Mentana, Battle of See GARIBALDI, GIUSEPPE.

meridionalisti See SOUTHERN QUESTION.

Merlin, Angelina (1889–1979)
journalist, active anti-Fascist, and feminist
A middle-school teacher who joined the Socialist Party (PSI) in 1919, Angelina (Lina) Merlin won attention with articles on worker issues published in labor union journals. Fascist authorities removed her from her teaching post in 1926 for subversive activities; she spent five years in political confinement. After her release she was active in the clandestine anti-Fascist movement. In 1943 she joined the RESISTANCE. She was a founder of the Gruppi di Difesa della Donna (Women Defense Groups) that mobilized women for participation in the armed resistance. After the war Merlin served in the Constituent Assembly that prepared the postwar CONSTITUTION (1946–48) and in the senate (1948–76). Issues of women's rights and public morality were her special concern. Both issues merged in the public campaign and parliamentary battle to abolish legalized prostitution. The controversial 1958 law that abolished public regulation of prostitution is still remembered as the Merlin Law (Legge Merlin).

Merlino, Francesco Saverio (1856–1930)
socialist theoretician and activist
Born in Naples, he joined the anarchist movement while still a student, received a law degree, and successfully defended anarchist prisoners accused of killing a policeman (1877–78). In 1884 Merlino fled abroad to avoid serving a jail sentence and spent the next 10 years traveling, making contacts with Italian workers in various countries, and familiarizing himself with the currents of socialist thought. He returned to Italy clandestinely in 1894, was apprehended, and served two years in jail. By that time he had abandoned anarchism and was an active participant in the international debate on the nature and prospects of socialism. His writings show Merlino trying to define a highly personal form of socialism that combined political militancy with the pursuit of concrete gains for workers. He rejected Marxist socialism for its authoritarian tendencies, materialism, and stress on class warfare, was attracted by and in turn influenced the revolutionary syndicalism of Georges Sorel, with whom he corresponded, emphasized the role of will and initiative, and called for a socialism based on grounds of social justice rather than material gain. In his view, socialism required a long period of gestation and would emerge gradually as a result of economic, cultural, and political transformations that required steady commitment to the ultimate revolutionary goal. Merlino's goal of radically transforming society was to be achieved gradually to avoid the opposing dangers of coercion and dilution. He rejected the drift toward reformist policies personified by ANDREA COSTA and attempted to infuse a stronger sense of discipline and organization into the workers' movement. Merlino's message was lost in the enthusiasm for political revolution that swept through the ranks of socialism in the wake of WORLD WAR I and the Russian Revolution.

Metastasio, Pietro (1698–1782)
poet, playwright, and librettist
Pietro Metastasio was born in Rome as Pietro Trapassi, the son of a small shopkeeper. His talent for poetic improvisation revealed itself at an early age and caught the attention of Gian Vincenzo Gravina (1664–1718), a noted scholar and literary critic, who took the youngster under his

wing and adopted him as his own son. It was Gravina who changed the boy's name to Metastasio, meaning transformed. He received a rigorous humanistic education, took minor orders, studied music and law, and became a full-time writer after the success of his first plays. He settled in Naples in 1719. A prolific writer with a seemingly inexhaustible capacity for turning out perfectly crafted, melodious verse, easy on the ear and inoffensive, Metastasio wrote melodramas of passion and intrigue, opera libretti, verses for special occasions, and *ariette* (little arias) suitable for drawing room entertainment. Familiarity with his verses was considered part of a proper education and a sign of social refinement, especially for young ladies who wanted to establish their marriage credentials. In 1730 Emperor Charles VI called Metastasio to Vienna to succeed APOSTOLO ZENO as court poet. Metastasio spent the rest of his life in Vienna, writing dramas for the court, odes for official occasions, lyrics for composers, and some works of literary criticism. As a literary critic he argued that theater should strive for the simplicity of ancient Greek drama, integrate music and the spoken word, convey morally uplifting messages in decorous forms, and avoid the excesses of the BAROQUE style. At their best, his verses express gentle human insight, tenderness, and delicacy of feeling; however, all too often they are superficial and perfunctory. Metastasio is often regarded as the typical poet of the ENLIGHTENMENT, but he was not receptive to the Enlightenment's aspirations for cultural renewal, and rejected an invitation to contribute to Diderot's *Encyclopédie*. Praised in his lifetime as the greatest of poets, Metastasio was soon forgotten or dismissed as a mere entertainer. He was nevertheless the voice of a culture that aspired to noble ideals.

mezzadria

Mezzadria occupies an intermediate position between direct cultivation, in which the land is owned and worked by the same person or family, and commercial farming, in which the owner pays transient laborers a daily wage to perform specified services. Often translated as "sharecropping," it is dissimilar from American sharecropping in one important respect. In the classic form of *mezzadria* that prevailed in central Italy, the *mezzadri* (sharecroppers) were protected by long-term leases on land and housing that gave them security and stability on the land, often for 20 years or longer. Contracts specified the kinds of crops to be grown and methods of cultivation. Tenant and landlord usually shared produce on a 50/50 basis, with frequent exceptions to the rule, usually in the landlord's favor. Landlords provided land suitable for cultivation, housing, some operating capital, and sometimes tools or machinery. The farmstead with housing and equipment was called a *podere* (holding). Tenant families typically supplied labor and tools, and were held collectively responsible for fulfilling contractual obligations. *Mezzadria* required large extended families working together in tightly organized and disciplined fashion. It was usually the oldest male member (*capoccia*) who organized work on the land, and the oldest woman (*massaia*) who was responsible for running the household. The *capoccia* and *massaia* had absolute authority in their respective domains, and their authority extended also to questions of marriage, for the number and character of individuals brought into the family affected the ability of the family as a whole to fulfill its obligations.

Sharecropping arrangements could be found everywhere, but *mezzadria* in its classic form existed in the central regions of MARCHES, TUSCANY, and UMBRIA. In the 19th century the system provided reasonable profits for the landowners and security for tenants. Both sides therefore regarded it as economically and socially desirable. By the beginning of the 20th century the system was in crisis. The type of mixed farming associated with *mezzadria* discouraged crop specialization, cash-starved tenants produced a variety of crops to minimize their recourse to market, and labor-intensive techniques raised costs of production. Labor organizers mobilized farmworkers and sharecroppers for collective action. As workers and tenants became more militant, *mezzadria* lost its social incentive: It was no longer a safeguard against class conflict. The system survived two world wars thanks in part to contractual and land legislation that kept people on the land. The demise of *mezzadria* came after WORLD WAR II, when it succumbed to the flight of people from the land, the modernization of farming, and the loosening of family ties.

Mezzogiorno   See SOUTHERN QUESTION.

Micca, Pietro   See SPANISH SUCCESSION, WAR OF THE.

Michelangelo Buonarroti (1475–1564)
sculptor, painter, architect, and writer regarded as the culmination of Renaissance art

Michelangelo (also Michelangiolo) was born in the small mountain village of Caprese in the Tuscan Apennines where his father, Lodovico Buonarroti, an impoverished gentleman, was serving as governor. The family moved back to FLORENCE soon after the boy's birth, and it was with Florentine political and cultural traditions that Michelangelo identified for his entire life. The boy's talent for sculpture manifested itself early, but family expectations stood in the way of an artistic career for the boy. Gentry like Michelangelo's parents regarded art as a form of manual labor, and therefore as socially demeaning. Parental reluctance overcome, in 1488 Michelangelo was apprenticed to the studio of the painter Domenico Ghirlandaio (1449–94), where he learned the technique of painting on fresco. After only a year of training, the boy was invited into the household of LORENZO DE MEDICI, where he developed his passion for marble sculpture by studying ancient relics and the art of DONATELLO. In Lorenzo's household he learned to identify with the Florentine political

Michelangelo *(Library of Congress)*

and cultural elites. The sculptures dating from this period show the combination of beauty of form and Christian piety that was the hallmark of Michelangelo's art.

After the death of Lorenzo in 1492 Michelangelo went to ROME, where he completed one of his best-known works, the *Pietà* that is now in St. Peter's Basilica. Back in Florence in 1501, he completed the *David* (1504) before being summoned back to Rome by Pope JULIUS II. Michelangelo never completed the pope's tomb that was his principal commission, but did finish the imposing figure of *Moses* that adorns Julius's tomb in the Church of San Pietro in Vincoli. A quarrel with the pope prompted Michelangelo to leave Rome, but he was back in 1508 to paint the ceiling of the Sistine Chapel (1508–11). This, his most ambitious and compelling work, would

Pietà, by Michelangelo *(Library of Congress)*

be crowned in 1541 by the completion of the vast fresco of the *Last Judgment* that surmounts the chapel's altar. Thus, in one grand sweep the paintings in the Sistine Chapel sum up the message of Christianity as perceived by Michelangelo, from the creation of the universe to the Day of Judgment.

Michelangelo's way of delivering the message of God's overwhelming power and stern justice made an indelible impression on contemporaries and confirmed his reputation as the leading artist of his time. He returned to Florence in 1516 to carry out architectural projects for the Medici (including the Laurentian Library attached to the Church of San Lorenzo), but shifted his attention to the family funerary monument in the attached chapel, with the four reclining figures of *Day, Night, Dawn,* and *Dusk* (1519–34). In 1534 Michelangelo left Florence to settle permanently in Rome. To this period belongs his

friendship with VITTORIA COLONNA, the sonnets inspired by her piety, frescoes in the Vatican's Pauline Chapel, the redesigning of St. Peter's Basilica with its towering dome, and the remodeling of Rome's Capitoline Hill. Two unfinished *Pietàs,* one meant for his own tomb, show Michelangelo striving to achieve a level of inner expression that seems to defy the capabilities of hand and stone. The art of Michelangelo reflects the tension between secular HUMANISM and religious faith that runs through Renaissance culture. It gave spiritual meaning to the human form, ultimately affirming the supremacy of faith. The art belongs to the world of the RENAISSANCE, CATHOLIC REFORMATION, and MANNERISM.

Michels, Roberto (1876–1936)
sociologist and political scientist who studied the functioning of political parties and became an apologist of fascism

Born in Cologne (Germany) to a manufacturing and military family of Italian ancestry on the father's side, Michels interrupted his education to serve in the German army, attended four different universities in Germany, France, and Italy, and completed his doctorate at the University of Marburg. He attributed his failure to obtain an academic appointment in Germany to his ties to the Social Democratic Party. Michels wrote articles for socialist publications, championed workers' rights, and called for a new sexual ethic to liberate women from the drudgery of domestic labor. ANNA KULISCIOFF introduced him to Italian socialists in 1902 and he joined the PSI that same year. However, Michels was more interested in the REVOLUTIONARY SYNDICALISM of Georges Sorel than the historical materialism and determinism of Karl Marx or the reformist tactics of Italian socialists. The socialist connection did not hinder his career in Italy. In 1907 he was appointed to teach political economy at the University of Turin, where he had studied previously. His analysis of how political parties function developed between 1905 and 1910, heavily influenced by the ideas of Max Weber on the nature of bureaucracy. In his *Sociologia del partito politico* (Sociology of the political party, 1912), Michels argued that political parties are essentially bureaucratic organizations run by party activists and professional politicians who put party interests ahead of all other concerns. Thus, Michels's "iron law of oligarchy" debunked the claims that parties, including the Socialist Party, stood for abstract principles of justice. Under pretense of furthering democracy and social justice, all political parties pursued their own organizational interests. This dispassionate analysis estranged Michels from both liberalism and socialism, drew him toward philosophical IDEALISM, and intellectual iconoclasts who fit no ready-made political label. This was the path that eventually brought him to FASCISM. Michels seems to have anticipated important aspects of Fascist ideology before 1914 and may have influenced Benito Mussolini's critique of socialism. Michels did not hold political posts under the regime, but was regarded as an important intellectual figure and precursor. He often lectured abroad, including in the United States. In 1927–28 he taught political sociology at the University of Chicago and lectured at other American colleges and universities.

migration

In the course of history the Italian peninsula has seen both the arrival (immigration) and departure (emigration) of people in large numbers, for settlement or relocation. Its central location and exposed coastline in the MEDITERRANEAN SEA, its climate, soil, and social organization, attracted Greeks, Phoenicians, and northern Europeans who invaded, settled, traded, and intermarried with the local populations. New arrivals in medieval times included Arabs, Germans, Normans, Spaniards, Greeks, Albanians, and Slavs.

A reverse outward flow of people developed in the late Middle Ages and early modern times as part of the commercial expansion that accompanied the Crusades and the rise of city-states. Venetian and Genoese settlers left a lasting imprint on the architecture, customs, and languages of eastern and western Mediterranean regions. Settlements ("colonies") of Italian mer-

chants and bankers formed in many cities of northern Europe. Lombard Street in the heart of London's business district derives its name from the Italian businessmen who did business there. In the 16th and 17th centuries Italian religious dissenters found refuge in Switzerland, France, Germany, the Netherlands, England, and Poland. Italian artists, musicians, and teachers were in demand everywhere in Europe from England to Russia. Itinerant artisans, peddlers, and street entertainers began to make their way toward France and the Catholic parts of central and eastern Europe in the late 16th century. By the 18th century stonecutters from Como, *figurinai* (makers of plaster statuettes) from LUCCA, and booksellers and organ grinders from the mountains of PARMA were familiar figures in the cities of northern and central Europe. In the 1820s Genoese seafarers and tradesmen settled in the United States, Brazil, and Argentina.

These trickles of ordinary workers anticipated the large-scale emigration of the late 19th century. The achievement of national unification in the 1860s contributed to the greatest wave of Italian emigration in history. In the wake of political unification came major economic dislocations, rising prices and taxes, agricultural crises, and business failures. The exodus affected first the mountain populations of Piedmont, Lombardy, and Venetia in the ALPS and of Liguria, Emilia, and Tuscany in the APENNINES. But by the 1880s emigration from the impoverished regions of the South exceeded emigration from the mountains of the North. All figures for this mass exodus are questionable, but it is estimated that there were about 20 million departures from the country between 1861 and 1940 and a net emigration of 7.7 million. At its most intense in 1901–10, an average of 603,000 emigrants left the country annually.

The outflow was mostly southern, rural, young, and male. Most emigrants claimed some nonagricultural occupational skill in construction, carpentry, manufacturing, or some other manual occupation. It was a rural but not predominantly peasant emigration, though it must be kept in mind that the line between peasant and non-peasant was a porous one everywhere in Italy and that peasants often possessed non-agricultural skills. Their major destinations before 1940 were North and South America, particularly the United States and Argentina. Except for the relatively few who left for political reasons, mostly anarchists and socialists, emigration was voluntary. It reflected individual decisions, but departures were organized to a degree. They often occurred in groups from the same or neighboring towns, destinations were chosen according to reports of employment opportunities, relatives and friends were forewarned of their arrival. Emigration "chains" thus developed that directed individuals from places of origin to predetermined destinations. *Paesani* (people from the same town) settled in the same neighborhoods because it was advantageous and reassuring to be surrounded by people of similar background.

The sense of a shared national identity was poorly developed among most emigrants. They left as Neapolitans, Sicilians, Piedmontese, or Venetians, only to discover that they were "Italian" after being labeled so by the immigration officer or hearing that some ethnic slur applied to all of them. Thus, Italians abroad have often displayed a stronger sense of national identity than Italians at home. Italians at home debated the effects of national emigration on emigrants and on themselves. Most welcomed emigration as a safety valve that kept the country socially stable. Emigrants' remittances in dollars and other valuable currencies helped keep the national economy afloat. Italians who deplored emigration thought that it drained the supply of workers, drove up wages, and was a source of national humiliation. Some deplored the lack of government assistance for Italians abroad and urged the government to acquire colonies where Italians could work under their own flag.

WORLD WAR I and the American Immigration Act of 1924 placed severe restrictions on the number of Italians allowed into the United States and ended the "golden age" of Italian emigration. FASCISM did not encourage emigration, reclaimed land to settle more people at home,

and promoted settlement in the African colonies. The Fascist regime appealed to Italians living abroad to support the homeland, promoted the diffusion of Italian language and culture, and instilled a sense of national pride among many emigrants. Political exiles often discovered to their dismay that Italian emigrants were not receptive to their anti-Fascist appeals.

WORLD WAR II and Italy's economic integration in Europe set the premises for a new wave of mass emigration that lasted from the early 1950s to the mid 1970s. The new emigration differed from the older one in many ways. It was still mostly southern (about 4.1 million people left the South in 1951–71), but many now migrated to the industrial cities of the North rather than going abroad. Of those who did go abroad, the most popular destinations were the countries of northern Europe and Argentina. Advances in elementary education meant that the new emigrants were also better educated. The new emigration accompanied an agricultural revolution that saw some 6 million agricultural jobs disappear between 1951 and 1971.

Internal migration from countryside to cities and from South to North posed its own special problems. Public housing, transportation, schools, and hospitals in many cities of the North, particularly GENOA, MILAN, and TURIN, struggled to keep up with the influx of new arrivals. Crime, drug addiction, the breakup of families, social unrest, and political terrorism were variously related to the phenomenon of mass migration. The economic expansion of the 1990s eased some of the pressure, but the urban crisis continues into the early years of the 21st century.

What seems definitely over is the phase of history during which Italians sought employment abroad. Although statistics show that unemployment at levels of 10–12 percent persists in some parts of the country, Italians no longer emigrate in large numbers. Government assistance and recourse to *lavoro nero* (unreported, sometimes illegal employment) alleviate the problem of unemployment. Jobs go begging in sectors of the economy, particularly agriculture, that are deemed undesirable by Italian workers. In the year 2001 the economy needed more than 200,000 foreign workers to fill jobs. There is a strong response from abroad to this demand. Estimates on the number of foreign workers in the country vary widely, but there seem to be about 1 million, with about half thought to be in the country illegally. Pressure from public opinion and the EUROPEAN UNION is behind recent Italian legislation to control immigration. Italy has resumed its historical role as an attractive destination for people from other parts of the world seeking a better life.

Milan, city of

Milan (population 1.3 million) is Italy's second-largest city after ROME. It is the capital of the region of LOMBARDY and the country's business center. As Mediolanum (the city in the middle), Milan was an important commercial and transportation hub of the late Roman Empire. Its main strategic asset has been its location at the center of the fertile Lombard plain. It was an attractive prize for Ostrogoths, Lombards, Byzantines, and Germans who fought over it in the Middle Ages. Milan began to organize itself as an independent commune in the 11th century, but then had to defend its independence from German emperors who considered it part of their domain. It headed the Lombard League formed at Pontida in 1167, which defeated the imperial forces at the Battle of Legnano in 1176. After that victory Milan's power extended gradually to the region of Lombardy. By the end of the 13th century Milan was the second-largest city in Italy after Venice, with a population of 90,000. Its trade and manufacturing grew as internal factions fought for control of the government. The VISCONTI FAMILY imposed their rule on the city near the end of the 14th century. From the rule of the Visconti, Milan passed to that of FRANCESCO SFORZA, and from the Sforzas to France in 1499. Spaniards ruled it (1535–1714), then Austrians (1714–96).

Under Austrian rule the city recovered from a long period of economic decline. The presence of such figures as CESARE BECCARIA, GIUSEPPE PARINI, and PIETRO VERRI made it a center of ENLIGHTEN-MENT culture. Urban renewal projects altered the medieval character of the city. Neoclassical architecture was the dominant style, exemplified in the designs of Giuseppe Piermarini (1734–1808), appointed state architect in 1770. His constructions include the Teatro alla Scala, Italy's premier opera house. In the Napoleonic period Milan served as capital of the nominally independent Italian republic (1800–05) and Kingdom of Italy (1805–14). Ambitious projects designed to make Milan the capital of an Italian state subject to France were never realized for lack of time.

During the RESTORATION Milan was the center of anti-Austrian agitations that culminated in the Five Days of March 18–23, 1848, when a popular insurrection forced the Austrians to evacuate the city. The memory of the Five Days, the presence of patriotic figures like CARLO CATTANEO and ALESSANDRO MANZONI, and broad support for national independence made Milan a political hotbed in the RISORGIMENTO. It assumed the role of business capital of the nation soon after national unification, as it developed its commercial ties with the rest of the nation and diversified its manufacturing activities beyond the traditional textile industries. Metallurgy, machinery, transportation, rubber, publishing, and electricity were the most dynamic sectors in the decades after national unification. Among the many construction projects of the postunification period, the most striking was the glass-covered Galleria Vittorio Emanuele that connects Piazza del Duomo with Piazza della Scala.

Milan's population grew from 240,000 in 1861 to about 600,000 in 1911. Workers were pushed out, the city center was gentrified, and took on the commercial and bourgeois character that it still retains. Relegated to the periphery and suburbs of the city, workers turned to socialism and collective organization. The economic crisis of the 1890s exacerbated social tensions and led to the bloody FATTI DI MAGGIO of 1898. The socialists won control of the municipal administration in 1914 and campaigned unsuccessfully to prevent Italy from going to war. After the war the city was the site of violent clashes between socialists and Fascists. BENITO MUSSOLINI headed the Fascist movement and propelled himself to power from his headquarters in the heart of the city.

The Fascist period witnessed the development of a vast metropolitan area gravitating economically and socially toward the city, but poorly integrated in terms of transportation and social services. Manufacturing took place in the suburbs where factories and tenements competed for space. Within the city itself old neighborhoods and picturesque but no longer functional canals made way for broad avenues, grandiose government buildings, and popular housing. The railroad station is perhaps the best example of the monumental style favored by the Fascist regime. Milan was the site of armed clashes between Fascists and anti-Fascists in the final months of World War II. In a gruesome climax, the bodies of Mussolini and some of his supporters were exposed to the fury of a mob in Milan's Piazzale Loreto.

Although heavily damaged by bombing in WORLD WAR II, Milan was quick to recover after the war, leading the country through the ECONOMIC MIRACLE of the 1950s. In those years, MIGRATION swelled its population and caused severe problems of overcrowding that were alleviated by extensive construction of popular housing, improvements in services, and public assistance. Milan is today a world center of fashion and industrial design. The city's annual *Fiera Campionaria* is a business event of international resonance. It is also home to UMBERTO BOSSI's autonomist Northern League, a movement that epitomizes Milanese perception and resentment of Rome as the corrupt, unproductive, and wasteful national capital. Ironically, the MANI PULITE scandal of the 1990s exposed Milan's own corruption. A paradoxical aspect of Milanese life today is its role as business capital and hotbed of radical movements of the Left and Right.

Milani, Don Lorenzo (1923–1967)
parish priest, writer, and social activist
Milani was born to a Florentine upper-class family and ordained as a priest in 1947. He was among the first postwar priests to call on the CATHOLIC CHURCH to take up the cause of the underprivileged. A profound religious creed based on his understanding of the principles of love and charity left in him no room for compromise. He was an outspoken critic of the religious hierarchy and the politics of the Christian Democratic Party (DC). After serving as priest in an industrial suburb of Florence, in 1958 he was appointed parish priest in the isolated mountain village of Barbiana in the Tuscan Apennines. From that remote post he launched an attack on church and government for neglecting the education of peasant children. He gained national attention with his zeal and his often intemperate pronouncements. His denuciation of the church's evangelical shortcomings in the book *Esperienze pastorali* (1960) brought on him an official censure from the Holy Office. His most controversial publication was *Lettera a una professoressa* (Letter to a Schoolteacher, 1967). That text charged that the standardized exams and formal expectations of the public school system discriminated against children from rural, underprivileged families. His critique of the schools as elitist and class-biased found a ready audience among the student protesters of 1968–69. Socially progressive and theologically conservative, Milani called on the clergy to fight against the political Left by taking up the cause of the poor and disinherited.

Millo, Enrico See ITALIAN-TURKISH WAR.

Minghetti, Marco (1818–1886)
Risorgimento patriot and political figure
Minghetti was born in Bologna to a family of wealthy landowners, studied science and literature at the University of Bologna, traveled widely in Europe to document political and economic conditions, and concluded that the political divisions impeded progress in Italy. In 1839 he participated in the first Congress of Italian Scientists, held in Pisa, that gathered scholars from all parts of the peninsula and helped cre-

ate a sense of common interests among them. Mighetti approached political issues from a moderate liberal perspective that called for education and reforms rather than revolution. Encouraged by the election of Pope PIUS IX in 1846, Minghetti joined the movement to liberalize papal government. During the REVOLUTION of 1848 he opposed the republicanism of GIUSEPPE MAZZINI and found refuge in Piedmont, where he continued his economic studies and eventually supported CAVOUR's policies. In 1859 he was instrumental in preparing the annexation of the Emilia-Romagna region to Piedmont as a first step toward national unification. As a member of the HISTORICAL RIGHT Minghetti served in the national parliament as minister of the interior (1860–61), prime minister and minister of finances (1862–64), minister of agriculture, industry, and commerce (1869), and again as prime minister and minister of finances (1873–76). During his first stint as prime minister he concluded the controversial September Convention with France (1864) that removed French troops from Rome and transferred the Italian capital from Turin to Florence. Critics charged that the transfer of the capital to Florence was an implicit renunciation of Rome as the national capital, and accused Minghetti of renouncing a major goal of the unification movement. While the September Convention made Minghetti unacceptable to the LIBERAL LEFT, his known preference for administrative decentralization also made him suspect within his own Historical Right. His major accomplishment, and one that he was most proud of, occurred during his second tenure as prime minister when he was able to announce in his very last speech that his government had balanced the national budget for the first time since national unification. Two days after the speech, on March 18, 1876, the opposition voted his government out of power. From then on Minghetti led the parliamentary opposition to the governments of the Liberal Left. He was also a prolific writer and commentator on art, literature, economics, and politics. The three volumes of his *I miei ricordi* (My Memories, 1888–90), published posthumously, cover his life up to 1859.

Misley, Enrico See MENOTTI, CIRO.

Modena, city of
Modena (population 177,000) is a provincial capital in the region of EMILIA-ROMAGNA situated on the Via Emilia, a modern road that traverses the Po Valley on the layout of the ancient Roman road with the same name. Originally founded by Ligurian populations, it became the Roman colony of Mutina in 183 B.C. It rose to power as an independent commune under the Canossa family in the 11th and 12th centuries. The ESTE FAMILY ruled it from the 13th century to the Napoleonic invasion of 1796. The CONGRESS OF VIENNA restored the Duchy of Modena to the Este family in 1814. Formally independent but in effect subject to Austria, the Estes ruled Modena until 1859. Under FRANCIS IV, in 1830, the Duchy of Modena incorporated the neighboring Duchy of Massa and Carrara, where orchestrated disturbances broke out in 1859 that enabled Cavour to goad Austria into declaring war on Piedmont. That decision set in motion the events that led to national unification (see WARS OF INDEPENDENCE, Second). Modena became part of united Italy in 1860. It has grown quietly and steadily into a prosperous city with a well-balanced economy. The agricultural, commercial, and manufacturing activities of the province complement one another. It is renowned for its wine, pork, and dairy products, for the Ferrari racing cars that are manufactured in the nearby town of Maranello, and as the birthplace and hometown of tenor Luciano Pavarotti.

modernism
Modernism affected all forms of religion in the western world, provoking fundamentalist reactions that reasserted the authority of the Bible and of historical interpretations against the revisionist ideas of modernist thinkers. The term itself came into use around 1904 when the debate between modernists and fundamentalists was fully underway. Modernists argued that to retain its spiritual meaning, religious dogma

must evolve as society changes and new needs develop. In Italy modernism found expression in the reviews *Rivista Storico-Critica delle Scienze Teologiche* (1905–10) and *Il Rinnovamento* (1907–09). The writer ANTONIO FOGAZZARO and the activist priest ROMOLO MURRI contributed to the elaboration and diffusion of modernist ideas in Italy. Italian modernism was sensitive to the issues of conscience generated by the conflict between CHURCH AND STATE, and to the challenge of socialism. Some modernists called for accommodation with the liberal state, while others wanted to organize Catholics politically so that they would control the liberal state. They accepted democracy as a means of mobilizing the Catholic vote, and acknowledged the justice of socialist concerns for the welfare of workers. At least by implication, Catholic modernists questioned adherence to tradition, the authority of bishops and pope, and believed in the fundamental compatibility of revealed and scientific truths. Hence their optimism that religion and science could join hands to improve the world. Pope PIUS X, who did not share their optimism, feared the challenge to the hierarchy, and put pastoral over social duties, condemned modernism as the "synthesis of all heresies" in the encyclical *Pascendi dominici gregis* (1907). Many modernist works were placed on the INDEX, and in 1910 all Catholic teachers of theology and sacred scripture were required to take an antimodernist oath. The papal condemnation silenced Italian modernists for the time being, but their ideas found an outlet later on in the movement of CHRISTIAN DEMOCRACY.

Molise

Molise (population 328,000) was part of the larger region of ABRUZZO until 1965. It borders with Abruzzo to the north, LATIUM to the west, CAMPANIA to the south, PUGLIA to the southeast, and the Adriatic Sea to the east. Campobasso, the regional capital, and Isernia, are its only two provinces. Only the region of VAL D'AOSTA is smaller than Molise in area and population.

Most of Molise's territory is mountainous or hilly, with the highest elevations of the interior exceeding 2,000 meters (6,560 feet) in elevation. The highly seasonal flow of its rivers and streams provides little support for agriculture. The mountainous terrain, poor agriculture, and depressed economy account for the high incidence of emigration from the region. The name of the region derives from that of Count Hugo of Mulhouse, a Norman lord who ruled over the area in the 11th century. In the 13th century it became part of the Kingdom of NAPLES, whose history it followed until it became part of the Kingdom of Italy in 1860. Molise's standard of living is one of the lowest in Italy. Some improvements in agriculture have taken place, mostly in the coastal region where irrigation, terrain, and communications lend themselves to large-scale cultivation of cereals, legumes, and potatoes. Small-scale manufacturing prevails in textiles, food processing, furniture, and building materials. Few motor roads and railroads serve the interior, where there are still Albanian- and Greek-speaking communities founded in the 15th century. Molise is the only Italian region to have no appreciable flow of tourists.

Monaco

The independent principality of Monaco, a small enclave on the Mediterranean coast of France near the Italian border, was historically tied to Italy for many centuries. From the 12th to the 15th century, the Grimaldi family and the Republic of GENOA claimed sovereignty over the territory. The Grimaldis asserted their independence in 1419 and ruled over Monaco until 1731, when the male line died out. The French Goyon-Matignon family, related to the Grimaldi by marriage, assumed the Grimaldi name, and their descendants still govern the principality. The current ruler, Prince Rainier III (born 1923), has governed since 1949. The small principality received outside protection from Spain (1542–1641) and France (1641–1793). France annexed Monaco in 1793, but the principality regained its independence in 1815 when it was placed under the protection of the Kingdom of SARDINIA. There was a minority movement for unification with Italy during the Risorgimento that involved about one-tenth of the population, mostly from the Italian-speaking towns of Mentone and Roccabruna, which took part in the REVOLUTIONS of 1848. The governing authorities promptly disavowed and suppressed the movement. When Italy became independent in 1861 Monaco returned to French protection as part of a general territorial settlement by the two governments. Of its current 29,972 inhabitants, approximately 12,000 speak French and 5,000 speak Italian.

Monarchist Party See PNF.

Monitore Italiano (Il) See FOSCOLO, UGO; JOURNALISM.

Monitore Napoletano (Il) See FONSECA, ELEONORA PIMENTEL DE.

Montale, Eugenio (1896–1981)
poet, essayist, literary and musical critic
Born and raised in Genoa, Montale drew inspiration from the atmosphere and landscape of his native city and region of LIGURIA. WORLD WAR I, in which he served as an infantry officer, interrupted the technical studies of his youth, and he later gave up the singing lessons that were supposed to prepare him for a career as a baritone. His literary formation is poorly documented, but early on he displayed the tendency to forsake rhetoric and theatricality for spare forms of expression. His politics in the 1920s inclined toward the democratic liberalism of PIERO GOBETTI, who published Montale's first collection of poems, *Ossi di sepia* (Cuttlefish bones, 1925), whose title and language evoke the stony, sun-drenched landscape of Liguria. In 1926 he moved to Florence where he worked in the pub-

lishing industry and served as director of a private library and cultural society until 1938 when he was forced out because he would not join the Fascist Party. His second major collection of poems, *Le occasioni* (The occasions) came out in 1939. In 1946 Montale began to work for the daily newspaper *Corriere della Sera* and in 1948 moved to Milan, where he spent the rest of his life. His volumes of poetry include *La bufera e altro* (The storm, etc., 1955), *Satura* (from the Latin for satire and medley, 1971), *Diario del '71 e del '72* (Diary of 1971 and 1972, 1974), and *Quaderno di quattro anni* (Four-year notebook, 1977). He was the 1975 recipient of the Nobel Prize in literature. Montale employed a deliberately obscure, concentrated language that was designed in part to camouflage his opposition to the Fascist regime, but which also captures and reflects the complexity of contemporary life. A pessimism that harks back to GIACOMO LEOPARDI, whom Montale greatly admired, informs his writings. That pessimism was an aspect of Montale's immense capacity for suffering. Montale rejected any political reading of his writings, but the pessimism can be seen as a reflection on the dramatic historical events of his time, evident, for instance, in the images of war in *La bufera e altro*. A sense of spirituality also emanates from his writings, but in the end Montale's poetry refuses the consolation of religion and acknowledges the mystery and unpredictability of human events. His *Collected Poems 1920–1954* (1998) is a bilibual edition of his major poems.

Montanelli, Giuseppe (1813–1862)
Risorgimento patriot and political writer
Montanelli was born in the Tuscan town of Fucecchio, studied and taught law at the University of Pisa where his liberal ideas won him popularity with the student body. Driven by a strong moral impulse, in 1843 he founded the Fratelli Italiani (Italian Brothers), an association that proposed national regeneration by spiritual reform. The liberal reforms of PIUS IX kindled his enthusiasm for the papacy and made him a fol-

lower of VINCENZO GIOBERTI's neo-Guelf movement. In 1848 he led a battalion of student volunteers in war against the Austrians, was wounded and taken prisoner at the battle of Curtatone. Released, he returned to Florence where he was elected to the revolutionary Tuscan assembly. His idea that an Italian constituent assembly should address the question of national unity was broadly debated. Montanelli saw a constituent assembly representing the different states and interests of the peninsula as the body best qualified to reconcile national unity with Italy's internal diversity. In 1849 he was part of a triumvirate that briefly governed in Tuscany, but lost his bid for the presidency to FRANCESCO DOMENICO GUERRAZZI who opposed convening a constituent assembly. The idea of a constituent assembly was rejected in 1848 and 1860 as cumbersome and divisive. After 1848 Montanelli supported neither the republican program of GIUSEPPE MAZZINI nor the monarchist program of CAVOUR. An expatriate in Paris, he wrote a book of memoirs and argued for a decentralized national state. Few followed his advice. He returned to Italy in 1859 to fight against Austria and to oppose, unsuccessfully, the union of Tuscany and Piedmont. As a member of the national parliament Montanelli was close to the HISTORICAL RIGHT. He backed the system of administrative decentralization proposed by MARCO MINGHETTI but never endorsed by parliament.

Montanelli, Indro (1909–2001)
independent journalist, historian, and political commentator

A descendant of GIUSEPPE MONTANELLI, Indro Montanelli was also born in Fucecchio, the son of an elementary school teacher and student of Sanskrit who named him after a Vedic goddess. Indro received degrees in law and political science, but pursued a career in JOURNALISM. In his youth he was attracted to the left fringes of fascism that called in vague terms for a radical social overhaul. He was a volunteer in the ETHIOPIAN WAR and was praised for his reports

from the frontlines. The product of Florentine intellectual circles known for their independence, he criticized the conservative bent of the regime and was expelled from the Fascist Party in 1937. He was arrested in German-occupied northern Italy in 1944 and sentenced to death. He escaped to Switzerland with the connivance of guards, and returned after the war to work for the Milanese daily *Corriere della Sera* until 1972. In 1974 he founded and directed *Il Giornale Nuovo* (which became *Il Giornale* in 1983). He stepped down in 1994 when that publication became part of SILVIO BERLUSCONI's media empire. Montanelli's legendary independence won him no political friends. Christian Democrats resented him for his condemnation of their party as the source of political corruption, while the left was affronted by his visceral anticommunism. His loathing of communism won out on the eve of the crucial national elections of 1976, when he urged voters to "hold their noses and vote for Christian Democracy." In June 1977 he was the victim of an armed attack by the RED BRIGADES as part of their campaign against prominent media figures. The collapse and discredit of both communism and Christian Democracy in the 1990s has vindicated his condemnations. Montanelli is also the author of works for the theater and of a multivolume history of Italy.

Montecatini See MONTEDISON.

Montecuccoli, Raimondo (1609–1680)
military commander, writer, and army reformer

This member of a military family from the mountains of the Duchy of MODENA stood out as an exceptionally capable and knowledgeable commander who rose through the ranks and learned the art of war on the battlefield. He relinquished the prospects of a career in the clergy to fight in Germany during the Thirty Years' War (1618–48) in the service of Holy

Roman Emperor Ferdinand II. As a prisoner of war (1639–42) he found time to reflect and write on the state of warfare. His main contribution was to grasp and make a persuasive case for the dominant roles that firearms were destined to play in war. He returned to Italy in 1643 to lead the troops of Duke Francis I of Modena against papal forces in the CastroWar (1641–43), a minor territorial dispute in which Montecuccoli prevailed but which divided the Italian states and invited further foreign intervention in Italian affairs. Montecuccoli returned to Germany to fight in the final campaigns of the Thirty Years' War, emerging at the end of that conflict as one of the most respected generals of the imperial army. In 1658 he became its leading commander. Under his direction, the imperial forces were reorganized around smaller, more mobile battalions, adopted standard uniforms and rank insignia, and increased the number of muskets and cannon. He led other successful campaigns against the Turks (1664) and the French (1675–80). His victory against the Turks was particularly beneficial to his career, raising him to a position of power second only to that of the emperor. Montecuccoli claimed that the true motivation of a military commander was to fight for glory, not gain. Shortly before his death he achieved his highest ambition, which was to be made a prince of the empire.

Monte dei Paschi See BANKING; SIENA, CITY OF.

Montedison

Montedison, the second-largest Italian private business after FIAT, is a large business conglomerate based in Milan active in chemicals, energy, agribusiness, and many other related and unrelated areas of production. Montedison was formed in 1966 from the merger of Montecatini (chemicals) and Edison (electricity) after the government's nationalization of the electrical industry (1962). Government payments to Edison shareholders helped pay Montecatini's debts and provided Montedison with the capital it needed to move into developing fields such as plastics and artificial fibers. The merger was promoted by Christian Democratic governments and opposed by the political parties of the Left, on the grounds of its high cost to taxpayers and its monopolistic dominance of the national market. By 1969 Montedison was doing the largest volume of business in the country. However, its growth was marked by recurring financial crises, which it met by recourse to complicated bank loans and other financial arrangements involving ENRICO CUCCIA's Mediobanca. When ENI, the state-owned energy holding company, bought its way into Montedison, the conglomerate technically lost its full private status. The economic crisis of the 1970s took its toll on Montedison. ENI pulled out in 1981and FIAT stepped in. In 1986 a group of investors led by the adventurous entrepreneur Raul Gardini attempted to inject new resources into Montedison. His plan to merge the chemical activities of Montedison and ENI led to the short-lived Enimont corporation formed in 1993. Enimont dissolved but left behind a trail of collusion and illicit deals that provided grist for the mill of the MANI PULITE investigation. Gardini committed suicide, and his empire collapsed. In 1995 Montedison was taken over by a financial holding company owned by several banks, which separated its chemical and electrical energy operations into two subsidiaries that took on the old names of Edison and Montecatini. Thus reorganized, Montedison once again attracted the attention of FIAT, which in July 2001 gained control of Montedison with a complicated financial deal that involved a French state-owned electrical company. This move was part of FIAT's ongoing strategy of diversifying its activities beyond automobile production. Its plan is to sell off Montedison's agricultural products business and concentrate on the production and distribution of electricity. Montedison's vicissitudes since its founding provide a revealing glimpse into the operations of large Italian firms, their connections with banks and political parties, and the rivalries among the top frequenters of what Italians call the *salotto buono* (drawing room) of the economy.

Montefeltro family

The Montefeltro family ruled the city-state of URBINO from the 13th to the 16th centuries. Family members showed military talent, generally in the service of the German emperors, receiving the title of counts from Emperor Frederick II (1194–1250). Although of Ghibelline origin, the family maintained good relations with the PAPACY when that institution was strong enough to threaten their hold on power and territory. Their traditional rivals and mortal enemies were the MALATESTA, who ruled over Rimini. The most prominent member of the family was Federico da Montefeltro (1422–82), who was educated by leading humanist scholars and is often seen as the ideal RENAISSANCE ruler, who combined intellectual accomplishments, physical prowess, and nobility of character. When he became lord of Urbino at age 22, Federico turned his attention to improving the city and turned the ducal palace into a splendid residence and a center for artists and scholars. For his loyalty to the papacy, Pope Sixtus IV named him duke in 1474. During his reign and that of his son Guidobaldo da Montefeltro (1472–1508), the relatively small city-state of Urbino emerged as a major center of Renaissance culture. The family lost control of Urbino when Guidobaldo died without leaving an heir.

Maria Montessori *(Library of Congress)*

Montessori, Maria (1870–1952)
physician, child psychologist, and education reformer

Born near Ancona (MARCHES) to a prominent family (her father was a military officer from a noble family and her mother was a niece of the liberal priest and scientist ANTONIO STOPPANI), Montessori showed early on an interest in scientific studies. At the University of Rome she studied mathematics, engineering, biology, and medicine. She was the first woman in Italy to receive a degree in medicine (1894). After graduation she lectured in anthropology at her alma mater and worked with mentally handicapped children. From 1898 to 1901 she served as director of a school for retarded children. It was there that she developed new methods of instruction, based on the manipulation of physical objects, that yielded encouraging results. Convinced that the same methods could be used to educate normal preschool children, in 1907 she opened the first *casa dei bambini* (children's home) as a daycare center in the working-class district of San Lorenzo in Rome. What came to be known as the Montessori method relies on the innate curiosity of children and their direct engagement with educational games, toys, utensils, plants, and animals to stimulate the imagination and motivate them to learn. Montessori redefined the role of the teacher from that of an instructor who imparts knowledge to that of guide who steers students toward individual discovery. She had some success in Italy at the preschool level, where the state played no educational role at the time. Privileged communities and groups established excellent preschools, but these enrolled only a small proportion of the population. Montessori's ideas made little headway at the elementary level where a state-mandated curriculum prevailed. There was more interest abroad, where the state played less of a role and liberal theories of education circulated freely. A Montessori school opened in Tarrytown, N.Y., in 1912; she herself opened an institute for the training of teachers in Barcelona in 1917 and one in London in 1919. When she returned to Italy in 1922 the government appointed her as inspector of schools and showed some interest in her ideas. Her experimental methods clashed, however, with the idealistic philosophy of education minister GIOVANNI GENTILE, who believed that a major goal of education was to inculcate patriotic values. Soon the Fascist regime turned toward a regimented system of education that was incompatible with Montessori's open-ended approach. The press eventually accused her of being a philosophical pacifist and mounted a campaign that forced her to leave the country in 1934. She settled in the Netherlands, where she died. The Montessori method gained enthusiastic support in the United States in the late 1950s and 1960s, and Montessori schools still function in America. In Italy her influence is greatest in districts that exert local autonomy, as is the case in the model preschools of Reggio Emilia.

Monteverdi, Claudio (1567–1643)
musician, first composer to establish opera as a new art form

Born in Cremona, Monteverdi studied music in his native city and started out as violinist, singer, and music master at the court of MANTUA. His first opera, *Orfeo* (1607), was written on the occasion of the marriage of the son of Mantua's duke. *Orfeo*'s immediate success has lasted through the centuries. All but one aria of *Arianna* (1608), Monteverdi's second opera for the Mantua court, has been lost. He was appointed master musician of St. Mark's Cathedral in Venice in 1613, a post that he kept for the rest of his life. His presence made Venice the operatic center of Italy, adding to the cultural distinction of the city and establishing its tradition of musical excellence. Monteverdi composed about 20 stage works for the Venetian theater, the most notable of which was *L'incoronazione di Poppea* (1643). The melodic richness and original orchestration of Monteverdi's music were perfectly suited to the expression of human character and sentiment that was his principal concern. His music endowed the spoken lines with greater expressiveness. Monteverdi developed the recitative passages into full-fledged arias, enlarged the orchestra, introduced ensembles, instrumental passages, and new string techniques. With these innovations, OPERA broke out from its court settings to become popular entertainment presented in theaters open to the public.

Monti, Vincenzo (1754–1828)
classicist poet who celebrated historical events and personalities

Born in a small town of the Po Valley that was part of the Papal States, Monti attended seminary school, studied law at the University of Padua to satisfy his family, but found his true passion in literature. His first published poems won him the patronage of the papal legate in Ferrara who took him to Rome. In Rome, employed as personal secretary to the pope's nephew, he composed the first poems destined to become famous, to celebrate mundane events, praise the papacy, and condemn the FRENCH REVOLUTION. But when NAPOLEON invaded Italy, Monti changed sides, moved to Milan, repudiated his past, and sang the virtues of French republicanism. When his enemies were not appeased, he found refuge in Paris. He returned to Italy in 1801. Now in Napoleon's favor, Monti was appointed to teach eloquence and poetry at the University of Pavia. In 1805 he was appointed official historian of Napoleon's kingdom of Italy. The years that followed were those of his greatest achievements. He poured out supremely well-crafted verses to celebrate Napoleon's victories, wrote dramas for the stage, and translated Homer's *Iliad* into Italian. The translation was a major linguistic achievement that confirmed his reputation as the outstanding literary figure of his time. Napoleon's downfall prompted Monti to switch allegiance once again. He collaborated with the Austrians, but his literary role changed in the remaining years of his life. In this final phase, with his best poetic productions behind him, Monti emerged as a linguist and literary critic. He engaged in the debate between classicists and romanticists as the standard-bearer of the former. Unlike most classicists, he did not resist change. Never a cultural conservative, Monti argued that the Italian language must change in response to scientific and cultural innovations and avoid confinement in the Tuscan forms inherited from Dante. Monti's political gyrations have obscured his literary significance. He may have personified the traditional role of the poet as an ornament of the court, but he was also an innovator and a writer of unmatched elegance.

Monti di Pietà   See BANKING.

Morandi, Giorgio (1890–1964)
painter known for the originality of his still lifes
Morandi who was born and spent most of his life in Bologna and its environs, taught print-mak-

ing and etching at the city's Academy of Fine Arts. His distinctive style developed in reaction to the flamboyance of FUTURISM, and the mysterious or "metaphysical" expressiveness of Giorgio di Chirico. Inspired by his study of early Renaissance painting, Morandi strove for a spare style of expression shorn of rhetoric and ornament. From 1922 on, Morandi painted landscapes, vases, and bottles, conveying his sense of the real through these inanimate objects. His paintings convey a sense of repose and an understated appreciation of the beauty inherent in objects of everyday life. Whatever his message, he did not verbalize it, but allowed his art to speak for itself. In his isolation, he was oblivious to politics. The Fascist regime under which he worked found nothing objectionable in his art and he was able to go his way undisturbed. Morandi can be cited as evidence that FASCISM imposed no artistic credo and allowed artists to follow their own individual inclinations as long as their art did not overtly challenge the regime.

Moravia, Alberto (1907–1990)
novelist, critic, journalist, and playwright, a cultural critic of bourgeois values
Born Alberto Pincherle in Rome into a wealthy family; his father, an architect, was Jewish and his mother Catholic. Privately taught by a family governess, he showed a precocious interest in literature, learned English, French, and German at an early age. Then, suffering from tuberculosis, he read a great deal on his own while interned in a sanatorium. Youthful unpublished writings prepared him for the novel that evoked strong reactions for and against. *Gli indifferenti* (The time of indifference, 1929), showed Moravia's clinical eye, psychological insight, and moral condemnation of bourgeois values. The regime regarded the novel with suspicion, fearing that it might be read as a condemnation of Italian society. He was nevertheless able to publish under a pseudonym and to live quietly under fascism. In 1941 he married the writer Elsa Morante (1912–85). The experience of forced flight from Rome in 1943–44

Alberto Moravia *(Library of Congress)*

inspired the novels *La romana* (The woman of Rome, 1947) and *La ciociara* (Two women, 1957), which depicted the harrowing experiences of women in wartime Italy. The theme of awakening sexuality features prominently in Moravia's writings and is particularly evident in the novels *Agostino* (1945) and *La disubbidienza* (Luca, 1948). Two volumes of short stories published in the 1950s show Moravia's sympathy for workers and his left-leaning political sympathies. By the 1960s Moravia had turned toward discussion of contemporary issues, including nuclear threats, lesbianism, feminism, and marital relations. He divorced his wife in 1962 and engaged in a long-term relationship with the feminist novelist,

poet, and playwright Dacia Maraini (born 1936) that lasted until 1983. A representative of literary NEOREALISM, Moravia's prose stands out for its clarity, descriptive precision, and psychological insight into his true-to-life characters.

Mori, Cesare (1872–1942)
police chief who led a successful campaign against the Mafia

A career civil servant, Mori worked his way up the law enforcement ladder and was appointed prefect in 1920. As prefect of Bologna (1921–22), he confronted widespread labor agitation with an evenly iron hand. Endowed with a strong sense of the state, and equally strict in dealing with owners and workers, socialists and Fascists, Mori made enemies on both sides. Eventually, Fascist pressure on government officials forced him out of Bologna, and he was transferred to the prefecture of Bari in the South. Mussolini valued his abilities and appointed him prefect of Palermo in 1924. From that post he took charge of the government's campaign against the MAFIA. Mori waged a no-holds-barred fight that resorted to legal and illegal means. The results are still controversial. The regime boasted that the Mafia was eliminated, but critics have pointed out that it only went underground, reduced the level of violence, and learned to operate quietly undercover, only to reemerge stronger after the collapse of the regime. The failure to uproot the Mafia is generally related not to Mori's intentions, but to the failure of the Fascist regime to address its underlying causes in the economic and social structures of the island. The regime hailed Mori's work as a great success and conferred senatorial rank on him (1928). Mori retired from public life the following year.

Moro, Aldo (1916–1978)
Christian Democratic leader, prime minister, victim of terrorism

Moro was one of the most influential political figures of post-1945 Italy. Born in the southern region of PUGLIA to a middle-class family of teachers, doctors, and lawyers, Moro was raised in a Catholic environment. Studious by temperament, he excelled in school, and was active in Catholic student organizations. He began to study law at the University of Bari, but in 1939 transferred to the University of Rome where he was national president of the Italian Catholic University Federation (FUCI). After serving in the army during the war, Moro taught law at the University of Bari (1945). He made his political debut in 1946 when he was elected to the national Constituent Assembly as a Christian Democrat. Elected to the chamber of deputies in 1948, he held that seat until his death 30 years later. His low-key demeanor disguised strong ambitions. He served as minister of justice (1955–57), minister of public instruction (1957–58), party secretary (1959–64, 1975–78), and was five times prime minister (1964–68). In his early days he was close to the progressive faction of the Christian Democratic Party (DC) led by GIUSEPPE DOSSETTI, but in time his political stance came to defy classification. Subtle to the point of being indecipherable, Moro's politics were reflected in the deliberate obscurity of his language, which was an essential part of a political high-wire act. As prime minister he prepared the OPENING TO THE LEFT that admitted Socialists into the governing coalition, while explaining to the public that what was happening was the "convergence of parallel lines." The members of parliament who supported Moro's course were known as Morotei, in contrast to the centrist Christian Democratic faction of the Dorotei who opposed collaboration with the Left.

Moro moved with the voters, and when they moved away from Christian Democracy and increasingly toward the Left, Moro as party secretary negotiated understandings that gave Communists an informal voice in government. He was working toward a HISTORIC COMPROMISE to make Christian Democrats and Communists partners in government. Moro found a willing interlocutor in Communist Party leader ENRICO BERLINGUER, but the prospect of collaboration between these two rival parties worried political conservatives and the extreme Left. Probably to sink the project, the RED BRIGADES, an extreme left-wing terrorist group, staged the daring kidnapping of Moro in the streets of Rome in March 1978. After holding him prisoner and interrogating him for 55 days while the police searched and the country agonized, they "executed" him and left his body in the trunk of a car in downtown Rome, at the exact midpoint between the headquarters of the Christian Democratic and Communist parties. When his kidnappers were eventually apprehended, their trial dragged on for years and left many questions unresolved. The Moro case has left a lasting legacy. Unresolved questions deal with the response of the major political parties to the kidnapping, possible involvement by secret services and the CIA, Moro's treatment and behavior at the hands of his kidnappers, and the motivations of the kidnappers themselves. Regardless of how the legacy of the Moro case plays out, of Moro himself it can be said that he was a talented negotiator in search of political compromise, but that it remains unclear whether he was pursuing a larger plan of national reconciliation or merely looking for ways to govern from day to day.

Morosini, Francesco (1618–1694)

Venetian military officer and political figure

A member of the Venetian nobility, Morosini began as a naval officer and took part in repeated campaigns against the Turks. These campaigns kept him in the eastern Mediterranean most of the time from 1639 to 1661. Back in Venice, he was responsible for building the system of fortifications on the mainland that protected the city from attack. Charges of misconduct that were apparently motivated by political jealousies were dropped, and he went back to campaign against the Turks after being exonerated. In 1687 he led a successful attack on the city of Athens that resulted in the destruction of the Parthenon when a Venetian mortar projectile blew up the gunpowder that the Turks had stored in the temple. His military successes earned him the nickname The Peloponnesian and gave him irresistible political ascendancy at home. He was elected doge (chief magistrate) of the Venetian republic in 1688. Continuing Turkish pressure on Venetian possessions in the eastern Mediterranean prompted Morosini's reappointment as chief military commander in 1693. He died before he could put into action a well-prepared plan to lure and destroy the Turkish navy in a pitched battle. Nevertheless, his plan relieved Turkish pressure on Venetian positions and secured Venice a foothold in the eastern Mediterranean until the fall of the republic in 1797. He was, in effect, the last commander who could carry out independent Venetian operations in the Mediterranean.

Mosca, Gaetano (1858–1941)
political theorist and critic of parliamentary democracy

Mosca was born in Palermo, studied and taught constitutional law and history of political theories and institutions at the universities of Turin, Milan, and Rome. He was elected to parliament in 1908, served as undersecretary in the ministry of colonies (1914–16), and was appointed senator in 1919. His studies and political experiences led him to formulate his theory that government is always run by organized, self-perpetuating minorities, which he called the "political class." The political class claims authority on the basis of some universal principles of government, but in reality represents the special interests of organized minorities. The universal principles that the political class invokes to justify their use of power are determined historically. Monarchs invoke the principles of divine right or legitimacy, while liberal democracies invoke majority rule. Whatever the ideological formula, government is based not on ideology but on the representation of organized interests. The thrust of his thinking was antidemocratic, because it pointed to the easy corruption and perversion of democratic rule, but not anti-liberal, because it upheld

constitutional government, civil liberties, and the rule of law. Mosca saw constitutional government as making possible the beneficent rule of qualified minorities. It is misleading to see him, as is often done, as a precursor and apologist for FASCISM. Mosca sympathized with fascism at first, seeing it as a corrective to the excesses of parliamentary democracy, but criticized it openly from 1925 when the regime began to subvert the very parliamentary system that he condemned in his writings. A certain similarity of views and claims of priority precipitated a bitter controversy with VILFREDO PARETO, another critic of parliamentary democracy. His treatise *Teorica dei governi* (1896) was translated into English as *The Ruling Class* (1939).

Moti del matese See ANARCHISM.

mountains, problem of the
References to Italy's "problem of the mountains" became part of the political vocabulary after 1945 when the governments of the Italian republic turned their attention to the country's many unsolved social problems. Article 44 of the CONSTITUTION of the Italian republic made the protection of mountainous areas and their populations a special responsibility of government. Unlike the SOUTHERN QUESTION (referred to at the time as the "Problem of the South") that was geographically specific, the Problem of the Mountains affected all regions. With approximately one-third of the national territory classified as mountainous, the problems of employment, housing, schooling, and transportation faced by people living in mountainous territories were most urgent. Government responses to the problem included tax exemptions, credit incentives, subsidies for public services, reforestation, agriculture, and tourism. Municipal administrations in mountain districts enjoy special autonomies for the protection of woods and pastures and for establishing agricultural cooperatives. The goal of special legislation is to provide

such services and amenities as will keep the populations in place, reduce emigration, and improve the natural environment. The prevalence of small landownership, tight ties of rural families, and influence of the clergy made for a socially conservative environment. The dominant Christian Democratic Party (DC) was particularly active in promoting measures to keep mountain populations in place, as voters from mountain districts tended to support DC candidates. These special measures have not prevented economic decline and severe depopulation of mountain areas. Budget reductions in the 1990s ended all but token gestures of relief. The future of mountain territories seems to lie in their attraction as places of recreation for vacationers and visitors.

Mozzoni, Anna Maria (1837–1920)
pioneer feminist, social activist, and patriot

The pioneer of the women's movement in Italy, Mozzoni was born and raised in Milan during the period of Austrian rule. In spite of the fact that the education of women had made more progress since the 18th century in the Austrian-ruled parts of Italy than anywhere else in the peninsula, Mozzoni identified with the movement for Italian independence. In the republican movement of GIUSEPPE MAZZINI she found the linkage between the cause of national liberation and the emancipation of women. In a publication of 1866, *Un passo avanti nella cultura femminile* (A step forward in the education of women), she argued that education was the key to the emancipation of women and that only coeducational instruction could give women the same opportunities as men. Women had to find employment outside the home in order to achieve full emancipation. Her awareness of the importance of work outside the home questioned the ideal of woman as wife and mother. In 1881 she founded the Lega promotrice degli interessi femminili (League for the Advancement of Women's Interests), which advocated for a broad range of feminist issues, including the right to vote and

the abolition of legal prostitution. She maintained close ties to the Italian Socialist Party (PSI), of which she was a founder, but did not join it, preferring to campaign for women's causes from a position of political independence. Mozzoni's *La liberazione della donna* (The liberation of women, 1975) is the classic text of Italian feminism.

MSI (Movimento Sociale Italiano)
political party of the post–World War II period, rooted in fascism

The Italian Social Movement derives its name from the ITALIAN SOCIAL REPUBLIC founded by Fascists during World War II. Supporters of that last Fascist government founded the MSI in Rome in 1946. Anticommunist, anti-American, and strongly nationalist, it became the political voice of neo-fascism in postwar elections, winning 2 percent of the national vote in the elections of 1948 but reaching 8.7 percent in those of 1972, running jointly with the vanishing Monarchist Party. The MSI vote came mostly from southern districts, suburban Rome, and border areas of northern Italy around Trent and Trieste. As a minority party, the MSI sought to form coalitions with the dominant Christian Democratic Party (DC). This policy of *inserimento* was partially successful at the local level in the 1950s. It was tried briefly at the national level in 1960 when the MSI delegation in parliament supported the government headed by FERDINANDO TAMBRONI. That development alarmed the Left and provoked street protests nationwide, brought down Tambroni's government, and ended all efforts at cooperation between Christian Democrats and the MSI. By the end of the 1960s, under the leadership of Giorgio Almirante (1914–88), a party founder who served as secretary from 1969 to 1987, the MSI forsook the policy of *inserimento*. Instead of seeking cooperation with moderates, Almirante stressed nationalism and social radicalism, called for national unity, a strong elective presidency, and an assertive foreign policy sensitive to the needs of developing countries. Almirante's departure and the political changes of the 1990s altered the party's prospects. Under the leadership of Gianfranco Fini, who became its secretary in January 1995, the MSI transformed into a new party, the Alleanza Nazionale (National Alliance). National Alliance has since been part of the governing coalitions headed by SILVIO BERLUSCONI.

Munich Conference

Hitler's demand that Czechoslovakia return to Germany the Sudetenland, a territory inhabited by German-speaking populations that the TREATY OF VERSAILLES had awarded to Czechoslovakia in 1919, precipitated an international crisis that brought Europe to the verge of war. The high-level meeting brought together Adolf Hitler for Germany, BENITO MUSSOLINI for Italy, Neville Chamberlain for Great Britain, and Edouard Daladier for France. Although Italian interests were not immediately at stake, Mussolini played an important role as mediator between Hitler, who demanded immediate cession of the Sudetenland, and Chamberlain and Daladier, who supposedly represented the Czechs, who were not allowed to participate. Mussolini took charge of the conference and, as the only participant with a working knowledge of all the languages spoken around the table, enjoyed an advantage in the discussions. The solution proposed by Mussolini and adopted by the conference had in reality been prepared by Hitler and his staff, who handed it to Mussolini shortly before the start of the conference. Not surprisingly, the Germans obtained the Sudetenland, but the conference may have prevented them from eliminating Czechoslovakia altogether, as Hitler may have wanted to do. German troops were allowed to occupy the contested territory, pending ratification of union with Germany by a popular plebiscite that was never held. The conference improved temporarily Mussolini's image as a pragmatic politician amenable to reason and compromise. The favorable reaction of Italian public opinion to his role as peacemaker displeased Mussolini, who preferred to be admired for his warlike achievements and to prepare Italians for future wars.

Murat, Joachim (1767–1815)
king of the Two Sicilies as King Joachim Napoleon (1808–1814)

The son of a southern French innkeeper, Murat abandoned seminary study to join the army, joined up with NAPOLEON in 1795, and served under him in Italy, Egypt, and all of the European campaigns. Strikingly handsome, dashing, and courageous, Murat made a name for himself in Napoleon's cavalry and rose quickly through the ranks. In 1800 he married Napoleon's sister Caroline Bonaparte, who advanced her intellectually shallow husband's career with intelligent coaching and intrigue. In 1808 Murat succeeded the emperor's brother JOSEPH BONAPARTE as king of the Two Sicilies. In Naples Murat promised constitutional reforms, built roads, cracked down on banditry, and expanded the Neapolitan army. He also encouraged trade against the provisions of Napoleon's Continental system, resisted his brother-in law's demands for money and troops, allowed the formation of secret societies, and encouraged expectations of Italian independence. Murat's policies, personal magnetism, generosity, and love of display won him popularity in Naples. He agreed to assume a command in Napoleon's 1812 invasion of Russia, but renounced his commission in December 1812 and returned to Naples. In 1814 he negotiated secretly with Great Britain and Russia to retain his throne, but convinced that they would not accept him indefinitely, decided to back Napoleon again during the One Hundred Days in 1815, when Napoleon escaped from ELBA and regained power. In March 1815 Murat issued a proclamation promising Italian independence if Italians would support his cause. The Austrians defeated his small force at the battle of Tolentino in May 1815. Murat escaped to France, from where he led an even smaller force to southern Italy in a hopeless attempt to regain his kingdom.

He was captured and shot by Neapolitan troops loyal to the Bourbon dynasty in October 1815. Murat's promises of constitutional monarchy and Italian independence resonated sufficiently with liberals to give rise to *murattismo,* a political movement that later in the century appealed particularly to Neapolitan liberals as an alternative to national unification without Piedmontese leadership.

Muratori, Lodovico Antonio
(1672–1750)
archivist, medievalist, and Enlightenment reformer

Born near Modena to a family of modest means, Muratori studied law and was ordained into the priesthood (1694) before taking up the study of antiquities for which he is known. While serving as curator of the Ambrosian Library in Milan (1695–1700) he published two volumes of *Anecdota* (1697–98), a selection of unpublished historical texts discovered in the library. In 1690 he was appointed archivist and librarian to the duke of Modena. He seldom left Modena after that appointment and devoted himself entirely to scholarly research. Three monumental publications resulted from his lifelong labors. The first was the *Rerum italicarum scriptores* (Of Italian writers, 1723–38), a 28-volume collection of chronicles written by Italians from the year 500 to 1500 covering the rise of independent communes and states. The second was the *Antiquitates italicae medii aevi* (Italian medieval antiquities, 1738–43), a series of 75 historical studies that explicated and commented on the *Rerum italicarum scriptores.* The third, written in Italian, was the 12 volumes of the *Annali della storia d'Italia* (Annals of Italian history, 1744–49), in which Muratori attempted to write a unified political history of the peninsula, looking for commonalities beneath the diversity of governments and events. Many other works of his were published posthumously. In his writings Muratori displayed scholarly rigor and detachment from the passions of his time, striving for a level of objectivity that

gives his work a modern tone. Nevertheless, Muratori was caught up in the issues of his time. He worked to restore Italian culture to the position of eminence it had occupied in earlier centuries, improve government, and reconcile the culture of Catholicism with that of the ENLIGHTENMENT. Because of his pioneering research, scholarly method, and respect for truth Muratori can be called the founder of modern Italian historiography.

Murri, Romolo (1870–1944)
Catholic modernist thinker and founder of Christian Democracy

Ordained a Catholic priest in 1893, Murri called on the Catholic laity to exercise the right to vote and take advantage of the constitutional liberties of the liberal state. He demanded universal suffrage, proportional representation, and far-reaching social reforms. Murri addressed himself primarily to Catholic elites, seminarians, and university students, an approach that aroused the hostility of rival Catholic organizers who banked on the support of the clerical hierarchy. He launched the journal *Cultura Sociale* (1898–1906) to propagate his views. The journal exposed and castigated the social inequities resulting from capitalist production and the social conservatism of traditional Catholicism. Rejecting also socialist materialism and historical determinism, Murri urged workers and employers to seek the solution to labor problems in CORPORATISM, relying on the cooperation of workers and owners. He called on the state to reduce military spending, enact social legislation, make taxes more equitable, and protect small landowners. Murri was a controversial figure. Tolerated by Pope LEO XIII, he was censured by his successor PIUS X. The new pope resented Murri's National Democratic League, founded in 1905 to give the Catholic laity an independent political voice, and his attempts to open a dialogue with Socialists. A series of open letters critical of Vatican diplomacy brought a formal papal condemnation and a suspension of his clerical prerogatives. Murri then accepted a RADICAL PARTY offer to run for parliament, was elected, and excommunicated a few days after his election in March 1909. He was not reelected in 1913 due to Catholic opposition. Distanced from the church, he married, campaigned for Italian intervention in WORLD WAR I against the wishes of the Vatican, worked as a journalist, and made his peace with FASCISM. Pope PIUS XII readmitted him into the church in 1943 when he was already terminally ill. The Italian Popular party (PPI) and the left wing of the Christian Democratic Party (DC) were inspired by his ideas.

Murtola, Gaspare See MARINO, GIAMBATTISTA.

Mussolini, Alessandra See MUSSOLINI, BENITO.

Mussolini, Benito (1883–1945)
political journalist, founder of the Fascist movement, and dictator

Mussolini was born to politics. A native of the political hotbed that was the Romagna region (he was born near Predappio in the province of Forlì), he grew up in a household dominated by the radical politics of his father, Alessandro, who was a blacksmith by trade and a political agitator by temperament. Socialism, anarchism, and anticlericalism were the political passions of the day. Alessandro named his first born after the Mexican leader Benito Juárez. With Alessandro putting more time into politics than blacksmithing, what degree of security the family enjoyed came mostly from the mother. Rosa Maltoni was a respected elementary school teacher, a devout Catholic, and a caring mother. Benito, the oldest of three children, was intelligent and temperamental. Withdrawn, stubborn, physically aggressive, resentful of authority and of people who put on airs of social superiority, he was often in trouble in and out of school. He was also sensitive, but his sensitivity was more for animals and

Benito Mussolini *(Library of Congress)*

music than for people. At age nine he was sent by his parents to a religious boarding school. He was expelled after two years for attacking a fellow student with a knife. He did better in a lay school, and in 1902 completed the course of study leading to certification as an elementary school teacher.

In keeping with his political beliefs, that same year he refused to report for military duty, became a draft dodger, and left Italy for Switzerland. After living from hand to mouth for more than two years, he took advantage of a political amnesty, returned to Italy, fulfilled his military obligation, and embarked on a career in political journalism. As a journalist he excelled, making a name for himself as a socialist revolutionary and opponent of moderate party leader FILIPPO TURATI. In 1911 Mussolini led popular protests against the ITALIAN-TURKISH WAR, was arrested, spent five months in jail, and gained a national reputation as a hard-liner who was not afraid to take to the streets. In 1912 he rose to the prestigious and powerful position of head editor of the Socialist Party's national newspaper *Avanti!*. Uncomfortable with the legal tactics of the Socialist Party (PSI) and hoping that war would provide a direct path to revolution, in October 1914 he openly challenged the party position that Italy stay out of the European conflict that had broken out in August. Expelled from the party, Mussolini launched his own newspaper, *Il Popolo d'Italia,* that ran the slogan "War Today, Revolution Tomorrow" and demanded Italian intervention in the war.

During the war he served as artillery instructor, was wounded, returned to his newspaper, called on the Italian people to support the war effort, and demanded large territorial gains for Italy. In March 1919 he founded the Fasci di Combattimento, from which the movement rose that would soon be known as FASCISM. Mussolini appealed to war veterans and to what he called the *trincerocrazia* (aristocracy of the trenches), proposed radical reforms, including the confiscation of war profits, land confiscation and redistribution, and abolition of the monarchy. Around the end of 1920, when the failed occupation of the factories signaled to him that the revolutionary moment had passed, he jettisoned the radical demands, turned moderate, and courted the support of outside groups, which regarded fascism as a patriotic law-and-order movement. Fascist squads took to the streets, beat and intimidated their political opponents, and seized control of some local administrations. His election to parliament in 1921, the transformation of the Fascist movement into a regular political party (Partito Nazionale Fascista, or PNF), and the conclusion of a pact of pacification with the socialists reassured the monarchy, army, business, and landowners that they had nothing to fear from a Fascist victory. In the last days of October 1922 Mussolini staged the "march on Rome" and was appointed prime minister by King VICTOR EMMANUEL III.

Mussolini's first government was a coalition of Fascists, nationalists, liberals, and Catholics. The consolidation of power in his hands was a gradual process. First he had to rein in undisciplined and turbulent followers, which he did by reorganizing the Fascist action squads as the Fascist Militia. The ACERBO LAW and the elections of 1924 gave him a parliament dominated by Fascists and their supporters. The Socialist leader GIACOMO MATTEOTTI protested the use of violence in the elections. The political crisis that followed Matteotti's assassination resulted in the complete elimination of political opposition. The year 1925 marked the beginning of Mussolini's personal dictatorship. Suspicious and often contemptuous toward collaborators, Mussolini saw to it that no rival personalities would threaten his hold on power. The process was not marked by the extreme violence that accompanied the seizure of power by Hitler or Stalin. Mussolini took charge of key ministries, mediated disputes, strengthened police surveillance, issued press directives, and took credit for every achievement.

His popularity rested on the achievement of a balanced budget, stable currency and prices, an economy seemingly immune to the oscillations of the free market, and the settlement of the historical conflict between CHURCH AND STATE. By the early 1930s the image of Mussolini as the indispensable Duce (Leader) was firmly in place. Faith in Mussolini (*mussolinismo*), rather than belief in the ideology of fascism, was the cement that held together the Fascist regime. Popular support for Mussolini crested in 1935–36 with the ETHIOPIAN WAR, willed by Mussolini and perceived by most Italians as the fulfillment of a legitimate colonial aspiration and the settling of an old score with Ethiopia. Military success confirmed Mussolini's faith in his own almost superhuman powers of intuition and political gamesmanship. After 1935 he and many Italians believed the propaganda slogan that Mussolini was always right. Few questioned the wisdom of his decisions to ally Fascist Italy with Nazi Germany and pursue an aggressive FOREIGN POLICY that put Italy on a collision course with Great Britain and other liberal democracies. Convinced that only he could make Italy a world power, Mussolini took personal charge of foreign policy. Intervention in the Spanish civil war (1936) and the invasion of ALBANIA (1939) were decisions in line with the pursuit of great-power status. The euphoria of success did not deprive Mussolini entirely of a sense of political realism. Still aware of Italy's limited economic and military capabilities, he maintained correct relations with Great Britain, acted as a mediator at the MUNICH CONFERENCE (1938), listened to advisers who were critical of Nazi Germany, and did not intervene when Germany invaded Poland in September 1939. His decision to declare war on France and Great Britain in June 1940 was based on the miscalculation that a German victory was assured in short order.

WORLD WAR II was the gamble that he lost. Faced with military defeat, the king, army, most of his supporters, and public opinion turned against him. On July 25, 1943, the Fascist Grand Council, the highest consultative body of the regime, called on the king to take over command of the armed forces. That vote of no confidence gave the king a pretext to order the arrest and detention of Mussolini. Liberated by German paratroopers in September, Mussolini was persuaded by Hitler to set up the government of the ITALIAN SOCIAL REPUBLIC in northern Italy where the German army was still in control. That puppet regime lasted until the end of the war in the final days of April 1945. On April 27, 1945, members of the Italian RESISTANCE captured Mussolini while he was trying to escape disguised in a German uniform, along with other prominent Fascists. Next day, they executed him and his mistress Clara Petacci, who had also been captured. Their bodies and those of other Fascist officials were put on public display in Milan, spat at and kicked by a jeering crowd. So intense were the passions aroused by Benito Mussolini that his remains were hidden, and 10 years passed before they were interred in the family vault in the cemetery of Predappio. The name of Mussolini was political anathema for decades. It returned to the political arena when his granddaughter Alessandra Mussolini (born 1962), daughter of his son Romano and a niece of actress Sofia Loren, was elected to parliament in April 1992 as a representative of the neo-fascist Italian Social Movement (MSI).

N

Nadi, Nedo See SPORTS.

Naples, city of

Naples (pop. 1,003,000) is the largest and most important city of southern Italy. It is a major port city, an industrial center, a cultural hub, and tourist attraction. Its origins go back to Greco-Roman times when it was called Neapolis, from which derives its modern Italian name of Napoli. In the Middle Ages the city was ruled by Goths, Byzantines, and Lombards, with intermittent periods as an independent duchy and commune. The Normans conquered it in 1139. The German emperor Frederick II of Hohenstaufen favored the city, founding a famous center of studies (1224) that became the University of Naples and has now been renamed after its founder. The French Angevins took over the city and made it the capital of the kingdom of Sicily in 1282. Under Spanish control from 1443 with King ALFONSO I, the city became the dominant metropolis of the South and one of the largest cities of Europe. The nobility gathered there, and built splendid palaces; the clergy erected magnificent churches, monasteries, and convents. Commoners flocked to new quarters, bringing the population to about 400,000 by the middle of the 17th century.

The intelligentsia participated fully in the cultural developments and debates of the 17th and 18th centuries. Eighteenth-century Naples was the musical capital of Italy and the birthplace of what came to be known as Italian OPERA. GAETANO FILANGIERI, ANTONIO GENOVESI, PIETRO GIANNONE, and GIAMBATTISTA VICO made their mark in philosophy, economics, jurisprudence, and science. Formidable opposition from nobility and clergy stymied the administrative and political reforms attempted by the BOURBON DYNASTY. The Bourbon rulers, particularly CHARLES III, gave Naples its modern appearance with ambitious urban renewal projects and the construction of landmark buildings, like the San Carlo Opera House and the royal residence of Capodimonte. Major improvements occurred also during the reign of JOACHIM MURAT. Naples was the capital of the KINGDOM OF THE TWO SICILIES until the unification of Italy in 1860. The loss of its status as a capital city and court center was only partly compensated by the decision of the HOUSE OF SAVOY to make it the residence of the heir to the throne, who had the title of prince of Naples.

Urban congestion, high unemployment, and deterioration of public services created major problems for the city in the following decades. A disastrous cholera epidemic in 1884 brought the city to a low point of its history. Living conditions were improved by a vast program of urban renewal that lasted until the outbreak of World War I. The image of Naples as a city of romance and sentiment was launched in the 1890s by the popularity of Neapolitan song, a melodious genre that became part of the national culture. The creation of an industrial zone in 1904 triggered an unregulated process of urban expansion that has never been brought under control. An urban plan approved in 1939 was never implemented. The city suffered extensive damage during WORLD WAR II. It was the site of the Four Days of Naples, a popular revolt that forced the occupying German army to evacuate the city before the arrival of the Allies. Spreading urban blight marred the economic expansion of the postwar years. The city's mayor in the 1950s and early 1960s was the colorful Achille Lauro (1887–1982), a wealthy shipowner and impenitent monarchist notorious for his unorthodox electoral practices, which included distributing packages of pasta free of charge on the eve of elections. His term of office saw unregulated residential and industrial expansion that overwhelmed public services and damaged the environment. Christian Democratic rule in the 1960s and 1970s was roundly blamed for the worsening plight of the city, but a stint of communist administration after 1975 did not improve matters. For all its urban problems, Naples remains the economic powerhouse and cultural center of the South, and a point of attraction for countless visitors every year.

Naples, Kingdom of   See TWO SICILIES, KINGDOM OF THE.

Napoleon I (1769–1821)
general and emperor who subjected Europe to French rule

Born in Ajaccio (Corsica) as Napoleone Bonaparte (or Buonaparte) to a family of Tuscan origin, he attended military schools in France and was commissioned as an artillery officer in 1785. His rapid career advancement occurred against the backdrop of the FRENCH REVOLUTION. Success in the field earned him promotion to the rank of general and command of an army of Italy, with which he invaded Italy in spring 1796. More loyal to Napoleon than to the French government, living off the land, moving quickly to catch the enemy by surprise, Napoleon's soldiers won quick victories over the opposing Austrian, Sardinian, Neapolitan, and papal armies. In October 1797 Napoleon signed the Treaty of Campo Formio with Austria, which ended the first round of Napoleon's Italian campaigns. The treaty abolished the independence of VENICE,

Napoleon Bonaparte *(Library of Congress)*

dividing Venetian territories between Austria and the French-controlled Cisalpine Republic of northern Italy, recently established by Napoleon. He lost control of Italy while away on his Egyptian campaign (1798–99), but regained it decisively in 1800 after defeating the Austrians at the Battle of Marengo (June 14, 1800).

In the following years Napoleon extended and consolidated French rule over all of continental Italy. His coronation as emperor of the French in Paris (December 2, 1804) was followed by his coronation as king of Italy in Milan (May 26, 1805). About one-third of the Italian peninsula, including the modern regions of Piedmont, Liguria, and Tuscany, was annexed to France, and the rest was securely under his control. Napoleon appointed his stepson EUGENE DE BEAUHARNAIS viceroy of the Kingdom of Italy (1805) to govern what formerly had been the Cisalpine Republic. In 1806 he also appointed his older brother JOSEPH BONAPARTE king of Naples to govern the southern part of the peninsula. The dispossessed BOURBONS retained control of the island of Sicily, where they ruled under British protection. JOACHIM MURAT, another of Napoleon's brothers-in law, succeeded to the throne of Naples in 1808 when Joseph was sent to occupy the Spanish throne. The PAPAL STATES were annexed to France in 1809.

With these territorial arrangements Napoleon put the entire Italian peninsula under direct or indirect French rule, with major and lasting consequences. Napoleon brought to Italy the systems of uniform law, centralized administration, public record keeping, government finance, taxation, and military conscription that prevailed in France. The revolutionary principle of the career open to talent gave educated Italians new opportunities for advancement in the army and public administration. Land reform in the Kingdom of Naples abolished peasant obligations and various aristocratic privileges. Restrictions that kept inherited lands off the market and in the hands of the aristocracy, or that subjected land to common rights that hindered its more productive use were also abolished. These land reforms meant the end of the feudal system that had prevailed for centuries.

Some of these reforms were overdue and generally welcomed while others were resented or welcomed by only a few. Taxes and military conscription were particularly resented by the peasantry, which rose up against the French in areas of the South. The trade restrictions of Napoleon's Continental System also aroused opposition because they favored the French at the expense of Italian manufacturers. Patriots longing for national independence formed SECRET SOCIETIES that opposed French rule. Murat would play on these sentiments to win support in the final months of Napoleonic rule, gaining for himself undeserved recognition as a champion of Italian independence. The strength of national sentiments in Napoleonic times can be exaggerated. When Napoleonic rule came to an end in 1815, most Italians wanted peace, not national independence. Except among restored monarchs, there was never enough anti-French sentiment in Italy to abandon Napoleonic reforms. Italians of later generations would remember the Napoleonic period as one of resurgence and progress, and would regard Napoleon with a mixture of admiration and resentment. Few doubt that Napoleonic rule brought the spirit of change to Italy and marked the beginning of its modern period.

Napoleon III (1808–1873)
emperor of the French (1852–1870)

Born Louis-Napoleon Bonaparte, and often referred to as Louis-Napoleon, this nephew of NAPOLEON I spent his life in the shadow of his uncle, whose accomplishments he sought to emulate. Expelled from France after the defeat of his uncle, Louis-Napoleon spent his youth and early adulthood in Germany, Switzerland, and Italy. In the latter, he plotted with liberal conspirators and took part in the REVOLUTIONS in 1830–31. In 1840 he was sentenced to life imprisonment in France for attempting to seize power, but escaped in 1846. He returned to France during the REVOLUTION of 1848. In December 1848 he was elected president of the French Republic on the popular appeal of his name and family background. His sympathy for the cause of Italian independence, which he had supported in his youth, did not prevent him from sending an army to put down the ROMAN REPUBLIC in 1849. In November 1852 he assumed the title of emperor of the French by popular plebiscite, and the numeration of Napoleon III to indicate the continuity of the family dynasty (Napoleon II would have been the son of Napoleon I, who died without occupying the throne).

Louis-Napoleon's interest in Italian affairs was partly due to his youthful association with Italian liberals, a romantic desire to emulate his uncle's achievements, and to the traditional rivalry between France and Austria for dominance of the Italian peninsula. He was receptive to CAVOUR's overtures for French support against Austria. In July 1858 they met secretly in the town of PLOMBIÈRES and agreed to a division of the spoils in case of war with Austria. Cavour provoked Austria into declaring war on Piedmont-Sardinia in April 1859, Louis Napoleon intervened in the conflict, and French troops defeated the Austrians at the battles of Magenta and Solferino. Intervention had consequences that Louis-Napoleon had not anticipated. His sudden and unannounced conclusion of an armistice with Austria after his initial victories angered Italian patriots who expected the complete defeat and expulsion of Austria from Italy. However, they took advantage of Austria's partial defeat to stir uprisings in central and southern Italy, which led to the unification of the country in 1860–61. That was not what Louis-Napoleon had in mind. He favored a kingdom of Italy in the north ruled by his ally and personal friend VICTOR EMMANUEL II, but he did not welcome a large Italian kingdom strong enough to act independently of France. He nevertheless accepted the fait accompli, gaining for France the territories of NICE and SAVOY as compensation.

Relations with the newly formed Kingdom of Italy were often tense because Louis-Napoleon insisted on protecting the pope's temporal power and political independence, largely to appease Catholic sentiment in France and the rest of Europe. In 1867 he dispatched troops to fight off an attempt to capture Rome led by GIUSEPPE GARIBALDI. While that encounter confirmed Napoleon's negative image among the most ardent Italian patriots, many Italians were still grateful for his earlier help. King Victor Emmanuel II had to be dissuaded from dragging Italy into war at Louis-Napoleon's side in the Franco-Prussian War of 1870. A recent proposal to erect a monument in Milan in honor of Napoleon III is a belated acknowledgment of the decisive role played by this often-indecisive ruler in the RISORGIMENTO.

Napolitano, Giorgio (1925–)
Communist Party leader, member of parliament, advocate of European Union

Born in Naples in 1925, Napolitano joined the Italian Communist Party (PCI) in 1945. He has held important posts in the party, including a seat on the party's central committee, and has emerged as a voice of moderation. He moved the party toward acceptance of Italian membership in NATO and the EUROPEAN UNION. Now an ex-communist, he speaks with authority on the SOUTHERN QUESTION, and on economic and foreign policy issues. He worked with little success to unify the Left before the demise of the Communist and Socialist parties, and guided the PCI in its transformation into the Democratic Party of the Left. He has served in the chamber of deputies (1953–63, 1968–96), was speaker of the chamber (1992–94), minister of the interior (1996–98), and head of the PCI parliamentary group (1981–86). He was also a member of the European parliament (1989–92) and remains active in the movement for European union. Along with GIORGIO AMENDOLA, Napolitano represents the most moderate, social democratic, and pro-western faction of the former PCI.

Nathan, Ernesto See FREEMASONRY.

National Alliance See MSI.

nationalism
ideology that exalts the national state as the ultimate object of political allegiance

Nationalism is an ideology that regards as natural a world order based on sovereign national states, with the citizens of each state sharing values that spring from a common language, territory, religion, customs, and traditions. Nationalism asserts that the bonds that hold the citizens together must be stronger than the differences of class, region, and of religion that are to be expected in a large assemblage. This way of thinking took shape in reaction to the cosmopolitanism of the ENLIGHTENMENT, found fertile soil in the culture of ROMANTICISM, and was propagated by governments in search of popular support.

Modern Italy is a prime example of a nation-state formed when the mind-set of nationalism was taking hold. The RISORGIMENTO meant that the will to be one nation prevailed over the political and cultural differences that divided Italians. Patriots unified the country politically, but their concept of *italianità,* the consciousness of being Italian, was not shared by most of the population. Developing the consciousness of a shared national identity was the work of many generations. The process took many forms. Governments used force to repress BRIGANDAGE and popular uprisings that were perceived as challenges to the integrity of the national state. The use of force may have preserved the state in moments of crisis, but it could not achieve the higher objective of "making Italians." That was done through the slow, gradual path of persuasion. EDUCATION carried out by schools, the ARMED FORCES, community groups, and cultural associations played the major role in the first 50 years of national unity.

Impatient nationalists looked for shortcuts. From their efforts and movements sprang the most extreme form of nationalism, which had little in common with the sense of national identity and patriotic pride of their Risorgimento precursors. IRREDENTISM fixated on seizing territories inhabited by Italian-speaking populations from Austria. COLONIALISM held out colonial empire as the crowning achievement and logical culmination of national independence, which would make Italians proud of their nation. ENRICO CORRADINI personified the "new nationalism" that rejected the slow pace and gradual measures of liberal government and called for a great collective enterprise that would galvanize the nation.

Corradini, LUIGI FEDERZONI, and others formed the Italian Nationalist Association in Florence in 1910. The group was small but influential, thanks to the support it received from big busi-

ness, which provided funds, intellectuals and students who articulated its views and staged demonstrations. It severed ties with liberals and moderate nationalists, and monopolized the political representation of nationalist sentiment. The ITALIAN-TURKISH WAR triggered an outburst of national sentiment that reached all strata of the population and made nationalism a more potent force. The National Association called for a strong executive, colonial expansion, tariffs to protect domestic producers, the reorganization of industry to favor large cartels, and curbs on the power of labor unions. Antisocialism was the dominant note of the nationalist program. The Socialist Party (PSI) was to be banned for its internationalism and promotion of internal agitation. With this program the Nationalist Association became the center of a coalition of conservative interests that won in local elections and sent their first representatives to parliament in 1913.

Nationalists welcomed WORLD WAR I and backed the interventionist policy of Prime Minister ANTONIO SALANDRA. On the issue of intervention, they were on the same side as the socialist BENITO MUSSOLINI, whom they otherwise did not fully trust because of his socialist past and rabble-rousing tactics. After the war the Nationalist Association looked to the monarchy to provide strong leadership, readied its own blue-shirted shock troops (the *Sempre Pronti,* or Minutemen), and kept a certain distance from FASCISM. The fateful merger of the National Association and the Fascist Party occurred in 1923 after the Fascists had come to power. The merger made the Fascists more conservative and the nationalists more radical. The Fascists abandoned their plans for radical reform, and the nationalists tied themselves to a regime that could not resist playing to mass sentiments in a way that nationalists did not share. Still, conservative nationalists like Federzoni and ALFREDO ROCCO had a fundamental impact on the Fascist state. Their legislation strengthened the powers of the police, repressed dissent, and enforced law and order.

WORLD WAR II created the conditions for the dismantling of the state created by Fascists and nationalists. Since World War II, nationalism has been associated with the extreme Right, and Italians have generally regarded it with suspicion. The strong popular sentiment in favor of the EUROPEAN UNION is one manifestation of the rejection of nationalism, as is the appeal of separatist or antistate movements. Italians today distinguish between patriotism defined as love of country, which most share, and nationalism defined as blind allegiance to the national state, which most associate with the experience of fascism. A seemingly paradoxical development of the period since 1945 is that nationalist rhetoric has declined, while education, sports, popular entertainment, and the mass media have created stronger cultural ties that cut across class and regional differences.

'Ndrangheta   See MAFIA.

Negri, Ada (1870–1945)
socially sensitive poet and novelist
Negri was born in the Lombard town of Lodi to a working-class family, experienced poverty early in life, and developed a lifelong sympathy for those who suffered similarly in life. Teaching in elementary and middle schools in Milan was her way out of poverty and into middle-class life. Her first published collections of poems, *Fatalità* (Fatalities, 1892) and *Tempeste* (Storms, 1895) showed her social sympathies and humanitarian spirit. Critics took note and recognized her as a type of writer familiar to the Italian reading public at the time. In the manner of EDMONDO DE AMICIS and other similar writers, Negri expressed a "socialism of the heart" that had no rigorous ideological basis and sympathized with the oppressed in a vaguely humanitarian way. Socialism for her was the movement that spoke for the poor. A controlled sentimentality marks all her writings. Her later poems, novels, and short stories were more introspective and lyrical. The autobiographical *Stella mattutina* (Morning Star, 1921) is a moving account of her childhood and of her life as a teacher. Mostly forgotten or ignored today, Negri was the recipient of many literary prizes and was made a member of the ITALIAN ACADEMY in 1940.

Negri, Antonio (1933–   )
Marxist intellectual, theoretician, and activist of the extra-parliamentary Left
Antonio (Toni) Negri is the best-known theoretician of the extra-parliamentary movements of the 1970s. Born in Padua, brought up in a Catholic environment and active in Catholic youth associations, a brilliant student, he rejected Catholicism and embraced Marxism after graduating from the University of Padua in 1955. His social activism drew him at first to DANILO DOLCI in Sicily and to living in a kibbutz in Israel. In 1958 he joined the Socialist Party (PSI) briefly, but abandoned it as too moderate. His Marxism combined anarchist and libertarian tendencies with a Leninist commitment to the initiative of revolutionary elites. The object was to overthrow capitalism and the political system that supported it by direct and violent action, based on an alliance of workers and intellectuals. In practice, while workers fought for higher wages and improvements in the workplace, it was university students and the privileged children of both sexes from bourgeois families who rallied to the ideas that Negri and other intellectuals put forth in revolutionary tracts and journals. Negri exerted influence as a professor at the University of Padua and as the chief inspirer of revolutionary publications and movements. He was particularly associated with *Autonomia Operaia* (Worker Autonomy), a movement that attempted to redress the emphasis placed by ANTONIO GRAMSCI on the factory as the decisive place of confrontation between capitalism and workers. *Autonomia* aimed at broadening the scope of social struggle beyond the factory and into the streets. Violent actions by members of the subproletariat, radicalized women, and the disaffected in general would destabilize government and bring down bourgeois society. Negri was

arrested along with others in April 1979 and charged with being the secret leader of the RED BRIGADES. That charge was never substantiated, and Negri insisted in his own defense that he had aided no acts of terrorism and had only exercised his right to reflect and speak freely on the issues of the day. He was released from prison in June 1983 because he enjoyed parliamentary immunity as a recently elected member of parliament on the Radical Party (PR) ticket. Negri took his seat amid a ruckus of protests, but fled abroad in September, before a parliamentary commission recommended that he be arrested again. The court continued to hear his case and in 1988 he was convicted of aiding and abetting terrorists. He returned to Italy in 1997 to serve the remainder of a 13-year jail sentence. Negri unquestionably advocated the violent overthrow of capitalism and the state, but his precise ties with terrorists and with specific acts of violence remain unclear. He is due to be released from jail in the year 2004.

Nenni, Pietro (1891–1980)
Socialist leader, anti-Fascist, and post–World War II government figure

Nenni's radical politics were rooted in the social struggles of his native Romagna region in the early years of the 20th century. Born in Faenza, he followed a political itinerary common in his region. As a republican activist, in 1911 he led protests against the ITALIAN-TURKISH WAR and shared a prison cell with the socialist BENITO MUSSOLINI. The two were once again on the same side in 1914–15, when they advocated Italian intervention in WORLD WAR I. The parting of the ways came after the war, when Mussolini launched FASCISM and Nenni, in 1921, joined the Socialist Party (PSI). Nenni became editor of the party newspaper *Avanti!* (1922–24). That same year he led the group of Socialists who asserted their independence from Moscow. An opponent of fascism, he fled to France. In the 1930s he emerged as the head of the Socialist Party in exile. In that capacity, in 1934 he backed the pact of unity with the Communist Party (PCI) to create a common front against fascism. The Nazi-Soviet Pact of 1939 brought on a challenge to his leadership and he was ousted as party secretary.

Restored to the leadership of the party in 1943, Nenni returned to Italy still committed to unity of action with the Communists. The unity was reflected in the name "Socialist Party of Proletarian Unity" that the PSI assumed from 1943 to 1947. Nenni's choice of alliance sanctioned his party's subordinate role to the PCI, which quickly garnered the most votes on the political Left. His alliance with the PCI provoked secessions on both the right and left flanks of the Socialist Party. GIUSEPPE SARAGAT led the secession of the right in 1947 to form the Social Democratic Party (PSDI). The left wing split off in 1964 to form the Socialist Party of Proletarian Unity (PSIUP), resurrecting the name that the PSI had assumed in 1943.

The Soviet invasion of Hungary in 1956 and the receding danger of a Fascist revival in Italy, which was Nenni's basic and recurring fear, led to the gradual distancing of his party from the Communists. His new tactic was to encourage the OPENING TO THE LEFT, or Socialist participation in governments headed by the Christian Democratic Party (DC). In 1963–68 he served as vice president of the council of ministers and as foreign minister in DC-PSI coalition governments. The crisis of center-left governments in the 1970s brought about his gradual retirement from politics. An enigmatic political figure whose career was marked by significant changes of course, Nenni was vulnerable to charges of political incoherence and opportunism. The key to his politics was his fear of fascism, which he saw as a recurring threat. His strategy was to second those trends that seemed most likely to avert that danger: communism from 1934 to 1956 and liberal democracy thereafter.

neofascism See MSI.

Neo-Guelfs See GIOBERTI, VINCENZO.

Neoplatonism

Neoplatonism was a current of RENAISSANCE thought that drew inspiration from the writings of Plato. Neoplatonists sought to understand nature and arrange human affairs according to principles different from those of Aristotelian philosophy, which prevailed in the world of learning. Aristotelian thought looked at physical properties and was based on empirical observation, experimentation, and logical deduction. Neoplatonism emphasized spiritual elements, intuitive understanding, and abstract reasoning. In the hands of Neoplatonists, mathematics was a tool for deciphering the secrets of nature but, not content with understanding nature, Neoplatonists addressed such issues as the nature of human bonds, justice, and beauty. Thus Neoplatonism influenced all fields from the arts to science and in all parts of Europe from the early 15th century into the 17th. Italian scholars played a key role in the rise of Neoplatonism as they became familiar with and translated into Latin previously unknown writings of Plato, brought to Italy early in the 15th century by Greek scholars from Byzantium. MARSILIO FICINO translated the entire available body of Plato's writings and founded the informal group known as the Platonic Academy, which met in Florence under Medici auspices from the 1460s to the early 1490s, and was revived briefly in the early 16th century. Interest in Plato's thought existed largely outside the universities. Thus, Neoplatonism was associated with a kind of counterculture and intellectualism that challenged established authority. At the heart of the Neoplatonist rebellion was the belief that accumulated knowledge obscured the simple universal principles of nature and social organization. Neoplatonists sought to clear the deck and start from scratch. The effort to simplify by going back to first principles had fruitful results in the political theories and scientific discoveries of the 16th and 17th centuries. However, Neoplatonic thought could also lead in different directions. HERMETISM, religious mysticism, and anti-intellectualism were also part of the Neoplatonic legacy.

Neorealism

Neorealism is a style of expression in art, literature, and cinema that emerged in the 1930s, flourished in the 1940s, and declined in the 1950s. The term came into use in the 1930s to describe any form of artistic expression inspired by late 19th-century authors, including Emile Zola in France and GIOVANNI VERGA in Italy. Neorealists regarded the social environment as the formative influence on personality and attempted to portray the psychology of characters by their actions and behavior.

After WORLD WAR II Neorealism was associated particularly with cinematography. Never an organized movement, Neorealism found expression in a number of critically acclaimed fictional films by such directors as VITTORIO DE SICA, Pietro Germi (1914–74), ROBERTO ROSSELLINI, and LUCHINO VISCONTI. Neorealist directors proposed a "cinema of reality" that was meant to be culturally valid and educational in the civic sense of the word. They did not, however, start from theoretical premises. Visconti's film *Ossessione* (Obsession, 1942) started the trend. Based on James Cain's novel *The Postman Always Rings Twice*, it tells a sordid story of sex and crime that had no discernible civic message. The film escaped Fascist censorship even though it did not conform to the regime's preference for stories of heroism or escapist entertainment. Neorealism flourished in the postwar climate of deprivation and social misery. Rossellini's *Roma città aperta* (Open City, 1945) and *Paisà* (1946), and De Sica's *Sciuscià* (Shoeshine, 1946) and *Ladri di biciclette* (Bicycle Thieves, 1948) are representative of the Neorealist style of cinematography.

These films focused on aspects of daily life in postwar Italy and showed how ordinary people coped with hardship. They were shot on site rather than in studios, avoided elaborate scenery, and used talented amateurs rather than professional actors. These techniques were intended initially to keep down costs of production, but directors soon saw that they were appropriate to the subjects and goals of Neorealism. Compelling views of street life, effective use of everyday speech, and expression of intimate insights were strengths of the new style. The style, however, was not uniform. Rossellini's films were cinematically spare and nonrhetorical, while De Sica's took on more intimate and lyrical tones. De Sica's *Miracolo a Milano* (Miracle in Milan, 1951) and *Umberto D* (1952) brought Neorealism to a conclusion. The first has been described as a Marxist fairy tale, in which the poor find salvation in a fanciful flight to heaven. The second tells the story of an impoverished pensioner who struggles in vain to hold onto a genteel and gentlemanly style of life. In the political context of the time, the social protest content of Neorealist films inevitably associated Neorealism with left-wing movements.

Whatever its politics, Neorealism was an artistic revolt against rhetoric, sentimentality, and sophistication. Critics hailed Neorealist films as innovative masterpieces, but public reactions were mixed. Many Italian viewers objected to the emphasis on the seamy aspects of life and the unflattering portrayals of Italians. The general reception was more favorable abroad, where Neorealist films did well at the box office. Neorealism's decline in the 1950s was the result of changing tastes and official policy. Audiences showed a distinct preference for Hollywood-style action, and the government was no longer willing to subsidize films that portrayed Italian life unfavorably. The legacy of Neorealism lives on in films that address social issues and call for socially responsible behavior.

Neri, Pompeo (1706–1776)
political adviser and Enlightenment reformer

Pompeo Neri was born in Florence, began his formal education in seminary, and completed it with a law degree from the University of Pisa (1726). He taught public law at the same institution from 1726 to 1735, when he began his career as a civil servant in the service of the MEDICI FAMILY. When the HABSBURG-LORRAINE DYNASTY took over the duchy of Tuscany in 1737,

Neri became secretary of state and chief adviser to the new rulers. In that capacity, he began the process of administrative reform that eventually made the Duchy of Tuscany a model of good government, according to the ideas of the ENLIGHTENMENT. His work in Tuscany was interrupted in 1748 when Empress Maria Theresa called him to Lombardy to complete a new *catasto* (census of land ownership) for purposes of taxation. Fiscal fairness and efficiency of collection were the guiding principles of his reforms. Neri returned to Tuscany 10 years later. Peter Leopold made him chief minister in 1765, charged with carrying out reforms to improve the public administration and stimulate the economy. Neri played a key role in the adoption of free trade in grains (1767), abolition of guilds, and reorganization of government that delegated important duties, including tax collection, to local administrations that represented taxpayers. Many of his reforms were still incomplete at the time of his death, and came to a halt when the outbreak of the French Revolution inspired fear of further change in the minds of monarchs.

Neri, Saint Philip   See BARONIO, CESARE.

Nervi, Pier Luigi   See ARCHITECTURE.

Niccolini, Giovanni Battista (1782–1861)
romantic writer noted for the patriotic tone of his works

This Tuscan writer and playwright, born near Pisa, achieved popularity with his plays that dramatized historical incidents and conveyed easily perceived patriotic messages. The subjects of two of his tragic plays, *Nabucco,* which told the story of the Babylonian ruler Nebuchadnezzar punished for his tyrannical use of power, and *Giovanni da Procida* (1817), which focused on the leader of the revolt of the Sicilian Vespers, inspired two popular operas by GIUSEPPE VERDI. His most popular play was *Arnaldo da Brescia*

(1843), which dramatized the story of the 12th-century religious radical who led a republican revolt against the pope. This play reflected Niccolini's strong ANTICLERICALISM and opposition to the PAPACY in 19th-century Italy. Niccolini's hatred of absolutism and papal power struck a chord among audiences during the RISORGIMENTO. Niccolini remained faithful to the republican radicalism that had been dominant before the REVOLUTION of 1848, when the movement for national unification turned moderate under CAVOUR's leadership. Literary critics have not been kind to Niccolini, dismissing him as a writer of minor talent who won success by catering to the tastes of a public easily stirred by patriotic rhetoric. His characters were political symbols that stirred patriotic sentiments.

Nice, city of (Nizza)

A port and resort city on the Mediterranean coast of France, Nice, formerly Nizza, has been part of France since 1860. Lombards, Franks, Neapolitans, the Ottomans, France, Spain, and the HOUSE OF SAVOY have fought over it in the course of its history. It passed under the rule of the Savoy dynasty in 1402 and remained there until 1860, with some interruptions in times of war when others occupied the city. The Italian government ceded it to France as part of the AGREEMENT OF PLOMBIÈRES negotiated by CAVOUR in return for French help in the war against Austria. The cession provoked a heated debate in the new Italian parliament, in the course of which GIUSEPPE GARIBALDI accused Cavour of having made him a foreigner in his own land by ceding his native city to France. The cession was ratified by a popular plebiscite that voted overwhelmingly in favor of union with France. Fascist propagandists claimed Nice for Italy prior to the outbreak of WORLD WAR II and Italian troops occupied the city during the war.

Nicholas V (Pope) See ALBERTI, LEON BATTISTA; MARTIN V.

Nicotera, Giovanni (1828–1894)
patriot, conspirator, and political figure of the Liberal Left

Nicotera was born near Catanzaro (Calabria) to a family of the nobility with ties through his mother to the democratic wing of the movement for national unification. His republican uncles, who conspired against the Bourbon monarchy, and his teacher LUIGI SETTEMBRINI inspired the young Nicotera to fight for the ROMAN REPUBLIC in 1849. After 1849 he found political refuge in Piedmont, where he consorted with republican revolutionaries hostile to the monarchy. He was with CARLO PISACANE in the unlucky expedition of June 1857 in which Pisacane lost his life. Nicotera, seriously wounded, was captured by Neapolitan troops. Charges leveled against him in 1877 that he had divulged sensitive information about the conspiracy to his interrogators became the basis of a clamorous trial while he was minister of the interior. In June 1860 the troops of GIUSEPPE GARIBALDI liberated him from a Neapolitan jail where he was serving a life sentence. From then on Nicotera was at Garibaldi's side, in the expeditions of 1862, 1866, and 1867. Like most republicans of his generation, Nicotera came to terms with the monarchy after national unification and was part of the LIBERAL LEFT. He was elected to parliament in 1862. He became minister of the interior when the Liberal Left came to power in 1876. During his two-year tenure in that post, he gained a reputation for authoritarian use of power and for using the country's security apparatus to win elections for candidates loyal to the government of AGOSTINO DEPRETIS. By 1891–92, when he again served as minister of the interior, Nicotera was a strong domestic law-and-order advocate close in spirit to FRANCESCO CRISPI.

Nievo, Ippolito (1831–1861)
novelist, poet, playwright, and Risorgimento patriot

Ippolito Nievo was born in Padua to a family of the upper middle class. The REVOLUTION of 1848 drew him to the republican movement of GIUSEPPE MAZZINI, to which he remained faithful when others defected to the monarchist side. He fought with GIUSEPPE GARIBALDI in 1859 and 1860, serving as a military administrator in Sicily. He died in a shipwreck in May 1861 on his way from Sicily to Naples. His many writings include verses and plays of patriotic and civic inspiration, plays and short stories that romanticize peasant life and popular customs, political tracts, and a diary. The most important of his many writings was the historical novel *Confessioni di un italiano* (The castle of Fratta), originally published posthumously in 1867 with the title *Confessioni di un ottuagenario* (Confessions of an octogenarian). It explores the course of events in Italy through the personal experiences of the fictional protagonist, a Venetian gentleman whose life spanned the period from the demise of the Venetian republic in 1797 to 1855 when Nievo began to write the novel. The opening sentence, in which the protagonist expressed the hope that, having been born a Venetian, he hoped to die an Italian, expressed Nievo's own longing for a national identity and set the tone for the book. Patriotic sentiment is what won admiration for the novel at first. Critics later discovered its literary merits, Nievo's talent for narrative, and his psychological insights. Nievo was a writer of considerable originality, whose premature death may have cut short a major literary career and silenced a voice sensitive to the political, social, and cultural problems inherent in the process of national unification.

Nigra, Costantino (1828–1907)
political figure, diplomat, scholar, and writer

Costantino Nigra was born in the small Piedmontese town of Villa Castelnuovo (Ivrea) to a family of the lower middle class (his father was an unlicensed medical practitioner). His family saw to it that he received a good education. Nigra interrupted his university studies in Turin to fight against the Austrians in 1848, was wounded in combat, returned to the university, and graduated with a law degree in 1849. His diplomatic career began in 1851 with a minor appointment in the Piedmontese Ministry of Foreign Affairs. Diligence, good looks, personal charm, and tactfulness eased his rise through the ranks. MASSIMO D'AZEGLIO and CAVOUR valued his services and speeded his progress. He was particularly valuable to Cavour as his chief contact with Emperor NAPOLEON III and Empress Eugénie in the late 1850s, when Cavour engineered the alliance with France against Austria. Nigra's charm is said to have softened the empress's opposition to her husband's policy of helping Piedmont. Nigra's reward was his appointment as Italian ambassador to Paris, a post that he held from 1860 to 1876. Influential and popular in Paris during the rest of the Second Empire, Nigra became a controversial figure after the downfall of Napoleon III in 1870. He was resented in France for supporting Italian neutrality in the Franco-Prussian War, and in Italy for being pro-French when Italian foreign policy veered toward Germany and Austria-Hungary. King VICTOR EMMANUEL II nurtured a strong dislike of Nigra. Questionable business deals may have accounted for the sizable fortune that Nigra accumulated in the booming Paris of the 1860s. He held on to his Paris post as long as the HISTORICAL RIGHT governed in Italy, and served as ambassador to St. Petersburg (1876–82), London (1882–85), and Vienna (1885–1904) before retiring to private life. Nigra excelled as a genial host and easily won the confidence of the powerful people with whom he associated in his ambassadorial capacity. He was made a count in 1882 and a senator in 1890. In 1892 he received the *Collare dell'Annunziata,* Italy's highest royal decoration, which made its recipients "cousins" of the king. His lifelong love of literature resulted in the publication of a collection of folk poetry, *I canti popolari in Piemonte* (Folk songs of Piedmont, 1888). His greatest contribution was as an intelligent executor of Cavour's foreign policy. A book of memoirs that he had completed disappeared mysteriously at the time of his death and has never been found.

Nitti, Francesco Saverio (1868–1953)
economist, promoter of southern economic development, and liberal leader

Nitti was born in Melfi in the region of BASILI-CATA. The son of a forestry inspector, he studied and taught finance at the University of Naples, and attracted public attention as a second-generation MERIDIONALISTA. His book *Nord e Sud* (North and South, 1900) addressed the burning political issue of the relationship between those two parts of the country. Nitti's sympathies were with the Radical Party (PR) and its program of rapid industrialization to solve the country's political and social problems. He was confident that Italy could compensate for its lack of coal and oil by developing its *carbone bianco* (white coal), an allusive name for the country's extensive hydroelectric resources. He also singled out the area of NAPLES as particularly promising for industrial development and was instrumental in passing legislation that had the desired result. Elected to parliament in 1904 for the PR, Nitti generally supported the progressive policies of GIOVANNI GIOLITTI, serving in one of his governments as minister of agriculture, industry, and commerce (1911–14).

Cooperation with Giolitti was short-lived and the two soon became bitter political rivals. Their rivalry weakened the liberal coalition that could have resisted the rise of the political Right. Nitti did not favor Italian intervention in WORLD WAR I, but when the country went to war he served as minister of finance in the government formed by VITTORIO EMANUELE ORLANDO (1917–19). He succeeded Orlando as prime minister (June 1919–June 1920) at a particularly difficult moment. Strikes, political turmoil, economic crisis, and the occupation of FIUME were his major challenges. Nitti, serving as both prime minister and minister of the interior responsible for law and order, took a strong stand against striking workers, demonstrators, and dissenters. His efforts to settle territorial disputes with neighboring Yugoslavia by negotiation, his refusal to accept Fiume from the self-proclaimed patriots and insubordinate troops who had occupied it against the wishes of the government, an amnesty for wartime deserters, and reduction of military spending cast him in the role of arch-villain in the eyes of nationalists and Fascists, who orchestrated a ferocious and at times highly personal smear campaign against him.

The adoption of proportional representation in national elections was an important and well-meaning political innovation of his prime ministry, but it further destabilized an already shaky political system. Far from helping moderate candidates of all parties, as Nitti had hoped, proportional representation weakened the liberal center and strengthened socialist and Catholic blocs with which he did not get along. Too controversial to form another government, Nitti stepped down and Giolitti took over. He fought against FASCISM from his seat in parliament. In 1924 the Fascists destroyed his home, and he fled the country for France. In 1943, still living in France, he was seized and imprisoned by German troops. After the war he founded the short-lived National Democratic Union Party. His politics now wavered from the Communist Party (PCI) to the populist UOMO QUALUNQUE (Everyman's Party). He became a senator in 1948. A public figure of exceptional intellect and technical competence, Nitti's political judgments and decisions were often perplexing and questionable.

Nobile, Umberto (1885–1978)
pioneer of Italian aviation, manufacturer, and explorer

A pioneer in the development of lighter-than-air aircraft, Nobile's ventures belong to the period between the two world wars when manufacturers and governments competed to develop new types of aircraft and achieve prestigious world records. Nobile was born near Naples, received degrees in electrical and industrial engineering from the University of Naples, and in 1911 entered the developing field of aeronautical engineering. During WORLD WAR I he served in the Italian army with the rank of lieutenant colonel, helping to develop airships modeled on

Umberto Nobile *(Library of Congress)*

explorer Roald Amundsen reached the North Pole on May 12, 1926. A competing American expedition, led by Richard E. Byrd, claimed to have reached the pole three days before Nobile's. Nobile's flight was nevertheless recognized as a major technological achievement. Lionized and honored in Italy and elsewhere, Nobile was encouraged by this first success to attempt a second and more ambitious expedition to the Arctic. The expedition ran into difficulties almost from the moment the dirigible *Italia* lifted off from Milan on April 15, 1928, with a crew of 18 on board. The *Italia* reached the North Pole on May 24. Disaster overtook the crew on the start of the return trip a day later, when bad weather and frozen controls forced the airship to crash onto the ice below. The dramatic attempts to rescue the survivors made international headlines. Nobile's reputation was severely shaken by the debacle. He resigned from the air force after an official government inquiry blamed him for the disaster. The rest of his life was anticlimactic. He designed dirigibles for the Soviet Union (1932–36), taught aeronautics at the University of Naples (1936–39) and in the United States until 1943. After the war he associated briefly with the Italian Communist Party (PCI), but politics did not interest him, and he dropped out.

After being cleared by a review of his case, he was restored to the air force and promoted to the rank of major-general. He resumed teaching at the University of Naples and spent his last years in Rome reading, writing, and trying to come to terms with the triumphs and ordeals of his career.

Germany's zeppelins. After the war he founded the Aeronautical Construction Factory, which manufactured dirigibles based on his own design, hoping to capture the promising American and Japanese markets. When the Fascists came to power in October 1922, Nobile was in the United States, but rushed back to Italy to look after the interests of his company, which was being eyed by the Fascists for possible purchase by the state. Nobile succeeded in fending off the Fascist overtures, but in the process incurred the enmity of prominent Fascist figures, including the young and ambitious ITALO BALBO, who looked upon the air force as his own special preserve. In 1925 Nobile began to plan the ventures with which his name would be associated forever: flights to the North Pole and the exploration of the Artic region by dirigible. A first flight carried out jointly with the Norwegian

nobility   See ARISTOCRACY.

nonexpedit   See CHURCH AND STATE.

Nono, Luigi (1924–1990)
innovative avant-garde composer
Luigi Nono was born in Venice and studied at the Venice Conservatory. He fell under the spell of Arnold Schoenberg (whose daughter he married)

and adopted electronic and serial music as his forms of expression. Drawn to the RESISTANCE movement, he became a member of the Italian Communist Party (PCI) after the war. Many of his musical works reflected his politics. His postwar compositions included *Il canto sospeso* (The suspended song, 1955), a setting to music of letters written by resistance fighters condemned to death, and *Suite: Intolleranza* (Intolerance Suite, 1960). *Intolleranza* is a sung and acted piece resembling OPERA that quotes communist liberation slogans and condemns all forms of authoritarianism. It pleased neither communists nor fascists, but it was the latter who staged noisy demonstrations at performances of the work. *A Specter Rises Over Europe* (1971) sets to music Karl Marx's *Communist Manifesto*. In time his music became less overtly political and more generally humanitarian. *Prometeo* (Prometheus, 1985) is widely regarded as a masterpiece of contemporary music. From the early 1960s on, Nono worked mainly from Germany. A striking feature of Nono's work is the search for novel sounds and visual effects contrived to elicit strong reactions. Nono sought to bring his music to popular audiences in factories and recreation halls; its reception in those locales is not documented.

Northern League   See BOSSI, UMBERTO.

Novara, Battle of   See WARS OF NATIONAL INDEPENDENCE; CHARLES ALBERT.

Novaro, Michele   See MAMELI, GOFFREDO.

Novecento movement

The Novecento (20th-Century) movement, or *novecentismo*, was a cultural trend of the 1920s that sought to align and harmonize the legacies of the past, particularly the classical and imperial legacy of ancient Rome, with the artistic, literary, and political sensitivities of the 20th century. FASCISM and communism shared the notion that art and politics are intimately intertwined. *Novecentismo* reinforced the concept of *romanità* (the cult of ancient Rome) that sustained the regime's cultural and political ambitions. The group that started the movement in October 1922 (the same month that the Fascists came to power) called itself the *Sette Pittori del Novecento* (Seven Painters of the 20th Century). Their intention was to launch a new art that would give fascism a distinct cultural identity. That art would reject romantic sentimentality, naturalistic representation, and psychological introspection in favor of a stern, controlled style of expression (classicism) that celebrated technical progress, modern dynamism, heroic action, and individual intelligence. Prominent among the founders were the literary critic MARGHERITA SARFATTI and the painter Mario Sironi (1885–1961). Sironi's murals were particularly successful examples of the fusion of past and present, classicism and heroic ethos, that was the aim of the *novecentisti*. In literature the chief *novecentista* was the writer and critic Massimo Bontempelli (1878–1960), who founded and led the literary review *900* (1926–29), for the express purpose of inserting Italian literature in the larger European context, where it could measure itself against competing currents. The desire to carry on a dialogue with currents like dadaism and surrealism that were considered alien to Italian culture was a major reason for the mixed reception that the movement received in Fascist circles. Hard-line Fascists damned its art as anarchist, internationalist, Leninist, and grotesque. Ironically, *novecentismo* lost political favor in the 1930s, just as the regime embarked on the policy of imperial expansion that was part of the cult of ancient Rome touted by the movement. By that time, some of its exponents, including Bontempelli, were distancing themselves from the regime. *Novecentismo* never became the official art movement of fascism that it aspired to be. Its presence attests instead to the regime's capacity for incorporating multiple styles of artistic expression.

Nuvolari, Tazio   See SPORTS.

Oberdan, Guglielmo See IRREDENTISM.

Occhetto, Achille See PCI.

Ochino, Bernardino (1487–1564)
Capuchin monk, theologian, preacher, and religious reformer

Ochino was born in Siena, took minor orders at an early age, and went on to study medicine, philosophy, and theology in Perugia. Dissatisfied with lax clerical discipline in minor orders, he joined the Capuchins in 1534. His exceptional devotion and learning paved the way to the highest post as general of the Capuchin Order (1538–42). As a preacher capable of stirring religious fervor in audiences, he was in high demand throughout Italy. It was therefore all the more shocking when he broke with the Catholic Church in 1542. After Luther's, his was the most clamorous defection from the church in the 16th century. Ochino's search for a more spiritual religion made him gravitate toward the evangelical movement that was taking root in northern Europe. The notion of justification by faith alone particularly appealed to Ochino. From that premise he condemned Catholic ritual, the sacraments, the authority of bishops, and the pope as the incarnation of the Antichrist. Called upon to justify his views before the ROMAN INQUISITION, Ochino fled to Geneva where Calvin welcomed him. In Geneva Ochino married a religious refugee from Lucca, but his stay in the Swiss city was soon marred by clashes with Calvin. He was in London from 1547 to 1553, when he was forced to leave by the government of the Catholic Queen Mary. From London he went to Strasbourg, and from there to Poland and Moravia, where he died. Ochino was a religious dissenter at war with all forms of authority, whether Protestant or Catholic. He was closest theologically to the anti-Trinitarians and Socinians who, also persecuted by everyone else, found refuge in eastern Europe.

Olivetti, Gino See CONFINDUSTRIA.

Olivetti S.p.A.
manufacturer of office machines and computers, known as a progressive employer

This major manufacturer of office machines began modestly as Italy's first manufacturer of typewriters. Camillo Olivetti (1868–1943) founded the firm in 1908 after an earlier successful start as a manufacturer of electrical gauges, which provided start-up capital for his typewriter business. Born to a family of Jewish merchants and landowners from the Piedmontese town of Ivrea, Olivetti married Luisa Revel in 1894 and later converted to her Waldensian Protestant faith. A pioneering industrial engineer in Italy, he was influenced by the example of American industrial production, which he observed and studied directly during several visits to the United States. However, Olivetti was also motivated by a paternal concern for the welfare of his workers, was active in the Italian Socialist Party (PSI), and wanted the workplace to provide financial security and social services for workers and their families. He adamantly refused to lay off workers in times of crisis, insisting that unemployment was a social scourge and a tragedy for workers. The town of Ivrea, in which he located his factories, became something of a company town, heavily dependent on the fortunes of the Olivetti family firm. The business had a slow start, employing only a few hundred workers in 1918 and about 4,000 workers in 1945. In between, however, Olivetti and his son Adriano (1901–60) laid the foundations for the enormous expansion that began in the 1950s. In the period between the two world wars, while the Fascist regime pursued the goal of national self-sufficiency (AUTARKY), the Olivetti company modernized its facilities, diversified its production, produced new models for office and home use, developed its own commercial network, and began to compete on foreign markets. Adriano assumed top managerial responsibilities in 1938, the year of the Fascist anti-Semitic legislation, which resulted in the removal of many Jewish managers, but the family retained control of the firm, even though Adriano, like his father, was rightly suspected of harboring anti-Fascist sentiments. In the final phases of World War II, Adriano actively collaborated with the RESISTANCE movement. The postwar expansion of the firm was facilitated by the fact that the physical plant emerged from the war with relatively little damage. The global expansion that transformed the family firm into an industrial giant occurred in the 1950s and 1960s, when Olivetti competed successfully for a share of world markets. The takeover of Underwood in 1960 gave Olivetti a secure foothold in the American market. In that same decade Olivetti began to compete in the production of computers. The social vision long associated with the Olivetti name passed with the death of Adriano, who shared his father's social ideals. In the last years of his life, Adriano launched his own movement to promote regionally balanced industrial development, urban planning, popular education, and social services for workers. He ran successfully for parliament

in 1958 on a personal ticket, but found that he lacked the party support needed to translate his vision into policy. Carlo de Benedetti, a business executive with a reputation for toughness, headed the Olivetti complex from 1978 to 1996. Large deficits incurred in the 1980s required major infusions of capital by international investors in the 1990s, which raised the prospect of international control of the company. In August 2003 Telecom Italia, a communicatioons firm, merged with Olivetti and gave its name to the reorganized enterprise. Telecom Italia has all but abandoned the business machines line to concentrate on the more promising fields of telecommunications and information technology.

Opening to the Left
inclusion of Socialists in governments dominated by Christian Democrats

In the wake of the ECONOMIC MIRACLE that transformed the Italian economy in the 1950s, of the mounting exodus of people from the countryside into the cities, and unequally distributed but very tangible improvements in the standard of living, the political system found a new equilibrium based on the inclusion in government of the Italian Socialist Party (PSI). The primary mover behind this "opening to the Left" was the Christian Democratic leader AMINTORE FANFANI, who served as both prime minister and foreign minister after the elections of 1958 gave the Christian Democrats a solid 42 percent of the national vote, not enough to govern alone but more than enough to dominate any governing coalition. Fear that an alliance with the Socialists would increase Fanfani's power, splits within the Christian Democratic Party (DC), the close relationship between the PSI and the Communist Party (PCI), and opposition from big business, the CATHOLIC CHURCH, and the United States delayed the inclusion of Socialists in the government until Fanfani's power was curbed, the Socialists distanced themselves from the Communists, the papacy of Pope John XXIII and the administration of U.S. president John F. Kennedy changed church and American policy, and big business was reassured by American support. The chief motivation was to give the Christian Democrats a more secure base in parliament and keep Communists away from the center of political power. On the Socialist side, it was party leader PIETRO NENNI who decided, after considerable hesitation, that it was time to be part of governing coalitions. The first center-left government was formed by Fanfani in March 1962 when the Socialists in parliament, who were not yet given ministerial posts, abstained from voting against it under the conditions that the electrical industry be nationalized, the school system reformed, and regional governments instituted. The government met only the first of these conditions. ALDO MORO formed the first government with the actual participation of Socialists and with Nenni as vice premier in December 1963, thus inaugurating the era of center-left coalitions that confronted student activism, labor militancy, political terrorism, and economic crisis through the 1960s and 1970s. The legalization of divorce and abortion, implementation of regional autonomy, and economic recovery were achievements of these center-left governments. The appointment of Socialist Party leader BETTINO CRAXI as prime minister in 1983 seemed a logical conclusion of what had matured in the previous 20 years, but by then it was also clear that the opening to the Left had not brought on the political renewal that many had expected. Political patronage in the public sector of the economy, government corruption, regional imbalances, and the inefficiency of public services plagued the political system that had led the country out of the postwar crisis and contributed to the downfall of the major political parties in the 1990s.

opera

Opera is a form of entertainment traceable to the RENAISSANCE interest in music and the theater of ancient Greece. An opera is a story set to music, staged, acted, and sung. A librettist (from *libretto,* or little book) writes the lyrics that are then set to music by the composer. Giulio Caccini (ca. 1546–1618) and Jacopo Peri (1561–1633) wrote the earliest opera for which the music has survived. Their *Euridice,* first performed in Florence's Palazzo Pitti in 1600 to celebrate the impending marriage of Henry IV of France to Marie de' Medici, set to music a text by the poet Ottavio Rinuccini (1562–1621). It was a retelling of the familiar Greek myth of Orpheus's love for Eurydice, changed to provide a happy ending to what originally was a tragic tale of lost love. The story of the two lovers combines dramatic action and deep emotional involvement, the two enduring characteristics of *opera seria* or tragic opera. Initially opera was a form of entertainment for the aristocracies of Florence and Rome that concerned itself with lofty, inspirational topics, and appealed to the tastes of musical connoisseurs.

Bolstered by the musical genius of CLAUDIO MONTEVERDI, opera won recognition as the most complete form of theater. It jumped from the courts and private theaters of Italy to those of Germany, France, and the rest of Europe, the last and most popular emanation of Italian Renaissance culture to win ascendancy abroad. Italian composers dominated the field in Monteverdi's time. The most notable were Francesco Cavalli (1602–76) who established opera in Venice, and Alessandro Scarlatti (1660–1725) and Niccolò Jommelli (1714–74), who helped launch the Neapolitan school of opera. The contribution of Naples to the tradition of Italian opera was particularly important, giving Italian opera lasting character and structure. Giovanni Battista Pergolesi (1710–36), Domenico Cimarosa (1749–1801), Niccola Piccinni (1728–1800), and Giovanni Paisiello (1740–1816) made Naples the musical center of 18th-century Italy. They were prolific composers of sacred and profane music. One of their great accomplishments was to give dignity to the *opera buffa* (comic opera), a lighter form of opera that appealed to popular audiences. *Opera buffa* forsook the heroic characters and inspirational motifs of *opera seria* in favor of earthy and sometimes wildly improbable but always amusing situations.

Neapolitan opera set the forms that became those of Italian opera in general. Individual arias, duets, trios, quartets, choruses, and ensembles became showpieces for the melodic inventiveness of composers and the bravura of singers. These showstoppers were strung together by long stretches of *recitativo* (recitative), lines spoken with minimal musical accompaniment. Melody counted more than harmony, sentiment more than character development. The strengths of Neapolitan opera were serenity, clarity, and simplicity. Serious or comic, opera took the world of entertainment by storm. Hundreds of public opera houses, several capable of accommodating thousands of spectators, went up in cities throughout Italy after the first was built in Venice in 1637. A remarkable phenomenon was that of the CASTRATI, the highly trained interpreters of male and female roles who became the first popular idols of the entertainment world. The art of bel canto (beautiful song) with its emphasis on purity of tone, breath control, agility in ornamentation, and sustained lyrical phrasing began with the castrati.

Opera bridged the gap between elite audiences and the general public. For all its popularity, opera was an economically risky business that attracted more than its share of improvisational and unscrupulous impresarios. Still, the potential for economic reward was sufficient to attract composers and performers of talent. With the help of government subsidies that opera has always needed, the 19th century was the golden age of Italian opera. Government help was not disinterested, however. Well aware of opera's popular following, the authorities wanted to make sure that what appeared on the opera stage posed no threat to established government, morality, and religious faith. Censorship was a fact of life for all composers until the liberal regime of united Italy lifted many restrictions. Composers were generally able to work their way around them.

The works of GIOACCHINO ROSSINI, VINCENZO BELLINI, GAETANO DONIZETTI, and GIUSEPPE VERDI dominated the world of opera in Italy and abroad

Arturo Toscanini *(Library of Congress)*

until challenged by French opera and the works of Richard Wagner in the latter part of the century. In Italy, Wagnerian composers like ARRIGO BOITO and ALFREDO CATALANI found a small but vocal and devoted following that challenged Verdi's overwhelming influence. It is a measure of the depth of musical talent in 19th-century Italy that composers of stature like Saverio Mercadante (1795–1870) and Amilcare Ponchielli (1834–86), the composer of *La Gioconda* (1876), were considered second rate. Ponchielli was also influential as professor of music at Milan's prestigious conservatory. His students included GIACOMO PUCCINI and PIETRO MASCAGNI, who carried Italian opera into the 20th century. Their operas, like those of RUGGIERO LEONCAVALLO and Umberto Giordano (1867–1948), expressed a more natural, colloquial idiom in which the music adhered closely to the spoken line. They often featured ordinary people caught in situations that audiences could relate to even when their driving passions were larger than life.

Puccini and his contemporaries were the last to compose in the tradition of Italian opera. With them ended the age of the composer and began that of the interpreter, when the tradition of Italian opera was kept alive, as it still is, by singers, conductors, and producers. Most important was the conductor Arturo Toscanini (1867–1957), whose talent was bolstered by the authority he derived from being the living link to the generations of Verdi and Puccini. ENRICO CARUSO was the first in a line of singers to catch and hold the imagination of audiences, thanks in part to the effective use of the phonograph. That was the invention that extended opera's lease on life by putting it within reach of millions of buyers who could listen to it in the privacy of their own homes. Caruso's most notable successors were the tenors Beniamino Gigli (1890–1957) and Luciano Pavarotti (1935–). What listeners heard and still hear is mostly the traditional repertory. Radical innovations appeared after World War II, but they did not fire popular enthusiasm in spite of the deliberate efforts of composers like LUIGI NONO and Nino Rota (1911–79) to write for mass audiences. By the 1950s Italian opera was losing its mass appeal and reverting to its historical origins as a form of art for the musically or vocally initiated.

Opera dei Congressi   See CATHOLIC ACTION.

Opera Nazionale Dopolavoro

The Opera Nazionale Dopolavoro (OND), usually referred to simply as the Dopolavoro, was designed and created by the Fascist regime to attract large strata of the population to FASCISM by providing assistance, instruction, and recreational opportunities. Dopolavoro means "after work," and the OND set out to organize the afterwork, or leisure, time of workers in "wholesome" ways, promoting their physical, mental, and spiritual well-being. The OND's activities were not overtly political, a fact that probably accounts for its popularity, but it did have political goal of broadening support for the regime.

Legislated into existence in April 1925, it was inaugurated on May 1, Italy's labor day, to underscore the Fascist regime's commitment to the well-being of workers and its ability to provide services that rival socialist and communist organizations could not deliver. Actually, Fascists had taken over many OND facilities forcibly from rival groups and integrated them into a nationwide network of clubs that also included recreational organizations from private industry and the national railroads. Initially limited to industry, after 1929 the OND reached out to rural men and women. Its membership expanded steadily, reaching 3,831,331 members in 1939 out of an estimated 13 million potential members. The OND's activities included the organization of sports activities and contests at the local and national levels; sponsoring of group trips; providing heavily discounted meals for members in firm cafeterias and restaurants; subsidizing performances of folk art, theater, music, and cinema; and providing opportunities for training in the manual arts. Women were encouraged to study nursing, hygiene, and domestic management. Plays were chosen for their patriotic content.

The "nationalization" of leisure time was actually a proud boast of the Fascist regime, which claimed that it was thus fulfilling its promise to bridge the gap between people and government. The Fascist Party coordinated the work of the OND's provincial sections until 1937, when the Fascist labor unions gained a voice in their administration. The party regained sole control of the OND in January 1943, a few months before the ouster of Mussolini and the fall of the regime in July. The OND's popularity assured its survival after the war, when its facilities and functions were taken over by ENAL (Ente Nazionale Assistenza Lavoratori), a government agency, and by ARCI (Associazione Ricreativa Culturale Italiana), with close ties the Communist Party (PCI).

opere pie See SOCIAL WELFARE.

Orano, Paolo (1875–1945)
journalist, Fascist propagandist, and anti-Semitic writer

Orano was born in Rome, took a degree in literature from the University of Rome (1895), taught philosophy in secondary schools, and entered politics as a journalist and member of the Socialist Party (PSI) in the 1890s. On the staff of *Avanti!* (1903–06), he left the paper and the party in 1906 to join REVOLUTIONARY SYNDICALISM. Following a familiar itinerary from left to right, as founder and editor of the review *La Lupa* (1910–11) he theorized the proto-Fascist merger of revolutionary syndicalism and NATIONALISM, an important step toward FASCISM. Close to BENITO MUSSOLINI, whose views he shared without reservations, Orano participated in the interventionist campaign that led to Italy's entry in WORLD WAR I. In the war he served as a propagandist on the front lines and as a press agent for the military in missions abroad. Elected to parliament in 1921, he joined the Fascist Party in 1922. Reelected to parliament in 1924 and 1928 and nominated to the senate in 1939, he served uninterruptedly until the fall of the Fascist regime in 1943. He also taught Fascist ideology and was appointed rector of the University of Perugia in 1939. A man of broad interests ranging from economics to the occult, Orano wrote political and literary biographies and books on AUTARKY, COLONIALISM, and FOREIGN POLICY, aspiring to the unofficial role and title of philosopher of fascism. In the late 1930s he emerged as an outspoken anti-Semite and supporter of the alliance with Nazi Germany. His book *Gli ebrei in Italia* (The Jews in Italy, 1937), authorized by Mussolini, signaled the beginning of the official anti-Semitic campaign. In it Orano argued that Italian anti-Semitism was different from Germany's, was political in nature, and dictated by Italian opposition to British imperialism, and the need to befriend the Muslim world to promote Italy's own colonial ambitions. Loyal to the end, Orano supported Mussolini's German-controlled ITALIAN SOCIAL REPUBLIC. Captured by Allied troops in 1944, he died in the Padula concentration camp for war prisoners.

Ordine Nuovo

An offshoot of the neo-Fascist Italian Social Movement (MSI), Ordine Nuovo (New Order) was founded in December 1954 by MSI members opposed to the party pursuit of an understanding with the dominant Christian Democratic Party (DC). Its founder and head until 1969 was Giuseppe Umberto (Pino) Rauti (born 1926). Originally envisaged as a study group to explore and propagate the ideology of the Right, it published the monthly review *Ordine Nuovo*. Its ideas derived largely from the writings of the political theorist JULIUS EVOLA. Strongest in Rome and parts of the South, the group had about 10,000 members in the 1960s. Its members turned to action in 1969 in response to spreading student unrest. They engaged in both legal and illegal activities. Acts of TERRORISM perpetrated by the group included the Piazza Fontana bombing of December 1969 in Milan (16 dead, 90 wounded) and the July 1970 bombing of the Rome-Messina train (6 dead, 100 wounded). These actions were part of what was called *strategia della tensione* (strategy of tension), which aimed at destabilizing the government and bringing about political change. Ordine Nuovo went underground in 1973 after being declared illegal. The Armed Revolutionary Nuclei were an offshoot of Ordine Nuovo responsible for the 1980 bombing of the Bologna train station that killed 85 people.

Oriani, Alfredo (1852–1909)
nationalist writer and political commentator

Oriani was born in Faenza (Emilia-Romagna) to a family of well-to-do property owners. He studied law in Rome and Naples, where he received a degree in jurisprudence (1872) but soon abandoned the practice of law. Most of his adult life was lived writing in seclusion in a family country house. He came to the attention of literary critics in the 1890s with his novels, written in a late-romantic vein, peopled by characters driven by irrepressible passions. In 1892 he ran for parliament unsuccessfully. That brief exposure to politics cured him of all ambition for a career in politics, but intensified the political passions that found an outlet in his writings. His fame rests on his political writings. In *Fino a Dogali* (Up to Dogali, 1889) he took up the cause of colonial expansion in the wake of a military setback suffered by Italian troops near the Ethiopian town of Dogali in 1887. *La lotta politica in Italia* (The political struggle in Italy, 1892) was a lively account of the causes of Italian political decadence from the fall of the Roman Empire to 1890, which deplored internal discord and called on the Italian nation to resume its civilizing mission in the world by building a modern colonial empire. Finally, *La rivolta ideale* (The revolt of ideals, 1908) was a call to Italians to pursue high ideals rather than material comforts. For all his vaunted idealism, Oriani was a vocal advocate of modernity and industrialization, his ideal nation being one where prosperity and order prevailed. His overriding concern was to improve Italy's standing among nations. Fame came to Oriani after his death, thanks largely to BENEDETTO CROCE, who drew attention to his writings. Nationalists picked up on his message and magnified his undeniable talent as a writer. The publication of his complete writings by the 1920s sealed his domestic reputation as a writer of genius, sponsored by BENITO MUSSOLINI, and prophet of national renewal. Needless to say, his political and literary reputation dipped after the fall of the Fascist regime, but his merits as a writer are now acknowledged.

Orlando, Vittorio Emanuele
(1860–1952)
legal expert, liberal member of parliament, and prime minister

Born in Palermo, Orlando followed in his father's footsteps to study law, but instead of pursuing a

Vittorio Emanuele Orlando *(Library of Congress)*

career as a practicing lawyer, decided early on to devote himself to teaching. Early publications won him an international reputation as a legal expert and brought him successive appointments as professor of constitutional law at the universities of Modena (1885), Messina (1886), Palermo (1889), and Rome (1901–31). In 1897 he won the first of successive elections that kept him in parliament until 1925. His firm grip on his electoral district in western Sicily gave credibility to allegations that he had close ties to the MAFIA. As a member of the liberal majorities of GIOVANNI GIOLITTI, Orlando was minister of public instruction (1903–05) and minister of justice (1907–09). Following the fall of Giolitti's government in 1909, Orlando took a back seat in parliament, but was called on again to hold the Ministry of Justice by ANTONIO SALANDRA (1914–16) and the Ministry of the Interior by PAOLO BOSELLI (1916–17). He became prime minister in October 1917 after the defeat of CAPORETTO. His political skills were instrumental in rallying parliament and the nation behind the successful effort to halt the Austrian advance. He was less successful after the end of the war, when he represented Italy at the PARIS PEACE CONFERENCE along with Foreign Minister SIDNEY SONNINO and presided over the start of demobilization. In April 1919 he clashed with President Woodrow Wilson over the issue of territorial compensations for Italy, especially over the disposition of FIUME, and led the Italian delegation out of the peace conference. Unable to hold his coalition together, he resigned as prime minister in June 1919. In 1922 he was called on twice to form a government, and twice failed. Seeing no way out of the parliamentary impasse, Orlando voted for BENITO MUSSOLINI's government after the march on Rome, expecting that the Fascists would govern constitutionally. He broke with the governing coalition and resigned his seat in 1925 when he realized that the Fascists were setting up a one-party dictatorship. In 1931 he resigned his university chair to avoid having to take a compulsory oath of loyalty to the Fascist regime. He returned to politics after the arrest of Mussolini in July 1943. He served as adviser to the king (1943–44), president of the chamber of deputies (1943–45), member of the Constituent Assembly (1946–47), and senator for life (1948–52). In his postwar career, he was often a critic of Christian Democracy (DC) and spoke against ratification of the PEACE TREATY because it sanctioned losses of territory and colonies. A highly emotional man who often broke into tears when speaking, Orlando was a frequent target of political critics and humorists, who charged that his tears were a substitute for firm political principles.

Orsini, Felice (1819–1858)
patriot political conspirator, and terrorist
Not related to the aristocratic family of the same name, Orsini was born in the papal states to a family of the lower middle class. His father managed property for a family of the nobility and conspired in the secret CARBONARI society. The son followed the father's example. After a difficult childhood spent in the care of an uncle, and marred by the boy's apparently accidental killing of a servant, Orsini avoided serving a jail sentence by taking first religious vows. From 1840 to 1843 he attended the University of Bologna, graduating with a law degree. Interested more in political conspiracy than in the practice of law, he joined Mazzini's YOUNG ITALY and founded a secret society of his own called the Conspiracy of the Sons of Death. In 1844 he was sentenced to a life term in jail but was released by the political amnesty of 1846. With his strong republican views Orsini fought for the republics of Venice and Rome in 1848–49. In Rome he stood out for the brutal efficiency of his repression of political dissidents and outlaws. In 1852–54 he conspired with GIUSEPPE MAZZINI in unsuccessful uprisings in central Italy. In December 1854 the Austrian police arrested him in Transylvania, where he was wandering in search of conspiratorial opportunities. Imprisoned, his harrowing escape from the heavily guarded castle of Mantua in 1856 became the stuff of legend and firmed up his reputation as a daredevil. No longer on friendly terms with Mazzini, Orsini now decided to strike out on his own. The result was a plot to assassinate NAPOLEON III, whom Orsini blamed for repressing the Roman Republic and not helping the cause of Italian unification. The attempt on January 4, 1858, left the emperor unharmed, but "Orsini's bombs" (manufactured by English collaborators) killed eight and wounded more than 150 bystanders. Before going to the guillotine Orsini wrote letters to Napoleon III and CAVOUR explaining his motives in respectful but firm language. Advisers dissuaded the French emperor from commuting the sentence of death to a life sentence. But his decision to allow publication of Orsini's letters prepared French public opinion for the emperor's change of policy in support of Italian unification.

Orsini family

The ancestry of this once-powerful family of the Roman aristocracy can be traced back to the 10th century. Their strongholds were in the territory north of Rome, where they came into frequent conflict with SIENA. With its close ties to the PAPACY and the highest levels of the religious hierarchy, the family played a major role in the affairs of the church and the PAPAL STATES from the 12th century. Popes Celestine III (1191–98), Nicholas III (1277–80), and Benedict XII (1334–42) belonged to the Orsini family. The Orsinis' feud with the rival COLONNA FAMILY was legendary, as each family sought political dominance and control of the papacy. A rivalry within the Orsini family facilitated the election of a French pope in 1305, and the removal of the papacy to the city of Avignon in southern France. The fortunes of the family improved with the return of the papacy to Rome in 1378. From then on they were careful to support the papacy against its enemies within and outside Italy, the exception being the period of Borgia rule when the Orsinis were temporarily out of papal favor. In 1511 they settled their long-standing feud with the Colonnas. Orsini family members held positions of prominence in the church and in the military. They distinguished themselves in defense of the pope during the SACK OF ROME (1527) and provided many com-manders and soldiers of fortune for the armies of Rome and other states. In 1718 Pope CLEMENT XI bestowed on the Orsinis the title of princes of the church and an official role in Vatican ceremonials. The family divided into many branches that responded differently to the events of their time. Although they were not strenuous defenders of the papacy in the struggles of the RISORGIMENTO, they were nevertheless prominent among the families of Rome's so-called black aristocracy that stuck by the pope and remained aloof from the affairs of the Italian court after 1870. Members of the family are still socially prominent and very much in the public eye.

Osservatore Cattolico (L') See MEDA, FILIPPO.

Osservatore Romano (L') See JOURNALISM.

Ottolenghi, Giuseppe See JEWS IN ITALY.

Ouchy, Treaty of See ITALIAN-TURKISH WAR.

OVRA See FASCISM.

P

P2 See PROPAGANDA 2.

Pacciardi, Randolfo (1889–1991)
*Republican Party leader, anti-Fascist fighter,
and minister of defense*

A lawyer, journalist, and politician of unwavering republican sentiments, Pacciardi was born
near Grosseto (Tuscany), was a veteran of WORLD
WAR I, and an opponent of the Fascist regime. He
worked against the regime as a political exile in
Switzerland, France, and the United States. In
the Spanish civil war (1936–39) he commanded
the famed Garibaldi Brigade, which performed
brilliantly at the Battle of Guadalajara (March
1937). Pacciardi's clashes with communist leaders of the anti-Fascist coalition in Spain convinced him that communists should be excluded
from any future anti-Fascist alliance. He was the
first postwar secretary of the Republican Party
(PRI), member of the Constituent Assembly and
of parliament, and served as defense minister
(1948–53). As defense minister he oversaw the
reorganization of the armed forces, and supported Italian membership in NATO and close
relations with the United States. He opposed any
opening to the parties of the Left, insisting on
excluding Communists and Socialists from government. On that issue he broke with the
Republican Party in 1963, dissenting from his
party's decision to seek a political alliance with
Socialists. That same year, calling for political
reforms, Pacciardi launched the movement
Nuova Repubblica. He was accused of envisaging
himself as the Italian De Gaulle when he proposed strengthening the presidency. He rejoined
the Republican Party in 1980 but never regained
his former influence. The campaign for constitutional reform that Pacciardi led in the 1960s
was being renewed and carried forward by others at the time of his death.

Pact of Steel

The Pact of Steel was the name given to the
diplomatic treaty that sealed the political and
military alliance between Fascist Italy and Nazi
Germany. GALEAZZO CIANO and Joachim von
Ribbentrop, respectively foreign ministers of Italy
and Germany, signed this diplomatic agreement
in Berlin on May 22, 1939. It marked the culmination of the AXIS alliance policy announced by
Mussolini in 1936 and strengthened a year later
by the signing of the ANTI-COMINTERN PACT. Ciano
and BENITO MUSSOLINI initially resisted German
pressures to sign a conclusive agreement binding on the two countries in case of war. They
were held back by their awareness that an
alliance with Germany was not popular in Italy,
and by Mussolini's desire for a tripartite alliance
that included Japan. Germany's military invasion of Czechoslovakia in March 1939, its growing military power, the acquiescence of France
and Great Britain to German actions, and their
apparent hostility toward Italy convinced Mussolini that a formal alliance with Germany was
in Italy's interest, and he instructed Ciano
accordingly. The German foreign ministry drew
up the text of the treaty with little input from
the Italians.

Brief and to the point, the Pact of Steel committed each side to support the other with all its
military resources if either was involved in conflict. Unlike most diplomatic agreements, this

one had none of the qualifying or limiting clauses that give signatories some freedom of action. Its designation as a Pact of Steel emphasized the totally binding character of the alliance between the two Fascist regimes and the definitive abandonment by Italy of its traditional strategy of balancing itself between rival blocs. Belatedly realizing that the agreement gave Germany too much latitude and might involve Italy in a war for which it was militarily unprepared, on June 5 Mussolini submitted a memorandum to Hitler stating that Italy needed peace for a period of three years. Hitler privately agreed to those terms, but the pact itself was never revised. When Germany found itself at war against France and Great Britain in September 1939, Mussolini invoked Italy's lack of military preparation to keep the country out of the war. Mussolini's subsequent decision to enter the conflict was based on the miscalculation of a quick German victory that would deprive Italy of its share of spoils if it did not intervene at the side of its ally.

See also WORLD WAR II.

Padua, city of (Padova)

Located in the Po Valley part of the region of VENETIA, the city of Padua (pop. 210,000) is a provincial capital of major economic importance, with sugar refineries, food processing plants, plastics, and engineering firms. A flourishing city in Roman times, it declined in the early Middle Ages, recovering from the 12th to the 14th centuries as a free commune. Internal discords did not impede its expansion at the expense of neighboring towns, in rivalry with neighboring VERONA and VENICE. Padua achieved its greatest prominence under the lordship of the native Carrara family (1338–1405). Venice ruled the city from the extinction of the main branch of Carrara family in 1405 until the fall of the Venetian republic in 1797. The city is rich in works of art by late medieval and Renaissance artists, which adorn its churches and museums, including murals by Giotto in the Scrovegni Chapel, sculptures by DONATELLO and Jacopo Sansovino (1486–1570), paintings by ANDREA MANTEGNA, TITIAN, GIOVANNI BATTISTA TIEPOLO, and TINTORETTO. The University of Padua, where GALILEO GALILEI lectured, was founded in 1222. It is the second-oldest university in Italy after Bologna's, and has been at the forefront of research and teaching in science and medicine.

Paganini, Niccolò (1782–1840)
composer, virtuoso violinist, and musical celebrity

Paganini was born in Genoa, where he made his debut as a child prodigy at age 13. For the next nine years he continued to perform and compose pieces for the violin designed to show off his mastery of the instrument. In 1805 he was appointed music master at the court of Lucca in the service of Napoleon's sister ELISA BONAPARTE BACIOCCHI. He left Lucca in 1809 to pursue fame and success outside Italy. From then on he lived the life of an itinerant artist, traveling tirelessly throughout Europe and leading the adventurous, disordered life that earned him a reputation as a mysterious figure and that fascinated audiences. He performed in the major courts of Europe but also went out of his way to reach a larger public in provincial towns where major artists had not performed before. His gaunt appearance, dark garb, flowing black hair, and piercing eyes reinforced his uncanny image. Legends grew up about him that depicted him as a devilish figure. Paganini seems to have deliberately cultivated this unconventional image, for in private he was genial and musically discerning. He created the figure of the romantic artist for the public, which came to equate an eccentric personality with genius. Critics scoffed, but audiences were enthralled by the image and by the bravura of his performances. Aside from such gimmicks as playing entire pieces on a single string, which were meant to amaze, Paganini made important contributions to music by expanding the role of the violin and developing new playing techniques. Many composers, including Berlioz, Liszt, Schumann, and Wagner, were influenced by this revolutionary figure. Paganini, who was also proverbial for his avarice, retired in 1835, apparently already suffering from the cancer of the larynx that caused his death five years later.

Pagano, Francesco Maria (1748–1799)
Neapolitan legal expert, writer, and political reformer

Pagano was born in the town of Brienza (Basilicata), earned a law degree, was appointed lecturer of ethics at the University of Naples in 1770, and won the chair of criminal law at the same university in 1777. Simultaneously, he also conducted a private law practice. Culminating in the publication of *Considerazioni sul processo criminale* (Considerations on the criminal trial, 1787), his work established him as an international authority on criminal law. An early sympathizer of the French Revolution, in 1794 Pagano took on the defense of Neapolitan Jacobins arrested on charges of conspiring with the French against the monarchy. Denounced as a liberal, in 1796 he was arrested, removed from his teaching post, and jailed. Released in 1798 for lack of evidence, he sought refuge in French-controlled Rome and Milan, but returned to Naples in 1799 after the proclamation of the PARTHENOPEAN REPUBLIC. He played an important role in the republic's legislative body, working on the new republic's constitution and supporting moderate reformers who wanted to deprive members of the nobility of their many privileges but not of their property. His opposition did not prevent the enactment of radical legislation, but delayed it long enough to prevent its application. When the monarchist forces counterattacked, Pagano first organized the fight against the armed bands led by Cardinal FABRIZIO RUFFO, then negotiated the surrender to the monarchy. Although the leaders of the republic were promised immunity, the monarchists reneged at the request of British admiral Horatio Nelson. Pagano was executed by hanging along with other leaders of the republic in October 1799. Radical critics and historians of the Left have blamed Pagano and other moderate reformers for the republic's failure to seize and redistribute land to the peasants to win mass support. A moderate school of thought sees Pagano as a patriot and forerunner of the RISORGIMENTO.

Paisiello, Giovanni See OPERA.

Pajetta, Gian Carlo (1911–1990)
Communist Party leader and parliamentary figure

In the surcharged political atmosphere of early 20th-century Turin where Pajetta was born to working-class parents, politics came easily to the youngster, who was expelled from school at age

Gian Carlo Pajetta *(Library of Congress)*

15 for anti-Fascist activities. He did not go abroad, but joined the Communist Party (PCI) underground and served as secretary of its youth organization until his arrest in 1933. Condemned to a 21-year prison term, he was freed in 1943 when the Fascist regime fell. He joined the RESISTANCE movement in a leading capacity and negotiated the official recognition of the movement by the Allies. The Allied command agreed to finance the resistance movement on condition that resistance fighters disarm and relinquish authority at the end of the war. Hard-line leftists subsequently denounced the agreement as a sellout, but Pajetta defended it as the best that could be obtained under the circumstances. He believed that any attempt to transform the fight against the Fascists into a communist revolution would have led to civil war. After the war Pajetta was a member of parliament, served as editor of the communist newspaper *L'Unità* and the review *Rinascita,* sat on the party's central committee, and contributed to the formulation of the party's foreign policy. Always outspoken, he was often an internal critic of the policies of party leader PALMIRO TOGLIATTI.

Paleario, Aonio (ca. 1503–1570)
humanist scholar and religious reformer drawn to Protestantism

Born in the southern town of Veroli (LATIUM) to a prominent local family, his real name was Antonio Della Paglia. After studying literature, philosophy, and theology, he was appointed to teach rhetoric in LUCCA (1546–55) and MILAN (1567–68). As early as 1542 (and again in 1559) he was accused of heresy for harboring ideas similar to those of the evangelical reformers of northern Europe, but had defended himself successfully. In Lucca he had found a government willing to defend him from the ROMAN INQUISITION and a group of similarly minded religious reformers. The enmity of ROME and FLORENCE prevailed, and Paleario was forced out of his refuge. His published view that church reform required the summoning of a council of believers and imposition of limits on papal authority brought on a third accusation of heresy. Arrested by order of the Inquisition, Paleario was taken to Rome, tried, found guilty, and hanged. For good measure, his remains were burned at the stake.

Palermo, city of

The port city of Palermo (pop. 679,000) is the administrative capital of the region of SICILY. It is located in the northwestern part of the island on the coast of the Tyrrhenian Sea, adjoining the fertile plain of the Conca d'Oro renowned for its citrus fruit groves. Its desirable location has made it a coveted prize for a long series of conquerors. Founded by the Phoenicians in the eighth century B.C., it became a Carthaginian stronghold. Rome seized it in 254–53 B.C. and ruled it for the next 800 years. In 440 A.D. it was overrun and sacked by the Goths. Byzantine rule lasted from 535 to 831. Under Arab rule (831–1072) Palermo prospered as the capital of an autonomous emirate of great economic and cultural vitality. It retained its preeminent status under Norman rule (1072–1194), and under the rule of the German Hohenstaufen dynasty (1194–1266). The Hohenstaufen ruler Frederick II (1220–50) made Palermo a center of culture. It was at his court that Tuscan became the literary language of choice and attained the distinction that would make it the basis of modern Italian. Palermo lost its leading role when French Angevin rulers made Naples their capital city. Hatred of the French ran so deep in the city that its inhabitants sparked the insurrection of the Sicilian Vespers (1282) that chased out the Angevins and brought in the Aragonese house of Spain, whose rule, however, did not arrest the decline of the city. In the centuries of Spanish rule, which lasted until 1711, the city changed character. It became the place of residence of the most important families of the Sicilian nobility, who embellished the city with many splendid palaces. The city lost much of its economic and cultural vitality. Its life revolved increasingly around royal and noble patronage, and around the churches and other religious establishments that sprouted everywhere in the city.

From the 15th century to the unification of Italy in 1860 the history of Palermo is essentially the history of Sicily and of the Kingdom of NAPLES that ruled the island for most of that time. It was the second-largest city in the kingdom, but far less important than Naples. The BOURBONS ruled from Naples and neglected the Sicilian capital, except in 1799 and 1806–14, when they took up residence in Palermo to escape from the French who dominated the mainland under NAPOLEON I. Resentment of Bourbon rule was rife in the 19th century. Palermo took the initiative in the revolutions of 1821 and 1848, hoping for Sicilian autonomy and independence from Naples. In 1860 Palermo saw combat between Garibaldi's volunteers fighting for Italian unification and Neapolitan troops trying to hold on to the island. Major urban renewal projects carried out in the decades after national unification have given the city much of its modern aspect. Building construction was a major economic activity as the city's population grew steadily from 194,000 in 1861 to 394,000 in 1921. Palermo suffered much damage from bombing in World War II before being taken by the Allies in July 1943. Since 1948 Palermo has been the seat of government of the autonomous region of Sicily. Its seaport and airport are important centers of Mediterranean traffic. It lags in industrial development, but tourism is an important resource. In recent years the city has been in the forefront in the campaign against the MAFIA, which nevertheless remains a powerful presence in its life.

Palestrina, Giovanni Pierluigi da (1525/26–1594)

sacred music composer and music master

Palestrina took his name from the town of Palestrina (Rome) where he was born. Little is known of his childhood, but by 1537 he was in Rome as a choirboy. In 1544 he was back in Palestrina as choirmaster and organist in the town's cathedral. Pope Julius III (1550–55), for-

merly the bishop of Palestrina, appointed his protégé chapel master of Saint Peter's in Rome (1551). Palestrina's first published work was a collection of four masses dedicated to Pope Julius (1554). These demonstrated Palestrina's mastery of counterpoint and polyphony, and established his reputation as the foremost composer of sacred music in Rome. He spent the rest of his life in Rome in various official posts and private employ. Palestrina's music must be considered in the context of the CATHOLIC REFORMATION unfolding at the time he was composing. Prior to Palestrina, music played in churches tended to lose sight of the religious texts that it was based on; it often went its own way, more for entertainment than inspiration. The Council of Trent was even considering eliminating music from religious ritual altogether, until it is said that the performance of Palestrina's *Missa Papae Marcelli* (1565), written in honor of Pope Marcellus II (1555), convinced the cardinals and the pope that music could conform to the devotional guidelines proposed by the council. In 1577 he undertook to rewrite the church's plainchant texts in conformity with the council's directives. The straitened financial circumstances of Palestrina's later years were alleviated by his second marriage to a wealthy widow in 1581. He continued to compose until the end of his life, leaving a large legacy of masses, motets, and hymns. Palestrina gave church music a new sound, one that was light, vibrant, and spiritual, much to the enrichment of Catholic ritual.

Palladio, Andrea (1508–1580)

architect and builder known for the classical style of his designs

Palladio's original name was Andrea di Pietro. The humanist Giangiorgio Trissino (1478–1550) bestowed on his friend the poetic name of Palladio, a reference to the palatial structures that he raised. Palladio was born in Padua, the son of a miller or cutter of millstones, studied in Vicenza, and worked as a stonemason until 1840, when he left for Rome to study the relics of ancient

Roman architecture. Palladio internalized the spirit of classical architecture with hundreds of drawings of Roman ruins, and applied his understanding imaginatively to create buildings of balance and restraint that answered the needs of his contemporaries. He worked mostly in Vicenza and Venice where he designed churches, public buildings, and private residences, always with an eye to combining stateliness with functionality. His buildings were sited to take advantage of the surroundings; flights of steps and columned entrances expressed the sense of dignity and grandeur that appealed to his clients, and the whole was symmetrically laid out for an impression of balance, repose, and permanence. The town hall of Vicenza (1549) is a good example of his civic architecture, while the private Villa Capra near Vicenza shows how Palladio built with an eye on location, design, theatrical effect, and comfort. Seventeen of the approximately 30 villas that he designed still survive. His *I quattro libri dell'architettura* (Four books of architecture, 1570), reissued many times and translated into English in 1716, influenced architectural design everywhere in Europe and the New World. Thomas Jefferson's residence at Monticello is a prime example of the Palladian influence in the neoclassical revival of the 18th century.

Pallavicino Trivulzio, Giorgio (1796–1878)

patriot, liberal reformer, and supporter of constitutional monarchy

A member of the Lombard aristocracy, born in Milan, he was drawn to liberal causes from his youth, joined the secret political opposition to Austrian rule, made contact with Piedmontese patriots conspiring to introduce liberal reforms, and participated in the unsuccessful REVOLUTION of 1821. Arrested after his return to Milan in December 1821, he confessed to his role and incriminated other conspirators, including FEDERICO CONFALONIERI. His release from jail in 1835, presumably granted for his earlier confession, did not endear him to other Italian patriots. When

the REVOLUTIONS of 1848 broke out, Pallavicino joined the revolutionary Lombard provisional government, advocated union with Piedmont, and opposed the republican members of the government. In the 1850s he was an exile in Turin and a member of the Piedmontese parliament. He played an important role in efforts to unite monarchists and republicans behind CAVOUR's program. Together with DANIELE MANIN, Pallavicino founded the ITALIAN NATIONAL SOCIETY that called for "independence and unification" under the constitutional monarchy of Piedmont. Pallavicino was an effective antagonist of GIUSEPPE MAZZINI, whom he abhorred for his republicanism and accused of fomenting social discord, but welcomed GIUSEPPE GARIBALDI, who he hoped would play a subordinate role in the national movement. Garibaldi's initiative in 1860 took him by surprise, but events eventually followed Pallavicino's script. He served as the king's representative in Naples after Garibaldi's liberation of the South and kept radical elements out of positions of power. He was made senator after national unification.

Panizzi, Antonio (1787–1879)

scholar, patriot, political exile, and chief librarian of London's British Museum

Panizzi was born in the town of Brescello (Reggio Emilia), studied law, and joined the secret society of the CARBONARI right after graduation. Implicated in the REVOLUTION of 1821, he fled abroad to avoid arrest. While in Lugano, Switzerland, he published a detailed denunciation of the illegalities committed by the government of FRANCIS IV of Modena against those accused of belonging to secret societies. Panizzi became a victim of the system when the government of Francis IV issued a death sentence against him. In May 1823 he left Lugano for London where he lived for most of the rest of his life. He took easily to British ways and became a naturalized citizen in 1832 without forsaking his interests and ties to Italy. His scholarship and learning were evident in the monumental editions of the writings of LUDOVICO ARIOSTO and Matteo Boiardo, published in 1830 and 1834 respectively. While pursuing his scholarly interests Panizzi also worked with the British Museum as assistant librarian (1831–37), keeper of books (1837–56), and chief librarian (1856–67). He was responsible for designing the reading room and galleries of the museum's library, and for developing and cataloging its collection. Well-connected, respected, and enterprising, he secured parliament's financial support for the library, which became at his insistence the one depository library entitled to receive copies of all books copyrighted in Great Britain. In spite of his demanding duties at the museum, Panizzi followed closely political developments in Italy. He raised money for the national movement, planned the escape of political prisoners, corresponded with patriots, and influenced British public opinion in favor of Italian independence. A moderate by temperament and conviction, Panizzi supported the policies of CAVOUR but also kept in touch with the more radical elements drawn to GIUSEPPE GARIBALDI and GIUSEPPE MAZZINI.

Pannella, Marco See RADICALISM.

Pantaleoni, Maffeo (1857–1924)
laissez-faire economist, free trader, and
government critic
This liberal economist may have inherited from his father Diomede Pantaleoni (1810–85) a taste for politics. He held teaching positions at the universities of Camerino, Venice, Bari, Naples, Geneva, and Rome. He left Italy for Switzerland in 1896 in self-imposed exile to protest the government's colonialist policies. Back in Italy, in 1901 he was elected to parliament as a member of the Radical Party (see RADICALISM) but resigned his seat after becoming involved in a bank scandal. From then on he gravitated toward conservative nationalist positions, favored Italian intervention in WORLD WAR I, was minister of finance in FIUME after the war, supported fascism,

and was nominated senator in 1923. Along with VILFREDO PARETO, Pantaleoni was part of a group of convinced free traders that in the 1890s publicized their views through the *Giornale degli Economisti.* His identification with socialism was based on socialist opposition to protective tariffs and special interests. It ended when he discovered that socialists supported free trade only as a political tactic and supported high tariffs when workers benefited from them. He was attracted to fascism for the same reason, again based on his perception that it favored free trade and economic laissez-faire. He did not live long enough to see fascism abandon the liberal economic policies of its first three years in power. Pantaleone is acknowledged today as the most important economist of his generation and as the founder of a particularly intransigent school of economics that insists on the scientific nature and universal validity of liberal economic principles.

Pantelleria

The island of Pantelleria (pop. 7,400) is located in the MEDITERRANEAN SEA approximately halfway between Tunisia and SICILY. Colonized by the Phoenicians and Carthaginians, it was taken over by Rome in 217 B.C. Arabs took over the island in the eighth century A.D., Normans in the 12th century, and the Aragonese in the 14th century. Pisan and Genoese forces occupied it off and on without ever being able to consolidate their hold. Its exposed position left the island vulnerable to attack by Turks and pirates, who sacked it repeatedly in the 15th and 16th centuries. Pantelleria's location in the Sicilian channel, the narrow body of water that separates Africa from Europe, underscores its strategic significance, which grew in Italian eyes when Italy acquired the colony of Libya in 1912. The Fascist regime's pursuit of a Mediterranean empire further magnified the strategic importance of Pantelleria, which the press often referred to as "Italy's Malta." The regime built major fortifications and underground facilities on the island, but as a naval and air base it was not strong enough to disrupt enemy operations during WORLD WAR II. Heavily bombed and all but cut off from Italy, its demoralized garrison surrendered in June 1943. The island's surrender removed the last obstacle to the Allied invasion of Sicily that occurred in July of that year.

Panunzio, Sergio (1886–1944)
political theoretician, university professor, and apologist for the Fascist regime

Born to a prominent and politically active family of Molfetta (Bari) in southern Italy, Panunzio received degrees in law (1908) and philosophy (1911) at the University of Naples, and taught law and political science at his alma mater and at the universities of Ferrara, Perugia, and Rome. Drawn to the study of social issues and REVOLUTIONARY SYNDICALISM in the early years of the 20th century, Panunzio changed his position around 1910, after concluding on the basis of his observations that working-class revolution was not likely to succeed. His political itinerary after that was similar to that of many social thinkers and activists who drifted in the direction of FASCISM. Panunzio joined the movement in 1921, but as early as 1919 he had collaborated with ITALO BALBO in the province of Ferrara. He was elected to parliament on the Fascist ticket in 1924. By then Panunzio had turned to CORPORATISM, which he understood to be a system of political representation based on occupational and economic criteria. The corporate state would give workers and management an equal voice in the operations of self-regulating corporate bodies in the various sectors of the economy, and representation at the highest levels of government. There was thus a democratic or populist aspect to Panunzio's version of the corporate state that was lacking in the authoritarian (and more decisive) prescriptions of politically influential theoreticians like ALFREDO ROCCO. The Fascist corporate state that emerged in the 1930s did not conform to Panunzio's views, but he continued nevertheless to revel in the role of social philosopher of the regime and touted fascism as the answer to the social problems of modern society.

Paoli, Pasquale See CORSICA; NAPOLEON I.

papacy

The papacy is the office held by the pope in his double capacity as head of the Roman Catholic Church and the sovereign state of Vatican City. According to Catholic doctrine, papal authority rests on Christ's delegation of authority to St. Peter, the first bishop of Rome. Popes claim that they have inherited that authority as St. Peter's successors in the HOLY SEE of Rome (Petrine doctrine). The historical origins of the papacy are complex, but it is useful to think of the office as developing from the decline of ancient Roman administration. When emperors could no longer protect the city, the bishops of Rome took on the duties of local government. Pope Gregory I (590–604) was an effective leader who solidified the authority and power of the Roman bishop over the city. The image of the pope as protector lives on in the Italian word *papa,* which means both pope and father. But the most important event in the early history of the papacy was the Donation of Pepin in 756, by which that Frankish ruler gave the pope land conquered from the Lombards, who were both his and the pope's enemies. From that donation emerged the PAPAL STATES that lasted until 1870. In that year the recently unified Kingdom of Italy seized from the pope all but the tiny enclave of Vatican City in Rome, thus putting an end to the more than millennial history of the papacy as head of a large state in central Italy. Papal opposition to Italian unification was motivated by the fear that loss of papal political power would make it impossible for the church to carry on with its spiritual mission. The resulting conflict of CHURCH AND STATE was troublesome for both sides. It intensified ANTICLERICALISM among patriotic Italians and set the papacy against all the perceived sins of modern civilization listed in the SYLLABUS OF ERRORS.

The papacy has long been a controversial institution for many Italians. In the RISORGIMENTO Italian patriots took up NICCOLÒ MACHIAVELLI's charge that the papacy was responsible for Italy's political disunity and weakness. The papacy and the Italian state have often disagreed on political, educational, family, and financial matters. On the other hand, in the course of history, the power of the papacy has at times protected Italy from outside intervention, made Italy more visible and influential abroad, and helped in times of crisis and reconstruction. The physical presence of the papacy in Rome, and the fact that in the last 500 years all but two popes have been Italians, has made the papacy particularly sensitive to what happens in Italy. It has favored those movements and governments that it deemed compatible with its interests and goals, and opposed others that threatened its security and prerogatives. It was often at odds with liberal governments in the early part of the 20th century. PIUS XI accepted fascism with reservations, glad that it settled the conflict of church and state but suspicious of its aspiration to control all aspects of life. PIUS XII gave unstinting support to CHRISTIAN DEMOCRACY and opposed COMMUNISM in the most difficult period of the cold war. His successors showed greater restraint, generally limiting their interventions to issues like divorce and abortion that touch directly on spiritual concerns. With JOHN PAUL II the papacy has shifted its focus from Italian to international affairs. Eastern Europe, Latin America, the so-called Third World, and doctrinal issues like clerical celibacy and the ordination of women matter far more to the papacy today than Italian politics. The change has been for the better. Anticlericalism is a spent force, and most Italians regard the papacy as a friendly presence and as a material and cultural asset.

Papal Guarantees, Law of   See ANTI-
CLERICALISM; CHURCH AND STATE; ROMAN QUESTION.

Papal States

From 756 to 1870 the Papal States, also called States of the Church (*Stati della Chiesa*) and Pontifical States (*Stati Pontifici*), were an independent and sovereign political entity under the rule of the PAPACY. The plural designation "states" indi-

cates their nature as a collection of territories held as fiefs by the pope. The makeup and territorial extent of these possessions varied through history. The original nucleus was various papal endowments in and around Rome, accumulated by bishops of Rome (popes) since the fourth century. In 754–56 Pepin the Short extended papal control to the exarchate of Ravenna and other lands in exchange for papal recognition of Pepin's title as king of the Franks. Charlemagne confirmed his father's donation in 774 and gave the papacy military protection. Papal scribes later forged the document known as the Donation of Constantine, claiming that papal territorial and secular authority came directly from the Roman emperor Constantine. For many centuries the Papal States were prone to internal discord and downright anarchy. Powerful clans like those of the COLONNA FAMILY and ORSINI FAMILY fought over land and for control of the papacy. German rulers sent their armies into Italy, factions of Guelfs and Ghibellines disrupted the life of towns. The proud "papal monarchy" of Innocent III (1198–1216) disintegrated into the papal wreckage of Boniface VIII (1294–1303).

It fell to the popes of the 15th century to resume the process of state-building. CESARE BORGIA conquered the Romagna and Marches for his father ALEXANDER VI. His successor JULIUS II personally led papal armies into battle to make sure that no one challenged papal authority over these coveted territories. FERRARA became part of the Papal States in 1598 and URBINO in 1631. On the minus side, Paul III ceded Parma and Piacenza to his relatives in 1545, permanently removing those territories from papal jurisdiction. NAPOLEON I actually abolished the Papal States twice. The French-controlled ROMAN REPUBLIC replaced papal rule in 1798. Papal rule was restored in 1801, only to be abolished again in 1809 when Napoleon incorporated into France what was left of papal territory.

In 1814–15 the CONGRESS OF VIENNA restored the papal state, now named in the singular form. Its borders were the old ones but not the administration, which was now unified over the entire territory. Reforms introduced by Cardinal ETTORE

CONSALVI alarmed the *zelanti,* traditionalists who feared that any innovation would only encourage more radical demands for change. After 1815 antagonism intensified between the northern regions of Romagna and Marches that had benefited from French rule and were more economically developed, and the southern provinces, including Rome, that relied on papal patronage. Secret societies sprung up everywhere. Liberals demanding change and a voice in government looked to the CARBONERIA, conservative supporters of papal absolutism turned to the Sanfedisti. Liberals tried revolution in 1821 and 1830, but conservatives prevailed.

The Papal States were a key component of the conservative alliance of "throne and altar" against revolution, until 1846 when, to everyone's amazement, the College of Cardinals elected a pope inclined to make liberal concessions. The election of PIUS IX raised the expectations of liberals and contributed powerfully to the climate of political euphoria behind the REVOLUTIONS of 1848. Pius IX spent the rest of his life trying to make up for the early political missteps of his pontificate. In so doing he veered to the opposite extreme, with serious consequences for the Papal States and church policy. His SYLLABUS OF ERRORS condemned the movement for Italian unification and all modern doctrines that inspired it, according to papal thinking. Opposition to Italian unification proved fatal for the Papal States. The pope lost most of his territory in 1860 to the army of VICTOR EMMANUEL II, the first king of united Italy. The Papal States shrank to the city of Rome and its environs, until that territory was also lost to the Italians in 1870. An aggrieved but unrelenting Pius IX proclaimed himself a "prisoner in the Vatican," the small enclave in Rome that he still controlled, refusing to recognize the Italian state. The conflict of CHURCH AND STATE was finally settled by negotiation in 1929 when, as part of a larger deal, papal policy renounced its claims to what had been the Papal States and accepted full sovereignty over Vatican City. In retrospect, the loss of temporal power in the Papal States has been of great advantage to the church, freeing it of troublesome political concerns and enhancing its international and spiritual role.

Papini, Giovanni (1881–1956)
writer and cultural critic

Papini's literary voice, witty, irreverent, and biting, is associated particularly with the Florentine cultural tradition. Born in Florence, Papini pursued his own interests. He attended university lectures but took no degree. He and GIUSEPPE PREZZOLINI founded and directed the review *Leonardo* (1903–07). They collaborated again later on *La Voce,* but Papini left that journal in 1913 to found the FUTURISM review *Lacerba* with ARDENGO SOFFICI. Papini was also editor of ENRICO CORRADINI's nationalist review *Il Regno.* These reference points place Papini in the rebellious counterculture movement that flourished in Italy before 1914. In literature, the revolt was directed against the dominance of GIOSUÈ CARDUCCI, GABRIELE D'ANNUNZIO, and GIOVANNI PASCOLI, all deemed hopelessly rhetorical and out of touch with the modern world. In politics, the revolt was against the cautiously progressive liberalism of GIOVANNI GIOLITTI. Influenced by the intuitivism of Henri Bergson and the pragmatism of Henry James, Papini participated in the "revolt against positivism" that attracted many intellectuals of his generation. Will and spontaneity were their vital elements, reason and calculation impediments to action. Rejection of philosophical POSITIVISM, science, and political liberalism was coupled in Papini's case with a strong NATIONALISM. Papini called for unity of will among Italians at home and for expansion abroad. Hence his antisocialism, blamed for domestic discord, and his endorsement of colonialism as the expression of the national will to power. In 1914–15 Papini joined the crusade for Italian intervention in WORLD WAR I on the side of BENITO MUSSOLINI. The antiestablishment rebel became part of the cultural establishment during the Fascist period. His enormously successful *Vita di Cristo* (Life of Christ, 1921) marked his conversion to Catholicism. He directed the important review *Il Frontespizio* (1928–40), taught literature at the University of Bologna, presided over cultural associations, and represented Italy abroad. Appointment to the Italian Academy in 1937 was the ultimate official distinction that the Fascist regime bestowed on Papini. Pride in Italian culture became a form of cultural AUTARKY, as expressed in his book *Italia mia* (1939). Papini's cultural chauvinism blended into overt racial thinking in the late 1930s. Sunk into deep depression by the events of WORLD WAR II and in poor health after the war, he continued to write to the end of his life for a public increasingly indifferent to what he had to say.

Pareto, Vilfredo (1848–1923)
sociologist, political economist, and critic of socialism and liberalism

Pareto was born in Paris where his parents found refuge after participating in the REVOLUTIONS of 1848. His mother was French and his father belonged to an upper-class Genoese family that supported GIUSEPPE MAZZINI. They returned to Genoa in 1854, and Pareto went on to take a degree in engineering at the Polytechnic Institute of Turin (1870). He took up the study of economics to satisfy his curiosity about business operations stimulated by his work as an industrial engineer. Influenced by the economist MAFFEO PANTALEONI, Pareto became a severe critic of economic protectionism and of the industrial interests behind it. His criticism extended to the liberal system of representative government that gave disproportionate power to special interests. In Pareto's analysis, big money and political ambition corrupted political democracy to the detriment of the general interest. The same principle of unrestrained competition in business that he argued for as an economist, he applied to social relations as a sociologist. His sociology was based on the observation that individuals are driven by nonrational motivations clothed in intellectually respectable garb by logically formulated ideologies. The student of social phe-

nomena who wants to understand what lies beyond appearances must be aware of the basic motivations (residues) that drive individuals and organized groups. In *Les systèmes socialistes* (1902), Pareto applied this analysis to the study of socialism, concluding that while socialists claimed to speak for the disenfranchised majority, their real objective was to replace the liberals as the ruling class. Politics was the struggle for power among elites carried out in the name of high ideals.

Pareto saw himself as an objective social scientist bent on discovering the immutable laws that govern social phenomena. His practical experience of public life was limited. In 1882 he ran and lost a race for a seat in the Italian parliament. The loss seems to have soured him on politics. In 1893 he accepted the chair of political economy at the University of Lausanne and remained in Switzerland for the rest of his life. His public lectures attracted much attention, and one of his auditors was the young BENITO MUSSOLINI who was an expatriate in the Swiss city. Although Fascist theoreticians appropriated his view of politics as a struggle for power among minorities, Pareto did not endorse fascism. In the year before his death he did write for Mussolini's review *Gerarchia* and accepted appointment to the Italian senate from the Fascist government. Pareto's three-volume work *Trattato di sociologia generale* (1916) has been translated into English as *Mind and Society* (1936) and *Treatise on General Sociology* (1963).

Parini, Giuseppe (1729–1799)
poet, moralist, and social critic

Parini was born in the small Lombard town of Bosisio (renamed Bosisio Parini after its illustrious citizen) to a family of small-scale silk manufacturers. At age nine he went to live with relatives in Milan, where he attended religious schools and studied without particular distinction. But his first collection of poems, published in 1752, the year of his graduation, won him recognition for the classical simplicity and conciseness of his language. He acquiesced to ordination in the priesthood in 1754 in order to meet a condition of inheritance from a religious aunt and to give himself status as an independent scholar and writer. After working as a private tutor and finding minor employment in classroom teaching and journalism, he finally landed a permanent position as professor of letters in Milan's Palatine schools. His public service in the years following his appointment was on committees to reorganize the schools and revise textbooks. In 1763 he published the first part of the long composition in verse that he continued to work on for the rest of his life, which is regarded as his masterpiece. *Il giorno* (The day) is divided into five parts corresponding to different phases of a typical day in the life of a young aristocrat. From *Il mattino* (Morning) when the young man wakes up late to a leisurely breakfast served to him in bed, to *La notte* (Night) when he retires late after having whiled his time away dancing and gambling, the poem mocks and ridicules the frivolous and corrupt ways of the nobility. The lesson for the imaginary pupil for whom this description is intended is that true nobility is not a matter of titles and riches, but of honesty, dedication to work, and civic service. It is a message that reflects both Parini's roots in the hardworking middle classes and the influence of ENLIGHTENMENT ideas of social usefulness. The poem has been read as social protest, but Parini was not at all interested in active protest. He placed his faith in progress by education and moral improvement.

Paris, Congress of See CRIMEAN WAR.

Paris Peace Conference (1919)

Representatives of France, Italy, Japan, the United Kingdom, and the United States met in Paris to set peace terms for the defeated countries of WORLD WAR I. The spirit of wartime collaboration among the victors dissolved into acrimony over the issue of Italian territorial claims. Italian claims against Austria-Hungary were settled quickly when the allies agreed to give Italy all the territory it had already occupied up to the Brenner Pass in the region of TRENTINO–ALTO ADIGE. The clash occurred when President Woodrow Wilson refused to accept territorial claims against the new state of Yugoslavia that, if granted, would have given Italy control of territories in ISTRIA and DALMATIA inhabited primarily by Slavic populations. Italian claims focused particularly on the disputed city of FIUME. In April 1919 President Wilson appealed directly to the Italian people to support his position in favor of national self-determination, bypassing the Italian delegation headed by Prime Minister VITTORIO EMANUELE ORLANDO and Foreign Minister SIDNEY SONNINO. The Italian delegates walked out of the conference in protest, thinking that their absence would bring all deliberations to a halt. They returned quietly two weeks later, when they saw that the conference was carrying on and setting peace terms for Germany without their participation. Italy thus lost out on some provisions of the Treaty of Versailles that was signed in June 1919. Italy nevertheless secured a share of German wartime reparations and a permanent seat on the council of the League of Nations. The Treaty of St. Germain with Austria that was signed in September 1919 gave Italy the Brenner frontier, a slice of Slovene-inhabited territory around the town of Tarvisio, control of the main railways from Trieste to the Austrian border, and the largest share of Austria-Hungary's merchant fleet. The issue of the eastern frontier with Yugoslavia was left unresolved, as were Italian claims to territory and spheres of influence in Asia Minor. The dispute unleashed a frenzy of nationalist passions in Italy. The press vilified President Wilson and demanded complete satisfaction of Italy's claims. Volunteers led by GABRIELE D'ANNUNZIO forcibly seized Fiume. BENITO MUSSOLINI supported the seizure, gaining national attention and support for the emerging Fascist movement. The border with Yugoslavia was settled by the Treaty of Rome (1924), which gave the city of Fiume to Italy and the hinterland to Yugoslavia.

Parma, city of

Parma (pop. 170,000), a provincial capital in the region of EMILIA-ROMAGNA, is a city of Roman origin. It prospered under Rome as an agricultural and transportation center located along the important Via Emilia that traversed the Po Valley in a southeast-northwest direction, from close to the Adriatic coast to the ALPS. After suffering devastation in the period of invasions in the early middle ages, it rose again to prominence under the lordship of its bishops in the 11th and 12th centuries. Its history as an independent commune ended in 1303. The Correggio, VISCONTI, and SFORZA families ruled it in succession until 1500 when the French occupied it, then turned it over to the PAPACY in 1512. Pope PAUL III made it the capital of the independent Duchy of Parma and Piacenza, which he bestowed on his natural son Pier Luigi Farnese. The FARNESE FAMILY ruled Parma until its direct line became extinct in 1731, after which it passed to CHARLES OF BOURBON, son of Philip V of Spain and ELISABETTA FARNESE, then from Charles to Austria, which added to it the Duchy of Guastalla (1738), and from Austria back to the Spanish BOURBONS in the person of Charles's brother Philip in 1748. Under Bourbon rule Parma was a cosmopolitan center of Enlightenment culture. Under its prime minister, GUILLAUME LÉON DU TILLOT, the duchy was at the vanguard of political reform. Incorporated into France by Napoleon I in 1808, it passed in 1814, through the CONGRESS OF VIENNA, to Marie Louise of Habsburg, second wife of Napoleon and daughter of the Austrian emperor, with the understanding that at her death it would revert to the Bourbons. The Bourbons were restored in 1847 in the person of CARLO LODOVICO of Lucca, who ruled in Parma as Carlo II (1847–49). The unsolved assassination of his son and successor, Carlo III, in 1854 was followed by a regency in the name of his son. Political dissent and domestic turmoil were features of life in the duchy throughout the 1850s. The duchy became part of the Kingdom of Italy in 1860. Its politics have gravitated toward the extremes of the political spectrum. The Po Valley lowlands have leaned to the Left, socialist until the rise of fascism and communist after the downfall of the regime. Conservative movements have done well in the higher elevations of the province. Politics have been no obstacle to Parma's economic progress. Its prosperity is based on a diversified economy that combines agriculture, commerce, and manufacturing. It is renowned for its cuisine and boasts such delicacies as prosciutto (cured ham) and Parmesan cheese (table and grating cheese).

Parmigianino See MANNERISM.

Parri, Ferruccio (1890–1981)
anti-Fascist leader, founder of the Action Party, and prime minister

This prominent anti-Fascist political figure was born in the town of Pinerolo (Turin). A decorated WORLD WAR I army officer, he actively opposed FASCISM, was imprisoned in 1927 for his political activities, and was a founder of the movement GIUSTIZIA E LIBERTÀ. In 1942 he founded the ACTION PARTY and joined the RESISTANCE movement in 1943. In the resistance, operating under the name of Maurizio, he served as military vice commander. Captured by the Germans in February 1945, he was released the following month as part of the secret deal behind the surrender of German troops in northern Italy in April 1945. He served as prime minister in June–November 1945 as a compromise candidate because the major parties could not agree on anyone else. He was an ideal interim candidate because of his undisputed personal prestige, and because as the head of a party that had little popular support he posed no threat to other figures. An austere intellectual figure, Parri seemed more suited to the classroom than to parliament. He was a member of the Constituent Assembly that framed the CONSTITUTION of the Italian republic, joined but quickly left the Republican Party (PRI), and was in parliament as an independent senator from 1948. In 1963 he was nominated senator for life in recognition of his outstanding services. After 1968 he headed a group of independent senators opposed to the OPENING TO THE LEFT. A political maverick to the end, Parri was respected and admired for his personal honesty, political coherence, and outspokenness.

Parthenopean Republic

This short-lived experiment in republican government occurred in Naples in 1799. It was inspired by the example of the FRENCH REVOLUTION and by the presence of the army of NAPOLEON I. When a French army reached Naples in January 1799, the Bourbon ruler FERDINAND I fled to Sicily with his court, abandoning his capital city and mainland provinces to the French and their supporters. The provisional government proclaimed the republic, promised to end aristocratic and clerical privileges, invoked the principles of the French Revolution, and appealed to the masses in the name of democracy. The reformers, known as JACOBINS because of their French sympathies, found little popular support. They had to contend with the attachment of the masses to the monarchy and the church and with the counterrevolutionary movement headed by Cardinal FABRIZIO RUFFO (1744–1827), who organized and led bands of armed peasants against the republic. His SANFEDISTI (Followers of the Holy Faith) recovered Naples for the king in June 1799, after the French army withdrew following military reverses in northern Italy. The loyalists inflicted bloody retribution on the Jacobins and their supporters. Although few of the victims were thinking in terms of national unity and independence, a later generation of patriots hailed them as the first martyrs of the RISORGIMENTO, thus giving the Parthenopean Republic a prominent place in the patriotic narrative.

partisans See RESISTANCE.

Partito d'Azione See ACTION PARTY.

Partito Operaio Italiano See LAZZARI, CONSTANTINO.

Pascoli, Giovanni (1855–1912)

poet, teacher, literary critic, and public figure

Born in San Mauro di Romagna, renamed San Mauro Pascoli after its famous son, Pascoli suffered through a traumatic childhood marked by the unsolved murder of his father, an agricultural manager, and the loss of his mother and siblings. He entered the University of Bologna in 1873, took time off from his studies to engage in political protest, was jailed for three months in 1879, resumed his studies and graduated with a degree in philology and classical languages in 1882. After holding several teaching positions, in 1906 he succeeded his former teacher GIOSUÈ CARDUCCI as professor of Italian literature at the University of Bologna, a position that he held for the rest of his life. Some of his best poetry appears in the collections entitled *Myricae* (1891) and *Canti di Castelvecchio* (Songs of Castelvecchio, 1903). The rustic home in Castelvecchio in the mountains of northern Tuscany near Lucca was Pascoli's favorite retreat. *Carmina* (1914), a prizewinning collection of poems that he wrote in Latin, was published posthumously. Pascoli's writings express love of nature, humanitarian ideals, and concern for the underprivileged. Initially attracted to militant socialism, Pascoli's political sentiments were transformed in several ways by the passage of time. His socialism mellowed after his imprisonment in 1879 into a sense of broad solidarity and brotherhood, far removed from notions of class conflict. Sensitive to the problems of emigrants, he came to regard colonial expansion as a legitimate answer to the problems of overpopulation, land scarcity, and poverty in Italy. Pascoli welcomed Italy's conquest of Libya as a legitimate assertion of national will and a means of solving Italy's social problems. He coined the phrase often cited by nationalists, "the great proletarian nation is on the move." COLONIALISM, monarchist sentiments, a strongly patriotic tone, and a social conscience mark him as belonging to the generation of pre-

war intellectuals who professed both nationalist and humanitarian sentiments.

Pasolini, Pier Paolo (1922–1975)
writer, film director, and social critic

The most controversial cultural figure of postwar
Italy was born to a family of the lower middle
class (his father was a military officer, his mother
a schoolteacher) in the FRIULI region of northern
Italy. Novelist, poet, literary critic, and film director, Pasolini made his debut in print in 1942 with
a collection of poems entitled *Poesie a Casarsa*,
written in Friulian dialect. The choice of dialect
was controversial in itself, and an indication of
Pasolini's abiding interest in popular culture as
a challenge to mainstream high culture. His first
publishing success came with the novel *Ragazzi
di vita* (1955), which peered into the seamy
world of Roman street boys that exerted a powerful, morbid attraction for Pasolini both as
writer and as a person. Sex scandals began to dog
Pasolini's life at about this time, caused his
expulsion from the Communist Party (PCI) and
ended his career as a schoolteacher. Repeated
brushes with the law and the courts followed. At
war with capitalism and bourgeois culture,
Pasolini lived his rebellion both artistically and
personally. In typical 1960s fashion, he mixed
Marx and Freud, but also showed an appreciation for the power of religion. His film *The Gospel
According to Saint Matthew* (1964) illustrates
Pasolini's handling of the themes of class struggle, personal liberation, and spiritual inspiration.
In the final years of his life he lashed out with
venomous power against the country's political
leadership, the miseries of urban life, and the
decadence of life in industrial society. At the root
of his rebellion was perhaps a romantic longing
and idealization of preindustrial society, evident
in his close studies of folk literature and popular
customs. He was found in a seedy Roman suburb
battered to death by a young man whom he had
picked up after leaving a gathering of Roman literary and society figures. His shocking death was
the tragic climax to a life of protest against social
controls and conventional morality.

Passaglia, Carlo (1812–1887)
*theologian and diplomatic negotiator who
worked to reconcile church and state*

Born near LUCCA, Passaglia entered the JESUIT
ORDER, gained a reputation as an expert theologian, and was one of Pope PIUS IX's principal advisers in the proclamation of the dogma of the
Immaculate Conception issued in 1854. But while
his theology was orthodox, his ideas of liberal
reform of the church proved incompatible with
his status as a Jesuit. In 1858 he left the Jesuit
Order for the secular priesthood and a papal
appointment as professor of philosophy at the
University of Rome. Because he enjoyed the confidence of both Pius IX and CAVOUR, Passaglia was
ideally positioned to act as intermediary between
the two in the conflict of CHURCH AND STATE. He
served as Cavour's official emissary in the negotiations that began in February 1861. Passaglia
was convinced that the pope could fulfill his
duties as head of the church without the temporal power that he enjoyed as head of the PAPAL
STATES. But he did not win papal support for his
views, and this first effort to negotiate a settlement of the conflict failed. Passaglia's position in
Rome was seriously compromised by his role as
Cavour's representative, and he had to leave the
city. In Turin where he found political refuge he
also found employment as university professor of
moral philosophy. Estranged from the church, he
continued to write and work for a peaceful settlement of the conflict of church and state. He
was reconciled with the church on his deathbed
when he renounced his unorthodox views.

Pastore, Giulio See SYNDICALISM.

Paul III (1468–1549)
pope (1534–1549)

Well-born, educated in the humanist tradition,
a sophisticated man of the world, and an astute
diplomat, Alessandro Farnese pursued an ecclesiastical career at his mother's urging. Pope
Alexander VI appointed him cardinal in 1493. In
the several posts that he held as papal legate and

bishop before and after his appointment as cardinal he showed more interest in worldly than in religious affairs. Nothing in his record prior to being elected pope indicated that he would be a vigorous and effective reformer. His top priority as pope was to summon a church council to confront the spread of Protestantism in northern Europe and promote church reform. In response to the threat of Turkish invasion from the east, the pope tried with little success to form a united Christian front by settling the conflict between Emperor Charles V and King Francis I of France. Opposition within and outside the church repeatedly stymied his efforts to summon a council. When the COUNCIL OF TRENT opened in 1545, it was no longer to heal the schism, but to define church doctrine, promote church reform, and take the offensive against Protestantism. To that end Paul III also gave papal approval to the JESUIT ORDER and established the ROMAN INQUISITION. His achievements as a reforming pope were obscured by his nepotism and sexual laxity. The most glaring case of both was his bestowal of the Duchy of PARMA and PIACENZA, formed out of papal lands, on his favorite son Pierluigi Farnese. Although Paul III did not live long enough to see the results of his initiatives, he did succeed in launching the process of reform known as the CATHOLIC REFORMATION.

Paul IV See JEWS IN ITALY.

Paul V (1552–1621)
pope (1605–1621)
Born Camillo Borghese to the prominent family of the Roman aristocracy, the future pope was created cardinal in 1596. His rather ordinary career in the papal administration, his scholarly temperament and personal piety gave little clue to the strong leadership that he provided as pope. A determined defender of church prerogatives, he placed the republic of Venice under interdict (papal condemnation) for infringing on the church's property rights and imprisoning

clerics in disregard of canon law. The incident triggered the antipapal writings of PAOLO SARPI in defense of the republic's sovereign powers. The first condemnation of GALILEO GALILEI's writings also occurred during the pontificate of Paul V. His intransigence provoked serious clashes with the English, French, and Russian governments. These actions were part of the pope's determined efforts to consolidate the international authority of the church and the reforms initiated by his predecessors. Paul V required bishops to reside in their sees, encouraged monastic orders, reformed church ritual, established homes and shelters for the poor, and encouraged missionary work within and outside Europe. An enthusiastic promoter of architects and urban constructions, he completed the building of St. Peter's Basilica, laid out the square in front of the basilica, and improved the city's water supply. Like most other popes of his period, Paul V was excessively prone to favor his relatives in public office and employment, but his most serious drawback was the lack of diplomatic tact that embroiled the church in difficult controversies and ultimately made it wholly reliant on the support of the HABSBURGS.

Paul VI (1897–1978)
pope (1963–1978)
Born Giovanni Battista Montini to a prominent family in the northern city of Brescia, he was educated by Jesuits and private tutors. Ordained a priest in 1920, he studied diplomacy in Rome and began his diplomatic career in 1923 as attaché to the papal embassy in Warsaw. After returning to Rome in 1924, he worked in the secretariat of state and served as chaplain to the Italian Association of Catholic University Students. PIUS XII appointed him substitute secretary of state and relied heavily on his advice. In the period 1946–55 Montini was considered to be the most influential Vatican figure after the pope. In 1955 Pius XII appointed Montini archbishop of Milan. For reasons that are still unclear, the pope did not make him cardinal, but that was

remedied by Pope JOHN XXIII in 1963. That same year he was elected pope, following the death of John XXIII. The central event of his pontificate was the conclusion of the council known as Vatican II, the reforms of which he backed and implemented. Paul VI was an effective innovator in many areas of church policy. He pursued the ecumenical dialogue with other churches and denominations to put Catholics in touch with non-Catholics. He traveled widely and drew attention to the problems of developing countries. He promoted the reform of church ritual, the ceremonial use of vernacular languages instead of Latin, and the greater involvement of clergy and laity in matters of local governance. However, he resisted demands for change on abortion and birth control, clerical celibacy, the ordination of women, or papal claims of infallibility and supremacy within the church and the Christian world. This fine balancing of tradition and innovation revealed Paul VI's diplomatic training and temper. In response to criticism that he was indecisive, he distinguished between reform and revolution. He was willing to implement the reform of Vatican II, but not to depart from the traditional teachings of the church on matters of morality and papal authority. He was also a staunch opponent of communism in Italy and on the world scene. JOHN PAUL II took up the course set by Paul VI of innovating in matters of church governance and politics while holding to tradition in matters of doctrine and morality.

Pavarotti, Luciano See MODENA, CITY OF; OPERA.

Pavese, Cesare (1908–1950)
novelist, poet, critic, and translator
Born to a family of the lower middle class in the Langhe region of Piedmont, Pavese took a degree in literature from the University of Turin in 1930 with a thesis on Walt Whitman. Arrested in 1935 on suspicion of antifascism, he spent 10 months in political confinement. The rest of his

adult life was outwardly uneventful. He worked for the publisher Giulio Einaudi as editor, reader, and translator. His classic translation of Melville's *Moby Dick* dates from 1932. Later, from his pen came translations of Whitman, Edgar Lee Masters, and Sinclair Lewis. Pavese never set foot on American soil, but admired America through the spirit of its writers. What he admired most was the American writers' grip on reality, their use of plain language, and avoidance of rhetorical flourishes. His own novels, however, were not written in the realist mode, but were peopled by mythological characters that he saw as archetypes of human personalities. The interest in American writing was really a protest against the culture of FASCISM, but a protest that in Pavese's case remained essentially literary. He did not join the antifascist RESISTANCE, but agonized over his own inability to move from the realm of thought to that of action. His political sympathies went to the Communist Party (PCI) and he wrote pieces of literary criticism for the party newspaper *L'Unità*. *Il compagno* (The Comrade, 1947) was one of his major novels. It told the story of a communist who overcomes his ingrained preference for the contemplative life to become a party activist. Pavese was fascinated by primitivism, nature, and rural life, and ambivalent toward mass politics, urban life, and industrial society. His diary *Il mestiere di vivere* (The Business of Living, 1952) is a dispassionate analysis of his inner life. His death by suicide in a Turin hotel was emblematic of his pessimism and sense of isolation.

Pavia, city of
This provincial capital (pop. 73,900) is surrounded by fertile land in the Lombard plain near the confluence of the Po and Ticino Rivers. Founded in pre-Roman times, it rose to prominence as capital of the Lombard kingdom in the seventh and eighth centuries A.D. It was the capital of the independent *Regnum Italicum* until the 11th century when it organized itself as a free commune. The origins of its famous university,

one of the oldest in Europe, go back to the 10th century, when it emerged as a center for the study of Roman law. Its jurists played the major role in preserving and applying Roman law to the needs of government in the Middle Ages. In the struggles of the 12th and 13th centuries, it generally sided with the imperial factions of the Ghibellines against its more powerful rival, Milan, under whose rule it fell in the 14th century. Its most important structures and monuments were built under Lombard rule and in the period of communal freedom. Its strategic importance made it an object of contention by the French, Spaniards, and Austrians, often with disastrous consequences for the city. In 1525, at the Battle of Pavia, fought near the town, Charles V defeated and captured his enemy King Francis I of France. The town was repeatedly besieged, captured, and sacked by rival armies, until the Spaniards established their hegemony over the entire region of LOMBARDY. Under Spanish rule (1559–1714) Pavia was secure from attack but lost much of its economic and political importance to Milan. It rose up against Napoleon I in 1796 and was an important center of resistance to Austrian rule in the RISORGIMENTO. Pavia has a diversified economy. It is still an agricultural center, but banking and commerce are also important. Shoe manufacturing, textile, chemical, and engineering industries are well established throughout the province.

Pavolini, Alessandro (1903–1945)
Fascist activist, journalist, cultural organizer, and party secretary

Born in Florence, Pavolini joined the Fascist Party in 1920, took part in street actions and in the march on Rome. He studied law and political science at the University of Florence while pursuing a career in the party. He achieved the office of *federale* (provincial leader) in 1929, was appointed to the party directorate in 1932, and elected to parliament in 1934. A protégé of GALEAZZO CIANO, he served as minister of popular culture from 1939 to 1943. In that capacity he directed Fascist propaganda, often clashing with party figures and journalists, whom he accused of undermining public morale by reporting news of military defeats during WORLD WAR II. Mussolini dismissed him in February 1943, but later that year appointed him party secretary in the ITALIAN SOCIAL REPUBLIC, the puppet government he set up in German-occupied northern Italy. In that final role Pavolini emerged as a die-hard Fascist who resorted to extreme measures to fight the anti-Fascist RESISTANCE. He urged Mussolini to crack down on Fascist turncoats, including Mussolini's son-in-law GALEAZZO CIANO. To win popular support for government he called for socialist measures and resistance to German interference in the political affairs of the Social Republic. The Black Brigades (*Brigate nere*) that he organized gained a reputation for brutality against partisans and civilians. He promised but failed to deliver a last-ditch defense of the Social Republic in the last days of the war. Pavolino was among the Fascist leaders captured and executed by partisans in the last days of the war.

Pazzi conspiracy See MEDICI, LORENZO DE'.

PCI (Partito Comunista Italiano)
Organized communism in Italy grew out of the internal disputes of the Italian Socialist Party (PSI). WORLD WAR I, the Russian Revolution of 1917, and the rise of FASCISM intensified the socialist debate over the strategy and prospects of revolution in Italy. Socialists who were inspired by the seizure of power by communists in Russia to do the same in Italy looked to Moscow for leadership and objected to the PSI's reluctance to join the Moscow-led Third Communist International (Comintern). These dissidents, led by AMADEO BORDIGA and ANTONIO GRAMSCI, bolted from the party at the annual party congress held in the city of LIVORNO in January 1921 and founded the Communist Party of Italy. The party was small, internally divided, and a victim of Fascist repression. It maintained a precarious presence

in Italy in the Fascist period by going underground. Most of its leaders fled abroad. The Soviet Union and France proved to be particularly hospitable to Italian communists in exile.

The leaders returned to Italy after the overthrow of Mussolini in July 1943 and played a major role in the RESISTANCE movement. Communist formations seized control of many cities and towns in northern Italy in the final days of the war. But with the Allies in firm military control of the country they stood no chance of seizing power at the national level. The tactic of cooperation with noncommunists was thus born out of necessity. Over the objections of hard-liners who favored more forceful approaches, Communist Party leader PALMIRO TOGLIATTI agreed to work with the Allies, church, monarchy, and other political parties. Known as the *svolta di Salerno,* the tactic of cooperation paid off temporarily. The PCI was part of the political coalitions that governed from 1945 to 1947.

The Italian Communist Party, called the "new party" to distinguish it from its Leninist predecessor of 1921, was a mass party with over 1.7 million members in 1945. It reached 2.6 million members a decade later. At the height of its power in the 1970s the PCI gathered more than one-third of the popular vote, coming close to but never overtaking the rival and politically dominant Christian Democratic Party (DC). It was the largest communist party outside the Soviet bloc and China. Manual workers and labor unions were its main, but by no means its sole, constituents. Members and voters came from a broad spectrum of society, with peasants and white-collar workers being well represented. The leadership was mostly of middle-class extraction, and intellectuals played important supporting roles. Its strongholds were the industrial cities, and the rural areas of northern and central Italy where *MEZZADRIA* and commercial farming dominated. In those areas, communist-controlled local administrations were often models of honest, efficient, and socially caring government. In the South, communism appealed largely to impoverished peasants eager for land and jobs.

This diverse social basis was a contributing factor to the strategy of gradual reform and "progressive democracy" adopted by Togliatti and his successors. Following that course, the party loosened its ties to the Soviet Union, accepted Italian membership in NATO, welcomed the EUROPEAN UNION, and professed complete acceptance of the rules of parliamentary politics and liberal democracy. The strategy of accommodation led to informal cooperation between PCI and DC. The HISTORIC COMPROMISE was supposed to formalize and seal their cooperation, but it never came to fruition. Extremists of the Left and Right resisted the Historic Compromise for different reasons. Diehard leftists denounced it as the *embourgeoisement* of the party (selling out to the class enemy, the bourgeoisie). They feared the complete transformation of the PCI into a party of government and law and order. Right-wing extremists saw it as creeping socialism. The extremists of left and right met in the phenomenon of TERRORISM.

The PCI weathered the crisis under the capable leadership of ENRICO BERLINGUER but did not reap the rewards of power sharing. In the 1980s it abandoned the policy of collaboration with the DC, without replacing it with a clear alternative course. Left to drift, it succumbed to domestic and international developments of the late 1980s and early 1990s. By then, the blue-collar workers, agricultural laborers, and unions that the party relied on for much of its support counted for less in the national economy. Italian society was more middle class, and consumerism was rampant. The passage of time eroded the memory of the anti-Fascist resistance on which much of the PCI appeal rested. The end of the cold war relieved the international tensions that divided communists and noncommunists. Communism collapsed globally in 1989–90. The PCI was still an important player in national and local politics, but the handwriting was on the wall. Its membership dropped to about 700,000 and its share of the popular vote fell from 34.4 percent in the elections of 1976 to 26.6 percent in the elections of 1987. Its last leader was Ochille Occhetto (born 1936). Chosen party secretary in 1988, Occhetto quickly decided to launch a "new course," announced his intention to dissolve the PCI, and create a new party of the Left. His resolution passed at the PCI's Twentieth Congress. The new party, also headed by Occhetto, was called the Democratic Party of the Left (Partito Democratico della Sinistra, or PDS). A dissenting minority refused to go along and launched Rifondazione Comunista (Communist Refounding), a party that adhered to traditional communist ideology, adopted a hard line on labor issues, and used obstructionist tactics in parliament with some success to advance its agenda.

PDS (Partito Democratico della Sinistra)

The Democratic Party of the Left was the principal successor of the disbanded PCI. It was founded in February 1991 after lengthy discussions, with a program that renounced communist ideology and espoused parliamentary democracy. Its membership of about 700,000 made it a party to be reckoned with, but lack of programmatic clarity, conflict within the ranks, and rivalries among its leaders diminished its clout. In the national elections of 1992 it gained only 17 percent of the popular vote, a decline of more than nine percentage points from the PCI's showing in 1987. After the national elections of 1994, in which the PDS suffered further losses, Occhetto resigned, and the party was led by MASSIMO D'ALEMA, who led the PDS to electoral success in the national elections of 1996 as the key party in the coalition of 13 parties known as the Ulivo (Olive Tree), which was politically dominant until the national elections of 2001. Under D'Alema's leadership the PDS distanced itself further from its communist roots. Since February 1998 it has called itself the Democratici di Sinistra (Democrats of the Left), an amorphous grouping of former communists and socialists that strives to be broadly representative. In the elections of May 2001 the Democrats of the Left competed against the coalition led by SILVIO BERLUSCONI. Their leader this time was Francesco Rutelli (born 1954), the young, attractive, but politically inexperienced mayor of Rome. Since Berlusconi's decisive victory, the Democrats of the Left have led the opposition, hoping to convince voters that they stand for a viable populist and compassionate approach to government.

Peace Treaty (World War II)

The Peace Treaty formally ending the state of war between Italy and the Allies was signed in Paris on February 10, 1947. Although the Allies had recognized Italy as a cobelligerent against Germany in October 1943, its earlier alliance and partnership with Germany against the Allies put it among the defeated nations, and as such it was treated in the peace negotiations. Italy had no voice in the final settlement, but it benefited by the start of the cold war that broke the unity of the wartime allies. France, Great Britain, and most particularly the United States were more disposed to leniency than the Soviet Union, which championed instead the territorial demands of its ally Yugoslavia at Italy's expense. While France was content with merely symbolic annexations of small Italian territories on its boundary, Yugoslavia received the major share of the former region of VENEZIA GIULIA, the islands of the upper Adriatic, and the Dalmatian cities of Pola and Zara. The disputed territory of TRIESTE was given to neither. It remained nominally autonomous as the Free Territory of Trieste, but divided into two zones. Zone A was under Allied control and Zone B under Yugoslav control. In 1954 Italy received Zone A (which included the city of Trieste) and Yugoslavia received Zone B. No change occurred in the border with Austria. The peace treaty deprived Italy of all its colonies, imposed severe limits on its armed forces, and called for Italian reparation payments to the Soviet Union, Albania, Ethiopia, Greece, and Yugoslavia. The treaty had major domestic repercussions. The loss of territories and colonies fed the propaganda of the political Right against the Italian Communist Party (PCI), which as an ally of the Soviet Union and Communist Yugo-slavia was seen as complicit in the loss of territory. The major beneficiary of anticommunist sentiment was the Christian Democratic Party (DC), but the neo-Fascist party (MSI) also used the Peace Treaty to its benefit by arguing that it was unfairly punitive, a sentiment shared by many who were not neo-fascists.

In retrospect, it cannot be argued that the Peace Treaty was punitive. Unlike Germany, Italy was not dismembered, though it had been an enemy for most of the war. Its territorial losses were minor and in some ways beneficial, for they conformed to the wishes of Slavic-speaking populations that were unfriendly to Italy. The loss of colonies also proved to be a blessing in disguise, for it relieved Italy of costly responsibilities and may have prevented the kind of conflicts that France faced in the colonies that it retained. Limitations on armaments enabled Italy to concentrate its scarce resources on more productive investments. Economic aid from the United States and the Marshall Plan more than made up for Italy's reparation payments. The relative leniency of the settlement facilitated Italy's transition from wartime enemy to peacetime collaborator of the western democracies.

Peano, Giuseppe   See SCIENCE.

peasantry   See AGRICULTURE; LAND REFORM; *MEZZADRIA*; MIGRATION; SOUTHERN QUESTION.

Pecorelli, Carmine   See ANDREOTTI, GIULIO.

Pella, Giuseppe   (1902–1981)
Christian Democratic leader, government figure, and economic expert
Pella was a prominent figure on the national scene in the 1950s and early 1960s. He was born to a peasant family in the region of Piedmont, received a degree in political economy from the University of Turin, and lobbied for textile interests in the 1930s. His close association with Christian Democratic leader ALCIDE DE GASPERI began shortly after World War II when Pella joined the Christian Democratic Party (DC) and was elected to the constituent assembly (1946–47) that drew up the CONSTITUTION of the Italian republic. He served in various government capacities, including minister of finance and budget minister, before forming his own government (in which he was also budget and foreign minister) in August 1953. During the five months that he was in power he confronted the crisis with Yugoslavia over the future of TRIESTE. His forceful response to the crisis, which included dispatching army divisions to the border, endeared him to Italian nationalists. He was done in politically by infighting within his own party and forced to step down in January 1954. In later governments he again held the posts of foreign minister (1957–58, 1959) and budget minister (1960–61). A steadying presence among Christian Democrats, Pella urged Italians to work hard and trust in their own ability to overcome economic adversity.

Pellico, Silvio   (1789–1854)
writer, educator, conspirator, and religiously motivated liberal patriot
Pellico, born in Piedmont, experienced a religious conversion after being arrested in Milan by the Austrian police in October 1820, on charges of conspiring against the government. Pellico had joined the secret society of the CARBONARI at the urging of his close friend and fellow conspirator Pietro Maroncelli (1795–1846), and had served as a secret courier between Milan and Turin prior to the uprisings of that year. Both Pellico and his friend served 10 years of their sentences in the Spielberg Castle (now in the Czech Republic), before being released in August 1830. Pellico's book, *Le mie prigioni* (My Prisons), published in 1832, was an immediate success. It is cast in the form of a pious meditation on his experience of life as a convict. Its tone of Christian resignation

and forgiveness in the face of suffering was controversial from the start. While devout Catholics admired the spirit of the book, embattled patriots found the author's stance too passive and submissive. Nevertheless, the book was widely read and quickly translated. It generated much sympathy for the cause of Italian independence, especially in Anglo–Saxon countries. The stance of victim seemed to suit Pellico's character. The Austrian chancellor, Prince Clemens von Metternich, is said to have resented and feared the book. Its popularity has overshadowed Pellico's other notable writings, particularly his once-popular tragic play *Francesca Da Rimini* (1815) and his book of exhortations to the young, *Dei doveri degli uomini* (On the Duties of Man, 1834). Pellico avoided political activity after his release from prison. Claiming that he had never condoned violence and civil strife, he devoted himself to writing and meditation, helped financially by family and friends. By the time of his death, he was an isolated and nearly forgotten figure. Later generations burnished his memory as a patriotic martyr, and it is in that light that he is chiefly remembered today.

Pelloux, Luigi Girolamo (1839–1924)
political and military figure close to the ruling House of Savoy

A native of the region of SAVOY ceded to France in 1860, Pelloux began his military career fighting in the wars of the RISORGIMENTO from 1859 to 1870. He was promoted to general in 1885 and received his first army corps command in 1896. Simultaneously active in politics, he represented the district of LIVORNO in the chamber of deputies from 1880 and was appointed to the senate in 1896. He served three times as war minister, with ANTONIO DI RUDINÌ in 1891–93, GIOVANNI GIOLITTI in 1892–93, and again with Rudinì in 1896–97. Acceptable to both liberals and conservatives, and well liked by the king, he seemed to be a good choice for prime minister in June 1898. In the wake of the antigovernment riots of the FATTI DI MAGGIO, the country needed a leader who could bring together the different factions. Pelloux seemed to be the man. As army commander in BARI he had dealt with street demonstrations without overreacting. But his appointment was also based on misunderstanding. King UMBERTO I and many conservatives felt that a firm hand was needed in government to correct abuses of parliamentary procedures by socialists and other opposition groups, which used filibustering and other obstructive practices against the majority. Pelloux shared those feelings and attempted to force through parliament measures to limit such practices, broaden the powers of the police, and restrict civil liberties. The measures were blocked in sessions more reminiscent of street brawling than parliamentary debate. The extreme Left adamantly refused to allow consideration of the bill, and when the president put the bill to a vote they smashed the ballot boxes. The government enacted the bill by decree as it had a right to do, pending approval of parliament within 30 days. The courts declared the bill null and void when the closing of parliament prevented the vote from taking place. The government was also embarrassed when Italy became the only western country to be refused extraterritorial rights by China in the wake of the Boxer rebellion. Pelloux stepped down in June 1900, opening the way to a liberal solution of the crisis. He was succeeded by GIUSEPPE SARACCO.

Pentarchy See LIBERAL LEFT.

Pepe, Guglielmo (1783–1855)
Neapolitan general and liberal patriot who fought for Italian independence

Pepe was born in the region of Calabria, began his military career under the BOURBONS, continued it during the PARTHENOPEAN REPUBLIC, and went on to serve in the armies of NAPOLEON I, JOSEPH BONAPARTE, and JOACHIM MURAT until 1815. The restored BOURBON monarchy kept him in service and entrusted him with the command of a division even though he was politically suspect. During the REVOLUTION of 1820–21 Murat sided with the insurgents, assumed command of the army, and pressured King FERDINAND I to grant a constitution. After the Austrians defeated his troops in 1821 and Ferdinand returned, Pepe went into political exile in France and Great Britain. He returned to Italy in 1848 to take command of the Neapolitan army corps sent to fight against the Austrians in northern Italy. When the Neapolitan government recalled the corps, Pepe refused to obey and continued to fight at the head of a force of about 2,000 soldiers, and as commander of the forces of the Venetian republic. Forced to capitulate in August 1849 and excluded from political amnesty, Pepe fled abroad once again. He settled for a while in Paris where he published his memoirs, then moved to Turin where he lived from 1851 to the end of his life. Well known and respected, he was an effective advocate of Italian independence in France and Great Britain where his writings were published and translated. His principal writings are *Memoirs of General Pepe* (1846) and *Narrative of Scenes and Events in Italy from 1847 to 1849* (1850).

Pergolesi, Giovanni Battista   See OPERA.

Peri, Jacopo   See OPERA.

Persano, Count Carlo Pellion di
(1806–1883)
navy admiral, collaborator of Cavour, navy commander in the war of 1866
Persano has the unfortunate distinction of being remembered as the commander who lost the most important engagement of the Italian navy between national unification and World War I. His advancement was slow but steady. He joined the Piedmontese navy in 1821, distinguished himself in raids against the pirate stronghold of Tripoli (1825), reached captain in 1848, and rear admiral in 1859. He performed a useful service for Prime Minister CAVOUR in 1860 by keeping an eye on GIUSEPPE GARIBALDI's movements. Garibaldi did not take umbrage, and gave Persano command of seized Neapolitan warships after the conquest of Naples. After participating in the campaign against the pope off the port of Ancona and against the resisting Neapolitan forces in Gaeta later that year, Persano was appointed vice admiral. As navy minister in the government headed by URBANO RATTAZZI (1862), he pushed for the modernization of the navy and the construction of ironclads. He was elected to the chamber of deputies (1860–65) and appointed to the senate (1865).

In May 1866 Persano was appointed chief admiral of the navy. It was in that capacity that he led the fleet against the Austrians during the third of the WARS OF INDEPENDENCE. Apparently concerned that his ships and crews were unprepared for action, he hesitated to take advantage of the numerical superiority of his fleet. On July 20, 1866, the Austrian navy attacked his ships while they were bombing enemy fortifications on the Adriatic island of Lissa. Persano made the unpardonable mistake of abandoning the flagship *Re d'Italia* for another vessel just before the engagement began, without telling anyone of his move. The Austrians moved quickly, while confusion reigned on the Italian side. In one hour Persano's fleet lost two ships, including the flagship, which was rammed, and 612 crew members. An inquiry conducted by the senate resulted in Persano's loss of rank, pension, and decorations. He never recovered from the disgrace and died in obscurity. The navy's poor performance fueled polemics against war and the military on the Left. The Right called for revenge, a strong military, and an expansionist foreign policy.

Pertini, Alessandro or Sandro
(1896–1996)
moderate socialist, anti-Fascist activist, and president of the republic
This colorful and popular political figure was born near Savona (Liguria), fought in WORLD WAR I, received a law degree, joined the Socialist

Party (PSI), and was an active anti-Fascist. Condemned to 10 years in jail in 1925, he escaped to France, returned clandestinely to Italy to carry on his political activities, and was captured. Freed in 1943, he joined the RESISTANCE, directed its final operations, and helped reorganize the Socialist Party. He was the party's first postwar secretary and editor of the party newspaper *Avanti!* (1945–46, 1950–52). An independent socialist, he was often at odds with the party leadership. A member of the constituent assembly (1946–47) and of parliament after 1948 both as deputy and senator for life, he served as president of the republic (1978–85). His grandfatherly demeanor, pipe-smoking image, plain speaking, and love of soccer appealed to the popular imagination. Pertini's reassuring presence in the office of president helped restore faith in government in the crisis that followed the kidnapping and assassination of ALDO MORO. Pertini was the most beloved political figure in Italy at a time when few politicians enjoyed public confidence.

Perugia, city of

Perugia (pop. 158,300) is the regional capital of UMBRIA. Picturesquely situated on a hilltop overlooking the TIBER RIVER, the city is an important cultural and commercial center located in the geographical center of the peninsula. The University of Perugia and the University for Foreigners are the two major institutions that give cultural luster to the city. Its people speak a particularly pure form of Italian. Important Etruscan remains attest to the pre-Roman origins of the town. The Romans took it over in the third century B.C. After the collapse of Roman administration, Goths and Byzantines ruled it in the fifth and sixth centuries A.D. The town managed to maintain its independence as a commune through complicated vicissitudes and expanded its control over nearby towns like Assisi and Gubbio while gradually gravitating toward papal control. Various lords ruled the city as nominal vassals of the pope, but often in conflict with Rome. Most prominent among these local potentates was the Baglioni family, whose contested

rule ended definitely in 1540. Papal control was consolidated with the construction of the 16th-century Fortezza Paolina that dominated the city until torn down during the REVOLUTIONS of 1848–49. In this center of political dissidence, liberals from Perugia organized resistance to papal rule and supported the movement for Italian independence. In 1859 the city suffered from reprisals after revolting unsuccessfully against papal rule. A year later it became part of the Kingdom of Italy. Until 1927, when the province of Terni was carved out of its territory, the province of Perugia covered the entire region of Umbria. The control of local politics by socialists and progressive Catholics began in the early years of the 20th century and ended in 1922. The Fascists made the city their headquarters for the march on Rome that brought them to power. The city gives its name to the famous Perugina chocolates that are manufactured nearby.

Perugino (ca. 1445–1523)

Renaissance painter known for the delicacy of his colors and graceful figures

Perugino (the "Perugian") was born Pietro di Cristoforo Vannucci in Città della Pieve, near the city that gave him his art name. Little is known about his apprenticeship; he may have worked in Verrocchio's studio in Florence. Summoned to Rome by the pope, he was part of a team that painted the original frescoes of the Sistine Chapel, some of which were later covered by Michelangelo's *Last Judgment.* Perugino's contribution still survives in the *Giving of the Keys to St. Peter* (1481), the first of his major works to exemplify his style. A painting from the same period, the *Crucifixion with Saints,* appears in the National Gallery of Art, Washington, D.C. In 1486 he returned to Florence, where he painted altarpieces, portraits, and frescoes for the next five years. After 1496 he worked mainly in Perugia, where his style matured. He made his influence felt by training a large number of apprentices and assistants, including RAPHAEL, whom Perugino outlived by three years. Perugino's spare landscapes and oval facial types are thought to be typically Umbrian. His paintings, often criticized for being too stylized, make an impact with their sense of intimacy. They avoid the grand effects typical of the high Renaissance style. According to Vasari, Perugino's religious paintings are secular in spirit because Perugino lacked the religious faith required to do justice to sacred subjects. If that is the case, the same can be said for many of Perugino's fellow artists.

Peruzzi, Ubaldino (1822–1891)
political figure who worked for Italian independence and unity

This member of a distinguished Florentine banking family was an important figure among the politically moderate Tuscan gentry working for Italian independence and unity. He studied law in Siena and engineering in Paris. His political debut was as a member of the Tuscan parliament during the REVOLUTION of 1848. Peruzzi was disappointed when, at Austria's urging, the restored ducal government ignored the constitution granted in 1848. He was not politically active in the 1850s, but when war broke out between Piedmont and Austria in 1859 he supported the cause of union with Piedmont and Italian unification. The city of Florence elected him as its representative in the national parliament in 1860. He served in the chamber of deputies until 1890 and in the senate in the last year of his life. He was minister of public works (1860–62) and minister of the interior (1862–64). He was also mayor of Florence (1870–78). All his efforts aimed at strengthening the moderate elements of the political leadership against the democratic currents of the RISORGIMENTO era. His politics and social paternalism were typical of the Tuscan upper classes to which he was born. Emilia Peruzzi, his wife, ran a prestigious salon frequented by the Florentine intelligentsia and seconded her husband's political work.

Pesaro, city of

Pesaro (pop. 89,400) is the capital of the province of Pesaro and Urbino in the region of MARCHES on the coast of the ADRIATIC SEA. A Roman settlement founded in 184 B.C., it was occupied by Goths, Byzantines, and Franks successively after the collapse of Roman administration. The city gained political importance as a Byzantine outpost from A.D. 544 to A.D. 752. In 754 the Franks donated it to the pope. Thus began the long period of direct and indirect papal rule that lasted until 1860, when Pesaro became part of the Kingdom of Italy. Pesaro was usually able to govern itself independently in the course of the Middle Ages by exploiting the political rivalries of popes and emperors. The MALATESTA FAMILY made Pesaro its stronghold and base of operations for control of the surrounding countryside. In 1445 the SFORZA FAMILY succeeded the Malatestas. In 1512 Pope JULIUS II bestowed Pesaro on his relatives, the dukes of URBINO, who ruled over Pesaro and Urbino until 1631, when the two cities became part of the PAPAL STATES. Pesaro has developed a balanced economy based on small-scale manufacturing (ceramics, copper ornaments), commercial and cultural activities, and tourism. The Rossini Conservatory and the Rossini Opera Festival make the city a center of musical culture.

Peter Leopold (1747–1792)
grand duke of Tuscany (1765–1790) and Holy Roman Emperor (1790–1792)

The third son of FRANCIS STEPHEN of Habsburg-Lorraine and Empress MARIA THERESA, Peter Leopold succeeded his father as grand duke of Tuscany in 1765 as Leopold I. Peter Leopold undertook an ambitious program of domestic reforms in the spirit of ENLIGHTENMENT philosophy that put the Grand Duchy of Tuscany in the forefront of enlightened government. Jealous of his prerogatives as a ruler, he appointed reform-minded collaborators like POMPEO NERI, FRANCESCO MARIA GIANNI, and VITTORIO FOSSOMBRONI to positions of power and heeded their advice. His reforms affected public administration, taxation, trade, and religion. The guiding principles of his administrative reforms were efficiency, accountability, and equality before the law. He abolished the death penalty and the use of torture in judicial proceedings, published state budgets, adopted free trade in grains and reduced other tariffs, suppressed guilds to encourage manufacturing, pressed for a new land survey to make taxation more equitable, expanded the powers of local government, and moved to curb the power of the church. In religious matters he supported the liturgical reforms introduced by Bishop SCIPIONE DE' RICCI. To conserve resources for his domestic programs, Peter Leopold all but abolished the Tuscan army and navy, relying for protection on the power of Austria. He abdicated the Tuscan throne in favor of his son FERDINAND III and succeeded to the imperial title as head of the AUSTRIAN EMPIRE on the death of his brother JOSEPH II, taking on the title of Leopold II. Important reforms left incomplete at the time of his abdication, including the land survey, a new land tax, and adoption of a representative assembly and constitution, were abandoned by his successor. Peter Leopold is perhaps the best example of Enlightened Absolutism that favored reform from above, but was also willing to move gradually toward representative forms of government. That approach encountered the mounting hostility of entrenched groups, particularly the nobility and clergy, and was further undermined by the fear that reforms would encourage revolutionary change. As Austrian emperor, Peter Leopold had to confront the international complications posed by the FRENCH REVOLUTION and had no opportunity to pursue domestic reforms similar to the ones he had adopted in Tuscany.

Petitti, Carlo Ilarione, Count of Roreto (1790–1850)
Piedmontese economic innovator and political liberal

Born to a family of the Piedmontese nobility with military traditions, Count Carlo chose instead to study economics and administration, graduating from the University of Genoa with a degree in civil and canon law. He held several posts in local administration before being called

on to serve on the council of state that advised King CHARLES ALBERT (1831). His interest in and progressive views on social problems such as alcoholism, pauperism, and social welfare earned him the distrust of conservative members of the council, who stymied his efforts to confront these issues and prevailed on the king to ignore his advice. Petitti found an ally in CAVOUR, with whom he collaborated as a member of the progressive Agrarian Association, until a more radical group forced out these moderates in 1846. Cavour's favorable review of Petitti's study *Des chemins de fer en Italie* (Of railroads in Italy, 1845) became a reference point for Italian patriots who argued that there could be no national system of transportation, and hence no economic progress, without political unity. Petitti was appointed to the newly created senate in 1848. Cavour and his moderate supporters carried on the fight for economic progress and political liberalization after Petitti's death.

Petrarch (1304–1374)
humanist scholar, poet, Latinist, and public figure

Christened Francesco Petracco, latinized as Petrarca to give the name classical dignity, and changed into Petrarch in the Anglo-Saxon world, Petrarch was born in Arezzo, the child of Florentine political exiles banished from their city in 1302. Petrarch spent his youth in Tuscany and, after 1312, lived with his family in France, near Avignon, where his father was employed at the papal court. Later, he attended the University of Montpellier and studied law at the Univerisity of Bologna. He studied the classics, perfected his Latin, and mastered the Italian language, in which he excelled as a poet. He may have been employed at the papal court after returning to Avignon in 1326. He lived stylishly, cultivating his poetic talent and good looks, both of which won him popularity. In 1327 he first saw Laura. Young, golden-haired, of noble birth, rich, married, and resistant to his advances, Laura became his lifelong obsession. He depicted her in verse both as a woman of flesh and blood and as the ideal of love itself, perhaps in imitation of Dante's Beatrice, and like Beatrice, able to lift her lover to a higher spiritual sphere. His love sonnets to Laura, written in Italian, won him immediate fame and have inspired endless imitators through the centuries, as has his use of *terza rima* (three-line stanzas rhymed ABA).

An enthusiastic traveler, Petrarch also wrote with great sensitivity about the beauty of nature, as in his famous description of a climb to the top of Mont Ventoux in southern France. For him Rome revived the ancient custom of crowning a poet with laurel, an honor that he received in 1341 during a ceremony held on the city's ancient Capitol. In Rome he fell under the spell of the popular leader COLA DI RIENZO (1313–54), who shared Petrarch's admiration for ancient Rome. Dreaming of reviving Rome's ancient glory, Cola ruled the city intermittently between 1347 and 1354, until murdered by a Roman crowd enraged by his self-glorification and by the hardships visited on the city by his visionary politics. Petrarch expressed his admiration for the ancient Roman republic in a long epic poem entitled *Africa,* written in Latin, which he considered to be his literary masterpiece. Friendship and support for Cola's project inspired Petrarch to write the ode *Italia mia,* expressing desire for Italian glory in his time, which he thought could be achieved under papal leadership. Bringing the papacy back to Rome from Avignon became Petrarch's political goal. As a prominent figure, he could not avoid other political commitments, which included serving the VISCONTI FAMILY of Milan as ambassador to Venice and the imperial court of Charles IV.

The death of Laura, other personal losses, and the onset of the Black Death in 1348 brought on an inner crisis noticeable in his *Secretum,* a book of confessions in the form of a dialogue with Saint Augustine. The book, kept secret during his life, is the first example of critical self-examination and spiritual autobiography at the dawn of modern times. It signals a turn toward spirituality, but also the awareness that the spiritual

and the carnal are locked in tragic conflict in the human psyche. He sought comfort and escape in books, particularly the ancient classics, which he collected and read avidly. Books, he claimed, were a refuge from the ugliness of the world of war, disease, and corruption in which he lived. The ideals that he found in the writers of ancient Rome, particularly in Cicero whom he admired above all others, inspired him to live a life of virtue. A master of Latin, Petrarch lamented his ignorance of classical Greek. He nevertheless prized Greek studies and thought Plato capable of lifting the mind from the earthly to the divine. His admiration for Plato spread to others and contributed to the rise of HUMANISM, of which Petrarch can be considered the founder. Although scholars rightly point out that Petrarch was in many ways a man of his times tied to what we call the medieval world, it is also true that his eye for the particular, his sensitivity and interest in people, the innovative literary style, and enthusiasm for using the models of the past to solve the problems of the present make him a figure that modern people can appreciate and admire.

Pezza, Michele See FRA DIAVOLO.

Physiocrats
eighteenth-century thinkers who developed the first school of economic thought
Physiocrats were Enlightenment thinkers inspired by the ideas of their founder François Quesnay (1694–1774). They applied the methods of rational analysis to the study of economic phenomena, believed that invariable natural laws governed the economy, that agriculture (land) was the ultimate source of individual and collective wealth, and that absolute free trade was needed to maintain fair prices and an optimal balance between supply and demand. Physiocrats disseminated these notions throughout Europe with the enthusiasm of missionaries. Because of their faith in the power of economic

laws, they were often referred to simply as "economists." Italians received their ideas with considerable skepticism. Thinkers like the Lombard PIETRO VERRI and the Neapolitan FERDINANDO GALLIANI questioned that the economy was governed by unvarying natural laws and expressed reservations about applying free-trade doctrines indiscriminately. Nevertheless, the governments of Lombardy and Tuscany followed Physiocratic advice to the extent that they sought to encourage trade with tariff reductions. In Austrian-ruled Lombardy, tariff reduction owed much to the interest that Emperor JOSEPH II took in Physiocratic doctrines. Progress toward free trade was most noticeable in Tuscany where POMPEO NERI took up the cause and influenced Grand Duke PETER LEOPOLD. Physiocratic doctrines lost much of their appeal in Italy and elsewhere after 1770, when the failure of several experiments and the need to raise revenue took precedence over theoretical issues.

Piacentini, Marcello See ARCHITECTURE.

Piacenza, city of

Piacenza (pop. 98,400) is a provincial capital in the region of EMILIA. Founded as a Roman colony in 218 B.C., it gained importance as a transportation center along the Roman Via Aemilia and for its proximity to the PO RIVER. The decline of Roman power ushered in a long period of turbulence during which Piacenza was occupied successively by Goths, Byzantines, Lombards, and Franks. Through these political changes the city grew in importance. It became a center of religious activities under Lombard rule (A.D. 570–774), a county seat under the Franks, and a bishopric under Holy Roman Emperor Otto III (996–1002). Piacenza supported the imperial side during the struggles between papacy and empire. After emerging from those struggles as an independent commune in 1090, Piacenza sided with the papacy. Internal discord played into the hands of the VISCONTI FAMILY of Milan,

who seized the city in 1335. FRANCESCO SFORZA took over the city in 1448, putting an end to a brief interlude of fractious republican government. Under papal rule from 1512, Pope PAUL III bestowed it as a papal fief on the FARNESE FAMILY, which ruled over both PARMA and Piacenza with interruptions until its extinction in 1731. The Duchy of Parma and Piacenza lost its independence in 1859 and became part of the Kingdom of Italy in 1860 at the conclusion of the RISORGIMENTO. Piacenza has lost the political importance it once had, but is a bustling regional market center with relatively little tourism.

Piave River, Battle of the See WORLD WAR I.

Piccinni, Niccolò See OPERA.

Piccolomini, Ottavio (1600–1650)
military commander in the service of the Habsburgs of Austria and Spain

Piccolomini, scion of a Sienese family prominent in the church, was born in Pisa. His father, Silvio Piccolomini, was a professional soldier who raised his son to follow in his footsteps. Ottavio first saw action in Lombardy at age 17 in the service of Spain. He held commands in central Europe during the Thirty Years' War (1618–48), during which he stood out for his pitiless treatment of Protestant enemies. Emperor Ferdinand II amply rewarded Piccolomini for his role in the assassination of his former patron, Count Albert Wallenstein (1583–1634), whose military victories and ambitions threatened the power of the emperor. Subsequently, Piccolomini's forces held off the French and saved Austria from Swedish invasion. He also fought in the Low Countries in the service of Spain. Gain was undoubtedly a motivation in Piccolomini's career, for among his other needs he had to satisfy a passion for gambling on a grand scale. However, Piccolomini was also driven by loyalty to the Catholic cause and to the HABSBURG DYNASTY as the defenders of Catholicism.

Pickler, Teresa See FOSCOLO, UGO.

Pico della Mirandola, Giovanni (1463–1494)
humanist philosopher concerned with unifying the various strands and traditions of Renaissance thought

Pico was born to the family of the counts of Mirandola from the Po Valley that had distinguished itself militarily. Pico studied philosophy at several Italian universities and in Paris. Familiar with both Latin and Greek, endowed with a prodigious memory and boundless intellectual curiosity, Pico's interests ranged far and wide. At the University of Padua, where he went in 1480, he studied Arabic philosophy and the Jewish kabbalah, a method of scriptural interpretation that ascribed hidden meanings to words and numbers. From the medieval notion of the unity of knowledge, he developed the idea that seemingly incompatible schools of thought could be reconciled and that all useful knowledge could be summed up in a finite number of propositions. That is what he tried to do in 1486, with the publication of 900 theses that he challenged others to debate. When the papal curia condemned some of his theses as heretical, Pico fled from Rome to France, where he was briefly imprisoned. Released, he went to Florence where he joined the circle of intellectuals close to LORENZO DE' MEDICI.

Unlike most Florentine Platonists who were interested only in Greek philosophy, Pico also showed a strong interest in Arabic and Jewish sources. His ultimate ambition was to unify rational and mystical schools of thought, as well as Christian and non-Christian sources, into a unified system of knowledge. He was sustained in this endeavor both by an enormous self-confidence that smacked of arrogance and by his faith in the human capacity for improvement and perfection. The potential for perfection was the message of his best-known work, *Oration on the Dignity of Man* (1489), which presented man as a creative being of unlimited power. No writing of the RENAISSANCE period better expresses the humanistic view that human nature has a potential for growth far beyond anything envisaged by Christianity with its doctrine of original sin. Pico was nevertheless a devout Christian who lived long enough to sympathize with the religious aims of GIROLAMO SAVONAROLA, but not long enough to become part of his movement. Because of his faith in human potential, Pico is often seen as the best representative of the spirit of HUMANISM.

Piedmont (Piemonte)
The region of Piedmont (pop. 4,287,500) in the northwest corner of the peninsula stretches from the ALPS to the Po Valley. It borders on France to the west and the regions of VALLE D'AOSTA to the northwest, LOMBARDY to the east, EMILIA-ROMAGNA to the southeast, and LIGURIA to the south. Its name, which means "at the foot of the mountains," does not indicate that the region in fact includes some of the highest elevations of the Italian Alps, which here reach 4,633 meters (15,196 feet) above sea level at Mount Rosa and 4,061 meters (13,320 feet) at the Gran Paradiso. The Gran Paradiso National Park, instituted in 1922, is the country's oldest natural preserve. The region is divided into the six provinces of TURIN (regional capital), Alessandria, Asti, Cuneo, Novara, and Vercelli. The PO RIVER originates in the Piedmontese Alps, traversing the mountains, hills, and plains of the region. The region's close association with the HOUSE OF SAVOY is an important element of its historical identity. Under the rule of the Savoy dynasty, Piedmont developed a tradition of military service unique among the Italian regions, as the Savoyard rulers enticed or coerced the Piedmontese nobility and their retainers to serve the state militarily and administratively. Because Piedmont was the most important territory in the Savoyard domain, its

name is often used as a synonym for or in conjunction with the Kingdom of SARDINIA (Kingdom of Piedmont-Sardinia), the official designation of all the territories ruled by the House of Savoy. Piedmont thus played a key role in the process of national unification with its diplomatic and military initiatives. It has also played an important economic role. Before national unification, Piedmont took the lead in railroad construction and in encouraging trade and manufacturing. Its progressive economic policies won it the support of economic liberals and modernizers throughout the peninsula, thus facilitating Piedmont's assumption of the lead role in the RISORGIMENTO. Wool and cotton manufacturing developed in the 1850s. Half a century later Piedmont led the way in the development of the machine and engineering industries. FIAT, the auto manufacturer founded in Turin in 1899, was the most successful of the new firms. Industrial growth was facilitated by established traditions of craftsmanship and the availability of relatively inexpensive hydroelectric power. Agriculture kept pace with the other sectors, developing commercial specializations in rice and wine grape production. The region's diversified agriculture sustains a well-developed food processing industry. While other regions boast of their cultural traditions, Piedmont takes quiet pride in its economic accomplishments and the practical outlook of its hardworking population.

Piermarini, Giuseppe See MILAN, CITY OF.

Piero della Francesca (ca. 1420–1492)
painter and art theoretician, known for the mathematical precision of his works

The precise birth date of this Umbrian painter is not known, but we do know that his period of activity (1439–78) coincided with major breakthroughs in the development of artistic techniques. In his writings he explained how the rules of geometry could be applied to give more accurate representations of natural objects and

Piero della Francesca *(Library of Congress)*

the human form. Accurate mathematical proportions were Piero's answer to the problem of realistic representation. The result was a technical perfection of form and perspective that astonished his contemporaries. None of this is to suggest that Piero's art lacked in feeling. On the contrary, he endowed his figures with an emotional intensity that may have been a reflection of his personality. Simplification was at the heart of his technique, but the end result visible in his best works is a unity of composition, an eye for overall effect, and meticulous planning and execution. The recently restored frescoes depicting the Legend of the True Cross in the Basilica of Saint Francis in Arezzo are a fine example of Piero's art. Failing eyesight forced him to abandon painting while still at the height of his creative powers, but not before he had raised art to a new level, paving the way for the masters of the mature RENAISSANCE.

Pigafetta, Antonio (unknown–1526)
seafarer and companion of the Portuguese explorer Magellan

Pigafetta's date of birth is not known, but he seems to have been born between 1480 and 1491 to an aristocratic family from Vicenza. Little is known about his early life, but he may have gained seafaring experience in the service of the Knights of St. John. In 1519, finding himself in Spain as part of a papal delegation to the Spanish court, Pigafetta volunteered to join Magellan on the first voyage around the world. Magellan apparently valued the company of a cultivated gentleman like Pigafetta, and the two became close friends. Pigafetta was wounded in the ambush that killed Magellan in the Philippines and was one of 18 survivors who returned to Europe at the end of the perilous three-year voyage. He wrote his account of the voyage at the urging of the GONZAGA FAMILY, completing his narrative in 1525. With its detailed descriptions of places, products, people, and customs around the globe, Pigafetta's work is a unique historical document, particularly for what it tells us about life in South America and the Pacific islands when Europeans first made contact with those places and populations. Pigafetta's account of the voyage is available in several English-language editions, the most recent being *The First Voyage around the World* (1995).

Pinocchio   See COLLODI, CARLO.

Pinturicchio   See PIUS II.

Pippi, Giulio   See MANNERISM.

Pirandello, Luigi (1867–1936)
playwright, novelist, and poet

Pirandello was born near Agrigento (Sicily) to a family that had made a considerable fortune in sulfur mining and supported the movement for

Luigi Pirandello *(Library of Congress)*

national unification. After completing his secondary studies in Palermo, Pirandello attended universities in Rome and Bonn, graduating in 1891 with a degree in linguistics. His career prospects as a writer took a turn for the worse when the family business went into decline in the late 1890s and his wife became mentally ill. Under the circumstance, Pirandello turned to teaching to support his family. From 1897 to 1922 he taught writing at a girls' school in Rome, conscientiously but without much enthusiasm. The literary writing that he did on the side was slow to win him recognition. A series of plays written and performed in 1916–17 established him as a major writer. The most important of these plays was *Cosi è, se vi pare* (It is so, if you think so, 1917). It explored Pirandello's favorite theme that reality is elusive and ultimately subjective, by telling the story of a woman who agrees to be different people to satisfy the contrasting perceptions of her held by her husband and mother. He returned to that theme in the even more famous and technically innovative *Sei personaggi in cerca d'autore* (Six characters in search of an author, 1921), a play that conveys the message that no representation can do justice to the complexity of human nature. In *Enrico IV* (Henry IV, 1922), a gentleman loses his mind after falling from a horse, imagines himself to be King Henry IV, and decides to hold on to that delusion after regaining his reason because the real world is not to his liking. Pirandello's achievements as a playwright won him the highest honors, including appointment to the Italian Academy in 1929 and the Nobel Prize for literature in 1934. His acceptance of recognitions by the Fascist regime has raised the question of his politics. Pirandello's contributions were not to FASCISM but to the world of culture. In that regard, his pessimism, the sense that reality is multifaceted, and the consequent lesson that activity is based on uncertainty, are far removed from the cult of action and power inherent in fascism.

Piranesi, Giovanni Battista (1720–1778)
architect and engraver, known for his representations of Rome and its environs

Piranesi was born in Venice, settled in Rome in 1740, and worked there for the rest of his life. Endowed with a powerful, irrepressible imagination, he turned all his energy and inventive powers toward representing Roman landscapes and antiquities in a series of etchings that became immensely popular with tourists. His commercial success enabled Piranesi to establish a business that was taken over by his sons. Reproduced in a variety of ways and circulating throughout Europe, Piranesi's *vedute* (views) reinforced the image of the Eternal City as the source and inspiration of classical art, a worthy rival of ancient Athens. Piranesi adopted different modes of representation, from the rigorously documentary to the wildly imaginative, always endowing his *vedute* with monumental dignity and richness of detail. Stylistically adaptive, he could express himself in the prevailing neoclassical style or with

the abandon typical of the romantic imagination that asserted itself in his lifetime.

Pirelli, Alberto (1882–1971)
cable and rubber industry pioneer, active in business and public life

Pirelli was the second-born son of Giovanni Battista Pirelli (1848–1932), who founded the Pirelli cable and rubber business in 1872. Along with his older brother Piero (1881–1956), Alberto inherited and expanded the family business to other areas in Italy and abroad by purchasing plantations and setting up commercial subsidiaries. During WORLD WAR I Alberto headed a government agency in charge of importing armaments. After the war, he served as an economic expert for the Italian delegation to the PARIS PEACE CONFERENCE and was involved in negotiations for the settlement of Italian war debts. In postwar politics he was a supporter of the liberal GIOVANNI GIOLITTI, whom he would have liked to have as prime minister in October 1922, when BENITO MUSSOLINI was appointed instead. He cooperated with the Fascist government in power in spite of his political reservations, and joined the Fascist Party in 1932. Under the regime, he served on various corporative agencies and was acting president of CONFINDUSTRIA (1934). Under fascism, Alberto Pirelli showed a remarkable capacity for getting along and profiting from a system of government that was not to his liking. His close identification with the regime required him to pull out of public life after the war, but he continued to run the family business quietly and effectively until his retirement in 1965, when his son Leopoldo took over. The Pirellis lost control of their vast business holdings in 1995 when an outsider, Marco Tronchetti Provera, was appointed business manager.

Pisa, city of

Pisa (pop. 92,000) is a provincial capital in the region of TUSCANY, situated on the banks of the Arno River approximately 10 kilometers from the Tyrrhenian Sea. Of Roman origin, it rose to prominence as a port city with trade connections

Campo dei Miracoli, Pisa, with its famously sloping campanile, the Leaning Tower (right) *(Library of Congress)*

in the western Mediterranean. In the 11th century, Pisa competed for territory with the neighboring city of LUCCA, challenged GENOA on the seas, conquered the island of SARDINIA, and fought off Muslim raiders. A self-governing commune after 1080, its strength was sapped by internal discords and by recurring conflicts with its neighbors. Its most important monuments, including the Duomo (cathedral church), the Campo dei Miracoli (Field of Miracles), and the famous Leaning Tower, date from the 11th and 12th centuries, when Pisa was at the height of its power as an independent republic. Its decline was due to unmanageable factional strife at home and recurring warfare with its neighbors. In 1284 the Genoese won a decisive naval victory over Pisa at the Battle of Meloria. As Genoa gained the upper hand on the seas, FLORENCE threatened Pisa on land, defeating it decisively in 1406 and taking it over in 1509. By then its port had silted up and its mercantile traditions were a distant memory. Under the rule of the MEDICI FAMILY and as part of the grand duchy of Tuscany, Pisa made a partial recovery as a cultural center. The University of Pisa, founded in the 14th century, became an important center of learning during the RENAISSANCE. Galileo, who was born in Pisa, studied and taught at the university, and is said to have conducted scientific experiments in the Duomo and Leaning Tower. In the 19th century, university faculty and students figured prominently in the struggles of the Risorgimento. Pisa's Scuola Normale is Italy's most prestigious institution of higher learning. Allied bombing inflicted heavy damage on the city during World War II. Its economy relies heavily on tourism, transportation, and light industry.

Pisacane, Carlo (1818–1857)
military figure, patriot, social commentator, and theorist

Pisacane was born to a distinguished Neapolitan family with a tradition of military and public service. Trained for a military career at Naples' prestigious Nunziatella Academy, his prospects for advancement were cut short by his own volatile temperament, liberal sentiments, and an affair with the wife of a fellow officer that may have been the reason for a mysterious attempt on Pisacane's life in 1847. When he recovered from a wound suffered in the attempt, the two lovers fled abroad where they lived precariously. His political ideas took form in Paris and London, where he made contact with Italian political exiles. He returned to Italy to join the REVOLUTION of 1848. After fighting and being wounded in the war against Austria in Lombardy, Pisacane assumed a military command for the ROMAN REPUBLIC, where he distinguished himself and established a close rapport with GIUSEPPE MAZZINI. In his *La guerra combattuta in Italia negli anni 1848–49* (The war fought in Italy in the years 1848–49), published posthumously, Pisacane argued that in order to succeed, the revolution must offer material incentives to the masses, particularly to the land-hungry, impoverished southern peasantry that he deemed ready for revolution. In June 1857 Pisacane sailed from Genoa for southern Italy with a small group of volunteers on a commandeered steamer, to arouse the people against the Bourbon regime of Naples. Landing near the town of Sapri in the region of CALABRIA, instead of being met by an enthusiastic populace, Pisacane and his companions were hunted down and killed or taken prisoner. Pisacane committed suicide rather than be captured. His tragic death assured him a place among the great figures of the RISORGIMENTO, but it was his posthumously published writings that had the greatest influence. Pisacane stressed the social inadequacies of the national movement, criticized its purely political character, and deplored its failure to reach out to the masses. Both socialists and anarchists claimed him as a precursor because of his critique of the national movement from a materialist perspective, and the importance that he attached to the individual act ("propaganda of the deed") as a means of arousing the political consciousness of the masses.

Pisciotta, Gaspare See GIULIANO, SALVATORE.

Pius II (1405–1464)
pope (1458–1464)

Baptized Enea Silvio Piccolomini, descended from a Sienese family of social standing, and educated in the humanist canon, the future pope gained a reputation as a writer of distinction with a talent for frivolous and erotic poetry. He embarked on an ecclesiastical career as private secretary to a cardinal who believed that ultimate authority should reside in a general council rather than in the pope. Whatever Piccolomini may have thought of that idea, that was not the course that he pursued. As a papal diplomatic envoy, bishop, and cardinal, Piccolomini shed the frivolous interests of his youth and became a devout servant of the church. To his former companions who deplored his transformation, he replied that they should reject Enea, his former self, and accept him as Pius the pope. One of his first acts as pope was to quash the movement to

empower a council. His easygoing manner ingratiated him to the Roman people. His main project, which became an obsession, was to organize a Christian crusade to roll back the Muslim Turks threatening Europe. It was a major disappointment that no government was willing to cooperate, except for the Venetians who hoped to make money by transporting the crusaders. Undeterred, Pius announced that he would act unilaterally and would personally lead a force of volunteers. Few showed up at the port of Ancona where Pius went to meet them. Already in poor health before undertaking the hard journey from Rome to Ancona, Pius died a few days after his arrival in that port city. His brief papacy caught the imagination of his contemporaries. The painter Pinturicchio (1454–1513) depicted the salient events of Pius's life, including the preparations for the crusade that never was, in the magnificent frescoes that adorn the Piccolomini Library in the Duomo of Siena. Another monument to his name is the town of Pienza near Siena. An unremarkable town when Pius was born there, he transformed it into a model city built according to the most advanced concepts of architectural and urban design of his time. Pius II is often thought of as a typical RENAISSANCE pope, learned and worldly. He would be better remembered as a religious idealist who failed in the one project that he hoped would earn him the rewards of heaven and a place in history.

Pius IV See BORROMEO, CARLO.

Pius V See INDEX; LÉPANTO, BATTLE OF.

Pius VI (1717–1799)
pope (1775–1799)

Giovanni Angelo Braschi from Cesena in the Romagna was elected pope at a most difficult time. Like his immediate predecessors, Pius VI was under pressure from various quarters to change the ways of the church. ENLIGHTENMENT thinkers depicted the CATHOLIC CHURCH as a bastion of ignorance and superstition, and many monarchs shared their views. None was more determined to impose clerical reforms than Austrian emperor JOSEPH II, who closed down monasteries, insisted on monitoring the education and behavior of the clergy, and expected the clergy to obey secular law. Pius's efforts to restrain Joseph were totally unsuccessful. More trouble came Pius's way after the outbreak of the FRENCH REVOLUTION in 1789. It was now the government of revolutionary France that demanded the complete allegiance of the French clergy, suppressed religious orders, arrested and executed members of the clergy, and expropriated church properties without compensation. Under the circumstances, Pius sided with the monarchs who were bent on invading France and suppressing the revolution, thus giving moral authority to the conservative coalition. Pius became the target of French hatred, with disastrous results. French retribution reached the pope when General Napoleon Bonaparte, the future NAPOLEON I, invaded Italy in 1796. After defeating the Austrians, Napoleon imposed on the pope the Treaty of Tolentino (February 1797). The pope lost territory, had to pay a large indemnity, surrender art works, and accept French tutelage. When Pius resisted French demands that he surrender his temporal power, the French army occupied Rome (February 1798), and evicted Pius from the city. Under house arrest in Siena and Florence, in March 1799 Pius, severely ill, was carted off to France, where he died in August of that year. His ordeal made him a martyr in the eyes of devout Catholics and enemies of the French Revolution. A man of amiable disposition, good intentions, and imposing presence, but lacking in fire and determination, Pius VI was overwhelmed by the revolutionary tide that swept through Europe.

Pius VII (1742–1823)

pope (1800–1823)

Also from Cesena like his predecessor PIUS VI, Gregorio Luigi Barnaba Chiaramonti was born to an aristocratic family. He was a compromise candidate, chosen after a seven-month interreg-

num, acceptable to the French because he had expressed confidence that revolutionary ideas could be reconciled with the teachings of religion. He chose his papal name in deference to his predecessor and former patron. By the time Pius VII was elected, NAPOLEON was ready to distance himself from the revolution, and eager to reach an understanding with the papacy and normalize relations with the church. The Concordat of 1801 settled the conflict between CHURCH AND STATE in France for the time being, without eliminating fundamental disagreements over freedom of worship, education, marriage, and family life. Above all, Pius valued the provisions of the agreement that restored papal authority over the French clergy in matters of appointments and discipline. On December 2, 1804, Pius VII anointed Napoleon emperor of the French in the Cathedral of Notre Dame in Paris, knowing ahead of time that Napoleon would choose to assert his independence by crowning himself, rather than having the pope place the crown on his head as was traditionally done. Relations deteriorated in the coming years as Napoleon's territorial ambitions extended in the direction of Rome, which was occupied by French troops in February 1808. In May 1809 Napoleon annexed the PAPAL STATES to France. When Pius VII denounced the occupation and excommunicated those responsible, he was summarily arrested and deported. Pius spent the remaining years of Napoleon's rule in captivity, refusing to acknowledge the legitimacy of Napoleon's actions, and calling on the clergy to respect papal authority against the emperor's commands. The defeat of Napoleon finally enabled Pius to return to Rome in May 1814. After the CONGRESS OF VIENNA, Pius VII set out to restore the temporal and spiritual powers of the papacy. With Cardinal ETTORE CONSALVI as secretary of state, Pius VII oversaw the reorganization of papal administration, took steps to revive the economy, and generally adopted conciliatory policies toward those who had supported Napoleonic rule. These moderate policies displeased political extremists on both sides. The decision to limit employment in the government posts to clerics was particularly galling to educated laymen, who found themselves excluded from careers in public administration. In the final years of his pontificate, Pius VII had to contend with the activities of dissident SECRET SOCIETIES. His successor, Pope Leo XII (1823–29), the candidate of the conservative faction, adopted repressive policies that put the papacy on a collision course with liberal elements.

Pius IX (1792–1878)
pope (1846–1878)

Giovanni Maria Mastai-Ferretti was a surprise choice as pope. His career had advanced steadily but unremarkably under mostly conservative popes since he was ordained in 1819. After serving on a mission to Chile for two years, he returned to Italy in 1825. Leo XII appointed him archbishop of Spoleto in 1827. GREGORY XVI transferred him to the bishopric of Imola in 1832 and made him a cardinal in 1840. In the politically difficult sees he was appointed to govern he showed diplomatic tact. His politics were nebulous, but he was regarded as pro-liberal and anti-Austrian. Whatever his politics, he was definitely amiable, handsome, and popular. The conclave chose him as a compromise between traditionalist and progressive aspirants to the papal throne, expecting him to steer a middle course between opposing factions and tendencies. He took the name of Pius out of reverence for Pius VII, who had suffered for his faith at the hands of Napoleon. Italians would always know him familiarly as *Pio Nono*. At the time of his election liberals were encouraged by his first acts in office, which included a relaxation of censorship, an amnesty for political prisoners, institution of a civic guard, plans for the creation of a council of ministers, introduction of lay people in the public administration, and planning for the construction of railroads (condemned by his predecessor as an unholy invention).

Enthusiasm for the new course buoyed the Neo-Guelf movement inspired by the writings of VINCENZO GIOBERTI and gave the impression that

Pius IX was an Italian patriot at heart, willing to lead a national crusade against Austria for the cause of national independence. Nothing could have been further from the truth. Pius IX may have been an Italian patriot in his own way, but he had no intention of countenancing revolution or war. He wished to proceed with reforms at his own cautious pace, resisted pressure from radical elements to go further, and broke completely with liberals during the revolution of 1848. After revolutionaries assassinated Prime Minister PELLEGRINO ROSSI, Pius abandoned Rome. From his refuge in Gaeta, he called on the Catholic powers to suppress the ROMAN REPUBLIC and restore papal rule to the city.

The experience of revolution and exile ended the pope's flirtation with liberalism. After his return to Rome in April 1850, Pius entrusted to Cardinal GIACOMO ANTONELLI, his secretary of state, the conduct of political matters, and turned his attention to the pastoral issues that had always mattered more to him than secular reforms. In 1854 Pius proclaimed the dogma of the Immaculate Conception, affirming that the Virgin Mary was conceived without original sin. It was a decisive step on the path of theological intransigence that would characterize his papacy for posterity. Later came the condemnation of modern civilization in the SYLLABUS OF ERRORS (1864), the convening of the First Vatican Council (1869–70) to organize the battle against secularism, and the proclamation of the doctrine of papal infallibility (1870).

The issue of Italian independence dogged Pius IX throughout his pontificate. Nationalism was on the list of the "errors" of modern civilization that the pope felt obliged to condemn. Believing that Italian unification would deprive the papacy of the territory and sovereignty that it needed to lead the church, Pius opposed unification with all the means at his disposal. The loss of Rome in September 1870 confirmed his fear that the Italian state was a mortal enemy of the papacy. Thus was born the ROMAN QUESTION that divided church and state in Italy for generations to come. Anticlericals directed their venom against Pius IX, whom they vilified as an enemy of Italy and of progress. Generations would have to pass before the reputation of Pius IX could recover. His beatification in 2002 under the pontificate of John Paul II was an acknowledgment of the depth of his faith, courage in the face of criticism, and adherence to the fundamentals of doctrine. Yet, at the same time that he was being beatified, Pius IX was again under attack for anti-Semitism. The controversy will not end soon.

Pius X (1835–1914)

pope (1903–1914)

Giuseppe Melchiorre Sarto, born to a farming family of modest means in a small town near Treviso in the northeastern corner of Italy, was able to study at considerable financial sacrifice to his family. He entered seminary at Padua in 1850 and was ordained a priest in 1858. The first 17 years of his ecclesiastical career were spent as parish priest in various small communities of the highly Catholic region of VENETIA. His exceptional ministry and devotion caught the attention of the bishop of Treviso, who appointed him spiritual director to a seminary. Named bishop of Mantua in 1884, he was appointed patriarch of Venice and made a cardinal in 1893. Elected pope in 1903, not without controversy, Pius X proved to be very different from his predecessor, LEO XIII. Whereas Leo had been a diplomat and an intellectual concerned with updating church policies to deal with the problems of industrial society, Pius was a pastoral pope interested primarily in the care of souls. His first challenge came from France, where the government adopted anticlerical legislation that infringed on the rights of the church. Pius protested vigorously and in 1906 broke off diplomatic relations, which were restored only in 1921. In the encyclical *Pascendi dominici gregi* (1907), Pius condemned MODERNISM as a set of heresies that threatened the spiritual mission of the church. He also affirmed ecclesiastical authority over the political activities of clergy and laity, instituted secret surveillance of the clergy, and disavowed CHRISTIAN

DEMOCRACY. In 1909 he excommunicated the priest ROMOLO MURRI for founding the Christian Democratic League, which was a political party in all but name. Pius was not against Catholics voting according to their Catholic consciences as long as they did so individually and not as an organized political party. He did relax the ban prohibiting Catholics from voting, thus allowing for the election to parliament for the first time since national unification of candidates who were openly Catholic. These proved to be useful allies for GIOVANNI GIOLITTI, who often relied on their votes. Pius thus initiated the process that allowed Catholics to participate in the political life of the Italian state. A highly popular pope known familiarly as *Papa Sarto* and as the "peasant pope," his picture was to be found in many homes. His image of saintliness earned him canonization in 1954.

Pius XI (1857–1939)

pope (1922–1939)

Born within the industrial orbit of Milan to a working-class family, Ambrogio Damiano Achille Ratti was ordained a priest in 1879 and continued with university studies in Rome. Of scholarly temperament, he taught in seminary, served as a librarian in Milan and as director of the Vatican Library in Rome. In 1919 he was sent as Vatican ambassador to Poland, where he witnessed the conflict between Poles and the Russian Red Army that nearly captured Warsaw. The experience left in him a lasting fear and revulsion for communism that would influence his decisions as pope. In 1921 he was appointed archbishop of Milan and made cardinal. He was elected pope in 1922 following the premature death of his predecessor, BENEDICT XV. His papacy was dominated by the rise and consolidation of FASCISM, which came to power in October 1922, nine months after his election. Pius XI, who like PIUS X was suspicious of politics, reversed Benedict's policy of encouragement for the Popular Party (PPI). He relied instead on diplomacy and on the efforts of his secretary of state, Cardinal

PIETRO GASPARRI, to address political problems. A shared anticommunism and hostility toward the Popular Party were the premises for the diplomatic dialogue that opened almost immediately between the Holy See and the Fascist government of BENITO MUSSOLINI. The crowning result of that effort was the settlement of the ROMAN QUESTION in 1929. The agreement did not, however, resolve all outstanding issues of CHURCH AND STATE. In the encyclical *Quadragesimo anno* (1931), written to commemorate the 40th anniversary of Leo XIII's *Rerum novarum*, Pius XI reaffirmed the principles of social cooperation and economic justice enunciated by his predecessor and defended Christian CORPORATISM against the Fascist version. Throughout the 1930s there was continued disagreement on matters of education and youth organization. While these issues were never fully resolved, they did not lead to a break because neither side was interested in open confrontation. Even more profound disagreements on war and racial policy seemed to be coming to a head in the last year of Pius XI's pontificate. The alliance between Fascist Italy and Nazi Germany was particularly troubling. In 1938, as the Italian and German regimes became increasingly racist, the pope instructed his advisers to prepare a statement condemning racial doctrines in general, and anti-Semitism in particular, noting that racism "ends by being uniquely the struggle against the Jews." Pius XI died in February 1939, before issuing the encyclical that had been prepared for him.

Pius XII (1876–1958)

pope (1939–1958)

Born to a family of the Roman nobility, Eugenio Pacelli was the first native Roman to be elected pope since 1721. A serious student with a special talent for foreign languages, he attended the University of Rome before going on to the seminary. Ordained in 1899, he earned a doctorate in theology, and taught canon law. His appointment in 1902 to the secretariat of state marked the beginning of his career in the Vatican diplomatic corps.

In 1917 Pacelli was appointed nuncio (papal envoy) to Bavaria and in 1920 nuncio to the German republic, a post that he held until 1929. Made cardinal in 1929, in 1930 he replaced Cardinal PIETRO GASPARRI as secretary of state. In 1935 he was appointed to the prestigious office of chief papal administrator (camerlengo), which he held concurrently with that of secretary of state until elected pope in March 1939. As secretary of state, he pursued a policy of accommodation with Nazi Germany, signing a concordat with Hitler in 1933 that safeguarded church interests in Germany.

The defining events of the pontificate of Pius XII were WORLD WAR II and the cold war. Anticommunism was the dominant passion of Pius XII's life. It explains his acceptance and qualified endorsement of FASCISM. Pius disapproved heartily of fascism as a political philosophy, rejected its cultural values, and was deeply suspicious of Hitler's motives. With war in the air, his principal concern at the time of his election was to work for peace. When war broke out in September 1939, he exerted himself to keep Italy neutral. But with all the great powers at war, his criticism of Hitler and Mussolini was muted and indirect. His main concern was to maintain absolute neutrality so as not to give the Fascist regimes reason for reprisals against the Vatican and the Catholic clergy. Italian bishops should support the government and the war effort. His condemnation of "atheistic communism" when Germany invaded Russia indicates the pope's approval of the German effort to crush communism in that country.

Pius XII has been severely criticized for failing to speak out against racial doctrines in general and against the Holocaust in particular. His defenders point out that doing so would have exposed the church to severe repression without helping the victims, that the pope lacked certain knowledge of events in eastern Europe, and that he did direct the clergy to help Jews and other victims of Nazi violence. He had no foreknowledge of the Nazi roundup of Roman Jews of October 1943, that occurred "under his very windows."

After the war, Pius XII played a major role in the campaign to contain the spread of communism. Condemning the Soviet takeover of Eastern Europe and working closely with the United States, he led a world crusade to contain and roll back communism. In Italy, he exhorted voters not to vote Communist on pain of excommunication and criticized the political independence of Prime Minister ALCIDE DE GASPERI and the Christian Democratic Party (DC). To the very end of his pontificate, Pius XII opposed any form of political collaboration between Catholics and Socialists or Communists. He gave no encouragement to reform movements within the church. Often attacked and vilified in the media, Pius XII lacked the popular touch. Nevertheless, his authority, austerity, and intellectual rigor won him many devoted admirers, who consider him a saintly figure.

Plombières, agreement of (1858)

The agreement between CAVOUR, prime minister of Piedmont-Sardinia, and NAPOLEON III rested on the interest shared by Piedmont-Sardinia and France to drive Austria out of Italy. The removal of Austrian influence would lead to Italian independence under Piedmontese leadership. Cavour was willing to leverage French support against Austria by ceding the territories of Nice and Savoy to France. An agreement along these lines was outlined at a secret meeting that took place between Cavour and the French emperor on July 20, 1858, near the resort town of Plombières in southern France. In return for the cession of Nice and Savoy, the emperor promised French military support for a war against Austria that would result in the annexation by Piedmont of the entire Po Valley, including Lombardy, Venetia, and part of the Papal States. This would result in the creation of a kingdom of upper Italy ruled by the HOUSE OF SAVOY. The pope would retain control of Rome and its surrounding territory, the remaining papal territory being incorporated in a kingdom of central Italy that would

also include Tuscany. The Kingdom of the Two Sicilies would not be affected by these changes. A dynastic alliance would be sealed by the marriage of Princess Clotilde, the daughter of King Victor Emmanuel II, to Prince Napoleon, the emperor's cousin. Piedmont would also have to agree to bear the financial costs of the war. Cavour had to provoke Austria into declaring war in order to win French public support for a war in Italy. The understanding was never ratified by either government, but served nevertheless as the basis for the French-Piedmontese alliance against Austria in the second of the WARS OF INDEPENDENCE. Matters did not turn out precisely as Cavour and Napoleon had hoped. Austria did declare war on Piedmont as intended, the French did intervene, but concluded an armistice before decisively defeating the Austrians. Cavour resigned temporarily. Piedmont received Lombardy, but not Venetia or the promised papal territory. The kingdom of central Italy never materialized. Napoleon had to wait until 1860 to obtain Nice and Savoy. Neither Cavour nor Napoleon envisaged a united Italy in 1858, but their understanding did set in motion the events that led to Italian unification. In that sense, Cavour and Piedmont received much more than what was promised by the agreement of Plombières.

PNF (Partito Nazionale Fascista)

See FASCISM.

PNM (Partito Nazionale Monarchico)

The National Monarchist Party was founded in 1946 for the purpose of restoring the monarchy abolished by the referendum of June 1946, a restoration that was illegal because the CONSTITUTION of the Italian republic ruled it out. Its electoral basis was mostly south of Rome. The wealthy ship owner Achille Lauro (1887–1982) led it in Naples, where he was elected mayor in 1952, 1956, and 1961, and senator in 1953. Voters represented a cross-section of society, from unemployed workers and peasants to wealthy landowners and aristocrats. Many supporters were sentimentally attached to the monarchy as a symbol of authority, paternalism, and national unity, but the party's showing at the polls did not reflect the strength of monarchist sentiment in the country in the immediate postwar years. In the referendum of 1946, nearly 10.7 million voters out of 23.4 million voted for the monarchy, but the PNF never gained more than the 6.9 percent of the popular vote it received in the elections of 1953. In 1948 a group of monarchists seceded to form the Popular Monarchist Party; the two parties were reunited in 1960. In the elections of 1968, the PNM won only 1.3 percent of the popular vote. The party tried unsuccessfully to become a partner of the governing Christian Democratic Party (DC). Declining interest in a monarchist restoration and communist inroads in the PNM's power base among southern workers and peasants were the major reasons for its losses. Before the elections of 1972, the PNM merged with the neo-Fascist Italian Social Movement (MSI) and formed a joint ticket (MSI-Destra Nazionale) that received 8.7 percent of the popular vote. It never ran again as an independent party. During its existence, the PNM opposed collaboration with communists and land reform, and hoped to keep peasants on the land as cheap labor. It failed in all respects.

Po River and Valley

About 400 miles long (650 km), the Po River is the longest in Italy. From its source in the Piedmontese ALPS to its outlet in the ADRIATIC SEA, the Po flows in an easterly direction through the regions of PIEDMONT, LOMBARDY, and EMILIA-ROMAGNA and touches the cities of TURIN, PAVIA, PIACENZA, Cremona, and FERRARA. Its major tributaries are the Dora Baltea, Tanaro, Ticino, Adda, Oglio, and Mincio Rivers. Past Ferrara, the river divides into several branches that enter the Adriatic Sea separately and form a large delta. Before national unification, the Po River for the most part marked the boundary between the

Austrian Empire to the north and the nominally independent central duchies and PAPAL STATES to the south. Frequent toll barriers impeded trade along its course. National unification made possible the economic integration of the entire Po Valley (Val Padana), which is today largely coterminous with the region of Emilia-Romagna, Emilia indicating its upper and Romagna its lowers parts. The province of BOLOGNA marks the approximate boundary between Emilia and Romagna. Extensive land drainage projects have reclaimed much land for agriculture in the Romagna since national unification. Sugar beets, grains, livestock, and fruit are cultivated intensely. The large numbers of day workers and sharecroppers organized in peasant leagues and labor associations have contributed to Romagna's image as a politically volatile region. Today, the Po Valley is Italy's most densely populated and prosperous area, with a highly developed agriculture and industry.

Politecnico (Il) See CATTANEO, CARLO.

Poliziano, Angelo (1454–1494)
humanist scholar and poet
Born Angelo Ambrogini, Poliziano derived the name by which he is known from the Tuscan town of Montepulciano where he was born. The murder of his father left an indelible impression on the young child, who found security in study and contemplation. At a young age he became proficient in Latin and Greek and showed great aptitude for writing verse in these ancient languages and the Tuscan vernacular. His translation of Homer's *Iliad* into Latin brought him to the attention of LORENZO DE' MEDICI, who took him into his household and appointed him tutor to his children (1473–78). His ordination into the priesthood (1477) and subsequent ecclesiastical appointments procured by Lorenzo gave Poliziano the economic security he needed to pursue a life of study and writing. His most productive years were the ones he spent in the

Angelo Poliziano *(Library of Congress)*

Medici household. His many writings from those years include the famous *Stanze* (1475) that display Poliziano's skill as a composer of Tuscan verse, his sensitivity for natural beauty, and melancholic appreciation for the fleeting joys of youth. After his appointment as professor of Latin and Greek (1480), Poliziano devoted himself primarily to scholarship, delving into the writings of Aristotle, corresponding and engaging in furious polemics with other humanists. His interest in and collections of popular verses and tales make Poliziano a pioneer in the study of folk literature.

Pollio, Alberto (1852–1914)
general and army chief of staff
Born in Caserta, Pollio studied at the military academies of Naples and Turin and was commissioned a lieutenant in the artillery in 1872. He was promoted to the rank of captain serving on the general staff in 1878, to major general in 1900, and lieutenant general in 1906. He also served as aide-de-camp to King UMBERTO I. In 1908 he was appointed army chief of staff, responsible for the readiness of the army in case of war. His rapid rise to the top of the military hierarchy and the strong connections to which that rise was attributed aroused considerable resentment among his peers. Pollio had little experience as a field commander. Rather, he was an expert in matters of military organization and command, an expertise that was largely based on studies of military figures and events, particularly his books on *Custoza 1866* (1903) and *Waterloo* (1906). Very much aware of the economic costs of maintaining a large army, Pollio campaigned hard and secured sizable increases in spending. Italy's membership in the Triple Alliance meant that he had to plan for war against France, but the ITALIAN-TURKISH WAR diverted his attention to Africa and interfered with preparations for fighting in Europe. Pollio's innovations included expansion of the army to nearly 1.4 million troops, improvements in pay, rations, and barracks, adoption of machine guns for infantry and cavalry units, army motorization, and use of aircraft for combat and reconnaissance. Inadequate funding and the war in Africa interfered with Pollio's plans for war in Europe. Pollio had to inform the Germans that Italy would no longer be able to send troops to its aid should it go to war against France. The TRIPLE ALLIANCE seemed to exclude the possibility of war with Austria, but Pollio took the precaution of ordering that fortifications be built along the northeastern frontier. Pollio died of a heart attack in July 1914, but his measures proved useful when the government declared war on Austria in May 1915.

Polo della Libertà
Literally the Liberty Pole but usually translated as Freedom Alliance, the Polo della Libertà (or simply *Il Polo*) was a political alliance of center-right parties headed in 1994–96 by SILVIO

BERLUSCONI's Forza Italia Party. Its main partners were UMBERTO BOSSI's Northern League and GIANFRANCO FINI's National Alliance. The coalition took advantage of the recent adoption of single-member constituencies, in which the winning party or coalition of parties got to represent an entire electoral district, to win a parliamentary majority and propel Berlusconi into the office of prime minister. The partnership was undermined from the beginning by major differences between the Northern League, which demanded government decentralization and regional autonomy, and the National Alliance, which stood for strong national government. Berlusconi's government lasted only seven months (May–December 1994). The Polo della Libertà lost votes in the elections of April 1996, and its parties were relegated to the role of opposition to the ruling center-left coalition. A center-right coalition similar to Polo della Libertà, but renamed Casa delle Libertà (House of Freedoms) won again in the elections of May 2001. This time the coalition was more stable. Berlusconi's Forza Italia won more votes than in 1994, while the troublesome Northern League lost votes. The coalition still governs the country.

Pomponazzi, Pietro (1462–1525)
Renaissance philosopher notable for his intellectual independence

Pomponazzi was born to a wealthy family of Mantua, received a degree in medicine from the University of Padua (1487), and taught natural philosophy (the precursor of modern science) at the same university (1495–1509). He then taught at the Universities of Ferrara (1510–12) and Bologna (1512–25). Pomponazzi is considered the major Aristotelian scholar of his time, but he was Aristotelian only in the sense that he believed in the importance of experimentation and empirical evidence, rather than in the sense of accepting Aristotle as the final authority. His guiding maxim was that the pursuit of truth implies a willingness to consider ideas that are philosophically heretical. The argument he advanced in *De immortalitate*

animae (On the immortality of the soul, 1516) that the Platonic concept of the soul as an entity separate from the body was absurd, because all the manifestations of the soul occurred through the senses, left him open to accusations of heresy. In later writings Pomponazzi pressed his argument to suggest that the soul is nothing more than a form of matter, and therefore perishable like the body. He also attempted a naturalistic explanation of miracles and questioned the role of free will in the larger scheme of natural law. All these potentially heretical views could have meant great trouble for Pomponazzi had he not enjoyed the protection of influential patrons and acknowledged the supreme authority of the CATHOLIC CHURCH in matters of faith. His intent to separate faith from reason is also a sign of the modernity of his thought.

Ponchielli, Amilcare   See OPERA.

Pontano, Giovanni, or Gioviano (1422–1503)
humanist writer, military and political figure active in Naples

Born in Umbria and educated in Perugia, in 1448 Pontano followed King ALFONSO I to Naples, where he spent the rest of his life. In Naples, under the adopted name of Gioviano, he became the central figure in the humanist circle that later became the Accademia Pontiana named after him. He was a loyal and effective servant of the monarchy, for which he carried out important diplomatic missions and served in war. Appointed prime minister in 1487, Pontano still held that office in 1495 when the invading French army occupied Naples in the course of the ITALIAN WARS. Pontano remained in Naples and submitted to the French, while the court found refuge in Sicily. His act of submission was interpreted as a betrayal, but may in fact have been agreed on with the king as a way of maintaining the continuity of government on the mainland. When the court returned to the capital, Pontano was retained in the service but never regained his former influence. He retired to private life in 1498 after the death of his beloved son. As a writer, Pontano was at his best in light-hearted satire, in verses celebrating nature and the joys of life, and as a memoirist. In *De amore coniugali* (Of married love), Pontano sang the pleasures of married and domestic life. His *De bello napolitano* (Naples at war) is an account of the conflict between the French and Spanish for control of Naples. Pontano was also interested in the study of nature, which he approached with a firm belief in the validity of astrology. Most original are five Socratic dialogues, published from 1467 to 1501, which cover topics discussed in Naples' learned circles.

Pontormo, Jacopo Carucci, called Il (1494–1556)

late Renaissance painter and exponent of the mannerist style

Born near Empoli, Pontormo studied with ANDREA DEL SARTO, whose delicate colors he complemented with an emphasis on clarity of line. Commissioned to decorate the MEDICI FAMILY villa at Poggio a Caiano, Pontormo painted his groundbreaking fresco *Vertumnus and Pomona* (1520–21), a pastoral scene of peasant figures depicted in a naturalistic manner that shows Pontormo's mastery of anatomy. The now severely damaged cycle of the *Passion* painted for the Certosa at Galluzzo, near Florence, shows Pontormo striving for effect with densely crowded scenes, and elongated, distorted figures. Pontormo's paintings opened the way to MANNERISM, of which he is the chief Tuscan exponent. In moving toward mannerism, Pontormo was encouraged by Michelangelo, who gave him cartoons to work on. Pontormo was reacting against the emphasized balance and clarity of the classical school dominant in his time. It was a timely reaction that pointed to the future of art, but a reaction that he also carried to excess. Some of his later paintings were painted over in the 18th century when the preference for the classical style revived. A moody and introverted personality, his paintings perhaps reflect the tensions and precarious balance of his emotions.

population

Reliable population figures are hard to come by for Italy before the 19th century. According to demographic estimates, the population of the peninsula rose from about 5.0 million in the year 1000 to 11 million in 1300. It dropped to 8 million due to epidemics of the 14th century. The recovery that began after 1400 brought the population to more than 13 million in 1600, but was interrupted by another round of epidemics (1630–31 in the North and 1656–57 in the South), with a net loss of about 2 million lives by the end of the century. The phase of population growth that began in the 18th century continues to this day.

The first national census (1861), adjusted to take into account today's political boundaries, registered a population of 25.8 million. The population rose to 29.3 million in 1881, 33.4 in 1901, 37.4 in 1921, 47.2 in 1951, 53.8 in 1971, and 57.1 million in 1991. In both the 19th and 20th centuries, national rates of growth have been moderate to low, averaging about 7 per thousand until the late 1960s. Nationally, high birth rates in the range of 37–32 per thousand population and death rates in the range of 30–21 per thousand prevailed before 1900. Although specific groups of the population, such as the aristocracy and religious minorities had low birth rates perhaps as early as the 18th century, the national birth rate did not reach levels below 20 per thousand until the 1950s. By 1971 the national birth rate had dropped to 9.4 per thousand. In 1999, with a birth rate of 9 per thousand and a death rate of 10 per thousand, the native population was actually declining. The estimated 1999 total stood at 57.4 million.

The phase of low growth has come somewhat later in Italy than in the countries of northern Europe. Within Italy, there have been major regional differences. Birth rates are highest in the South. EMIGRATION has affected the population as a whole, with an estimated net loss of some 8.6 million people from 1861 to 1971. Since then, immigration has exceeded emigration, leading to an estimated presence of some 1 million to 2 million legal and illegal immigrants in the year 2001. These figures indicate that population growth in Italy has followed a course very similar to that of Europe as a whole, marked by moderate rates of increase from about 1850 to 1950, by slow growth or stability after 1950, and by reliance on immigrants in recent years to make up for natural population losses and to meet the needs of the economy.

positivism

The notion that factual observation, experimentation, and verification are the only way to acquire reliable knowledge is rooted in the ideas of 17th-century scientific thought. The French philosopher Auguste Comte (1798–1857) brought this mind-set to the study of society. According to Comte, positivism was the "positive philosophy" of the scientific age, and "sociology" the social science that addressed social issues. Acceptance of positivism encountered obstacles in Italy. The CATHOLIC CHURCH and the prevailing lay school of philosophical IDEALISM, each for different reasons, rejected the materialism of the positivist school. Empiricism and objective observation did not sit well with intellectuals imbued with the sentimental ethos of romanticism, as many were in Italy. Positivism did appeal to an influential minority. The social investigations of, among others, CARLO CATTANEO, CESARE LOMBROSO, PAOLO MANTEGAZZA, and PASQUALE VILLARI were very much in the spirit of positivism. FREEMASONRY and anticlerical associations spread the message to the rest of society. These figures envisaged positivism as essential to the modernization of Italian society and the formation of a strong national community. Their high priest was the philosopher ROBERTO ARDIGÒ, who sought to make positivism more appealing by distancing it from its strictly materialist foundations. Further to the

Left, positivism also appealed to socialists, who often used its weapons to bring attention to the inadequacies of government social policy. As elsewhere in Europe, in Italy the debate over the merits of positivism tended to focus on the Darwinian controversy over the descent of man after Darwin's *Origin of Species* appeared in Italian in 1864. Condemned by the church, Darwin's theory of evolution was defended by secular writers as a way of combating clerical influence. The cultural debate thus took on political overtones that facilitated acceptance of the new philosophy. At the grass roots of society, the cultural war between positivists and antipositivists often took the form of a fight between village priests and local medical doctors, the latter seeing themselves as representatives of the culture of science against superstition and organized religion. With the outcome of the struggle still undecided in society at large, a revolt against positivism began to take shape among intellectuals. BENEDETTO CROCE led the antipositivist campaign in the name of a revived idealism capable of making room for the role of will and moral values. Croce's onslaught had some success, but the influence of positivism continues to make itself felt in Italian social science.

PPI (Partito Popolare Italiano)

The founding of the Italian Popular Party in January 1919 was made possible by the complete revocation by Pope BENEDICT XV of the papal ban on voting in national elections by Italian Catholics. Its roots went back to the movement of Christian Democracy (see DC) launched in the 1890s and inspired by the social principles of Pope LEO XIII. Although founded with Vatican approval, the PPI was nonconfessional and formally independent from the CATHOLIC CHURCH. It opposed socialism, liberalism, freemasonry, and anticlericalism as ideologies incompatible with Christian principles, but expressed willingness to cooperate with outside individuals and groups willing to accept its program. The program was in many ways quite radical. Politically, the PPI called for the adoption of universal suffrage for men and women, proportional representation, an elective senate, government decentralization, and local autonomies. Its social program, based on the principle of social solidarity, called for cooperation across class lines, protection of small property holdings, pro-family legislation, sickness and disability insurance. A well-organized and active labor union base backed these demands and negotiated aggressively on behalf of sharecroppers and small landowners. In the elections of 1919 the *popolari* won 100 out of 508 seats in the lower house of parliament. LUIGI STURZO was the PPI's founder and inspirational figure, but the party was internally divided between right-wing conservatives and left-wing progressives, who disagreed on goals and tactics. Sturzo, who was a priest, could not sit in parliament. The PPI's parliamentary leader was the more conservative Stefano Cavazzoni (1881–1951), who actually joined the first Fascist government formed by BENITO MUSSOLINI in October 1922 as minister of labor. Progressives and conservatives disagreed on many issues, not the least important being how to deal with FASCISM. PPI support for the Fascist government was based on the premise that once in power, fascism would shed its propensity for violence and become a party of law and order. When that did not happen, the PPI went over to the opposition. In the meantime, the recently elected Pope PIUS XI reversed his predecessor's policy, turned against the PPI, and opened negotiations with the Fascist government to settle the ROMAN QUESTION. The Vatican pressured Sturzo to resign as party secretary, the right wing of the party defected to Mussolini, and the party disbanded in 1925–26. The Christian Democratic Party would pick up after WORLD WAR II where the PPI had left off, but in a more moderate vein and without the PPI's radical social program.

PR (Partito Radicale) See RADICALISM.

Praga, Emilio See SCAPIGLIATURA.

prefects

Prefects were key figures in the system of centralized government introduced in Italy by the Napoleonic administrations of the early 19th century. Pre-Napoleonic precedents for giving broad powers to appointed local officials (intendants) are found, however, in the centralized administration developed by the monarchy of the Kingdom of SARDINIA. The system was modified during the RESTORATION period along the lines of the French model. The CONSTITUTION of 1848 of the Kingdom of Sardinia made intendants political appointees responsible to the Ministry of the Interior and gave them authority over both civilian and military affairs. The powers of these local officials, who were designated first as governors and later as prefects, were broadened and consolidated in the Kingdom of Italy by the administrative reforms of 1859–65 that were part of the process of political unification.

Prefects played an important role as political organizers for governments in power. As governments changed, so did the prefects, who were expected to enforce political directives and organize voter support for the government in power. Prefects served as the local eyes and ears of the national government. The concentration of power in the hands of prefects was the system's reply to demands for administrative decentralization. It was up to the discretion of prefects to decide how to enforce the law in light of local conditions. Prefects played such an important role that the government of the unified state was sometimes called a "prefectocracy." The Fascist state officially acknowledged the power of prefects, but the Fascist Party was nevertheless able to infringe on those powers by appointing its own local officials. Fascist *federali* (local party secretaries) and *podestà* (appointed officials replacing elective mayors) coexisted somewhat uneasily with prefects for most of the Fascist period. The Italian republic has retained the prefect in spite of the widespread sentiment against the office, attributable to its close identification with the strong state reminiscent of fascism. Fear of communism, of social instability, and domestic discord in the difficult postwar years contributed to their retention. Their powers have nevertheless been limited by the rise of competing institutions. Political parties, labor unions, and other pressure groups with access to government circumscribe the role of prefects in informal but effective ways.

presidents   See GOVERNMENT.

Preziosi, Giovanni   (1881–1945)
Fascist racial theoretician and anti-Semite
Preziosi came to politics via the priesthood, which he left at a young age, a career in journalism, and an interest in demography and emigration dating from the first years of the 20th century. Firsthand knowledge of the hardships experienced by Italian immigrants in the United States may account for the feelings of extreme NATIONALISM that characterized Preziosi's writings. Back in Italy, he joined the Nationalist Association and campaigned for Italy's intervention in WORLD WAR I. The interventionist campaign marked the start of a lifelong preoccupation with the suspected political intrigues of international finance, which he later came to identify with the role of "international Jewry." These views he aired through the review *La Vita Italiana* (1913–43), which was Preziosi's personal publication. In 1920 he published the first Italian edition of the *Protocols of the Elders of Zion*. He joined the Fascist Party that same year, but never won BENITO MUSSOLINI's confidence. The Duce did not share Preziosi's doctrinaire anti-Semitism. Furthermore, he kept his distance to avoid the evil eye that he suspected Preziosi of having. Preziosi did enjoy the support of ROBERTO FARINACCI and other prominent Fascists who viewed anti-Semitism as an ideology that reinforced their image as intransigent Fascists. Preziosi became prominent in the late 1930s when the Axis alliance took shape, and anti-Semitism became official policy in Italy. Made a minister of state in 1938, he was a staunch supporter of Hitler and the German alliance. He was unrepentant to the end of his life, which came when he committed suicide with his wife a few days before the final collapse of Mussolini's regime in northern Italy at the end of WORLD WAR II.

Prezzolini, Giuseppe   (1882–1981)
antiliberal writer and journalist identified
with fascism
Born in Perugia, Prezzolini was part of the group of Florentine writers who revolted against the cultural influence of POSITIVISM. Rejecting the strict determinism of political ideologies based on social science, Prezzolini joined with other anti-rationalist intellectuals to publicize an alternate view of life that stressed instead the role of will, motivation, and choice. Their inspiration came from various sources, including the intuitionism of Henri Bergson and the pragmatism of William James. It was not their intent to elaborate a new philosophy, but rather to experience life as a journey of possibilities. Together with GIOVANNI PAPINI, Prezzolini cofounded the review *Leonardo* (1903–07). He then launched and directed *La Voce* (1908–16), served as Roman correspondent for Mussolini's *Il Popolo d'Italia* (1915–16), worked for the government in an academic capacity for the remainder of WORLD WAR I, and for the League of Nations after the war. His relationship to the Fascist regime was an ambiguous one. While admiring the iconoclastic and innovative spirit of FASCISM, Prezzolini was at the same time critical of the bureaucratic regimentation that was inseparable from fascism. His known political reservations toward fascism may actually have helped his academic career. In 1930 he was appointed professor of Italian literature at Columbia University, where he also served as director of the government-sponsored Casa Italiana until 1940. In these capacities, he was an intelligent propagandist for the regime. He continued to write profusely back in Italy after WORLD WAR II, but his most creative contributions are to be found in his writings dating from before

1914. See his *Fascism* (1926) and *The Case of the Casa Italiana* (1976).

PRI (Partito Repubblicano Italiano)

A Republican Party inspired by the ideas of GIUSEPPE MAZZINI was formed in 1895. Its principal goal was to keep alive the republican ideal, cooperate with progressive parties, and fight for honest government. They called for the abolition of the monarchy as the source of political corruption and attacked the army, courts, big business, and other groups as partners and beneficiaries of the monarchist system. The party did well enough in elections to help defend parliament when it came under attack in 1898–1900. During the era of GIOVANNI GIOLITTI the Republican Party often cooperated with Socialists and Radicals and promoted popular associations and initiatives to keep the republican spirit alive. In 1914–15 it came out in favor of Italian intervention in WORLD WAR I. This first Republican Party dissolved under FASCISM in 1925–26. It revived after the fall of the Fascist regime. Its republican ideal was realized in June 1946 when Italians voted out the monarchy and instituted the Italian republic. The new Republican Party was still a minority party. Campaigning against government corruption, it also favored the American alliance, free market policies, cooperation with the dominant Christian Democratic Party (DC), and the bridging of differences between the parties of the center and those of the Left. On that last point, however, those republicans who favored cooperation with the parties of the Left had to overcome the resistance of many party members who opposed it. As a key component of the various four-party coalitions of Christian Democrats, Liberals, Republicans, and Social Democrats that governed until the late 1980s, the PRI wielded power out of proportion to its electoral strength, which reached a maximum 5.1 percent of the popular vote in the elections of 1983. Part of its influence was due to the personal prestige of its leaders, which included RANDOLFO PACCIARDI and Ugo La Malfa.

In 1981, party leader GIOVANNI SPADOLINI became the first non–Christian Democrat to hold the office of prime minister. The PRI survived the political crises and reforms of the 1990s to remain politically viable as one of several tiny splinter parties in the new electoral system.

Prinetti-Barrère Agreements See FOREIGN POLICY.

Prodi, Romano (1940–)
economist, prime minister, and European Union leader

Romano Prodi has played an important part in public life in administrative and political roles. An economics professor at the University of Bologna, where he was known as an advocate of privatization, Prodi established ties with the Christian Democratic Party (DC), served twice as chief manager of the giant state holding company IRI between 1982 and 1994, was a founder of the center-left Olive Tree coalition, and led it to a narrow victory in the elections of 1996. Following the elections, Prodi formed his own government, which survived until October 1998. As prime minister, he took on the challenge of curbing public spending and reducing the public debt to meet the criteria for admission to the euro monetary zone. He defines his political philosophy as "Catholic humanism," enjoys the support of the vast network of Catholic associations, but does not identify politically with the CATHOLIC CHURCH. Prodi has held appointments at Harvard University and the London School of Economics, speaks English and French fluently, and is respected in Italy and abroad for his economic expertise. A strong Europeanist, he has headed the European Commission since September 1999, presiding over the European Union at a time when its functions are expanding from the purely economic to the economic and political. His main concern has been to set goals and develop new approaches to governing Europe. His term as president of the European Commission expires in 2004.

Propaganda 2 (or Propaganda Due)

Secret Masonic lodge, whose discovery
precipitated a major political scandal

The existence of this secret Masonic lodge was discovered in May 1981 by police searching the home of businessman Licio Gelli (1919–   ) in connection with the investigation into the activities of banker Michele Sindona (1920–86). The search brought to light the names of 953 members of the lodge referred to as Propaganda 2 (P2), including names of government ministers, members of parliament, admirals, generals, judges, businessmen, and journalists. The press immediately voiced the suspicion that the lodge was engaged in a political conspiracy against the state and the parties of the Left, which were making a bid to share power with the dominant Christian Democratic Party (DC). Gelli's long-standing ties to right-wing groups and his many contacts with high-placed personalities in Italy and abroad lent credence to the charges of political conspiracy. Communists and socialists in particular carried on a loud campaign calling for a parliamentary investigation, which was entrusted to the Christian Democratic deputy Tina Anselmi (1927–   ). The ensuing scandal forced the resignation of the Christian Democratic government headed by Arnaldo Forlani (1925–   ) and led to the appointment of the first non–Christian Democrat to head a postwar cabinet, the republican leader GIOVANNI SPADOLINI.

PSDI (Partito Social Democratico Italiano)

See NENNI, PIETRO; PSI; SARAGAT, GIUSEPPE.

PSI (Partito Socialista Italiano)

The term socialism entered political discourse in the 1820s to describe the belief that individuals ought to put the collective or social interest ahead of their own personal or "egotistic" interest. That attitude was in turn rooted in the traditions of worker guilds and the Jacobin ideology of the FRENCH REVOLUTION. Nineteenth-century versions of collective theory gave socialism its modern ideological basis. Marxism was the most influential

of the 19th-century elaborations. Marxist socialism was introduced in Italy in the 1860s, where it collided with competing ideologies of collective action. These included the associational movement of GIUSEPPE MAZZINI, the antiauthoritarian anarchism of MICHAEL BAKUNIN, and the "propaganda of the deed" approach of CARLO PISACANE that called on the few to lead the revolution of the many. In addition to these diverse ideologies, Italian socialists were also hampered by the late development of industrial manufacturing.

Without the factories of the Industrial Revolution, there was no urban working class to answer the call of socialism. Italian socialists turned their attention to the masses of precariously employed rural day workers (*braccianti*) and sharecroppers (*mezzadri*) concentrated in those areas of the country where commercial agriculture flourished. Italian socialism reached out to this rural working class. The socialist program tried to reconcile and unify the demands of this rural proletariat with those of urban workers employed in industries that were starting to develop in the 1890s. The Italian Socialist Party, founded in stages from 1892 to 1895, took on the task of giving political voice and leverage to this working-class constituency. It faced serious internal divisions from the beginning. The skilled workers represented by COSTANTINO LAZZARI were organized in trade unions that sought to improve wages, benefits, and working conditions through collective bargaining. Other workers, with less bargaining power, were organized territorially in chambers of labor that were more militant politically, brought together skilled and unskilled workers, and often took to the streets. Rural day laborers organized in peasant leagues and cooperatives sought control of both wages and hiring practices; they too were prone to take direct action that often resulted in major disorders.

The political strategy of the Socialist Party, as elaborated by a leadership that was heavily intellectual and of middle-class extraction, reflected the heterogeneous nature of the movement. That strategy envisaged the simultaneous pursuit of gradual reforms and of revolution. ANDREA COSTA, the most prestigious figure among first-generation socialists, abandoned revolution to pursue universal suffrage and concrete economic gains by working with parliament. The leadership split among "minimalists" who sought reforms and "maximalists" who insisted on talking the language of revolution. FILIPPO TURATI and ENRICO FERRI represented, respectively, the reformist and revolutionary souls of the PSI before 1914. Turati's reformism prevailed at the national level where the PSI's parliamentary delegation often supported the liberal governments headed by GIOVANNI GIOLITTI in return for the extension of voting rights, preferential treatment of worker cooperatives in awarding government contracts, social welfare measures, and government neutrality in labor disputes.

This complex tactic brought the party electoral success, but did not satisfy young socialist firebrands who charged that the party was straying from the path of revolution. Their leader in 1911–14 was BENITO MUSSOLINI, who took with him a small group of radical socialists when he was expelled from the PSI in 1914. The issue that provoked the schism was that of Italian intervention or neutrality in WORLD WAR I. These breakaway socialists formed the nucleus of what became FASCISM. The PSI opposed Italian participation in the war and, when the government went to war, pledged to "neither support nor sabotage" the war effort.

In the turbulent postwar years the PSI once again vacillated between reform and revolution. In 1921 its left wing defected to form the Communist Party of Italy (PCI). Another split occurred in 1923 when Giacinto Menotti Serrati (1876–1926), leader of the maximalist current, urged cooperation with the Communist Party. This time the defectors were the moderates who formed the Partito Socialista Unitario (PSU). It was the denunciation of Fascist violence and intimidation in the elections of 1924 by PSU secretary GIACOMO MATTEOTTI that precipitated the crisis that led to the banning of all opposition parties in Fascist Italy.

The PSI maintained a presence abroad after Fascist repression forced it to cease operations in Italy. It was reconstituted in 1943 and, with the

name of Partito Socialista Italiano d'Unità Proletaria (PSIUP), played a role in the RESISTANCE. Led by PIETRO NENNI, the PSI participated in center-left governing coalitions (1945–47) that brought together Christian Democrats, Communists, and Socialists. Nenni's controversial policy of close collaboration with the Communist Party brought on the first postwar party split as GIUSEPPE SARAGAT and followers split to form the anticommunist Social Democratic Party of Italy (PSDI). At that point, the party reclaimed its former name, Partito Socialista Italiano (PSI).

In the elections of 1948 the PSI and PCI formed a joint ticket, but losses of seats to the benefit of the PCI persuaded the party to run independently in 1953, when it emerged from those elections as the country's third-largest party, with more than 3.4 million votes. The PSI distanced itself further from the Communist Party and pursued the dialogue with the dominant Christian Democratic Party (DC) that led to the OPENING TO THE LEFT in 1963. That decision caused still another defection and led to the creation of the PSIUP, a party of the Left that opposed the compromise with Christian Democracy, and to the temporary reunification of PSI and PSDI (1966–69). The clear victory of the currents that favored cooperation with the Christian Democrats and participation in governing coalitions culminated in the emergence of BETTINO CRAXI as party leader and the corruption scandals of TANGENTOPOLI that engulfed the party in the early 1990s. The electoral reforms of those same years dealt the final blows to the PSI, which dissolved formally in 1994. Socialists went off in different directions, some forming small splinter parties of little consequence, others joining larger parties of the Left, center, and Right. The PSI, carrier of a glorious if troubled tradition, did not survive quite long enough to celebrate the full 100th anniversary of its founding.

PSIUP (Partito Socialista Italiano d'Unità Proletaria)

The Italian Socialist Party of Proletarian Unity was the official name that the Italian Socialist

Party (PSI) assumed when it was reconstituted in 1943. It dropped that name in 1947 when it split into two factions headed, respectively, by PIETRO NENNI and GIUSEPPE SARAGAT. The name was taken up again by the left wing that split from the PSI in 1963 to protest its alliance with the governing Christian Democratic Party (see OPENING TO THE LEFT). Led by the hard-line leftist Lelio Basso (1903–78), the PSIUP won 4.5 percent of the popular vote in the elections of 1968. Its electoral strength declined and the party disappeared in the 1970s. During its brief existence, the PSIUP raised important questions of Italian political life. It insisted on the revolutionary mission of socialism and rejected Socialist participation in government as a deviation that would corrupt the party. The PSIUP favored instead a policy of close collaboration with the Communist Party (PCI) and a common front against the dominant Christian Democratic Party (DC). The PSIUP directed its message to young militants and tried to serve as a bridge toward the New Left, without being able to arrest the New Left's drift toward the extra-parliamentary modes of protest of the 1970s. The defection of the PSIUP had important consequences for the PSI, weakening it at the crucial moment when it became an ally of the DC and opening the way to a new generation of pragmatic Socialists led by BETTINO CRAXI.

PSU (Patito Socialista Unitario) See PSI.

Pucci, Emilio (1914–1992)
sportsman and fashion innovator known for the casual elegance of his designs
Born to a somewhat impoverished family of the Florentine nobility, Emilio Pucci, marquis of Barsento, participated as a skier in the 1934 winter Olympics, attended college in the United States, and struck up a friendship with Edda Ciano, wife of Galeazzo CIANO and daughter of BENITO MUSSOLINI. He served in the Italian armed forces during WORLD WAR II. In 1943 he helped Edda Ciano and her children escape into Switzerland and was

instrumental in saving the precious Ciano diaries that provide a unique glimpse of the backstairs of political life in Fascist Italy. After the war Pucci launched the sportswear and informal-wear lines that made him famous. His trademark was the use of simple lines and colorful patterns that flattered the wearer. Priceless exposure and publicity came when international glamour figures like Jackie Kennedy wore Pucci creations. Youthful image is a central attraction of Pucci designs. His success gave Italian fashion the international appeal that it still enjoys.

Puccini, Giacomo (1858–1924)
last composer to work in the tradition of 19th-century Italian opera
Regarded as the last of the truly popular Italian opera composers, Puccini was born in LUCCA to a family of professional musicians, sang in local church choirs as a child, and began composing in earnest at age 17. In 1880 he entered the prestigious Milan Conservatory, where he completed his musical education over the next three years. His first major success was the opera *Manon Lescaut* (1893). His next production, *La Bohème* (1896), was not an immediate success, but soon became and still remains the most popular of all his operas. *Tosca* (1900), *Madama Butterfly* (1906), and *La fanciulla del West* (The girl of the golden West, 1910) also found favor with the public. WORLD WAR I found him at work on the lightest of his operas, *La rondine* (The swallow, 1917) and the three one-act operas *Il tabarro* (The cloak), *Suor Angelica,* and *Gianni Schicchi,* that are usually performed and known collectively as *Il trittico* (1919). Puccini's final opera, *Turandot* (1926), was still unfinished when he died in 1924 after undergoing an operation for throat cancer. While the public enthused over Puccini's music, music critics were often lukewarm or downright hostile. They objected to Puccini's choice of subjects, which were deemed vulgar or sentimental, and to the music, which they found cloying or lacking in depth. In effect, Puccini had to contend with changing musical tastes and a new genera-

Giacomo Puccini *(Library of Congress)*

tion of Italian composers who preferred orchestral to vocal music and Germanic harmony to Italian melody. Puccini was nevertheless attentive and receptive to musical innovation, had a keen sense of theater, and knew how to reach audiences emotionally. He was particularly adept at portraying feminine characters that are striking for their pathos, as in *Boheme* and *Madama Butterfly,* or for their steel, as in *Fanciulla del West, Tosca,* and *Turandot.* But what all his heroines have in common is that they are loyal and that they live and die for love. Puccini preferred to steer clear of politics, was suspicious of parties, and was patriotic in an elemental way that made

him root for strong government. His music generally avoided grand effects and sought to recreate worlds of intimate emotions.

Puglia

The region of Puglia (pop. 4.1 million), once known as Apulia, lies in the southeastern part of the peninsula where it forms the boot's "heel." Its most prominent feature is the flat plain known as the Tavoliere that served in times past as a large winter grazing ground for sheep coming down from the mountains in winter. At its northern end lies the Gargano, a steep promontory that juts out into the Adriatic Sea like a spur. The region's five provinces are BARI, which is also the regional capital, Brindisi, Foggia, Lecce, and Taranto. Large "farming towns" that traditionally served as bedroom communities for peasants commuting to work on nearby land dominate the countryside. Farming, often conducted on a large commercial scale, and related food processing industries are still the backbone of the regional economy. The large estates (*latifundia*) that once dominated the region were mostly broken up by land reform in the 1950s. Lack of water in this mostly dry region has been only partly alleviated by the construction of an extensive aqueduct that was long in the making (1906–39). Industrial manufacturing in the region has been stimulated by the government's policy of encouraging public and private investment in the South. Government support made possible the construction of a gigantic steel mill at Taranto and chemical plants around Brindisi. These and other public concerns are now in crisis in the competitive economic environment of globalization and the EUROPEAN UNION. Fishing, shipping, and tourism are also important resources. All in all, the region enjoys a relatively high standard of living compared to other regions of the South. The ports of Bari, Brindisi, and Taranto facilitate trade and communications with Greece and the former Yugoslavia. The strategic importance of the region is a function of its proximity to the Balkans and the eastern Mediterranean.

Q

Quadragesimo anno See PIUS XI.

Quadrilateral See MANTUA, CITY OF.

Qualunquismo See UOMO QUALUNQUE (L').

Quanta cura See PIUS IX.

Quasimodo, Salvatore (1901–1968)
Sicilian poet, translator of the classics, and Nobel laureate

Quasimodo was born in Modica (Sicily), studied engineering, and until the late 1920s worked at various jobs, some menial, in the private and public sectors to earn a living while continuing to study and write. In 1939 he was appointed professor of Italian literature at Milan's Musical Conservatory, a position that he held for the rest of his life. His first published volume of poetry, *Acque e terre* (Waters and land, 1930), an example of literary HERMETICISM, won him critical acclaim as evidence that a new voice had emerged in Italian poetry. Its often obscure, spare language avoided rhetorical flourishes and conveyed delicate images in melodious sounds. Quasimodo stood out in sharp contrast to GABRIELE D'ANNUNZIO and the dominant literary tradition that reveled in grandiloquent gestures and images, but he also made it clear that he owed much to d'Annunzio's use of language and that he saw himself as working within the tradition of Italian letters. *Ed è subito sera* (And at once it's

Salvatore Quasimodo *(Library of Congress)*

evening, 1942), is the title of the one-volume collection of all his poems up to the year of publication. Always intimately distant from the Fascist regime, Quasimodo's poetry took a new turn during WORLD WAR II. His postwar compositions were much more explicit and accessible than the prewar works. The poetry of the first period is personal, while that of the second social. Critics had mixed reactions to Quasimodo's second manner. The award of the 1959 Nobel Prize for literature to Quasimodo took the literary world by surprise, because Quasimodo was little known outside Italy, and some felt that other Italian writers were more deserving. In any case, Quasimodo's victory was more than personal, for it focused world attention on postwar Italian literature that until then had received little notice outside the country.

Quirinal Palace

The Quirinal Palace takes its name from the Roman hill on which it is located. Construction of this vast structure began in 1574 and was finally completed in the 1730s. The length of time it took to complete and the fact that several architects were responsible for its design may account for the building's lack of unity. However, what the palace lacks in architectural distinction it makes up for in historical interest. Pope GREGORY XIII, who initiated the project, envisaged the hilltop Quirinal as a summer residence where popes could find some relief from the stifling heat of the lower city. Instead, the Quirinal became the regular residence of the papal court until the seizure of Rome by the Italian army in September 1870. It then served as the official residence of the royal court, although individual monarchs usually resided in a less formal and more comfortable private residence. When the monarchy was abolished and the Italian republic was born in June 1946, the Quirinal Palace became the official residence of the presidents of the Italian republic. It is the site of formal state occasions and, because of its official status and for security reasons, it is not regularly open to the public.

Quota 90

The campaign to halt the devaluation of the Italian CURRENCY was BENITO MUSSOLINI's pet project. The Duce put the political prestige of the regime on the line to attain the goal of revaluation. The "battle of the lira," as the press dubbed the campaign, was prompted by the rapid devaluation of the lira, which lost 30 percent of its value between January 1925 and July 1926. That same month Mussolini announced his intention to revaluate the currency, eventually settling on the exchange rate of 92.46 lire to the pound sterling as the goal of the campaign. That was the exchange rate that the press turned into the military-sounding slogan of Quota 90. While the issue of political prestige was important, the campaign also reflected a widespread desire to halt the erosive effects of inflation on wages, fixed incomes, and savings. The stabilizing effects were deemed socially beneficial, and therefore desirable enough to overcome the fears of economic recession and the objections of exporters who feared loss of their markets from such steep revaluation. The campaign against inflation was an expression of the Fascist regime's pursuit of economic and social stability even if that meant taking the momentum out of economic growth. The deflationary policy, in fact, produced an economic recession in Italy some two years before the onset of the Great Depression. Quota 90 also oriented the national economy toward the policy of AUTARKY that the regime adopted in the 1930s.

R

Racial Laws See FARINACCI, ROBERTO; FASCISM; JEWS IN ITALY; PIUS XI; PIUS XII; PREZIOSI, GIOVANNI.

Radicalism (Radical Parties)

The term *radical* applies to currents, groups, or parties located left of center, but distinct from the main parties of the Left, republicans, socialists, and communists. In Italian politics, radicals have preferred the republic as a form of government, but have accepted the monarchy, pressed for social legislation, but rejected socialist and communist appeals to class interests and class conflict, wanted active government, but embraced free-market and laissez-faire economics.

Three parties have adopted the radical designation in Italian politics. Members of the governing LIBERAL LEFT, who wanted to differentiate their positions from those of the governing majority, formed the first Radical Party in 1878. Their leader was the charismatic FELICE CAVALLOTTI, and their program called for lowering taxes on low-income payers, administrative decentralization, broadening the suffrage, and IRREDENTISM in foreign policy.

The second Radical Party was founded in Rome in 1904. It was grounded ideologically in the philosophy of POSITIVISM, from which it drew its faith in the inevitability of progress, the ability of science and rational analysis to provide answers to economic and social problems, and of government to implement solutions. Anticlericalism was also a strong feature of its program, radicals looking upon clerical influence as incompatible with science and progress. The Radical Party at times supported GIOVANNI GIOLITTI's progressive policies, especially legislation designed to promote economic development and broadening the franchise. FRANCESCO SAVERIO NITTI was a prominent radical whose notion of "industrial democracy" defined the party's faith in the inevitability of economic and political progress. The party was quite small (its membership never exceeded 6,000), its organization patchy, and its leadership unremarkable, but it polled 7–14 percent of the votes in elections between 1904 and 1913, giving it considerable leverage in the coalition governments of those years. Giolitti had to resign in 1914 when the party withdrew its support. It favored Italian intervention in WORLD WAR I, but disappeared after the war, overwhelmed by Catholic and Socialist landslides.

Born from a small splinter group that separated from the LIBERAL PARTY in the 1950s, the third Radical Party evolved during the 1960s, shaped by its charismatic leader, Marco Pannella (born 1930). Pannella first gained national attention by staging hunger strikes in support of DIVORCE legislation. He and his small party have attracted attention by unconventional tactics, including acts of civil disobedience, and by championing causes that the main political parties have hesitated to embrace. Feminism, gay rights, legalization of contraceptives, abortion on demand, use of marijuana, conscientious objection to military service, prison reform, abolition of life imprisonment, of antiterrorist laws, and of the right to own guns, the banning of nuclear power, and breaking up the state communications monopoly, are all causes for which the Radical Party has campaigned, with mixed success. It delights in playing the role of maverick, occasionally running unconventional figures for parliament. In the elections of 1987 it ran the Hungarian-born porn queen and stripper Ilona Staller (born 1950), better known as Cicciolina, who represented the party in parliament until 1992. Too small to play a significant role in parliament (it has never polled more than 3.5 percent of the vote and has been on the verge of extinction since the early 1990s), the Radical Party has made extensive use of the constitutional right to call for popular referenda. Antiestablishment, strongly anticlerical, environmentalist, libertarian, and irreverent, the Radical Party has carved out a special role for itself that gives it visibility and significance out of all proportion to its numerical strength. The tradition of championing progressive causes with demonstrations and acts of civil disobedience continues under the presidency of Emma Bonino (born 1948), a member of the Italian parliament since 1976.

Radicati di Passerano, Alberto (1698–1737)

Piedmontese social philosopher, religious dissident, and political exile

Radicati was born into a family of the Piedmontese nobility with whom he was in conflict from an early age. Caught in an unhappy marriage and wrongly accused of having poisoned his wife, Radicati was spared from prosecution by the protection of King VICTOR AMADEUS II. The young man was encouraged by the king's struggle with the papacy over questions of jurisdictional sovereignty to vent his own nonconformist views. Radicati mistook the king's grudging acceptance of the WALDENSIANS, a Protestant minority, for a commitment to full-fledged religious toleration. Radicati would have liked to see the Piedmontese monarchy imitate Louis XIV of France and other European monarchs, who were curbing clerical privileges, instituting political reforms, and strengthening the state. But while

Victor Amadeus shared some of these goals, he was appalled by Radicati's apparent attraction to Protestantism. Twice banned from the kingdom, in 1726 and again in 1728, Radicati found refuge in England and Holland, where he did embrace Protestantism. Radicati's submission to Victor Amadeus of his manuscript *Discours moraux, historiques et politiques* (1728), setting forth his ideas on religion and social organization, was the reason for his second and final banishment from Piedmont. Carrying John Locke's theory that ideas and values are acquired through the senses to an extreme if logical conclusion, Radicati proceeded to question the validity of all forms of tradition and received knowledge. He rejected organized religion, the family, private property, social hierarchy, and external authority as institutions incompatible with a truly egalitarian society of the kind that he believed Christ had preached. In a more realistic vein, he found British constitutional monarchy to be the best possible form of government in an imperfect world. Even that was far too radical a conclusion for the Piedmontese monarchy. Though Radicati is sometimes regarded as Italy's first ENLIGHTENMENT figure, the extremism of his ideas makes him something of an anomaly even among his contemporaries who were open to innovation.

Raggi, Secret Society of the See SECRET SOCIETIES.

RAI (Radio Audizioni Italiane)

Italy's national broadcasting system developed slowly from a modest beginning in 1924, when the first radio station went on the air broadcasting from Rome. Since the start of radio broadcasting coincided closely with the advent to power of FASCISM, it devolved on the Fascist regime to develop a national system of broadcasting. GUGLIELMO MARCONI, inventor of wireless telegraphy and a pioneer in radio broadcasting, used his prestige and influence to prod the government into licensing private broadcasters. Mussolini decided instead to establish a government agency to take charge of the sector, with the proviso that it could license private broadcasters subject to public regulation. In 1927 the government authorized the formation of EIAR (Ente Italiano Audizioni Radiofoniche), formally autonomous but subject to strict government regulation with regard to political broadcasting. Under EIAR, radio broadcasting became the major means of mass communication. RAI, EIAR's successor after the fall of the regime, became part of the state holding company IRI, and when television broadcasting began in Italy in 1954, reached out to control the new medium. It continued the prewar tradition of political subservience by favoring the new party in power, the Christian Democratic Party (DC). In the 1950s RAI programming fulfilled an important social function by devoting much on-air time to spreading literacy, providing Italian language lessons, lessening regional antagonisms, and fostering a sense of national identity. Other political parties and private pressure groups eager to gain entry into the mass communications market challenged the DC monopoly. In 1974 the constitutional court proclaimed the state monopoly illegal. In subsequent years local private radio and television stations began to appear throughout the country. Much of this new broadcasting was by *radio pirate* (pirate radios) and *radio libere* (free radios), stations that were politically radical and provided information that challenged the official versions of events. In 1976 RAI launched a second national television channel, this one controlled by the Socialist Party (PSI). A third channel, reflecting the views of the Communist Party (PCI), went on the air in 1979. Private commercial broadcasting developed in the 1980s. It successfully challenged RAI's control of communications, bringing the Italian broadcasting scene in closer alignment with the American free-market model. Private radio and television have become a major means for the diffusion of American popular culture in music, fashions, and behavior. RAI nevertheless continues to control a large share of radio and television broadcasting, making the Italian system a hybrid of public and private organization.

Rame, Franca See FO, DARIO.

Ramusio, Giovanni Battista (1485–1557)
Venetian humanist scholar, public servant, and geographer

Ramusio was born to a patrician family of Treviso, received his education in PADUA and VENICE, and served the Venetian republic as senate secretary and ambassador. In that latter capacity he may have traveled to distant places, including Egypt and northern Africa. Wherever he went, he indulged his passion for collecting ancient artifacts and natural objects, which he then organized and displayed in his villa near Padua. His most important work is the three-volume account of the navigations and voyages of his time, *Delle navigazioni e viaggi* (1550–59), the last volume of which was published posthumously. It contains the earliest existing accounts of famous geographical voyages and explorations by early travelers, including descriptions of Marco Polo's trips to China and of Magellan's circumnavigation of the globe. Ramusio's book is a primary source for all subsequent accounts of early modern geographic explorations by Europeans.

Rapallo, Treaty of

Representatives of Italy and Yugoslavia signed this diplomatic agreement on November 12, 1920, in an effort to settle the disputed boundary between the two countries and decide the future of the city of FIUME that had been occupied by Italian free-corps troops led by GABRIELE D'ANNUNZIO. The treaty provided that Fiume would become a free state, Italy would receive the city of Zara and some Adriatic islands, and would renounce claims to the larger territory of DALMATIA. The agreement reflected the policy of accommodation with the new state of Yugoslavia favored by Foreign Minister CARLO SFORZA. But the compromise solution did not please the Fascist government that came to power in October 1922. The new government negotiated a new treaty with Yugoslavia, the Treaty of Rome of January 27, 1924, which gave Fiume to Italy but granted economic rights to Yugoslavia in the city and ceded nearby Port Baros.

Raphael Sanzio (1483–1520)
painter and architect, who set the style for Renaissance art at its most refined

Little is known about Raphael's early life, except that he was born in URBINO, that his father was a painter, and that he probably entered PERUGINO's workshop after his father's death in 1494. Driven by intense curiosity and desire to excel, Raphael studied closely the major artists of his period, absorbed their methods and style, and transformed what he learned into something uniquely his own. He worked in FLORENCE, Urbino, and PERUGIA, but his most accomplished works are in ROME, where he was summoned to work in 1508. Most notable are his frescoes in the Vatican, where he was responsible for decorating several rooms. Of particular interest are the four scenes in the Stanza della Segnatura (1509–11), including the renowned *School of Athens,* which illustrate aspects of Christian and Platonic doctrine. In 1514 he succeeded DONATO BRAMANTE as chief architect of St. Peter's. Pope Leo X, a connoisseur of art, was an admirer and patron of Raphael's art. The art conveyed Raphael's uncanny ability to portray character by focusing in on the revealing moment and the expressive gesture. His several paintings of the Virgin Mary are most affecting representations of feminine grace and maternal love. The ability to convey character, classical clarity and simplicity, and the aura of serenity that pervades his works, make Raphael's art the best expression of HUMANISM in the visual arts.

Rassegna Settimanale See FRANCHETTI, LEOPOLDO.

Rattazzi, Urbano (1808–1873)
parliamentary leader of the center-left liberals and prime minister

Rattazzi studied law at the University of Turin and practiced successfully before turning his attention to politics in 1847. Active in the local affairs of Casale Monferrato, Rattazzi drew up a petition urging King CHARLES ALBERT to institute the civic guard, a typical liberal demand on the eve of the REVOLUTIONS of 1848. He was elected to the first Piedmontese parliament in 1848 and served as minister of education, agriculture, and commerce in 1848–49. In parliament he sat with the constitutional Left and helped draw up the plan for the union of Lombardy and Piedmont, a union undone by Austria's defeat of Piedmont in 1849. In subsequent legislatures he emerged as leader of the center-left liberals. In that capacity, he formed the political alliance with Prime Minister CAVOUR known as the *connubio* (cohabitation). Subsequently criticized as a glaring example of unprincipled political opportunism that marked the start of the practice of TRANSFORMISM, the intent of the alliance was to prevent the conservative faction in parliament from passing legislation restricting freedom of the press. By collaborating with Cavour, Rattazzi differentiated himself from the extreme LIBERAL LEFT and from the parliamentary conservatives headed by LUIGI FEDERICO MENABREA. Rattazzi's relations with Cavour were often tense, as the two competed for the ear of King Victor Emmanuel II and the support of parliament. Rattazzi benefited from his close relationship with the king, who often turned to Rattazzi to contain Cavour. But Rattazzi also cultivated the democratic Left that opposed both Cavour and the king. His was a politically ambiguous and dangerous position that could easily be misunderstood by all sides. GIUSEPPE GARIBALDI misunderstood it in 1862 and 1867 when he calculated that, with Rattazzi serving as prime minister, the government would not oppose his attempts to seize Rome from the pope. Rattazzi's tardy disavowal of Garibaldi's attempts led to the disastrous clashes of Aspromonte and Mentana.

Rattazzi's equivocal behavior on those occasions lost him the support of both Left and Right, forcing him to resign as prime minister and permanently tarnishing his political reputation.

Rauti, Giuseppe Umberto (Pino)   See
ORDINE NUOVO.

Red Brigades
left-wing revolutionary group committed to political violence, active in the 1970s

The Red Brigades (Brigate Rosse) were a clandestine group of the extreme Left founded in Milan in 1969 by students and workers in revolt against the politics of accommodation and compromise pursued by the Communist Party (PCI). They were not the only group to adopt TERRORISM as a political tactic, but they were by far the best organized and most effective. From 1970 to 1988 the Red Brigades' several hundred members carried out more than 500 attacks on people and property, including murders and kidnappings. "Kneecappings" (shootings in the knees) against prominent political, business, law enforcement, and cultural figures became a favorite form of nonlethal violence perpetrated by *brigatisti*. Their most spectacular action was the 1978 kidnapping and murder of ALDO MORO. The violence aimed at destabilizing the Italian state, provoking an overreaction by the government or the political Right, discrediting the Communist Party, or possibly pressuring it into abandoning its policy of collaboration with the dominant Christian Democratic Party (DC). The Red Brigades believed that Italian society was ready for a communist revolution and that public opinion would support acts of revolutionary violence. Their inspiration came from the Italian RESISTANCE, Third World anticolonial movements, and the struggle that was then being waged by the Viet Cong for the liberation of Vietnam. Public sympathy for the Red Brigades waned as their level of violence escalated, and it became clear that the state was strong enough to resist their attacks. The murder of Aldo Moro was a decisive turning point. Loss of public support, defections by informants, new antiterrorist laws, and a strong antiterrorist response organized by General ALBERTO DALLA CHIESA resulted in the death, capture, arrest, and imprisonment of the most prominent leaders, including Renato Curcio (born 1941), a founder of the movement. By the early 1980s the Red Brigades' network was almost completely disrupted. Isolated acts of violence continued into the late 1980s, when the movement was no longer politically significant. In retrospect, the flare-up of violence epitomized by the Red Brigades appears as a last desperate effort by leftist extremists to salvage the myth of communist revolution.

Red Week

Red Week (*la settimana rossa*) of June 7–14, 1914, began with a series of demonstrations by anarchists, republicans, and revolutionary syndicalists to protest police shootings of workers and antimilitarist demonstrators in Ancona. PIETRO NENNI and BENITO MUSSOLINI were among its principal organizers. The socialist General Confederation of Labor called a general strike in support of the demonstrations. Without central organization, the violence spread spontaneously to various provinces of the MARCHES and EMILIA-ROMAGNA regions, where local revolutionary committees seized power, declared independent republics, issued their own currencies, abolished taxes, ransacked the homes of wealthy people, interrupted railways and telegraphs, and for several days held off troops sent to restore order. The Socialist Party (PSI) tried to disassociate itself from the violence, but its image as a dangerous revolutionary force was strengthened by the presence of socialists among the insurrectionists. The difficulty experienced by army and police in restoring law and order convinced members of the propertied classes and groups on the political Right that they should take steps to defend themselves from the violence of the Left. This type of political confrontation would escalate and set the stage for the rise of FASCISM after WORLD WAR I.

Redi, Francesco (1626–1698)
pioneer scientist, anatomist, and literary figure

Born in Arezzo into a family of the nobility, Redi first studied in Florence with the Jesuits, then went on to receive doctorates in philosophy and medicine from the University of Pisa in 1647. Redi is noted for his contributions to both science and literature. An accomplished linguist and avid collector of books and manuscripts, he soon came to the attention of the Grand Duke FERDINAND II who called him to his service as his own private physician and collector. Redi spent most of his adult life at the Florentine court where he used his influence and contacts to publicize the experimental methods of the new science. Redi experimented widely in all fields of natural science. His experiments on rotting carcasses disproved the then prevalent notion of spontaneous generation, showing that all forms of animal life are born from the eggs of other living animals of the same species. He studied the digestive system, blood circulation, intestinal parasites, insect reproduction, the properties of glass and crystals, and of salts. If he had a predilection, it was for the smallest forms of life, which he studied with the aid of the microscope. The study and practice of medicine took up much of his time, with great success and profit. His most important contribution to medicine was to challenge the prevalent practice of prescribing a multitude of substances to deal with illnesses. He argued that the best and safest approach was to limit prescriptions to a few, well-known remedies, whose effectiveness he confirmed by experimentation. He also showed that traditional remedies like administering violent laxatives and the bleeding of patients could do more harm than good. The physician, Redi argued, should limit himself to removing obstacles to the healing powers of nature. Redi's insights revolutionized the practice of medicine and laid the foundation of modern medical practice. He was also a literary stylist who presented his findings in elegant language that made science accessible and enjoyable for a broad literary public. Of his nonscientific writings, the best known is a 1,000-line poem entitled *Bacchus in Tuscany* (1685), an amusing description of the joys of wine drinking. Redi was fortunate enough to have his many talents amply recognized and rewarded in his lifetime. Although always in frail health, he lived into old age admired and revered by his contemporaries, and leaving a large fortune to his heirs.

regionalism

Regionalism is an ideology that calls for stronger regional governments and a smaller role for the national government. Unlike federalism, in which the power of constituent subnational entities, like the American states, is constitutionally protected, in regionalism, powers are delegated to regional administrations by the central government. Federalism gives the national government only those powers that are delegated to it by the constitution, others remaining within the purview of the state. The opposite is true in regionalism. Regionalism has been an issue in Italy since national unification. Regionalists argue that Italian regions are entitled to administrative autonomy by virtue of their diverse cultures and needs, distinct geographical characteristics, and their history as independent states before national unification. Regionalists also argue that devolving power to regional administrations will make for more democratic government and for the more efficient delivery of public services. Their arguments found little reception at the level of government after national unification, when it was feared that giving power to the regions might undermine the fragile unity of the new state. The Fascist regime rejected regionalism in principle as incompatible with the centralizing policies of the regime. Strong political support for regionalism emerged after World War II.

The issue of regionalism featured prominently in the discussions that preceded the adoption of the CONSTITUTION of the Italian republic in 1948. The constitution declared that the republic was "one and indivisible," but recognized the regions as autonomous entities entitled to certain constitutionally defined powers. The constitution listed SICILY, SARDINIA, the TRENTINO–ALTO ADIGE, FRIULI–VENEZIA GIULIA, and VALLE D'AOSTA as "special regions" entitled to administrative autonomy because of their linguistic, ethnic, and cultural characteristics. They were the first to receive their own councils, limited fiscal autonomy, and control over local administrations, police, schools, transportation, and land use. Administrative autonomy for the other 15 "ordinary regions" was delayed until the early 1970s when center-left governments began to carry out a process of administrative decentralization for the whole country. In 1975–77 parliament passed a series of laws that gave real powers to regional councils, including powers of taxation, economic planning, health, education, social services, and leisure activities.

Political parties control elected regional governments, sometimes singly, but mostly in coalitions of various parties. Regional politics have benefited minor parties like the Republican (PRI) and Social Democratic (PSDI), who do well by staying in touch with local needs and running locally popular candidates. The most vehement critics of regionalism come from the political Right. The Italian Social Movement (MSI) opposes regionalism as a threat to national unity and an encouragement to regional SEPARATISM. Such fears are confirmed by the separatist aspirations of some regionalists, like supporters of the NORTHERN LEAGUE, who have argued at times for breaking up the country into separate political units. However linked they may be politically, regionalism and separatism are conceptually distinct, and one need not lead logically to the other. The contrary argument is also made, namely, that regionalism strengthens national ties by reducing domestic frictions and making for more effective use of public powers.

religion See CATHOLIC CHURCH.

Renaissance

The Renaissance is a cultural phenomenon. Like all cultural phenomena, it cannot be dated pre-cisely, but the dates 1350 to 1550 may do as an approximation of its flowering in Italy. Those two centuries saw innovative trends in art, literature, political thought, and in the understanding of nature that are at the heart of Renaissance culture. It began in the city-states of central and northern Italy, Florence foremost among them. Towns offered resources and patrons for the artists and scholars who pioneered and developed the new trends. Together, they fostered the culture of HUMANISM, which sought to recover the culture of ancient Greece and Rome to forge new approaches to the problems of their time. The past provided the ideas and the models, hence the term Renaissance (*rinascenza* or *rinascimento* in Italian), which means rebirth.

Searching for ancient manuscripts and artifacts to recover the lost knowledge of the ancients became the passionate concern of humanists. The search was stimulated by the arrival of Greek scholars before and after the capture of Constantinople by the Turks in 1453. Renaissance culture acknowledged its debt to Greek and Islamic influences from Eastern Europe, but applied them creatively to deal with contemporary problems. The motive behind the interest in the classical past was the urgent need to address problems of government, social organization, population, and environment that Europeans faced after the wars, epidemics, and social and political breakdowns of the first half of the 14th century. As the traditional institutions of church and empire went into decline, and the feudal order approached its final phase, new forms of economic, political, and social life were poised to take over. The momentum shifted from the countryside to the towns, and Italian towns were ideally situated to take advantage of the new possibilities. A few, like GENOA, LUCCA, and SIENA, were relatively untouched by the new trends, but FLORENCE, MILAN, VENICE, ROME, and others as far south as NAPLES, reacted creatively.

It was to these towns that banking, manufacturing, and trade brought the wealth needed to sustain the work of thousands of artists and scholars. And it was the concentration of wealth in the hands of relatively few families that made private patronage of the arts possible. Renaissance culture would not have flourished without the patronage of families like the MEDICI of Florence, the ESTE of Ferrara, the MONTEFELTRO of Urbino, the GONZAGA of Mantua, the SFORZA of Milan, or the aristocratic families of Venice. Governments were also interested in encouraging the new culture. The role of government was nowhere more evident than in Rome. Starting with the pontificate of MARTIN V, popes patronized artists generously in their efforts to make the city attractive and revive the lucrative pilgrimage trade, which was the equivalent of modern tourism. What humanists did naturally reflected the needs of their patrons. Paintings and sculptures that were lifelike and true to nature caught the eye of the observers and flattered the patrons who were their subjects.

Whether the subjects were religious or profane, the new art techniques were a powerful tools of propaganda. The trend toward a more realistic representation of people and objects begins with the paintings of Giotto (ca. 1267–1337) and the sculptures of Nicola Pisano (1220–1287), reaching ultimate development in the works of TITIAN and MICHELANGELO. Perspective drawing, a notable advance of the period, owed much to the renewed study of mathematics and geometry. The study of anatomy was partly motivated by artists' desire to understand the human form from the inside out. In architecture, the inspiration of classical models and the development of new construction techniques gathered momentum in the centuries from BRUNELLESCHI TO PALLADIO. Architects and engineers, who were often one and the same, applied their talents to the design and construction of impressive churches, civic structures, and opulent private palaces.

Political philosophers and commentators thought of the state as a sovereign power driven by its own interests and needs, answerable to no higher authority, be it the CATHOLIC CHURCH or the HOLY ROMAN EMPIRE. This secular strain of political thought culminates in MACHIAVELLI, the first advocate of the modern state. Change was real, but not as rapid or as pervasive as we some-

times imagine. It did not affect all segments of society equally, and some it did not reach until centuries later. The good deportment and manners proposed by BALDASSARRE CASTIGLIONE and GIOVANNI DELLA CASA in their manuals of etiquette were meant not for ordinary folks, but for those who frequented princely courts. Among the arts, music was the last to feel the effects of the new culture, perhaps because of its ties with religious ritual. The secular madrigal and OPERA are innovations of the late 16th century. Even in the visual arts, religious themes dominated throughout the Renaissance, largely because the church and religious organizations were the most important patrons. Religion retained its popular appeal even as humanist scholars condemned the corruption of church and clergy. Florence in the 1490s experienced the revivalist movement led by GIROLAMO SAVONAROLA with its bonfires of the vanities, which included the works of humanist scholars and artists.

Thus, in many ways the culture of the Renaissance shows no clear break with that of earlier centuries. Early humanist figures like BOCCACCIO and PETRARCH saw themselves as improving upon rather than rejecting the earlier culture. New concepts of government also owed much to the medieval recovery of the legacy of ancient Roman law. In philosophy, Aristotelian influences remained as strong as in medieval times, although during the Renaissance they were challenged by rival systems drawing inspiration from the philosophy of Plato and other pre-Christian thinkers. Italian states and the state system that prevailed in the peninsula were propped up by methods and skills of diplomacy honed in the course of many centuries.

The crowning achievement of Renaissance diplomacy was the PEACE OF LODI, which sought to bring tranquillity to the peninsula by maintaining a balance of power among the principal states. The collapse of that equilibrium in the 1490s and the so-called Italian Wars, or Wars of Italy, that occurred intermittently from 1494 to the peace of CATEAU-CAMBRÉSIS (1559). ultimately undermined the structural foundation of the Italian Renaissance. While it lasted, the Renaissance did see a clustering and flowering of creative talent that begs explanation. Materialistic explanations, like that proposed by Karl Marx, who saw the Renaissance as the consequence of wealth accumulations attributable to Italy's lead in trade and business organization, draw attention to the material basis of Renaissance culture, but do not explain the phenomenon itself. The historian FRANCESCO GUICCIARDINI thought that the competition among city-states was a major cause of cultural creativity.

Undoubtedly the most influential study of the Renaissance is Jacob Burckhardt's *The Civilization of the Renaissance in Italy,* first published in 1860. In that seminal work, the Swiss historian attributed the greatness of Renaissance culture to the spirit of individualism that he saw as its animating force. In Burckhardt's analysis, the joyous rediscovery of the self and of the particular in nature was a conceptual breakthrough that changed the course of history, making the Renaissance the cradle of modern civilization. More recently, the German historian Hans Baron has argued in *The Crisis of the Early Italian Renaissance* (1955) that it was the threat to the survival of political liberty in Florence in the early part of the 15th century that stimulated public discourse over the nature and role of government, thus giving birth to what Baron called civic humanism. Other historians have looked at the humanist passion for collecting, describing, and classifying classical artifacts as the distinctive feature of the Renaissance. From that perspective, Renaissance culture was preoccupied primarily with making rational sense of the natural world, thus laying the intellectual foundations of modern science. No single theory seems capable of explaining the flowering of learning and artistic creativity that marked the Renaissance, while all seem to point to important contributing causes and features. Burckhardt's view may still be the most persuasive: the Renaissance, or the "early modern period" as historians now prefer to call that time in history, may indeed mark the beginning of modern western culture.

Reni, Guido (1575–1642)
painter of the Renaissance school in the post-Renaissance period

Reni was born in BOLOGNA and belonged to the school of art centered there. Inspired by Annibale Carracci (1560–1609), another Bolognese painter, Reni sought to strike the perfect balance between the expression of individuality and respect for the canons of classical art. Around 1602 Reni went to Rome, where he was captivated by recent archaeological discoveries of early Christianity. His paintings from this period show early Christian martyrs like St. Cecilia and St. Sebastian showing unflappable composure while undergoing torture. Portraying their classical serenity in the face of intense pain and emotion was Reni's way of expressing the "perfect idea" of art. His later paintings, carried out in Bologna and Genoa, are overtly religious and sentimental, showing devotional figures like the *Mater Dolorosa* and *Ecce Homo* typical of the popular piety associated with the CATHOLIC REFORMATION. Reni's art is often described as "academic" because of its deliberate and self-conscious striving for the ideal of perfection, understood as a synthesis of the profane and the religious, of the restrained and the expressive.

Repubblica (La) See JOURNALISM.

Republican Party See PRI.

Rerum novarum See LEO XIII.

resistance

Resistance to FASCISM took many forms and evolved in time. At the most basic level, many Italians resisted fascism by ignoring its precepts. The most common form of resistance had little to do with political ideology or organized activity. It expressed itself in daily behavior: the refusal to have large families, as the regime called for, or valuing peace over war. In a political context, however, the term *resistance* refers to the opposition that was organized politically and ideologically. In that specific sense, it operated openly as long as it could, and went underground in 1925–26 when the Fascist regime suppressed civil liberties. At that time, anti-Fascists who persisted in their opposition to the regime (many chose instead to retire from public life and keep silent) went underground in Italy or fled abroad. Most of those who stayed in Italy to fight the regime served jail terms, were confined to remote locations, or had their movements restricted and monitored. During the entire regime, about 5,000 dissidents were jailed, and about 10,000 sentenced to *confino*, which meant isolation in a remote community, usually in the South or the islands.

Internal resistance virtually ceased by 1932, but anti-Fascist exiles continued to oppose the regime from abroad. France, the Soviet Union, and the United States had the largest concentrations of anti-Fascist political exiles. The Anti-fascist Concentration, founded in France by PIETRO NENNI in 1927, appealed to anti-Fascists of all political persuasions who believed in fighting fascism by legal, nonviolent means. GIUSTIZIA E LIBERTÀ, founded by CARLO ROSSELLI, also in France, did not renounce violence and rejected cooperation with communists. Some 4,000 Italian anti-Fascists of all political persuasions fought against the forces of General Franco in the Spanish civil war (1936–39). Communists who found refuge in the Soviet Union agreed to cooperate with noncommunists only after the rise of Hitler in 1933 convinced them of the need to form a common front against fascism. Italian anti-Fascists in the United States found limited support among Italian-Americans, but were instrumental in turning American public opinion against the Fascist regime in the late 1930s.

Within Italy, discontent with the regime mounted in the late 1930s as Fascist FOREIGN POLICY embroiled the country in war. Armed

resistance developed during WORLD WAR II, after Mussolini was ousted from power, Italy surrendered to the Allies, and the Germans occupied most of the country. In NAPLES a popular revolt forced the Germans to evacuate the city after four days of street fighting (September 28–October 1, 1943). But it was in the central and northern regions of the peninsula, where the German occupation lasted until the very last days of the war, that the resistance had time to develop fully. Officers and troops from the disbanded army sometime took the initiative. Political exiles from abroad returned home to join or lead bands forming in the mountains. Cells known as *Gruppi di Azione Patriottica* (GAP) carried out guerrilla actions in the cities. One of these actions in Rome provoked a German reprisal known as the massacre of the FOSSE ARDEATINE.

The fighters came to be known as partisans (*partigiani*), meaning those who took sides standing up for their anti-Fascist beliefs. Young men and women joined the resistance to rid the country of diehard Fascists, expel German troops occupying the country, and give voice to the people. The resistance was thus simultaneously anti-Fascist, patriotic, and revolutionary. But the motivations varied, and many joined to avoid being drafted by the Fascists or being sent to Germany as forced laborers. For whatever motives, some 250,000 Italians took an active part in the resistance, while many times that number provided shelter and support for the partisans. The number of participants rose rapidly in the last weeks or days of the war, when as many as 500,000 may have taken part in the final operations.

Direction for the movement came from the Comitato di Liberazione Nazionale per l'Alta Italia (CLNAI), which represented the major political parties. The ACTION PARTY, Christian Democratic Party (DC), Communist Party (PCI), Liberal Party (PLI), and Socialist Party (PSI) were all represented, but the PCI was the most influential. In January 1944 the CLNAI declared itself the governing authority in German-occupied territory. The Allies and the Italian government in the South contested that claim, but eventually agreed to deal with the CLNAI as a de facto government in the North. In the summer of 1944 the resistance was strong enough to liberate sizable areas in the ALPS and APENNINES, but was forced to relinquish those gains by the slow pace of the Allied advance and by the onset of winter. The final surrender of German forces in northern Italy at the end of April 1945 enabled partisan formations to liberate many northern cities before the arrival of Allied troops.

The sense of pride shared by many Italians in the achievements of the resistance, its record of suffering and sacrifice, the fact that Italians of different political persuasions came together to fight against fascism, made the resistance a symbol of national resolve. The Italian republic celebrates the "values of the resistance" as the source of its commitment to political democracy and social justice. In the 1990s the "myth of the resistance" came under attack from several quarters. As the historian RENZO DE FELICE argued, since the danger of a Fascist resurgence was remote, antifascism was no longer a valid foundation of democratic ideology. The passage of time and the gradual disappearance of the generation that took part in the resistance are changing the landscape of politics and public life in Italy.

Respighi, Ottorino (1879–1936)
composer and conductor who turned Italy's musical attention from opera to symphonic music

Respighi was born in Bologna, studied at the Bologna music lyceum until 1899, and continued to study with Rimsky-Korsakov in St. Petersburg and Max Bruch in Berlin. Along the way, he assimilated a variety of influences, including the influence of Brahms, Debussy, and Richard Strauss. He served as professor of composition at the Santa Cecilia Academy in Rome from 1913 until his death and as musical director of that institute in 1923–25. In 1932 he was appointed to the ITALIAN ACADEMY, the highest

official recognition for artistic and professional achievement. His most famous compositions are the symphonic poems *The Fountains of Rome* (1917), *The Pines of Rome* (1924), and *Roman Festivals* (1929) that form an orchestral triptych. These compositions display to the fullest Respighi's talent for subtle orchestration and rendering of atmospheric effects. Although remembered primarily for his symphonic music, Respighi made various attempts to establish himself as an opera composer. From the comic opera *Re Enzo* (King Enzo) (1905), his first composition for the stage, to the posthumously performed tragic opera *Lucrezia* (1937) completed by his wife, he wrote a total of 11 compositions for voice, including the opera *La fiamma* (The flame, 1933), a medieval witch's tale that is considered to be his operatic masterpiece. In his vocal compositions Respighi sought the perfect fit between music and words, aiming for expressiveness rather than melodic appeal. Critics have acknowledged Respighi's talent for orchestration while faulting him for lack of originality, seeing him as an imitator rather than an originator. In the Italian musical tradition Respighi marks the point of departure from 19th-century melodic composition to 20th-century orchestral coloring and expressiveness.

Restoration (1815–1848)
The principles of legitimacy (government by established hereditary monarchies) and balance of power (no state strong enough to threaten the status quo) adopted by the CONGRESS OF VIENNA (1815) governed international relations during the Restoration period. This "Congress System," also called the "Concert of Europe," was designed to prevent the recurrence of revolution and war not by restoring the precise political arrangements that existed before the French Revolution, but rather by fostering respect for traditional institutions and conducting international relations in the spirit of nonideological diplomacy that had prevailed before the outbreak of the FRENCH REVOLUTION. Popular support for the sys-

tem would come from religion, which was the ultimate bond of society in the Restoration period. Applied to Catholic Italy, these principles meant restoring the monarchies deposed by NAPOLEON I, including the papal monarchy, making some territorial adjustments to discourage future French designs on the Italian peninsula, including strengthening the Austrian presence in northern Italy by making LOMBARDY and VENETIA part of the empire, and giving Austria the role of dominant power and policeman previously exercised by France. Restoration governments, while conservative in outlook, were not opposed to gradual change. Most governments experimented with administrative reforms for the sake of efficiency of government, encouraged educational reforms and economic innovation, and allowed limited freedom of expression. But they also feared that reforms would only whet the appetite for more change, and were unalterably opposed to revolution. They could not accommodate groups that challenged the principle of absolute monarchy, and that called for constitutions, government accountability, the expulsion of Austria, national independence and unity. The stability of Restoration Italy was seriously undermined by the presence of groups that called for some or all of these changes. SECRET SOCIETIES did so in the REVOLUTIONS of 1821 and 1831, prompting governments to adopt ever more restrictive policies and to rely ultimately on Austrian military power for their own survival. But the effectiveness of secret societies was limited by their own secret nature and by the justified fear that the masses would not support their call for change. GIUSEPPE MAZZINI broke through that barrier when he called for popular involvement and the adoption of democratic principles by the movement for national unification. Mounting dissatisfaction with Austrian dominance, resentment of governments seemingly deaf to calls for change, the election in 1846 of a seemingly liberal pope in the person of PIUS IX, encouragement of liberal reforms in the Kingdom of Sardinia and, finally, the success of revolution in Paris in February 1848, brought to Italy the revolutions of 1848–49 and the demise of Restoration government as envisaged by the Congress of Vienna.

revolutionary syndicalism

Revolutionary syndicalism derived from the doctrines of the French social theorist Georges Sorel and spread from France to Italy in the first decade of the 20th century. A version of socialism disavowed by most socialists, revolutionary syndicalism rejected historical materialism, stressed the motivational power of ideals ("myths," in their terminology) and called on workers to overthrow bourgeois society and capitalism by launching a general strike to paralyze production and bring down the state. Revolutionary syndicalists initially believed that workers organized in labor unions (*sindacati*) were the force most likely to carry out a socialist revolution. These ideas were propagated in Italy by ARTURO LABRIOLA and influenced some labor organizers, most notably EDMONDO ROSSONI, the future head of the Fascist labor movement. But the failure of the general strike of September 1904 and other labor setbacks convinced the revolutionary syndicalists that socialism lacked revolutionary potential. They concluded that the "myth" of nationalism carried a greater charge and was therefore more likely to lead to revolution. Revolutionary syndicalism's turn toward nationalism separated the ideology from the socialist tradition and launched it on the path of eventual encounter with FASCISM. AGOSTINO LANZILLO, PAOLO ORANO, and SERGIO PANUNZIO were revolutionary syndicalists who were later hailed as precursors of fascism. There were ideological similarities between revolutionary syndicalism and fascism. Both rejected bourgeois society, believed in revolutionary violence and in a strong economic role for the state. The Fascist regime developed or transformed revolutionary syndicalism into Fascist CORPORATISM. But corporatism benefited business more than labor, and Fascist ideology was more interested in national power and imperial expansion than in social justice. Mussolini was not a revolutionary syndicalist, and Rossoni, who had been at one time and retained the labor orientation of syndicalism, was forced out as head of the Fascist labor movement in 1928.

revolutions

Popular uprisings against government have punctuated modern Italian history. Directed against native and foreign powers alike, they occurred in protest against taxes, high prices, scarcity of food, military conscription, or for positive goals like national independence and unity, or in the name of ideologies promising a different political and social order. But not all popular uprisings rise to the level of full-scale revolutions. Although revolutions are often initiated by organized minorities and reach a majority of the people only in later stages, they must have some degree of popular support, a broad geographical base, and a program of change (ideology) that appeals to many different groups. Thus defined, revolutions are actually quite rare in the modern history of western nations, Italy included. In 1796–99 Italian JACOBINS succeeded in overthrowing governments with the help of the French. The changes that came to Italy during the Napoleonic era were revolutionary in many ways, but were handed down from above by NAPOLEON I and his officials.

The RISORGIMENTO was another matter. Although historians generally acknowledge that specific revolts and insurgencies of the struggle for national unification were generally the work of minorities, these minorities were active throughout the country, could count on some degree of support from different social groups, and raised questions of principle that affected the very nature of government and social relations. In 1820–21 revolutionaries in NAPLES, TURIN, and MILAN demanded constitutions to limit the power of absolute monarchs, and allow political representation and freedom of expression. In 1831 revolutions making similar demands broke out in PARMA, MODENA, and the PAPAL STATES. These revolutions were the work of liberals speaking for the tax-paying, educated middle classes, but also involved significant numbers of city workers. Educated Italians everywhere shared the desire for national independence that was demanded by the revolutionaries. GIUSEPPE MAZZINI's secret revolutionary network reached deep into Italian society from north to south. Peasants generally supported the traditional institutions of monarchy and religion, and showed little interest in the activities of middle-class liberals, but did not actively oppose revolution in 1820–21 and 1831. These revolutions were defeated not by lack of popular support, but by the military intervention from Austria.

The revolutions of 1848–49 presented Austria with a far more serious challenge as revolution broke out in many parts of the empire and in Vienna itself. Italy was engulfed by revolution from Sicily to the Alps, and hopeful revolutionaries hailed the advent of the "springtime of the people." Palermo gave the signal in January 1848, and its example was quickly followed by Naples, Milan, Venice, Florence, and Rome. From these centers revolution spread to the provinces and the countryside. Independence from foreign powers and constitutional government were once again the principal demands of the revolutionaries. The rulers of the Two Sicilies, Piedmont, and Tuscany, as well as the pope granted CONSTITUTIONS that promised representation and civil liberties. In the Five Days of Milan (March 18–22, 1848) insurgents forced Austrian troops to evacuate the Lombard capital. Venetians did likewise in their city. CHARLES ALBERT declared war against Austria (see WARS OF NATIONAL INDEPENDENCE), and his troops were joined by contingents of Neapolitan, Roman, and Tuscan troops. Republicans, monarchists, and VINCENZO GIOBERTI's neo-Guelfs joined the national crusade for independence. The revolution turned radical at the end of 1848, when PIUS IX was compelled to abandon Rome, and the ROMAN REPUBLIC was proclaimed. It took the combined forces of Austria, France, Naples, and

Spain to put down these revolutions. The revolutionaries did not achieve their objectives, but the events of 1848 left a lasting legacy that sustained the movement for national unification until its completion in 1870. For other movements of revolutionary character after national unification, see ANARCHISM, BRIGANDAGE, FASCISM, PCI, PSI, and RESISTANCE.

Ricasoli, Bettino (1809–1880)
Tuscan nobleman, Risorgimento figure, and Italian prime minister

This member of one of the oldest families of the Tuscan nobility divided his time between improving the family estate around the castle of Brolio in the Chianti region and working for political reform in the Grand Duchy of Tuscany. He transformed the Brolio estate into a model farm that he ran with almost military discipline. In Brolio, Ricasoli developed the formula that still governs the commercial production of Chianti wine. In public life he advocated constitutional government, economic and educational reforms. An early supporter of REVOLUTION in 1848, he broke with the democratic faction headed by FRANCESCO DOMENICO GUERRAZZI and retired to Brolio for the next decade, during which he once again devoted himself to agricultural improvements and land reclamation. Ricasoli returned to public life in 1859 as head of the provisional government that carried out the union of Tuscany with Piedmont, an important moment in the history of the RISORGIMENTO and a crucial step toward the political unification of the peninsula. He served as Italian prime minister after the death of CAVOUR in June 1861, but did not get along well with King VICTOR EMMANUEL II and stepped down in March 1862. Prime minister again in 1866–67, Ricasoli faced the double challenge of leading the country at war with Austria (see WARS OF NATIONAL INDEPENDENCE) and confronting a major fiscal crisis. An attempt to resolve the conflict between church and state, a matter of great concern to Ricasoli, foundered on the opposition of intransigent anticlericals in parliament. Called the Iron Baron because of his strong resolve, he struck many people as downright obstinate and intractable. A figure for moments of crisis, Ricasoli was poorly suited to the give-and-take of parliamentary politics. He played no public role after 1867, living out his last years in the solitude of Brolio.

Ricci, Matteo (1552–1610)
Jesuit missionary to China, noted mathematician, astronomer, and linguist

Ricci was born in Macerata, joined the JESUIT ORDER in 1571, and undertook missionary work in the Far East, where he served in India, Macao, and China, which he reached in 1582. Chinese officials showed interest in the samples of western technology, such as clocks, lenses, maps, and astronomical measuring instruments that Ricci had brought with him. The interest was reciprocal. A quick learner of languages, Ricci soon developed a command of the Chinese language and classics that improved his standing in China. But his attempts to enter the city of Beijing were rebuffed until 1601, when he was finally admitted into the imperial capital. In Beijing he served as court astronomer and mathematician, and translated western works of science into Chinese. He made some converts, founded the first Christian congregation in Beijing, corrected Chinese translations of Christian writings, and familiarized many educated Chinese with the precepts of Christianity. Educated Chinese respected him for his learning and for what many thought were magical powers. He developed a system of memorization ("the Memory Palace") that enabled Chinese students to excel in civil service exams required for careers in the imperial administration. His reports improved European knowledge of China and argued for acceptance of Confucian rites on the ground that Confucianism was not a religion, and that therefore Confucian practices were compatible with the Christian faith. In 1597 he was named superior of the Jesuit mission in China, where he ended his life.

Ricci, Scipione de' (1741–1820)
clergyman, bishop of Prato and Pistoia, and religious innovator

Born to a Florentine patrician family. Ricci studied for the clergy in Pisa and Rome, being influenced in the process by the reform ideas of JANSENISM. Appointed bishop of Prato and Pistoia in 1780 with the backing of Grand Duke PETER LEOPOLD, he took steps to improve the education of the clergy and stimulate lay interest in religious practices. These included a reform of religious orders, adoption of a new catechism, simplification of ritual, abolition of the cult of relics, reduction in the number of religious festivities, and the use of Italian instead of Latin for parts of the mass. In 1786 he prevailed on a diocesan synod to adopt resolutions that affirmed the autonomy of local churches from the pope and the authority of an ecumenical council over that of the pope. The grand duke supported Ricci's positions against the wishes of the pope, the majority of bishops, and of the faithful, but the grand duke's abdication in 1790 left Ricci without political support. Hostile demonstrations broke out, and Ricci was compelled to back down. The pope officially condemned Ricci's views in 1795 and Ricci reluctantly made a formal act of submission to papal authority in 1799. Ricci gave up all hope of reform in 1805 when it became clear that NAPOLEON I had no interest in promoting religious reform. Reforming clergy nevertheless took up Ricci's ideas, many of which were actually enacted in the 1960s by the church council of Vatican II.

Ricotti Magnani, Cesare See ARMED FORCES.

Rifondazione Comunista See ALEMA, MASSIMO D'; PCI.

Righi, Augusto See MARCONI, GUGLIELMO.

Rigola, Rinaldo See SYNDICALISM.

Rinnovamento Italiano See DINI, LAMBERTO.

Rinucccini, Ottavio See OPERA.

Risorgimento

The term Risorgimento (resurgence) expressed the hope of Italian patriots that Italy could regain its past strength and glory by becoming politically independent and united. Eighteenth-century writers who deplored the political divisions and economic backwardness of the Italian peninsula were the first to use the term in that sense. CAVOUR named his progressive newspaper *Il Risorgimento,* giving further currency to the term as the struggle for national independence got underway. It was left to MASSIMO D'AZEGLIO to define the Risorgimento as "the period that witnessed the affirmation of the unity and independence of Italy" (1866).

The complex events that constitute the Risorgimento make it difficult to date the movement, except in the narrowest political terms. Since the pursuit of political independence and unity implies the existence of a sense of national identity, the origins of the movement can be traced to the first literary sources that reflect similarities of language and culture. Nineteenth-century patriots regarded DANTE, founder of the Italian language, as the symbol of Italy's cultural unity. For them, culture came before politics. It is certainly the case that writers and literature have played an important role in defining an Italian identity. The most notable 18th-century writer to do so was VITTORIO ALFIERI, but ALESSANDRO MANZONI and GIOSUÈ CARDUCCI in the 19th century have at least an equal claim to the role of national inspirers. But while writers voiced an ideal that was shared by literate minorities, it was the FRENCH REVOLUTION and its Napoleonic aftermath that gave the movement a political dimension. Italian JACOBINS seized on the revolutionary ideals of liberty, equality, and fraternity to demand independence. The changes brought on by NAPOLEON I (1796–1814) reduced political divisions, introduced needed reforms, and provided Italians with military experience that would be put to use in the struggle for national independence. But French military conscription and taxation also provoked anti-French sentiments and intensified Italian desire for national independence.

The CONGRESS OF VIENNA (1815) ignored such expectations, divided the peninsula into eight separate states, and replaced French with Austrian domination. It thus set the stage for the movement for national independence that began with the REVOLUTIONS of 1821 and ended with the entry of the Italian army in ROME on September 20, 1870, and the proclamation of Rome as the capital of the united Kingdom of Italy. Between 1821 and 1870, the Risorgimento can be divided into three distinct phases. The first (1821–49) was dominated by SECRET SOCIETIES, principally the CARBONERIA, by the activities of GIUSEPPE MAZZINI and his YOUNG ITALY, rebellions that kept alive the ideal of independence, the temporary success and ultimate failure of the REVOLUTIONS of 1848–49. This preparatory phase is important for at least two reasons: It trained the generation that carried on the fight after 1848, and it brought the "Question of Italy" to the attention of Europe and America. In the second phase (1849–61) CAVOUR and the kingdom of SARDINIA took up the cause of Italian independence, alliance with France made possible a successful war against Austria (see WARS OF NATIONAL INDEPENDENCE), diplomacy set the pace, and GIUSEPPE GARIBALDI launched the daring expedition of the Thousand (1860) that made possible the unification of North and South. This was the heroic moment of the Risorgimento that became a cherished and inspiring memory of future generations.

The second phase concluded on March 17, 1861, when VICTOR EMMANUEL II was proclaimed king of Italy. Unity was not complete, however, because ROME was still under papal and VENETIA under Austrian rule. The acquisition of Venetia in 1866 (see WARS OF NATIONAL INDEPENDENCE) and Rome in 1870 completed the third and final phase of the Risorgimento (1861–70). Political unification was the principal aim, but many Italian patriots saw the Risorgimento as something more than political and territorial. The most radical envisaged the Risorgimento as a revolutionary event. It was to be a spiritual experience shared by all Italians, the making not just of a state with one government and one set of laws, but of a nation backed by the will of the people, the beginning of a new and glorious phase of national history harking back to the glories of ancient Rome and the Renaissance. The inability of the Italian state to live up to these high expectations became a burning political issue after unification. The difficulties that the new kingdom faced in pursuit of these goals marked the transition from the "era of poetry" of the Risorgimento period to the "era of prose" of post-Risorgimento Italy.

Rivista Enciclopedica Italiana See LA FARINA, GIUSEPPE.

Robilant, Count Carlo di See MEDITERRANEAN AGREEMENTS.

Rocco, Alfredo (1875–1935)
legal expert, social theorist, and Fascist legislator

Ranked among the most influential legislators of the Fascist regime, Rocco was both a scholar and political activist. He taught at the Universities of Parma, Urbino, Macerata, and Padua and published studies on commercial and penal law before turning to politics and emerging as a spokesman for the Italian Nationalist Association (see NATIONALISM) in 1914. An unrelenting critic of LIBERALISM, Rocco searched for the root causes of Italy's spiritual and political malaise in the Giolittian era. He did not blame Italy's weakness on GIOVANNI GIOLITTI, for whom he actually professed admiration, but rather on the principle of individualism that was at the core of liberal ideology. From that premise, Rocco went on to condemn capitalism, democracy, and socialism, which he saw as logical outgrowths of liberalism, and looked to the state as the necessary power needed to counteract the antisocial and centrifugal tendencies of individualism. In Rocco's thinking, individual rights had no basis in natural law, but were rather a concession that state law made to the individual. What the state gave, the state could take away; "reason of state" took precedence over individual rights. Rocco favored Italian intervention in WORLD WAR I on the side of the Entente powers to curb the power of Austria and improve Italy's chances of expansion in the Mediterranean and the Balkans. He was an unapologetic expansionist, who regarded imperialism as an unavoidable and desirable consequence of nationalism.

After the war, Rocco advocated the merging of the Nationalist Association and the Fascist movement, which he regarded as a more effective guardian of the authority and power of the state. He was elected to parliament as a Nationalist in 1921. BENITO MUSSOLINI appointed him to several posts in the government he formed after the march on Rome (1922–24), including the posts of undersecretary in the ministries of the treasury and finance. After the elections of 1924 Rocco was elected president of the Chamber of Deputies, and held that post until January 1925, when Mussolini appointed him minister of justice. It was in that capacity that Rocco made his most important contribution as primary architect of the Fascist regime. The legislative measures that he framed and pushed through parliament signaled the end of liberalism, gave all power to the state, and created the institutions through which the Fascist state could reach out, organize, and regiment the masses. Ironically, one of the casualties of Rocco's reforms was the Fascist Party itself, which lost its auton-omy and took its place as an institution subordinate to the government and to Benito Mussolini. Rocco could not have reached the position of power that he enjoyed without Mussolini's unconditional support. He enjoyed that support because Mussolini had faith in his judgment and loyalty; both believed that "everything must be within the state, nothing outside the state, and nothing against the state." That was the governing principle of the regime that Rocco more than anyone else was responsible for translating into law. His work done, Mussolini dismissed him from his post in July 1932. Rocco returned to academic life, as president of the University of Rome until his death.

rococo

The term rococo (rococcò in Italian) probably derives from the French rocaille and coquille (rock and shell), which were ornamental forms popular in Italian BAROQUE architecture. Although rococo is sometimes traced to the influence of GIAN LORENZO BERNINI, the taste for this type of ornamentation spread from France to the rest of Europe in the 18th century. In Italy it met the opposition of the classical school, which emphasized symmetry and simplicity and was particularly entrenched in Tuscany and Venice, and the prevalence of baroque architecture, which emphasized monumentality over prettiness. Thus, in Italy the inroads made by the rococo style were perceived as a decline of the standards of good taste and a sign of artistic decadence.

Romagna See EMILIA-ROMAGNA.

Romagnosi, Gian Domenico (1761–1835)
social philosopher, legal expert, economist, educator and legislator

Born in Salsomaggiore (Parma), Romagnosi studied in Piacenza and received a law degree from the University of Parma (1786), after which he practiced law, served in the judiciary, and pursued scholarly interests. His first publication, *Genesi del diritto penale* (Origins of penal law, 1791), provided a historical account of the state's emergence as sole dispenser of justice. In it, Romagnosi used the historical method to make the case for the principle of equality before the law, a principle that he deemed to be fundamental politically and socially. The title of his most influential work, *Introduzione allo studio del diritto pubblico universale* (Introduction to the study of universal public law, 1805), reflects Romagnosi's faith in the universal applicability of the law. Romagnosi's influence was greatest during the Napoleonic period when he taught law at the Universities of Parma, Pavia, and Milan. His support for NAPOLEON I and known preference for constitutional monarchy made him suspect in the eyes of the Austrian government of Lombardy during the RESTORATION. In 1817 he was deprived of his chair at the University of Milan. Allowed to teach privately, Romagnosi soon attracted a group of devoted reform-minded followers. The most notable personality among them was the young CARLO CATTANEO, who venerated Romagnosi as an inspirational figure without equal. Arrested on charges of treason after the REVOLUTION of 1821, Romagnosi defended himself capably on technical grounds and was released. Forbidden to teach, he continued to exert great influence through his writings. His conviction that knowledge had to be socially useful reflected Romagnosi's grounding in the thought of the ENLIGHTENMENT, but his interest in and teaching of GIAMBATTISTA VICO also showed that Romagnosi wanted to supplement the abstract rationalism of the Enlightenment with an understanding of the historical process. His far-ranging interests in law, government, and history appealed to a young generation of intellectuals poised between the culture of the Enlightenment and the emerging culture of ROMANTICISM. Romagnosi was the link between those two cultures and phases of history.

Roman Catholic Church   See CATHOLIC CHURCH.

Roman Inquisition   See INQUISITION, ROMAN.

Roman Question

Papal opposition to Italian unification was motivated by secular and religious concerns that are discussed under the heading of CHURCH AND STATE. The Roman Question stemmed from the seizure of church territory and assets by the Italian state in 1859–60. But these seizures did not deprive the papal government of all territory. ROME and its immediate environs remained under papal sovereignty until September 1870. The kingdom of Italy, founded in 1861, claimed Rome as its capital but refrained from taking the city as long as France, a Catholic power friendly to the pope, and whose diplomatic support was also important to the Italian government, was able to protect papal sovereignty over the city.

That changed when Prussia defeated France in the Franco-Prussian War of 1870. Taking advantage of the removal of French troops, the Italian army occupied Rome in September 1870, ending papal temporal power and forcing Pius IX to retreat to the Vatican enclave within the city. There he proclaimed himself a prisoner and refused the settlement offered unilaterally by the Italian government with the Law of Papal Guarantees (May 1871). That law guaranteed the pope political sovereignty, full freedom to exercise his powers as head of the CATHOLIC CHURCH, and compensation for seized property. The persisting papal refusal to recognize the Kingdom of Italy and papal prohibition against participation in national politics by Italian Catholics announced in the *non expedit* pronouncement of 1874 exacerbated feelings of anticlericalism among patriotic Italians. Papal policy aimed at regaining control of Rome by international diplomacy and pressure on the Italian government by Catholic powers, particularly by Austria-Hungary, which had also opposed Italian unification. It was partly to outmaneuver papal diplomacy and placate Austria-Hungary that Italy joined the TRIPLE ALLIANCE in 1882. Relations between Italy and the Vatican reached a low point in the 1880s and 1890s during the pontificate of LEO XIII with frequent and ugly confrontations by clericals and anticlericals in the press and in the streets.

Relations began to improve slowly under PIUS X, who did not renounce claims to Rome but did relax the *non expedit* enough to allow Catholics to vote selectively for candidates acceptable to the church from 1904 to 1913. Negotiations to resolve the Roman Question and other outstanding issues began in 1919. The Fascist government of BENITO MUSSOLINI took them up and, after laborious negotiations, concluded the Lateran Treaty and Concordat with the Holy See in February 1929. With the Lateran Treaty the Italian government recognized Roman Catholicism as the official religion of the state, the political sovereignty of the Holy See, and provided financial compensations to the papacy for its losses. The Concordat dealt with religious issues. It regulated the role of ecclesiastics in Italian society, recognized the legal validity and sanctity of religious marriages (thereby banning DIVORCE), allowed the teaching of Catholic doctrine in public schools, and acknowledged the legitimacy of Catholic nonpolitical youth organizations. Differences of interpretation over the role of youth organizations surfaced quickly, as did the divorce issue after WORLD WAR II, but for all intents and purposes the signing of the Lateran Treaty and Concordat put an end to the Roman Question.

Roman Republic (1798–1799)

This short-lived experiment in republican government, one of several occurring simultaneously in Italy, was a consequence of the first invasion of Italy by NAPOLEON I in 1796–97. The republic was proclaimed after the French seized the city in retaliation for the murder of a French general. Roman JACOBINS who supported the French proclaimed the republic, planted liberty trees, adopted a constitution, and passed legislation abolishing feudal obligations and curbing clerical power. Freedom of the press and of association allowed newspapers and political clubs to spring up in Rome and the provinces. Pope Pius

VI went into exile and died in France shortly thereafter. Sympathy for the pope facilitated the formation of the anti-Napoleonic coalition that defeated the French in the summer of 1799 and overthrew the republic. Papal rule was restored in 1800. When the French occupied Rome again in 1808 they were no longer interested in republicanism. France was by then a monarchy, Napoleon had the title of emperor, and Rome became part of the French empire. In 1811 Napoleon bestowed the title of king of Rome on his infant son and presumptive heir.

Roman Republic (1849)

This experiment in republican government was carried out in the context of the REVOLUTIONS of 1848–49. Only the government of the United States of America recognized the Roman Republic, but the republic proclaimed on February 9, 1849, attracted a great deal of international attention and was at the center of European politics for several months. Patriots from other parts of Italy and Europe came to Rome in the fall of 1848 after Roman conspirators assassinated Prime Minister PELLEGRINO ROSSI and Pope PIUS IX left the city. Many were attracted by the prospect of carrying on the revolution in Rome after suffering setbacks elsewhere. Prominent among the arrivals were GIUSEPPE MAZZINI and GIUSEPPE GARIBALDI. Their presence transformed an ordinary revolutionary event into a founding moment of the struggle for national independence. Mazzini took charge of politics and diplomacy, while Garibaldi emerged as its most colorful and charismatic military defender. The governing triumvirate introduced universal suffrage and civil liberties, encouraged popular participation in public life with rallies and ceremonies, provided work for the unemployed, and called the people to arms in defense of the republic. The republican constitution was the most democratic document to come out of the struggle for national unification. But the republic stood little chance against the combined forces of the antirevolutionary coalition. The defenders held at bay troops sent by France, Austria, Spain, and the KINGDOM OF THE TWO SICILIES until the first days of July 1849, when they were forced to leave the city or surrender. Garibaldi with several thousand volunteers left the city hoping to reach Venice, still holding out against the Austrians, but was forced to disband the surrounded remnants of his force on the territory of the REPUBLIC OF SAN MARINO. The republican experiment was an important episode in the history of the RISORGIMENTO: it set a democratic precedent for others to follow, served as a training ground for many of its leaders, added to the roster of martyrs, and showed that there were Italians willing to fight for their national independence.

romanità See FASCISM; ROME, CITY OF.

Romano, Giulio See MANNERISM.

romanticism

Rejecting the abstract reasoning, materialism, and determinism of ENLIGHTENMENT culture, romanticism valued instead individual spontaneity and creativity, the emotional nature of human beings, validity of spiritual values, appeal of religion, cult of historical traditions and institutions, the uniqueness of national cultures and identities. Romanticism and classicism denoted different kinds of sensibilities that found expression in literature and the visual arts. Classicism, associated with the Enlightenment, valued clarity, balance, composure, and restraint, while romanticism looked for the fantastic, the extreme, and the enigmatic.

There was room for diversity within romanticism, depending on which themes and traits were emphasized and how they were related to one another. For instance, the cult of history and tradition could exalt the role of traditional institutions like the monarchy and the CATHOLIC CHURCH, or of national character carried by lan-

guage, popular customs, and folk culture. In the former case, the result could be intransigent conservatism, in the latter a revolutionary attitude bent on gaining cultural and political independence for nationalities under foreign rule, like the Italian. The Savoyard philosopher Joseph de Maistre (1754–1821) spoke for intransigent conservatives when he upheld traditional monarchy and religion against all forms of change, while Italian patriots revered the equally religious ALESSANDRO MANZONI, who found in Catholicism the key to the Italian national character.

Although contemporaries saw a precursor of romanticism in the Neapolitan GIAMBATTISTA VICO, romanticism was born in England and Germany. It was a product of the northern European imagination that reached Italy in 1816 with the publication of Madame de Staël's essay *Sulla maniera e l'utilità delle traduzioni* (On the manner and usefulness of translations). The essay urged Italians to familiarize themselves with the writings of other nations in order to enrich their own culture. Romanticists welcomed the advice as a way of restoring dynamism to what they perceived to be a static culture, while classicists resented it as a slur on the dominant Italian tradition of classical letters. In the ensuing controversy, romanticists fought an uphill battle against the classicists entrenched in the schools and in the world of letters. Romanticism was never the uncontested master of literature and the arts in Italy. The influence of classicism is evident even on writers like UGO FOSCOLO and GIACOMO LEOPARDI, who do display traits of the romantic imagination, but whose carefully crafted, austere style shows more classical restraint than romantic effusion.

Romantic sensibility was nevertheless very much in evidence among educated Italians of GIUSEPPE MAZZINI's generation, who turned the romantic cult of individual self-expression into a call for political revolution. All major Italian writers of the romantic period, including ALEARDO ALEARDI, GIOVANNI BERCHET, GIUSEPPE GIUSTI, GIOVANNI BATTISTA NICCOLINI, SILVIO PELLICO, and NICCOLÒ TOMMASEO, contributed with their writings to the movement for Italian independence (see RISORGIMENTO). Italian romanticism thus took on revolutionary connotations that made the whole movement politically suspect in the eyes of conservatives. Austrian authorities quickly shut down the Milanese weekly *Il Conciliatore* (1818–19) because it sided with the romanticists in literary matters. Its repression in turn encouraged its supporters to become political conspirators, thus contributing to the REVOLUTIONS of 1820–21. In Italy, romanticism assumed a politically revolutionary role that it generally did not have in northern Europe, where romanticists tended to avoid politics or split evenly in opposite camps.

Rome, city of

Rome (pop. 2.6 million) is the capital of Italy and of the region of LATIUM. Italy's most populous and largest city lies on the banks of the Tiber River, approximately 25 miles from the sea and the ancient port city of Ostia. Tradition dates the founding to 753 B.C., by Latin-speaking settlers who early on showed a tendency to seize territory, livestock, and women from their neighbors. It emancipated itself from Etruscan domination in 509 B.C., when it replaced the monarchy that had ruled it from the founding with a republican form of government. By around 260 B.C. it controlled most of the Italian peninsula. It then turned its attention to the rival powers of Carthage and the Greek city-states, defeating the Carthaginians in the Punic Wars (264–146 B.C.) and the Greeks in the Macedonian Wars (215–168 B.C.). Those victories gave Rome control of most of the MEDITERRANEAN SEA and opened the way to further expansion. The Roman Empire, proclaimed by Augustus, who ruled from 27 B.C. to A.D. 14, lasted for almost 500 years and stretched from the British Isles to the Persian Gulf. Rome was the imperial capital until A.D. 331, when Emperor Constantine moved the capital to Byzantium on the Bosporus. For many centuries Rome was the largest and most polyglot city of the ancient world, with approximately 1 million inhabitants in the third century

A.D., when it was surrounded by the Aurelian Walls, that today mark the periphery of the center of the city.

Its decline began the following century and continued in the fifth and sixth centuries. The Christian bishops of the city halted the decline, reorganized the city, and made it the seat of the PAPACY. Most notable in that respect was the pontificate of Gregory I (590–604), during which Rome asserted its independence from what remained of the imperial power and guided the spread of Christianity in western Europe. As the seat of the papacy and center of the Roman Catholic Church, Rome regained some of its former importance. Under papal rule, Rome became a political as well as a spiritual power in the Middle Ages and a center of culture during the RENAISSANCE. It remained subject to the power of the papacy until 1870. Association with empire and papacy has made Rome an irresistible symbol of power and greatness. Artists, pilgrims, and tourists of all conditions and descriptions have flocked to the city, attracted by its artistic and religious treasures. Italian patriots hoped that the Rome of the People would follow in the glorious footsteps of the Rome of the Caesars and the Rome of the Popes. The ROMAN REPUBLIC of 1849 was an attempt to make that vision a reality. In 1862 and 1867 GIUSEPPE GARIBALDI tried and failed to take the city by force. The army took the city in September 1870 against the token military resistance and vehement moral protest of the papacy (see ROMAN QUESTION).

Rapid population growth brought the problems of urban congestion, inadequate public services, and municipal corruption to the capital. It adjusted gradually to its role as national capital, relying heavily on government employment and tourism as its economic mainstays. FASCISM made *romanità* (cult of Roman greatness) an integral part of its ideology and popular appeal, transforming parts of the city to highlight the relics of its ancient imperial past. The city experienced its greatest expansion after World War II without changing its traditional economic base. Industrial manufacturing has never been important, but building construction, food processing, publishing, and entertainment, especially film-making, are economically significant. Rome is also an important cultural center, with some of the world's richest museums and galleries, the public University of Rome (*La Sapienza*), the private Catholic University, and the Technical Institute (*Politecnico*).

Rome, Treaties of See EUROPEAN UNION; FIUME; PARIS PEACE CONFERENCE.

Romiti, Cesare See FIAT.

Rosa, Salvator (1615–1673)
unconventional artist whose style and adventurous life appealed to the romantic imagination

Rosa was born in Arenella (Naples) to a family of painters, pursued no regular course of studies, and worked mostly in Naples, Rome, and Florence. His imagination was receptive to the influence of northern European artists, evident in his fantastic landscapes of menacing forests and cliffs, which he may have painted on the spot. He is considered an innovator in landscape painting, but landscapes were not his sole interest. Animated battle scenes, witches, bandits, and anything dark and mysterious, appealed to his imagination. His works reveal a tormented view of nature and humanity, at odds with the idealized representations of classical artists of his time. Frantic movement, violence, and mystery are hallmarks of Rosa's art. As a writer he is remembered for his *Satires*, which ridiculed prevalent tastes in music and painting, popular vices, papal corruption, and war. His attacks on the academic culture of his time and an unstable temperament made him many enemies, who disparaged his abilities as a painter and leveled against him charges of immorality. Later generations saw him as the prototype of the romantic genius, highly original, individualistic, and creatively unconventional.

Salvator Rosa *(Library of Congress)*

Rosmini-Serbati, Antonio (1797–1855)
liberal Catholic theologian and political philosopher

Rosmini was born in Rovereto (Trent), completed his studies at the University of Padua, and was ordained into the priesthood in 1821. In 1828 he founded the Institute of the Brethren of Charity (Rosminians), a religious order devoted to education and charity, which received papal approval in 1839. But Rosmini's fame rests largely on his writings, starting with his *Nuovo saggio sull'origine dell'idee* (New essay on the origin of ideas, 1830), which addressed the issue of the nature of knowledge. Starting with the innate concept of being, Rosmini concluded that knowledge revealed by faith is valid because it is planted in the human mind by God. From that philosophical premise, Rosmini proceeded to develop a plan for the renovation of society. The power of the state was to be limited to the protection of individual rights, the role of the family, and the preservation of private property. The body of the faithful should choose the leaders of the CATHOLIC CHURCH by popular election. This was the message of his controversial *Delle cinque piaghe della chiesa* (The five wounds of the holy church, 1848), which was condemned and placed on the INDEX. The JESUIT ORDER led the attack against Rosmini, who was accused of holding Jansenist doctrines incompatible with clerical authority. Rosmini also envisaged a role for the pope as permanent head of a federation of Italian states, a view shared by VINCENZO GIOBERTI and closely associated in 1848 with the idea of national revolution. But Rosmini was no revolutionary, and generally shied away from public life. A diplomatic mission that he undertook in 1848 at King CHARLES ALBERT's request to mediate a dispute with Pope PIUS IX failed. After the assassination of PELLEGRINO ROSSI in 1849, Rosmini turned down an invitation to head a papal government. His moderate views pleased neither revolutionaries nor conservatives. Revolutionaries feared that the democratic reforms that he proposed might strengthen the church that they wanted to topple, while conservatives feared that the same democratic reforms would hasten the downfall of the church. The philosophical current of neo-Thomism, which sought to apply the teachings of Thomas Aquinas to modern society, was in part a reaction to Rosimi's challenge to the church.

shared those sentiments but, while Nello expressed his politics in scholarship, Carlo chose the course of active participation in politics. Nello published important works on MICHAEL BAKUNIN and Mazzini (1927) and CARLO PISACANE (1932). Like the historian GAETANO SALVEMINI who influenced them, both brothers adopted a form of democratic socialism that kept them apart from the socialist mainstream in Italy. In 1925, after the murder of GIACOMO MATTEOTTI, Carlo joined Salvemini, ERNESTO ROSSI, and other anti-Fascists to found the review *Non Mollare!* (Don't Give Up!). In 1926 he collaborated with the socialist PIETRO NENNI on *Il Quarto Stato* (The Fourth Estate), another short-lived but influential anti-Fascist publication. In 1927 he was tried for having planned the flight abroad of socialist leader FILIPPO TURATI. Jailed, Carlo escaped to France in 1929. In France he published *Socialismo liberale* (Liberal socialism, 1930), an eloquent statement of his political creed. Soon after his arrival in France, Carlo also launched the movement Giustizia e Libertà (Justice and Liberty), an alliance of republicans and democratic socialists that attracted some of the most illustrious figures of the noncommunist opposition to FASCISM. A volunteer fighter against Franco in the Spanish civil war, where he was wounded, Rosselli regarded the armed fight against fascism as a prelude to armed opposition to fascism in Italy. Both brothers were high on the list of enemies of the regime. Members of an extreme right-wing group with ties to the French secret service assassinated both brothers in Normandy, where they were vacationing together.

Rosselli, Carlo (1899–1937), and Rosselli, Nello (1900–1937)
anti-Fascist activists and political exiles, assassinated by Fascist agents in France
The Rosselli brothers were born in Rome to a distinguished Jewish family from Tuscany that in the 19th century had befriended GIUSEPPE MAZZINI and identified with the tradition of republican, democratic politics. Both Carlo and Nello

Rossellini, Roberto (1906–1977)
film director, writer, and television producer
Rossellini was born to an upper-class Roman family. The son of a builder of movie houses, he was drawn to the world of cinema from an early age. In the late 1930s he turned to scriptwriting and filmmaking. Well-connected in Roman circles, he was part of the group of young actors and directors that gravitated to Vittorio Mus-

solini, the Duce's son. He directed a trilogy of war films, including *La nave bianca* (Hospital Ship, 1942), which combined a semi-documentary style with the sentimentalism of a love story. It was a harbinger of things to come, as Rossellini was eager to move away from the heroic tone of Fascist cinema and determined to find a new voice shorn of rhetoric and close to the lives of ordinary people. The postwar trilogy, *Roma città aperta* (Rome, Open City, 1945), *Paisà* (1946), and *Germania anno zero* (Germany Zero Year, 1947) established Rossellini as the most original figure of Italian cinema. With their gritty depictions of life amid the ruins of WORLD WAR II, these films inaugurated the era of Neorealism and set the tone for the most notable achievements of Italian cinema in the postwar era. But Rossellini was never entirely at ease with Neorealism. Perhaps it was the intellectual influence of BENEDETTO CROCE's idealism that made him leery of the materialistic premises of Neorealism. The films that Rossellini made in the late 1940s show him in a more introspective mood, intent on exploring the private lives and psychological mechanisms of his characters. The most notable and controversial film of this period was *Stromboli, terra di Dio* (Stromboli, 1950), which dealt with the theme of adultery and featured the actress Ingrid Bergman, with whom Rossellini was carrying on a notorious affair. By then Rossellini had become a public figure. Due both to his success as a film director and his private escapades, his life was the subject of intense curiosity and scrutiny by the media. His later films met with far less box office success than his earlier ones. *Il generale Della Rovere* (General Della Rovere, 1959), starring VITTORIO DE SICA, a film that told the story of a wartime impostor who ended up a hero in spite of himself, was one of his last productions for the theater. In the 1960s Rossellini turned his attention to French and Italian television, for which he made several historical documentaries on prominent figures and moments of western civilization. At the time of his death he was working on a television biography of Karl Marx.

Rossi, Alessandro (1819–1998)
industrialist, economic protectionist, and philanthropist

Born in Schio (Vicenza), at age 20 Rossi took over from his father as manager of the family woolen manufacturing business, enlarging it and transforming it into a leading producer of woolen textiles. In the first decades of national unification, Rossi personified the successful captain of industry who, from modest beginnings, rose to prominence with hard work and ingenuity. He was among the first to transform a family venture into a shareholding enterprise that raised capital through the stock market. That decision enabled his firm to weather the economic downturn of the early 1870s and made him an advocate of large-scale manufacturing. Rossi called for protective tariffs to preserve national markets for domestic producers, especially against French and American competitors gaining footholds in Italy. Economic protectionism made Rossi an ally of those political groups of the LIBERAL LEFT concerned with job protection, but not a supporter of their leader, FRANCESCO CRISPI, who was distrusted by Rossi. With others on the constitutional Left, Rossi carried on a dialogue to explore the possibilities of an alliance of business and labor in the interests of national production. Sensitive to the problem of class tensions, Rossi sought ways of alleviating the plight of workers. To that end, he launched philanthropic enterprises in his mills, encouraged workers to save, and backed private charities. His paternalism was rather the exception than the rule among Italian entrepreneurs of his generation.

Rossi, Ernesto (1897–1967)
anti-Fascist activist, social democrat, economist, and political commentator

Rossi was born in Caserta (Naples), the son of an army officer. Of strong patriotic sentiments, Rossi advocated Italian intervention in WORLD WAR I. He studied law in Florence and taught economics. He joined the anti-Fascist movement in 1923, working with CARLO ROSELLI and NELLO

ROSSELLI, GIOVANNI AMENDOLA, RICCARDO BAUER, and GAETANO SALVEMINI, with whom he was particularly close. His economic interests also drew him close to LUIGI EINAUDI, to whose review *Riforma Sociale* Rossi contributed articles. He was a cofounder and militant member of Carlo Rosselli's Giustizia e Libertà. His attempt to organize armed resistance to FASCISM within Italy led to his conviction and sentencing, along with Bauer, to a 20-year prison term. He spent 13 years in jail and political confinement, until liberated in 1943 after the fall of the regime. After the war he was undersecretary for reconstruction in the government of FERRUCCIO PARRI. His most important postwar role, however, was as a public debater and writer. Critical of big business, the CATHOLIC CHURCH, and the dominant Christian Democratic Party (DC), Rossi was an outspoken and effective critic of government inefficiency and corruption. *L'Astrolabio,* a respected monthly review that he launched in 1963, was his last journalistic venture. Rossi was widely admired for his political independence and forthright denunciations of public mismanagement.

Rossi, Pellegrino (1797–1848)

law expert, economist, diplomat, active in Swiss, French, and Italian politics

Rossi was born in Carrara (Tuscany), and studied and taught law at the University of Bologna (1812–14). In favor of Italian independence, he served the government of JOACHIM MURAT as commissary general in the Romagna. In that capacity he drew up Murat's proclamation of March 30, 1815, promising Italian independence in return for support in his fight against Austria. Murat's defeat a few days later persuaded Rossi to seek refuge in Switzerland, where he became a citizen (1820) and served in the Swiss diet (1820–33). His proposal for a new constitution for the Swiss federation (1832) attempted to reconcile the autonomy of the cantons with a stronger federal government. The proposal was rejected, and Rossi left for France, where he taught political economy at the Collège de

France (1834) and served as French ambassador at the papal court (1845–48). King Louis Philippe bestowed on him the title of count in recognition of his distinguished diplomatic service. The REVOLUTION of 1848 and the overthrow of Louis Philippe marooned Rossi in Rome, where he put himself at the service of Pope PIUS IX with the intention of furthering the liberal reforms promised by the pope at the start of his pontificate. First as minister of the interior in charge of the police (April 1848), then as prime minister (September 1848), he attempted to enact administrative reforms to make government more representative without compromising the principle of papal power. His compromise approach pleased neither absolutists nor democrats. A political realist to the bone, Rossi did not hide his contempt for popular agitators and politicians. Democratic conspirators assassinated him on November 15, 1848, while he was on his way to present his proposals to the Roman parliament. One of the more amazing political careers of 19th-century Europe thus ended in tragedy. Rossi's death was the last straw for Pius IX, who fled from Rome a few days later, leaving the city and the revolutionaries to their fate.

Rossini, Gioacchino Antonio (1792–1868)

operatic composer and stage director notable for melodic inventiveness and sense of theater

Rossini was born in Pesaro, then under papal rule, to a family that had some connections with the musical world. His parents were itinerant operatic performers in provincial theaters and the young Rossini grew up in the world of entertainment. A recalcitrant student, Rossini had little regular schooling but developed an interest in music after his father taught him to play the horn. In his early teens Rossini studied at Bologna's Music Lyceum where his musical talent was recognized. His first opera, *La cambiale di matrimonio* (The promise of marriage, 1810) was produced in Venice. Rossini's debut coincided with the crisis of traditional *opera seria* that dealt with classical subjects, relied on simple orchestration, and showed little interest in character delineation and development. Sheer melodic beauty, orchestral brilliance, choral effects, scenic appeal, and attention to character were very evident in *Tancredi* and *L'italiana in Algeri,* both produced in Venice in 1813. They were followed by the perennially popular *Barber of Seville* (1816), which is considered his masterwork. With these operas Rossini captured the admiration of both the public and critics and became the dominant figure of the operatic stage. His sparkling, light-hearted music, devoid of political overtones, pleased a public seeking respite and diversion from the drama of the Napoleonic Wars and their aftermath. In 1822 Rossini married the soprano Isabella Colibran (1785–1845) and left Italy for Vienna, where he was acclaimed. In 1824 he went to Paris to direct the Théâtre des Italiens. In Paris he composed at the request of King Charles X, who was one of Rossini's admirers and who granted him a life pension. The last opera that he wrote, *William Tell,* was produced at the Paris Opera in 1829. In the next four decades he produced some minor vocal and instrumental works. Basking in his reputation as a musical genius, Rossini devoted himself mainly to entertaining lavishly in his luxurious Paris apartment, proffering advice to younger composers, enjoying grand cuisine, and gaining a great deal of weight in the process. Although he took no discernible interest in political causes, including that of Italian unification, united Italy claimed him as one of Italy's glories and buried him in the Church of Santa Croce in Florence, alongside other prominent Italians. An incredibly prolific composer, in the short span of his productive life Rossini composed over 40 operas.

Rossoni, Edmondo (1884–1965)
revolutionary syndicalist and Fascist labor leader

Rossoni, born in the province of Ferrara, was formed by the tense labor relation and sur-charged politics of his native Romagna region. He emerged as a local strike leader in 1904, moved on to Milan, and in that city joined the group of revolutionary syndicalists gathered around ARTURO LABRIOLA. Always at the forefront of the labor struggle, Rossoni regarded the national General Confederation of Labor (see CGII) and the Socialist Party (PSI) as too prone to compromise with management. Rossoni was indifferent to theoretical issues and unalterably opposed to parliamentary politics, but he was a tireless propagandist and an inflammatory speaker in front of peasant and worker audiences. Vehement condemnations of bosses, priests, politicians, and patriotism were the staples that he pitched regularly and with great success. He left the country in 1908 to avoid facing a variety of charges that would have sent him to jail. In France, Brazil, Canada, and the United States he was an active organizer of Italian emigrants. Rossoni admired the tactics of the Industrial Workers of the World (Wobblies) and supported the 1912 labor strike in the mills of Lawrence, Massachusetts. The New York Italian-language newspaper *Il Proletario* was his mouthpiece. But his experiences in the United States also convinced him that workers could gain from aggressive negotiating tactics like those practiced by the American Federation of Labor. Another American lesson was that there was little substance to the Marxist notion of the international solidarity of workers. Workers, according to Rossoni, were nationalists at heart, and therefore more likely to bond with other workers of the same nationality and to regard others as competitors.

He returned to Italy in 1914 in a chastened mood, skeptical that workers could pull off a successful revolution, and open to the notion that war might do what the workers could not. Thus, he favored Italian intervention in WORLD WAR I, supported the interventionist campaign of BENITO MUSSOLINI, and embarked on the path that would eventually bring him and his movement to FASCISM. The formal merger occurred in January 1922, when Rossoni and his followers joined the Fascist Party. Rossoni's decision to merge may have been motivated by the desire to prevent fascism from being dominated by its conservative supporters. Rossoni hoped to give the labor movement that he led a decisive voice in the Fascist system, but what he encountered instead was systematic and effective opposition not only from business but also from competing personalities and currents within fascism itself. Opposed by GIUSEPPE BOTTAI, ROBERTO FARINACCI, and party secretary AUGUSTO TURATI, and regarded with suspicion by Mussolini, Rossoni fought a losing battle. In 1928 he was forced to resign as head of the regime's principal labor union, the General Confederation of Fascist Syndicates. Rossoni continued to serve the regime in various capacities. He was a member of the Fascist Grand Council (1930–43), undersecretary of state (1932–35), and minister of agriculture and forestry (1935–39). In that last capacity he contributed to the implementation of the economic campaign in pursuit of AUTARKY. But Rossoni's ability to influence the social orientation of the Fascist regime ended in 1928 with his dismissal as head of the labor movement. On July 25, 1943, he voted for the Fascist Grand Council motion that called for Mussolini's resignation. After the war, he lived quietly in the resort town of Viareggio.

Rota, Nino See OPERA.

Rovani, Giuseppe See SCAPIGLIATURA.

Rubattino, Raffaele (1810–1881)
*shipping industry pioneer, patriot, and
advocate of colonial expansion*
Rubattino was born in Genoa to a well-off merchant family. He completed his secondary education in his native city, joined Mazzini's YOUNG ITALY, and started several business ventures that also served his political interests. His interest in maritime commerce began as an insurer in 1837.

He founded his own shipping company in 1838, and in 1841 started a transportation business between Genoa and Milan. In addition to moving people and goods, Rubattino also smuggled propaganda and political suspects. He was the first Italian ship owner to commit his company to steam navigation. After expanding his activities in the Mediterranean until 1848, Rubattino looked to the Atlantic trade. With the help of Cavour and financial subsidies from the Piedmontese government, in 1852 Rubattino launched the Transatlantic Shipping Company. The merger of Rubattino's company with the shipping business run by the Florio family of Sicily resulted in the formation of *Navigazione Generale Italiana* (1881), Italy's largest shipping organization. Rubattino never separated his business from his political interests. One of his ships transported CARLO PISACANE's ill-fated expedition of 1857 to Naples, and two of his ships transported GIUSEPPE GARIBALDI's Thousand on their luckier venture to Sicily in 1860. Rubattino's degree of complicity in these ventures is still the subject of debate. In 1869 Rubattino purchased the Bay of Assab concession on the Red Sea that, when acquired by the government in 1882, served as the point of penetration for Italian COLONIALISM.

Rudinì, Antonio Starabba, marchese di
(1839–1908)
*Sicilian patriot and political figure of the
conservative Right*
Marchese di Rudinì was born in Palermo to a family of the Sicilian aristocracy. Compromised with the Bourbon government by his participation in the Sicilian uprising of April 1860, he had to leave the island before the arrival of GIUSEPPE GARIBALDI's Thousand that ended Bourbon rule. Appointed to posts in the Italian foreign ministry after national unification, he left that ministry in 1864 to serve as the elected mayor of Palermo. In that capacity he emerged as the man of law and order who was instrumental in putting down the

popular uprising of September 1866, when pro-Bourbon insurgents took temporary control of the city. That same year he was appointed prefect of the city in recognition of his role. In 1868 he was appointed prefect of Naples. Elected to parliament, he sat with the Historical Right, which he led after the death of MARCO MINGHETTI in 1886. Rudinì emerged as an outspoken critic of his fellow Sicilian FRANCESCO CRISPI, whom he succeeded as prime minister. His government (February 1891–May 1892) reduced expenditures, opposed colonial expansion, and renewed the TRIPLE ALLIANCE while trying to improve relations with France, which had seriously deteriorated under Crispi. He succeeded Crispi as prime minister for a second time after Italy's defeat at ADOWA in March 1896, and again renounced colonial expansion, reduced expenditures, and endeavored to improve relations with France. He was in office when the popular uprisings of May 1898 (FATTI DI MAGGIO) broke out. His severe repression of these disturbances, reminiscent of his actions in 1866, turned against him both the Left and the Right in parliament. The Left blamed him for the repression, and the Right for the alleged permissiveness that they claimed had promoted the uprisings. He resigned as prime minister in June 1898, but retained his seat in parliament until the end of his life.

Ruffo, Cardinal Fabrizio See
PARTHENOPEAN REPUBLIC.

Russo, Vincenzo (1770–1799)
Neapolitan jurist and revolutionary influenced by the ideas of the Enlightenment

Russo was born in Palma Campania (Naples), studied in seminary, and received a law degree from the University of Naples. A political radical of republican convictions, he joined societies sympathetic to the FRENCH REVOLUTION. Arrested in 1794, he escaped jail by revealing some details of his activities, then sought refuge in Milan and Switzerland. He returned to Italy in 1796 in the wake of NAPOLEON's first invasion, distinguishing himself among Jacobins in Rome and Naples for his republican fervor and journalistic writings. In Rome he wrote his most important work, *Pensieri politici* (Political thoughts, 1798), in which he grounded his defense of republicanism as the only democratic form of government in a philosophy of human nature based on the ideas of Jean-Jacques Rousseau. But Russo was not content with mere theoretical speculation. Also interested in the practical application of political theories, he sought to influence public opinion, and participated in the work of the legislative commission that was preparing the constitution of the PARTHENOPEAN REPUBLIC. High on the list of enemies of the Bourbon regime, he was arrested and hanged during the reaction of 1799, a martyr of the first wave of revolutions inspired by the ideals of liberty, equality, and fraternity.

Russolo, Luigi See FUTURISM.

S

Saba, Umberto (1883–1957)

poet with a highly individual voice who drew inspiration from ordinary events and figures

For over 50 years the largely self-educated Saba (he never completed secondary school) observed and expressed in rhyme and meter his own and others' experiences in poetic language easily accessible to the general reader. He was born in Trieste to a Jewish mother and an Italian Catholic father who abandoned the family early on. His real name was Umberto Poli, but he adopted the name of Saba ("bread" in Hebrew) to acknowledge his Jewish heritage. Through his father he obtained Italian citizenship in Austrian-ruled Trieste. In 1903 he moved to Pisa, where he took courses at the university. The mental traumas caused by a difficult childhood and by his Jewish identity in a milieu where anti-Semitism was rife were partially resolved by Saba's discovery of Nietszche's admiration for the isolated individual and of Freudian psychology. Saba actually reveled in the mix of Italian, Jewish, and Slavic influences that he experienced in Trieste. Two years of service in the Italian army (1907–08) awakened in him a sense of camaraderie and empathy for ordinary folks. After WORLD WAR I Saba owned and managed a well-stocked bookstore in Trieste that appealed to a discerning clientele. In plain language, his poems describe and reflect on people close to him, ordinary objects, street scenes, and events of daily life. The sense of melancholy that permeates his poetry never degenerates into despair. Saba actually derives and communicates a sense of comfort from the ordinariness of life. Not interested in literary experimentation for its own sake, Saba used poetry as a means of self-exploration and for answering existential questions. He explained himself and his poetry in *Storia e cronistoria del Canzoniere* (History and chronicle of the songbook, 1948).

Sack of Rome

The siege, capture, and wholesale looting of the city of Rome by the troops of Emperor CHARLES V on May 6–14, 1527, was a shocking act that drove home the harsh reality that Italy had become a defenseless pawn at the mercy of greater powers. The inhabitants were left helpless in the hands of a violent soldiery that had been left unpaid for months and had degenerated into an undisciplined and lawless mob. Murder, rape, and theft went on for a whole week, while Pope CLEMENT VII watched helplessly from the ramparts of the Castel Sant'Angelo where he and his court found refuge. The marauding troops were mostly Lutheran mercenaries from Germany hired by Emperor Charles, himself a good Catholic, to punish the pope for having defected to the French side in the French-Spanish struggle for control of Italy. Some 4,000 people are thought to have perished in Rome. Clement had to come to terms with the emperor, paying a large ransom and surrendering territory. The emperor's victory and the pope's humiliating defeat also compelled the French to come to terms with Charles. The Treaty of Chambrai (1529) would confirm Spanish political dominance of the Italian peninsula.

Sadoleto, Jacopo (1477–1547)
humanist scholar, clergyman, and religious reformer critical of papal power

Sadoleto was born in Modena to a family in government service, studied in Ferrara and Rome, and pursued a career in papal administration. He was appointed bishop in 1517 and made cardinal in 1536. At the courts of LEO X and CLEMENT VII, Sadoleto, with his learning and elegant style, excelled as the secretary in charge of writing papal documents. He also carried out important diplomatic missions for these two popes and for PAUL III. When the sack of Rome occurred in 1527, Sadoleto was safe in his diocese of Carpentras in southern France, where he had moved to take up his duties as bishop. Interested in education, he wrote a treatise on the schooling of boys (1533). Sadoleto was the leading figure in a papal commission that in 1536–37 recommended limiting the power of the pope. He participated in the initial sessions of the Council of Trent as a moderate Catholic who hoped to maintain a dialogue and avoid any complete break with Protestants. An admirer of Erasmus of Rotterdam, Sadoleto favored reforms within the CATHOLIC CHURCH, but was not prepared to make concessions to Protestants on doctrinal grounds. His death may have deprived the Council of Trent of a voice of moderation. His principal concern as a scholar was to reconcile Christian belief and the culture of HUMANISM.

Saint Germain, Treaty of See PARIS PEACE CONFERENCE.

Salandra, Antonio (1853–1931)
conservative political leader, legal and economic expert, prime minister during World War I

Salandra was born to a family of the southern gentry in the town of Troia in the region of Puglia. After receiving a law degree from the University of Naples (1872), he went into private practice. In 1879 he was appointed professor of business law and administration at the University of Rome, a post that he held for the rest of his life. His political debut came in 1886 when he was elected to parliament as a "conservative liberal" in the tradition of the HISTORICAL RIGHT and a political ally of SIDNEY SONNINO. He gained experience in government serving in various capacities, including minister of agriculture (1899–1900), minister of finance (1906), and treasury minister (1909–10). Sonnino's failure to form parliamentary coalitions strong enough to support his policies may have influenced Salandra to move closer to the liberal course adopted by GIOVANNI GIOLITTI. Salandra was Giolitti's successor as prime minister when the latter stepped down in March 1914. Salandra's government was regarded as transitional, but the outbreak of World War I kept Salandra in office much longer than had been foreseen. Initially undecided, Salandra eventually came to favor Italian participation in the war on the side of Great Britain, France, and Russia. His declaration that Italian policy was guided by "sacred egoism" left him open to the accusation that he was indifferent to the ideals and principles of government at stake in the conflict. But in reality Salandra was only voicing an attitude shared by European leaders at the time, before American idealism and wartime propaganda transformed the war into a struggle for democratic ideals. Salandra and Foreign Minister Sonnino negotiated the PACT OF LONDON and brought Italy into the war in May 1915. Although Salandra's war cabinet had full powers to govern, Salandra did not have an easy time once the country was at war. Dissatisfaction with the conduct of military operations weakened Salandra's government, and he stepped down as prime minister in May 1916. After the war, he was a member of the Italian peace delegation at the PARIS PEACE CONFERENCE. In 1923 Benito Mussolini named him ambassador to the League of Nations. He retired from politics in 1925 but was nominated senator in 1928. Salandra spent the last years of his life working on books of memoirs. See his *Italy and the Great War: From Neutrality to Intervention* (1932).

Salgari, Emilio (1863–1911)
novelist, writer of adventure stories situated in exotic lands

Salgari (also pronounced Sálgari) was born in Verona, never finished naval studies in Venice, returned to his native city, and later moved to Turin to take up writing. A tireless and prolific writer, Salgari published 85 novels and 130 short stories that established him as Italy's most popular writer of his generation. His novels were organized in series that dealt with jungles, pirates, and the American Far West, the works in each series being connected by the same characters facing hardship and deadly challenges. Salgari distinguished clearly between good and bad characters, with the roles of heroes and villains distributed among both Europeans and natives. His heroes, who carried names like Sandokan, Tremal Naik, Yanez, and Kammamuri, were honest, loyal, generous, and protective toward the weak. There are few messages of European superiority in Salgari's writings. Nevertheless, his publications at a time when COLONIALISM was in the air stimulated Italian popular interest in far-off, exotic places. *I misteri della Jungla nera* (The mysteries of the black jungle, 1895), *I pirati della Malesia* (The pirates of Malaysia, 1896), *Il corsaro nero* (The black pirate, 1899), *Iolanda, la figlia del corsaro nero* (Yolanda, the daughter of the black pirate, 1905), and *Sulle frontiere del Far West* (On the Far West frontiers, 1908), were among Salgari's more popular novels. Although they had a special appeal for the young, Salgari's writings appealed to people of all ages. His popularity did not make him a rich man. Frustrated by financial need and family problems, Salgari committed suicide.

Salieri, Antonio See DA PONTE, LORENZO.

Salò, Republic of See ITALIAN SOCIAL REPUBLIC.

Salutati, Coluccio (1331–1406)
pioneering humanist scholar, linguist, teacher, and public official

Salutati is remembered primarily for his role as chancellor of the Florentine republic from 1375 to 1406. In that office, he placed his humanist learning at the service of the state, establishing by personal example and with his writings a connection between scholarship and public service. He reached the office of chancellor in Florence after serving a long apprenticeship. After studying in Bologna, where his father was a political exile and where he came to know and admire GIOVANNI BOCCACCIO and PETRARCH, Salutati worked as a notary public in his native town of Stignano (1350–67), served as chancellor of the town of Todi (Umbria) (1367), was at the papal court in Rome (1367–70), and held the office of chancellor in LUCCA (1370–75). After 1475 he lived in Florence. During the 30 years that he was chancellor, Florence experienced domestic unrest and war against Rome and Milan. With his writings and personal example of dedication to public service, Salutati rallied the intelligentsia behind the government of the republic. Implicit in his treatises and letters is the assumption that HUMANISM is not merely learning for its own sake, but a school of life. His writings were credited with upholding the republic as effectively as if they were military forces. His voluminous correspondence is a mine of information on the events and personalities of his time. Among his notable writings, *De saeculo et religione* (On the world and religious life, 1381) addresses the issue of religious contemplation and the active life, *De fato, fortuna et caso* (On fate, fortune and accident, 1396–99) speaks to the issue of free will, *De tyranno* (On the tyrant, 1400) makes a case for the elimination of tyrants who threaten liberty, and the unfinished *De laboribus Herculis* (On the labors of Hercules, 1401) magnifies the role of the heroic figure, and makes a case for poetry as a medium for moral instruction. Salutati also promoted the study of classical Greek and Latin as indispensable scholarly tools for the recovery of the learning and wisdom of the ancients. An inspiring teacher, his many pupils included the outstanding humanist LEONARDO BRUNI. His writings, example, and influence make Salutati the founder of the *studia humanitatis.*

Salvator Rosa See ROSA, SALVATORE.

Salvemini, Gaetano (1873–1957)
historian, teacher, political figure, and anti-Fascist expatriate
Salvemini was born in the southern town of Molfetta (Puglia) to a family of modest means, received his early education in Catholic schools, and completed his university studies in Florence (1894). His writings on the history of medieval FLORENCE, the FRENCH REVOLUTION, and GIUSEPPE MAZZINI established him as a historian of note. Appointed professor of medieval and modern history at the University of Messina (1901), Salvemini lost his wife and five children in the earthquake that leveled that city in 1908. At the time Salvemini looked to the Italian Socialist Party (PSI), but as a MERIDIONALISTA he also chastised the party for its alliance with northern industry and indifference to the plight of the South. Also an uncompromising critic of GIOVANNI GIOLITTI, Salvemini put his hopes of political reform on universal suffrage and the organization of peasants and workers on a national basis. In 1916 he was appointed professor of modern history at the University of Florence, where he remained until 1925 when Fascist persecution forced him to leave the country. Initially silent toward FASCISM, Salvemini joined the opposition after the murder of GIACOMO MATTEOTTI, when it became clear that the Fascists were determined to establish a one-party dictatorship. A cofounder of Giustizia e Libertà with CARLO and NELLO ROSSELLI in Paris, in 1934 Salvemini accepted an offer to teach Italian civilization at Harvard University. In addition to teaching and writing, Salvemini toured the United States in his campaign to alert American public opinion and political leaders to the dangers of fascism. His writings on that subject include *The Fascist Dictatorship in Italy* (1927) and *Under the Axe of Fascism* (1936). These are works both historical and political that show the compatibility of scholarly accuracy and political commitment. Salvemini was the principal founder of the Mazzini Society, founded in New York City in 1939, to promote unity among Italian-Americans in the fight against fascism. *What to Do with Italy* (1943), a book that Salvemini coauthored with Giorgio La Piana, another Harvard professor, outlined a plan for the reconstruction of postwar Italy along social democratic lines. The victory of the Christian Democratic Party (DC) in postwar elections alarmed him, but life in the United States, which he admired, and the experience of fascism, which he detested, had taught him to appreciate the merits of political democracy. He remained in the United States until 1949, when he returned to Italy to resume his teaching position in Florence. Like a prophet of old, Salvemini was at his best when calling for the infusion of moral values in public life.

Sanfedisti See PAPAL STATES; PARTHENOPEAN REPULIC; SECRET SOCIETIES.

San Giuliano, Antonino Paternò Castello, Marquis of (1852–1914)
diplomat, colonial and foreign policy expert
San Giuliano was born in Catania to a family of the Sicilian nobility. Before turning to politics, San Giuliano studied economics and sociology, publishing articles on agriculture, industry, population, labor legislation, and emigration in various journals. After being elected to parliament in 1882, he aligned himself with SIDNEY SONNINO and the conservatives who identified with the old HISTORICAL RIGHT. Foreign policy attracted his attention from the early years of the 20th century, when the polarization of European powers into TRIPLE ALLIANCE and Triple Entente camps convinced him that Italy could best advance its national interest by balancing itself between the two competing blocs. He thus favored a policy of friendship toward France, while remaining faithful to Italy's commitments to Austria and

Germany. San Giuliano served as foreign minister (1905–06), ambassador to London (1906–09), ambassador to Paris (1909–10), and foreign minister (1910–14). An advocate of colonial expansion, his diplomacy cleared the way for the ITALIAN-TURKISH WAR and the acquisition of Libya. He opposed Austrian expansion in the Balkans, supported Italian economic penetration of Montenegro, and the independence of Albania. When World War I broke out, San Giuliano adopted a policy of watchful neutrality and resisted pressures from both Triple Entente and Triple Alliance powers to draw Italy into the war. He did not rule out intervention, but insisted on obtaining maximum concessions for Italian participation in the war. His successor, Baron SIDNEY SONNINO, followed the negotiating strategy set by San Giuliano, who retired seriously ill in October 1914.

San Marino, Republic of

The independent Republic of San Marino is one of two minuscule sovereign states surrounded by Italian territory (the other is the HOLY SEE). San Marino is the name of the capital (pop. 4,400), but the republic itself is commonly referred to as San Marino. It covers 60 square kilometers of territory in the region of the Marches, near the Adriatic Sea. In 1997 its population was estimated to be 24,700 and its workforce at 15,600. However, many of its inhabitants have emigrated, and it is estimated that some 20,000 San Marinesi live abroad. Italian is the official language and the population is overwhelmingly Roman Catholic. Tourism has replaced farming as the republic's principal source of income. The republic receives some 3.5 million visitors a year and the tourist industry employs about 60 percent of the workforce. The republic has been self-governing since the Middle Ages. According to tradition, Marino, a Christian stonecutter, escaped persecution by the soldiers of Emperor Diocletian, and founded the first community in A.D. 301. Its first statute dates from 1263. The PAPAL STATES, which surrounded the territory of San Marino, recognized the independent republic in 1631. Its independence was subsequently acknowledged by NAPOLEON I in 1797, by the CONGRESS OF VIENNA in 1815, and by the Italian state in 1862. It was occupied briefly by papal forces in the 18th century and suffered from bombing in WORLD WAR II. Otherwise, governments have respected San Marino's independence and policy of neutrality in war. In 1849 San Marino gave temporary refuge to GIUSEPPE GARIBALDI and his volunteers fighting for Italian independence, a gesture that earned San Marino the goodwill of Italian patriots. It is governed by a constitution that dates from 1600. Modified to take into account changing circumstances, the constitution gives voting rights to citizens who are 18 or older (women won the right to vote in 1960), provides for a legislative council of 60 members elected every five years, and an executive of two regents (*capitani reggenti*) who serve for six-month terms and check on one another. San Marino issues its own coins and stamps (which are sought after by collectors), but Italian currency circulated freely until replaced by the euro in 2002. A basic treaty that is periodically reviewed governs relations with Italy. Although San Marino generally follows the Italian diplomatic lead, it has its own seat in the United Nations and its own diplomatic representatives in about 70 states.

Sannazzaro, Jacopo (1457–1530)
(or Sannazaro)
scholar and poet active in Naples, leading figure of southern humanism

This descendant of a noble Lombard family was born and lived most of his adult life in Naples, where for many years he was attached to the royal court. He wrote poetry and prose in both Latin and Italian. *De partu virginis* (On the virgin birth, 1526) is a poem in elegant Latin that tells the story of the annunciation and birth of Christ. His most famous work is the autobiographical novel *Arcadia* (1504), which in poetry and prose tells the story of an unrequited lover who seeks refuge and solace in the imaginary, idyllic land of Arcadia. The vision of an ideal land ruled by simplicity and virtue had enormous appeal for writers of Sannazzaro's time and set a literary fashion for generations to come. The Arcadian movement (see ACADEMIES) that was partly inspired by Sannazzaro set out to rejuvenate customs by presenting images of pastoral societies uncorrupted by wealth, power, and social refinements. Thomas More and other northern European writers added a dash of religious fervor to Sannazzaro's elegant style and came up with socially radical, utopian visions of just societies. Sannazzaro's popularity went into decline in the 18th century, when literature was expected to provide realistic and psychologically valid descriptions of life. To appreciate the originality of Sannazzaro's work one must considered it in its proper historical context.

Sant'Elia, Antonio See ARCHITECTURE; FUTURISM.

Sapeto, Giuseppe (1811–1895)
missionary, explorer, scholar, and advocate of colonial expansion

Sapeto played a major role in drawing the attention of European powers to the possibilities for colonial expansion in East Africa. Born near Genoa, at the age of 18 he entered the Lazarist Order of Saint Vincent de Paul. He served in Lebanon and Egypt in the 1830s as a missionary for that order, and began to explore inland from the Red Sea and Indian Ocean in the 1840s and 1850s. His reports drew the attention of the French government, which was interested in establishing a presence in East Africa. French settlement of Somaliland occurred, however, later in the 1880s. In the 1850s Sapeto left his religious order to devote himself entirely to the study of Arabic and advocacy of European colonization. His knowledge of Arabic led to his appointment as curator of oriental manuscripts at the Bibliothèque Nationale in Paris, but he left that post to teach languages in Florence and Genoa until his retirement in 1891; he was acknowledged as an orientalist of stature in Europe. After the opening of the Suez Canal in 1869, he urged the Italian government and private groups to establish an Italian presence in East Africa. He proposed the purchase of Assab Bay to the government, but the shipping company of RUBATTINO carried out the deal instead as a private purchase backed by the government. This was the first step on the road toward colonial empire for Italy, resulting in the creation of the colony of Eritrea (see COLONIALISM).

Saracco, Giuseppe (1821–1907)
parliamentary leader and prime minister

Born in Piedmont and a lawyer by profession, Saracco was a member of parliament from 1849 to the end of his life. First in the chamber of deputies from 1849 to 1865, then, failing to be reelected, in the senate to the end of his life, Saracco held a variety of posts under successive prime ministers. The experience gave him a secure understanding of parliamentary dynamics. He became president of the senate in 1898 and was prime minister in 1900–01 during the political crisis that followed the popular disturbances of 1898 (see FATTI DI MAGGIO), the attempts to curb the independence of parliament and the press during the reaction of 1899, and the assassination of King UMBERTO I in 1900. Saracco's prime ministry also coincided with the start of the reign of the new and inexperienced King VICTOR EMMANUEL III. Saracco was the right candidate for the moment. Respected for his integrity, common sense, and financial savvy, he protected the prerogatives of parliament and generally kept the country on a liberal course. His handling of a workers' strike in Genoa brought him criticism from the Left for being too repressive and from the Right for being too permissive. He resigned as prime minister but kept the presidency of the senate until 1904. The last of the old political guard with roots in the RISORGIMENTO, Saracco's resignation as prime minister opened the way to the new era of GIOVANNI GIOLITTI.

Saragat, Giuseppe (1898–1988)
*Socialist leader, member of parliament, and
president of the Italian republic*

Saragat joined the Unitary Socialist Party (see
PSI) in 1922, was elected to its directorate in
1925, and was driven into political exile in 1926
by FASCISM. In his years of exile, first in Austria
and then in France, he studied socialist theory
and organization and was active in the anti-Fascist RESISTANCE. He returned to Italy in 1943, but
was arrested a few months later in Rome by the
German forces that had taken over the city. After
escaping, he rejoined the resistance movement
and sat on the Socialist Party's national committee. After the war he served as ambassador to
Paris (1945–46) and was president of the Constituent Assembly that drew up the CONSTITUTION
of the Italian republic. Opposed to the policy of
socialist cooperation with the Communist Party
(PCI), Saragat split with PIETRO NENNI and led dissidents out of the Socialist Party. He later
founded the Italian Social Democratic Party
(PSDI), which collaborated with the dominant
Christian Democratic Party (DC) and held the PSI
out of power until the OPENING TO THE LEFT of the
early 1960s. Saragat led the PSDI as its secretary
general from 1952 to 1963 and was foreign minister in 1963–64. In foreign policy, he was
unswervingly pro-NATO and pro-American. Parliament elected him to the largely honorific office
of president of the republic in 1964, and he
served his full seven-year term until 1971.

Sardinia

Sardinia (pop. 1.7 million) is an autonomous
region and the second-largest island in the
MEDITERRANEAN SEA after Sicily. Surrounded by
the Tyrrhenian Sea, it is separated from the island
of Corsica to the north by the Straits of Bonifacio, and lies in close proximity to smaller islands
of Asinara, Caprera, La Maddalena, San Pietro,
and Sant'Antioco. Life on the island has been
shaped by distance from the Italian mainland,
distinct dialect and customs, a largely agrarian
economy, and traditions of self-reliance. A rather
mysterious prehistoric population has left evidence of settlement in the form of *nuraghe,* trun-
cated round stone towers that may have served
as strongholds of which several thousand remain
throughout the island. The Phoenicians used Sardinia as a base for their trade in the western
Mediterranean. The rule of Greeks, Romans,
Muslims, Pisans, Genoese, Spaniards, Piedmontese, and Italians has often met local resistance,
sometimes in the form of brigandage. Recognizing Sardinia's unique character and special needs,
the constitution of the Italian republic accorded
autonomous status to the region. Since 1949 Sardinia has chosen its own regional parliament and
administered its own internal affairs. The port
city of Cagliari on the south coast is the regional
capital. Nuoro, Oristano, and Sassari are the
other major towns and provincial capitals. Agriculture and pastoral activities have been modernized, and the production of cheeses and wines
occurs on an industrial scale. Tourism is an
important resource along stretches of the coast,
particularly in the northeast along the so-called
Costa Esmeralda (Emerald Coast). Urbanization,
however, has occurred more in the interior than
the coastal areas, due perhaps to the historic need
to establish towns in locations secure from outside attack. Most of the island's once prosperous
mining industry has succumbed to international
competition. There is still some coal mining
around the appropriately named town of Carbo-
nia in the southwest part of the island. Considered part of the Italian South, the island is
nevertheless economically better off than most
southern regions.

Sardinia, Kingdom of

The name "Kingdom of Sardinia" came into
being in 1720 when the dukes of the HOUSE OF
SAVOY ceded control of Sicily to Austria in return
for Sardinia. The coveted royal title was part of
the bargain. With the title, King of Sardinia, VIC-
TOR AMADEUS II and his descendants ruled over
the island, the mainland regions of PIEDMONT
and SAVOY, and the district of NICE. In 1815 the

Kingdom of Sardinia also included the region of LIGURIA, formerly the Republic of Genoa. In this enlarged form, the Kingdom of Sardinia played a major role in the process of Italian unification with judicious use of diplomacy and military force. The constitutional monarchy introduced by King Charles Albert in 1848 made the kingdom a magnet for liberals in Italy and abroad. In 1859 the Kingdom of Sardinia, with the decisive military help of France, successfully challenged Austrian dominance in Italy and annexed the region of Lombardy. In 1860 it took advantage of uprisings in central Italy to annex MODENA, PARMA, TUSCANY, and the Romagna (part of the PAPAL STATES). Following the annexation of the KINGDOM OF THE TWO SICILIES, Victor Emmanuel II of Sardinia became the first king of Italy in March 1861. The laws and administrative practices of the Kingdom of Sardinia became those of the Kingdom of Italy.

Sarfatti-Grassini, Margherita
(1883–1961)
influential writer and cultural figure, confidante and biographer of Benito Mussolini

Born to a well-off Venetian Jewish family, she joined the Italian Socialist Party (PSI) while still in her teens and campaigned for the rights of women and workers. In 1898 she married the lawyer Cesare Sarfatti, who was also active in the socialist movement. They became friends and supporters of BENITO MUSSOLINI when he was serving as editor of the socialist newspaper *Avanti!* Like Mussolini, they broke with the Socialist Party over the issue of Italian intervention in WORLD WAR I. The death of a son in the war strengthened the feelings of patriotism and cemented the alliance with Mussolini. By the time Margherita and Mussolini became lovers, probably in 1921, she had already made herself indispensable to him as a political and literary collaborator. She is credited with inspiring in Mussolini the cult of ancient Roman power (*romanità*) that guided fascism in power. In 1921

Margherita Sarfatti-Grassini *(Library of Congress)*

Mussolini put her in charge of his journal *Gerarchìa*. In 1926 she published *Dux,* an admiring and uncritical biography of the Fascist dictator that was a great commercial success. Sarfatti urged Mussolini to set the cultural course of the regime by embracing modernism in the arts. The artistic success and political favor enjoyed by the NOVECENTO MOVEMENT in the late 1920s owed much to Sarfatti's championing efforts. The contradiction between the traditionalist cult of ancient Rome and modernism in art was never resolved in either Sarfatti's or Mussolini's mind. Her influence waned in the 1930s. The relationship with Mussolini ended painfully for her in 1934. The final break came when the regime's anti-Semitic campaign of the late 1930s made her politically unacceptable. In forced exile, she lived in Argentina, the United States, and France, returning to Italy after the war.

Sarpi, Paolo (1552–1623)
scholar, public official, critic of the papacy, and
defender of the Venetian republic

A Servite friar ordained in 1565, Sarpi rose from humble beginnings in a merchant family from the Friuli region to high position as a scholar and public official of the Republic of VENICE. A man of many accomplishments, Sarpi made his mark as a theologian, philosopher, historian, canon lawyer, and scientist. In his young days as a student and visitor to Rome, he became acquainted with religious reformers critical of papal authority. Cardinal CARLO BORROMEO recruited him at age 22 for his group of religious reformers active in the archdiocese of Milan. Sarpi's apprenticeship for public life continued in the 1590s in the aristocratic circles of Venice, which welcomed him because his known antipapal feelings coincided with those of Venetian patricians resentful of clerical interference in the affairs of the republic. In 1606 the Venetian government appointed him to the new post of state consultant of theology and canon law. In that capacity, Sarpi defended the Venetian state under an interdict by Pope PAUL V. He argued that the state was politically sovereign and free to act in its own interest in all matters pertaining to church-state relations. He is thus seen as an early advocate of the modern concept of "reason of state." Sarpi also urged the Venetian government to conclude an alliance with France and the Protestant powers against Catholic Spain and the papacy. After an assassination attempt allegedly instigated by the pope, Sarpi was given official protection by the Venetian government. Papal persecution greatly enhanced Sarpi's popularity in Protestant countries, where he was seen as a Protestant in disguise. While Sarpi's theology remains unclear, he did take positions popular among Protestants, such as denouncing papal authority, the INQUISITION, and clerical wealth and corruption. In his celebrated *History of the Council of Trent* (1619), he documented the backstairs politics and political deals that he blamed for the council's failure to enact far-reaching religious reforms. The book is considered to be Sarpi's masterpiece and is still regarded as a valid contribution to the religious history of the 16th century. Also highly regarded, and even more controversial, is the work entitled *Pensieri* (Thoughts), written secretly and not intended for publication (portions were published in 1910 and 1969). The *Pensieri* betray a materialist cast of mind highly critical of all revealed knowledge, probably related to Sarpi's interest in the science of his time. The secrecy and ambiguity of his theological beliefs suggest that he was an accomplished dissembler with views far ahead of his time. Nineteenth-century Italian patriots admired Sarpi's anticlericalism, his defense of state sovereignty, and rejection of clerical authority in secular affairs. Along with GIORDANO BRUNO and TOMMASO CAMPANELLA, Sarpi was seen, and is still regarded by many, as a forerunner of modern secular culture.

Savonarola, Girolamo (1452–1498)
Dominican friar, religious and political
reformer hostile to Medici and papal rule

Born in Ferrara, the son of a doctor, Savonarola was well educated in medicine, philosophy, and the arts. Although well versed in secular humanistic studies, Savonarola nevertheless looked at the world with religious intransigence. Two of his early writings, *De ruina mundi* (On the ruin of the world, 1472) and *De ruina Ecclesiae* (On the ruin of the church, 1475) expressed his fears that the Christian world had lost its way. In 1475 he experienced a religious conversion, entered the monastery of Saint Dominic in Bologna, and a year later was admitted to the Dominican Order. His fame as a powerful preacher and theologian spread rapidly. He was in Florence in 1482–85, and was invited back in 1490 by none other than LORENZO DE' MEDICI, who must soon have regretted his decision. Savonarola became prior of the Dominican monastery of San Marco in 1491. He preached vehemently against secularism, materialism, and frivolity, targeting the Medici and the clergy as responsible for the corruption of city life. Savonarola's sermons insisted on the need to return to the simple Christianity of the gospels and predicted an apocalyptic fate for the city if the Florentines did not mend their ways. The enemies of the Medici, angry that they had been frozen out of government, listened attentively.

According to Savonarola, a ruler from across the Alps would inflict retribution on the unrepentant. That prediction seemed to come true in 1494 when Charles VIII led a French army into Italy and the Medici were forced out of Florence. Savonarola was part of the delegation that negotiated the agreement whereby the French spared the city from attack in return for territorial and financial concessions. Savonarola undertook a campaign to purify the city with public denunciations of sinners and the burning of books and art works deemed immoral ("bonfires of the vanities") and called for a new constitution to limit the power of the most prominent families.

Savonarola also intensified his attacks on the clergy and the pope, ALEXANDER VI, whom he accused of corrupting the church. The pope revoked the friar's license to preach, and when Savonarola ignored the ban, excommunicated him (1497), thereby giving his Florentine enemies the pretext they were seeking to challenge him publicly. Savonarola retorted by declaring that Alexander was no true pope. Street fights ensued between Savonarola's followers, the *piagnoni* (weepers), and his enemies, the *arrabbiati* (enraged). In April 1498, Savonarola was arrested and tried. On May 22, 1498, he was burned at the stake in Piazza della Signoria in front of a cheering crowd. Savonarola came to be seen as a martyr to the cause of popular government and religious reform. He also exposed the growing gap between popular religiosity and the elite culture of secular HUMANISM.

Savoy, House of

The dynasty that would eventually rule the Kingdom of Italy began as an obscure feudal lordship in the alpine region of SAVOY. Its first historical figure was the semilegendary Count Umberto Biancamano (Whitehand), who lived in the 11th century and acquired the family's first possessions in the region of PIEDMONT, including the city of Turin. From the Savoy capital of Chambéry where they resided, his descendants expanded their possessions in Italy by war, marriage, and diplomacy. Their ambitions, however, were not confined to Italy. Taking advantage of Savoy's position in the ALPS at the juncture of Italy, France, and Switzerland, the *sabaudi* (Savoyards), as the dynasty is called, looked in all three directions. Their acquisitions included the Swiss city of Geneva (1285) and the seaport of NICE (1388). Eager to establish themselves among the titled families of the Christian world, they acquired the title of dukes (1416). Among the many titles of nobility accumulated by this dynasty was that of kings of Jerusalem, Cyprus, and Armenia. After a series of serious military reverses during the Italian Wars of the early 16th century, which resulted in the permanent loss of Geneva (1533), the dynasty's fortunes rose again under the ambitious and capable EMANUEL PHILIBERT, who transferred the capital from Chambéry to Turin.

That move signaled a permanent shift of their designs toward Italy, since the French monarchy and the Swiss cantons were now strong enough to resist Savoyard expansion. The dynasty followed an opportunistic course of action, taking advantage of wars among the great powers, arranging advantageous marriages, aligning themselves with this or that power, sometimes changing sides in the course of a war. Its policy of piecemeal expansion has been called the "policy of the artichoke," because the Savoyards nibbled away at Italian territories one at a time, the way one eats an artichoke one leaf at a time. The acquisition of the island of SARDINIA (1720) brought with it the title of kings of Sardinia, given as part of the swap of the wealthier island of Sicily claimed by Austria. In spite of their Sardinian title, Savoyard power was still based primarily on their mainland possessions of Piedmont and Savoy.

In the 17th and 18th centuries, the dynasty built a modern absolutist state strong enough to pursue an independent foreign policy and hold its own against the rival powers of Austria and France. The close bond between the dynasty and the army was a key feature of the Savoyard state. Particularly notable in this respect was the contribution of Victor Amadeus II (1675–1730), who restructured and centralized the state administration, carried out a land census, improved the collection of taxes, compelled the nobility to serve the state, curbed the power of the clergy, and encouraged education. The absolutist state created by Victor Amadeus remained unchanged until the end of the 18th century, when the dynasty was swept up in wars triggered by the FRENCH REVOLUTION. Charles Emmanuel IV (1796–1802) lost all his mainland possessions to NAPOLEON I and resigned in favor of his brother VICTOR EMMANUEL I, who held on to Sardinia under the protection of the British navy. He followed a conservative course in the early years of the RESTORATION, as did his brother and successor CHARLES FELIX, the last ruler of the direct Savoyard line.

His successor, CHARLES ALBERT, came from the lateral family branch of the Savoia-Carignano. Hesitantly, he encouraged reform, challenged Austria, and in 1848 granted the CONSTITUTION that made the government a limited monarchy. The dynasty's championing of the cause of Italian independence led to the acquisition of the crown of Italy when the country was unified in 1861. Charles Albert's son and successor, VICTOR EMMANUEL II, became the first king of Italy. In 1860 he had to surrender the ancestral region of Savoy to France as part of the price of French support against Austria during the wars of the RISORGIMENTO. The dynasty ruled in Italy until 1946, under the successive reigns of Victor Emmanuel II, UMBERTO I, VICTOR EMMANUEL III, and UMBERTO II. Seriously compromised with the Fascist regime and discredited by military defeat in WORLD WAR II the monarchy was abolished by popular vote in June 1946. Umberto II went into exile without formally renouncing the family's claim to the throne. His male descendants were banned from entering Italian soil until 2002, when the Italian parliament lifted the ban.

Savoy, region of

Savoy (*Savoie* in French) is an alpine region located at the junction of France, Italy, and Switzerland. The important Little Saint Bernard and Mont Cenis passes between France and Italy are located in the region. The Mont Cenis railroad tunnel, opened in 1871 and one of the world's longest at about eight miles, connects Turin and Savoy's regional capital of Chambéry. The ancient seat of the HOUSE OF SAVOY, this region was part of the KINGDOM OF SARDINIA until 1860, when it became part of France. The cession was part of a larger deal that also involved the cession of Nice, in return for French recognition of Italy's political unification. France had long coveted Savoy, and had annexed it in 1792 in the course of the wars of the FRENCH REVOLUTION. Restored to the House of Savoy by the CONGRESS OF VIENNA (1815), the Savoyards became increasingly restive and disillusioned by the Italian orientation of the House of Savoy. Both geographically and linguistically, Savoy looked toward France rather than Italy, and the WARS OF NATIONAL INDEPENDENCE imposed a heavy financial and military burden that was resented by many Savoyards. The plebiscite that sanctioned the cession to France therefore reflected the true state of popular sentiment in the region. Not everyone in Italy accepted the cession with equanimity. Italian nationalists periodically claimed Savoy for Italy, but only the Fascist government demanded its return.

Scalabrini, Giovanni Battista (1839–1905)

cleric and social worker active among Italian emigrants

Scalabrini was born in the town of Mornasco in the province of Como (Piedmont), was ordained into the priesthood in 1863 and became bishop of Piacenza in 1875. He was an active organizer of the Catholic movement (see DC) in his bishopric and took a conciliatory position in the ongoing conflict between church and state that pegged him as a Catholic liberal. His most notable achievement was as promoter and developer of a vast Catholic assistance network among Italian emigrants, culminating in the creation in 1914 of a Pontifical College of Emigration located in the Vatican. That was an important development in what was described at the time as the "conquest of emigration" by competing political groups. Thanks to the efforts of Scalabrini, and other Catholic leaders like Bishop Geremia Bonomelli (1831–1914), Catholic organizational efforts succeeded in winning the battle against socialist and government-sponsored initiatives. Catholic organizational efforts were most successful among Italian immigrants in the United States, where Scalabrini's Congregation of the Missionaries of San Carlo was active. Criticism that the Italian government was indifferent to the plight of Italian emigrants resulted in passage of the Migration Act of 1901 that established government norms for the protection of emigrants (see MIGRATION).

Scalfaro, Oscar Luigi (1918–)

Christian Democratic leader, member of parliament, president of the republic

Scalfaro was born in Novara (Piedmont), received a law degree from the Catholic University of Milan, and was elected to Italy's constituent assembly in 1946. He represented the Christian Democratic Party (DC) in parliament without interruption from 1948 until he was elected president of the republic in 1992. Always in the background, he held significant posts, including the ministries of education, transport, and home affairs. He became the ninth president following the sudden resignation of FRANCESCO COSSIGA, and his presidency (1992–99) was marked by MAFIA political assassinations, the political scandal of TANGETOPOLI, the demise of the party system in existence since 1945, and far-reaching political reforms. Scalfaro's low-key personality disguised considerable political tact. He broadened the powers of his office, insisted that prime ministers consult with him before making major decisions, and called on capable technocrats like CARLO AZEGLIO CIAMPI and LAMBERTO DINI to confront the government's financial problems. He also took the daring step of appointing MASSIMO D'ALEMA, the first former communist to serve as prime minister. He has been criticized for not showing more enthusiasm for political reforms favored by a majority of voters, but there were solid achievements during his presidency. Constitutional reforms did occur, state finances improved, Italy moved toward full integration in Europe, and the economy prospered.

Scapigliatura

The term *scapigliatura* derives from *scapigliato*, which has the multiple meaning of disheveled, disorderly, and loose. In the late 19th century it was applied to a literary movement of protest based in MILAN, where members of the intelligentsia felt the cultural and social tensions that followed national unification and the beginnings of industrialization. The novelist Giuseppe Rovani (1818–74) was considered its leader, but the movement brought together too many divergent personalities to be identified with any single one. Nevertheless, in Rovani's major work, the novel *Cento anni*, first published in newspaper installments in 1857–58, one detects characteristics common to the Scapigliatura movement. The novel, cast in the form of a memoir by a 90-year-old man, narrates real and imagined events from the period 1750–1850 in down-to-earth language, with realistic attention to detail and motivation. It avoids the sentimentalism of romantic literature, which the *scapigliati* ascribed largely to the influence of ALESSANDRO MANZONI, and demystifies the process of national unification in the spirit of social and psychological realism. In the hands of later *scapigliati*, such as Emilio Praga (1839–75) and Arrigo Boito (1842–1918), the revolt against social conventions became explicit. In the case of Praga, the revolt took on the tone of an angry polemic that sought to shock readers out of their complacent acceptance of social conventions. Boito's rejection of established canons manifested itself as a preoccupation with the eternal conflict between good and evil, resulting in agonized appraisals of the human condition and culminating in the musical masterpiece, the opera *Mefistofele* (1868), which Boito composed in the manner of Richard Wagner to protest the ascendancy of the widely revered GIUSEPPE VERDI. Scapigliatura triumphed in the troubled decade 1860–70, but its influence continued into the late 1890s, when it yielded to the hedonistic, sensual trend (decadentism) associated with GABRIELE D'ANNUNZIO. The term also applies to a current in the visual arts that rejected the prevailing neoclassic canons dominant in Italian painting in the first half of the 19th century.

Scarlatti, Domenico See OPERA.

Scelba, Mario (1901–1991)

Christian Democratic leader and prime minister, known for his strict law-and-order policies

Born to a working-class family of Caltagirone (Sicily), which would later manage the estate of a local baron, Scelba came to the attention of LUIGI STURZO, the founder of the Catholic Popular Party (see PPI), who encouraged him to study. After completing preparatory studies in his native town, Scelba went on to study law in Rome and received a law degree in 1924. His political career began as personal secretary to Sturzo, until the party was disbanded and Sturzo forced into exile in 1924. Scelba earned a modest living practicing law, remained active in the Catholic movement, and refused to join the Fascist Party. He was a founder of the Christian Democratic Party (DC) in 1943, held his first government post in 1945, and was a member of the constituent assembly that prepared and adopted the CONSTITUTION of the Italian republic. He went on to serve in the Chamber of Deputies (1948–1968) and the senate after 1968. As minister of the interior (1947–53), he reorganized the police and dealt severely with street rioters. During street clashes in March 1950 hundreds of demonstrators and police were injured and some 7,000 protestors were arrested. His fast-moving squads of riot police mounted on jeeps left behind by the American army were the most visible evidence of the government's resolve to resist popular pressures and bring order to the

streets. Scelba became the man most hated by the political Left, vilified and demonized relentlessly in the press. He was the controversial leader of the conservative wing of the Christian Democratic Party that refused any form of dialogue with socialists and communists. As prime minister (1954–55) he cultivated strong ties with the United States and negotiated the return of TRIESTE to Italy. He served again as minister of the interior (1960–61), but his political career faded in the 1960s with the OPENING TO THE LEFT. He headed the Christian Democratic Party in 1966–68 and served as president of the European Parliament in 1970–72. Perhaps more than any other figure of his generation, Scelba personified the centrist policy of opposition to the forces of the Left, attachment to the church, and loyalty to the western alliance.

Schanzer, Carlo See GENOA, CONFERENCE(S) OF.

scholasticism

As a method of intellectual inquiry, scholasticism operated by positing an argument (*quaestio*), a counter-argument (*disputatio*), and a reasoned resolution (*sententia*). Central to scholasticism as a philosophy was the notion that faith and reason are compatible and complementary. Faith, based on acceptance and proper understanding of Scripture, was the foundation of knowledge. Reasoned interpretations of Scripture sanctioned by the church clarified the nature and message of faith. Scholasticism regarded Scripture as the source of revealed knowledge and faith, and the writings of Aristotle as the ultimate reasoned confirmation of the validity of the knowledge revealed in Scripture. In the scholastic tradition, theology was considered the highest form of rational inquiry because it reasoned about the nature of the divine and thereby allowed the mind to connect with God. The reconciliation of faith and reason, of divine and natural law, was the supreme achievement of Thomas Aquinas (1225–74). His philosophy (Thomism) dominated the culture of the late Middle Ages, for a while excluding alternate ways of thinking from the universities and religious schools. Renaissance HUMANISM was at least in part a revolt against the intellectual dominance of scholasticism. PETRARCH and LORENZO VALLA questioned it, and NEOPLATONISM asserted the primacy of spiritual understanding over reasoned knowledge. Renaissance humanism approached ancient texts critically and raised issues of private and public conduct that were foreign to scholasticism. But Renaissance culture did not reject scholasticism entirely. Scholasticism still held out in universities and religious schools, and its influence remained great in the study of law, politics, and nature in the 15th century. Much later, GIORDANO BRUNO, TOMMASO CAMPANELLA, and GALILEO would question its reliance on metaphysics and Aristotle in the study of physical nature ("natural philosophy"). Since the 19th century an updated version of scholasticism called neo-scholasticism or neo-Thomism has been the official philosophy of the CATHOLIC CHURCH, which seeks to apply the thinking of Aquinas to the solution of modern problems.

Scialoja, Antonio (1817–1877)
Neapolitan economist, liberal patriot in the struggle for national unification, and government figure

Scialoja was born in the town of San Giovanni a Teduccio (Naples) to a family in the pasta manufacturing business. A student of political economy, he won scholarly recognition with the publication of *Principi di economia sociale esposti in ordine cronologico* (Principles of political economy explained in chronological order, 1840). That publication won him appointment to the recently established chair of political economy at the University of Turin. He returned to Naples during the revolution of 1848. In the revolutionary government he held the post of minister of agriculture and commerce. Condemned to life in exile after the revolution was suppressed, Scialoja resumed his teaching and scholarly activities in Turin. His publication *Note e confronti dei bilanci del Regno di Napoli e degli Stati Sardi*

(Notes and comparisons on the budgets of the Kingdom of Naples and the Sardinian states, 1857) argued that the liberal financial and budgetary practices of the KINGDOM OF SARDINIA, subject to parliamentary scrutiny, were preferable to those of the absolutist KINGDOM OF THE TWO SICILIES. He returned to Naples in 1860 to hold the position of minister of finances in the provisional government of GIUSEPPE GARIBALDI. Scialoja went on to serve in the national parliament, in the chamber of deputies (1860–65) and in the senate from 1865 until his death. In the national government he served as minister of finances (1866) and minister of education (1870–72). As finance minister he grappled with a huge deficit, aggravated by the cost of the war of 1866 against Austria (see WARS OF NATIONAL INDEPENDENCE), which he tried to stem by adopting the policy of nonconvertibility of the CURRENCY (*corso forzoso*). In the last years of his life he served as financial adviser to the Egyptian government.

Sciascia, Leonardo (1921–1989)
Sicilian writer, political activist, social commentator and critic

This writer was born in the town of Racalmuto, province of Agrigento (Sicily), trained as an elementary school teacher, taught, worked as a school administrator, and served in the ministry of education in Rome. He retired from public service in 1968 to devote himself full time to writing. His first book, *Le favole della dittatura* (Fables of the Dictatorship, 1950), was a satire on the Fascist regime. He has made Sicily the focal point of his literary and political reflections. He was an active member of the Italian Communist Party (PCI) until the late 1970s when he joined the Radical Party (PR), representing it in both the Italian and the European parliaments. Sciascia's first full-length novel was *Il giorno della civetta* (The day of the owl, 1961). Written in his favorite form as a detective novel, it relates how an honest policeman's efforts to solve a MAFIA crime were thwarted by the influence of families with powerful connections. Preoccupation with the Mafia recurs in many of Sciascia's writings.

He sees the strength of the Mafia in its connections with powerful political figures and in the culture of silence (*omertà*) that protects the *mafiosi*. Members of the Mafia emerge from Sciascia's writings as belonging to a culture apart, marked by distrust of the state and its agents, sustained by a particular concept of honor, rooted in centuries of oppression by outside powers, the latest of which is the Italian state. Sciascia's writings reflect a profound pessimism, which some see as typically Sicilian, in the capacity of reason to deal with the problems of society. Yet Sciascia never surrenders to complete despair, leaving open the possibility of dialogue, mutual understanding, and ultimate resolution. His own political activism springs from his faith in the power of reason as a guide to action. Many of his novels and essays have been translated into English.

science

Modern science is a by-product of the secular culture of the RENAISSANCE, which separated the study of nature from a general philosophical speculation that made no clear distinction between the religious and the secular (see SCHOLASTICISM). The founders of modern science pursued the study of "natural philosophy," arguing that observation and reasoning, not revealed knowledge, were the indispensable guides to the study of nature. The attention to detail evident in the drawings of the human body made by LEONARDO DA VINCI reveal the concern for accuracy of observation that is characteristic of modern science. GALILEO's use of the telescope to study the appearance and behavior of celestial objects and his use of mathematics to explain the behavior of falling objects exemplify how accurate observation and rigorous reasoning could be put to the service of science. Scientific thought ran into obstacles in Italy after Galileo's run-in with the CATHOLIC CHURCH over his advocacy of the heliocentric model of the solar system.

Galileo's trial and imprisonment deterred other scientists from engaging in open speculation and theorizing that might run contrary to the teachings of the church. But that is not the only reason for the slow progress of scientific inquiry in Italy after Galileo. It is also true that Leonardo and Galileo functioned more as isolated geniuses than as teachers and organizers of schools of thought. Neither left disciples behind who could carry on their work. The Italian environment of the 17th century did not encourage innovation. Scientists found it hard to communicate across a politically divided peninsula and governments had neither the resources nor the inclination to subsidize independent inquiry or the practical application of scientific and technological skills. Except in the fields of military fortification and land reclamation, where technological talent was in demand, scientists and engineers were seldom called upon to discharge public functions.

The history of scientific investigation in Italy is usually a tale of isolated individual work with little impact or follow-up in society at large. ULISSE ALDROVANDI, AMADEO AVOGADRO, ENRICO FERMI, LUIGI GALVANI, GUGLIELMO MARCONI, EVANGELISTA TORRICELLI, and ALESSANDRO VOLTA are all Italian scientists whose findings received more attention abroad than in their own country. But while the peninsula was relegated to the periphery of European science after Galileo, it was never so distant from the center as to lose touch with the latest developments. Most of the ACADEMIES that proliferated in the peninsula during and after the 16th century paid scant attention to the natural sciences, but scientific ideas managed to circulate by various other channels. The interest in science and technology that accompanied the ENLIGHTENMENT had some echoes in Italy. The era of Galvani and Volta also produced Giambattista Beccaria (1716–81), a physicist who championed Benjamin Franklin's electrical theories and conducted his own studies of electricity in the atmosphere.

In the 19th century, the Milanese review *Annali Universali di Statistica* (1824–71) reported on scientific findings from other countries and encouraged Italians to address social issues by gathering and studying statistical data. Italian scientists held nine national congresses from 1839 to 1847 sponsored by various governments. Government sponsorship ceased after the REVOLUTIONS OF 1848 raised fears that cultural contacts, even the collection of statistics across state boundaries, could have dangerous political repercussions. National unification did not improve matters much. Three national scientific congresses were held in 1862, 1873, and 1875, before the idea of such gatherings was dropped altogether. Lack of resources and tight national budgets were principally responsible for the neglect of science. Not even the physicist Carlo Matteucci (1811–68), who served as minister of public education in 1862–64, could find funds to organize research.

But another reason for the low priority accorded to science was the humanistic orientation of educated Italians, who preferred law schools to schools of science and engineering. What little research there was occurred in universities, in poorly equipped laboratories dependent on the resourcefulness of individual professors. Nevertheless, universities did turn out well-trained scientists, engineers, and doctors. Giuseppe Peano (1858–1932) in mathematics, Antonio Pacinotti (1841–1912) and Galileo Ferraris (1847–1897) in the developing field of electricity, Stanislao Cannizzaro (1826–1910) in chemistry, Pietro Angelo Secchi (1818–78) and Giovanni Battista Donati (1826–73) in astronomy were among the scientists who gained international recognition in their respective disciplines during what is usually considered a low point of Italian science. In a more dubious and controversial area of science, the skull-measuring exercises of CESARE LOMBROSO and his followers gave authority to the pseudoscience of phrenology. The notion at the heart of phrenology that physiological features control behavior influenced eugenics and contributed to the development of racial theories. A more benign contribution was made by PAOLO MANTEGAZZA with his widely read books on personal hygiene and sex education.

The lessons of WORLD WAR I, which had shown the national importance of scientific research, were heeded slowly. The Fascist government established the National Council for Research in the 1930s, with a regular budget and an administrative structure headed by the famed GUGLIEMO MARCONI. The council's immediate charge was to encourage research in pursuit of national economic self-sufficiency (see AUTARKY). The adoption of anti-Semitic policies by the Fascist regime in the 1930s led to the voluntary expatriation of several prominent or promising scientists, including ENRICO FERMI, Salvatore Luria (1912–91), RITA LEVI-MONTALCINO, and Emilio Segrè (1905–89). The National Council survived the fall of the Fascist regime and to this day continues to function as the highest coordinating body for scientific research.

The American example of successful collaboration by government, universities, and private enterprise served as the model for the organization of Italian science after WORLD WAR II. A ministry of national research was established in 1962. From 1963 to 1975 state funding for research increased modestly from 0.4 percent to 1 percent of GNP. Italian industry benefited mostly from the application of technological research conducted elsewhere. The 1980s saw the development of nuclear and space programs. National investment in scientific research remains far below the average within the EUROPEAN UNION. Organizational weaknesses have not prevented Italian researchers from making important contributions in molecular science, medicine, genetics, and many other areas of research, but public and private funding remains low by western standards.

Scoccimarro, Mauro (1895–1972)
opponent of the Fascist regime, Communist Party leader, and government figure of the reconstruction period

Scoccimarro joined the Italian Socialist Party (PSI) in 1917 and the Italian Communist Party (PCI) at the time of its founding in 1921. In 1923 he was appointed to the party's executive and

Mauro Scoccimarro *(Library of Congress)*

central committees, where he tried unsuccessfully to mediate differences between the currents headed by AMADEO BORDIGA and ANTONIO GRAMSCI. In 1928 a special tribunal of the Fascist regime condemned Scoccimarro and 21 other Communist detainees to 20 years in jail. After his liberation following the fall of the Fascist regime in 1943 he headed a provisional party directorate in Rome. In 1944 he unsuccessfully opposed the policy of cooperation with the monarchy advocated by PALMIRO TOGLIATTI. In the first postwar governments headed successively by FERRUCCIO PARRI and ALCIDE DE GASPERI, Scoccimarro held the post of minister of finances (1945–47). In that capacity he pressed for a progressive system of taxation and monetary conversion that would have amounted to a form of wealth redistribution. The Christian Democratic

Party (DC) successfully resisted that plan. Scoccimarro was a member of the Communist Party's national directorate, and served in the constituent assembly that drew up the CONSTITUTION of the Italian republic (1945–47), and in the Senate from 1948.

Scorza, Carlo (1897–1988)
Fascist leader, youth organizer, and last Fascist Party secretary

Born in the Calabrian town of Paola (Cosenza) the 10th of 12 children, Scorza's political career began in LUCCA where he had relocated at age 15 in search of work. After finishing three years of study at a technical school, in 1916 Scorza joined the army, where he rose to the rank of lieutenant and won three bronze medals for bravery. In 1920 he joined the local Fascist cell and was put in charge of its action squads that took the fight to the streets. Under his aggressive leadership the Fascist squads cleared Lucca of political opponents and Scorza became the uncontested Fascist *ras* (leader) of the province. He took part in the march on Rome and was elected to parliament in 1924. Dogged by rumors of financial misconduct, out of political favor because of his strong anticlerical views and intemperate conduct, Scorza was forced out of Lucca in 1932. He emerged from obscurity and regained prominence during WORLD WAR II as a hard-liner willing to resort to extreme measures to carry on the war. BENITO MUSSOLINI appointed Scorza secretary of the Fascist Party in April 1943 when Italy's invasion and military defeat appeared inevitable. As party secretary Scorza played an ambiguous role in the events that led to Mussolini's ouster. He knew ahead of time of the Fascist plot to remove Mussolini, but took no steps to prevent it; he urged Mussolini to arrest the dissidents, but acquiesced in the coup. Arrested by resistance fighters in 1945, he escaped from jail under mysterious circumstances and fled to Argentina. He returned to Italy in 1955 and lived the rest of his life in quiet obscurity in the countryside of Florence.

Secchi, Pietro See SCIENCE.

Secolo (Il) See JOURNALISM.

secret societies

The term secret societies refers to clandestine organizations committed to political causes and plotting against established governments in the last years of Napoleonic government and during the RESTORATION. Lack of freedom of expression, fear of government, and a long tradition of organizational secrecy among all social groups, created an atmosphere conducive to conspiracy, in which secret societies thrived. Their secret rituals, symbolism, and organizational structure suggest connections with 18th-century FREEMASONRY, but secret societies were much more political and conspiratorial than freemasonry, and more open to members of modest economic condition, including some manual workers. Secret societies were hierarchical, structured around ascending levels of membership, each level being more radical in outlook than the preceding. Full disclosure of a society's goals was reserved for members of the topmost levels.

From 1808–10 to 1815, secret societies were directed primarily against the authoritarian government of NAPOLEON I. Launched perhaps by dissident French officers, these secret societies embraced the cause of Italian independence and republicanism, and sometimes cooperated with Austria and Great Britain against Napoleonic rule. The most radical of the early secret societies, the Società dei Raggi (Society of Rays), founded in the 1790s, was committed to economic egalitarianism and suspicious of private property. It reflected the Jacobin views of FILIPPO MICHELE BUONARROTI I, who went on to found or run a number of equally radical secret societies, including the Adelfi, Filadelfi, Apofasimeni, and Veri Italiani (True Italians), all strongly republican and antimonarchist, economically egalitarian, international, and for Italian independence. The best known and most active of the progres-

sive secret societies was the CARBONERIA, which accepted constitutional monarchy, political representation, and a moderate social program in all except its highest and most exclusive levels of membership.

Against these variously liberal and radical secret societies, there were others that espoused conservative causes and were the self-proclaimed champions of traditional and ruling dynasties, particularly the BOURBONS of Naples. Conservative and liberal societies may have worked together against Napoleon, but became political enemies after Napoleon was deposed in 1815. They went by such names as Amicizia Cristiana (Christian Friendship), Calderari, and Trinitari, but less is known about them than about their liberal counterparts. Governments feared all secret societies, called them "sects" and their members "sectarians," and outlawed them.

Liberal secret societies turned against Austrian rule. The more moderate ones hoped to win over Italian rulers to the cause of national independence, and may have had some success in the case of King CHARLES ALBERT of Piedmont. An effort was made in 1818–20 to bring together or improve coordination among liberal secret societies, with little apparent success. The failure of the REVOLUTIONS of 1820–21 and 1830 revealed the organizational inadequacies of secret societies. Their isolation, inability to reach out beyond their ranks, lack of coordination, and organizational confusion pointed to the need for different forms of political organization. GIUSEPPE MAZZINI responded by launching YOUNG ITALY and a program of national education for all levels of society. The ideal of popular revolution gradually eroded the secret societies' culture of conspiracy.

Segni, Antonio (1891–1972)
*legal expert, Christian Democratic leader,
president of the Italian republic*

Segni was born in Sassari (Sardinia) to a family of wealthy landowners, received a law degree from the University of Rome (1913), taught law at the university level, and in 1919 joined the

Italian Popular Party (PPI). In 1924 he was appointed to the party's national council. FASCISM forced him out of public life, but he suffered no persecution and his academic career flourished under the regime. In 1943, the last year of the regime, he was appointed rector of the University of Sassari. He resumed his political activities in 1944–45 when he organized the Christian Democratic Party (DC) in Sardinia and served as undersecretary of agriculture in the first postwar governments. He was elected to the constituent assembly that drew up the CONSTITUTION of the Italian republic (1946–47) and was a member of parliament from 1948. As minister of agriculture (1946–51) Segni was responsible for sweeping land reforms involving the expropriation of large tracts of land and their distribution to peasant families willing and able to cultivate them. These reforms broke up many of the large estates (*latifundia*) of the South and Segni's own properties in Sardinia. He also served as minister of public instruction (1951–54), prime minister (1955–57), minister of defense (1958–59), prime minister (1959–60), and foreign minister (1960–63). In 1962 parliament elected Segni president of the republic over the rival candidacy of GIUSEPPE SARAGAT, who was favored by the Left. Saragat succeeded him when Segni resigned from the presidency in 1964 after suffering a nearly fatal stroke. His son, Mario Segni (born 1939), also a Christian Democrat, was a major promoter of the government reforms of the early 1990s that changed the electoral and party system in existence since 1945.

Segrè, Emilio See SCIENCE.

Sella, Quintino (1827–1884)
engineer, mathematician, political figure, and finance minister

Sella was born in Biella (Piedmont) to a family of pioneers of the Italian woolens industry. He received a degree in engineering from the University of Turin (1847) and spent the next 10 years studying and traveling abroad to familiarize himself with the science and technology of his time. He was elected to parliament in 1860 and remained there until his death. A leader of the HISTORICAL RIGHT, Sella made his mark in politics as minister of finances, holding that post at several different times under different prime ministers. Balancing the budget to achieve monetary stability at home and consolidate Italy's credit abroad became Sella's obsession. He worked strenuously to contain government expenditures (his well-known personal parsimony was the object of frequent jokes) but, constrained by the costs of war and unavoidable domestic expenditures, he resorted to massive tax increases. He did so in 1862, 1864–65, and 1869–73, always drawing on himself the ire from such unpopular measures. His reliance on indirect taxes that weighed disproportionately on consumers and low-income people was attacked as insensitive and unfair. Sella responded to such criticisms with the argument that paying taxes increased the sense of public responsibility and made for a more patriotic citizenry. Riots followed the introduction of the most unpopular tax, the MACINATO (grist tax), in 1869. An exacting administrator, Sella demanded and obtained precise, verifiable figures from his subordinates. His efforts were principally responsible for the achievement of a balanced budget in 1876, when he was no longer in the government. That was the crowning achievement of the Historical Right just before it fell from power. Sella led the Historical Right after 1876 when it was in opposition.

separatism
The belief that separation or secession from the national government in Rome is in the best interest of certain parts or regions runs through the history of Italy since national unification (see RISORGIMENTO). It is rooted historically in the presence of independent states before national unification, the strong bonds that unite Italians

to their native cities and regions (CAMPANILISMO), economic and cultural differences between North and South, and the regional base of many political movements. Resentment of centrally imposed taxes, military conscription, and law enforcement measures played a role in the post-unification phenomenon of BRIGANDAGE in the South. National governments repressed brigandage and other forms of armed resistance by force, but also adopted peaceful measures to win over the people. The compulsory teaching of the Italian language in all schools, discouragement of local dialects, and adoption of uniform teaching curricula for the whole nation were part of the national effort to discourage and repress separatist tendencies.

War and economic crisis account for several separatist movements in the 20th century. The acquisition at the end of WORLD WAR I of territories inhabited predominantly by Germanic and Slavic minorities created the potential for separatist movements to emerge in the region of TRENTINO–ALTO ADIGE and the new provinces of the northeast bordering on Yugoslavia. The Fascist regime repressed any separatist tendencies in these areas, but Italy's defeat in WORLD WAR II allowed separatists to challenge Italian rule. The support of separatist elements facilitated Yugoslavia's seizure of Italian territory. The German-speaking populations of the Alto Adige carried on a low-level guerrilla warfare that lasted into the 1970s. Their separatist aspirations were never fulfilled, but they did obtain cultural, economic, and political concessions that defused the separatist movement. Separatist sentiment backed the exploits of the Sicilian outlaw SALVATORE GIULIANO in the aftermath of World War II.

The constitution of the Italian republic implicitly acknowledged the gravity of the separatist phenomenon by designating the border regions of Trentino–Alto Adige, FRIULI–VENEZIA GIULIA, and VALLE D'AOSTA, and the islands of SICILY and SARDINIA, as autonomous regions. Historically, separatist movements have done best in border regions inhabited by ethnic minorities or in economically depressed areas like the South and the islands. But in the last 20 years of the 20th century the most vocal separatist groups emerged in some of the most prosperous and culturally homogeneous regions of the North. This was the phenomenon of the *leghe* (leagues) that, at its most extreme, demanded separation from the rest of Italy and political independence for the North. UMBERTO BOSSI, the outspoken leader of the movement, called for the creation of an ill-defined independent nation called Padania, centered on the Po Valley. In 1996 Bossi proposed a formal separation of North and South along the lines of the Czech-Slovak split. His demands prompted vigorous rebuttals from the government, most political parties, and even from the pope. Since then the movement has lost support at the polls and scaled down its demands to calls for a redistribution of the powers of government in favor of the regions. While it is unlikely that separatists will achieve their most extreme objectives, separatist sentiments will continue to agitate Italian politics for the foreseeable future.

September Convention   See CHURCH AND STATE; MINGHETTI, MARCO.

Serao, Matilde (1856–1927)
Neapolitan novelist, journalist, and social commentator

Born in Greece to an Italian father and Greek mother, Serao arrived with her family in Naples at the age of four, studied at a school for teachers, and was licensed to teach. She worked instead for two years as a telegraph employee while beginning to write for local newspapers. In Rome, where she moved in 1882 to write for journals and newspapers, she met and in 1885 married Edoardo Scarfoglio (1860–1917), another prominent journalist with whom she cofounded and edited several newspapers, the most famous of which was *Il Mattino* of Naples (1892). Their stormy marriage ended in separation in 1902 and their professional relationship ended in 1904 when she left *Il Mattino* to found her own newspaper, *Il Giorno*. Late romanticism, French naturalism, and Italian VERISMO, all of which were alive in the period of her career, influenced her writing. She was perhaps at her best when describing the appalling living conditions of poor Neapolitans in *Il ventre di Napoli* (The underbelly of Naples, 1884), feminine psychology in *La virtù di Checchina* (The virtue of Checchina, 1884), social foibles in *Il paese di Cuccagna* (The land of plenty, 1891), which denounced the popular craze for playing the lottery, and the corruption of political life in *La conquista di Roma* (The conquest of Rome, 1885). Her antiwar novel *Mors tua* (Your death, 1926), the last of her writings, is said to have infuriated Benito Mussolini and cost her the Nobel Prize.

Sereni, Emilio (1907–1977)
scholar and political figure of the Left, active in the anti-Fascist resistance

Born in Rome, Sereni joined the Italian Communist Party (PCI) in 1928, operating in the anti-Fascist underground until 1930, when he was arrested and sentenced to 15 years in prison. Amnestied in 1936, he fled abroad, but was arrested again when he returned in 1943. Freed in the political confusion of that year, he joined the RESISTANCE movement, in which he served as political commissar for the region of Lombardy. He was a member of parliament from 1946, serving both in the chamber of deputies and in the senate, always as a member of the Communist Party. In addition to his political activities, Sereni was a scholar of note. He taught at the University of Rome and in 1966 was appointed editor of the review, *Critica Marxista*. An expert in agrarian history, he published studies on the rise of capitalist agriculture in the Po Valley, labor relations in the countryside, and forms of land tenure and use. His *Storia del paesaggio agrario italiano* (1976), published in English as

History of the Italian Agricultural Landscape (1997), is a classic of Marxist historiography.

Serrati, Giacinto See PSI.

Settembrini, Luigi (1813–1876)
Neapolitan liberal reformer, writer, political prisoner, and exile

Settembrini was born in Naples to a family of liberal traditions. He studied law but preferred to devote himself to writing, frequented literary circles, and taught literature in Catanzaro from 1835. In that city he joined the SECRET SOCIETY Sons of Young Italy, founded by Benedetto Musolino (1809–85), that conspired to unify Italy as an egalitarian social republic. Arrested in 1839, Settembrini was detained in prison until 1841 when he was released for lack of evidence against him. He was the anonymous author of the pamphlet *Protesta del popolo delle Due Sicilie* (Protest of the people of the Two Sicilies, 1847) that accused the BOURBONS of misgoverning. Suspected of being the author and fearing imprisonment, Settembrini sought English protection on the island of MALTA. He returned to Naples in 1848, after the king had granted a constitution, and briefly held the ministry of public instruction in the short-lived constitutional government. After resigning that post, he joined other conspirators to form a secret society for Italian unity. A death sentence imposed on him in 1849 was commuted to life imprisonment. Released in 1859 on condition that he go into permanent exile in America, he sailed on a ship that was hijacked by other conspirators who took it to Ireland, from where Settembrini made his way to London and eventually to Piedmont, where he joined the thousands of other Italian political exiles who had found refuge there. After Italy was unified Settembrini was appointed school inspector and professor of literature at the University of Naples. He now spoke out against the policy of administrative centralization of the national government and called for autonomy for the South. In 1873 he was appointed senator. His writings include the two volumes of his incomplete memoirs, *Ricordanze* (Recollections, 1878–79), published posthumously.

Severini, Gino See FUTURISM.

Sforza, Carlo (1872–1952)
diplomat, opponent of the Fascist regime, political exile, and foreign minister

Count Carlo Sforza, descended from the historic SFORZA FAMILY, was born in the ancestral residence of Montignoso near Massa Carrara, entered diplomatic service in 1896, became chief assistant to Foreign Minister SAN GIULIANO (1910), was ambassador to Beijing (1911–15) and to Serbia (1915–18). In 1919 he was appointed to the senate. As foreign minister in the last government of GIOVANNI GIOLITTI (1920–21), Sforza negotiated the TREATY OF RAPALLO, which earned him the enmity of nationalists and Fascists who accused him of yielding to Yugoslavia's territorial demands. Appointed ambassador to Paris at the beginning of 1922, he resigned from that post soon after BENITO MUSSOLINI became prime minister in October 1922. He chose voluntary exile rather than to cooperate or acquiesce in the victory of fascism. He was an active anti-Fascist in France, Belgium, Great Britain, and the United States, where he headed the Mazzini Society. After returning to Italy in 1944 in the wake of the Allied invasion, he opposed the monarchy. The enmity of Winston Churchill is said to have prevented his appointment as foreign minister in 1944, but he did hold that post for four years (1947–51) in the governments headed by ALCIDE DE GASPERI, working to regain international confidence for Italy, American friendship, and integration in Europe. During his tenure Italy ratified the PEACE TREATY, subscribed to the Marshall Plan, joined NATO, and took the first steps toward European economic integration. Senator for life as of 1948, he remained active in government and public life to the end of his life. Sforza combined moral rigor with an aristocratic disdain for popularity that made him more respected than loved. His book *Contemporary Italy. Its Intellectual and Moral Origins* (1944) reflects his personality and politics.

Sforza, Caterina (1462–1509)
strong-willed, uninhibited Renaissance figure who caught the popular imagination

The illegitimate but acknowledged daughter of Galeazzo Maria Sforza (see SFORZA FAMILY), Caterina was brought up and educated at her father's court. Early on she showed more disposition for the active life than for study. As an acknowledged member of her powerful family and physically attractive, she made a desirable match for Girolamo Riario, the favorite nephew and chief adviser to Pope Sixtus IV (1471–84). This political marriage proved to be also a love match that produced seven children in 11 years. The couple lived at the papal court, receiving from the pope the towns of Imola and Rimini as papal fiefs. They retreated to Imola after the pope's death, in fear for their lives as resented outsiders. In Imola, where they were chronically short of money and surrounded by a none-too-friendly population, they tried to build a power base that would give them security against their many enemies. When Girolamo was assassinated in 1488, Caterina carried on with the help of a series of advisers and lovers. Gossipers charged that the only thing she was afraid of was a cold bed. Neither Caterina's courage nor her able diplomacy could ward off the depredations of her territory by French armies during the invasion of 1494. She also had to confront the territorial ambitions of neighboring VENICE and the PAPAL STATES. She succumbed to the papal armies of CESARE BORGIA, became his prisoner in January 1500, and never returned to power. Although Caterina's role in history was a minor one, her strong, uninhibited personality caught the attention of her contemporaries and of posterity. She is often ranked among the great women of the RENAISSANCE.

Sforza, Francesco (1401–1466)
most prominent member of the Sforza family, soldier of fortune, duke of Milan

Duke Francesco Sforza I of Milan was the most respected and feared of the Renaissance CONDOTTIERI. From his father, Muzio, he inherited a company of mercenary soldiers. With that force at his command he carved out a personal fief in the town of Fermo in the modern region of MARCHES. Francesco served in the pay of Naples, Venice, the Papal States, and Milan, managing to maintain his reputation for integrity and reliability even as he changed sides. Forcing his way into the VISCONTI FAMILY by way of marriage in 1443, he supplanted his in-laws as ruler of Milan in 1450, with the hereditary title of duke. The PEACE OF LODI, which he promoted, gave him the period of peace that he needed to consolidate his rule. Not particularly popular with the Milanese, he preferred to live in his large castle in PAVIA, where he indulged his passion for hunting and the outdoors. The dynasty that he launched retained political and social prominence long after it had ceased to be a ruling family. The imposing Sforza Castle and Ospedale Maggiore of Milan and the Certosa (cathedral church) of Pavia are his most celebrated architectural legacies.

Sforza, Ludovico (Il Moro)
See SFORZA FAMILY.

Sforza family
renowned military family of the Renaissance period that came to power in Milan

This family of renowned condottieri rose from obscurity in the span of two generations. The ascent began with Muzio Attendolo (1369–1424), who honed his military skills in the tur-

Ludovico Sforza *(Library of Congress)*

bulent politics of his native Romagna region. The nickname of Sforza (from *sforzare,* to force), given to him because of his physical strength and stubbornness, became the family surname. His son FRANCESCO SFORZA won even greater military renown, married into the VISCONTI FAMILY, and eventually replaced his in-laws as ruler of MILAN. At his death the Duchy of Milan passed to his oldest son Galeazzo Maria (1444–76), who had neither military ability nor political tact. He fancied himself a protector of artists and scholars, but his lasting legacy was the introduction of rice-growing in the region of LOMBARDY, with lasting impact on the cuisine of northern Italy. His arbitrary and often brutal ways, and the high taxes that he levied, made him unpopular. Three disgruntled subjects assassinated him after he had ruled for 10 years. His successor was Gian

Galeazzo (1469–94), who was only eight when his father died. Real power was in the hands of Gian Galeazzo's uncle Ludovico (1451–1508), nicknamed Ludovico il Moro (The Moor) because of his dark complexion. Ludovico was formally invested with the title of duke of Milan at Gian Galeazzo's death in 1494. A lover of luxury and display, he turned his court into a great center of the arts. LEONARDO DA VINCI was among the prominent artists whom Ludovico patronized. He also improved agriculture and animal husbandry, often at the expense of small landowners whose lands he expropriated to build his model farms. Historians remember him chiefly as the ruler who invited the French into Italy, thus initiating four centuries of foreign domination. But the French deposed him and he died their prisoner. Sforza rule in Milan continued with his two sons, but Ludovico's son Francesco (1495–1535) was the last Sforza to hold the title of duke of Milan. The family line continued. A lateral branch took up residence in the republic of LUCCA. Giovanni Sforza (1846–1922) was a distinguished historian. His son Carlo SFORZA was a prominent 20th-century political figure. The last descendant, fittingly named Muzia after the founder of the dynasty, died in 1980.

Siccardi Laws See AZEGLIO, MASSIMO D'.

Sicily

The island of Sicily (pop. 5.1 million) is Italy's southernmost region. It is separated from the Italian mainland by the Strait of Messina, and is surrounded by the smaller Lipari Islands (Isole Eolie, in Italian), Ustica, the Egadi Islands, PANTELLERIA, and the distant Pelagie Islands that are closer to Africa than to Europe. The climate is temperate, the hilly and mountainous interior mostly dry, with rivers that flow irregularly and unpredictably depending on rainfall. Population is unevenly distributed between the thickly settled coastal regions and almost uninhabited inland regions. The regions of the interior are the

principal sources of emigration toward the coastal regions, the rest of Italy, and foreign lands. Agriculture and tourism are the major economic resources of the island. Europe's most active volcano, Mount Etna, near the city of Catania, is a place of special interest both for its volcanic activity and for the diverse natural environment of its slopes. The *Conca d'oro* (Golden Bowl) off the northern coast is a particularly fertile area, with extensive production of citrus fruit and vegetables. Petroleum refineries are found off the southern and eastern coasts, while engineering, pharmaceuticals, electrochemical, building, and food processing industries cluster along the west coast from Messina to Catania.

Sicily's central location in the MEDITERRANEAN SEA has made it a historic crossroad, meeting place, and melting pot of Mediterranean cultures. Its modern name derives from the *siculi*, the original inhabitants about whom virtually nothing is known because later occupants wiped out all but their name. Phoenicians founded the capital city of PALERMO in the eighth and seventh centuries B.C. The ancient Greeks, who called the island Trinacria because of its triangular shape, made Sicily an extension of Greece. Siracusa was a major power of Greater Greece, a town as prosperous and powerful as any on the Greek mainland. Under Rome, which took it from Carthage, Sicily became the breadbasket of the empire. Its history of multicultural settlement continued in the Middles Ages with the arrival of Goths, Byzantines, Arabs, Normans, and Spaniards. Italian administration is the last in a long series of political presences that have come from abroad.

All these presences have left their imprint on the architecture, language, cuisine, customs, and landscape of the island. Yet, from so many influences comes a distinct insular culture. The proverbial attachment of Sicilians to their traditional ways and their distrust of outsiders are rooted in the experiences of a people conquered by outsiders, who have treated the island like a land conquest. The German Frederick II (1197–1250) may have been the exception, for he loved the island and made it the base of his empire. In the revolt of the Sicilian Vespers (1282) the people rose up and slaughtered their Norman rulers. Sicilian resentment of Bourbon rule played an important role in the RISORGIMENTO, as many Sicilians were willing to replace a hated dynasty with national government. The origins of the MAFIA, with which the island is unfortunately and unfairly identified in the public mind, are related to the suspicion of government authority rooted in the experience of quasi-colonial rule. SEPARATISM has been an underlying current that surfaces in moments of political crisis. It exploded with particular virulence in the aftermath of WORLD WAR II, but was partly allayed by the broad administrative autonomy given to Sicily and other "special regions" by the CONSTITUTION of the Italian republic.

Sidoli, Giuditta Bellerio (1804–1871)
patriot and political exile, friend of Giuseppe Mazzini and other conspirators

Born Giuditta Bellerio to a family of the Milanese aristocracy, she received a good education, and in 1820 married Giovanni Sidoli (1795–1828), a political conspirator from a wealthy merchant family of Reggio Emilia. Compromised by his participation in the REVOLUTIONS of 1820–21, Bellerio and his young bride went into exile, where he died. The widowed Giuditta returned to Reggio Emilia, but was in turn compromised by her active participation in the revolution of 1831 and exiled. In Marseilles she met, became intimate with, and had a child by GIUSEPPE MAZZINI, helping him in his political work and providing inspiration and support for Italian political exiles. She returned to Italy in 1833 in the vain hope of being allowed to rejoin her four children, whom she had left in the care of her in-laws. The child she had with Mazzini was left in the care of friends in France and died in infancy. Unable to rejoin her children in Reggio Emilia, Sidoli moved from city to city, always under police surveillance. Allowed to reside in

Florence, she opened a salon frequented by liberals and became a close friend and confidante of GINO CAPPONI. After 1848, still persecuted by the police, she lived in Parma (1851–52), then moved and settled in Turin, where she spent the rest of her life. Her Turin salon was again a center of political activity open to patriots of all political persuasions. Mazzini was an occasional secret visitor, but their romantic relationship had ended long before. Mazzini regarded Giuditta Sidoli as the only romantic love of his life.

Siena, city of
Siena (pop. 56,400) is a provincial capital in Tuscany. A town of Etruscan origin, it dominates the surrounding countryside from its hilltop position, and maintains its medieval aspect as a clustered town of narrow, winding streets. A Roman colony, Siena grew in importance during the Middle Ages under the rule of its bishops and as a free commune (1147). In the 13th century Siena became one of Europe's major banking centers. The banking tradition continues to this day with the activities of the Monte dei Paschi, a financial institution with a global reach. The free commune, or Republic of Siena, engaged in a centuries-long struggle with neighboring Florence for control of territory, a struggle that sapped Siena of its economic resources and ended with the victory of Florence in 1555 and the absorption of the city by the Grand Duchy of TUSCANY. Before succumbing to its more powerful neighbor, however, Siena experienced the RENAISSANCE in its own way. The 13th-century Piazza del Campo and Palazzo Pubblico, with its bold and elegant Torre del Mangia, constitute a unique architectural ensemble. The Duomo and its piazza demonstrate the enduring influence of the Gothic style in Sienese architecture. The *Allegory of Good and Bad Government* by Ambrogio Lorenzetti in the Palazzo Pubblico is a series of frescoes that shows how an orderly society should be governed and what it should look like. The Sienese express their attachment to city tra-

ditions in the annual festivities of the Palio that culminate in the famous horse race in which the different neighborhoods (*contrade*) run against each other. There is relatively little industrial manufacturing in or around the city. Agriculture, banking, commerce, and tourism account for the city's prosperity. Cultural activities are also important. They revolve around academies (including the Chigiana Musical Academy), museums, and schools (including the University of Siena and the University for Foreigners).

SIFAR (Servizio Informazioni Forze Armate) See DE LORENZO, GIOVANNI.

Sighele, Scipio (1868–1913)
sociologist and political activist, known for his studies of mass psychology

Sighele was born in Brescia, received a law degree from the University of Rome, but showed more interest in teaching and social research than in the practice of law. His publications on legal aspects of infanticide, criminal complicity, political crimes, and crowd psychology gained him international attention and a teaching appointment at the University of Brussels (1899–1902). The work for which Sighele is best known is *La folla delinquente* (The criminal crowd, 1891), also published in French as *La foule criminelle: Essai de psychologie collective* (1892). Written to assess responsibility for criminal acts committed by individuals who are part of a crowd, it is actually a pioneering study that points to the irrational motivations and unpremeditated nature of criminal crowd behavior. Individuals may be swayed by rational calculation, but crowds respond to emotional stimuli. The notion that individuals and groups behave differently, that groups are governed by passions and prejudices that clever leaders can manipulate to their advantage, raised serious questions about the validity of political liberalism and democracy, which are predicated on the assumption of human rationality and cal-

culations of pains and pleasures, benefits and deprivations. Sighele's account of crowd psychology anticipated the work of the French sociologist Gustave LeBon who, in his *Psychologie des foules* (1896), popularized the notion that groups are suggestible. LeBon is thought to have influenced BENITO MUSSOLINI and Adolf Hitler. Sighele regarded LeBon as a plagiarist, but in fact both shared ideas that were part of the cultural climate of the time. Sighele was attracted to NATIONALISM and IRREDENTISM. He agitated for the union of the TRENTINO to Italy and was expelled from that region by the Austrian authorities in 1911. Sighele's political ideal was a populist nationalism, with government enjoying broad popular support.

Signorelli, Luca (ca. 1450–1523)
painter who raised Renaissance art to a new level of realism and emotional intensity

Signorelli was born in Cortona (Tuscany) but the date of birth is unknown. First mentioned as a painter in 1470, he is thought to have been influenced by PIERO DELLA FRANCESCA. But the originality and power of Signorelli's style were apparent to his contemporaries. He combines monumentality of conception with attention to detail, clarity of line with effective use of chiaroscuro shadings; figures suggest motion, facial expressions suggest character. The frescoes of the *Last Judgment* (1499–1503) in the cathedral of Orvieto are Signorelli's masterpiece. Particularly striking in these scenes are the depictions of the figure of the Antichrist who brings a false message of redemption and of the writhing figures of sinners tormented for eternity. RAPHAEL and MICHELANGELO are said to have studied these frescoes. In addition to superb craftsmanship, these paintings also express the spiritual unease and anxiety felt by many Christians at the time. Signorelli's art seems poised uneasily between traditional religion and the new culture of HUMANISM. His world is that of Christianity on the eve of the Protestant Reformation.

signoria

Competition for political power among rival clans, economic conflicts, and frequent warfare tested the ability of Italian city-states to govern themselves through representative institutions in the late Middle Ages. In the 12th and 13th centuries city governments instituted the office of *podestà* to deal with domestic discord. The *podestà* was a foreigner elected or appointed for a specific period of time to manage the affairs of the city in conjunction with other government bodies. The *podestà* was in no sense a lord (*signore*) because his powers were temporary and limited, but recourse to this office is a sign of the severity of internal discord that was also responsible for the rise of *signorie*. The *signori* themselves came from different strata of society. The ESTE FAMILY of Ferrara and the VISCONTI FAMILY of Milan belonged to the old feudal or military nobility, but the MEDICI FAMILY of Florence emerged from the merchant class, and the SFORZA were originally mercenary soldiers. The emergence of a *signoria* did not necessarily eliminate the trappings of representative government. Florence was still officially a republic under Medici rule, and the Medici were at first careful to preserve the semblance of representative government. LUCCA experienced the rule of Paolo Guinigi for only a bried time (1400–30) before reclaiming its republican constitution. Not all *signorie* were established by force, for in some cases town governments voluntarily put themselves under the protection of a powerful lord. But whatever their origin or form, the reality of the *signorie* was that power was heavily concentrated in the hands of one family and their retainers. Power passed from one generation to the next through the family line, the retention and passage of power often being legitimized by the theoretically superior authority of popes or emperors. The ruling family was not necessarily isolated because their retainers could number in the thousands, forming a privileged elite that identified its interests with those of the ruling family. The republics of GENOA and VENICE were never *signorie*. They retained their representative forms of government, but empowered a relatively small number of families of aristocratic origin. The golden age of the Italian *signorie* ended with the French invasion of 1494. The native ruling dynasties that survived the upheavals of the Italian Wars were wholly dependent on the support of outside powers like France and Spain.

Silone, Ignazio (1900–1978)

writer and political activist who broke with communism and condemned fascism

Ignazio Silone was the pen name of Secondino Tranquilli, who was born near the town of L'Aquila in the region of Abruzzo to a family of small landowners and factory workers. Before devoting himself entirely to literary writing, Silone was a journalist and a militant socialist and communist. He joined the Socialist Party (PSI) at an early age and in 1919–20 was in charge of party youth groups and publications. In January 1921 he was a founding member of the Italian Communist Party (PCI). A member of the communist inner circle, Silone was in charge of propaganda and of a vast and active underground resistance movement that covered several countries. Arrested in Italy, Spain, and France, he established himself as a tireless opponent of fascism. In 1927 he was appointed to the PCI's central committee. But at about that time he began to experience a political crisis that led to an open break with the PCI and communism. He broke with the PCI in 1930–31, apparently in protest over the party's blind adherence to political directives from Moscow. From 1930 to 1945 he lived in Switzerland and carried on his political battle with his writings. His novels *Fontamara* (1930) and *Pane e vino* (Bread and wine, 1937) feature peasant characters from Silone's native Abruzzo abused and suffering under Fascist rule. *La scuola dei dittatori* (The school for dictators, 1938) is an impassioned condemnation of all totalitarian ideologies. *The Living Thoughts of Mazzini* (1939) is a very personal and deeply felt account of that 19th-century figure. After returning to Italy at the end of World War II, his writings became less

Ignazio Silone *(Hulton/Archive)*

political and more introspective, culminating in his profession of Christian faith in *L'avventura d'un povero cristiano* (The story of a humble Christian, 1968). Recent revelations identify Silone as an informant secretly working for the Fascist police against his Communist comrades in the late 1920s, before his open break with the Communist Party. The revelations have caused a furor in Italy and have added fuel to the ongoing debate over the role of ANTIFASCISM in Italian life.

Sindona, Michele   See BANCO AMBROSIANO, SCANDAL OF; PROPAGANDA 2.

Sinistra Liberale   See LIBERAL LEFT.

Sironi, Mario   See NOVECENTO MOVEMENT.

Sixtus IV   See JULIUS II; MONTEFELTRO FAMILY.

Social Democratic Party   See PSDI.

social welfare

Unlike charity, which is essentially a private matter usually rooted in religious convictions, social welfare (*previdenza sociale*) is a secular concept that looks to government as the provider of services. In Italy social welfare dates from the latter part of the 19th century, when government began to provide health and unemployment benefits for certain groups of people. Before that, poor relief was mostly the responsibility of religious charities (*opere pie*), but criticism of their activities by CESARE BECCARIA and other reformers produced the first regulatory legislation in 18th-century Lombardy and Tuscany. Later legislation by NAPOLEON I regulated all private charities, but these provisions were largely revoked during the subsequent RESTORATION period. In the movement for national unification, GIUSEPPE MAZZINI called on government to support workers' efforts at collective organization and self-help.

After national unification the religious charities became a favorite target of anticlerical elements resentful of their power, but governments recognized and licensed private relief efforts of the *opere pie*. Legislation sponsored by the anticlerical FRANCESCO CRISPI in the 1890s assigned principal responsibility for poor relief to the local administrations (*comuni*), which were chronically strapped for funds. Government in those years also sought to encourage mutual aid societies and savings institutions among workers. The presence of organized socialist and Catholic opposition groups spurred the government to be more active in the early years of the 20th century. In 1901–14 the governments of prime ministers GIUSEPPE ZANARDELLI and GIOVANNI GIOLITTI passed laws to regulate the employment of women and children (1902, 1907, 1909), curb the spread of malaria (1903), assist the unemployed (1902), insure workers against disability, old age, and job-related accidents (1903, 1904, 1913), provide a weekly day of rest (1907), give benefits to pregnant women and mothers (1912), and underwrite life insurance policies (1912). Workers generally could choose their coverage from among competing public and private plans, which by 1914 reached some 4 million workers.

Further advances during WORLD WAR I and the immediate postwar years increased both the number of beneficiaries and the level of benefits. Agricultural workers who had been previously uninsured were now covered for work-related accidents (1917), unemployment insurance was extended to all workers (1919), and war veterans received additional benefits. In the aftermath of the war, employer organizations protested against the increased costs of welfare. They found a political ally in FASCISM, which initially privatized life insurance coverage and excluded certain categories of agricultural workers from accident insurance. But the Fascist regime changed course in 1925, extending accident insurance, disability, retirement, and general health coverage to additional sectors of the population. Improved health coverage for mothers and newborns, summer camps for children, subsidies for early marriages and large families were aspects of the regime's policy of demographic expansion, physical fitness, and preparation for war. The law specified that workers and employers had to contribute equally toward the financial cost of social programs.

These social welfare programs were the basis for the more comprehensive cradle-to-grave measures that came after WORLD WAR II. The strong representation of varied segments of the citizenry through political parties, labor unions, and other organized interest groups has been largely responsible for the expansion of social welfare to levels previously unimaginable. State legislation guaranteed citizens a variety of social services and prerogatives, including medical care, unemployment and disability benefits, old-age pensions, low-income housing, paid vacations, and end-of-the-year bonuses. Workers and employers shared the costs, but political pressures gradually shifted an increasing share of the financial burden toward employers. The expansion of social services provided ample opportunities for critics, who deplored their high cost, bureaucratic inefficiency and mismanagement, political interference, and corrupt practices. Italy still has one of the most comprehensive systems of social insurance, but domestic and international pressures are forcing significant retrenchments.

socialism See PSI.

Società Nazionale Italiana

Promoted by the republican DANIELE MANIN and the monarchist GIORGIO PALLAVICINO, the Italian National Society set out to unify the movement for national unification with a moderate program that had the backing of the movement's most influential figures. With Pallavicino as its president and GIUSEPPE GARIBALDI its vice president, it appealed to monarchists and republicans willing to cooperate with the monarchy. Its monarchist program assured it the tacit support of CAVOUR and King VICTOR EMMANUEL II. Excluded from its ranks were GIUSEPPE MAZZINI and his followers, who rejected the monarchy in principle. The society was founded in August 1857 after a long period of gestation marked by bitter polemics. Its slogan "Italy and Victor Emmanuel" acknowledged Victor Emmanuel's claim to the throne of Italy. It launched an intensive propaganda effort on behalf of the king on the one hand, while on the other it worked on Cavour and the king to make room for popular participation in the national movement. In practice, that meant accepting volunteer troops with Garibaldi at their head. Giuseppe La Farina, its ambitious and resourceful secretary, mediated disagreements among its fractious members, and between them and the Piedmontese government. The society operated openly in the Kingdom of Sardinia and secretly in the other states of Italy. Its network played a decisive role in mobilizing public sentiment and support for Piedmont in the war against Austria in 1859 (see WARS OF INDEPENDENCE). The National Society united moderate patriots willing to accept the monarchy to the exclusion of hard-line republicans and radical extremists.

Society of Jesus See JESUIT ORDER.

Soderini, Piero (1452–1522)
opponent of Medici power and chief official of the Florentine republic
Soderini belonged to a distinguished family of the Florentine aristocracy that resented MEDICI FAMILY rule of the city. Nevertheless, Piero served the Medici as ambassador to the French court in 1493. His diplomatic mission failed when the French king Charles VIII invaded Italy in 1494. The invasion resulted in the expulsion of the Medici from Florence and the creation of the Florentine republic (1494–1512). Now an opponent of the Medici, in 1502 Soderini was elected for life to the newly created office of *gonfaloniere,* or chief executive, of the republic. With his reputation for firmness, Soderini was expected to provide continuity and stability, but his decisions made him many powerful enemies. His greatest success was the capitulation of Pisa (1509) after a long and costly war. He followed the advice of NICCOLÒ MACHIAVELLI to institute a popular militia for the defense of the republic, but many aristocratic families resented its existence and the militia did not perform well militarily. His alliance with France brought on him the enmity of Spain and of the papacy of Julius II, who led a war against the French and their allies, princi-

pally Florence and Pisa. Soderini left Florence in a great hurry in 1512 at the approach of enemy troops. The republic was overthrown and Medici rule restored. Soderini was given refuge in Rome by Pope LEO X who, himself a Medici and an opponent of Soderini, trusted that his act of generosity would contribute to the political pacification of Florence.

Sodoma, Giovanni Antonio Bazzi, called See MANNERISM.

Soffici, Ardengo (1879–1964)
writer, painter, and literary critic of illiberal convictions and outlook
Soffici, born near Florence, belonged to a pre-1914 Tuscan avant-garde group that sought to inject movement and dynamism in what they regarded as the outmoded and static culture of liberal Italy. Along with GIOVANNI PAPINI and GIUSEPPE PREZZOLINI, Soffici was an editor and contributor to the review *La Voce,* but Papini and Soffici broke away to found the review *Lacerba* (1912), to be free from Prezzolini's dominance and speak more assertively. Their intent to transform culture through literature involved the difficult gambit of drawing inspiration from foreign models while simultaneously asserting Italian uniqueness. Soffici, who lived in Paris from 1900 to 1907, was particularly receptive to French artistic and literary stimuli. His writings helped familiarize Italians with French impressionism, cubism, and symbolism. Although Soffici thought of himself as apolitical, his paintings and writings expressed hostility toward materialism, liberalism, and socialism. The novel *Lemmonio Boreo* (1912) described how the protagonist went out into the world to fight injustice and corruption. It was a call on individuals of strong conscience to take matters into their own hands against the impotence of the law and public institutions. That call later reverberated strongly among Fascists, who also imagined themselves as champions of a just order in a corrupt society.

Soffici fought as a volunteer in WORLD WAR I and later sympathized with FASCISM. He maintained a certain distance from fascism even as he found official approval for his denunciations of art that was anti-Italian, liberal, and democratic in spirit.

Solaro della Margarita, Count Clemente (1792–1869)
Piedmontese diplomat, supporter of absolute monarchy

Solaro della Margarita was born in Cuneo to a family of the old feudal nobility of Piedmont. The experience of political persecution at the hands of French revolutionaries and JACOBINS turned him irrevocably against the culture of the ENLIGHTENMENT, on which he blamed all social disorders, and made him a die-hard supporter of absolute monarchy and papal power. His diplomatic career began in 1816, when he was appointed to the post of embassy secretary in Naples and continued with his appointment as chargé d'affaires in Madrid (1825–34). As foreign minister under King CHARLES ALBERT (1835–47), Solaro worked to improve relations with the PAPACY, supported the Carlist conservatives in Spain against their liberal opponents, and sought to maintain freedom of action for Piedmont, especially against Austria and France. He liked Austria for its form of government, but resented its interference in Italian affairs. Although averse to change, he favored the territorial expansion of Piedmont as long as it did not involve making liberal concessions, and he opposed Italian unification because it meant dispossessing legitimate monarchies and infringing on the historical rights of the papacy. Solaro regarded the papacy and Catholicism as the greatest glories of Italy. His political usefulness diminished as Charles Albert decided to court the support of liberals and play an active role in Italian affairs. In the Piedmontese parliament, where he sat from 1848 to 1860 as a member of the extreme right, he opposed the policies of CAVOUR. Convinced that liberalism served the interests of ambitious individuals and organized minorities, Solaro proposed universal suffrage as a way to protect the majority, which he regarded as inherently conservative.

Soldati, Mario (1906–1999)
writer, film director, and interpreter of American culture for the Italian public

Soldati, born in Turin, began to publish in the late 1920s and attracted much attention with his commentary on American life, *America, primo amore* (America, first love, 1935). Based on his experience of American life as a graduate student and instructor at Columbia University in the early years of the Great Depression, it presented America as a land of raw energy and little culture, consumed by materialism, wild and chaotic. Such a view catered to anti-American feelings prevalent at the time when the book was published, feelings that had much to do with the influence of FASCISM. But one could also sense Soldati's fascination with America, and his book intensified the curiosity of intellectuals, prompting downright admiring evaluations by such writers as CESARE PAVESE and ELIO VITTORINI. What really fascinated Soldati was the interaction between two dissimilar cultures attracted to one another as opposites attract. The mutual incomprehension of the two cultures is the theme of Soldati's novels *Le lettere da Capri* (The Capri letters, 1953) and *La sposa americana* (The American bride, 1978). Soldati was also an acute observer of Italian life, who dug deeply into his personal experiences. His appreciation of the pleasures of life and nature, and a sharp eye for psychological nuances, impart a realistic touch to his writings. Soldati was also a film director , an occasional actor, and a stimulating public personality.

Solferino and San Martino, Battles of
See WARS OF NATIONAL INDEPENDENCE.

Solo Operation See DE LORENZO, GIOVANNI.

Somalia See COLONIALISM.

Sonnino, Giorgio Sidney (1847–1922)
conservative leader, foreign minister during
World War I, and Italian representative at the
Paris Peace Conference

Sonnino was born in Pisa to a successful Jewish businessman and a Protestant English mother. This parentage, unusual for an Italian at the time, is often cited as a clue if not a cause of Sonnino's complex character and politics. Sonnino developed into an ardent Italian patriot who was quick to criticize the inadequacies of the Italian state. He was among the first to recognize the existence of, and denounce the indifference of the state toward, the SOUTHERN QUESTION. He deplored the disenfranchisement of the majority of Italians and called for universal suffrage, denounced government corruption and disregard of civil rights. After a stint in the practice of law and in the foreign service (1867–73), he turned to journalism. His *Rassegna Settimanale* (Weekly review, 1878–82) called for sweeping political reforms to curb the power of the governing minorities. After his election to parliament in 1880, Sonnino emerged as a leader of the opposition to the governing LIBERAL LEFT. He was a strict constitutionalist who called for strong government and resistance to the pressure of special interests. The combination of authoritarianism and constitutionalism makes him a conservative liberal. In 1897 Sonnino called for "going back to the constitution," which meant restoring the royal prerogative to appoint and dismiss prime ministers without consulting parliament. That stand put him at odds with most liberals and with liberal leader GIOVANNI GIOLITTI, whose policies Sonnino often contested. Sonnino served as treasury minister (1889), minister of finances (1893–96), prime minister (1906, 1909–10), and foreign minister (1914–19). As prime minister he could not enact any of the reforms for which he had fought in his career, but he seconded Giolitti's successful efforts to enact the electoral reform bill of 1912, which

enfranchised most males. ANTONIO SALANDRA called on Sonnino to become minister of foreign affairs in October 1914, following the death of the MARQUIS OF SAN GIULIANO. Sonnino negotiated the PACT OF LONDON that brought Italy into WORLD WAR I on the side of Great Britian, France, and Russia. At the Paris Peace Conference Sonnino insisted on a broad interpretation of terms of the Pact of London that included the contested city of FIUME. Sonnino thus clashed with President Woodrow Wilson, who did not feel bound by the Pact of London and wanted Fiume to go to Yugoslavia. Sonnino signed the Treaty of Versailles reluctantly, stepped down as foreign minister, and refused to run for his seat in parliament in the elections of November 1919. His appointment to the senate in 1920 did not lessen his sense that his public life had ended in failure.

Southern Question

Growing awareness of the socioeconomic and cultural differences between North and South gave rise to the Southern Question (*questione del mezzogiorno*) soon after national unification. Few northerners had a clear perception of those differences when the country was unified in 1860–61. The differences in the standards of living of northerners and southerners were not glaring at the time, because most Italians were impoverished. But North and South did differ already in their potential for economic progress. The area in question was that of the former KINGDOM OF THE TWO SICILIES. They had inadequate transportation facilities, industries that survived only because of high protective tariffs, agriculture that suffered from intensive deforestation, soil erosion, poorly run large estates, tiny landholdings for most peasants, chronic unemployment and underemployment, and high crime rates.

Those few northerners who understood what conditions were like blamed the "problem of the South" on bad government. They believed that efficient government was all that was needed to unlock what they thought were the natural riches of the South. Thinking along those lines,

CAVOUR decided that Piedmontese laws and methods of government should be applied immediately to the provinces of the former Kingdom of the Two Sicilies. The reaction to the application of new laws and their enforcement by military means took the form of BRIGANDAGE. That was a clear indication that the integration of these recently acquired territories in the unified state would be a difficult operation. The Neapolitan historian PASQUALE VILLARI publicized the issue in his *Lettere meridionali* (Letters from the South, 1875).

Villari's wakeup call was followed by the urgings of other *meridionalisti*, or advocates for the South, not all of whom were southerners. LEOPOLDO FRANCHETTI and SIDNEY SONNINO were Tuscans who published groundbreaking studies on the economic and administrative conditions of the Neapolitan provinces and Sicily (1875–76). Southern *meridionalisti* included PASQUALE TURIELLO, GIUSTINO FORTUNATO, GAETANO SALVEMINI, and FRANCESCO SAVERIO NITTI. Each had a particular view of the problems of the South and its relationship to the rest of the country, but they also had much in common. They called on government to be mindful to the special needs of the South, encourage its industrialization, and give southerners a stronger voice in running their own affairs. Salvemini banked heavily on universal suffrage to give the South the same political clout as the North. Nitti's economic analysis was directly responsible for the first special laws to promote the industrialization of NAPLES (1904).

WORLD WAR I interrupted these early efforts to confront the Southern Question. Fascism was reluctant to admit that the question existed at all, for to acknowledge it implied that the country was internally divided. Nevertheless, the policy of LAND REFORM, the construction of dams and aqueducts, public health measures, and construction of popular housing did benefit the South in the Fascist period. But the most energetic efforts to deal with the Question of the South occurred after WORLD WAR II. Land reform, special laws for the southern regions, and the CASSA PER IL MEZZOGIORNO (Fund for the South)

were part of a plan of intensive government intervention to close the economic gap between North and South. The definition of the South was extended to include parts of central Italy, like the *maremma* of southern Tuscany, and the islands of Sardinia and Sicily.

These measures, and large-scale MIGRATION to the industrial cities of the North and foreign countries (more than 4 million people have left the South since 1945), have alleviated but not resolved the Southern Question. There have been major improvements in education, public health, transportation, and tourism. The South is no longer the uniformly depressed area that it was at the beginning of the 20th century. There are oases of economic prosperity in all its regions. But southern unemployment is double the national average, crime rates are high, clientelism rampant, and public services inadequate. The recent tendency to ascribe the Southern Question to northern attitudes toward the South has had the unintended effect of making the issue a matter of perception and semantics rather than of social realities. At the same time, many northerners have come to look upon programs for the South as forms of preferential treatment. Charges that programs for the South are a cover for wasteful spending and government collusion with the Mafia are part of the political rhetoric of northern SEPARATISM. These programs have been cut back, the Fund for the South has been abolished, free trade and privatization are now relied on to stimulate the economic growth of all depressed areas. The results of these changes are still unclear but, acknowledged or not, the Question of the South remains Italy's most pressing public issue.

Sozzini, Lelio (or Socini) (1525–1562), and Fausto (1539–1604)
religious expatriates and reformers, highly regarded in the Evangelical movement

Lelio and Fausto Sozzini, uncle and nephew, belonged to a family of lawyers from Siena, but forsook the legal profession to participate in the movement for religious reform underway in Europe. A learned contributor to the theological controversies that swirled around Europe, Lelio left Italy in 1544 to escape the Inquisition. He pursued his theological interests in Switzerland in close rapport with Heinrich Bullinger and John Calvin. His writings had a decisive influence on Fausto, who after his uncle's death made them the basis of the creed subsequently known as Socinianism (also referred to as Old Unitarianism). The creed rejected the Catholic doctrine of the Holy Trinity, regarded Scripture as authoritative but subject to rational interpretation, and the sacraments as symbolic acts devoid of intrinsic power. Fausto turned down an invitation from the Medici to be a family secretary and left Italy for Basel in 1575. When his ideas encountered opposition in Switzerland he moved on to Poland, where he became the leader and chief theologian of the anti-Trinitarians and organized them into the fellowship of the Polish Brethren, who lived in communities, renounced war, and refused to keep serfs. The movement was stamped out in Poland by Catholic persecution around 1640, but some Socinians found refuge in Holland where they continued to participate in the religious reform movement.

Spadolini, Giovanni (1925–1994)
noted scholar, Republican Party leader, and prime minister

Spadolini broke the Christian Democratic monopoly on the prime ministry when he formed his own government in June 1981. This lifelong bachelor was born in Florence, earned a law degree from the University of Florence in 1947, and there became a professor of history in 1950. An expert on RISORGIMENTO history, Spadolini's broad intellectual interests led him in different directions. Scholarly activities and the academic life were too small to contain him. Moving into journalism, he wrote for various newspapers, and in 1963 became editor in chief of the authoritative Milanese daily *Corriere della*

Sera. The combination of serious scholarship and journalism made Spadolini an influential commentator and opinion maker. He was elected to parliament in 1972 as an independent, running on the ticket of the small but prestigious Republican Party (PRI), favorite home of intellectuals from outside the political Left. Before becoming head of the Republican Party in 1979, he held several government posts relating to culture and education. In 1980 he launched the *Fondazione Nuova Antologia,* a foundation that promotes the publication of historical studies and documents. As prime minister (1981–82), Spadolini had to confront the severe problems of political terrorism, organized crime, political conspiracies against the state, and the scandal of the BANCO AMBROSIANO. When his coalition government fell, he went on to serve as defense minister (1983–87) and speaker of the senate (1987), and was made senator for life in 1991. He always acquitted himself well and was one of the few political figures of the time to escape charges of favoritism or personal corruption.

Spallanzani, Lazzaro (1729–1799)
scientist, mathematician, traveler, known for his pioneering work in physiology

Considered a founder of modern zoology, Spallanzani's interests actually ranged far and wide. He was born in the town of Scandiano (Modena), was educated by Jesuits, studied mathematics and physics at the University of Bologna, took religious orders, taught Greek, logic, and physics in Modena and Reggio Emilia. Influenced by ANTONIO VALLISNIERI, he turned his attention to the natural sciences. He studied human blood circulation, described the functioning of the heart, role of capillaries, and noted the presence of white blood cells. From his observations, he concluded that the circulatory system was self-contained. In studying animal digestion, he noted the role of stomach acids. In animal reproduction, he noted the phenomenon of parthenogenesis and the various stages of embryonic development in the egg. He also experimented with artificial insemination in animals. An enthusiastic traveler, Spallanzani visited Constantinople, the Balkans, Romania, Hungary, Switzerland, and southern Italy. Wherever he went, he took copious notes on the landscape, vegetation, minerals, and life forms. He collected samples, classified them, and showcased them in his personal museum. The vast reach of his interests suggests a mind of immense curiosity led in many different directions.

Spanish Succession, War of the (1701–1714)

The death in 1700 of the last Habsburg monarch of Spain, the childless Charles II, left the Spanish throne open to the claims of candidates backed by rival European powers. Louis XIV of France secured the Spanish throne for his grandson Philip, heir to the French throne, who ruled Spain as Philip V (1700–46) and established the Spanish branch of the BOURBON dynasty. Fearing French domination if the thrones of France and Spain became united, the rival Habsburg dynasty formed a coalition that included England and Holland. On their side, the French lined up Spain, Bavaria, Portugal, and SAVOY. War between the two coalitions broke out in 1701. Fighting began that same year in northern Italy, where Habsburg forces commanded by EUGENE OF SAVOY defeated the French. Alarmed by the defeat of his French allies and enticed by Habsburg promises of territorial concessions, VICTOR AMADEUS II of Savoy changed sides in 1703. The French retaliated by occupying Piedmont and laying siege to the citadel of Turin, which was saved when a Savoyard soldier named Pietro Micca (1677–1706) sacrificed himself to blow up a tunnel that would have allowed the French to penetrate inside. Patriotic legend would later see Micca as a martyr of Italian independence. In 1707 the French were expelled and fighting ended in Italy. The war continued in the rest of Europe until the treaties of Rastadt (1713) and Utrecht (1714) put an end to the fighting. Philip V formally renounced his right to the French crown, thus eliminating the prospect of a dynastic union between France and Spain, fear of which had precipitated the war. Victor Amadeus received extensive territorial compensations in Piedmont, and received also the island of SICILY, which he exchanged reluctantly in 1720 for the island of SARDINIA and the royal title of king of Sardinia that his descendants held until 1861. Thus was born the KINGDOM OF SARDINIA destined to play the leading role in the movement for Italian unification. Although Spain maintained a foothold in Italy, and further improved its position in 1735 when it regained title to Naples and Sicily, the stage was set for Austrian dominance in the peninsula. It would be consolidated by the outcomes of the War of the Polish Succession (1733–35) and the WAR OF THE AUSTRIAN SUCCESSION.

Spaventa, Bertrando (1817–1883)
historian and philosopher, founder of the Italian school of neoidealism

The most influential of Italy's 19th-century philosophers was born near Chieti (Abruzzo), was pressured into the priesthood by his family (1840), but pursued a career in teaching as a private tutor and as head of his own private school in Naples (1846–50). A proponent of liberal education and a severe critic of the Jesuits, Spaventa sympathized with the revolutionaries of 1848. He left Naples in 1850 and taught sporadically in Turin, Modena, and Bologna, before going back to Naples in 1861. The philosophy course that he taught at the University of Naples examined the relationship between Italian and European philosophy. Its message was that Italian thinkers of the Renaissance had anticipated all aspects of modern thought, but that the Catholic Church had later stifled Italian thought and caused Italy to fall behind the other countries of Europe. Unified Italy, free of clerical influences, had the resources to catch up with the rest of Europe. He took issue with VINCENZO GIOBERTI and others who hypothesized an Italian cultural primacy. Their lack of realism, he argued, contributed to Italy's cultural backwardness. Although an admirer of Kant and Hegel and German IDEAL-

ISM, Spaventa did not believe that German philosophy could be automatically transplanted into Italy. His view was that Italians should develop their own school of modern philosophy by building on the foundations set by GIORDANO BRUNO, TOMMASO CAMPANELLA, and BERNARDINO TELESIO. Spaventa's teaching was contested in his later years by a younger generation of scholars attracted to the rival school of philosophical POSITIVISM. Embittered by the opposition and by the defeat in 1876 of the HISTORICAL RIGHT with which he identified politically, Spaventa withdrew from public life and spent his final years in obscurity. His most enduring legacy was the Hegelian concept of the "ethical state" as the product of historical necessity. Spaventa envisioned the state as an impartial arbiter of social conflicts, an abstract entity above all political passions. His ideas had a deep influence on his nephew BENEDETTO CROCE and on GIOVANNI GENTILE. Gentile published the lecture notes of Spaventa's influential course as *La filosofia italiana nelle sue relazioni con la filosofia europea* (Italian philosophy and its relations with European philosophy, 1908).

Spaventa, Silvio (1822–1893)
liberal opponent of the Bourbon monarchy in Naples and political figure of united Italy

Silvio Spaventa, younger brother of Bertrando, studied law but followed in his brother's footsteps to study philosophy. He shared his brother's philosophical views and political allegiance, but did not immerse himself totally in the study of philosophy. More of a political activist than his brother, he took up the cause of revolution in 1848, and after 1848 conspired to bring down Bourbon rule in Naples. He was imprisoned in 1849 and condemned to death, but the sentence was commuted to life imprisonment (1852), then to permanent exile (1859). He returned to Naples in 1860 after the Bourbons were ousted to collaborate with the provisional government of GIUSEPPE GARIBALDI. A supporter of union with Piedmont and of constitutional monarchy, Spaventa served as minister of the

interior in charge of the police and domestic security. Elected to the first national parliament in 1861, he held the important post of general secretary in the ministry of the interior, and in that capacity played an important role in the repression of BRIGANDAGE. He held other government posts, including the ministry of public works (1873–76), for as long as the HISTORICAL RIGHT remained in power. As minister of public works he favored the controversial nationalization of the railroads that brought down the last government of the Right. He was appointed to the senate in 1889. Throughout his career, Spaventa remained aloof from special interests and pressure groups, personifying that vision of the state as the impartial arbiter of social conflicts that was central to the ideology of the Historical Right.

Spinola, Ambrogio (1569–1630)
military commander in the service of Spain who distinguished himself in the wars against the Netherlands

Spinola belonged to one of Genoa's most distinguished families. But instead of serving the Genoese republic as his ancestors had done, Ambrogio found fame and fortune serving the Spanish Crown, with which his family had business connections, in the long and bloody wars to retain possession of the Netherlands. His military talent did not reveal itself immediately. He was an excellent student of mathematics, and seemed likely to pursue a mercantile career like other Genoese aristocrats. Thwarted in Genoa by the rival house of Doria, he entered Spanish service in 1599 with an offer to raise and equip an army at his own expense. Skilled in the art of siege warfare, for which he relied on the expertise of Italian engineers, Spinola won victories and gained a reputation as a formidable commander. Much in his debt, the Spanish government rewarded Spinola generously, and Spinola was in turn generous with members of his family who gained a privileged place in the Spanish court. Spinola, who in 1605 was put in charge of all imperial troops in the Low Countries, was soon credited with being the real power behind the Spanish throne. The Dutch agreed to a truce in 1609. Spinola took the field again when the THIRTY YEARS' WAR broke out. His greatest success was the capture of the city of Breda (1625), but he lost political favor for his conciliatory policy toward the Protestants and lost his command in the Netherlands. Appointed governor of Milan and commander of imperial forces in Italy (1629), Spinola was unable to capture the key fortress of Casale in Piedmont defended by French and assorted Italian troops. He resigned his commission and retired to his private estates, where he died a few months later. Spinola was one of many talented CONDOTTIERI who found fortune abroad at a time when Italian states could no longer afford them opportunities for advancement.

Spirito, Ugo (1896–1979)
philosopher and economic theorist, proponent of Fascist corporatism and collectivism

Spirito was born in Arezzo (Tuscany), studied with Giovanni Gentile, took degrees in law and philosophy, taught at various universities, including the University of Rome, and emerged as a theorist of an extreme form of Fascist CORPORATISM that Spirito called a form of communism. According to Spirito, FASCISM was in a position to resolve the conflict between management and labor endemic to industrial society by expropriating large-scale property, vesting it in state corporations, and giving management and labor a voice in economic decision making through the same corporations. State corporations should own the means of production and manage production in the general interest. Spirito's corporatism, regarded as too radical by nearly everyone else, was successfully opposed by big business and by more moderate Fascist corporatists, including GIUSEPPE BOTTAI, who openly criticized Spirito's position at a semiofficial conference on corporatism held in Ferrara in 1932. The regime's corporative reforms reflected more moderate views and resulted in the formation of state corporations that had few decision-making powers. Spir-

ito's ideas appealed to young Fascist radicals who wanted to revive the revolutionary spirit that they saw in the early Fascist movement of 1919.

Spontini, Gasparo (1774–1851)
opera composer and musical director

Born in the town of Majolati (Marches), Spontini's parents intended him for the priesthood, but his musical talent drew him to the theater. He studied at the Naples conservatory, where he began by writing light operas in the fashion popular at the time. In 1803 Spontini left for Paris, where he became a protégé of the Empress Josephine and a favorite of Napoleon I. The imperial court appreciated his talent for writing in the grand manner on lofty subjects. His greatest success was the opera *La Vestale* (The vestal virgin, 1807). Set in ancient Rome, it tells the story of a priestess condemned to death for neglecting her public duty, but rescued at the last minute by miraculous intervention. Its dramatically effective weaving of public concerns and private sentiments touched a nerve with audiences poised between ENLIGHTENMENT ideals of public duty and romantic notions of self-fulfillment. Public and critics alike acclaimed Spontini as a musical genius, opening for him a career that continued during the Restoration period in France, Germany, and Italy. But, erratic and quarrelsome, Spontini had difficult relations with patrons and colleagues. He spent the last years of his life in Naples isolated and in poor health, devoting himself to works of charity.

sports

Athletic display has a long history going back to ancient Greece and Rome, but the origins of modern sport go no further back than the 19th century. What is considered here is the modern phenomenon of regulated, competitive individual or group athletic activity offered to a large public for personal improvement and recreation. Italy's first sport associations were the rifle and shooting clubs (*tiri a segno*) that sprang up in the RISORGIMENTO to train Italians in the use of firearms and prepare them for the wars of national independence. Fencing and equitation, long practiced by the nobility, also became more popular and organized in the 19th century for patriotic reasons. But while these initiatives qualify as sport in retrospect, the word and the concept of sport as a means of personal improvement and entertainment entered the Italian language from English in the 1870s. English visitors and residents formed Italy's first soccer clubs in the 1880s. The first Italian national championship game was played in Genoa in 1908 and the first international championship in Milan in 1910. The first Italian bicycling association was the Veloce Club of Milan founded in 1870. That sport, originally inspired by the French, was slow to take hold because of the high cost of bicycles, but became increasingly popular as the cost dropped. The first national bicycling organization, the Unione velocipedistica italiana, was founded in 1887. The Italian Touring Club was founded in 1894 to popularize the new sport. The first *Giro d'Italia* (Tour of Italy) was held in 1909. Soccer and bicycling were already emerging as Italy's most popular sports, but Olympic games also attracted attention. Italian athletes competed in the Olympic games of 1896, 1900, 1908, and 1912, with the legendary fencing master Nedo Nadi (1894–1940) winning his first of many Olympic medals in 1912. The press covered auto races and aircraft exhibits and flying demonstrations. The cult of the machine propagated by FUTURISM and the interests of manufacturers fueled interest in sports.

Private organization of sports was the norm until the advent of FASCISM, when the state took over. Fascism realized the value of sports as an instrument of national mobilization. The regime touted physical fitness and athletic success as evidence that the people were ready and fit for the lethal kind of combat it had in mind. Many organizations of the regime were involved in the promotion of sports. The Fascist Party and the OPERA NAZIONALE DOPOLAVORO actively promoted individual and group athletics, government funds built athletic facilities, and the regime's propaganda magnified the achievements of Ital-

ian athletes and organizations. The names of Alfredo Binda (1902–86), Costante Girardengo (1893–1978), and Learco Guerra (1902–63) in bicycling, of Tazio Nuvolari (1892–1953) in auto racing, of PRIMO CARNERA in boxing, became household words. Not directly part of the history of sport, but similar to sporting events in the public interest they generated, were the aerial feats and explorations of ITALO BALBO, FRANCESCO DE PINEDO, and UMBERTO NOBILE. Italy's strong showing in the Olympic games of 1932 and 1936, and its World Cup victories of 1934 and 1938 reinforced the message of Fascist propaganda that the regime had transformed the Italian people physically and spiritually. Italian youth met once a year in Rome to compete and be recognized for their athletic prowess. The Fascist regime's interest in sports was directly related to its glorification of war as the ultimate form of competition, but there were also other reasons behind the effort to popularize sports. Italian industry also benefited from the popularity of sports as the producer of the machines and services involved in sporting events.

Sports underwent major changes after WORLD WAR II. ARCI (Associazione Ricreativa Culturale Italiana) carried to new heights the popularization of sports begun by the Dopolavoro. Private initiative dominated the organization of sports after the war. The most striking phenomenon of the sporting scene in the immediate postwar years was the rivalry between bicycle racing champions Gino Bartali and Fausto Coppi. The public identified the religiously observant and good family man Bartali with the Christian Democratic Party (DC) and the secularist philanderer Coppi with the Communist Party (PCI). The Bartali-Coppi rivalry reflected the larger rivalry on the political scene, which had rejected the international ambitions of fascism, had turned inward, and was wholly absorbed by domestic concerns. The 1950s saw the decline of the bicycle both in sports and as a means of conveyance. Soccer gained popularity, aided by the ease and low cost of playing it and, not least, by the introduction in 1947 of legalized national betting (*Totocalcio*) and the well-publicized winning of fabulous sums. It was estimated that by 1975, 35 percent of all Italians had bought into the national pastime. That was only one measure of the growing popularity of mass sports. Public schools, Catholic organizations, and political parties sponsored clubs and built sporting facilities. Volunteer workers contributed time and labor. The percentage of Italians actively participating in sporting activities rose from 2–3 percent in the 1950s to 22 percent in the 1980s. By the end of the 1980s Italians were spending more on sports per capita than any other European nationality. Sports were big business, and business tycoons like Gianni Agnelli of FIAT and SILVIO BERLUSCONI financed favorite soccer teams. In Berlusconi's case, success in sports and politics went together. His political movement Forza Italia (Go, Italy) echoes the chant of sports enthusiasts. According to recent polls the most popular sports and pastimes in Italy are soccer, hunting, fishing, basketball, volleyball, tennis, and winter sports. At the start of the 21st century sports are, and appear likely to remain, an integral part of Italian life and culture.

Sraffa, Piero (1898–1983)
Marxist theoretician, economist, and founding figure of the Italian Communist Party
The son of a professor at the Bocconi University in Milan, Sraffa was close to ANTONIO GRAMSCI and other founders of Italian communism. Sraffa contributed to the Marxist journal *Ordine Nuovo* while a student at the University of Turin, but by 1921 he was already separating himself from that group. In 1921 he visited Cambridge and became part of the group of economists gravitating to John Maynard Keynes. He became a fellow of Trinity College in 1927 and remained there for the rest of his career. His writings attracted the attention of economists and sparked debates and investigations of the nature of competition in capitalist systems, criticized the foundations of classical economics, and argued that in capitalist systems distribution is governed by the struggle over wages and profits. On the question of political tactics, Sraffa urged fellow Marx-

ists to set aside doctrinal differences and form a united front against FASCISM, advice that went unheeded in the 1920s when it might have contained the spread of fascism. Sraffa initially made his reputation as a Marxist economist by publishing seminal articles, then brought his ideas together in *Production of Commodities by Means of Commodities* (1960).

Staller, Ilona See RADICALISM.

Stampa (La) See JOURNALISM.

Stampa, Gaspara (1523–1554)
Venetian poet, entertainer, and social figure
Gaspara Stampa was born in Padua to a family rich in poetic talent. The career of her older brother Baldassare Stampa (1521–44), also a poet, was cut short by his premature death. Gaspara grew up in Venice, frequented its literary circles, and was accepted in Venetian society as a *cortigiana onorata* (respectable courtesan), meaning that she had a steady relationship as an unmarried woman. Her romantic passion for a Venetian nobleman gave her that status and inspired much of her writing. Some critics have ascribed the originality of her love poetry to a superficial culture that kept her from being an imitator. Others point out that the condescending verdict ignored the great merit of her poetry, which is her feeling for the musicality of language. The positive reevaluation of Stampa's writings is part of the ongoing revisionism inspired by the feminist movement (see FEMINISM).

Starace, Achille (1889–1945)
important figure of the Fascist regime, political organizer, Fascist Party secretary, and head of the Fascist Militia
Born in the southern town of Gallipoli (Puglia) to a middle-class family, Starace belonged to the generation shaped by the experience of WORLD WAR I. For Starace, the war was a moment of

self-discovery. A volunteer fighter, he won promotion to captain and several medals for bravery in action. It has been suggested that Starace's wartime exploits were trumped up to advance his political career. The war brought out Starace's predilection for authority, order, and action, and gave him the military skills that he put to use after the war fighting those whom he regarded as Italy's internal enemies, namely, socialists and communists. When the war ended, Starace did not return to the South but joined the Fascist movement, and in 1920 he founded the *fascio* of TRENT in the recently acquired region of Venezia Tridentina (now TRENTINO–ALTO ADIGE). He led punitive expeditions against anti-Fascists in various regions, including his native Puglia, and was responsible for the torching of the Milan headquarters of the socialist newspaper *Avanti!* In 1921–23 he was a vice secretary of the Fascist Party. Elected to parliament in 1924, he resumed the position of party vice secretary in 1926 and held it until 1931 when BENITO MUSSOLINI appointed him party secretary. During his years as party secretary (1931–39), Starace became notorious, and was often ridiculed in private, for his insistence on regimentation, absolute discipline, and blind loyalty to Mussolini. Some of the regime's most unpopular campaigns were ascribed to Starace, including the campaigns to abolish the use of the polite *lei* as a form of address, to purge the Italian language of all foreign words, replace the traditional handshake with the Fascist salute, require Italians to devote their Saturdays to community or party work (*sabato fascista*), wear uniforms, and engage in physical exercise. Starace was the nation's disciplinarian, but all his initiatives had the full approval of Mussolini, who valued Starace precisely because he was a loyal organizer rather than an initiator. Starace's most notable political trait was his utter loyalty to Mussolini, whom he revered as supreme leader and demigod. By 1939 Starace was so discredited that his removal as party secretary became inevitable. Appointed wartime head of the Fascist Militia, he held that post until May 1941, when his removal was motivated by trumped up charges of personal corruption and, ironically, lack of Fascist style. He reemerged at Mussolini's side during the period of the ITALIAN SOCIAL REPUBLIC, and was among the Fascist leaders captured and executed by resistance fighters in the last days of the war. After having been shown Mussolini's body hanging in Milan's Piazzale Loreto, Starace gave his last Fascist salute to the Duce in front of the firing squad.

statistics

The collection of reliable facts and figures on population, economic activity, consumption, and social customs and practices is a key aspect of modern administration in government, business, and all other forms of social organization. Eighteenth-century governments made the first attempts to collect reliable data on population and property for purposes of taxation and military conscription. In Italy, the governments of Austrian LOMBARDY and of the Grand Duchy of TUSCANY undertook to carry out land censuses, but were obstructed by large property owners and peasants who distrusted government authorities. Efforts by the Napoleonic administrations to gather vital statistics met with greater success, and compiled banks of information that were utilized and enlarged in the RESTORATION period. The Lombard reformers MELCHIORRE GIOIA and GIAN DOMENICO ROMAGNOSI argued that quantified knowledge was needed to address economic and social problems. Preunification statistics reflected existing political division, followed no uniform criteria, and gave no overall view of conditions in the Italian peninsula. The *Annuario economico statistico per l'Italia,* published in Turin in 1853, offered the first national overview. That publication reflected the thinking of CAVOUR and his collaborator Pietro Maestri (1816–71) that there could be no economic progress without accurate statistics. Maestri was in charge of Italy's statistical services until his death. Luigi Bodio (1840–1920), who succeeded Maestri and served as general director of statistical services until 1898, centralized the collection of statistics within his office and published the *Annuario statistico italiano* (1873), the first of many yearbooks published by the government. Bodio's faith that all problems could be solved with accurate statistical knowledge is a prime example of the cultural influence of POSITIVISM in the latter part of the 19th century. A statistician of international stature, Bodio was the real founder of Italy's Ufficio Centrale di Statistica, which was expanded in 1926 and given its current name of Istituto Centrale di Statistica (ISTAT). The office is politically independent. Its many publications include the aggregated figures of the population censuses that have been taken every 10 years since 1861 in the first year of every decade (there were no population censuses in 1891 for lack of funds and in 1941 because the country was at war, but a special census was taken in 1936). The systematic collection of statistical data has helped identify regional economic imbalances, public health problems, educational inadequacies, and many other social problems requiring public attention.

Statuto See CONSTITUTIONS.

Stoppani, Antonio (1824–1891)
liberal priest, writer, and geologist
Stoppani belonged to the minority of Catholic clergy who deplored the political divisions of the peninsula and openly supported the movement for national unification against papal policy. He participated in the REVOLUTION of 1848 in Milan and in the Third WAR OF NATIONAL INDEPENDENCE as a medical volunteer. He taught geology at various institutions of higher learning from 1861 to 1883 and served as director of the Museum of Natural History in Milan. An authority on the geology of his native Lombardy, his most popular publication was the book *Il Bel Paese* (*The Beautiful Land*), published in 1875. It is a description of the Italian peninsula seen as a unified, integrated whole, where mountains and plains, forests and fields, water and land, north and south come together in complementary ways to form *il bel paese*. Cast in the form of a dialogue,

the book described sites of geological interest and exotic appeal, such as volcanoes, hot springs, mud baths, and oil wells. Stoppani's writings on the subject of oil wells sparked public interest in oil exploration when oil deposits were discovered in the APENNINES. Stoppani used the interest to encourage Italians to make better use of the natural richness of their land and close the economic gap between Italy and the more economically advanced countries. In so doing, he perpetuated the myth of Italy as a naturally wealthy land held back by human negligence, but he also linked scientific discourse to patriotic sentiment.

Stradella, Alessandro (1644–1682)
composer and colorful figure who appealed to the romantic imagination
It is impossible to separate fact from fiction in accounts of Stradella's life. He enlivened the musical scene in Venice with operas, cantatas, oratorios, and instrumental music, and the social scene with his escapades. His light touch and gift for melody made him highly popular. His operas are no longer performed but were highly regarded in their time and he is thought to have influenced George Frideric Handel and 18th-century opera. He was supposedly assassinated at the behest of a jealous husband with whose wife Stradella had eloped. In the eyes of posterity the life of Stradella, like that of his older contemporary SALVATOR ROSA, reflected the turbulence and passion of a dark period of Italian history and contributed to the myth of the Italian as an irrepressible individualist. That image caught on abroad, especially in the Anglo-Saxon world, in the 18th century, was reinforced by ROMANTICISM, and is still common. In 1844 the German composer Friedrich von Flotow made Stradella the subject of an opera.

Stradivari, Antonio (1644–1737)
maker of string instruments known for the perfection of his violins
Antonio Stradivari, or Antonius Stradivarius, was born in or near the city of Cremona (Lom-

bardy), where he worked for his entire life. He began to make stringed instruments in 1667, probably in the workshop of Niccolò Amati (1596–1684). He opened his own shop in 1680 and was soon renowned for superb craftsmanship and inventiveness. He made at least 1,116 instruments, including 540 violins, bringing the violin to near perfection. He improved the construction and design with meticulous care for arching, choice of wood, joining of parts, design of the scroll, and varnishing. His two sons carried on the business that he established, also producing instruments of the finest quality. Stradivari violins are today the most prized and sought-after instruments in the world.

Stresa Conference(s)

The town of Stresa (Piedmont) on the western shore of Lake Maggiore was the site of two international conferences in the 1930s. The representatives of 15 European nations attended the first, held in 1932, to discuss economic collaboration. They failed to revive international trade, as governments gave in to economic pressures to reduce imports and protect national markets. In Italy and Germany, economic protectionism paved the way to the policy of AUTARKY. The second Stresa conference took place in April 1935. The prime ministers of France, Great Britain, and Italy met at this conference to discuss relations with Nazi Germany. France and Great Britain worried over German rearmament, while Italy was concerned over Hitler's plans to unify Austria and Germany. It was the British who convened the conference, but it was Mussolini who pressed hardest for a binding agreement to contain Germany for fear that an enlarged Germany would threaten Italy's security and its influence in the BALKANS. The agreement condemned German rearmament, reaffirmed the commitment of the three governments to keep peace in Europe, and maintained the independence of Austria. But it lacked provisions for enforcement, and convinced Mussolini that France and Great Britain would not stand up to Germany. Mussolini interpreted the statement in the final communiqué

that the three governments would oppose any change in the status quo *in Europe* as giving Italy tacit permission to go ahead with its war plans against Ethiopia. Thus, the pleasant town of Stresa was the site of two conferences that in different ways paved the way to WORLD WAR II.

Stringher, Bonaldo See BANK OF ITALY.

Strozzi family

This was a vast family of Florentine origin with branches present in many cities in Italy and elsewhere in Europe. The founder, Strozza di Ubaldino, was an active merchant and banker in Florence around the middle of the 13th century. His descendants survived the banking crisis of the 14th century that ruined some of Italy's leading bankers. The Strozzi were rivals of the MEDICI FAMILY in Florentine politics and were driven into exile by Cosimo. They returned in 1466 to cooperate with Lorenzo and rally around the Medici as part of the aristocratic oligarchy that ran the state. The Medici and Strozzi families intermarried in 1508 while they were both in exile during the period of the Florentine republic. When the Medici returned to Florence in 1512, the Strozzi were again part of the governing elite, but the two families drifted apart and ended on opposite sides again when the Strozzi sided with the faction that backed a second restoration of the republic in 1527–30. But the Strozzi were playing on both sides, did not live in the city while the republicans governed, and returned only after the Medici came back in 1530. After trying unsuccessfully to broker a peace between the Medici and the aristocratic opposition, the Strozzi broke with the Medici for good and emerged as the leaders of the exiled opposition. Giovan Battista Strozzi (1489–1538), led the opposition, was defeated in battle, and committed suicide in a Florentine jail. His sons Piero (1510–58) and Leone (1515–54) distinguished themselves as commanders in the service of the French monarchy in continued opposition to Medici rule. Both were killed in action. Among the aristocratic families of Florence, the Strozzi were second in importance only to the Medici.

Sturzo, Luigi (1871–1959)
Catholic political organizer, founder and leader of Christian Democracy, anti-Fascist exile

Sturzo was born in Caltagirone (Sicily) to a family of the lower nobility, was ordained a priest (1894), and continued his theological studies in Rome, where he was also a social worker. Inspired by the principles of social solidarity enunciated by Pope LEO XIII in the encyclical *Rerum novarum,* Sturzo joined the Christian Democratic movement to give Catholics a voice in national politics. He returned to Caltagirone to organize Catholics for political action, was elected to city government, and in 1905 announced his intention to found a party inspired by Christian principles, independent of the church, and committed to democracy and social justice. He directed his call to peasants, workers, and students. His program met with papal opposition at the time and could be implemented only after Pope BENEDICT XV definitely lifted the ban against Catholics voting in national elections. The Italian Popular Party (PPI) founded in January 1919 was Sturzo's party. He was its secretary, set its course, and was caught between it and the course set by the papal curia. The most contentious issue was how to deal with the emerging phenomenon of FASCISM. Sturzo was strongly anti-Fascist, but his unwillingness to cooperate with either liberals or socialists allowed the Fascists to take advantage of these political divisions to march into power in October 1922. Thereafter, Sturzo's opposition to fascism clashed with the policy of accommodation pursued by Pope PIUS XI. Embarrassed by Sturzo's double status as priest and political activist, and urged on by BENITO MUSSOLINI who wanted to be rid of a troublesome political enemy, the pope pressured Sturzo into resigning as party secretary in July 1923. In October 1924 he went into political exile, from where he tried without success to

organize an anti-Fascist Catholic party. In 1940 he moved to the United States, where he carried on an intense anti-Fascist campaign through the press outside the ranks of secular anti-Fascist groups. Discouraged for political reasons from returning to Italy immediately after the war, he waited until 1946 to repatriate. Sturzo was not at all in accord with the Christian Democratic Party (DC) that controlled the government after the war. He thought that the new party lacked a sense of direction, was too inclined to cooperate with the parties of the Left, and too timid in its social policies. When he was made a senator for life in 1952, he joined a small group of independents. Although he did not play a formal role in the Christian Democratic Party after the war, Sturzo was a source of inspiration for dissident Christian Democrats.

Suckert, Kurt Erich See MALAPARTE, CURZIO.

Svevo, Italo (1861–1928)
novelist and playwright whose narrative style combined realism and psychological understanding of characters

Born Ettore Schmitz in Trieste to a family of merchants, Svevo's writing vocation was a well-kept secret until he met James Joyce in 1907. Joyce, who had recently taken up residence in the city, recognized Svevo's writing talent and encouraged him to persevere. He did so and completed several novels while continuing to look after the family's glassware business. His writings caught the attention of French literary critics, who recognized his originality. Svevo was then welcomed in Paris as a new voice among writers. Initially Svevo had been influenced by French 19th-century realists like Balzac, Flaubert, and Zola. Eventually, Svevo fused realism with a Freudian approach that enabled him to delve into the complex motivations of his characters. The fusion is most successful in Svevo's acclaimed novel *La coscienza di Zeno* (Confessions of Zeno, 1923). While Svevo dismissed Freudian psychoanalysis as therapeutically useless, he did admire Freud's understanding of human motivation. Svevo's Triestine background helps explain his delayed recognition in Italy, where critics initially objected to his plain style and occasional lapses from correct use of the language. Svevo wrote in Italian to reach a larger audience, but his first language was the Triestine dialect, and German was the language that he used for business purposes. The pseudonym Italo Svevo that he chose (Italo meaning Italian and Svevo referring to his Swabian or German ancestry) points to his understanding of himself as the product of different cultures. It is the cosmopolitan, timeless quality of Svevo's writings that accounts perhaps for his great popularity outside Italy, where he has been hailed as the real initiator of the modernist novel. He died in a car accident. All his major works have been translated into English.

Syllabus of Errors (1864)

Pope PIUS IX issued this controversial document as an appendage to the encyclical *Quanta cura* in December 1864. The encyclical condemned religious liberalism, but the Syllabus strayed into the secular realm to list and condemn the principal errors of modern civilization that the pope regarded as being incompatible with the Christian faith. Rationalism, free thought, bible societies, religious freedom, public (secular) education, socialism, Protestantism, and the separation of church and state were some of the listed errors. The 80th and last of the errors was the belief that "The Roman Pontiff can and ought to reconcile himself to, and agree with, progress, liberalism, and civilization as lately introduced." Papal opposition to the RISORGIMENTO largely motivated this sweeping condemnation of modern civilization, for the movement for national unification aimed at depriving the pope of his temporal powers and eliminating the PAPAL STATES. Pius IX was ultimately responsible for a document, which had been several years in the making and incorporated denunciations leveled in earlier pronouncements. The document's standing was unclear. It created divisions among Catholics, some accepting it as an infallible pronouncement, others regarding it only as an instrument of guidance. It certainly inflamed ANTICLERICALISM and made it more difficult to resolve the conflict between CHURCH AND STATE. It placed the Catholic Church on a collision course with modern science, political democracy, and popular movements. The papal position was partly rectified by Pius IX's successor, LEO XIII, and more thoroughly by PAUL VI with the reforms of the 1960s.

syndicalism

In Italian the term *sindacalismo* (from the French *syndicalisme*) refers to the organization of workers in labor unions for the purpose of protecting their interests. Syndicalism is synonymous with organized labor, but with a militant connotation that emphasizes class struggle and opposition to capitalism. The militancy is due in part to the fact that workers had to struggle in order to gain the right to organize. Before national unification, worker associations were legal only in the KINGDOM OF SARDINIA, where the constitution of 1848 provided for freedom of association. National unification extended that freedom to the entire nation in principle. In reality, workers were often denied that right if their association was deemed to be politically subversive or a threat to public order. The police were often authorized to close down worker associations that were politically suspect. Troops were often called out to disperse assemblies of workers and street demonstrations. Only mutual aid societies engaged in philanthropic activities functioned more or less undisturbed. Labor organizations based on the principles of class solidarity and resistance against business or government faced an uphill battle. COSTANTINO LAZZARI formed the Partito Operaio Italiano (Italian Workers' Party) in 1882. It was the first party to be based on labor organizations and it demanded the right to strike and to organize nationally, and called on government to reduce unemployment. It was suppressed in 1886. Chambers of labor were formed in the 1890s. These associations brought together workers in a given territory regardless of occupation or skill levels. Leagues of peasant workers also formed in the 1890s. Together, the chambers of labor and peasant leagues gave the labor movement a mass basis that was often more demanding, militant, and aggressive than the leadership of the movement. Trade unions of skilled workers and their national federations were usually more moderate. Many of these organizations gravitated toward the Partito dei Lavoratori Italiani (1892), renamed Partito Socialista dei Lavoratori Italiani in 1893, and Partito Socialista Italiano (PSI) in 1895.

The Socialist Party thus came to be closely identified with the labor movement, but party and labor leaders often disagreed on what tactics labor should follow to achieve its ends or what should be the relationship between the party and the labor movement. On one extreme were the REVOLUTIONARY SYNDICALISTS, who believed that socialism would come to power by violent means by launching a general strike that would bring down the state. On the other were the reformers who argued for a piecemeal approach. Organized workers would gain by using the tactics of negotiation, and power of the vote and parliament, to improve their lot within the framework of the liberal state. Eventually, they would also gain control of the apparatus of political power and achieve socialism by peaceful means. The reformists dominated the Confederazione Generale del Lavoro (General Confederation of Labor or CGL) founded in 1906. Steered by Rinaldo Rigola (1868–1954) and Ludovico D'Aragona (1876–1961), its membership grew from 190,000 in 1906 to 2.2 million in 1920. Its principal constituents were industrial workers, but agricultural workers were also well represented, with about one-third of its membership in 1920. Under the double blows of economic recession and Fascist violence, its membership dropped to 1.1 million in 1921. It was forced out of existence in 1925–26 by Fascist legislation that deprived it and all non-Fascist organizations of the right to conclude legally binding collective contracts. FASCISM in effect abolished freedom of association and assigned the representation of workers to government-sponsored syndicates.

The CGL's successor was the Confederazione Generale Italiana del Lavoro (Italian General Confederation of Labor or CGIL), founded with the Pact of Rome in June 1944 immediately after the liberation of the city by Allied troops. With the support of all major political parties, it turned its attention to the urgent problems of economic reconstruction. It rebuilt the organization of labor from the ground into a powerful national labor union that called for far-reaching structural reforms of the system of production, including LAND REFORM. But the CGIL was torn by internal divisions that were aggravated by the cold war and by the political split between the Christian Democratic Party (DC) and the parties of the Left. In 1948 the Christian Democrats bolted from the CGIL, and a year later founded their own Confederazione Italiana Sindacati Lavoratori (Italian Confederation of Worker Unions or CISL). Its leader was Giulio Pastore (1902–69), a Christian Democrat who avoided political ties. The CISL pursued wage increases, maximum employment, and price controls. There was also a third independent labor union, the Unione Italiana del Lavoro (Italian Union of Labor or UIL), formed in 1949 by republicans and social democrats, and a smaller organization formed by neo-fascists. Wages were kept relatively low by a divided labor movement before and during the ECONOMIC MIRACLE. Rank-and-file members turned militant in the 1960s, setting the stage for the confrontations of 1968–69 and the bitter labor disputes of the 1970s.

Throughout the 1970s the labor unions strengthened their bargaining position vis-à-vis management and government. In 1975 the government agreed to link wage increases automatically to the rate of inflation. This was perhaps the most significant of the many gains of labor, which also included improvements in health care and pensions, housing and education subsidies. These gains did not bring peace to the labor scene, which was marked by strikes, high rates of absenteeism, and violence. By the end of the decade labor faced a strong reaction from management. Rampant inflation threatened the entire economy. Industries had to restructure in the face of mounting global competition and government had to rein in spending to deal with huge deficits. Workers in the vast public sector organized militant shop-floor committees known as *comitati di base* (COBAS) that engaged in obstructionist tactics, and staged walkouts and loud demonstrations. Unions in the private sector responded in an ambivalent manner. On the one hand the leadership spoke of intransigent resistance against all attempts to roll back the gains of labor. On the other, negotiators on both sides behaved pragmatically and found acceptable compromises at the shop level.

The decline in industrial employment throughout the 1980s rendered workers more cautious and unions more willing to compromise. The services and white-collar professions that did grow were not good grounds for union recruitment. Wage indexing was abolished in 1992. The political crisis of the 1990s deprived the unions of the party support that had helped them win many victories. Labor unions are still active in the early years of the 21st century, but without the mass base and political clout that had made them formidable players a few decades before. Yet, many of the gains in pensions, wages, housing, medical care, and job security endure in spite of the retrenchments of recent years, contributing to the high standard of living of most organized workers.

T

Tambroni, Fernando (1901–1963)
political figure associated with an early experiment in conservative government

Born in Ascoli Piceno (Marches), Tambroni was a prominent member of the Christian Democratic Party (DC), which he represented in the constituent assembly (1946–47) and the Chamber of Deputies (1948–63). He held several government posts, most notably the ministry of the interior (1955–59). In March 1960 he headed a Christian Democratic government that was supported by the right-wing Monarchist Party and the neofascist Italian Social Movement (MSI). Fear that reliance on these parties might signal a turn to the Right motivated the demonstrations and riots that broke out (July 7–14). Ten people were killed in Genoa, where the government had authorized a meeting of the Italian Social Movement. While the popular protests were clearly orchestrated by the parties of the Left, fears of a turn to the Right were widespread. Public pressure and lack of support within his own party forced Tambroni to resign on July 19. The resignation ended his political career. More significantly, the failed experiment in center-right government cleared the way for the OPENING TO THE LEFT that brought the Socialist Party (PSI) into the government and set the political course for 30 years.

Tangentopoli See MANI PULITE.

Tanlongo, Bernardo See BANCA ROMANA, SCANDAL OF.

Tanucci, Bernardo (1698–1783)
eighteenth-century administrator and political reformer

The Tuscan-born Tanucci served as minister of justice (1752) and minister of foreign affairs and of the royal household (1754) to King CHARLES OF BOURBON in Naples. When Charles left Naples to assume the crown of Spain in 1759, Tanucci became regent during the minority of King FERDINAND I. As regent, Tanucci stepped up his attempts at reform in the spirit of ENLIGHTENMENT notions of good government. He moved to strengthen the power of the monarchy by curtailing the privileges and powers of the ARISTOCRACY and the CATHOLIC CHURCH. Strong resistance from these entrenched groups stymied his efforts, but he did reform penal law, carried out a land census, reapportioned taxes, reorganized the food supply to avoid shortages, expelled the JESUIT ORDER from the kingdom (1773), and abolished the yearly gift of a white mare (*chinea*) that was the symbol of the king's vassalage to the pope (1776). The cultural life of the city gained from the construction of the San Carlo Opera House, archaeological excavations in Pompeii, and government patronage of scholarship. The rising conservatism of the court, attributed to the influence of Queen MARIE CAROLINE, prompted Tanucci to resign from office in 1776. Nevertheless, efforts at reform continued in Naples until the outbreak of the FRENCH REVOLUTION.

Taparelli d'Azeglio, Luigi See CIVILTÀ CATTOLICA (LA).

Tarchiani, Alberto (1885–1964)
journalist, anti-Fascist political exile, and diplomat

Born in Rome, Tarchiani started in 1903 as a political journalist, and went on to become New York correspondent for several Italian newspapers. He interrupted his career in journalism to serve as a volunteer in WORLD WAR I. From 1919 to 1925 he was editor in chief of the prestigious Milanese daily *Corriere della Sera*. His known anti-Fascist views forced him to leave the country. In Paris, where he lived until 1940, he was active in anti-Fascist circles, helped political prisoners escape from Italian jails, and was a founding member of the movement GIUSTIZIA E LIBERTÀ. Following the German invasion of France in 1940, Tarchiani relocated to the United States, where he served as secretary of the anti-Fascist Mazzini Society (1940–43). He landed with American troops at Anzio in January 1944. The Italian Republican Party (PRI), to which Tarchiani belonged, cultivated close ties with the American government. That connection, and his familiarity with the United States, made Tarchiani the logical choice for the post of Italian ambassador to Washington (1945–55). In that capacity, he lobbied effectively to secure financial aid for the postwar reconstruction of the country, invoking the need to stop communism and protect America's strategic interests in the Mediterranean. A staunch anticommunist, Tarchiani supported and may have pressed for Prime Minister ALCIDE DE GASPERI's decision of May 1947 to expel communists from the Italian government. He also pressed for Italy's entry in NATO.

Tartaglia (1499–1557)
mathematician, engineer, pioneering figure of the scientific revolution

Baptized Niccolò Fontana, Tartaglia was born in Brescia, which was then part of the Republic of VENICE, the son of a mail rider. The nickname of Tartaglia (Stammerer) was given to him because he suffered from a speech impediment that

Tartaglia *(Library of Congress)*

resulted from a saber wound. Largely self-taught, he earned a living by teaching mathematics privately. In spite of his speech defect, he excelled in public disputations, through which he won recognition of his gifts as a mathematician. In 1535 he stunned his peers by solving different types of cubic equations algebraically. Suspicious of other mathematicians and prone to quarrel, Tartaglia was shunned in his later years. In a famous quarrel, he accused GIROLAMO CARDANO of plagiarism, perhaps because Cardano had divulged mathematical information that Tartaglia hoped to use for his own advancement. Tartaglia's inventive mind came up with ways to salvage sunken ships at great depths, build better fortifications, and calculate the trajectory of artillery fire. He is considered to be the founder of the modern science of ballistics.

Tasca, Angelo (1892–1960)
founding figure of Italian communism, communist dissident, anti-Fascist and anti-Stalinist

This enigmatic and tortured figure of the political Left was born in the province of Cuneo (Piedmont), the son of a railway mechanic who was a single father. Tasca's socialism derived from the influence of his father and from his own intellectual interests. Admitted to the University of Turin in 1911, he made contact with other young radicals, including ANTONIO GRAMSCI and PALMIRO TOGLIATTI. Tasca shared their desire to rejuvenate Italian socialism, but he also had his own ideas. He wanted to preserve the unity of the socialist movement, believed that moderate socialists had a role to play in the party, and distrusted those who wanted to give all power to the party or to workers' councils. With some hesitation, he joined his companions who seceded from the Socialist Party (PSI) in January 1921 and formed the Communist Party of Italy (see PCI). Tasca tried to rally all leftists against FASCISM, but was unsuccessful. Fascist persecution forced him to leave Italy in 1926. He moved to France, where he remained active in party affairs, continued the work for a united front against fascism, and spoke out against the policies of the Moscow-dominated Third International. His opposition to Stalin within the Third International brought about his expulsion from the party in 1929. Bitter and disillusioned, Tasca broke permanently with communism, developed a deep suspicion of Soviet motives and methods, and returned to socialism. His anticommunism grew more pronounced in time, isolating him from the majority of Socialists who followed PIETRO NENNI's policy of collaboration with communists. After the German invasion of France in 1940, Tasca collaborated with the Vichy regime. He was convinced that a complete German victory was imminent and hoped to influence Vichy's social policies toward some form of national collectivism. WORLD WAR II ended Tasca's political career. His personal discovery of religion and militant anticommunism made him an intransigent cold war warrior. His book *The Rise of Italian Fascism* (1938), written under the pseudonym of Angelo Rossi, is a classic account of the Fascist regime.

Tasso, Torquato (1544–1595)
celebrated poet, narrator of chivalric epics, major figure of Italian literature

Tasso was born in Sorrento but left southern Italy for the North as a child to accompany his father into political exile. At age 18 he published his first successful work, the chivalric poem *Rinaldo*. After studying in URBINO, PADUA, and BOLOGNA, he took up service at the court of the ESTE FAMILY in Ferrara, where he did most of his creative work. He wrote the pastoral drama *Aminta* (1573) to amuse, but his talent was fully revealed by the masterpiece that assured him literary fame and immortality. That masterpiece was the epic poem *Gerusalemme liberata* (Jerusalem Delivered), which he finished in 1575 but did not publish until 1581. Using an eight-line rhyming scheme (*ottava rima*), in it Tasso tells the story of the First Crusade and the capture of Jerusalem in 1099. It revolves around the deeds of the historical figure of Godfrey of Bouillon, but Tasso surrounds that historical figure with a set of fictional characters and imaginary exploits. The figure of Rinaldo reappears from his earlier poem by that name, presented now as an ancestor of the Este family in a gesture of flattery to his patrons. In 20 cantos, Tasso spins out a tale of love and war, praising the Christian knights for their courage and virtue, but also showing the complexity of human emotions, conflicts between duty and passion, achieving a lofty tone, and expressing a melancholy, lyrical spirit unprecedented in the chivalric literature. The tone, heroic, solemn, and grand, reflects the sense of urgency of Christian Europe. The Turks were threatening from the East, Christians were torn by religious strife, and the CATHOLIC CHURCH was engaged in long and agonizing reform. Tasso also faced his own personal drama. Restless, dissatisfied, at times physically ill, he was emotionally unstable, prey to uncontrollable outbursts, and convinced that hidden enemies dogged him at every step. His behavior landed him in jail in 1577 and 1579. Released in 1586, he wandered from city to city. His fame assured him the support of various patrons, including that of Pope Clement VIII (1592–1605). Tasso spent his final years in Rome under papal protection. In 1593 he published *Gerusalemma conquistata* (Jerusalem Conquered, 1593), a revised version of his masterpiece that was not well received. Tasso's combination of extraordinary talent and emotional instability appealed to the romantic imagination that saw in him the personification of literary genius. There is a modern translation of *Gerusalemme liberata* (2000) by Anthony M. Esolen.

Taviani, Paolo Emilio (1912–2001)
resistance fighter, Christian Democratic leader, and parliamentary figure

Taviani was born in Genoa, earned degrees in economics, legal studies, history, and political science at the University of Genoa, and at that school taught economics. In 1931–34 he was president of the Federation of Catholic University Students (FUCI). He was detained in 1943 for his anti-Fascist sentiments, escaped, joined the RESISTANCE, and led the fight that liberated Genoa from Nazi occupation in April 1945. He served in the constituent assembly (1946–47) and was a member of parliament from 1948 until his death, serving first in the chamber of deputies (1948–76) and then in the senate. He held major government posts from the early 1950s to the mid-1970s. As defense minister (1953–57) he bolstered the armed forces and initiated the clandestine organization known as Gladio that was designed to thwart any communist attempt to seize power by force. Understandable in the cold war context of the 1950s, the revelation that the organization still functioned in the early 1990s caused a political uproar; it was abolished in 1993. Taviani also served as finance minister (1959–60), treasury minister (1960–62), interior minister (1962–68, 1973–74), minister for the South (1968–72), and budget minister (1972–73). In the 1970s Taviani took a hard line against TERRORISM and opposed all efforts to negotiate for the release of ALDO MORO. In 1991 President Francesco Cossiga appointed him senator for life. Taviani's presence and longevity in many different governments illustrate the underlying stability and continuity of power during the period of Christian Democratic hegemony.

taxation

Tax revenues provide the financial resources that governments need to meet their obligations. These obligations include ensuring security for their citizens, encouraging economic growth, undertaking public works, and providing social services such as education, health care, and pensions. Modern governments provide services in all these areas with varying degrees of comprehensiveness. Historically, however, the single most important reason for taxation has been war. RENAISSANCE states spent much on war, and displayed great ingenuity in levying taxes to provide for it. They used direct taxes such as the tithe (*decima*), which required payment of one-10th of one's income, and property taxes based on the value of land. To ascertain the value of land the Florentine state carried out a land census (*catasto*) over the strong opposition of landowners who did not want the government to know what they owned. These taxes were based on the wealth of individuals or families, and therefore theoretically were the most fair. But since direct taxes were difficult to assess and collect, Renaissance governments also adopted indirect taxes on consumption (*gabelle*), particularly on salt, which was a commodity in great demand for the preservation of food and feeding of animals, and taxes on the transportation of goods (*dazi*), which were collected on the road or at the city gates when farmers came to the city to sell their produce. There were also stamp taxes for legal documents, "hearth taxes" (*focatici*) levied on families, and poll taxes levied on individuals. Clergy and religious associations were exempt from most taxes. The nobility was not, but generally found ways not to pay proportionately to their wealth. Governments often farmed out the collection of taxes to private individuals or associations, which took a percentage of the revenue for their services.

Renaissance states thus developed a system of taxation that survived into modern times with relatively few changes in principle. Renaissance states, however, did develop and pass on systems that differed greatly in detail and complexity, the greatest difference being found in the tax systems of the city states of central and northern Italy on the one hand, and the tax system of the Kingdom of Naples (see KINGDOM OF THE TWO SICILIES) on the other. Naples relied heavily on indirect taxation, the nobility of the kingdom enjoyed substantial tax privileges, and the bureaucracy of this large state found it much more difficult to assess the value of property and collect taxes than the bureaucracies of the smaller states to the north. Lax enforcement of tax laws in the South was not due simply to administrative inefficiency; it was also a policy calculated to minimize social resentment and political disaffection.

National unification simplified the overall picture by extending the taxation system of the KINGDOM OF SARDINIA to the rest of the country, adopting new uniform laws, minimizing exemptions, and providing strict enforcement. Taxation was uppermost on the agenda of the national government because of the need to meet the extraordinary expenses of national unification, balance the budget, and establish sound credit for the state. The result was an increase in taxes that caused widespread disenchantment and downright revolt against the national government, particularly in the South (see BRIGANDAGE). High taxes probably were also a factor in the massive EMIGRATION experienced by the country's poorest areas. The most resented tax was the grist tax (MACINATO), which weighed heavily on people of modest means who could least afford to pay it. The needs of government were many. Repayment of debts took over 40 percent of tax revenues. Military expenditures were next in line, absorbing nearly 25 percent of government revenues between 1862 and 1913, according to one estimate. In spite of its flaws, especially heavy reliance on indirect taxes that

fell disproportionately on the poorest taxpayers, the tax system of the liberal state provided enough revenue to meet the goals of government. WORLD WAR I changed all that by requiring massive borrowing and higher taxes to meet its unexpected costs, which affected national budgets long after the war was over. Antitaxation sentiment played a part in the rise of FASCISM, which came to power promising to rein in public expenditures, reduce the cost of government, and encourage private initiative. Taxation remained moderate until the late 1930s when the regime raised direct taxes on incomes, property, and dividends and introduced a general sales tax to help pay for its expansionist policies.

Nevertheless, budget deficits piled up immediately before and during WORLD WAR II. Postwar governments held the line on spending and taxes through the 1950s to stimulate recovery and help the private sector. In 1951 Finance Minister EZIO VANONI introduced a system based on individual annual income declarations that relied on taxpayer honesty. It never achieved its intended objective of efficient and equitable taxation. In the 1960s government expenditures caught up with and began to exceed revenues. Fiscal reforms in the early 1970s introduced a value-added tax on consumer products, a comprehensive tax on incomes, and uniform municipal taxes to provide for local needs. The system was much simplified by these reforms. It is still in place, with glaring problems that challenge the ingenuity of experts and the political resolve of governments. The tax burden falls unevenly on different categories of taxpayers (automatic payroll deductions subject wage earners to the full rigor of the law), relies heavily on regressive consumer taxes (Italians pay a lot more taxes than they realize because the value added tax is rolled into the price of products), evasions are a problem, and thousands of special laws make the tax code confusingly complex. Legislation chips away at exemptions, adjusts rates, and passes special laws, without overhauling the system. In the 1990s tax issues became political issues, feeding regional resentments and complicating the process of economic integration in Europe.

Governments have met the economic requirements for membership in the EUROPEAN UNION by cutting public expenditures. Taxpayers have generally accepted fiscal discipline as a necessary condition for membership in Europe.

Telecom Italia See OLIVETTI S.P.A.

Terni Steelworks See INDUSTRIALIZATION.

Terracini, Umberto Elia (1895–1983)
Communist Party founder and leader, party dissident, and hard-liner

Terracini was born in Genoa but the family moved to Turin in 1899 following the death of his father. He received a law degree from the University of Turin, where he also met and bonded with future communist leaders ANTONIO GRAMSCI and PALMIRO TOGLIATTI. Terracini joined the Socialist Party (PSI) in 1916. That same year he was arrested and sentenced to four months in jail for distributing antiwar propaganda. After his release he was drafted and served in the Italian army until 1919. In 1919–20 he was part of the *Ordine Nuovo* group and encouraged the occupation of the factories by workers. He broke away from the Socialist Party and was a founder of the Italian Communist Party (PCI) in 1921. In 1926 he was arrested and sentenced to 23 years in jail on charges of plotting against the state. While in jail, he was expelled from the Communist Party for his criticism of the Nazi-Soviet pact of 1939, but was later readmitted. Liberated in September 1943, he participated in the RESISTANCE in a political capacity. After the war he served in the constituent assembly (1946–47) and was appointed "senator by right" in 1948 on the basis of his anti-Fascist credentials. He was president of the Communist group in the senate from 1958 to 1972. An outspoken critic of the Christian Democratic Party (DC), Terracini argued that the Constitution envisioned a sharing of power by all political parties represented in parliament rather than dominance by one party.

Umberto Terracini *(Library of Congress)*

terrorism

The use of violence against constituted governments or other institutions is a political tactic often employed by clandestine groups that are denied or reject recourse to legal means of persuasion. Terrorist acts include assassinating or maiming political opponents, deliberate killing of civilians, kidnappings, destruction of physical property, and other acts of intimidation. In the 19th century SECRET SOCIETIES often targeted prominent figures for political assassination. GIUSEPPE MAZZINI argued that the use of violence against targeted political opponents was legitimate when the law banned peaceful forms of political opposition. Later in the century, anarchists justified and carried out political assassinations to intimidate rulers or in retaliation for the use of state violence against protesters.

The assassination in 1900 of King UMBERTO I by the anarchist Gaetano Bresci (1869–1901) was the most sensational of several political assassinations carried out by Italian political malcontents at the time. The most widespread recurrence of political terrorism in Italy dates from 1944–45. The RESISTANCE movement used terrorist tactics against Fascists and their supporters in the final stages of WORLD WAR II, often in retaliation for acts of violence committed against them. From the 1950s to the 1970s separatists in the German-speaking areas of the TRENTINO–ALTO ADIGE used terrorist tactics to achieve secession or autonomy for their region. At the other end of the country, the MAFIA uses political assassination and acts of violence against civilians to weaken government authority and secure control of territory for illegal activities.

But the most notorious cases of political terrorism since 1945 are tied to the activities of right-wing and left-wing extremists. Right wingers (neo-fascists) are blamed for one of the country's most sensational acts of terrorism. The explosion of a bomb in Milan's Piazza Fontana in December 1969 that killed 16 people and injured 90 set off repeated acts of terrorism in the 1970s. This act inaugurated the *strategia della tensione* (strategy of tension) that relied on the indiscriminate use of violence to create a sense of general insecurity in the country, undermine the authority of government, and provoke the army into staging a military coup that, in the thinking of the terrorists, would reveal the repressive nature of the capitalist system. The new type of terrorism no longer limited itself to targeting individuals (although many prominent political and cultural figures did become its victims), but struck at anonymous crowds without distinction. Right-wing groups like ORDINE NUOVO seem to have favored the indiscriminate terrorism that prevailed until 1974, but in the murky world of the so-called extra-parliamentary opposition groups, it is not always possible to distinguish between Left and Right.

The most dangerous groups seem to be those that combine Marxist-Leninist ideological fanaticism with the neo-fascist glorification of violence as a form of political therapy. During what came to be known as the *anni di piombo* (years of lead) from about 1975 to 1980, the most effective and notorious terrorist organization was that of the RED BRIGADES, which in 1978 staged and carried out the highly dramatic kidnapping and murder of the Christian Democratic leader ALDO MORO. The ensuing government crackdown on terrorist groups and the changing nature of Italian society in the 1990s reduced political terrorism to the level of a nuisance rather than a threat. Government responses included substituting single-judge trials for jury trials to speed up proceedings and avoid intimidation of jurors, holding secret hearings, protecting the anonymity of prosecutors, creating witness protection programs, and training special antiterrorist police units, the so-called *teste di cuoio* (leather heads), named from the leather headgear designed to protect them and prevent their identification. The response of government to terrorism has been particularly effective because it has avoided extreme reactions that might have posed a serious threat to civil liberties. In spite of fears to the contrary voiced by opposition groups, nothing remotely comparable to the Fascist regime's use of repressive measures against its domestic opponents has occurred. Italians today show little support for political extremism of either Left or Right. From the perspective of 2004, the *strategia della tensione* has failed in its intended goals of polarizing society and destabilizing government.

Thousand, the See GARIBALDI, GIUSEPPE.

Tiber River See LATIUM; ROME, CITY OF.

Ticino

The Swiss canton of Ticino (Tessin) is located on the southern slope of the Alps bordering on Italy. This territory shared the history of LOMBARDY until the 16th century when Swiss armies wrested it from the duchy of Milan. The Ticino became an autonomous canton of the Swiss Confederation in 1803. Most of its 250,000 inhabitants are Italian-speaking Roman Catholics. A mountainous region, with Bellinzona as its capital, the Ticino Canton spreads out over the valley of the Ticino River as it flows southward from the Alps into Lago Maggiore, from where the river continues south to join the Po River near Pavia. The town of Locarno located in its territory was the site of an important international conference in 1925. Lugano is another popular resort town within the canton. Unlike other Italian-speaking territories of the Alps, the Ticino Canton has never had a significant irredentist movement seeking unification with Italy. Occasional public references to its Italian character in the press and in parliament hinted at a Fascist territorial interest in this region.

Tiepolo, Giovanni Battista (1696–1770)
Venetian painter and decorator, last of the great Venetian artists

Of working-class parents, Tiepolo was apprenticed at the age of 14 to learn painting. He looked upon his work as a trade, and later in his own shop, surrounded himself with apprentices who painted in his own style in a manner that makes it difficult to distinguish their work from his. His fame spread throughout Europe and drew him away from Venice. In Würzburg (Bavaria) where he went in 1750 he decorated the archbishop's palace with frescoes illustrating the life of Emperor Frederick I. In 1762 he went to Madrid, where he spent the rest of his life. There, he decorated the royal palace with frescoes depicting the provinces of Spain and its rise as an imperial power. Ceiling sky scenes are Tiepolo's hallmark. With allegorical figures floating on banks of clouds, light blues and pinks, these scenes draw the viewer upward and suggest a connection between the human and the divine. His works emanate a sense of serenity that has been attributed to the deceptive sense of stability and prosperity of the Venetian republic in its waning days. A prolific painter, Tiepolo's oil paintings can be seen in many museums throughout Europe and North America.

Tintoretto (1518–1594)
Venetian painter and decorator known for the dynamism of his style, and the drama and monumentality of his representations

Originally named Jacopo Robusti, he was given the name of Tintoretto (little dyer) from his father's trade (*tintore*). He seems to have studied under Titian, with whom he did not get along well. Tintoretto was known for his volatile temperament, but he also seems to have borrowed and copied shamelessly from contemporary artists. Yet, even his early works show distinctive hallmarks, such as successful use of light effects and a dramatic style of visual narrative. The contorted figures, agonized expressions, and long perspectives of his mature works suggest movement in the direction of MANNERISM. His best-known canvases belong to the series that he painted off and on for the Scuola di San Rocco (1564–87). These illustrate the lives of Venetian saints, scenes from the New Testament, and include an enormous *Crucifixion*. Other late canvases that he painted include those for the Ducal Palace and the Church of San Giorgio Maggiore. Paintings for the former include his vision of *Paradise,* which is the largest of all his works. Outstanding among the paintings for San Giorgio Maggiore are the *Last Supper* and *Entombment.* Painted in the early 1590s, these works represent Tintoretto's last style, which is marked by a strong sense of mystery and spirituality.

Titian (ca. 1485–1576)
(Tiziano Vecellio)
leading painter who extended the influence of the Venetian school to the rest of Italy and Europe

Titian (Tiziano Vecellio) was born in the alpine village of Pieve di Cadore (Belluno). He moved to Venice to be apprenticed as a mosaicist and

Titian, in a portrait of Agostino Carraci, 1587 *(Library of Congress)*

painter. He was also assistant to the painter Giorgione (ca. 1478–1510) and completed some of his works when Giorgione died. Titian's reputation and career rose quickly after he received his first independent commission in 1511. In 1516 he was named the official painter of the Republic of VENICE. Equally proficient with religious, secular, and mythological subjects, Titian was the ideal artist to depict the glories of Venice. In addition to painting for the government he also took on many commissions from churches and private patrons, including the ESTE FAMILY and GONZAGA FAMILY, King Francis I of France, Emperor CHARLES V, and Pope PAUL III. His talents included that of winning the esteem of the most powerful personages of his time. Charles V appointed him court painter and bestowed on

him a title of nobility. His portraits of Paul III (1546) and Charles V (1548) are among his best works of portraiture, a branch of painting to which he was increasingly drawn as he grew older. Titian did most of his work in Venice, but he was in Rome in 1545–46 and in Germany in the early 1550s. Titian's talent and long active life assured him a place among the towering artists of his age. TINTORETTO, VERONESE, Rubens, and Velasquez felt his influence.

Tittoni, Romolo   See BANCO DI ROMA.

Tittoni, Tommaso (1855–1931)
economist, political figure, and diplomat, four times foreign minister
Tittoni belonged to a prominent Roman family with ties to the Vatican. He served in the chamber of deputies from 1886 and in the senate from 1902, was prefect of Perugia (1898) and Naples (1900), ambassador to London (1906), Paris (1910–16), president of the senate (1920–29), and president of the Italian Academy (1929–30). In his capacity as foreign minister in four different governments (1903–05, 1906–09, 1919–20) he followed a cautious policy designed to improve Italy's position without creating international complications. In 1903–05 he worked to improve relations with France within the framework of Italy's obligations as a member of the TRIPLE ALLIANCE. In 1906–09 he worked to strengthen Italy's influence in the Balkans, but was undermined by Austria's surprise annexation of Bosnia-Herzegovina in 1908. As ambassador to Paris, Tittoni worked quietly to bring Italy into WORLD WAR I on the side of Great Britain and France. Once again foreign minister after the war, he led the Italian delegation at the Paris Peace Conference where he tried unsuccessfully to settle the question of FIUME by diplomatic negotiation. Tittoni was a conservative sympathizer of fascism, which he kept at a discreet distance. His appointment as first president of the Italian Academy showed BENITO MUSSOLINI's high regard for him.

Toeplitz, Giuseppe See BANKING.

Togliatti, Palmiro (1893–1964)
Communist Party founder and leader during
and after World War II

Togliatti was born in Genoa on Palm Sunday (hence the name Palmiro), but the family moved to Sardinia in 1908. He entered the University of Turin in 1911 and received a degree in jurisprudence (1915). While at the university he joined the Socialist Party (PSI) and met ANTONIO GRAMSCI, with whom he struck up a close ideological and political relationship. Although opposed to Italian intervention, Togliatti served in World War I as a volunteer. In 1919 he and Gramsci founded the review *Ordine Nuovo*. In 1921 he joined the newly founded Communist Party (PCI), worked as a party journalist, and in 1922 rose to a position on the party's central committee. In 1924 he and Gramsci wrested control of the party from AMADEO BORDIGA.

When Gramsci was arrested in 1926, Togliatti assumed the leadership of the party, but shortly thereafter he went into political exile in Moscow, where he remained for most of the time until 1944. In the Soviet Union he managed to survive by staying on Josef Stalin's good side. Writing under the name of Ercole Ercoli, he was an effective propagandist for the Soviet line on how to deal with FASCISM, which he analyzed with exceptional subtlety in spite of the ideological constraints to which he was subjected as a Communist. The recognition that the strength of the Fascist regime derived from the popular support that it enjoyed led him to propose a strategy of combating fascism by changing public opinion. That strategy was in turn based on Gramsci's concept of the importance of cultural factors in modern politics.

Upon his return to Italy in March 1944 he moved quickly to establish the Communist Party as a legitimate contender for power within the framework of political democracy. The move, known as the *svolta di Salerno*, directed Communists to collaborate with other political parties in the process of postwar reconstruction. The fate of the monarchy would be decided by popular vote after the war, but in the meantime, Communists would collaborate with the monarchist government of PIETRO BADOGLIO. Togliatti participated in postwar governments, most notably as minister of justice in 1945 and 1946–47. The "new party" envisaged by Togliatti was to be a mass party rather than a party of workers; it would accept the ground rules of political democracy without abandoning its fight for social justice; it would seek to persuade rather than coerce.

Thus, Togliatti set the course for an "Italian road to socialism" that met resistance from hardliners within the party and from outside skeptics who did not trust his intentions. He was a member of parliament from 1948 until his death. Countrywide protests followed an attempt on his life in July 1948 that left him seriously wounded.

Palmiro Togliatti *(Library of Congress)*

In the years that followed he opposed Italy's participation in NATO, led the parliamentary battle against the so-called *legge truffa* (swindle law) of 1953 that would have benefited the Christian Democrats, and led the party through the period of de-Stalinization that followed the revelations of Stalin's brutality in 1956. Just before his death he penned the so-called Yalta Memorandum that declared the Italian Communist Party independent of the Soviet Union, and proposed a new polycentric model of international organization for socialism called "Unity in Diversity." He died a few days before he was to release the memorandum, which was later adopted and published by the Italian Communist Party.

Tolentino, Treaty of   See PIUS VI.

Tommaseo, Niccolò (1802–1874)
writer, linguist, and political figure
Tommaseo was born in Sebenico (Sibenik) in DALMATIA but identified fully with Italian culture. Proud of his Slavic ancestry he looked upon Dalmatia as a natural bridge between the Slavic and Latin worlds. He completed his studies at the University of Padua, where he struck up a stormy friendship with and was influenced by the liberal Catholicism of ANTONIO ROSMINI-SERBATI. Literary taste and impulsive character attracted Tommaseo to ROMANTICISM, which he defended in his usual intemperate manner against the attacks of the classicists, even though his style owed much to the latter. Drawn to Tuscany by his intense desire to study spoken Italian, he took up residence in Florence in 1827. His *Dizionario dei sinonimi* (Dictionary of synonyms, 1830) reveals a fine sensitivity and grasp of the subtleties of language. In 1834 he left Florence for Paris to avoid complications with the police who were aware of his liberal sentiments. In France he published a commentary on the affairs of Italy, a volume of verses, a historical novel, a study of Venetian diplomacy in the 16th century, and wrote the novel *Fede e bellezza*

(Faith and beauty, 1840). That novel, clearly his major literary work, was published one year after he returned to Italy. A pioneering figure in the study of popular customs and folk literature, Tommaseo researched and published a groundbreaking study in this field, the *Canti popolari toscani, corsi, illirici, greci* (Tuscan, Corsican, Illyrian, and Greek popular songs, 1841–42). In 1848 he was a member of the revolutionary government of Venice, where he had lived since 1839. Forced into exile after the revolution was put down, he lived, unhappily, on the island of Corfu. There he wrote the political tract *Rome et le monde* (Rome and the world, 1851), which urged the PAPACY to give up its temporal power and accept Italian independence. However, a republican at heart, Tommaseo objected to unification under the Piedmontese monarchy and favored a decentralized confederation of states. His dislike of monarchy notwithstanding, he lived in Turin from 1854 to 1859, grateful for the freedom to write that he enjoyed there and appreciative of the religiosity of its inhabitants. In Piedmont he carried on work on the monumental *Dizionario della lingua italiana* (Dictionary of the Italian language, 1858–79), which was completed posthumously. Tommaseo spent the last years of his life in Florence, blind and in poor health. His vast legacy as a writer, scholar, and political figure spread across many fields, testimony to frenetic and unfocused activity, so that there is no single work that gives the measure of his genius. Tommaseo's writings hinted at the inner demons that troubled him all his life, the often shocking details of which are revealed in the posthumously published *Diario intimo* (Intimate Diary, 1938).

Toniolo, Giuseppe (1845–1918)
economist and Catholic political activist, inspirer of Christian Democracy
Toniolo personified the tradition of social Catholicism of his native town of Treviso (Venetia). He received a law degree from the University of Padua (1867) and stayed on at that school

after graduation to teach political economy until 1873. He subsequently taught at the universities of Venice and Pisa, staying in that latter post until his death. His political activity was informed by the principles of social solidarity enunciated in Pope LEO XIII's encyclical *Rerum novarum*. Toniolo applied those principles to economic relations. In his writings he proposed a system of production based on state-recognized corporations of workers and managers and a national parliament representative of the economic interests of capital and labor. It was Toniolo's intent to strike a balance between the extremes of socialist collectivism and liberal individualism. Immediate reforms that he proposed to alleviate the plight of workers included profit-sharing, compulsory holidays, a shorter workday, protections for women and children in the workplace, and encouragement of small property ownership. He called on Catholics to make their presence felt politically and socially. The founding in 1889 of the Catholic Union of Social Studies was a first step in that direction designed to involve Catholic intellectuals. Within the Catholic movement Toniolo occupied a middle position between the radical activism of ROMOLO MURRI and outright conservatives. His conviction that social reforms should reflect principles of Christian ethics endeared him to Pope PIUS X, who supported Toniolo's work. After the pope dissolved the OPERA DEI CONGRESSI (1903), Toniolo became head of the Popular Union of Italian Catholics, which was faithful to the pope. Toniolo relied on faith to motivate Catholics in public life; his work was more in the nature of an apostolate than a militant crusade. The sobriquet of "God's Economist" applied to him by his followers is particularly fitting.

Torricelli, Evangelista (1608–1647)
pioneer of modern science particularly interested in technological discoveries and applications

Regarded as the foremost Italian scientist of his generation, Torricelli followed in the footsteps of GALILEO, whom he served as secretary in 1641–42. He was born in Faenza (Emilia), was trained by local Jesuits in mathematics and philosophy, and completed his studies in Rome under the famed Galilean scholar and teacher Benedetto Castelli (1577–1643). In 1642, the grand duke of Tuscany FERDINAND II appointed Torricelli court mathematician. A physicist less mathematical and more experimental than Galileo, Torricelli's experiments led to his invention of a device (later called a barometer) that measured changes in air pressure using a column of mercury enclosed in a glass tube. An important by-product of his experiments was the creation of an artificial vacuum, which was considered impossible by scientists who followed the prevailing views of Aristotle. He also invented a microscope, devised improvements for the telescope, and made important contributions to the understanding of hydraulics, which found practical application in land drainage. Torricelli showed more interest in practical applications than theoretical speculation, which may have been a strategy for survival in an environment where independent thought could lead to accusations of heresy. Like other Italian scientists who came after Galileo, Torricelli was able to carry on his experiments without interference from religious or political authorities by speaking carefully and avoiding controversial issues. The scientific tradition survived in Italy thanks in part to the cautious behavior so well exemplified by Torricelli.

Toscanelli, Paolo dal Pozzo (1397–1482)
pioneer of modern science, mathematician, astronomer, cosmographer, and mapmaker

Toscanelli was born in Florence, the son of a prominent physician. He studied at the University of Padua where he received a degree in medicine (1424). He lived most of the rest of his life in Florence at the center of a community of scholars and artists equally interested in science and art. His reputation as a distinguished mathematician spread beyond Florence. He carried out and recorded exact astronomical observations that enabled him to map out the orbits of comets. A leading cosmographer, he tried to comprehend the Earth in its totality. On the basis of calculations and travelers' reports he concluded that the landmass of Europe and Asia covered about two-thirds of the surface of the Earth (about 230 degrees of latitude), and that it was therefore possible to reach Asia from Europe by traveling no more than 130 degrees westward. The calculation was wrong, but according to tradition, it inspired Christopher Columbus to undertake his transatlantic journeys aiming to reach Asia after seeking Toscanelli's advice. Toscanelli is therefore credited as being the true inspirer of the idea that led to Columbus's accidental landfall in America and the opening of the American continent to European colonization.

Toscanini, Arturo See OPERA.

transformism

Transformism (*trasformismo*) refers to the practice of political parties and personalities to resolve differences and seek accords on specific issues while ignoring or circumventing differences of programs and ideologies. The term is often used in a pejorative sense to indicate lack of programmatic coherence and the prevalence of wheeling and dealing in the Italian political process. Critics argue that transformism is an enduring characteristic of Italian politics, that it corrupts government, encourages unprincipled behavior, and favors the rise of politicians adroit at manipulating parliament. The term was coined to describe the methods of AGOSTINO DEPRETIS, and it has been in circulation ever since. A less critical view of transformism sees it as a legitimate political tool, particularly appropriate when employed to bridge ideological or party differences that might otherwise paralyze the political system. Giovanni Giolitti employed transformist practices to win the support of socialists and Catholic deputies for his liberal reforms. A "transformist" alliance among liberals, socialists, and Catholics might

have prevented FASCISM from coming to power. The transformation of the Italian Communist Party (PCI) from a revolutionary to a reformist party can also be seen as a successful transformist operation. The practices associated with transformism are neither necessarily bad nor exclusively Italian. Transformism is a pragmatic response to long-term problems. It seeks to avoid head-on confrontations among parties in favor of workable accommodations. Transformist practices are typical of systems of political representation that seek to accommodate diverse interest groups.

Tremellius, John (1510–1580)
classical scholar and religious reformer,
author of an authoritative translation of
the Bible

Tremellius was born in Ferrara to a Jewish family, but converted to Catholicism in 1538. Committed to the cause of religious reform and influenced by PETER MARTYR VERMIGLI, he turned to Protestantism and left Italy in 1542. After sojourning in Basle and Strasbourg, he settled in England, where King Edward VI favored him and appointed him to teach Hebrew at Cambridge (1549). Tremellius returned to Europe after the death of King Edward (1553), eventually settled in Metz, and spent the last years of his life teaching Hebrew in Sedan. His greatest achievement was the translation of the Bible from Hebrew into Latin. It became the standard version of the Bible after its posthumous publication in 1590.

Trent, city of (Trento)
Trent (pop. 105,900) is the major city and regional capital of TRENTINO–ALTO ADIGE. A city of strategic importance, it commands access to the upper part of the Adige River valley. It was founded in Roman times, but it became important in the Middle Ages as the capital of a principality that served as a buffer state between the Italian states and the Germanic Empire. The

bishops who ruled the principality generally sided with the German emperors against the PAPACY. Its location midway between Italy and Germany made it a convenient meeting place for the COUNCIL OF TRENT, whose long duration and large gathering of prelates stimulated building construction and gave the town the look of a modern city. The principality was formally independent until 1801 when it was absorbed by the HABSBURG EMPIRE, of which it remained a part until 1918, with the brief interruption of 1809–13 when it was part of NAPOLEON's kingdom of Italy. A movement calling for administrative autonomy within the Austrian Empire developed in the city in the 19th century and turned increasingly toward union with Italy as the imperial government ignored its demands for autonomy and for an Italian university. The erection in 1896 of the monument to Dante in the heart of the city was the occasion for demonstrations calling for union with Italy. The liberation and acquisition of Trent and TRIESTE was Italy's major territorial goal in World War I. Italian troops occupied the city in the very last days of WORLD WAR I. Trent's economy is favored by its location on important lines of communication, its role as an administrative capital, and the presence of a university.

Trent, Council of (1545–1563)

ecumenical gathering called to reconcile Catholics and Protestants and to promote church reform

The need to call an ecumenical council to deal with the problems of the CATHOLIC CHURCH was strongly felt in the early 16th century, but papal fears that such a council might call into question the authority of the pope and the uncertainties created by the wars between CHARLES V and Francis I delayed its opening until 1545. It was finally convened by Pope PAUL III, but the clash of factions, fear of epidemics, and war caused several interruptions from 1547 to 1562. The council dealt simultaneously with questions of doctrine and practice, affirmed the validity of traditional interpretations of dogma alongside that of the Bible, and upheld the doctrine of salvation by faith and good works, and the validity of all sacraments; it established norms to improve the education and conduct of priests, required bishops to reside in their sees, prohibited the simultaneous holding of more than one clerical office, and established the INDEX. The Council of Trent did not heal the schism between Catholics and Protestants, but it did formulate the doctrinal and organizational norms of the Catholic Church that are still valid today. Implementing the decisions of the council was the work of many decades. The Spanish monarchy proved to be the papacy's most reliable ally in the long struggle to impose uniformity on church practices. At least 40 years, more than the lifespan of one generation at the time, passed before the reforms were felt at the parish level. The keeping of regular parish records, a duty that the council assigned to parish priests, began in Italy only in the first years of the 17th century.

Trentino–Alto Adige

An alpine region, the Trentino–Alto Adige (pop. 936,300) borders on Austria, Switzerland, and the regions of LOMBARDY and VENETIA. In the Austrian Empire before its annexation by Italy at the end of World War I, the region was called the Lower Tyrol. The Adige River that crosses it from north to south forms a natural corridor between Mediterranean and central Europe. A railway mainline and a modern highway facilitate communications. Of the region's two provinces, the northern one of Bolzano (Bözen) in the Alto Adige (Upper Adige) has a population (465,300) two-thirds of whom are German-speaking and less than one-third Italian-speaking. A smaller minority of about 5 percent living in the Val Gardena speaks a dialect derived directly from Latin that is called Ladin. The rural population of the Alto Adige has a strong attachment to the land, encouraged by an unusual form of land inheritance known as *maso chiuso*, which keeps family properties intact by passing them on undivided to the eldest son. Within the province, Merano (Meran) is a renowned holiday resort. Further north is the Brenner Pass that leads into the Austrian Tyrol. During the Fascist period, this part of the region was subjected to a coercive process of "Italianization." In 1939 the Italian and German governments agreed to a program, only partially executed, of compensated relocation for inhabitants who opted (the *Optanten*) to live in Germany. The southern province of the Trentino, population 477,900, where the regional capital of TRENT in located, is almost entirely Italian-speaking. The region has enjoyed special autonomous status since 1948, and the Italian parliament has passed special legislation to protect the rights and cultural identity of the German and Ladin-speaking populations. The region as a whole enjoys a standard of living above the national average, based on a diversified mix of agricultural, commercial, and industrial activities and tourism. Vineyards and producers turn out high-quality wines, and the region's extensive forests satisfy about 17 percent of Italy's lumber needs. Livestock-breeding sustains a well-developed dairy industry. The region relies heavily on hydroelectric power produced by harnessing its extensive water resources.

Treves, Claudio (1869–1933)

Socialist journalist, party leader, and member of parliament

Treves was born in Turin, received a degree in medicine in 1891, and that same year began his collaboration with the socialist review *Critica Sociale* and his long association with the review's editor FILIPPO TURATI, leaving behind the republicanism of his earlier years. In the 1890s he was a political organizer among Italian workers in Switzerland. From 1909 to 1912 he was editor-in-chief of the socialist daily *Avanti!* Always associated with the moderate reformist wing of the Italian Socialist Party (PSI), he was ousted from that post when the reformists lost control of the party in 1912. BENITO MUSSOLINI and other party extremists attacked Treves for support of the

government during the ITALIAN-TURKISH WAR. The defeat of Treves opened the way to Benito Mussolini, who soon took over the editorship of *Avanti!* and became the young man to watch in the Socialist Party. Treves was a member of parliament from 1906 to 1926, when he left the country following the loss of parliamentary immunity decreed by the Fascist government. He lived in Paris until his death, active in the anti-Fascist opposition movement.

Trieste, city of

Trieste (pop. 215,100) is the principal city and administrative capital of the region of FRIULI–VENEZIA GIULIA and a major Adriatic seaport. Originally an Illyrian settlement, it was later ruled by the Romans, who made it an important commercial center, and by Goths, Byzantines, Lombards, Franks, Venetians, Spaniards, French, and Austrians in a complicated history that denotes its importance as a gateway between the Mediterranean world and central Europe. HABSBURG domination began in the 16th century and, with some interruptions, ended in 1918 when the city was occupied by Italian troops at the end of WORLD WAR I and annexed by Italy, to the enthusiasm of the city's Italian residents and the concern of its non-Italian ones. *Trento e Trieste* was the Italian patriotic slogan of World War I, when the liberation of the two cities from Austrian rule and union with Italy drove the Italian war effort. Italians keenly felt the loss of Trieste to the Germans in 1943 and to the Yugoslavs in 1945. But the Anglo-American allies forced the Yugoslavs to give up the city. In 1946 they set up the Free Territory of Trieste, divided it into Zone A under Anglo-American administration and Zone B under Yugoslav administration. In 1954 Zone A (including the city of Trieste) was assigned to Italy and Zone B to Yugoslavia.

Declared a free port in 1719, Trieste became the major seaport of the Austrian Empire. Habsburg rule made Trieste a shipping center and the point of embarkation for millions of central European emigrants to the New World. Navigation, insurance, and banking companies made it their headquarters. Part of a multinational empire, Trieste became a cosmopolitan city where Germans, Italians, Slavs, Greeks, and Jews met and mixed. The disappearance of the Austrian Empire in 1918 deprived Trieste of access to central Europe and the Balkans, the principal sources of its traffic. The subsequent economic downturn was exacerbated by the efforts of the Fascist regime to eliminate the Slavic presence in the city. The city's economic prospects have improved since it was returned to Italy in 1954. Italian policy seeks to improve Trieste's historic ties to central Europe and accepts its cosmopolitan character. The expansion of the EUROPEAN UNION augurs well for the return of Trieste to its former role as a commercial center.

Tripartite Pact

Representatives of the three governments signed this pact in Berlin on September 27, 1940. Germany and Italy were already allies at war against Great Britain, but Japan was still a noncombatant. According to the provisions of the pact, Japan recognized the leadership of Germany and Italy in creating a new order in Europe, and the two European powers recognized the leadership of Japan in creating a new order in Greater East Asia. They further agreed to assist one another in all ways, including military, should any one of them be attacked by another power not involved in the ongoing European conflict or in the war between China and Japan. The Tripartite Pact was a logical corollary to the ANTI-COMINTERN PACT signed by the three governments in 1937. The Tripartite Pact made it clear that the three signatory powers were willing to cooperate militarily in any conflict that extended beyond Europe. Although it had no enforcement clauses, the pact transformed a European into a global conflict when Germany and Italy declared war on the United States after the Japanese attack on Pearl Harbor. However, the Japanese did not declare war on the Soviet Union after the German attack. At the time it was signed, the three

powers hoped that the prospect of war against all three would keep the United States out of the war until Great Britain was defeated.

Triple Alliance

The Triple Alliance was formed in 1882 when Italy joined the Dual Alliance that Germany and Austria-Hungary had concluded in 1879. Italy's principal motivation for joining these two European powers was to avoid diplomatic isolation, the consequences of which had been brought painfully home by France's recent acquisition of Tunis, coveted as a colony by Italy's government because of its proximity to Sicily and the presence of a large Italian population. By concluding this alliance the Italian government also hoped to isolate the papacy, which refused to recognize the Italian state and sought the support of Austria-Hungary and Germany. The treaty of the Triple Alliance signed on May 20, 1882, provided that Germany and Austria-Hungary would support the existing order in Italy, that is, the unified state and the monarchy, and would come to her aid if France attacked Italy. Italy in turn promised to go to the aid of her allies if France or Russia attacked either.

The alliance was of limited practical use for Italy because France had no intention of fighting Italy after the acquisition of Tunis, but it did raise Italy's status as a European power. It excluded any hostility toward Great Britain, which Italy could not afford to antagonize because it was vulnerable to British attack in the MEDITERRANEAN SEA. Italy's ongoing conflicts of interest with Austria in the Balkans and over the *terre irredente* (see IRREDENTISM) undermined relations with its partners, who were always much closer to one another than to Italy. Italy also resented the lack of support from its two partners over its colonial ambitions in North Africa. The agreements with Great Britain, France, and Russia concluded between 1900 and 1909 indicated Italy's desire to maintain some freedom of action as the European powers lined up into the two rival blocs of Triple Alliance and Triple Entente.

The Triple Alliance was renewed six times between 1882 and 1912, but when Germany and Austria-Hungary went to war against the Triple Entente powers in August 1914, Italy proclaimed its neutrality. After failing to obtain satisfactory pledges of territorial concessions from Austria-Hungary in return for Italian neutrality in the conflict, Italy concluded the PACT OF LONDON with the Entente powers and declared war against Austria-Hungary in May 1915, thus becoming a combatant in WORLD WAR I.

Tripolitania See COLONIALISM.

Tronchetti Provera, Marco See PIRELLI, ALBERTO.

Troya, Carlo (1784–1858)
historian and political figure active in the liberal reform movement

Troya was born in Naples, entered journalism and government service, and served as royal intendant of BASILICATA during the REVOLUTION of 1820–21 when he supported demands for constitutional government. Subsequently exiled, he traveled in Italy, studying and gathering documents for his many studies of medieval Italy. An authority on Dante, Troya published several groundbreaking studies, including the five-volume *Codice diplomatico longobardo* (Lombard diplomatic law code, 1852–55) and the four-volume *Storia d'Italia nel medioevo* (History of Italy in the Middle Ages, 1839–55). A moderate liberal who sympathized with the Neo-Guelfs and looked for a peaceful solution to the question of national independence, Troya served as president of the Neapolitan cabinet during the REVOLUTION of 1848. Appointed to head the government in April, Troya mediated between the king, who had granted the constitution reluctantly, and liberals who wanted to broaden the suffrage and further limit the power of the king, managing in the process to avoid a break with either side.

Troya expanded the suffrage and agreed reluctantly to Piedmontese requests for Neapolitan troops in the war against Austria. But Troya could not carry on his balancing act for long. Faced by an anti-Neapolitan movement in Sicily, peasant uprisings in the southern provinces, and an insurrection in the capital, Troya resigned in May 1848.

Turati, Augusto (1888–1955)
journalist, Fascist organizer, and national Fascist Party secretary

Born in Parma, Augusto Turati never completed his law studies at the city university, volunteered for military service in WORLD WAR I, joined the Fascist Party, and emerged as the Fascist *ras* (local boss) of the city of Brescia (Lombardy), where he worked as a journalist. Turati showed a distinct sympathy for workers, resisted employer demands, distrusted BENITO MUSSOLINI's accommodating politics, and cultivated the image of an independent Fascist. In March 1925 Fascist metalworker unions in Brescia staged a strike to obtain cost of living increases that spread to other parts of the country and gave Turati national visibility. Emerging from the GIACOMO MATTEOTTI crisis, Mussolini needed new faces in positions of responsibility. In March 1926 he appointed Turati as party vice secretary to succeed the hard-liner ROBERTO FARINACCI who had taken on the legal defense of the Fascists accused of Matteotti's murder. Turati carried on a major purge of party activists, replacing them with more docile members recruited in part from the state bureaucracy. Turati's idea was to make the party a responsible mainstay of government, but instead of making the party more independent and influential, his measures made it a more docile instrument in Mussolini's hands. Turati also favored the dismantling of EDMONDO ROSSONI's national labor union, thus further weakening the labor movement that he had previously championed. Embroiled in a public dispute that cast doubt on the financial honesty of Arnaldo Mussolini, the dictator's brother, and subjected to a press campaign of personal vilification, Turati resigned as party secretary in September 1930. He was expelled from the party in 1933, but readmitted in 1937 without ever again holding political office. Condemned after the war for his Fascist activities, he was never jailed and was eventually amnestied. Turati is seen as the last party secretary who tried to give the Fascist Party a role independent of Mussolini.

Turati, Filippo (1857–1932)
early leader and chief political strategist of the
Italian Socialist Party

A man of many talents and high ideals, Filippo Turati (no relation to AUGUSTO TURATI) was born in Canzo, a small town north of MILAN, to a relatively well-off middle-class family. He received a degree in law from the University of Bologna in 1877, but instead of practicing law, he joined the artists and writers of the Milanese SCAPIGLIATURA movement, who delighted in their role of cultural rebels. His political convictions matured slowly, but he did move steadily toward SOCIALISM via republicanism, POSITIVISM, and broad humanitarian ideals. His socialism was of the gradual, reformist variety that relied on the use of the vote and peaceful political means to transform capitalism and bring about a socially just society. His relationship with ANNA KULISCIOFF, whom he met in 1885, played an important role in his political maturation, to the point that it is difficult to separate them politically and intellectually. In 1891 they founded *Critica Sociale,* a serious review that contributed to the diffusion of Marxist ideas in Italy. He was elected to parliament in 1896. Although Turati did not encourage street uprisings, a military tribunal sentenced him to serve 12 years in jail for fomenting the FATTI DI MAGGIO of 1898. Released in 1900, he resumed his parliamentary seat and announced a policy of socialist collaboration with other progressive parties, including the liberals. That decision laid the basis for his collaboration with GIOVANNI GIOLITTI, who responded with policies and practical concessions that favored workers

and their parliamentary representatives. However, Turati steadfastly refused to participate in Giolitti's governments, and their collaboration never developed into a partnership. Turati lost control of the Socialist Party (PSI) in 1912 to extremists who demanded more confrontational tactics. He favored Italian neutrality in World War I, but came around to supporting the war effort after CAPORETTO. After the war he opposed socialists who wanted revolution, fearing that the use of violence by socialists would provoke a violent reaction. In 1922 Turati was expelled from the Socialist Party because he favored forming a united front with other parties against FASCISM. He then founded the small *Partito Socialista Unitario,* whose secretary was GIACOMO MATTEOTTI. An opponent of the Fascist regime and leader of the AVENTINE SECESSION, Turati fled Italy in 1926 and went to Paris, where he was active in the anti-Fascist movement until his death.

Turiello, Pasquale (1836–1902)
journalist, political writer and activist
known for anti-liberal, authoritarian,
and nationalistic creed

Turiello was born and lived all of his life in Naples. A lawyer by profession, in 1862 he turned to teaching and journalism. His role as spokesman for the political Right belied his beginnings on the opposite side of the political spectrum as a volunteer fighting for GIUSEPPE GARIBALDI in 1866–67. Populist sympathies help explain Turiello's political itinerary. Noting the deteriorating conditions of the southern peasantry after national unification, he denounced the growing gap between the government and the people in his *Governo e governati in Italia* (Government and the governed in Italy, 1882). Blaming the practices and philosophy of liberal government for public indifference to the lot of the poor, Turiello became an outspoken critic of parliament, called on the monarchy to exert the full prerogatives allowed it by the constitution, and urged colonial expansion to alleviate the land question.

Turin, city of (Torino)

Turin (pop. 901,000) is the regional capital of PIEDMONT. Located on the Po River at the foot of the Alps, it was an important military post that controlled access to the rich Po Valley. Fought over and claimed by various powers since Roman times, the HOUSE OF SAVOY brought it under its control in the 13th century and made it its point of entry into Italy. Turin's Military Academy, once one of Europe's most prestigious military schools, is evidence of the city's long association with the expansionist policies of the Savoy dynasty. It was the capital of the KINGDOM OF SARDINIA from 1713 to 1861, and of the kingdom of Italy from 1861 to 1865. Public administration, industry, and commerce gave the city new life in the 18th and 19th centuries. Major riots broke out in the city to protest the transfer of the national capital to Florence in 1865. Workers and student radicals at the University of Turin came together in 1919–22 to create an extremely active and aggressive labor movement (see ANTONIO GRAMSCI) that was dismantled during the Fascist period. Today Turin is one of the anchors, along with MILAN and GENOA, of Italy's "industrial triangle," the most economically developed (and congested) area of the country. It is home to the FIAT conglomerate. The country's largest producer of motor vehicles dominates the economic and cultural life of the city, but the engineering, textile, food, electronics, and printing industries are also well represented in the economy of the province. Turin's population soared in the years of the ECONOMIC MIRACLE, when industrial growth attracted emigrants, mostly from Italy's South. The city was once again the scene of large-scale labor protests in the 1970s. Management regained the upper hand in the 1980s. The city's labor scene was relatively quiet in the 1990s, but the financial crisis of FIAT and thousands of layoffs are causing feelings of unease and uncertainty about the future in the early years of the 21st century.

Tuscany

The region of Tuscany (pop. 3,536,400), Italy's fifth largest, is located in the central part of the peninsula. The APENNINE MOUNTAINS that form its northern border shade off toward the east and south into hilly terrain. The broad Maremma plain, once infested by malaria and almost uninhabited but now reclaimed, covers the extreme southern part of the region. Small and medium-sized family farms prevail in the mountains and hills, while the south has relatively large farms. The economy is diversified, with areas of intensive industrial manufacturing around the towns of LIVORNO, LUCCA, and Prato. Tourism is a major resource for the entire region. Popular seaside resorts like Viareggio and Forte dei Marmi line the coastal region of the Versilia. Prized marble is extracted from the quarries of the Apuan Alps, a lateral branch of the Apennines. Its nine provincial capitals (Arezzo, FLORENCE, Grosseto, LIVORNO, Lucca, Massa-Carrara, PISA, Pistoia, SIENA) recall some of the most glorious names of the Middle Ages and Renaissance. The name of the region derives from *Tuscia,* the term that Roman administrators used for the region, from which come the forms *Tuscania* and *Toscana.* All refer to the Etruscans, who were the regions' first historical inhabitants. Ruled successively by Goths, Byzantines, Lombards, and Franks, its towns were among the first in Italy to become independent communes in the 11th century. Tuscany played a leading role in the cultural revival of the late Middle Ages and RENAISSANCE. Its poets and artists established Tuscan as the most prestigious of the Italian dialects and made it the national language of modern Italy. Tuscany became the regional state of the Grand Duchy of Tuscany under MEDICI FAMILY rule in the 16th century. After the extinction of the Medici dynasty, the House of HABSBURG-LORRAINE ruled the grand duchy until 1859. A year later Tuscany became part of the Kingdom of Italy. Of all the Italian regions, Tuscany is the one that is closest to the national averages in family size, income, standard of living, and in most other respects.

Two Sicilies, Kingdom of the

The unusual name of Kingdom of the Two Sicilies derived from the ancient custom of using the name Sicily for both the island itself and that part of the southern mainland that coincides today roughly with the region of CALABRIA. And because a lighthouse (faro) stood by the Strait of Messina that separates the mainland from the island, the entire territory was referred to in Latin as Sicily *citra et ultra farum* and in Italian as Sicily *al di qua e al di là dal faro* (on this and that side of the lighthouse). This state stood at an international crossroad. As the passegeway between the East and continental Europe, it was contested by every major power with imperial ambitions. Byzantines, Muslims, Normans, Germans, and Spaniards made it a base for their operations. To the Normans it was a jumping-off point for their conquest of the Near East during the Crusades. The German emperor Frederick II (1220–50) made Sicily the center of his empire. His court in Palermo became a center of learning and culture. Writers made Tuscan the language of his court and gave it the distinction it needed to become the national language. Naples and Sicily were joined in the 15th and 16th centuries to form a single political unit with two autonomous parts. Thereafter the Kingdom of Naples and the Kingdom of Sicily were held together as possessions of the Spanish monarchy. After losing the mainland territory to Austria during the WAR OF THE SPANISH SUCCESSION, the Spanish crown regained possession of both the Kingdom of Naples and the Kingdom of Sicily in 1734, with both being ruled by King CHARLES OF BOURBON. The designation Kingdom of the Two Sicilies became official in 1816 when King FERDINAND I decreed the administrative centralization of all the provinces of the kingdom. The decision to centralize power in the hands of the royal bureaucracy caused Sicilian separatists to take up arms against Naples in the REVOLUTIONS of 1820–21 and 1848. Tension between Sicily and the mainland was a serious internal weakness of the kingdom. The term *Kingdom of Naples* (Regno di Napoli) is often used incorrectly as a synonym for the Kingdom of the Two Sicilies (Regno delle Due Sicilie). The Kingdom of the Two Sicilies ceased to exist in 1860 when it fell to the volunteers led by GIUSEPPE GARIBALDI and to the regular troops of the KINGDOM OF SARDINIA, becoming part of the Kingdom of Italy.

Tyrrhenian Sea See MEDITERRANEAN SEA.

U

Uccialli, Treaty of

Treaty of friendship between the Italian diplomat and explorer Pietro Antonelli (1853–1901), signing for the king of Italy, and the Ethiopian chieftain Ras Menelik (1844–1913) on May 2, 1889. In return for Italy's friendship, a loan of 2 million lire, and Italian recognition of Menelik's title of *negus neghesti* (king of kings, or emperor of Ethiopia), Menelik agreed to allow the Italians to retain the highlands above the territory of Eritrea that the Italians had previously occupied and to avail himself of the Italian government in all his dealings with foreign powers. The Italian interpretation, that this amounted to Menelik's recognition of an Italian protectorate over all of Ethiopia, was challenged by Menelik, who argued that the claim of a protectorate was based on a mistranslation of the language he had agreed to in the Amharic text. Menelik used Italian help to establish himself as emperor over rival chieftains, while the Italians expanded their territory and obtained recognition of their protectorate from all European powers except Russia. Defeat at the BATTLE OF ADOWA in 1896 halted Italian designs on Ethiopia until the ETHIOPIAN WAR of 1935–36 made Ethiopia an Italian colony.

UDR (Unione Democratica per la Repubblica) See COSSIGA, FRANCESCO.

UIL (Unione Italiana dei Lavoratori) See CGIL; SYNDICALISM.

Ulivo Coalition See PDS.

Umberto I (1844–1900)
king of Italy (1878–1900)

Umberto succeeded to the Italian throne in 1878 at the death of his father, King VICTOR EMMANUEL II. Like all male members of the HOUSE OF SAVOY Umberto received a strict military education and rose through the ranks from captain at age 14 to general at 22. He saw active duty and won a gold medal for bravery in action in the war of 1866 against Austria. Before coming to the throne he served as military commander of the Naples area and of an army corps in Rome. In 1868 he married his first cousin, Margherita of Savoia (1851–1926). Popular in the first years of his reign because of the concern shown for flood, earthquake, and cholera victims, and for the courage shown in the face of attempts on his life, opposition to him mounted as he supported repressive measures at home and expansionist policies abroad. He favored the TRIPLE ALLIANCE, COLONIALISM, and building a large army and navy. In 1898–99 he backed conservative proposals to assert the right of the monarchy to govern without the consent of parliament. He also made the mistake of decorating the general who led the bloody repression of workers in Milan during the FATTI DI MAGGIO of 1898. By then his earlier reputation as the *Re Buono* (Good or Kind King) was severely tarnished. The anarchist Gaetano Bresci (1869–1901), a returning emigrant from Paterson, New Jersey, assassinated Umberto on July 29, 1900, to avenge the victims of the

King Umberto I *(Library of Congress)*

army massacres of May 1898. Umberto's only son succeeded him as VICTOR EMMANUEL III. Umberto's policies reflected his narrow military upbringing and limited understanding of social realities. A well-intentioned monarch, he would have been better suited to the task of national consolidation and reconciliation, which he undertook in the last months of his life, than to the maintenance of law and order.

Umberto II (1904–1983)
last king of Italy (1946) and royal exile

The last king of Italy was the only son of King VICTOR EMMANUEL III and Elena of Montenegro

(1873–1952). His accession to the throne was delayed by the long reign of his father. As prince of Naples (the official title of the heir to the throne), Umberto's duties were almost entirely ceremonial. In 1930 he married Maria José (1907–2001), daughter of King Albert I of Belgium. They had four children, but the marriage was not a happy one and they separated in 1947. Following the traditions of his house, Umberto pursued a military career, achieving the title of army general in 1938. In June 1940 he was given nominal command of the troops facing France, then was out of the public eye for the rest of the war. As the war turned against Italy, Umberto discreetly cultivated an anti-Fascist image, aided by his wife who was more openly critical of the Fascist regime. On June 5, 1944, he assumed the title of lieutenant general of the kingdom, which gave him the royal prerogatives of government, but not the royal title. He assumed the title of king on May 9, 1946, when Victor Emmanuel abdicated, hoping thereby to save the monarchy in the upcoming referendum of June 2, 1946. Umberto left the country quietly on June 13 for exile in Portugal after a majority voted for the republic. He never formally abdicated and spent the rest of his life in dignified exile. He is buried in the family vault in Hautecombe Abbey, in the French region of Savoy, where the dynasty originated. In 1948 the Italian government passed a law permanently banning Umberto and his male descendants from the country. The ban was lifted in 2002.

Umbria

The landlocked region of Umbria (pop. 835,500) is surrounded in the heart of the peninsula by the regions of the Marches on the north and northeast, Tuscany on the west and northwest, and Latium to the south. Lake Trasimeno near the Tuscan border is a large, shallow body of water that sustains a small fishing industry. This mostly mountainous and hilly region has a population density about half the national average. Under the idyllic appearance lies an economy that is fairly static. Its two provinces of Perugia and Terni have many towns of artistic and historic importance, but no major urban centers. The region therefore retains its traditional rural aspect, with villages situated on hilltops and mountainsides, small sharecropping farms scattered throughout, and about 13 percent of the working population employed in agriculture. There is small craft production of pottery, laces, and wood and copper items. Large industrial complexes are limited to the Terni area in the extreme south of the region, where steel, chemicals, food, and textile factories are located. The region's enormous tourist potential awaits the building of better transportation links and hotels to be fully realized. Assisi, the birthplace of Saint Francis, with its frescoed medieval churches, Gubbio with its picturesque location and folk rituals, Orvieto with its splendid cathedral, are just three of the region's minor towns that are of major interest. The regions' dialects reflect the influence of the surrounding regions, those closest to Tuscan being the ones spoken in the western and central areas. The region's central location and lack of natural defenses have made it vulnerable to attack. After the collapse of Roman administration, it was devastated by Goths and ruled by Lombards, Byzantines, and Franks before being assigned to papal rule by Charlemagne in 774. But conflicts between towns and the rural nobility, and among rival towns, disrupted the region for centuries, until Pope Innocent III consolidated papal rule in 1198. No strong *signoria* emerged in the region in spite of efforts by the MALATESTA, MONTEFELTRO, ORSINI, and VISCONTI families to replace papal rule. Pope Paul III eliminated the last vestiges of local independence and imposed a uniform administration on the region. From then on the history of the region was the same as that of the PAPAL STATES.

Ungaretti, Giuseppe See HERMETISM.

Unione Popolare dei Cattolici Italiani
See TONIOLO, GIUSEPPE.

Unità (L') See PCI.

Uomo Qualunque (L')
The journalist and playwright Guglielmo Giannini (1891–1960) launched L'Uomo Qualunque, or Average Man's Movement, in 1945, naming it after a satirical weekly that he had founded in 1944. In 1946 Giannini organized the movement politically under the name Fronte dell'Uomo Qualunque, which won 5.4 percent of the popular vote in the first postwar elections of June 1946. It sent a delegation of 30 that included Giannini to the national parliament. The movement did particularly well in Rome, where it was born, and in parts of the South. It did not survive the next electoral test in 1948 and disappeared from the political scene shortly thereafter. Most of its voters rallied to the Christian Democratic Party (DC) to keep the Communist Party (PCI) out of government. The movement also opposed purging the public administration of former Fascists. That stand reflected the background of many *qualunquisti* who were white-collar workers fearful that a thorough purge would result in their eviction from government and public administration. Beyond that fairly narrow social base, however, the movement attracted voters who were generally suspicious of big government and political parties. It expressed faith in the wisdom of the common people and claimed to voice their aspiration that the state could perform its administrative functions without the interference of political parties. The fear of party politics was largely a legacy of 20 years of Fascist propaganda against political openness. The movement's anti-party posture was roundly condemned at the time and since. The term *qualunquismo* has become part of the Italian political vocabulary and is generally used as a pejorative, similar to the American term populism, meaning a disingenuous catering to popular resentments and prejudices.

Urban VIII (1568–1644)
pope (1623–1644)

Maffeo Barberini was born to a Florentine family, studied law in Pisa, and pursued a successful career in papal service. In 1604 he was appointed papal nuncio (ambassador) to the French court, which instilled in him false confidence that he could influence the affairs of France; he was made a cardinal in 1606 and appointed bishop of Spoleto in 1608. A highly cultivated if somewhat vain man, he was an elegant writer and a discerning patron of the arts. Elected pope, he saw to it that his many relatives benefited financially from his elevation, but kept them away from positions of power in the papal administration. His low profile during the Thirty Years' War fueled charges that he had not done enough to defend the Catholic side, and rumors that he secretly desired the defeat of the Catholic HABSBURGS, whom he disliked. Urban is remembered for his generous patronage of distinguished artists such as GIAN LORENZO BERNINI and GUIDO RENI, and the construction of splendid palaces (including Rome's Palazzo Barberini) and churches, primarily the completion of the new Basilica of Saint Peter and the start of the colonnade that embraces its vast square. Because much of the material needed for these construction projects was quarried from the city's ancient ruins, Romans quipped that *quod non facerunt barbari facerunt Barberini* (what the barbarians didn't do, the Barberinis did). Not surprisingly, he nearly depleted the treasury and left papal finances in disarrary. Initially a friend and admirer of GALILEO, Urban turned against him and backed the Inquisition's condemnation of the *Dialogue on the Great World Systems* that resulted in the scientist's incarceration for life. Political intrigue and Urban's offended pride that Galileo might have been secretly lampooning him in his writings are blamed for the abandonment of his old friend and professed admirer.

Urban did intercede on Galileo's behalf to mitigate the terms of his imprisonment and allow him to spend the remaining years of his life in the comfort of his own home. But he clamped down on dissenters within the church, condemned JANSENISM, created new religious orders, and reformed the liturgy.

Urbino, city of

Founded by the Romans who called it *Urvinum Metaurense* after the Metauro River on which it is located, Urbino is part of the region of MARCHES. In 774 the Carolingian rulers donated the town to the PAPACY, which thenceforth claimed it as part of its patrimony. It became an independent commune in the 11th century, but became a fief of the MONTEFELTRO FAMILY in 1213. Pope Eugenius IV (1431–47) made it a duchy in 1443. Under the rule of the Montefeltro, the duchy of Urbino became a center of RENAISSANCE culture and humanist learning far more significant than its small size and modest political role might indicate. The 15th-century Ducal Palace is the city's architectural gem. On it the Montefeltro lavished their fortune, bringing to it the best artists and builders of their time. Cesare BORGIA occupied the town in 1502–03 to reassert the papal claim to sovereignty, then assigned it to the Della Rovere family, which held it with some interruptions until 1631 when Urbino became part of the PAPAL STATES. As a papal city Urbino lost its importance, turning into a local trade center with some small-scale manufacturing activities. The vestiges of its Renaissance past and the cultural activities connected with the University of Urbino, including foreign programs, bring large numbers of visitors to the city. The National Gallery located in the Ducal Palace is one of the most important art galleries of Italy, with paintings by the greatest masters of the Renaissance.

V

Valiani, Leo (1909–1999)
journalist, scholar, and political commentator

A historian who has also played a role in shaping history, Valiani was born in FIUME when that city was still part of the AUSTRIAN EMPIRE, and became an Italian citizen when the city was annexed by Italy in 1924. Valiani, a communist and a Jew, developed an immediate dislike for the Fascist regime, joined the opposition, and was jailed repeatedly for his politics. Valiani distanced himself from communism in 1939 to protest the conclusion of the Nazi-Soviet Non-Aggression Pact. When the Fascist regime collapsed in July 1943, Valiani helped organize the RESISTANCE and was a member of the Committee of National Liberation that functioned as a provisional government in German-occupied northern Italy. Although he enjoyed the support of American and British military authorities, he did not accede to American requests that BENITO MUSSOLINI be handed over to the Allies, and may have ordered the Italian resistance to execute him. Valiani stayed out of party politics after the war, but played a role in drafting the CONSTITUTION of the Italian republic. He was appointed senator for life in recognition of his public service, but held no public posts. A columnist for the newspaper *Corriere della Sera,* he was a severe critic of the system of government he had helped create, deploring its instability, lack of direction, and public acceptance of political corruption and organized crime. He saw at least a partial remedy for political instability in a strong presidency. His journalistic and scholarly writings range far and wide, covering the history of the resistance, socialism, contemporary politics, and foreign policy.

Valla, Lorenzo (1407–1457)
(or Della Valle)
humanist scholar and classical linguist

Valla, born in Rome, left his native city in 1429, to teach at the University of Pavia. In 1435 he went to Naples, where he was personal secretary to King ALFONSO I. He returned to Rome in 1448 to teach and serve as papal secretary. Often embroiled in controversy, he used his learning as a weapon in the battle for cultural innovation, based on his admiration and love of classical antiquity. His *De elegantia Linguae Latinae* (On the elegance of the Latin language, ca. 1440) argued for the superiority of classical over medieval Latin. His stands on moral and religious questions left him open to charges of heresy. On the question of what constitutes virtuous conduct, he took issue with the prevalent Stoic model of renunciation in favor of the Epicurean view that virtue consists of the judicious pursuit of pleasure. On the question of salvation, Valla questioned the relevance of free will and asserted the power of God's will. Valla is best remembered for his demonstration that the document called the Donation of Constantine, on which the church based its claim to territorial sovereignty, was a medieval forgery. Valla's text stimulated ANTICLERICALISM at a time when the PAPACY was working to regain spiritual and political authority. Valla was in the service of the Neapolitan court after 1435 when he wrote many of his writings, and political animosities between the Neapolitan crown and the papacy may account for the anticlerical tone of Valla's writings. But Valla, genuinely interested in religious reform, emphasized that knowledge of classical scholarship helped in the task of religious reform, and hoped that the papacy would lead the way. The questions raised by Valla anticipate those of a later generation of religious reformers who would launch the Protestant Reformation and carry their attack on the church much further than Valla was prepared to do.

Valle d'Aosta

Valle d'Aosta (pop. 120,300) is a mountainous, thinly populated region tucked into the northwestern corner of the peninsula, bordered by Switzerland to the north, France to the west, and the region of PIEDMONT to the east and south. Part of Piedmont until 1948, Valle d'Aosta is today the smallest of the Italian regions. The Romans founded the city of Aosta, the capital that gives its name to the region, in the first century B.C. as an outpost to control traffic across the ALPS. Striking examples of Roman architecture can still be seen in the city. The importance of the region as a point of transit increased with the opening in 1964 of a tunnel to Switzerland under the Gran San Bernardo mountain complex and of the Mont Blanc tunnel to France in 1965. Tourism, particularly winter sports, is the main source of employment, but there is also a significant production of wine grapes and a sizable textile industry. Energy is provided by a system of hydroelectric power that takes full advantage of the abundant waters of the region's rivers and streams. The iron deposits of Cogne were once a significant resource for the Italian steel industry, but can no longer be worked economically. The region was under the political control of the HOUSE OF SAVOY from the 11th century and became part of the Kingdom of Italy in 1861. It is one of the regions mentioned by the constitution of the Italian republic (1948) as entitled to special autonomous status because of its geography and bilingual nature. The constitution guarantees one seat in the senate to the region, which otherwise might have no representation in parliament because of its small population. Italian and French are the official languages of the region, but the inhabitants also speak a dialect of Provençal origin.

Valletta, Vittorio See FIAT.

Vallisnieri, Antonio, Sr. (1661–1730)
scientific investigator and promoter of the new culture of science

Vallisnieri was born to a family of the local nobility in the town of Tresilico (Modena), was educated by Jesuits, and studied medicine, surgery, anatomy, botany, and chemistry at the University of Bologna. He taught medicine at the University of Padua from 1700 until his death. A passionate experimenter, he argued that experimentation was fully compatible with respect for traditional medicine. He studied insects, worms, birds, eels, various plants, fossils, and natural phenomena like hot springs, volcanoes, and earthquakes. He explained the presence of marine fossils in the APENNINES by positing the emergence of the mountains from the sea due to volcanic eruptions in prehistoric times. He advanced the understanding of animal physiology with insightful contributions to the study of the reproductive system by tracing the origins of embryos in the eggs, describing the separation of the eggs from the ovaries, their movement to the uterus, and noted the phenomenon of extrauterine pregnancies. He chose to present his findings in Italian, rather than Latin as was still customary in his time, to reach a wider audience. Both a scientist and a publicist of the new science, Vallisnieri made important contributions to the study of animals, vegetables, and minerals, carrying on an intensive correspondence with the major scientists of his time.

Vannucci, Pietro See PERUGINO.

Vanoni, Ezio (1903–1956)
political figure, legislator, and planner of postwar economic reconstruction

A member of the Christian Democratic Party (DC), Vanoni played a major role in the reconstruction of the Italian economy after WORLD WAR

II. He was a professor of finance before the war, joined the RESISTANCE in 1943, was elected to the constituent assembly in 1946 and to parliament in 1948 and 1953. As minister of finance (1948–53) Vanoni was responsible for a reform of TAXATION and in 1954 formulated the so-called Vanoni Plan for the reconstruction of the economy. Vanoni, who had been a socialist in his youth, was inspired by the Christian principle of social responsibility to formulate a plan that wanted controlled economic growth, balanced budgets, full employment, and reduction of regional disparities. The plan envisaged an active role for the government, which was to set economic goals and monitor the private sector, and was inspired by a vision of social justice within the framework of a market economy. Socialists dared the Christian Democrats to implement Vanoni's plan, while Communists found it inadequate. In any case, the plan foundered on the opposition of free-market advocates and was voted down in parliament. In retrospect, Vanoni's plan may seem to have been a missed opportunity. The mix of public and private enterprise that developed in the absence of a plan increased the state's financial burden but did not yield the social benefits envisaged by Vanoni.

Vasari, Giorgio (1511–1574)

painter, architect, art critic, and historian

Vasari was born in Arezzo, the child of a potter, and was fortunate enough to attract the attention of a high prelate who tutored for the MEDICI FAMILY and took charge of the young man's education. The clergyman introduced his protégé into the Medici household, giving the young Vasari the opportunity to move into the most exclusive circles of Florentine society. Vasari developed into an accomplished and prolific painter. He worked in Florence, where he executed paintings in the Palazzo Vecchio and painted portraits of the Medici, and in the Vatican. His architectural projects include the extensive redesign and renovation of the center of Florence, with the building of the Uffizi as a long gallery of government offices. Although an

Giorgio Vasari *(Library of Congress)*

important artistic figure in his own right, Vasari is chiefly remembered as the author of the *Vite de' più eccellenti architetti, pittori e scultori italiani da Cimabue insino a' tempi nostri* (Lives of the most excellent Italian architects, painters and sculptors from Cimabue to our times; 1550, rev. 1568). Called the first history of modern art, this collection of biographies spans the course of Italian art from the 13th century to Vasari's time. It formulated the interpretative canon that sees art as developing steadily and linearly from the first attempts to paint realistically, culminating in the work of MICHELANGELO. Implicit in Vasari's interpretation is the notion that Renaissance art is a supreme achievement of skill and imagination.

Vatican City See HOLY SEE; PAPACY.

Vatican Councils See JOHN XXIII, PAUL VI; PIUS IX.

Vatican Museum See CLEMENT XIV.

Velletri, Battle of See AUSTRIAN
SUCCESSION, WAR OF THE.

Venetia (Veneto)

The region of Venetia, or Veneto in Italian (pop.
4,512,000), occupies part of northeastern Italy,
bordered on the east by the region of Friuli–
Venezia Giulia and stretching northward from
the shores of the upper Adriatic Sea to the border with Austria. VENICE is the regional capital.
Other major cities and provincial capitals are
Belluno, PADUA, Rovigo, Treviso, VERONA, and
Vicenza. The geography of the region is a study
in contrasts, as its alpine areas give way to hills,
hills to plains, rivers that empty into lakes, and
carry soil to the large delta of the Po River. Much
of the land that was once part of lagoons has
been reclaimed and supports an intensive, market-oriented agriculture that produces sugar
beets, corn, wheat, and fruit and the raising of
cattle and pigs. Small and medium-sized firms
predominate in the manufacturing of textiles,
shoes, furniture, and household appliances. In
the absence of large industrial cities, manufacturing establishments are distributed widely over
the region's territory, thus avoiding the worst
aspects of urban concentrations. Chemical plants
and oil refineries cluster around the industrial
complex of Porto Marghera near Venice. Hydroelectric plants utilizing the water resources of the
mountains sustain the region's industrial production. The artistic, historic, and natural attractions of the region draw millions of tourists, who
are well served by excellent transportation facilities. Winter sports, seaside resorts, and spas are
popular. As an area of transit, the region has been
exposed in the course of its history to incursions
from the east and north, changing hands many
times until its towns, led by Verona, began to
form communal leagues in the 12th century.
From then on, the history of the region was
dominated by conflicts among rival cities, until
Venice gained control of the region in the 15th

century and imposed order. The region then followed the fortunes of the Venetian republic until
its demise in 1797, when it became a possession
of the HABSBURGS. With the brief Napoleonic
interruption of 1805–13, Venetia was part of the
Austrian Empire, as part of the Kingdom of Lombardy-Venetia set up by the CONGRESS OF VIENNA.
It became part of the Kingdom of Italy in 1866,
following the Third WAR OF NATIONAL INDEPEN-
DENCE. The religious traditions of the region sustain many of the region's social activities and a
progressive Catholic political movement.

Venezia Giulia See FRIULI–VENEZIA GIULIA.

Venezia Tridentina See TRENTINO–ALTO
ADIGE.

Venice, city of

Archaeological evidence points to permanent
human settlement of the islands of the Venice
lagoon from as early as the second century A.D.
when the island of Torcello was inhabited by
mainlanders seeking refuge from military incursions. The attractiveness of the lagoon islands as
places of refuge increased during the early Middle Ages, when the decline of Roman imperial
power left the populations of the mainland even
more vulnerable to attack. By the 10th century
Venice had definitely begun its ascent as a sea
power, and Venetians seized opportunities for
sea trade offered by their location at the head of
the Adriatic Sea. A series of victorious expeditions opened the way to its penetration of markets in the eastern Mediterranean regions.
Venice also took advantage of the Crusades to
consolidate its control of eastern Mediterranean
routes. In 1082 the Republic of Venice concluded
a treaty with the Byzantine emperor Alexius
Comnenus that allowed Venetian merchants to
conduct business throughout the empire without paying tribute, and assigned to them a special quarter in Constantinople. Statutes dating
from 1172, 1178, and 1220 gave the right to

Panoramic view of the Grand Canal, Venice, ca. 1909 *(Library of Congress)*

elect the doge, or head of the republic, to a small number of citizens, curtailed the powers of the doge, and gave ultimate power to representative councils, including the senate. These provisions made Venice an aristocratic republic in which only a limited number of wealthy families had access to political office. By the end of the 13th century, commoners were completely excluded from government.

In the course of its maritime expansion Venice came into conflict with other city-states, particularly with the rival republic of GENOA, with which Venice had to share access to the eastern Mediterranean. In the 14th century the Venetian government turned its attention to the mainland where it sought to halt the growth of powers that threatened its security from that direction. Venice took advantage of the decline of Milanese power under the rule of the VISCONTI FAMILY to seize important towns, including Padua and Verona at the beginning of the 15th century. Its mainland territory was rounded out by 1453, the year that also saw the fall of Constantinople to the Turks. That event, and the shifting of trade routes to the Atlantic as a result of Portuguese and Spanish explorations, including the European discovery of America, marked the decline of Venetian maritime trade and power. But the decline was gradual, and Venice was still a Mediterranean power to be reckoned with for most of the 16th century. The Venetian republic ceased to exist with the Treaty of Campoformio (1797), by which France and Austria divided the possessions of the republic among themselves, with Austria gaining the city of Venice and its Adriatic possessions, including ISTRIA and DAL-

MATIA. The Republic of Venice became a lingering historical memory powerful enough to inspire Venetian revolutionaries in 1848–49. For a few months Venice reclaimed its independence, calling itself the Repubblica di San Marco after its patron saint.

The legacy of Venice's grand past lives on in the city's palaces, churches, museums, and monuments. The approximately 14 million tourists who visit the city of canals and bridges seldom realize that what they are experiencing are the fruits of one of the western world's longest and most successful ventures in imperial expansion. What they may not also realize is that behind the historic vestiges of its past lies a city in crisis. Decaying housing, the gradual sinking of the land, and periodic flooding (*acqua alta*) are the visible signs of a decline that has been going on for decades. The stable population of the historic center has shrunk from 150,000 to 70,000. The other 275,400 inhabitants that the census lists for the municipality (*comune*) of Venice live on the mainland, where many have moved in recent decades to find jobs, better housing, and services. Glass-blowing and lacemaking are still practiced on the islands of the lagoon, but most industrial activity occurs around the mainland settlements of Mestre and Porto Marghera. Chemical plants, oil refineries, shipyards, and textile factories cluster around Porto Marghera. Mestre has become largely a bedroom community for workers in Venice and other towns in the region of VENETIA. The plight of the city is due to the double impact of the sinking of its foundations, possibly caused by the excessive extraction of water from the subsoil, and the simultaneous rise of the sea level, possibly related to global warming. Plans to confront the city's urgent problems run into the obstacles of high cost and bureaucratic inertia. In 2003 the Italian government gave the greenlight to the construction of a complex, costly, and controversial system of sea barriers and locks designed to protect the city from flooding.

Venturi, Lionello (1885–1961)
art critic and historian

The son of distinguished art historian Adolfo Venturi (1856–1941), Lionello Venturi followed in his father's footsteps as a scholar and art critic. From 1915 to 1932 he taught art history at the University of Turin. Refusing to take the oath of allegiance to the Fascist regime that was required of all academics that year, he resigned from his post and moved with his family to Paris. He lived in Paris and the United States, holding a variety of academic positions. In 1945 he returned to Italy and held the chair of art history at the University of Rome until his retirement in 1955. His first studies, published in 1907 and 1913, dealt with Venetian painting. He is remembered for the reevaluation of primitive art brought about by the publication of *Il gusto dei primitivi* (1926). In that book, Venturi formulated an aesthetic that made possible the appreciation of forms of art that did not conform to classical canons. He followed up with the publication in 1936 of studies of Cézanne, the French impressionists, and a magisterial *History of Art Criticism* published in English. His son, Franco Venturi (1914–94), also a distinguished scholar, was a historian of the Italian ENLIGHTENMENT, and a member of the anti-Fascist RESISTANCE.

Verdi, Giuseppe (1813–1901)
opera composer, patriotic figure, and popular icon

Italy's most famous composer was born into a family of innkeepers in the hamlet of Roncole, near Busseto (Parma). His parents bought him

Giuseppe Verdi *(Library of Congress)*

a spinet and arranged for music lessons when his passion for music manifested itself at age seven or eight. Music instruction followed in Busseto, where he graduated with honors from the local gymnasium in 1827. The famed Milan Conservatory refused him admission in 1832. His first works, composed for the local orchestra, made a favorable impression and won him entry into the homes of prominent families. Antonio Barezzi befriended the young composer, took him into his home, and helped him financially. After studying privately in Milan (1832–35), Verdi was appointed music director in Busseto, a post that he held from 1836 to 1839. In 1836 he married Barezzi's daughter, Margherita, and three years later they moved to Milan, the city that was emerging as Italy's musical capital. Within the next two years, his wife and child died, and his first two operas, *Oberto* (1839) and *Un giorno di regno* (King for a day, 1840), made little impression.

Verdi's first great success came with the opera *Nabucco* (1842), and was followed by a similarly successful production of *I Lombardi alla prima crociata* (The Lombards on the first Crusade) the following year. All these were produced at the Teatro alla Scala. The success of *Ernani* in Venice in 1844 confirmed his reputation as the upcoming master of the operatic stage. His rich melodic vein was appreciated, but what distinguished the young Verdi was a vigorous, earthy style and a robust sound noticeably different from the light manner and delicate orchestration of his predecessors. Verdi's early period concludes with *La Battaglia di Legnano* (The Battle of Legnano, 1849) which, depicting the victory of Italians over Germans in the Middle Ages, was perfomed in revolutionary Rome to frenzied acclaim. Verdi's patriotic spirit endeared him and his music to the generation that fought in the RISORGIMENTO.

His later operas show greater psychological insight and mastery of technical musical matters. The operas of the middle period from 1850 to the mid-1860s are more introspective, more intent on exploring the private world of emotions than venting public sentiments. *Rigoletto* (1851) explores the tragic consequences of the love that the hunchback court jester Rigoletto has for his daughter. *Il Trovatore* (The troubadour, 1853) is a strong theatrical statement of love, jealousy, and revenge. With *La Traviata* (1853), Verdi for the first and only time in his career tackled a subject drawn from his own time, giving a sympathetic account of the intimate anguish of a high-class Parisian courtesan trapped in her frivolous life. *Simon Boccanegra* (1857) looks at the private tribulations of a 14th-century figure. The operas of Verdi's final period, *Don Carlos* (1867), *Aida* (1871), *Otello* (1887), and *Falstaff* (1893), reach new levels of musical inventiveness and subtlety, making Verdi that rare artistic figure whose creative powers grow and mature with advancing age. In the course of a career that spanned more than half a century, Verdi's music reflected the changing tastes and voiced the aspirations of generations of Italians. The epitaph composed by GABRIELE D'ANNUNZIO described Verdi as the one who "wept and rejoiced for us all."

Verga, Giovanni (1840–1922)
Sicilian novelist and playwright, leading exponent of the school of literary realism

Verga was born in Catania to a family of the impoverished Sicilian nobility that sympathized with the movement for national independence. The precarious financial conditions of the family may account for the pessimism that pervades Verga's writings and his determined pursuit of financial security and social respectability. His interest in writing manifested itself even before he entered the University of Catania in 1858 to study law. Verga decided to devote himself entirely to writing before completing his law studies. The favorable reception of his first writings convinced him to move to Florence (1865–71) and then to Milan (1871–93), where he was close to members of the SCAPIGLIATURA movement. Contact with the literary rebels that made up that movement influenced the tone of novels like *Una peccatrice* (A sinning woman, 1866), *Eva* (1873), and *Eros* (1875) that were critical of middle-class values and expressed Verga's lasting preoccupation with the power of sexual passions. The discovery of French naturalism turned Verga's interest toward the world of Sicilian middle-class and peasant characters, which he had approached in some of his early writings. He described the world of ordinary people without sentimentality. His true-to-life descriptions make him the most notable representative of the Italian version of naturalism called VERISMO. He sees tragedy in the hopeless struggles of people who must confront insurmountable odds built into the nature of things. Verga's harsh view of life is barely relieved by a sense of sympathy for his characters. His view of the severe code of honor of Sicilians confirmed northern notions of southerners as people driven by uncontrollable passions and instincts.

His major writings are the novels *I Malavoglia* (The house by the medlar tree, 1881) and *Mastro Don Gesualdo* (1889), and the collections of short stories entitled *Vita dei campi* (Life in the fields, 1880) and *Novelle rusticane* (1883). *Vita dei campi* contains the short story *Cavalleria rusticana* that inspired PIETRO MASCAGNI to compose his highly successful opera with the same title. D. H. Lawrence translated *Novelle rusticane* into English as *Little Novels of Sicily* (1925).

Veri Italiani See SECRET SOCIETIES.

verismo

Verismo, derived from *verità* (truth), took hold in Italian culture in the last two decades of the 19th century, influenced by philosophical POSITIVISM and by French literary naturalism as seen in the writings of Gustave Flaubert and Emile Zola. The writer and critic Luigi Capuana (1839–1915) was its most influential publicist and propagator, but the greatest practitioner of the veristic mode was Capuana's close friend GIOVANNI VERGA. Writers of the verismo school favored regional subjects through which they could best approach the everyday language and manners of peasants, workers, and ordinary middle-class figures. Plain language and the use of dialectal expressions are characteristics of the verismo school evident in the writings of authors as diverse as the young GABRIELE D'ANNUNZIO, MATILDE SERAO, and Renato Fucini (1843–1921) in his short stories and descriptions of life in rural Tuscany. Precisely because verismo could encompass and accommodate such diversity, it is best thought of as a current or trend rather than as a well-defined school of writing. Critics and historians see it as a reaction against the sentimental mode of writing rooted in ROMANTICISM and as an effort to capture the essence of a traditional rural world threatened by industrialization and urbanization. It must be remembered, however, that the inspiration to write in a naturalistic way came precisely from the currents of philosophical positivism that were part of the process of modernization at the time.

Vermigli, Pietro Martire (1499–1562)
religious reformer, humanist scholar, convert to Protestantism

Known in the English-speaking world simply as Peter Martyr, Vermigli was born in Florence to a family of modest means as Pietro Mariano Vermigli. He studied with Augustinian friars, and took on the name of Pietro Martire at the time of his induction in the Augustinian Order (1518). He went on to study philosophy and theology at the University of Padua and was ordained into the priesthood (1525). After obtaining a doctorate in theology (1526), he was an itinerant preacher in northern Italy and resumed his studies in Bologna, becoming an authority on ancient Hebrew, Aramaic, Syriac, and Amharic. With his exceptional linguistic competence and theological training, Vermigli felt qualified to interpret Scripture and propose religious reforms, particularly of monastic orders. Assigned to various posts as abbot, he was in Spoleto (1533–37), NAPLES (1537–40), and LUCCA (1540–42). It was particularly in Naples and Lucca that Vermigli began to gravitate toward notions of religious reform associated with Protestantism. Simplification of ritual, clerical marriage, the Eucharist as a mere symbolic act, a return to the spirit of early Christianity, and involvement of the laity in church matters were some of Vermigli's positions that brought about his conversion to a radical Protestantism akin to that of the Swiss reformers Ulrich Zwingli and Heinrich Bullinger. Keeping one step ahead of the INQUISITION, Vermigli left Lucca for Zurich and went from there to Strasbourg, where he taught the Old Testament until 1547. He left Strasbourg for England to teach at Oxford and collaborate with Archbishop Cramner in drawing up the Second Book of Common Prayer, which formed the basis of the Anglican faith. In 1548 he played a leading role in an unsuccessful effort to unify the various Protestant churches of Europe. When the Catholic Queen Mary assumed the

English throne in 1553, Vermigli returned to the Continent, first to Strasbourg (1553–57), then to Zurich to teach the Old Testament. There, in the last years of his life, he fully developed his evangelical ideas and published some of his most important work of biblical exegesis. His exceptional learning based on humanistic and religious texts and his activism as a religious reformer make Vermigli one of the most important figures of the evangelical movement. His European stature at the time makes his neglect in current memory and scholarship all the more perplexing.

Verona, city of

Verona (pop. 257,500) is located in the region of VENETIA on the banks of the Adige River. An important transportation point since ancient times, Verona rose to prominence during the Roman period. After experiencing domination by Goths, Lombards, Franks, and Germans, it became a free commune in the 13th century. Under the SIGNORIA of the Della Scala, or Scaligeri, family (1282–1387) the city enjoyed a period of power and prosperity. MILAN and VENICE fought for control of the city after the fall of the Scaligeri, with Venice annexing the city and its territory in 1405. From then on Verona followed the history of its region under Venetian rule. Under Austrian rule (1814–66) it was a stronghold of the fortified area known as the Quadrilatero that anchored the Austrian military presence in northern Italy. In 1822 the city hosted the conference of the European great powers to put down the revolution that had broken out in Spain in 1820–21. It was the last conference summoned to enforce the provisions of the Treaty of Vienna and the Quadruple Alliance. Verona and the region became part of the Kingdom of Italy in 1866. The province has a diversified economy based on agriculture, industry, and tourism. Its horticultural products and wines are popular in Italy and abroad. Rich in monuments that cover every century from antiquity to the present, Verona is also an important cultural center. The summer opera season in the Arena, the city's ancient Roman amphitheater, is a major cultural event.

Veronese, Paolo (ca. 1528–1588)
painter and decorator known for his
animated compositions and lavish use
of colors

Called Veronese because he was born and trained in the city of VERONA, Paolo Caliari won fame in Venice where he was working in 1553. He was influenced by TITIAN in Venice and by RAPHAEL in Rome, where he journeyed in 1560. Veronese made distinctive use of opulent colors, painted grand scenes crowded with figures and objects, loved light, pleasure, and elegance. His religious paintings exude a worldly, sensuous charm that did not sit well with religious authorities in the age of the CATHOLIC REFORMATION. Summoned by the Inquisition in 1573 to answer for one of his works, he defended himself ably by invoking the license allowed artists and fools and was required only to change the title of the incriminated painting, *Christ in the House of Levi.* The Venetian government had no such qualms, and commissioned him to redecorate the Ducal Palace after it was damaged by fire in 1577. Veronese painted the magnificent *Triumph of Venice* and *Venice Ruling with Justice and Peace,* flattering allegorical representations of Venice at the height of its power and splendor. In the exuberance of Veronese's works, one senses the worldliness of 16th-century Venetian culture deliberately presenting itself as a rival to the austere image of papal authority.

Verrazzano, Giovanni da
(ca. 1480–ca. 1527)
Florentine explorer of the North American
coast in the service of France

Giovanni da Verrazzano (also spelled Verrazano) was born near Florence to an established family, received an excellent education, and sought fame and fortune abroad. In 1524 he sailed in the service of Francis I of France to search for a northwest passage to Asia, explored the coast of North

America from North Carolina to Maine, and continued on to Nova Scotia and Newfoundland, from where he sailed back to Europe. He was the first to enter New York Bay, but quickly concluded that the Hudson River, named after Henry Hudson who explored it 85 years later, was not the sought passage to Asia. Considered a failure at the time, the voyage nevertheless established French territorial claims to North America. Much about Verrazzano's life is conjectural. However, the once-disputed claim that he was the first European to sail into New York Harbor seems valid. According to one version of his death, he was killed in a fight with natives in the Lesser Antilles during a second voyage to the New World. According to another version, he was executed by order of Emperor CHARLES V after being captured by Spaniards off Cadiz. The suspension bridge that spans the narrows between Brooklyn and Staten Island at the entrance to New York Bay is named after him.

Verri, Pietro (1728–1797)
Lombard writer, economist, and
Enlightenment reformer
Born to a family of the Milanese aristocracy, Verri personified the ideal of the intellectual committed to public service. After being schooled by religious orders, Verri attended a lay school for the nobility in Parma. Steered by his father, a senator, toward a law degree and a position at the imperial court in Vienna (1752), he resided in the Austrian capital and was an officer in the Austrian army during the Seven Years' War. Back in Milan in 1760, Verri was the key figure of a group of intellectuals that included his brother, the writer and classicist scholar Alessandro Verri (1741–1816), and CESARE BECCARIA.

Inclined toward political reform, Verri and his group used the press, including the brilliant review *Il Caffè* (1764–66), to propagate ENLIGHTENMENT notions of good government, public administration, and economic policy. Verri addressed issues of immediate concern to his generation and grounded his recommendations on concrete evidence. In government he supported a strong monarchy capable of bringing about reforms that were opposed by entrenched interests. Those entrenched interests included the aristocracy to which he belonged by birth, but which he condemned in his writings as lacking in education and public spirit. Enlightened intellectuals had a moral obligation to cooperate with reforming monarchs to achieve a society of the common good. Once that goal is established, it is the task of legislators to devise appropriate laws for its achievement.

The key to government reform was to make taxation more equitable and efficient. To that end, Verri engaged in a long and partially successful battle to eliminate the farming out (collection) of taxes to private individuals and centralize it instead in the hands of government officials. In his *Discorso sulla felicità* (Discourse on happiness, 1781), Verri argued that public and private happiness could be achieved by maximizing pleasures and minimizing pains. This philosophical materialism unconnected to religion sustained an optimistic faith in human perfectibility and progress. Verri set out his thoughts on economic matters in his *Meditazioni sulla economia politica* (Meditations on political economy, 1771). It proposed the abolition of restrictions on production and trade, free circulation of property, and a balanced economy based on agriculture, manufacturing, and trade. Verri was not an absolute laissez-faire economist because he did believe in the usefulness of indirect government intervention in economic matters, but he did anticipate the idea of Adam Smith that wealth consists not in the accumulation of precious metals but in a net increase in production. In his later years Verri acknowledged that a strong but constitutional monarch might be a more effective ruler than the absolutist JOSEPH II, who had undermined his efforts at reform by acting unilaterally and impolitically.

Verrocchio, Andrea del See BOTTICELLI, SANDRO.

Versailles, Treaty of   See PARIS PEACE CONFERENCE.

Vespucci, Amerigo (1454–1512)
businessman, scholar, and navigator who gave his name to the New World

The explorer who gave his name to the American continent was born to a merchant family of Florence that had seen better days, absorbed the culture of humanism from his surroundings, and was part of the cultural elite of the city. A protégé of LORENZO DE' MEDICI, Vespucci was often entrusted with missions to look after that family's business interests abroad. In 1492 he went to Seville on such an errand and decided to go into business for himself in that Spanish port city as an outfitter and supplier of ships. The contact with seafarers heightened Vespucci's interest in travel, which had already developed in Florence with his study of astronomy and cartography. Vespucci followed news of the voyages of CHRISTOPHER COLUMBUS and fitted out the explorer's third voyage of 1498. A year later he joined a Spanish expedition headed for the New World, broke off from the main body to conduct his own exploration of the coast of modern Brazil, but was forced to turn back to Europe when his ship suffered damage. A second voyage in 1501, this time for King Manuel I of Portugal (1495–1521), was more successful. Vespucci was able to explore the coast of South America to a point far south, concluding that the landmass he was exploring was a new continent. Still, Vespucci thought that a westward passage to the Orient could be found, and with that goal in mind planned further explorations. In 1508, back in Spanish service, he received the title and honors of pilot-major of Spain, charged with training ship pilots for further exploration. Vespucci died of malaria before he could start on a third voyage of his own. His few surviving letters reveal a mind ready to draw conclusions on the basis of independent observation, skeptical of received knowledge and religious authority. Vespucci did not name America after himself. It was an obscure and misinformed German clergyman, Martin Wadseemüller, who erroneously attributed to Vespucci the discovery of the new continent and named it America in his treatise *Cosmographia* (1507). The popularity of that work, and the desire of the Portuguese to magnify their role in the discovery of the New World, prevented the error from being corrected.

Vico, Giambattista (1668–1744)
Neapolitan thinker, precursor of 19th-century romanticism and historical philosophy

The son of a Neapolitan bookseller, Vico was educated by clergymen, studied law at the University of Naples, and indulged his real interest by reading philosophy in his spare time. In 1699 he was appointed professor of rhetoric at the University of Naples. Recognition came slowly. For much of his life Vico lived in straitened circumstances, burdened by a large family and by a feeling of estrangement from his contemporaries, who considered him an intellectual crank and loose cannon. But, far from being estranged, Vico was very much a part of intellectual life in Naples and of the philosophical debates of his time. In the ongoing controversy between "ancients" and "moderns" about the relative merits of tradition and innovation, Vico leaned toward the former. He was familiar with and admired the scientific and mathematical thought of his time, but did not believe that progress was brought about by reason alone. In *De antiquissima Italorum sapientia* (On the ancient wisdom of the Italians, 1710) he identified the wisdom of the ancient Romans with their habit of seeking truth in the nature of things rather than in abstractions, and with their awareness that a full understanding of reality exists only in the mind of God.

His doubts about the ability of reason alone to grasp reality found complete expression in his major work *La scienza nuova* (The new science, 1725). That work sketches the transformation of society from a primitive state (the age of gods or myths) in which the poetic imagination prevailed, through the age of heroes (Homeric age), dominated by the cult of the exceptional individual, to the age of men in which reason becomes manifest. Each age has its own culture, or forms of sensitivity and thought. According to Vico, history does not proceed linearly through these three stages from one to the next. The course of history is cyclical; it is characterized by "flux" and "reflux," each new age representing both something new and a return to the primitive past, just as the Middle Ages represented a compromise between the refinements of classical civilization and the crude customs of the barbarians.

Throughout his work Vico relies on the study of language and law to reveal the nature of culture, and sees history (the study of the real) as the "new science" that alone can fulfill that role. The challenge to the primacy of reason, rejection of the notion of steady progress, and recourse to history as the ultimate discipline endeared Vico to 19th-century philosophy. It was the revaluation of Vico's thought by the French historian Jules Michelet that brought the almost forgotten Neapolitan scholar to the attention of Michelet's contemporaries and created the image of Vico as a precursor of modern culture. Vico's *Autobiography* (translated in 1944) is a good starting point for a study of this intriguing figure.

Victor Amadeus II See CLEMENT XI; SAVOY, HOUSE OF.

Victor Emmanuel I (1759–1824)
(Vittorio Emanuele I)
king of Sardinia (1802–1821)

Victor Emmanuel became king of Sardinia in 1802, when his older brother Carlo Emanuele IV abdicated the throne. He fought tenaciously against Napoleon but, defeated, he retreated to the island of Sardinia, where he ruled under protection of the British navy without renouncing his claims to the mainland territories. The CONGRESS OF VIENNA restored to him all his territories, plus the region of Liguria, formerly part of the abolished Republic of GENOA. Victor

Emmanuel ruled over his enlarged state like an absolute monarch, abolishing the reforms introduced during the Napoleonic period, restoring the old forms of government, the privileges of the ARISTOCRACY and clergy, including clerical control of education, and removing or demoting civil servants and military officers who had risen in rank under Napoleon. But he did retain administrative reforms designed to improve the functioning of government, the collection of taxes and tariffs, and management of the public debt. His strong sense of dynastic pride came into play in his dealing with Austria, whose dominance in the peninsula he resisted to the best of his ability. He opposed political initiatives that he feared would consolidate Austrian power in Italy and hoped to acquire Austrian LOMBARDY. His ideological absolutism was actually at odds with Metternich's more practical conservatism. When revolution broke out in 1821, he abdicated in favor of his brother CHARLES FELIX rather than grant the constitution demanded by insurgents. But this strenuous defender of royal power was also a stickler for legal procedures; his ideal was absolute power, not arbitrary government.

Victor Emmanuel II (1820–1878)
(Vittorio Emanuele II)
last king of Sardinia (1849–1860), first king of Italy (1861–1878)

Victor Emmanuel II succeeded to the Sardinian throne after the abdication of his father, Charles Albert, who stepped down in 1849 after being defeated by the Austrians in the first WAR OF NATIONAL INDEPENDENCE. He was able to negotiate a peace agreement that allowed him to retain the CONSTITUTION (Statuto) that provided for a representative parliament and civil liberties. Victor Emmanuel thus attracted the sympathies and support of Italian liberals who favored both national independence and constitutional government.

Although inclined by upbringing and temperament to govern personally, Victor Emmanuel was shrewd enough to realize that it was to the advantage of the monarchy to show respect for the constitution and work with parliament. By working, however reluctantly, with CAVOUR as his prime minister, he showed his willingness to respect the prerogatives of parliament. But he could still conduct his own personal diplomacy behind the prime minister's back, as he did in 1860 when he let GIUSEPPE GARIBALDI loose in Sicily. His amicable relationship with the French emperor NAPOLEON III also helped the cause of Italian unification. Like all male members of his dynasty, he received a strict military education and was exposed to the risks of battle, for which he showed exceptional courage. But while his personal courage is not in question, there are grave doubts about his military judgment. His tendency to appoint subservient commanders and to issue orders that interfered with military operations made him a troublesome presence on the field of battle.

Like Cavour, he may have been a late convert to the cause of Italian unification, as opposed to that of independence. National unification may have been the unintended consequence of the policy of Piedmontese territorial expansion eagerly pursued by both king and prime minister. After the death of Cavour in 1861, Victor Emmanuel asserted himself more forcefully in choosing ministers, conducting foreign and military policy, and ignoring parliament, without ever reverting to the methods of an absolute monarch. He preferred to work behind weak ministers like URBANO RATTAZZI, or to appoint to political office generals bound to him by their military oath. Personally devout to the point of bigotry, he was troubled by the conflict of CHURCH AND STATE that turned Pope PIUS IX and many Catholics against him and the Italian state. He traveled reluctantly to Rome after its capture in 1870 to take possession of the city as the new capital of the Kingdom of Italy, and never felt at home living in the QUIRINAL PALACE. In 1873 he paid an official state visit to Vienna, thus taking a giant step toward allaying the anti-Austrian animosities of the RISORGIMENTO, giving Italy greater security in Europe, and laying the ground for the

TRIPLE ALLIANCE that would be consummated by his son and successor UMBERTO I.

Victor Emmanuel II remains an enigmatic and controversial figure. The official image of Victor Emmanuel as the *Re Galantuomo* (Honest King) hardly does justice to his character. He was above all a man of contradictions: inordinately proud of his long royal lineage, he did not hide his plebeian tastes; an absolutist ruler by temperament who accepted constitutional monarchy; a religious man driven by earthy appetites; a political enemy of the church but a devout Catholic; impulsive and calculating. One constant trait ruled this man of contradictory impulses: a basic common sense kept him in touch with reality and held him back ultimately from his most reckless schemes.

Victor Emmanuel III (1869–1947)
(Vittorio Emanuele III)
king of Italy (1900–1946)

Victor Emmanuel came to the throne in 1900 following the assassination of his father, UMBERTO I; his long reign lasted until 1946. He was born in Naples, given the title of Prince of Naples, spent his youth in the city, and there attended a military academy, to endear the national dynasty to the Neapolitans. After traveling in eastern Europe and the Near East, in 1896 he married Princess Elena of Montenegro (1873–1952), daughter of the ruler of that Balkan kingdom. They had five children, including Umberto, the second born, who as the only male ruled briefly as UMBERTO II following his father's resignation.

In the first years of his rule, Victor Emmanuel III lived up to the expectation that he would show due regard for the prerogatives of parliament. He was more than willing to let GIOVANNI GIOLITTI take charge of parliament. In foreign policy, it was known that he disapproved of the policy of colonial expansion backed by his father. He supported Italy's membership in the TRIPLE ALLIANCE, but also favored cordial relations with Great Britain and France. When Italy went to war in 1915, true to the military traditions of his forebears, he left for the front line and spent the war years close to the troops. He is credited with insisting that the army make a stand to halt the Austrian advance on the Piave River after the disaster of CAPORETTO.

Fear of the consequences of social revolution for the country, and the dynasty, governed his political behavior in the turbulent aftermath of war. That fear, and his lack of faith in liberal politicians, led him to support BENITO MUSSOLINI's bid for power. That fateful decision tied the monarchy to FASCISM. Relations between Mussolini and the king were cordial, but the undercurrent of distrust and hostility between the monarchy and the Fascist regime was stronger than their personal bond. Victor Emmanuel retreated into himself, and was publicly silent when the regime curtailed his royal prerogatives. In 1928 the Fascist Grand Council asserted its right to interfere in the succession to the throne. In 1938 Mussolini obtained parity of military command with the king. Victor Emmanuel welcomed the additional titles of emperor (1936) and of king of Albania (1939) that came to him from the territorial conquests of the regime. Deeply distrustful and openly contemptuous of Hitler, he expressed his reservations privately, approved of the alliance with Nazi Germany, and when a German victory seemed certain nine months into WORLD WAR II, had no reservations about going to war on Germany's side.

Only in the face of certain and impending military defeat did Victor Emmanuel assert his authority as the head of state. In July 1943 he dimissed Mussolini and authorized the secret surrender to the Allies of September 1943. In the chaotic days that followed the announcement of the armistice, Victor Emmanuel abandoned Rome with a retinue of generals and high officials and sought the protection of the Allies in the occupied South. That move contributed to the country's ordeal in the coming days. The army, left with ambiguous and contradictory orders, was leaderless. It could neither mount an effective resistance against the Germans, who

King Victor Emmanuel III *(Library of Congress)*

were now its enemies, nor win the trust of the Allies. The people were left to themselves to decide between the enemies and friends of the past and of the present. Most chose simply to wait out the crisis and survive.

The decision to abandon the capital dealt the final and irreparable blow to the king's personal prestige. He continued to reign in name only in the puppet state known as the *Regno del Sud* (Kingdom of the South) controlled by the Allies. There he stubbornly clung to the trappings of royal authority devoid of real power. He resigned in favor of his son UMBERTO II one month before the general elections and plebiscite of June 1946, hoping that his resignation would improve the monarchy's chances of survival. It did not. The House of Savoy ceased to rule, and Italy became a republic. Victor Emmanuel and Queen Elena left the country immediately for exile in Egypt, where he lived out the rest of his years reading, fishing, and collecting stamps. Collecting was Victor Emmanuel's lifelong passion. His contribution to numismatics is a lasting legacy. He amassed the largest collection of Italian coins and published a 20-volume descriptive catalog of the same. Whatever his shortcomings as a monarch, Victor Emmanuel's *Corpus nummorum italicorum* (1910–40) is a monument to his erudition and to the acquisitive temperament that enabled him to enlarge the family fortune in good and bad times.

Vieusseux, Gian Pietro (1779–1863)
publisher, cultural promoter, and guiding liberal figure

Born of Swiss parents in the town of Oneglia, Vieusseux was a successful businessman who made a fortune in wheat trading before settling into the publishing business in Florence in 1819. His first venture in that city was the opening of a reading room (*gabinetto di lettura*) where subscribers could read publications not readily available in Italy at the time. The Gabinetto Scientifico-Letterario Gian Pietro Vieusseux promoted the circulation of ideas and drew Italian intellectual circles into the European cultural mainstream. Later transformed into a permanent institution, the Gabinetto still functions as a library and cultural institute. Vieusseux took advantage of the relative mildness and tolerance of the Tuscan government to launch other initiatives that could not succeed without some degree of freedom of expression. Most important was the *Antologia*, a review covering science, literature, and the arts, that Vieusseux launched in 1820 with the help of GINO CAPPONI and other prominent Tuscan moderates. It soon began to address issues such as legal reform, custom union projects intended to create a single market in Italy, free trade, civil liberties, and public education. While seemingly nonpolitical, these projects had strong political implications that pointed to independence and unity. Vieusseux was careful not to criticize the government openly, but it became increasingly clear that the reforms discussed in the *Antologia* could not be enacted without changes in government policies. Tuscan landowners backed Vieusseux's *Giornale Agrario,* founded in 1827, a publication that promoted improvements in the land tenure system of MEZZADRIA that was the basis of Tuscan agriculture. The period of political tolerance ended when the revolution of 1830–31 prompted the Tuscan government to clamp down on dissenters. The *Antologia* ceased publication in 1833. Its disappearance marked the end of an era when moderate liberals like Vieusseux expected governments to grant meaningful reforms.

Villafranca, Armistice of See WARS OF NATIONAL INDEPENDENCE.

Villa Giulia, Armistice of See WORLD WAR I.

Villari, Pasquale (1826–1917)
patriotic writer, historian, publicist, and advocate for southern Italy

Villari was forced to leave his native Naples after being implicated in the REVOLUTION of 1848, which he supported. A political exile in Tuscany, he taught history at the University of Pisa (1859–65) and at the Institute for Advanced Studies in Florence (1865–1913). After national unification he served in the Chamber of Deputies (1870–76, 1880–82) and in the senate from 1883 to the end of his life, was minister of public education (1891–92), and first president of the DANTE ALIGHIERI SOCIETY (1896–1903). An expert on conditions in the South, his *Lettere meridionali* (Letters from the South, 1878) helped bring the SOUTHERN QUESTION to national attention. His biographies of GIROLAMO SAVONAROLA and NICCOLÒ MACHIAVELLI, and histories of Florence and Italy in the Middle Ages, stand out for both scholarship and literary merit. As a historian Villari coupled respect for factual accuracy, called for by the school of philosophical POSITIVISM to which he adhered, with the expression of patriotic and anticlerical sentiments. Villari influenced a whole generation with his writings, teaching, and vigorous public debates.

Vinci, Leonardo da See LEONARDO DA VINCI.

Visconti, Luchino (1906–1974)
Neorealist film director known for his treatment of literary and historical subjects

Count Luchino Visconti, descended from a lateral branch of the VISCONTI FAMILY of Milan, is regarded as the founder of cinematic NEOREALISM. His remarkable career began in the twilight years of FASCISM, which Visconti is thought to have opposed from within by proposing realistic depictions of life at odds with the heroic rhetoric of the regime. His first film, *Ossessione* (1942), was an adaptation to an Italian setting of the American novel *The Postman Always Rings Twice* by James Cain. The film gave a disheartening view of rural life steeped in poverty and moral degradation, totally different from the Fascist view of rural life as the cradle of strength and virtue. Realistic depictions of life characterized Visconti's postwar films. *La terra trema* (1948), based on the novel *The House by the Medlar Tree* by GIOVANNI VERGA, shows a family of fishermen driven to ruin by the unscrupulousness of men and the calamities of nature. The human drama of the 1950s emigration of southerners to the cities of northern Italy inspired *Rocco and His Brothers* (1960). Visconti displayed an uncanny talent for re-creating a particular locale or period by focusing the camera on the small but revealing detail. His later productions looked to the past. *The Leopard* (1963), based on the novel by Giuseppe di Lampedusa, depicts the decline of an aristocratic Sicilian family in the 50 years after national unification. *Death in Venice* (1971)

and *The Innocent* (1976), based, respectively, on novels by Thomas Mann and GABRIELE D'ANNUNZIO, are introspective explorations of emotions and identity. The preoccupation with characters in crisis and moments of decline has been ascribed to the crisis in modern times of the aristocratic element to which he belonged by birth and temperament. Visconti's filmmaking can also be seen as reflecting the changes of mood and sensitivity of the postwar generations.

Visconti family
The origins of this powerful family of Lombard lords can be traced as far back as the 10th century, when they first appear as vassals of German emperors ruling Lombardy at that time. The family lordship over MILAN dates from the 1270s when Ottone Visconti (1207–95) seized control of the city and established the family rule that lasted for the next two centuries. The Visconti earned a reputation for dealing ruthlessly with their enemies and rivals, but they also showed superior administrative and military skills, and were on occasion generous and discerning patrons of the arts. FRANCESCO PETRARCA was one of their protégés. Gian Galeazzo (1351–1402), greatest of the Visconti, seized power from another family member in 1385. Ten years later he obtained from the Holy Roman Emperor the title of duke of Milan and official recognition as legitimate ruler of a hereditary state. A typical RENAISSANCE despot, Gian Galeazzo centralized government, reformed the administration, and enlarged his dominions by war and diplomacy. His enlarged state eventually posed a threat to his neighbors, prompting Florence, Venice, and the Papal States to form a common front against him. Contemporaries suspected that he aimed at unifying the entire peninsula under his rule. But if that was his intention, it was cut short by his sudden death by natural causes at age 51. His less capable successors held onto power for a while longer. A short-lived Ambrosian Republic was set up at the death of Filippo Maria Visconti

(1392–1447), followed by the rise to power of the condottiere FRANCESCO SFORZA, who had served Filippo Maria and married his only daughter and heir.

Visconti-Venosta, Emilio (1829–1914)
Risorgimento patriot, career diplomat, and foreign minister

Visconti-Venosta was descended from the Venosta family that traced its lineage back to 12th-century Lombardy. In the 15th century they were authorized to add the VISCONTI surname to their own. Their patent of nobility was confirmed in 1816; the title of marquis was bestowed on them in 1876. Emilio fought against the Austrians in the Milanese uprising of 1848, when he met and collaborated with GIUSEPPE MAZZINI. But in 1853 he abandoned the republican movement and gravitated toward CAVOUR, whose legacy he cultivated and furthered. In 1859–60 he worked to bring about the union of Lombardy to the KINGDOM OF SARDINIA. He held the post of foreign minister in 1863–64, 1866–67, 1869–73, 1873–76, 1896–98, and 1899–1901. In early missions he demonstrated the tact expected of a diplomat. He negotiated the SEPTEMBER CONVENTION, steered government through the crises of 1866–67 and 1870–71. When he returned to the foreign ministry in 1896 after an absence of 20 years he reversed the policy of colonial expansion that had led to the humiliating defeat of ADOWA. He performed a final diplomatic service for the country by heading the Italian delegation at the Algeciras Conference (1906) where he cast Italy in the role of peacemaker. Visconti-Venosta opposed the TRIPLE ALLIANCE, but agreed to work with it. He set a cautious foreign policy course that aimed at giving Italy international security in a system of relations based on the balance-of-power principle. Italy was to maintain a low international profile, be ready to seize opportunities for expansion abroad without taking undue risks, avoid isolation, and maintain maximum freedom of action. It was a measure of Visconti-Venosta's diplomatic ability that he was able to juggle such seemingly incompatible objectives while maintaining a reputation for reliability and trustworthiness.

Vittorini, Elio   See HERMETISM.

Vittorio Veneto, Battle of   See WORLD WAR I.

Vivaldi, Antonio (1676–1741)
composer known for his vivacious style in orchestral and vocal music

Even in the years of its decline, VENICE threw off sparks that illuminated the dusk. One of these was Antonio Vivaldi, the son of a violinist, who became one of the most influential composers of his generation. Ordained into the priesthood in 1703, he came to be known as Venice's Red Priest for his flaming red hair. A priest he was, but not cut out for a life of clerical celibacy. Appointed music teacher to an orphanage for girls, his interest in his pupils went well beyond their musical education. He gave further cause for scandal by refusing to say mass and living the high life. The flamboyance of his personal life is reflected in his music, the inventiveness of which is often at war with the rules of composition. As long as inventiveness was prized, Vivaldi's reputation soared, making him the outstanding figure of Italian BAROQUE music. His reputation suffered in the later part of his life when musical taste shifted toward strict adherence to the rules. He had many imitators and admirers, including Johann Sebastian Bach who transcribed several of Vivaldi's string concertos for the keyboard. He composed some 550 concerti, including *L'estro armonico* (1711), *La stravaganza* (1712), *The Four Seasons* (1725), and *La cetra* (1727). He also wrote for the voice, his operas being greatly admired for their vigorous and imaginative instrumentation. Financially hard-pressed and in disgrace because of his unrepentant lifestyle, he left Venice in 1740 and died in Vienna the following year in dire poverty.

Voce (La) See PREZZOLINI, GIUSEPPE.

Volpe, Gioacchino (1876–1971)
historian and public figure known for his nationalist leanings

Volpe was a scholar of medieval and modern history. He was born in the province of L'Aquila (Abruzzo), taught history in Milan (1906–24) and at the University of Rome (1924–40). He also presided over important cultural associations and reviews. His relationship to FASCISM is the subject of debate. Once considered inseparable from the regime, historians now see him rather as a sympathizer who saw fascism as the legitimate heir of the Italian patriotic tradition rooted in the RISORGIMENTO. That was the message of his major work *Italia moderna* (Modern Italy, 1943–52) and it challenged the liberal interpretation of BENEDETTO CROCE, who saw fascism as a break from Italy's liberal traditions. Whatever his feelings about fascism, Volpe was prominent and influential in his writings and in his official capacities. He served in parliament from 1924 to 1929 and contributed to the process of constitutional revision and government reform underway in those years. Volpe was the most prominent historian of the Fascist period, an eminent scholar whose support gave intellectual credibility to the Fascist regime.

Volpi, Giuseppe (1877–1947)
industrialist, promoter of colonial expansion, and collaborator of the Fascist regime

Volpi was that fairly rare figure in history who combines the qualities of the successful businessman with those of the consummate politician. He was born in Venice to a respectable middle-class family of patriotic sentiments. Following the death of his father (a civil engineer) in 1898, he decided to abandon to study of law that he had undertaken at the University of Padua and devote himself to a career in business. The timing was propitious, as the Italian economy was about to embark on a period of sustained growth that lasted into the 1920s. Following the mercantile traditions of his beloved Venice, Volpi turned his attention to the Balkans, emerging rapidly as Italy's most successful importer/exporter in that region, and one who believed that business and government must march together to achieve success. Investments in promising industries like tobacco, mining, navigation, and hydroelectricity rounded out his holdings. Volpi, never known for false modesty, liked to boast that he had millions to burn. He also had good contacts with prominent political figures as dissimilar as GIOVANNI GIOLITTI and, later, BENITO MUSSOLINI. Giolitti entrusted him with the peace negotiations with the Ottoman Empire that ended the ITALIAN-TURKISH WAR. During WORLD WAR I, after a brief stint on the front line, he sat on the committee for national mobilization. After the war he played a leading role in promoting the national organization of business interests.

In 1921 Giolitti appointed him governor of Libya, where he presided over the consolidation of Italian rule in that colony. In 1922 the last pre-Fascist government appointed him to the senate. In 1925 Mussolini appointed him minister of finances. In that capacity he negotiated the settlement of Italy's wartime debts with the United States, reined in an inflationary economy, and, at Mussolini's insistence, carried out the revaluation of the currency that culminated in the policy of QUOTA 90. Mussolini dismissed him in 1928, after he had rendered invaluable service to the regime with his economic expertise and influence. From 1934 to 1943 he was president of CONFINDUSTRIA, Italy's most powerful business pressure group and the official representative of all industrial employers. He also found time to help revitalize the economy of Venice by promoting the industrialization of its environs and inaugurating the famous Biennale cultural exposition that continues to attract. Volpi was never a Fascist in the ideological sense, but he did remain faithful to the regime until it became clear that it faced military defeat. In the political trials that followed WORLD WAR II, Volpi was found not guilty of complicity with the regime. His death in 1947 attracted little attention for one who had played such a prominent public role.

Volta, Alessandro (1745–1827)

scientist who pioneered in the study of
electricity, gases, and meteorology

Volta was born in Como (Lombardy) to a family of the local aristocracy with close ties to the church. Educated by Jesuits, he resisted their pressure to enter the priesthood, and family pressure to become a lawyer. His interest in the natural sciences led him to correspond with other scientists and undertake his own experiments to determine the nature of electricity. He traveled extensively in Italy and the rest of Europe in the 1770s and 1780s. In 1778 he was appointed to the chair of experimental physics at the University of Pavia. There he carried on his most important experiments and, in the process, made the school an important center for the study of the natural sciences. In the 1790s Volta challenged the theory proposed by LUIGI GALVANI that the electrical charges he had noticed in experiments with animals were generated in the animals' tissues. Volta correctly argued that the electricity noticed by Galvani originated from a metallic arc. In 1800 he invented the voltaic cell (sometimes also called the galvanic cell), a device that converts chemical into electrical energy. Volta was the recipient of many honors and distinctions in his lifetime, including a pension and decoration from NAPOLEON I. The volt, a unit that measures the strength of an electrical current, is named after Volta.

W

Waldensians (or Waldenses)

The theory that the Waldensians were named after Peter Waldo, their 12th-century founder, is ascribed to papal writers who wanted to deny that the Waldensians might have been direct descendants of early Christians. The Italian term *valdesi* used to describe them may derive from the fact that they lived in mountain valleys (*valli*). Whatever their origin, the Waldensians were lay religious dissenters who renounced property, practiced poverty, proclaimed the priesthood of all believers, accepted the Bible as their sole guide, denounced papal authority, the mass, and other forms of Christian ritual. In 1184 they were condemned as heretics and persecuted after disobeying a papal prohibition against preaching. But they persevered and survived in their mountain strongholds above Turin, but also in the southern region of Calabria. After the Waldensians embraced Protestantism, a series of persecutions inflicted severe losses on their communities. The Waldensians of Calabria were massacred in 1561. In Piedmont, EMANUEL PHILIBERT granted them limited religious toleration that same year, but it was revoked by his successors. In 1655 Charles Emmanuel II of Savoy (1634–75), launched a persecution of the Waldensians to repress a rebellion and impose religious uniformity. On that occasion Oliver Cromwell lodged a diplomatic protest, and John Milton wrote a famous sonnet denouncing the persecution. Piedmontese policy wavered thereafter from persecution to grudging acceptance. Toleration was the official policy of the Napoleonic regime. The Piedmontese government after 1848 and the Italian government after 1861 embraced freedom of religion, which guaranteed Waldensians the right to worship their own way. The Waldensian Church today belongs to the World Council of Churches. Waldensians choose their own administrators, pastors, and lay ministers, but their original doctrines and moral intransigence have given way to modern interpretations and attitudes that make for peaceful coexistence with the world around them.

Wars of National Independence

These wars saw the KINGDOM OF SARDINIA, its allies, and formations of volunteers fighting against the forces of the AUSTRIAN EMPIRE. The First War of National Independence broke out during the REVOLUTION of 1848. After Milanese insurgents had forced imperial troops to evacuate Milan and the imperial government in Vienna was on the verge of collapsing as a result of revolution in that city, on March 23, 1848, King CHARLES ALBERT marched his army from Piedmont into Austrian Lombardy. Pledging support for the cause of Italian independence, he proclaimed the union of Lombardy and Venetia with his kingdom. The Austrian forces under the octagenarian Marshall Radetsky held out, struck back, and forced Charles Albert's forces back into Piedmont after defeating them at the first battle of Custoza on July 23–25, 1848. The Armistice of Salasco (August 8, 1848) put on end to the fighting, but hostilities broke out again when the Piedmontese denounced the armistice on March 12, 1849. This time the Piedmontese forces were defeated decisively at the battle of Novara fought on March 23, 1849. Charles Albert resigned from the throne in favor of his son, who became King VICTOR EMMANUEL II. Radetsky and the imperial government agreed to a settlement that allowed Piedmont to retain the constitution of 1848. The Piedmontese agreed to withdraw all their troops behind their own borders, demobilize, pay an indemnity, and promise future peace and cooperation between the Kingdom of Sardinia and the Austrian Empire. The decisive defeat of Piedmont-Sardinia in this conflict did not prevent that state from pursuing the cause of Italian independence in the years to come. In fact, the retention of the constitution and the fact that after the war it became a haven for political refugees from other Italian states strengthened Piedmont's claim to champion the cause of Italian unity.

The Second War of Independence broke out in April 1859. Having secured a promise of military help from France with the secret AGREEMENT OF PLOMBIÈRES, Prime Minister CAVOUR of Piedmont-Sardinia succeeded in provoking Austria into declaring war on Piedmont. On April 29 Austrian forces crossed the border into Piedmont and could conceivably have defeated the outnumbered Piedmontese by moving rapidly before the arrival of the French. But their slow advance allowed the French emperor NAPOLEON III to have a large army in place by June. Also fighting on the French-Piedmontese side were volunteer units commanded by GIUSEPPE GARIBALDI. The French contributed almost 150,000 troops, the Piedmontese 80,000, and Garibaldi's volunteers numbered about 10,000. The French bore the brunt of the fighting at the bloody battles of Magenta (June 4) and Solferino (June 24). At Solferino the Piedmontese army prevailed in the related engagement of San Martino. Garibaldi, operating independently in the mountains, was able to take his forces deep into enemy territory by outmaneuvering his opponents. The war ended unexpectedly when Napoleon III and Austrian emperor Francis Joseph signed the Armisitice of Villafranca on July 5, 1859. Napoleon's motivations for this unexpected decision are not entirely clear, but he may have been influenced by the high losses suffered by his army, by a Prussian mobilization on France's bor-

der on the Rhine River, and by concern that the Italian unification movement was gathering too much momentum as a result of the war. Napoleon had agreed that Piedmont should annex the regions of LOMBARDY and VENETIA, but not other territories. In the event, the Piedmontese had to settle for Lombardy. The acquisition of additional territory in the Romagna and central Italy was an indirect result of this war, which was not foreseen when military operations ceased. A chagrined Cavour resigned as prime minister, but returned to power in January 1860 to oversee the decisive push toward Italian unity that occurred that year.

Italy acquired the region of Venetia as a result of the Third War of Independence that was fought in 1866. This time Italy was allied with Prussia against Austria. Military operations began on June 16, with the Austrians forced to divide their forces on two distant fronts. On the Italian front Italian troops heavily outnumbered the Austrians, but a confusing command structure, and poor planning and organization nullified their numerical advantage. The Austrian army prevailed at the second battle of Custoza fought on June 24, 1866. The Austrian navy inflicted severe losses on the Italian fleet at the battle of Lissa fought on July 20, 1866. But Prussia's decisive victories that same month forced Austria to cede Venetia to Italy. At Austria's insistence the cession occurred indirectly, since the Austrians refused to hand over Venetia to the Italians, handing it over instead to France, which then turned it over to Italy. That gesture of disdain contributed to keeping animosities between Austria and Italy alive and sustained Italian IRREDENTISM until WORLD WAR I, when Italy went to war against Austria to acquire the Trentino–Alto Adige, Istria, and Trieste. For that reason Italy's role in the first world conflict was sometimes referred to as the fourth war of independence.

witchcraft

The belief in witchcraft can be traced to the Christian condemnation of pagan deities in the early Middle Ages. The association of witchcraft with the devil and evildoing is a later development, dating perhaps from the 12th or 13th centuries. The oldest references to witchcraft trials in Italy date from 1385–90 in the city of MILAN. Early in the next century the belief spread that witches consorted regularly in nocturnal gatherings with the devil. Belief in regular gatherings became a central part of witchcraft lore, and the fact that these gatherings were imagined to occur in isolated mountain recesses associated the practice of witchcraft with rural populations. Old women were thought to be particularly susceptible to such devilish summonses. Indeed, many confessed witches were old women who claimed special powers because of their imagined relations with the devil.

Religious authorities looked upon witchcraft as the work of the devil and sought to ban or uproot it. Pope Innocent VIII (1484–92) condemned witchcraft in a bull of 1484. The papal condemnation brought the problem to public attention and may have played a role in stimulating the witchhunts that swept through Europe in the 16th and 17th centuries. By then witchcraft was also associated with the spread of religious heresies, a connection that loomed large in the thinking of religious inquisitors with the rise of Protestantism. But the witch craze had a more limited impact on Italy than in the rest of Europe. There are two principal reasons for the relative rarity of witch trials in Italy. One is that the CATHOLIC CHURCH was able to crack down on and silence suspected individuals and groups without recourse to civil authorities. The other reason is the attitude of intellectual skepticism that permeated Italian culture under the influence of HUMANISM. Intellectuals associated belief in witchcraft with ignorance, questioned the credibility of tales and confessions, thought that confessed witches were delusionary, and in need of medical attention rather than deserving of punishment.

Challenged by the learned, belief in witchcraft remained firmly rooted in the general population. In 16th-century FRIULI self-proclaimed enemies of witches called *benandanti* (do-gooders) set out to fight witches using their own arts, until the authorities forced them to confess that they too were witches. Belief in witchcraft and magic has survived into modern times. Witchcraft practices to detect and cure diseases were still common in most parts of Italy in the 19th century. Recourse to *stregoni* (witch doctors) for health reasons was not unheard of in the latter part of the 20th century. The spread of satanic cults in Italy is a recent phenomenon that causes much concern in religious circles.

World War I

Italy did not immediately join the European conflict that broke out in August 1914. The government chose not to join in war its partners in the Triple Alliance, Austria-Hungary and Germany. It argued that it was not bound to do so by the essentially defensive nature of the alliance, by the failure of its partners to give them adequate notice of their intention to go to war, and to discuss territorial compensations for Italy. The fundamental problem was that Italy's territorial aspirations could only be satisfied at the expense of Austria-Hungary, which held Italian-speaking parts of ISTRIA and the TRENTINO regions, including the cities of TRENT and TRIESTE, places that had acquired enormous symbolic value in the eyes of Italian nationalists. Austria-Hungary's reluctance to part with these territories gave an advantage to the Entente Powers on the other side of the conflict. Great Britain and France in particular were quite willing to promise Italy lands that belonged to Austria-Hungary in return for Italian participation in the war on their side. Their territorial promises were at the heart of the PACT OF LONDON signed on April 26, 1915, that led to an Italian declaration of war against Austria-Hungary on May 24, 1915.

Fighting in the mountainous territory of the Alps against a well-entrenched enemy was hard and costly in human lives. The tactics adopted by the Italian commander in chief, General LUIGI CADORNA, were similar to those adopted by generals in other armies. But Cadorna insisted more than most on carrying out frontal assaults against prepared positions. Italian troops pounded away at enemy lines in 11 major offensives from May 1915 to October 1917, advancing slowly and gaining territory with an enormous cost in lives. The other side struck back suddenly on October 24, 1917, exactly 29 months to the day after Italy had gone to war. In what has come to be known as the BATTLE OF CAPORETTO, near the town of that name, combined German and Austro-Hungarian forces infiltrated behind the Italian lines, causing a panic that sent the Italians reeling all the way back to the Piave River. There they regrouped, preventing another breakthrough that might have knocked Italy out of the war.

Soon after Caporetto, General ARMANDO DIAZ replaced Cadorna. The new commander in chief enjoyed good rapport with the troops and the government. His appointment was part of a wider effort to bolster civilian morale and broaden support for the war. Public opinion did rally behind the war effort, which came to a victorious conclusion a year after the Caporetto debacle. The army resumed the offensive on October 24, 1918, the anniversary of the Battle of Caporetto. The final engagement of the war, the Battle of Vittorio Veneto, was timed to break the back of the exhausted Austro-Hungarians. On November 3, 1918, the two sides agreed to a cessation of hostilities and signed the Armistice of Villa Giusti. The war ended on the Western Front on November 11 with the surrender of the Germans. To fight the war Italy mobilized about 6 million men. Casualties have been estimated at about 600,000 dead and about twice that number wounded. The Italian government borrowed heavily to finance the war effort, leaving the country heavily indebted at the end of the war, particularly toward the United States.

The war had a major impact on the country. The debate that preceded the decision to go to war made it clear that public opinion was deeply divided on the issue of intervention. King VICTOR EMMANUEL III decided constitutionally but impolitically to go to war without consulting parliament. At war's end the bitter polemics between neutralists and interventionists broke out anew, poisoning the political atmosphere. Nationalists demanded full implementation of the territorial promises of the Pact of London, plus the annexation of FIUME and other territories not explicitly mentioned in the agreement. A rift developed between Italy and its wartime allies at the PARIS PEACE CONFERENCE. GABRIELE D'ANNUNZIO, voicing the grievances of nationalists, spoke of a "mutilated victory," claiming that Italy had won the war but lost the peace. Exasperated nationalist feelings, fear of Bolshevism and communist revolution, economic dislocations, charges of war profiteering against big business, and of draft dodging against many who had not served, created an atmosphere conducive to FASCISM. The problems of victory proved to be as difficult as those of defeat.

World War II

As it had done in 1914, Italy delayed joining the conflict. But the similarities end there. In September 1939, when the German invasion of Poland plunged Europe into war, the conduct of Italian foreign policy was in the hands of one man, BENITO MUSSOLINI, who never entertained the possibility of negotiating with the two warring sides to get the best deal for Italy. The PACT OF STEEL that Germany and Italy had signed in May proclaimed the full ideological, political, and military alignment of Mussolini and Hitler and their respective regimes. Mussolini's decision to not intervene immediately on the side of his ally was based on several considerations. Some of his political and military advisers urged him to hold back, he himself was well aware that the country was unprepared for a large-scale military conflict, and aware also of the risks of jumping into a conflict of unpredictable duration. Germany's imminent victory over France, Great Britain's isolation, and the conviction that Italy had to participate before the war was over to claim its share of gains at the peace table, convinced Mussolini that Italy must intervene.

Italy declared war on Great Britain and France on June 10, 1940. There was little fighting on the French front in the Alps because of France's rapid surrender, and the inability of Italian troops to make much headway in that short a time. The Italian plan was to wage a separate "parallel war" alongside Germany on fronts of its own choosing. In North Africa, Italian troops attempted an invasion of Egypt from the colony of Libya. The objective was the Suez Canal. Launched in the hot summer after much delay due to inadequate preparation, this offensive sputtered and came to a halt in the desert well short of its goal. A British counterattack sent them reeling back into Libya with enormous losses of prisoners and equipment. On October 28, 1940, Italian troops attacked Greece from Albania, expecting a quick victory. The Greeks struck back with British support, forcing the Italians to fight a tough defensive war in the mountains to hang on to Albania. On November 10 a surprise British attack on the Taranto naval base inflicted severe damage on Italian warships. By 1941, Italians had to call in German help in North Africa and the Balkans. German and Italian troops occupied Yugoslavia and Greece in the spring, but later that same year the Italians surrendered Ethiopia to the British. Mussolini insisted on committing a large expeditionary force in the fighting against the Soviet Union to show that Italy was a major combatant. The war in Africa continued with alternating fortunes until May 1943, when Germans and Italians were forced out of their last stronghold in Tunisia and retreated to the European continent. The Allies followed up their victory in Africa with the invasion of Sicily, carried out and completed in July–August 1943.

The loss of Sicily and imminent invasion of the mainland had immediate political repercussions. Fascist dissidents and King VICTOR EMMANUEL III engineered a coup that ousted Mussolini from power on July 25, 1943. Mussolini was seized and imprisoned. General PIETRO BADOGLIO replaced Mussolini as head of the government and began secret negotiations for an armistice with the Allies. A strong German reaction followed the announcement of the armistice on September 8. They disarmed regular Italian army troops. Many were transported to prisoner of war camps in Germany. Others, left leaderless, tried to make their way home as best they could. A few units resisted the Germans, but the bulk of the army disintegrated practically overnight.

While Allied forces occupied the South, German forces occupied the North, liberated Mussolini, and set him up as head of the puppet government, the ITALIAN SOCIAL REPUBLIC, that continued to fight alongside Germany. The country was left at the mercy of Germans and Allies. The Germans halted the Allied advance along the Gustav line that ran just north of Naples. The Allies broke through and took Rome on June 4, 1944, after fighting the bloody battles of Anzio and Monte Cassino. Their progress north was stopped again in the fall. Unable to capitalize on a breakthrough into the Po Valley, they paused for the winter along the Gothic line that roughly followed the crest of the Apennine Mountains north of Florence. In this final phase of the war, regular units of a partially reconstituted Italian army and formations of the RESISTANCE movement joined the Allies in the final battles against German troops and Italians fighting for Mussolini and the Italian Social Republic. Thus, the last phase of World War II was for Italy also a civil war that saw Italians fighting on both sides. Hostilities ended the last week of April 1945 with the surrender of German forces in Italy. Resistance fighters captured and executed Mussolini on April 28, 1945.

Italian casualties in World War II are estimated at 205,000 military and 25,000 civilians before the armistice of 1943, and at 225,000 civilians and military from September 1943 to May 1945. These figures are hard to verify given the chaotic conditions of the country after 1943 and the difficulty of distinguishing between combatants and civilians. Different estimates point to as many as 650,000 military and civilian casualties. Physical destruction was extensive in many cities like Genoa, Milan, and Turin that were subjected to heavy Allied bombardments. The transportation system also suffered heavily, but much of the country's industrial apparatus was saved, thanks perhaps to Mussolini's policy of cooperation with the Germans after 1943 and the rapidity of the Allied advance in the last week of the war. The war had major political consequences. The most important was regime change. There can be little doubt that FASCISM would not have been uprooted without its utter military defeat in the war. The monarchy, fatally compromised by its association with fascism, was voted out of existence and replaced by a republican form of government in 1946. The PEACE TREATY was not harsh, but it did impose condi-

tions and limitations that affected government and the economy. In FOREIGN POLICY, Italy renounced war and scaled down its ambitions. The experience of war had a lasting impact on public attitudes. Italians were not necessarily less patriotic after the war, but they identified the national interest with international cooperation and friendly diplomacy. Social solidarity, European cooperation, and openness to the outside world replaced earlier notions of national primacy and great-power status.

Y

Young Europe See MAZZINI, GIUSEPPE.

Young Italy

GIUSEPPE MAZZINI founded Young Italy in July 1831 in the French port city of Marseilles, where he had settled after leaving Italy because he was a political suspect. As its name indicates, it aimed to attract the young to the cause of Italian independence and unity. Young Italy's republicanism reflected Mazzini's antimonarchist sentiments and democratic convictions. It was a secret society pledged to carry on its fight by peaceful means and by armed insurrection. Its clandestine publication smuggled into Italy, also called *Young Italy,* urged the Italian people to rise up against Austria and conservative governments. Members were expected to be ready for insurrection, ready to strike at tyrants, and be prepared for martyrdom. There are no reliable figures on the number of members, but it is likely that they numbered in the thousands. It was based on a network of mostly urban secret cells that covered many regions of the peninsula. Young Italy faced a serious crisis after a conspiracy to stir up revolt in SAVOY and parts of Italy failed in February 1834. Mazzini, who had moved from Marseilles to Switzerland to direct the conspiracy, was forced to leave Switzerland three years later. From London, he launched a second version of Young Italy in the early 1840s. Sometimes referred to as the second Young Italy, this association emphasized education, social commitment, and long-term preparation for revolution. It sought to win workers to the cause of national revolution. Young Italy engaged in political conspiracy even in its new version, but it was most successful as an instrument of political education and propaganda. As such, it contributed to the political climate that led to the REVOLUTIONS of 1848. Many of its new members later accepted the monarchy and, after national unification, rose to positions of prominence in business and government.

Z

Zaccagnini, Benigno (1913–1989)

*Christian Democratic leader, member of
parliament, and prime minister*

Zaccagnini was born in Faenza (Emilia-Romagna),
received a degree in medicine, and practiced pediatrics before devoting himself to politics, which was
his passion. Always close to the CATHOLIC CHURCH,
he shunned the Fascist regime and joined the
RESISTANCE in 1943 as a leader of the emerging
Christian Democratic Party (DC). He was elected
to the constituent assembly in 1946 and to parliament in 1948, serving in the chamber of deputies
until 1983 and in the senate thereafter, always as
a Christian Democrat. He was minister of labor
and social welfare (1959–60) and public works
(1960–63). Throughout his career he maintained
a reputation for honesty and integrity that earned
him the endearing nickname of *Onesto Zac.* Deeply
involved in DC affairs and chosen party secretary
in 1975, he engineered the electoral recovery of
the elections of 1976 that gave his party a new
lease on life. He was a close friend of ALDO MORO,
whose policies he supported. It was particularly
painful for Zaccagnini to have to uphold the hard
line that his party took against making concessions
to the RED BRIGADES after they kidnapped Moro,
who was later killed. That episode brought Zaccagnini's political career to a disappointing end.

Zanardelli, Giuseppe (1826–1903)

*government figure and political reformer
known for his liberal sentiments*

Born in Brescia (Lombardy), Zanardelli interrupted his law studies to fight against the Austrians in 1848. His disillusionment with King
CHARLES ALBERT that year turned him into a permanent critic of the Piedmontese monarchy.
After working as a journalist in the 1850s, he
volunteered to fight under GIUSEPPE GARIBALDI.
He was elected to parliament continuously from
1860 until his death. In the course of a long and
distinguished parliamentary career, he served as
minister of public works (1876–77), of the interior (1878), justice (1881–83, 1887–91, 1897–98),
president of the chamber of deputies (1892–94,
1897–99), and prime minister (1901–03). An
opponent of the governing HISTORICAL RIGHT,
Zanardelli was also an internal critic of the LIBERAL
LEFT to which he belonged after it came to power
in 1876. A member of the dissident group known
as the Pentarchy, he defended civil liberties, condemned the political practice of TRANSFORMISM,
and called for government accountability. His
consistent position on these and other reform
issues earned him a reputation for honesty and
integrity that was reinforced by his readiness to
resign from government posts on matters of
principle. His major accomplishment was the
preparation and adoption of the new legal code
of 1890 that abolished the death penalty, gave
workers the right to strike, provided for freedom
of association, speech, and religion. Zanardelli
was an anticlerical who viewed the CATHOLIC
CHURCH as a threat to liberty and the state. His
appointment as prime minister marked the
beginning of a new liberal course in politics. GIOVANNI GIOLITTI served as Zanardelli's interior minister and succeeded him as prime minister when
Zanardelli resigned for health reasons. Already
the most powerful parliamentary figure before
becoming prime minister, Giolitti continued his

predecessor's liberal policies with a stronger sense of political realism that allowed him to translate Zanardelli's principles into liberal practice.

Zavattini, Cesare See DE SICA, VITTORIO.

Zelanti See CONSALVI, ETTORE.

Zeno, Apostolo (1668–1750)
Venetian playwright, court poet, and scholar who called for a return to classical models
A member of the Venetian aristocracy, Zeno was prominent in the cultural renewal movement centered on the ACADEMIES. Inspired by Racine and other French writers, Zeno turned to the myths and historical figures of ancient Greece and Rome for subjects suitable to the solemn sentiments he wished to convey. His carefully crafted, harmonious verse was ideally suited for musical composition, and prominent composers, including Domenico Scarlatti and ANTONIO VIVALDI, used them as librettos for their operas. His comic plays were based on characters drawn from COMMEDIA DELL'ARTE, but his contemporaries found these lighter subjects less appealing than his serious dramas. The 36 plays that he wrote include the popular *Lucio Vero* (1700), *Merope* (1711), *Alessandro Severo* (1716), and *Semiramide* (1725). Zeno was also an erudite historian. From 1718 to 1728 he served as court poet and historian at the imperial court in Vienna. In his later years, Zeno suffered and resented the indignity of seeing his fame obscured by PIETRO METASTASIO, his more popular successor who used him as a model.

Zoagli, Adelaide See MAMELI, GOFFREDO.

Zoli, Adone (1887–1960)
prominent Christian Democrat, government figure, and financial expert
Born in Cesena (Emilia-Romagna) into a family of small landowners, Zoli was raised as a practicing Catholic. He took a law degree from the University of Bologna, served as an officer in World War I, opened a law practice in Florence after the war, and joined the Italian Popular Party (PPI) in 1919. During the Fascist period Zoli kept out of the public eye, pursued his professional interests with considerable success, and raised a family. In 1943 he joined the RESISTANCE movement in Tuscany. Arrested and jailed in 1943–44, he avoided a death sentence by escaping from prison. He joined the Christian Democratic Party (DC) and served as vice mayor of Florence in 1944–46. In 1948 he was elected to the senate. He served as interim minister of justice and minister of public instruction (1951–53), minister of finance (1954), and budget minister (1956–57). As prime minister (1957–58), he headed the first postwar government constituted solely of Christian Democrats. His government survived with the help of the neo-Fascist Italian Social Movement (MSI), a potentially embarrassing situation that Zoli defused with great tact and diplomacy. A notable event of his ministry was the decision to allow the physical remains of BENITO MUSSOLINI, kept until then in secret locations, to be buried in the Mussolini family vault in the cemetery of Predappio. Zoli is also buried in that cemetery, a few steps away from the tomb of the former dictator. Zoli was appreciated for his honesty, common sense, and good-natured wit. An advocate of fiscal austerity and tight spending, he avoided political grandstanding, valued sound administration, and personified the kind of low-key political figure who steered the economy in the years of the ECONOMIC MIRACLE.

CHRONOLOGY

753 B.C.

Rome founded as an Etruscan settlement ruled by kings (traditional date).

508

Romans overthrow the monarchy and adopt a republican form of government dominated by the patrician upper class.

450

The plebeian (popular) majority wins right to elect their own representatives (tribunes) and to have written laws.

201

Rome defeats Carthage in the Second Punic War (218–201 B.C.) and gains control of western Mediterranean Sea.

168

Rome extends its rule to Greece and Egypt.

88

Roman citizenship extended to free inhabitants of the Italian peninsula.

48

Julius Caesar defeats rivals and becomes master of Rome.

44

Conspirators assassinate Julius Caesar.

27

Roman Senate bestows the title of Augustus (The Revered) on Caesar's nephew Octavian; Augustus is considered the first Roman emperor; the Roman Republic becomes the Roman Empire; a period begins of relative peace that lasts for almost 200 years (Pax Romana).

A.D. 117

The Roman Empire reaches its greatest extent under Emperor Trajan (98–117 A.D.): from Scotland to the Persian Gulf and from Germany to North Africa.

235

Period of political instability starts; army elects emperors; epidemics; insecurity on the frontiers of the empire.

284

Emperor Diocletian eliminates the last traces of republican government, gives absolute power to the office of emperor, reforms the army, reorganizes defense of the frontiers, launches major persecution of Christians, and decentralizes the administration of the empire. He abdicates in 305 A.D. and retires to private life.

313

Emperor Constantine (306–37 A.D.) grants religious toleration to Christians; moves the capital from Rome to Byzantium (renamed Constantinople).

395

Death of Emperor Theodosius I (379–95), last Roman emperor to rule over both eastern and western parts of the empire. As imperial power weakens, the papacy rises in the west.

476

Odoacer, ruler of the Visigoths, deposes Romulus Augustulus, last Roman emperor of the west.

493

Theodoric (d. 526) defeats Odoacer and begins period of Ostrogoth rule that lasts until 552.

568

Lombard invasion of northern Italy.

590

Pope Gregory I (590–604) consolidates papal power in Rome, defends city from Lombards, initiates church reforms.

712

King Liutprand comes to the throne. During his reign (712–44) Lombard domination extends to southern Italy.

754

Pope Stephen II calls on Pepin the Short and his Frankish knights to protect the papacy from the Lombards.

800

Pope Leo III bestows title of Holy Roman Emperor on Charlemagne; prized for the authority it confers, the title lasts until 1806 when Napoleon abolishes it.

827

First Saracen landing in Sicily marks the beginning of Muslim invasions.

888

Feudal warfare results in coronation of Berengar I (d. 924) as king of Italy.

900

First Magyar invasion of Italy; repeated in 924.

902

Arabs complete conquest of Sicily.

951

Otto I of Saxony (d. 973) defeats Berengar II and becomes king of Italy as vassal of the Holy Roman Emperor; begins period of Saxon rule in Italy.

962

Otto I made Holy Roman Emperor; claims right to choose the pope.

1029

First Norman settlement in southern Italy.

1046

Henry III of Saxony (1039–56) enforces imperial right to elect the pope and begins process of church reform.

1054

The Latin (Catholic) Church separates from the Eastern (Orthodox) Church.

1061

Normans begin conquest of Sicily and southern Italy; completed by 1091.

1077

Pope Gregory VII (1073–85) claims papal authority over secular rulers and forces Emperor Henry IV to humble himself before the pope at the Castle of Canossa.

1095

Pope Urban II (1088–99) calls on Frankish nobility to lead the First Crusade.

1125

Conflict between Guelfs (supporters of the pope) and Ghibellines (supporters of the emperor) facilitates the rise of the first independent communes, forerunners of later city-states.

1152

Pope Eugenius III (1147–53) calls on German emperor Frederick I (Barbarossa) to protect papacy from Norman lords and rebellious Roman populace led by religious reformer Arnaldo da Brescia (d. 1154).

1162

Frederick I destroys the rebellious town of Milan.

1167

Lombard towns take the Oath of Pontida, form the Lombard League against the emperor.

1176

The Lombard League defeats Frederick I at the Battle of Legnano.

1183

At the Peace of Constance Frederick I grants communes the right to administer their own affairs in return for payment of an annual tribute and a loyalty oath from their freely elected town governments.

1198

Frederick II, grandson of Frederick I, becomes Holy Roman Emperor at age three as a ward of Pope Innocent III (1198–1216). Papal monarchy achieves height of power under Innocent III.

1265

Birth of Dante Alighieri (d. 1321). In *De monarchia* he makes the case that the spiritual and secular powers are distinct; the *Divine Comedy* sums up medieval culture and becomes the classic work of the Italian language and literature.

1266

Charles of Anjou (Angevins) rules as king of Naples and Sicily (1266–85) after defeating and killing the last German emperor to rule in medieval Italy, King Manfred, at the Battle of Benevento.

1282

The uprising of the Sicilian Vespers topples Angevin rule in Sicily and brings in the ruling house of Aragon.

1302

Pope Boniface VIII (1294–1303) issues the Bull *Unam Sanctam* asserting absolute papal sovereignty over secular rulers.

1303

Pope Boniface is taken prisoner by troops of King Philip the Fair of France.

1309

Pope Clement V moves the papacy to Avignon, beginning the so-called Babylonian Captivity of the Church in France (1309–78).

1347

Cola Di Rienzo is installed as chief of the Roman Republic in the popes' absence in Avignon; deposed that same year, he returns to power and is killed by a mob in 1354; Catherine of Siena (1347–80) leads a religious revival and calls for the return of the pope to Rome.

1348

The Black Death epidemic devastates towns and countryside.

1376

Pope Gregory XI (1370–78) brings the papacy back to Rome.

1378

A contested papal election causes the Great Schism; rival claimants to the papal throne keep the church divided until 1417.

1385

Beginning of Visconti rule in Milan.

1417

Pope Martin V (1417–31) ends the Great Schism; begins reconstruction of Rome as the religious capital of western Christianity and major center of Renaissance culture.

1434

Start of the personal rule of Cosimo de' Medici in Florence.

1442

Alfonso I seizes the throne of Naples, establishes Spanish rule in southern Italy.

1450

Francesco Sforza becomes duke of Milan.

1454–1455

The Peace of Lodi and the Italic League introduce a period of relative peace and stability among the Italian states.

1469

The personal rule of Lorenzo de' Medici begins; Florence dominates as a center of Renaissance culture.

1492

Lorenzo de' Medici dies; Christopher Columbus crosses the Atlantic and initiates period of sustained European exploration and settlement of the American continent; shift of trade routes from the Mediterranean to the Atlantic hurts economies of the Italian city-states.

1494

Charles VIII leads the first French invasion of Italy; the religious reformer Girolamo Savonarola leads the revolt that drives the Medici from Florence.

1499

Louis XII leads the second French invasion of Italy, claims the duchy of Milan, establishes French rule in northern Italy.

1504

The Peace of Blois recognizes French possession of Milan and Spanish possession of Naples.

1513

Niccolò Machiavelli writes *The Prince,* seen as the fundamental text of modern government.

1517

Martin Luther challenges the papacy and begins the Protestant Reformation.

1525

The Spanish/imperial forces of Emperor Charles V defeat the French at the Battle of Pavia; the French defeat sets the stage for Spanish dominance of the Italian peninsula.

1527

German/imperial troops of Charles V carry out the Sack of Rome.

1529

Charles V restores Medici rule to Florence; it will last until the Medici line becomes extinct in 1737.

1534

Pope Paul III (1534–49) begins process of Catholic Reformation to halt spread of Protestantism.

1540

Paul III authorizes the constitution of the Jesuit Order.

1544

Paul III opens the Council of Trent that lasts until 1563; the *Professio Fidei Tridentinae* (1564) outlines the council's plan for church reform.

1559

Treaty of Cateau-Cambrésis between France and Spain confirms Spanish hegemony in Italy; Prince Emanuel Philibert strengthens royal power of the House of Savoy and lays the foundation for the modern state in Piedmont-Sardinia.

1572

Battle of Lépanto halts Turkish advance in the western Mediterranean.

1573

Venice surrenders the island of Cyprus to the Turks, beginning its withdrawal from the eastern Mediterranean.

1601

House of Savoy begins pullout from French territories and redirects its attention to Italy.

1633

The church condemns Galileo Galilei for his advocacy of the heliocentric solar system.

1647

The Masaniello insurrection against Spanish rule breaks out in Naples; suppressed the following year.

1701

The War of the Spanish Succession breaks out; Victor Amadeus II of Piedmont enters the war on the side of France, but switches in 1703 to the winning side.

1714

War of the Spanish Succession ends; the Treaty of Rastatt makes Austria the dominant power in

Italy; Victor Amadeus II receives territory in Lombardy and the island of Sicily, and the title of king.

1718

Victor Amadeus II exchanges Sicily for Sardinia and receives the title king of Sardinia.

1732

The extinction of the Farnese family gives the Duchy of Parma to Charles of Bourbon.

1734

Charles of Bourbon conquers Naples and Sicily; Charles assumes the Neapolitan throne; the Bourbons rule Naples until 1860.

1737

The extinction of the Medici family gives the grand duchy of Tuscany to Francis Stephen of Habsburg-Lorraine; House of Habsburg-Lorraine rules Tuscany until 1859.

1738

The Treaty of Vienna ends the War of the Polish Succession (1733–35); Spain receives Naples and Sicily, Austria receives Tuscany and Parma; Piedmont gains territory from Austrian Lombardy.

1748

The Treaty of Aix-la-Chapelle ends the War of the Austrian Succession; Austria cedes Parma and Piacenza to the Bourbons and more territory to Piedmont, but retains dominant position in Italy.

1754

Charles of Bourbon leaves Naples to become king of Spain; Naples ruled by a regency council during the minority of his son, King Ferdinand IV, who assumes personal rule in 1767.

1765

Peter Leopold of Habsburg-Lorraine becomes grand duke of Tuscany; sets an example of Enlightenment reform.

1773

Pope Clement XIV abolishes the Jesuit Order.

1775

Pope Pius VI condemns the Freemasons.

1789

The outbreak of the French Revolution ends the era of Enlightened Reform.

1796

Napoleon Bonaparte (Napoleon I) invades Italy, defeats Piedmont, annexes Nice and Savoy, occupies Austrian Lombardy and parts of the Papal States, compels the pope and the dukes of Modena and Parma to sue for peace.

1797

Napoleon defeats Austria in northern Italy; establishes the French-controlled Cisalpine Republic; suppresses the aristocratic Republic of Genoa; Austria recognizes the Cisalpine Republic and annexes Venetian territory (Treaty of Campoformio); Republic of Venice ceases to exist.

1799

An anti-French coalition of the great powers and a popular uprising put down the pro-French Parthenopean Republic in Naples; the French hold onto Piedmont; Piedmontese court escapes to Sardinia.

1800

Napoleon returns to Italy; defeats the Austrians at the Battle of Marengo; restores the Ligurian and Cisalpine Republics.

1801

The Treaty of Luneville sanctions French control of Italy; an enlarged Cisalpine Republic is renamed the Italian Republic.

1802

France annexes Piedmont and parts of Tuscany; Bonaparte becomes president of the Italian Republic.

1805

Napoleon renames the Italian Republic the Kingdom of Italy; assumes title of king of Italy, appoints son-in-law Eugène de Beauharnais as his viceroy, annexes the region of Liguria to France; Giuseppe Mazzini is born in Genoa.

1806

Joseph Bonaparte becomes king of Naples; the Bourbons flee to Sicily protected by the British navy.

1807

Giuseppe Garibaldi is born in Nice.

1808

Joachim Murat replaces Joseph Bonaparte as king of Naples; Napoleon occupies Rome; France annexes Tuscany, Parma, and Piacenza; the Carboneria society becomes active in Naples.

1809

Napoleon has Pope Pius VII arrested; declares an end to the temporal power of the pope; annexes Rome and all papal territory to France; Austria cedes the Trentino–Alto Adige and Trieste to France, which also annexes Istria and Dalmatia.

1810

Camillo Benso, count of Cavour, is born in the family palace in Turin.

1812–15

After Napoleon's defeat in Russia Murat joins the anti-Napoleonic coalition; Austria invades Lombardy; Napoleon is defeated decisively at Waterloo; Murat conspires against Austria, is captured, and executed; Congress of Vienna restores Bourbons to Naples, House of Savoy to Kingdom of Sardinia, pope to the Papal States, Tuscany to the House of Habsburg-Lorraine; Austria regains all Italian territories lost to Napoleon; Kingdom of Sardinia annexes Genoa and Liguria; secret societies become active; Restoration period begins.

1820

A military revolt forces King Ferdinand I of Naples to grant a constitution.

1821

Insurgents in Piedmont demand a constitution; King Victor Emmanuel I abdicates the throne; Charles Albert (regent) grants the constitution but is forced to retract it; Charles Felix becomes king of Sardinia; Piedmontese and Austrian troops put down the revolt.

1827

Alessandro Manzoni publishes first version of *I promessi sposi;* novel becomes a patriotic text.

1831

Revolts break out in Bologna, Modena, and Parma; Gregory XVI elected pope, calls on Austria to put down the revolts; Charles Albert becomes king of Sardinia; Giuseppe Mazzini founds Young Italy in Marseilles.

1843

Vincenzo Gioberti publishes *On the Moral and Civil Primacy of the Italians;* that patriotic text sustains the Neo-Guelf movement.

1846

Pius IX is elected pope; his election encourages liberals who expect him to lead a national movement for reform and independence; Neo-Guelf movement gathers momentum.

1848

A popular uprising in Palermo in January is the first of a series of revolutions that sweep through Italy and the rest of Europe. Ferdinand II of Naples grants the first constitution, followed by Leopold II of Tuscany, Charles Albert of Piedmont, and Pius IX; insurgents evict the Austrians from Milan in five days of street fighting; Charles Albert wages war on Austria, invades Lombardy in the first of the Wars of Independence; insurgents expel the Austrians from Venice and proclaim the independent Republic of St. Mark; Leopold leaves Tuscany; Pius IX leaves Rome; Austrians counterattack, drive Charles Albert's army back into Piedmont.

1849

Garibaldi and Mazzini go to Rome to fight for the Roman Republic; a French expeditionary force occupies Rome and restores it to the pope; Piedmont-Sardinia and Venice capitulate to the Austrians; Charles Albert abdicates in favor of his son Victor Emmanuel II; Piedmont-Sardinia is the only state that retains a constitution.

1850

The Piedmont parliament passes the Siccardi laws that curb the power of the clergy; Piedmont-Sardinia welcomes anti-Austrian political exiles from other Italian states.

1852

Cavour becomes prime minister of Piedmont-Sardinia.

1855

Piedmont-Sardinia joins Great Britain and France in an anti-Russian alliance and sends 15,000 troops to fight in the Crimean War.

1857

The Italian National Society based in Turin calls on all patriots to unite behind Victor Emmanuel II and his dynasty, the House of Savoy.

1858

Cavour and Napoleon III negotiate the secret Agreement of Plombières to wage war against Austria.

1859

Piedmont provokes Austria into declaring war; French-Piedmontese forces defeat the Austrians in the Second War of National Independence, win control of Lombardy; revolutionary governments seize control of the Central Duchies; Piedmont annexes Lombardy.

1860

Revolutionary governments request union of Central Duchies with Piedmont; Garibaldi's expedition of the Thousand liberates Sicily and Naples, which also request union with Piedmont; Piedmontese forces invade the Papal States and seize the regions of the Marches, Umbria, and part of Latium, leaving only Rome to the pope. Plebiscites sanction the unification of Italy under the House of Savoy.

1861

Kingdom of Italy is officially proclaimed (March 17, 1861), minus Rome and Venice; the first national elections produce a parliamentary majority for the Historical Right; Cavour dies unexpectedly on June 6, leaving his work unfinished.

1862

Brigandage breaks out in the South; army stops Garibaldi's first attempt to take Rome from the pope.

1864

Italian and French governments stipulate the September Convention concerning the status of Rome; Pius IX issues the *Syllabus of Errors* condemning all manifestations of liberalism.

1866

Italy and Prussia conclude an alliance against Austria; Italy fights the Third War of Independence, gains Venice and the Venetia region.

1867

French troops stop Garibaldi's second attempt to take Rome.

1869

Imposition of the macinato (grist tax) causes riots and disorders; first Italian colonial settlement established in Eritrea.

1870

Italian government takes advantage of the Franco-Prussian War to take Rome from the pope; beginning of the Roman Question and intensification of the conflict of church and state.

1872

Mazzini dies; anarchism and socialism on the rise.

1874

Pius IX issues the *non expedit* decree forbidding Catholics to vote and participate in national politics.

1876

The Historical Right loses control of parliament to the Liberal Left; Agostino Depretis becomes prime minister.

1878

Pius IX and Victor Emmanuel II die; Umberto I succeeds to the throne; Leo XIII is elected pope; parliament passes first tariff law providing protection for domestic manufacturers.

1881

Alcide De Gasperi, future leader of Christian Democracy (DC) and prime minister, is born in the region of the Trentino under Austrian rule.

1882

Electoral reform broadens the suffrage; Italy becomes the partner of Germany and Austria-Hungary in the Triple Alliance; Garibaldi dies.

1883

Benito Mussolini is born in Predappio, the son of a blacksmith and an elementary school teacher.

1885

Italian troops occupy the port city of Massawa on the Red Sea in Eritrea, a decisive step toward colonialism.

1887

A stronger tariff law and denunciation of commercial treaties with France introduce heavy economic protectionism of domestic market; Triple Alliance is renewed with clauses that provide compensations for Italy should Austria acquires territory in the Balkans; Francesco Crispi becomes prime minister.

1889

Italians claim that the Treaty of Uccialli gives Italy a protectorate over Ethiopia, but Ethiopians reject that interpretation; a new penal code abolishes the death penalty.

1891

Pope Leo XIII issues the encyclical *Rerum novarum* acknowledging seriousness of social problems and calling for cooperation across class lines.

1892

Italian Workers' Party is formed in Genoa, renamed Italian Socialist Party (PSI) in 1895.

1893

Bank scandals rock the economy and the government; parliament enacts laws to regulate collective bargaining; the popular agitation of the Fasci Siciliani spreads in Sicily; Crispi declares martial law.

1894

Military operations against insurgents continue in Sicily and central Italy; government enacts bank reforms; founding of the Banca Commerciale Italiana.

1896

Ethiopians destroy an Italian military expedition at the battle of Adowa; domestic crisis ensues; government scales back African designs.

1898

Severe popular disturbances throughout Italy; bloody clashes in Milan (fatti di maggio); government disbands all Catholic, radical, and socialist organizations; General Luigi Pelloux appointed prime minister.

1899

The government submits to parliament bills expanding powers of police and curtailing civil liberties; stymied in parliament, the prime minister adopts the provisions on an emergency basis, creating a constitutional crisis.

1900

Supreme Court declares the government measures unconstitutional; new elections strengthen opposition parties; Gaetano Bresci, an anarchist, assassinates King Umberto I; Victor Emmanuel III succeeds to the throne.

1901

Giuseppe Zanardelli, the new prime minister, initiates the era of liberal reform; the era will take its name from his successor, Giovanni Giolitti, who served as minister of the interior in Zanardelli's cabinet.

1902

The Prinetti-Barrère agreements ease tensions between Italy and France.

1903
Giolitti becomes prime minister; Leo XIII dies and is succeeded by Pius X.

1904
Socialists call first general strike; Giolitti adopts policy of government neutrality in labor conflicts; parliament passes special laws to promote the economic development of the South.

1906
Socialist chambers of labor and agrarian leagues form the General Confederation of Labor (CGL), the first national labor union.

1907
Pius X condemns modernism; Giosuè Carducci receives the Nobel Prize in literature.

1908
Earthquake destroys city of Messina, killing more than 100,000.

1910
Founding of the Italian Nationalist Association.

1911
Italy fights the Italian-Turkish War; acquires the colony of Libya and the Dodecanese Islands in the Aegean Sea.

1912
New electoral law enfranchises most males; Turkey cedes Libya and agrees to temporary Italian occupation of Dodecanese Islands.

1913
New elections; the Gentiloni Pact allows Catholic voters to support liberal candidates who are not anticlerical.

1914
Antonio Salandra replaces Giolitti as prime minister; Red Week takes the country to the brink of civil war; government announces Italian neutrality at outbreak of World War I; public opinion divided on issue of intervention; Benito Mussolini expelled from the Socialist Party (PSI) because he favors intervention; Bendict XV elected pope.

1915
Italian government signs Pact of London with France, Great Britain, and Russia; declares war on Austria-Hungary; Benedict XV opposes Italian intervention in the war.

1916
Italian forces capture city of Gorizia after heavy fighting; declare war against Germany; Paolo Boselli succeeds Salandra as head of a government of national unity.

1917
Italian army retreats after the defeat of Caporetto; Vittorio Emanuele Orlando is the new prime minister; General Armando Diaz replaces Luigi Cadorna as commander in chief; antiwar riots break out in Turin.

1918
Italian army regroups along the Piave River, launches final offensive, occupies Trent and Trieste; fighting on the Italian front ends on November 4.

1919
Italian representatives abandon Paris Peace Conference to protest the decision to give the city of Fiume and Dalmatia to Yugoslavia; Gabriele D'Annunzio occupies Fiume with irregular forces; Francesco Saverio Nitti become prime minister; elections based on proportional representation give major gains to the Socialist Party (PSI) and the Catholic Popular Party (PPI); year of intense political and social conflicts; Mussolini founds fascism.

1920
Giolitti forms his last government; labor unrest climaxes in September when workers forcibly occupy factories in Milan, Turin, and other industrial cities; then begins to subside.

1921
In national elections, Fascists elected to parliament for first time; Mussolini reorganizes the Fascist movement as the National Fascist Party (PNF); Fascist action squads attack political opponents; Ivanoe Bonomi replaces Giolitti as prime minister.

1922

Fascists stage the "march on Rome" at the end of October; Mussolini is appointed prime minister; parliament authorizes his government to rule by decree; Pius XI is the new pope.

1923

Parliament adopts Acerbo Law, abolishes proportional representation; the government negotiates the acquisition of Fiume with Yugoslavia.

1924

Fascists and their supporters win in national elections and control parliament; socialist leader Giacomo Matteotti charges electoral fraud, is killed by Fascist toughs; major government crisis ensues; opposition leaves parliament, asks King Victor Emmanuel III to dismiss Mussolini; Victor Emmanuel refuses.

1925

Mussolini assumes full powers, begins personal dictatorship; opposition groups disbanded, civil liberties restricted.

1926

Special laws ban political opposition, strengthen executive branch of government, establish censorship, secret police (OVRA), and special courts to deal with political opponents; anti-Fascists go abroad; Grazia Deledda receives the Nobel Prize in literature.

1927

Fascist regime begins reform of state along principles of corporatism.

1929

The Holy See and Italian government settle the Roman Question.

1932

Appointment of Achille Starace as party secretary signals a hardening of the regime; experts prepare contingency plans for war against Ethiopia.

1933

Italy, France, Great Britain, and Germany sign Four-Power Pact for peaceful revision of the international status quo.

1934

Mussolini foils Hitler's first attempt to annex Austria, denounces racial ideology; Pirandello receives the Nobel Prize in literature.

1935

At the Stresa Conference, Italy, France, and Great Britain vow to protect Austrian independence and peace in Europe; the Ethiopian War begins in October when Italian troops cross the border from Eritrea and Somalia; League of Nations calls for economic sanctions against Italy; Germany sides with Italy.

1936

Mussolini declares military victory in Ethiopia and proclaims the Italian Empire; sends troops to fight for General Franco in the Spanish civil war; beginning of the Rome-Berlin Axis.

1937

Italy joins the Anti-Comintern Pact and leaves the League of Nations; French Fascists kill the anti-Fascist brothers Carlo and Nello Rosselli.

1938

Italy acquiesces in Germany's annexation of Austria, adopts anti-Semitic measures; Mussolini plays role of mediator at Munich Conference.

1939

Italy occupies Albania; concludes Pact of Steel with Nazi Germany; declares its "non-belligerence" when Germany invades Poland, starting World War II; Pius XII is the new pope.

1940

Italy declares war on France and Great Britain; military reverses follow in Africa and Greece; signs the Tripartite Pact with Germany and Japan.

1941

Germany intervenes to support Italian forces in Africa and Balkans; Italy intervenes in war against the Soviet Union and sends a large expeditionary force; declares war on the United States after the Japanese attack on Pearl Harbor.

1942

Italian-German forces advance into Egypt from Libya but are forced back; Russian counteroffensive overwhelms German and Italian forces; Italian cities heavily bombed.

1943

Italian and German forces abandon Africa; strikes break out in industrial cities of the North; American-British forces invade Sicily and the southern mainland; King Victor Emmanuel III removes Mussolini from power, appoints General Pietro Badoglio to succeed him as prime minister; Badoglio agrees to unconditional surrender to the Allies and signs a secret armistice; king and government leave Rome to avoid capture by the Germans, put themselves under the protection of the Allies in the occupied South; Italian army, left without orders, disintegrates; Germans free Mussolini, who sets up the puppet government of the Italian Social Republic in the area of northern Italy controlled by the Germans; Badoglio's government declares war against Germany; Allied offensive stalls north of Naples.

1944

The resistance movement develops in German-occupied Italy; Allies take Rome in June and advance as far north as Florence; political parties emerge in the South, agree to work with the monarchy until the end of the war; Victor Emmanuel III steps aside and appoints his son Umberto II as his lieutenant.

1945

Germany surrenders to the Allies; resistance fighters execute Mussolini and other Fascist leaders, take control of cities in the North. Alcide De Gasperi becomes prime minister; his first government includes communists and socialists.

1946

In first elections by universal suffrage, with women voting, Italians vote to abolish the monarchy, elect a constituent assembly to write a constitution for the Italian republic; the republic is proclaimed on June 2; Umberto II leaves the country for exile; Enrico De Nicola becomes interim president of the republic.

1947

Italy signs the Peace Treaty; De Gasperi expels socialists and communists from the government; parliament approves the new constitution, which incorporates previous agreements with the Holy See.

1948

The Constitution of the Italian republic goes into effect on January 1; Christian Democracy (DC) wins absolute majority in national elections; Marshall Plan funds and anti-inflationary and free-market policies of Luigi Einaudi shape the economic reconstruction of the country; Einaudi becomes the first constitutionally chosen president of the republic.

1949

Italy joins NATO after heated national debate in which Left and Right oppose membership.

1950

The Cassa per il Mezzogiorno (Fund for the South) provides for special measures to promote the economic development of the southern regions; the labor movement splits along political lines.

1951

First Festival of San Remo launches yearly review of popular music.

1952

Italy joins the European Coal and Steel Community, first step toward European economic integration.

1953

Christian Democrats lose absolute majority in national elections, never to regain it.

1954

Italy and Yugoslavia agree to division of contested territory; Trieste returns to Italy; RAI begins regular television broadcasting in January.

1955

Giovanni Gronchi becomes president of the republic; Italy is admitted to the United Nations.

1957

Treaty of Rome establishes the European Economic Community (Common Market) and European Economic Energy Commission.

1958

National elections strengthen DC and other center parties; legal brothels abolished; John XXIII is the new pope.

1959

Salvatore Quasimodo becomes Nobel poet laureate.

1960

National protests bring down the center-right government headed by Fernando Tambroni; Olympic Games held in Rome.

1962

Aldo Moro proposes the political "Opening to the Left"; Socialists support government formed by Amintore Fanfani; electrical industry nationalized; Antonio Segni becomes president of the republic; Second Vatican Council (Vatican II) opens discussion of church reform.

1963

DC loses votes in national elections; Aldo Moro forms first center-left government that includes Socialists; Paul VI is the new pope.

1964

Rumors circulate of a military coup by General Giovanni De Lorenzo; Segni resigns as president

for health reasons; his successor is the Social Democratic leader Giuseppe Saragat.

1968

Student protests against universities and Vietnam War intensify; the Socialist Party loses votes in national elections, imperiling the Opening to the Left; the European Economic Community goes into effect.

1969

Parliament passes law legalizing divorce; in the Autunno caldo (Hot Autumn) angry strikers walk out of factories; worker and student demonstrators take to the streets; a deadly bomb explosion in Milan sets off the long period of political terrorism.

1970

Parliament approves laws granting administrative autonomy to the regions, protecting worker rights and privileges, and legalizing divorce.

1971

Giovanni Leone becomes president of the republic.

1972

Political crisis forces early elections, with gains for the neo-Fascist party (MSI) and losses for Socialist Party (PSI); Communist Party (PCI) pushes for the Historic Compromise to share power with Christian Democrats (DC).

1973

Communist Party leader Enrico Berlinguer formally proposes the Historic Compromise; Middle East oil crisis wreaks havoc on the Italian economy, dramatizing its total dependence on Middle East oil.

1974

Voters in national referendum reject effort to repeal the divorce law.

1975

Voting age lowered from 21 to 18; Communists score victories in local elections; wages indexed to keep pace with inflation automatically; Eugenio Montale receives Nobel Prize for literature.

1976

Lockheed business scandal rocks the government and forces early elections; Communists register major electoral gains, intensify drive to share power at the national level; chemical accident at Seveso triggers major debate on pollution and government responsibility for preservation of the environment.

1978

Communists support government headed by Christian Democratic leader Aldo Moro; Red Brigades capture and kill Moro; President Leone forced out of office by political scandal, is succeeded by socialist Sandro Pertini; parliament passes law legalizing abortion; Paul VI is succeeded by Pope John Paul I, who dies after only 33 days in office; John Paul II is elected pope.

1979

Political crisis in the wake of the Moro affair forces early elections; Communists suffer significant losses; the lira joins the European Monetary System.

1980

Communists renounce goal of Historic Compromise but call for unofficial partnership with DC; terrorism intensifies; major earthquake kills thousands in southern Italy; management scores first significant victories against organized labor.

1981

Republican Party leader Giovanni Spadolini forms the first postwar government not headed by a Christian Democrat; national referendum approves legalized abortion; P2 Masonic lodge scandal breaks out.

1982

Security forces rescue kidnapped American general James Lee Dozier; Italy wins soccer World Cup; General Alberto Della Chiesa is killed by Mafia operators.

1983

Early national elections result in major losses for Christian Democrats, gains for Socialists; Bettino Craxi forms first postwar government headed by a Socialist.

1984

New Concordat with the Holy See supersedes the agreements of 1929 incorporated in the Constitution of the Republic.

1985

Craxi initiatives in Middle East signal a more active foreign policy; Francesco Cossiga becomes president of the republic; national referendum repeals wage indexation measure passed in 1975.

1987

Communist Party (PCI) vote drops to 26.6 percent.

1991

PCI splits into Democratic Party of the Left (PDS), which renounces communism, and Communist Refoundation, which adheres to the communist line; Umberto Bossi founds the separatist Northern League.

1992

Oscar Luigi Scalfaro becomes president of the republic; Christian Democrats and Socialists lose votes in national elections; Democratic Party of the Left gains 16.1 percent of popular vote in the first elections since its founding; the Northern League gains 8.7 percent of the vote; the Mani Pulite (Clean Hands) investigation of political corruption begins.

1993

National referendum shows that a majority of voters want electoral reform; parliament adopts the uninominal (winner-takes-all) system of electoral representation for 75 percent of seats in parliament.

1994

Christian Democratic Party (DC) dissolves; media magnate Silvio Berlusconi launches the Forza

Italia (Go Italy) movement and forms the Freedom Alliance coalition, which wins a parliamentary majority in national elections; Berlusconi's government lasts seven months; Massimo D'Alema becomes PDS secretary.

1995

Lamberto Dini forms a nonpolitical government of "technicians" to rein in public spending and meet the conditions for admittance to the European Monetary Union; national referendum approves existing media system, rejects antitrust restrictions and limits on advertising.

1996

In national elections the center-left Olive Tree coalition headed by Romano Prodi wins more votes than the center-right Freedom Alliance coalition headed by Berlusconi; Prodi forms the new government, continues policies of tight spending and reduction of public debt initiated by Dini.

1998

Crash of American jet into ski lift in northern Italy creates friction with the United States over issue of responsibility; D'Alema replaces Prodi as prime minister; Prodi becomes president of the European Commission; Italy is admitted to the European Monetary Union.

1999

Public opinion splits on NATO bombing of Serbia; the D'Alema government supports intervention to remain true to NATO, Catholics and left-wingers oppose it. Italian forces participate in military operations; Carlo Azeglio Ciampi becomes president of the republic.

2000

Italian peacekeeping troops deployed in Kosovo; Giuliano Amato replaces D'Alema as prime minister.

2001

National elections give Forza Italia a decisive parliamentary majority after it promises to enact major reforms; Berlusconi forms his second government; strong police reaction to demonstrations against G8 summit in Genoa countered by antigovernment protests.

2002

The Berlusconi government skirmishes with the European Union over issue of national sovereignty; mass demonstrations held against a government proposal to give employers more freedom to hire and fire workers.

2003

Berlusconi supports American intervention in Iraq, contends with mounting campaign to put him on trial for corrupt business practices; parliament passes law exonerating Berlusconi from prosecution while in office; Berlusconi assumes presidency of the European Union; national debate continues over policies toward European Union, organized labor, pensions, and privatization of government-run enterprises; Italian food giant Parmalat files for bankruptcy in what potentially may be Europe's biggest case of corporate fraud.

2004

Constitutional court rescinds law granting prosecutorial immunity to Berlusconi and other top officials. Berlusconi's trial resumes in April; Italian civilian killed in Iraq.

APPENDIXES

APPENDIX I
Maps

APPENDIX II
Rulers and Statesmen of Italy, 1861 to the Present

APPENDIX I

MAPS

Holy Roman Empire, 1215–1250

Renaissance Italy, 1490

Unification of Italy, 1859–1870

Italy after the Congress of Vienna, 1815

Expansion of the Italian Empire, 1922–1939

Present-Day Italy

HOLY ROMAN EMPIRE, 1215–1250

Baltic Sea

North Sea

Prussia

County of Holstein

Slavinia

Duchy of Pomerania

KINGDOM OF POLAND

Friesland

Duchy of Saxony

March of Brandenburg

March of Lausitz

Duchy of Silesia

Brabant

Flanders

Duchy of Lower Lorraine

Hainault

Landgravate of Thuringia

March of Meissen

Opol and Ratibor

Franconia

KINGDOM OF BOHEMIA

March of Moravia

Duchy of Upper Lorraine

KINGDOM OF FRANCE

Duchy of Swabia

Duchy of Bavaria

Duchy of Austria

County of Burgundy

Duchy of Styria

KINGDOM OF HUNGARY

KINGDOM OF BURGUNDY

Duchy of Carinthia

Savoy

Patriarchate of St. Peter

March of Carniola

March of Verona

KINGDOM OF ITALY

Emilia

Provence

Romagna

Adriatic Sea

Tuscany

March of Ancona

Corsica

Duchy of Spoleto

Patrimony of St. Peter

Mediterranean Sea

Sardinia

KINGDOM OF SICILY

N

▨	Holy Roman Empire, 1250
—·—·—	Boundary of kingdom
·········	Boundary of duchy or march

0   100 miles
0   100 km

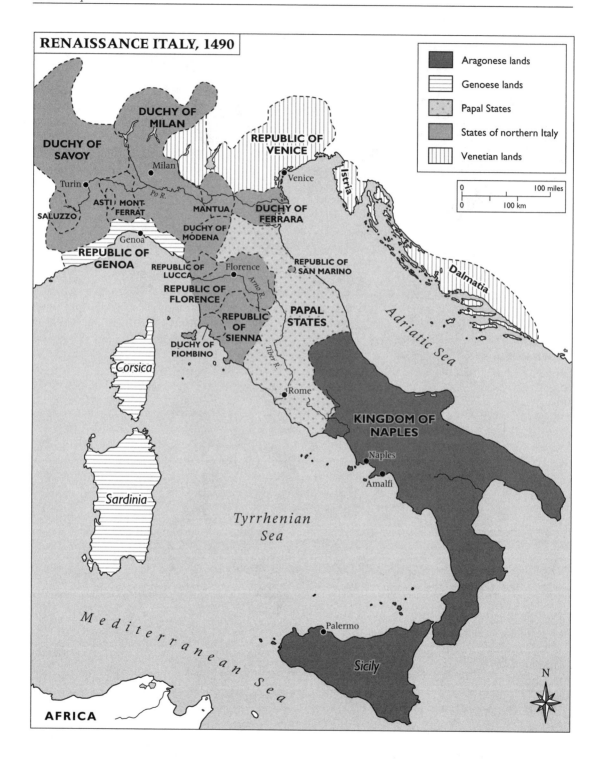

RENAISSANCE ITALY, 1490

Aragonese lands

Genoese lands

Papal States

States of northern Italy

Venetian lands

0   100 miles
0   100 km

DUCHY OF SAVOY

DUCHY OF MILAN

REPUBLIC OF VENICE

Turin

Milan

Venice

Istria

ASTI   MONT-FERRAT

Po R.

MANTUA

DUCHY OF FERRARA

SALUZZO

DUCHY OF MODENA

Genoa

Dalmatia

REPUBLIC OF GENOA

REPUBLIC OF LUCCA

Florence

REPUBLIC OF SAN MARINO

Arno R.

Adriatic Sea

REPUBLIC OF FLORENCE

PAPAL STATES

REPUBLIC OF SIENNA

DUCHY OF PIOMBINO

Corsica

Tiber R.

Rome

KINGDOM OF NAPLES

Naples

Amalfi

Sardinia

Tyrrhenian Sea

Mediterranean Sea

Palermo

Sicily

AFRICA

N

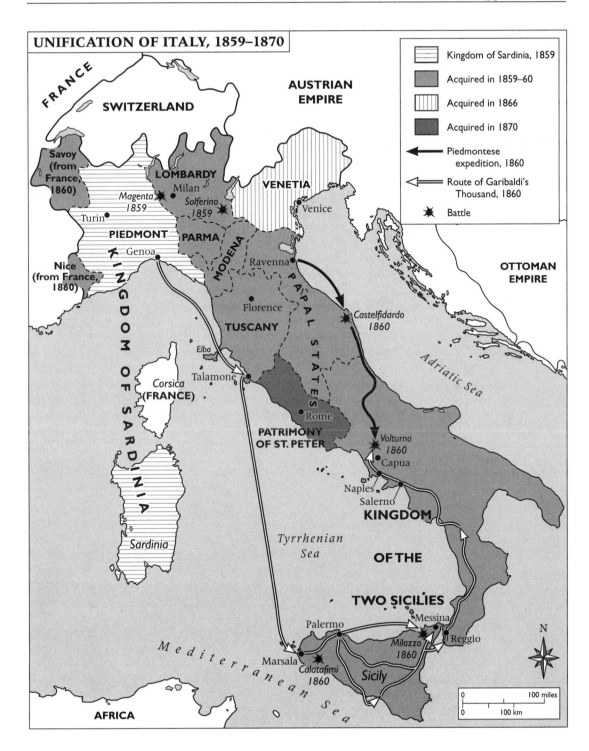

UNIFICATION OF ITALY, 1859–1870

Legend:
- Kingdom of Sardinia, 1859
- Acquired in 1859–60
- Acquired in 1866
- Acquired in 1870
- ← Piedmontese expedition, 1860
- ⇐ Route of Garibaldi's Thousand, 1860
- ✳ Battle

FRANCE

SWITZERLAND

AUSTRIAN EMPIRE

Savoy (from France, 1860)

LOMBARDY

Milan

Magenta 1859

VENETIA

Venice

Turin

PIEDMONT

PARMA

Solferino 1859

MODENA

OTTOMAN EMPIRE

Nice (from France, 1860)

KINGDOM OF SARDINIA

Genoa

Ravenna

PAPAL STATES

Florence

TUSCANY

Castelfidardo 1860

Adriatic Sea

Elba

Talamone

Corsica (FRANCE)

Rome

PATRIMONY OF ST. PETER

Volturno 1860

Capua

Naples

Salerno

KINGDOM

Sardinia

Tyrrhenian Sea

OF THE

TWO SICILIES

Palermo

Messina

Milazzo 1860

Reggio

Marsala

Calatafimi 1860

Sicily

Mediterranean Sea

AFRICA

N

0   100 miles
0   100 km

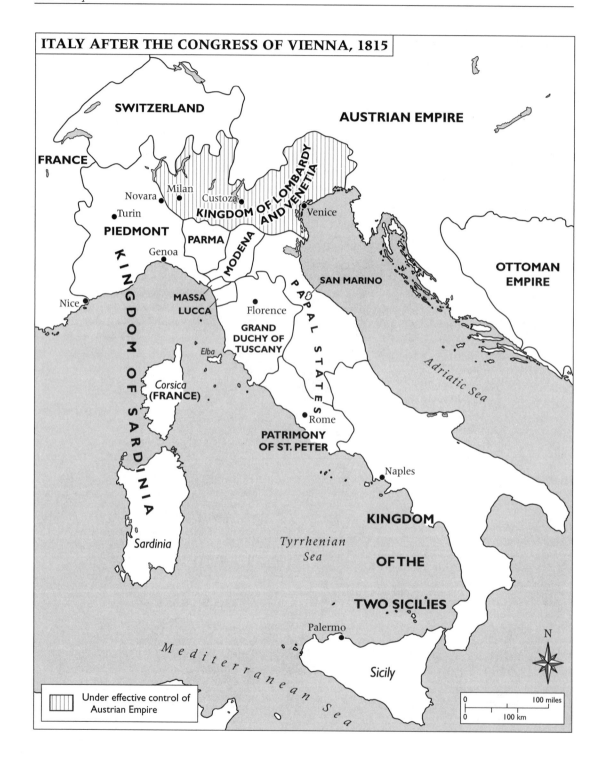

ITALY AFTER THE CONGRESS OF VIENNA, 1815

SWITZERLAND

AUSTRIAN EMPIRE

FRANCE

•Novara •Milan Custoza•

KINGDOM OF LOMBARDY AND VENETIA

•Venice

•Turin

PIEDMONT

PARMA

MODENA

OTTOMAN EMPIRE

K I N G D O M   O F   S A R D I N I A

•Genoa

MASSA LUCCA

Nice•

Florence•

GRAND DUCHY OF TUSCANY

Elba

SAN MARINO

P A P A L   S T A T E S

Adriatic Sea

Corsica (FRANCE)

•Rome

PATRIMONY OF ST. PETER

Sardinia

•Naples

KINGDOM

Tyrrhenian Sea

OF THE

TWO SICILIES

Palermo•

N

Sicily

M e d i t e r r a n e a n   S e a

0 — 100 miles
0 — 100 km

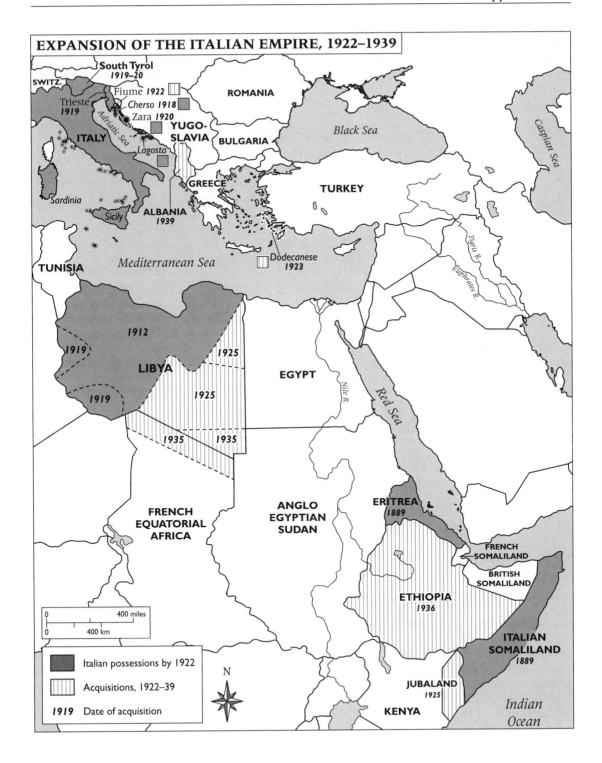

PRESENT-DAY ITALY

SWITZER-
LAND

FRANCE

AUSTRIA

HUNGARY

SLOVENIA

CROATIA

BOSNIA-HERZEGOVINA

A   L   P   S

Trento

Udine

Como
Bergamo

Milan
Brescia
Verona

Venice
Padua

Trieste

Turin

Piacenza

Po R.

Parma
Modena

Bologna

SAN
MARINO

Genoa

La Spezia

*Ligurian
Sea*

Lucca
Pisa
Florence
Livorno

Arno R.

Ancona

Adriatic Sea

MONACO

Perugia

*Elba
(ITALY)*

Tiber R.

*Corsica
(FRANCE)*

Viterbo
L'Aquila
Pescara

Strait of Bonifacio

VATICAN
CITY

★ Rome

Campobasso

Anzio
Cassino

Foggia

Olbia

Calore R.

Bari

Sassari

Alghero

Tirso R.

Naples
Salerno

Bradano R.

Brindisi

Potenza

Taranto

Macomer

Sardinia

Sele R.

*Tyrrhenian
Sea*

*Gulf of
Taranto*

Iglesias

Cagliari

Cosenza
Catanzaro

Mediterranean Sea

Ionian Sea

Palermo

Messina

Reggio di Calabria

Sicily

Dittaino R.

Strait of Messina

Strait of Sicily

Salso R.

Catania

Siracusa

N

ALGERIA

TUNISIA

*Pantelleria I.
(ITALY)*

0   100 miles

0   100 km

APPENDIX II

Kingdom of Italy

Reign	Name
Kings (Savoia dynasty)	
17 Mar 1861–9 Jan 1878	Victor Emmannuel II
9 Jan 1878–29 Jul 1900	Umberto I
29 Jul 1900–9 May 1946	Victor Emmanuel III
9 May 1946–18 Jun 1946	Umberto II

Italian Social Republic (counter-government at Lake Garda)

Provisional Head of State	
15 Sep 1943–28 Apr 1945	Benito Mussolini

Italian Republic

Term	Name
Provisional Heads of State	
18 Jun 1946–1 Jul 1946	Alcide De Gasperi (acting)
1 Jul 1946–1 Jan 1948	Enrico De Nicola

Presidents

Term	Name
1 Jan 1948–12 May 1948	Enrico De Nicola
12 May 1948–11 May 1955	Luigi Einaudi
11 May 1955–11 May 1962	Giovanni Gronchi
11 May 1962–6 Dec 1964	Antonio Segni
6 Dec 1964–29 Dec 1964	Cesare Merzagora (acting)
29 Dec 1964–29 Dec 1971	Giuseppe Saragat
29 Dec 1971–15 Jun 1978	Giovanni Leone
15 Jun 1978–9 Jul 1978	Amintore Fanfani (acting)
9 Jul 1978–29 Jun 1985	Sandro Pertini
29 Jun 1985–28 Apr 1992	Francesco Cossiga
(acting to 3 Jul 1985)	
28 Apr 1992–28 May 1992	Giovanni Spadolini (acting)
28 May 1992–15 May 1999	Oscar Luigi Scalfaro
15 May 1999–18 May 1999	Nicola Mancino (acting)
18 May 1999–	Carlo Azeglio Ciampi

Prime ministers (presidents of the Council of Ministers)

Term	Name
17 Mar 1861–6 Jun 1861	Camillo Benso, conte di Cavour
6 Jun 1861–4 Mar 1862	Bettino Ricasoli, conte di Brolio (1st time)
4 Mar 1862–9 Dec 1862	Urbano Rattazzi (1st time)
9 Dec 1862–24 Mar 1863	Luigi Carlo Farini
24 Mar 1863–23 Sep 1864	Marco Minghetti (1st time)
23 Sep 1864–17 Jun 1866	Alfonso Ferrero, marchese di La Marmora
17 Jun 1866–11 Apr 1867	Bettino Ricasoli, conte di Brolio (2nd time)
11 Apr 1867–27 Oct 1867	Urbano Rattazzi (2nd time)
27 Oct 1867–12 Dec 1869	Conte Luigi Federico Menabrea
12 Dec 1869–10 Aug 1873	Giovanni Lanza
10 Aug 1873–25 Mar 1876	Marco Minghetti (2nd time)
25 Mar 1876–23 Mar 1878	Agostino Depretis (1st time)
23 Mar 1878–18 Dec 1878	Benedetto Cairoli (1st time)
18 Dec 1878–12 Jul 1879	Agostino Depretis (2nd time)
12 Jul 1879–28 May 1881	Benedetto Cairoli (2nd time)
28 May 1881–29 Jul 1887	Agostino Depretis (3rd time)
8 Aug 1887–9 Feb 1891	Francesco Crispi (1st time)
9 Feb 1891–15 May 1892	Antonio Starabba, marchese di Rudinì (1st time)
15 May 1892–10 Dec 1893	Giovanni Giolitti (1st time)
10 Dec 1893–10 Mar 1896	Francesco Crispi (2nd time)
10 Mar 1896–29 Jun 1898	Antonio Starabba, marchese di Rudinì (2nd time)
29 Jun 1898–24 Jun 1900	Luigi Pelloux
24 Jun 1900–15 Feb 1901	Giuseppe Saracco
15 Feb 1901–3 Nov 1903	Giuseppe Zanardelli
3 Nov 1903–27 Mar 1905	Giovanni Giolitti (2nd time)
27 Mar 1905–8 Feb 1906	Alessandro Fortis
8 Feb 1906–29 May 1906	Barone Sidney Sonnino (1st time)
29 May 1906–10 Dec 1909	Giovanni Giolitti (3rd time)
10 Dec 1909–30 Mar 1910	Barone Sidney Sonnino (2nd time)
30 Mar 1910–27 Mar 1911	Luigi Luzzatti
27 Mar 1911–21 Mar 1914	Giovanni Giolitti (4th time)
21 Mar 1914–19 Jun 1916	Antonio Salandra
19 Jun 1916–30 Oct 1917	Paolo Boselli
30 Oct 1917–23 Jun 1919	Vittorio Emanuele Orlando
23 Jun 1919–16 Jun 1920	Francesco Saverio Nitti
16 Jun 1920–4 Jul 1921	Giovanni Giolitti (5th time)
4 Jul 1921–25 Feb 1922	Ivanoe Bonomi (1st time)
25 Feb 1922–31 Oct 1922	Luigi Facta
31 Oct 1922–25 Jul 1943	Benito Mussolini
27 Jul 1943–9 Jun 1944	Pietro Badoglio

Prime ministers (presidents of the Council of Ministers) *(continued)*

Term	Name
9 Jun 1944–21 Jun 1945	Ivanoe Bonomi (2nd time)
21 Jun 1945–10 Dec 1945	Ferruccio Parri
10 Dec 1945–17 Aug 1953	Alcide De Gasperi
17 Aug 1953–18 Jan 1954	Giuseppe Pella
18 Jan 1954–9 Feb 1954	Amintore Fanfani (1st time)
9 Feb 1954–6 Jul 1955	Mario Scelba
6 Jul 1955–19 May 1957	Antonio Segni (1st time)
19 May 1957–1 Jul 1958	Adone Zoli
1 Jul 1958–15 Feb 1959	Amintore Fanfani (2nd time)
15 Feb 1959–25 Mar 1960	Antonio Segni (2nd time)
25 Mar 1960–26 Jul 1960	Fernando Tambroni
26 Jul 1960–21 Jun 1963	Amintore Fanfani (3rd time)
21 Jun 1963–5 Dec 1963	Giovanni Leone (1st time)
5 Dec 1963–25 Jun 1968	Aldo Moro (1st time)
25 Jun 1968–13 Dec 1968	Giovanni Leone (2nd time)
13 Dec 1968–7 Aug 1970	Mariano Rumor (1st time)
7 Aug 1970–18 Feb 1972	Emilio Colombo
18 Feb 1972–4 Jul 1973	Giulio Andreotti (1st time)
4 Jul 1973–2 Nov 1974	Mariano Rumor (2nd time)
2 Nov 1974–29 Jul 1976	Aldo Moro (2nd time)
29 Jul 1976–5 Aug 1979	Giulio Andreotti (2nd time)
5 Aug 1979–18 Oct 1980	Francesco Cossiga
18 Oct 1980–28 Jun 1981	Arnaldo Forlani
28 Jun 1981–30 Nov 1982	Giovanni Spadolini
30 Nov 1982–4 Aug 1983	Amintore Fanfani (4th time)
4 Aug 1983–18 Apr 1987	Bettino Craxi
18 Apr 1987–29 Jul 1987	Amintore Fanfani (5th time)
29 Jul 1987–13 Apr 1988	Giovanni Goria
13 Apr 1988–23 Jul 1989	Ciriaco De Mita
23 Jul 1989–28 Jun 1992	Giulio Andreotti (3rd time)
28 Jun 1992–29 Apr 1993	Giuliano Amato (1st time)
29 Apr 1993–11 May 1994	Carlo Azeglio Ciampi
11 May 1994–17 Jan 1995	Silvio Berlusconi (1st time)
17 Jan 1995–18 May 1996	Lamberto Dini
18 May 1996–21 Oct 1998	Romano Prodi
21 Oct 1998–26 Apr 2000	Massimo D'Alema
26 Apr 2000–11 Jun 2001	Giuliano Amato (2nd time)
11 Jun 2001–	Silvio Berlusconi (2nd time)

BIBLIOGRAPHY

This is a bibliography of English-language books likely to be found in most college and general reference libraries. Preference is given to studies published in the last 50 years, but older works of enduring value and relevance are also listed. In the sections below, books are arranged by type, chronological period, topic, and methodology. A short list of primary works available in English translation concludes the bibliography. Readers are advised to consult the entire bibliography since titles that straddle different categories are listed only once, in the category that seems most appropriate.

GENERAL REFERENCE

The titles in this section direct the reader to general sources of information similar to what this reference work provides. Students should be aware that no single work covers the entire field of Italian studies exhaustively. It is therefore advisable to look at several sources when looking for general information or researching a topic. The World Wide Web carries many useful sites on Italy. Links to them are available on the Web site of the Society for Italian Historical Studies at http://faculty.valenciacc.edu/ckillinger/sihs.

Bibliographies

Bull, Martin J. *Contemporary Italy: A Research Guide.* Westport, Conn.: Greenwood Press, 1996.

Cassels, Alan. *Italian Foreign Policy, 1918–1945: A Guide to Research and Research Materials.* Wilmington, Del.: Scholarly Resources, 1981.

Coppa, Frank J., and William Roberts, eds. *Modern Italian History: An Annotated Bibliography.* New York: Greenwood Press, 1990.

Cordasco, Francesco. *The Italian Emigration to the United States, 1880–1930.* Fairview, N.J.: Junius-Vaughn Press, 1990.

Delzell, Charles F. *Italy in Modern Times.* Washington, D.C.: American Historical Association, 1964.

———. *Italy in the Twentieth Century.* Washington, D.C.: American Historical Association, 1980.

Lange, Peter, ed. *Studies on Italy 1943–1975.* Select Bibliography of American and British Materials in Political Science, Economics, Sociology and Anthropology. Turin: Fondazione Giovanni Agnelli, 1977.

Lovett, Clara M., ed. *Contemporary Italy: A Selective Bibliography.* Washington, D.C.: Library of Congress, 1985.

Sponza, Lucio, and Diego Zancani, eds. *Italy.* World Bibliographical Series. Oxford and Santa Barbara, Calif.: Clio Press, 1995.

Stych, F. S. *How to Find Out about Italy.* Oxford: Pergamon Press, 1970.

Tommasi, Silvano M., ed. *National Directory of Research Centers, Repositories and Organizations of Italian Culture in the United States.* Turin: Fondazione Giovanni Agnelli, 1980.

Varley, Douglas H. *A Bibliography of Italian Colonization in Africa with a Section on Abyssinia.* Reprint, 1936. Folkstone and London: Dawson's of Pall Mall, 1970.

A comprehensive bibliography organized by topics is available online for a fee: *Early Modern Italy: A Comprehensive Bibliography of Works in English and French* at www.EarlyModernItaly.com.

Dictionaries and Encyclopedias

Avery, Catherine D., ed. *The New Century Italian Renaissance Encyclopedia.* New York: Appleton-Century-Crofts, 1972.

Bondanella, Peter, ed. *Dictionary of Italian Literature.* 2d ed. Westport, Conn.: Greenwood Press, 1996.

Cannistraro, Philip V., ed. *Historical Dictionary of Fascist Italy.* Westport, Conn.: Greenwood Press, 1982.

Coppa, Frank J., ed. *Dictionary of Modern Italian History*. Westport, Conn.: Greenwood Press, 1985.

Cosenza, Mario Emilio. *Biographical and Bibliographical Dictionary of the Italian Humanists and of the World of Classical Scholarship in Italy, 1300–1800*. 6 vols. Boston: G. K. Hall, 1962–67.

Gilbert, Mark F., and K. Robert Nilsson. *The Historical Dictionary of Modern Italy*. Lanham, Md.: Scarecrow Press, 1999.

Hale, J. R., ed. *Dictionary of the Italian Renaissance*. London: Thames and Hudson, 1981.

Kelly, John M. D., ed. *The Oxford Dictionary of Popes*. Oxford: Oxford University Press, 1986.

Moliterno, Gino, ed. *Encyclopedia of Contemporary Italian Culture*. London: Routledge, 2000.

GENERAL SURVEYS AND TEXTBOOKS

Selections of Documents

Clough, Shepard B., and Salvatore Saladino, eds. *A History of Modern Italy. Documents, Readings, and Commentary*. New York: Columbia University Press, 1968.

Mack Smith, Denis, ed. *The Making of Italy, 1796–1866*. New York: Holmes and Meier, 1988.

Salomone, William A., ed. *Italy from the Risorgimento to Fascism: An Inquiry into the Origins of the Totalitarian State*. Garden City, N.Y.: Anchor Books, 1970.

Series Surveys

Longman History of Italy. London: Longman.

   Hay, Denys, and John Law. *Italy in the Age of the Renaissance, 1380–1530*. 1989.

   Cochrane, Eric. *Italy, 1530–1630*. 1988.

   Sella, Domenico. *Italy in the Seventeenth Century*. 1997.

   Carpanetto, Dino, and Giuseppe Ricuperati. *Italy in the Age of Reason, 1685–1789*. 1987.

   Hearder, Harry. *Italy in the Age of the Risorgimento, 1790–1870*. 1983.

   Clark, Martin. *Modern Italy, 1871–1995*. 2d ed. 1996.

The Short Oxford History of Italy. Oxford: Oxford University Press.

   Davis, John A., ed. *Italy in the Nineteenth Century, 1796–1900*. 2000.

   Lyttelton, Adrian, ed. *Liberal and Fascist Italy, 1900–1945*. 2002.

   McCarthy, Patrick, ed. *Italy since 1945*. 2000.

Single-Volume Surveys

Absalom, Roger. *Italy since 1800: A Nation in the Balance?* London: Longman, 1995.

Black, Christopher. *Early Modern Italy. A Social History*. London: Routledge, 2001.

Bobbio, Norberto. *Ideological Profile of Twentieth-Century Italy*. Princeton, N.J.: Princeton University Press, 1995.

Bosworth, Richard J. B. *Italy and the Wider World, 1860–1960*. London: Routledge, 1996.

Croce, Benedetto. *A History of Italy, 1871–1915*. Oxford: Clarendon Press, 1929.

Di Scala, Spencer M. *Italy: From Revolution to Republic: 1700 to the Present* 3rd ed. Boulder, Colo.: Westview Press, 2004.

Domenico, Roy P. *Remaking Italy in the Twentieth Century*. Lanham, Md.: Rowman and Littlefield, 2002.

Doumanis, Nicholas. *Italy*. London: Arnold, 2001.

Duggan, Christopher. *A Concise History of Italy*. Cambridge: Cambridge University Press, 1994.

Dunnage, Jonathan. *Twentieth-Century Italy: A Social History*. London: Longman, 2002.

Hanlon, Gregory. *Early Modern Italy, 1550–1800*. New York: St. Martin's Press, 2000.

Procacci, Giuliano. *History of the Italian People*. New York: Harper and Row, 1971.

Mack Smith, Denis. *Italy: A Political History*. Ann Arbor: University of Michigan Press, 1997.

———. *Italy and Its Monarchy*. New Haven, Conn.: Yale University Press, 1989.

Salvatorelli, Luigi. *A Concise History of Italy from Prehistoric Times to Our Own Day*. New York: Oxford University Press, 1940.

Seton-Watson, Christopher. *Italy from Liberalism to Fascism, 1870–1925*. London: Methuen, 1967.

Tannenbaum, Edward R., and Emiliana P. Noether, eds. *Modern Italy: A Topical History since 1861*. New York: New York University Press, 1974.

Trevelyan, Janet Penrose. *A Short History of the Italian People from the Barbarian Invasions to the Present Day*. Rev. ed. London: Allen and Unwin, 1956.

Woolf, Stuart. *A History of Italy, 1700–1860*. London: Methuen, 1979.

CHRONOLOGICAL PERIODS

Renaissance and Reformation (1350–1600)

Baron, Hans. *The Crisis of the Early Italian Renaissance: Civic Humanism and Republican Liberty in an*

Age of Classicism and Tyranny. 2 vols. Princeton, N.J.: Princeton University Press, 1955.

Bentley, Jerry H. *Politics and Culture in Renaissance Naples.* Princeton, N.J.: Princeton University Press, 1987.

Black, Christopher F. *Italian Confraternities in the Sixteenth Century.* Cambridge: Cambridge University Press, 1989.

Burckhardt, Jacob. *The Civilization of the Renaissance in Italy.* 2 vols. New York: Harper and Row, 1975.

Burke, Peter. *The Historical Anthropology of Early Modern Italy. Essays on Perception and Communication.* Cambridge: Cambridge University Press, 1987.

———. *The Italian Renaissance: Culture and Society in Italy.* Princeton, N.J.: Princeton University Press, 1999.

Chamberlain, Eric Russell. *The Sack of Rome.* London: Batsford, 1979.

Church, Frederic C. *The Italian Reformers, 1534–1564.* New York: Columbia University Press, 1932.

D'Amico, John F. *Renaissance Humanism in Papal Rome. Humanists and Churchmen on the Eve of the Reformation.* Baltimore: Johns Hopkins University Press, 1983.

De Leon-Jones, Karen Silva. *Giordano Bruno and the Kabbalah: Prophets, Magicians, and Rabbis.* New Haven, Conn.: Yale University Press, 1997.

Garin, Eugenio. *Italian Humanism: Philosophy and Civic Life in the Renaissance.* New York: Harper and Row, 1965.

Gilbert, Felix. *Machiavelli and Guicciardini: Politics and History in Sixteenth-Century Florence.* Princeton, N.J.: Princeton University Press, 1965.

Ginzburg, Carlo. *The Cheese and the Worms: The Cosmos of a Sixteenth-Century Miller.* Baltimore: Johns Hopkins University Press, 1980.

———. *The Night Battles: Witchcraft and Agrarian Cults in the Sixteenth and Seventeenth Centuries.* Baltimore: Johns Hopkins University Press, 1983.

Goldthwaite, Richard A. *The Building of Renaissance Florence: An Economic and Social History.* Baltimore: Johns Hopkins University Press, 1980.

Grendler, Paul F. *The Roman Inquisition and the Venetian Press, 1540–1605.* Princeton, N.J.: Princeton University Press, 1977.

Gundersheimer, Werner L. *Ferrara: The Style of a Renaissance Despotism.* Princeton, N.J.: Princeton University Press, 1973.

Hale, J. R. *Florence and the Medici: The Pattern of Control.* London: Thames and Hudson, 1977.

Hay, Denys, and John Law. *Italy in the Age of the Renaissance, 1380–1530.* London: Longman, 1989.

Headley, John M., and John B. Tomaro, eds. *San Carlo Borromeo: Catholic Reform and Ecclesiastical Politics in the Second Half of the Sixteenth Century.* Washington, D.C.: Folger Shakespeare Library, 1988.

James, Frank A. *Peter Martyr Vermigli and Predestination: The Augustinian Inheritance of an Italian Reformer.* Oxford: Clarendon Press, 1998.

Kristeller, Paul Oscar. *Renaissance Thought: The Classic, Scholastic, and Humanist Strains.* New York: Harper Torchbooks, 1961.

Mallett, Michael Edward. *The Borgias: The Rise and Fall of a Renaissance Dynasty.* London: Bodley Head, 1969.

Martin, John. *Venice's Hidden Enemies: Italian Heretics in a Renaissance City.* Berkeley: University of California Press, 1993.

Martin, Ruth. *Witchcraft and the Inquisition in Venice, 1550–1650.* New York: Basil Blackwell, 1989.

Mattingly, Garrett. *Renaissance Diplomacy.* Boston: Houghton Mifflin, 1955. Reprint Dover Publications 1988.

Phillips, William D. *The Worlds of Christopher Columbus.* Cambridge: Cambridge University Press, 1992.

Pocock, John G. A. *The Machiavellian Moment: Florentine Political Thought and the Atlantic Republican Tradition.* Princeton, N.J.: Princeton University Press, 1975.

Pullan, Brian. *Rich and Poor in Renaissance Venice: The Social Institutions of a Catholic State to 1620.* Cambridge, Mass.: Harvard University Press, 1971.

Ridolfi, Roberto. *The Life of Francesco Guicciardini.* New York: Knopf, 1968.

———. *The Life of Niccolò Machiavelli.* Cambridge: Cambridge University Press, 1992.

Ruggiero, Guido. *Binding Passions: Tales of Magic, Marriage, and Power at the End of the Renaissance.* New York: Oxford University Press, 1993.

Ryder, Alan. *The Kingdom of Naples under Alfonso the Magnanimous: The Making of a Modern State.* Oxford: Clarendon Press, 1976.

Stephens, J. N. *The Italian Renaissance: The Origins of Intellectual and Artistic Change before the Reformation.* London: Longman, 1990.

Stinger, Charles L. *The Renaissance in Rome.* Bloomington: Indiana University Press, 1985.

Terpstra, Nicholas, ed. *The Politics of Ritual Kinship: Confraternities and Social Order in Early Modern Italy.* Cambridge: Cambridge University Press, 2000.

Weinstein, Donald. *Savonarola and Florence: Prophecy and Patriotism in the Renaissance.* Princeton, N.J.: Princeton University Press, 1970.

———. *The Captain's Concubine: Love, Honor, and Violence in Renaissance Tuscany.* Baltimore: Johns Hopkins University Press, 2000.

Wootton, David. *Paolo Sarpi: Between Renaissance and Enlightenment.* New York: Cambridge University Press, 1983.

Zimmerman, T. C. Price. *Paolo Giovio: The Historian and the Crisis of Sixteenth-Century Italy.* Princeton, N.J.: Princeton University Press, 1995.

The Seventeenth Century

Acton, Harold M. *The Last Medici.* Rev. ed. London: Thames and Hudson, 1980.

Astarita, Tommaso. *The Continuity of Feudal Power. The Caracciolo di Brienza in Spanish Naples.* Cambridge: Cambridge University Press, 1992.

———. *Village Justice. Community, Family, and Popular Culture in Early Modern Italy.* Baltimore: Johns Hopkins University Press, 1999.

Burke, Peter. *Venice and Amsterdam: A Study of Seventeenth-Century Elites.* London: Temple Smith, 1994.

———. *Vico.* Oxford: Oxford University Press, 1985.

Calabria, Antonio. *The Finances of the Kingdom of Naples in the Time of Spanish Rule.* Cambridge: Cambridge University Press, 1991.

Cipolla, Carlo M. *Faith, Reason, and the Plague in Seventeenth-Century Tuscany.* Ithaca, N.Y.: Cornell University Press, 1979.

Davis, Robert C. *Shipbuilders of the Venetian Arsenal: Workers and Workplace in the Preindustrial City.* Baltimore: Johns Hopkins University Press, 1991.

Sella, Domenico. *Crisis and Continuity: The Economy of Spanish Lombardy in the Seventeenth Century.* Cambridge, Mass.: Harvard University Press, 1979.

Villari, Rosario. *The Revolt of Naples.* Cambridge: Polity Press, 1993.

The Enlightenment (1685–1789)

Acton, Harold M. *The Bourbons of Naples: 1734–1825.* London: Methuen, 1956.

Childs, J. Rives. *Casanova: A New Perspective.* New York: Paragon House, 1988.

Cochrane, Eric W. *Tradition and Enlightenment in the Tuscan Academies, 1690–1800.* Chicago: University of Chicago Press, 1961.

Dooley, Brendan M. *Science, Politics, and Society in Eighteenth-Century Italy: The Giornale de' letterati d'Italia and Its World.* New York: Garland, 1991.

Ferrone, Vincenzo. *The Intellectual Roots of the Italian Enlightenment: Newtonian Science, Religion, and Politics in the Early Eighteenth Century.* Atlantic Highlands, N.J.: Humanities Press, 1995.

Gross, Hanns. *Rome in the Age of Enlightenment.* Cambridge: Cambridge University Press, 1990.

Imbruglia, Girolamo, ed. *Naples in the Eighteenth Century: The Birth and Death of a Nation State.* Cambridge: Cambridge University Press, 2000.

Italian Institute, London. *Art and Ideas in 18th-Century Italy.* Rome: Edizioni di Storia e Letteratura, 1960.

Johns, Christopher M. S. *Papal Art and Cultural Politics: Rome in the Age of Clement XI.* Cambridge: Cambridge University Press, 1993.

Levy, Miriam J. *Governance and Grievance: Habsburg Policy and Tyrol in the Eighteenth Century.* West Lafayette, Ind.: Purdue University Press, 1988.

McCalman, Iain. *The Last Alchemist: Count Cagliostro, Master of Magic in the Age of Reason.* New York: HarperCollins, 2003.

Steegmuller, Francis. *A Woman, a Man, and Two Kingdoms: The Story of Madame D'Epinay and the Abbé Galiani.* New York: Knopf, 1991.

Symcox, Geoffrey. *Victor Amadeus II: Absolutism in the Savoyard State, 1675–1730.* Berkeley: University of California Press, 1983.

Venturi, Franco. *Italy and the Enlightenment: Studies in a Cosmopolitan Century.* London: Longman, 1972.

The French Revolution and Napoleon (1789–1815)

Broers, Michael. *Politics and Religion in Napoleonic Italy: The War against God.* Cambridge: Cambridge University Press, 2001.

Connelly, Owen. *The Gentle Bonaparte: A Biography of Joseph Bonaparte, Napoleon's Elder Brother.* New York: Macmillan, 1968.

Ferrero, Guglielmo. *The Gamble: Bonaparte in Italy, 1796–1797.* New York: Walker, 1961.

Finley, Milton. *The Most Monstrous of Wars: The Napoleonic Guerrilla War in Southern Italy, 1806–1811.* Columbia: University of South Carolina Press, 1994.

Gregory, Desmond. *Napoleon's Italy.* Madison, N.J.: Fairleigh Dickinson University Press, 2001.

Heriot, Angus. *The French in Italy, 1796–1799.* London: Chatto and Windus, 1957.

Rath, John R. *The Fall of the Napoleonic Kingdom of Italy.* New York: Columbia University Press, 1941.

Rosselli, John. *Lord William Bentinck and the British Occupation of Sicily, 1811–1814.* Cambridge: Cambridge University Press, 1956.

Schneid, Frederick C. *Napoleon's Italian Campaigns, 1805–1815.* Westport, Conn.: Praeger, 2002.

———. *Napoleon's Kingdom of Italy: Army, State, and Society, 1800–1815.* Boulder, Colo.: Westview Press, 1995.

The Restoration (1815–1848)

Acton, Harold M. *The Last Bourbons of Naples, 1825–1861.* London: Methuen, 1961.

Brady, Joseph H. *Rome and the Neapolitan Revolution of 1821: A Study in Papal Neutrality.* New York: Columbia University Press, 1937.

Ellis, John Tracy. *Cardinal Consalvi and Anglo-Papal Relations, 1814–1824.* Washington, D.C.: Catholic University Press of America, 1942.

Laven, David. *Venice and Venetia under the Habsburgs, 1815–1835.* Oxford: Oxford University Press, 2002

Rath, R. John. *The Provisional Austrian Regime in Lombardy-Venetia, 1814–1815.* Austin: University of Texas Press, 1969.

Reinerman, Alan J. *Austria and the Papacy in the Age of Metternich.* Vol. 1, *Between Conflict and Cooperation.* Washington, D.C.: Catholic University Press of America, 1979.

———. *Austria and the Papacy in the Age of Metternich.* Vol. 2, *Revolution and Reaction, 1830–1838.* Washington, D.C.: Catholic University Press of America, 1989.

Robinson, John M. *Cardinal Consalvi, 1757–1824.* New York: St. Martin's Press, 1987.

Wicks, Margaret C. W. *The Italian Exiles in London 1816–1848.* Manchester: Manchester University Press, 1937.

The Risorgimento to 1861

Beales, Derek. *The Risorgimento and the Unification of Italy.* London: Allen and Unwin, 1971.

Coppa, Frank J. *Camillo di Cavour.* New York: Twayne, 1973.

Davis, John A., and Paul Ginsborg, eds. *Society and Politics in the Age of the Risorgimento.* Cambridge: Cambridge University Press, 1991.

Ginsborg, Paul. *Daniele Manin and the Venetian Revolution of 1848–49.* Cambridge: Cambridge University Press, 1979.

Greenfield, Kent Roberts. *Economics and Liberalism in the Risorgimento: A Study of Nationalism in Lombardy, 1814–1848.* Rev. ed. Baltimore: Johns Hopkins University Press, 1965.

Grew, Raymond A. *A Sterner Plan for Italian Unity: The Italian National Society in the Risorgimento.* Princeton, N.J.: Princeton University Press, 1963.

Hearder, Harry. *Cavour.* London: Longman, 1994.

Hibbert, Christopher. *Garibaldi and His Enemies.* Boston: Little, Brown, 1965.

Hughes, Steven C. *Crime, Disorder and the Risorgimento: The Politics of Policing in Bologna.* Cambridge: Cambridge University Press, 1994.

Jenks, William A. *Francis Joseph and the Italians, 1849–1859.* Charlottesville: University of Virginia Press, 1978.

LoRomer, David G. *Merchants and Reform in Livorno, 1814–1868.* Berkeley: University of California Press, 1987.

Lovett, Clara M. *Carlo Cattaneo and the Politics of the Risorgimento, 1820–1860.* The Hague: Martin Nijhoff, 1972.

———. *The Democratic Movement in Italy, 1830–1876.* Cambridge, Mass.: Harvard University Press, 1982.

———. *Giuseppe Ferrari and the Italian Revolution.* Chapel Hill: University of North Carolina Press, 1979.

Mack Smith, Denis. *Cavour.* New York: Knopf, 1985.

———. *Cavour and Garibaldi, 1860: A Study in Political Conflict.* Cambridge: Cambridge University Press, 1954.

———. *Garibaldi: A Great Life in Brief.* New York: Knopf, 1956.

———. *Mazzini.* New Haven, Conn.: Yale University Press, 1994.

———. *Victor Emanuel, Cavour, and the Risorgimento.* New York: Oxford University Press, 1972.

Marshall, Ronald. *Massimo d'Azeglio: An Artist in Politics, 1798–1866*. London: Oxford University Press, 1966.

Megaro, Gaudens. *Vittorio Alfieri: Forerunner of Italian Nationalism*. New York: Columbia University Press, 1930.

Noether, Emiliana P. *Seeds of Italian Nationalism, 1700–1815*. New York: Columbia University Press, 1951.

Riall, Lucy. *Sicily and the Unification of Italy: Liberal Policy and Local Power*. Oxford: Clarendon Press, 1998.

Ridley, Jasper. *Garibaldi*. London: Constable, 1974.

Romani, George T. *The Neapolitan Revolution of 1820–1821*. Evanston, Ill.: Northwestern University Press, 1950.

Sarti, Roland. *Mazzini: A Life for the Religion of Politics*. Westport, Conn.: Praeger, 1997.

Trevelyan, George M. *Garibaldi's Defense of the Roman Republic, 1848–49*. London: Longmans, Green, 1907.

———. *Garibaldi and the Thousand*. London: Longmans, Green, 1909.

———. *Garibaldi and the Making of Italy: June–November 1860*. London: Longmans, Green, 1911.

Whyte, Arthur J. *The Early Life and Letters of Cavour, 1810–1848*. London: Oxford University Press, 1925.

———. *The Political Life and Letters of Cavour, 1848–1861*. London: Oxford University Press, 1930.

Woolf, S. J., ed. *The Italian Risorgimento*. New York: Barnes and Noble, 1969.

Consolidation of National Unity (1861–1901)

Cardoza, Anthony L. *Aristocrats in Bourgeois Italy: The Piedmontese Nobility, 1861–1930*. Cambridge: Cambridge University Press, 1997.

Croce, Benedetto. *A History of Italy, 1871–1915*. Oxford: Clarendon Press, 1929.

Drake, Richard. *Byzantium for Rome: The Politics of Nostalgia in Umbertian Italy, 1878–1900*. Chapel Hill: University of North Carolina Press, 1980.

Duggan, Christopher. *Francesco Crispi, 1818–1901: From Nation to Nationalism*. Oxford: Oxford University Press, 2002.

Gooch, John. *Army, State, and Society in Italy, 1870–1915*. London: St. Martin's Press, 1989.

Haywood, Geoffrey A. *Failure of a Dream: Sidney Sonnino and the Rise and Fall of Liberal Italy, 1847–1922*. Florence: Olschki, 1999.

Jacobitti, Edmund E. *Revolutionary Humanism and Historicism in Modern Italy*. New Haven, Conn.: Yale University Press, 1981.

Jensen, Richard Bach. *Liberty and Order: The Theory and Practice of Italian Public Security Policy, 1848 to the Crisis of the 1890s*. New York: Garland Publishers, 1991.

Morris, Jonathan. *The Political Economy of Shopkeeping in Milan, 1885–1922*. Cambridge: Cambridge University Press, 1993.

Patriarca, Silvana. *Numbers and Nationhood: Writing Statistics in Nineteenth-Century Italy*. Cambridge: Cambridge University Press, 1996.

Roberts, David D. *Benedetto Croce and the Uses of Historicism*. Berkeley: University of California Press, 1987.

Snowden, Frank M. *Naples in the Time of Cholera, 1884–1911*. Cambridge: Cambridge University Press, 1995.

Thayer, John A. *Italy and the Great War: Politics and Culture, 1870–1915*. Madison: University of Wisconsin Press, 1964.

The Giolittian Period (1901–1914)

Coppa, Frank J. *Planning, Protectionism, and Politics in Liberal Italy: Economics and Politics in the Giolittian Age*. Washington, D.C.: Catholic University Press of America, 1971.

De Grand, Alexander J. *The Hunchback's Tailor: Giovanni Giolitti and Liberal Italy from the Challenge of Mass Politics to the Rise of Fascism, 1882–1922*. Westport, Conn.: Praeger, 2001.

Salomone, A. William. *Italy in the Giolittian Era: Italian Democracy in the Making, 1900–1914*. 2d ed. Philadelphia: University of Pennsylvania Press, 1960.

War and the Postwar Crisis (1914–1922)

Burgwyn, H. James. *The Legend of the Mutilated Victory: Italy, the Great War, and the Paris Peace Conference, 1915–1919*. Westport, Conn.: Greenwood Press, 1993.

Cardoza, Anthony L. *Agrarian Elites and Italian Fascism: The Province of Bologna, 1901–1926*. Princeton, N.J.: Princeton University Press, 1982.

Corner, Paul. *Fascism in Ferrara, 1915–1925*. Oxford: Oxford University Press, 1975.

Falls, Cyril. *Caporetto, 1917*. London: Weidenfeld and Nicolson, 1966.

Jones, Simon Mark. *Domestic Factors in Italian Intervention in the First World War*. New York: Garland, 1986.

Kelikian, Alice A. *Town and Country under Fascism: The Transformation of Brescia, 1915–1926*. Oxford: Clarendon Press, 1986.

Ledeen, Michael A. *The First Duce: D'Annunzio at Fiume*. Baltimore: Johns Hopkins University Press, 1977.

Morselli, Mario. *Caporetto, 1917: Victory or Defeat?* London: Frank Cass, 2002.

Renzi, William A. *In the Shadow of the Sword: Italy's Neutrality and Entrance into the Great War, 1914–1915*. New York: Lang, 1987.

Schindler, John R. *Isonzo: The Forgotten Sacrifice of the Great War*. Westport, Conn.: Praeger, 2001.

Snowden, Frank M. *The Fascist Revolution in Tuscany, 1919–1922*. New York: Cambridge University Press, 1989.

Spriano, Paolo. *The Occupation of the Factories: Italy, 1920*. London: Pluto Press, 1975.

Fascism (1922–1943)

Adler, Franklin H. *Italian Industrialists from Liberalism to Fascism. The Political Development of the Industrial Bourgeoisie, 1906–1934*. Cambridge: Cambridge University Press, 1995.

Ben-Ghiat, Ruth. *Fascist Modernities: Italy, 1922–1945*. Berkeley: University of California Press, 2001.

Berezin, Mabel. *Making the Fascist Self: Political Culture of Interwar Italy*. Ithaca, N.Y.: Cornell University Press, 1997.

Cannistraro, Philip V., and Brian R. Sullivan. *Il Duce's Other Woman*. New York: William Morrow, 1993.

Chabod, Federico. *History of Italian Fascism*. London: Weidenfeld and Nicolson, 1963.

De Grand, Alexander J. *Italian Fascism: Its Origins and Development*. Lincoln: University of Nebraska Press, 1982.

De Grazia, Victoria. *The Culture of Consent: Mass Organization of Leisure in Fascist Italy*. Cambridge: Cambridge University Press, 1981.

Duggan, Christopher. *Fascism and the Mafia*. New Haven, Conn.: Yale University Press, 1989.

Falasca-Zamponi, Simonetta. *Fascist Spectacle: The Aesthetics of Power in Mussolini's Italy*. Berkeley: University of California Press, 1997.

Forgacs, David, ed. *Rethinking Italian Fascism: Capitalism, Populism and Culture*. London: Lawrence and Wishart, 1986.

Fornari, Harry. *Mussolini's Gadfly: Roberto Farinacci*. Nashville, Tenn.: Vanderbilt University Press, 1971.

Gaudens, Megaro. *Mussolini in the Making*. Boston: Houghton, 1938.

Gentile, Emilio. *The Sacralization of Politics in Fascist Italy*. Cambridge, Mass.: Harvard University Press, 1996.

Germino, Dante. *The Italian Fascist Party in Power: A Study in Totalitarian Rule*. Minneapolis: University of Minnesota Press, 1959.

Hay, James. *Popular Film Culture in Fascist Italy: The Passing of the Rex*. Bloomington: Indiana University Press, 1987.

Kirkpatrick, Ivone. *Mussolini: A Study in Power*. New York: Hawthorn, 1964.

Koon, Tracy H. *Believe, Obey, Fight: Political Socialization of Youth in Fascist Italy, 1922–1943*. Chapel Hill: University of North Carolina Press, 1985.

Lyttelton, Adrian. *The Seizure of Power: Fascism in Italy, 1919–1929*. 2d ed. Princeton, N.J.: Princeton University Press, 1987.

Mack Smith, Denis. *Mussolini*. New York: Knopf, 1982.

Morgan, Philip. *Italian Fascism, 1919–1945*. New York: St. Martin's Press, 1995.

Moseley, Ray. *Mussolini's Shadow: The Double Life of Count Galeazzo Ciano*. New Haven, Conn.: Yale University Press, 1999.

Pinkus, Karen. *Bodily Regimes: Italian Advertising under Fascism*. Minneapolis: University of Minnesota Press, 1995.

Pollard, John F. *The Fascist Experience in Italy*. London: Routledge, 1998.

Roberts, David D. *The Syndicalist Tradition and Italian Fascism*. Chapel Hill: University of North Carolina Press, 1979.

Sarti, Roland, ed. *The Ax Within: Italian Fascism in Action*. New York: New Viewpoints, 1974.

———. *Fascism and the Industrial Leadership in Italy, 1919–1940.* Berkeley: University of California Press, 1971.

Schmitz, David F. *The United States and Fascist Italy, 1922–1940.* Chapel Hill: University of North Carolina Press, 1988.

Segrè, Claudio G. *Italo Balbo: A Fascist Life.* Berkeley: University of California Press, 1987.

Stone, Marla Susan. *The Patron State: Culture and Politics in Fascist Italy.* Princeton, N.J.: Princeton University Press, 1998.

Tannenbaum, Edward R. *The Fascist Experience: Italian Society and Culture, 1922–1945.* New York: Basic Books, 1972.

Thompson, Doug. *State Control in Fascist Italy: Culture and Conformity, 1925–1943.* Manchester: Manchester University Press, 1991.

Tinghino, John. *Edmondo Rossoni from Revolutionary Syndicalist to Fascism.* New York: Peter Lang, 1990.

World War II, Fall of the Fascist Regime, and Armed Resistance (1940–1945)

Absalom, Roger. *A Strange Alliance: Aspects of Escape and Survival in Italy, 1943–1945.* Florence: Olschki, 1991.

Brooks, Thomas R. *The War North of Rome: June 1944–May 1945.* New York: Sarpedon, 1996.

Cervi, Mario. *The Hollow Legions: Mussolini's Blunder in Greece, 1940–1941.* Garden City, N.Y.: Doubleday, 1971.

Davis, Melton S. *Who Defends Rome? The Forty-Five Days, July 25–September 8, 1943.* New York: Dial Press, 1972.

Deakin, F. W. *The Brutal Friendship: Mussolini, Hitler and the Fall of Italian Fascism.* New York: Harper and Row, 1962.

Domenico, Roy P. *Italian Fascists on Trial, 1943–1948.* Chapel Hill: University of North Carolina Press, 1991.

Ellwood, David W. *Italy 1943–1945.* New York: Holmes and Meier, 1985.

Graham, Dominick, and Shelford Bidwell. *Tug of War: The Battle for Italy, 1943–45.* New York: St. Martin's Press, 1986.

Harris, C. R. S. *Allied Military Administration of Italy, 1943–1945.* London: HMSO, 1957.

Knox, MacGregor. *Hitler's Italian Allies: Royal Armed Forces, Fascist Regime, and the War, 1940–1943.* Cambridge: Cambridge University Press, 2000.

———. *Mussolini Unleashed, 1939–1941: Politics and Strategy in Fascist Italy's Last War.* Cambridge: Cambridge University Press, 1982.

Miller, James A. *The United States and Italy, 1940–1950: The Politics of Diplomacy and Stabilization.* Chapel Hill: University of North Carolina Press, 1986.

Orgill, Douglas. *The Gothic Line: The Italian Campaign, August 1944.* New York: Norton, 1967.

Raspin, Angela. *The Italian War Economy, 1940–1943.* New York: Garland, 1986.

Smyth, Howard McGaw. *Secrets of the Fascist Era: How Uncle Sam Obtained Some of the Top-Level Documents of Mussolini's Period.* Carbondale: Southern Illinois University Press, 1975.

Steinberg, Jonathan. *All or Nothing: The Axis and the Holocaust 1941–1943.* London: Routledge, 1990.

Strawson, John. *The Italian Campaign.* London: Secker and Warburg, 1987.

Political Culture since 1945

Bosworth, Richard J. B., and Patrizia Dogliani, eds. *Italian Fascism: History, Memory and Representation.* New York: St. Martin Press, 1999.

Bull, Anna Cento. *Social Identities and Political Cultures in Italy: Catholic, Communist and 'Leghist' Communities between Civicness and Localism.* Oxford: Berghahn Books, 2001.

Burnett, Stanton, and Luca Mantovani. *The Italian Guillotine: Operation Clean Hands and the Overthrow of Italy's First Republic.* Lanham, Md.: Rowman and Littlefield, 1998.

Duggan, Christopher, and Christopher Wagstaff, eds. *Italy in the Cold War: Politics, Culture, and Society, 1948–1958.* Oxford: Berg Publishers, 1995.

Ferraresi, Franco. *Threats to Democracy: The Radical Right in Italy after the War.* Princeton, N.J.: Princeton University Press, 1996.

Gilbert, Mark. *The Italian Revolution: The End of Politics, Italian Style?* Boulder, Colo.: Westview Press, 1995.

Ginsborg, Paul. *A History of Contemporary Italy: Society and Politics, 1943–1988.* London: Penguin, 1990.

Gundle, Stephen. *Between Hollywood and Moscow: The Italian Communists and the Challenge of Mass Culture, 1943–1991.* Durham, N.C.: Duke University Press, 2000.

———, and Simon Parker, eds. *The New Italian Republic: From the Fall of the Berlin Wall to Berlusconi.* London: Routledge, 1996.

Harper, John L. *America and the Reconstruction of Italy, 1945–1948*. Cambridge: Cambridge University Press, 1986.

Kertzer, David I. *Politics and Symbols: The Italian Communist Party and the Fall of Communism*. New Haven, Conn.: Yale University Press, 1996.

Koff, Sondra Z., and Stephen P. Koff. *Italy: From the First to the Second Republic*. London: Routledge, 2000.

Lumley, Robert. *States of Emergency: Cultures of Revolt in Italy, 1968 to 1978*. London: Verso, 1990.

Moss, David. *The Politics of Left-Wing Violence in Italy, 1969–1985*. New York: St. Martin's Press, 1989.

Passerini, Luisa. *Fascism in Popular Memory: The Cultural Experience of the Turin Working Class*. Cambridge: Cambridge University Press, 1987.

Putnam, Robert. *Making Democracy Work: Civic Traditions in Modern Italy*. Princeton, N.J.: Princeton University Press, 1993.

Sabetti, Filippo. *The Search for Good Government: Understanding the Paradox of Italian Democracy*. Montreal: McGill-Queen's University Press, 2000.

Sassoon, Donald. *Contemporary Italy: Politics, Economics, and Society since 1945*. 2d ed. New York: Longman, 1997.

———. *The Strategy of the Italian Communist Party: From the Resistance to the Historic Compromise*. New York: St. Martin's Press, 1981.

Sniderman, P. M., et al. *The Outsider: Prejudice and Politics in Italy*. Princeton, N.J.: Princeton University Press, 2001.

Stille, Alexander. *Excellent Cadavers: The Mafia and the Death of the First Italian Republic*. New York: Pantheon Books, 1995.

Urban, Joan Barth. *Moscow and the Italian Communist Party: From Togliatti to Berlinguer*. Ithaca, N.Y.: Cornell University Press, 1986.

TOPICS

Antifascism

Battaglia, Roberto. *The Story of the Italian Resistance*. London: Odhams Press, 1957.

Delzell, Charles F. *Mussolini's Enemies: The Italian Anti-Fascist Resistance*. Princeton, N.J.: Princeton University Press, 1961.

Killinger, Charles. *Gaetano Salvemini: A Biography*. Westport, Conn.: Praeger, 2002.

Pugliese, Stanislao. *Carlo Rosselli: Socialist, Heretic and Anti-Fascist Exile*. Cambridge, Mass.: Harvard University Press, 1999.

Rosengarten, Frank. *The Italian Anti-Fascist Press, 1919–1945*. Cleveland: Case Western Reserve University Press, 1968.

Antiliberalism and Nationalism

Adamson, Walter L. *Avant-Garde Florence: From Modernism to Fascism*. Cambridge, Mass.: Harvard University Press, 1993.

Bellamy, Richard. *Modern Italian Social Theory: Ideology and Politics from Pareto to the Present*. Oxford: Polity Press, 1987.

Berghaus, Günter. *Futurism and Politics: Between Anarchist Rebellion and Fascist Reaction, 1909–1944*. Providence, R.I.: Berghahn Books, 1996.

Bonadeo, Alfredo. *D'Annunzio and the Great War*. Madison-Teaneck, N.J.: Fairleigh Dickinson University Press, 1995.

Cunsolo, Ronald S. *Italian Nationalism: From Its Origins to World War II*. Malabar, Fla.: Krieger, 1990.

De Grand, Alexander J. *The Italian Nationalist Association and the Rise of Fascism in Italy*. Lincoln: University of Nebraska Press, 1978.

Finocchiaro, Maurice A. *Beyond Right and Left: Democratic Elitism in Mosca and Gramsci*. New Haven, Conn.: Yale University Press, 1999.

Gregor, A. James. *Young Mussolini and the Intellectual Origins of Fascism*. Berkeley: University of California Press, 1979.

Hamilton, Alastair. *The Appeal of Fascism: A Study of Intellectuals and Fascism, 1919–1945*. New York: Avon, 1971.

Harris, Henry S. *The Social Philosophy of Giovanni Gentile*. Urbana: University of Illinois Press, 1960.

Hughes, H. Stuart. *Consciousness and Society: The Reorientation of European Thought, 1890–1930*. Rev. ed. New York: Vintage Books, 1977.

Lyttleton, Adrian, ed. *Italian Fascisms from Pareto to Gentile*. New York: Harper Torchbooks, 1975.

Meisel, James H. *The Myth of the Ruling Class: Gaetano Mosca and the "Elite."* Ann Arbor: University of Michigan Press, 1958.

Nye, Robert A. *The Anti-Democratic Sources of Elite Theory: Pareto, Mosca, Michels*. London: SAGE, 1977.

Patrucco, Armand. *The Critics of the Italian Parliamentary System, 1860–1915*. New York: Garland, 1992.

Pick, Daniel. *Faces of Degeneration: A European Disorder, c. 1848–c. 1918*. Cambridge: Cambridge University Press, 1989.

Roth, Jack J. *The Cult of Violence: Sorel and the Sorelians*. Berkeley: University of California Press, 1980.

Sternhell, Zeev. *The Birth of Fascist Ideology: From Cultural Rebellion to Political Revolution*. Princeton, N.J.: Princeton University Press, 1994.

Wohl, Robert. *The Generation of 1914*. Cambridge, Mass.: Harvard University Press, 1979.

Woodhouse, John. *Gabriele d'Annunzio: Defiant Archangel*. Oxford: Clarendon Press, 1998.

Art and Architecture

Alloway, Lawrence. *The Venice Biennale, 1895–1968*. Greenwich, Conn.: New York Graphic Society, 1968.

Boime, Albert. *The Art of the Macchia and the Risorgimento: Representing Culture and Nationalism in Nineteenth-Century Italy*. Chicago: University of Chicago Press, 1993.

Braun, Emily. *Mario Sironi and Italian Modernism: Art and Politics under Fascism*. Cambridge: Cambridge University Press, 2000.

Broude, Norma. *The Macchiaioli. Italian Painters of the Nineteenth Century*. New Haven, Conn.: Yale University Press, 1987.

Carver, Norman F. *Italian Hill Towns*. Kalamazoo, Mich.: Documan Press, 1980.

Chastel, André. *Italian Art: Architecture, Painting and Sculpture from the Early Christian Period to the Present Day*. New York: Harper and Row, 1963.

Doordan, Dennis P. *Building Modern Italy: Italian Architecture, 1914–1936*. New York: Princeton Architectural Press, 1988.

Hartt, Frederick. *History of Italian Renaissance Art*. 3d ed. New York: Abrams, 1987.

Haskell, Francis. *Patrons and Painters: A Study in the Relations between Italian Art and Society in the Age of the Baroque*. New Haven, Conn.: Yale University Press, 1980.

Hulten, Pontus, and Germano Celant, eds. *Italian Art, 1900–1945*. New York: Rizzoli, 1989.

Humphreys, Richard. *Futurism*. Cambridge: Cambridge University Press, 1999.

Meeks, Carroll L. V. *Italian Architecture, 1750–1914*. New Haven, Conn.: Yale University Press, 1966.

Olson, Roberta J. M., ed. *Ottocento: Romanticism and Revolution in 19th-Century Italian Painting*. New York: American Federation of Arts, 1992.

Ostrow, Steven. *Art and Spirituality in Counter-Reformation Rome: The Sistine and Pauline Chapels in S. Maria Maggiore*. Cambridge: Cambridge University Press, 1996.

Varriano, John L. *Italian Baroque and Rococo Architecture*. New York: Oxford University Press, 1986.

Wittkower, Rudolf. *Art and Architecture in Italy, 1600–1750*. New York: Penguin Books, 1980.

Yarwood, Doreen. *The Architecture of Italy*. New York: Harper and Row, 1969.

Church and State, Papacy, Catholicism

Binchy, Daniel A. *Church and State in Fascist Italy*. London: Oxford University Press, 1941.

Carrillo, Elisa. *De Gasperi: The Long Apprenticeship*. Notre Dame, Ind.: University of Notre Dame Press, 1965.

Carroll, Michael P. *Madonnas That Maim: Popular Catholicism in Italy since the Fifteenth Century*. Baltimore: Johns Hopkins University Press, 1992.

———. *Veiled Threats: The Logic of Popular Catholicism in Italy*. Baltimore: Johns Hopkins University Press, 1996.

Coppa, Frank J. *Cardinal Giacomo Antonelli and Papal Politics in European Affairs*. Albany: SUNY Press, 1990.

———. *The Modern Papacy since 1789*. New York: Longman, 1998.

———. *Pope Pius IX: Crusader in a Secular Age*. Boston: Twayne, 1979.

Hales, E. E. Y. *Pio Nono: Creator of the Modern Papacy*. New York: P. J. Kenedy, 1954.

———. *Revolution and Papacy, 1769–1846*. Notre Dame, Ind.: University of Notre Dame Press, 1966.

Halperin, William S. *Italy and the Vatican at War: A Study of Their Relations from the Outbreak of the Franco-Prussian War to the Death of Pius IX*. Chicago: University of Chicago Press, 1939.

———. *The Separation of Church and State in Italian Thought from Cavour to Mussolini*. Chicago: University of Chicago Press, 1937.

Jemolo, Arturo Carlo. *Church and State in Italy, 1850–1960*. Oxford: Basil Blackwell, 1960.

Kent, Peter C. *The Pope and the Duce: The International Impact of the Lateran Agreements.* New York: St. Martin's Press, 1981.

Kertzer, David I. *Comrades and Christians: Religion and Political Struggle in Communist Italy.* New York: Cambridge University Press, 1980.

———. *The Kidnappping of Edgardo Mortara.* New York: Knopf, 1997.

———. *The Popes against the Jews: The Vatican's Role in the Rise of Modern Anti-Semitism.* New York: Knopf, 2001.

Moloney, John N. *The Emergence of Political Catholicism in Italy: Partito Popolare 1919–1926.* London: Croom Helm, 1977.

Poggi, Gianfranco. *Catholic Action in Italy: The Sociology of a Sponsored Organization.* Stanford, Calif.: Stanford University Press, 1967.

Pollard, John F. *The Vatican and Fascism, 1919–1932: A Study in Conflict.* Cambridge: Cambridge University Press, 1985.

Webster, Richard A. *Christian Democracy in Italy: 1860–1960.* London: Hollis and Carter, 1961.

———. *The Cross and the Fasces: Christian Democracy and Fascism in Italy.* Stanford, Calif.: Stanford University Press, 1960.

Zuccotti, Susan. *Under His Very Windows: The Vatican and the Holocaust in Italy.* New Haven, Conn.: Yale University Press, 2000.

Cities

Bolton, Glorney. *Roman Century: A Portrait of Rome as the Capital of Italy, 1870–1970.* New York: Viking Press, 1970.

Bondanella, Peter. *The Eternal City: Roman Images in the Modern World.* Chapel Hill: University of North Carolina Press, 1987.

Brucker, Gene A. *Florence: The Golden Age, 1138–1737.* New York: Abbeville Press, 1983.

Cochrane, Eric W. *Florence in the Forgotten Centuries, 1527–1800.* Chicago: University of Chicago Press, 1973.

Dandelet, Thomas James. *Spanish Rome, 1500–1700.* New Haven, Conn.: Yale University Press, 2001.

Fried, Robert C. *Planning the Eternal City: Roma Politics and Planning since World War II.* New Haven, Conn.: Yale University Press, 1973.

Hibbert, Christopher. *Florence: The Biography of a City.* New York: Norton, 1993.

Logan, Oliver. *Culture and Society in Venice, 1470–1790: The Renaissance and Its Heritage.* New York: Charles Scribner's Sons, 1972.

Plant, Margaret. *Venice: Fragile City, 1797–1997.* New Haven, Conn.: Yale University Press, 2003.

Pollack, Martha D. *Turin, 1564–1680: Urban Design, Military Culture, and the Creation of the Absolutist Capital.* Chicago: University of Chicago Press, 1991.

Tobriner, Stephen. *The Genesis of Noto: An Eighteenth-Century Sicilian City.* Berkeley: University of California Press, 1980.

Zorzi, Alvise. *Venice, the Golden Age, 1697–1797.* New York: Abbeville Press, 1983.

Colonialism

Askew, William C. *Europe and Italy's Acquisition of Libya, 1911–1912.* Durham, N.C.: Duke University Press, 1942.

Barker, A. J. *The Civilizing Mission: A History of the Italo-Ethiopian War.* Cambridge, Mass.: Harvard University Press, 1978.

Del Boca, Angelo. *The Ethiopian War, 1935–1941.* Chicago: University of Chicago Press, 1965.

Hess, Robert L. *Italian Colonialism in Somalia.* Chicago: University of Chicago Press, 1966.

Larebo, Haile. *The Building of an Empire: Italian Land Policy and Practice in Ethiopia, 1935–1941.* New York: Oxford University Press, 1994.

Mack Smith, Denis. *Mussolini's Roman Empire.* New York: Viking, 1976.

Robertson, Esmonde M. *Mussolini as Empire Builder: Europe and Africa, 1932–1936.* New York: St. Martin's Press, 1977.

Sbacchi, Alberto. *Legacy of Bitterness: Ethiopia and Fascist Italy, 1935–1941.* Lawrenceville, N.J.: Red Sea Press, 1997.

Schaefer, Ludwig F., ed. *The Ethiopian Crisis: Touchstone of Appeasement?* Boston: D.C. Heath, 1961.

Segrè, Claudio G. *Fourth Shore: The Italian Colonization of Libya.* Chicago: University of Chicago Press, 1974.

Webster, Richard A. *Industrial Imperialism in Italy, 1908–1915.* Berkeley: University of California Press, 1974.

Economy

Allen, Kevin, and Andrew Stevenson. *An Introduction to the Italian Economy.* London: Robertson, 1974.

Clough, Shepard B. *The Economic History of Modern Italy*. New York: Columbia University Press, 1964.

Cohen, Jon, and Giovanni Federico. *The Growth of the Italian Economy, 1820–1960*. Cambridge: Cambridge University Press, 2001.

Forsyth, Douglas J. *The Crisis of Liberal Italy: Monetary and Financial Policy, 1914–1922*. Cambridge: Cambridge University Press, 1993.

King, Russell. *Land Reform: The Italian Experience*. London: Butterworth, 1973.

Schramm, Albert. *Railways and the Formation of the Italian State in the Nineteenth Century*. Cambridge: Cambridge University Press, 1997.

Toniolo, Gianni. *An Economic History of Liberal Italy, 1850–1918*. London: Routledge, 1990.

Zamagni, Vera. *The Economic History of Italy, 1860–1990*. Oxford: Clarendon Press, 1993.

Education, Public Administration, and Social Services

Barbagli, Marzio. *Educating for Unemployment: Politics, Labor Markets and the School System, 1859–1973*. New York: Columbia University Press, 1982.

Cappelletti, Mauro. *The Italian Legal System: An Introduction*. Stanford, Calif.: Stanford University Press, 1967.

Cavallo, Sandra. *Charity and Power in Early Modern Italy: Benefactors and Their Motives in Turin, 1541–1789*. Cambridge: Cambridge University Press, 1995.

Davis, John A. *Conflict and Control: Law and Order in Nineteenth-Century Italy*. Atlantic Highlands, N.J.: Humanities Press, 1988.

Fried, Robert C. *The Italian Prefects: A Study in Administrative Politics*. New Haven, Conn.: Yale University Press, 1963.

Gibson, Mary. *Prostitution and the State in Italy, 1860–1915*. New Brunswick, N.J.: Rutgers University Press, 1986.

Grendler, Paul F. *Schooling in Renaissance Italy: Literacy and Learning, 1300–1600*. Baltimore: Johns Hopkins University Press, 1989.

Malatesta, Maria. *Society and the Professions in Italy, 1860–1914*. Cambridge: Cambridge University Press, 1995.

Quine, Maria Sophia. *Italy's Social Revolution: Charity and Welfare from Liberalism to Fascism*. New York: Palgrave, 2002.

Sievert, James. *The Origins of Nature Conservation in Italy*. New York: Peter Lang, 2000.

Emigration

Baily, Samuel L. *Immigrants in the Lands of Promise: Italians in Buenos Aires and New York City, 1870–1914*. Ithaca, N.Y.: Cornell University Press, 1999.

Bianco, Carla. *The Two Rosetos*. Bloomington: Indiana University Press, 1974.

Boyd-Caroli, Betty. *Italian Repatriation from the United States, 1900–1914*. New York: Center for Migration Studies, 1973.

Briggs, John. *An Italian Passage: Immigrants to Three American Cities*. New Haven, Conn.: Yale University Press, 1978.

Chapman, Charlotte Gower. *Milocca: A Sicilian Village*. Cambridge: Schenkman, 1971.

Cinel, Dino. *From Italy to San Francisco: The Immigrant Experience*. Stanford, Calif.: Stanford University Press, 1982.

———. *The National Integration of Return Migration, 1870–1929*. New York: Cambridge University Press, 1991.

Douglas, William A. *Emigration in a South Italian Town: An Anthropological History*. New Brunswick, N.J.: Rutgers University Press, 1984.

Foerster, Robert F. *The Italian Emigration of Our Time*. Cambridge, Mass.: Harvard University Press, 1919.

Gabaccia, Donna. *Italy's Many Diasporas*. London and Seattle: UCL Press and University of Washington Press, 2000.

Sponza, Lucio. *Italian Immigrants in Nineteenth-Century Britain: Realities and Images*. Leicester: Leicester University Press, 1988.

Ethnic and Religious Minorities

Caracciolo, Nicola. *Uncertain Refuge: Italy and the Jews During the Holocaust*. Urbana: University of Illinois Press, 1995.

Carter, Donald Martin. *States of Grace: Senegalese in Italy and the New European Migration*. Minneapolis: University of Minnesota Press, 1997.

Cole, Jeffrey. *The New Racism in Europe: A Sicilian Ethnography*. Cambridge: Cambridge University Press, 1997.

Cole, John W., and Eric R. Wolf. *The Hidden Frontier: Ecology and Ethnicity in an Alpine Valley*. New York: Academic Press, 1974.

De Felice, Renzo. *The Jews in Fascist Italy: A History.* New York: Enigma Books, 2001.

Dubin, Lois C. *The Port Jews of Habsburg Trieste: Absolutist Politics and Enlightenment Culture.* Stanford, Calif.: Stanford University Press, 1999.

Hsia, R. Po-chia. *Trent 1475: Stories of a Ritual Murder Trial.* New Haven, Conn.: Yale University Press, 1992.

Hughes, H. Stuart. *Prisoners of Hope: The Silver Age of Italian Jews, 1924–1974.* Cambridge, Mass.: Harvard University Press, 1983.

Michaelis, Meir. *Mussolini and the Jews: German-Italian Relations and the Jewish Question in Italy, 1922–1945.* Oxford: Clarendon Press, 1978.

Novak, Bogdan C. *Trieste, 1941–1954: The Ethnic, Political, and Ideological Struggle.* Chicago: University of Chicago Press, 1970.

Roth, Cecil. *The History of the Jews in Italy.* Philadelphia: The Jewish Publication Society of America, 1946.

Rusinow, Dennison I. *Italy's Austrian Heritage, 1919–1946.* Oxford: Clarendon Press, 1969.

Sluga, Glenda. *The Problem of Trieste and the Yugoslav Border: Difference, Identity and Sovereignty in Twentieth-Century Europe.* Albany: SUNY Press, 2001.

Sniderman, Paul M., et al. *The Outsider: Prejudice and Politics in Italy.* Princeton, N.J.: Princeton University Press, 2000.

Stille, Alexander. *Benevolence and Betrayal: Five Italian Jewish Families under Fascism.* New York: Summit Books, 1991.

Zuccotti, Susan. *The Italians and the Holocaust: Persecution, Rescue, and Survival.* New York: Basic Books, 1987.

Family and Reproduction

Geltmaker, Ty. *Tired of Living: Suicide in Italy from National Unification to World War I, 1860–1915.* New York: Peter Lang, 2002.

Horn, David G. *Social Bodies: Science, Reproduction, and Italian Modernity.* Princeton, N.J.: Princeton University Press, 1994.

Ipsen, Carl. *Dictating Demography: The Problem of Population in Fascist Italy.* Cambridge: Cambridge University Press, 1996.

Kertzer, David I. *Family Life in Central Italy, 1880–1910. Sharecropping, Wage Labor and Coresidence.* New Brunswick, N.J.: Rutgers University Press, 1984.

———. *Sacrificed for Honor: Italian Infant Abandonment and the Politics of Reproductive Control.* Boston: Beacon Press, 1993.

———, and Dennis P. Hogan. *Family, Political Economy, and Demographic Change: The Transformation of Life in Casalecchio, Italy, 1861–1921.* Madison: University of Wisconsin Press, 1989.

———. *The Family in Italy from Antiquity to the Present.* Edited by David I. Kertzer and Richard P. Saller. New Haven, Conn.: Yale University Press, 1991.

Livi-Bacci, Massimo. *A History of Italian Fertility during the Last Two Centuries.* Princeton, N.J.: Princeton University Press, 1977.

Pitkin, Donald. *The House That Giacomo Built: History of an Italian Family, 1898–1978.* New York: Cambridge University Press, 1985.

Schneider, Jane C., and Peter T. Schneider. *Festival of the Poor: Fertility Decline and the Ideology of Class in Sicily, 1860–1980.* Tucson: University of Arizona Press, 1996.

Whitaker, Elizabeth Dixon. *Measuring Mamma's Milk: Fascism and the Medicalization of Maternity in Italy.* Ann Arbor: University of Michigan Press, 2000.

Foreign Relations

Albrecht-Carrié, René. *Italy at the Paris Peace Conference.* New York: Columbia University Press, 1938.

Alcock, Antony E. *The History of the South Tyrol Question.* London: Michael Joseph, 1970.

Baer, George W. *The Coming of the Italian-Ethiopian War.* Cambridge, Mass.: Harvard University Press, 1967.

Barros, James. *The Corfù Incident of 1923: Mussolini and the League of Nations.* Princeton, N.J.: Princeton University Press, 1965.

Bosworth, Richard J. B. *Italy and the Approach of the First World War.* London: Macmillan, 1983.

———. *Italy, the Least of the Great Powers: Italian Foreign Policy before the First World War.* London: Cambridge University Press, 1979.

Burgwyn, H. James. *Italian Foreign Policy in the Interwar Period, 1918–1940.* Westport, Conn.: Praeger, 1997.

Bush, John W. *Venetia Redeemed: Franco-Italian Relations, 1864–1866.* Syracuse, N.Y.: Syracuse University Press, 1967.

Caracciolo, Luciano, and Michel Korinman, eds. *Italy and the Balkans*. Washington, D.C.: Center for Strategic and International Studies, 1998.

Cassels, Alan. *Mussolini's Early Diplomacy*. Princeton, N.J.: Princeton University Press, 1970.

Chabod, Federico. *Italian Foreign Policy: The Statecraft of the Founders*. Princeton, N.J.: Princeton University Press, 1996.

Coverdale, John F. *Italian Intervention in the Spanish Civil War*. Princeton, N.J.: Princeton University Press, 1975.

Halperin, S. William. *Diplomat under Stress: Visconti-Venosta and the Crisis of July 1870*. Chicago: University of Chicago Press, 1963.

Harris, Brice. *The United States and the Italo-Ethiopian Crisis*. Stanford, Calif.: Stanford University Press, 1964.

Kallis, Aristotle A. *Fascist Ideology: Territory and Expansionism in Italy and Germany, 1922–1945*. London: Routledge, 2000.

Kogan, Norman. *The Politics of Italian Foreign Policy*. New York: Praeger, 1963.

Ledeen, Michael A. *Universal Fascism: The Theory and Practice of the Fascist International, 1928–1936*. New York: Fertig, 1972.

Lowe, C. J., and Frank Marzari. *Italian Foreign Policy, 1870–1940*. London: Routledge and Kegan Paul, 1971.

Sadkovich, James J. *Italian Support for Croatian Separatism, 1927–1931*. New York: Garland Press, 1987.

Salerno, Reynolds M. *Vital Crossroads: Mediterranean Origins of the Second World War, 1935–1940*. Ithaca, N.Y.: Cornell University Press, 2002.

Toscano, Mario. *The Origins of the Pact of Steel*. Baltimore: Johns Hopkins University Press, 1967.

Villari, Luigi. *Italian Foreign Policy under Mussolini*. New York: Devin-Adair, 1956.

Willis, F. Roy. *Italy Chooses Europe*. New York: Oxford University Press, 1971.

Wiskemann, Elizabeth. *The Rome-Berlin Axis: A History of the Relations between Hitler and Mussolini*. London: Oxford University Press, 1949.

Geography

Bethemont, Jacques, and Jean Pelletier. *Italy: A Geographical Introduction*. London: Longman, 1983.

King, Russell. *The Industrial Geography of Italy*. New York: St. Martin's Press, 1985.

McNeill, J. R. *The Mountains of the Mediterranean World: An Environmental History*. Cambridge: Cambridge University Press, 1992.

Walker, D. S. *A Geography of Italy*. 2d ed. London: Methuen, 1967.

Literature

Brand, Peter, and Lino Pertile, eds. *The Cambridge History of Italian Literature*. Cambridge: Cambridge University Press, 1996.

Caesar, Michael, and Peter Hansworth, eds. *Writers and Society in Contemporary Italy: A Collection of Essays*. Leamington Spa, U.K.: Berg, 1984.

Cairns, Christopher. *Italian Literature: The Dominant Themes*. New York: Barnes and Noble, 1977.

Colquhoun, Archibald. *Manzoni and His Times*. London: Dent, 1954.

Giudice, Gaspare. *Pirandello: A Biography*. London: Oxford University Press, 1975.

Kennard, Joseph. *A Literary History of the Italian People*. New York: Macmillan, 1941.

Radcliff-Umstead, Douglas. *Ugo Foscolo*. New York: Twayne Publishers, 1970.

Whitfield, John Humphreys. *A Short History of Italian Literature*. 2d ed. Manchester, U.K.: Manchester University Press, 1980.

Wilkins, Ernest Hatch. *A History of Italian Literature*. Cambridge, Mass.: Harvard University Press, 1974.

Military

Hanlon, Gregory. *The Twilight of a Military Tradition: Italian Aristocrats and European Conflicts, 1560–1800*. New York: Holmes and Meier, 1998.

Mallett, Robert. *The Italian Navy and Fascist Expansionism, 1935–1940*. London: Frank Cass, 1998.

Sweet, John J. T. *Iron Arm: The Mechanization of Mussolini's Army, 1920–1940*. Westport, Conn.: Greenwood Press, 1980.

Taylor, Frederic Lewis. *The Art of War in Italy, 1494 to 1529*. Cambridge: Cambridge University Press, 1921.

Trease, Geoffrey. *The Condottieri: Soldiers of Fortune*. London: Thames and Hudson, 1970.

Trye, Rex. *Mussolini's Soldiers*. Shrewsbury, U.K.: Airlife Publishing, 1995.

Whittam, John. *The Politics of the Italian Army, 1861–1918*. London: Croon Helm, 1977.

Music

Budden, Julian. *Puccini: His Life and Works.* Oxford: Oxford University Press, 2002.

———. *The Operas of Verdi.* 3 vols. Oxford: Oxford University Press, 1973–1981.

Galatopoulos, Stelios. *Bellini: Life, Times, Music, 1801–1835.* London: Sanctuary Publishing, 2002.

———. *Italian Opera.* London: Dent, 1971.

Heriot, Angus. *The Castrati in Opera.* New York: Da Capo Press, 1974.

Martin, George. *Verdi: His Music, Life, and Times.* London: Macmillan, 1965.

Mallach, Alan. *Pietro Mascagni and His Operas.* Boston: Northeastern University Press, 2002.

Phillips-Matz, Mary Jane. *Puccini: A Biography.* Boston: Northeastern University Press, 2002.

———. *Verdi: A Biography.* Oxford: Oxford University Press, 1993.

Rosselli, John. *Music and Musicians in Nineteenth-Century Italy.* Portland, Ore.: Amadeus Press, 1991.

———. *The Opera Industry in Italy from Cimarosa to Verdi: The Role of the Impresario.* Cambridge: Cambridge University Press, 1984.

———. *Singers of Italian Opera: The History of a Profession.* Cambridge: Cambridge University Press, 1992.

Sachs, Harvey. *Music in Fascist Italy.* New York: Norton, 1988.

Tambling, Jeremy. *Opera and the Culture of Fascism.* Oxford: Clarendon Press, 1996.

Weaver, William. *The Golden Century of Italian Opera.* New York: Thames and Hudson, 1980.

Weinstock, Herbert. *Donizetti and the World of Opera in Italy, Paris, and Vienna in the First Half of the Nineteenth Century.* New York: Pantheon Books, 1963.

———. *Rossini: A Biography.* New York: Alfred A. Knopf, 1968.

Regionalism, the South, and Rural Italy

Arlacchi, Pino. *Mafia Business: The Mafia Ethic and the Spirit of Capitalism.* London: Verso, 1986.

Banfield, Edward C. *The Moral Basis of a Backward Society.* New York: Free Press, 1958.

Bell, Rudolph M. *Fate and Honor, Family and Village: Demographic and Cultural Change in Rural Italy since 1800.* Chicago: University of Chicago Press, 1979.

Blok, Anton. *The Mafia of a Sicilian Village, 1860–1960: A Study of Violent Peasant Entrepreneurs.* New York: Harper Torchbooks, 1973.

Chandler, Billy. *King of the Mountain: The Life and Death of Giuliano the Bandit.* DeKalb: Northern Illinois University Press, 1988.

Croce, Benedetto. *History of the Kingdom of Naples.* Chicago: University of Chicago Press, 1965.

Davis, James C. *Rise from Want: A Peasant Family in the Machine Age.* Philadelphia: University of Pennsylvania Press, 1986.

Davis, John A. *Merchants, Monopolists, and Contractors: A Study of Economic Activity in Bourbon Naples, 1815–1860.* New York: Arno Press, 1981.

Dickie, John. *Darkest Italy: The Nation and Stereotypes of the Mezzogiorno, 1860–1900.* New York: St. Martin's Press, 1999.

Fentress, James. *Rebels and Mafiosi: Death in a Sicilian Landscape.* Ithaca, N.Y.: Cornell University Press, 2000.

Galt, Anthony H. *Far from the Church Bells: Settlement and Society in an Apulian Town.* New York: Cambridge University Press, 1991.

Hess, Henner. *Mafia and Mafiosi: Origin, Power, and Myth.* New York: New York University Press, 1998.

Levy, Carl, ed. *Italian Regionalism: History, Identity, and Politics.* Oxford: Berg, 1996.

Lopreato, Joseph. *Peasants No More: Social Change in an Underdeveloped Society.* San Francisco: Chandler, 1967.

Lumley, Robert, and Jonathan Morris, eds. *The New History of the Italian South: The Mezzogiorno Revisited.* Exeter: University of Exeter Press, 1997.

Mack Smith, Denis. *A History of Sicily.* Vol. 1., *Medieval Sicily, 800–1713.* New York: Viking Press, 1968.

———. *A History of Sicily.* Vol. 2, *Modern Sicily after 1713.* New York: Viking Press, 1968.

McArdle, Frank. *Altopascio: A Study in Tuscan Rural Society, 1587–1784.* New York: Cambridge University Press.

Moe, Nelson. *The View from Vesuvius: Italian Culture and the Southern Question.* Berkeley, Calif.: University of California Press, 2003.

Pantaleone, Michele. *The Mafia and Politics.* New York: Coward-McCann, 1966.

Petrusewicz, Marta. *Latifundium. Moral Economy and Material Life in a European Periphery.* Ann Arbor: University of Michigan Press, 1996.

Pratt, Jeff. *The Rationality of Rural Life: Economic and Cultural Change in Tuscany.* Chur, Switzerland: Harwood Academic Publishers, 1994.

Riall, Lucy. *Sicily and the Unification of Italy: Liberal Policy and Local Power, 1859–1866.* Oxford: Clarendon Press, 1998.

Sabetti, Philip. *Political Authority in a Sicilian Village.* New Brunswick, N.J.: Rutgers University Press, 1984.

Sarti, Roland. *Long Live the Strong: A History of Rural Society in the Apennine Mountains.* Amherst: University of Massachusetts Press, 1985.

Schacter, Gustav. *The Italian South: Economic Development in Mediterranean Europe.* New York: Random House, 1965.

Schneider, Jane, ed. *Italy's Southern Question: Orientalism in One Country.* Oxford: Berg, 1998.

Schneider, Jane, and Peter Schneider. *Cultural and Political Economy in Western Sicily.* New York: Academic Press, 1976.

Sereni, Emilio. *History of the Italian Agricultural Landscape.* Princeton, N.J.: Princeton University Press, 1997.

Silverman, Sydel. *Three Bells of Civilization: The Life of an Italian Hill Town.* New York: Columbia University Press, 1975.

Snowden, Frank M. *Violence and Great Estates in the South of Italy: Apulia, 1900–1922.* New York: Cambridge University Press, 1986.

White, Caroline. *Patrons and Partisans: A Study of Politics in Two Southern Italian Comuni.* New York: Columbia University Press, 1980.

Science

Dooley, Brendan M. *Science and the Marketplace in Early Modern Italy.* Lanham, Md.: Lexington Books, 2001.

Findlen, Paula. *Possessing Nature: Museums, Collecting, and Scientific Culture in Early Modern Italy.* Berkeley: University of California Press, 1994.

Freedberg, David. *The Eye of the Lynx: Galileo, His Friends, and the Beginnings of Modern Natural History.* Chicago: University of Chicago Press, 2002.

Gibson, Mary. *Born to Crime: Cesare Lombroso and the Origins of Biological Criminology.* Westport, Conn.: Praeger, 2002.

Guarnieri, Patrizia. *A Case of Child Murder: Law and Science in Nineteenth-Century Tuscany.* Cambridge: Polity Press, 1993.

Pancaldi, Giuliano. *Darwin in Italy: Science across Cultural Frontiers.* Bloomington: Indiana University Press, 1991.

———. *Volta: Science and Culture in the Age of Enlightenment.* Princeton, N.J.: Princeton University Press, 2003.

Randall, John Herman. *The School of Padua and the Emergence of Modern Science.* Padua: Editrice Antenore, 1961.

Segre, Michael. *In the Wake of Galileo.* New Brunswick, N.J.: Rutgers University Press, 1991.

Wightman, W. P. D. *Science and the Renaissance: An Introduction to the Study of the Emergence of the Sciences in the Sixteenth Century.* Edinburgh: Oliver and Boyd, 1962.

Social Conditions, Socialism, Labor, Popular Movements

Agocs, Sandor. *The Troubled Origins of the Italian Catholic Labor Movement, 1878–1914.* Detroit: Wayne State University Press, 1988.

Barkan, Joanne. *Visions of Emancipation: The Italian Workers' Movement since 1945.* New York: Praeger, 1984.

Bell, Donald H. *Sesto San Giovanni: Workers, Culture, and Politics in an Italian Town: 1880–1922.* New Brunswick, N.J.: Rutgers University Press, 1986.

Cammett, John M. *Antonio Gramsci and the Origins of Italian Communism.* Stanford, Calif.: Stanford University Press, 1967.

Davis, John A., ed. *Gramsci and Italy's Passive Revolution.* London: Croom Helm, 1979.

De Grand, Alexander J. *In Stalin's Shadow: Angelo Tasca and the Crisis of the Left in Italy and France, 1910–1945.* DeKalb: Northern Illinois University Press, 1986.

———. *The Italian Left in the Twentieth Century: A History of the Socialist and Communist Parties.* Bloomington: Indiana University Press, 1989.

Di Scala, Spencer M. *Dilemmas of Italian Socialism: The Politics of Filippo Turati.* Amherst: University of Massachusetts Press, 1980.

———. *Renewing Italian Socialism: Nenni to Craxi.* New York: Oxford University Press, 1988.

Drake, Richard. *Apostles and Agitators: Italy's Marxist Revolutionary Tradition.* Cambridge, Mass.: Harvard University Press, 2003.

Eisenstein, Elizabeth L. *The First Professional Revolutionist: Filippo Michele Buonarroti (1761–1837).* Cambridge, Mass.: Harvard University Press, 1959.

Filippelli, Ronald L. *American Labor and Postwar Italy, 1943–1953: A Study of Cold War Politics.* Stanford, Calif.: Stanford University Press, 1989.

Fiori, Giuseppe. *Antonio Gramsci: Life of a Revolutionary.* New York: Dutton, 1971.

Gonzales, Manuel G. *Andrea Costa and the Rise of Socialism in the Romagna.* Lanham, Md.: University Press of America, 1979.

Hobsbawm, Eric J., and Giorgio Napolitano. *The Italian Road to Socialism.* Westport, Conn.: Lawrence Hill, 1977.

Hostetter, Richard. *The Italian Socialist Movement.* Vol. 1, *Origins, 1860–1882.* Princeton, N.J.: Van Nostrand, 1958.

Joll, James. *Antonio Gramsci.* New York: Viking, 1978.

Miller, James Edward. *From Elite to Mass Politics: Italian Socialism in the Giolittian Era.* Kent, Ohio: Kent State University Press, 1990.

Pernicone, Nunzio. *Italian Anarchism, 1864–1892.* Princeton, N.J.: Princeton University Press, 1993.

Piccone, Paul. *Italian Marxism.* Berkeley: University of California Press, 1983.

Procacci, Giuliano. *The Italian Working Class from Risorgimento to Fascism.* Cambridge, Mass.: Harvard University Center for European Studies, 1979.

Ravindranathan, T. R. *Bakunin and the Italians.* Kingston, Ont.: McGill-Queens University Press, 1988.

Surace, Samuel J. *Ideology, Economic Change, and the Working Classes: The Case of Italy.* Berkeley: University of California Press, 1966.

Tarrow, Sidney G. *Peasant Communism in Southern Italy.* New Haven, Conn.: Yale University Press, 1967.

Tilly, Louise A. *Politics and Class in Milan, 1881–1901.* New York: Oxford University Press, 1992.

Williams, Gwyn A. *Proletarian Order: Antonio Gramsci and the Origins of Italian Communism, 1911–1921.* London: Pluto Press, 1975.

Terrorism

Drake, Richard. *The Aldo Moro Murder Case.* Cambridge, Mass.: Harvard University Press, 1995.

———. *The Revolutionary Mystique and Terrorism in Contemporary Italy.* Bloomington: Indiana University Press, 1989.

Meade, Robert C., Jr. *Red Brigades: The Story of Italian Terrorism.* London: Macmillan, 1989.

Pisano, Vittorfranco S. *The Dynamics of Subversion and Violence in Contemporary Italy.* Stanford, Calif.: Hoover Institution Press, 1987.

Wagner-Pacifici, Erica. *The Moro Morality Play: Terrorism as Social Drama.* Chicago: Chicago University Press, 1986.

Weinberg, Leonard, and William Lee Eubank. *The Rise and Fall of Italian Terrorism.* Boulder, Colo.: Westview Press, 1987.

Women

Baernstein, P. Renée. *A Convent Tale: A Century of Sisterhood in Spanish Milan.* New York: Routledge, 2002.

Budani, Donna M. *Italian Women's Narratives of Their Experiences during World War II.* Lewiston, N.Y.: Edwin Mellen Press, 2003.

Chiavola-Birnbaum, Lucia. *Liberazione della donna: Feminism in Italy.* Middletown, Conn.: Wesleyan University Press, 1986.

Chojnacka, Monica. *Working Women of Early Modern Venice.* Baltimore, Md.: Johns Hopkins University Press, 2001.

Corneliesen, Ann. *Women of the Shadows: A Study of the Wives and Mothers of Southern Italy.* New York: Vintage Books, 1977.

De Grazia, Victoria. *How Fascism Ruled Women: Italy, 1922–1945.* Berkeley: University of California Press, 1992.

Deiss, Joseph J. *The Roman Years of Margaret Fuller.* New York: Crowell, 1969.

Gabaccia, Donna, and Franca Iacovetto, eds. *Women; Gender, and Transnational Lives: Italian Women Around the World.* Toronto: University of Toronto Press, 2002.

Hellman, Judith A. *Journeys among Women: Feminism in Five Italian Cities.* New York: Oxford University Press, 1987.

Panizza, Letizia, and Sharon Wood, eds. *A History of Women's Writing in Italy.* Cambridge: Cambridge University Press, 2000.

Pickering-Iazzi, Robin, ed. *Mothers of Invention: Women, Italian Fascism, and Culture.* Minneapolis: University of Minnesota Press, 1995.

———. *Politics of the Visible: Writing Women, Culture, and Fascism.* Minneapolis: University of Minnesota Press, 1997.

Reeder, Linda. *Widows in White: Migration and the Transformation of Rural Italian Women, Sicily, 1880–1920.* Toronto: University of Toronto Press, 2003.

Slaughter, Jane. *Women and the Italian Resistance, 1943–1945.* Denver, Colo.: Arden Press, 1997.

Sperling, Jutta G. *Convents and the Body Politic in Late Renaissance Venice.* Chicago: University of Chicago Press, 1999.

Wilson, Perry R. *The Clockwork Factory: Women and Work in Fascist Italy.* Oxford: Clarendon Press, 1993.

———. *Peasant Women and Politics in Fascist Italy: The Massaie Rurali Section of the PNF.* Cambridge: Cambridge University Press, 2002.

Zappi, Elda Gentili. *If Eight Hours Seem Too Few: Mobilization of Women Workers in the Italian Rice Fields.* Albany: SUNY Press, 1991.

APPROACHES

Comparative Studies

Bessel, Richard, ed. *Fascist Italy and Nazi Germany: Comparisons and Contrasts.* Cambridge: Cambridge University Press, 1996.

Dal Lago, Enrico, and Rick Halpern, eds. *The American South and the Italian Mezzogiorno: Essays in Comparative History.* New York: Palgrave, 2002.

De Grand, Alexander J. *Fascist Italy and Nazi Germany: The 'Fascist' Style of Rule.* London: Routledge, 1995.

De Grazia, Victoria, and Ellen Furlough, eds. *The Sex of Things: Gender and Consumption in Historical Perspective.* Berkeley: University of California Press, 1996.

Delzell, Charles F., ed. *Mediterranean Fascism, 1919–1945.* New York: Harper and Row, 1970.

Doyle, Don Harrison. *Nations Divided: America, Italy, and the Southern Question.* Athens: University of Georgia Press, 2002.

Hobsbawm, Eric J. *Primitive Rebels: Studies in Archaic Forms of Social Movement in the Nineteenth and Twentieth Centuries.* Manchester: Manchester University Press, 1959.

Knox, MacGregor. *Common Destiny: Dictatorship, Foreign Policy, and War in Fascist Italy and Nazi Germany.* Cambridge: Cambridge University Press, 2000.

Kolinsky, Martin. *Continuity and Change in European Society: France, Germany, and Italy since 1870.* New York: St. Martin's Press, 1974.

Lange, Peter M. *Unions, Change and Crisis: French and Italian Union Strategy and the Political Economy, 1945–1980.* Boston: Allen and Unwin, 1982.

———, and Maurizio Vannicelli, eds. *The Communist Parties of Italy, France, and Spain: Postwar Change and Continuity.* London: Unwin and Allen, 1981.

Loubère, Leo A. *The Red and the White: The History of Wine in France and Italy in the Nineteenth Century.* Albany: SUNY Press, 1978.

Maier, Charles S. *Recasting Bourgeois Europe: Stabilization in France, Germany, and Italy in the Decade after World War I.* Princeton, N.J.: Princeton University Press, 1975.

Meyer, Donald. *Sex and Power: The Rise of Women in America, Russia, Sweden, and Italy.* Middletown, Conn.: Wesleyan University Press, 1987.

Nolte, Ernst. *Three Faces of Fascism: Action Française, Italian Fascism, National Socialism.* New York: Holt, Rinehart and Winston, 1966.

Quine, Maria Sophia. *Population Politics in Twentieth-Century Europe.* London: Routledge, 1996.

Samuels, Richard J. *Machiavelli's Children: Leaders and Their Legacies in Italy and Japan.* Ithaca, N.Y.: Cornell University Press, 2003.

Stuart Hughes, H. *The United States and Italy.* 3d ed. Cambridge, Mass.: Harvard University Press, 1979.

Tilly, Charles, Louise Tilly, and Richard Tilly. *The Rebellious Century, 1830–1930.* Cambridge, Mass.: Harvard University Press, 1975.

Cultural Studies

Allen, Beverly, and Mary Russo, eds. *Revisioning Italy: National Identity and Global Culture.* Minneapolis: University of Minnesota Press, 1997.

Dundees, Alan, and Alessandro Falassi. *La terra in piazza: An Interpretation of the Palio of Siena.* Berkeley: University of California Press, 1975.

Forgacs, David. *Italian Culture in the Industrial Era, 1880–1980.* Manchester: Manchester University Press, 1990.

Forgacs, David, and Robert Lumley, eds. *Italian Cultural Studies: An Introduction.* Oxford: Oxford University Press, 1996.

Lumley, Robert, ed. *Italian Journalism: A Critical Anthology.* Manchester: Manchester University Press, 1996.

Historiography

Bosworth, Richard. *The Italian Dictatorship: Problems and Perspectives in the Interpretation of Mussolini and Fascism.* London: Arnold, 1998.

De Felice, Renzo. *Interpretations of Fascism.* Cambridge, Mass.: Harvard University Press, 1977.

Riall, Lucy. *The Italian Risorgimento: State, Society and National Unification.* London: Routledge, 1994.

PRIMARY SOURCES

This section includes selected memoirs, diaries, documents, and other firsthand accounts by participants in historical events.

Abba, Giuseppe. *The Diary of One of Garibaldi's Thousands.* London: Oxford University Press, 1962.

Alfieri, Vittorio. *The Life of Vittorio Alfieri Written by Himself.* Lawrence: University of Kansas Press, 1953.

Amendola, Giorgio. *The Life I Chose.* New York: Karz Publications, 1979.

Badoglio, Pietro. *Italy in the Second World War.* New York: Oxford University Press, 1948.

———. *The War in Abyssinia.* London: Methuen, 1937.

Azeglio, Massimo d'. *Things I Remember.* London: Oxford University Press, 1966.

Balabanoff, Angelica. *My Life As a Rebel.* London: Hamish Hamilton, 1938.

Bosco, Giovanni (Don). *Memoirs of the Oratory of Saint Francis of Sales from 1815 to 1855: The Autobiography of Don Giovanni Bosco.* New Rochelle, N.Y.: Don Bosco Publications, 1989.

Bragadin, Marcantonio A. *The Italian Navy in World War II.* Annapolis, Md.: U.S. Naval Institute, 1957.

Cellini, Benvenuto. *Autobiography.* New York: Dodd, Mead, 1961.

Ciano, Galeazzo. *Diary, 1937–1943.* New York: Enigma Books, 2002.

Corti, Eugenio. *Few Returned; Twenty-Eight Days on the Russian Front, Winter 1942–1943.* Columbia: University of Missouri Press, 1997.

Corvo, Max. *The O.S.S. in Italy, 1942–1945: A Personal Memoir.* New York: Praeger, 1990.

Croce, Benedetto. *An Autobiography.* Oxford: Clarendon Press, 1028.

———. *Croce, the King and the Allies: Extracts from a Diary.* London: Allen, 1950.

Garibaldi, Giuseppe. *Autobiography.* 3 vols. London: Walter Smith and Innes, 1889.

Germanetto, Giovanni. *Memoirs of a Barber.* New York: International Publishers, 1935.

Giolitti, Giovanni. *Memoirs of My Life.* London: Chapman and Dodd, 1923.

Mussolini, Benito. *Fascism: Doctrine and Institutions.* New York: H. Fertig, 1968.

———. *My Rise and Fall.* New York: Da Capo Press, 1998.

Pellico, Silvio. *My Prisons.* London: Oxford University Press, 1963.

Pesce, Giovanni. *And No Quarter: An Italian Partisan in World War II.* Athens: Ohio University Press, 1972.

Russell, Odo. *The Roman Question: Extracts from the Despatches of Odo Russell from Rome, 1858–1870.* London: Chapman and Hall, 1962.

Salandra, Antonio. *Italy and the Great War: From Neutrality to Intervention.* London: Arnold, 1932.

Segre, Dan Vittorio. *Memoirs of a Fortunate Jew: An Italian Story.* Bethesda, Md.: Adler & Adler, 1987.

Silj, Alessandro. *Never Again without a Rifle: The Origins of Italian Terrorism.* New York: Karz Publishers, 1979.

Tittoni, Tommaso. *Italy's Foreign and Colonial Policy.* London: Smith Elder, 1914.

Verdi, Giuseppe. *Letters of Giuseppe Verdi.* London: Gollancz, 1971.

Vico, Giambattista. *The Autobiography.* Ithaca, N.Y.: Cornell University Press, 1944.

Visconti-Venosta, Giovanni. *Memoirs of Youth: Things Seen and Known, 1847–1860.* Boston: Houghton Mifflin, 1914.

Volpi, Giuseppe, and Bonaldo Stringher. *The Financial Reconstruction of Italy.* New York: The Italian Historical Society, 1927.

INDEX